Collins
ITALIAN
DICTIONARY
ESSENTIAL EDITION

Published by Collins
An imprint of HarperCollins Publishers
Westerhill Road
Bishopbriggs
Glasgow G64 2QT

First Edition 2018

10 9 8 7 6 5 4 3 2

© HarperCollins Publishers 2018

ISBN 978-0-00-827075-9

Collins® is a registered trademark of
HarperCollins Publishers Limited

collinsdictionary.com

Typeset by
Davidson Publishing Solutions, Glasgow

Printed and bound by
CPI Group (UK) Ltd, Croydon, CR0 4YY

A catalogue record for this book is
available from the British Library.

If you would like to comment on any
aspect of this book, please contact us
at the given address or online.
E-mail: dictionaries@harpercollins.co.uk
 facebook.com/collinsdictionary
 @collinsdict

Acknowledgements
We would like to thank those authors
and publishers who kindly gave
permission for copyright material to
be used in the Collins Corpus. We would
also like to thank Times Newspapers
Ltd for providing valuable data.

INDICE

CONTENTS

INTRODUZIONE

Vi ringraziamo di aver scelto questo dizionario e ci auguriamo che si riveli uno strumento utile e piacevole da usare nello studio, in vacanza e sul lavoro.

In questa introduzione troverete alcuni suggerimenti per aiutarvi a trarre il massimo beneficio dal vostro nuovo dizionario, ricco non solo per il suo ampio lemmario ma anche per il gran numero di informazioni contenute in ciascuna voce.

All'inizio del dizionario troverete l'elenco delle abbreviazioni usate nel testo e una guida alla pronuncia. Troverete inoltre un utile elenco delle forme dei verbi irregolari inglesi e italiani, seguito da una sezione finale con i numeri, l'ora e la data.

COME USARE IL DIZIONARIO COLLINS GEM

Per imparare ad usare in modo efficace il dizionario è importante comprendere la funzione delle differenziazioni tipografiche, dei simboli e delle abbreviazioni usati nel testo. Vi forniamo pertanto qui di seguito alcuni chiarimenti in merito a tali convenzioni.

I LEMMI

Sono le parole in **neretto** elencate in ordine alfabetico. Il primo e l'ultimo lemma di ciascuna pagina appaiono al margine superiore.

Dove opportuno, informazioni sull'ambito d'uso o il livello di formalità di certe parole vengono fornite tra parentesi in corsivo e spesso in forma abbreviata dopo l'indicazione della categoria grammaticale (es. (*Comm*), (*col*)).

In certi casi più parole con radice comune sono raggruppate sotto lo stesso lemma. Tali parole appaiono in neretto ma in un carattere leggermente ridotto (es. **acceptance**).

Esempi d'uso del lemma sono a loro volta in neretto ma in un carattere diverso dal lemma (es. **cold** [kəuld] **to be ~**).

LA TRASCRIZIONE FONETICA

La trascrizione fonetica che illustra la corretta pronuncia del lemma è tra parentesi quadre e segue immediatamente il lemma (es. **knee** [niː]). L'elenco dei simboli fonetici è alle pagine x–xi.

LE TRADUZIONI

Le traduzioni sono in carattere tondo e,quando il lemma ha più di un significato, le traduzioni sono separate da un punto e virgola. Spesso diverse traduzioni di un lemma sono introdotte da una o più parole in corsivo tra parentesi tonde: la loro funzione è di chiarire a quale significato del lemma si riferisce la traduzione. Possono essere sinonimi, indicazioni di ambito d'uso o di registro del lemma (es. **party** *(Pol)*, *(team)*, *(celebration)*; **laid-back** *(col)* ecc.).

LE 'PAROLE CHIAVE' ⭕

Un trattamento particolare è stato riservato a quelle parole che, per frequenza d'uso o complessità, necessitano una strutturazione più chiara ed esauriente (es. **da**, **di**, **avere** in italiano, **at**, **to**, **be**, **this** in inglese). Frecce e numeri vi guidano attraverso le varie distinzioni grammaticali e di significato; ulteriori informazioni sono fornite in corsivo tra parentesi.

INFORMAZIONI GRAMMATICALI

Le parti del discorso (noun, adjective ecc.) sono espresse da abbreviazioni convenzionali in corsivo *(n, adj* ecc.) e seguono la trascrizione fonetica del lemma.

Eventuali ulteriori informazioni grammaticali, come ad esempio le forme di un verbo irregolare o il plurale irregolare di un sostantivo, precedono tra parentesi la parte del discorso (es. **give** *(pt* **gave**, *pp* **given**) *vt*; **man** […] *(pl* **men**) *n*).

INTRODUCTION

We are delighted that you have decided to buy this dictionary and hope you will enjoy and benefit from using it at school, at home, on holiday or at work.

This introduction gives you a few tips on how to get the most out of your dictionary – not simply from its comprehensive wordlist but also from the information provided in each entry. This will help you to read and understand modern Italian, as well as communicate and express yourself in the language.

The dictionary begins by listing the abbreviations used in the text and illustrating the sounds shown by the phonetic symbols. You will also find Italian and English verb tables, followed by a section on numbers and time expressions.

USING YOUR DICTIONARY

A wealth of information is presented in the dictionary, using various typefaces, sizes of type, symbols, abbreviations and brackets. The various conventions and symbols used are explained in the following sections.

HEADWORDS

The words you look up in a dictionary – 'headwords' – are listed alphabetically. They are printed in **bold type** for rapid identification. The two headwords appearing at the top of each page indicate the first and last word dealt with on the page in question.

Information about the usage or form of certain headwords is given in brackets after the part of speech. This usually appears in abbreviated form and in italics (e.g.(*fam*), (*Comm*)).

Where appropriate, words related to headwords are grouped in the same entry (e.g. **illustrare**, **illustrazione**) in a slightly smaller bold type than the headword.

Common expressions in which the headword appears are shown in a different bold roman type (e.g. **freddo, -a aver ~**).

PHONETIC SPELLINGS

Where the phonetic spelling of headwords (indicating their pronunciation) is given, it will appear in square brackets immediately after the headword (e.g. **calza** ['kaltsa]). A list of these symbols is given on pages x–xi.

Headword translations are given in ordinary type and, where more than one
meaning or usage exists, these are separated by a semicolon. You will often find
other words in italics in brackets before the translations. These offer suggested
contexts in which the headword might appear (e.g. **duro** (*pietra*) or (*lavoro*)) or
provide synonyms (e.g. **duro** (*ostinato*)).

KEYWORDS 🔘

Special status is given to certain Italian and English words which are considered
as 'key' words in each language. They may, for example, occur very frequently or
have several types of usage (e.g. **da**, **di**, **avere** in Italian, **at**, **to**, **be**, **this** in English).
A combination of arrows and numbers helps you to distinguish different parts
of speech and different meanings. Further helpful information is provided in
brackets and italics.

GRAMMATICAL INFORMATION
Parts of speech are given in abbreviated form in italics after the phonetic
spellings of headwords (e.g. *vt*, *av*, *cong*).

Genders of Italian nouns are indicated as follows: *sm* for a masculine and *sf* for
a feminine noun. Feminine and irregular plural forms of nouns are also shown
(e.g. **uovo**, (*pl f* **uova**); **dottore**, **-essa**).

Feminine adjective endings are given, as are plural forms (e.g. **opaco**, **-a**,
-chi, **-che**).

abréviation	*ab(b)r*	abbreviation
abbreviazione	*abbr*	abbreviation
aggettivo	*adj*	adjective
amministrazione	*Admin*	administration
avverbio	*adv*	adverb
aeronautica, viaggi aerei	*Aer*	flying, air travel
aggettivo	*ag*	adjective
agricoltura	*Agr*	agriculture
amministrazione	*Amm*	administration
anatomia	*Anat*	anatomy
architettura	*Archit*	architecture
articolo determinativo	*art def*	definite article
articolo indeterminativo	*art indef*	indefinite article
attributivo	*attrib*	attributive
ausiliare	*aus, aux*	auxiliary
Australia	*Aust*	Australia
automobile	*Aut*	motor car and motoring
avverbio	*av*	adverb
aeronautica, viaggi aerei	*Aviat*	flying, air travel
biologia	*Biol*	biology
botanica	*Bot*	botany
inglese britannico	*BRIT*	British English
consonante	*C*	consonant
chimica	*Chim, Chem*	chemistry
familiare (! da evitare)	*col(!)*	colloquial usage (! particularly offensive)
commercio, finanza	*Comm*	commerce, finance
comparativo	*compar*	comparative
informatica	*Comput*	computing
congiunzione	*cong, conj*	conjunction
edilizia	*Constr*	building
sostantivo usato come aggettivo, ma mai con funzione predicativa	*cpd*	compound element: noun used as adjective and which cannot follow the noun it qualifies

ABBREVIAZIONI		ABBREVIATIONS
cucina	*Cuc, Culin*	cookery
davanti a	*dav*	before
articolo determinativo	*def art*	definite article
determinativo; articolo, aggettivo dimostrativo o indefinito	*det*	determiner: article, demonstrative
diminutivo	*dimin*	diminutive
diritto	*Dir*	law
economia	*Econ*	economics
edilizia	*Edil*	building
elettricità, elettronica	*Elettr, Elec*	electricity, electronics
esclamazione	*escl, excl*	exclamation
femminile	*f*	feminine
familiare (! da evitare)	*fam(!)*	colloquial usage (! particularly offensive)
ferrovia	*Ferr*	railways
senso figurato	*fig*	figurative use
fisiologia	*Fisiol*	physiology
fotografia	*Fot*	photography
verbo inglese la cui particella è inseparabile dal verbo	*fus*	(phrasal verb) where the particle cannot be separated from the main verb
nella maggior parte dei sensi; generalmente	*gen*	in most or all senses; generally
geografia, geologia	*Geo*	geography, geology
geometria	*Geom*	geometry
storia, storico	*Hist*	history, historical
impersonale	*impers*	impersonal
articolo indeterminativo	*indef art*	indefinite article
informatica	*Inform*	computing
insegnamento, sistema scolastico e universitario	*Ins*	schooling, schools and universities
invariabile	*inv*	invariable
irregolare	*irreg*	irregular
grammatica, linguistica	*Ling*	grammar, linguistics

ABBREVIAZIONI

ABBREVIATIONS

maschile	*m*	masculine
matematica	*Mat(h)*	mathematics
termine medico, medicina	*Med*	medical term, medicine
il tempo, meteorologia	*Meteor*	the weather, meteorology
maschile o femminile	*m/f*	masculine or feminine
esercito, linguaggio militare	*Mil*	military matters
musica	*Mus*	music
sostantivo	*n*	noun
nautica	*Naut*	sailing, navigation
numerale (aggettivo, sostantivo)	*num*	numeral adjective or noun
Nuova Zelanda	*NZ*	New Zealand
	o.s.	oneself
peggiorativo	*peg, pej*	derogatory, pejorative
fotografia	*Phot*	photography
fisiologia	*Physiol*	physiology
plurale	*pl*	plural
politica	*Pol*	politics
participio passato	*pp*	past participle
preposizione	*prep*	preposition
pronome	*pron*	pronoun
psicologia, psichiatria	*Psic, Psych*	psychology, psychiatry
tempo passato	*pt*	past tense
qualcosa	*qc*	something
qualcuno	*qn*	someone
religione, liturgia	*Rel*	religions, church service
sostantivo	*s*	noun
	sb	somebody
insegnamento, sistema scolastico e universitario	*Scol*	schooling, schools and universities
singolare	*sg*	singular
soggetto (grammaticale)	*sog*	(grammatical) subject
	sth	something
congiuntivo	*sub*	subjunctive
soggetto (grammaticale)	*subj*	(grammatical) subject

superlativo	*superl*	superlative
termine tecnico, tecnologia	*Tecn, Tech*	technical term, technology
telecomunicazioni	*Tel*	telecommunications
tipografia	*Tip*	typography, printing
televisione	*TV*	television
tipografia	*Typ*	typography, printing
università	*Univ*	university
inglese americano	*US*	American English
vocale	*V*	vowel
verbo	*vb*	verb
verbo o gruppo verbale con funzione intransitiva	*vi*	verb or phrasal verb used intransitively
verbo pronominale o riflessivo	*vpr*	pronominal or reflexive verb
verbo o gruppo verbale con funzione transitiva	*vt*	verb or phrasal verb used transitively
zoologia	*Zool*	zoology
marchio registrato	®	registered trademark
introduce un'equivalenza culturale	≈	introduces a cultural equivalent

TRASCRIZIONE FONETICA

CONSONANTI		CONSONANTS
p, b, t, d, k, g sono seguite da un'aspirazione in inglese.		**p, b, t, d, k, g** are not aspirated in Italian.

padre	p	**p**u**pp**y
bam**b**ino	b	**b**a**b**y
tu**tt**o	t	**t**en**t**
da**d**o	d	**d**a**dd**y
cane **ch**e	k	**c**or**k k**iss **ch**ord
gola **gh**iro	g	**g**a**g g**uess
sano	s	**s**o ri**c**e ki**ss**
svago e**s**ame	z	cou**s**in bu**zz**
scena	ʃ	**sh**eep **s**ugar
	ʒ	plea**s**ure bei**g**e
pe**c**e lan**c**iare	tʃ	**ch**ur**ch**
giro **g**ioco	dʒ	**j**udge **g**eneral
a**f**a **f**aro	f	**f**arm ra**ff**le
vero bra**v**o	v	**v**ery re**v**
	θ	**th**in ma**th**s
	ð	**th**at o**th**er
letto a**l**a	l	**l**itt**l**e ba**ll**
g**l**i	ʎ	mi**lli**on
rete a**r**co	r	**r**at **r**a**r**e
ramo ma**dr**e	m	**m**u**mm**y co**mb**
no fu**m**ante	n	**n**o ra**n**
gnomo	ɲ	ca**ny**on
	ŋ	si**ng**ing ba**n**k
	h	**h**at re**h**eat
bu**i**o **pi**acere	j	**y**et
uomo g**u**aio	w	**w**all be**w**ail
	x	lo**ch**

VARI		MISCELLANEOUS
per l'inglese: la 'r' finale viene pronunciata se seguita da una vocale	r	
precede la sillaba accentata	'	precedes the stressed syllable

PHONETIC TRANSCRIPTION

VOCALI		VOWELS
La messa in equivalenza di certi suoni indica solo una rassomiglianza approssimativa.		The pairing of some vowel sounds only indicates approximate equivalence.

vino idea	i i:	heel bead
	ɪ	hit pity
stella edera	e	
epoca eccetto	ɛ	set tent
mamma amore	a æ	bat apple
	ɑː	after car calm
	ɑ̃	fiancé
	ʌ	fun cousin
müsli	y	
	ə	over above
	əː	urn fern work
rosa occhio	ɔ	wash pot
	ɔː	born cork
ponte ognuno	o	
föhn	ø	
utile zucca	u	full soot
	uː	boon lewd

DITTONGHI		DIPHTHONGS
	ɪə	beer tier
	ɛə	tear fair there
	eɪ	date plaice day
	aɪ	life buy cry
	au	owl foul now
	əu	low no
	ɔɪ	boil boy oily
	uə	poor tour

ITALIAN PRONUNCIATION

VOWELS

Where the vowel **e** or the vowel **o** appears in a stressed syllable it can be either open [ɛ],[ɔ] or closed [e],[o]. As the open or closed pronunciation of these vowels is subject to regional variation, the distinction is of little importance to the user of this dictionary. Phonetic transcription for headwords containing these vowels will therefore only appear where other pronunciation difficulties are present.

CONSONANTS

c before 'e' or 'i' is pronounced like the '*tch*' in match.

ch is pronounced like the '*k*' in 'kit'.

g before 'e' or 'i' is pronounced like the '*j*' in 'jet'.

gh is pronounced like the '*g*' in 'get'.

gl before 'e' or 'i' is normally pronounced like the '*lli*' in 'million', and in a few cases only like the '*gl*' in 'glove'.

gn is pronounced like the '*ny*' in 'canyon'

sc before 'e' or 'i' is pronounced '*sh*'.

z is pronounced like the '*ts*' in 'stetson', or like the '*d's*' in 'bird's-eye'.

Headwords containing the above consonants and consonantal groups have been given full phonetic transcription in this dictionary.

NB All double written consonants in Italian are fully sounded:
e.g. the *tt* in 'tutto' is pronounced as in 'h*at* *t*rick'.

ITALIAN VERB FORMS

a Gerund **b** Past participle **c** Present **d** Imperfect **e** Past historic **f** Future
g Conditional **h** Present subjunctive **i** Imperfect subjunctive **j** Imperative

1 **abbattere** e abbattei, abbattesti
(doesn't have alternative forms -etti,
-ette, -ettero)

2 **accendere** b acceso e accesi,
accendesti

3 **accludere** b accluso e acclusi,
accludesti

4 **accorgersi** b accorto e mi
accorsi, ti accorgesti

5 **aggiungere** b aggiunto
e aggiunsi, aggiungesti

6 **andare** c vado, vai, va, andiamo,
andate, vanno f andrò *etc.* h vada
j va'!, vada!, andate!, vadano!

7 **apparire** b apparso c appaio,
appari *or* apparisci, appare *or*
apparisce, appaiono *or*
appariscono e apparvi *or* apparsi,
apparisti, apparve *or* apparì *or*
apparse, apparvero *or* apparirono
or apparsero h appaia *or*
apparisca

8 **appendere** b appeso e appesi,
appendesti

9 **aprire** b aperto c apro e aprii,
apristi h apra

10 **ardere** b arso e arsi, ardesti

11 **assistere** b assistito e assistei *or*
assistetti, assistesti

12 **assumere** b assunto e assunsi,
assumesti

13 **AVERE** c ho, hai, ha, abbiamo,
avete, hanno e ebbi, avesti, ebbe,
avemmo, aveste, ebbero f avrò
etc. h abbia *etc.* j abbi!, abbia!,
abbiate!, abbiano!

14 **baciare** *when the ending begins
with* -e, *the* i *is dropped* → bacerò
(*not* bacierò)

15 **bagnare** c bagniamo, bagniate
h bagniamo, bagniate (*not*
bagnamo, bagnate)

16 **bere** a bevendo b bevuto c bevo
etc. d bevevo *etc.* e bevvi *or*
bevetti, bevesti f berrò *etc.* h beva
etc. i bevessi *etc.*

17 **bollire** c bollo *or* bollisco, bolli *or*
bollisci *etc.*

18 **cadere** e caddi, cadesti f cadrò
etc.

19 **cambiare** *drops the* i *of the root if
the ending starts with* i (cambi,
cambino *not* cambii, cambiino (*cf.*
inviare)

20 **caricare** *when* c *in the root is
followed by* -i *or* -e *an* h *should be
inserted* (*i.e.* carichi, carichiamo,
caricherò)

21 **chiedere** b chiesto e chiesi,
chiedesti

22 **chiudere** b chiuso e chiusi,
chiudesti

23 **cogliere** b colto c colgo, colgono
e colsi, cogliesti h colga

24 **compiere** b compiuto e compii,
compisti

25 **confondere** b confuso e confusi,
confondesti

26 **conoscere** b conosciuto
e conobbi, conoscesti

27 **consigliare** *when the ending begins
with* -i, *the* i *of the root is dropped* →
consigli (*not* consiglii)

28 **correre** b corso e corsi, corresti

29 **CREDERE** a credendo b creduto
c credo, credi, crede, crediamo,
credete, credono d credevo,
credevi, credeva, credevamo,

credevate, credevano **e** credei *or* credetti, credesti, credé *or* credette, credemmo, credeste, crederono *or* credettero **f** crederò, crederai, crederà, crederemo, crederete, crederanno **g** crederei, crederesti, crederebbe, crederemmo, credereste, crederebbero **h** creda, creda, creda, crediamo, crediate, credano **i** credessi, credessi, credesse, credessimo, credeste, credessero **j** credi!, creda!, credete!, credano!

30 **crescere b** cresciuto **e** crebbi, crescesti

31 **cucire** *when c or g in the root is followed by -o or -a an i should be inserted (i.e. cucio, cucia)*

32 **cuocere b** cotto **c** cuocio, cuociamo, cuociono **e** cossi, cocesti

33 **dare b** do, dai, dà, diamo, date, danno **e** diedi *or* detti, desti **f** darò *etc.* **h** dia *etc.* **i** dessi *etc.* **j** da'!, dai!, date!, diano!

34 **decidere b** deciso **e** decisi, decidesti

35 **deludere b** deluso **e** delusi, deludesti

36 **difendere b** difeso **e** difesi, difendesti

37 **dipingere b** dipinto **e** dipinsi, dipingesti

38 **dire a** dicendo **b** detto **c** dico, dici, dice, diciamo, dite, dicono **d** dicevo *etc.* **e** dissi, dicesti **f** dirò *etc.* **h** dica, diciamo, diciate, dicano **i** dicessi *etc.* **j** di'!, dica!, dite!, dicano!

39 **dirigere b** diretto **e** diressi, dirigesti

40 **discutere b** discusso **e** discussi, discutesti

41 **disfare** *like* fare *but* **c** disfo, disfi *etc.* **f** disferò, disferai *etc.* **i** disfi, disfi *etc. (regular forms)*

42 **distinguere b** distinto **e** distinsi, distinguesti

43 **dividere b** diviso **e** divisi, dividesti

44 **dolere c** dolgo, duoli, duole, dolgono **e** dolsi, dolesti **f** dorrò *etc.* **h** dolga

45 **DORMIRE a** dormendo **b** dormito **c** dormo, dormi, dorme, dormiamo, dormite, dormono **d** dormivo, dormivi, dormiva, dormivamo, dormivate, dormivano **e** dormii, dormisti, dormì, dormimmo, dormiste, dormirono **f** dormirò, dormirai, dormirà, dormiremo, dormirete, dormiranno **g** dormirei, dormiresti, dormirebbe, dormiremmo, dormireste, dormirebbero **h** dorma, dorma, dorma, dormiamo, dormiate, dormano **i** dormissi, dormissi, dormisse, dormissimo, dormiste, dormissero **j** dormi!, dorma!, dormite!, dormano!

46 **dovere c** devo *or* debbo, devi, deve, dobbiamo, dovete, devono *or* debbono **f** dovrò *etc.* **h** debba, dobbiamo, dobbiate, devano *or* debbano

47 **esigere b** esatto (*not common*) **e** esigei *or* esigetti, esigesti

48 **espellere b** espulso **e** espulsi, espellesti

49 **esplodere b** esploso **e** esplosi, esplodesti

50 **esprimere b** espresso **e** espressi, esprimesti

51 **ESSERE b** stato **c** sono, sei, è, siamo, siete, sono **d** ero, eri, era, eravamo, eravate, erano **e** fui, fosti, fu, fummo, foste, furono **f** sarò *etc.* **h** sia *etc.* **i** fossi, fossi, fosse, fossimo, foste, fossero **j** sii!, sia!, siate!, siano!

52 **evadere b** evaso **e** evasi, evadesti

53 **fare a** facendo **b** fatto **c** faccio, fai, fa, facciamo, fate, fanno **d** facevo *etc.* **e** feci, facesti **f** farò *etc.* **h** faccia *etc.* **i** facessi *etc.* **j** fa'!, faccia!, fate!, facciano!

54 **fingere b** finto **e** finsi, fingesti

55 **FINIRE a** finendo **b** finito **c** finisco, finisci, finisce, finiamo, finite, finiscono **d** finivo, finivi, finiva, finivamo, finivate, finivano **e** finii, finisti, finì, finimmo, finiste, finirono **f** finirò, finirai, finirà, finiremo, finirete, finiranno **g** finirei, finiresti, finirebbe, finiremmo, finireste, finirebbero **h** finisca, finisca, finisca, finiamo, finiate, finiscano **i** finissi, finissi, finisse, finissimo, finiste, finissero **j** finisci!, finisca!, finite!, finiscano!

56 **friggere b** fritto **e** frissi, friggesti

57 **giacere b** giaciuto **e** giacqui, giacesti

58 **godere f** godrò, godrai *etc.* **g** godrei, godresti *etc.*

59 **immergere b** immerso **e** immersi, immergesti

60 **inviare c** (tu) invii **f** (essi) inviino

61 **leggere b** letto **e** lessi, leggesti

62 **mangiare** *when the ending begins with -e, the i is dropped* → mangerò (*not* mangierò)

63 **mettere b** messo **e** misi, mettesti

64 **mordere b** morso **e** morsi, mordesti

65 **morire b** morto **c** muoio, muori, muore, moriamo, morite, muoiono **f** morirò *or* morrò *etc.* **h** muoia

66 **muovere b** mosso **e** mossi, muovesti

67 **nascere b** nato **e** nacqui, nascesti

68 **nascondere b** nascosto **e** nascosi, nascondesti

69 **nuocere b** nuociuto **c** nuoccio, nuoci, nuoce, nociamo *or* nuociamo, nuocete, nuocciono **d** nuocevo *etc.* **e** nocqui, nuocesti **f** nuocerò *etc.* **g** nuoccia

70 **offrire b** offerto **c** offro **e** offersi *or* offrii, offristi **h** offra

71 **parere b** parso **c** paio, paiamo, paiono **e** parvi *or* parsi, paresti **f** parrò *etc.* **h** paia, paiamo, paiate, paiano

72 **PARLARE a** parlando **b** parlato **c** parlo, parli, parla, parliamo, parlate, parlano **d** parlavo, parlavi, parlava, parlavamo, parlavate, parlavano **e** parlai, parlasti, parlò, parlammo, parlaste, parlarono **f** parlerò, parlerai, parlerà, parleremo, parlerete, parleranno **g** parlerei, parleresti, parlerebbe, parleremmo, parlereste, parlerebbero **h** parli, parli, parli, parliamo, parliate, parlino **i** parlassi, parlassi, parlasse, parlassimo, parlaste, parlassero **j** parla!, parli!, parlate!, parlino!

73 **perdere b** perso *or* perduto **e** persi, perdesti

74 **piacere b** piaciuto **c** piaccio, piacciamo, piacciono **e** piacqui, piacesti **h** piaccia *etc.*

75 **piangere b** pianto **e** piansi, piangesti

76 **piovere b** piovuto **e** piovve

77 **porre a** ponendo **b** posto **c** pongo, poni, pone, poniamo, ponete, pongono **d** ponevo *etc.* **e** posi, ponesti **f** porrò *etc.* **h** ponga, poniamo, poniate, pongano **i** ponessi *etc.*

78 **potere c** posso, puoi, può, possiamo, potete, possono

f potrò *etc.* **h** possa, possiamo, possiate, possano

79 **prefiggersi b** prefisso **e** mi prefissi, ti prefiggesti

80 **pregare** *when g in the root is followed by* -i *or* -e *an* h *should be inserted (i.e.* preghi, preghiamo, pregherò)

81 **prendere b** preso **e** presi, prendesti

82 **prevedere** *like* vedere *but* **f** prevederò, prevederai *etc.* **g** prevederei *etc.*

83 **proteggere b** protetto **e** protessi, proteggesti

84 **pungere b** punto **e** punsi, pungesti

85 **radere b** raso **e** rasi, radesti

86 **redimere b** redento **e** redensi, redimesti

87 **reggere b** retto **e** ressi, reggesti

88 **rendere b** reso **e** resi, rendesti

89 **ridere b** riso **e** risi, ridesti

90 **ridurre a** riducendo **b** ridotto **c** riduco *etc.* **d** riducevo *etc.* **e** ridussi, riducesti **f** ridurrò *etc.* **h** riduca *etc.* **i** riducessi *etc.*

91 **riempire a** riempiendo **c** riempio, riempi, riempie, riempiono

92 **riflettere b** riflettuto *or* riflesso

93 **rimanere b** rimasto **c** rimango, rimangono **e** rimasi, rimanesti **f** rimarrò *etc.* **h** rimanga

94 **risolvere b** risolto **e** risolsi, risolvesti

95 **rispondere b** risposto **e** risposi, rispondesti

96 **rivolgere b** rivolto **e** rivolsi, rivolgesti

97 **rompere b** rotto **e** ruppi, rompesti

98 **salire c** salgo, sali, salgono **h** salga

99 **sapere c** so, sai, sa, sappiamo, sapete, sanno **e** seppi, sapesti **f** saprò *etc.* **h** sappia *etc.* **j** sappi!, sappia!, sappiate!, sappiano!

100 **scegliere b** scelto **c** scelgo, scegli, sceglie, scegliamo, scegliete, scelgono **e** scelsi, scegliesti **h** scelga, scegliamo, scegliate, scelgano **j** scegli!, scelga!, scegliamo!, scegliete!, scelgano!

101 **scendere b** sceso **e** scesi, scendesti

102 **scindere b** scisso **e** scissi, scindesti

103 **sciogliere b** sciolto **c** sciolgo, sciogli, scioglie, sciogliamo, sciogliete, sciolgono **e** sciolsi, sciogliesti **h** sciolga, sciogliamo, sciogliate, sciolgano **j** sciogli!, sciolga!, sciogliamo!, sciogliete!, sciolgano!

104 **sconfiggere b** sconfitto **e** sconfissi, sconfiggesti

105 **scrivere b** scritto **e** scrissi, scrivesti

106 **scuotere b** scosso **e** scossi, scuotesti

107 **sedere c** siedo, siedi, siede, siedono **h** sieda

108 **solere b** solito **e** soglio, suoli, suole, sogliamo, solete, sogliono **h** soglia *(regular imperfect, gerund, past participle; no other verb forms)*

109 **sorgere b** sorto **e** sorse, sorsero

110 **spandere b** spanto **e** spansi, spandesti

111 **spargere b** sorto **e** sorse, sorsero

112 **sparire e** sparii, sparisti

113 **spegnere b** spento **c** spengo, spengono **e** spensi, spegnesti **h** spenga

114 spingere b spinto e spinsi, spingesti

115 sporgere b sporto e sporsi, sporgesti

116 stare b stato c sto, stai, sta, stiamo, state, stanno e stetti, stesti f starò *etc.* h stia *etc.* i stessi *etc.* j sta'!, stia!, state!, stiano!

117 stringere b stretto e strinsi, stringesti

118 succedere b successo e successi, succedesti

119 tacere b taciuto c taccio, tacciono e tacqui, tacesti h taccia

120 tendere b teso e tesi, tendesti

121 tenere c tengo, tieni, tiene, tengono e tenni, tenesti f terrò *etc.* h tenga

122 togliere b tolto c tolgo, togli, toglie, togliamo, togliete, tolgono e tolsi, togliesti h tolga j togli!, tolga!, togliamo!, togliete!, tolgano!

123 trarre a traendo b tratto c traggo, trai, trae, traiamo, traete, traggono d traevo *etc.* e trassi, traesti f trarrò *etc.* h tragga i traessi *etc.*

124 udire c odo, odi, ode, odono h oda

125 uscire c esco, esci, esce, escono h esca

126 valere b valso c valgo, valgono e valsi, valesti f varrò *etc.* h valga

127 vedere b visto *or* veduto e vidi, vedesti f vedrò *etc.*

128 venire b venuto c vengo, vieni, viene, vengono e venni, venisti f verrò *etc.* h venga

129 vincere b vinto e vinsi, vincesti

130 vivere b vissuto e vissi, vivesti

131 volere c voglio, vuoi, vuole, vogliamo, volete, vogliono e volli, volesti f vorrò *etc.* h voglia *etc.* j *not common*

ENGLISH VERB FORMS

PRESENT	PT	PP	PRESENT	PT	PP
arise	arose	arisen	feel	felt	felt
awake	awoke	awoken	fight	fought	fought
be (am, is, are; being)	was, were	been	find	found	found
			flee	fled	fled
bear	bore	born(e)	fling	flung	flung
beat	beat	beaten	fly	flew	flown
become	became	become	forbid	forbade	forbidden
begin	began	begun	forecast	forecast	forecast
bend	bent	bent	forget	forgot	forgotten
bet	bet, betted	bet, betted	forgive	forgave	forgiven
bid (at auction, cards)	bid	bid	forsake	forsook	forsaken
			freeze	froze	frozen
bid (say)	bade	bidden	get	got	got, (US) gotten
bind	bound	bound			
bite	bit	bitten	give	gave	given
bleed	bled	bled	go (goes)	went	gone
blow	blew	blown	grind	ground	ground
break	broke	broken	grow	grew	grown
breed	bred	bred	hang	hung	hung
bring	brought	brought	hang (execute)	hanged	hanged
build	built	built	have (has; having)	had	had
burn	burnt, burned	burnt, burned			
			hear	heard	heard
burst	burst	burst	hide	hid	hidden
buy	bought	bought	hit	hit	hit
can	could	(been able)	hold	held	held
cast	cast	cast	hurt	hurt	hurt
catch	caught	caught	keep	kept	kept
choose	chose	chosen	kneel	knelt, kneeled	knelt, kneeled
cling	clung	clung			
come	came	come	know	knew	known
cost	cost	cost	lay	laid	laid
cost (work out price of)	costed	costed	lead	led	led
			lean	leant, leaned	leant, leaned
creep	crept	crept			
cut	cut	cut	leap	leapt, leaped	leapt, leaped
deal	dealt	dealt			
dig	dug	dug	learn	learnt, learned	learnt, learned
do (does)	did	done			
draw	drew	drawn	leave	left	left
dream	dreamed, dreamt	dreamed, dreamt	lend	lent	lent
			let	let	let
drink	drank	drunk	lie (lying)	lay	lain
drive	drove	driven	light	lit, lighted	lit, lighted
dwell	dwelt	dwelt	lose	lost	lost
eat	ate	eaten	make	made	made
fall	fell	fallen	may	might	—
feed	fed	fed	mean	meant	meant

PRESENT	PT	PP	PRESENT	PT	PP
meet	met	met	spell	spelt,	spelt,
mistake	mistook	mistaken		spelled	spelled
mow	mowed	mown,	spend	spent	spent
		mowed	spill	spilt,	spilt,
must	(had to)	(had to)		spilled	spilled
pay	paid	paid	spin	spun	spun
put	put	put	spit	spat	spat
quit	quit, quitted	quit,	split	split	split
		quitted	spoil	spoiled,	spoiled,
read	read	read		spoilt	spoilt
rid	rid	rid	spread	spread	spread
ride	rode	ridden	spring	sprang	sprung
ring	rang	rung	stand	stood	stood
rise	rose	risen	steal	stole	stolen
run	ran	run	stick	stuck	stuck
saw	sawed	sawed,	sting	stung	stung
		sawn	stink	stank	stunk
say	said	said	stride	strode	stridden
see	saw	seen	strike	struck	struck,
seek	sought	sought			stricken
sell	sold	sold	strive	strove	striven
send	sent	sent	swear	swore	sworn
sew	sewed	sewn	sweep	swept	swept
shake	shook	shaken	swell	swelled	swollen,
shear	sheared	shorn,			swelled
		sheared	swim	swam	swum
shed	shed	shed	swing	swung	swung
shine	shone	shone	take	took	taken
shoot	shot	shot	teach	taught	taught
show	showed	shown	tear	tore	torn
shrink	shrank	shrunk	tell	told	told
shut	shut	shut	think	thought	thought
sing	sang	sung	throw	threw	thrown
sink	sank	sunk	thrust	thrust	thrust
sit	sat	sat	tread	trod	trodden
slay	slew	slain	wake	woke,	woken,
sleep	slept	slept		waked	waked
slide	slid	slid	wear	wore	worn
sling	slung	slung	weave	wove,	woven,
slit	slit	slit		weaved	weaved
smell	smelt,	smelt,	wed	wedded,	wedded,
	smelled	smelled		wed	wed
sow	sowed	sown,	weep	wept	wept
		sowed	win	won	won
speak	spoke	spoken	wind	wound	wound
speed	sped,	sped,	wring	wrung	wrung
	speeded	speeded	write	wrote	written

I NUMERI

		NUMBERS
uno(a)	1	one
due	2	two
tre	3	three
quattro	4	four
cinque	5	five
sei	6	six
sette	7	seven
otto	8	eight
nove	9	nine
dieci	10	ten
undici	11	eleven
dodici	12	twelve
tredici	13	thirteen
quattordici	14	fourteen
quindici	15	fifteen
sedici	16	sixteen
diciassette	17	seventeen
diciotto	18	eighteen
diciannove	19	nineteen
venti	20	twenty
ventuno	21	twenty-one
ventidue	22	twenty-two
ventitré	23	twenty-three
ventotto	28	twenty-eight
trenta	30	thirty
quaranta	40	forty
cinquanta	50	fifty
sessanta	60	sixty
settanta	70	seventy
ottanta	80	eighty
novanta	90	ninety
cento	100	a hundred
cento uno, centouno	101	a hundred and one
duecento	200	two hundred
mille	1 000	a thousand
milleduecentodue	1 202	one thousand two hundred and two
cinquemila	5000	five thousand
un milione	1 000 000	a million

I NUMERI

NUMBERS

primo(a)	first, 1st
secondo(a)	second, 2nd
terzo(a)	third, 3rd
quarto(a)	fourth, 4th
quinto(a)	fifth, 5th
sesto(a)	sixth, 6th
settimo(a)	seventh
ottavo(a)	eighth
nono(a)	ninth
decimo(a)	tenth
undicesimo(a)	eleventh
dodicesimo(a)	twelfth
tredicesimo(a)	thirteenth
quattordicesimo(a)	fourteenth
quindicesimo(a)	fifteenth
sedicesimo(a)	sixteenth
diciassettesimo(a)	seventeenth
diciottesimo(a)	eighteenth
diciannovesimo(a)	nineteenth
ventesimo(a)	twentieth
ventunesimo(a)	twenty-first
ventiduesimo(a)	twenty-second
ventitreesimo(a)	twenty-third
ventottesimo(a)	twenty-eighth
trentesimo(a)	thirtieth
centesimo(a)	hundredth
centunesimo(a)	hundred-and-first
millesimo(a)	thousandth
milionesimo(a)	millionth

FRAZIONI

mezzo
terzo
due terzi
quarto
quinto
zero virgola cinque, 0,5
tre virgola quattro, 3,4
dieci per cento
cento per cento

FRACTIONS

half
third
two thirds
quarter
fifth
(nought) point five, 0.5
three point four, 3.4
ten per cent
a hundred per cent

ESEMPI

abita al numero dieci
si trova nel capitolo sette, a pagina sette
abita al terzo piano
arrivò quarto
scala uno a venticinquemila

EXAMPLES

he lives at number 10
it's in chapter 7, on page 7
he lives on the 3rd floor
he came in 4th
scale 1:25,000

L'ORA

THE TIME

che ora è?, che ore sono?	*what time is it?*
è..., sono...	*it's...*
mezzanotte	midnight
l'una (di notte)	one o'clock (in the morning), one (a.m.)
le tre del mattino	three o'clock (in the morning), three (a.m.)
l'una e cinque	five past one
l'una e dieci	ten past one
l'una e un quarto, l'una e quindici	a quarter past one, one fifteen
l'una e venticinque	twenty-five past one, one twenty-five
l'una e mezzo or mezza, l'una e trenta	half past one, one thirty
le due meno venticinque, l'una e trentacinque	twenty-five to two, one thirty-five
le due meno venti, l'una e quaranta	twenty to two, one forty
le due meno un quarto, l'una e tre quarti	a quarter to two, one forty-five
le due meno dieci, l'una e cinquanta	ten to two, one fifty
le dodici, mezzogiorno	twelve o'clock, midday, noon
l'una, le tredici	one o'clock (in the afternoon), one (p.m.)
le sette (di sera), le diciannove	seven o'clock (in the evening), seven (p.m.)
a che ora?	*at what time?*
a mezzanotte	at midnight
all'una, alle tredici	at one o'clock
fra venti minuti	in twenty minutes
venti minuti fa	twenty minutes ago

LA DATA	**DATES**
oggi	today
ogni giorno, tutti i giorni	every day
ieri	yesterday
stamattina	this morning
domani notte; domani sera	tomorrow night
l'altroieri notte; l'altroieri sera	the night before last
l'altroieri	the day before yesterday
ieri notte; ieri sera	last night
due giorni/sei anni fa	two days/six years ago
domani pomeriggio	tomorrow afternoon
dopodomani	the day after tomorrow
tutti i giovedì, di or il giovedì	every Thursday, on Thursdays
ci va di or il venerdì	he goes on Fridays
'chiuso il mercoledì'	'closed on Wednesdays'
dal lunedì al venerdì	from Monday to Friday
per giovedì, entro giovedì	by Thursday
un sabato di marzo	one Saturday in March
tra una settimana	in a week's time
martedì a otto	a week next or on Tuesday
questa/la prossima/la scorsa settimana	this/next/last week
tra due settimane, tra quindici giorni	in two weeks or a fortnight
lunedì a quindici	two weeks on Monday
il primo/l'ultimo venerdì del mese	the first/last Friday of the month
il mese prossimo	next month
l'anno scorso	last year
il primo giugno	the 1st of June, June first
il due ottobre	the 2nd of October or October 2nd
sono nato nel 1987	I was born in 1987
il suo compleano è il 5 giugno	his birthday is on 5th June (BRIT) or June 5th (US)
il 18 agosto	on 18th August (BRIT) or August 18th (US)
nel 2016	in 2016
nella primavera del '94	in the Spring of '94
dal 19 al 3	from the 19th to the 3rd
quanti ne abbiamo oggi?	what's the date? or what date is it today?
oggi è il 15	today's date is the 15th or today is the 15th

1988 – millenovecentottantotto	1988 – nineteen eighty-eight
2016 – duemilasedici	2016 – two thousand and sixteen
10 anni esatti	10 years to the day
alla fine del mese	at the end of the month
la settimana del 30/7	week ending 30/7
giornalmente *or* al giorno	daily
settimanalmente *or* alla settimana	weekly
mensilmente, al mese	monthly
annualmente *or* all'anno	annually
due volte alla settimana/al mese/all'anno	twice a week/month/year
bimestralmente	bi-monthly
nel 4 a.C.	in 4 B.C. *or* B.C. 4
nel 79 d.C.	in 79 A.D. *or* A.D. 79
nel tredicesimo secolo	in the 13th century
negli anni '80	in *or* during the 80s
nel 1990 e rotti	in 1990 something

LA DATA NELLE LETTERE
9 ottobre 2016

HEADINGS OF LETTERS
9th October 2016 *or* 9 October 2016

Italiano – Inglese

Italian – English

a

A *abbr* (= *autostrada*) ≈ M (*BRIT*)

◯ **PAROLA CHIAVE**

a (*a* + *il* = **al**, *a* + *lo* = **allo**, *a* + *l'* = **all'**, *a* + *la* = **alla**, *a* + *i* = **ai**, *a* + *gli* = **agli**, *a* + *le* = **alle**) *prep*
1 (*stato in luogo*) at; (: *in*) in; **essere alla stazione** to be at the station; **essere a casa/a scuola/a Roma** to be at home/at school/in Rome; **è a 10 km da qui** it's 10 km from here, it's 10 km away
2 (*moto a luogo*) to; **andare a casa/a scuola/alla stazione** to go home/to school/to the station
3 (*tempo*) at; (*epoca, stagione*) in; **alle cinque** at five (o'clock); **a mezzanotte/Natale** at midnight/Christmas; **al mattino** in the morning; **a maggio/primavera** in May/spring; **a cinquant'anni** at fifty (years of age); **a domani!** see you tomorrow!
4 (*complemento di termine*) to; **dare qc a qn** to give sb sth
5 (*mezzo, modo*) with; by; **a piedi/cavallo** on foot/horseback; **fatto a mano** made by hand, handmade; **una barca a motore** a motorboat; **a uno a uno** one by one; **all'italiana** the Italian way, in the Italian fashion
6 (*rapporto*) a, per; (: *con prezzi*) at; **prendo 2000 euro al mese** I get 2000 euro a *o* per month; **pagato a ore** paid by the hour; **vendere qc a 2 euro il chilo** to sell sth at 2 euros a *o* per kilo

abbagli'ante [abbaʎˈʎante] *ag* dazzling; **abbaglianti** *smpl* (*Aut*): **accendere gli abbaglianti** to put one's headlights on full (*BRIT*) *o* high (*US*) beam
abbagli'are [abbaʎˈʎare] /27/ *vt* to dazzle; (*illudere*) to delude

abbai'are /19/ *vi* to bark
abbando'nare /72/ *vt* to leave, abandon, desert; (*trascurare*) to neglect; (*rinunciare a*) to abandon, give up; **abbandonarsi** *vpr* to let o.s. go; **abbandonarsi a** (*ricordi, vizio*) to give o.s. up to
abbas'sare /72/ *vt* to lower; (*radio*) to turn down; **abbassarsi** *vpr* (*chinarsi*) to stoop; (*livello, sole*) to go down; (*fig: umiliarsi*) to demean o.s.; **~ i fari** (*Aut*) to dip (*BRIT*) *o* dim (*US*) one's lights
ab'basso *escl*: **~ il re!** down with the king!
abbas'tanza [abbas'tantsa] *av* (*a sufficienza*) enough; (*alquanto*) quite, rather, fairly; **non è ~ furbo** he's not shrewd enough; **un vino ~ dolce** quite a sweet wine; **averne ~ di qn/qc** to have had enough of sb/sth
ab'battere /1/ *vt* (*muro, casa, ostacolo*) to knock down; (*albero*) to fell; (: *vento*) to bring down; (*bestie da macello*) to slaughter; (*cane, cavallo*) to destroy, put down; (*selvaggina, aereo*) to shoot down; (*fig: malattia, disgrazia*) to lay low; **abbattersi** *vpr* (*avvilirsi*) to lose heart; **abbat'tuto, -a** *ag* (*fig*) depressed
abba'zia [abbat'tsia] *sf* abbey
'abbia *vb vedi* **avere**
abbi'ente *ag* well-to-do, well-off; **abbienti** *smpl*: **gli abbienti** the well-to-do
abbiglia'mento [abbiʎʎa'mento] *sm* dress *no pl*; (*indumenti*) clothes *pl*; (*industria*) clothing industry
abbi'nare /72/ *vt*: **~ (con** *o* **a)** to combine (with)
abboc'care /20/ *vi* (*pesce*) to bite; (*tubi*) to join; **~ (all'amo)** (*fig*) to swallow the bait
abbona'mento *sm* subscription; (*alle ferrovie ecc*) season ticket; **fare l'~ (a)** to take out a subscription (to)
abbo'nare /72/ *vt* to deduct; **abbonarsi** *vpr*: **abbonarsi a un giornale** to take out a subscription to a newspaper; **abbonarsi al teatro/alle ferrovie** to take out a season ticket for the theatre/the train
abbon'dante *ag* abundant, plentiful; (*giacca*) roomy
abbon'danza [abbon'dantsa] *sf* abundance; plenty
abbor'dabile *ag* (*persona*) approachable; (*prezzo*) reasonable
abbotto'nare /72/ *vt* to button up, do up
abbracci'are [abbrat'tʃare] /14/ *vt* to embrace; (*persona*) to hug, embrace; (*professione*) to take up; (*contenere*) to include; **abbracciarsi** *vpr* to hug *o* embrace (one another); **ab'braccio** *sm* hug, embrace
abbrevi'are /19/ *vt* to shorten; (*parola*) to abbreviate

abbreviazi'one [abbrevjat'tsjone] *sf* abbreviation

abbron'zante [abbron'dzante] *ag* tanning, sun *cpd*

abbron'zare [abbron'dzare] /72/ *vt* to tan; **abbronzarsi** *vpr* to tan, get a tan

abbron'zato, -a [abbron'dzato] *ag* (sun) tanned

abbrusto'lire /55/ *vt* (*pane*) to toast; (*caffè*) to roast; **abbrustolirsi** *vpr* to toast; (*fig, al sole*) to soak up the sun

abbuf'farsi /72/ *vpr* (*fam*): **~ (di qc)** to stuff o.s. (with sth)

abdi'care /20/ *vi* to abdicate; **~ a** to give up, renounce

a'bete *sm* fir (tree); **~ rosso** spruce

'abile *ag* (*idoneo*): **~ (a qc/a fare qc)** fit (for sth/to do sth); (*capace*) able; (*astuto*) clever; (*accorto*) skilful; **~ al servizio militare** fit for military service; **abilità** *sf inv* ability; cleverness; skill

a'bisso *sm* abyss, gulf

abi'tante *smf* inhabitant

abi'tare /72/ *vt* to live in, dwell in ▷ *vi*: **~ in campagna/a Roma** to live in the country/ in Rome; **dove abita?** where do you live?; **abitazi'one** *sf* residence; house

'abito *sm* dress *no pl*; (*da uomo*) suit; (*da donna*) dress; (*abitudine, disposizione, Rel*) habit; **abiti** *smpl* (*vestiti*) clothes; **in ~ da sera** in evening dress

abitu'ale *ag* usual, habitual; (*cliente*) regular

abitual'mente *av* usually, normally

abitu'are /72/ *vt*: **~ qn a** to get sb used o accustomed to; **abituarsi a** to get used to, accustom o.s. to

abitudi'nario, -a *ag* of fixed habits ▷ *sm/f* creature of habit

abi'tudine *sf* habit; **aver l'~ di fare qc** to be in the habit of doing sth; **d'~** usually; **per ~** from o out of habit

abo'lire /55/ *vt* to abolish; (*Dir*) to repeal

abor'tire /55/ *vi* (*Med*) to miscarry, have a miscarriage; (: *deliberatamente*) to have an abortion; (*fig*) to miscarry, fail; **a'borto** *sm* miscarriage; abortion

ABS [abi'esse] *sigla m* (= *Anti-Blockier System*) ABS = **anti-lock braking system**

'abside *sf* apse

abu'sare /72/ *vi*: **~ di** to abuse, misuse; (*approfittare, violare*) to take advantage of; **~ dell'alcool/dei cibi** to drink/eat to excess

abu'sivo, -a *ag* unauthorized, unlawful; (*occupante*) **~** (*di una casa*) squatter

　Attenzione! In inglese esiste la parola *abusive*, che però vuol dire *ingiurioso*.

a.C. *abbr* (= *avanti Cristo*) BC

a'cacia, -cie [a'katʃa] *sf* (*Bot*) acacia

ac'cadde *vb vedi* **accadere**

acca'demia *sf* (*società*) learned society; (*scuola: d'arte, militare*) academy

acca'dere /18/ *vb impers* to happen, occur

accal'dato *ag* hot

accalo'rarsi /61/ *vpr* (*fig*) to get excited

accampa'mento *sm* camp

accam'pare /72/ *vt* to encamp; **accamparsi** *vpr* to camp

acca'nirsi /55/ *vpr* (*infierire*) to rage; (*ostinarsi*) to persist; **acca'nito, -a** *ag* (*odio, gelosia*) fierce, bitter; (*lavoratore*) assiduous; (*giocatore, fumatore*) inveterate

ac'canto *av* near, nearby; **~ a** *prep* near, beside, close to

accanto'nare /72/ *vt* (*problema*) to shelve; (*somma*) to set aside

accappa'toio *sm* bathrobe

accarez'zare [akkaret'tsare] /72/ *vt* to caress, stroke, fondle; (*fig*) to toy with

acca'sarsi /27/ *vpr* to set up house; to get married

accasci'arsi [akkaʃ'ʃarsi] /14/ *vpr* to collapse; (*fig*) to lose heart

accat'tone, -a *sm/f* beggar

accaval'lare /72/ *vt* (*gambe*) to cross

acce'care [attʃe'kare] /20/ *vt* to blind ▷ *vi* to go blind

ac'cedere [at'tʃɛdere] /29/ *vi*: **~ a** to enter; (*richiesta*) to grant, accede to

accele'rare [attʃele'rare] /72/ *vt* to speed up ▷ *vi* (*Aut*) to accelerate; **~ il passo** to quicken one's pace; **accelera'tore** *sm* (*Aut*) accelerator

ac'cendere [at'tʃendere] /2/ *vt* (*fuoco, sigaretta*) to light; (*luce, televisione*) to put o switch o turn on; (*Aut: motore*) to switch on; (*Comm: conto*) to open; (*fig: suscitare*) to inflame, stir up; **accen'dino, accendi'sigaro** *sm* (*cigarette*) lighter

accen'nare [attʃen'nare] /72/ *vt* (*Mus*) to pick out the notes of; to hum ▷ *vi*: **~ a** (*fig*) (*alludere a*) to hint at; (*far atto di*) to make as if; **~ un saluto** (*con la mano*) to make as if to wave; (*col capo*) to half nod; **accenna a piovere** it looks as if it's going to rain

ac'cenno [at'tʃenno] *sm* (*cenno*) sign; nod; (*allusione*) hint

accensi'one [attʃen'sjone] *sf* (*vedi accendere*) lighting; switching on; opening; (*Aut*) ignition

ac'cento [at'tʃento] *sm* accent; (*Fonetica, fig*) stress; (*inflessione*) tone (of voice)

accentu'are [attʃentu'are] /72/ *vt* to stress, emphasize; **accentuarsi** *vpr* to become more noticeable

accerchi'are [attʃer'kjare] /19/ *vt* to surround, encircle

accerta'mento [attʃerta'mento] *sm* check; assessment

accer'tare [attʃer'tare] /72/ vt to ascertain; (verificare) to check; (reddito) to assess; **accertarsi** vpr: **accertarsi (di qc/che)** to make sure (of sth/that)

ac'ceso, -a [at'tʃeso] pp di **accendere** ▷ ag lit; on; open; (colore) bright

acces'sibile [attʃes'sibile] ag (luogo) accessible; (persona) approachable; (prezzo) reasonable

ac'cesso [at'tʃɛsso] sm (anche Inform) access; (Med) attack, fit; (impulso violento) fit, outburst

acces'sorio, -a [attʃes'sɔrjo] ag secondary; **accessori** smpl accessories

ac'cetta [at'tʃetta] sf hatchet

accet'tabile [attʃet'tabile] ag acceptable

accet'tare [attʃet'tare] /72/ vt to accept; **~ di fare qc** to agree to do sth; **accettazi'one** sf acceptance; (locale di servizio pubblico) reception; **accettazione bagagli** (Aer) check-in (desk)

acchiap'pare [akkjap'pare] /72/ vt to catch

acciaie'ria [attʃaje'ria] sf steelworks sg

acci'aio [at'tʃajo] sm steel

acciden'tato, -a [attʃiden'tato] ag (terreno ecc) uneven

accigli'ato, -a [attʃiʎ'ʎato] ag frowning

ac'cingersi [at'tʃindʒersi] /54/ vpr: **~ a fare** to be about to do

acciuf'fare [attʃuf'fare] /72/ vt to seize, catch

acci'uga, -ghe [at'tʃuga] sf anchovy

ac'cludere /3/ vt to enclose

accocco'larsi /72/ vpr to crouch

accogli'ente [akkoʎ'ʎɛnte] ag welcoming, friendly

ac'cogliere /23/ vt (ricevere) to receive; (dare il benvenuto) to welcome; (approvare) to agree to, accept; (contenere) to hold, accommodate

ac'colgo ecc vb vedi **accogliere**

ac'colsi ecc vb vedi **accogliere**

accoltel'lare /72/ vt to knife, stab

accomoda'mento sm agreement, settlement

accomo'dante ag accommodating

accomo'dare /72/ vt to repair; **accomodarsi** vpr (sedersi) to sit down; (fig: risolversi: situazione) to work out; **si accomodi!** (venga avanti) come in!; (si sieda) take a seat!

accompagna'mento [akkompaɲɲa'mento] sm (Mus) accompaniment

accompa'gnare [akkompaɲ'ɲare] /15/ vt to accompany, come o go with; (Mus) to accompany; (unire) to couple; **~ la porta** to close the door gently

accompagna'tore, -'trice sm/f companion; **~ turistico** courier

acconcia'tura [akkontʃa'tura] sf hairstyle

accondiscen'dente [akkondiʃʃen'dɛnte] ag affable

acconsen'tire /17/ vi: **~ (a)** to agree o consent (to)

acconten'tare /72/ vt to satisfy; **accontentarsi** vpr: **accontentarsi di** to be satisfied with, content o.s. with

ac'conto sm part payment; **pagare una somma in ~** to pay a sum of money as a deposit

acco'rato, -a ag heartfelt

accorci'are [akkor'tʃare] /14/ vt to shorten; **accorciarsi** vpr to become shorter

accor'dare /72/ vt to reconcile; (colori) to match; (Mus) to tune; (Ling): **~ qc con qc** to make sth agree with sth; (Dir) to grant; **accordarsi** vpr to agree, come to an agreement; (colori) to match

ac'cordo sm agreement; (armonia) harmony; (Mus) chord; **essere d'~** to agree; **andare d'~** to get on well together; **d'~!** all right!, agreed!; **~ commerciale** trade agreement

ac'corgersi [ak'kɔrdʒersi] /4/ vpr: **~ di** to notice; (fig) to realize

ac'correre /28/ vi to run up

ac'corto, -a pp di **accorgersi** ▷ ag shrewd; **stare ~** to be on one's guard

accos'tare /72/ vt (avvicinarsi a) to approach; (socchiudere: imposte) to half-close; (: porta) to leave ajar ▷ vi: (Naut) to come alongside; **accostarsi** vpr: **accostarsi a** to draw near, approach; (idee politiche) to come to agree with; **~ qc a** (avvicinare) to bring sth near to, put sth near to

accredi'tare /72/ vt (notizia) to confirm the truth of; (Comm) to credit; (diplomatico) to accredit

ac'credito sm (Comm: atto) crediting; (: effetto) credit

accucci'arsi [akkut'tʃarsi] /14/ vpr (cane) to lie down

accu'dire /55/ vi: **~ a** to attend to

accumu'lare /72/ vt to accumulate; **accumularsi** vpr to accumulate; (Finanza) to accrue

accu'rato, -a ag (diligente) careful; (preciso) accurate

ac'cusa sf accusation; (Dir) charge; **la pubblica ~** the prosecution

accu'sare /72/ vt: **~ qn di qc** to accuse sb of sth; (Dir) to charge sb with sth; **~ ricevuta di** (Comm) to acknowledge receipt of

accusa'tore, -'trice sm/f accuser ▷ sm (Dir) prosecutor

a'cerbo, -a [a'tʃerbo] *ag* bitter; (*frutta*) sour, unripe; (*persona*) immature

'acero ['atʃero] *sm* maple

a'cerrimo, -a [a'tʃerrimo] *ag* very fierce

a'ceto [a'tʃeto] *sm* vinegar

ace'tone [atʃe'tone] *sm* nail varnish remover

'A.C.I. ['atʃi] *sigla m* (= *Automobile Club d'Italia*) ≈ AA (BRIT)

'acido, -a ['atʃido] *ag* (*sapore*) acid, sour; (*Chim*) acid ▷ *sm* (*Chim*) acid

'acino ['atʃino] *sm* berry; **~ d'uva** grape

'acne *sf* acne

'acqua *sf* water; (*pioggia*) rain; **acque** *sfpl* (*di mare, fiume ecc*) waters; **fare ~** (*Naut*) to leak, take in water; **~ in bocca!** mum's the word!; **~ corrente** running water; **~ dolce** fresh water; **~ minerale** mineral water; **~ potabile** drinking water; **~ salata** o **salmastra** salt water; **~ tonica** tonic water

a'cquaio *sm* sink

acqua'ragia [akkwa'radʒa] *sf* turpentine

a'cquario *sm* aquarium; **A~** Aquarius

acquas'cooter [akkwas'cuter] *sm inv* Jet Ski®

a'cquatico, -a, -ci, -che *ag* aquatic; (*sport, sci*) water *cpd*

acqua'vite *sf* brandy

acquaz'zone [akkwat'tsone] *sm* cloudburst, heavy shower

acque'dotto *sm* aqueduct; waterworks *pl*, water system

acque'rello *sm* watercolour

acqui'rente *smf* purchaser, buyer

acquis'tare /72/ *vt* to purchase, buy; (*fig*) to gain; **a'cquisto** *sm* purchase; **fare acquisti** to go shopping

acquo'lina *sf*: **far venire l'~ in bocca a qn** to make sb's mouth water

a'crobata, -i, -e *sm/f* acrobat

a'culeo *sm* (*Zool*) sting; (*Bot*) prickle

a'cume *sm* acumen, perspicacity

a'custico, -a, -ci, -che *ag* acoustic ▷ *sf* (*scienza*) acoustics *sg*; (*di una sala*) acoustics *pl*; **apparecchio ~** hearing aid; **cornetto ~** ear trumpet

a'cuto, -a *ag* (*appuntito*) sharp, pointed; (*suono, voce*) shrill, piercing; (*Mat, Ling, Med*) acute; (*Mus*) high-pitched; (*fig: dolore, desiderio*) intense; (: *perspicace*) acute, keen

a'dagio [a'dadʒo] *av* slowly ▷ *sm* (*Mus*) adagio; (*proverbio*) adage, saying

adatta'mento *sm* adaptation

adat'tare /72/ *vt* to adapt; (*sistemare*) to fit; **adattarsi** *vpr*: **adattarsi (a)** (*ambiente, tempi*) to adapt (to); (*essere adatto*) to be suitable (for)

a'datto, -a *ag*: **~ (a)** suitable (for), right (for)

addebi'tare /72/ *vt*: **~ qc a qn** to debit sb with sth

ad'debito *sm* (*Comm*) debit

adden'tare /72/ *vt* to bite into

adden'trarsi /72/ *vpr*: **~ in** to penetrate, go into

addestra'mento *sm* training

addes'trare /72/ *vt* to train

ad'detto, -a *ag*: **~ a** (*persona*) assigned to; (*oggetto*) intended for ▷ *sm* employee; (*funzionario*) attaché; **~ commerciale/stampa** commercial/press attaché; **gli addetti ai lavori** authorized personnel; (*fig*) those in the know

ad'dio *sm, escl* goodbye, farewell

addirit'tura *av* (*veramente*) really, absolutely; (*perfino*) even; (*direttamente*) directly, right away

addi'tare /72/ *vt* to point out; (*fig*) to expose

addi'tivo *sm* additive

addizi'one *sf* addition

addob'bare /72/ *vt* to decorate; **ad'dobbo** *sm* decoration

addolo'rare /72/ *vt* to pain, grieve; **addolorarsi** *vpr*: **addolorarsi (per)** to be distressed (by)

addolo'rato, -a *ag* distressed, upset; **l'Addolorata** (*Rel*) Our Lady of Sorrows

ad'dome *sm* abdomen

addomesti'care /20/ *vt* to tame

addomi'nale *ag* abdominal; **(muscoli) addominali** stomach muscles

addormen'tare /72/ *vt* to put to sleep; **addormentarsi** *vpr* to fall asleep, go to sleep

ad'dosso *av* on; **~ a** (*sopra*) on; (*molto vicino*) right next to; **mettersi ~ il cappotto** to put one's coat on; **stare ~ a qn** (*fig*) to breathe down sb's neck; **dare ~ a qn** (*fig*) to attack sb

adegu'are /72/ *vt*: **~ qc a** to adjust sth to; **adeguarsi** *vpr* to adapt

adegu'ato, -a *ag* adequate; (*conveniente*) suitable; (*equo*) fair

a'dempiere /24/ *vt* to fulfil, carry out

ade'rente *ag* adhesive; (*vestito*) close-fitting ▷ *smf* follower

ade'rire /55/ *vi* (*stare attaccato*) to adhere, stick; **~ a** to adhere to, stick to; (*fig: società, partito*) to join; (*opinione*) to support; (*richiesta*) to agree to

adesi'one *sf* adhesion; (*fig*) agreement, acceptance; **ade'sivo, -a** *ag, sm* adhesive

a'desso *av* (*ora*) now; (*or ora, poco fa*) just now; (*tra poco*) any moment now

adia'cente [adja'tʃente] *ag* adjacent

adi'bire /55/ *vt* (*usare*): **~ qc a** to turn sth into

adole'scente [adoleʃʃente] *ag, smf* adolescent

adope'rare /72/ *vt* to use

do'rare /72/ vt to adore; (Rel) to adore, worship

dot'tare /72/ vt to adopt; (decisione, provvedimenti) to pass; **adot'tivo, -a** ag (genitori) adoptive; (figlio, patria) adopted; **adozio'ne** sf adoption; **adozione a distanza** child sponsorship

dri'atico, -a, -ci, -che ag Adriatic ▷ sm: **l'A~, il mare A~** the Adriatic, the Adriatic Sea

DSL sigla m ADSL = **asymmetric digital subscriber line**

du'lare /72/ vt to flatter

'dultero, -a ag adulterous ▷ sm/f adulterer (adulteress)

'dulto, -a ag adult; (fig) mature ▷ sm adult, grown-up

'ereo, -a ag air cpd; (radice) aerial ▷ sm aerial; (aeroplano) plane; **~ da caccia** fighter (plane); **~ di linea** airliner; **~ a reazione** jet (plane); **ae'robica** sf aerobics sg;

aero'nautica sf (scienza) aeronautics sg; **aeronautica militare** air force

ero'porto sm airport

ero'sol sm inv aerosol

'fa sf sultriness

ffabile ag affable

ffaccen'dato, -a [affatt∫en'dato] ag (persona) busy

ffacci'arsi [affat't∫arsi] /14/ vpr: **~ (a)** to appear (at)

ffa'mato, -a ag starving; (fig): **~ (di)** eager (for)

ffan'noso, -a ag (respiro) difficult; (fig) troubled, anxious

ffare sm (faccenda) matter, affair; (Comm) piece of business, (business) deal; (occasione) bargain; (Dir) case; (fam: cosa) thing; **affari** smpl (Comm) business sg; **ministro degli Affari Esteri** Foreign Secretary (BRIT), Secretary of State (US)

ffasci'nante [affa∫∫i'nante] ag fascinating

ffasci'nare [affa∫∫i'nare] /72/ vt to bewitch; (fig) to charm, fascinate

ffati'care /20/ vt to tire; **affaticarsi** vpr (durar fatica) to tire o.s. out; **affati'cato, -a** ag tired

ffatto av completely; **non ... ~** not ... at all; **niente ~** not at all

ffer'mare /72/ vt (dichiarare) to maintain, affirm; **affermarsi** vpr to assert o.s., make one's name known; **affer'mato, -a** ag established, well-known; **affermazi'one** sf affirmation, assertion; (successo) achievement

ffer'rare /72/ vt to seize, grasp; (fig: idea) to grasp; **afferrarsi** vpr: **afferrarsi a** to cling to

affet'tare /72/ vt (tagliare a fette) to slice; (ostentare) to affect

affetta'trice [affetta'trit∫e] sf meat slicer

affet'tivo, -a ag emotional, affective

af'fetto sm affection; **affettu'oso, -a** ag affectionate

affezio'narsi [affettsjo'narsi] /72/ vpr: **~ a** to grow fond of

affezio'nato, -a [affettsjo'nato] ag: **~ a qn/qc** fond of sb/sth; (attaccato) attached to sb/sth

affia'tato, -a ag: **essere affiatati** to work well together o get on

affib'bi'are /19/ vt (fig: dare) to give

affi'dabile ag reliable

affida'mento sm (Dir: di bambino) custody; (fiducia): **fare ~ su qn** to rely on sb; **non dà nessun ~** he's not to be trusted

affi'dare /72/ vt: **~ qc o qn a qn** to entrust sth o sb to sb; **affidarsi** vpr: **affidarsi a** to place one's trust in

affi'lare /72/ vt to sharpen

affi'lato, -a ag (gen) sharp; (volto, naso) thin

affinché [affin'ke] cong in order that, so that

affit'tare /72/ vt (dare in affitto) to let, rent (out); (prendere in affitto) to rent; **af'fitto** sm rent; (contratto) lease

af'fliggere [af'flidd∫ere] /104/ vt to torment; **affliggersi** vpr to grieve

af'flissi ecc vb vedi **affliggere**

afflosci'arsi [afflo∫'∫arsi] /14/ vpr to go limp

afflu'ente sm tributary

affo'gare /80/ vt, vi to drown

affol'lare /72/ vt, **affol'larsi** vpr to crowd; **affol'lato, -a** ag crowded

affon'dare /72/ vt to sink

affran'care /20/ vt to free, liberate; (Amm) to redeem; (lettera) to stamp; (: meccanicamente) to frank (BRIT), meter (US)

af'fresco, -schi sm fresco

affret'tare /72/ vt to quicken; **affrettarsi** vpr to hurry; **affrettarsi a fare qc** to hurry o hasten to do sth

affret'tato, -a ag (veloce: passo, ritmo) quick, fast; (frettoloso: decisione) hurried, hasty; (: lavoro) rushed

affron'tare /72/ vt (pericolo ecc) to face; (nemico) to confront; **affrontarsi** vpr (reciproco) to confront each other

affumi'cato, -a ag (prosciutto, aringa ecc) smoked

affuso'lato, -a ag tapering

Af'ghanistan sm: **l'~** Afghanistan

a'foso, -a ag sultry, close

'Africa sf: **l'~** Africa; **afri'cano, -a** ag, sm/f African

a'genda [a'dʒɛnda] *sf* diary

> Attenzione! In inglese esiste la parola *agenda*, che però vuol dire *ordine del giorno*.

a'gente [a'dʒɛnte] *sm* agent; **~ di cambio** stockbroker; **~ di polizia** police officer; **~ segreto** secret agent; **agen'zia** *sf* agency; (*succursale*) branch; **agenzia di collocamento** employment agency; **agenzia immobiliare** estate agent's (office) (*BRIT*), real estate office (*US*); **agenzia di stampa** press agency; **agenzia viaggi** travel agency

agevo'lare [adʒevo'lare] /72/ *vt* to facilitate, make easy

agevolazi'one [adʒevolat'tsjone] *sf* (*facilitazione economica*) facility; **~ di pagamento** payment on easy terms; **agevolazioni creditizie** credit facilities; **agevolazioni fiscali** tax concessions

a'gevole [a'dʒevole] *ag* easy; (*strada*) smooth

aggranci'are [aggan'tʃare] /14/ *vt* to hook up; (*Ferr*) to couple

ag'geggio [ad'dʒeddʒo] *sm* gadget, contraption

agget'tivo [addʒet'tivo] *sm* adjective

agghiacci'ante [aggjat'tʃante] *ag* chilling

aggior'nare [addʒor'nare] /72/ *vt* (*opera, manuale*) to bring up-to-date; (*seduta ecc*) to postpone; **aggiornarsi** *vpr* to bring (o keep) o.s. up-to-date; **aggior'nato, -a** *ag* up-to-date

aggi'rare [addʒi'rare] /72/ *vt* to go round; (*fig: ingannare*) to trick; **aggirarsi** *vpr* to wander about; **il prezzo s'aggira sul milione** the price is around the million mark

aggi'ungere [ad'dʒundʒere] /5/ *vt* to add; (*Inform*) **grazie per avermi aggiunto (come amico)** thanks for the add

aggi'unsi *ecc* [ad'dʒunsi] *vb vedi* **aggiungere**

aggrap'parsi /72/ *vpr*: **~ a** to cling to

aggra'vare /72/ *vt* (*aumentare*) to increase; (*appesantire: anche fig*) to weigh down, make heavy; (*pena*) to make worse; **aggravarsi** *vpr* to worsen, become worse

aggre'dire /55/ *vt* to attack, assault

aggressi'one *sf* aggression; (*atto*) attack, assault

aggres'sivo, -a *ag* aggressive

aggres'sore *sm* aggressor, attacker

aggrot'tare /72/ *vt*: **~ le sopracciglia** to frown

aggrovigli'are /27/ *vt* to tangle; **aggrovigliarsi** *vpr* (*fig*) to become complicated

aggu'ato *sm* trap; (*imboscata*) ambush; **tendere un ~ a qn** to set a trap for sb

agguer'rito, -a *ag* fierce

agi'ato, -a [a'dʒato] *ag* (*vita*) easy; (*persona*) well-off, well-to-do

'agile ['adʒile] *ag* agile, nimble

'agio ['adʒo] *sm* ease, comfort; **agi** *smpl* comforts; **mettersi a proprio ~** to make o.s. at home *o* comfortable; **dare ~ a qn di fare qc** to give sb the chance of doing sth

a'gire [a'dʒire] /55/ *vi* to act; (*esercitare un'azione*) to take effect; (*Tecn*) to work, function; **~ contro qn** (*Dir*) to take action against sb

agi'tare [adʒi'tare] /72/ *vt* (*bottiglia*) to shake; (*mano, fazzoletto*) to wave; (*fig: turbare*) to disturb; (: *incitare*) to stir (up); (: *dibattere*) to discuss; **agitarsi** *vpr* (*mare*) to be rough; (*malato, dormitore*) to toss and turn; (*bambino*) to fidget; (*emozionarsi*) to get upset; (*Pol*) to agitate; **agi'tato, -a** *ag* rough; restless; fidgety; upset, perturbed

'aglio ['aʎʎo] *sm* garlic

a'gnello [aɲ'ɲɛllo] *sm* lamb

'ago (*pl* **aghi**) *sm* needle

ago'nistico, -a, -ci, -che *ag* athletic; (*fig*) competitive

agopun'tura *sf* acupuncture

a'gosto *sm* August

a'grario, -a *ag* agrarian, agricultural; (*riforma*) land *cpd*

a'gricolo, -a *ag* agricultural, farm *cpd*; **agricol'tore** *sm* farmer; **agricol'tura** *sf* agriculture, farming

agri'foglio [agri'fɔʎʎo] *sm* holly

agritu'rismo *sm* farm holidays *pl*

agro'dolce *ag* bittersweet; (*salsa*) sweet and sour

a'grume *sm* (*spesso al pl: pianta*) citrus; (: *frutto*) citrus fruit

a'guzzo, -a [a'guttso] *ag* sharp

'ahi *escl* (*dolore*) ouch!

'Aia *sf*: **L'~** The Hague

AIDS ['aids] *abbr m, abbr f* AIDS

airbag *sm inv* air bag

ai'rone *sm* heron

aiu'ola *sf* flower bed

aiu'tante *smf* assistant ▷ *sm* (*Mil*) adjutant; (*Naut*) master-at-arms; **~ di campo** aide-de-camp

aiu'tare /72/ *vt* to help; **~ qn (a fare)** to help sb (to do); **aiutarsi** *vpr* to help each other; **~ qn in qc/a fare qc** to help sb with sth/to do sth; **può aiutarmi?** can you help me?

ai'uto *sm* help, assistance, aid; (*aiutante*) assistant; **venire in ~ di qn** to come to sb's aid; **~ chirurgo** assistant surgeon

'ala (*pl* **ali**) *sf* wing; **fare ~** to fall back, make way; **~ destra/sinistra** (*Sport*) right/left wing

ala'bastro *sm* alabaster

a'lano *sm* Great Dane

'alba *sf* dawn

alba'nese *ag, smf, sm* Albanian

Alba'nia *sf*: l'~ Albania

albe'rato, -a *ag* (*viale, piazza*) lined with trees, tree-lined

al'bergo, -ghi *sm* hotel; ~ della gioventù youth hostel

'albero *sm* tree; (*Naut*) mast; (*Tecn*) shaft; ~ genealogico family tree; ~ a gomiti crankshaft; ~ maestro mainmast; ~ di Natale Christmas tree; ~ di trasmissione transmission shaft

albi'cocca, -che *sf* apricot

'album *sm* album; ~ da disegno sketch book

al'bume *sm* albumen

'alce ['altʃe] *sm* elk

'alcol *sm inv* = alcool

al'colico, -a, -ci, -che *ag* alcoholic ▷ *sm* alcoholic drink

alcoliz'zato, -a [alkolid'dzato] *sm/f* alcoholic

'alcool *sm inv* alcohol

al'cuno, -a *det* (*dav sm*: alcun + C, V, alcuno + s impura, gn, pn, ps, x, z; *dav sf*: alcuna + C, alcun' +V: nessuno): non ... ~ no, not any; alcuni, e *det pl, pron pl* some, a few; non c'è alcuna fretta there's no hurry, there isn't any hurry; senza alcun riguardo without any consideration

alfa'betico, -a, -ci, -che *ag* alphabetical

alfa'beto *sm* alphabet

'alga, -ghe *sf* seaweed *no pl*, alga

'algebra ['aldʒebra] *sf* algebra

Alge'ria [aldʒe'ria] *sf*: l'~ Algeria; alge'rino, -a *ag, sm/f* Algerian

ali'ante *sm* (*Aer*) glider

'alibi *sm inv* alibi

a'lice [a'litʃe] *sf* anchovy

ali'eno, -a *ag* (*avverso*): ~ (da) opposed (to), averse (to) ▷ *sm/f* alien

alimen'tare /72/ *vt* to feed; (*Tecn*) to feed, supply; (*fig*) to sustain ▷ *ag* food *cpd*; alimentari *smpl* foodstuffs; (*anche:* negozio di alimentari) grocer's shop; alimentazi'one *sf* feeding; supplying; sustaining; (*cibi*) diet

a'liquota *sf* share; ~ d'imposta tax rate

alis'cafo *sm* hydrofoil

'alito *sm* breath

all. *abbr* (= *allegato*) encl.

allaccia'mento [allattʃa'mento] *sm* (*Tecn*) connection

allacci'are [allat'tʃare] /14/ *vt* (*scarpe*) to tie, lace (up); (*cintura*) to do up, fasten; (*luce, gas*) to connect; (*amicizia*) to form

allaccia'tura [allattʃa'tura] *sf* fastening

alla'gare /80/ *vt*, alla'garsi *vpr* to flood

allar'gare /80/ *vt* to widen; (*vestito*) to let out; (*aprire*) to open; (*fig: dilatare*) to extend; allargarsi *vpr* (*gen*) to widen; (*scarpe, pantaloni*) to stretch; (*fig: problema, fenomeno*) to spread

allar'mare /72/ *vt* to alarm

al'larme *sm* alarm; ~ aereo air-raid warning

allat'tare /72/ *vt* to (breast-)feed

alle'anza [alle'antsa] *sf* alliance

alle'arsi /72/ *vpr* to form an alliance; alle'ato, -a *ag* allied ▷ *sm/f* ally

alle'gare /80/ *vt* (*accludere*) to enclose; (*Dir: citare*) to cite, adduce; (*denti*) to set on edge; alle'gato, -a *ag* enclosed ▷ *sm* enclosure; (*di e-mail*) attachment; in allegato enclosed

allegge'rire [alleddʒe'rire] /55/ *vt* to lighten, make lighter; (*fig: lavoro, tasse*) to reduce

alle'gria *sf* gaiety, cheerfulness

al'legro, -a *ag* cheerful, merry; (*un po' brillo*) merry, tipsy; (*vivace: colore*) bright ▷ *sm* (*Mus*) allegro

allena'mento *sm* training

alle'nare /72/ *vt*, alle'narsi *vpr* to train; allena'tore *sm* (*Sport*) trainer, coach

allen'tare /72/ *vt* to slacken; (*disciplina*) to relax; allentarsi *vpr* to become slack; (*ingranaggio*) to work loose

aller'gia, -'gie [aller'dʒia] *sf* allergy; al'lergico, -a, -ci, -che [al'lɛrdʒiko] *ag* allergic

alles'tire /55/ *vt* (*cena*) to prepare; (*esercito, nave*) to equip, fit out; (*spettacolo*) to stage

allet'tante *ag* attractive, alluring

alle'vare /72/ *vt* (*animale*) to breed, rear; (*bambino*) to bring up

allevi'are /19/ *vt* to alleviate

alli'bito, -a *ag* pale; disconcerted; astounded

alli'evo *sm* pupil; (*apprendista*) apprentice; ~ ufficiale cadet

alliga'tore *sm* alligator

alline'are /72/ *vt* (*persone, cose*) to line up; (*Tip*) to align; (*fig: economia, salari*) to adjust, align; allinearsi *vpr* to line up; (*fig: a idee*): allinearsi a to come into line with

al'lodola *sf* (sky)lark

alloggi'are [allod'dʒare] /62/ *vt* to accommodate ▷ *vi* to live; al'loggio *sm* lodging, accommodation (BRIT), accommodations (US)

allonta'nare /72/ *vt* to send away, send off; (*impiegato*) to dismiss; (*pericolo*) to avert, remove; (*estraniare*) to alienate; allontanarsi *vpr*: allontanarsi (da) to go away (from); (*estraniarsi*) to become estranged (from)

al'lora av (in quel momento) then ▷ cong (in questo caso) well then; (dunque) well then, so; **la gente d'~** people then o in those days; **da ~ in poi** from then on

al'loro sm laurel

'alluce ['allutʃe] sm big toe

alluci'nante [allutʃi'nante] ag awful; (fam) amazing

allucinazi'one [allutʃinat'tsjone] sf hallucination

al'ludere /35/ vi: **~ a** to allude to, hint at

allu'minio sm aluminium (BRIT), aluminum (US)

allun'gare /80/ vt to lengthen; (distendere) to prolong, extend; (diluire) to water down; **allungarsi** vpr to lengthen; (ragazzo) to stretch, grow taller; (sdraiarsi) to lie down, stretch out

al'lusi ecc vb vedi **alludere**

allusi'one sf hint, allusion

alluvi'one sf flood

al'meno av at least ▷ cong: **(se) ~** if only; **(se) ~ piovesse!** if only it would rain!

a'logeno, -a [a'lɔdʒeno] ag: **lampada alogena** halogen lamp

a'lone sm halo

'Alpi sfpl: **le ~** the Alps

alpi'nismo sm mountaineering, climbing; **alpi'nista, -i, -e** sm/f mountaineer, climber

al'pino, -a ag Alpine; mountain cpd; **alpini** smpl (Mil) Italian Alpine troops

alt escl halt!, stop!

alta'lena sf (a funi) swing; (in bilico) seesaw

al'tare sm altar

alter'nare /72/ vt, **alter'narsi** vpr to alternate; **alterna'tivo, -a** ag alternative

al'terno, -a ag alternate; **a giorni alterni** on alternate days, every other day

al'tero, -a ag proud

al'tezza [al'tettsa] sf height; (di tessuto) width, breadth; (di acqua, pozzo) depth; (di suono) pitch; (Geo) latitude; (titolo) highness; (fig: nobiltà) greatness; **essere all'~ di** to be on a level with; (fig) to be up to o equal to

al'ticcio, -a, -ci, -ce [al'tittʃo] ag tipsy

alti'tudine sf altitude

'alto, -a ag high; (persona) tall; (tessuto) wide, broad; (sonno, acque) deep; (suono) high(-pitched); (Geo) upper; (: settentrionale) northern ▷ sm top (part) ▷ av high; (parlare) aloud, loudly; **il palazzo è ~ 20 metri** the building is 20 metres high; **ad alta voce** aloud; **a notte alta** in the dead of night; **in ~** up, upwards; at the top; **dall'~ in o al basso** up and down; **degli alti e bassi** (fig) ups and downs; **alta fedeltà** high fidelity, hi-fi; **alta finanza/società** high finance/ society; **alta moda** haute couture; **alta definizione** (TV) high definition; **alta velocità** (Ferr) high speed rail system

altopar'lante sm loudspeaker

altopi'ano (pl **altipiani**) sm upland plain, plateau

altret'tanto, -a ag, pron as much; (pl) as many ▷ av equally; **tanti auguri! — grazie, ~ a te** all the best! — thank you, the same to you

altri'menti av otherwise

PAROLA CHIAVE

'altro, -a det **1** (diverso) other, different; **questa è un'altra cosa** that's another o a different thing

2 (supplementare) other; **prendi un altro cioccolatino** have another chocolate; **hai avuto altre notizie?** have you had any more o any other news?

3 (nel tempo): **l'altro giorno** the other day; **l'altr'anno** last year; **l'altro ieri** the day before yesterday; **domani l'altro** the day after tomorrow; **quest'altro mese** next month

4: **d'altra parte** on the other hand

▶ pron **1** (persona, cosa diversa o supplementare): **un altro, un'altra** another (one); **lo farà un altro** someone else will do it; **altri, e** others; **gli altri** (la gente) others, other people; **l'uno e l'altro** both (of them); **aiutarsi l'un l'altro** to help one another; **da un giorno all'altro** from day to day; (nel giro di 24 ore) from one day to the next; (da un momento all'altro) any day now

2 (sostantivato: solo maschile) something else; (: in espressioni interrogative) anything else; **non ho altro da dire** I have nothing else o I don't have anything else to say; **più che altro** above all; **se non altro** at least; **tra l'altro** among other things; **ci mancherebbe altro!** that's all we need!; **non faccio altro che lavorare** I do nothing but work; **contento? — altro che!** are you pleased? — I certainly am!; vedi anche **senza; noialtri; voialtri; tutto**

al'trove av elsewhere, somewhere else

altru'ista, -i, -e ag altruistic

a'lunno, -a sm/f pupil

alve'are sm hive

al'zare [al'tsare] /72/ vt to raise, lift; (issare) to hoist; (costruire) to build, erect; **alzarsi** vpr to rise; (dal letto) to get up; (crescere) to grow tall (o taller); **~ le spalle** to shrug one's shoulders; **alzarsi in piedi** to stand up, get to one's feet

a'maca, -che sf hammock

amalga'mare /72/ vt, **amalga'marsi** vpr to amalgamate

a'mante *ag*: ~ **di** (*musica ecc*) fond of ▷ *smf* lover (mistress)

a'mare /72/ *vt* to love; (*amico, musica, sport*) to like; **amarsi** *vpr* to love each other

amareggi'ato, -a [amared'dʒato] *ag* upset, saddened

ama'rena *sf* sour black cherry

ama'rezza [ama'rettsa] *sf* bitterness

a'maro, -a *ag* bitter ▷ *sm* bitterness; (*liquore*) bitters *pl*

amaz'zonico, -a, -ci, -che [amad'dzɔniko] *ag* Amazonian; Amazon *cpd*

ambasci'ata [ambaʃ'ʃata] *sf* embassy; (*messaggio*) message; **ambascia'tore, -'trice** *sm/f* ambassador (ambassadress)

ambe'due *ag inv*: ~ **i ragazzi** both boys ▷ *pron inv* both

ambienta'lista, -i, -e *ag* environmental ▷ *sm/f* environmentalist

ambien'tare /72/ *vt* to acclimatize; (*romanzo, film*) to set; **ambientarsi** *vpr* to get used to one's surroundings

ambi'ente *sm* environment; (*fig: insieme di persone*) milieu; (*stanza*) room

am'biguo, -a *ag* ambiguous

ambizi'one [ambit'tsjone] *sf* ambition; **ambizi'oso, -a** *ag* ambitious

'ambo *ag inv* both ▷ *sm* (*al gioco*) double

'ambra *sf* amber; ~ **grigia** ambergris

ambu'lante *ag* itinerant ▷ *sm* peddler

ambu'lanza [ambu'lantsa] *sf* ambulance; **chiamate un ~** call an ambulance

ambula'torio *sm* (*studio medico*) surgery

A'merica *sf*: **l'~** America; **l'~ latina** Latin America; **ameri'cano, -a** *ag, sm/f* American

ami'anto *sm* asbestos

ami'chevole [ami'kevole] *ag* friendly

ami'cizia [ami'tʃittsja] *sf* friendship; **amicizie** *sfpl* (*amici*) friends

a'mico, -a, -ci, -che *sm/f* friend; (*amante*) boyfriend (girlfriend); **~ del cuore** *o* **intimo** bosom friend; **aggiungere come ~** (*Internet*) to friend

'amido *sm* starch

ammac'care /20/ *vt* (*pentola*) to dent; (*persona*) to bruise; **ammacca'tura** *sf* dent; bruise

ammaes'trare /72/ *vt* (*animale*) to train

ammai'nare /72/ *vt* to lower, haul down

amma'larsi /72/ *vpr* to fall ill; **amma'lato, -a** *ag* ill, sick ▷ *sm/f* sick person; (*paziente*) patient

ammanet'tare /72/ *vt* to handcuff

ammas'sare /72/ *vt* (*ammucchiare*) to amass; (*raccogliere*) to gather together; **ammassarsi** *vpr* to pile up; to gather

ammat'tire /55/ *vi* to go mad

ammaz'zare [ammat'tsare] /72/ *vt* to kill; **ammazzarsi** *vpr* (*uccidersi*) to kill o.s.; (*rimanere ucciso*) to be killed; **ammazzarsi di lavoro** to work o.s. to death

am'mettere /63/ *vt* to admit; (*riconoscere: fatto*) to acknowledge, admit; (*permettere*) to allow, accept; (*supporre*) to suppose

amminis'trare /72/ *vt* to run, manage; (*Rel, Dir*) to administer; **amministra'tore** *sm* administrator; (*di condominio*) flats manager; **amministratore delegato** managing director; **amministrazi'one** *sf* management; administration

ammi'raglio [ammi'raʎʎo] *sm* admiral

ammi'rare /72/ *vt* to admire; **ammirazi'one** *sf* admiration

am'misi *ecc vb vedi* **ammettere**

ammobili'ato, -a *ag* furnished

am'mollo *sm*: **lasciare in ~** to leave to soak

ammo'niaca *sf* ammonia

ammo'nire /55/ *vt* (*avvertire*) to warn; (*rimproverare*) to admonish; (*Dir*) to caution

ammonizi'one [ammonit'tsjone] *sf* (*monito: anche Sport*) warning; (*rimprovero*) reprimand; (*Dir*) caution

ammon'tare /72/ *vi*: ~ **a** to amount to ▷ *sm* (*totale*) amount

ammorbi'dente *sm* fabric softener

ammorbi'dire /55/ *vt* to soften

ammortizza'tore [ammortiddza'tore] *sm* (*Aut, Tecn*) shock absorber

ammucchi'are [ammuk'kjare] /19/ *vt* to pile up, accumulate

ammuf'fire /55/ *vi* to go mouldy (BRIT) *o* moldy (US)

ammuto'lire /55/ *vi* to be struck dumb

amne'sia *sf* amnesia

amnis'tia *sf* amnesty

'amo *sm* (*Pesca*) hook; (*fig*) bait

a'more *sm* love; **amori** *smpl* love affairs; **il tuo bambino è un ~** your baby's a darling; **fare l'~ o all'~** to make love; **per ~ o per forza** by hook or by crook; **amor proprio** self-esteem, pride

amo'roso, -a *ag* (*affettuoso*) loving, affectionate; (*d'amore: sguardo*) amorous; (: *poesia, relazione*) love *cpd*

'ampio, -a *ag* wide, broad; (*spazioso*) spacious; (*abbondante: vestito*) loose; (: *gonna*) full; (: *spiegazione*) ample, full

am'plesso *sm* intercourse

ampli'are /19/ *vt* (*ingrandire*) to enlarge; (*allargare*) to widen; **ampliarsi** *vpr* to grow, increase

amplifica'tore *sm* (*Tecn, Mus*) amplifier

ampu'tare /72/ *vt* (*Med*) to amputate

A.N. *sigla f* (*Pol*) = **Alleanza Nazionale**

anabbagli'ante [anabbaʎ'ʎante] *ag* (*Aut*) dipped; **anabbaglianti** *smpl* dipped *or* dimmed headlights

anaboliz'zante *sm* anabolic steroid

anal'colico, -a, -ci, -che ag non-alcoholic ▷ sm soft drink

analfa'beta, -i, -e ag, smf illiterate

anal'gesico, -a, -ci, -che [anal'dʒeziko] ag, sm analgesic

a'nalisi sf inv analysis; (Med: esame) test; ~ **del sangue** blood test

analiz'zare [analid'dzare] /72/ vt to analyse; (Med) to test

a'nalogo, -a, -ghi, -ghe ag analogous

'ananas sm inv pineapple

anar'chia [anar'kia] sf anarchy; **a'narchico, -a, -ci, -che** ag anarchic(al) ▷ sm/f anarchist

anarco-insurreziona'lista ag anarcho-revolutionary

'A.N.A.S. sigla f (= Azienda Nazionale Autonoma delle Strade) national roads department

anato'mia sf anatomy

'anatra sf duck

'anca, -che sf (Anat) hip

'anche ['anke] cong (inoltre, pure) also, too; (perfino) even; **vengo anch'io!** I'm coming too!; ~ **se** even if

an'cora av still; (di nuovo) again; (di più) some more; (persino): ~ **più forte** even stronger; **non** ~ not yet; ~ **una volta** once more, once again; ~ **un po'** a little more; (di tempo) a little longer

an'dare /6/ sm: **a lungo** ~ in the long run ▷ vi to go; ~ **a** (essere adatto) to suit; **il suo comportamento non mi va** (piace) I don't like the way he behaves; **ti va di** ~ **al cinema?** do you feel like going to the cinema?; ~ **a cavallo** to ride; ~ **in macchina/aereo** to go by car/plane; ~ **a fare qc** to go and do sth; ~ **a pescare/sciare** to go fishing/skiing; **andarsene** to go away; **questa camicia va lavata** this shirt needs a wash o should be washed; ~ **a male** to go bad; **come va?** (lavoro, progetto) how are things?; **come va? — bene, grazie!** how are you? — fine, thanks!; **va fatto entro oggi** it's got to be done today; **ne va della nostra vita** our lives are at stake; **an'data** sf going; (viaggio) outward journey; **biglietto di sola andata** single (BRIT) o one-way ticket; **biglietto di andata e ritorno** return (BRIT) o round-trip (US) ticket

andrò ecc vb vedi **andare**

a'neddoto sm anecdote

a'nello sm ring; (di catena) link; **anelli** smpl (Ginnastica) rings

a'nemico, -a, -ci, -che ag anaemic

aneste'sia sf anaesthesia

anfeta'mina sf amphetamine

'angelo ['andʒelo] sm angel; ~ **custode** guardian angel

anghe'ria [ange'ria] sf vexation

angli'cano, -a ag Anglican

anglo'sassone ag Anglo-Saxon

'angolo sm corner; (Mat) angle; ~ **cottura** (di appartamento ecc) cooking area

an'goscia, -sce [an'goʃʃa] sf deep anxiety, anguish no pl

an'guilla sf eel

an'guria sf watermelon

'anice ['anitʃe] sm (Cuc) aniseed; (Bot) anise

'anima sf soul; (abitante) inhabitant; ~ **gemella** soul mate; **non c'era** ~ **viva** there wasn't a living soul

ani'male sm, ag animal; ~ **domestico** pet

anna'cquare /72/ vt to water down, dilute

annaffi'are /19/ vt to water; **annaffia'toio** sm watering can

an'nata sf year; (importo annuo) annual amount; **vino d'**~ vintage wine

anne'gare /80/ vt, vi to drown

anne'rire /55/ vt to blacken ▷ vi to become black

annien'tare /72/ vt to annihilate, destroy

anniver'sario sm anniversary; ~ **di matrimonio** wedding anniversary

'anno sm year; **quanti anni hai? — ho 40 anni** how old are you? — I'm 40 (years old)

anno'dare /72/ vt to knot, tie; (fig: rapporto) to form

annoi'are /19/ vt to bore; **annoiarsi** vpr to be bored

🔹 Attenzione! In inglese esiste il verbo to annoy, che però vuol dire dare fastidio a.

anno'tare /72/ vt (registrare) to note, note down; (commentare) to annotate

annu'ale ag annual

annu'ire /55/ vi to nod; (acconsentire) to agree

annul'lare /72/ vt to annihilate, destroy; (contratto, francobollo) to cancel; (matrimonio) to annul; (sentenza) to quash; (risultati) to declare void

annunci'are [annun'tʃare] /14/ vt to announce; (dar segni rivelatori) to herald

an'nuncio [an'nuntʃo] sm announcement; (fig) sign; ~ **pubblicitario** advertisement; **annunci economici** classified advertisements, small ads; **annunci mortuari** (colonna) obituary column

'annuo, -a ag annual, yearly

annu'sare /72/ vt to sniff, smell; ~ **tabacco** to take snuff

a'nomalo, -a ag anomalous

a'nonimo, -a ag anonymous ▷ sm (autore) anonymous writer (o painter ecc); **società anonima** (Comm) joint stock company

anores'sia sf anorexia

ano'ressico, -a, -ci, -che ag anorexic

anor'male ag abnormal ▷ smf subnormal person

'**ANSA** *sigla f* (= *Agenzia Nazionale Stampa Associata*) *national press agency*

'**ansia** *sf* anxiety

ansi'mare /72/ *vi* to pant

ansi'oso, -a *ag* anxious

'**anta** *sf* (*di finestra*) shutter; (*di armadio*) door

An'tartide *sf*: l'~ Antarctica

an'tenna *sf* (*Radio*, *TV*) aerial; (*Zool*) antenna, feeler; (*Naut*) yard; ~ **parabolica** satellite dish

ante'prima *sf* preview; ~ **di stampa** (*Inform*) print preview

anteri'ore *ag* (*ruota*, *zampa*) front *cpd*; (*fatti*) previous, preceding

antiade'rente *ag* non-stick

antibi'otico, -a, -ci, -che *ag, sm* antibiotic

anti'camera *sf* anteroom; **fare ~** to be kept waiting

antici'pare [antitʃi'pare] /72/ *vt* (*consegna*, *visita*) to bring forward, anticipate; (*somma di denaro*) to pay in advance; (*notizia*) to disclose ▷ *vi* to be ahead of time; **an'ticipo** *sm* anticipation; (*di denaro*) advance; **in anticipo** early, in advance

an'tico, -a, -chi, -che *ag* (*quadro*, *mobili*) antique; (*dell'antichità*) ancient; **all'antica** old-fashioned

anticoncezio'nale [antikontʃettsjo'nale] *sm* contraceptive

anticonfor'mista, -i, -e *ag, smf* nonconformist

anti'corpo *sm* antibody

antidolo'rifico, -ci *sm* painkiller

anti'doping *sm inv, ag inv* drug testing; **test ~ drugs** (*BRIT*) o **drug** (*US*) test

an'tifona *sf* (*Mus, Rel*) antiphon; **capire l'~** (*fig*) to take the hint

anti'forfora *ag inv* anti-dandruff

anti'furto *sm* anti-theft device

anti'gelo [anti'dʒɛlo] *ag inv* antifreeze *cpd* ▷ *sm* (*per motore*) antifreeze; (*per cristalli*) de-icer

antiglobalizza'zione [antiglobaliddza'tsjone] *ag* anti-globalization

An'tille *sfpl*: **le ~** the West Indies

antin'cendio [antin'tʃɛndjo] *ag inv* fire *cpd*

anti'nebbia *sm inv* (*anche*: **faro ~**) (*Aut*) fog lamp

antin'fiammatorio, -a *ag, sm* anti-inflammatory

antio'rario *ag*: **in senso ~** anticlockwise

anti'pasto *sm* hors d'œuvre

antipa'tia *sf* antipathy, dislike; **anti'patico, -a, -ci, -che** *ag* unpleasant, disagreeable

antipro'iettile *ag inv* bulletproof

antiquari'ato *sm* antique trade; **un pezzo d'~** an antique; **anti'quario** *sm* antique

dealer; **anti'quato, -a** *ag* antiquated, old-fashioned

anti'rughe [anti'ruge] *ag inv* (*crema*, *prodotto*) anti-wrinkle

antitraspi'rante *ag* antiperspirant

anti'vipera *ag inv*: **siero ~** remedy for snake bites

antivi'rale *ag* antiviral

anti'virus [anti'virus] *sm inv* antivirus software *no pl*

antolo'gia, -'gie [antolo'dʒia] *sf* anthology

anu'lare *ag* ring *cpd* ▷ *sm* ring finger

'**anzi** ['antsi] *av* (*invece*) on the contrary; (*o meglio*) or rather, or better still

anzi'ano, -a [an'tsjano] *ag* old; (*Amm*) senior ▷ *sm/f* old person; senior member

anziché [antsi'ke] *cong* rather than

a'patico, -a, -ci, -che *ag* apathetic

'**ape** *sf* bee

aperi'tivo *sm* apéritif

aperta'mente *av* openly

a'perto, -a *pp di* **aprire** ▷ *ag* open ▷ *sm*: **all'~** in the open (air)

aper'tura *sf* opening; (*ampiezza*) width; (*Fot*) aperture; ~ **alare** wing span; ~ **mentale** open-mindedness

ap'nea *sf*: **immergersi in ~** to dive without breathing apparatus

a'postrofo *sm* apostrophe

ap'paio *ecc vb vedi* **apparire**

ap'palto *sm* (*Comm*) contract; **dare/prendere in ~ un lavoro** to let out/undertake a job on contract

appan'nare /72/ *vt* (*vetro*) to mist; **appannarsi** *vpr* to mist over; to grow dim

apparecchi'are [apparek'kjare] /19/ *vt* to prepare; (*tavola*) to set ▷ *vi* to set the table

appa'recchio [appa'rekkjo] *sm* piece of apparatus, device; (*aeroplano*) aircraft *inv*; ~ **acustico** hearing aid; ~ **televisivo/telefonico** television set/telephone

appa'rente *ag* apparent

appa'rire /7/ *vi* to appear; (*sembrare*) to seem, appear

apparta'mento *sm* flat (*BRIT*), apartment (*US*)

appar'tarsi /72/ *vpr* to withdraw

apparte'nere /121/ *vi*: ~ **a** to belong to

ap'parvi *ecc vb vedi* **apparire**

appassio'nare /72/ *vt* to thrill; (*commuovere*) to move; **appassionarsi** *vpr*: **appassionarsi a qc** to take a great interest in sth; **appassio'nato, -a** *ag* passionate; (*entusiasta*): **appassionato (di)** keen (on)

appas'sire /55/ *vi* to wither; **appas'sito, -a** *ag* dead

ap'pello *sm* roll-call; (*implorazione, Dir*) appeal; **fare ~ a** to appeal to

ap'pena *av* (*a stento*) hardly, scarcely; (*solamente, da poco*) just ▷ *cong* as soon as; **(non) ~ furono arrivati ...** as soon as they had arrived ...; **~ ... che** *o* **quando** no sooner ... than

ap'pendere /8/ *vt* to hang (up)

appen'dice [appen'ditʃe] *sf* appendix; **romanzo d'~** popular serial; **appendi'cite** *sf* appendicitis

Appen'nini *smpl*: **gli ~** the Apennines

appesan'tire /55/ *vt* to make heavy; **appesantirsi** *vpr* to grow stout

appe'tito *sm* appetite

appic'care /20/ *vt*: **~ il fuoco a** to set fire to, set on fire

appicci'care [appittʃi'kare] /20/ *vt* to stick; **appiccicarsi** *vpr* to stick; (*fig: persona*) to cling

appiso'larsi /72/ *vpr* to doze off

applau'dire /45/ *vt*, *vi* to applaud; **ap'plauso** *sm* applause *no pl*

appli'care /20/ *vt* to apply; (*regolamento*) to enforce; **applicarsi** *vpr* to apply o.s.; **applicazi'one** *sf* application; **applicazione per il cellulare** mobile app

appoggi'are [appod'dʒare] /62/ *vt* (*fig: sostenere*) to support; **~ qc a qc** (*mettere contro*) to lean *o* rest sth against sth; **appoggiarsi** *vpr*: **appoggiarsi a** to lean against; (*fig*) to rely upon; **ap'poggio** *sm* support

apposita'mente *av* (*apposta*) on purpose; (*specialmente*) specially

ap'posito, -a *ag* appropriate

ap'posta *av* on purpose, deliberately

appos'tarsi /72/ *vpr* to lie in wait

ap'prendere /81/ *vt* (*imparare*) to learn; **appren'dista, -i, -e** *sm/f* apprentice

apprensi'one *sf* apprehension

apprez'zare [appret'tsare] /72/ *vt* to appreciate

appro'dare /72/ *vi* (*Naut*) to land; (*fig*): **non ~ a nulla** to come to nothing

approfit'tare /72/ *vi*: **~ di** (*situazione*) to make the most of; (*persona*) to take advantage of

approfon'dire /55/ *vt* to deepen; (*fig*) to study in depth

appropri'ato, -a *ag* appropriate

approssima'tivo, -a *ag* approximate, rough; (*impreciso*) inexact, imprecise

appro'vare /72/ *vt* (*condotta, azione*) to approve of; (*candidato*) to pass; (*progetto di legge*) to approve

appunta'mento *sm* appointment; (*amoroso*) date; **darsi ~** to arrange to meet (one another); **ho un ~ con...** I have an appointment with ...; **vorrei prendere un ~** I'd like to make an appointment

ap'punto *sm* note; (*rimprovero*) reproach ▷ *av* (*proprio*) exactly, just; **per l'~!, ~!** exactly!

apribot'tiglie [apribot'tiʎʎe] *sm inv* bottleopener

a'prile *sm* April

a'prire /9/ *vt* to open; (*via, cadavere*) to open up; (*gas, luce, acqua*) to turn on ▷ *vi* to open; **aprirsi** *vpr* to open; **aprirsi a qn** to confide in sb, open one's heart to sb

apris'catole *sm inv* tin (*BRIT*) *o* can opener

APT *sigla f* (= *Azienda di Promozione*) ≈ tourist board

aquagym [akwa'dʒim] *sf* aquarobics

'aquila *sf* (*Zool*) eagle; (*fig*) genius

aqui'lone *sm* (*giocattolo*) kite; (*vento*) North wind

A/R *abbr* (= *andata e ritorno*) (*biglietto*) return (ticket) (*BRIT*), round-trip ticket (*US*)

A'rabia Sau'dita *sf*: **l'~** Saudi Arabia

'arabo, -a *ag*, *sm/f* Arab ▷ *sm* (*Ling*) Arabic

a'rachide [a'rakide] *sf* peanut

ara'gosta *sf* crayfish; spiny lobster

a'rancia, -ce [a'rantʃa] *sf* orange; **aranci'ata** *sf* orangeade; **aranci'one** *ag inv*: **(color) arancione** bright orange

a'rare /72/ *vt* to plough (*BRIT*), plow (*US*)

a'ratro *sm* plough (*BRIT*), plow (*US*)

a'razzo [a'rattso] *sm* tapestry

arbi'trare /72/ *vt* (*Sport*) to referee; to umpire; (*Dir*) to arbitrate

arbi'trario, -a *ag* arbitrary

'arbitro *sm* arbiter, judge; (*Dir*) arbitrator; (*Sport*) referee; (: *Tennis, Cricket*) umpire

ar'busto *sm* shrub

archeolo'gia [arkeolo'dʒia] *sf* arch(a)eology; **arche'ologo, -a, -gi, -ghe** *sm/f* arch(a)eologist

architet'tare [arkitet'tare] /72/ *vt* (*fig: ideare*) to devise; (: *macchinare*) to plan, concoct

archi'tetto [arki'tetto] *sm* architect; **architet'tura** [arkitet'tura] *sf* architecture

ar'chivio [ar'kivjo] *sm* archives *pl*; (*Inform*) file

'arco *sm* (*arma, Mus*) bow; (*Archit*) arch; (*Mat*) arc

arcoba'leno *sm* rainbow

arcu'ato, -a *ag* curved, bent

'ardere /10/ *vt*, *vi* to burn

ar'desia *sf* slate

'area *sf* area; (*Edil*) land, ground; **~ di rigore** (*Sport*) penalty area; **~ di servizio** (*Aut*) service area

a'rena *sf* arena; (*per corride*) bullring; (*sabbia*) sand

are'narsi /72/ *vpr* to run aground

argente'ria [ardʒente'ria] *sf* silverware, silver

Argen'tina [ardʒen'tina] *sf*: l'~ Argentina; **argen'tino, -a** *ag*, *sm/f* Argentinian

ar'gento [ar'dʒento] *sm* silver; ~ **vivo** quicksilver

ar'gilla [ar'dʒilla] *sf* clay

'argine ['ardʒine] *sm* embankment, bank; (*diga*) dyke, dike

argo'mento *sm* argument; (*motivo*) motive; (*materia, tema*) subject

'aria *sf* air; (*espressione, aspetto*) air, look; (*Mus: melodia*) tune; (: *di opera*) aria; **all'~ aperta** in the open (air); **mandare all'~ qc** to ruin o upset sth

'arido, -a *ag* arid

arieggi'are [arjed'dʒare] /62/ *vt* (*cambiare aria*) to air; (*imitare*) to imitate

ari'ete *sm* ram; (*Mil*) battering ram; **A~** Aries

a'ringa, -ghe *sf* herring *inv*

arit'metica *sf* arithmetic

'arma, -i *sf* weapon, arm; (*parte dell'esercito*) arm; **alle armi!** to arms!; **chiamare alle armi** to call up (*BRIT*), draft (*US*); **sotto le armi** in the army (o forces); ~ **atomica/ nucleare** atomic/nuclear weapon; ~ **da fuoco** firearm; **armi di distruzione de massa** weapons of mass destruction

arma'dietto *sm* (*di medicinali*) medicine cabinet; (*in palestra ecc*) locker; (*in cucina*) (kitchen) cupboard

ar'madio *sm* cupboard; (*per abiti*) wardrobe; ~ **a muro** built-in cupboard

ar'mato, -a *ag*: ~ (**di**) (*anche fig*) armed (with) ▷ *di* (*Mil*) army; (*Naut*) fleet; **rapina a mano armata** armed robbery

arma'tura *sf* (*struttura di sostegno*) framework; (*impalcatura*) scaffolding; (*Storia*) armour *no pl*, suit of armour

armis'tizio [armis'tittsjo] *sm* armistice

armo'nia *sf* harmony

ar'nese *sm* tool, implement; (*oggetto indeterminato*) thing, contraption; **male in** ~ (*malvestito*) badly dressed; (*di salute malferma*) in poor health; (*di condizioni economiche*) down-at-heel

'arnia *sf* hive

a'roma, -i *sm* aroma; fragrance; **aromi** *smpl* (*Cuc*) herbs and spices; **aromatera'pia** *sf* aromatherapy

'arpa *sf* (*Mus*) harp

arrabbi'are /19/ *vi* (*cane*) to be affected with rabies; **arrabbiarsi** *vpr* (*essere preso dall'ira*) to get angry, fly into a rage; **arrabbi'ato, -a** *ag* rabid, with rabies; (*persona*) furious, angry

arrampi'carsi /20/ *vpr* to climb (up)

arran'giare [arran'dʒare] /62/ *vt* to arrange; **arrangiarsi** *vpr* to manage, do the best one can

arreda'mento *sm* (*studio*) interior design; (*mobili ecc*) furnishings *pl*

arre'dare /72/ *vt* to furnish

ar'rendersi /88/ *vpr* to surrender

arres'tare /72/ *vt* (*fermare*) to stop, halt; (*catturare*) to arrest; **arrestarsi** *vpr* (*fermarsi*) to stop; **ar'resto** *sm* (*cessazione*) stopping; (*fermata*) stop; (*cattura, Med*) arrest; **subire un arresto** to come to a stop o standstill; **mettere agli arresti** to place under arrest; **arresti domiciliari** house arrest *sg*

arre'trare /72/ *vt*, *vi* to withdraw; **arre'trato, -a** *ag* (*lavoro*) behind schedule; (*paese, bambino*) backward; (*numero di giornale*) back *cpd*; **arretrati** *smpl* arrears

arric'chire [arrik'kire] /55/ *vt* to enrich; **arricchirsi** *vpr* to become rich

arri'vare /72/ *vi* to arrive; (*accadere*) to happen, occur; ~ **a** (*livello, grado ecc*) to reach; **lui arriva a Roma alle 7** he gets to o arrives at Rome at 7; **non ci arrivo** I can't reach it; (*fig: non capisco*) I can't understand it

arrive'derci [arrive'dertʃi] *escl* goodbye!

arri'vista, -i, -e *sm/f* go-getter

ar'rivo *sm* arrival; (*Sport*) finish, finishing line

arro'gante *ag* arrogant

arros'sire /55/ *vi* (*per vergogna, timidezza*) to blush; (*per gioia*) to flush

arros'tire /55/ *vt* to roast; (*pane*) to toast; (*ai ferri*) to grill

ar'rosto *sm*, *ag inv* roast

arroto'lare /72/ *vt* to roll up

arroton'dare /72/ *vt* (*forma, oggetto*) to round; (*stipendio*) to add to; (*somma*) to round off

arrugg'nito, -a [arruddʒin'nito] *ag* rusty

'arsi *vb vedi* **ardere**

'arte *sf* art; (*abilità*) skill

ar'teria *sf* artery; ~ **stradale** main road

'artico, -a, -ci, -che *ag* Arctic

articolazi'one [artikolat'tsjone] *sf* (*Anat, Tecn*) joint

ar'ticolo *sm* article; ~ **di fondo** (*Stampa*) leader, leading article

artifici'ale [artifi'tʃale] *ag* artificial

artigia'nato [artidʒa'nato] *sm* craftsmanship; craftsmen *pl*

artigi'ano, -a [arti'dʒano] *sm/f* craftsman/-woman

ar'tista, -i, -e *sm/f* artist; **un lavoro da** ~ (*fig*) a professional piece of work; **ar'tistico, -a, -ci, -che** *ag* artistic

ar'trite *sf* (*Med*) arthritis

a'scella [aʃ'ʃella] *sf* (*Anat*) armpit

ascen'dente [aʃʃen'dɛnte] *sm* ancestor; (*fig*) ascendancy; (*Astr*) ascendant

ascen'sore [aʃʃen'sore] *sm* lift

a'scesso [aʃˈʃɛsso] *sm* (*Med*) abscess

asciugaca'pelli [aʃʃugakaˈpelli] *sm* hair dryer

asciuga'mano [aʃʃugaˈmano] *sm* towel

asciu'gare [aʃʃuˈgare] /80/ *vt* to dry; **asciugarsi** *vpr* to dry o.s.; (*diventare asciutto*) to dry

asci'utto, -a [aʃʃutto] *ag* dry; (*fig: magro*) lean; (: *burbero*) curt; **restare a bocca asciutta** (*fig*) to be disappointed

ascol'tare /72/ *vt* to listen to

as'falto *sm* asphalt

'Asia *sf*: l'~ Asia; **asi'atico, -a, -ci, -che** *ag*, *sm/f* Asiatic, Asian

a'silo *sm* refuge, sanctuary; ~ (**d'infanzia**) nursery(-school); ~ **nido** crèche; ~ **politico** political asylum

'asino *sm* donkey, ass

ASL *sigla f* (= *Azienda Sanitaria Locale*) local health centre

'asma *sf* asthma

as'parago, -gi *sm* asparagus *no pl*

aspet'tare /72/ *vt* to wait for; (*anche Comm*) to await; (*aspettarsi*) to expect ▷ *vi* to wait

as'petto *sm* (*apparenza*) aspect, appearance, look; (*punto di vista*) point of view; **di bell'~** good-looking

aspira'polvere *sm inv* vacuum cleaner

aspi'rare /72/ *vt* (*respirare*) to breathe in, inhale; (*apparecchi*) to suck (up) ▷ *vi*: ~ **a** to aspire to

aspi'rina *sf* aspirin

'aspro, -a *ag* (*sapore*) sour, tart; (*odore*) acrid, pungent; (*voce, clima, fig*) harsh; (*superficie*) rough; (*paesaggio*) rugged

assaggi'are [assadˈdʒare] /62/ *vt* to taste; **assag'gini** [assadˈdʒini] *smpl* (*Cuc*) *selection of first courses*

as'sai *av* (*molto*) a lot, much; (: *con ag*) very; (*a sufficienza*) enough ▷ *ag inv* (*quantità*) a lot of, much; (*numero*) a lot of, many; ~ **contento** very pleased

as'salgo *ecc vb vedi* **assalire**

assa'lire /98/ *vt* to attack, assail

assal'tare /72/ *vt* (*Mil*) to storm; (*banca*) to raid; (*treno, diligenza*) to hold up

as'salto *sm* attack, assault

assassi'nare /72/ *vt* to murder; (*Pol*) to assassinate; (*fig*) to ruin; **assas'sino, -a** *ag* murderous ▷ *sm/f* murderer; assassin

'asse *sm* (*Tecn*) axle; (*Mat*) axis ▷ *sf* board; ~ **da stiro** ironing board

assedi'are /19/ *vt* to besiege

asse'gnare [asseɲˈɲare] /15/ *vt* to assign, allot; (*premio*) to award

as'segno [asˈseɲɲo] *sm* allowance; (*anche*: ~ **bancario**) cheque (BRIT), check (US); **contro ~** cash on delivery; ~ **circolare** bank draft; ~ **di malattia** *o* **di invalidità** sick pay/disability benefit; ~ **sbarrato** crossed cheque; ~ **di viaggio** travel(l)er's cheque; ~ **a vuoto** dud cheque; **assegni familiari** ≈ child benefit *sg*

assem'blea *sf* assembly

assen'tarsi /72/ *vpr* to go out; **as'sente** *ag* absent; (*fig*) faraway, vacant; **as'senza** *sf* absence

asse'tato, -a *ag* thirsty, parched

assicu'rare /72/ *vt* (*accertare*) to ensure; (*infondere certezza*) to assure; (*fermare, legare*) to make fast, secure; (*fare un contratto di assicurazione*) to insure; **assicurarsi** *vpr*: **assicurarsi (di)** (*accertarsi*) to make sure (of); **assicurarsi (contro)** (*il furto ecc*) to insure o.s. (against); **assicurazi'one** *sf* assurance; insurance

assi'eme *av* (*insieme*) together ▷ *prep*: ~ **a** (together) with

assil'lare /72/ *vt* to pester, torment

assis'tente *smf* assistant; ~ **sociale** social worker; ~ **di volo** (*Aer*) steward (stewardess); **assis'tenza** *sf* assistance; **assistenza ospedaliera** free hospital treatment; **assistenza sanitaria** health service; **assistenza sociale** welfare services *pl*; **as'sistere** /11/ *vt* (*aiutare*) to assist, help; (*curare*) to treat ▷ *vi*: **assistere (a qc)** (*essere presente*) to be present (at sth), attend (sth)

'asso *sm* ace; **piantare qn in** ~ to leave sb in the lurch

associ'are [assoˈtʃare] /14/ *vt* to associate; **associarsi** *vpr* to enter into partnership; **associarsi a** to become a member of, join; (*dolori, gioie*) to share in; ~ **qn alle carceri** to take sb to prison

associazi'one [assotʃatˈtsjone] *sf* association; (*Comm*) association, society; ~ **a** *o* **per delinquere** (*Dir*) criminal association

as'solsi *ecc vb vedi* **assolvere**

assoluta'mente *av* absolutely

asso'luto, -a *ag* absolute

assoluzi'one [assolutˈtsjone] *sf* (*Dir*) acquittal; (*Rel*) absolution

as'solvere /94/ *vt* (*Dir*) to acquit; (*Rel*) to absolve; (*adempiere*) to carry out, perform

assomigli'are [assomiʎˈʎare] /27/ *vi*: ~ **a** to resemble, look like; **assomigliarsi** *vpr* to look alike; (*nel carattere*) to be alike

asson'nato, -a *ag* sleepy

asso'pirsi /55/ *vpr* to doze off

assor'bente *ag* absorbent ▷ *sm*: ~ **igienico/esterno** sanitary towel; ~ **interno** tampon

assor'bire /17/ *vt* to absorb

assor'dare /72/ *vt* to deafen

assorti'mento *sm* assortment; **assor'tito, -a** *ag* assorted; (*colori*) matched, matching

assuefazi'one [assuefat'tsjone] *sf* (*Med*) addiction

as'sumere /12/ *vt* (*impiegato*) to take on, engage; (*responsabilità*) to assume, take upon o.s.; (*contegno, espressione*) to assume, put on; (*droga*) to consume

as'sunsi *ecc vb vedi* **assumere**

assurdità *sf inv* absurdity; **dire delle ~** to talk nonsense; **as'surdo, -a** *ag* absurd

'**asta** *sf* pole; (*modo di vendita*) auction

as'temio, -a *ag* teetotal ▷ *sm/f* teetotaller
▮ Attenzione! In inglese esiste la parola *abstemious*, che però vuol dire *moderato*.

aste'nersi /121/ *vpr*: **~ (da)** to abstain (from), refrain (from); (*Pol*) to abstain (from)

aste'risco, -schi *sm* asterisk

'**astice** ['astitʃe] *sm* lobster

astig'matico, -a, -ci, -che *ag* astigmatic

asti'nenza [asti'nɛntsa] *sf* abstinence; **essere in crisi di ~** to suffer from withdrawal symptoms

as'tratto, -a *ag* abstract

'**astro...** *prefisso* astro; **astrolo'gia** [astrolo'dʒia] *sf* astrology; **astro'nauta, -i, -e** *sm/f* astronaut; **astro'nave** *sf* space ship; **astrono'mia** *sf* astronomy; **astro'nomico, -a, -ci, -che** *ag* astronomic(al)

as'tuccio [as'tuttʃo] *sm* case, box, holder

as'tuto, -a *ag* astute, cunning, shrewd

A'tene *sf* Athens

'ateo, -a *ag, sm/f* atheist

at'lante *sm* atlas

at'lantico, -a, -ci, -che *ag* Atlantic ▷ *sm*: **l'A~, l'Oceano A~** the Atlantic, the Atlantic Ocean

at'leta, -i, -e *sm/f* athlete; **at'letica** *sf* athletics *sg*; **atletica leggera** track and field events *pl*; **atletica pesante** weightlifting and wrestling

atmos'fera *sf* atmosphere

a'tomico, -a, -ci, -che *ag* atomic; (*nucleare*) atomic, atom *cpd*, nuclear

'atomo *sm* atom

'atrio *sm* entrance hall, lobby

a'troce [a'trotʃe] *ag* (*che provoca orrore*) dreadful; (*terribile*) atrocious

attac'cante *smf* (*Sport*) forward

attacca'panni *sm* hook, peg; (*mobile*) hall stand

attac'care /20/ *vt* (*unire*) to attach; (*cucire*) to sew on; (*far aderire*) to stick (on); (*appendere*) to hang (up); (*assalire: anche fig*) to attack; (*iniziare*) to begin, start; (*fig: contagiare*) to pass on ▷ *vi* to stick, adhere; **attaccarsi** *vpr* to stick, adhere; (*trasmettersi*

per contagio) to be contagious; (*afferrarsi*): **attaccarsi (a)** to cling (to); (*fig: affezionarsi*): **attaccarsi (a)** to become attached (to); **~ discorso** to start a conversation;

at'tacco, -chi *sm* (*azione offensiva: anche fig*) attack; (*Med*) attack, fit; (*Sci*) binding; (*Elettr*) socket

atteggia'mento [atteddʒa'mento] *sm* attitude

at'tendere /120/ *vt* to wait for, await ▷ *vi*: **~ a** to attend to

atten'dibile *ag* (*scusa, storia*) credible; (*fonte, testimone, notizia*) reliable

atten'tato *sm* attack; **~ alla vita di qn** attempt on sb's life

attenta'tore, -'trice *sm/f* bomber; **~ suicida** suicide bomber

at'tento, -a *ag* attentive; (*accurato*) careful, thorough ▷ *escl* be careful!; **stare ~ a qc** to pay attention to sth; **attenzi'one** [atten'tsjone] *sf* attention ▷ *escl* watch out!, be careful!; **attenzi'oni** *sfpl* (*premure*) attentions; **fare attenzione a** to watch out for; **coprire qn di attenzioni** to lavish attention on sb

atter'raggio [atter'raddʒo] *sm* landing

atter'rare /72/ *vt* to bring down ▷ *vi* to land

at'tesa *sf* waiting; (*tempo trascorso aspettando*) wait; **essere in ~ di qc** to be waiting for sth

at'tesi *ecc vb vedi* **attendere**

at'teso, -a *pp di* **attendere**

'attico, -ci *sm* attic

attil'lato, -a *ag* (*vestito*) close-fitting

'attimo *sm* moment; **in un ~** in a moment

atti'rare /72/ *vt* to attract

atti'tudine *sf* (*disposizione*) aptitude; (*atteggiamento*) attitude

attività *sf inv* activity; (*Comm*) assets *pl*

at'tivo, -a *ag* active; (*Comm*) profit-making, credit *cpd* ▷ *sm* (*Comm*) assets *pl*; **in ~** in credit

'atto *sm* act; (*azione, gesto*) action, act, deed; (*Dir: documento*) deed, document; **atti** *smpl* (*di congressi ecc*) proceedings; **mettere in ~** to put into action; **fare ~ di fare qc** to make as if to do sth; **~ di nascita/morte** birth/death certificate

at'tore, -'trice *sm/f* actor (actress)

at'torno *av* round, around, about ▷ *prep*: **~ a** round, around, about

attrac'care /20/ *vt, vi* (*Naut*) to dock, berth

at'tracco, -chi *sm* (*Naut*) docking; (: *luogo*) berth

at'trae *ecc vb vedi* **attrarre**

attra'ente *ag* attractive

at'traggo *ecc vb vedi* **attrarre**

at'trarre /123/ *vt* to attract

at'trassi *ecc vb vedi* **attrarre**

attraver'sare /72/ vt to cross; (*città, bosco, fig: periodo*) to go through; (*fiume*) to run through

attra'verso prep through; (*da una parte all'altra*) across

attrazi'one [attrat'tsjone] sf attraction

attrezza'tura sf equipment *no pl*; rigging

at'trezzo sm tool, instrument; (*Sport*) piece of equipment

àt'trice [at'tritʃe] sf vedi **attore**

attu'ale ag (*presente*) present; (*di attualità*) topical

▌ Attenzione! In inglese esiste la parola *actual*, che però vuol dire *effettivo*.

attualità sf inv topicality; (*avvenimento*) current event; **attual'mente** av at the moment, at present

▌ Attenzione! In inglese esiste la parola *actually*, che però vuol dire *effettivamente* oppure *veramente*.

attu'are /72/ vt to carry out; **attuarsi** vpr to be realized

attu'tire /55/ vt to deaden, reduce

'audio sm (*TV, Radio, Cine*) sound

audiovi'sivo, -a ag audiovisual

audizi'one [audit'tsjone] sf hearing; (*Mus*) audition

augu'rare /72/ vt to wish; **augurarsi qc** to hope for sth

au'gurio sm (*good wish*); **auguri** smpl best wishes; **fare gli auguri a qn** to give sb one's best wishes; **tanti auguri!** best wishes!; (*per compleanno*) happy birthday!

'aula sf (*scolastica*) classroom; (*universitaria*) lecture theatre; (*di edificio pubblico*) hall

aumen'tare /72/ vt, vi to increase; **~ di peso** (*persona*) to put on weight; **la produzione è aumentata del 50%** production has increased by 50%; **au'mento** sm increase

au'rora sf dawn

ausili'are ag, sm, smf auxiliary

Aus'tralia sf: **l'~** Australia; **australi'ano, -a** ag, sm/f Australian

'Austria sf: **l'~** Austria; **aus'triaco, -a, -ci, -che** ag, sm/f Austrian

au'tentico, -a, -ci, -che ag authentic, genuine

au'tista, -i sm driver

'auto sf inv car

autoabbron'zante ag self-tanning

autoade'sivo, -a ag self-adhesive ▷ sm sticker

autobio'grafico, -a, -ci, -che ag autobiographic(al)

'autobus sm inv bus

auto'carro sm lorry (*BRIT*), truck

autocertificazi'one [autotʃertifikat'tsjone] sf self-declaration

autodistrut'tivo, -a ag self-destructive

auto'gol sm inv own goal

au'tografo, -a ag, sm autograph

auto'grill® sm inv motorway café

auto'matico, -a, -ci, -che ag automatic ▷ sm (*bottone*) snap fastener; (*fucile*) automatic

auto'mobile sf (*motor*) car; **automobi'lista, -i, -e** sm/f motorist

autono'leggio [autono'leddʒo] sm car hire

autono'mia sf autonomy; (*di volo*) range; **au'tonomo, -a** ag autonomous; independent

autop'sia sf post-mortem (examination), autopsy

auto'radio sf inv (*apparecchio*) car radio; (*autoveicolo*) radio car

au'tore, -'trice sm/f author

autoreg'gente [autored'dʒɛnte] ag: **calze autoreggenti** hold ups

auto'revole ag authoritative; (*persona*) influential

autoricari'cabile ag: **scheda ~** top-up card

autori'messa sf garage

autorità sf inv authority

autoriz'zare [autorid'dzare] /72/ vt (*permettere*) to authorize; (*giustificare*) to allow, sanction

autos'contro sm dodgem car (*BRIT*), bumper car (*US*)

autoscu'ola sf driving school

autos'tima sf self-esteem

autos'top sm hitchhiking; **autostop'pista, -i, -e** sm/f hitchhiker

autos'trada sf motorway (*BRIT*), highway (*US*); **~ informatica** information superhighway

---

❋ **AUTOSTRADE**
❋
❋ You have to pay to use Italian motorways.
❋ They are indicated by an "A" followed by a
❋ number on a green sign. The speed limit
❋ on Italian motorways is 130 kph.

---

auto'velox® sm inv (*police*) speed camera

autovet'tura sf (*motor*) car

au'tunno sm autumn

avam'braccio [avam'brattʃo] (*pl f* **avambraccia**) sm forearm

avangu'ardia sf vanguard

a'vanti av (*stato in luogo*) in front; (*moto: andare, venire*) forward; (*tempo: prima*) before ▷ prep (*luogo*): **~ a** before, in front of; (*tempo*): **~ Cristo** before Christ ▷ escl (*entrate*) come (*o go*) in!; (*Mil*) forward!; (*coraggio*) come on! ▷ sm inv (*Sport*) forward; **~ e indietro** backwards and forwards; **andare ~** to go forward; (*continuare*) to go on; (*precedere*) to go (on) ahead; (*orologio*) to be fast; **essere ~ negli studi** to be well advanced with one's studies

avan'zare [avan'tsare] /72/ *vt* (*spostare in avanti*) to move forward, advance; (*domanda*) to put forward; (*promuovere*) to promote; (*essere creditore*): **~ qc da qn** to be owed sth by sb ▷ *vi* (*andare avanti*) to move forward, advance; (*progredire*) to make progress; (*essere d'avanzo*) to be left, remain

ava'ria *sf* (*guasto*) damage; (: *meccanico*) breakdown

a'varo, -a *ag* avaricious, miserly ▷ *sm* miser

🔵 **PAROLA CHIAVE**

a'vere /13/ *sm* (Comm) credit; **gli averi** (*ricchezze*) wealth *sg*
▶*vt* **1** (*possedere*) to have; **ha due bambini/una bella casa** she has (got) two children/a lovely house; **ha i capelli lunghi** he has (got) long hair; **non ho da mangiare/bere** I've (got) nothing to eat/drink, I don't have anything to eat/drink
2 (*indossare*) to wear, have on; **aveva una maglietta rossa** he was wearing *o* he had on a red T-shirt; **ha gli occhiali** he wears *o* has glasses
3 (*ricevere*) to get; **hai avuto l'assegno?** did you get *o* have you had the cheque?
4 (*età, dimensione*) to be; **ha 9 anni** he is 9 (years old); **la stanza ha 3 metri di lunghezza** the room is 3 metres in length; *vedi* **fame; paura; sonno** *ecc*
5 (*tempo*): **quanti ne abbiamo oggi?** what's the date today?; **ne hai per molto?** will you be long?
6 (*fraseologia*): **avercela con qn** to be angry with sb; **cos'hai?** what's wrong *o* what's the matter (with you)?; **non ha niente a che vedere *o* fare con me** it's got nothing to do with me
▶*vb aus* **1** to have; **aver bevuto/mangiato** to have drunk/eaten
2 (+ *da* + *infinito*): **avere da fare qc** to have to do sth; **non hai che da chiederlo** you only have to ask him

aviazi'one [avjat'tsjone] *sf* aviation; (*Mil*) air force

'avido, -a *ag* eager; (*peg*) greedy

avo'cado *sm* avocado

a'vorio *sm* ivory

Avv. *abbr* = **avvocato**

avvantaggi'are [avvantad'dʒare] /62/ *vt* to favour; **avvantaggiarsi** *vpr*: **avvantaggiarsi negli affari/sui concorrenti** to get ahead in business/of one's competitors

avvele'nare /72/ *vt* to poison

av'vengo *ecc vb vedi* **avvenire**

avveni'mento *sm* event

avve'nire /128/ *vi, vb impers* to happen, occur ▷ *sm* future

av'venni *ecc vb vedi* **avvenire**

avven'tato, -a *ag* rash, reckless

avven'tura *sf* adventure; (*amorosa*) affair

avventu'rarsi /72/ *vpr* to venture

avventu'roso, -a *ag* adventurous

avve'rarsi /72/ *vpr* to come true

av'verbio *sm* adverb

avverrò *ecc vb vedi* **avvenire**

avver'sario, -a *ag* opposing ▷ *sm* opponent, adversary

avver'tenza [avver'tentsa] *sf* (*ammonimento*) warning; (*cautela*) care; (*premessa*) foreword; **avvertenze** *sfpl* (*istruzioni per l'uso*) instructions

avverti'mento *sm* warning

avver'tire /45/ *vt* (*avvisare*) to warn; (*rendere consapevole*) to inform, notify; (*percepire*) to feel

avvi'are /60/ *vt* (*mettere sul cammino*) to direct; (*impresa, trattative*) to begin, start; (*motore*) to start; **avviarsi** *vpr* to set off, set out

avvici'nare [avvitʃi'nare] /72/ *vt* to bring near; (*trattare con: persona*) to approach; **avvicinarsi** *vpr*: **avvicinarsi (a qn/qc)** to approach (sb/sth), draw near (to sb/sth)

avvi'lito, -a *ag* discouraged

avvin'cente [avvin'tʃente] *ag* enthralling

avvi'sare /72/ *vt* (*far sapere*) to inform; (*mettere in guardia*) to warn; **av'viso** *sm* warning; (*annuncio*) announcement; (*affisso*) notice; (*inserzione pubblicitaria*) advertisement; **a mio avviso** in my opinion; **avviso di chiamata** (*servizio*) call waiting; (*segnale*) call waiting signal; **avviso di garanzia** (*Dir*) notification (*of impending investigation and of the right to name a defence laywer*)

▍ Attenzione! In inglese esiste la parola *advice*, che però vuol dire *consiglio*.

avvis'tare /72/ *vt* to sight

avvi'tare /72/ *vt* to screw down (*o* in)

avvo'cato, -'essa *sm/f* (*Dir*) barrister (BRIT), lawyer; (*fig*) defender, advocate

av'volgere [av'vɔldʒere] /96/ *vt* to roll up; (*avviluppare*) to wrap up; **avvolgersi** *vpr* (*avvilupparsi*) to wrap o.s. up; **avvol'gibile** *sm* roller blind (BRIT), blind

av'volsi *ecc vb vedi* **avvolgere**

avvol'toio *sm* vulture

aza'lea [addza'lɛa] *sf* azalea

azi'enda [ad'dzjɛnda] *sf* business, firm, concern; **~ agricola** farm

azi'one [at'tsjone] *sf* action; (*Comm*) share

a'zoto [ad'dzɔto] *sm* nitrogen

azzar'dare [addzar'dare] /72/ *vt* (*soldi, vita*) to risk, hazard; (*domanda, ipotesi*) to hazard, venture; **azzardarsi** *vpr*: **azzardarsi a fare** to dare (to) do

az'zardo [ad'dzardo] *sm* risk

azzec'care [attsek'kare] /20/ *vt* (*risposta, pronostico*) to get right

azzuf'farsi [attsuf'farsi] /72/ *vpr* to come to blows

az'zurro, -a [ad'dzurro] *ag* blue ▷ *sm* (*colore*) blue; **gli azzurri** (*Sport*) the Italian national team

'babbo *sm* (*fam*) dad, daddy; **B~ Natale** Father Christmas

baby'sitter ['beɪbɪsitəʳ] *sm inv, f inv* baby-sitter

'bacca, -che *sf* berry

baccalà *sm* dried salted cod; (*fig: peg*) dummy

bac'chetta [bak'ketta] *sf* (*verga*) stick, rod; (*di direttore d'orchestra*) baton; (*di tamburo*) drumstick; **~ magica** magic wand

ba'checa, -che [ba'kɛka] *sf* (*mobile*) showcase, display case; (*Università, in ufficio*) notice board (*BRIT*), bulletin board (*US*)

baci'are [ba'tʃare] /14/ *vt* to kiss; **baciarsi** *vpr* to kiss (one another)

baci'nella [batʃi'nɛlla] *sf* basin

ba'cino [ba'tʃino] *sm* basin; (*Mineralogia*) field, bed; (*Anat*) pelvis; (*Naut*) dock; **~ d'utenza** catchment area

'bacio ['batʃo] *sm* kiss

'baco, -chi *sm* worm; **~ da seta** silkworm

ba'dante *smf* care worker

ba'dare /72/ *vi* (*fare attenzione*) to take care, be careful; **~ a** (*occuparsi di*) to look after, take care of; (*dar ascolto*) to pay attention to; **bada ai fatti tuoi!** mind your own business!

'baffi *smpl* moustache *sg*; (*di animale*) whiskers; **leccarsi i ~** to lick one's lips; **ridere sotto i ~** to laugh up one's sleeve

bagagli'aio [bagaʎ'ʎajo] *sm* luggage van (*BRIT*) o car (*US*); (*Aut*) boot (*BRIT*), trunk (*US*)

ba'gaglio [ba'gaʎʎo] *sm* luggage *no pl*, baggage *no pl*; **fare/disfare i bagagli** to pack/unpack; **~ a mano** hand luggage

bagli'ore [baʎ'ʎore] *sm* flash, dazzling light; **un ~ di speranza** a (sudden) ray of hope

ba'gnante [baɲ'ɲante] smf bather
ba'gnare [baɲ'ɲare] /15/ vt to wet; (inzuppare) to soak; (innaffiare) to water; (fiume) to flow through; (: mare) to wash, bathe; **bagnarsi** vpr to get wet; (al mare) to go swimming o bathing; (in vasca) to have a bath
ba'gnato, -a [baɲ'ɲato] ag wet
ba'gnino [baɲ'ɲino] sm lifeguard
'bagno ['baɲɲo] sm bath; (locale) bathroom; (toilette) toilet; **bagni** smpl (stabilimento) baths; **fare il ~** to have a bath; (nel mare) to go swimming o bathing; **fare il ~ a qn** to give sb a bath; **mettere a ~** to soak
bagnoma'ria [baɲɲoma'ria] sm: **cuocere a ~** to cook in a double saucepan (BRIT) o double boiler (US)
bagnoschi'uma [baɲɲoskj'uma] sm inv bubble bath
'baia sf bay
balbet'tare /72/ vi to stutter, stammer; (bimbo) to babble ▷ vt to stammer out
bal'canico, -a, -ci, -che ag Balkan
bal'cone sm balcony
bal'doria sf: **fare ~** to have a riotous time
ba'lena sf whale
ba'leno sm flash of lightning; **in un ~** in a flash
bal'lare /72/ vt, vi to dance
balle'rina sf dancer; ballet dancer; (scarpa) ballet shoe
balle'rino sm dancer; ballet dancer
bal'letto sm ballet
'ballo sm dance; (azione) dancing no pl; **essere in ~** (fig: persona) to be involved; (: cosa) to be at stake
balne'are ag seaside cpd; (stagione) bathing
'balsamo sm (aroma) balsam; (lenimento, fig) balm; (per capelli) conditioner
bal'zare [bal'tsare] /72/ vi to bounce; (lanciarsi) to jump, leap; **'balzo** sm bounce; jump, leap; (del terreno) crag
bam'bina sf vedi **bambino**
bam'bino, -a sm/f child
'bambola sf doll
bambù sm bamboo
ba'nale ag banal, commonplace
ba'nana sf banana
'banca, -che sf bank; **~ (di) dati** data bank
banca'rella sf stall
banca'rotta sf bankruptcy; **fare ~** to go bankrupt
ban'chetto [ban'ketto] sm banquet
banchi'ere [ban'kjɛre] sm banker
ban'china [ban'kina] sf (di porto) quay; (per pedoni, ciclisti) path; (di stazione) platform; **~ cedevole** (Aut) soft verge (BRIT) o shoulder (US)

'banco, -chi sm bench; (di negozio) counter; (di mercato) stall; (di officina) (work)bench; (Geo, banca) bank; **~ di corallo** coral reef; **~ degli imputati** dock; **~ di prova** (fig) testing ground; **~ dei testimoni** witness box (BRIT) o stand (US); **~ dei pegni** pawnshop; **~ di nebbia** bank of fog
'Bancomat® sm inv automated banking; (tessera) cash card; (sportello automatico) cashpoint
banco'nota sf banknote
'banda sf band; (di stoffa) band, stripe; (lato, parte) side; **~ larga** broadband
bandi'era sf flag, banner
ban'dito sm outlaw, bandit
'bando sm proclamation; (esilio) exile, banishment; **~ alle ciance!** that's enough talk!; **~ di concorso** announcement of a competition
bar sm inv bar
'bara sf coffin
ba'racca, -che sf shed, hut; (peg) hovel; **mandare avanti la ~** to keep things going
ba'rare /72/ vi to cheat
'baratro sm abyss
ba'ratto sm barter
ba'rattolo sm (di latta) tin; (di vetro) jar; (di coccio) pot
'barba sf beard; **farsi la ~** to shave; **farla in ~ a qn** (fig) to do sth to sb's face; **servire qn di ~ e capelli** (fig) to teach sb a lesson; **che ~!** what a bore!
barbabi'etola sf beetroot (BRIT), beet (US); **~ da zucchero** sugar beet
barbi'ere sm barber
bar'bone sm (cane) poodle; (vagabondo) tramp
'barca, -che sf boat; **~ a motore** motorboat; **~ a remi** rowing boat; **~ a vela** sailing boat (BRIT), sailboat (US)
barcol'lare /72/ vi to stagger
ba'rella sf (lettiga) stretcher
ba'rile sm barrel, cask
ba'rista, -i, -e sm/f barman (barmaid); (proprietario) bar owner
ba'rocco, -a, -chi, -che ag, sm baroque
ba'rometro sm barometer
ba'rone sm baron; **baro'nessa** sf baroness
'barra sf bar; (Naut) helm; (linea grafica) line, stroke
bar'rare /72/ vt to bar
barri'care /20/ vt to barricade; **barricarsi** vpr to barricade o.s.
barri'era sf barrier; (Geo) reef
ba'ruffa sf scuffle
barzel'letta [bardzel'letta] sf joke, funny story
ba'sare /72/ vt to base, found; **basarsi** vpr: **basarsi su** (fatti, prove) to be based

o founded on; (*persona*) to base one's arguments on

'basco, -a, -schi, -sche *ag* Basque ▷ *sm* (*copricapo*) beret

'base *sf* base; (*fig: fondamento*) basis; (*Pol*) rank and file; **di ~** basic; **in ~ a** on the basis of, according to; **a ~ di caffè** coffee-based

'baseball ['beizbɔ:l] *sm* baseball

ba'silica, -che *sf* basilica

ba'silico *sm* basil

'basket ['basket] *sm* basketball

bas'sista, -i, -e *sm/f* bass player

'basso, -a *ag* low; (*di statura*) short; (*meridionale*) southern ▷ *sm* bottom, lower part; (*Mus*) bass; **la bassa Italia** southern Italy

bassorili'evo *sm* bas-relief

bas'sotto, -a *ag* squat ▷ *sm* (*cane*) dachshund

'basta *escl* (that's) enough!, that will do!

bas'tardo, -a *ag* (*animale, pianta*) hybrid, crossbreed; (*persona*) illegitimate, bastard (!) ▷ *sm/f* illegitimate child, bastard (*peg*)

bas'tare /72/ *vi, vb impers* to be enough, be sufficient; **~ a qn** to be enough for sb; **basta chiedere** *o* **che chieda a un vigile** you have only to *o* need only ask a police officer; **basta così, grazie** that's enough, thanks

basto'nare /72/ *vt* to beat, thrash

baston'cino [baston'tʃino] *sm* (*Sci*) ski pole; **bastoncini di pesce** fish fingers

bas'tone *sm* stick; **~ da passeggio** walking stick

bat'taglia [bat'taʎʎa] *sf* battle; fight

bat'tello *sm* boat

bat'tente *sm* (*imposta: di porta*) wing, flap; (: *di finestra*) shutter; (*batacchio: di porta*) knocker; (: *di orologio*) hammer; **chiudere i battenti** (*fig*) to shut up shop

'battere /1/ *vt* to beat; (*grano*) to thresh; (*percorrere*) to scour ▷ *vi* (*bussare*) to knock; (*pioggia, sole*) to beat down; (*cuore*) to beat; (*Tennis*) to serve; (*urtare*): **~ contro** to hit *o* strike against; **battersi** *vpr* to fight; **~ le mani** to clap; **~ i piedi** to stamp one's feet; **~ a macchina** to type; **~ bandiera italiana** to fly the Italian flag; **~ in testa** (*Aut*) to knock; **in un batter d'occhio** in the twinkling of an eye

batte'ria *sf* battery; (*Mus*) drums *pl*

bat'terio *sm* bacterium

batte'rista, -i, -e *sm/f* drummer

bat'tesimo *sm* (*rito*) baptism; christening

battez'zare [batted'dzare] /72/ *vt* to baptize; to christen

batti'panni *sm inv* carpet-beater

battis'trada *sm inv* (*di pneumatico*) tread; (*di gara*) pacemaker

'battito *sm* beat, throb; **~ cardiaco** heartbeat

bat'tuta *sf* blow; (*di macchina da scrivere*) stroke; (*Mus*) bar; beat; (*Teat*) cue; (*frase spiritosa*) witty remark; (*di caccia*) beating; (*Polizia*) combing, scouring; (*Tennis*) service

ba'tuffolo *sm* wad

ba'ule *sm* trunk; (*Aut*) boot (BRIT), trunk (US)

'bava *sf* (*di animale*) slaver, slobber; (*di lumaca*) slime; (*di vento*) breath

bava'glino [bavaʎ'ʎino] *sm* bib

ba'vaglio [ba'vaʎʎo] *sm* gag

'bavero *sm* collar

ba'zar [bad'dzar] *sm inv* bazaar

BCE *sigla f* (= *Banca centrale europea*) ECB

be'ato, -a *ag* blessed; (*fig*) happy; **~ te!** lucky you!

bec'care /20/ *vt* to peck; (*fig: raffreddore*) to catch; **beccarsi** *vpr* (*fig*) to squabble; **beccarsi qc** to catch sth

beccherò *ecc* [bekke'rɔ] *vb vedi* **beccare**

'becco, -chi *sm* beak, bill; (*di caffettiera ecc*) spout; lip

Be'fana *sf* old woman who, according to legend, brings children their presents at the Epiphany; (*Epifania*) Epiphany; **befana** hag, witch

---

● **BEFANA**
●
● Marking the end of the traditional 12 days
● of Christmas on 6 January, the *Befana*, or
● the feast of the Epiphany, is a national
● holiday in Italy. It is named after the old
● woman who, legend has it, comes down
● the chimney the night before, bringing
● gifts to children who have been good
● during the year and leaving lumps of coal
● for those who have not.

---

bef'fardo, -a *ag* scornful, mocking

'begli ['beʎʎi], **'bei** *ag vedi* **bello**

beige [bɛʒ] *ag inv* beige

bel *ag vedi* **bello**

be'lare /72/ *vi* to bleat

'belga, -gi, -ghe *ag, smf* Belgian

'Belgio ['bɛldʒo] *sm*: **il ~** Belgium

'bella *sf* (*Sport*) decider; *vedi* **bello**

bel'lezza [bel'lettsa] *sf* beauty

 PAROLA CHIAVE

'bello, -a (*ag: dav sm* **bel** + C, **bell'** + V, **bello** + *s impura, gn, pn, ps, x, z, pl* **bei** + C, **begli** + *s impura ecc o* V) *ag* **1** (*oggetto, donna, paesaggio*) beautiful, lovely; (*uomo*) handsome; (*tempo*) beautiful, fine, lovely; **le belle arti** fine arts

2 (*quantità*): **una bella cifra** a considerable sum of money; **un bel niente** absolutely nothing

3 (*rafforzativo*): **è una truffa bella e buona!** it's a real fraud!; **è bell'e finito** it's already finished

▶ *sm* **1** (*bellezza*) beauty; (: *tempo*) fine weather

2: adesso viene il bello now comes the best bit; **sul più bello** at the crucial point; **cosa fai di bello?** are you doing anything interesting?

▶ *av*: **fa bello** the weather is fine, it's fine

'**belva** *sf* wild animal

belve'dere *sm inv* panoramic viewpoint

benché [ben'ke] *cong* although

'**benda** *sf* bandage; (*per gli occhi*) blindfold; **ben'dare** /72/ *vt* to bandage; to blindfold

'**bene** *av* well; (*completamente, affatto*): **è ben difficile** it's very difficult ▷ *ag inv*: **gente ~** well-to-do people ▷ *sm* good; **beni** *smpl* (*averi*) property *sg*, estate *sg*; **io sto ~/ poco ~** I'm well/not very well; **va ~** all right; **volere un ~ dell'anima a qn** to love sb very much; **un uomo per ~** a respectable man; **fare ~** to do the right thing; **fare ~ a** (*salute*) to be good for; **fare del ~ a qn** to do sb a good turn; **beni di consumo** consumer goods

bene'detto, -a *pp di* **benedire** ▷ *ag* blessed, holy

bene'dire /38/ *vt* to bless; to consecrate

benedu'cato, -a *ag* well-mannered

benefi'cenza [benefi'tʃɛntsa] *sf* charity

bene'ficio [bene'fitʃo] *sm* benefit; **con ~ d'inventario** (*fig*) with reservations

be'nessere *sm* well-being

benes'tante *ag* well-to-do

be'nigno, -a [be'niɲɲo] *ag* kind, kindly; (*critica ecc*) favourable; (*Med*) benign

benve'nuto, -a *ag*, *sm* welcome; **dare il ~ a qn** to welcome sb

ben'zina [ben'dzina] *sf* petrol (BRIT), gas (US); **fare ~** to get petrol *o* gas; **rimanere senza ~** to run out of petrol *o* gas; **~ verde** unleaded petrol; **benzi'naio** *sm* petrol (BRIT) *o* gas (US) pump attendant

'**bere** /16/ *vt* to drink; **darla a ~ a qn** (*fig*) to fool sb

ber'lina *sf* (*Aut*) saloon (car) (BRIT), sedan (US)

Ber'lino *sf* Berlin

ber'muda *smpl* (*calzoncini*) Bermuda shorts

ber'noccolo *sm* bump; (*inclinazione*) flair

ber'retto *sm* cap

berrò *ecc vb vedi* **bere**

ber'saglio [ber'saʎʎo] *sm* target

bescia'mella [beʃʃa'mɛlla] *sf* béchamel sauce

bes'temmia *sf* curse; (*Rel*) blasphemy; **bestemmi'are** /19/ *vi* to curse, swear; to blaspheme ▷ *vt* to curse, swear at; to blaspheme

'**bestia** *sf* animal; **andare in ~** (*fig*) to fly into a rage; **besti'ale** *ag* beastly; animal *cpd*; (*fam*): **fa un freddo bestiale** it's bitterly cold; **besti'ame** *sm* livestock; (*bovino*) cattle *pl*

be'tulla *sf* birch

be'vanda *sf* drink, beverage

'**bevo** *ecc vb vedi* **bere**

be'vuto, -a *pp di* **bere**

'**bevvi** *ecc vb vedi* **bere**

bianche'ria [bjanke'ria] *sf* linen; **~ intima** underwear; **~ da donna** ladies' underwear, lingerie; **~ femminile** lingerie

bi'anco, -a, -chi, -che *ag* white; (*non scritto*) blank ▷ *sm* white; (*intonaco*) whitewash ▷ *sm/f* white, white man (woman); **in ~** (*foglio, assegno*) blank; **in ~ e nero** (TV, Fot) black and white; **mangiare in ~** to follow a bland diet; **pesce in ~** boiled fish; **andare in ~** (*non riuscire*) to fail; **notte bianca** *o* **in ~** sleepless night; **~ dell'uovo** egg-white

biasi'mare /72/ *vt* to disapprove of, censure

'**Bibbia** *sf* (*anche fig*) Bible

bibe'ron *sm inv* feeding bottle

'**bibita** *sf* (soft) drink

biblio'teca, -che *sf* library; (*mobile*) bookcase

bicarbo'nato *sm*: **~ (di sodio)** bicarbonate (of soda)

bicchi'ere [bik'kjɛre] *sm* glass

bici'cletta [bitʃi'kletta] *sf* bicycle; **andare in ~** to cycle

bidè *sm inv* bidet

bi'dello, -a *sm/f* (Ins) janitor

bi'done *sm* drum, can; (*anche*: **~ dell'immondizia**) (dust)bin; (*fam*: *truffa*) swindle; **fare un ~ a qn** (*fam*) to let sb down; to cheat sb

bien'nale *ag* biennial

◦ BIENNALE DI VENEZIA
◦
◦ Dating back to 1895, the *Biennale di*
◦ *Venezia* is an international festival of the
◦ contemporary arts. It takes place every
◦ two years in the "Giardini Pubblici". The
◦ various countries taking part each put on
◦ exhibitions in their own pavilions. There is
◦ a section dedicated to the work of young
◦ artists, as well as a special exhibition
◦ organized around a specific theme for
◦ that year.

bifami'liare *ag* (*villa, casetta*) semi-detached

bifor'carsi /20/ *vpr* to fork

bigiotte'ria [bidʒotte'ria] *sf* costume jewellery (BRIT) o jewelry (US); (*negozio*) jeweller's (shop) (BRIT) o jewelry store (US: *selling only costume jewellery*)

bigliet'taio, -a *sm/f* (*nei treni*) ticket inspector; (*in autobus ecc*) conductor

bigliette'ria [biʎʎette'ria] *sf* (*di stazione*) ticket office; booking office; (*di teatro*) box office

bigli'etto [biʎ'ʎetto] *sm* (*per viaggi, spettacoli ecc*) ticket; (*cartoncino*) card; **~ di banca** (bank)note; (*anche*: **~ d'auguri/da visita**) greetings/visiting card; **~ di andata e ritorno** return (BRIT) o round-trip (US) ticket; **~ di sola andata** single (ticket); **~ elettronico** e-ticket

bignè [biɲ'ɲɛ] *sm inv* cream puff

bigo'dino *sm* roller, curler

bi'gotto, -a *ag* over-pious ▷ *sm/f* church fiend

bi'kini *sm inv* bikini

bi'lancia, -ce [bi'lantʃa] *sf* (*pesa*) scales *pl*; (*: di precisione*) balance; **B~** Libra; **~ commerciale/dei pagamenti** balance of trade/payments

bi'lancio [bi'lantʃo] *sm* (*Comm*) balance (sheet); (*statale*) budget; **fare il ~ di** (*fig*) to assess; **~ consuntivo** (final) balance; **~ preventivo** budget

biliar'dino *sm* pinball

bili'ardo *sm* billiards *sg*; (*tavolo*) billiard table

bi'lingue *ag* bilingual

bilo'cale *sm* two-room flat (BRIT) o apartment (US)

'bimbo, -a *sm/f* little boy (girl)

bi'nario, -a *ag* (*sistema*) binary ▷ *sm* (*railway*) track o line; (*piattaforma*) platform; **~ morto** dead-end track

bi'nocolo *sm* binoculars *pl*

bio... *prefisso* bio; **biocarbu'rante** *sm* biofuel; **biodegra'dabile** *ag* biodegradable; **biodi'namico, -a, -ci, -che** *ag* biodynamic; **biogra'fia** *sf* biography; **biolo'gia** *sf* biology

bio'logico, -a, -ci, -che *ag* (*scienze, fenomeni ecc*) biological; (*agricoltura, prodotti*) organic; **guerra biologica** biological warfare

bi'ondo, -a *ag* blond, fair

biotecnolo'gia [bioteknolo'dʒia] *sf* biotechnology

bipo'lare *ag* bipolar

biri'chino, -a [biri'kino] *ag* mischievous ▷ *sm/f* scamp, little rascal

bi'rillo *sm* skittle (BRIT), pin (US)

'biro® *sf inv* biro®

'birra *sf* beer; **~ chiara/scura** lager/stout; **a tutta ~** (*fig*) at top speed; **birre'ria** *sf* ≈ bierkeller

bis *escl, sm inv* encore

bis'betico, -a, -ci, -che *ag* ill-tempered, crabby

bisbigli'are [bizbiʎ'ʎare] /27/ *vt, vi* to whisper

'bisca, -sche *sf* gambling house

'biscia, -sce ['biʃʃa] *sf* snake; **~ d'acqua** water snake

biscot'tato, -a *ag* crisp; **fette biscottate** rusks

bis'cotto *sm* biscuit

bisessu'ale *ag, smf* bisexual

bises'tile *ag*: **anno ~** leap year

bis'nonno, -a *sm/f* great grandfather/grandmother

biso'gnare [bizoɲ'ɲare] /15/ *vb impers*: **bisogna che tu parta/lo faccia** you'll have to go/do it; **bisogna parlargli** we'll (*o* I'll) have to talk to him

bi'sogno [bi'zoɲɲo] *sm* need; **ha ~ di qualcosa?** do you need anything?

bis'tecca, -che *sf* steak, beefsteak

bisticci'are [bistit'tʃare] /14/ *vi* to quarrel, bicker; **bisticciarsi** *vpr* to quarrel, bicker

'bisturi *sm inv* scalpel

'bivio *sm* fork; (*fig*) dilemma

biz'zarro, -a [bid'dzarro] *ag* bizarre, strange

blate'rare /72/ *vi* to chatter

blin'dato, -a *ag* armoured

bloc'care /20/ *vt* to block; (*isolare*) to isolate, cut off; (*porto*) to blockade; (*prezzi, beni*) to freeze; (*meccanismo*) to jam; **bloccarsi** *vpr* (*motore*) to stall; (*freni, porta*) to jam, stick; (*ascensore*) to get stuck, stop

blocchè'rò *ecc* [blokke'rɔ] *vb vedi* **bloccare**

bloc'chetto [blok'ketto] *sm* notebook; (*di biglietti*) book

'blocco, -chi *sm* block; (*Mil*) blockade; (*dei fitti*) restriction; (*quadernetto*) pad; (*fig: unione*) coalition; (*il bloccare*) blocking; isolating, cutting-off; blockading; freezing; jamming; **in ~** (*nell'insieme*) as a whole; (*Comm*) in bulk; **~ cardiaco** cardiac arrest; **~ stradale** road block

blog [blog] *sm inv* blog

'bloggare /80/ *vi* to blog

blogo'sfera *sf* blogosphere

blu *ag inv, sm inv* dark blue

'blusa *sf* (*camiciotto*) smock; (*camicetta*) blouse

'boa *sm inv* (*Zool*) boa constrictor; (*sciarpa*) feather boa ▷ *sf* buoy

bo'ato *sm* rumble, roar

bob [bɔb] *sm inv* bobsleigh

'bocca, -che *sf* mouth; **in ~ al lupo!** good luck!

boc'caccia, -ce [bok'kattʃa] *sf* (*malalingua*) gossip; **fare le boccacce** to pull faces

boc'cale *sm* jug; **~ da birra** tankard

boc'cetta [bot'tʃetta] *sf* small bottle

'boccia, -ce ['bottʃa] *sf* bottle; (*da vino*) decanter, carafe; (*palla di legno, metallo*) bowl; **gioco delle bocce** bowls *sg*

bocci'are [bot'tʃare] /14/ *vt* (*proposta, progetto*) to reject; (*Ins*) to fail; (*Bocce*) to hit

bocci'olo [bot'tʃɔlo] *sm* bud

boc'cone *sm* mouthful, morsel

boicot'tare /72/ *vt* to boycott

'bolla *sf* bubble; (*Med*) blister; **~ di consegna** (*Comm*) delivery note; **~ papale** papal bull

bol'lente *ag* boiling; boiling hot

bol'letta *sf* bill; (*ricevuta*) receipt; **essere in ~** to be hard up

bollet'tino *sm* bulletin; (*Comm*) note; **~ meteorologico** weather forecast; **~ di spedizione** consignment note

bolli'cina [bolli'tʃina] *sf* bubble

bol'lire /17/ *vt, vi* to boil

bolli'tore *sm* boiler; (*Cuc: per acqua*) kettle

'bollo *sm* stamp; **~ per patente** driving licence tax; **~ postale** postmark

'bomba *sf* bomb; **~ atomica** atom bomb; **~ a mano** hand grenade; **~ ad orologeria** time bomb

bombarda'mento *sm* bombardment; bombing

bombar'dare /72/ *vt* to bombard; (*da aereo*) to bomb

'bombola *sf* cylinder

bombo'letta *sf* spray can

bomboni'era *sf* box of sweets (*as souvenir at weddings, first communions etc*)

bo'nifico, -ci *sm* (*riduzione, abbuono*) discount; (*versamento a terzi*) credit transfer

bontà *sf* goodness; (*cortesia*) kindness; **aver la ~ di fare qc** to be good o kind enough to do sth

borbot'tare /72/ *vi* to mumble

'borchia ['bɔrkja] *sf* stud

bor'deaux [bor'dɔ] *ag inv, sm inv* maroon

'bordo *sm* (*Naut*) ship's side; (*orlo*) edge; (*striscia di guarnizione*) border, trim; **a ~ di** (*nave, aereo*) aboard, on board; (*macchina*) in

bor'ghese [bor'geze] *ag* (*spesso peg*) middle-class; bourgeois; **abito ~** civilian dress

'borgo, -ghi *sm* (*paesino*) village; (*quartiere*) district; (*sobborgo*) suburb

boro'talco *sm* talcum powder

bor'raccia, -ce [bor'rattʃa] *sf* canteen, water-bottle

'borsa *sf* bag; (*anche*: **~ da signora**) handbag; (*Econ*): **la B~ (valori)** the Stock Exchange; **~ dell'acqua calda** hot-water

bottle; **~ nera** black market; **~ della spesa** shopping bag; **~ di studio** grant; **borsel'lino** *sm* purse; **bor'setta** *sf* handbag

'bosco, -schi *sm* wood

bos'niaco, -a, -ci, -che *ag, sm/f* Bosnian

'Bosnia-Erze'govina ['bɔsnja erdze'govina] *sf*: **la ~** Bosnia-Herzegovina

Bot, bot *sigla m inv* (= *buono ordinario del Tesoro*) short-term Treasury bond

bo'tanico, -a, -ci, -che *ag* botanical ▷ *sm* botanist ▷ *sf* botany

'botola *sf* trap door

'botta *sf* blow; (*rumore*) bang

'botte *sf* barrel, cask

bot'tega, -ghe *sf* shop; (*officina*) workshop

bot'tiglia [bot'tiʎʎa] *sf* bottle; **bottiglie'ria** *sf* wine shop

bot'tino *sm* (*di guerra*) booty; (*di rapina, furto*) loot

'botto *sm* bang; crash; **di ~** suddenly

bot'tone *sm* button; **attaccare (un) ~ a qn** to buttonhole sb

bo'vino, -a *ag* bovine; **bovini** *smpl* cattle

box [bɔks] *sm inv* (*per cavalli*) horsebox; (*per macchina*) lock-up; (*per macchina da corsa*) pit; (*per bambini*) playpen

boxe [bɔks] *sf* boxing

'boxer ['bɔkser] *sm inv* (*cane*) boxer ▷ *smpl* (*mutande*): **un paio di ~** a pair of boxer shorts

BR *sigla fpl* = **Brigate Rosse**

brac'cetto [brat'tʃetto] *sm*: **a ~** arm in arm

braccia'letto [brattʃa'letto] *sm* bracelet, bangle

bracci'ata [brat'tʃata] *sf* (*nel nuoto*) stroke

'braccio ['brattʃo] *sm* (*pl f* **braccia**) (*Anat*) arm; (*pl m* **bracci**) (*di gru, fiume*) arm; (*di edificio*) wing; **~ di mare** sound; **bracci'olo** *sm* (*appoggio*) arm

'bracco, -chi *sm* hound

'brace ['bratʃe] *sf* embers *pl*

braci'ola [bra'tʃɔla] *sf* (*Cuc*) chop

'branca, -che *sf* branch

'branchia ['brankja] *sf* (*Zool*) gill

'branco, -chi *sm* (*di cani, lupi*) pack; (*di uccelli, pecore*) flock; (*peg: di persone*) gang, pack

bran'dina *sf* camp bed (BRIT), cot (US)

'brano *sm* piece; (*di libro*) passage

Bra'sile *sm*: **il ~** Brazil; **brasili'ano, -a** *ag, sm/f* Brazilian

'bravo, -a *ag* (*abile*) clever, capable, skilful; (*buono*) good, honest; (*: bambino*) good; (*coraggioso*) brave; **~!** well done!; (*al teatro*) bravo!

bra'vura *sf* cleverness, skill

Bre'tagna [bre'taɲɲa] *sf*: **la ~** Brittany

bre'tella *sf* (*Aut*) link; **bretelle** *sfpl* (*di calzoni*) braces

bret(t)one *ag*, *smf* Breton
'**breve** *ag* brief, short; **in ~** in short
brevet'tare /72/ *vt* to patent
bre'vetto *sm* patent; **~ di pilotaggio** pilot's licence (BRIT) *o* license (US)
'**bricco, -chi** *sm* jug; **~ del caffè** coffeepot
bri'ciola ['britʃola] *sf* crumb
bri'ciolo ['britʃolo] *sm* (*fig*) bit
'**briga, -ghe** *sf* (*fastidio*) trouble, bother; **pigliarsi la ~ di fare qc** to take the trouble to do sth
bri'gata *sf* (*Mil*) brigade; (*gruppo*) group, party; **le Brigate Rosse** (*Pol*) the Red Brigades
'**briglia** ['briʎʎa] *sf* rein; **a ~ sciolta** at full gallop; (*fig*) at full speed
bril'lante *ag* bright; (*anche fig*) brilliant; (*che luccica*) shining ▷ *sm* diamond
bril'lare /72/ *vi* to shine; (*mina*) to blow up ▷ *vt* (*mina*) to set off
'**brillo, -a** *ag* merry, tipsy
'**brina** *sf* hoarfrost
brin'dare /72/ *vi:* **~ a qn/qc** to drink to *o* toast sb/sth
'**brindisi** *sm inv* toast
bri'oche [bri'ɔʃ] *sf inv* brioche (bun)
bri'tannico, -a, -ci, -che *ag* British
'**brivido** *sm* shiver; (*di ribrezzo*) shudder; (*fig*) thrill
brizzo'lato, -a [brittso'lato] *ag* (*persona*) going grey; (*barba, capelli*) greying
'**brocca, -che** *sf* jug
'**broccoli** *smpl* broccoli *sg*
'**brodo** *sm* broth; (*per cucinare*) stock; **~ ristretto** consommé
bron'chite [bron'kite] *sf* (*Med*) bronchitis
bronto'lare /72/ *vi* to grumble; (*tuono, stomaco*) to rumble
'**bronzo** ['brondzo] *sm* bronze
'**browser** ['brauzer] *sm inv* (*Inform*) browser
brucia'pelo [brutʃa'pelo]: **a ~** *av* point-blank
bruci'are [bru'tʃare] /14/ *vt* to burn; (*scottare*) to scald ▷ *vi* to burn; **bruciarsi** *vpr* to burn o.s.; (*fallire*) to ruin one's chances; **~ le tappe** *o* **i tempi** (*fig*) to shoot ahead; **bruciarsi la carriera** to put an end to one's career
'**bruco, -chi** *sm* grub; (*di farfalla*) caterpillar
'**brufolo** *sm* pimple, spot
'**brullo, -a** *ag* bare, bleak
'**bruno, -a** *ag* brown, dark; (*persona*) dark(-haired)
'**brusco, -a, -schi, -sche** *ag* (*sapore*) sharp; (*modi, persona*) brusque, abrupt; (*movimento*) abrupt, sudden
bru'sio *sm* buzz, buzzing
bru'tale *ag* brutal

'**brutto, -a** *ag* ugly; (*cattivo*) bad; (*malattia, strada, affare*) nasty, bad; **~ tempo** bad weather
Bru'xelles [bry'sɛl] *sf* Brussels
BSE [biesse'e] *sigla f* BSE
'**buca, -che** *sf* hole; (*avvallamento*) hollow; **~ delle lettere** letterbox
buca'neve *sm inv* snowdrop
bu'care /20/ *vt* (*forare*) to make a hole (*o* holes) in; (*pungere*) to pierce; (*biglietto*) to punch; **bucarsi** *vpr* (*con eroina*) to mainline; **~ una gomma** to have a puncture
bu'cato *sm* (*operazione*) washing; (*panni*) wash, washing
'**buccia, -ce** ['buttʃa] *sf* skin, peel
bucherò *ecc* [buke'rɔ] *vb vedi* **bucare**
'**buco, -chi** *sm* hole
bud'dismo *sm* Buddhism
bu'dino *sm* pudding
'**bue** *sm inv* ox; (*anche:* **carne di ~**) beef
bu'fera *sf* storm
'**buffo, -a** *ag* funny; (*Teat*) comic
bu'gia, -'gie [bu'dʒia] *sf* lie; **dire una ~** to tell a lie; **bugi'ardo, -a** *ag* lying, deceitful ▷ *sm/f* liar
'**buio, -a** *ag* dark ▷ *sm* dark, darkness
'**bulbo** *sm* (*Bot*) bulb; **~ oculare** eyeball
Bulga'ria *sf:* **la ~** Bulgaria; '**bulgaro, -a** *ag*, *sm/f*, *sm* Bulgarian
buli'mia *sf* bulimia; **bu'limico, -a, -ci, -che** *ag* bulimic
bul'lismo *sm* bullying
bul'lone *sm* bolt
buona'notte *escl* good night! ▷ *sf:* **dare la ~ a** to say good night to
buona'sera *escl* good evening!
buongi'orno [bwon'dʒorno] *escl* good morning (*o* afternoon)!
buongus'taio, -a *sm/f* gourmet

 PAROLA CHIAVE

bu'ono, -a (*ag: dav sm* **buon** + C *o* V, **buono** + *s impura, gn, pn, ps, z; dav sf* **buon'** + V) *ag*
1 (*gen*) good; **un buon pranzo/ristorante** a good lunch/restaurant; **(stai) buono!** behave!
2 (*benevolo*): **buono (con)** good (to), kind (to)
3 (*giusto, valido*) right; **al momento buono** at the right moment
4 (*adatto*): **buono a/da** fit for/to; **essere buono a nulla** to be no good *o* use at anything
5 (*auguri*): **buon anno!** happy New Year!; **buon appetito!** enjoy your meal!; **buon compleanno!** happy birthday!; **buon divertimento!** have a nice time!; **buona fortuna!** good luck!; **buon riposo!** sleep

well!; **buon viaggio!** bon voyage!, have a good trip!
6: a buon mercato cheap; **di buon'ora** early; **buon senso** common sense; **alla buona** *ag* simple
▶ *av* in a simple way, without any fuss
▶ *sm* **1** (*bontà*) goodness, good
2 (*Comm*) voucher, coupon; **buono di cassa** cash voucher; **buono di consegna** delivery note; **buono del Tesoro** Treasury bill

buon'senso *sm* = **buon senso**
burat'tino *sm* puppet
'burbero, -a *ag* surly, gruff
buro'cratico, -a, -ci, -che *ag* bureaucratic
burocra'zia [burokrat'tsia] *sf* bureaucracy
bur'rasca, -sche *sf* storm
'burro *sm* butter
bur'rone *sm* ravine
bus'sare /72/ *vi* to knock
'bussola *sf* compass
'busta *sf* (*da lettera*) envelope; (*astuccio*) case; **in ~ aperta/chiusa** in an unsealed/ sealed envelope; **~ paga** pay packet
busta'rella *sf* bribe, backhander
bus'tina *sf* (*piccola busta*) envelope; (*di cibi, farmaci*) sachet; (*Mil*) forage cap; **~ di tè** tea bag
'busto *sm* bust; (*indumento*) corset, girdle; **a mezzo ~** (*fotografia, ritratto*) half-length
but'tare /72/ *vt* to throw; (*anche:* **~ via**) to throw away; **buttarsi** *vpr* (*saltare*) to jump; **~ giù** (*scritto*) to scribble down; (*cibo*) to gulp down; (*edificio*) to pull down, demolish; (*pasta, verdura*) to put into boiling water; **buttarsi dalla finestra** to jump out of the window
byte ['bait] *sm inv* byte

C

ca'bina *sf* (*di nave*) cabin; (*da spiaggia*) beach hut; (*di autocarro, treno*) cab; (*di aereo*) cockpit; (*di ascensore*) cage; **~ di pilotaggio** cockpit; **~ telefonica** callbox, (tele)phone box *o* booth
cabi'nato *sm* cabin cruiser
ca'cao *sm* cocoa
'caccia ['kattʃa] *sf* hunting; (*con fucile*) shooting; (*inseguimento*) chase; (*cacciagione*) game ▷ *sm inv* (*aereo*) fighter; (*nave*) destroyer; **~ grossa** big-game hunting; **~ all'uomo** manhunt
cacci'are [kat'tʃare] /14/ *vt* to hunt; (*mandar via*) to chase away; (*ficcare*) to shove, stick ▷ *vi* to hunt; **cacciarsi** *vpr*: **~ fuori qc** to whip *o* pull sth out; **~ un urlo** to let out a yell; **dove s'è cacciata la mia borsa?** where has my bag got to?; **cacciarsi nei guai** to get into trouble; **caccia'tore** *sm* hunter; **cacciatore di frodo** poacher
caccia'vite [kattʃa'vite] *sm inv* screwdriver
'cactus *sm inv* cactus
ca'davere *sm* (*dead*) body, corpse
'caddi *ecc vb vedi* **cadere**
ca'denza [ka'dɛntsa] *sf* cadence; (*andamento ritmico*) rhythm; (*Mus*) cadenza
ca'dere /18/ *vi* to fall; (*denti, capelli*) to fall out; (*tetto*) to fall in; **questa gonna cade bene** this skirt hangs well; **lasciar ~** (*anche fig*) to drop; **~ dal sonno** to be falling asleep on one's feet; **~ dalle nuvole** (*fig*) to be taken aback
cadrò *ecc vb vedi* **cadere**
ca'duta *sf* fall; **la ~ dei capelli** hair loss
caffè *sm inv* coffee; (*locale*) café; **~ corretto** coffee with liqueur; **~ in grani** coffee beans; **~ macchiato** coffee with a dash of milk; **~ macinato** ground coffee
caffel'latte *sm inv* white coffee
caffetti'era *sf* coffeepot

'**cagna** ['kaɲɲa] sf (Zool, peg) bitch

CAI sigla m = **Club Alpino Italiano**

cala'brone sm hornet

cala'maro sm squid

cala'mita sf magnet

calamità sf inv calamity, disaster

ca'lare /72/ vt (far discendere) to lower; (Maglia) to decrease ▷ vi (discendere) to go (o come) down; (tramontare) to set, go down; **~ di peso** to lose weight

cal'cagno [kal'kaɲɲo] sm heel

cal'care /20/ sm (incrostazione) (lime)scale

'**calce** ['kaltʃe] sm: **in ~** at the foot of the page ▷ sf lime; **~ viva** quicklime

cal'cetto [kal'tʃetto] sm (calcio-balilla) table football; (calcio a cinque) five-a-side (football)

calci'are [kal'tʃare] /14/ vt, vi to kick; **calcia'tore** sm footballer

'**calcio** ['kaltʃo] sm (pedata) kick; (sport) football, soccer; (di pistola, fucile) butt; (Chim) calcium; **~ d'angolo** (Sport) corner (kick); **~ di punizione** (Sport) free kick; **~ di rigore** penalty

calco'lare /72/ vt to calculate, work out, reckon; (ponderare) to weigh (up); **calcola'tore, -'trice** ag calculating ▷ sm calculator; (fig) calculating person ▷ sf: **calcolatore elettronico** computer; **calcola'trice** sf calculator

'**calcolo** sm (anche Mat) calculation; (infinitesimale ecc) calculus; (Med) stone; **fare i propri calcoli** (fig) to weigh the pros and cons; **per ~** out of self-interest

cal'daia sf boiler

'**caldo, -a** ag warm; (molto caldo) hot; (fig: appassionato) keen; hearty ▷ sm heat; **ho ~** I'm warm; I'm hot; **fa ~** it's warm; it's hot

caleidos'copio sm kaleidoscope

calen'dario sm calendar

'**calibro** sm (di arma) calibre, bore; (Tecn) callipers pl; (fig) calibre; **di grosso ~** (fig) prominent

'**calice** ['kalitʃe] sm goblet; (Rel) chalice

Cali'fornia sf California; **californi'ano, -a** ag Californian

calligra'fia sf (scrittura) handwriting; (arte) calligraphy

'**callo** sm callus; (ai piedi) corn

'**calma** sf calm

cal'mante sm tranquillizer

cal'mare /72/ vt to calm; (lenire) to soothe; **calmarsi** vpr to grow calm, calm down; (vento) to abate; (dolori) to ease

'**calmo, -a** ag calm, quiet

'**calo** sm (Comm: di prezzi) fall; (: di volume) shrinkage; (: di peso) loss

ca'lore sm warmth; (intenso) heat; **essere in ~** (Zool) to be on heat

calo'ria sf calorie

calo'rifero sm radiator

calo'roso, -a ag warm

calpes'tare /72/ vt to tread on, trample on; **"è vietato ~ l'erba"** "keep off the grass"

ca'lunnia sf slander; (scritta) libel

cal'vizie [kal'vittsje] sf baldness

'**calvo, -a** ag bald

'**calza** ['kaltsa] sf (da donna) stocking; (da uomo) sock; **fare la ~** to knit; **calze di nailon** nylons, (nylon) stockings

calza'maglia [kaltsa'maʎʎa] sf tights pl; (per danza, ginnastica) leotard

calzet'tone [kaltset'tone] sm heavy knee-length sock

cal'zino [kal'tsino] sm sock

calzo'laio [kaltso'lajo] sm shoemaker; (che ripara scarpe) cobbler

calzon'cini [kaltson'tʃini] smpl shorts; **~ da bagno** (swimming) trunks

cal'zone [kal'tsone] sm trouser leg; (Cuc) savoury turnover made with pizza dough; **calzoni** smpl (pantaloni) trousers (BRIT), pants (US)

camale'onte sm chameleon

cambia'mento sm change; **cambiamenti climatici** climate change sg

cambi'are /19/ vt to change; (modificare) to alter, change; (barattare): **~ (qc con qn/ qc)** to exchange (sth with sb/for sth) ▷ vi to change, alter; **cambiarsi** vpr (variare abito) to change; **~ casa** to move (house); **~ idea** to change one's mind; **~ treno** to change trains

cambiava'lute sm inv exchange office

'**cambio** sm change; (modifica) alteration, change; (scambio, Comm) exchange; (corso dei cambi) rate (of exchange); (Tecn, Aut) gears pl; **in ~ di** in exchange for; **dare il ~ a qn** to take over from sb

'**camera** sf room; (anche: **~ da letto**) bedroom; (Pol) chamber, house; **~ ardente** mortuary chapel; **~ d'aria** inner tube; (di pallone) bladder; **C~ di Commercio** Chamber of Commerce; **C~ dei Deputati** Chamber of Deputies, ≈ House of Commons (BRIT), ≈ House of Representatives (US); **~ a gas** gas chamber; **~ a un letto/a due letti/ matrimoniale** single/twin-bedded/double room; **~ oscura** (Fot) dark room

▌ Attenzione! In inglese esiste la parola *camera*, che però significa *macchina fotografica*.

came'rata, -i, -e sm/f companion, mate ▷ sf dormitory

cameri'era sf (domestica) maid; (che serve a tavola) waitress; (che fa le camere) chambermaid

cameri'ere *sm* (man)servant; (*di ristorante*) waiter

came'rino *sm* (*Teat*) dressing room

'camice ['kamitʃe] *sm* (*Rel*) alb; (*per medici ecc*) white coat

cami'cetta [kami'tʃetta] *sf* blouse

ca'micia, -cie [ka'mitʃa] *sf* (*da uomo*) shirt; (*da donna*) blouse; **~ di forza** straitjacket; **~ da notte** (*da donna*) nightdress; (*da uomo*) nightshirt

cami'netto *sm* hearth, fireplace

ca'mino *sm* chimney; (*focolare*) fireplace, hearth

'camion *sm inv* lorry (BRIT), truck (US)

camio'nista, -i *sm* lorry driver (BRIT), truck driver (US)

cam'mello *sm* (*Zool*) camel; (*tessuto*) camel hair

cammi'nare /72/ *vi* to walk; (*funzionare*) to work, go

cam'mino *sm* walk; (*sentiero*) path; (*itinerario, direzione, tragitto*) way; **mettersi in ~** to set o start off

camo'milla *sf* camomile; (*infuso*) camomile tea

ca'moscio [ka'moʃʃo] *sm* chamois; **di ~** (*scarpe, borsa*) suede *cpd*

cam'pagna [kam'paɲɲa] *sf* country, countryside; (*Pol, Comm, Mil*) campaign; **in ~** in the country; **andare in ~** to go to the country; **fare una ~** to campaign; **~ pubblicitaria** advertising campaign

cam'pana *sf* bell; (*anche:* **~ di vetro**) bell jar; **~ (per la raccolta del vetro)** bottle bank; **campa'nello** (*all'uscio, da tavola*) bell

campa'nile *sm* bell tower, belfry

cam'peggio *sm* camping; (*terreno*) camp site; **fare (del) ~** to go camping

camper ['kamper] *sm inv* motor caravan (BRIT), motor home (US)

campio'nario, -a *ag*: **fiera campionaria** trade fair ▷ *sm* collection of samples

campio'nato *sm* championship

campi'one, -'essa *sm/f* (*Sport*) champion ▷ *sm* (*Comm*) sample

'campo *sm* field; (*Mil*) field; (*: accampamento*) camp; (*spazio delimitato: sportivo ecc*) ground; field; (*di quadro*) background; **i campi** (*campagna*) the countryside; **~ da aviazione** airfield; **~ di battaglia** (*Mil, fig*) battlefield; **~ di concentramento** concentration camp; **~ di golf** golf course; **~ profughi** refugee camp; **~ sportivo** sports ground; **~ da tennis** tennis court; **~ visivo** field of vision

'Canada *sm*: **il ~** Canada; **cana'dese** *ag, smf* Canadian ▷ *sf* (*anche:* **tenda canadese**) ridge tent

ca'naglia [ka'naʎʎa] *sf* rabble, mob; (*persona*) scoundrel, rogue

ca'nale *sm* (*anche fig*) channel; (*artificiale*) canal

'canapa *sf* hemp; **~ indiana** (*droga*) cannabis

cana'rino *sm* canary

cancel'lare [kantʃel'lare] /72/ *vt* (*con la gomma*) to rub out, erase; (*con la penna*) to strike out; (*annullare*) to annul, cancel; (*disdire*) to cancel

cancelle'ria [kantʃelle'ria] *sf* chancery; (*quanto necessario per scrivere*) stationery

can'cello [kan'tʃello] *sm* gate

'cancro *sm* (*Med*) cancer; **C~** Cancer

candeg'gina [kanded'dʒina] *sf* bleach

can'dela *sf* candle; **~ (di accensione)** (*Aut*) spark(ing) plug

cande'labro *sm* candelabra

candeli'ere *sm* candlestick

candi'dare /72/ *vt* to present as candidate; **candidarsi** *vpr* to present o.s. as candidate

candi'dato, -a *sm/f* candidate; (*aspirante a una carica*) applicant

'candido, -a *ag* white as snow; (*puro*) pure; (*sincero*) sincere, candid

can'dito, -a *ag* candied

'cane *sm* dog; (*di pistola, fucile*) cock; **fa un freddo ~** it's bitterly cold; **non c'era un ~** there wasn't a soul; **~ da caccia** hunting dog; **~ da guardia** guard dog; **~ lupo** alsatian; **~ pastore** sheepdog

ca'nestro *sm* basket

can'guro *sm* kangaroo

ca'nile *sm* kennel; (*di allevamento*) kennels *pl*; **~ municipale** dog pound

'canna *sf* (*pianta*) reed; (*: indica, da zucchero*) cane; (*bastone*) stick, cane; (*di fucile*) barrel; (*di organo*) pipe; (*fam: Droga*) joint; **~ fumaria** chimney flue; **~ da pesca** (fishing) rod; **~ da zucchero** sugar cane

cannel'loni *smpl* pasta tubes stuffed with sauce and baked

cannocchi'ale [kannok'kjale] *sm* telescope

can'none *sm* (*Mil*) gun; (*: Storia*) cannon; (*tubo*) pipe, tube; (*piega*) box pleat; (*fig*) ace

can'nuccia, -ce [kan'nuttʃa] *sf* (drinking) straw

ca'noa *sf* canoe

'canone *sm* canon, criterion; (*mensile, annuo*) rent; fee

canot'taggio [kanot'taddʒo] *sm* rowing

canotti'era *sf* vest

ca'notto *sm* small boat, dinghy; canoe

can'tante *smf* singer

can'tare /72/ *vt, vi* to sing; **cantau'tore, -'trice** *sm/f* singer-composer

canti'ere *sm* (*Edil*) (building) site; (*anche:* **~ navale**) shipyard

can'tina sf cellar; (bottega) wine shop;
~ sociale cooperative winegrowers'
association

 Attenzione! In inglese esiste la parola
canteen, che però significa mensa.

'canto sm song; (arte) singing; (Rel) chant;
chanting; (Poesia) poem, lyric; (parte di una
poesia) canto; (parte, lato): **da un ~** on the
one hand; **d'altro ~** on the other hand

canzo'nare [kantso'nare] /72/ vt to tease

can'zone [kan'tsone] sf song; (Poesia)
canzone

'caos sm inv chaos; **ca'otico, -a, -ci, -che**
ag chaotic

CAP sigla m = **codice di avviamento postale**

ca'pace [ka'patʃe] ag able, capable; (ampio,
vasto) large, capacious; **sei ~ di farlo?** can
you o are you able to do it?; **capacità** sf inv
ability; (Dir, di recipiente) capacity

ca'panna sf hut

capan'none sm (Agr) barn; (fabbricato
industriale) (factory) shed

ca'parbio, -a ag stubborn

ca'parra sf deposit, down payment

ca'pello sm hair; **capelli** smpl (capigliatura)
hair sg

ca'pezzolo [ka'pettsolo] sm nipple

ca'pire /55/ vt to understand

capi'tale ag (mortale) capital; (fondamentale)
main cpd, chief cpd ▷ sf (città) capital ▷ sm
(Econ) capital

capi'tano sm captain

capi'tare /72/ vi (giungere casualmente)
to happen to go, find o.s.; (accadere) to
happen; (presentarsi: cosa) to turn up,
present itself ▷ vb impers to happen; **mi è
capitato un guaio** I've had a spot of trouble

capi'tello sm (Archit) capital

ca'pitolo sm chapter

capi'tombolo sm headlong fall, tumble

'capo sm head; (persona) head, leader;
(: in ufficio) head, boss; (: in tribù) chief; (di
tavolo, scale) head, top; (di filo) end; (Geo)
cape; **andare a ~** to start a new paragraph;
da ~ over again; **~ di bestiame** head inv
of cattle; **~ di vestiario** item of clothing;
Capo'danno sm New Year; **capo'giro**
sm dizziness no pl; **capola'voro, -i** sm
masterpiece; **capo'linea** (pl **capilinea**) sm
terminus; **capostazi'one** (pl **capistazione**)
sm station master; **capo'tavola** (mpl
capitavola, fpl **capotavola**) smf (persona)
head of the table; **sedere a capotavola** to
sit at the head of the table; **capo'volgere**
/96/ vt to overturn; (fig) to reverse;
capovolgersi vpr to overturn; (barca) to
capsize; (fig) to be reversed

'cappa sf (mantello) cape, cloak; (del camino)
hood

cap'pella sf (Rel) chapel

cap'pello sm hat

'cappero sm caper

cap'pone sm capon

cap'potto sm (over)coat

cappuc'cino [kapput'tʃino] sm (frate)
Capuchin monk; (bevanda) cappuccino

cap'puccio [kap'puttʃo] sm (copricapo)
hood; (della biro) cap

'capra sf (she-)goat

ca'priccio [ka'prittʃo] sm caprice, whim;
(bizza) tantrum; **fare i capricci** to be very
naughty; **capricci'oso, -a** ag capricious,
whimsical; naughty

Capri'corno sm Capricorn

capri'ola sf somersault

capri'olo sm roe deer

'capro sm: **~ espiatorio** scapegoat

ca'prone sm billy-goat

'capsula sf capsule; (di arma, per bottiglie)
cap

cap'tare /72/ vt (Radio, TV) to pick up;
(cattivarsi) to gain, win

carabini'ere sm member of Italian military
police force

CARABINIERI

Originally part of the armed forces,
the Carabinieri are police who now have
civil as well as military duties, such as
maintaining public order. They include
paratroop units and mounted divisions
and report to either the Minister of
the Interior or the Minister of Defence,
depending on the function they are
performing.

---

ca'raffa sf carafe

Ca'raibi smpl: **il mar dei ~** the Caribbean
(Sea)

cara'mella sf sweet

ca'rattere sm character; (caratteristica)
characteristic, trait; **avere un buon ~**
to be good-natured; **~ jolly** wild card;
caratte'ristico, -a, -ci, -che ag
characteristic ▷ sf characteristic, trait

car'bone sm coal

carbu'rante sm (motor) fuel

carbura'tore sm carburettor

carce'rato, -a [kartʃe'rato] sm/f prisoner

'carcere ['kartʃere] sm prison; (pena)
imprisonment

carci'ofo [kar'tʃɔfo] sm artichoke

cardel'lino sm goldfinch

car'diaco, -a, -ci, -che ag cardiac,
heart cpd

cardi'nale ag, sm cardinal

'cardine sm hinge

'**cardo** *sm* thistle
ca'**rente** *ag:* ~ **di** lacking in
cares'**tia** *sf* famine; (*penuria*) scarcity, dearth
ca'**rezza** [ka'rettsa] *sf* caress
'**carica** *sf vedi* **carico**
caricabatte'**ria** *sm inv* (*Elettr*) battery charger
cari'**care** /20/ *vt* (*merce*) to load; (*orologio*) to wind up; (*batteria, Mil*) to charge; (*Inform*) to load
'**carico, -a, -chi, -che** *ag* (*fucile*) loaded; (*orologio*) wound up; (*batteria*) charged; (*colore*) deep; (*caffè, tè*) strong; ~ **di** (*che porta un peso*) loaded o laden with ▷ *sm* (*il caricare*) loading; (*ciò che si carica*) load; (*fig: peso*) burden, weight; **persona a** ~ dependent; **essere a** ~ **di qn** (*spese ecc*) to be charged to sb
'**carie** *sf* (*dentaria*) decay
ca'**rino, -a** *ag* (*grazioso*) lovely, pretty, nice; (*simpatico*) nice
cari'**tà** *sf* charity; **per** ~! (*escl di rifiuto*) good heavens, no!
carnagi'**one** [karna'dʒone] *sf* complexion
'**carne** *sf* flesh; (*bovina, ovina ecc*) meat; ~ **di manzo/maiale/pecora** beef/pork/mutton; ~ **in scatola** tinned o canned meat; ~ **tritata** o **macinata** mince (*BRIT*), hamburger meat (*US*), minced (*BRIT*) o ground (*US*) meat
carne'**vale** *sm* carnival; **C~**; *see note* "**Carnevale**"

* **CARNEVALE**

* *Carnevale* is the name given to the period
* between Epiphany (6 January) and the
* beginning of Lent, when people throw
* parties, put on processions with
* spectacular floats, build bonfires in the
* "piazze" and dress up in fabulous costumes
* and masks. Building to a peak just before
* Lent, *Carnevale* culminates in the festivities
* of *Martedì grasso* (Shrove Tuesday).

'**caro, -a** *ag* (*amato*) dear; (*costoso*) dear, expensive; **è troppo** ~ it's too expensive
ca'**rogna** [ka'roɲɲa] *sf* carrion; (*fig: fam*) swine
ca'**rota** *sf* carrot
caro'**vana** *sf* caravan
car'**poni** *av* on all fours
car'**rabile** *ag* suitable for vehicles; "**passo ~**" "keep clear"
carreggi'**ata** [karred'dʒata] *sf* carriageway (*BRIT*), roadway
car'**rello** *sm* trolley; (*Aer*) undercarriage; (*Cine*) dolly; (*di macchina da scrivere*) carriage

carri'**era** *sf* career; **fare** ~ to get on; **a gran** ~ at full speed
carri'**ola** *sf* wheelbarrow
'**carro** *sm* cart, wagon; ~ **armato** tank; ~ **attrezzi** (*Aut*) breakdown van
car'**rozza** [kar'rɔttsa] *sf* carriage, coach
carrozze'**ria** [karrottse'ria] *sf* body, coachwork (*BRIT*); (*officina*) coachbuilder's workshop (*BRIT*), body shop
carroz'**zina** [karrot'tsina] *sf* pram (*BRIT*), baby carriage (*US*)
'**carta** *sf* paper; (*al ristorante*) menu; (*Geo*) map; plan; (*documento*) card; (*costituzione*) charter; **carte** *sfpl* (*documenti*) papers, documents; **alla** ~ (*al ristorante*) à la carte; ~ **assegni** bank card; ~ **assorbente** blotting paper; ~ **bollata** o **da bollo** official stamped paper; ~ (**da gioco**) playing card; ~ **di credito** credit card; ~ **fedeltà** loyalty card; ~ (**geografica**) map; ~ **d'identità** identity card; ~ **igienica** toilet paper; ~ **d'imbarco** (*Aer, Naut*) boarding card; ~ **da lettere** writing paper; ~ **libera** (*Amm*) unstamped paper; ~ **stradale** road map; ~ **da pacchi** wrapping paper; ~ **da parati** wallpaper; ~ **verde** (*Aut*) green card; ~ **vetrata** sandpaper; ~ **da visita** visiting card
car'**taccia, -ce** [kar'tattʃa] *sf* waste paper
carta'**pesta** *sf* papier-mâché
car'**tella** *sf* (*scheda*) card; (*custodia: di cartone, Inform*) folder; (: *di uomo d'affari ecc*) briefcase; (: *di scolaro*) schoolbag, satchel; ~ **clinica** (*Med*) case sheet
cartel'**lino** *sm* (*etichetta*) label; (*su porta*) notice; (*scheda*) card; **timbrare il** ~ (*all'entrata*) to clock in; (*all'uscita*) to clock out; ~ **di presenza** clock card, timecard
car'**tello** *sm* sign; (*pubblicitario*) poster; (*stradale*) sign, signpost; (*in dimostrazioni*) placard; (*Econ*) cartel; ~ **stradale** sign; cartel'**lone** *sm* (*della tombola*) scoring frame; (*Teat*) playbill; **tenere il cartellone** (*spettacolo*) to have a long run; **cartellone pubblicitario** advertising poster
car'**tina** *sf* (*Aut, Geo*) map
car'**toccio** [kar'tɔttʃo] *sm* paper bag
cartolarizzazi'**one** [kartolariddza'tsjone] *sf* securitization
cartole'**ria** *sf* stationer's (shop)
carto'**lina** *sf* postcard; ~ **postale** ready-stamped postcard
car'**tone** *sm* cardboard; (*Arte*) cartoon; **cartoni animati** (*Cine*) cartoons
car'**tuccia, -ce** [kar'tuttʃa] *sf* cartridge
'**casa** *sf* house; (*specialmente la propria casa*) home; (*Comm*) firm, house; **essere a** ~ to be at home; **vado a** ~ **mia/tua** I'm going home/to your house; **vino della** ~ house wine; ~ **di cura** nursing home; ~ **editrice**

publishing house; **C~ delle Libertà** *centre-right coalition*; **~ di riposo** (old people's) home, care home; **~ dello studente** student hostel; **case popolari** ≈ council houses (*o flats*) (BRIT), ≈ public housing units (US)

ca'sacca, -che *sf* military coat; (*di fantino*) blouse

casa'lingo, -a, -ghi, -ghe *ag* household, domestic; (*fatto a casa*) home-made; (*semplice*) homely; (*amante della casa*) home-loving ▷ *sf* housewife

cas'care /20/ *vi* to fall; **cas'cata** *sf* fall; (*d'acqua*) cascade, waterfall

cascherò *ecc* [kaske'rɔ] *vb vedi* cascare

'casco (*pl* **caschi**) *sm* helmet; (*del parrucchiere*) hair-dryer; (*di banane*) bunch; **~ blu** (*Mil*) blue helmet (*UN soldier*)

casei'ficio [kazei'fitʃo] *sm* creamery

ca'sella *sf* pigeonhole; **~ email** mailbox; **~ postale** post office box

ca'sello *sm* (*di autostrada*) tollgate

ca'serma *sf* barracks

ca'sino *sm* (*fam: confusione*) row, racket; (*casa di prostituzione*) brothel

casinò *sm inv* casino

'caso *sm* chance; (*fatto, vicenda*) event, incident; (*possibilità*) possibility; (*Med, Ling*) case; **a ~** at random; **per ~** by chance, by accident; **in ogni ~, in tutti i casi** in any case, at any rate; **nel ~ che** should the opportunity arise; **nel ~ che** in case; **~ mai** if by chance; **~ limite** borderline case

caso'lare *sm* cottage

'caspita *escl* (*di sorpresa*) good heavens!; (*di impazienza*) for goodness' sake!

'cassa *sf* case, crate, box; (*bara*) coffin; (*mobile*) chest; (*involucro: di orologio ecc*) case; (*macchina*) cash register, till; (*luogo di pagamento*) cash desk, checkout (counter); (*fondo*) fund; (*istituto bancario*) bank; **~ automatica prelievi** automatic telling machine, cash dispenser; **~ continua** night safe; **mettere in ~ integrazione** ≈ to lay off; **~ mutua** *o* **malattia** health insurance scheme; **~ di risparmio** savings bank; **~ toracica** (*Anat*) chest

cassa'forte (*pl* **casseforti**) *sf* safe

cassa'panca (*pl* **cassapanche** *o* **cassepanche**) *sf* settle

casseru'ola, casse'rola *sf* saucepan

cas'setta *sf* box; (*per registratore*) cassette; (*Cine, Teat*) box-office takings *pl*; **film di ~** box-office draw; **~ delle lettere** letterbox; **~ di sicurezza** strongbox

cas'setto *sm* drawer

cassi'ere, -a *sm/f* cashier; (*di banca*) teller

casso'netto *sm* wheelie-bin

cas'tagna [kas'taɲɲa] *sf* chestnut

cas'tagno [kas'taɲɲo] *sm* chestnut (tree)

cas'tano, -a *ag* chestnut (brown)

cas'tello *sm* castle; (*Tecn*) scaffolding

casti'gare /80/ *vt* to punish; **cas'tigo, -ghi** *sm* punishment; **mettere/essere in castigo** to punish/be punished

cas'toro *sm* beaver

casu'ale *ag* chance *cpd*; (*Inform*) random *cpd*

catalizza'tore [kataliddza'tore] *sm* (*anche fig*) catalyst; (*Aut*) catalytic converter

ca'talogo, -ghi *sm* catalogue

catarifran'gente [katarifran'dʒɛnte] *sm* (*Aut*) reflector

ca'tarro *sm* catarrh

ca'tastrofe *sf* catastrophe, disaster; **catastro'fista, -i, -e** *ag, smf* doom-monger

catego'ria *sf* category

ca'tena *sf* chain; **~ di montaggio** assembly line; **catene da neve** (*Aut*) snow chains; **cate'nina** *sf* (*gioiello*) (thin) chain

cate'ratta *sf* cataract; (*chiusa*) sluice gate

ca'tino *sm* basin

ca'trame *sm* tar

'cattedra *sf* teacher's desk; (*di università*) chair

catte'drale *sf* cathedral

catti'veria *sf* wickedness, malice; (*di bambino*) naughtiness; (*azione*) spiteful act; (*parole*) malicious *o* spiteful remark

cat'tivo, -a *ag* bad; (*malvagio*) bad, wicked; (*turbolento: bambino*) bad, naughty; (*: mare*) rough; (*odore, sapore*) nasty, bad

cat'tolico, -a, -ci, -che *ag, sm/f* (Roman) Catholic

cattu'rare /72/ *vt* to capture

'causa *sf* cause; (*Dir*) lawsuit, case, action; **a ~ di, per ~ di** because of; **fare** *o* **muovere ~ a qn** to take legal action against sb

cau'sare /72/ *vt* to cause

cau'tela *sf* caution, prudence

'cauto, -a *ag* cautious, prudent

cauzi'one [kaut'tsjone] *sf* security; (*Dir*) bail

'cava *sf* quarry

caval'care /20/ *vt* (*cavallo*) to ride; (*muro*) to sit astride; (*ponte*) to span; **caval'cata** *sf* ride; (*gruppo di persone*) riding party

cavalca'via *sm inv* flyover

cavalci'oni [kaval'tʃoni]: **a ~ di** *prep* astride

cavali'ere *sm* rider; (*feudale, titolo*) knight; (*soldato*) cavalryman; (*al ballo*) partner

caval'letta *sf* grasshopper

caval'letto *sm* (*Fot*) tripod; (*da pittore*) easel

ca'vallo *sm* horse; (*Scacchi*) knight; (*Aut: anche*: **~ vapore**) horsepower; (*dei pantaloni*) crotch; **a ~** on horseback; **a ~ di** astride, straddling; **~ di battaglia** (*fig*) hobbyhorse; **~ da corsa** racehorse; **~ a dondolo** rocking horse

ca'vare /72/ vt (togliere) to draw out, extract, take out; (: giacca, scarpe) to take off; (: fame, sete, voglia) to satisfy; **cavarsela** to get away with it; to manage, get on all right

cava'tappi sm inv corkscrew

ca'verna sf cave

'cavia sf guinea pig

cavi'ale sm caviar

ca'viglia [ka'viʎʎa] sf ankle

'cavo, -a ag hollow ▷ sm (Anat) cavity; (grossa corda) rope, cable; (Elettr, Tel) cable

cavo'letto sm: **~ di Bruxelles** Brussels sprout

cavolfi'ore sm cauliflower

'cavolo sm cabbage; **non m'importa un ~** (fam) I don't give a hoot

'cazzo ['kattso] sm (fam!: pene) prick (!); **non gliene importa un ~** (fig: fam!) he doesn't give a damn about it; **fatti i cazzi tuoi** (fig: fam!) mind your own damn business

C.C.D. sigla m (= Centro Cristiano Democratico) party originating from Democrazia Cristiana

C.D. sm inv (= compact disc) CD; (lettore) CD player

CD-Rom [tʃidi'rɔm] sigla m inv CD-Rom

C.d.U. sigla m (= Cristiano Democratici Uniti) United Christian Democrats (Italian centre-right political party)

ce [tʃe] pron, av vedi **ci**

Ce'cenia [tʃe'tʃenja] sf Chechnya; **ce'ceno, -a** ag, sm/f Chechen

'ceco, -a, -chi, -che ['tʃɛko] ag, sm/f, sm Czech; **la Repubblica Ceca** the Czech Republic

'cedere ['tʃɛdere] /29/ vt (concedere: posto) to give up; (Dir) to transfer, make over ▷ vi (cadere) to give way, subside; **~ (a)** to surrender (to), yield (to), give in (to)

'cedola ['tʃɛdola] sf (Comm) coupon; voucher

'ceffo ['tʃɛffo] sm (peg) ugly mug

ceffone [tʃef'fone] sm slap, smack

cele'brare [tʃele'brare] /72/ vt to celebrate

'celebre ['tʃɛlebre] ag famous, celebrated

ce'leste [tʃe'lɛste] ag celestial; heavenly; (colore) sky-blue

'celibe ['tʃɛlibe] ag single, unmarried

'cella ['tʃɛlla] sf cell; **~ frigorifera** cold store

'cellula ['tʃɛllula] sf (Biol, Elettr, Pol) cell; **cellu'lare** sm cellphone

cellu'lite [tʃellu'lite] sf cellulite

cemen'tare [tʃemen'tare] /72/ vt (anche fig) to cement

ce'mento [tʃe'mento] sm cement; **~ armato** reinforced concrete

'cena ['tʃena] sf dinner; (leggera) supper

ce'nare [tʃe'nare] /72/ vi to dine, have dinner

'cenere ['tʃenere] sf ash

'cenno ['tʃenno] sm (segno) sign, signal; (gesto) gesture; (col capo) nod; (con la mano) wave; (allusione) hint, mention; (breve esposizione) short account; **far ~ di sì/no** to nod (one's head)/shake one's head

censi'mento [tʃensi'mento] sm census

cen'sura [tʃen'sura] sf censorship; censor's office; (fig) censure

cente'nario, -a [tʃente'narjo] ag (che ha cento anni) hundred-year-old; (che ricorre ogni cento anni) centennial, centenary cpd ▷ sm/f centenarian ▷ sm centenary

cen'tesimo, -a [tʃen'tɛzimo] ag, sm hundredth; (di euro, dollaro) cent

cen'tigrado, -a [tʃen'tigrado] ag centigrade; **20 gradi centigradi** 20 degrees centigrade

cen'timetro [tʃen'timetro] sm centimetre

centi'naio [tʃenti'najo] (pl f **centinaia**) sm: **un ~ (di)** a hundred; about a hundred

'cento ['tʃɛnto] num a hundred, one hundred

cento'mila [tʃɛnto'mila] num a o one hundred thousand; **te l'ho detto ~ volte** (fig) I've told you a thousand times

cen'trale [tʃen'trale] ag central ▷ sf: **~ elettrica** electric power station; **~ eolica** wind farm; **~ telefonica** (telephone) exchange; **centrali'nista** smf operator; **centra'lino** sm (telephone) exchange; (di albergo ecc) switchboard; **centraliz'zato, -a** [tʃentralid'dzato] ag central

cen'trare [tʃen'trare] /72/ vt to hit the centre (BRIT) o center (US) of; (Tecn) to centre

cen'trifuga [tʃen'trifuga] sf spin-dryer

'centro ['tʃɛntro] sm centre; **~ civico** civic centre; **~ commerciale** shopping centre; (città) commercial centre; **~ di permanenza temporanea** reception centre

centro'destra [tʃentro'dɛstra] sm (Pol) centre right

centrosi'nistra [tʃentrosi'nistra] sm (Pol) centre left

'ceppo ['tʃeppo] sm (di albero) stump; (pezzo di legno) log

'cera ['tʃera] sf wax; (aspetto) appearance

ce'ramica (pl **ceramiche**) [tʃe'ramika] sf ceramic; (Arte) ceramics sg

cerbi'atto [tʃer'bjatto] sm (Zool) fawn

cercaper'sone [tʃerkaper'sone] sm inv bleeper

cer'care [tʃer'kare] /20/ vt to look for, search for ▷ vi: **~ di fare qc** to try to do sth

cercherò ecc [tʃerke'rɔ] vb vedi **cercare**

'cerchia [tʃerkja] sf circle

cer'chietto [tʃer'kjetto] sm (per capelli) hairband

'cerchio ['tʃerkjo] *sm* circle; (*giocattolo, di botte*) hoop
cere'ale [tʃere'ale] *sm* cereal
ceri'monia [tʃeri'mɔnja] *sf* ceremony
ce'rino [tʃe'rino] *sm* wax match
'cernia ['tʃɛrnja] *sf* (*Zool*) stone bass
cerni'era [tʃer'njɛra] *sf* hinge; **~ lampo** zip (fastener) (BRIT), zipper (US)
'cero ['tʃero] *sm* (church) candle
ce'rotto [tʃe'rɔtto] *sm* sticking plaster
certa'mente [tʃerta'mente] *av* certainly
certifi'cato [tʃertifi'kato] *sm* certificate; **~ medico/di nascita/di morte** medical/birth/death certificate

 PAROLA CHIAVE

'certo, -a ['tʃɛrto] *ag* (*sicuro*): **certo (di/che)** certain *o* sure (of/that)
▶ *det* **1** (*tale*) certain; **un certo signor Smith** a (certain) Mr Smith
2 (*qualche: con valore intensivo*) some; **dopo un certo tempo** after some time; **un fatto di una certa importanza** a matter of some importance; **di una certa età** past one's prime, not so young
▶ *pron*: **certi, e** (*pl*) some
▶ *av* (*certamente*) certainly; (*senz'altro*) of course; **di certo** certainly; **no (di) certo!, certo che no!** certainly not!; **sì certo** yes indeed, certainly

cer'vella [tʃer'vɛlla] *sfpl* brains
cer'vello [tʃer'vɛllo] (*pl* **cervelli**) *sm* (*Anat*) brain; **~ elettronico** computer
'cervo, -a ['tʃervo] *sm/f* stag (hind) ▷ *sm* deer; **~ volante** stag beetle
ces'puglio [tʃes'puʎʎo] *sm* bush
ces'sare [tʃes'sare] /72/ *vi, vt* to stop, cease; **~ di fare qc** to stop doing sth
ces'tino [tʃes'tino] *sm* basket; (*per la carta straccia*) wastepaper basket; (*Inform*) recycle bin; **~ da viaggio** (*Ferr*) packed lunch (*o* dinner)
'cesto ['tʃesto] *sm* basket
'ceto ['tʃeto] *sm* (social) class
cetrio'lino [tʃetrio'lino] *sm* gherkin
cetri'olo [tʃetri'ɔlo] *sm* cucumber
Cfr. *abbr* (= *confronta*) cf
C.G.I.L. *sigla f* (= *Confederazione Generale Italiana del Lavoro*) trades union organization
chat'line [tʃæt'laen] *sf inv* chat room
chat'tare [tʃat'tare] /72/ *vi* (*online*) to chat; **chat'tata** [tʃat'tata] *sf* chat

 PAROLA CHIAVE

che [ke] *pron* **1** (*relativo: persona: soggetto*) who; (: *oggetto*) whom, that; (: *cosa, animale*) which, that; **il ragazzo che è venuto** the boy who came; **l'uomo che io vedo** the man (whom) I see; **il libro che è sul tavolo** the book which *o* that is on the table; **il libro che vedi** the book (which *o* that) you see; **la sera che ti ho visto** the evening I saw you
2 (*interrogativo, esclamativo*) what; **che (cosa) fai?** what are you doing?; **a che (cosa) pensi?** what are you thinking about?; **non sa che (cosa) fare** he doesn't know what to do; **ma che dici!** what are you saying!
3 (*indefinito*): **quell'uomo ha un che di losco** there's something suspicious about that man; **un certo non so che** an indefinable something
▶ *det* **1** (*interrogativo: tra tanti*) what; (: *tra pochi*) which; **che tipo di film preferisci?** what sort of film do you prefer?; **che vestito ti vuoi mettere?** what (*o* which) dress do you want to put on?
2 (*esclamativo: seguito da aggettivo*) how; (: *seguito da sostantivo*) what; **che buono!** how delicious!; **che bel vestito!** what a lovely dress!
▶ *cong* **1** (*con proposizioni subordinate*) that; **credo che verrà** I think he'll come; **voglio che tu studi** I want you to study; **so che tu c'eri** I know (that) you were there; **non che sia sbagliato, ma ...** not that it's wrong, but ...
2 (*finale*) so that; **vieni qua, che ti veda** come here, so (that) I can see you
3 (*temporale*): **arrivai che eri già partito** you had already left when I arrived; **sono anni che non lo vedo** I haven't seen him for years
4 (*in frasi imperative, concessive*): **che venga pure!** let him come by all means!; **che tu sia benedetto!** may God bless you!
5 (*comparativo: con più, meno*) than; *vedi anche* **più; meno; così** ecc

chemiotera'pia [kemjotera'pia] *sf* chemotherapy
chero'sene [kero'zɛne] *sm* kerosene

 PAROLA CHIAVE

chi [ki] *pron* **1** (*interrogativo: soggetto*) who; (: *oggetto*) who, whom; **chi è?** who is it?; **di chi è questo libro?** whose book is this?, whose is this book?; **con chi parli?** who are you talking to?; **a chi pensi?** who are you thinking about?; **chi di voi?** which of you?; **non so a chi rivolgermi** I don't know who to ask
2 (*relativo*) whoever, anyone who; **dillo a chi vuoi** tell whoever you like

3 (*indefinito*): **chi ... chi ...** some ... others ...; **chi dice una cosa, chi dice un'altra** some say one thing, others say another

chiacchie'rare [kjakkje'rare] /72/ *vi* to chat; (*discorrere futilmente*) to chatter; (*far pettegolezzi*) to gossip; **chi'acchiere** *sfpl*: **fare due** o **quattro chiacchiere** to have a chat

chia'mare [kja'mare] /72/ *vt* to call; (*rivolgersi a qn*) to call (in), send for; **chiamarsi** *vpr* (*aver nome*) to be called; **come ti chiami?** what's your name?; **mi chiamo Paolo** my name is Paolo, I'm called Paolo; **~ alle armi** to call up; **~ in giudizio** to summon; **chia'mata** *sf* (*Tel*) call; (*Mil*) call-up

chia'rezza [kja'rettsa] *sf* clearness, clarity

chia'rire [kja'rire] /55/ *vt* to make clear; (*fig: spiegare*) to clear up, explain

chi'aro, -a ['kjaro] *ag* clear; (*luminoso*) clear, bright; (*colore*) pale, light

chi'asso ['kjasso] *sm* uproar, row

chi'ave ['kjave] *sf* key ⊳ *ag inv* key *cpd*: **~ d'accensione** (*Aut*) ignition key; **~ inglese** monkey wrench; **~ di volta** keystone; **~ USB** (*Inform*) USB key

chia'vetta [kja'vetta] *sf* (*Inform*) dongle

chi'azza ['kjattsa] *sf* stain, splash

'**chicco, -chi** ['kikko] *sm* grain; (*di caffè*) bean; **~ d'uva** grape

chi'edere ['kjedere] /21/ *vt* (*per sapere*) to ask; (*per avere*) to ask for ⊳ *vi*: **~ di qn** to ask after sb; (*al telefono*) to ask for o want sb; **chiedersi** *vpr*: **chiedersi (se)** to wonder (whether); **~ qc a qn** to ask sb sth; to ask sb for sth

chi'esa ['kjeza] *sf* church

chi'esi *ecc* ['kjezi] *vb vedi* **chiedere**

'**chiglia** ['kiʎʎa] *sf* keel

'**chilo** ['kilo] *sm* kilo; **chilo'grammo** *sm* kilogram(me); **chi'lometro** *sm* kilometre

'**chimico, -a, -ci, -che** ['kimiko] *ag* chemical ⊳ *sm/f* chemist

chi'nare [ki'nare] /72/ *vt* to lower, bend; **chinarsi** *vpr* to stoop, bend

chi'occiola ['kjɔttʃola] *sf* snail; (*di indirizzo e-mail*) at (symbol); **scala a ~** spiral staircase

chi'odo ['kjɔdo] *sm* nail; (*fig*) obsession; **~ di garofano** (*Cuc*) clove

chi'osco, -schi ['kjɔsko] *sm* kiosk, stall

chi'ostro ['kjɔstro] *sm* cloister

chiro'mante [kiro'mante] *smf* palmist

chirur'gia [kirur'dʒia] *sf* surgery; **~ estetica** cosmetic surgery; **chi'rurgo, -ghi** o **-gi** *sm* surgeon

chissà [kis'sa] *av* who knows, I wonder

chi'tarra [ki'tarra] *sf* guitar

chitar'rista, -i, -e [kitar'rista] *sm/f* guitarist, guitar player

chi'udere ['kjudere] /22/ *vt* to close, shut; (*luce, acqua*) to put off, turn off; (*definitivamente: fabbrica*) to close down, shut down; (*strada*) to close; (*recingere*) to enclose; (*porre termine a*) to end ⊳ *vi* to close, shut; to close down, shut down, to end; **chiudersi** *vpr* to shut, close; (*ritirarsi: anche fig*) to shut o.s. away; (*ferita*) to close up

chi'unque [ki'unkwe] *pron* (*relativo*) whoever; (*indefinito*) anyone, anybody; **~ sia** whoever it is

'**chiusi** *ecc* ['kjusi] *vb vedi* **chiudere**

chi'uso, -a ['kjuso] *pp di* **chiudere** ⊳ *sf* (*di corso d'acqua*) sluice, lock; (*recinto*) enclosure; (*di discorso ecc*) conclusion, ending; **chiu'sura** *sf* closing; shutting; closing o shutting down; enclosing; putting o turning off; ending; (*dispositivo*) catch; fastening; fastener; **chiusura lampo**® zip (fastener) (BRIT), zipper (US)

 PAROLA CHIAVE

ci [tʃi] (*dav lo, la, li, le, ne diventa* **ce**) *pron* **1** (*personale: complemento oggetto*) us; (: *a noi, complemento di termine*) (to) us; (: *riflessivo*) ourselves; (: *reciproco*) each other, one another; (: *impersonale*): **ci si veste** we get dressed; **ci ha visti** he's seen us; **non ci ha dato niente** he gave us nothing; **ci vestiamo** we get dressed; **ci amiamo** we love one another o each other

2 (*dimostrativo, di ciò, su ciò, in ciò ecc*) about (o on o of) it; **non so cosa farci** I don't know what to do about it; **che c'entro io?** what have I got to do with it?

▶ *av* (*qui*) here; (*lì*) there; (*moto attraverso luogo*): **ci passa sopra un ponte** a bridge passes over it; **non ci passa più nessuno** nobody comes this way any more; **esserci** *vedi* **essere**

C.I. *abbr* = **carta d'identità**

cia'batta [tʃa'batta] *sf* slipper; (*pane*) ciabatta

ciam'bella [tʃam'bɛlla] *sf* (*Cuc*) ring-shaped cake; (*salvagente*) rubber ring

ci'ao ['tʃao] *escl* (*all'arrivo*) hello!; (*alla partenza*) cheerio! (BRIT), bye!

cias'cuno, -a [tʃas'kuno] (*dav sm*: **ciascun** + C, V, **ciascuno** + s impura, gn, pn, ps, x, z; *dav sf*: **ciascuna** + C, **ciascun'** + V) *det* every, each; (*ogni*) every ⊳ *pron* each (one); (*tutti*) everyone, everybody

ci'barie [tʃi'barje] *sfpl* foodstuffs

cibernauta, -i, -e [tʃiber'nauta] *sm/f* Internet surfer

ciberspazio [tʃiberˈspattsjo] *sm* cyberspace

'**cibo** [ˈtʃibo] *sm* food

ci'cala [tʃiˈkala] *sf* cicada

cica'trice [tʃikaˈtritʃe] *sf* scar

'**cicca, -che** [ˈtʃikka] *sf* cigarette end

'**ciccia** [ˈtʃittʃa] *sf* (*fam*) fat

cicci'one, -a [tʃitˈtʃone] *sm/f* (*fam*) fatty

cicla'mino [tʃiklaˈmino] *sm* cyclamen

ci'clismo [tʃiˈklizmo] *sm* cycling; **ci'clista, -i, -e** *sm/f* cyclist

'**ciclo** [ˈtʃiklo] *sm* cycle; (*di malattia*) course

ciclomo'tore [tʃiklomoˈtore] *sm* moped

ci'clone [tʃiˈklone] *sm* cyclone

ci'cogna [tʃiˈkoɲɲa] *sf* stork

ci'eco, -a, -chi, -che [ˈtʃɛko] *ag* blind ▷ *sm/f* blind man/woman

ci'elo [ˈtʃɛlo] *sm* sky; (*Rel*) heaven

'**cifra** [ˈtʃifra] *sf* (*numero*) figure, numeral; (*somma di denaro*) sum, figure; (*monogramma*) monogram, initials *pl*; (*codice*) code, cipher

'**ciglio** [ˈtʃiʎʎo] *sm* (*margine*) edge, verge; (*pl(f) ciglia: delle palpebre*) (eye)lash; (eye) lid; (*sopracciglio*) eyebrow

'**cigno** [ˈtʃiɲɲo] *sm* swan

cigo'lare [tʃigoˈlare] /72/ *vi* to squeak, creak

'**Cile** [ˈtʃile] *sm*: **il ~** Chile; **ci'leno, -a** [tʃiˈlɛno] *ag*, *sm/f* Chilean

cili'egia, -gie *o* **-ge** [tʃiˈljɛdʒa] *sf* cherry

cilie'gina [tʃiljeˈdʒina] *sf* glacé cherry

cilin'drata [tʃilinˈdrata] *sf* (*Aut*) (cubic) capacity; **una macchina di grossa ~** a big-engined car

ci'lindro [tʃiˈlindro] *sm* cylinder; (*cappello*) top hat

'**cima** [ˈtʃima] *sf* (*sommità*) top; (*di monte*) top, summit; (*estremità*) end; **in ~ a** at the top of; **da ~ a fondo** from top to bottom; (*fig*) from beginning to end

'**cimice** [ˈtʃimitʃe] *sf* (*Zool*) bug; (*puntina*) drawing pin (*BRIT*), thumbtack (*US*)

cimini'era [tʃimiˈnjɛra] *sf* chimney; (*di nave*) funnel

cimi'tero [tʃimiˈtero] *sm* cemetery

'**Cina** [ˈtʃina] *sf*: **la ~** China

cin'cin, cin cin [tʃinˈtʃin] *escl* cheers!

'**cinema** [ˈtʃinema] *sm inv* cinema

ci'nese [tʃiˈnese] *ag*, *smf*, *sm* Chinese *inv*

'**cinghia** [ˈtʃingja] *sf* strap; (*cintura, Tecn*) belt

cinghi'ale [tʃinˈgjale] *sm* wild boar

cinguet'tare [tʃingwetˈtare] /72/ *vi* to twitter

'**cinico, -a, -ci, -che** [ˈtʃiniko] *ag* cynical ▷ *sm/f* cynic

cin'quanta [tʃinˈkwanta] *num* fifty; **cinquan'tesimo, -a** *num* fiftieth

cinquan'tina [tʃinkwanˈtina] *sf* (*serie*): **una ~ (di)** about fifty; (*età*): **essere sulla ~** to be about fifty

'**cinque** [ˈtʃinkwe] *num* five; **avere ~ anni** to be five (years old); **il ~ dicembre 2008** the fifth of December 2008; **alle ~ (ora)** at five (o'clock)

cinque'cento [tʃinkweˈtʃento] *num* five hundred ▷ *sm*: **il C~** the sixteenth century

cin'tura [tʃinˈtura] *sf* belt; **~ di salvataggio** lifebelt (*BRIT*), life preserver (*US*); **~ di sicurezza** (*Aut*, *Aer*) safety *o* seat belt

cintu'rino [tʃintuˈrino] *sm* strap; **~ dell'orologio** watch strap

ciò [tʃɔ] *pron* this; that; **~ che** what; **~ nonostante** *o* **nondimeno** nevertheless, in spite of that

ci'occa, -che [ˈtʃɔkka] *sf* (*di capelli*) lock

ciocco'lata [tʃokkoˈlata] *sf* chocolate; (*bevanda*) (hot) chocolate; **cioccola'tino** *sm* chocolate

cio'è [tʃoˈɛ] *av* that is (to say)

ci'otola [ˈtʃɔtola] *sf* bowl

ci'ottolo [ˈtʃɔttolo] *sm* pebble; (*di strada*) cobble(stone)

ci'polla [tʃiˈpolla] *sf* onion; (*di tulipano ecc*) bulb

cipol'lina [tʃipolˈlina] *sf*: **cipolline sottaceto** pickled onions

ci'presso [tʃiˈprɛsso] *sm* cypress (tree)

'**cipria** [ˈtʃiprja] *sf* (face) powder

'**Cipro** [ˈtʃipro] *sm* Cyprus

'**circa** [ˈtʃirka] *av* about, roughly ▷ *prep* about, concerning; **a mezzogiorno ~** about midday

'**circo, -chi** [ˈtʃirko] *sm* circus

circo'lare [tʃirkoˈlare] /72/ *vi* to circulate; (*Aut*) to drive (along), move (along) ▷ *ag* circular ▷ *sf* (*Amm*) circular; (*di autobus*) circle (line); **circolazi'one** *sf* circulation; (*Aut*): **la circolazione** (the) traffic

'**circolo** [ˈtʃirkolo] *sm* circle

circon'dare [tʃirkonˈdare] /72/ *vt* to surround; **circondarsi** *vpr*: **circondarsi di** to surround o.s. with

circonvallazi'one [tʃirkonvallatˈtsjone] *sf* ring road (*BRIT*), beltway (*US*); (*per evitare una città*) by-pass

circos'petto, -a [tʃirkosˈpɛtto] *ag* circumspect, cautious

circos'tante [tʃirkosˈtante] *ag* surrounding, neighbouring

circos'tanza [tʃirkosˈtantsa] *sf* circumstance; (*occasione*) occasion

cir'cuito [tʃirˈkuito] *sm* circuit

C.I.S.L. *sigla f* (= *Confederazione Italiana Sindacati Lavoratori*) trades union organization

cis'terna [tʃisˈtɛrna] *sf* tank, cistern

'**cisti** [ˈtʃisti] *sf inv* cyst

cis'tite [tʃis'tite] sf cystitis

ci'tare [tʃi'tare] /72/ vt (Dir) to summon; (autore) to quote; (a esempio, modello) to cite

ci'tofono [tʃi'tɔfono] sm entry phone; (in uffici) intercom

città [tʃit'ta] sf inv town; (importante) city; ~ **universitaria** university campus

cittadi'nanza [tʃittadi'nantsa] sf citizens pl; (Dir) citizenship

citta'dino, -a [tʃitta'dino] ag town cpd; city cpd ▷ sm/f (di uno Stato) citizen; (abitante di città) town dweller, city dweller

ci'uccio ['tʃuttʃo] sm (fam) comforter, dummy (BRIT), pacifier (US)

ci'uffo ['tʃuffo] sm tuft

ci'vetta [tʃi'vetta] sf (Zool) owl; (fig: donna) coquette, flirt ▷ ag inv: **auto/nave ~** decoy car/ship

'civico, -a, -ci, -che ['tʃiviko] ag civic; (museo) municipal, town cpd; city cpd

ci'vile [tʃi'vile] ag civil; (non militare) civilian; (nazione) civilized ▷ sm civilian

civiltà [tʃivil'ta] sf civilization; (cortesia) civility

'clacson sm inv (Aut) horn

clandes'tino, -a ag clandestine; (Pol) underground, clandestine; (immigrato) illegal ▷ sm/f stowaway; (anche: **immigrato ~**) illegal immigrant

'classe sf class; **di ~** (fig) with class; of excellent quality; **~ operaia** working class; **~ turistica** (Aer) economy class

'classico, -a, -ci, -che ag classical; (tradizionale: moda) classic(al) ▷ sm classic; (autore) classical author

clas'sifica, -che sf classification; (Sport) placings pl

classifi'care /20/ vt to classify; (candidato, compito) to grade; **classificarsi** vpr to be placed

'clausola sf (Dir) clause

clavi'cembalo [klavi'tʃembalo] sm harpsichord

cla'vicola sf (Anat) collarbone

clic'care /20/ vi (Inform): **~ su** to click on

cli'ente smf customer, client

'clima, -i sm climate; **climatizza'tore** sm air conditioner

'clinico, -a, -ci, -che ag clinical ▷ sf (scienza) clinical medicine; (casa di cura) clinic, nursing home; (settore d'ospedale) clinic

clo'nare /72/ vt to clone; **clona'zione** [klonat'tsjone] sf cloning

'cloro sm chlorine

club sm inv club

cm abbr (= centimetro) cm

c.m. abbr (= corrente mese) inst.

coalizi'one [koalit'tsjone] sf coalition

'COBAS sigla mpl (= Comitati di base) independent trades unions

'coca sf (bibita) Coke; (droga) cocaine

coca'ina sf cocaine

cocci'nella [kottʃi'nɛlla] sf ladybird (BRIT), ladybug (US)

cocci'uto, -a [kot'tʃuto] ag stubborn, pigheaded

'cocco, -chi sm (pianta) coconut palm; (frutto): **noce di ~** coconut ▷ sm/f (fam) darling

cocco'drillo sm crocodile

cocco'lare /72/ vt to cuddle, fondle

cocerò ecc [kotʃe'rɔ] vb vedi **cuocere**

co'comero sm watermelon

'coda sf tail; (fila di persone, auto) queue (BRIT), line (US); (di abiti) train; **con la ~ dell'occhio** out of the corner of one's eye; **mettersi in ~** to queue (up) (BRIT), line up (US); to join the queue o line; **~ di cavallo** (acconciatura) ponytail

co'dardo, -a ag cowardly ▷ sm/f coward

'codice ['kɔditʃe] sm code; **~ di avviamento postale** postcode (BRIT), zip code (US); **~ a barre** bar code; **~ civile** civil code; **~ fiscale** tax code; **~ penale** penal code; **~ segreto** (di tessera magnetica) PIN (number); **~ della strada** highway code

coe'rente ag coherent

coe'taneo, -a ag, sm/f contemporary

'cofano sm (Aut) bonnet (BRIT), hood (US); (forziere) chest

'cogliere ['kɔʎʎere] /23/ vt (fiore, frutto) to pick, gather; (sorprendere) to catch, surprise; (bersaglio) to hit; (fig: momento opportuno ecc) to grasp, seize, take; (: capire) to grasp; **~ sul fatto** o **in flagrante/alla sprovvista** to catch red-handed/unprepared

co'gnato, -a [koɲ'ɲato] sm/f brother-in-law/sister-in-law

co'gnome [koɲ'ɲome] sm surname

coinci'denza [kointʃi'dɛntsa] sf coincidence; (Ferr, Aer, di autobus) connection

coin'cidere [koin'tʃidere] /34/ vi to coincide

coin'volgere [koin'vɔldʒere] /96/ vt: **~ in** to involve in

cola'pasta sm inv colander

co'lare /72/ vt (liquido) to strain; (pasta) to drain; (oro fuso) to pour ▷ vi (sudore) to drip; (botte) to leak; (cera) to melt; **~ a picco** vt (nave) to sink

colazi'one [kolat'tsjone] sf breakfast; lunch; **fare ~** to have breakfast (o lunch)

co'lera sm (Med) cholera

'colgo ecc vb vedi **cogliere**

'colica sf (Med) colic

co'lino sm strainer

'colla *prep + det vedi* **con** ▷ *sf* glue; (*di farina*) paste

collabo'rare /72/ *vi* to collaborate; ~ **a** to collaborate on; (*giornale*) to contribute to; **collabora'tore, -'trice** *sm/f* collaborator; (*di giornale, rivista*) contributor; **collaboratore esterno** freelance; **collaboratrice familiare** home help

col'lana *sf* necklace; (*collezione*) collection, series

col'lant [kɔ'lã] *sm inv* tights *pl*

col'lare *sm* collar

col'lasso *sm* (*Med*) collapse

collau'dare /72/ *vt* to test, try out

col'lega, -ghi, -ghe *sm/f* colleague

collega'mento *sm* connection; (*Mil*) liaison

colle'gare /80/ *vt* to connect, join, link; **collegarsi** *vpr* (*Radio, TV*) to link up; **collegarsi con** (*Tel*) to get through to

col'legio [kol'lɛdʒo] *sm* college; (*convitto*) boarding school; ~ **elettorale** (*Pol*) constituency

'collera *sf* anger

col'lerico, -a, -ci, -che *ag* quick-tempered, irascible

col'letta *sf* collection

col'letto *sm* collar

collezio'nare [kollettsjo'nare] /72/ *vt* to collect

collezi'one [kollet'tsjone] *sf* collection

col'lina *sf* hill

col'lirio *sm* eyewash

'collo *prep + det vedi* **con** ▷ *sm* neck; (*di abito*) neck, collar; (*pacco*) parcel; ~ **del piede** instep

colloca'mento *sm* (*impiego*) employment; (*disposizione*) placing, arrangement

collo'care /20/ *vt* (*libri, mobili*) to place; (*Comm: merce*) to find a market for

collocazi'one [kollokat'tsjone] *sf* placing; (*di libro*) classification

col'loquio *sm* conversation, talk; (*ufficiale, per un lavoro*) interview; (*Ins*) preliminary oral exam

col'mare /72/ *vt*: ~ **di** (*anche fig*) to fill with; (*dare in abbondanza*) to load *o* overwhelm with

co'lombo, -a *sm/f* dove; pigeon

co'lonia *sf* colony; (*per bambini*) holiday camp; (**acqua di**) ~ (eau de) cologne

co'lonna *sf* column; ~ **sonora** (*Cine*) sound track; ~ **vertebrale** spine, spinal column

colon'nello *sm* colonel

colo'rante *sm* colouring

colo'rare /72/ *vt* to colour; (*disegno*) to colour in

co'lore *sm* colour; **a colori** in colour, colour *cpd*; **farne di tutti i colori** to get up to all sorts of mischief

colo'rito, -a *ag* coloured; (*viso*) rosy, pink; (*linguaggio*) colourful ▷ *sm* (*tinta*) colour; (*carnagione*) complexion

'colpa *sf* fault; (*biasimo*) blame; (*colpevolezza*) guilt; (*azione colpevole*) offence; (*peccato*) sin; **di chi è la ~?** whose fault is it?; **è ~ sua** it's his fault; **per ~ di** through, owing to; **col'pevole** *ag* guilty

col'pire /55/ *vt* to hit, strike; (*fig*) to strike; **rimanere colpito da qc** to be amazed *o* struck by sth

'colpo *sm* (*urto*) knock; (*fig: affettivo*) blow, shock; (: *aggressivo*) blow; (*di pistola*) shot; (*Med*) stroke; (*furto*) raid; **di ~** suddenly; **fare ~** to make a strong impression; **il motore perde colpi** the engine is misfiring; ~ **d'aria** chill; ~ **in banca** bank job *o* raid; ~ **basso** (*Pugilato, fig*) punch below the belt; ~ **di fulmine** love at first sight; ~ **di grazia** coup de grâce; ~ **di scena** (*Teat*) coup de théâtre; (*fig*) dramatic turn of events; ~ **di sole** sunstroke; **colpi di sole** (*nei capelli*) highlights; ~ **di Stato** coup d'état; ~ **di telefono** phone call; ~ **di testa** (*sudden*) impulse *o* whim; ~ **di vento** gust (of wind)

'colsi *ecc vb vedi* **cogliere**

coltel'lata *sf* stab

col'tello *sm* knife; ~ **a serramanico** clasp knife

colti'vare /72/ *vt* to cultivate; (*verdura*) to grow, cultivate

'colto, -a *pp di* **cogliere** ▷ *ag* (*istruito*) cultured, educated

'coma *sm inv* coma

comanda'mento *sm* (*Rel*) commandment

coman'dante *sm* (*Mil*) commander, commandant; (*di reggimento*) commanding officer; (*Naut, Aer*) captain

coman'dare /72/ *vi* to be in command ▷ *vt* to command; (*imporre*) to order, command; ~ **a qn di fare** to order sb to do

combaci'are [komba'tʃare] /14/ *vi* to meet; (*fig: coincidere*) to coincide

com'battere /1/ *vt*, *vi* to fight

combi'nare /72/ *vt* to combine; (*organizzare*) to arrange; (*fam: fare*) to make, cause; **combinazi'one** *sf* combination; (*caso fortuito*) coincidence; **per combinazione** by chance

combus'tibile *ag* combustible ▷ *sm* fuel

⊙ **PAROLA CHIAVE**

'come *av* **1** (*alla maniera di*) like; **ti comporti come lui** you behave like him *o* like he does; **bianco come la neve** (as) white as snow; **come se** as if, as though

2 (*in qualità di*) as a; **lavora come autista** he works as a driver

3 (*interrogativo*) how; **come ti chiami?** what's your name?; **come sta?** how are you?; **com'è il tuo amico?** what is your friend like?; **come?** (*prego?*) pardon?, sorry?; **come mai?** how come?; **come mai non ci hai avvertiti?** how come you didn't warn us?

4 (*esclamativo*): **come sei bravo!** how clever you are!; **come mi dispiace!** I'm terribly sorry!

▶ *cong* **1** (*in che modo*) how; **mi ha spiegato come l'ha conosciuto** he told me how he met him

2 (*correlativo*) as; (*con comparativi di maggioranza*) than; **non è bravo come pensavo** he isn't as clever as I thought; **è meglio di come pensassi** it's better than I thought

3 (*appena che, quando*) as soon as; **come arrivò, iniziò a lavorare** as soon as he arrived, he set to work; *vedi anche* **così; tanto**

'**comico, -a, -ci, -che** *ag* (*Teat*) comic; (*buffo*) comical ▷ *sm* (*attore*) comedian, comic actor

cominci'are [komin'tʃare] /14/ *vt, vi* to begin, start; **~ a fare/col fare** to begin to do/by doing

comi'tato *sm* committee

comi'tiva *sf* party, group

co'mizio [ko'mittsjo] *sm* (*Pol*) meeting, assembly

com'media *sf* comedy; (*opera teatrale*) play; (: *che fa ridere*) comedy; (*fig*) playacting *no pl*

commemo'rare /72/ *vt* to commemorate

commen'tare /72/ *vt* to comment on; (*testo*) to annotate; (*Radio, TV*) to give a commentary on

commerci'ale [kommer'tʃale] *ag* commercial, trading; (*peg*) commercial

commercia'lista, -i, -e [kommertʃa'lista] *sm/f* (*laureato*) graduate in economics and commerce; (*consulente*) business consultant

commerci'ante [kommer'tʃante] *smf* trader, dealer; (*negoziante*) shopkeeper

commerci'are [kommer'tʃare] /14/ *vi*: **~ in** to deal *o* trade in ▷ *vt* to deal *o* trade in

com'mercio [kom'mertʃo] *sm* trade, commerce; **essere in ~** (*prodotto*) to be on the market *o* on sale; (*persona*) to be in business; **~ all'ingrosso/al dettaglio** wholesale/retail trade

com'messo, -a *pp di* **commettere** ▷ *sm/f* shop assistant (*BRIT*), sales clerk (*US*) ▷ *sm* (*impiegato*) clerk; **~ viaggiatore** commercial traveller

commes'tibile *ag* edible

com'mettere /63/ *vt* to commit

com'misi *ecc vb vedi* **commettere**

commissari'ato *sm* (*Amm*) commissionership; (: *sede*) commissioner's office; (: *di polizia*) police station

commis'sario *sm* commissioner; (*di pubblica sicurezza*) ≈ (police) superintendent (*BRIT*), ≈ (police) captain (*US*); (*Sport*) steward; (*membro di commissione*) member of a committee *o* board

commissi'one *sf* (*incarico*) errand; (*comitato, percentuale*) commission; (*Comm: ordinazione*) order; **commissioni** *sfpl* (*acquisti*) shopping *sg*; **~ d'esame** examining board; **commissioni bancarie** bank charges

com'mosso, -a *pp di* **commuovere**

commo'vente *ag* moving

commozi'one [kommot'tsjone] *sf* emotion, deep feeling; **~ cerebrale** (*Med*) concussion

commu'overe /66/ *vt* to move, affect; **commuoversi** *vpr* to be moved

como'dino *sm* bedside table

comodità *sf inv* comfort; convenience

'**comodo, -a** *ag* comfortable; (*facile*) easy; (*conveniente*) convenient; (*utile*) useful, handy ▷ *sm* comfort; convenience; **con ~** at one's convenience *o* leisure; **fare il proprio ~** to do as one pleases; **far ~** to be useful *o* handy

compa'gnia [kompaɲ'ɲia] *sf* company; (*gruppo*) gathering

com'pagno, -a [kom'paɲɲo] *sm/f* (*di classe, gioco*) companion; (*Pol*) comrade

com'paio *ecc vb vedi* **comparire**

compa'rare /72/ *vt* to compare

compara'tivo, -a *ag, sm* comparative

compa'rire /7/ *vi* to appear

com'parvi *ecc vb vedi* **comparire**

compassi'one *sf* compassion, pity; **avere ~ di qn** to feel sorry for sb, pity sb

com'passo *sm* (*pair of*) compasses *pl*; callipers *pl*

compa'tibile *ag* (*scusabile*) excusable; (*conciliabile, Inform*) compatible

compa'tire /55/ *vt* (*aver compassione di*) to sympathize with, feel sorry for; (*scusare*) to make allowances for

com'patto, -a *ag* compact; (*roccia*) solid; (*folla*) dense; (*fig: gruppo, partito*) united

compen'sare /72/ *vt* to compensate for, make up for; **~ qn di** (*rimunerare*) to pay *o* remunerate sb for; (*risarcire*) to pay compensation to sb for; (*fig: fatiche, dolori*) to reward sb for; **com'penso** *sm* compensation; payment, remuneration; reward; **in compenso** (*d'altra parte*) on the other hand

compe'rare /72/ vt = comprare

'compere sfpl: fare ~ to do the shopping

compe'tente ag competent; (mancia) apt, suitable

com'petere /45/ vi to compete, vie; (Dir: spettare): ~ a to lie within the competence of; **competizi'one** sf competition

compi'angere [kom'pjandʒere] /75/ vt to sympathize with, feel sorry for

'compiere /24/ vt (concludere) to finish, complete; (adempiere) to carry out, fulfil; **compiersi** vpr (avverarsi) to be fulfilled, come true; ~ **gli anni** to have one's birthday

compi'lare /72/ vt to compile; (modulo) to complete, fill in (BRIT), fill out (US)

'compito sm (incarico) task, duty; (dovere) duty; (Ins) exercise; (: a casa) piece of homework; **fare i compiti** to do one's homework

comple'anno sm birthday

complessità sf complexity

comples'sivo, -a ag (globale) comprehensive, overall; (totale: cifra) total

com'plesso, -a ag complex ▷ sm (Psic, Edil) complex; (Mus: corale) ensemble; (: orchestrina) band; (: di musica pop) group; **in o nel ~** on the whole; ~ **alberghiero** hotel complex; ~ **edilizio** building complex; ~ **vitaminico** vitamin complex

completa'mente av completely

comple'tare /72/ vt to complete

com'pleto, -a ag complete; (teatro, autobus) full ▷ sm suit; **al ~** full; ~ **da sci** ski suit

compli'care /20/ vt to complicate; **complicarsi** vpr to become complicated

'complice ['komplitʃe] smf accomplice

complicità [komplitʃi'ta] sf inv complicity; **un sorriso/uno sguardo di ~** a knowing smile/look

complimen'tarsi /72/ vpr: ~ **con** to congratulate

compli'mento sm compliment; **complimenti** smpl (cortesia eccessiva) ceremony sg; (ossequi) regards, compliments; **complimenti!** congratulations!; **senza complimenti!** don't stand on ceremony!; make yourself at home!; help yourself!

complot'tare /72/ vi to plot, conspire

com'plotto sm plot, conspiracy

com'pone ecc vb vedi **comporre**

compo'nente smf member ▷ sm component

com'pongo ecc vb vedi **comporre**

componi'mento sm (Dir) settlement; (Ins) composition; (poetico, teatrale) work

com'porre /77/ vt (musica, testo) to compose; (mettere in ordine) to arrange; (Dir: lite) to settle; (Tip) to set; (Tel) to dial;

comporsi vpr: **comporsi di** to consist of, be composed of

comporta'mento sm behaviour

compor'tare /72/ vt (implicare) to involve; **comportarsi** vpr to behave

com'posi ecc vb vedi **comporre**

composi'tore, -'trice sm/f composer; (Tip) compositor, typesetter

com'posto, -a pp di **comporre** ▷ ag (persona) composed, self-possessed; (: decoroso) dignified; (formato da più elementi) compound ▷ sm compound

com'prare /72/ vt to buy

com'prendere /81/ vt (contenere) to comprise, consist of; (capire) to understand

compren'sibile ag understandable

comprensi'one sf understanding

compren'sivo, -a ag (prezzo): ~ **di** inclusive of; (indulgente) understanding

> Attenzione! In inglese esiste la parola comprehensive, che però in genere significa completo.

com'preso, -a pp di **comprendere** ▷ ag (incluso) included

com'pressa sf vedi **compresso**

com'presso, -a pp di **comprimere** ▷ sf (Med: garza) compress; (: pastiglia) tablet

com'primere /50/ vt (premere) to press; (Fisica) to compress; (fig) to repress

compro'messo, -a pp di **compromettere** ▷ sm compromise

compro'mettere /63/ vt to compromise; **compromettersi** vpr to compromise o.s.

com'puter sm inv computer

comu'nale ag municipal, town cpd; **consiglio/palazzo ~** town council/hall

Co'mune sm (Amm) town council; (sede) town hall

co'mune ag common; (consueto) common, everyday; (di livello medio) average; (ordinario) ordinary ▷ sf (di persone) commune; **fuori del ~** out of the ordinary; **avere in ~** to have in common, share; **mettere in ~** to share

comuni'care /20/ vt (notizia) to pass on, convey; (malattia) to pass on; (ansia ecc) to pass on; (trasmettere: calore ecc) to transmit, communicate; (Rel) to administer communion to ▷ vi to communicate

comuni'cato sm communiqué; ~ **stampa** press release

comunicazi'one [komunikat'tsjone] sf communication; (annuncio) announcement; (Tel): ~ **(telefonica)** (telephone) call; **dare la ~ a qn** to put sb through; **ottenere la ~** to get through

comuni'one sf communion; ~ **dei beni** (Dir) joint ownership of property

comu'nismo sm communism

comunità *sf inv* community; **C~ Economica Europea** European Economic Community

co'munque *cong* however, no matter how ▷ *av* (*in ogni modo*) in any case; (*tuttavia*) however, nevertheless

con *prep* (*nei seguenti casi* **con** *può fondersi con l'articolo definito,* con + il = **col**, con + la = **colla**, con + gli = **cogli**, con + l = **coi**, con + le = **colle**) with; **partire col treno** to leave by train; **~ mio grande stupore** to my great astonishment; **~ tutto ciò** for all that

con'cedere [kon'tʃɛdere] /29/ *vt* (*accordare*) to grant; (*ammettere*) to admit, concede; **concedersi qc** to treat o.s. to sth, allow o.s. sth

concen'trare [kontʃen'trare] /72/ *vt*, **concen'trarsi** *vpr* to concentrate

concentrazi'one *sf* concentration

conce'pire [kontʃe'pire] /55/ *vt* (*bambino*) to conceive; (*progetto, idea*) to conceive (of); (*metodo, piano*) to devise

con'certo [kon'tʃɛrto] *sm* (*Mus*) concert; (*: componimento*) concerto

con'cessi *ecc* [kon'tʃɛssi] *vb vedi* **concedere**

con'cetto [kon'tʃɛtto] *sm* (*pensiero, idea*) concept; (*opinione*) opinion

concezi'one [kontʃet'tsjone] *sf* conception

con'chiglia [kon'kiʎʎa] *sf* shell

conci'are [kon'tʃare] /14/ *vt* (*pelli*) to tan; (*tabacco*) to cure; (*fig: ridurre in cattivo stato*) to beat up; **conciarsi** *vpr* (*sporcarsi*) to get in a mess; (*vestirsi male*) to dress badly

concili'are [kontʃi'ljare] /19/ *vt* to reconcile; (*contravvenzione*) to pay on the spot; (*sonno*) to be conducive to, induce; **conciliarsi qc** to gain *o* win sth (for o.s.); **conciliarsi qn** to win sb over; **conciliarsi con** to be reconciled with

con'cime [kon'tʃime] *sm* manure; (*chimico*) fertilizer

con'ciso, -a [kon'tʃizo] *ag* concise, succinct

concitta'dino, -a [kontʃitta'dino] *sm/f* fellow citizen

con'cludere /3/ *vt* to conclude; (*portare a compimento*) to conclude, finish, bring to an end; (*operare positivamente*) to achieve ▷ *vi* (*essere convincente*) to be conclusive; **concludersi** *vpr* to come to an end, close

concor'dare /72/ *vt* (*prezzo*) to agree on; (*Ling*) to make agree ▷ *vi* to agree

con'corde *ag* (*d'accordo*) in agreement; (*simultaneo*) simultaneous

concor'rente *ag* competing; (*Mat*) concurrent ▷ *smf* competitor; (*Ins*) candidate; **concor'renza** *sf* competition

concorrenzi'ale [konkorren'tsjale] *ag* competitive

con'correre /28/ *vi*: **~ (in)** (*Mat*) to converge *o* meet (in); **~ (a)** (*competere*) to compete (for); (*Ins: a una cattedra*) to apply (for); (*partecipare: a un'impresa*) to take part (in), contribute (to); **con'corso, -a** *pp di* **concorrere** ▷ *sm* competition; (*esame*) competitive examination; **concorso di colpa** (*Dir*) contributory negligence

con'creto, -a *ag* concrete

con'danna *sf* condemnation; sentence; conviction

condan'nare /72/ *vt* (*disapprovare*) to condemn; (*Dir*): **~ a** to sentence to; **~ per** to convict of

conden'sare /72/ *vt* to condense

condi'mento *sm* seasoning; dressing

con'dire /55/ *vt* to season; (*insalata*) to dress

condi'videre /43/ *vt* to share

condizio'nale [kondittsjo'nale] *ag* conditional ▷ *sm* (*Ling*) conditional ▷ *sf* (*Dir*) suspended sentence

condizio'nare [kondittsjo'nare] /72/ *vt* to condition; **ad aria condizionata** air-conditioned; **condiziona'tore** *sm* air conditioner

condizi'one [kondit'tsjone] *sf* condition

condogli'anze [kondoʎ'ʎantse] *sfpl* condolences

con'dominio *sm* joint ownership; (*edificio*) jointly-owned building

con'dotta *sf vedi* **condotto**

con'dotto, -a *pp di* **condurre** ▷ *sf* (*modo di comportarsi*) conduct, behaviour; (*di un affare ecc*) handling; (*di acqua*) piping; (*incarico sanitario*) country medical practice controlled by a local authority

condu'cente [kondu'tʃɛnte] *sm* driver

con'duco *ecc vb vedi* **condurre**

con'durre /90/ *vt* to conduct; (*azienda*) to manage; (*accompagnare: bambino*) to take; (*automobile*) to drive; (*trasportare: acqua, gas*) to convey, conduct; (*fig*) to lead ▷ *vi* to lead

con'dussi *ecc vb vedi* **condurre**

confe'renza [konfe'rɛntsa] *sf* (*discorso*) lecture; (*riunione*) conference; **~ stampa** press conference

con'ferma *sf* confirmation

confer'mare /72/ *vt* to confirm

confes'sare /72/ *vt*, **confes'sarsi** *vpr* to confess; **andare a confessarsi** (*Rel*) to go to confession

con'fetto *sm* sugared almond; (*Med*) pill

▌ Attenzione! In inglese esiste la parola *confetti*, che però significa *coriandoli*.

confet'tura *sf* (*gen*) jam; (*di arance*) marmalade

confezio'nare [konfettsjo'nare] /72/ *vt* (*vestito*) to make (up); (*merci, pacchi*) to package

confezi'one [konfet'tsjone] *sf* (*di abiti: da uomo*) tailoring; (*: da donna*) dressmaking;

(*imballaggio*) packaging; **~ regalo** gift pack; **confezioni per signora** ladies' wear *no pl*; **confezioni da uomo** menswear *no pl*

confic'care /20/ *vt*: **~ qc in** to hammer *o* drive sth into; **conficcarsi** *vpr* to stick

confi'dare /72/ *vi*: **~ in** to confide in, rely on ▷ *vt* to confide; **confidarsi con qn** to confide in sb

configu'rare /72/ *vt* (*Inform*) to set

configurazi'one [konfigurat'tsjoni] *sf* configuration; (*Inform*) setting

confi'nare /72/ *vi*: **~ con** to border on ▷ *vt* (*Pol*) to intern; (*fig*) to confine

CONFIN'DUSTRIA *sigla f* (= *Confederazione Generale dell'Industria Italiana*) *employers' association* ≈ CBI (BRIT)

con'fine *sm* boundary; (*di paese*) border, frontier

confis'care /20/ *vt* to confiscate

con'flitto *sm* conflict; **~ d'interessi** conflict of interests

conflu'enza [konflu'entsa] *sf* (*di fiumi*) confluence; (*di strade*) junction

con'fondere /25/ *vt* to mix up, confuse; (*imbarazzare*) to embarrass; **confondersi** *vpr* (*mescolarsi*) to mingle; (*turbarsi*) to be confused; (*sbagliare*) to get mixed up

confor'tare /72/ *vt* to comfort, console

confron'tare /72/ *vt* to compare

con'fronto *sm* comparison; **in** *o* **a ~ di** in comparison with, compared to; **nei miei** (*o* **tuoi** *ecc*) **confronti** towards me (*o* you *ecc*)

con'fusi *ecc vb vedi* **confondere**

confusi'one *sf* confusion; (*imbarazzo*) embarrassment; **far ~** (*chiasso*) to make a racket

con'fuso, -a *pp di* **confondere** ▷ *ag* (*vedi confondere*) confused; embarrassed

conge'dare [kondʒe'dare] /72/ *vt* to dismiss; (*Mil*) to demobilize; **congedarsi** *vpr* to take one's leave

con'gegno *sm* device, mechanism

conge'lare [kondʒe'lare] /72/ *vt* to freeze; **congela'tore** *sm* freezer

congesti'one [kondʒes'tjone] *sf* congestion

conget'tura [kondʒet'tura] *sf* conjecture

con'giungere [kon'dʒundʒere] /5/ *vt*, **con'giungersi** *vpr* to join (together)

congiunti'vite [kondʒunti'vite] *sf* conjunctivitis

congiun'tivo [kondʒun'tivo] *sm* (*Ling*) subjunctive

congi'unto, -a [kon'dʒunto] *pp di* **congiungere** ▷ *ag* (*unito*) joined ▷ *sm/f* relative

congiunzi'one [kondʒun'tsjone] *sf* (*Ling*) conjunction

congi'ura [kon'dʒura] *sf* conspiracy

congratu'larsi /72/ *vpr*: **~ con qn per qc** to congratulate sb on sth

congratulazi'oni [kongratulat'tsjoni] *sfpl* congratulations

con'gresso *sm* congress

C.O.N.I. *sigla m* (= *Comitato Olimpico Nazionale Italiano*) Italian Olympic Games® Committee

coni'are /19/ *vt* to mint, coin; (*fig*) to coin

co'niglio [ko'niλλo] *sm* rabbit

coniu'gare /80/ *vt* (*Ling*) to conjugate; **coniugarsi** *vpr* to get married

'coniuge ['kɔnjudʒe] *smf* spouse

connazio'nale [konnattsjo'nale] *smf* fellow-countryman/woman

connessi'one *sf* connection

con'nettere /63/ *vt* to connect, join ▷ *vi* (*fig*) to think straight

'cono *sm* cone; **~ gelato** ice-cream cone

co'nobbi *ecc vb vedi* **conoscere**

cono'scente [konoʃʃente] *smf* acquaintance

cono'scenza [konoʃʃentsa] *sf* (*il sapere*) knowledge *no pl*; (*persona*) acquaintance; (*facoltà sensoriale*) consciousness *no pl*; **perdere ~** to lose consciousness

co'noscere [ko'noʃʃere] /26/ *vt* to know; **ci siamo conosciuti a Firenze** we (first) met in Florence; **conoscersi** *vpr* to know o.s.; (*reciproco*) to know each other; (*incontrarsi*) to meet; **~ qn di vista** to know sb by sight; **farsi ~** (*fig*) to make a name for o.s.; **conosci'uto, -a** *pp di* **conoscere** ▷ *ag* well-known

con'quista *sf* conquest

conquis'tare /72/ *vt* to conquer; (*fig*) to gain, win

consa'pevole *ag*: **~ di** aware of

'conscio, -a, -sci, -sce ['kɔnʃo] *ag*: **~ di** aware *o* conscious of

consecu'tivo, -a *ag* consecutive; (*successivo: giorno*) following, next

con'segna [kon'seɲɲa] *sf* delivery; (*merce consegnata*) consignment; (*custodia*) care, custody; (*Mil: ordine*) orders *pl*; (*: punizione*) confinement to barracks; **dare qc in ~ a qn** to entrust sth to sb; **pagamento alla ~** cash on delivery

conse'gnare [konseɲ'ɲare] /15/ *vt* to deliver; (*affidare*) to entrust, hand over; (*Mil*) to confine to barracks

consegu'enza [konse'gwentsa] *sf* consequence; **per** *o* **di ~** consequently

con'senso *sm* approval, consent; **~ informato** informed consent

consen'tire /45/ *vi*: **~ a** to consent *o* agree to ▷ *vt* to allow, permit

con'serva *sf* (*Cuc*) preserve; **~ di frutta** jam; **~ di pomodoro** tomato purée

conser'vante *sm* (*per alimenti*) preservative
conser'vare /72/ *vt* (*Cuc*) to preserve; (*custodire*) to keep; (: *dalla distruzione ecc*) to preserve, conserve
conserva'tore, -'trice *sm/f* (*Pol*) conservative
conserva'torio *sm* (*di musica*) conservatory
conservazi'one [konservat'tsjone] *sf* preservation; conservation
conside'rare /72/ *vt* to consider; (*reputare*) to consider, regard; **considerarsi** *vpr* to consider o.s.
consigli'are [konsiʎ'ʎare] /27/ *vt* (*persona*) to advise; (*metodo, azione*) to recommend, advise, suggest; **con'siglio** *sm* (*suggerimento*) advice *no pl*, piece of advice; (*assemblea*) council; **consiglio d'amministrazione** board; **Consiglio d'Europa** Council of Europe; **il Consiglio dei Ministri** (*Pol*) ≈ the Cabinet
consis'tente *ag* thick; solid; (*fig*) sound, valid
con'sistere /11/ *vi*: ~ **in** to consist of
conso'lare /72/ *vt* to console, comfort ▷ *vt* (*confortare*) to console, comfort; (*rallegrare*) to cheer up; **consolarsi** *vpr* to be comforted; to cheer up
conso'lato *sm* consulate
consolazi'one [konsolat'tsjone] *sf* consolation, comfort
'console *sm* consul
conso'nante *sf* consonant
'consono, -a *ag*: ~ **a** consistent with, consonant with
con'sorte *smf* consort
consta'tare /72/ *vt* to establish, verify
consu'eto, -a *ag* habitual, usual
consu'lente *smf* consultant
consul'tare /72/ *vt* to consult; **consultarsi** *vpr*: **consultarsi con qn** to seek the advice of sb
consul'torio *sm*: ~ **familiare** family planning clinic
consu'mare /72/ *vt* (*logorare: abiti, scarpe*) to wear out; (*usare*) to consume, use up; (*mangiare, bere*) to consume; (*Dir*) to consummate; **consumarsi** *vpr* to wear out; to be used up; (*anche fig*) to be consumed; (*combustibile*) to burn out
con'tabile *ag* accounts *cpd*, accounting ▷ *smf* accountant
contachi'lometri [kontaki'lɔmetri] *sm inv* ≈ mileometer
conta'dino, -a *sm/f* countryman/woman; farm worker; (*peg*) peasant
contagi'are [konta'dʒare] /62/ *vt* to infect
contagi'oso, -a *ag* infectious; contagious
conta'gocce [konta'gottʃe] *sm inv* (*Med*) dropper
contami'nare /72/ *vt* to contaminate

con'tante *sm* cash; **pagare in contanti** to pay cash; **non ho contanti** I haven't got any cash
con'tare /72/ *vt* to count; (*considerare*) to consider ▷ *vi* to count, be of importance; ~ **su qn** to count o rely on sb; ~ **di fare qc** to intend to do sth; **conta'tore** *sm* meter
contat'tare /72/ *vt* to contact
con'tatto *sm* contact
'conte *sm* count
conteggi'are [konted'dʒare] /62/ *vt* to charge, put on the bill
con'tegno [kon'teɲɲo] *sm* (*comportamento*) behaviour; (*atteggiamento*) attitude; **darsi un** ~ to act nonchalant; (*ricomporsi*) to pull o.s. together
contemporanea'mente *av* simultaneously; at the same time
contempo'raneo, -a *ag, sm/f* contemporary
conten'dente *smf* opponent, adversary
conte'nere /121/ *vt* to contain; **conteni'tore** *sm* container
conten'tezza [konten'tettsa] *sf* contentment
con'tento, -a *ag* pleased, glad; ~ **di** pleased with
conte'nuto *sm* contents *pl*; (*argomento*) content
con'tessa *sf* countess
contes'tare /72/ *vt* (*Dir*) to notify; (*fig*) to dispute
con'testo *sm* context
continen'tale *ag, smf* continental
conti'nente *ag* continent ▷ *sm* (*Geo*) continent; (: *terra ferma*) mainland
contin'gente [kontin'dʒɛnte] *ag* contingent ▷ *sm* (*Comm*) quota; (*Mil*) contingent
continua'mente *av* (*senza interruzione*) continuously, nonstop; (*ripetutamente*) continually
continu'are /72/ *vt* to continue (with), go on with ▷ *vi* to continue, go on; ~ **a fare qc** to go on o continue doing sth
continuità *sf* continuity
con'tinuo, -a *ag* (*numerazione*) continuous; (*pioggia*) continual, constant; (*Elettr: corrente*) direct; **di** ~ continually
'conto *sm* (*calcolo*) calculation; (*Comm, Econ*) account; (*di ristorante, albergo*) bill; (*fig: stima*) consideration, esteem; **fare i conti con qn** to settle one's account with sb; **fare** ~ **su qn** to count o rely on sb; **rendere** ~ **a qn di qc** to be accountable to sb for sth; **tener** ~ **di qn/qc** to take sb/sth into account; **per** ~ **di** on behalf of; **per** ~ **mio** as far as I'm concerned; **a conti fatti, in fin dei conti** all things considered; ~ **corrente** current account; ~ **alla rovescia** countdown

con'torno sm (linea) outline, contour; (ornamento) border; (Cuc) vegetables pl

contrabbandi'ere, -a sm/f smuggler

contrab'bando sm smuggling, contraband; **merce di ~** contraband, smuggled goods pl

contrab'basso sm (Mus) (double) bass

contraccambi'are /19/ vt (favore ecc) to return

contraccet'tivo, -a [kontrattʃet'tivo] ag, sm contraceptive

contrac'colpo sm rebound; (di arma da fuoco) recoil; (fig) repercussion

contrad'dire /38/ vt to contradict; **contraddirsi** vpr to contradict o.s.; (uso reciproco: persone) to contradict each other o one another; (: testimonianze ecc) to be contradictory

contraf'fare /41/ vt (persona) to mimic; (alterare: voce) to disguise; (: firma) to forge, counterfeit

contraria'mente av: ~ a contrary to

contrari'are /19/ vt (contrastare) to thwart, oppose; (irritare) to annoy, bother

con'trario, -a ag opposite; (sfavorevole) unfavourable ▷ sm opposite; **essere ~ a qc** (persona) to be against sth; **al ~** on the contrary; **in caso ~** otherwise; **avere qualcosa in ~** to have some objection

contrasse'gnare [kontrasseɲ'ɲare] /15/ vt to mark

contras'tare /72/ vt (avversare) to oppose; (impedire) to bar; (negare: diritto) to contest, dispute ▷ vi: ~ **(con)** (essere in disaccordo) to contrast (with); (lottare) to struggle (with)

contrat'tacco sm counterattack

contrat'tare /72/ vt, vi to negotiate

contrat'tempo sm hitch

con'tratto, -a pp di **contrarre** ▷ sm contract

contravvenzi'one sf contravention; (ammenda) fine

contrazi'one [kontrat'tsjone] sf contraction; (di prezzi ecc) reduction

contribu'ente sm/f taxpayer; ratepayer (BRIT), property tax payer (US)

contribu'ire /55/ vi to contribute

'contro prep against; **~ di me/lui** against me/him; **pastiglie ~ la tosse** throat lozenges; **~ pagamento** (Comm) on payment; **controfi'gura** sf (Cine) double

control'lare /72/ vt (accertare) to check; (sorvegliare) to watch, control; (tenere nel proprio potere, fig: dominare) to control; **controllarsi** vpr to control o.s.; **con'trollo** sm check; watch; control; **controllo delle nascite** birth control; **control'lore** sm (Ferr, Aut) (ticket) inspector

contro'luce [kontro'lutʃe] sf inv (Fot) backlit shot ▷ av: **(in) ~** against the light; (fotografare) into the light

contro'mano av: **guidare ~** to drive on the wrong side of the road; (in un senso unico) to drive the wrong way up a one-way street

controprodu'cente [kontroprodu'tʃɛnte] ag counterproductive

contro'senso sm (contraddizione) contradiction in terms; (assurdità) nonsense

controspio'naggio [kontrospio'naddʒo] sm counterespionage

contro'versia sf controversy; (Dir) dispute

contro'verso, -a ag controversial

contro'voglia [kontro'vɔʎʎa] av unwillingly

contusi'one sf (Med) bruise

convale'scente [konvaleʃ'ʃɛnte] ag, smf convalescent

convali'dare /72/ vt (Amm) to validate; (fig: sospetto, dubbio) to confirm

con'vegno [kon'veɲɲo] sm (incontro) meeting; (congresso) convention, congress; (luogo) meeting place

conve'nevoli smpl civilities

conveni'ente ag suitable; (vantaggioso) profitable; (: prezzo) cheap

▌ Attenzione! In inglese esiste la parola convenient, che però significa comodo.

conve'nire /128/ vi (riunirsi) to gather, assemble; (concordare) to agree; (tornare utile) to be worthwhile ▷ vb impers: **conviene fare questo** it is advisable to do this; **conviene andarsene** we should go; **ne convengo** I agree

con'vento sm (di frati) monastery; (di suore) convent

convenzio'nale [konventsjo'nale] ag conventional

convenzi'one [konven'tsjone] sf (Dir) agreement; (nella società) convention

conver'sare /72/ vi to have a conversation, converse

conversazi'one [konversat'tsjone] sf conversation; **fare ~** to chat, have a chat

conversi'one sf conversion; **~ ad U** (Aut) U-turn

conver'tire /45/ vt (trasformare) to change; (Inform, Pol, Rel) to convert; **convertirsi** vpr: **convertirsi (a)** to be converted (to)

con'vesso, -a ag convex

convin'cente [konvin'tʃɛnte] ag convincing

con'vincere [kon'vintʃere] /129/ vt to convince; **convincersi** vpr: **convincersi (di qc)** to convince o.s. (of sth); **~ qn di qc** to convince sb of sth; **~ qn a fare qc** to persuade sb to do sth

convi'vente *smf* common-law husband/ wife

con'vivere /130/ *vi* to live together

convo'care /20/ *vt* to call, convene; (*Dir*) to summon

convulsi'one *sf* convulsion

coope'rare /72/ *vi*: ~ **(a)** to cooperate (in); **coopera'tiva** *sf* cooperative

coordi'nare /72/ *vt* to coordinate

co'perchio [ko'pɛrkjo] *sm* cover; (*di pentola*) lid

co'perta *sf* cover; (*di lana*) blanket; (*da viaggio*) rug; (*Naut*) deck

coper'tina *sf* (*Stampa*) cover, jacket

co'perto, -a *pp di* **coprire** ▷ *ag* covered; (*cielo*) overcast ▷ *sm* place setting; (*posto a tavola*) place; (*al ristorante*) cover charge; ~ **di** covered in *o* with

coper'tone *sm* (*Aut*) rubber tyre

coper'tura *sf* (*anche Econ, Mil*) cover; (*di edificio*) roofing

'copia *sf* copy; **brutta/bella** ~ rough/final copy

copi'are /19/ *vt* to copy

copincol'lare /72/ *vt* to copy and paste

copin'collo *sm* copy and paste

copi'one *sm* (*Cine, Teat*) script

'coppa *sf* (*bicchiere*) goblet; (*per frutta, gelato*) dish; (*trofeo*) cup, trophy; ~ **dell'olio** oil sump (*BRIT*) *o* pan (*US*)

'coppia *sf* (*di persone*) couple; (*di animali, Sport*) pair

coprifu'oco, -chi *sm* curfew

copri'letto *sm* bedspread

copripiu'mino *sm inv* duvet cover

co'prire /9/ *vt* to cover; (*occupare: carica, posto*) to hold; **coprirsi** *vpr* (*cielo*) to cloud over; (*vestirsi*) to wrap up, cover up; (*Econ*) to cover o.s.; **coprirsi di** (*macchie, muffa*) to become covered in

coque [kɔk] *sf*: **uovo alla** ~ boiled egg

co'raggio [ko'raddʒo] *sm* courage, bravery; ~**!** (*forza!*) come on!; (*animo!*) cheer up!

co'rallo *sm* coral

Co'rano *sm* (*Rel*) Koran

co'razza [ko'rattsa] *sf* armour; (*di animali*) carapace, shell; (*Mil*) armour(-plating)

'corda *sf* cord; (*fune*) rope; (*spago, Mus*) string; **dare** ~ **a qn** to let sb have his (*o* her) way; **tenere sulla** ~ **qn** to keep sb on tenterhooks; **tagliare la** ~ to slip away, sneak off; **corde vocali** vocal cords

cordi'ale *ag* cordial, warm ▷ *sm* (*bevanda*) cordial

'cordless ['kɔːdlɪs] *sm inv* cordless phone

cor'done *sm* cord, string; (*linea: di polizia*) cordon; ~ **ombelicale** umbilical cord

Co'rea *sf*: **la** ~ Korea

coreogra'fia *sf* choreography

cori'andolo *sm* (*Bot*) coriander; **coriandoli** *smpl* confetti *no pl*

cor'nacchia [kor'nakkja] *sf* crow

corna'musa *sf* bagpipes *pl*

cor'netta *sf* (*Mus*) cornet; (*Tel*) receiver

cor'netto *sm* (*Cuc*) croissant; (*gelato*) cone

cor'nice [kor'nitʃe] *sf* frame; (*fig*) background, setting

cornici'one [korni'tʃone] *sm* (*di edificio*) ledge; (*Archit*) cornice

'corno *sm* (*pl f* **corna** *Zool*) horn; (*pl m* **corni** *Mus*) horn; **fare le corna a qn** to be unfaithful to sb

Corno'vaglia [korno'vaʎʎa] *sf*: **la** ~ Cornwall

cor'nuto, -a *ag* (*con corna*) horned; (*fam!: marito*) cuckolded ▷ *sm* (*fam!*) cuckold; (*: insulto*) bastard (*!*)

'coro *sm* chorus; (*Rel*) choir

co'rona *sf* crown; (*di fiori*) wreath

'corpo *sm* body; (*militare, diplomatico*) corps *inv*; **prendere** ~ to take shape; **a** ~ **a** ~ hand-to-hand; ~ **di ballo** corps de ballet; ~ **insegnante** teaching staff

corpora'tura *sf* build, physique

cor'reggere [kor'reddʒere] /87/ *vt* to correct; (*compiti*) to correct, mark

cor'rente *ag* (*fiume*) flowing; (*acqua del rubinetto*) running; (*moneta, prezzo*) current; (*comune*) everyday ▷ *sm*: **essere al ~ (di)** to be well-informed (about) ▷ *sf* (*movimento di liquido*) current, stream; (*spiffero*) draught; (*Elettr, Meteor*) current; (*fig*) trend, tendency; **la vostra lettera del 5 ~ mese** (*in lettere commerciali*) in your letter of the 5th inst.; ~ **alternata (c.a.)** alternating current (AC); ~ **continua (c.c.)** direct current (DC); **corrente'mente** *av* commonly; **parlare una lingua correntemente** to speak a language fluently

'correre /28/ *vi* to run; (*precipitarsi*) to rush; (*partecipare a una gara*) to race, run; (*fig: diffondersi*) to go round ▷ *vt* (*Sport: gara*) to compete in; (*rischio*) to run; (*pericolo*) to face; ~ **dietro a qn** to run after sb; **corre voce che ...** it is rumoured that ...

cor'ressi *ecc vb vedi* **correggere**

correzi'one [korret'tsjone] *sf* correction; marking; ~ **di bozze** proofreading

corri'doio *sm* corridor; (*in aereo, al cinema*) aisle

corri'dore *sm* (*Sport*) runner; (*: su veicolo*) racer

corri'era *sf* coach (*BRIT*), bus

corri'ere *sm* (*diplomatico, di guerra, postale*) courier; (*spedizioniere*) carrier

corri'mano *sm* handrail

corrispon'dente *ag* corresponding ▷ *smf* correspondent

corrispon'denza [korrispon'dɛntsa] *sf*
correspondence

corris'pondere /95/ *vi* (*equivalere*): ~ **(a)** to
correspond (to) ▷ *vt* (*stipendio*) to pay; (*fig:
amore*) to return

cor'rodere /49/ *vt* to corrode

cor'rompere /97/ *vt* to corrupt; (*comprare*)
to bribe

cor'roso, -a *pp di* **corrodere**

cor'rotto, -a *pp di* **corrompere** ▷ *ag*
corrupt

corru'gare /80/ *vt* to wrinkle; ~ **la fronte**
to knit one's brows

cor'ruppi *ecc vb vedi* **corrompere**

corruzi'one [korrut'tsjone] *sf* corruption;
bribery

'corsa *sf* running *no pl*; (*gara*) race; (*di
autobus, taxi*) journey, trip; **fare una ~**
to run, dash; (*Sport*) to run a race;
~ **campestre** cross-country race

'corsi *ecc vb vedi* **correre**

cor'sia *sf* (*Aut, Sport*) lane; (*di ospedale*) ward

'Corsica *sf*: **la ~** Corsica

cor'sivo *sm* cursive (writing); (*Tip*) italics *pl*

'corso, -a *pp di* **correre** ▷ *sm* course; (*strada
cittadina*) main street; (*di unità monetaria*)
circulation; (*di titoli, valori*) rate, price; **in ~**
in progress, under way; (*annata*) current;
~ **d'acqua** river; stream; (*artificiale*)
waterway; ~ **d'aggiornamento** refresher
course; ~ **serale** evening class

'corte *sf* (court)yard; (*Dir, regale*) court; **fare
la ~ a** qn to court sb; ~ **marziale** court-martial

cor'teccia, -ce [kor'tettʃa] *sf* bark

corteggi'are [korted'dʒare] /62/ *vt* to
court

cor'teo *sm* procession

cor'tese *ag* courteous; **corte'sia** *sf*
courtesy; **per cortesia, dov'è ...?** excuse
me, please, where is ...?

cor'tile *sm* (court)yard

cor'tina *sf* curtain; (*anche fig*) screen

'corto, -a *ag* short; **essere a ~ di qc** to be
short of sth; ~ **circuito** short-circuit

'corvo *sm* raven

'cosa *sf* thing; (*faccenda*) affair, matter,
business *no pl*; **(che) ~?** what?; **(che)
cos'è?** what is it?; **a ~ pensi?** what are you
thinking about?

'coscia, -sce ['kɔʃʃa] *sf* thigh; ~ **di pollo**
(*Cuc*) chicken leg

cosci'ente [koʃʃɛnte] *ag* conscious; ~ **di**
conscious *o* aware of

PAROLA CHIAVE

così *av* **1** (*in questo modo*) like this, (in) this
way; (*in tal modo*) so; **le cose stanno così**
this is the way things stand; **non ho detto**

così! I didn't say that!; **come stai? — (e)
così** how are you? — so-so; **e così via** and
so on; **per così dire** so to speak; **così sia**
amen

2 (*tanto*) so; **così lontano** so far away;
un ragazzo così intelligente such an
intelligent boy

▶ *ag inv* (*tale*): **non ho mai visto un film così**
I've never seen such a film

▶ *cong* **1** (*perciò*) so, therefore

2: **così ... come** as ... as; **non è così bravo
come te** he's not as good as you; **così ...
che** so ... that

cosid'detto, -a *ag* so-called

cos'metico, -a, -ci, -che *ag, sm* cosmetic

cos'pargere [kos'pardʒere] /111/ *vt*: ~ **di** to
sprinkle with

cos'picuo, -a *ag* considerable, large

cospi'rare /72/ *vi* to conspire

'cossi *ecc vb vedi* **cuocere**

'costa *sf* (*tra terra e mare*) coast(line);
(*litorale*) shore; (*Anat*) rib; **la C~ Azzurra** the
French Riviera

cos'tante *ag* constant; (*persona*) steadfast
▷ *sf* constant

cos'tare /72/ *vi, vt* to cost; ~ **caro** to be
expensive, cost a lot

cos'tata *sf* (*Cuc*) large chop

costeggi'are [kosted'dʒare] /62/ *vt* to be
close to; to run alongside

costi'ero, -a *ag* coastal, coast *cpd*

costitu'ire /55/ *vt* (*comitato, gruppo*) to
set up, form; (*elementi, parti: comporre*) to
make up, constitute; (: *rappresentare*) to
constitute; (*Dir*) to appoint; **costituirsi** *vpr*:
costituirsi (alla polizia) to give o.s. up (to
the police)

costituzi'one [kostitut'tsjone] *sf* setting
up; building up; constitution

'costo *sm* cost; **a ogni** *o* **qualunque ~, a
tutti i costi** at all costs

'costola *sf* (*Anat*) rib

cos'toso, -a *ag* expensive, costly

cos'tringere [kos'trindʒere] /117/ *vt*: ~ **qn
a fare qc** to force sb to do sth

costru'ire /55/ *vt* to construct, build;
costruzi'one *sf* construction, building

cos'tume *sm* (*uso*) custom; (*foggia di vestire,
indumento*) costume; ~ **da bagno** bathing
o swimming costume (*BRIT*), swimsuit; (*da
uomo*) bathing *o* swimming trunks *pl*

co'tenna *sf* bacon rind

coto'letta *sf* (*di maiale, montone*) chop; (*di
vitello, agnello*) cutlet

co'tone *sm* cotton; ~ **idrofilo** cotton wool
(*BRIT*), absorbent cotton (*US*)

'cotta *sf* (*fam: innamoramento*) crush

'cottimo *sm*: **lavorare a ~** to do piecework

'cotto, -a pp di cuocere ▷ ag cooked; (fam: innamorato) head-over-heels in love; ben ~ (carne) well done

cot'tura sf cooking; (in forno) baking; (in umido) stewing

co'vare /72/ vt to hatch; (fig: malattia) to be sickening for; (: odio, rancore) to nurse ▷ vi (fuoco, fig) to smoulder

'covo sm den

co'vone sm sheaf

'cozza ['kɔttsa] sf mussel

coz'zare [kot'tsare] /72/ vi: ~ contro to bang into, collide with

CPT sigla m inv = **Centro di Permanenza Temporanea**

crac'care /20/ vt (Inform) to crack

'crampo sm cramp; ho un ~ alla gamba I've got cramp in my leg

'cranio sm skull

cra'tere sm crater

cra'vatta sf tie

cre'are /72/ vt to create

'crebbi ecc vb vedi crescere

cre'dente smf (Rel) believer

cre'denza [kre'dɛntsa] sf belief; (armadio) sideboard

'credere /29/ vt to believe ▷ vi: ~ in, ~ a to believe in; ~ qn onesto to believe sb (to be) honest; ~ che to believe o think that; credersi furbo to think one is clever

'credito sm (anche Comm) credit; (reputazione) esteem, repute; comprare a ~ to buy on credit

'crema sf cream; (con uova, zucchero ecc) custard; ~ pasticciera confectioner's custard; ~ solare sun cream

cre'mare /72/ vt to cremate

'crepa sf crack

cre'paccio [kre'pattʃo] sm large crack, fissure; (di ghiacciaio) crevasse

crepacu'ore sm broken heart

cre'pare /72/ vi (fam: morire) to snuff it (BRIT), kick the bucket; ~ dalle risa to split one's sides laughing

crêpe [krɛp] sf inv pancake

cre'puscolo sm twilight, dusk

'crescere ['kreʃʃere] /30/ vi to grow ▷ vt (figli) to raise

'cresima sf (Rel) confirmation

'crespo, -a ag (capelli) frizzy; (tessuto) puckered ▷ sm crêpe

'cresta sf crest; (di polli, uccelli) crest, comb

'creta sf chalk; (argilla) clay

creti'nata sf (fam): dire/fare una ~ to say/ do a stupid thing

cre'tino, -a ag stupid ▷ sm/f idiot, fool

CRI sigla f = **Croce Rossa Italiana**

'cric sm inv (Tecn) jack

cri'ceto [kri'tʃeto] sm hamster

crimi'nale ag, smf criminal

criminalità sf crime; ~ organizzata organized crime

'crimine sm (Dir) crime

crip'tare /72/ vt (TV: programma) to encrypt

crisan'temo sm chrysanthemum

'crisi sf inv crisis; (Med) attack, fit; ~ di nervi attack o fit of nerves

cris'tallo sm crystal; cristalli liquidi liquid crystals

cristia'nesimo sm Christianity

cristi'ano, -a ag, sm/f Christian

'cristo sm: C~ Christ

cri'terio sm criterion; (buon senso) (common) sense

'critica, -che sf vedi critico

criti'care /20/ vt to criticize

'critico, -a, -ci, -che ag critical ▷ sm critic ▷ sf criticism; la critica (attività) criticism; (persone) the critics pl

cro'ato, -a ag, sm/f Croatian, Croat

Cro'azia [kro'attsja] sf Croatia

croc'cante ag crisp, crunchy

'croce ['krotʃe] sf cross; in ~ (di traverso) crosswise; (fig) on tenterhooks; la C~ Rossa the Red Cross

croci'ato, -a [kro'tʃato] ag cross-shaped ▷ sf crusade

croci'era [kro'tʃɛra] sf (viaggio) cruise; (Archit) transept

crol'lare /72/ vi to collapse; 'crollo sm collapse; (di prezzi) slump, sudden fall; crollo in Borsa slump in prices on the Stock Exchange

cro'mato, -a ag chromium-plated

'cromo sm chrome, chromium

'cronaca, -che sf (Stampa) news sg; (: rubrica) column; (TV, Radio) commentary; fatto o episodio di ~ news item; ~ nera crime news sg; crime column

'cronico, -a, -ci, -che ag chronic

cro'nista, -i sm (Stampa) reporter

cro'nometro sm chronometer; (a scatto) stopwatch

'crosta sf crust

cros'tacei [kros'tatʃei] smpl shellfish

cros'tata sf (Cuc) tart

cros'tino sm (Cuc) croûton; (: da antipasto) canapé

cruci'ale [kru'tʃale] ag crucial

cruci'verba sm inv crossword (puzzle)

cru'dele ag cruel

'crudo, -a ag (non cotto) raw; (aspro) harsh, severe

cru'miro sm (peg) blackleg (BRIT), scab

'crusca sf bran

crus'cotto sm (Aut) dashboard

CSI sigla f (= Comunità di Stati Indipendenti) CIS

CSM [tʃiesse'emme] sigla m (= consiglio superiore della magistratura) Magistrates' Board of Supervisors

'**Cuba** sf Cuba; **cu'bano, -a** ag, sm/f Cuban

cu'betto sm: **~ di ghiaccio** ice cube

'**cubico, -a, -ci, -che** ag cubic

cu'bista, -i, -e ag (Arte) Cubist ▷ sf podium dancer, dancer who performs on stage in a club

'**cubo, -a** ag cubic ▷ sm cube; **elevare al ~** (Mat) to cube

cuc'cagna [kuk'kaɲɲa] sf: **paese della ~** land of plenty; **albero della ~** greasy pole (fig)

cuc'cetta [kut'tʃetta] sf (Ferr) couchette; (Naut) berth

cucchiai'ata [kukkja'jata] sf spoonful

cucchia'ino [kukkja'ino] sm teaspoon; coffee spoon

cucchi'aio [kuk'kjajo] sm spoon

'**cuccia, -ce** ['kuttʃa] sf dog's bed; **a ~!** down!

'**cucciolo** ['kuttʃolo] sm cub; (di cane) puppy

cu'cina [ku'tʃina] sf (locale) kitchen; (arte culinaria) cooking, cookery; (le vivande) food, cooking; (apparecchio) cooker; **~ componibile** fitted kitchen; **cuci'nare** /72/ vt to cook

cu'cire [ku'tʃire] /31/ vt to sew, stitch; **cuci'trice** sf stapler

cucù cuckoo

'**cuffia** sf bonnet, cap; (da infermiera) cap; (da bagno) (bathing) cap; (per ascoltare) headphones pl, headset

cu'gino, -a [ku'dʒino] sm/f cousin

 PAROLA CHIAVE

'**cui** pron **1** (nei complementi indiretti: persona) whom; (: oggetto, animale) which; **la persona/le persone a cui accennavi** the person/people you were referring to o to whom you were referring; **i libri di cui parlavo** the books I was talking about o about which I was talking; **il quartiere in cui abito** the district where I live; **la ragione per cui** the reason why
2 (inserito tra articolo e sostantivo) whose; **la donna i cui figli sono scomparsi** the woman whose children have disappeared; **il signore, dal cui figlio ho avuto il libro** the man from whose son I got the book

culi'naria sf cookery

'**culla** sf cradle

cul'lare /72/ vt to rock

'**culmine** sm top, summit

'**culo** sm (fam !) arse (BRIT !), ass (US !); (fig: fortuna): **aver ~** to have the luck of the devil

'**culto** sm (religione) religion; (adorazione) worship, adoration; (venerazione: anche fig) cult

cul'tura sf culture; (conoscenza) education, learning; **cultu'rale** ag cultural

cultu'rismo sm body-building

cumula'tivo, -a ag cumulative; (prezzo) inclusive; (biglietto) group cpd

'**cumulo** sm (mucchio) pile, heap; (Meteor) cumulus

cu'netta sf (scolo) gutter; (avvallamento) dip

cu'ocere ['kwɔtʃere] /32/ vt (alimenti) to cook; (mattoni ecc) to fire ▷ vi to cook; **~ al forno** (pane) to bake; (arrosto) to roast; **cu'oco, -a, -chi, -che** sm/f cook; (di ristorante) chef

cu'oio sm leather; **~ capelluto** scalp

cu'ore sm heart; **cuori** smpl (Carte) hearts; **avere buon ~** to be kind-hearted; **stare a ~ a qn** to be important to sb

'**cupo, -a** ag dark; (suono) dull; (fig) gloomy, dismal

'**cupola** sf dome; (più piccola) cupola

'**cura** sf care; (Med: trattamento) (course of) treatment; **aver ~ di** (occuparsi di) to look after; **a ~ di** (libro) edited by; **~ dimagrante** diet

cu'rare /72/ vt (malato, malattia) to treat; (: guarire) to cure; (aver cura di) to take care of; (testo) to edit; **curarsi** vpr to take care of o.s.; (Med) to follow a course of treatment; **curarsi di** to pay attention to

curio'sare /72/ vi to look round, wander round; (tra libri) to browse; **~ nei negozi** to look o wander round the shops

curiosità sf inv curiosity; (cosa rara) curio, curiosity

curi'oso, -a ag curious; **essere ~ di** to be curious about

cur'sore sm (Inform) cursor

'**curva** sf curve; (stradale) bend, curve

cur'vare /72/ vt to bend ▷ vi (veicolo) to take a bend; (strada) to bend, curve; **curvarsi** vpr to bend; (legno) to warp

'**curvo, -a** ag curved; (piegato) bent

cusci'netto [kuʃʃi'netto] sm pad; (Tecn) bearing ▷ ag inv: **stato ~** buffer state; **~ a sfere** ball bearing

cu'scino [kuʃʃino] sm cushion; (guanciale) pillow

cus'tode smf keeper, custodian

cus'todia sf care; (Dir) custody; (astuccio) case, holder

custo'dire /55/ vt (conservare) to keep; (assistere) to look after, take care of; (fare la guardia) to guard

C.V. abbr (= cavallo vapore) h.p.

cyberca'ffè [tʃiberka'fe] sm inv cybercafé

cyber'nauta, -i, -e sm/f Internet surfer

cyber'spazio sm cyberspace

d

○ **PAROLA CHIAVE**

da (da + il = **dal**, da + lo = **dallo**, da + l' = **dall'**, da + la = **dalla**, da + i = **dai**, da + gli = **dagli**, da + le = **dalle**) prep **1** (agente) by; **dipinto da un grande artista** painted by a great artist **2** (causa) with; **tremare dalla paura** to tremble with fear
3 (stato in luogo) at; **abito da lui** I'm living at his house o with him; **sono dal giornalaio** I'm at the newsagent's; **era da Francesco** she was at Francesco's (house)
4 (moto a luogo) to; (moto per luogo) through; **vado da Pietro/dal giornalaio** I'm going to Pietro's (house)/to the newsagent's; **sono passati dalla finestra** they came in through the window
5 (provenienza, allontanamento) from; **arrivare/partire da Milano** to arrive/depart from Milan; **scendere dal treno/dalla macchina** to get off the train/out of the car; **si trova a 5 km da qui** it's 5 km from here
6 (tempo: durata) for; (: a partire da: nel passato) since; (: nel futuro) from; **vivo qui da un anno** I've been living here for a year; **è dalle 3 che ti aspetto** I've been waiting for you since 3 (o'clock); **da oggi in poi** from today onwards; **da bambino** as a child, when I (o he ecc) was a child
7 (modo, maniera) like; **comportarsi da uomo** to behave like a man; **l'ho fatto da me** I did it (by) myself
8 (descrittivo): **una macchina da corsa** a racing car; **una ragazza dai capelli biondi** a girl with blonde hair; **un vestito da 100 euro** a 100 euro dress

dà vb vedi **dare**

dac'capo av (di nuovo) (once) again; (dal principio) all over again, from the beginning

'dado sm (da gioco) dice o die; (Cuc) stock cube (BRIT), bouillon cube (US); (Tecn) (screw) nut; **dadi** smpl (game of) dice; **giocare a dadi** to play dice

'daino sm (fallow) deer inv; (pelle) buckskin

dal'tonico, -a, -ci, -che ag colour-blind

'dama sf lady; (nei balli) partner; (gioco) draughts sg (BRIT), checkers sg (US)

damigi'ana [dami'dʒana] sf demijohn

da'nese ag Danish ▷ smf Dane ▷ sm (Ling) Danish; **Dani'marca** sf: **la Danimarca** Denmark

dannazi'one [dannat'tsjone] sf damnation

danneggi'are [danned'dʒare] /62/ vt to damage; (rovinare) to spoil; (nuocere) to harm

'danno sm damage; (a persona) harm, injury; **danni** smpl (Dir) damages; **dan'noso, -a** ag: **dannoso (a o per)** harmful (to), bad (for)

Da'nubio sm: **il ~** the Danube

'danza ['dantsa] sf: **la ~** dancing; **una ~** a dance; **dan'zare** /72/ vt, vi to dance

dapper'tutto av everywhere

dap'prima av at first

'dare /33/ sm (Comm) debit ▷ vt to give; (produrre: frutti, suono) to produce ▷ vi (guardare): **~ su** to look (out) onto; **darsi** vpr: **darsi a** to dedicate o.s. to; **~ da mangiare a qn** to give sb something to eat; **~ per certo qc** to consider sth certain; **~ per morto qn** to give sb up for dead; **darsi al bere** to take to drink; **darsi al commercio** to go into business; **darsi per vinto** to give in

'data sf date; **~ di nascita** date of birth; **~ di scadenza** expiry date; **~ limite d'utilizzo** o **di consumo** (Comm) best-before date

'dato, -a ag (stabilito) given ▷ sm datum; **dati** smpl data pl; **~ che** given that; **è un ~ di fatto** it's a fact; **dati sensibili** sense data

da'tore, -'trice sm/f: **~ di lavoro** employer

'dattero sm date (Bot)

dattilogra'fia sf typing

datti'lografo, -a sm/f typist

da'vanti av in front; (dirimpetto) opposite ▷ ag inv front ▷ sm front; **~ a** in front of; (dirimpetto a) facing, opposite; (in presenza di) before, in front of

davan'zale [davan'tsale] sm windowsill

dav'vero av really, indeed

d.C. abbr (= dopo Cristo) A.D.

'dea sf goddess

'debbo ecc vb vedi **dovere**

'debito, -a ag due, proper ▷ sm debt; (Comm: dare) debit; **a tempo ~** at the right time

'debole ag weak, feeble; (suono) faint; (luce) dim ▷ sm weakness; **debo'lezza** sf weakness

debut'tare /72/ *vi* to make one's début
deca'denza [deka'dɛntsa] *sf* decline; (*Dir*) loss, forfeiture
decaffei'nato, -a *ag* decaffeinated
decapi'tare /72/ *vt* to decapitate, behead
decappot'tabile *ag*, *sf* convertible
de'cennio [de'tʃɛnnjo] *sm* decade
de'cente [de'tʃɛnte] *ag* decent, respectable, proper; (*accettabile*) satisfactory, decent
de'cesso [de'tʃɛsso] *sm* death
de'cidere [de'tʃidere] /34/ *vt*: ~ qc to decide on sth; (*questione, lite*) to settle sth; **decidersi** *vpr*: **decidersi (a fare)** to decide (to do), make up one's mind (to do); ~ **di fare/che** to decide to do/that; ~ **di qc** (*cosa*) to determine sth
deci'frare [detʃi'frare] /72/ *vt* to decode; (*fig*) to decipher, make out
deci'male [detʃi'male] *ag* decimal
'decimo, -a ['dɛtʃimo] *num* tenth
de'cina [de'tʃina] *sf* ten; (*circa dieci*): **una ~ (di)** about ten
de'cisi *ecc* [de'tʃizi] *vb vedi* **decidere**
decisi'one [detʃi'zjone] *sf* decision; **prendere una ~** to make a decision
deci'sivo, -a [detʃi'zivo] *ag* (*gen*) decisive; (*fattore*) deciding
de'ciso, -a [de'tʃizo] *pp di* **decidere**
decli'nare /72/ *vi* (*pendio*) to slope down; (*fig: diminuire*) to decline ▷ *vt* to decline
declinazi'one *sf* (*Ling*) declension
de'clino *sm* decline
decodifica'tore *sm* (*Tel*) decoder
decol'lare /72/ *vi* (*Aer*) to take off; **de'collo** *sm* take-off
deco'rare /72/ *vt* to decorate; **decorazi'one** *sf* decoration
de'creto *sm* decree; ~ **legge** *decree with the force of law*
'dedica, -che *sf* dedication
dedi'care /20/ *vt* to dedicate; **dedicarsi** *vpr*: **dedicarsi a** to devote o.s. to
dediche'rò *ecc* [dedike'rɔ] *vb vedi* **dedicare**
'dedito, -a *ag*: ~ **a** (*studio ecc*) dedicated *o* devoted to; (*vizio*) addicted to
de'duco *ecc* [de'duko] *vb vedi* **dedurre**
de'durre /90/ *vt* (*concludere*) to deduce; (*defalcare*) to deduct
de'dussi *ecc* [de'dussi] *vb vedi* **dedurre**
defici'ente [defi'tʃɛnte] *ag* (*insufficiente*) insufficient; ~ **di** (*mancante*) deficient in ▷ *smf* (*peg: cretino*) idiot
'deficit ['dɛfitʃit] *sm inv* (*Econ*) deficit
defi'nire /55/ *vt* to define; (*risolvere*) to settle; **defini'tivo, -a** *ag* definitive, final ▷ *sf*: **in definitiva** (*dopotutto*) when all is said and done; (*dunque*) hence; **definizi'one** *sf* definition; (*di disputa, vertenza*) settlement

defor'mare /72/ *vt* (*alterare*) to put out of shape; (*corpo*) to deform; (*pensiero, fatto*) to distort; **deformarsi** *vpr* to lose its shape
de'forme *ag* deformed; disfigured
de'funto, -a *ag* late *cpd* ▷ *sm/f* deceased
degene'rare [dedʒene'rare] /72/ *vi* to degenerate
de'gente [de'dʒɛnte] *smf* (*ricoverato in ospedale*) in-patient
deglu'tire /55/ *vt* to swallow
de'gnare [deɲ'ɲare] /15/ *vt*: ~ **qn della propria presenza** to honour sb with one's presence; **degnarsi** *vpr*: **degnarsi di fare qc** to deign *o* condescend to do sth
'degno, -a [deɲo] *ag* dignified; ~ **di** worthy of; ~ **di lode** praiseworthy
de'grado *sm*: ~ **urbano** urban decline
'delega, -ghe *sf* (*procura*) proxy
dele'terio, -a *ag* damaging; (*per salute ecc*) harmful
del'fino *sm* (*Zool*) dolphin; (*Storia*) dauphin; (*fig*) probable successor
deli'cato, -a *ag* delicate; (*salute*) delicate, frail; (*fig: gentile*) thoughtful, considerate; (: *che dimostra tatto*) tactful
delin'quente *smf* criminal, delinquent; ~ **abituale** regular offender, habitual offender; **delin'quenza** *sf* criminality, delinquency; **delinquenza minorile** juvenile delinquency
deli'rare /72/ *vi* to be delirious, rave; (*fig*) to rave
de'lirio *sm* delirium; (*ragionamento insensato*) raving; (*fig*): **andare/mandare in ~** to go/ send into a frenzy
de'litto *sm* crime
delizi'oso, -a [delit'tsjoso] *ag* delightful; (*cibi*) delicious
delta'plano *sm* hang-glider; **volo col ~** hang-gliding
delu'dente *ag* disappointing
de'ludere /35/ *vt* to disappoint; **delusi'one** *sf* disappointment; **de'luso, -a** *pp di* **deludere**
'demmo *vb vedi* **dare**
demo'cratico, -a, -ci, -che *ag* democratic
democra'zia [demokrat'tsia] *sf* democracy
demo'lire /55/ *vt* to demolish
de'monio *sm* demon, devil; **il D~** the Devil
de'naro *sm* money
densità *sf inv* density
'denso, -a *ag* thick, dense
den'tale *ag* dental
'dente *sm* tooth; (*di forchetta*) prong; **al ~** (*Cuc: pasta*) al dente; **denti del giudizio** wisdom teeth; **denti da latte** milk teeth; **denti'era** *sf* (*set of*) false teeth *pl*
denti'fricio [denti'fritʃo] *sm* toothpaste

den'tista, -i, -e *sm/f* dentist

'dentro *av* inside; (*in casa*) indoors; (*fig: nell'intimo*) inwardly ▷ *prep*: **~ (a)** in; **piegato in ~** folded over; **qui/là ~** in here; there; **~ di sé** (*pensare, brontolare*) to oneself

de'nuncia, -ce *o* **-cie** [de'nuntʃa] *sf* denunciation; declaration; **~ del reddito** (*income*) tax return

denunci'are [denun'tʃare] /14/ *vt* to denounce; (*dichiarare*) to declare; **~ qn/qc (alla polizia)** to report sb/sth to the police

denu'trito, -a *ag* undernourished

denutrizi'one [denutrit'tsjone] *sf* malnutrition

deodo'rante *sm* deodorant

depe'rire /55/ *vi* to waste away

depi'larsi /72/ *vpr*: **~ (le gambe)** (*con rasoio*) to shave (one's legs); (*con ceretta*) to wax (one's legs)

depila'torio, -a *ag* hair-removing *cpd*, depilatory

dépli'ant [depli'ã] *sm inv* leaflet; (*opuscolo*) brochure

deplo'revole *ag* deplorable

de'pone, de'pongo *ecc vb vedi* **deporre**

de'porre /77/ *vt* (*depositare*) to put down; (*rimuovere: da una carica*) to remove; (: *re*) to depose; (*Dir*) to testify

depor'tare /72/ *vt* to deport

de'posi *ecc vb vedi* **deporre**

deposi'tare /72/ *vt* (*gen, Geo, Econ*) to deposit; (*lasciare*) to leave; (*merci*) to store; **depositarsi** *vpr* (*sabbia, polvere*) to settle

de'posito *sm* deposit; (*luogo*) warehouse; depot; (: *Mil*) depot; **~ bagagli** left-luggage office

deposizi'one [depozit'tsjone] *sf* deposition; (*da una carica*) removal

depra'vato, -a *ag* depraved ▷ *sm/f* degenerate

depre'dare /72/ *vt* to rob, plunder

depressi'one *sf* depression

de'presso, -a *pp di* **deprimere** ▷ *ag* depressed

deprez'zare [depret'tsare] /72/ *vt* (*Econ*) to depreciate

depri'mente *ag* depressing

de'primere /50/ *vt* to depress

depu'rare /72/ *vt* to purify

depu'tato, -a *sm/f* (*Pol*) deputy, ≈ Member of Parliament (*BRIT*), ≈ Congressman/woman (*US*)

deragli'are [deraʎ'ʎare] /27/ *vi* to be derailed; **far ~** to derail

de'ridere /89/ *vt* to mock, deride

de'risi *ecc vb vedi* **deridere**

de'riva *sf* (*Naut, Aer*) drift; **andare alla ~** (*anche fig*) to drift

deri'vare /72/ *vi*: **~ da** to derive from ▷ *vt* to derive; (*corso d'acqua*) to divert

derma'tologo, -a, -gi, -ghe *sm/f* dermatologist

deru'bare /72/ *vt* to rob

des'crivere /105/ *vt* to describe; **descrizi'one** *sf* description

de'serto, -a *ag* deserted ▷ *sm* (*Geo*) desert; **isola deserta** desert island

deside'rare /72/ *vt* to want, wish for; (*sessualmente*) to desire; **~ fare/che qn faccia** to want *o* wish to do/sb to do; **desidera fare una passeggiata?** would you like to go for a walk?

desi'derio *sm* wish; (*più intenso, carnale*) desire

deside'roso, -a *ag*: **~ di** longing *o* eager for

desi'nenza [dezi'nɛntsa] *sf* (*Ling*) ending, inflexion

de'sistere /11/ *vi*: **~ da** to give up, desist from

'desktop ['dɛsktop] *sm inv* (*Inform*) desktop

deso'lato, -a *ag* (*paesaggio*) desolate; (*persona: spiacente*) sorry

'dessi *ecc vb vedi* **dare**

'deste *ecc vb vedi* **dare**

desti'nare /72/ *vt* to destine; (*assegnare*) to appoint, assign; (*indirizzare*) to address; **~ qc a qn** to intend to give sth to sb, intend sb to have sth; **destina'tario, -a** *sm/f* (*di lettera*) addressee

destinazi'one [destinat'tsjone] *sf* destination; (*uso*) purpose

des'tino *sm* destiny, fate

destitu'ire /55/ *vt* to dismiss, remove

'destra *sf vedi* **destro**

destreggi'arsi [destred'dʒarsi] /62/ *vpr* to manoeuvre (*BRIT*), maneuver (*US*)

des'trezza [des'trettsa] *sf* skill, dexterity

'destro, -a *ag* right, right-hand ▷ *sf* (*mano*) right hand; (*parte*) right (side); (*Pol*): **la destra** the right; **a destra** (*essere*) on the right; (*andare*) to the right

dete'nuto, -a *sm/f* prisoner

deter'gente [deter'dʒɛnte] *ag* (*crema, latte*) cleansing ▷ *sm* cleanser

⬛ Attenzione! In inglese esiste la parola *detergent*, che però significa *detersivo*.

determi'nare /72/ *vt* to determine

determina'tivo, -a *ag* determining; **articolo ~** (*Ling*) definite article

determi'nato, -a *ag* (*gen*) certain; (*particolare*) specific; (*risoluto*) determined, resolute

deter'sivo *sm* detergent

detes'tare /72/ *vt* to detest, hate

de'trae, de'traggo *ecc vb vedi* **detrarre**

de'trarre /123/ *vt*: **~ (da)** to deduct (from), take away (from)

de'trassi *ecc vb vedi* **detrarre**

'detta *sf*: **a ~ di** according to

det'taglio [det'taʎʎo] *sm* detail; (*Comm*):
il ~ retail; al ~ (*Comm*) retail; separately

det'tare /72/ *vt* to dictate; ~ **legge** (*fig*) to
lay down the law; **det'tato** *sm* dictation

'detto, -a *pp di* **dire** ▷ *ag* (*soprannominato*)
called, known as; (*già nominato*) above-
mentioned ▷ *sm* saying; ~ **fatto** no sooner
said than done

deva'stare /72/ *vt* to devastate; (*fig*) to
ravage

devi'are /19/ *vi*: ~ (**da**) to turn off (from)
▷ *vt* to divert; **deviazi'one** *sf* (*anche Aut*)
diversion

'devo *ecc vb vedi* **dovere**

de'volvere /94/ *vt* (*Dir*) to transfer, devolve

de'voto, -a *ag* (*Rel*) devout, pious;
(*affezionato*) devoted; **devozi'one** *sf* devoutness;
(*anche Rel*) devotion

dezip'pare [dedzip'pare] /72/ *vt* (*Inform*)
to unzip

○ **PAROLA CHIAVE**

di (*di* + *il* = **del**, *di* + *lo* = **dello**, *di* + *l'* = **dell'**, *di*
+ *la* = **della**, *di* + *i* = **dei**, *di* + *gli* = **degli**, *di* + *le*
= **delle**) *prep* **1** (*possesso, specificazione*) of;
(*composto da, scritto da*) by; **la macchina di
Paolo/di mio fratello** Paolo's/my brother's
car; **un amico di mio fratello** a friend of my
brother's, one of my brother's friends; **un
quadro di Botticelli** a painting by Botticelli
2 (*caratterizzazione, misura*) of; **una casa
di mattoni** a brick house, a house made
of bricks; **un orologio d'oro** a gold watch;
un bimbo di 3 anni a child of 3, a 3-year-old
child

3 (*causa, mezzo, modo*) with; **tremare di
paura** to tremble with fear; **morire di
cancro** to die of cancer; **spalmare di burro**
to spread with butter

4 (*argomento*) about, of; **discutere di sport**
to talk about sport

5 (*luogo, provenienza*) from; out of; **essere di
Roma** to be from Rome; **uscire di casa** to
come out of *o* leave the house

6 (*tempo*) in; **d'estate/d'inverno** in (the)
summer/winter; **di notte** by night, at
night; **di mattina/sera** in the morning/
evening; **di lunedì** on Mondays

▶ *det* (*una certa quantità di*) some; (*: negativo*)
any; (*interrogativo*) any; some; **del pane**
(some) bread; **delle caramelle** (some)
sweets; **degli amici miei** some friends of
mine; **vuoi del vino?** do you want some *o*
any wine?

dia'bete *sm* diabetes *sg*

dia'betico, -a, -ci, -che *ag, sm/f* diabetic

---

dia'framma, -i *sm* (*divisione*) screen; (*Anat,
Fot: contraccettivo*) diaphragm

di'agnosi [di'aɲɲozi] *sf* diagnosis *sg*

diago'nale *ag, sf* diagonal

dia'gramma, -i *sm* diagram

dia'letto *sm* dialect

di'alisi *sf* dialysis *sg*

di'alogo, -ghi *sm* dialogue

di'amante *sm* diamond

di'ametro *sm* diameter

diaposi'tiva *sf* transparency, slide

di'ario *sm* diary

diar'rea *sf* diarrhoea

di'avolo *sm* devil

di'battito *sm* debate, discussion

'dice ['ditʃe] *vb vedi* **dire**

di'cembre [di'tʃembre] *sm* December

dice'ria [ditʃe'ria] *sf* rumour, piece of gossip

dichia'rare [dikja'rare] /72/ *vt* to declare;
dichiararsi *vpr* to declare o.s.; (*innamorato*)
to declare one's love; **dichiararsi vinto**
to admit defeat; **dichiarazi'one** *sf*
declaration; **dichiarazione dei redditi**
statement of income; (*modulo*) tax return

dician'nove [ditʃan'nɔve] *num* nineteen

dicias'sette [ditʃas'sette] *num* seventeen

dici'otto [di'tʃɔtto] *num* eighteen

dici'tura [ditʃi'tura] *sf* words *pl*, wording

'dico *ecc vb vedi* **dire**

didasca'lia *sf* (*di illustrazione*) caption; (*Cine*)
subtitle; (*Teat*) stage directions *pl*

di'dattico, -a, -ci, -che *ag* didactic; (*metodo,
programma*) teaching; (*libro*) educational

di'eci ['djɛtʃi] *num* ten

'diedi *ecc vb vedi* **dare**

'diesel ['di:zəl] *sm inv* diesel engine

dies'sino, -a *sm/f* member of the DS political
party

di'eta *sf* diet; **essere a ~** to be on a diet

di'etro *av* behind; (*in fondo*) at the back
▷ *prep* behind; (*tempo: dopo*) after ▷ *sm* back,
rear ▷ *ag inv* back *cpd*; **le zampe di ~** the
hind legs; **~ richiesta** on demand; (*scritta*)
on application

di'fendere /36/ *vt* to defend; **difendersi** *vpr*
(*cavarsela*) to get by; **difendersi da/contro**
to defend o.s. from/against; **difendersi
dal freddo** to protect o.s. from the cold;
difen'sore, -a *sm/f* defender; **avvocato
difensore** counsel for the defence (*BRIT*) *o*
defense (*US*); **di'fesa** *sf vedi* **difeso**

'difesi *ecc vb vedi* **difendere**

di'fetto *sm* (*mancanza*): ~ **di** lack of;
shortage of; (*di fabbricazione*) fault, flaw,
defect; (*morale*) fault, failing, defect; (*fisico*)
defect; **far ~** to be lacking; **in ~** at fault;
in the wrong; **difet'toso, -a** *ag* defective,
faulty

diffe'rente *ag* different

diffe'renza [diffe'rentsa] *sf* difference; **a ~ di** unlike

diffe'rire /55/ *vt* to postpone, defer ▷ *vi* to be different

diffe'rita *sf*: **in ~** (*trasmettere*) prerecorded

dif'ficile [dif'fitʃile] *ag* difficult; (*persona*) hard to please, difficult (to please); (*poco probabile*): **è ~ che sia libero** it is unlikely that he'll be free ▷ *sm* difficult part; difficulty; **difficoltà** *sf inv* difficulty

diffi'dente *ag* suspicious, distrustful

diffi'denza *sf* suspicion, distrust

dif'fondere /25/ *vt* (*luce, calore*) to diffuse; (*notizie*) to spread, circulate; **diffondersi** *vpr* to spread

dif'fusi *ecc vb vedi* **diffondere**

dif'fuso, -a *pp di* **diffondere** ▷ *ag* (*fenomeno, notizia, malattia ecc*) widespread

'diga, -ghe *sf* dam; (*portuale*) breakwater

dige'rente [didʒe'rɛnte] *ag* (*apparato*) digestive

dige'rire [didʒe'rire] /55/ *vt* to digest; **digesti'one** *sf* digestion; **diges'tivo, -a** *ag* digestive ▷ *sm* (*after-dinner*) liqueur

digi'tale [didʒi'tale] *ag* digital; (*delle dita*) finger *cpd*, digital ▷ *sf* (*Bot*) foxglove

digi'tare [didʒi'tare] /72/ *vt* (*dati*) to key (in)

digiu'nare [didʒu'nare] /72/ *vi* to starve o.s.; (*Rel*) to fast; **digi'uno, -a** *ag*: **essere digiuno** not to have eaten ▷ *sm* fast; **a digiuno** on an empty stomach

dignità [diɲɲi'ta] *sf inv* dignity

'DIGOS *sigla f* (= *Divisione Investigazioni Generali e Operazioni Speciali*) *police department dealing with political security*

digri'gnare [digriɲ'ɲare] /15/ *vt*: **~ i denti** to grind one's teeth

dilapi'dare /72/ *vt* to squander, waste

dila'tare /72/ *vt* to dilate; (*gas*) to cause to expand; (*passaggio, cavità*) to open (up); **dilatarsi** *vpr* to dilate; (*Fisica*) to expand

dilazio'nare [dilattsjo'nare] /72/ *vt* to delay, defer

di'lemma, -i *sm* dilemma

dilet'tante *smf* dilettante; (*anche Sport*) amateur

dili'gente [dili'dʒɛnte] *ag* (*scrupoloso*) diligent; (*accurato*) careful, accurate

dilu'ire /55/ *vt* to dilute

dilun'garsi /80/ *vpr* (*fig*): **~ su** to talk at length on *o* about

dilu'viare /19/ *vb impers* to pour (down)

di'luvio *sm* downpour; (*inondazione, fig*) flood

dima'grante *ag* slimming *cpd*

dima'grire /55/ *vi* to get thinner, lose weight

dime'nare /72/ *vt* to wave, shake; **dimenarsi** *vpr* to toss and turn; (*fig*) to struggle; **~ la coda** (*cane*) to wag its tail

dimensi'one *sf* dimension; (*grandezza*) size

dimenti'canza [dimenti'kantsa] *sf* forgetfulness; (*errore*) oversight, slip; **per ~** inadvertently

dimenti'care /20/ *vt* to forget; **dimenticarsi** *vpr*: **dimenticarsi di qc** to forget sth

dimesti'chezza [dimesti'kettsa] *sf* familiarity

di'mettere /63/ *vt*: **~ qn da** to dismiss sb from; (*dall'ospedale*) to discharge sb from; **dimettersi** *vpr*: **dimettersi (da)** to resign (from)

dimez'zare [dimed'dzare] /72/ *vt* to halve

diminu'ire /55/ *vt* to reduce, diminish; (*prezzi*) to bring down, reduce ▷ *vi* to decrease, diminish; (*rumore*) to die down, die away; (*prezzi*) to fall, go down

diminu'tivo, -a *ag, sm* diminutive

diminuzi'one [diminut'tsjone] *sf* decreasing, diminishing

di'misi *ecc vb vedi* **dimettere**

dimissi'oni *sfpl* resignation *sg*; **dare** *o* **presentare le ~** to resign, hand in one's resignation

dimos'trare /72/ *vt* to demonstrate, show; (*provare*) to prove, demonstrate; **dimostrarsi** *vpr*: **dimostrarsi molto abile** to show o.s. *o* prove to be very clever; **dimostra 30 anni** he looks about 30 (years old); **dimostrazi'one** *sf* demonstration; proof

di'namico, -a, -ci, -che *ag* dynamic ▷ *sf* dynamics *sg*

dina'mite *sf* dynamite

'dinamo *sf inv* dynamo

dino'sauro *sm* dinosaur

din'torno *av* round; **dintorni** *smpl* outskirts; **nei dintorni di** in the vicinity *o* neighbourhood of

'dio (*pl* **dei**) *sm* god; **D~** God; **gli dei** the gods; **D~ mio!** my God!

diparti'mento *sm* department

dipen'dente *ag* dependent ▷ *smf* employee; **~ statale** state employee

di'pendere /8/ *vi*: **~ da** to depend on; (*finanziariamente*) to be dependent on; (*derivare*) to come from, be due to

di'pesi *ecc vb vedi* **dipendere**

di'pingere [di'pindʒere] /37/ *vt* to paint

di'pinsi *ecc vb vedi* **dipingere**

di'pinto, -a *pp di* **dipingere** ▷ *sm* painting

di'ploma, -i *sm* diploma

diplo'matico, -a, -ci, -che *ag* diplomatic ▷ *sm* diplomat

diploma'zia [diplomat'tsia] *sf* diplomacy

di'porto *sm*: **imbarcazione da ~** pleasure craft

dira'dare /72/ vt to thin (out); (visite) to reduce, make less frequent; (diradarsi vpr to disperse; (nebbia) to clear (up)

'dire /38/ vt to say; (segreto, fatto) to tell; ~ **qc a qn** to tell sb sth; ~ **a qn di fare qc** to tell sb to do sth; ~ **di sì/no** to say yes/no; **si dice che ...** they say that ...; **si direbbe che ...** it looks (o sounds) as though ...; **dica, signora?** (in un negozio) yes, Madam, can I help you?

di'ressi ecc vb vedi **dirigere**

di'retta sf: **in ~** (trasmettere) live; **un incontro di calcio in ~** a live football match

di'retto, -a pp di **dirigere** ▷ ag direct ▷ sm (Ferr) through train

diret'tore, -'trice sm/f (di azienda) director, manager(manageress); (di scuola elementare) head (teacher) (BRIT), principal (US); ~ **d'orchestra** conductor; ~ **vendite** sales director o manager; **direzi'one** sf board of directors; management; (senso: anche fig) direction; **in direzione di** in the direction of, towards

diri'gente smf executive; (Pol) leader ▷ ag: **classe ~** ruling class; **di'rigere** /39/ vt to direct; (impresa) to run, manage; (Mus) to conduct; **dirigersi** vpr: **dirigersi verso** o **a** to make o head for

dirim'petto av opposite; ~ **a** opposite, facing

di'ritto, -a ag straight; (onesto) straight, upright ▷ av straight, directly ▷ sm right side; (Tennis) forehand; (Maglia) plain stitch; (prerogativa) right; (leggi, scienza): **il ~** law; **diritti** smpl (tasse) duty sg; **stare ~** to stand up straight; **aver ~ a qc** to be entitled to sth; **andare ~** to go straight on; **diritti (d'autore)** royalties

dirotta'mento sm: ~ **(aereo)** hijack

dirot'tare /72/ vt (nave, aereo) to change the course of; (aereo: sotto minaccia) to hijack; (traffico) to divert ▷ vi (nave, aereo) to change course; **dirotta'tore, -'trice** sm/f hijacker

di'rotto, -a ag (pioggia) torrential; (pianto) unrestrained; **piovere a ~** to pour; **piangere a ~** to cry one's heart out

di'rupo sm crag, precipice

di'sabile smf person with a disability ▷ ag disabled; **i disabili** people with disabilities

disabi'tato, -a ag uninhabited

disabitu'arsi /72/ vpr: ~ **a** to get out of the habit of

disac'cordo sm disagreement

disadat'tato, -a ag (Psic) maladjusted

disa'dorno, -a ag plain, unadorned

disagi'ato, -a [diza'dʒato] ag poor, needy; (vita) hard

di'sagio [di'zadʒo] sm discomfort; (disturbo) inconvenience; (fig: imbarazzo) embarrassment; **essere a ~** to be ill at ease

disappro'vare /72/ vt to disapprove of; **disapprovazi'one** sf disapproval

disap'punto sm disappointment

disar'mare /72/ vt, vi to disarm; **di'sarmo** sm (Mil) disarmament

di'sastro sm disaster

disas'troso, -a ag disastrous

disat'tento, -a ag inattentive; **disattenzi'one** sf carelessness, lack of attention

disavven'tura sf misadventure, mishap

dis'capito sm: **a ~ di** to the detriment of

dis'carica, -che sf (di rifiuti) rubbish tip o dump

di'scendere [diʃ'ʃɛndere] /101/ vt to go (o come) down ▷ vi to go (o come) down; (strada) to go down; (smontare) to get off; ~ **da** (famiglia) to be descended from; ~ **dalla macchina/dal treno** to get out of the car/out of o off the train; ~ **da cavallo** to dismount, get off one's horse

di'scesa [diʃ'ʃesa] sf descent; (pendio) slope; **in ~** (strada) downhill cpd, sloping; ~ **libera** (Sci) downhill (race)

disci'plina [diʃʃi'plina] sf discipline

'disco, -schi sm disc; (Sport) discus; (fonografico) record; (Inform) disk; ~ **orario** (Aut) parking disc; ~ **rigido** (Inform) hard disk; ~ **volante** flying saucer

disco'grafico, -a, -ci, -che ag record cpd, recording cpd ▷ sm record producer; **casa discografica** record(ing) company

dis'correre /28/ vi: ~ **(di)** to talk (about)

dis'corso, -a pp di **discorrere** ▷ sm speech; (conversazione) conversation, talk

disco'teca, -che sf (raccolta) record library; (luogo di ballo) disco(theque)

dis'count [dis'kaunt] sm inv (supermercato) cut-price supermarket

discre'panza [diskre'pantsa] sf discrepancy

dis'creto, -a ag discreet; (abbastanza buono) reasonable, fair

discriminazi'one [diskriminat'tsjone] sf discrimination

dis'cussi ecc vb vedi **discutere**

discussi'one sf discussion; (litigio) argument; **fuori ~** out of the question

dis'cutere /40/ vt to discuss, debate; (contestare) to question ▷ vi (litigare) to argue; (conversare): ~ **(di)** to discuss

dis'detto, -a pp di **disdire** ▷ sf (di prenotazione ecc) cancellation; (sfortuna) bad luck

dis'dire /38/ vt (prenotazione) to cancel; ~ **un contratto d'affitto** (Dir) to give notice (to quit)

dise'gnare [disɲɲnare] /15/ vt to draw; (*progettare*) to design; (*fig*) to outline; **disegna'tore, -'trice** sm/f designer

di'segno [di'zeɲɲo] sm drawing; (*su stoffa ecc*) design; (*fig: schema*) outline; **~ di legge** (*Dir*) bill

diser'bante sm weedkiller

diser'tare /72/ vt, vi to desert

dis'fare /41/ vt to undo; (*valigie*) to unpack; (*meccanismo*) to take to pieces; (*neve*) to melt; **disfarsi** vpr to come undone; (*neve*) to melt; **~ il letto** to strip the bed; **disfarsi di qn** (*liberarsi*) to get rid of sb; **dis'fatto, -a** pp di **disfare**

dis'gelo [diz'dʒɛlo] sm thaw

dis'grazia [diz'grattsja] sf (*sventura*) misfortune; (*incidente*) accident, mishap

disgu'ido sm hitch; **~ postale** error in postal delivery

disgus'tare /72/ vt to disgust

dis'gusto sm disgust; **disgus'toso, -a** ag disgusting

disidra'tare /72/ vt to dehydrate

disimpa'rare /72/ vt to forget

disinfet'tante ag, sm disinfectant

disinfet'tare /72/ vt to disinfect

disini'bito, -a ag uninhibited

disinstal'lare /72/ vt (*software*) to uninstall

disinte'grare /72/ vt, vi to disintegrate; **disintegrarsi** vpr to disintegrate

disinteres'sarsi /72/ vpr: **~ di** to take no interest in; **disinte'resse** sm indifference; (*generosità*) unselfishness

disintossi'care /20/ vt (*alcolizzato, drogato*) to treat for alcoholism (*o drug* addiction); **disintossicarsi** vpr to clear out one's system; (*alcolizzato, drogato*) to be treated for alcoholism (*o drug addiction*); **disintossicazione** sf detox

disin'volto, -a ag casual, free and easy

dismi'sura sf excess; **a ~** to excess, excessively

disoccu'pato, -a ag unemployed ▷ sm/f unemployed person; **disoccupazi'one** sf unemployment

diso'nesto, -a ag dishonest

disordi'nato, -a ag untidy; (*privo di misura*) irregular, wild; **di'sordine** sm (*confusione*) disorder, confusion; (*sregolatezza*) debauchery; **disordini** smpl (*Pol: ecc*) disorder sg; (*tumulti*) riots

disorien'tare /72/ vt to disorientate

disorien'tato, -a ag disorientated

dis'pari ag inv odd, uneven

dis'parte: **in ~** av (*da lato*) aside, apart; **tenersi** o **starsene in ~** to keep to o.s., hold aloof

dispendi'oso, -a ag expensive

dis'pensa sf pantry, larder; (*mobile*) sideboard; (*Dir*) exemption; (*Rel*) dispensation; (*fascicolo*) number, issue

dispe'rato, -a ag (*persona*) in despair; (*caso, tentativo*) desperate

disperazi'one sf despair

dis'perdere /73/ vt (*disseminare*) to disperse; (*Mil*) to scatter, rout; (*fig: consumare*) to waste, squander; **disperdersi** vpr to disperse; to scatter; **dis'perso, -a** pp di **disperdere** ▷ sm/f missing person

dis'petto sm spite no pl, spitefulness no pl; **fare un ~ a qn** to play a (nasty) trick on sb; **a ~ di** in spite of; **dispet'toso, -a** ag spiteful

dispia'cere [dispja'tʃere] /74/ sm (*rammarico*) regret, sorrow; (*dolore*) grief ▷ vi: **~ a** to displease ▷ vb impers: **mi dispiace (che)** I am sorry (that); **le dispiace se...?** do you mind if ...?; **dispiaceri** smpl (*preoccupazioni*) troubles, worries

dis'pone ecc vb vedi **disporre**

dispo'nibile ag available

dis'porre /77/ vt (*sistemare*) to arrange; (*preparare*) to prepare; (*Dir*) to order; (*persuadere*): **~ qn a** to incline o dispose sb towards ▷ vi (*decidere*) to decide; (*usufruire*): **~ di** to use, have at one's disposal; (*essere dotato*): **~ di** to have

dis'posi ecc vb vedi **disporre**

disposi'tivo sm (*meccanismo*) device

disposizi'one [dispozit'tsjone] sf arrangement, layout; (*stato d'animo*) mood; (*tendenza*) bent, inclination; (*comando*) order; (*Dir*) provision, regulation; **a ~ di qn** at sb's disposal

dis'posto, -a pp di **disporre**

disprez'zare [dispret'tsare] /72/ vt to despise

dis'prezzo [dis'prɛttso] sm contempt

'disputa sf dispute, quarrel

dispu'tare /72/ vt (*contendere*) to dispute, contest; (*gara*) to take part in ▷ vi to quarrel; **~ di** to discuss; **disputarsi qc** to fight for sth

'disse vb vedi **dire**

dissente'ria sf dysentery

dissen'tire /45/ vi: **~ (da)** to disagree (with)

disse'tante ag refreshing

'dissi vb vedi **dire**

dissimu'lare /72/ vt (*fingere*) to dissemble; (*nascondere*) to conceal

dissi'pare /72/ vt to dissipate; (*scialacquare*) to squander, waste

dissu'adere /88/ vt: **~ qn da** to dissuade sb from

dissu'asore sm: **~ di velocità** (*Aut*) speed bump

distac'care /20/ vt to detach, separate; (*Sport*) to leave behind; **distaccarsi** vpr to

be detached; (*fig*) to stand out;
distaccarsi da (*fig*: *allontanarsi*) to grow
away from

dis'tacco, -chi *sm* (*separazione*) separation;
(*fig*: *indifferenza*) detachment; (*Sport*):
vincere con un ~ di ... to win by a
distance of ...

dis'tante *av* far away ▷ *ag*: **essere ~ (da)** to
be a long way (from)

dis'tanza [dis'tantsa] *sf* distance

distanzi'are [distan'tsjare] /19/ *vt* to
space out, place at intervals; (*Sport*) to
outdistance; (*fig*: *superare*) to outstrip,
surpass

dis'tare /72/ *vi*: **distiamo pochi chilometri
da Roma** we are only a few kilometres
(away) from Rome; **quanto dista il centro
da qui?** how far is the town centre?

dis'tendere /120/ *vt* (*coperta*) to spread
out; (*gambe*) to stretch (out); (*mettere a
giacere*) to lay; (*rilassare*: *muscoli, nervi*) to
relax; **distendersi** *vpr* (*rilassarsi*) to relax;
(*sdraiarsi*) to lie down

dis'teso, -a *pp di* **distendere** ▷ *sf* expanse,
stretch

distil'lare /72/ *vt* to distil

distille'ria *sf* distillery

dis'tinguere /42/ *vt* to distinguish;
distinguersi *vpr* (*essere riconoscibile*) to be
distinguished; (*emergere*) to stand out, be
conspicuous, distinguish o.s.

dis'tinta *sf* (*nota*) note; (*elenco*) list; **~ di
versamento** pay-in slip

distin'tivo, -a *ag* distinctive; distinguishing
▷ *sm* badge

dis'tinto, -a *pp di* **distinguere** ▷ *ag*
(*dignitoso ed elegante*) distinguished;
distinti saluti (*in lettera*) yours faithfully

distinzi'one [distin'tsjone] *sf* distinction

dis'togliere [dis'tɔʎʎere] /122/ *vt*: **~ da** to
take away from; (*fig*) to dissuade from

distorsi'one *sf* (*Med*) sprain; (*Fisica, Ottica*)
distortion

dis'trarre /123/ *vt* to distract; (*divertire*)
to entertain, amuse; **distrarsi** *vpr* (*non
fare attenzione*) to be distracted, let one's
mind wander; (*svagarsi*) to amuse o enjoy
o.s.; **dis'tratto, -a** *pp di* **distrarre** ▷ *ag*
absent-minded; (*disattento*) inattentive;
distrazi'one *sf* absent-mindedness;
inattention; (*svago*) distraction,
entertainment

dis'tretto *sm* district

distribu'ire /55/ *vt* to distribute; (*Carte*)
to deal (out); (*posta*) to deliver; (*lavoro*) to
allocate, assign; (*ripartire*) to share out;
distribu'tore *sm* (*di benzina*) petrol (BRIT)
o gas (US) pump; (*Aut, Elettr*) distributor;
(*automatico*) vending machine

distri'care /20/ *vt* to disentangle, unravel;
districarsi *vpr* (*tirarsi fuori*): **districarsi da**
to get out of, disentangle o.s. from

dis'truggere [dis'truddʒere] /83/ *vt* to
destroy; **distruzi'one** *sf* destruction

distur'bare /72/ *vt* to disturb, trouble;
(*sonno, lezioni*) to disturb, interrupt;
disturbarsi *vpr* to put o.s. out; **dis'turbo**
sm trouble, bother, inconvenience;
(*indisposizione*) (slight) disorder, ailment

disubbidi'ente *ag* disobedient;
disubbi'dire /55/ *vi*: **disubbidire (a qn)** to
disobey (sb)

disu'mano, -a *ag* inhuman

di'tale *sm* thimble

'dito (*pl f* **dita**) *sm* finger; (*misura*) finger,
finger's breadth; **~ (del piede)** toe

'ditta *sf* firm, business

ditta'tore *sm* dictator

ditta'tura *sf* dictatorship

dit'tongo, -ghi *sm* diphthong

di'urno, -a *ag* day *cpd*, daytime *cpd*

'diva *sf vedi* **divo**

di'vano *sm* sofa; (*senza schienale*) divan;
~ letto bed settee, sofa bed

divari'care /20/ *vt* to open wide

di'vario *sm* difference

dive'nire /128/ *vi* = **diventare**

diven'tare /72/ *vi* to become; **~ famoso/
professore** to become famous/a teacher

diversifi'care /20/ *vt* to diversify, vary;
to differentiate; **diversificarsi** *vpr*:
diversificarsi (per) to differ (in)

diversità *sf inv* difference, diversity;
(*varietà*) variety

diver'sivo *sm* diversion, distraction

di'verso, -a *ag* (*differente*): **~ (da)** different
(from); **diversi, e** *det pl, pron pl* several,
various; (*Comm*) sundry; several people,
many (people)

diver'tente *ag* amusing

diverti'mento *sm* amusement, pleasure;
(*passatempo*) pastime, recreation

diver'tire /45/ *vt* to amuse, entertain;
divertirsi *vpr* to amuse o enjoy o.s.

di'videre /43/ *vt* (*anche Mat*) to divide;
(*distribuire, ripartire*) to divide (up), split
(up); **dividersi** *vpr* (*persone*) to separate;
(*ramificarsi*) to fork

divi'eto *sm* prohibition; **"~ di sosta"** (*Aut*)
"no waiting"

divinco'larsi /72/ *vpr* to wriggle, writhe

di'vino, -a *ag* divine

di'visa *sf* (*Mil*: *ecc*) uniform; (*Comm*) foreign
currency

di'visi *ecc vb vedi* **dividere**

divisi'one *sf* division

'divo, -a *sm/f* star

divo'rare /72/ *vt* to devour

divorzi'are [divor'tsjare] /19/ vi: ~ **(da qn)** to divorce (sb)

di'vorzio [di'vɔrtsjo] sm divorce

divul'gare /80/ vt to divulge, disclose; (rendere comprensibile) to popularize

dizio'nario sm dictionary

DJ [di'dʒei] sigla m, sigla f (= Disc Jockey) DJ

do sm (Mus) C; (: solfeggiando la scala) do(h)

dobbi'amo vb vedi **dovere**

D.O.C. [dɔk] sigla (= denominazione di origine controllata) label guaranteeing the quality of wine

'doccia, -ce ['dɔttʃa] sf (bagno) shower; **fare la ~** to have a shower

docciaschi'uma [dottʃas'kjuma] sm inv shower gel

do'cente [do'tʃɛnte] ag teaching ▷ smf teacher; (di università) lecturer

'docile ['dɔtʃile] ag docile

documen'tare /72/ vt to document; **documentarsi** vpr: **documentarsi (su)** to gather information o material (about)

documen'tario, -a sm documentary

docu'mento sm document; **documenti** smpl (d'identità ecc) papers

dodi'cesimo, -a [dodi'tʃɛzimo] num twelfth

'dodici ['doditʃi] num twelve

do'gana sf (ufficio) customs pl; (tassa) (customs) duty; **passare la ~** to go through customs; **dogani'ere** sm customs officer

'doglie ['dɔʎʎe] sfpl (Med) labour sg (BRIT), labour pains

'dolce ['doltʃe] ag sweet; (carattere, persona) gentle, mild; (fig: mite: clima) mild; (non ripido: pendio) gentle ▷ sm (sapore dolce) sweetness, sweet taste; (Cuc: portata) sweet, dessert; (: torta) cake; **dolcifi'cante** sm sweetener

do'lere /44/ vi to be sore

'dollaro sm dollar

Dolo'miti sfpl: **le ~** the Dolomites

do'lore sm (fisico) pain; (morale) sorrow, grief; **dolo'roso, -a** ag painful; sorrowful, sad

'dolsi ecc vb vedi **dolere**

do'manda sf (interrogazione) question; (richiesta) demand; (: cortese) request; (Dir: richiesta scritta) application; (Econ): **la ~** demand; **fare una ~ a qn** to ask sb a question; **fare ~ (per un lavoro)** to apply (for a job)

doman'dare /72/ vt (per avere) to ask for; (per sapere) to ask; (esigere) to demand; **domandarsi** vpr to wonder; to ask o.s.; **~ qc a qn** to ask sb for sth; to ask sb sth

do'mani av tomorrow ▷ sm: **il ~** (il futuro) the future; (il giorno successivo) the next day; **~ l'altro** the day after tomorrow

do'mare /72/ vt to tame

doma'tore, -'trice sm/f (gen) tamer; **~ di cavalli** horsebreaker; **~ di leoni** lion tamer

domat'tina av tomorrow morning

do'menica, -che sf Sunday; **di o la ~** on Sundays

do'mestico, -a, -ci, -che ag domestic ▷ sm/f servant, domestic

domi'cilio [domi'tʃiljo] sm (Dir) domicile, place of residence

domi'nare /72/ vt to dominate; (fig: sentimenti) to control, master ▷ vi to be in the dominant position

do'nare /72/ vt to give, present; (per beneficenza ecc) to donate ▷ vi (fig): **~ a** to suit, become; **~ sangue** to give blood; **dona'tore, -'trice** sm/f donor; **donatore di sangue/di organi** blood/organ donor

dondo'lare /72/ vt (cullare) to rock; **dondolarsi** vpr to swing, sway; **'dondolo** sm: **sedia/cavallo a dondolo** rocking chair/horse

'donna sf woman; **~ di casa** housewife; home-loving woman; **~ di servizio** maid

donnai'olo sm ladykiller

'donnola sf weasel

'dono sm gift

'doping sm doping

'dopo av (tempo) afterwards; (: più tardi) later; (luogo) after, next ▷ prep after ▷ cong (temporale): **~ aver studiato** after having studied ▷ ag inv: **il giorno ~** the following day; **~ mangiato va a dormire** after having eaten o after a meal he goes for a sleep; **un anno ~** a year later; **~ di me/lui** after me/ him; **~, a ~!** I see you later!

dopo'barba sm inv after-shave

dopodo'mani av the day after tomorrow

doposcì [dopoʃ'ʃi] sm inv après-ski outfit

dopo'sole sm inv: **(lozione/crema) ~** aftersun (lotion/cream)

dopo'tutto av (tutto considerato) after all

doppi'aggio [dop'pjaddʒo] sm (Cine) dubbing

doppi'are /19/ vt (Naut) to round; (Sport) to lap; (Cine) to dub

'doppio, -a ag double; (fig: falso) double-dealing, deceitful ▷ sm (quantità): **il ~ (di)** twice as much (o many), double the amount (o number) of; (Sport) doubles pl ▷ av double

doppi'one sm duplicate (copy)

doppio'petto sm double-breasted jacket

dormicchi'are [dormik'kjare] /19/ vi to doze

dormigli'one, -a [dormiʎ'ʎone] sm/f sleepyhead

dor'mire /45/ vi to sleep; **andare a ~** to go to bed; **dor'mita** sf: **farsi una dormita** to have a good sleep

dormi'torio sm dormitory

dormi'veglia [dormi'veʎʎa] sm drowsiness

'**dorso** sm back; (di montagna) ridge, crest; (di libro) spine; **a ~ di cavallo** on horseback

do'sare /72/ vt to measure out; (Med) to dose

'**dose** sf quantity, amount; (Med) dose

do'tato, -a ag: **~ di** (attrezzature) equipped with; (bellezza, intelligenza) endowed with; **un uomo ~** a gifted man

'**dote** sf (di sposa); (assegnata a un ente) endowment; (fig) gift, talent

Dott. abbr (= dottore) Dr

dotto'rato sm degree; **~ di ricerca** doctorate, doctor's degree

dot'tore, -'essa sm/f doctor

> ◆ **DOTTORE**
> ◆
> ◆ In Italy, anyone who has a degree in any
> ◆ subject can use the title dottore. Thus a
> ◆ person who is addressed as dottore is not
> ◆ necessarily a doctor of medicine.

dot'trina sf doctrine

Dott.ssa abbr (= dottoressa) Dr

'**dove** av (gen) where; (in cui) where, in which; (dovunque) wherever ▷ cong (mentre, laddove) whereas; **~ sei?/vai?** where are you?/are you going?; **dimmi dov'è** tell me where it is; **di dov'è?** where are you from?; **per ~ si passa?** which way should we go?; **la città ~ abito** the town where o in which I live; **siediti ~ vuoi** sit wherever you like

do'vere /46/ sm (obbligo) duty ▷ vt (essere debitore): **~ qc (a qn)** to owe (sb) sth ▷ vi (seguito dall'infinito, obbligo) to have to; **devo partire domani** (intenzione) I'm (due) to leave tomorrow; **dev'essere tardi** (probabilità) it must be late; **lui deve farlo** he has to do it, he must do it; **quanto le devo?** how much do I owe you?; **è dovuto partire** he had to leave; **ha dovuto pagare** he had to pay; **rivolgersi a chi di ~** to apply to the appropriate authority o person; **come si deve** (bene) properly; **una persona come si deve** a respectable person

dove'roso, -a ag (right and) proper

dovrò ecc vb vedi **dovere**

do'vunque av (in qualunque luogo) wherever; (dappertutto) everywhere; **~ io vada** wherever I go

do'vuto, -a ag (causato): **~ a** due to

doz'zina [dod'dzina] sf dozen; **una ~ di uova** a dozen eggs

dozzi'nale [doddzi'nale] ag cheap, second-rate

'**drago, -ghi** sm dragon

'**dramma, -i** sm drama; **dram'matico, -a, -ci, -che** ag dramatic

'**drastico, -a, -ci, -che** ag drastic

'**dritto, -a** ag, av = **diritto**

'**droga, -ghe** sf (sostanza aromatica) spice; (stupefacente) drug; **droghe pesanti/ leggere** hard/soft drugs

dro'gare /80/ vt to drug; **drogarsi** vpr to take drugs

dro'gato, -a sm/f drug addict

droghe'ria [droge'ria] sf grocer's (shop) (BRIT), grocery (store) (US)

drome'dario sm dromedary

DS [di'ɛsse] smpl (= Democratici di Sinistra) Democrats of the Left (Italian left-wing party)

'**dubbio, -a** ag (incerto) doubtful, dubious; (ambiguo) dubious ▷ sm (incertezza) doubt; **avere il ~ che** to be afraid that, suspect that; **mettere in ~ qc** to question sth

dubi'tare /72/ vi: **~ di** to doubt; (risultato) to be doubtful of

Du'blino sf Dublin

'**duca, -chi** sm duke

du'chessa [du'kessa] sf duchess

'**due** num two

due'cento [due'tʃɛnto] num two hundred ▷ sm: **il D~** the thirteenth century

due'pezzi [due'pettsi] sm (costume da bagno) two-piece swimsuit; (abito femminile) two-piece suit

'**dunque** cong (perciò) so, therefore; (riprendendo il discorso) well (then) ▷ sm inv: **venire al ~** to come to the point

du'omo sm cathedral

▌Attenzione! In inglese esiste la parola dome, che però significa cupola.

dupli'cato sm duplicate

'**duplice** ['duplitʃe] ag double, twofold; **in ~ copia** in duplicate

du'rante prep during

du'rare /72/ vi to last; **~ fatica a** to have difficulty in

du'rezza [du'rettsa] sf hardness; stubbornness; harshness; toughness

'**duro, -a** ag (pietra, lavoro, materasso, problema) hard; (persona: ostinato) stubborn, obstinate; (: severo) harsh, hard; (voce) harsh; (carne) tough ▷ sm/f hardness; (difficoltà) hard part; (persona) tough one ▷ av: **tener ~** to stand firm, hold out; **~ d'orecchi** hard of hearing

DVD [divu'di] sm inv DVD; (lettore) DVD player

e

E *abbr* (= *est*) E

e (*dav V spesso* **ed**) *cong* and; **e lui?** what about him?; **e compralo!** well buy it then!

è *vb vedi* **essere**

eb'bene *cong* well (then)

'ebbi *ecc vb vedi* **avere**

e'braico, -a, -ci, -che *ag* Hebrew, Hebraic ▷ *sm* (*Ling*) Hebrew

e'breo, -a *ag* Jewish ▷ *sm/f* Jewish person, Jew

EC *abbr* (= *Eurocity*) fast train connecting Western European cities

ecc. *abbr* (= *eccetera*) etc

eccel'lente [ettʃel'lɛnte] *ag* excellent

ec'centrico, -a, -ci, -che [et'tʃɛntriko] *ag* eccentric

ecces'sivo, -a [ettʃes'sivo] *ag* excessive

ec'cesso [et'tʃɛsso] *sm* excess; **all'~** (*gentile, generoso*) to excess, excessively; **~ di velocità** (*Aut*) speeding

ec'cetera [et'tʃetera] *av* et cetera, and so on

ec'cetto [et'tʃetto] *prep* except, with the exception of; **~ che** except, other than; **~ che (non)** unless

eccezio'nale [ettʃettsjo'nale] *ag* exceptional

eccezi'one [ettʃet'tsjone] *sf* exception; (*Dir*) objection; **a ~ di** with the exception of, except for; **d'~** exceptional

ecci'tare [ettʃi'tare] /72/ *vt* (*curiosità, interesse*) to excite, arouse; (*folla*) to incite; **eccitarsi** *vpr* to get excited; (*sessualmente*) to become aroused

'ecco *av* (*per dimostrare*): **~ il treno!** here's *o* here comes the train!; (*dav pronome*): **eccomi!** here I am!; **eccone uno!** here's one (of them)!; (*dav pp*): **~ fatto!** there, that's it done!

ec'come *av* rather; **ti piace?** — **~!** do you like it? — I'll say! *o* and how! *o* rather! (*BRIT*)

e'clisse *sf* eclipse

'eco (*pl m* **echi**) *sm o* **echo**

ecogra'fia *sf* (*Med*) ultrasound

ecolo'gia [ekolo'dʒia] *sf* ecology

eco'logico, -a, -ci, -che [eko'lɔdʒiko] *ag* ecological

eco'mafia *sf* mafia involved in crimes related to the environment, in particular the illegal disposal of waste

econo'mia *sf* economy; (*scienza*) economics *sg*; (*risparmio, azione*) saving; **fare ~** to economize, make economies; **eco'nomico, -a, -ci, -che** *ag* economic; (*poco costoso*) economical

'ecstasy ['ɛkstasi] *sf inv* ecstasy

'edera *sf* ivy

e'dicola *sf* newspaper kiosk *o* stand (*US*)

edi'ficio [edi'fitʃo] *sm* building

e'dile *ag* building *cpd*

Edim'burgo *sf* Edinburgh

edi'tore, -'trice *ag* publishing *cpd* ▷ *sm/f* publisher

> Attenzione! In inglese esiste la parola *editor*, che però significa *redattore*.

edizi'one [edit'tsjone] *sf* edition; (*tiratura*) printing; **~ straordinaria** special edition

edu'care /20/ *vt* to educate; (*gusto, mente*) to train; **~ qn a fare** to train sb to do; **edu'cato, -a** *ag* polite, well-mannered; **educazi'one** *sf* education; (*familiare*) upbringing; (*comportamento*) (good) manners *pl*; **educazione fisica** (*Ins*) physical training *o* education

educherò *ecc* [eduke'rɔ] *vb vedi* **educare**

effemi'nato, -a *ag* effeminate

efferve'scente [efferveʃ'ʃente] *ag* effervescent

effet'tivo, -a *ag* (*reale*) real, actual; (*impiegato, professore*) permanent; (*Mil*) regular ▷ *sm* (*Mil*) strength; (*di patrimonio ecc*) sum total

effetto *sm* effect; (*Comm: cambiale*) bill; (*fig: impressione*) impression; **in effetti** in fact, actually; **effetti personali** personal effects, personal belongings; **~ serra** greenhouse effect

effi'cace [effi'katʃe] *ag* effective

effici'ente [effi'tʃente] *ag* efficient

E'geo [e'dʒɛo] *sm*: **l'~, il mare ~** the Aegean (Sea)

E'gitto [e'dʒitto] *sm*: **l'~** Egypt; **egizi'ano, -a** [edʒit'tsjano] *ag, sm/f* Egyptian

'egli ['eʎʎi] *pron* he; **~ stesso** he himself

ego'ismo *sm* selfishness, egoism; **ego'ista, -i, -e** *ag* selfish, egoistic ▷ *sm/f* egoist

Egr. *abbr* = **egregio**

e'gregio, -a, -gi, -gie [e'grɛdʒo] *ag* (*nelle lettere*): **E~ Signore** Dear Sir

E.I. *abbr* = **Esercito Italiano**

elabo'rare /72/ vt (progetto) to work out, elaborate; (dati) to process

elasticiz'zato, -a [elastitʃid'dzato] ag stretch cpd

e'lastico, -a, -ci, -che ag elastic; (fig: andatura) springy; (: decisione, vedute) flexible ▷ sm (gommino) rubber band; (per il cucito) elastic no pl

ele'fante sm elephant

ele'gante ag elegant

e'leggere [e'lɛddʒere] /61/ vt to elect

elemen'tare ag elementary; **le (scuole) elementari** sfpl primary (BRIT) o grade (US) school

ele'mento sm element; (parte componente) element, component, part; **elementi** smpl (della scienza ecc) elements, rudiments

ele'mosina sf charity, alms pl; **chiedere l'~** to beg

elen'care /20/ vt to list

elenche'rò ecc [elenke'rɔ] vb vedi **elencare**

e'lenco, -chi sm list; **~ telefonico** telephone directory

e'lessi ecc vb vedi **eleggere**

eletto'rale ag electoral, election cpd

elet'tore, -'trice sm/f voter, elector

elet'trauto sm inv workshop for car electrical repairs; (tecnico) car electrician

elettri'cista, -i [elettri'tʃista] sm electrician

elettrici'tà [elettritʃi'ta] sf electricity

e'lettrico, -a, -ci, -che ag electric(al)

elettriz'zante [elettrid'dzante] ag (fig) electrifying, thrilling

elettriz'zare [elettrid'dzare] /72/ vt to electrify; **elettrizzarsi** vpr to become charged with electricity

e'lettro... prefisso: **elettrodo'mestico, -a, -ci, -che** ag: **apparecchi elettrodomestici** domestic (electrical) appliances; **elet'tronico, -a, -ci, -che** ag electronic

elezi'one [elet'tsjone] sf election; **elezioni** sfpl (Pol) election(s)

'elica, -che sf propeller

eli'cottero sm helicopter

elimi'nare /72/ vt to eliminate

elisoc'corso sm helicopter ambulance

el'metto sm helmet

elogi'are [elo'dʒare] /62/ vt to praise

elo'quente ag eloquent

e'ludere /35/ vt to evade

e'lusi ecc vb vedi **eludere**

e-'mail [e'mɛil] sf inv (messaggio, sistema) e-mail ▷ ag inv email; **indirizzo ~** email address

emargi'nato, -a [emardʒi'nato] sm/f outcast; **emarginazione** [emardʒinat'tsjone] sf marginalization

embri'one sm embryo

emenda'mento sm amendment

emer'genza [emer'dʒɛntsa] sf emergency; **in caso di ~** in an emergency

e'mergere [e'mɛrdʒere] /59/ vi to emerge; (sommergibile) to surface; (fig: distinguersi) to stand out

e'mersi ecc vb vedi **emergere**

e'mettere /63/ vt (suono, luce) to give out, emit; (onde radio) to send out; (assegno, francobollo, ordine) to issue

emi'crania sf migraine

emi'grare /72/ vi to emigrate

emis'fero sm hemisphere; **~ boreale/ australe** northern/southern hemisphere

e'misi ecc vb vedi **emettere**

emit'tente ag (banca) issuing; (Radio) broadcasting, transmitting ▷ sf (Radio) transmitter

emorra'gia, -'gie [emorra'dʒia] sf haemorrhage

emor'roidi sfpl haemorrhoids pl (BRIT), hemorrhoids pl (US)

emo'tivo, -a ag emotional

emozio'nante [emottsjo'nante] ag exciting, thrilling

emozio'nare [emottsjo'nare] /72/ vt (appassionare) to excite; (commuovere) to move; (agitare) to make nervous; **emozionarsi** vpr to be excited; to be moved; to be nervous; **emozionato, -a** [emottsjo'nato] ag (commosso) moved; (agitato) nervous; (elettrizzato) excited

emozi'one [emot'tsjone] sf emotion; (agitazione) excitement

enciclope'dia [entʃiklope'dia] sf encyclop(a)edia

endove'noso, -a ag (Med) intravenous

'E.N.E.L. sigla m (= Ente Nazionale per l'Energia Elettrica) national electricity company

ener'getico, -a, -ci, -che [ener'dʒɛtiko] ag (risorse, crisi) energy cpd; (sostanza, alimento) energy-giving

ener'gia, -'gie [ener'dʒia] sf (Fisica) energy; (fig) strength, vigour; **~ eolica** wind power; **~ solare** solar energy, solar power; **e'nergico, -a, -ci, -che** [e'nɛrdʒiko] ag energetic, vigorous

'enfasi sf emphasis; (peg) bombast, pomposity

en'nesimo, -a ag (Mat, fig) nth; **per l'ennesima volta** for the umpteenth time

e'norme ag enormous, huge

'ente sm (istituzione) body, board, corporation; (Filosofia) being; **~ pubblico** public body; **~ di ricerca** research organization

en'trambi, -e pron pl both (of them) ▷ ag pl: **~ i ragazzi** both boys, both of the boys

en'trare /72/ vi to enter, go (o come) in;
~ **in** (luogo) to enter, go (o come) into; (trovar posto, poter stare) to fit into; (essere ammesso a: club ecc) to join, become a member of;
~ **in automobile** to get into the car; **far** ~ **qn** (visitatore ecc) to show sb in; **questo non c'entra** (fig) that's got nothing to do with it; **en'trata** sf entrance, entry; **dov'è l'entrata?** where's the entrance?; **entrate** sfpl (Comm) receipts, takings; (Econ) income sg

'**entro** prep (temporale) within

entusias'mare /72/ vt to excite, fill with enthusiasm; **entusiasmarsi** vpr: **entusiasmarsi (per qc/qn)** to become enthusiastic (about sth/sb); **entusi'asmo** sm enthusiasm; **entusi'asta, -i, -e** ag enthusiastic ▷ sm/f enthusiast

e'olico, -a, -chi, -che ag wind; **energia eolica** wind power

epa'tite sf hepatitis

epide'mia sf epidemic

Epifa'nia sf Epiphany

epiles'sia sf epilepsy

epi'lettico, -a, -ci, -che ag, sm/f epileptic

epi'sodio sm episode

'**epoca, -che** sf (periodo storico) age, era; (tempo) time; (Geo) age

ep'pure cong and yet, nevertheless

EPT sigla m (= Ente Provinciale per il Turismo) district tourist bureau

equa'tore sm equator

equazi'one [ekwat'tsjone] sf (Mat) equation

e'questre ag equestrian

equi'librio sm balance, equilibrium; **perdere l'~** to lose one's balance

e'quino, -a ag horse cpd, equine

equipaggia'mento [ekwipaddʒa'mento] sm (operazione: di nave) equipping, fitting out; (: di spedizione, esercito) equipping, kitting out; (attrezzatura) equipment

equipaggi'are [ekwipad'dʒare] /62/ vt (di persone) to man; (di mezzi) to equip; **equipaggiarsi** vpr to equip o.s.; **equi'paggio** sm crew

equitazi'one [ekwitat'tsjone] sf (horse-) riding

equiva'lente ag, sm equivalent

e'quivoco, -a, -ci, -che ag equivocal, ambiguous; (sospetto) dubious ▷ sm misunderstanding; **a scanso di equivoci** to avoid any misunderstanding; **giocare sull'~** to equivocate

'**equo, -a** ag fair, just

'**era** ecc vb vedi **essere**

'**erba** sf grass; **in ~** (fig) budding; **erbe aromatiche** herbs; ~ **medica** lucerne; **er'baccia, -ce** sf weed

erboriste'ria sf (scienza) study of medicinal herbs; (negozio) herbalist's (shop)

e'rede smf heir(-ess); **eredità** sf (Dir) inheritance; (Biol) heredity; **lasciare qc in eredità a qn** to leave o bequeath sth to sb; **eredi'tare** /72/ vt to inherit; **eredi'tario, -a** ag hereditary

ere'mita, -i sm hermit

er'gastolo sm (Dir: pena) life imprisonment

'**erica** sf heather

er'metico, -a, -ci, -che ag hermetic

'**ernia** sf (Med) hernia

'**ero** vb vedi **essere**

'**eroe** sm hero

ero'gare /80/ vt (somme) to distribute; (gas, servizi) to supply

e'roico, -a, -ci, -che ag heroic

ero'ina sf heroine; (droga) heroin

erosi'one sf erosion

e'rotico, -a, -ci, -che ag erotic

er'rato, -a ag wrong

er'rore sm error, mistake; (morale) error; **per ~** by mistake; **ci dev'essere un ~** there must be some mistake; ~ **giudiziario** miscarriage of justice

eruzi'one [erut'tsjone] sf eruption

esacer'bare [ezatʃer'bare] /72/ vt to exacerbate

esage'rare [ezadʒe'rare] /72/ vt to exaggerate ▷ vi to exaggerate; (eccedere) to go too far

esal'tare /72/ vt to exalt; (entusiasmare) to excite, stir

e'same sm examination; (Ins) exam, examination; **fare un ~ di coscienza** to search one's conscience; ~ **di guida** driving test; ~ **del sangue** blood test

esami'nare /72/ vt to examine

esaspe'rare /72/ vt to exasperate; (situazione) to exacerbate

esatta'mente av exactly; accurately, precisely

esat'tezza [ezat'tettsa] sf exactitude, accuracy, precision

e'satto, -a pp di **esigere** ▷ ag (calcolo, ora) correct, right, exact; (preciso) accurate, precise; (puntuale) punctual

esau'dire /55/ vt to grant, fulfil

esauri'ente ag exhaustive

esauri'mento sm exhaustion; ~ **nervoso** nervous breakdown

esau'rire /55/ vt (stancare) to exhaust, wear out; (provviste, miniera) to exhaust; **esaurirsi** vpr to exhaust o.s., wear o.s. out; (provviste) to run out; **esau'rito, -a** ag exhausted; (merci) sold out; **registrare il tutto esaurito** (Teat) to have a full house; **e'sausto, -a** ag exhausted

'**esca** (pl **esche**) sf bait

'esce ['ɛʃʃe] *vb vedi* **uscire**

eschi'mese [eski'mese] *ag, smf* Inuit

'esci ['ɛʃʃi] *vb vedi* **uscire**

escla'mare /72/ *vi* to exclaim, cry out

esclama'tivo, -a *ag*: **punto ~** exclamation mark

esclamazi'one [esklamat'tsjone] *sf* exclamation

es'cludere /3/ *vt* to exclude

es'clusi *ecc vb vedi* **escludere**

esclusi'one *sf* exclusion; **a ~ di, fatta ~ per** except (for), apart from; **senza ~ (alcuna)** without exception; **procedere per ~ to** follow a process of elimination; **senza ~ di colpi** (*fig*) with no holds barred; **~ sociale** social exclusion

esclu'siva *sf vedi* **esclusivo**

esclusiva'mente *av* exclusively, solely

esclu'sivo, -a *ag* exclusive ▷ *sf* (*Dir, Comm*) exclusive *o* sole rights *pl*

es'cluso, -a *pp di* **escludere**

'esco *vb vedi* **uscire**

escogi'tare [eskodʒi'tare] /72/ *vt* to devise, think up

'escono *vb vedi* **uscire**

escursi'one *sf* (*gita*) excursion, trip; (: *a piedi*) hike, walk; (*Meteor*): **~ termica** temperature range

esecuzi'one [ezekut'tsjone] *sf* execution, carrying out; (*Mus*) performance; **~ capitale** execution

esegu'ire /45/ *vt* to carry out, execute; (*Mus*) to perform, execute

e'sempio *sm* example; **per ~** for example, for instance; **fare un ~** to give an example; **esem'plare** *ag* exemplary ▷ *sm* example; (*copia*) copy

eserci'tare [ezertʃi'tare] /72/ *vt* (*professione*) to practise (BRIT), practice (US); (*allenare: corpo, mente*) to exercise, train; (*diritto*) to exercise; (*influenza, pressione*) to exert; **esercitarsi** *vpr* to practise; **esercitarsi nella guida** to practise one's driving

e'sercito [e'zertʃito] *sm* army

eser'cizio [ezer'tʃittsjo] *sm* practice; exercising; (*fisico: di matematica*) exercise; (*Econ*): **~ finanziario** financial year; **in ~** (*medico ecc*) practising (BRIT), practicing (US)

esi'bire /55/ *vt* to exhibit, display; (*documenti*) to produce, present; **esibirsi** *vpr* (*attore*) to perform; (*fig*) to show off; **esibizi'one** *sf* exhibition; (*di documento*) presentation; (*spettacolo*) show, performance

esi'gente [ezi'dʒɛnte] *ag* demanding

e'sigere [e'zidʒere] /47/ *vt* (*pretendere*) to demand; (*richiedere*) to demand, require; (*imposte*) to collect

'esile *ag* (*persona*) slender, slim; (*stelo*) thin; (*voce*) faint

esili'are /19/ *vt* to exile; **e'silio** *sm* exile

esis'tenza [ezis'tɛntsa] *sf* existence

e'sistere /11/ *vi* to exist

esi'tare /72/ *vi* to hesitate

'esito *sm* result, outcome

'esodo *sm* exodus

esone'rare /72/ *vt*: **~ qn da** to exempt sb from

e'sordio *sm* debut

esor'tare /72/ *vt*: **~ qn a fare** to urge sb to do

e'sotico, -a, -ci, -che *ag* exotic

es'pandere /110/ *vt* to expand; (*confini*) to extend; (*influenza*) to extend, spread; **espandersi** *vpr* to expand; **espansi'one** *sf* expansion; **espansione di memoria** (*Inform*) memory upgrade; **espan'sivo, -a** *ag* expansive, communicative

espatri'are /19/ *vi* to leave one's country

espedi'ente *sm* expedient

es'pellere /48/ *vt* to expel

esperi'enza [espe'rjɛntsa] *sf* experience

esperi'mento *sm* experiment

es'perto, -a *ag, sm/f* expert

espi'rare /72/ *vt, vi* to breathe out

es'plicito, -a [es'plitʃito] *ag* explicit

es'plodere /49/ *vi* (*anche fig*) to explode ▷ *vt* to fire

esplo'rare /72/ *vt* to explore

esplosi'one *sf* explosion

es'pone *ecc vb vedi* **esporre**

es'pongo, es'poni *ecc vb vedi* **esporre**

es'porre /77/ *vt* (*merci*) to display; (*quadro*) to exhibit, show; (*fatti, idee*) to explain, set out; (*porre in pericolo, Fot*) to expose; **esporsi** *vpr*: **esporsi a** (*sole, pericolo*) to expose o.s. to; (*critiche*) to lay o.s. open to

espor'tare /72/ *vt* to export

es'pose *ecc vb vedi* **esporre**

esposizi'one [espozit'tsjone] *sf* displaying; exhibiting; setting out; (*anche Fot*) exposure; (*mostra*) exhibition; (*narrazione*) explanation, exposition

es'posto, -a *pp di* **esporre** ▷ *ag*: **~ a nord** facing north ▷ *sm* (*Amm*) statement, account; (: *petizione*) petition

espressi'one *sf* expression

espres'sivo, -a *ag* expressive

es'presso, -a *pp di* **esprimere** ▷ *ag* express ▷ *sm* (*lettera*) express letter; (*anche*: **treno ~**) express train; (*anche*: **caffè ~**) espresso

es'primere /50/ *vt* to express; **esprimersi** *vpr* to express o.s.

es'pulsi *ecc vb vedi* **espellere**

espulsi'one *sf* expulsion

es'senza [es'sɛntsa] *sf* essence; **essenzi'ale** *ag* essential ▷ *sm*: **l'essenziale** the main *o* most important thing

⊙ **PAROLA CHIAVE**

'essere /51/ *sm* being; **essere umano** human being

▶ *vb copulativo* **1** (*con attributo, sostantivo*) to be; **sei giovane/simpatico** you are o you're young/nice; **è medico** he is o he's a doctor **2** (+ *di: appartenere*) to be; **di chi è la penna?** whose pen is it?; **è di Carla** it is o it's Carla's, it belongs to Carla

3 (+ *di: provenire*) to be; **è di Venezia** he is o he's from Venice

4 (*data, ora*): **è il 15 agosto** it is o it's the 15th of August; **è lunedì** it is o it's Monday; **che ora è?, che ore sono?** what time is it?; **è l'una** it is o it's one o'clock; **sono le due** it is o it's two o'clock

5 (*costare*): **quant'è?** how much is it?; **sono 20 euro** it's 20 euros

▶ *vb aus* **1** (*attivo*): **essere arrivato/venuto** to have arrived/come; **è già partita** she has already left

2 (*passivo*) to be; **essere fatto da** to be made by; **è stata uccisa** she has been killed **3** (*riflessivo*): **si sono lavati** they washed, they got washed

4 (+ *da* + *infinito*): **è da farsi subito** it must be done o it is to be done immediately

▶ *vi* **1** (*esistere, trovarsi*) to be; **sono a casa** I'm at home; **essere in piedi/seduto** to be standing/sitting

2: **esserci**: **c'è** there is; **ci sono** there are; **che c'è?** what's the matter?, what is it?; **ci sono!** (*ho capito*) I get it!

▶ *vb impers*: **è tardi/Pasqua** it's late/Easter; **è possibile che venga** he may come; **è così** that's the way it is

'essi *pron mpl vedi* **esso**

'esso, -a *pron* it; (*riferito a persona: soggetto*) he (she); (: *complemento*) him (her)

est *sm* east

es'tate *sf* summer

esteri'ore *ag* outward, external

es'terno, -a *ag* (*porta, muro*) outer, outside; (*scala*) outside; (*alunno, impressione*) external ▷ *sm* outside, exterior ▷ *sm/f* (*allievo*) day pupil; **esterni** *smpl* (*Cine*) location shots; "**per uso ~**" "for external use only"; **all'~** outside

'estero, -a *ag* foreign ▷ *sm*: **all'~** abroad

es'teso, -a *pp di* **estendere** ▷ *ag* extensive, large; **scrivere per ~** to write in full

es'tetico, -a, -ci, -che *ag* aesthetic ▷ *sf* (*disciplina*) aesthetics *sg*; (*bellezza*) attractiveness; **este'tista, -i, -e** *sm/f* beautician

es'tinguere /42/ *vt* to extinguish, put out; (*debito*) to pay off; **estinguersi** *vpr* to go out; (*specie*) to become extinct

es'tinsi *ecc vb vedi* **estinguere**

estin'tore *sm* (*fire*) extinguisher

estinzi'one *sf* putting out; (*di specie*) extinction

estir'pare /72/ *vt* (*pianta*) to uproot, pull up; (*fig: vizio*) to eradicate

es'tivo, -a *ag* summer *cpd*

es'torcere [es'tortʃere] /106/ *vt*: ~ **qc (a qn)** to extort sth (from sb)

estradizi'one [estradit'tsjone] *sf* extradition

es'trae, es'traggo *ecc vb vedi* **estrarre**

es'traneo, -a *ag* foreign ▷ *sm/f* stranger; **rimanere ~ a qc** to take no part in sth

es'trarre /123/ *vt* to extract; (*minerali*) to mine; (*sorteggiare*) to draw

es'trassi *ecc vb vedi* **estrarre**

estrema'mente *av* extremely

estre'mista, -i, -e *sm/f* extremist

estremità *sf inv* extremity, end ▷ *sfpl* (*Anat*) extremities

es'tremo, -a *ag* extreme; (*ultimo: ora, tentativo*) final, last ▷ *sm* extreme; (*di pazienza, forza*) limit, end; **estremi** *smpl* (*Amm: dati essenziali*) details, particulars; **l'E~ Oriente** the Far East

estro'verso, -a *ag*, *sm* extrovert

età *sf inv* age; **all'~ di 8 anni** at the age of 8, at 8 years of age; **ha la mia ~** he (o she) is the same age as me o as I am; **raggiungere la maggiore ~** to come of age; **essere in ~ minore** to be under age

'etere *sm* ether

eternità *sf* eternity

e'terno, -a *ag* eternal

etero'geneo, -a [etero'dʒɛneo] *ag* heterogeneous

eterosessu'ale *ag*, *smf* heterosexual

'etica *sf vedi* **etico**

eti'chetta [eti'ketta] *sf* label; (*cerimoniale*): **l'~** etiquette

'etico, -a, -ci, -che *ag* ethical ▷ *sf* ethics *sg*

eti'lometro *sm* Breathalyzer®

etimolo'gia, -'gie [etimolo'dʒia] *sf* etymology

Eti'opia *sf*: **l'~** Ethiopia

'etnico, -a, -ci, -che *ag* ethnic

e'trusco, -a, -schi, -sche *ag*, *sm/f* Etruscan

'ettaro *sm* hectare (10,000 m²)

'etto *abbr m* (= *ettogrammo*) 100 grams

'etto *abbr m* (= *ettogrammo*) 100 grams

'euro *sm inv* (*divisa*) euro

Eu'ropa *sf*: **l'~** Europe

europarlamen'tare *smf* Member of the European Parliament, MEP

euro'peo, -a *ag*, *sm/f* European

euta'na'sia *sf* euthanasia

evacu'are /72/ *vt* to evacuate

e'vadere /52/ *vi* (*fuggire*): ~ **da** to escape from ▷ *vt* (*sbrigare*) to deal with, dispatch; (*tasse*) to evade

evapo'rare /72/ vi to evaporate

e'vasi ecc vb vedi **evadere**

evasi'one sf (vedi evadere) escape; dispatch; ~ **fiscale** tax evasion

eva'sivo, -a ag evasive

e'vaso, -a pp di **evadere** ▷ sm escapee

e'vento sm event

eventu'ale ag possible

> Attenzione! In inglese esiste la parola *eventual*, che però significa *finale*.

eventual'mente av if necessary

> Attenzione! In inglese esiste la parola *eventually*, che però significa *alla fine*.

evi'dente ag evident, obvious

evidente'mente av evidently; (palesemente) obviously, evidently

evi'tare /72/ vt to avoid; ~ **di fare** to avoid doing; ~ **qc a qn** to spare sb sth

evoluzi'one [evolut'tsjone] sf evolution

e'volversi /94/ vpr to evolve

ev'viva escl hurrah!; ~ **il re!** long live the king!, hurrah for the king!

ex prefisso ex-, former

'extra ag inv first-rate; top-quality ▷ sm inv extra; **extracomuni'tario, -a** ag non-EU ▷ sm/f non-EU citizen (often referred to non-European immigrant)

extrater'restre ag, smf extraterrestrial

fa vb vedi **fare** ▷ sm inv (Mus) F; (: solfeggiando la scala) fa ▷ av: **10 anni fa** 10 years ago

'fabbrica sf factory; **fabbri'care** /20/ vt to build; (produrre) to manufacture, make; (fig) to fabricate, invent

> Attenzione! In inglese esiste la parola *fabric*, che però significa *stoffa*.

fac'cenda [fat'tʃɛnda] sf matter, affair; (cosa da fare) task, chore

fac'chino [fak'kino] sm porter

'faccia, -ce ['fattʃa] sf face; (di moneta, medaglia) side; ~ **a** ~ face to face

facci'ata [fat'tʃata] sf façade; (di pagina) side

fac'cina [fat'tʃina] sf (Inform) emoticon

'faccio ecc ['fattʃo] vb vedi **fare**

fa'cessi ecc [fa'tʃessi] vb vedi **fare**

fa'cevo ecc [fa'tʃevo] vb vedi **fare**

'facile ['fatʃile] ag easy; (disposto): ~ **a** inclined to, prone to; (probabile): **è ~ che piova** it's likely to rain

facoltà sf inv faculty; (autorità) power

facolta'tivo, -a ag optional; (fermata d'autobus) request cpd

'faggio ['faddʒo] sm beech

fagi'ano [fa'dʒano] sm pheasant

fagio'lino [fadʒo'lino] sm French (BRIT) o string bean

fagi'olo [fa'dʒɔlo] sm bean

'fai vb vedi **fare**

'fai-da-'te sm inv DIY, do-it-yourself

'falce ['faltʃe] sf scythe; **falci'are** /14/ vt to cut; (fig) to mow down

falcia'trice [faltʃa'tritʃe] sf (per fieno) reaping machine; (per erba) mowing machine

'falco, -chi sm hawk

'falda sf layer, stratum; (di cappello) brim; (di cappotto) tails pl; (di monte) lower slope; (di tetto) pitch

fale'gname [faleɲ'ɲame] *sm* joiner
falli'mento *sm* failure; bankruptcy
fal'lire /55/ *vi* (*Dir*) to go bankrupt; (*non riuscire*): **~ (in)** to fail (in) ▷ *vt* (*colpo, bersaglio*) to miss
'fallo *sm* error, mistake; (*imperfezione*) defect, flaw; (*Sport*) foul; fault; **senza ~** without fail
falò *sm inv* bonfire
falsifi'care /20/ *vt* to forge; (*monete*) to forge, counterfeit
'falso, -a *ag* false; (*errato*) wrong; (*falsificato*) forged; fake; (: *oro, gioielli*) imitation *cpd* ▷ *sm* forgery; **giurare il ~** to commit perjury
'fama *sf* fame; (*reputazione*) reputation, name
'fame *sf* hunger; **aver ~** to be hungry
fa'miglia [fa'miʎʎa] *sf* family
famili'are *ag* (*della famiglia*) family *cpd*; (*ben noto*) familiar; (*rapporti, atmosfera*) friendly; (*Ling*) informal, colloquial ▷ *smf* relative, relation
fa'moso, -a *ag* famous, well-known
fa'nale *sm* (*Aut*) light, lamp; (*luce stradale, Naut*) light; (*di faro*) beacon
fa'natico, -a, -ci, -che *ag* fanatical; (*del teatro, calcio ecc*): **~ di** o **per** mad o crazy about ▷ *sm/f* fanatic; (*tifoso*) fan
'fango, -ghi *sm* mud
'fanno *vb vedi* fare
fannul'lone *sm/f* idler, loafer
fantasci'enza [fantaʃʃɛntsa] *sf* science fiction
fanta'sia *sf* fantasy, imagination; (*capriccio*) whim, caprice ▷ *ag inv*: **vestito ~** patterned dress
fan'tasma, -i *sm* ghost, phantom
fan'tastico, -a, -ci, -che *ag* fantastic; (*potenza, ingegno*) imaginative
fan'tino *sm* jockey
fara'butto *sm* crook
fard *sm inv* blusher

PAROLA CHIAVE

'fare /53/ *sm* **1** (*modo di fare*): **con fare distratto** absent-mindedly; **ha un fare simpatico** he has a pleasant manner
2: **sul far del giorno/della notte** at daybreak/nightfall

▷ *vt* **1** (*fabbricare, creare*) to make; (: *casa*) to build; (: *assegno*) to make out; **fare un pasto/una promessa/un film** to make a meal/promise/a film; **fare rumore** to make a noise
2 (*effettuare: lavoro, attività, studi*) to do; (: *sport*) to play; **cosa fa?** (*adesso*) what are you doing?; (*di professione*) what do you do?; **fare psicologia/italiano** (*Ins*) to do psychology/Italian; **fare un viaggio** to go on a trip o journey; **fare una passeggiata** to go for a walk; **fare la spesa** to do the shopping
3 (*funzione*) to be; (*Teat*) to play, be; **fare il medico** to be a doctor; **fare il malato** (*fingere*) to act the invalid
4 (*suscitare: sentimenti*): **fare paura a qn** to frighten sb; **(non) fa niente** (*non importa*) it doesn't matter
5 (*ammontare*): **3 più 3 fa 6** 3 and 3 are o make 6; **fanno 6 euro** that's 6 euros; **Roma fa oltre 2.000.000 di abitanti** Rome has over 2,000,000 inhabitants; **che ora fai?** what time do you make it?
6 (+ *infinito*): **far fare qc a qn** (*obbligare*) to make sb do sth; (*permettere*) to let sb do sth; **fammi vedere** let me see; **far partire il motore** to start (up) the engine; **far riparare la macchina/costruire una casa** to get o have the car repaired/a house built
7: **farsi: farsi una gonna** to make o.s. a skirt; **farsi un nome** to make a name for o.s.; **farsi la permanente** to get a perm; **farsi tagliare i capelli** to get one's hair cut; **farsi operare** to have an operation
8 (*fraseologia*): **farcela** to succeed, manage; **non ce la faccio più** I can't go on; **ce la faremo** we'll make it; **me l'hanno fatta!** (*imbrogliare*) I've been done!; **lo facevo più giovane** I thought he was younger; **fare sì/no con la testa** to nod/shake one's head
▷ *vi* **1** (*agire*) to act, do; **fate come volete** do as you like; **fare presto** to be quick; **fare da** to act as; **non c'è niente da fare** it's no use; **saperci fare con qn/qc** to know how to deal with sb/sth; **faccia pure!** go ahead!
2 (*dire*) to say; **"davvero?" fece** "really?" he said
3: **fare per** (*essere adatto*) to be suitable for; **fare per fare qc** to be about to do sth; **fece per andarsene** he made as if to leave
4: **farsi: si fa così** you do it like this, this is the way it's done; **non si fa così!** (*rimprovero*) that's no way to behave!; **la festa non si fa** the party is off
5: **fare a gara con qn** to compete with sb; **fare a pugni** to come to blows; **fare in tempo a fare** to be in time to do
▷ *vb impers*: **fa bel tempo** the weather is fine; **fa caldo/freddo** it's hot/cold; **fa notte** it's getting dark
▷ *vpr* **1** (*diventare*) to become; **farsi prete** to become a priest; **farsi grande/vecchio** to grow tall/old
2 (*spostarsi*): **farsi avanti/indietro** to move forward/back
3 (*fam: drogarsi*) to be a junkie

far'falla sf butterfly

fa'rina sf flour

farma'cia, -'cie [farma'tʃia] sf pharmacy; (negozio) chemist's (shop) (BRIT), pharmacy; **farma'cista, -i, -e** [farma'tʃista] sm/f chemist (BRIT), pharmacist

'farmaco, -ci o **-chi** sm drug, medicine

'faro sm (Naut) lighthouse; (Aer) beacon; (Aut) headlight

'fascia, -sce ['faʃʃa] sf band, strip; (Med) bandage; (di sindaco, ufficiale) sash; (parte di territorio) strip, belt; (di contribuenti ecc) group, band; **essere in fasce** (anche fig) to be in one's infancy; **~ oraria** time band

fasci'are [faʃ'ʃare] /14/ vt to bind; (Med) to bandage

fa'scicolo [faʃ'ʃikolo] sm (di documenti) file, dossier; (di rivista) issue, number; (opuscolo) booklet, pamphlet

'fascino ['faʃʃino] sm charm, fascination

fa'scismo [faʃ'ʃizmo] sm fascism

'fase sf phase; (Tecn) stroke; **essere fuori ~** (motore) to be rough

fa'stidio sm bother, trouble; **dare ~ a qn** to bother o annoy sb; **sento ~ allo stomaco** my stomach's upset; **avere fastidi con la polizia** to have trouble o bother with the police; **fastidi'oso, -a** ag annoying, tiresome; (schifiltoso) fastidious

▎ Attenzione! In inglese esiste la parola *fastidious*, che però significa *pignolo*.

'fata sf fairy

fa'tale ag fatal; (inevitabile) inevitable; (fig) irresistible

fa'tica, -che sf hard work, toil; (sforzo) effort; (di metalli) fatigue; **a ~** with difficulty; **fare ~ a fare qc** to find it difficult to do sth; **fati'coso, -a** ag tiring, exhausting; (lavoro) laborious

'fatto, -a pp di **fare** ▷ ag: **un uomo ~** a grown man ▷ sm fact; (azione) deed; (avvenimento) event, occurrence; (di romanzo, film) action, story; **~ a mano/in casa** hand-/home-made; **cogliere qn sul ~** to catch sb red-handed; **il ~ sta** o **è che** the fact remains o is that; **in ~ di** as for, as far as … is concerned; **coppia/unione di ~** long-standing relationship

fat'tore sm (Agr) farm manager; (Mat: elemento costitutivo) factor; **~ di protezione** (di lozione solare) factor

fatto'ria sf farm; (casa) farmhouse

▎ Attenzione! In inglese esiste la parola *factory*, che però significa *fabbrica*.

fatto'rino sm errand boy; (di ufficio) office boy; (d'albergo) porter

fat'tura sf (Comm) invoice; (di abito) tailoring; (malia) spell

fattu'rato sm (Comm) turnover

'fauna sf fauna

'fava sf broad bean

'favola sf (fiaba) fairy tale; (d'intento morale) fable; (fandonia) yarn; **favo'loso, -a** ag fabulous; (incredibile) incredible

fa'vore sm favour; **per ~** please; **fare un ~ a qn** to do sb a favour; **favo'rire** /55/ vt to favour; (il commercio, l'industria, le arti) to promote, encourage; **vuole favorire?** won't you help yourself?; **favorisca in salotto** please come into the sitting room

fax sm inv fax; **mandare qc via ~** to fax sth

fazzo'letto [fattso'letto] sm handkerchief; (per la testa) (head)scarf; **~ di carta** tissue

feb'braio sm February

'febbre sf fever; **aver la ~** to have a high temperature; **~ da fieno** hay fever

'feci ecc ['fetʃi] vb vedi **fare**

fecondazi'one [fekondat'tsjone] sf fertilization; **~ artificiale** artificial insemination; **fe'condo, -a** ag fertile

fede sf (credenza) belief, faith; (Rel) faith; (fiducia) faith, trust; (fedeltà) loyalty; (anello) wedding ring; (attestato) certificate; **aver ~ in qn** to have faith in sb; **in buona/cattiva ~** in good/bad faith; **"in ~"** (Dir) "in witness whereof"; **fe'dele** ag: **fedele (a)** faithful (to) ▷ sm/f follower; (Rel) the faithful; **i fedeli** (Rel) the faithful

'federa sf pillowslip, pillowcase

fede'rale ag federal

'fegato sm liver; (fig) guts pl, nerve

'felce ['feltʃe] sf fern

fe'lice [fe'litʃe] ag happy; (fortunato) lucky; **felicità** sf happiness

felici'tarsi [felitʃi'tarsi] /72/ vpr (congratularsi): **~ con qn per qc** to congratulate sb on sth

fe'lino, -a ag, sm feline

'felpa sf sweatshirt

'femmina sf (Zool, Tecn) female; (figlia) girl, daughter; (spesso peg) woman; **femmi'nile** ag feminine; (sesso) female; (lavoro, giornale) woman's, women's; (moda) women's ▷ sm (Ling) feminine

'femore sm thighbone, femur

fe'nomeno sm phenomenon

feri'ale ag: **giorno ~** weekday

'ferie sfpl holidays (BRIT), vacation sg (US); **andare in ~** to go on holiday o vacation

fe'rire /55/ vt to injure; (deliberatamente: Mil: ecc) to wound; (colpire) to hurt; **ferirsi** vpr to hurt o.s., injure o.s.; **fe'rito, -a** sm/f wounded o injured man/woman ▷ sf injury; wound

fer'maglio [fer'maʎʎo] sm clasp; (per documenti) clip

fer'mare /72/ vt to stop, halt; (Polizia) to detain, hold ▷ vi to stop; **fermarsi** vpr to stop, halt; **fermarsi a fare qc** to stop to do sth

fer'mata sf stop; ~ **dell'autobus** bus stop

fer'menti smpl: ~ **lattici** probiotic bacteria

fer'mezza [fer'mettsa] sf (fig) firmness, steadfastness

'**fermo, -a** ag still, motionless; (veicolo) stationary; (orologio) not working; (saldo: anche fig) firm; (voce, mano) steady ▷ escl stop!; keep still! ▷ sm (chiusura) catch, lock; (Dir): ~ **di polizia** police detention

fe'roce [fe'rɔtʃe] ag (animale) fierce, ferocious; (persona) cruel, fierce; (fame, dolore) raging; **le bestie feroci** wild animals

ferra'gosto sm (festa) feast of the Assumption; (periodo) August holidays pl (BRIT) o vacation (US)

⁂ FERRAGOSTO

- Ferragosto, 15 August, is a national holiday.
- Marking the feast of the Assumption, its
- origins are religious but in recent years it
- has simply become the most important
- public holiday of the summer season.
- Most people take some extra time off
- work and head out of town to the holiday
- resorts. Consequently, most of industry
- and commerce grinds to a standstill.

ferra'menta sfpl: **negozio di ~** ironmonger's (BRIT), hardware shop o store (US)

'**ferro** sm iron; **una bistecca ai ferri** a grilled steak; ~ **battuto** wrought iron; ~ **di cavallo** horseshoe; ~ **da stiro** iron; **ferri da calza** knitting needles

ferro'via sf railway (BRIT), railroad (US); **ferrovi'ario, -a** ag railway cpd (BRIT), railroad cpd (US); **ferrovi'ere** sm railwayman (BRIT), railroad man (US)

'**fertile** ag fertile

'**fesso, -a** pp di **fendere** ▷ ag (fam: sciocco) crazy, cracked

fes'sura sf crack, split; (per gettone, moneta) slot

'**festa** sf (religiosa) feast; (pubblica) holiday; (compleanno) birthday; (onomastico) name day; (ricevimento) celebration, party; **far ~** to have a holiday; (far baldoria) to live it up; **far ~ a qn** to give sb a warm welcome

festeggi'are [fested'dʒare] /62/ vt to celebrate; (persona) to have a celebration for

fes'tivo, -a ag (atmosfera) festive; **giorno ~** holiday

'**feto** sm foetus (BRIT), fetus (US)

'**fetta** sf slice

fettuc'cine [fettut'tʃine] sfpl (Cuc) ribbon-shaped pasta

FF.SS. abbr = **Ferrovie dello Stato**

FI sigla = **Firenze** ▷ abbr (= Forza Italia) Italian centre-right political party

fi'aba sf fairy tale

fi'acca sf weariness; (svogliatezza) listlessness

fi'acco, -a, -chi, -che ag (stanco) tired, weary; (svogliato) listless; (debole) weak; (mercato) slack

fi'accola sf torch

fi'ala sf phial

fi'amma sf flame

fiam'mante ag (colore) flaming; **nuovo ~** brand new

fiam'mifero sm match

fiam'mingo, -a, -ghi, -ghe ag Flemish ▷ sm/f Fleming ▷ sm (Ling) Flemish; **i Fiamminghi** the Flemish

fi'anco, -chi sm side; (Mil) flank; **di ~** sideways, from the side; **a ~ a ~** side by side

fi'asco, -schi sm flask; (fig) fiasco; **fare ~** to fail

fia'tare /72/ vi (fig: parlare): **senza ~** without saying a word

fi'ato sm breath; (resistenza) stamina; **avere il ~ grosso** to be out of breath; **prendere ~** to catch one's breath

'**fibbia** sf buckle

'**fibra** sf fibre; (fig) constitution

fic'care /20/ vt to push, thrust, drive; **ficcarsi** vpr (andare a finire) to get to

ficcherò ecc [fikke'rɔ] vb vedi **ficcare**

'**fico, -chi** sm (pianta) fig tree; (frutto) fig; ~ **d'India** prickly pear; ~ **secco** dried fig

fiction ['fikʃon] sf inv TV drama

> Attenzione! In inglese esiste la parola *fiction*, che però significa *narrativa* oppure *finzione*.

fidanza'mento [fidantsa'mento] sm engagement

fidan'zarsi [fidan'tsarsi] /72/ vpr to get engaged; **fidan'zato, -a** sm/f fiancé (fiancée)

fi'darsi /72/ vpr: ~ **di** to trust; **fi'dato, -a** ag reliable, trustworthy

fi'ducia [fi'dutʃa] sf confidence, trust; **incarico di ~** position of trust, responsible position; **persona di ~** reliable person

fie'nile sm barn; hayloft

fi'eno sm hay

fi'era sf fair

fi'ero, -a ag proud; (audace) bold

'**fifa** sf (fam): **aver ~** to have the jitters

fig. abbr (= figura) fig

'**figlia** ['fiʎʎa] sf daughter

figli'astro, -a [fiʎ'ʎastro] sm/f stepson/daughter

'**figlio** ['fiʎʎo] sm son; (senza distinzione di sesso) child; ~ **di papà** spoilt, wealthy young man; ~ **unico** only child

figura | 66

fi'gura *sf* figure; *(forma, aspetto esterno)* form, shape; *(illustrazione)* picture, illustration; **far ~** to look smart; **fare una brutta ~** to make a bad impression

figu'rare *vi* to appear ▷ *vt:* **figurarsi qc** to imagine sth; **figurarsi** *vr:* **figurati!** imagine that!; **ti do noia?** — **ma figurati!** am I disturbing you? — not at all!

figu'rina *sf* figurine; *(cartoncino)* picture card

'fila *sf* row, line; *(coda)* queue; *(serie)* series, string; **di ~** in succession; **fare la ~** to queue; **in ~ indiana** in single file

fi'lare /72/ *vt* to spin ▷ *vi (baco, ragno)* to spin; *(formaggio fuso)* to go stringy; *(discorso)* to hang together; *(fam: amoreggiare)* to go steady; *(muoversi a forte velocità)* to go at full speed; **~ diritto** *(fig)* to toe the line; **~ via** to dash off

filas'trocca, -che *sf* nursery rhyme

filate'lia *sf* philately, stamp collecting

fi'letto *sm (di vite)* thread; *(di carne)* fillet

fili'ale *ag* filial ▷ *sf (di impresa)* branch

film *sm inv* film

'filo *sm (anche fig)* thread; *(filato)* yarn; *(metallico)* wire; *(di lama, rasoio)* edge; **con un ~ di voce** in a whisper; **per ~ e per segno** in detail; **~ d'erba** blade of grass; **~ interdentale** dental floss; **~ di perle** string of pearls; **~ spinato** barbed wire

fi'lone *sm (di minerali)* seam, vein; *(pane)* ≈ Vienna loaf; *(fig)* trend

filoso'fia *sf* philosophy; **fi'losofo, -a** *sm/f* philosopher

fil'trare /72/ *vt, vi* to filter

'filtro *sm* filter; **~ dell'olio** *(Aut)* oil filter

fi'nale *ag* final ▷ *sm (di libro, film)* end, ending; *(Mus)* finale ▷ *sf (Sport)* final; **final'mente** *av* finally, at last

fi'nanza [fi'nantsa] *sf* finance; **finanze** *sfpl (di individuo, Stato)* finances

finché [fin'ke] *cong (per tutto il tempo che)* as long as; *(fino al momento in cui)* until; **aspetta ~ io (non) sia ritornato** wait until I get back

'fine *ag (lamina, carta)* thin; *(capelli, polvere)* fine; *(vista, udito)* keen, sharp; *(persona: raffinata)* refined, distinguished; *(osservazione)* subtle ▷ *sf* end ▷ *sm* aim, purpose; *(esito)* result, outcome; **in o alla ~** in the end, finally; **secondo ~** ulterior motive

fi'nestra *sf* window; **fines'trino** *sm* window

'fingere ['findʒere] /54/ *vt* to feign; *(supporre)* to imagine, suppose; **fingersi** *vpr:* **fingersi ubriaco/pazzo** to pretend to be drunk/crazy; **~ di fare** to pretend to do

fi'nire /55/ *vt* to finish ▷ *vi* to finish, end; **~ di fare** *(compiere)* to finish doing; *(smettere)* to

stop doing; **~ in galera** to end up o finish up in prison

finlan'dese *ag* Finnish ▷ *smf* Finn ▷ *sm (Ling)* Finnish; **Fin'landia** *sf:* **la Finlandia** Finland

'fino, -a *ag (capelli, seta)* fine; *(oro)* pure; *(fig: acuto)* shrewd ▷ *av (spesso troncato in fin: pure, anche)* even ▷ *prep (spesso troncato in fin):* **fin quando?** till when?; **fin qui** as far as here; **~ a** *(tempo)* until, till; *(luogo)* as far as, (up) to; **fin da domani** from tomorrow onwards; **fin da ieri** since yesterday; **fin dalla nascita** from o since birth

fi'nocchio [fi'nɔkkjo] *sm* fennel; *(fam, peg: omosessuale)* queer (!)

fi'nora *av* up till now

'finsi *ecc vb vedi* **fingere**

'finto, -a *pp di* **fingere** ▷ *ag* false; *(fiori)* artificial ▷ *sf* pretence

finzi'one [fin'tsjone] *sf* pretence , sham

fi'occo, -chi *sm (di nastro)* bow; *(di stoffa, lana)* flock; *(di neve)* flake; *(Naut)* jib; **coi fiocchi** *(fig)* first-rate; **fiocchi di avena** oatflakes; **fiocchi di granoturco** cornflakes

fi'ocina ['fjɔtʃina] *sf* harpoon

fi'oco, -a, -chi, -che *ag* faint, dim

fi'onda *sf* catapult

fio'raio, -a *sm/f* florist

fi'ore *sm* flower; **fiori** *smpl (Carte)* clubs; **a fior d'acqua** on the surface of the water; **aver i nervi a fior di pelle** to be on edge; **fior di latte** cream; **fiori di campo** wild flowers

fioren'tino, -a *ag* Florentine

fio'retto *sm (Scherma)* foil

fio'rire /55/ *vi (rosa)* to flower; *(albero)* to blossom; *(fig)* to flourish

Fi'renze [fi'rentse] *sf* Florence

'firma *sf* signature

▌ Attenzione! In inglese esiste la parola *firm*, che però significa *ditta*.

fir'mare /72/ *vt* to sign; **un abito firmato** a designer suit

fisar'monica, -che *sf* accordion

fis'cale *ag* fiscal, tax *cpd*; **medico ~** doctor employed by Social Security to verify cases of sick leave

fischi'are [fis'kjare] /19/ *vi* to whistle ▷ *vt* to whistle; *(attore)* to boo, hiss; **fischi'etto** *sm (strumento)* whistle; **'fischio** *sm* whistle

'fisco *sm* tax authorities *pl*, ≈ Inland Revenue (BRIT), ≈ Internal Revenue Service (US)

'fisica *sf vedi* **fisico**

'fisico, -a, -ci, -che *ag* physical ▷ *sm/f* physicist ▷ *sm* physique

fisiotera'pia *sf* physiotherapy; **fisiotera'pista** *smf* physiotherapist

fis'sare /72/ *vt* to fix, fasten; *(guardare intensamente)* to stare at; *(data, condizioni)*

to fix, establish, set; (*prenotare*) to book;
fissarsi *vpr*: **fissarsi su** (*sguardo, attenzione*)
to focus on; (*fig: idea*) to become obsessed
with

'fisso, -a *ag* fixed; (*stipendio, impiego*) regular
▷ *av*: **guardare ~ qn/qc** to stare at sb/sth;
telefono ~ landline

'fitta *sf vedi* **fitto**

fit'tizio, -a *ag* fictitious, imaginary

'fitto, -a *ag* thick, dense; (*pioggia*) heavy
▷ *sm* depths *pl*, middle; (*affitto, pigione*) rent
▷ *sf* sharp pain; **una fitta al cuore** (*fig*) a
pang of grief; **nel ~ del bosco** in the heart *o*
depths of the wood

fi'ume *sm* river

fiu'tare /72/ *vt* to smell, sniff; (*animale*) to
scent; (*fig: inganno*) to get wind of, smell;
~ tabacco to take snuff; **~ cocaina** to snort
cocaine

fla'grante *ag*: **cogliere qn in ~** to catch sb
red-handed

fla'nella *sf* flannel

flash [flaʃ] *sm inv* (*Fot*) flash; (*giornalistico*)
newsflash

'flauto *sm* flute

fles'sibile *ag* pliable; (*fig: che si adatta*)
flexible

flessibili'tà *sf* (*anche fig*) flexibility

flessi'one *sf* (*gen*) bending; (*Ginnastica:
a terra*) sit-up; (: *in piedi*) forward bend;
(: *sulle gambe*) knee-bend; (*diminuzione*)
slight drop, slight fall; (*Ling*) inflection;
fare una ~ to bend; **una ~ economica** a
downward trend in the economy

'flettere /92/ *vt* to bend

'flipper *sm inv* pinball machine

F.lli *abbr* (= *fratelli*) Bros

'flora *sf* flora

'florido, -a *ag* flourishing; (*fig*) glowing with
health

'floscio, -a, -sci, -sce ['floʃʃo] *ag* (*cappello*)
floppy, soft; (*muscoli*) flabby

'flotta *sf* fleet

'fluido, -a *ag*, *sm* fluid

flu'oro *sm* fluorine

'flusso *sm* flow; (*Fisica, Med*) flux; **~ e
riflusso** ebb and flow

fluvi'ale *ag* river *cpd*, fluvial

FMI *sigla m* (= *Fondo Monetario Internazionale*)
IMF

'foca, -che *sf* (*Zool*) seal

fo'caccia, -ce [fo'kattʃa] *sf* kind of pizza;
(*dolce*) bun

'foce ['fotʃe] *sf* (*Geo*) mouth

foco'laio *sm* (*Med*) centre (BRIT) *o* center
(US) of infection; (*fig*) hotbed

foco'lare *sm* hearth, fireside; (*Tecn*) furnace

'fodera *sf* (*di vestito*) lining; (*di libro, poltrona*)
cover

'fodero *sm* (*di spada*) scabbard; (*di pugnale*)
sheath; (*di pistola*) holster

'foga *sf* enthusiasm, ardour

'foglia ['fɔʎʎa] *sf* leaf; **~ d'argento/d'oro**
silver/gold leaf

'foglio ['fɔʎʎo] *sm* (*di carta*) sheet (of paper);
(*di metallo*) sheet; **~ di calcolo** (*Inform*)
spreadsheet; **~ rosa** (*Aut*) provisional
licence; **~ di via** (*Dir*) expulsion order;
~ volante pamphlet

'fogna ['foɲɲa] *sf* drain, sewer

föhn [føːn] *sm inv* hair-dryer

folkso'nomia *sf* (*Inform*) folksonomy

'folla *sf* crowd, throng

'folle *ag* mad, insane; (*Tecn*) idle; **in ~** (*Aut*)
in neutral

fol'lia *sf* folly, foolishness; foolish act;
(*pazzia*) madness, lunacy

'folto, -a *ag* thick

fon *sm inv* = **föhn**

fondamen'tale *ag* fundamental, basic

fonda'mento *sm* foundation;
fondamenta *sfpl* (*Edil*) foundations

fon'dare /72/ *vt* to found; (*fig: dar base*):
~ qc su to base sth on

fon'dente *ag*: **cioccolato ~** plain *o* dark
chocolate

'fondere /25/ *vt* (*neve*) to melt; (*metallo*)
to fuse, melt; (*fig: colori*) to merge, blend;
(: *imprese, gruppi*) to merge ▷ *vi* to melt;
fondersi *vpr* to melt; (*fig: partiti, correnti*) to
unite, merge

'fondo, -a *ag* deep ▷ *sm* (*di recipiente,
pozzo*) bottom; (*di stanza*) back; (*quantità di
liquido che resta, deposito*) dregs *pl*; (*sfondo*)
background; (*unità immobiliare*) property,
estate; (*somma di denaro*) fund; (*Sport*)
long-distance race; **fondi** *smpl* (*denaro*)
funds; **a notte fonda** at dead of night; **in ~
a** at the bottom of; at the back of; (*strada*)
at the end of; **in ~** (*fig*) after all, all things
considered; **andare fino in ~ a** (*fig*) to
examine thoroughly; **andare a ~** (*nave*) to
sink; **conoscere a ~** to know inside out; **dar
~ a** (*provvisti, soldi*) to use up; **~ a perduto**
(*Comm*) without security; **~ comune di
investimento** investment trust; **fondi di
caffè** coffee grounds; **fondi di magazzino**
old *o* unsold stock *sg*

fondo'tinta *sm inv* (*cosmetico*) foundation

fo'netica *sf* phonetics *sg*

fon'tana *sf* fountain

'fonte *sf* spring, source; (*fig*) source ▷ *sm*:
~ battesimale (*Rel*) font; **~ energetica**
source of energy

fo'raggio [fo'raddʒo] *sm* fodder, forage

fo'rare /72/ *vt* to pierce, make a hole in;
(*pallone*) to burst; (*biglietto*) to punch; **~ una
gomma** to burst a tyre (BRIT) *o* tire (US)

'forbici ['fɔrbitʃi] *sfpl* scissors

'forca, -che *sf* (*Agr*) fork, pitchfork; (*patibolo*) gallows *sg*

for'chetta [for'ketta] *sf* fork

for'cina [for'tʃina] *sf* hairpin

fo'resta *sf* forest

foresti'ero, -a *ag* foreign ▷ *sm/f* foreigner

'forfora *sf* dandruff

'forma *sf* form; (*aspetto esteriore*) form, shape; (*Dir: procedura*) procedure; (*per calzature*) last; (*stampo da cucina*) mould; **mantenersi in ~** to keep fit

formag'gino [formad'dʒino] *sm* processed cheese

for'maggio [for'maddʒo] *sm* cheese

for'male *ag* formal

for'mare /72/ *vt* to form, shape, make; (*numero di telefono*) to dial; (*fig: carattere*) to form, mould; **formarsi** *vpr* to form, take shape; **for'mato** *sm* format, size; **formazi'one** *sf* formation; (*fig: educazione*) training; **formazione continua** continuing education; **formazione permanente** lifelong learning; **formazione professionale** vocational training

for'mica¹, -che *sf* ant

formica²® ['fɔrmika] *sf* (*materiale*) Formica®

formi'dabile *ag* powerful, formidable; (*straordinario*) remarkable

'formula *sf* formula; **~ di cortesia** (*nelle lettere*) letter ending

formu'lare /72/ *vt* to formulate; to express

for'naio *sm* baker

for'nello *sm* (*elettrico, a gas*) ring; (*di pipa*) bowl

for'nire /55/ *vt*: **~ qn di qc, ~ qc a qn** to provide *o* supply sb with sth, supply sth to sb

'forno *sm* (*di cucina*) oven; (*panetteria*) bakery; (*Tecn: per calce ecc*) kiln; (: *per metalli*) furnace; **~ a microonde** microwave oven

'foro *sm* (*buco*) hole; (*Storia*) forum; (*tribunale*) (law) court

'forse *av* perhaps, maybe; (*circa*) about; **essere in ~** to be in doubt

'forte *ag* strong; (*suono*) loud; (*spesa*) considerable, great; (*passione, dolore*) great, deep ▷ *av* strongly; (*velocemente*) fast; (*a voce alta*) loud(ly); (*violentemente*) hard ▷ *sm* (*edificio*) fort; (*specialità*) forte, strong point; **essere ~ in qc** to be good at sth

for'tezza [for'tettsa] *sf* (*morale*) strength; (*luogo fortificato*) fortress

for'tuito, -a *ag* fortuitous, chance *cpd*

for'tuna *sf* (*destino*) fortune, luck; (*buona sorte*) success, fortune; (*eredità, averi*) fortune; **per ~** luckily, fortunately; **di ~** makeshift, improvised; **atterraggio di ~** emergency landing; **fortu'nato, -a** *ag* lucky, fortunate; (*coronato da successo*) successful

'forza ['fɔrtsa] *sf* strength; (*potere*) power; (*Fisica*) force ▷ *escl* come on!; **forze** *sfpl* (*fisiche*) strength *sg*; (*Mil*) forces; **per ~** against one's will; (*naturalmente*) of course; **a viva ~** by force; **a ~ di** by dint of; **per causa di ~ maggiore** due to circumstances beyond one's control; **la ~ pubblica** the police *pl*; **forze dell'ordine** the forces of law and order; **~ di pace** peacekeeping force; **le forze armate** the armed forces; **F~ Italia** *moderate right-wing party*

for'zare [for'tsare] /72/ *vt* to force; **~ qn a fare** to force sb to do

for'zista, -i, -e [for'tsista] *ag* of Forza Italia ▷ *sm/f* member (*o* supporter) of Forza Italia

fos'chia [fos'kia] *sf* mist, haze

'fosco, -a, -schi, -sche *ag* dark, gloomy

'fosforo *sm* phosphorous

'fossa *sf* pit; (*di cimitero*) grave; **~ biologica** septic tank

fos'sato *sm* ditch; (*di fortezza*) moat

fos'setta *sf* dimple

'fossi *ecc vb vedi* **essere**

'fossile *ag, sm* fossil (*cpd*)

'fosso *sm* ditch; (*Mil*) trench

'foste *ecc vb vedi* **essere**

'foto *sf inv* photo ▷ *prefisso*: **~ ricordo** souvenir photo; **~ tessera** passport(-type) photo; **foto'camera** *sf*: **fotocamera digitale** digital camera; **foto'copia** *sf* photocopy; **fotocopi'are** /19/ *vt* to photocopy; **fotoco'pia'trice** [fotokopja'tritʃe] *sf* photocopier; **fotofo'nino** *sm* camera phone; **fotogra'fare** /72/ *vt* to photograph; **fotogra'fia** *sf* (*procedimento*) photography; (*immagine*) photograph; **fare una fotografia** to take a photograph; **una fotografia a colori/in bianco e nero** a colour/black and white photograph; **foto'grafico, -a, -ci, -che** *ag* photographic; **macchina fotografica** camera; **fo'tografo, -a** *sm/f* photographer; **fotoro'manzo** *sm* romantic picture story; **fotovol'taico, -a, -ci, -che** *ag* photovoltaic; **pannelli fotovoltaici** solar panels

fou'lard [fu'lar] *sm inv* scarf

fra *prep* = **tra**

'fradicio, -a, -ci, -ce ['fraditʃo] *ag* (*molto bagnato*) soaking (wet); **ubriaco ~** blind drunk

'fragile ['fradʒile] *ag* fragile; (*fig: salute*) delicate

'fragola *sf* strawberry

fra'grante *ag* fragrant

frain'tendere /120/ *vt* to misunderstand

fram'mento sm fragment

'frana sf landslide; (fig: persona): **essere una ~** to be useless

fran'cese [fran'tʃeze] ag French ▷ smf Frenchman/woman ▷ sm (Ling) French; **i Francesi** the French

'Francia ['frantʃa] sf: **la ~** France

'franco, -a, -chi, -che ag (Comm) free; (sincero) frank, open, sincere ▷ sm (moneta) franc; **farla franca** (fig) to get off scot-free; **~ di dogana** duty-free; **prezzo ~ fabbrica** ex-works price

franco'bollo sm (postage) stamp

'frangia, -ge ['frandʒa] sf fringe

frappé sm milk shake

'frase sf (Ling) sentence; (locuzione, espressione, Mus) phrase; **~ fatta** set phrase

'frassino sm ash (tree)

frastagli'ato, -a [frastaʎ'ʎato] ag (costa) indented, jagged

frastor'nare /72/ vt to daze; (confondere) to bewilder

frastu'ono sm hubbub, din

'frate sm friar, monk

fratel'lastro sm stepbrother; (con genitore in comune) half brother

fra'tello sm brother; **fratelli** smpl brothers; (nel senso di fratelli e sorelle) brothers and sisters

fra'terno, -a ag fraternal, brotherly

frat'tempo sm: **nel ~** in the meantime, meanwhile

frat'tura sf fracture; (fig) split, break

frazi'one [frat'tsjone] sf fraction; (anche: **~ di comune**) hamlet

'freccia, -ce ['frettʃa] sf arrow; **~ di direzione** (Aut) indicator

fred'dezza [fred'dettsa] sf coldness

'freddo, -a ag, sm cold; **fa ~** it's cold; **aver ~** to be cold; **a ~** (fig) deliberately; **freddo'loso, -a** ag sensitive to the cold

fre'gare /80/ vt to rub; (fam: truffare) to take in, cheat; (: rubare) to swipe, pinch; **fregarsene** (fam!): **chi se ne frega?** who gives a damn (about it)?

fregherò ecc [frege'rɔ] vb vedi **fregare**

fre'nare /72/ vt (veicolo) to slow down; (cavallo) to rein in; (lacrime) to restrain, hold back ▷ vi to brake; **frenarsi** vpr (fig) to restrain o.s., control o.s.

'freno sm brake; (morso) bit; **tenere a ~** to restrain; **~ a disco** disc brake; **~ a mano** handbrake

frequen'tare /72/ vt (scuola, corso) to attend; (locale, bar) to go to, frequent; (persone) to see (often); **frequen'tato, -a** ag (locale) busy; **fre'quente** ag frequent; **di frequente** frequently

fres'chezza [fres'kettsa] sf freshness;

'fresco, -a, -schi, -sche ag fresh; (temperatura) cool; (notizia) recent, fresh ▷ sm: **godere il fresco** to enjoy the cool air; **stare fresco** (fig) to be in for it; **mettere al fresco** to put in a cool place

'fretta sf hurry, haste; **in ~** in a hurry; **in ~ e furia** in a mad rush; **aver ~** to be in a hurry

'friggere ['friddʒere] /56/ vt to fry ▷ vi (olio ecc) to sizzle

'frigido, -a ['fridʒido] ag (Med) frigid

'frigo, -ghi sm fridge

frigo'bar sm inv minibar

frigo'rifero, -a ag refrigerating ▷ sm refrigerator

fringu'ello sm chaffinch

'frissi ecc vb vedi **friggere**

frit'tata sf omelet(te); **fare una ~** (fig) to make a mess of things

frit'tella sf (Cuc) fritter

'fritto, -a pp di **friggere** ▷ ag fried ▷ sm fried food; **~ misto** mixed fry

frit'tura sf: **~ di pesce** mixed fried fish

'frivolo, -a ag frivolous

frizi'one [frit'tsjone] sf friction; (di pelle) rub, rub-down; (Aut) clutch

friz'zante [frid'dzante] ag (anche fig) sparkling

fro'dare /72/ vt to defraud, cheat

'frode sf fraud; **~ fiscale** tax evasion

'fronda sf (leafy) branch; (di partito politico) internal opposition; **fronde** sfpl (di albero) foliage sg

fron'tale ag frontal; (scontro) head-on

'fronte sf (Anat) forehead; (di edificio) front, façade ▷ sm (Mil, Pol, Meteor) front; **a ~, di ~** facing, opposite; **di ~ a** (posizione) opposite, facing, in front of; (a paragone di) compared with

fronti'era sf border, frontier

'frottola sf fib

fru'gare /80/ vi to rummage ▷ vt to search

frugherò ecc [fruge'rɔ] vb vedi **frugare**

frul'lare /72/ vt (Cuc) to whisk ▷ vi (uccelli) to flutter; **frul'lato** sm milk shake; fruit drink; **frulla'tore** sm electric mixer

fru'mento sm wheat

fru'scio [fruʃ'ʃio] sm rustle; rustling; (di acque) murmur

'frusta sf whip; (Cuc) whisk

frus'tare /72/ vt to whip

frus'trato, -a ag frustrated

'frutta sf fruit; (portata) dessert; **~ candita/ secca** candied/dried fruit

frut'tare /72/ vi to bear dividends, give a return

frut'teto sm orchard

frutti'vendolo, -a sm/f greengrocer (BRIT), produce dealer (US)

'frutto sm fruit; (fig: risultato) result(s); (Econ: interesse) interest; (: reddito) income; **frutti di mare** seafood sg; **frutti di bosco** berries

FS abbr (= Ferrovie dello Stato) Italian railways

fu vb vedi **essere** ▷ ag inv: **il fu Paolo Bianchi** the late Paolo Bianchi

fuci'lare [futʃi'lare] /72/ vt to shoot

fu'cile [fu'tʃile] sm rifle, gun; (da caccia) shotgun, gun

'fucsia sf fuchsia

'fuga, -ghe sf escape, flight; (di gas, liquidi) leak; (Mus) fugue; **~ di cervelli** brain drain

fug'gire [fud'dʒire] /31/ vi to flee, run away; (fig: passar veloce) to fly ▷ vt to avoid

'fui vb vedi **essere**

fu'liggine [fu'liddʒine] sf soot

'fulmine sm bolt of lightning; **fulmini** smpl lightning sg

fu'mare /72/ vi to smoke; (emettere vapore) to steam ▷ vt to smoke; **fuma'tore, -'trice** sm/f smoker

fu'metto sm comic strip; **giornale a fumetti** comic

'fummo vb vedi **essere**

'fumo sm smoke; (vapore) steam; (il fumare tabacco) smoking; **fumi** smpl (industriali ecc) fumes; **vendere ~** to deceive, cheat; **i fumi dell'alcool** the after-effects of drink; **~ passivo** passive smoking; **fu'moso, -a** ag smoky; (fig) muddled

'fune sf rope, cord; (più grossa) cable

'funebre ag (rito) funeral; (aspetto) gloomy, funereal

fune'rale sm funeral

'fungere ['fundʒere] /5/ vi: **~ da** to act as

'fungo, -ghi sm fungus; (commestibile) mushroom; **~ velenoso** toadstool

funico'lare sf funicular railway

funi'via sf cable railway

'funsi ecc vb vedi **fungere**

funzio'nare [funtsjo'nare] /72/ vi to work, function; (fungere): **~ da** to act as

funzio'nario [funtsjo'narjo] sm official; **~ statale** civil servant

funzi'one [fun'tsjone] sf function; (carica) post, position; (Rel) service; **in ~** (meccanismo) in operation; **in ~ di** (come) as; **fare la ~ di qn** (farne le veci) to take sb's place

fu'oco, -chi sm fire; (fornello) ring; (Fot, Fisica) focus; **dare ~ a qc** to set fire to sth; **far ~** (sparare) to fire; **al ~!** fire!; **~ d'artificio** firework

fuorché [fwor'ke] cong, prep except

fu'ori av outside; (all'aperto) outdoors, outside; (fuori di casa, Sport) out; (esclamativo) get out! ▷ prep: **~ (di)** out of, outside ▷ sm outside; **lasciar ~ qc/qn** to leave sth/sb out; **far ~ qn** (fam) to kill sb, do

sb in; **essere ~ di sé** to be beside oneself; **~ luogo** (inopportuno) out of place, uncalled for; **~ mano** out of the way, remote; **~ pericolo** out of danger; **~ uso** old-fashioned; obsolete; **fuorigi'oco** sm offside; **fuoris'trada** sm (Aut) cross-country vehicle

'furbo, -a ag clever, smart; (peg) cunning

fu'rente ag: **~ (contro)** furious (with)

fur'fante sm rascal; scoundrel

fur'gone sm van

'furia sf (ira) fury, rage; (fig: impeto) fury, violence; (: fretta) rush; **a ~ di** by dint of; **andare su tutte le furie** to fly into a rage; **furi'bondo, -a** ag furious

furi'oso, -a ag furious

'furono vb vedi **essere**

fur'tivo, -a ag furtive

'furto sm theft; **~ con scasso** burglary

'fusa sfpl: **fare le ~** to purr

fu'seaux smpl leggings

'fusi ecc vb vedi **fondere**

fu'sibile sm (Elettr) fuse

fusi'one sf (di metalli) fusion, melting; (colata) casting; (Comm) merger; (fig) merging

'fuso, -a pp di **fondere** ▷ sm (Filatura) spindle; **~ orario** time zone

fus'tino sm (di detersivo) tub

'fusto sm stem; (Anat, di albero) trunk; (recipiente) drum, can

fu'turo, -a ag, sm future

g

G8 [dʒi'ɔtto] *sm* (= *Gruppo degli Otto*) G8

G2o [dʒi'venti] *sm* (= *Gruppo dei Venti*) G2o

'gabbia *sf* cage; (*da imballaggio*) crate; **~ dell'ascensore** lift (BRIT) o elevator (US) shaft; **~ toracica** (*Anat*) rib cage

gabbi'ano *sm* (sea)gull

gabi'netto *sm* (*Med: ecc*) consulting room; (*Pol*) ministry; (*di decenza*) toilet, lavatory; (*Ins: di fisica ecc*) laboratory

gaffe [gaf] *sf inv* blunder, boob

ga'lante *ag* gallant, courteous; (*avventura, poesia*) amorous

ga'lassia *sf* galaxy

ga'lera *sf* (*Naut*) galley; (*prigione*) prison

'galla *sf*: **a ~** afloat; **venire a ~** to surface, come to the surface; (*fig: verità*) to come out

galleggi'are [galled'dʒare] /62/ *vi* to float

galle'ria *sf* (*traforo*) tunnel; (*Archit, d'arte*) gallery; (*Teat*) circle; (*strada coperta con negozi*) arcade

'Galles *sm*: **il ~** Wales; **gal'lese** *ag* Welsh ▷ *smf* Welshman/woman ▷ *sm* (*Ling*) Welsh; **i Gallesi** the Welsh

gal'lina *sf* hen

'gallo *sm* cock

galop'pare /72/ *vi* to gallop

ga'loppo *sm* gallop; **al** o **di ~** at a gallop

'gamba *sf* leg; (*asta: di lettera*) stem; **in ~** (*in buona salute*) well; (*bravo, sveglio*) bright, smart; **prendere qc sotto ~** (*fig*) to treat sth too lightly

gambe'retto *sm* shrimp

'gambero *sm* (*di acqua dolce*) crayfish; (*di mare*) prawn

'gambo *sm* stem; (*di frutta*) stalk

'gamma *sf* (*Mus*) scale; (*di colori, fig*) range

'gancio ['gantʃo] *sm* hook

'gara *sf* competition; (*Sport*) competition; contest; match; (: *corsa*) race; **fare a ~ to** compete, vie

ga'rage [ga'raʒ] *sm inv* garage

garan'tire /55/ *vt* to guarantee; (*debito*) to stand surety for; (*dare per certo*) to assure

garan'zia [garan'tsia] *sf* guarantee; (*pegno*) security

gar'bato, -a *ag* courteous, polite

gareggi'are [gared'dʒare] /62/ *vi* to compete

garga'rismo *sm* gargle; **fare i gargarismi** to gargle

ga'rofano *sm* carnation; **chiodo di ~** clove

'garza ['gardza] *sf* (*per bende*) gauze

gar'zone [gar'dzone] *sm* (*di negozio*) boy

gas *sm inv* gas; **a tutto ~** at full speed; **dare ~** (*Aut*) to accelerate

ga'solio *sm* diesel (oil)

ga's(s)ato, -a *ag* fizzy

gast'rite *sf* gastritis

gastrono'mia *sf* gastronomy

gatta *sf* cat, she-cat

gat'tino *sm* kitten

gatto *sm* cat, tomcat; **~ delle nevi** (*Aut, Sci*) snowcat; **~ selvatico** wildcat

gazza ['gaddza] *sf* magpie

gel [dʒɛl] *sm inv* gel

ge'lare [dʒe'lare] /72/ *vt, vi, vb impers* to freeze

gelate'ria [dʒelate'ria] *sf* ice-cream shop

gela'tina [dʒela'tina] *sf* gelatine; **~ esplosiva** gelignite; **~ di frutta** fruit jelly

ge'lato, -a [dʒe'lato] *ag* frozen ▷ *sm* ice cream

'gelido, -a ['dʒɛlido] *ag* icy, ice-cold

'gelo ['dʒɛlo] *sm* (*temperatura*) intense cold; (*brina*) frost; (*fig*) chill

gelo'sia [dʒelo'sia] *sf* jealousy

ge'loso, -a [dʒe'loso] *ag* jealous

'gelso ['dʒɛlso] *sm* mulberry (tree)

gelso'mino [dʒelso'mino] *sm* jasmine

ge'mello, -a [dʒe'mɛllo] *ag, sm/f* twin; **gemelli** *smpl* (*di camicia*) cufflinks; **Gemelli** Gemini *sg*

'gemere ['dʒɛmere] /29/ *vi* to moan, groan; (*cigolare*) to creak

'gemma ['dʒɛmma] *sf* (*Bot*) bud; (*pietra preziosa*) gem

gene'rale [dʒene'rale] *ag, sm* general; **in ~** (*per sommi capi*) in general terms; (*di solito*) usually, in general

gene'rare [dʒene'rare] /72/ *vt* (*dar vita*) to give birth to; (*produrre*) to produce; (*causare*) to arouse; (*Tecn*) to produce, generate; **generazi'one** *sf* generation

'genere ['dʒɛnere] *sm* kind, type, sort; (*Biol*) genus; (*merce*) article, product; (*Ling*) gender; (*Arte, Letteratura*) genre; **in ~** generally, as a rule; **il ~ umano** mankind; **generi alimentari** foodstuffs

ge'nerico, -a, -ci, -che [dʒe'nɛriko] *ag* generic; (*vago*) vague, imprecise

'genero ['dʒɛnero] *sm* son-in-law

gene'roso, -a [dʒene'roso] *ag* generous

ge'netico, -a, -ci, -che [dʒe'nɛtiko] *ag* genetic ▷ *sf* genetics *sg*

gen'giva [dʒen'dʒiva] *sf* (Anat) gum

geni'ale [dʒe'njale] *ag* (persona) of genius; (idea) ingenious, brilliant

'genio ['dʒɛnjo] *sm* genius; **andare a ~ a qn** to be to sb's liking, appeal to sb

geni'tore [dʒeni'tore] *sm* parent, father o mother; **genitori** *smpl* parents

gen'naio [dʒen'najo] *sm* January

ge'noma [dʒe'nɔma] *sm* genome

'Genova ['dʒɛnova] *sf* Genoa

'gente ['dʒɛnte] *sf* people *pl*

gen'tile [dʒen'tile] *ag* (persona, atto) kind; (: garbato) courteous, polite; (nelle lettere): **G~ Signore** Dear Sir; **G~ Signor Fernando Villa** (sulla busta) Mr Fernando Villa

genu'ino, -a [dʒenu'ino] *ag* (prodotto) natural; (persona, sentimento) genuine, sincere

geogra'fia [dʒeogra'fia] *sf* geography

geolo'gia [dʒeolo'dʒia] *sf* geology

ge'ometra, -i, -e [dʒe'ɔmetra] *smf* (professionista) surveyor

geome'tria [dʒeome'tria] *sf* geometry

ge'ranio [dʒe'ranjo] *sm* geranium

gerar'chia [dʒerar'kia] *sf* hierarchy

'gergo, -ghi ['dʒɛrgo] *sm* jargon; slang

geria'tria [dʒerja'tria] *sf* geriatrics *sg*

Ger'mania [dʒer'manja] *sf*: **la ~** Germany; **la ~ occidentale/orientale** West/East Germany

'germe ['dʒɛrme] *sm* germ; (fig) seed

germogli'are [dʒermoʎ'ʎare] /27/ *vi* to sprout; (germinare) to germinate

gero'glifico, -ci [dʒero'glifiko] *sm* hieroglyphic

ge'rundio [dʒe'rundjo] *sm* gerund

'gesso ['dʒɛsso] *sm* chalk; (Scultura, Med, Edil) plaster; (statua) plaster figure; (minerale) gypsum

gesti'one [dʒes'tjone] *sf* management

ges'tire [dʒes'tire] /55/ *vt* to run, manage

'gesto ['dʒɛsto] *sm* gesture

Gesù [dʒe'zu] *sm* Jesus

gesu'ita, -i [dʒezu'ita] *sm* Jesuit

get'tare [dʒet'tare] /72/ *vt* to throw; (anche: **~ via**) to throw away o out; (Scultura) to cast; (Edil) to lay; (acqua) to spout; (grido) to utter; **gettarsi** *vpr*: **gettarsi in** (fiume) to flow into; **~ uno sguardo su** to take a quick look at

'getto ['dʒɛtto] *sm* (di gas, liquido, Aer) jet; **a ~ continuo** uninterruptedly; **di ~** (fig) straight off, in one go

get'tone [dʒet'tone] *sm* token; (per giochi) counter; (: roulette ecc) chip; **~ telefonico** telephone token

ghiacci'aio [gjat'tʃajo] *sm* glacier

ghiacci'ato, -a *ag* frozen; (bevanda) ice-cold

ghi'accio ['gjattʃo] *sm* ice

ghiacci'olo [gjat'tʃɔlo] *sm* icicle; (tipo di gelato) ice lolly (BRIT), popsicle (US)

ghi'aia ['gjaja] *sf* gravel

ghi'anda ['gjanda] *sf* (Bot) acorn

ghi'andola ['gjandola] *sf* gland

ghi'otto, -a ['gjotto] *ag* greedy; (cibo) delicious, appetizing

ghir'landa [gir'landa] *sf* garland, wreath

'ghiro ['giro] *sm* dormouse

'ghisa ['giza] *sf* cast iron

già [dʒa] *av* already; (ex, in precedenza) formerly ▷ *escl* of course!, yes indeed!

gi'acca, -che ['dʒakka] *sf* jacket; **~ a vento** windcheater (BRIT), windbreaker (US)

giacché [dʒak'ke] *cong* since, as

giac'cone [dʒak'kone] *sm* heavy jacket

gia'cere [dʒa'tʃere] /57/ *vi* to lie

gi'ada ['dʒada] *sf* jade

giagu'aro [dʒa'gwaro] *sm* jaguar

gi'allo [dʒ'allo] *ag* yellow; (carnagione) sallow ▷ *sm* yellow; (anche: **romanzo ~**) detective novel; (anche: **film ~**) detective film; **~ dell'uovo** yolk

Gia'maica [dʒa'maika] *sf*: **la ~** Jamaica

Giap'pone [dʒap'pone] *sm*: **il ~** Japan; **giappo'nese** *ag, smf, sm* Japanese *inv*

giardi'naggio [dʒardi'naddʒo] *sm* gardening

giardini'ere, -a [dʒardi'njɛre] *sm/f* gardener

giar'dino [dʒar'dino] *sm* garden; **~ d'infanzia** nursery school; **~ pubblico** public gardens *pl*, (public) park; **~ zoologico** zoo

giavel'lotto [dʒavel'lotto] *sm* javelin

giga *sm inv* (Inform) gig

giga'byte [dʒiga'bait] *sm inv* gigabyte

gi'gante, -'essa [dʒi'gante] *sm/f* giant ▷ *ag* giant, gigantic; (Comm) giant-size

'giglio ['dʒiʎʎo] *sm* lily

gilè [dʒi'lɛ] *sm inv* waistcoat

gin [dʒin] *sm inv* gin

gine'cologo, -a, -gi, -ghe [dʒine'kɔlogo] *sm/f* gynaecologist

gi'nepro [dʒi'nepro] *sm* juniper

gi'nestra [dʒi'nɛstra] *sf* (Bot) broom

Gi'nevra [dʒi'nevra] *sf* Geneva

gin'nastica [dʒin'nastika] *sf* gymnastics *sg*; (esercizio fisico) keep-fit exercises *pl*; (Ins) physical education

gi'nocchio [dʒi'nɔkkjo] (*pl f* **ginocchia**) *sm* knee; **stare in ~** to kneel, be on one's knees; **mettersi in ~** to kneel (down)

gio'care [dʒo'kare] /20/ *vt* to play; (scommettere) to stake, wager, bet; (ingannare) to take in ▷ *vi* to play; (a roulette *ecc*) to gamble; (*fig*) to play a part, be important; **~ a** (*gioco*, *sport*) to play; (*cavalli*) to bet on; **~ carsi la carriera** to put one's career at risk; **gioca'tore, -'trice** *sm/f* player; gambler

gio'cattolo [dʒo'kattolo] *sm* toy

giocherò *ecc* [dʒoke'rɔ] *vb vedi* **giocare**

gioco, -chi ['dʒɔko] *sm* game; (*divertimento*, *Tecn*) play; (*al casinò*) gambling; (*Carte*) hand; (*insieme di pezzi ecc necessari per un gioco*) set; **per ~** for fun; **fare il doppio ~ con qn** to double-cross sb; **~ d'azzardo** game of chance; **~ degli scacchi** chess set; **i Giochi Olimpici** the Olympic Games®

giocoli'ere [dʒoko'ljɛre] *sm* juggler

gi'oia ['dʒɔja] *sf* joy, delight; (*pietra preziosa*) jewel, precious stone

gioielle'ria [dʒojelle'ria] *sf* jeweller's (BRIT) *o* jeweler's (US) craft; (*negozio*) jewel(l)er's (shop)

gioiell'ere, -a [dʒojel'ljɛre] *sm/f* jeweller

gioi'ello [dʒo'jɛllo] *sm* jewel, piece of jewellery (BRIT) *o* jewelry (US); **gioielli** *smpl* (*anelli*, *collane ecc*) jewellery *sg*; **i miei gioielli** my jewels *o* jewellery; **i gioielli della Corona** the crown jewels

Gior'dania [dʒor'danja] *sf*: **la ~** Jordan

giorna'laio, -a [dʒorna'lajo] *sm/f* newsagent (BRIT), newsdealer (US)

gior'nale [dʒor'nale] *sm* (news)paper; (*diario*) journal, diary; (*Comm*) journal; **~ di bordo** (*Naut*) ship's log; **~ radio** radio news *sg*

giornali'ero, -a [dʒorna'ljɛro] *ag* daily; (*che varia*: *umore*) changeable ▷ *sm* day labourer (BRIT) *o* laborer (US)

giorna'lismo [dʒorna'lizmo] *sm* journalism

giorna'lista, -i, -e [dʒorna'lista] *smf* journalist

gior'nata [dʒor'nata] *sf* day; **~ lavorativa** working day

gi'orno ['dʒorno] *sm* day; (*opposto alla notte*) day, daytime; (*luce del giorno*) daylight; **al ~** per day; **di ~** by day; **al ~ d'oggi** nowadays

gi'ostra ['dʒɔstra] *sf* (*per bimbi*) merry-go-round; (*torneo storico*) joust

gi'ovane ['dʒovane] *ag* young; (*aspetto*) youthful ▷ *sm* youth, young man ▷ *sf* girl, young woman; **i giovani** young people

gio'vare [dʒo'vare] /72/ *vi*: **~ a** (*essere utile*) to be useful to; (*far bene*) to be good for ▷ *vb impers* (*essere bene*, *utile*) to be useful; **giovarsi** *vpr*: **giovarsi di qc** to make use of sth

giovedì [dʒove'di] *sm inv* Thursday; **di** *o* **il ~** on Thursdays

gioventù [dʒoven'tu] *sf* (*periodo*) youth; (*i giovani*) young people *pl*, youth

gip [dʒip] *sigla m inv* (= giudice per le indagini preliminari) judge for preliminary enquiries

gira'dischi [dʒira'diski] *sm inv* record player

gi'raffa [dʒi'raffa] *sf* giraffe

gi'rare [dʒi'rare] /72/ *vt* (*far ruotare*) to turn; (*percorrere*, *visitare*) to go round; (*Cine*) to shoot; (: *come regista*) to make; (*Comm*) to endorse ▷ *vi* to turn; (*più veloce*) to spin; (*andare in giro*) to wander, go around; **girarsi** *vpr* to turn; **~ attorno a** to go round; to revolve round; **far ~ la testa a qn** to make sb dizzy; (*fig*) to turn sb's head

girar'rosto [dʒirar'rɔsto] *sm* (*Cuc*) spit

gira'sole [dʒira'sole] *sm* sunflower

gi'revole [dʒi'revole] *ag* revolving, turning

gi'rino [dʒi'rino] *sm* tadpole

'giro ['dʒiro] *sm* (*circuito*, *cerchio*) circle; (*di chiave*, *manovella*) turn; (*viaggio*) tour, excursion; (*passeggiata*) stroll, walk; (*in macchina*) drive; (*in bicicletta*) ride; (*Sport*: *della pista*) lap; (*di denaro*) circulation; (*Carte*) hand; (*Tecn*) revolution; **fare un ~** to go for a walk (*o* a drive *o* a ride); **andare in ~** to go about, walk around; **prendere in ~** (*fig*) to take sb for a ride; **a stretto ~ di posta** by return of post; **nel ~ di un mese** in a month's time; **essere nel ~** (*fig*) to belong to a circle (of friends); **~ d'affari** (*Comm*) turnover; **~ di parole** circumlocution; **~ di prova** (*Aut*) test drive; **~ turistico** sightseeing tour; **giro'collo** *sm*: **a girocollo** crewneck *cpd*

gironzo'lare [dʒirondzo'lare] /72/ *vi* to stroll about

'gita ['dʒita] *sf* excursion, trip; **fare una ~** to go for a trip, go on an outing

gi'tano, -a [dʒi'tano] *sm/f* gipsy

giù [dʒu] *av* down; (*dabbasso*) downstairs; **in ~** downwards; down; **~ di lì** (*pressappoco*) thereabouts; **bambini dai 6 anni in ~** children aged 6 and under; **~ per**: **cadere ~ per le scale** to fall down the stairs; **essere ~** (*fig*: *di salute*) to be run down; (: *di spirito*) to be depressed

giub'botto [dʒub'bɔtto] *sm* jerkin; **~ antiproiettile** bulletproof vest; **~ salvagente** life jacket

giudi'care [dʒudi'kare] /20/ *vt* to judge; (*accusato*) to try; (*lite*) to arbitrate in; **~ qn/ qc bello** to consider sb/sth (to be) beautiful

gi'udice ['dʒuditʃe] *sm* judge; **~ conciliatore** justice of the peace; **~ istruttore** examining (BRIT) *o* committing (US) magistrate; **~ popolare** member of a jury

giu'dizio [dʒu'dittsjo] *sm* judgment; (*opinione*) opinion; (*Dir*) judgment, sentence; (: *processo*) trial; (: *verdetto*) verdict; **aver ~** to be wise o prudent; **citare in ~** to summons

gi'ugno ['dʒuɲɲo] *sm* June

gi'ungere ['dʒundʒere] /5/ *vi* to arrive ▷ *vt* (*mani ecc*) to join; **~ a** to arrive at, reach

gi'ungla ['dʒungla] *sf* jungle

gi'unsi *ecc* ['dʒunsi] *vb vedi* **giungere**

giura'mento [dʒura'mento] *sm* oath; **~ falso** perjury

giu'rare [dʒu'rare] /72/ *vt* to swear ▷ *vi* to swear, take an oath

giu'ria [dʒu'ria] *sf* jury

giu'ridico, -a, -ci, -che [dʒu'ridiko] *ag* legal

giustifi'care [dʒustifi'kare] /20/ *vt* to justify; **giustificazi'one** *sf* justification; (*Ins*) (note of) excuse

gius'tizia [dʒus'tittsja] *sf* justice; **giustizi'are** /19/ *vt* to execute, put to death

gi'usto, -a ['dʒusto] *ag* (*equo*) fair, just; (*vero*) true, correct; (*adatto*) right, suitable; (*preciso*) exact, correct ▷ *av* (*esattamente*) exactly, precisely; (*per l'appunto, appena*) just; **arrivare ~** to arrive just in time; **ho ~ bisogno di te** you're just the person I need

glaci'ale [gla'tʃale] *ag* glacial

gli [ʎi] *det mpl* (*dav V, s impura, gn, pn, ps, x, z*) the ▷ *pron* (*a lui*) to him; (*a esso*) to it; (*in coppia con lo, la, li, le, ne, a lui, a lei, a loro ecc*): **~ele do** I'm giving them to him (o her o them); *vedi anche* **il**

glo'bale *ag* overall

'globo *sm* globe

'globulo *sm* (*Anat*): **~ rosso/bianco** red/white corpuscle

glocalizzazi'one [glokaliddza'tsjone] *sf* glocalization

'gloria *sf* glory

'gnocchi ['ɲɔkki] *smpl* (*Cuc*) small dumplings *made of semolina pasta or potato*

'gobba *sf* (*Anat*) hump; (*protuberanza*) bump

'gobbo, -a *ag* hunchbacked; (*ricurvo*) round-shouldered ▷ *sm/f* hunchback

'goccia, -ce ['gottʃa] *sf* drop; **goccio'lare** /72/ *vi, vt* to drip

go'dere /58/ *vi*: **~ (di)** (*compiacersi*) to be delighted (at), rejoice (at); **~ di** (*trarre vantaggio*) to benefit from ▷ *vt* to enjoy; **godersi la vita** to enjoy life; **godersela** to have a good time, enjoy o.s.

godrò *ecc vb vedi* **godere**

'goffo, -a *ag* clumsy, awkward

gol [gɔl] *sm inv* (*Sport*); = **goal**

'gola *sf* (*Anat*) throat; (*golosità*) gluttony, greed; (*di camino*) flue; (*di monte*) gorge; **fare ~** (*anche fig*) to tempt

golf *sm inv* (*Sport*) golf; (*maglia*) cardigan

'golfo *sm* gulf

go'loso, -a *ag* greedy

gomi'tata *sf*: **dare una ~ a qn** to elbow sb; **farsi avanti a (forza o furia di) gomitate** to elbow one's way through; **fare a gomitate per qc** to fight to get sth

'gomito *sm* elbow; (*di strada ecc*) sharp bend

go'mitolo *sm* ball

'gomma *sf* rubber; (*per cancellare*) rubber, eraser; (*di veicolo*) tyre (BRIT), tire (US); **~ da masticare** chewing gum; **~ a terra** flat tyre; **gom'mone** *sm* rubber dinghy

gonfi'are /19/ *vt* (*pallone*) to blow up, inflate; (*dilatare, ingrossare*) to swell; (*fig: notizia*) to exaggerate; **gonfiarsi** *vpr* to swell; (*fiume*) to rise; **'gonfio, -a** *ag* swollen; (*stomaco*) bloated; (*vela*) full; **gonfi'ore** *sm* swelling

'gonna *sf* skirt; **~ pantalone** culottes *pl*

goo'glare [gu'glare] /72/ *vt* (*Inform*) to google

'gorgo, -ghi *sm* whirlpool

gorgogli'are [gorgoʎ'ʎare] /27/ *vi* to gurgle

go'rilla *sm inv* gorilla; (*guardia del corpo*) bodyguard

'gotico, -a, -ci, -che *ag, sm* Gothic

'gotta *sf* gout

gover'nare /72/ *vt* (*stato*) to govern, rule; (*pilotare, guidare*) to steer; (*bestiame*) to tend, look after

go'verno *sm* government

GPL [dʒipi'ɛlle] *sigla m* (= *Gas di Petrolio Liquefatto*) LPG

GPS [dʒipi'ɛsse] *sigla m* GPS

graci'dare [gratʃi'dare] /72/ *vi* to croak

'gracile ['gratʃile] *ag* frail, delicate

gradazi'one [gradat'tsjone] *sf* (*sfumatura*) gradation; **~ alcolica** alcoholic content, strength

gra'devole *ag* pleasant, agreeable

gradi'nata *sf* flight of steps; (*in teatro, stadio*) tiers *pl*

gra'dino *sm* step; (*Alpinismo*) foothold

gra'dire /55/ *vt* (*accettare con piacere*) to accept; (*desiderare*) to wish, like; **gradisce una tazza di tè?** would you like a cup of tea?

'grado *sm* (*Mat, Fisica: ecc*) degree; (*stadio*) degree, level; (*Mil, sociale*) rank; **essere in ~ di fare** to be in a position to do

gradu'ale *ag* gradual

graf'fetta *sf* paper clip

graffi'are /19/ *vt* to scratch; **graffiarsi** *vpr* to get scratched; (*con unghie*) to scratch o.s.

'graffio *sm* scratch

gra'fia *sf* spelling; (*scrittura*) handwriting

'grafico, -a, -ci, -che *ag* graphic ▷ *sm* graph; (*persona*) graphic designer

gram'matica, -che *sf* grammar

'grammo *sm* gram(me)

'grana *sf* (*granello, di minerali, corpi spezzati*) grain; (*fam: seccatura*) trouble; (: *soldi*) cash ▷ *sm inv* cheese similar to Parmesan

gra'naio sm granary, barn

gra'nata sf (proiettile) grenade

Gran Bre'tagna [granbre'taɲɲa] sf: la ~ Great Britain

'granchio ['grankjo] sm crab; (fig) blunder; **prendere un ~** (fig) to blunder

'grande (qualche volta **gran** + C, **grand'** + V) ag (grosso, largo, vasto) big, large; (alto) tall; (lungo) long; (in sensi astratti) great ▷ smf (persona adulta) adult, grown-up; (chi ha ingegno e potenza) great man/woman; **fare le cose in ~** to do things in style; **una gran bella donna** a very beautiful woman; **non è una gran cosa** o **un gran che** it's nothing special; **non ne so gran che** I don't know very much about it

gran'dezza [gran'dettsa] sf (dimensione) size; magnitude; (fig) greatness; **in ~ naturale** lifesize

grandi'nare /72/ vb impers to hail

'grandine sf hail

gra'nello sm (di cereali, uva) seed; (di frutta) pip; (di sabbia, sale ecc) grain

gra'nito sm granite

'grano sm (in quasi tutti i sensi) grain; (frumento) wheat; (di rosario, collana) bead; **~ di pepe** peppercorn

gran'turco sm maize

'grappa sf rough, strong brandy

'grappolo sm bunch, cluster

gras'setto sm (Tip) bold (type)

'grasso, -a ag fat; (cibo) fatty; (pelle) greasy; (terreno) rich; (fig: guadagno, annata) plentiful ▷ sm (di persona, animale) fat; (sostanza che unge) grease

'grata sf grating

gra'ticola sf grill

'gratis av free, for nothing

grati'tudine sf gratitude

'grato, -a ag grateful; (gradito) pleasant, agreeable

gratta'capo sm worry, headache

grattaci'elo [gratta'tʃɛlo] sm skyscraper

gratta e 'sosta sm inv scratch card used to pay for parking

gratta e 'vinci [grattae'vintʃi] sm (lotteria) lottery; (biglietto) scratchcard

grat'tare /72/ vt (pelle) to scratch; (raschiare) to scrape; (pane, formaggio, carote) to grate; (fam: rubare) to pinch ▷ vi (stridere) to grate; (Aut) to grind; **grattarsi** vpr to scratch o.s.; **grattarsi la pancia** (fig) to twiddle one's thumbs

grat'tugia [grat'tudʒa], **-gie** sf grater; **grattugi'are** /62/ vt to grate; **pane grattugiato** breadcrumbs pl

gra'tuito, -a ag free; (fig) gratuitous

'grave ag (danno, pericolo, peccato ecc) grave, serious; (responsabilità) heavy, grave; (contegno) grave, solemn; (voce, suono) deep, low-pitched; (Ling): **accento ~** grave accent; **un malato ~** a person who is seriously ill

grave'mente av (ammalato, ferito) seriously

gravi'danza [gravi'dantsa] sf pregnancy

gravità sf seriousness; (anche Fisica) gravity

gra'voso, -a ag heavy, onerous

'grazia ['grattsja] sf grace; (favore) favour; (Dir) pardon

'grazie ['grattsje] escl thank you!; **~ mille!** o **tante!** o **infinite!** thank you very much!; **~ a** thanks to

grazi'oso, -a [grat'tsjoso] ag charming, delightful; (gentile) gracious

'Grecia ['grɛtʃa] sf: **la ~** Greece; **'greco, -a, -ci, -che** ag, sm/f, sm Greek

'gregge ['greddʒe] (pl **greggi**) sm flock

'greggio, -a, -gi, -ge ['greddʒo] ag raw, unrefined; (diamante) rough, uncut; (tessuto) unbleached

grembi'ule sm apron; (sopravveste) overall

'grembo sm lap; (ventre della madre) womb

'grezzo, -a ['greddzo] ag = **greggio**

gri'dare /72/ vi (per chiamare) to shout, cry (out); (strillare) to scream, yell ▷ vt to shout (out), yell (out); **~ aiuto** to cry o shout for help

'grido (pl f **grida**) sm shout, cry; scream, yell; (pl m **gridi**: di animale) cry; **di ~** famous

'grigio, -a, -gi, -gie ['gridʒo] ag, sm grey

'griglia ['griʎʎa] sf (per arrostire) grill; (Elettr) grid; (inferriata) grating; **alla ~** (Cuc) grilled

gril'letto sm trigger

'grillo sm (Zool) cricket; (fig) whim

'grinta sf grim expression; (Sport) fighting spirit

gris'sino sm bread-stick

Groen'landia sf: **la ~** Greenland

gron'daia sf gutter

gron'dare /72/ vi to pour; (essere bagnato): **~ di** to be dripping with ▷ vt to drip with

'groppa sf (di animale) back, rump; (fam: dell'uomo) back, shoulders pl

gros'sezza [gros'settsa] sf size; thickness

gros'sista, -i, -e smf (Comm) wholesaler

'grosso, -a ag big, large; (di spessore) thick; (grossolano: anche fig) coarse; (grave, insopportabile) serious, great; (tempo, mare) rough ▷ sm: **il ~ di** the bulk of; **un pezzo ~** (fig) a VIP, a bigwig; **farla grossa** to do something very stupid; **dirle grosse** to tell tall stories (BRIT) o tales (US); **sbagliarsi di ~** to be completely wrong

'grotta sf cave; grotto

grot'tesco, -a, -schi, -sche ag grotesque

gro'viglio [gro'viʎʎo] sm tangle; (fig) muddle

gru sf inv crane

'gruccia, -ce ['gruttʃa] sf (per camminare) crutch; (per abiti) coat-hanger

'grumo sm (di sangue) clot; (di farina ecc) lump

'gruppo sm group; **~ sanguigno** blood group

GSM sigla m (= Global System for Mobile Communication) GSM

guada'gnare [gwadaɲ'ɲare] /15/ vt (ottenere) to gain; (soldi, stipendio) to earn; (vincere) to win; (raggiungere) to reach

gua'dagno [gwa'daɲɲo] sm earnings pl; (Comm) profit; (vantaggio, utile) advantage, gain; **~ lordo/netto** gross/net earnings pl

gu'ado sm ford; **passare a ~** to ford

gu'ai escl: **~ a te** (o lui ecc) **!** woe betide you (o him ecc)!

gu'aio sm trouble, mishap; (inconveniente) trouble, snag

gua'ire /55/ vi to whine, yelp

gu'ancia, -ce ['gwantʃa] sf cheek

guanci'ale [gwan'tʃale] sm pillow

gu'anto sm glove

guarda'linee sm inv (Sport) linesman

guar'dare /72/ vt (con lo sguardo: osservare) to look at; (: film, televisione) to watch; (custodire) to look after, take care of ▷ vi to look; (badare): **~ a** to pay attention to; (luoghi: esser orientato): **~ a** to face; **guardarsi** vpr to look at o.s.; **guardarsi da** (astenersi) to refrain from; (stare in guardia) to beware of; **guardarsi dal fare** to take care not to do; **guarda di non sbagliare** try not to make a mistake; **~ a vista qn** to keep a close watch on sb

guarda'roba sm inv wardrobe; (locale) cloakroom

gu'ardia sf (individuo, corpo) guard; (sorveglianza) watch; **fare la ~ a qc/qn** to guard sth/sb; **stare in ~** (fig) to be on one's guard; **il medico di ~** the doctor on call; **~ carceraria** (prison) warder (BRIT) o guard (US); **~ del corpo** bodyguard; **~ di finanza** (corpo) customs pl; (persona) customs officer; **~ medica** emergency doctor service

guardi'ano, -a sm/f (di carcere) warder; (di villa ecc) caretaker; (di museo) custodian; (di zoo) keeper; **~ notturno** night watchman

guarigi'one [gwari'dʒone] sf recovery

gua'rire /55/ vt (persona, malattia) to cure; (ferita) to heal ▷ vi to recover, be cured; to heal (up)

guar'nire /55/ vt (ornare: abiti) to trim; (Cuc) to garnish

guasta'feste smf inv spoilsport

guas'tare /72/ vt to spoil; **guastarsi** vpr (cibo) to go bad; (meccanismo) to break down; (tempo) to change for the worse

gu'asto, -a ag (non funzionante) broken; (: telefono ecc) out of order; (andato a male) bad, rotten; (: dente) decayed, bad; (fig: corrotto) depraved ▷ sm breakdown; (avaria) failure; **~ al motore** engine failure

gu'erra sf war; (tecnica: atomica, chimica ecc) warfare; **fare la ~ (a)** to wage war (against); **~ mondiale** world war; **~ preventiva** preventive war

'gufo sm owl

gu'ida sf (persona) guide; (libro) guide(book); (comando, direzione) guidance, direction; (Aut) driving; (tappeto: di tenda, cassetto) runner; **~ a destra/sinistra** (Aut) right-/left-hand drive; **~ telefonica** telephone directory; **~ turistica** tourist guide

gui'dare /72/ vt to guide; (squadra, rivolta) to lead; (auto) to drive; (aereo, nave) to pilot; **sa ~?** can you drive?; **guida'tore, -'trice** sm/f (conducente) driver

guin'zaglio [gwin'tsaʎʎo] sm leash, lead

'guscio ['guʃʃo] sm shell

gus'tare /72/ vt (cibi) to taste; (: assaporare con piacere) to enjoy, savour; (fig) to enjoy, appreciate ▷ vi: **~ a** to please; **non mi gusta affatto** I don't like it at all

'gusto sm taste; (sapore) taste, flavour (BRIT), flavor (US); (godimento) enjoyment; **al ~ di fragola** strawberry-flavoured; **mangiare di ~** to eat heartily; **prenderci ~: ci ha preso ~** he's acquired a taste for it, he's got to like it; **gus'toso, -a** ag tasty; (fig) agreeable

H, h ['akka] *sf o m inv (lettera)* H, h ▷ *abbr* (= *ora*) hr; (= *etto, altezza*) h; **H come hotel** ≈ H for Harry (BRIT), H for How (US)
ha, hai [a, ai] *vb vedi* **avere**
ha'cker ['haker] *sm inv* hacker
hall [hɔːl] *sf inv* hall, foyer
ham'burger [am'burger] *sm inv (carne)* hamburger; (*panino*) burger
'handicap ['handikap] *sm inv* handicap; **handicap'pato, -a** *ag* disabled, handicapped (!) ▷ *sm/f* disabled person
'hanno ['anno] *vb vedi* **avere**
hard dis'count [ardis'kaunt] *sm inv* discount supermarket
hard 'disk [ar'disk] *sm inv* hard disk
'hardware ['ardwer] *sm inv* hardware
ha'scisc, hascisch [aʃʃiʃ] *sm inv* hashish
'hashtag ['aʃteg] *sm inv (su Twitter)* hashtag
Ha'waii [a'vai] *sfpl*: **le ~** Hawaii *sg*
help [ɛlp] *sm inv (Inform)* help
'herpes ['ɛrpes] *sm (Med)* herpes *sg*; **~ zoster** shingles *sg*
'hi-fi ['haifai] *sm inv, ag inv* hi-fi
ho [ɔ] *vb vedi* **avere**
'hobby ['hɔbi] *sm inv* hobby
'hockey ['hɔki] *sm* hockey; **~ su ghiaccio** ice hockey
'home page ['houm'pɛidʒ] *sf inv* home page
'Hong Kong ['ɔkɔg] *sf* Hong Kong
'hostess ['houstis] *sf inv* air hostess (BRIT) *o* stewardess
'hot dog ['hɔtdɔg] *sm inv* hot dog
ho'tel *sm inv* hotel
'humour ['jumor] *sm inv (sense of)* humour
'humus *sm* humus
'husky ['aski] *sm inv (cane)* husky

i *det mpl* the
'ibrido, -a *ag, sm* hybrid
IC *abbr* (= *Intercity*) Intercity
'ICI ['itʃi] *sigla f* (= *Imposta Comunale sugli Immobili*) ≈ Council Tax
i'cona *sf (Rel, Inform, fig)* icon
i'dea *sf* idea; (*opinione*) opinion, view; (*ideale*) ideal; **dare l'~ di** to seem, look like; **neanche** *o* **neppure per ~!** certainly not!; **~ fissa** obsession
ide'ale *ag, sm* ideal
ide'are /72/ *vt (immaginare)* to think up, conceive; (*progettare*) to plan
i'dentico, -a, -ci, -che *ag* identical
identifi'care /20/ *vt* to identify; **identificarsi** *vpr*: **identificarsi (con)** to identify o.s. (with)
identità *sf inv* identity
ideolo'gia, -'gie [ideolo'dʒia] *sf* ideology
idio'matico, -a, -ci, -che *ag* idiomatic; **frase idiomatica** idiom
idi'ota, -i, -e *ag* idiotic ▷ *sm/f* idiot
'idolo *sm* idol
idoneità *sf* suitability
i'doneo, -a *ag*: **~ a** suitable for, fit for; (*Mil*) fit for; (*qualificato*) qualified for
i'drante *sm* hydrant
idra'tante *ag* moisturizing ▷ *sm* moisturizer
i'draulico, -a, -ci, -che *ag* hydraulic ▷ *sm* plumber
idroe'lettrico, -a, -ci, -che *ag* hydroelectric
i'drofilo, -a *ag*: **cotone ~** cotton wool (BRIT), absorbent cotton (US)
i'drogeno [i'drɔdʒeno] *sm* hydrogen
idrovo'lante *sm* seaplane
i'ena *sf* hyena
i'eri *av, sm* yesterday; **il giornale di ~** yesterday's paper; **l'altro** the day before yesterday; **~ sera** yesterday evening

igi'ene [i'dʒɛne] *sf* hygiene; ~ **pubblica** public health; **igi'enico, -a, -ci, -che** *ag* hygienic; (*salubre*) healthy

i'gnaro, -a [iɲ'ɲaro] *ag*: ~ **di** unaware of, ignorant of

i'gnobile [iɲ'ɲɔbile] *ag* despicable, vile

igno'rante [iɲɲo'rante] *ag* ignorant

igno'rare [iɲɲo'rare] /72/ *vt* (*non sapere, conoscere*) to be ignorant o unaware of, not to know; (*fingere di non vedere, sentire*) to ignore

i'gnoto, -a [iɲ'ɲɔto] *ag* unknown

 PAROLA CHIAVE

il (*pl(m)* **i**; *diventa* **lo** (*pl* **gli**) *davanti a s impura, gn, pn, ps, x, z;* **f** *la* (*pl* **le**)) *det m* **1** the; **il libro/lo studente/l'acqua** the book/the student/the water; **gli scolari** the pupils
2 (*astrazione*): **il coraggio/l'amore/la giovinezza** courage/love/youth
3 (*tempo*): **il mattino/la sera** in the morning/evening; **il venerdì** (*abitualmente*) on Fridays; (*quel giorno*) on (the) Friday; **la settimana prossima** next week
4 (*distributivo*) a, an; **2 euro il chilo/paio** 2 euros a o per kilo/pair
5 (*partitivo*) some, any; **hai messo lo zucchero?** have you added sugar?; **hai comprato il latte?** did you buy (some o any) milk?
6 (*possesso*): **aprire gli occhi** to open one's eyes; **rompersi la gamba** to break one's leg; **avere i capelli neri/il naso rosso** to have dark hair/a red nose
7 (*con nomi propri*): **il Petrarca** Petrarch; **il Presidente Bush** President Bush; **dov'è la Francesca?** where's Francesca?
8 (*con nomi geografici*): **il Tevere** the Tiber; **l'Italia** Italy; **il Regno Unito** the United Kingdom; **l'Everest** Everest

ille'gale *ag* illegal
illeg'gibile [illed'dʒibile] *ag* illegible
ille'gittimo, -a [ille'dʒittimo] *ag* illegitimate
il'leso, -a *ag* unhurt, unharmed
illimi'tato, -a *ag* boundless; unlimited
ill.mo *abbr* = **illustrissimo**
il'ludere /35/ *vt* to deceive, delude; **illudersi** *vpr* to deceive o.s., delude o.s.
illumi'nare /72/ *vt* to light up, illuminate; (*fig*) to enlighten; **illuminarsi** *vpr* to light up; ~ **a giorno** to floodlight; **illuminazi'one** *sf* lighting; illumination; floodlighting; (*fig*) flash of inspiration
il'lusi *ecc vb vedi* **illudere**
illusi'one *sf* illusion; **farsi delle illusioni** to delude o.s.; ~ **ottica** optical illusion

il'luso, -a *pp di* **illudere**
illus'trare /72/ *vt* to illustrate; **illustrazi'one** *sf* illustration
il'lustre *ag* eminent, renowned; **illus'trissimo, -a** *ag* (*negli indirizzi*) very revered
i'mam [i'mam] *sm inv* imam
imbal'laggio [imbal'laddʒo] *sm* packing *no pl*
imbal'lare /72/ *vt* to pack; (*Aut*) to race
imbalsa'mare /72/ *vt* to embalm
imbambo'lato, -a *ag* (*sguardo, espressione*) vacant, blank
imbaraz'zante [imbarat'tsante] *ag* embarrassing, awkward
imbaraz'zare [imbarat'tsare] /72/ *vt* (*mettere a disagio*) to embarrass; (*ostacolare: movimenti*) to hamper
imbaraz'zato, -a [imbarat'tsato] *ag* embarrassed; **avere lo stomaco ~** to have an upset stomach
imba'razzo [imba'rattso] *sm* (*disagio*) embarrassment; (*perplessità*) puzzlement, bewilderment; ~ **di stomaco** indigestion
imbar'care /20/ *vt* (*passeggeri*) to embark; (*merci*) to load; **imbarcarsi** *vpr*: **imbarcarsi su** to board; **imbarcarsi per l'America** to sail for America; **imbarcarsi in** (*fig: affare*) to embark on
imbarcazi'one [imbarkat'tsjone] *sf* (*small*) boat, (*small*) craft *inv*; ~ **di salvataggio** lifeboat
im'barco, -chi *sm* embarkation; loading; boarding; (*banchina*) landing stage
imbas'tire /55/ *vt* (*cucire*) to tack; (*fig: abbozzare*) to sketch, outline
imbat'tersi /72/ *vpr*: ~ **in** (*incontrare*) to bump o run into
imbat'tibile *ag* unbeatable, invincible
imbavagli'are [imbavaʎ'ʎare] /27/ *vt* to gag
imbe'cille [imbe'tʃille] *ag* idiotic ▷ *smf* idiot; (*Med*) imbecile
imbian'care /20/ *vt* to whiten; (*muro*) to whitewash ▷ *vi* to become o turn white
imbian'chino [imbjan'kino] *sm* (*house*) painter, painter and decorator
imboc'care /20/ *vt* (*bambino*) to feed; (*entrare: strada*) to enter, turn into
imbocca'tura *sf* mouth; (*di strada, porto*) entrance; (*Mus, del morso*) mouthpiece
imbos'cata *sf* ambush
imbottigli'are [imbottiʎ'ʎare] /27/ *vt* to bottle; (*Naut*) to blockade; (*Mil*) to hem in; **imbottigliarsi** *vpr* to be stuck in a traffic jam
imbot'tire /55/ *vt* to stuff; (*giacca*) to pad; **imbottirsi** *vpr* (*rimpinzarsi*): **imbottirsi di**

to stuff o.s. with; **imbot'tito, -a** *ag* stuffed; *(giacca)* padded; **panino imbottito** filled roll

imbra'nato, -a *ag* clumsy, awkward ▷ *sm/f* clumsy person

imbrogli'are [imbroʎ'ʎare] /27/ *vt* to mix up; *(fig: raggirare)* to deceive, cheat; *(: confondere)* to confuse, mix up; **imbrogli'one, -a** *sm/f* cheat, swindler

imbronci'ato, -a *ag* sulky

imbu'care /20/ *vt* to post

imbur'rare /72/ *vt* to butter

im'buto *sm* funnel

imi'tare /72/ *vt* to imitate; *(riprodurre)* to copy; *(assomigliare)* to look like

immagazzi'nare [immagaddzi'nare] /72/ *vt* to store

immagi'nare [immadʒi'nare] /72/ *vt* to imagine; *(supporre)* to suppose; *(inventare)* to invent; **s'immagini!** don't mention it!, not at all!; **immaginazi'one** *sf* imagination; *(cosa immaginata)* fancy

im'magine [im'madʒine] *sf* image; *(rappresentazione grafica, mentale)* picture

imman'cabile *ag* certain; unfailing

im'mane *ag* *(smisurato)* huge; *(spaventoso, inumano)* terrible

immangi'abile [imman'dʒabile] *ag* inedible

immatrico'lare /72/ *vt* to register; **immatricolarsi** *vpr* (*Ins*) to matriculate, enrol

imma'turo, -a *ag* *(frutto)* unripe; *(persona)* immature; *(prematuro)* premature

immedesi'marsi /72/ *vpr*: **~ in** to identify with

immediata'mente *av* immediately, at once

immedi'ato, -a *ag* immediate

im'menso, -a *ag* immense

im'mergere [im'mɛrdʒere] /59/ *vt* to immerse, plunge; **immergersi** *vpr* to plunge; *(sommergibile)* to dive, submerge; *(dedicarsi a)*: **immergersi in** to immerse o.s. in

immeri'tato, -a *ag* undeserved

immersi'one *sf* immersion; *(di sommergibile)* submersion, dive; *(di palombaro)* dive

im'mettere /63/ *vt*: **~ (in)** to introduce (into); **~ dati in un computer** to enter data on a computer

immi'grato, -a *sm/f* immigrant

immi'nente *ag* imminent

immischi'are [immis'kjare] /19/ *vt*: **~ qn in** to involve sb in; **immischiarsi** *vpr*: **immischiarsi in** to interfere o meddle in

im'mobile *ag* motionless, still; **immobili'are** *ag* *(Dir)* property *cpd*

immon'dizia [immon'dittsja] *sf* dirt, filth; *(spesso al pl: spazzatura, rifiuti)* rubbish *no pl*, refuse *no pl*

immo'rale *ag* immoral

immor'tale *ag* immortal

im'mune *ag* *(esente)* exempt; *(Med, Dir)* immune

immu'tabile *ag* immutable; unchanging

impacchet'tare [impakket'tare] /72/ *vt* to pack up

impacci'ato, -a *ag* awkward, clumsy; *(imbarazzato)* embarrassed

im'pacco, -chi *sm* *(Med)* compress

impadro'nirsi /55/ *vpr*: **~ di** to seize, take possession of; *(fig: apprendere a fondo)* to master

impa'gabile *ag* priceless

impa'lato, -a *ag* *(fig)* stiff as a board

impalca'tura *sf* scaffolding

impalli'dire /55/ *vi* to turn pale; *(fig)* to fade

impa'nato, -a *ag* *(Cuc)* coated in breadcrumbs

impanta'narsi /72/ *vpr* to sink (in the mud); *(fig)* to get bogged down

impappi'narsi /72/ *vpr* to stammer, falter

impa'rare /72/ *vt* to learn

impar'tire /55/ *vt* to bestow, give

imparzi'ale [impar'tsjale] *ag* impartial, unbiased

impas'sibile *ag* impassive

impas'tare /72/ *vt* *(pasta)* to knead

impastic'carsi /20/ *vpr* to pop pills

im'pasto *sm* *(l'impastare: di pane)* kneading; *(: di cemento)* mixing; *(pasta)* dough; *(anche fig)* mixture

im'patto *sm* impact

impau'rire /55/ *vt* to scare, frighten ▷ *vi* *(anche:* **impaurirsi***)* to become scared o frightened

impazi'ente [impat'tsjente] *ag* impatient

impaz'zata [impat'tsata] *sf*: **all'~** *(precipitosamente)* at breakneck speed

impaz'zire [impat'tsire] /55/ *vi* to go mad; **~ per qn/qc** to be crazy about sb/sth

impec'cabile *ag* impeccable

impedi'mento *sm* obstacle, hindrance

impe'dire /55/ *vt* *(vietare)*: **~ a qn di fare** to prevent sb from doing; *(ostruire)* to obstruct; *(impacciare)* to hamper, hinder

impe'gnare [impeɲ'ɲare] /15/ *vt* *(obbligare)* to oblige; **impegnarsi** *vpr* *(vincolarsi)*: **impegnarsi a fare** to undertake to do; *(mettersi risolutamente)*: **impegnarsi in qc** to devote o.s. to sth; **impegnarsi con qn** *(accordarsi)* to come to an agreement with sb

impegna'tivo, -a *ag* binding; *(lavoro)* demanding, exacting

impe'gnato, -a ag (occupato) busy; (fig: romanzo, autore) committed, engagé

im'pegno [im'peɲɲo] sm (obbligo) obligation; (promessa) promise, pledge; (zelo) diligence, zeal; (compito: d'autore) commitment

impel'lente ag pressing, urgent

impen'narsi /72/ vpr (cavallo) to rear up; (Aer) to go into a climb; (fig) to bridle

impensie'rire /55/ vt to worry; **impensierirsi** vpr to worry

impera'tivo, -a ag, sm imperative

impera'tore, -'trice sm/f emperor (empress)

imperdo'nabile ag unforgivable, unpardonable

imper'fetto, -a ag imperfect ▷ sm (Ling) imperfect (tense)

imperi'ale ag imperial

imperi'oso, -a ag (persona) imperious; (motivo, esigenza) urgent, pressing

imperme'abile ag waterproof ▷ sm raincoat

im'pero sm empire; (forza, autorità) rule, control

imperso'nale ag impersonal

imperso'nare /72/ vt to personify; (Teat) to play, act (the part of)

imper'territo, -a ag unperturbed, undaunted; impassive

imperti'nente ag impertinent

'impeto sm (moto, forza) force, impetus; (assalto) onslaught; (fig: impulso) impulse; (: slancio) transport; **con ~** energetically; vehemently

impet'tito, -a ag stiff, erect

impetu'oso, -a ag (vento) strong, raging; (persona) impetuous

impi'anto sm (installazione) installation; (apparecchiature) plant; (sistema) system; **~ elettrico** wiring; **~ di riscaldamento** heating system; **~ sportivo** sports complex; **impianti di risalita** (Sci) ski lifts

impic'care /20/ vt to hang; **impiccarsi** vpr to hang o.s.

impicci'are [impit'tʃare] /14/ vt to hinder; **impicciarsi** vpr (immischiarsi): **impicciarsi (in)** to meddle (in), interfere (in); **impicciati degli affari tuoi!** mind your own business!

impicci'one, -a [impit'tʃone] sm/f busybody

impie'gare /80/ vt (usare) to use, employ; (spendere: denaro, tempo) to spend; (investire) to invest; **impie'gato, -a** sm/f employee

impi'ego, -ghi sm (uso) use; (occupazione) employment; (posto di lavoro) (regular) job, post; (Econ) investment

impieto'sire /55/ vt to move to pity; **impietosirsi** vpr to be moved to pity

impigli'are [impiʎ'ʎare] /27/ vt to catch; **impigliarsi** vpr to get caught up o entangle

impi'grire /55/ vt to make lazy ▷ vi (anche: **impigrirsi**) to grow lazy

impli'care /20/ vt to imply; (coinvolgere) to involve; **implicarsi** vpr: **implicarsi (in)** to become involved (in)

im'plicito, -a [im'plitʃito] ag implicit

implo'rare /72/ vt to implore; (pietà ecc) to beg for

impolve'rare /72/ vt to cover with dust; **impolverarsi** vpr to get dusty

im'pone ecc vb vedi **imporre**

impo'nente ag imposing, impressive

im'pongo ecc vb vedi **imporre**

impo'nibile ag taxable ▷ sm taxable income

impopo'lare ag unpopular

im'porre /77/ vt to impose; (costringere) to force, make; (far valere) to impose, enforce; **imporsi** vpr (persona) to assert o.s.; (cosa: rendersi necessario) to become necessary; (aver successo: moda, attore) to become popular; **~ a qn di fare** to force sb to do, make sb do

impor'tante ag important; **impor'tanza** sf importance; **dare importanza a qc** to attach importance to sth; **darsi importanza** to give o.s. airs

impor'tare /72/ vt (introdurre dall'estero) to import ▷ vi to matter, be important ▷ vb impers (essere necessario) to be necessary; (interessare) to matter; **non importa!** it doesn't matter!; **non me ne importa!** I don't care!

im'porto sm (total) amount

importu'nare /72/ vt to bother

im'posi ecc vb vedi **imporre**

imposizi'one [impozit'tsjone] sf imposition; (ordine) order, command; (onere, imposta) tax

imposses'sarsi /72/ vpr: **~ di** to seize, take possession of

impos'sibile ag impossible; **fare l'~** to do one's utmost, do all one can

im'posta sf (di finestra) shutter; (tassa) tax; **~ sul reddito** income tax; **~ sul valore aggiunto** value added tax (BRIT), sales tax (US)

impos'tare /72/ vt (imbucare) to post; (resoconto, rapporto) to plan; (problema) to set out; (avviare) to begin, start off; **~ la voce** (Mus) to pitch one's voice

impostazi'one [impostat'tsjone] sf (di lettera) posting (BRIT), mailing (US); (di problema, questione) formulation, statement; (di lavoro) organization, planning; (di attività) setting up; (Mus: di voce) pitch; **impostazioni** sfpl (di computer) settings

impo'tente *ag* weak, powerless; (*anche Med*) impotent

imprati'cabile *ag* (*strada*) impassable; (*campo da gioco*) unplayable

impre'care /20/ *vi* to curse, swear; **~ contro** to hurl abuse at

imprecazi'one [imprekat'tsjone] *sf* abuse, curse

impre'gnare [impreɲ'ɲare] /15/ *vt*: **~ (di)** (*imbevere*) to soak o impregnate (with); (*riempire*) to fill (with)

imprendi'tore *sm* (*industriale*) entrepreneur; (*appaltatore*) contractor; **piccolo ~** small businessman

im'presa *sf* (*iniziativa*) enterprise; (*azione*) exploit; (*azienda*) firm, concern

impressio'nante *ag* impressive; upsetting

impressio'nare /72/ *vt* to impress; (*turbare*) to upset; (*Fot*) to expose; **impressionarsi** *vpr* to be easily upset

impressi'one *sf* impression; (*fig: sensazione*) sensation, feeling; (*stampa*) printing; **fare ~** (*colpire*) to impress; (*turbare*) to frighten, upset; **fare buona/cattiva ~ a** to make a good/bad impression on

impreve'dibile *ag* unforeseeable; (*persona*) unpredictable

impre'visto, -a *ag* unexpected, unforeseen ▷ *sm* unforeseen event; **salvo imprevisti** unless anything unexpected happens

imprigio'nare [impridʒo'nare] /72/ *vt* to imprison

impro'babile *ag* improbable, unlikely

im'pronta *sf* (*di piede, mano*) print; (*fig*) mark, stamp; **~ di carbonio** carbon footprint; **~ digitale** fingerprint

improvvisa'mente *av* suddenly; unexpectedly

improvvi'sare /72/ *vt* to improvise

improv'viso, -a *ag* (*imprevisto*) unexpected; (*subitaneo*) sudden; **all'~** unexpectedly; suddenly

impru'dente *ag* unwise, rash

impu'gnare [impuɲ'ɲare] /15/ *vt* to grasp, grip; (*Dir*) to contest

impul'sivo, -a *ag* impulsive

im'pulso *sm* impulse

impun'tarsi /72/ *vpr* to stop dead, refuse to budge; (*fig*) to be obstinate

impu'tato, -a *sm/f* (*Dir*) accused, defendant

PAROLA CHIAVE

in (*in + il* = **nel**, *in + lo* = **nello**, *in + l'* = **nell'**, *in + la* = **nella**, *in + i* = **nei**, *in + gli* = **negli**, *in + le* = **nelle**) *prep* **1** (*stato in luogo*) in; **vivere in Italia/città** to live in Italy/town; **essere in casa/ufficio** to be at home/the office; **se fossi in te** if I were you

2 (*moto a luogo*) to; (: *dentro*) into; **andare in Germania/città** to go to Germany/town; **andare in ufficio** to go to the office; **entrare in macchina/casa** to get into the car/go into the house

3 (*tempo*) in; **nel 1989** in 1989; **in giugno/estate** in June/summer

4 (*modo, maniera*) in; **in silenzio** in silence; **in abito da sera** in evening dress; **in guerra** at war; **in vacanza** on holiday; **Maria Bianchi in Rossi** Maria Rossi née Bianchi

5 (*mezzo*) by; **viaggiare in autobus/treno** to travel by bus/train

6 (*materia*) made of; **in marmo** made of marble, marble *cpd*; **una collana in oro** a gold necklace

7 (*misura*) in; **siamo in quattro** there are four of us; **in tutto** in all

8 (*fine*): **dare in dono** to give as a gift; **spende tutto in alcool** he spends all his money on drink; **in onore di** in honour of

inabi'tabile *ag* uninhabitable

inacces'sibile [inatt'ʃes'sibile] *ag* (*luogo*) inaccessible; (*persona*) unapproachable

inaccet'tabile [inattʃet'tabile] *ag* unacceptable

ina'datto, -a *ag*: **~ (a)** unsuitable o unfit (for)

inadegu'ato, -a *ag* inadequate

inaffi'dabile *ag* unreliable

inami'dato, -a *ag* starched

inar'care /20/ *vt* (*schiena*) to arch; (*sopracciglia*) to raise

inaspet'tato, -a *ag* unexpected

inas'prire /55/ *vt* (*disciplina*) to tighten up, make harsher; (*carattere*) to embitter; **inasprirsi** *vpr* to become harsher; to become bitter; to become worse

inattac'cabile *ag* (*anche fig*) unassailable; (*alibi*) cast-iron

inatten'dibile *ag* unreliable

inat'teso, -a *ag* unexpected

inattu'abile *ag* impracticable

inau'dito, -a *ag* unheard of

inaugu'rare /72/ *vt* to inaugurate, open; (*monumento*) to unveil

inaugurazi'one [inaugurat'tsjone] *sf* inauguration; unveiling

incal'lito, -a *ag* calloused; (*fig*) hardened, inveterate; (: *insensibile*) hard

incande'scente [inkandeʃ'ʃente] *ag* incandescent, white-hot

incan'tare /72/ *vt* to enchant, bewitch; **incantarsi** *vpr* (*rimanere intontito*) to be spellbound; to be in a daze; (*meccanismo: bloccarsi*) to jam; **incan'tevole** *ag* charming, enchanting

in'canto sm spell, charm, enchantment; (asta) auction; **come per** ~ as if by magic; **mettere all'**~ to put up for auction

inca'pace [inka'patʃe] ag incapable

incarce'rare [inkartʃe'rare] /72/ vt to imprison

incari'care /20/ vt: ~ **qn di fare** to give sb the responsibility of doing; **incaricarsi** vpr: **incaricarsi di** to take care o charge of

in'carico, -chi sm task, job

incarta'mento sm dossier, file

incar'tare /72/ vt to wrap (in paper)

incas'sare /72/ vt (merce) to pack (in cases); (gemma: incastonare) to set; (Econ: riscuotere) to collect; (Pugilato: colpi) to take, stand up to; **in'casso** sm cashing, encashment; (introito) takings pl

incas'trare /72/ vt to fit in, insert; (fig: intrappolare) to catch; **incastrarsi** vpr (combaciare) to fit together; (restare bloccato) to become stuck

incate'nare /72/ vt to chain up

in'cauto, -a ag imprudent, rash

inca'vato, -a ag hollow; (occhi) sunken

incendi'are [intʃen'djare] /19/ vt to set fire to; **incendiarsi** vpr to catch fire, burst into flames

in'cendio [in'tʃendjo] sm fire

inceneri'tore [intʃeneri'tore] sm incinerator

in'censo [in'tʃenso] sm incense

incensu'rato, -a [intʃensu'rato] ag (Dir): **essere** ~ to have a clean record

incenti'vare [intʃenti'vare] /72/ vt (produzione, vendite) to boost; (persona) to motivate

incen'tivo [intʃen'tivo] sm incentive

incep'pare [intʃep'pare] /72/ vt to obstruct; **incepparsi** vpr to jam

incer'tezza [intʃer'tettsa] sf uncertainty

in'certo, -a [in'tʃerto] ag uncertain; (irresoluto) undecided, hesitating ▷ sm uncertainty

in'cetta [in'tʃetta] sf buying up; **fare** ~ **di qc** to buy up sth

inchi'esta [in'kjɛsta] sf investigation, inquiry

inchi'nare [inki'nare] /72/ vt to bow; **inchinarsi** vpr to bend down; (per riverenza) to bow; (: donna) to curtsy

inchio'dare [inkjo'dare] /72/ vt to nail (down); ~ **la macchina** (Aut) to jam on the brakes

inchi'ostro [in'kjɔstro] sm ink; ~ **simpatico** invisible ink

inciam'pare [intʃam'pare] /72/ vi to trip, stumble

inci'dente [intʃi'dɛnte] sm accident; ~ **automobilistico** o **d'auto** car accident; ~ **diplomatico** diplomatic incident

in'cidere [in'tʃidere] /34/ vi: ~ **su** to bear upon, affect ▷ vt (tagliare incavando) to cut into; (Arte) to engrave; to etch; (canzone) to record

in'cinta [in'tʃinta] ag f pregnant

incipri'are [intʃi'prjare] /19/ vt to powder; **incipriarsi** vpr to powder one's face

in'circa [in'tʃirka] av: **all'**~ more or less, very nearly

in'cisi ecc [in'tʃizi] vb vedi **incidere**

incisi'one [intʃi'zjone] sf cut; (disegno) engraving; etching; (registrazione) recording; (Med) incision

in'ciso, -a [in'tʃizo] pp di **incidere** ▷ sm: **per** ~ incidentally, by the way

inci'tare [intʃi'tare] /72/ vt to incite

inci'vile [intʃi'vile] ag uncivilized; (villano) impolite

incl. abbr (= incluso) encl.

incli'nare /72/ vt to tilt; **inclinarsi** vpr (barca) to list; (aereo) to bank

in'cludere /3/ vt to include; (accludere) to enclose; **in'cluso, -a** pp di **includere** ▷ ag included; enclosed

incoe'rente ag incoherent; (contraddittorio) inconsistent

in'cognito, -a [in'kɔɲɲito] ag unknown ▷ sm: **in** ~ incognito ▷ sf (Mat, fig) unknown quantity

incol'lare /72/ vt to glue, gum; (unire con colla) to stick together

inco'lore ag colourless

incol'pare /72/ vt: ~ **qn di** to charge sb with

in'colto, -a ag (terreno) uncultivated; (trascurato: capelli) neglected; (persona) uneducated

in'colume ag safe and sound, unhurt

incom'benza [inkom'bɛntsa] sf duty, task

in'combere /29/ vi (sovrastare minacciando): ~ **su** to threaten, hang over

incominci'are [inkomin'tʃare] /14/ vi, vt to begin, start

incompe'tente ag incompetent

incompi'uto, -a ag unfinished, incomplete

incom'pleto, -a ag incomplete

incompren'sibile ag incomprehensible

inconce'pibile [inkontʃe'pibile] ag inconceivable

inconcili'abile [inkontʃi'ljabile] ag irreconcilable

inconclu'dente ag inconclusive; (persona) ineffectual

incondizio'nato, -a [inkondittsjo'nato] ag unconditional

inconfon'dibile ag unmistakable

inconsa'pevole ag: ~ **di** unaware of, ignorant of

in'conscio, -a, -sci, -sce [in'kɔnʃo] *ag* unconscious ▷ *sm* (*Psic*): **l'~ the** unconscious

inconsis'tente *ag* insubstantial; (*dubbio*) unfounded

inconsu'eto, -a *ag* unusual

incon'trare /72/ *vt* to meet; (*difficoltà*) to meet with; **incontrarsi** *vpr* to meet

in'contro *av*: ~ **a** (*verso*) towards ▷ *sm* meeting; (*Sport*) match; meeting; ~ **di calcio** football match

inconveni'ente *sm* drawback, snag

incoraggia'mento [inkoraddʒa'mento] *sm* encouragement

incoraggi'are [inkorad'dʒare] /62/ *vt* to encourage

incornici'are [inkorni'tʃare] /14/ *vt* to frame

incoro'nare /72/ *vt* to crown

in'correre /28/ *vi*: ~ **in** to meet with, run into

incosci'ente [inkoʃʃɛnte] *ag* (*inconscio*) unconscious; (*irresponsabile*) reckless, thoughtless

incre'dibile *ag* incredible, unbelievable

in'credulo, -a *ag* incredulous, disbelieving

incremen'tare /72/ *vt* to increase; (*dar sviluppo a*) to promote

incre'mento *sm* (*sviluppo*) development; (*aumento numerico*) increase, growth

incresci'oso, -a [inkreʃʃoso] *ag* (*incidente ecc*) regrettable

incrimi'nare /72/ *vt* (*Dir*) to charge

incri'nare /72/ *vt* to crack; (*fig: rapporti, amicizia*) to cause to deteriorate; **incrinarsi** *vpr* to crack; to deteriorate

incroci'are [inkro'tʃare] /14/ *vt* to cross; (*incontrare*) to meet ▷ *vi* (*Naut, Aer*) to cruise; **incrociarsi** *vpr* (*strade*) to cross, intersect; (*persone, veicoli*) to pass each other; ~ **le braccia/le gambe** to fold one's arms/cross one's legs

in'crocio [in'krotʃo] *sm* (*anche Ferr*) crossing; (*di strade*) crossroads

incuba'trice [inkuba'tritʃe] *sf* incubator

'incubo *sm* nightmare

incu'rabile *ag* incurable

incu'rante *ag*: ~ (**di**) heedless (of), careless (of)

incurio'sire /55/ *vt* to make curious; **incuriosirsi** *vpr* to become curious

incursi'one *sf* raid

incur'vare /72/ *vt* to bend, curve; **incurvarsi** *vpr* to bend, curve

incusto'dito, -a *ag* unguarded, unattended

in'cutere /40/ *vt*: ~ **timore/rispetto a qn** to strike fear into sb/command sb's respect

'indaco *sm* indigo

indaffa'rato, -a *ag* busy

inda'gare /80/ *vt* to investigate

in'dagine [in'dadʒine] *sf* investigation, inquiry; (*ricerca*) research, study; ~ **di mercato** market survey

indebi'tare /72/ *vt*: ~ **qn** to get sb into debt; **indebitarsi** *vpr* to run o get into debt

indebo'lire /55/ *vt, vi* (*anche*: **indebolirsi**) to weaken

inde'cente [inde'tʃɛnte] *ag* indecent

inde'ciso, -a [inde'tʃizo] *ag* indecisive; (*irresoluto*) undecided

indefi'nito, -a *ag* (*anche Ling*) indefinite; (*impreciso, non determinato*) undefined

in'degno, -a [in'deɲɲo] *ag* (*atto*) shameful; (*persona*) unworthy

indemoni'ato, -a *ag* possessed (by the devil)

in'denne *ag* unhurt, uninjured

indenniz'zare [indennid'dzare] /72/ *vt* to compensate

indetermina'tivo, -a *ag* (*Ling*) indefinite

'India *sf*: **l'~** India; **indi'ano, -a** *ag* Indian ▷ *sm/f* (*d'India*) Indian; (*d'America*) Native American, (American) Indian

indi'care /20/ *vt* (*mostrare*) to show, indicate; (: *col dito*) to point to, point out; (*consigliare*) to suggest, recommend; **indica'tivo, -a** *ag* indicative ▷ *sm* (*Ling*) indicative (mood); **indicazi'one** *sf* indication; (*informazione*) piece of information

'indice ['inditʃe] *sm* (*Anat: dito*) index finger, forefinger; (*fig*) sign; (*nei libri*) index; ~ **di gradimento** (*Radio, TV*) popularity rating

indicherò *ecc* [indike'rɔ] *vb vedi* **indicare**

indi'cibile [indi'tʃibile] *ag* inexpressible

indietreggi'are [indjetred'dʒare] /62/ *vi* to draw back, retreat

indi'etro *av* back; (*guardare*) behind, back; (*andare, cadere: anche*: **all'~**) backwards; **rimanere ~** to be left behind; **essere ~** (*col lavoro*) to be behind; (*orologio*) to be slow; **rimandare qc ~** to send sth back

indi'feso, -a *ag* (*città, confine*) undefended; (*persona*) defenceless

indiffe'rente *ag* indifferent

in'digeno, -a [in'didʒeno] *ag* indigenous, native ▷ *sm/f* native

indigesti'one [indidʒes'tjone] *sf* indigestion

indi'gesto, -a [indi'dʒɛsto] *ag* indigestible

indi'gnare [indiɲ'ɲare] /15/ *vt* to fill with indignation; **indignarsi** *vpr* to be (o get) indignant

indimenti'cabile *ag* unforgettable

indipen'dente *ag* independent

in'dire /38/ *vt* (*concorso*) to announce; (*elezioni*) to call

indi'retto, -a ag indirect

indiriz'zare [indirit'tsare] /72/ vt (dirigere) to direct; (mandare) to send; (lettera) to address

indi'rizzo [indi'rittso] sm address; (direzione) direction; (avvio) trend, course

indis'creto, -a ag indiscreet

indis'cusso, -a ag unquestioned

indispen'sabile ag indispensable, essential

indispet'tire /55/ vt to irritate, annoy ▷ vi (anche: **indispettirsi**) to get irritated o annoyed

individu'ale ag individual

individu'are /72/ vt (dar forma distinta a) to characterize; (determinare) to locate; (riconoscere) to single out

indi'viduo sm individual

indizi'ato, -a ag suspected ▷ sm/f suspect

in'dizio [in'dittsjo] sm (segno) sign, indication; (Polizia) clue; (Dir) piece of evidence

'indole sf nature, character

indolen'zito, -a [indolen'tsito] ag stiff, aching; (intorpidito) numb

indo'lore ag painless

indo'mani sm: l'~ the next day, the following day

Indo'nesia sf: l'~ Indonesia

indos'sare /72/ vt (mettere indosso) to put on; (avere indosso) to have on; **indossa'tore, -'trice** sm/f model

indottri'nare /72/ vt to indoctrinate

indovi'nare /72/ vt (scoprire) to guess; (immaginare) to imagine, guess; (il futuro) to foretell; **indovi'nello** sm riddle

indubbia'mente av undoubtedly

in'dubbio, -a ag certain, undoubted

in'duco ecc vb vedi **indurre**

indugi'are [indu'dʒare] /62/ vi to take one's time, delay

in'dugio [in'dudʒo] sm (ritardo) delay; senza ~ without delay

indul'gente [indul'dʒɛnte] ag indulgent; (giudice) lenient

indu'mento sm article of clothing, garment

indu'rire /55/ vt to harden ▷ vi (anche: **indurirsi**) to harden, become hard

in'durre /90/ vt: ~ qn a fare qc to induce o persuade sb to do sth; ~ qn in errore to mislead sb

in'dussi ecc vb vedi **indurre**

in'dustria sf industry; **industri'ale** ag industrial ▷ sm industrialist

inecce'pibile [inettʃe'pibile] ag unexceptionable

i'nedito, -a ag unpublished

ine'rente ag: ~ a concerning, regarding

i'nerme ag unarmed, defenceless

inerpi'carsi /72/ vpr: ~ (su) to clamber (up)

i'nerte ag inert; (inattivo) indolent, sluggish

ine'satto, -a ag (impreciso) inexact; (erroneo) incorrect; (Amm: non riscosso) uncollected

inesis'tente ag non-existent

inesperi'enza [inespe'rjɛntsa] sf inexperience

ines'perto, -a ag inexperienced

inevi'tabile ag inevitable

i'nezia [i'nɛttsja] sf trifle, thing of no importance

infagot'tare /72/ vt to bundle up, wrap up; **infagottarsi** vpr to wrap up

infal'libile ag infallible

infa'mante ag defamatory

in'fame ag infamous; (fig: cosa, compito) awful, dreadful

infan'gare /80/ vt to cover with mud; (fig: nome, reputazione) to sully; **infangarsi** vpr to get covered in mud; to be sullied

infan'tile ag child cpd; childlike; (adulto, azione) childish; **letteratura ~** children's books pl

in'fanzia [in'fantsja] sf childhood; (bambini) children pl; **prima ~** babyhood, infancy

infari'nare /72/ vt to cover with (o sprinkle with o dip in) flour; **infarina'tura** sf (fig) smattering

in'farto sm (Med): ~ **(cardiaco)** coronary

infasti'dire /55/ vt to annoy, irritate; **infastidirsi** vpr to get annoyed o irritated

infati'cabile ag tireless, untiring

in'fatti cong as a matter of fact, actually

> Attenzione! In inglese esiste l'espressione in fact, che però vuol dire in effetti.

infatu'arsi /72/ vpr: ~ **di** o **per** to become infatuated with, fall for

infe'dele ag unfaithful

infe'lice [infe'litʃe] ag unhappy; (sfortunato) unlucky, unfortunate; (inopportuno) inopportune, ill-timed; (mal riuscito: lavoro) bad, poor

inferi'ore ag lower; (per intelligenza, qualità) inferior ▷ sm/f inferior; ~ **a** (numero, quantità) less o smaller than; (meno buono) inferior to; ~ **alla media** below average; **inferiorità** sf inferiority

inferme'ria sf infirmary; (di scuola, nave) sick bay

infermi'ere, -a sm/f nurse

infermità sf inv illness; infirmity; ~ **mentale** mental illness; (Dir) insanity

in'fermo, -a ag (ammalato) ill; (debole) infirm

infer'nale ag infernal; (proposito, complotto) diabolical

in'ferno sm hell

inferri'ata sf grating

infes'tare /72/ vt to infest

infet'tare /72/ vt to infect; **infettarsi** vpr to become infected; **infezi'one** sf infection

infiam'mabile ag inflammable

infiam'mare /72/ vt to set alight; (fig, Med) to inflame; **infiammarsi** vpr to catch fire; (Med) to become inflamed; **infiammazi'one** sf (Med) inflammation

infie'rire /55/ vi: ~ **su** (fisicamente) to attack furiously; (verbalmente) to rage at

infi'lare /72/ vt (ago) to thread; (mettere: chiave) to insert; (: vestito) to slip o put on; (strada) to turn into, take; **infilarsi** vpr: **infilarsi in** to slip into; (indossare) to slip on; ~ **un anello al dito** to slip a ring on one's finger; ~ **l'uscio** to slip in; to slip out

infil'trarsi /72/ vpr to penetrate, seep through; (Mil) to infiltrate

infil'zare [infil'tsare] /72/ vt (infilare) to string together; (trafiggere) to pierce

'infimo, -a ag lowest

in'fine av finally; (insomma) in short

infinità sf infinity; (in quantità): **un'~ di** an infinite number of

infi'nito, -a ag infinite; (Ling) infinitive ▷ sm infinity; (Ling) infinitive; **all'~** (senza fine) endlessly

infinocchi'are [infinok'kjare] /19/ vt (fam) to hoodwink

infischi'arsi [infis'kjarsi] /19/ vpr: ~ **di** not to care about

in'fisso sm fixture; (di porta, finestra) frame

inflazi'one [inflat'tsjone] sf inflation

in'fliggere [in'fliddʒere] /104/ vt to inflict

in'flissi ecc vb vedi **infliggere**

influ'ente ag influential; **influ'enza** sf influence; (Med) influenza, flu; **influenza aviaria** bird flu; **influenza suina** swine flu

influen'zare [influen'tsare] /72/ vt to influence, have an influence on

influ'ire /55/ vi: ~ **su** to influence

in'flusso sm influence

infon'dato, -a ag unfounded, groundless

in'fondere /25/ vt: ~ **qc in qn** to instill sth in sb

infor'mare /72/ vt to inform, tell; **informarsi** vpr: **informarsi** (di o su) to inquire (about)

infor'matico, -a, -ci, -che ag computer cpd ▷ sf computer science

informa'tivo, -a ag informative

infor'mato, -a ag informed; **tenersi ~** to keep o.s. (well-)informed

informa'tore sm informer

informazi'one [informat'tsjone] sf piece of information; **informazioni** sfpl information sg; **chiedere un'~** to ask for (some) information

in'forme ag shapeless

informico'larsi /72/ vpr: **mi si è informicolata una gamba** I've got pins and needles in my leg

infortu'nato, -a ag injured, hurt ▷ sm/f injured person

infor'tunio sm accident; ~ **sul lavoro** industrial accident, accident at work

infra'dito sm inv (calzatura) flip flop (BRIT), thong (US)

infrazi'one [infrat'tsjone] sf: ~ **a** breaking of, violation of

infredda'tura sf slight cold

infreddo'lito, -a ag cold, chilled

infu'ori av out; **all'~** outwards; **all'~ di** (eccetto) except, with the exception of

infuri'are /19/ vi to rage; **infuriarsi** vpr to fly into a rage

infusi'one sf infusion

in'fuso, -a pp di **infondere** ▷ sm infusion

Ing. abbr = **ingegnere**

ingaggi'are [ingad'dʒare] /62/ vt (assumere con compenso) to take on, hire; (Sport) to sign on; (Mil) to engage

ingan'nare /72/ vt to deceive; (fisco) to cheat; (eludere) to dodge, elude; (fig: tempo) to while away ▷ vi (apparenza) to be deceptive; **ingannarsi** vpr to be mistaken, be wrong

in'ganno sm deceit, deception; (azione) trick; (menzogna, frode) cheat, swindle; (illusione) illusion

inge'gnarsi [indʒeɲ'ɲarsi] /15/ vpr to do one's best, try hard; ~ **per vivere** to live by one's wits

inge'gnere [indʒeɲ'ɲɛre] sm engineer; ~ **civile/navale** civil/naval engineer; **ingegne'ria** sf engineering; **ingegnere genetica** genetic engineering

in'gegno [in'dʒeɲɲo] sm (intelligenza) intelligence, brains pl; (capacità creativa) ingenuity; (disposizione) talent; **inge'gnoso, -a** ag ingenious, clever

ingelo'sire /55/ vt to make jealous ▷ vi (anche: **ingelosirsi**) to become jealous

in'gente [in'dʒɛnte] ag huge, enormous

ingenuità [indʒenui'ta] sf ingenuousness

in'genuo, -a [in'dʒɛnuo] ag naïve

> ⚠ Attenzione! In inglese esiste la parola *ingenious*, che però significa *ingegnoso*.

inge'rire [indʒe'rire] /55/ vt to ingest

inges'sare [indʒes'sare] /72/ vt (Med) to put in plaster; **ingessa'tura** sf plaster

Inghil'terra [ingil'tɛrra] sf: **l'~** England

inghiot'tire [ingjot'tire] /17/ vt to swallow

ingial'lire [indʒal'lire] /55/ vi to go yellow

inginocchi'arsi [indʒinok'kjarsi] /19/ vpr to kneel (down)

ingiù [in'dʒu] av down, downwards

ingi'uria [in'dʒurja] *sf* insult; *(fig: danno)* damage

ingius'tizia [indʒus'tittsja] *sf* injustice

ingi'usto, -a [in'dʒusto] *ag* unjust, unfair

in'glese *ag* English ▷ *smf* Englishman/ woman ▷ *sm* (Ling) English; **gli Inglesi** the English; **andarsene** *o* **filare all'~** to take French leave

ingoi'are /19/ *vt* to gulp (down); *(fig)* to swallow (up)

ingol'fare /72/ *vt*, **ingol'farsi** *vpr* to flood

ingom'brante *ag* cumbersome

ingom'brare /72/ *vt* (strada) to block; *(stanza)* to clutter up

in'gordo, -a *ag*: **~ di** greedy for; *(fig)* greedy *o* avid for

in'gorgo, -ghi *sm* blockage, obstruction; *(anche:* **~ stradale)** traffic jam

ingoz'zare [ingot'tsare] /72/ *vt* (persona) to stuff; **ingozzarsi** *vpr*: **ingozzarsi (di)** to stuff o.s. (with)

ingra'naggio [ingra'naddʒo] *sm* (Tecn) gear; *(di orologio)* mechanism; **gli ingranaggi della burocrazia** the bureaucratic machinery

ingra'nare /72/ *vi* to mesh, engage ▷ *vt* to engage; **~ la marcia** to get into gear

ingrandi'mento *sm* enlargement; extension

ingran'dire /55/ *vt* (anche Fot) to enlarge; *(estendere)* to extend; *(Ottica, fig)* to magnify ▷ *vi* (anche: **ingrandirsi**) to become larger *o* bigger; *(aumentare)* to grow, increase; *(espandersi)* to expand

ingras'sare /72/ *vt* to make fat; *(animali)* to fatten; *(lubrificare)* to oil, lubricate ▷ *vi* (anche: **ingrassarsi**) to get fat, put on weight

in'grato, -a *ag* ungrateful; *(lavoro)* thankless, unrewarding

ingredi'ente *sm* ingredient

in'gresso *sm* (porta) entrance; *(atrio)* hall; *(l'entrare)* entrance, entry; *(facoltà di entrare)* admission; **"~ libero"** "admission free"

ingros'sare /72/ *vt* to increase; *(folla, livello)* to swell ▷ *vi* (anche: **ingrossarsi**) to increase; to swell

in'grosso *av*: **all'~** (Comm) wholesale; *(all'incirca)* roughly, about

ingua'ribile *ag* incurable

'inguine *sm* (Anat) groin

ini'bire /55/ *vt* to forbid, prohibit; *(Psic)* to inhibit; **inibirsi** *vpr* to restrain o.s.

ini'bito, -a *ag* inhibited ▷ *sm/f* inhibited person

iniet'tare /72/ *vt* to inject; **iniezi'one** *sf* injection

ininterrotta'mente *av* non-stop, continuously

ininter'rotto, -a *ag* unbroken; *(rumore)* uninterrupted

inizi'ale [init'tsjale] *ag*, *sf* initial

inizi'are [init'tsjare] /19/ *vi*, *vt* to begin, start; **~ qn a** to initiate sb into; *(pittura ecc)* to introduce sb to; **~ a fare qc** to start doing sth

inizia'tiva [inittsja'tiva] *sf* initiative; **~ privata** private enterprise

i'nizio [i'nittsjo] *sm* beginning; **all'~** at the beginning, at the start; **dare ~ a qc** to start sth, get sth going

innaffi'are *ecc* = **annaffiare** *ecc*

innamo'rare /72/ *vt* to enchant; **innamorarsi** *vpr*: **innamorarsi (di qn)** to fall in love (with sb) **innamo'rato, -a** *ag*: **innamorato (di)** (che nutre amore) in love (with); **innamorato di** (appassionato) very fond of ▷ *sm/f* lover; *(anche scherzoso)* sweetheart

innanzi'tutto [innantsi'tutto] *av* first of all

in'nato, -a *ag* innate

innatu'rale *ag* unnatural

inne'gabile *ag* undeniable

innervo'sire /55/ *vt*: **~ qn** to get on sb's nerves; **innervosirsi** *vpr* to get irritated *o* upset

innes'care /20/ *vt* to prime

'inno *sm* hymn; **~ nazionale** national anthem

inno'cente [inno'tʃɛnte] *ag* innocent

in'nocuo, -a *ag* innocuous, harmless

innova'tivo, -a *ag* innovative

innume'revole *ag* innumerable

inol'trare /72/ *vt* (Amm) to pass on, forward

i'noltre *av* besides, moreover

inon'dare /72/ *vt* to flood

inoppor'tuno, -a *ag* untimely, ill-timed; *(poco adatto)* inappropriate; *(momento)* inopportune

inorri'dire /55/ *vt* to horrify ▷ *vi* to be horrified

inosser'vato, -a *ag* (non notato) unobserved; *(non rispettato)* not observed, not kept

inossi'dabile *ag* stainless

INPS *sigla m* (= Istituto Nazionale Previdenza Sociale) social security service

inqua'drare /72/ *vt* (foto, immagine) to frame; *(fig)* to situate, set

inqui'eto, -a *ag* restless; *(preoccupato)* worried, anxious

inqui'lino, -a *sm/f* tenant

inquina'mento *sm* pollution

inqui'nare /72/ *vt* to pollute

insabbi'are /19/ *vt* (fig: pratica) to shelve; **insabbiarsi** *vpr* (arenarsi: barca) to run aground; *(fig: pratica)* to be shelved

insac'cati *smpl* (*Cuc*) sausages

insa'lata *sf* salad; **~ mista** mixed salad; **~ russa** (*Cuc*) Russian salad (*comprised of cold diced cooked vegetables in mayonnaise*); **insalati'era** *sf* salad bowl

insa'nabile *ag* (*piaga*) which cannot be healed; (*situazione*) irremediable; (*odio*) implacable

insa'puta *sf*: **all'~ di qn** without sb knowing

insedi'are /19/ *vt* (*Amm*) to install; **insediarsi** *vpr* to take up office; (*colonia, profughi ecc*) to settle

in'segna [in'sɛɲɲa] *sf* sign; (*emblema*) sign, emblem; (*bandiera*) flag, banner

insegna'mento [inseɲɲa'mento] *sm* teaching

inse'gnante [inseɲ'ɲante] *ag* teaching ▷ *smf* teacher; **~ di sostegno** teaching assistant

inse'gnare [inseɲ'ɲare] /15/ *vt, vi* to teach; **~ a qn qc** to teach sb sth; **~ a qn a fare qc** to teach sb (how) to do sth

insegui'mento *sm* pursuit, chase

insegu'ire /45/ *vt* to pursue, chase

insena'tura *sf* inlet, creek

insen'sato, -a *ag* senseless, stupid

insen'sibile *ag* (*anche fig*) insensitive

inse'rire /55/ *vt* to insert; (*Elettr*) to connect; (*allegare*) to enclose; (*annuncio*) to put in, place; **inserirsi** *vpr* (*fig*): **inserirsi in** to become part of

inservi'ente *smf* attendant

inserzi'one [inser'tsjone] *sf* insertion; (*avviso*) advertisement; **fare un'~ sul giornale** to put an advertisement in the newspaper

insetti'cida, -i [insetti'tʃida] *sm* insecticide

in'setto *sm* insect

insi'curo, -a *ag* insecure

insi'eme *av* together ▷ *prep*: **~ a o con** together with ▷ *sm* whole; (*Mat, servizio, assortimento*) set; (*Moda*) ensemble, outfit; **tutti ~** all together; **tutto ~** all together; (*in una volta*) at one go; **nell'~** on the whole; **d'~** (*veduta ecc*) overall

in'signe [in'siɲɲe] *ag* (*persona*) famous, distinguished; (*città, monumento*) notable

insignifi'cante [insiɲɲifi'kante] *ag* insignificant

insinu'are /72/ *vt* (*fig*) to insinuate, imply; **~ qc in** (*introdurre*) to slip o slide sth into; **insinuarsi** *vpr*: **insinuarsi in** to seep into; (*fig*) to creep into; to worm one's way into

in'sipido, -a *ag* insipid

insis'tente *ag* insistent; (*pioggia, dolore*) persistent

in'sistere /11/ *vi*: **~ su qc** to insist on sth; **~ in qc/a fare** (*perseverare*) to persist in sth/in doing

insoddis'fatto, -a *ag* dissatisfied

insoffe'rente *ag* intolerant

insolazi'one [insolat'tsjone] *sf* (*Med*) sunstroke

inso'lente *ag* insolent

in'solito, -a *ag* unusual, out of the ordinary

inso'luto, -a *ag* (*non risolto*) unsolved

in'somma *av* (*in breve, in conclusione*) in short; (*dunque*) well ▷ *escl* for heaven's sake!

in'sonne *ag* sleepless; **in'sonnia** *sf* insomnia, sleeplessness

insonno'lito, -a *ag* sleepy, drowsy

insoppor'tabile *ag* unbearable

in'sorgere [in'sordʒere] /109/ *vi* (*ribellarsi*) to rise up, rebel; (*apparire*) to come up, arise

in'sorsi *ecc vb vedi* **insorgere**

insospet'tire /55/ *vt* to make suspicious ▷ *vi* (*anche*: **insospettirsi**) to become suspicious

inspi'rare /72/ *vt* to breathe in, inhale

in'stabile *ag* (*carico, indole*) unstable; (*tempo*) unsettled; (*equilibrio*) unsteady

instal'lare /72/ *vt* to install

instan'cabile *ag* untiring, indefatigable

instau'rare /72/ *vt* to establish, introduce

insuc'cesso [insut'tʃesso] *sm* failure, flop

insuffici'ente [insuffi'tʃɛnte] *ag* insufficient; (*compito, allievo*) inadequate; **insuffici'enza** *sf* insufficiency; inadequacy; (*Ins*) fail; **insufficienza di prove** (*Dir*) lack of evidence; **insufficienza renale** renal insufficiency

insu'lina *sf* insulin

in'sulso, -a *ag* (*sciocco*) inane, silly; (*persona*) dull, insipid

insul'tare /72/ *vt* to insult, affront

in'sulto *sm* insult, affront

intac'care /20/ *vt* (*fare tacche*) to cut into; (*corrodere*) to corrode; (*fig: cominciare ad usare: risparmi*) to break into; (*: ledere*) to damage

intagli'are [intaʎ'ʎare] /27/ *vt* to carve

in'tanto *av* (*nel frattempo*) meanwhile, in the meantime; (*per cominciare*) just to begin with; **~ che** while

inta'sare /72/ *vt* to choke (up), block (up); (*Aut*) to obstruct, block; **intasarsi** *vpr* to become choked o blocked

intas'care /20/ *vt* to pocket

in'tatto, -a *ag* intact; (*puro*) unsullied

intavo'lare /72/ *vt* to start, enter into

inte'grale *ag* complete; (*pane, farina*) wholemeal (*BRIT*), wholewheat (*US*); **calcolo ~** (*Mat*) integral calculus

inte'grante *ag*: **parte ~** integral part

inte'grare /72/ *vt* to complete; (*Mat*) to integrate; **integrarsi** *vpr* (*persona*) to become integrated

integra'tore *sm*: **integratori alimentari** nutritional supplements

integrità *sf* integrity

'integro, -a *ag* (*intatto, intero*) complete, whole; (*retto*) upright

intelaia'tura *sf* frame; (*fig*) structure, framework

intel'letto *sm* intellect; **intellettu'ale** *ag*, *smf* intellectual

intelli'gente [intelli'dʒɛnte] *ag* intelligent

intem'perie *sfpl* bad weather *sg*

in'tendere /120/ *vt* (*comprendere*) to understand; (*udire*) to hear; (*significare*) to mean; (*avere intenzione*): **~ fare qc** to intend *o* mean to do sth; **intendersi** *vpr* (*conoscere*): **intendersi di** to know a lot about, be a connoisseur of; (*accordarsi*) to get on (well); **intendersela con qn** (*avere una relazione amorosa*) to have an affair with sb; **intendi'tore, -'trice** *sm/f* connoisseur, expert

inten'sivo, -a *ag* intensive

in'tenso, -a *ag* intense

in'tento, -a *ag* (*teso, assorto*): **~ (a)** intent (on), absorbed (in) ▷ *sm* aim, purpose

intenzio'nale [intentsjo'nale] *ag* intentional

intenzi'one [inten'tsjone] *sf* intention; (*Dir*) intent; **avere ~ di fare qc** to intend to do sth, have the intention of doing sth

interat'tivo, -a *ag* interactive

intercet'tare [intertʃet'tare] /72/ *vt* to intercept

intercity [inter'siti] *sm inv* (*Ferr*) ≈ intercity (train)

inter'detto, -a *pp di* **interdire** ▷ *ag* forbidden, prohibited; (*sconcertato*) dumbfounded ▷ *sm* (*Rel*) interdict

interes'sante *ag* interesting; **essere in stato ~** to be expecting (a baby)

interes'sare /72/ *vt* to interest; (*concernere*) to concern, be of interest to; (*far intervenire*): **~ qn a** to draw sb's attention to ▷ *vi*: **~ a** to interest, matter to; **interessarsi** *vpr* (*mostrare interesse*): **interessarsi a** to take an interest in, be interested in; (*occuparsi*): **interessarsi di** to take care of

inte'resse *sm* (*anche Comm*) interest

inter'faccia, -ce [inter'fattʃa] *sf* (*Inform*) interface

interfe'renza [interfe'rɛntsa] *sf* interference

interfe'rire /55/ *vi* to interfere

interiezi'one [interjet'tsjone] *sf* exclamation, interjection

interi'nale *ag*: **lavoro ~** temporary work (*through an agency*)

interi'ora *sfpl* entrails

interi'ore *ag* inner *cpd*; **parte ~** inside

inter'medio, -a *ag* intermediate

inter'nare /72/ *vt* (*arrestare*) to intern; (*Med*) to commit (to a psychiatric facility)

inter'nauta *smf* Internet user

internazio'nale [internattsjo'nale] *ag* international

'Internet ['internet] *sf* Internet; **in ~** on the Internet

in'terno, -a *ag* (*di dentro*) internal, interior, inner; (: *mare*) inland; (*nazionale*) domestic; (*allievo*) boarding ▷ *sm* inside, interior; (*di paese*) interior; (*fodera*) lining; (*di appartamento*) flat (*BRIT*) *o* apartment (*US*) (number); (*Tel*) extension ▷ *sm/f* (*Ins*) boarder; **interni** *smpl* (*Cine*) interior shots; **all'~** inside; **Ministero degli Interni** Ministry of the Interior, ≈ Home Office (*BRIT*), ≈ Department of the Interior (*US*)

in'tero, -a *ag* (*integro, intatto*) whole, entire; (*completo, totale*) complete; (*numero*) whole; (*non ridotto: biglietto*) full; (*latte*) full-cream

interpel'lare /72/ *vt* to consult

interpre'tare /72/ *vt* to interpret; **in'terprete** *smf* interpreter; (*Teat*) actor (actress), performer; (*Mus*) performer; **farsi interprete di** to act as a spokesman for

interregio'nale [interredʒo'nale] *sm* train that travels between two or more regions of Italy

interro'gare /80/ *vt* to question; (*Ins*) to test; **interrogazi'one** *sf* questioning *no pl*; (*Ins*) oral test

inter'rompere /97/ *vt* to interrupt; (*studi, trattative*) to break off, interrupt; **interrompersi** *vpr* to break off, stop

interrut'tore *sm* switch

interruzi'one [interrut'tsjone] *sf* interruption; break

interur'bano, -a *ag* inter-city ▷ *sf* long-distance call

inter'vallo *sm* interval; (*spazio*) space, gap

interve'nire /128/ *vi* (*partecipare*): **~ a** to take part in; (*intromettersi, anche Pol*) to intervene; (*Med: operare*) to operate; **inter'vento** *sm* participation; (*intromissione*) intervention; (*Med*) operation; **fare un intervento nel corso di** (*dibattito, programma*) to take part in

inter'vista *sf* interview; **intervis'tare** /72/ *vt* to interview

intes'tare /72/ *vt* (*lettera*) to address; (*proprietà*): **~ a** to register in the name of; **~ un assegno a qn** to make out a cheque to sb

intestato, -a *ag* (*proprietà, casa, conto*) in the name of; (*assegno*) made out to; **carta intestata** headed paper

intes'tino *sm* (*Anat*) intestine

intimidazi'one [intimidat'tsjone] *sf* intimidation

intimi'dire /55/ *vt* to intimidate ▷ *vi* (*anche*: **intimidirsi**) to grow shy

intimità *sf* intimacy; privacy; (*familiarità*) familiarity

'intimo, -a ag intimate; (affetti, vita) private; (fig: profondo) inmost ▷ sm (persona) intimate o close friend; (dell'animo) bottom, depths pl; **parti intime** (Anat) private parts

in'tingolo sm sauce; (pietanza) stew

intito'lare /72/ vt (canto) to give a title to; (dedicare) to dedicate; **intitolarsi** vpr (libro, film) to be called

intolle'rabile ag intolerable

intolle'rante ag intolerant

in'tonaco, -ci o **-chi** sm plaster

into'nare /72/ vt (canto) to start to sing; (armonizzare) to match; **intonarsi** vpr (colori) to go together; **intonarsi a** (carnagione) to suit; (abito) to go with, match

inton'tito, -a ag stunned, dazed; **~ dal sonno** stupid with sleep

in'toppo sm stumbling block, obstacle

in'torno av around; **~ a** (attorno a) around; (riguardo, circa) about

intossi'care /20/ vt to poison; **intossicazi'one** sf poisoning

intralci'are [intral'tʃare] /14/ vt to hamper, hold up

intransi'tivo, -a ag, sm intransitive

intrapren'dente ag enterprising, go-ahead

intra'prendere /81/ vt to undertake

intrat'tabile ag intractable

intratte'nere /121/ vt to entertain; (chiacchierando) to engage in conversation; **intrattenersi** vpr to linger; **intrattenersi su qc** to dwell on sth

intrave'dere /127/ vt to catch a glimpse of; (fig) to foresee

intrecci'are [intret'tʃare] /14/ vt (capelli) to plait, braid; (intessere: anche fig) to weave, interweave, intertwine

intri'gante ag scheming ▷ smf schemer, intriguer

in'trinseco, -a, -ci, -che ag intrinsic

in'triso, -a ag: **~ (di)** soaked (in)

intro'durre /90/ vt to introduce; (chiave ecc): **~ qc in** to insert sth into; (persona: far entrare) to show in; **introdursi** vpr (moda, tecniche) to be introduced; **introdursi in** (persona: penetrare) to enter; (entrare furtivamente) to steal o slip into; **introduzi'one** sf introduction

in'troito sm income, revenue

intro'mettersi /63/ vpr to interfere, meddle; (interporsi) to intervene

in'truglio [in'truʎʎo] sm concoction

intrusi'one sf intrusion; interference

in'truso, -a sm/f intruder

intu'ire /55/ vt to perceive by intuition; (rendersi conto) to realize; **in'tuito** sm intuition; (perspicacia) perspicacity

inu'mano, -a ag inhuman

inumi'dire /55/ vt to dampen, moisten; **inumidirsi** vpr to become damp o wet

i'nutile ag useless; (superfluo) pointless, unnecessary

inutil'mente av (senza risultato) in vain; (senza utilità, scopo) unnecessarily

inva'dente ag (fig) interfering, nosey

in'vadere /52/ vt to invade; (affollare) to swarm into, overrun; (acque) to flood

inva'ghirsi [inva'girsi] /55/ vpr: **~ di** to take a fancy to

invalidità sf infirmity; disability; (Dir) invalidity

in'valido, -a ag (infermo) infirm, invalid; (al lavoro) disabled; (Dir: nullo) invalid ▷ sm/f invalid; person with a disability

in'vano av in vain

invasi'one sf invasion

inva'sore, invadi'trice [invadi'tritʃe] ag invading ▷ sm/f invader

invecchi'are [invek'kjare] /19/ vi (persona) to grow old; (vino, popolazione) to age; (moda) to become dated ▷ vt to age; (far apparire più vecchio) to make look older

in'vece [in'vetʃe] av instead; (al contrario) on the contrary; **~ di** instead of

inve'ire /55/ vi: **~ contro** to rail against

inven'tare /72/ vt to invent; (pericoli, pettegolezzi) to make up, invent

inven'tario sm inventory; (Comm) stocktaking no pl

inven'tore, -'trice sm/f inventor

invenzi'one [inven'tsjone] sf invention; (bugia) lie, story

inver'nale ag winter cpd; (simile all'inverno) wintry

in'verno sm winter

invero'simile ag unlikely

inversi'one sf inversion; reversal; **"divieto d'~"** (Aut) "no U-turns"

in'verso, -a ag opposite; (Mat) inverse ▷ sm contrary, opposite; **in senso ~** in the opposite direction; **in ordine ~** in reverse order

inver'tire /45/ vt to invert, reverse; **~ la marcia** (Aut) to do a U-turn

investi'gare /80/ vt, vi to investigate; **investiga'tore, -'trice** sm/f investigator, detective; **investigatore privato** private investigator

investi'mento sm (Econ) investment

inves'tire /45/ vt (denaro) to invest; (veicolo: pedone) to knock down; (: altro veicolo) to crash into; (apostrofare) to assail; (incaricare): **~ qn di** to invest sb with

invi'are /60/ vt to send; **invi'ato, -a** sm/f envoy; (Stampa) correspondent; **inviato speciale** (Pol) special envoy; (di giornale) special correspondent

in'vidia *sf* envy; **invidi'are** /19/ *vt*: **invidiare qn (per qc)** to envy sb (for sth); **invidiare qc a qn** to envy sb sth; **invidi'oso, -a** *ag* envious

in'vio, -'vii *sm* sending; *(insieme di merci)* consignment; *(tasto)* Return (key), Enter (key)

invipe'rito, -a *ag* furious

invi'sibile *ag* invisible

invi'tare /72/ *vt* to invite; **~ qn a fare** to invite sb to do; **invi'tato, -a** *sm/f* guest; **in'vito** *sm* invitation

invo'care /20/ *vt* (*chiedere: aiuto, pace*) to cry out for; (*appellarsi: la legge, Dio*) to appeal to, invoke

invogli'are [invoʎ'ʎare] /27/ *vt*: **~ qn a fare** to tempt sb to do, induce sb to do

involon'tario, -a *ag* (*errore*) unintentional; (*gesto*) involuntary

invol'tino *sm* (*Cuc*) roulade

in'volto *sm* (*pacco*) parcel; (*fagotto*) bundle

in'volucro *sm* cover, wrapping

inzup'pare [intsup'pare] /72/ *vt* to soak; **inzupparsi** *vpr* to get soaked

'io *pron* I ▷ *sm*: **l'io** the ego, the self; **io stesso(a)** I myself

i'odio *sm* iodine

l'onio *sm*: **lo ~, il mar ~** the Ionian (Sea)

iper'mercato *sm* hypermarket

ipertensi'one *sf* high blood pressure, hypertension

iper'testo *sm* hypertext; **ipertestu'ale** *ag* (*Inform*): **collegamento o link ipertestuale** hyperlink

ip'nosi *sf* hypnosis; **ipnotiz'zare** /72/ *vt* to hypnotize

ipocri'sia *sf* hypocrisy

i'pocrita, -i, -e *ag* hypocritical ▷ *smf* hypocrite

ipo'teca, -che *sf* mortgage

i'potesi *sf inv* hypothesis

'ippico, -a, -ci, -che *ag* horse *cpd* ▷ *sf* horseracing

ippocas'tano *sm* horse chestnut

ip'podromo *sm* racecourse

ippo'potamo *sm* hippopotamus

'ipsilon *sf o m inv* (*lettera*) Y, y; (*: dell'alfabeto greco*) epsilon

IR *abbr* (*= Interregionale*) long distance train which stops frequently

ira'cheno, -a [ira'kɛno] *ag, sm/f* Iraqi

l'ran *sm*: **l'~** Iran

irani'ano, -a *ag, sm/f* Iranian

l'raq *sm*: **l'~** Iraq

'iride *sf* (*arcobaleno*) rainbow; (*Anat, Bot*) iris

'iris *sm inv* iris

Ir'landa *sf*: **l'~** Ireland; **l'~ del Nord** Northern Ireland, Ulster; **la Repubblica d'~** Eire, the Republic of Ireland; **irlan'dese** *ag*

Irish ▷ *smf* Irishman/woman; **gli Irlandesi** the Irish

iro'nia *sf* irony; **i'ronico, -a, -ci, -che** *ag* ironic(al)

irragio'nevole [irrad͡ʒo'nevole] *ag* irrational; (*persona, pretese, prezzo*) unreasonable

irrazio'nale [irrattsjo'nale] *ag* irrational

irre'ale *ag* unreal

irrego'lare *ag* irregular; (*terreno*) uneven

irremo'vibile *ag* (*fig*) unshakeable, unyielding

irrequi'eto, -a *ag* restless

irresis'tibile *ag* irresistible

irrespon'sabile *ag* irresponsible

irri'gare /80/ *vt* (*annaffiare*) to irrigate; (*fiume ecc*) to flow through

irrigi'dire [irrid͡ʒi'dire] /55/ *vt* to stiffen; **irrigidirsi** *vpr* to stiffen

irri'sorio, -a *ag* derisory

irri'tare /72/ *vt* (*mettere di malumore*) to irritate, annoy; (*Med*) to irritate; **irritarsi** *vpr* (*stizzirsi*) to become irritated o annoyed; (*Med*) to become irritated

ir'rompere /97/ *vi*: **~ in** to burst into

irru'ente *ag* (*fig*) impetuous, violent

ir'ruppi *ecc vb vedi* **irrompere**

irruzi'one [irrut'tsjone] *sf*: **fare ~ in** to burst into; (*polizia*) to raid

is'crissi *ecc vb vedi* **iscrivere**

is'critto, -a *pp di* **iscrivere** ▷ *smf* member; **per o in ~** in writing

is'crivere /105/ *vt* to register, enter; (*persona*): **~ (a)** to register (in), enrol (in); **iscriversi** *vpr*: **iscriversi (a)** (*club, partito*) to join; (*università*) to register o enrol (at); (*esame, concorso*) to register o enter (for); **iscrizi'one** *sf* (*epigrafe ecc*) inscription; (*a scuola, società ecc*) enrolment, registration; (*registrazione*) registration

Is'lam *sm*: **l'~** Islam

Is'landa *sf*: **l'~** Iceland

islan'dese *ag* Icelandic ▷ *smf* Icelander ▷ *sm* (*Ling*) Icelandic

'isola *sf* island; **~ pedonale** (*Aut*) pedestrian precinct

isola'mento *sm* isolation; (*Tecn*) insulation

iso'lante *ag* insulating ▷ *sm* insulator

iso'lare /72/ *vt* to isolate; (*Tecn*) to insulate; (*: acusticamente*) to soundproof; **isolarsi** *vpr* to isolate o.s.; **iso'lato, -a** *ag* isolated; insulated ▷ *sm* (*edificio*) block

ispet'tore, -'trice *sm/f* inspector

ispezio'nare [ispettsjo'nare] /72/ *vt* to inspect

'ispido, -a *ag* bristly, shaggy

ispi'rare /72/ *vt* to inspire

Isra'ele *sm*: **l'~** Israel; **israeli'ano, -a** *ag, sm/f* Israeli

is'sare /72/ *vt* to hoist

istan'taneo, -a *ag* instantaneous ▷ *sf* (*Fot*) snapshot

is'tante *sm* instant, moment; **all'~, sull'~** instantly, immediately

is'terico, -a, -ci, -che *ag* hysterical

isti'gare /80/ *vt* to incite

is'tinto *sm* instinct

istitu'ire /55/ *vt* (*fondare*) to institute, found; (*porre: confronto*) to establish; (*intraprendere: inchiesta*) to set up

isti'tuto *sm* institute; (*di università*) department; (*ente, Dir*) institution; **~ di bellezza** beauty salon; **~ di credito** bank, banking institution; **~ di ricerca** research institute

istituzi'one [istitut'tsjone] *sf* institution

'istmo *sm* (*Geo*) isthmus

'istrice ['istritʃe] *sm* porcupine

istru'ito, -a *ag* educated

istrut'tore, -'trice *sm/f* instructor ▷ *ag*: **giudice ~** examining (*BRIT*) *o* committing (*US*) magistrate

istruzi'one [istrut'tsjone] *sf* (*gen*) training; (*Ins, cultura*) education; (*direttiva*) instruction; **istruzioni** *sfpl* (*norme*) instructions; **istruzioni per l'uso** instructions (for use); **~ obbligatoria** (*Ins*) compulsory education

l'talia *sf*: **l'~** Italy

itali'ano, -a *ag* Italian ▷ *sm/f* Italian ▷ *sm* (*Ling*) Italian; **gli Italiani** the Italians

itine'rario *sm* itinerary

'ittico, -a, -ci, -che *ag* fish *cpd*; fishing *cpd*

lugos'lavia *sf* = **Jugoslavia**

'I.V.A. *sigla f* (= *imposta sul valore aggiunto*) VAT

jazz [dʒaz] *sm* jazz

jeans [dʒinz] *smpl* jeans

Jeep® [dʒip] *sm inv* jeep

'jogging ['dʒɔgiŋ] *sm* jogging; **fare ~** to go jogging

'jolly ['dʒɔli] *sm inv* joker

joys'tick [dʒois'tik] *sm inv* joystick

ju'do [dʒu'dɔ] *sm* judo

Jugos'lavia [jugoz'lavja] *sf* (*Storia*): **la ~** Yugoslavia; **la ex-~** former Yugoslavia; **jugos'lavo, -a** *ag, sm/f* (*Storia*) Yugoslav(ian)

K l

K, k ['kappa] *sf o m inv (lettera)* K, k ▷ *abbr*
(= *kilo-, chilo-*) k; *(Inform)* K; **K come**
Kursaal ≈ K for King
kami'kaze [kami'kaddze] *sm inv* kamikaze
kara'oke [kara'oke] *sm inv* karaoke
kara'tè *sm* karate
ka'yak [ka'jak] *sm inv* kayak
'Kenia ['kɛnja] *sm*: **il ~** Kenya
kg *abbr* (= *chilogrammo*) kg
'killer *sm inv* gunman, hired gun
kitsch [kitʃ] *sm* kitsch
'kiwi ['kiwi] *sm inv* kiwi (fruit)
km *abbr* (= *chilometro*) km
K.'O. [kappa'ɔ] *sm inv* knockout
ko'ala [kɔ'ala] *sm inv* koala (bear)
koso'varo, -a *ag, sm/f* Kosovan
'Kosovo *sm* Kosovo
'krapfen *(Cuc) sm inv* doughnut
Ku'wait [ku'vait] *sm*: **il ~** Kuwait

l *abbr* (= *litro*) l
l' *det vedi* **la; lo; il**
la *det f (dav V* **l'***)* the ▷ *pron (dav V* **l'**: *oggetto:*
persona) her; (: *cosa)* it; (: *forma di cortesia)*
you; *vedi anche* **il**
là *av* there; **di là** (*da quel luogo*) from there;
(*in quel luogo*) in there; (*dall'altra parte*) over
there; **di là di** beyond; **per di là** that way;
più in là further on; (*tempo*) later on; **fatti
in là** move up; **là dentro/sopra/sotto** in/
up o on/under there; *vedi anche* **quello**
'labbro *sm (pl f* **labbra***) (Anat)* lip
labi'rinto *sm* labyrinth, maze
labora'torio *sm (di ricerca)* laboratory;
(*di arti, mestieri*) workshop; **~ linguistico**
language laboratory
labori'oso, -a *ag (faticoso)* laborious;
(*attivo*) hard-working
'lacca, -che *sf* lacquer
'laccio ['lattʃo] *sm* noose; (*legaccio, tirante*)
lasso; (*di scarpa*) lace; **~ emostatico**
tourniquet
lace'rare [latʃe'rare] /72/ *vt* to tear to
shreds, lacerate; **lacerarsi** *vpr* to tear
'lacrima *sf* tear; **in lacrime** in tears;
lacri'mogeno, -a *ag*: **gas lacrimogeno**
tear gas
la'cuna *sf (fig)* gap
'ladro *sm* thief
laggiù [lad'dʒu] *av* down there; (*di là*) over
there
la'gnarsi [laɲ'ɲarsi] /15/ *vpr*: **~ (di)** to
complain (about)
'lago, -ghi *sm* lake
la'guna *sf* lagoon
'laico, -a, -ci, -che *ag (apostolato)* lay;
(*vita*) secular; (*scuola*) non-denominational
▷ *sm/f* layman/woman
'lama *sf* blade ▷ *sm inv (Zool)* llama; (*Rel*)
lama

lamen'tare /72/ vt to lament; **lamentarsi** vpr (emettere lamenti) to moan, groan; (rammaricarsi): **lamentarsi (di)** to complain (about)

lamen'tela sf complaining no pl

la'metta sf razor blade

'lamina sf (lastra sottile) thin sheet (o layer o plate); **~ d'oro** gold leaf; gold foil

'lampada sf lamp; **~ a petrolio/a gas** oil/ gas lamp; **~ da tavolo** table lamp

lampa'dario sm chandelier

lampa'dina sf light bulb; **~ tascabile** pocket torch (BRIT), flashlight (US)

lam'pante ag (fig: evidente) crystal clear, evident

lampeggi'are [lamped'dʒare] /62/ vi (luce, fari) to flash ▷ vb impers: **lampeggia** there's lightning; **lampeggia'tore** sm (Aut) indicator

lampi'one sm street light o lamp (BRIT)

'lampo sm (Meteor) flash of lightning; (di luce, fig) flash

lam'pone sm raspberry

'lana sf wool; **~ d'acciaio** steel wool; **pura ~ vergine** pure new wool; **~ di vetro** glass wool

lan'cetta [lan'tʃetta] sf (indice) pointer, needle; (di orologio) hand

'lancia, -ce ['lantʃa] sf (arma) lance; (: picca) spear; (di pompa antincendio) nozzle; (imbarcazione) launch; **~ di salvataggio** lifeboat

lanciafi'amme [lantʃa'fjamme] sm inv flamethrower

lanci'are [lan'tʃare] /14/ vt to throw, hurl, fling; (Sport) to throw; (far partire: automobile) to get up to full speed; (bombe) to drop; (razzo, prodotto, moda) to launch; **lanciarsi** vpr: **lanciarsi contro/su** to throw o hurl o fling o.s. against/on; **lanciarsi in** (fig) to embark on

lanci'nante [lantʃi'nante] ag (dolore) shooting, throbbing; (grido) piercing

'lancio ['lantʃo] sm throwing no pl; throw; dropping no pl; drop; launching no pl; launch; **~ del disco** (Sport) throwing the discus; **~ del peso** (Sport) putting the shot

'languido, -a ag (fiacco) languid, weak; (tenero, malinconico) languishing

lan'terna sf lantern; (faro) lighthouse

'lapide sf (di sepolcro) tombstone; (commemorativa) plaque

'lapsus sm inv slip

'lardo sm bacon fat, lard

lar'ghezza [lar'gettsa] sf width; breadth; looseness; generosity; **~ di vedute** broad-mindedness

'largo, -a, -ghi, -ghe ag wide; broad; (maniche) wide; (abito: troppo ampio) loose; (fig) generous ▷ sm width; breadth; (mare aperto): **il ~** the open sea ▷ sf: **stare o tenersi alla larga (da qn/qc)** to keep one's distance (from sb/sth), keep away (from sb/sth); **~ due metri** two metres wide; **~ di spalle** broad-shouldered; **di larghe vedute** broad-minded; **su larga scala** on a large scale; **di manica larga** generous, open-handed; **al ~ di Genova** off (the coast of) Genoa; **farsi ~ tra la folla** to push one's way through the crowd

'larice ['laritʃe] sm (Bot) larch

larin'gite [larin'dʒite] sf laryngitis

'larva sf larva; (fig) shadow

la'sagne [la'zaɲɲe] sfpl lasagna sg

lasci'are [laʃʃare] /14/ vt to leave; (abbandonare) to leave, abandon, give up; (cessare di tenere) to let go of ▷ vb aus: **~ qn fare qc** to let sb do sth; **lasciarsi** vpr (persone) to part; (coppia) to split up; **~ andare o correre o perdere** to let things go their own way; **~ stare qc/qn** to leave sth/sb alone; **lasciarsi andare/truffare** to let o.s. go/be cheated

'laser ['lazer] ag, sm inv: **(raggio) ~** laser (beam)

lassa'tivo, -a ag, sm laxative

'lasso sm: **~ di tempo** interval, lapse of time

lassù av up there

'lastra sf (di pietra) slab; (di metallo, Fot) plate; (di ghiaccio, vetro) sheet; (radiografica) X-ray (plate)

lastri'cato sm paving

late'rale ag lateral, side cpd; (uscita, ingresso ecc) side cpd ▷ sm (Calcio) half-back

la'tino, -a ag, sm Latin

lati'tante smf fugitive (from justice)

lati'tudine sf latitude

'lato, -a ag (fig) wide, broad; **in senso ~** broadly speaking ▷ sm side; (fig) aspect, point of view

'latta sf tin (plate); (recipiente) tin, can

lat'tante ag unweaned

'latte sm milk; **~ detergente** cleansing milk o lotion; **~ intero** full-cream milk; **~ a lunga conservazione** UHT milk, long-life milk; **~ magro o scremato** skimmed milk; **~ secco o in polvere** dried o powdered milk; **~ solare** suntan lotion; **latti'cini** smpl dairy o milk products

lat'tina sf (di birra ecc) can

lat'tuga, -ghe sf lettuce

'laurea sf degree; **~ in ingegneria** engineering degree; **~ in lettere** ≈ arts degree

● **LAUREA**

● The laurea is awarded to students who
● successfully complete their degree
● courses. Traditionally, this takes between
● four and six years; a major element of the

* final examinations is the presentation
* and discussion of a dissertation. A shorter,
* more vocational course of study, taking
* from two to three years, is also available;
* at the end of this time students receive a
* diploma called the *laurea breve*.

laure'are /72/ *vt* to confer a degree on;
  laurearsi *vpr* to graduate
laure'ato, -a *ag, sm/f* graduate
'lauro *sm* laurel
'lauto, -a *ag* (*pranzo, mancia*) lavish
'lava *sf* lava
la'vabo *sm* washbasin
la'vaggio [la'vaddʒo] *sm* washing *no pl*;
  ~ del cervello brainwashing *no pl*; **~ a secco**
  dry-cleaning
la'vagna [la'vaɲɲa] *sf* (*Geo*) slate; (*di scuola*)
  blackboard; **~ interattiva** interactive
  whiteboard
la'vanda *sf* (*anche Med*) wash; (*Bot*)
  lavender; **lavande'ria** *sf* laundry;
  lavanderia automatica launderette;
  lavanderia a secco dry-cleaner's;
  lavan'dino *sm* sink
lavapi'atti *smf inv* dishwasher
la'vare /72/ *vt* to wash; **lavarsi** *vpr* to
  wash, have a wash; **~ a secco** to dry-clean;
  lavarsi le mani/i denti to wash one's
  hands/clean one's teeth
lava'secco *sf o m inv* dry-cleaner's
lavasto'viglie [lavasto'viʎʎe] *sf o m inv*
  (*macchina*) dishwasher
lava'trice [lava'tritʃe] *sf* washing machine
la'vello *sm* (kitchen) sink
lavo'rare /72/ *vi* to work; (*fig: bar, studio ecc*)
  to do good business ▷ *vt* to work; **~ a**
  work on; **~ a maglia** to knit; **lavorarsi qn**
  (*fig: convincere*) to work on sb; **lavora'tivo,
  -a** *ag* working; **lavora'tore, -'trice** *sm/f*
  worker ▷ *ag* working
la'voro *sm* work; (*occupazione*) job, work *no
  pl*; (*opera*) piece of work, job; (*Econ*) labour;
  che ~ fa? what do you do?; **lavori forzati**
  hard labour *sg*; **~ interinale** *o* **in affitto**
  temporary work
le *det fpl* the ▷ *pron* (*oggetto*) them; (: *a lei, a
  essa*) (to) her; (: *forma di cortesia*) (to) you;
  vedi anche **il**
le'ale *ag* loyal; (*sincero*) sincere; (*onesto*) fair
'lecca 'lecca *sm inv* lollipop
leccapi'edi *smf inv* (*peg*) toady, bootlicker
lec'care /20/ *vt* to lick; (*gatto: latte ecc*) to
  lick up *o* lap up; (*fig*) to flatter; **leccarsi i baffi**
  to lick one's lips
leccherò *ecc* [lekke'rɔ] *vb vedi* **leccare**
'leccio ['lettʃo] *sm* holm oak, ilex
leccor'nia *sf* titbit, delicacy
'lecito, -a ['letʃito] *ag* permitted, allowed

'lega, -ghe *sf* league; (*di metalli*) alloy
le'gaccio [le'gattʃo] *sm* string, lace
le'gale *ag* legal ▷ *sm* lawyer; **legaliz'zare**
  /72/ *vt* to legalize; (*documento*) to
  authenticate
le'game *sm* (*corda, fig: affettivo*) tie, bond;
  (*nesso logico*) link, connection
le'gare /80/ *vt* (*prigioniero, capelli, cane*) to
  tie (up); (*libro*) to bind; (*Chim*) to alloy; (*fig:
  collegare*) to bind, join ▷ *vi* (*far lega*) to unite;
  (*fig*) to get on well
le'genda [le'dʒɛnda] *sf* (*di carta geografica
  ecc*); = **leggenda**
'legge ['leddʒe] *sf* law
leg'genda [led'dʒɛnda] *sf* (*narrazione*)
  legend; (*di carta geografica ecc*) key, legend
'leggere ['leddʒere] /61/ *vt*, *vi* to read
legge'rezza [leddʒe'rettsa] *sf* lightness;
  thoughtlessness; fickleness
leg'gero, -a [led'dʒɛro] *ag* light; (*agile,
  snello*) nimble, agile, light; (*tè, caffè*) weak;
  (*fig: non grave, piccolo*) slight; (: *spensierato*)
  thoughtless; (: *incostante*) fickle; free and
  easy; **alla leggera** thoughtlessly
leg'gio, -'gii [led'dʒio] *sm* lectern; (*Mus*)
  music stand
legherò *ecc* [lege'rɔ] *vb vedi* **legare**
legisla'tivo, -a [ledʒizla'tivo] *ag* legislative
legisla'tura [ledʒizla'tura] *sf* legislature
le'gittimo, -a [le'dʒittimo] *ag* legitimate;
  (*fig: giustificato, lecito*) justified, legitimate;
  legittima difesa (*Dir*) self-defence (BRIT),
  self-defense (US)
'legna ['leɲɲa] *sf* firewood
'legno ['leɲɲo] *sm* wood; (*pezzo di
  legno*) piece of wood; **di ~** wooden;
  ~ compensato plywood
le'gume *sm* (*Bot*) pulse; **legumi** *smpl* pulses
'lei *pron* (*soggetto*) she; (*oggetto: per dare
  rilievo, con preposizione*) her; (*forma di
  cortesia: anche*: **L~**) you ▷ *sm*: **dare del ~
  a qn** to address sb as "lei"; **~ stessa** she
  herself; you yourself

lenta'mente *av* slowly
'lente *sf* (*Ottica*) lens *sg*; **~ d'ingrandimento**
  magnifying glass; **lenti** *sfpl* (*occhiali*) lenses;
  lenti a contatto, lenti corneali contact
  lenses; **lenti (a contatto) morbide/rigide**
  soft/hard contact lenses
len'tezza [len'tettsa] *sf* slowness
len'ticchia [len'tikkja] *sf* (*Bot*) lentil

len'tiggine [len'tiddʒine] *sf* freckle
'lento, -a *ag* slow; *(molle: fune)* slack; *(non stretto: vite, abito)* loose ▷ *sm (ballo)* slow dance
'lenza ['lɛntsa] *sf* fishing line
lenzu'olo [len'tswɔlo] *sm* sheet
le'one *sm* lion; **L~** Leo
lepo'rino, -a *ag*: **labbro ~** harelip
'lepre *sf* hare
'lercio, -a, -ci, -ce ['lɛrtʃo] *ag* filthy
lesi'one *sf (Med)* lesion; *(Dir)* injury, damage; *(Edil)* crack
les'sare /72/ *vt (Cuc)* to boil
'lessi *ecc vb vedi* **leggere**
'lessico, -ci *sm* vocabulary; *(dizionario)* lexicon
'lesso, -a *ag* boiled ▷ *sm* boiled meat
'le'tale *ag* lethal; fatal
leta'maio *sm* dunghill
le'tame *sm* manure, dung
le'targo, -ghi *sm* lethargy; *(Zool)* hibernation
'lettera *sf* letter; **lettere** *sfpl (letteratura)* literature *sg*; *(studi umanistici)* arts (subjects); **alla ~** literally; **in lettere** in words, in full
letteral'mente *av* literally
lette'rario, -a *ag* literary
lette'rato, -a *ag* well-read, scholarly
lettera'tura *sf* literature
let'tiga, -ghe *sf (barella)* stretcher
let'tino *sm* cot (BRIT), crib (US); *(per il sole)* sun lounger; **~ solare** sunbed
'letto, -a *pp di* **leggere** ▷ *sm* bed; **andare a ~** to go to bed; **~ a castello** bunk beds *pl*; **~ a una piazza/a due piazze** *o* **matrimoniale** single/double bed
let'tore, -'trice *sm/f* reader; *(Ins)* (foreign language) assistant (BRIT), (foreign) teaching assistant (US) ▷ *sm (Tecn)*: **~ di libri digitali** e-reader; **~ ottico (di caratteri)** optical character reader; **~ CD/DVD** CD/DVD player; **~ MP3/MP4** MP3/MP4 player
let'tura *sf* reading

> Attenzione! In inglese esiste la parola *lecture*, che però significa *lezione* oppure *conferenza*.

leuce'mia [leutʃe'mia] *sf* leukaemia
'leva *sf* lever; *(Mil)* conscription; **far ~ su qn** to work on sb; **~ del cambio** *(Aut)* gear lever
le'vante *sm* east; *(vento)* East wind; **il L~** the Levant
le'vare /72/ *vt (occhi, braccio)* to raise; *(sollevare, togliere: tassa, divieto)* to lift; *(: indumenti)* to take off, remove; *(rimuovere)* to take away; *(: dal di sopra)* to take off; *(: dal di dentro)* to take out
leva'toio, -a *ag*: **ponte ~** drawbridge

lezi'one [let'tsjone] *sf* lesson; *(all'università, sgridata)* lecture; **fare ~** to teach; to lecture; **dare una ~ a qn** to teach sb a lesson; **lezioni private** private lessons
li *pron (oggetto)* them
lì *av* there; **di** *o* **da lì** from there; **per di lì** that way; **di lì a pochi giorni** a few days later; **lì per lì** there and then; at first; **essere lì (lì) per fare** to be on the point of doing, be about to do; **lì dentro** in there; **lì sotto** under there; **lì sopra** on there; up there; *vedi anche* **quello**
liba'nese *ag*, *sm/f* Lebanese *inv*
Li'bano *sm*: **il ~** the Lebanon
'libbra *sf (peso)* pound
li'beccio [li'bettʃo] *sm* south-west wind
li'bellula *sf* dragonfly
libe'rale *ag*, *sm/f* liberal
liberaliz'zare [liberalid'dzare] /72/ *vt* to liberalize
libe'rare /72/ *vt (rendere libero: prigioniero)* to release; *(: popolo)* to free, liberate; *(sgombrare: passaggio)* to clear; *(: stanza)* to vacate; *(produrre: energia)* to release; **liberarsi** *vpr*: **liberarsi di qc/qn** to get rid of sth/sb; **liberazi'one** *sf (di prigioniero)* release, freeing; *(di popolo)* liberation; rescuing

LIBERAZIONE

- The *Liberazione* is a national holiday which
- falls on 25 April. It commemorates the
- liberation of Italy in 1945 from German
- forces and Mussolini's government and
- marks the end of the war on Italian soil.

'libero, -a *ag* free; *(strada)* clear; *(non occupato: posto ecc)* vacant; free; not taken; empty; not engaged; **~ di fare qc** free to do sth; **~ da** free from; **~ arbitrio** free will; **~ professionista** self-employed professional person; **~ scambio** free trade; **libertà** *sf inv* freedom; *(tempo disponibile)* free time ▷ *sfpl (licenza)* liberties; **essere in libertà provvisoria/vigilata** to be released without bail/be on probation
'Libia *sf*: **la ~** Libya; **'libico, -a, -ci, -che** *ag*, *sm/f* Libyan
li'bidine *sf* lust
li'braio *sm* bookseller
li'brarsi /72/ *vpr* to hover
libre'ria *sf (bottega)* bookshop; *(mobile)* bookcase

> Attenzione! In inglese esiste la parola *library*, che però significa *biblioteca*.

li'bretto *sm* booklet; *(taccuino)* notebook; *(Mus)* libretto; **~ degli assegni** chequebook; **~ di circolazione** *(Aut)* logbook; **~ di risparmio** (savings) bankbook, passbook; **~ universitario** student's report book

'libro sm book; **~ di cassa** cash book; **~ mastro** ledger; **~ paga** payroll; **~ di testo** textbook

li'cenza [li'tʃɛntsa] sf (permesso) permission, leave; (di pesca, caccia, circolazione) permit, licence; (Mil) leave; (Ins) school-leaving certificate; (libertà) liberty; licence; (sfrenatezza) licentiousness; **andare in ~** (Mil) to go on leave

licenzia'mento [litʃentsja'mento] sm dismissal

licenzi'are [litʃen'tsjare] /19/ vt (impiegato) to dismiss; (Comm: per eccesso di personale) to make redundant; (Ins) to award a certificate to; **licenziarsi** vpr (impiegato) to resign, hand in one's notice; (Ins) to obtain one's school-leaving certificate

li'ceo [li'tʃɛo] sm (Ins) secondary (BRIT) o high (US) school (for 14- to 19-year-olds)

'lido sm beach, shore

'Liechtenstein ['liktənstain] sm: **il ~** Liechtenstein

li'eto, -a ag happy, glad; **"molto ~"** (nelle presentazioni) "pleased to meet you"

li'eve ag light; (di poco conto) slight; (sommesso: voce) faint, soft

lievi'tare /72/ vi (anche fig) to rise ▷ vt to leaven

li'evito sm yeast; **~ di birra** brewer's yeast

'ligio, -a, -gi, -gie ['lidʒo] ag faithful, loyal

'lilla, lillà sm inv lilac

'lima sf file; **~ da unghie** nail file

limacci'oso, -a [limat'tʃoso] ag slimy; muddy

li'mare /72/ vt to file (down); (fig) to polish

limi'tare /72/ vt to limit, restrict; (circoscrivere) to bound, surround; **limitarsi** vpr: **limitarsi nel mangiare** to limit one's eating; **limitarsi a qc/a fare qc** to limit o.s. to sth/to doing sth

'limite sm limit; (confine) border, boundary; **~ di velocità** speed limit

limo'nata sf lemonade (BRIT), (lemon) soda (US); (spremuta) lemon squash (BRIT), lemonade (US)

li'mone sm (pianta) lemon tree; (frutto) lemon

'limpido, -a ag (acqua) limpid, clear; (cielo) clear

'lince ['lintʃe] sf lynx

linci'are [lin'tʃare] /14/ vt to lynch

'linea sf line; (di mezzi pubblici di trasporto: itinerario) route; (: servizio) service; **a grandi linee** in outline; **mantenere la ~** to look after one's figure; **aereo di ~** airliner; **nave di ~** liner; **volo di ~** scheduled flight;

~ aerea airline; **~ di partenza/d'arrivo** (Sport) starting/finishing line; **~ di tiro** line of fire

linea'menti smpl features; (fig) outlines

line'are ag linear; (fig) coherent, logical

line'etta sf (trattino) dash; (d'unione) hyphen

lin'gotto sm ingot, bar

'lingua sf (Anat, Cuc) tongue; (idioma) language; **mostrare la ~** to stick out one's tongue; **di ~ italiana** Italian-speaking; **~ madre** mother tongue; **una ~ di terra** a spit of land

lingu'aggio [lin'gwaddʒo] sm language

lingu'etta sf (di strumento) reed; (di scarpa, Tecn) tongue; (di busta) flap

'lino sm (pianta) flax; (tessuto) linen

li'noleum sm inv linoleum, lino

liposuzi'one [liposut'tsjone] sf liposuction

liqui'dare /72/ vt (società, beni, persona: uccidere) to liquidate; (persona: sbarazzarsene) to get rid of; (conto, problema) to settle; (Comm: merce) to sell off, clear; **liquidazi'one** sf liquidation; (di conto) settlement; (di merce) clearance sale

liquidità sf liquidity

'liquido, -a ag, sm liquid; **~ per freni** brake fluid

liqui'rizia [likwi'rittsja] sf liquorice

li'quore sm liqueur

'lira sf (unità monetaria) lira; (Mus) lyre; **~ sterlina** pound sterling

'lirico, -a, -ci, -che ag lyric(al); (Mus) lyric; **cantante/teatro ~** opera singer/house

Lis'bona sf Lisbon

'lisca, -sche sf (di pesce) fishbone

lisci'are [liʃ'ʃare] /14/ vt to smooth; (fig) to flatter

'liscio, -a, -sci, -sce ['liʃʃo] ag smooth; (capelli) straight; (mobile) plain; (bevanda alcolica) neat; (fig) straightforward, simple ▷ av: **andare ~** to go smoothly; **passarla liscia** to get away with it

'liso, -a ag worn out, threadbare

'lista sf (elenco) list; **~ elettorale** electoral roll; **~ delle spese** shopping list; **~ dei vini** wine list; **~ delle vivande** menu

lis'tino sm list; **~ dei cambi** (foreign) exchange rate; **~ dei prezzi** price list

'lite sf quarrel, argument; (Dir) lawsuit

liti'gare /80/ vi to quarrel; (Dir) to litigate

li'tigio [li'tidʒo] sm quarrel

lito'rale ag coastal, coast cpd ▷ sm coast

'litro sm litre

livel'lare /72/ vt to level, make level

li'vello sm level; (fig) level, standard; **ad alto ~** (fig) high-level; **~ del mare** sea level

'livido, -a ag livid; (per percosse) bruised, black and blue; (cielo) leaden ▷ sm bruise

Li'vorno sf Livorno, Leghorn

'lizza ['littsa] *sf* lists *pl*; **scendere in ~** to enter the lists

lo *det m* (*dav s impura, gn, pn, ps, x, z*; *dav V* **l'**) the ▷ *pron* (*dav V* **l'**, *oggetto: persona*) him; (: *cosa*) it; **lo sapevo** I knew it; **lo so** I know; **sii buono, anche se lui non lo è** be good, even if he isn't; *vedi anche* **il**

lo'cale *ag* local ▷ *sm* room; (*luogo pubblico*) premises *pl*; **~ notturno** nightclub; **località** *sf inv* locality

lo'canda *sf* inn

locomo'tiva *sf* locomotive

locuzi'one [lokut'tsjone] *sf* phrase, expression

lo'dare /72/ *vt* to praise

'lode *sf* praise; (*Ins*): **laurearsi con 110 e ~** ≈ to graduate with first-class honours (*BRIT*), ≈ to graduate summa cum laude (*US*)

'loden *sm inv* (*stoffa*) loden; (*cappotto*) loden overcoat

lo'devole *ag* praiseworthy

loga'ritmo *sm* logarithm

log'garsi /72/ *vpr* (*Inform*) to log in

'loggia, -ge ['lɔddʒa] *sf* (*Archit*) loggia; (*circolo massonico*) lodge; **loggi'one** *sm* (*di teatro*): **il loggione** the Gods *sg*

'logico, -a, -ci, -che ['lɔdʒiko] *ag* logical

logo'rare /72/ *vt* to wear out; (*sciupare*) to waste; **logorarsi** *vpr* to wear out; (*fig*) to wear o.s. out

'logoro, -a *ag* (*stoffa*) worn out, threadbare; (*persona*) worn out

Lombar'dia *sf*: **la ~** Lombardy

lom'bata *sf* (*taglio di carne*) loin

lom'brico, -chi *sm* earthworm

londi'nese *ag* London *cpd* ▷ *smf* Londoner

'Londra *sf* London

lon'gevo, -a [lon'dʒevo] *ag* long-lived

longi'tudine [londʒi'tudine] *sf* longitude

lonta'nanza [lonta'nantsa] *sf* distance; absence

lon'tano, -a *ag* (*distante*) distant, faraway; (*assente*) absent; (*vago: sospetto*) slight, remote; (*tempo: remoto*) far-off, distant; (*parente*) distant, remote ▷ *av* far; **è lontana la casa?** is it far to the house?, is the house far from here?; **è ~ un chilometro** it's a kilometre away or a kilometre from here; **più ~** farther; **da o di ~** from a distance; **~ da** a long way from; **è molto ~ da qui?** is it far from here?; **alla lontana** slightly, vaguely

lo'quace [lo'kwatʃe] *ag* talkative, loquacious; (*fig: gesto ecc*) eloquent

'lordo, -a *ag* dirty, filthy; (*peso, stipendio*) gross

'loro *pron pl* (*oggetto, con preposizione*) them; (*complemento di termine*) to them; (*soggetto*) they; (*forma di cortesia: anche:* **L~**) you;

to you; **il (la) ~, i (le) ~** *det* their; (*forma di cortesia: anche:* **L~**) your ▷ *pron* theirs; (*forma di cortesia: anche:* **L~**) yours; **~ stessi(e)** they themselves; you yourselves

'losco, -a, -schi, -sche *ag* (*fig*) shady, suspicious

'lotta *sf* struggle, fight; (*Sport*) wrestling; **~ libera** all-in wrestling; **lot'tare** /72/ *vi* to fight, struggle; to wrestle

lotte'ria *sf* lottery; (*di gara ippica*) sweepstake

'lotto *sm* (*gioco*) (state) lottery; (*parte*) lot; (*Edil*) site

● **LOTTO**

● The *Lotto* is an official lottery run by the
● Italian Finance Ministry. It consists of
● a weekly draw of numbers and is very
● popular.

lozi'one [lot'tsjone] *sf* lotion

lubrifi'cante *sm* lubricant

lubrifi'care /20/ *vt* to lubricate

luc'chetto [luk'ketto] *sm* padlock

lucci'care [luttʃi'kare] /20/ *vi* to sparkle; (*oro*) to glitter; (*stella*) to twinkle

'luccio ['luttʃo] *sm* (*Zool*) pike

'lucciola ['luttʃola] *sf* (*Zool*) firefly; glow-worm

'luce ['lutʃe] *sf* light; (*finestra*) window; **alla ~ di** by the light of; **fare ~ su qc** (*fig*) to shed o throw light on sth; **~ del sole/della luna** sun/moonlight

lucer'nario [lutʃer'narjo] *sm* skylight

lu'certola [lu'tʃertola] *sf* lizard

luci'dare [lutʃi'dare] /72/ *vt* to polish

lucida'trice [lutʃida'tritʃe] *sf* floor polisher

'lucido, -a ['lutʃido] *ag* shining, bright; (*lucidato*) polished; (*fig*) lucid ▷ *sm* shine, lustre; (*per scarpe ecc*) polish; (*disegno*) tracing

'lucro *sm* profit, gain

'luglio ['luʎʎo] *sm* July

'lugubre *ag* gloomy

'lui *pron* (*soggetto*) he; (*oggetto: per dare rilievo, con preposizione*) him; **~ stesso** he himself

lu'maca, -che *sf* slug; (*chiocciola*) snail

lumi'noso, -a *ag* (*che emette luce*) luminous; (*cielo, colore, stanza*) bright; (*sorgente*) of light, light *cpd*; (*fig: sorriso*) bright, radiant

'luna *sf* moon; **~ nuova/piena** new/full moon; **~ di miele** honeymoon

'luna park *sm inv* amusement park, funfair

lu'nare *ag* lunar, moon *cpd*

lu'nario *sm* almanac; **sbarcare il ~** to make ends meet

lu'natico, -a, -ci, -che *ag* whimsical, temperamental

lunedì *sm inv* Monday; **di** *o* **il ~** on Mondays
lun'ghezza [lun'gettsa] *sf* length; **~ d'onda** (*Fisica*) wavelength
'lungo, -a, -ghi, -ghe *ag* long; (*lento: persona*) slow; (*diluito: caffè, brodo*) weak, watery, thin ▷ *sm* length ▷ *prep* along; **~ 3 metri** 3 metres long; **a ~** for a long time; **a ~ andare** in the long run; **di gran lunga** (*molto*) by far; **andare in ~** *o* **per le lunghe** to drag on; **saperla lunga** to know what's what; **in ~ e in largo** far and wide, all over; **~ il corso dei secoli** throughout the centuries
lungo'mare *sm* promenade
lu'notto *sm* (*Aut*) rear *o* back window; **~ termico** heated rear window
lu'ogo, -ghi *sm* place; (*posto: di incidente ecc*) scene, site; (*punto, passo di libro*) passage; **in ~ di** instead of; **in primo ~** in the first place; **aver ~** to take place; **dar ~ a** to give rise to; **~ comune** commonplace; **~ di nascita** birthplace; (*Amm*) place of birth; **~ di provenienza** place of origin
'lupo, -a *sm/f* wolf/she-wolf
'luppolo *sm* (*Bot*) hop
'lurido, -a *ag* filthy
lusin'gare /80/ *vt* to flatter
Lussem'burgo *sm* (*stato*): **il ~** Luxembourg ▷ *sf* (*città*) Luxembourg
'lusso *sm* luxury; **di ~** luxury *cpd*; **lussu'oso, -a** *ag* luxurious
lus'suria *sf* lust
lus'trino *sm* sequin
'lutto *sm* mourning; **essere in/portare il ~** to be in/wear mourning

m

m. *abbr* = **mese**; **metro**; **miglia**; **monte**
ma *cong* but; **ma insomma!** for goodness sake!; **ma no!** of course not!
'macabro, -a *ag* gruesome, macabre
macché [mak'ke] *escl* not at all!, certainly not!
macche'roni [makke'rɔni] *smpl* macaroni *sg*
'macchia ['makkja] *sf* stain, spot; (*chiazza di diverso colore*) spot, splash, patch; (*tipo di boscaglia*) scrub; **darsi/vivere alla ~** (*fig*) to go into/live in hiding; **macchi'are** /19/ *vt* (*sporcare*) to stain, mark; **macchiarsi** *vpr* (*persona*) to get o.s. dirty; (*stoffa*) to stain; to get stained *o* marked
macchi'ato, -a [mak'kjato] *ag* (*pelle, pelo*) spotted; **~ di** stained with; **caffè ~** coffee with a dash of milk
'macchina ['makkina] *sf* machine; (*motore, locomotiva*) engine; (*automobile*) car; (*fig: meccanismo*) machinery; **andare in ~** (*Aut*) to go by car; (*Stampa*) to go to press; **~ da cucire** sewing machine; **~ fotografica** camera; **~ da presa** cine *o* movie camera; **~ da scrivere** typewriter; **~ a vapore** steam engine
macchi'nario [makki'narjo] *sm* machinery
macchi'nista, -i [makki'nista] *sm* (*di treno*) engine-driver; (*di nave*) engineer
Mace'donia [matʃe'dɔnja] *sf* Macedonia
mace'donia [matʃe'dɔnja] *sf* fruit salad
macel'laio [matʃel'lajo] *sm* butcher
macelle'ria *sf* butcher's (shop)
ma'cerie [ma'tʃɛrje] *sfpl* rubble *sg*, debris *sg*
ma'cigno [ma'tʃiɲɲo] *sm* (*masso*) rock, boulder
maci'nare [matʃi'nare] /72/ *vt* to grind; (*carne*) to mince (BRIT), grind (US)
macrobi'otico, -a *ag* macrobiotic ▷ *sf* macrobiotics *sg*

Ma'donna *sf* (*Rel*) Our Lady

mador'nale *ag* enormous, huge

'madre *sf* mother; (*matrice di bolletta*) counterfoil ▷ *ag inv* mother *cpd*; **ragazza ~** unmarried mother; **scena ~** (*Teat*) principal scene; (*fig*) terrible scene

madre'lingua *sf* mother tongue, native language

madre'perla *sf* mother-of-pearl

ma'drina *sf* godmother

maestà *sf inv* majesty

ma'estra *sf vedi* **maestro**

maes'trale *sm* north-west wind, mistral

ma'estro, -a *sm/f* (*Ins: anche:* **~ di scuola** *o* **elementare**) primary (*BRIT*) *o* grade school (*US*) teacher; (*esperto*) expert ▷ *sm* (*artigiano, fig: guida*) master; (*Mus*) maestro ▷ *ag* (*principale*) main; (*di grande abilità*) masterly, skilful; **maestra d'asilo** nursery teacher; **~ di cerimonie** master of ceremonies

'mafia *sf* Mafia

'maga, -ghe *sf* sorceress

ma'gari *escl* (*esprime desiderio*): **~ fosse vero!** if only it were true! **ti piacerebbe andare in Scozia? — ~!** would you like to go to Scotland? — I certainly would! ▷ *av* (*anche*) even; (*forse*) perhaps

magaz'zino [magad'dzino] *sm* warehouse; **grande ~** department store

⚠ Attenzione! In inglese esiste la parola *magazine*, che però significa *rivista*.

'maggio ['maddʒo] *sm* May

maggio'rana [maddʒo'rana] *sf* (*Bot*) (sweet) marjoram

maggio'ranza [maddʒo'rantsa] *sf* majority

maggior'domo [maddʒor'dɔmo] *sm* butler

maggi'ore [mad'dʒore] *ag* (*comparativo: più grande*) bigger, larger; taller; greater; (*: più vecchio: sorella, fratello*) older, elder; (*: di grado superiore*) senior; (*: più importante: Mil, Mus*) major; (*superlativo*) biggest, largest; tallest; greatest; oldest, eldest ▷ *smf* (*di grado*) superior; (*di età*) elder; (*Mil*) major; (*: Aer*) squadron leader; **la maggior parte** the majority; **andare per la ~** (*cantante, attore ecc*) to be very popular; **maggio'renne** *ag* of age ▷ *smf* person who has come of age

ma'gia [ma'dʒia] *sf* magic; **'magico, -a, -ci, -che** *ag* magic; (*fig*) fascinating, charming, magical

magis'trato [madʒis'trato] *sm* magistrate

'maglia ['maʎʎa] *sf* stitch; (*lavoro ai ferri*) knitting *no pl*; (*tessuto, Sport*) jersey; (*maglione*) jersey, sweater; (*di catena*) link; (*di rete*) mesh; **~ diritta/rovescia** plain/ purl; **magli'etta** *sf* (*canottiera*) vest; (*tipo camicia*) T-shirt

magli'one [maʎ'ʎone] *sm* jumper, sweater

ma'gnetico, -a, -ci, -che *ag* magnetic

ma'gnifico, -a, -ci, -che [maɲ'nifiko] *ag* magnificent, splendid; (*ospite*) generous

ma'gnolia [maɲ'nɔlja] *sf* magnolia

'mago, -ghi *sm* (*stregone*) magician, wizard; (*illusionista*) magician

ma'grezza [ma'grettsa] *sf* thinness

'magro, -a *ag* (*very*) thin, skinny; (*carne*) lean; (*formaggio*) low-fat; (*fig: scarso, misero*) meagre, poor; (*: meschino: scusa*) poor, lame; **mangiare di ~** not to eat meat

'mai *av* (*nessuna volta*) never; (*talvolta*) ever; **non ... ~** never; **~ più** never again; **come ~?** why (*o* how) on earth? **chi/dove/quando ~?** whoever/wherever/whenever?

mai'ale *sm* (*Zool*) pig; (*carne*) pork

mail ['meil] *sf inv* = **e-mail**

maio'nese *sf* mayonnaise

'mais *sm* maize

mai'uscolo, -a *ag* (*lettera*) capital; (*fig*) enormous, huge

mala'fede *sf* bad faith

malan'dato, -a *ag* (*persona: di salute*) in poor health; (*: di condizioni finanziarie*) badly off; (*trascurato*) shabby

ma'lanno *sm* (*disgrazia*) misfortune; (*malattia*) ailment

mala'pena *sf*: **a ~** hardly, scarcely

ma'laria *sf* (*Med*) malaria

ma'lato, -a *ag* ill, sick; (*gamba*) bad; (*pianta*) diseased ▷ *sm/f* sick person; (*in ospedale*) patient; **malat'tia** *sf* (*infettiva ecc*) illness, disease; (*cattiva salute*) illness, sickness; (*di pianta*) disease

mala'vita *sf* underworld

mala'voglia [mala'vɔʎʎa] *sf*: **di ~** *av* unwillingly, reluctantly

Mala'ysia *sf* Malaysia

mal'concio, -a, -ci, -ce [mal'kontʃo] *ag* in a sorry state

malcon'tento *sm* discontent

malcos'tume *sm* immorality

mal'destro, -a *ag* (*inabile*) inexpert, inexperienced; (*goffo*) awkward

'male *av* badly ▷ *sm* (*ciò che è ingiusto, disonesto*) evil; (*danno, svantaggio*) harm; (*sventura*) misfortune; (*dolore fisico, morale*) pain, ache; **sentirsi ~** to feel ill; **aver mal di cuore/fegato** to have a heart/liver complaint; **aver mal di denti/d'orecchi/ di testa** to have toothache/earache/a headache; **aver mal di gola** to have a sore throat; **aver ~ ai piedi** to have sore feet; **far ~** (*dolere*) to hurt; **far ~ alla salute** to be bad for one's health; **far del ~ a qn** to hurt *o* harm sb; **restare** *o* **rimanere ~** to be sorry;

to be disappointed, to be hurt; **trattar ~ qn** to ill-treat sb; **andare a ~** to go off o bad; **come va? — non c'è ~** how are you? — not bad; **di ~ in peggio** from bad to worse; **mal d'auto** carsickness; **mal di mare** seasickness

male'detto, -a pp di **maledire** ▷ ag cursed, damned; (fig fam) damned, blasted

male'dire /38/ vt to curse; **maledizi'one** sf curse; **maledizione!** damn it!

maledu'cato, -a ag rude, ill-mannered

maleducazi'one [maledukat'tsjone] sf rudeness

ma'lefico, -a, -ci, -che ag (influsso, azione) evil

ma'lessere sm indisposition, slight illness; (fig) uneasiness

malfa'mato, -a ag notorious

malfat't'ore, -'trice sm/f wrongdoer

mal'fermo, -a ag unsteady, shaky; (salute) poor, delicate

mal'grado prep in spite of, despite ▷ cong although; **mio o tuo** ecc ~ against my (o your ecc) will

ma'ligno, -a [ma'liɲɲo] ag (malvagio) malicious, malignant; (Med) malignant

malinco'nia sf melancholy, gloom; **malin'conico, -a, -ci, -che** ag melancholy

malincu'ore: a ~ av reluctantly, unwillingly

malin'teso, -a ag misunderstood; (riguardo, senso del dovere) mistaken, wrong ▷ sm misunderstanding; **c'è stato un ~** there's been a misunderstanding

ma'lizia [ma'littsja] sf (malignità) malice; (furbizia) cunning; (espediente) trick; **malizi'oso, -a** ag malicious; cunning; (vivace, birichino) mischievous

malme'nare /72/ vt to beat up

ma'locchio [ma'lɔkkjo] sm evil eye

ma'lora sf: **andare in ~** to go to the dogs

ma'lore sm (sudden) illness

mal'sano, -a ag unhealthy

'malta sf (Edil) mortar

mal'tempo sm bad weather

'malto sm malt

maltrat't'are /72/ vt to ill-treat

malu'more sm bad mood; (irritabilità) bad temper; (discordia) ill feeling; **di ~** in a bad mood

'malva sf (Bot) mallow ▷ ag, sm inv mauve

mal'vagio, -a, -gi, -gie [mal'vadʒo] ag wicked, evil

malvi'vente sm criminal

malvolenti'eri av unwillingly, reluctantly

'mamma sf mum(my); **~ mia!** my goodness!

mam'mella sf (Anat) breast; (di vacca, capra ecc) udder

mam'mifero sm mammal

ma'nata sf (colpo) slap; (quantità) handful

man'canza [man'kantsa] sf lack; (carenza) shortage, scarcity; (fallo) fault; (imperfezione) failing, shortcoming; **per ~ di tempo** through lack of time; **in ~ di meglio** for lack of anything better

man'care /20/ vi (essere insufficiente) to be lacking; (venir meno) to fail; (sbagliare) to be wrong, make a mistake; (non esserci) to be missing, not to be there; (essere lontano): **~ (da)** to be away (from) ▷ vt to miss; **~ di** to lack; **~ a** (promessa) to fail to keep; **tu mi manchi** I miss you; **mancò poco che morisse** he very nearly died; **mancano ancora 10 sterline** we're still £10 short; **manca un quarto alle 6** it's a quarter to 6

mancherò ecc [manke'rɔ] vb vedi **mancare**

'mancia, -ce ['mantʃa] sf tip; **~ competente** reward

manci'ata [man'tʃata] sf handful

man'cino, -a [man'tʃino] ag (braccio) left; (persona) left-handed; (fig) underhand

manda'rancio [manda'rantʃo] sm clementine

man'dare /72/ vt to send; (far funzionare: macchina) to drive; (emettere) to send out; (: grido) to give, utter, let out; **~ avanti** (fig: famiglia) to provide for; (: fabbrica) to run, look after; **~ giù** to send down; (anche fig) to swallow; **~ via** to send away; (licenziare) to fire

manda'rino sm mandarin (orange); (cinese) mandarin

man'data sf (quantità) lot, batch; (di chiave) turn; **chiudere a doppia ~** to double-lock

man'dato sm (incarico) commission; (Dir: provvedimento) warrant; (di deputato ecc) mandate; (ordine di pagamento) postal o money order; **~ d'arresto** warrant for arrest

man'dibola sf mandible, jaw

'mandorla sf almond; **'mandorlo** sm almond tree

'mandria sf herd

maneggi'are [maned'dʒare] /62/ vt (creta, cera) to mould, work, fashion; (arnesi, utensili) to handle; (: adoperare) to use; (fig: persone, denaro) to handle, deal with; **ma'neggio** sm moulding; handling; use; (intrigo) plot, scheme; (per cavalli) riding school

ma'nesco, -a, -schi, -sche ag free with one's fists

ma'nette sfpl handcuffs

manga'nello sm club

mangi'are [man'dʒare] /62/ vt to eat; (intaccare) to eat into o away; (Carte, Scacchi ecc) to take ▷ vi to eat ▷ sm eating; (cibo) food; (cucina) cooking; **mangiarsi le parole**

to mumble; **mangiarsi le unghie** to bite one's nails

man'gime [man'dʒime] *sm* fodder

'**mango, -ghi** *sm* mango

ma'nia *sf* (*Psic*) mania; (*fig*) obsession, craze; **ma'niaco, -a, -ci, -che** *ag* suffering from a mania; **maniaco (di)** obsessed (by), crazy (about)

'**manica, -che** *sf* sleeve; (*fig: gruppo*) gang, bunch; (*Geo*): **la M~, il Canale della M~** the (English) Channel; **essere di ~ larga/stretta** to be easy-going/strict; **~ a vento** (*Aer*) wind sock

mani'chino [mani'kino] *sm* (*di sarto, vetrina*) dummy

'**manico, -ci** *sm* handle; (*Mus*) neck

mani'comio *sm* psychiatric hospital; (*fig*) madhouse

mani'cure *sf* o *m inv* manicure ▷ *sf inv* manicurist

mani'era *sf* way, manner; (*stile*) style, manner; **maniere** *sfpl* (*comportamento*) manners; **in ~ che** so that; **in ~ da** so as to; **in tutte le maniere** at all costs

manifes'tare /72/ *vt* to show, display; (*esprimere*) to express; (*rivelare*) to reveal, disclose ▷ *vi* to demonstrate; **manifestazi'one** *sf* show, display, expression; (*sintomo*) sign, symptom; (*dimostrazione pubblica*) demonstration; (*cerimonia*) event

mani'festo, -a *ag* obvious, evident ▷ *sm* poster, bill; (*scritto ideologico*) manifesto

ma'niglia [ma'niʎʎa] *sf* handle; (*sostegno: negli autobus ecc*) strap

manipo'lare /72/ *vt* to manipulate; (*alterare: vino*) to adulterate

man'naro, -a *ag*: **lupo ~** werewolf

'**mano, -i** *sf* hand; (*strato: di vernice ecc*) coat; **a ~** by hand; **di prima ~** (*notizia*) first-hand; **di seconda ~** second-hand; **man ~ little by little, gradually; **man ~ che** as; **darsi o stringersi la ~** to shake hands; **mettere le mani avanti** (*fig*) to safeguard o.s.; **restare a mani vuote** to be left empty-handed; **venire alle mani** to come to blows; **mani in alto!** hands up!

mano'dopera *sf* labour

ma'nometro *sm* gauge, manometer

mano'mettere /63/ *vt* (*alterare*) to tamper with; (*aprire indebitamente*) to break open illegally

ma'nopola *sf* (*dell'armatura*) gauntlet; (*guanto*) mitt; (*di impugnatura*) hand-grip; (*pomello*) knob

manos'critto, -a *ag* handwritten ▷ *sm* manuscript

mano'vale *sm* labourer

mano'vella *sf* handle; (*Tecn*) crank

ma'novra *sf* manoeuvre (BRIT), maneuver (US); (*Ferr*) shunting

man'sarda *sf* attic

mansi'one *sf* task, duty, job

mansu'eto, -a *ag* gentle, docile

man'tello *sm* cloak; (*fig: di neve ecc*) blanket, mantle; (*Zool*) coat

mante'nere /121/ *vt* to maintain; (*adempiere: promesse*) to keep, abide by; (*provvedere a*) to support, maintain; **mantenersi** *vpr*: **mantenersi calmo/giovane** to stay calm/young

'**Mantova** *sf* Mantua

manu'ale *ag* manual ▷ *sm* (*testo*) manual, handbook

ma'nubrio *sm* handle; (*di bicicletta ecc*) handlebars *pl*; (*Sport*) dumbbell

manutenzi'one [manuten'tsjone] *sf* maintenance, upkeep; (*d'impianti*) ~ maintenance, servicing

'**manzo** ['mandzo] *sm* (*Zool*) steer; (*carne*) beef

'**mappa** *sf* (*Geo*) map; **mappa'mondo** *sm* map of the world; (*globo girevole*) globe

mara'tona *sf* marathon

'**marca, -che** *sf* (*Comm: di prodotti*) brand; (*contrassegno, scontrino*) ticket, check; **prodotti di (gran) ~** high-class products; **~ da bollo** official stamp

mar'care /20/ *vt* (*munire di contrassegno*) to mark; (*a fuoco*) to brand; (*Sport: gol*) to score; (: *avversario*) to mark; (*accentuare*) to stress; **~ visita** (*Mil*) to report sick

marcherò *ecc* [marke'rɔ] *vb vedi* **marcare**

mar'chese, -a [mar'keze] *sm/f* marquis o marquess/marchioness

marchi'are [mar'kjare] /19/ *vt* to brand

'**marcia, -ce** ['martʃa] *sf* (*anche Mus, Mil*) march; (*funzionamento*) running; (*il camminare*) walking; (*Aut*) gear; **mettere in ~** to start; **mettersi in ~** to get moving; **far ~ indietro** (*Aut*) to reverse; (*fig*) to back-pedal

marciapi'ede [martʃa'pjɛde] *sm* (*di strada*) pavement (BRIT), sidewalk (US); (*Ferr*) platform

marci'are [mar'tʃare] /14/ *vi* to march; (*andare, treno, macchina*) to go; (*funzionare*) to run, work

'**marcio, -a, -ci, -ce** ['martʃo] *ag* (*frutta, legno*) rotten, bad; (*Med*) festering; (*fig*) corrupt, rotten

mar'cire [mar'tʃire] /55/ *vi* (*andare a male*) to go bad, rot; (*suppurare*) to fester; (*fig*) to rot, waste away

'**marco, -chi** *sm* (*unità monetaria*) mark

'**mare** *sm* sea; **in ~** at sea; **andare al ~** (*in vacanza ecc*) to go to the seaside; **il ~ del Nord** the North Sea

ma'rea *sf* tide; **alta/bassa ~** high/low tide

mareggi'ata [mared'dʒata] *sf* heavy sea

mare'moto *sm* seaquake

maresci'allo [mareʃʃallo] *sm* (*Mil*) marshal; (*sottufficiale*) warrant officer

marga'rina *sf* margarine

marghe'rita [marge'rita] *sf* (ox-eye) daisy, marguerite

'margine ['mardʒine] *sm* margin; (*di bosco, via*) edge, border

mariju'ana [mæri'wa:nə] *sf* marijuana

ma'rina *sf* navy; (*costa*) coast; (*quadro*) seascape; **~ mercantile** merchant navy (*BRIT*) o marine (*US*); **~ militare** ≈ Royal Navy (*BRIT*), ≈ Navy (*US*)

mari'naio *sm* sailor

mari'nare /72/ *vt* (*Cuc*) to marinate; **~ la scuola** to play truant

ma'rino, -a *ag* sea *cpd*, marine

mario'netta *sf* puppet

ma'rito *sm* husband

ma'rittimo, -a *ag* maritime, sea *cpd*

marmel'lata *sf* jam; (*di agrumi*) marmalade

mar'mitta *sf* (*recipiente*) pot; (*Aut*) silencer; **~ catalitica** catalytic converter

'marmo *sm* marble

mar'motta *sf* (*Zool*) marmot

maroc'chino, -a [marok'kino] *ag*, *sm/f* Moroccan

Ma'rocco *sm*: **il ~** Morocco

mar'rone *ag inv* brown ▷ *sm* (*Bot*) chestnut

> Attenzione! In inglese esiste la parola *maroon*, che però indica un altro colore, il rosso bordeaux.

mar'supio *sm* (*Zool*) pouch, marsupium

martedì *sm inv* Tuesday; **di** o **il ~** on Tuesdays; **~ grasso** Shrove Tuesday

martel'lare /72/ *vt* to hammer ▷ *vi* (*pulsare*) to throb; (: *cuore*) to thump

mar'tello *sm* hammer; (*di uscio*) knocker; **~ pneumatico** pneumatic drill

'martire *smf* martyr

mar'xista, -i, -e *ag*, *smf* Marxist

marza'pane [martsa'pane] *sm* marzipan

'marzo ['martso] *sm* March

mascal'zone [maskal'tsone] *sm* rascal, scoundrel

mas'cara *sm inv* mascara

ma'scella [maʃʃella] *sf* (*Anat*) jaw

'maschera ['maskera] *sf* mask; (*travestimento*) disguise; (*per un ballo ecc*) fancy dress; (*Teat, Cine*) usher/usherette; (*personaggio del teatro*) stock character; **masche'rare** /72/ *vt* to mask; (*travestire*) to disguise; (*fig: celare*) to hide, conceal; (*Mil*) to camouflage; **mascherarsi** *vpr*: **mascherarsi da** to disguise o.s. as; to dress up as; (*fig*) to masquerade as

mas'chile [mas'kile] *ag* masculine; (*sesso, popolazione*) male; (*abiti*) men's; (*per ragazzi, scuola*) boys'

mas'chilista, -i, -e *ag*, *smf* (*uomo*) (male) chauvinist, sexist; (*donna*) sexist

'maschio, -a ['maskjo] *ag* (*Biol*) male; (*virile*) manly ▷ *sm* (*anche Zool, Tecn*) male; (*uomo*) man; (*ragazzo*) boy; (*figlio*) son

masco'lino, -a *ag* masculine

'massa *sf* mass; (*di gente*) mass, multitude; (*Elettr*) earth; **una ~ di** (*di errori ecc*) heaps of, masses of; **in ~** (*Comm*) in bulk; (*tutti insieme*) en masse; **adunata in ~** mass meeting; **manifestazione/cultura di ~** mass demonstration/culture

mas'sacro *sm* massacre, slaughter; (*fig*) mess, disaster

massaggi'are [massad'dʒare] /62/ *vt* to massage

mas'saggio [mas'saddʒo] *sm* massage; **~ cardiaco** cardiac massage

mas'saia *sf* housewife

masse'rizie [masse'rittsje] *sfpl* (household) furnishings

mas'siccio, -a, -ci, -ce [mas'sittʃo] *ag* (*oro, legno*) solid; (*palazzo*) massive; (*corporatura*) stout ▷ *sm* (*Geo*) massif

'massima *sf* vedi **massimo**

massi'male *sm* maximum; (*Comm*) ceiling, limit

'massimo, -a *ag*, *sm* maximum ▷ *sf* (*sentenza, regola*) maxim; (*Meteor*) maximum temperature; **in linea di massima** generally speaking; **al ~** at (the) most

'masso *sm* rock, boulder

masteriz'zare [masterid'dzare] /72/ *vt* (*CD, DVD*) to burn

masterizza'tore [masteriddza'tore] *sm* CD burner o writer

masti'care /20/ *vt* to chew

'mastice ['mastitʃe] *sm* mastic; (*per vetri*) putty

mas'tino *sm* mastiff

ma'tassa *sf* skein

mate'matico, -a, -ci, -che *ag* mathematical ▷ *sm/f* mathematician ▷ *sf* mathematics *sg*

materas'sino *sm* mat; **~ gonfiabile** air bed

mate'rasso *sm* mattress; **~ a molle** spring o interior-sprung mattress

ma'teria *sf* (*Fisica*) matter; (*Tecn, Comm*) material, matter *no pl*; (*disciplina*) subject; (*argomento*) subject matter, material; **in ~ di** (*per quanto concerne*) on the subject of; **materie prime** raw materials

materi'ale *ag* material; (*fig: grossolano*) rough, rude ▷ *sm* material; (*insieme di strumenti ecc*) equipment *no pl*, materials *pl*

maternità *sf* motherhood, maternity; (*reparto*) maternity ward

ma'terno, -a *ag* (*amore, cura ecc*) maternal, motherly; (*nonno*) maternal; (*lingua, terra*) mother *cpd*

ma'tita *sf* pencil; **matite colorate** coloured pencils; **~ per gli occhi** eyeliner (pencil)

ma'tricola *sf* (*registro*) register; (*numero*) registration number; (*nell'università*) freshman, fresher

ma'trigna [ma'trinɲa] *sf* stepmother

matrimoni'ale *ag* matrimonial, marriage *cpd*

matri'monio *sm* marriage, matrimony; (*durata*) marriage, married life; (*cerimonia*) wedding

mat'tina *sf* morning

'matto, -a *ag* mad, crazy; (*fig: falso*) false, imitation ▷ *sm/f* madman/woman; **avere una voglia matta di qc** to be dying for sth

mat'tone *sm* brick; (*fig*): **questo libro/film è un ~** this book/film is heavy going

matto'nella *sf* tile

matu'rare /72/ *vi* (*anche*: **maturarsi**) (*frutta, grano*) to ripen; (*ascesso*) to come to a head; (*fig: persona, idea, Econ*) to mature ▷ *vt* to ripen, to (make) mature

maturità *sf* maturity; (*di frutta*) ripeness, maturity; (*Ins*) school-leaving examination, ≈ GCE A-levels (*BRIT*)

ma'turo, -a *ag* mature; (*frutto*) ripe, mature

max. *abbr* (= *massimo*) max

maxis'chermo [maksis'kermo] *sm* giant screen

'mazza ['mattsa] *sf* (*bastone*) club; (*martello*) sledge-hammer; (*Sport: da golf*) club; (: *da baseball, cricket*) bat

maz'zata [mat'tsata] *sf* (*anche fig*) heavy blow

'mazzo ['mattso] *sm* (*di fiori, chiavi ecc*) bunch; (*di carte da gioco*) pack

me *pron* me; **me stesso, me stessa** myself; **sei bravo quanto me** you are as clever as I (am) *o* as me

mec'canico, -a, -ci, -che *ag* mechanical ▷ *sm* mechanic

mecca'nismo *sm* mechanism

me'daglia [me'daʎʎa] *sf* medal

me'desimo, -a *ag* same; (*in persona*): **io ~** I myself

'media *sf* vedi **medio**

medi'ante *prep* by means of

media'tore, -'trice *sm/f* mediator; (*Comm*) middle man, agent

medi'care /20/ *vt* to treat; (*ferita*) to dress

medi'cina [medi'tʃina] *sf* medicine; **~ legale** forensic medicine

'medico, -a, -ci, -che *ag* medical ▷ *sm* doctor; **~ generico** general practitioner, GP

medie'vale *ag* medieval

'medio, -a *ag* average; (*punto, ceto*) middle; (*altezza, statura*) medium ▷ *sm* (*dito*) middle finger ▷ *sf* average; (*Mat*) mean; (*Ins: voto*) end-of-term average; **medie** *sfpl* vedi **scuola media**; **licenza media** *leaving certificate awarded at the end of 3 years of secondary education*; **in media** on average

medi'ocre *ag* mediocre; poor

medi'tare /72/ *vt* to ponder over, meditate on; (*progettare*) to plan, think out ▷ *vi* to meditate

mediter'raneo, -a *ag* Mediterranean; **il (mare) M~** the Mediterranean (Sea)

me'dusa *sf* (*Zool*) jellyfish

mega *sm inv* (*Inform*) meg

mega'byte *sm inv* (*Inform*) megabyte

me'gafono *sm* megaphone

'meglio ['meʎʎo] *av, ag inv* better; (*con senso superlativo*) best ▷ *sm* (*la cosa migliore*): **il ~** the best (thing); **faresti ~ ad andartene** you had better leave; **alla ~** as best one can; **andar di bene in ~** to get better and better; **fare del proprio ~** to do one's best; **per il ~** for the best; **aver la ~ su qn** to get the better of sb

'mela *sf* apple; **~ cotogna** quince

mela'grana *sf* pomegranate

melan'zana [melan'dzana] *sf* aubergine (*BRIT*), eggplant (*US*)

melato'nina *sf* melatonin

'melma *sf* mud, mire

'melo *sm* apple tree

melo'dia *sf* melody

me'lone *sm* (*musk*) melon

'membro *sm* (*pl m* **membri**) member; (*pl f* **membra**) (*arto*) limb

memo'randum *sm inv* memorandum

me'moria *sf* memory; **memorie** *sfpl* (*opera autobiografica*) memoirs; **a ~** (*imparare, sapere*) by heart; **a ~ d'uomo** within living memory

mendi'cante *smf* beggar

 PAROLA CHIAVE

'meno *av* **1** (*in minore misura*) less; **dovresti mangiare meno** you should eat less, you shouldn't eat so much

2 (*comparativo*): **meno ... di** not as ... as, less ... than; **sono meno alto di te** I'm not as tall as you (are), I'm less tall than you (are); **meno ... che** not as ... as, less ... than; **meno che mai** less than ever; **è meno intelligente che ricco** he's more rich than intelligent; **meno fumo più mangio** the less I smoke the more I eat

3 (*superlativo*) least; **il meno dotato degli studenti** the least gifted of the students;

è quello che compro meno spesso it's the one I buy least often
4 (*Mat*) minus; **8 meno 5** 8 minus 5, 8 take away 5; **sono le 8 meno un quarto** it's a quarter to 8; **meno 5 gradi** 5 degrees below zero, minus 5 degrees; **mille euro in meno** a thousand euros less
5 (*fraseologia*): **quanto meno poteva telefonare** he could at least have phoned; **non so se accettare o meno** I don't know whether to accept or not; **fare a meno di qc/qn** to do without sth/sb; **non potevo fare a meno di ridere** I couldn't help laughing; **meno male!** thank goodness!; **meno male che sei arrivato** it's a good job that you've come
▶ *ag inv* (*tempo, denaro*) less; (*errori, persone*) fewer; **ha fatto meno errori di tutti** he made fewer mistakes than anyone, he made the fewest mistakes of all
▶ *sm inv* **1**: **il meno** (*il minimo*) the least; **parlare del più e del meno** to talk about this and that
2 (*Mat*) minus
▶ *prep* (*eccetto*) except (for), apart from; **a meno che, a meno di** unless; **a meno che non piova** unless it rains; **non posso, a meno di prendere ferie** I can't, unless I take some leave

meno'pausa *sf* menopause
'mensa *sf* (*locale*) canteen; (: *Mil*) mess; (: *nelle università*) refectory
men'sile *ag* monthly ▷ *sm* (*periodico*) monthly (magazine); (*stipendio*) monthly salary
'mensola *sf* bracket; (*ripiano*) shelf; (*Archit*) corbel
'menta *sf* mint; (*anche: ~ piperita*) peppermint; (*bibita*) peppermint cordial; (*caramella*) mint, peppermint
men'tale *ag* mental; **mentalità** *sf inv* mentality
'mente *sf* mind; **imparare/sapere qc a ~** to learn/know sth by heart; **avere in ~ qc** to have sth in mind; **passare di ~ a qn** to slip sb's mind
men'tire /17/ *vi* to lie
'mento *sm* chin
'mentre *cong* (*temporale*) while; (*avversativo*) whereas
menù *sm inv* (set) menu; **~ turistico** set *o* tourists' menu
menzio'nare [mentsjo'nare] /72/ *vt* to mention
men'zogna [men'tsɔɲɲa] *sf* lie
mera'viglia [mera'viʎʎa] *sf* amazement, wonder; (*persona, cosa*) marvel, wonder; **a ~** perfectly, wonderfully; **meravigli'are** /27/

vt to amaze, astonish; **meravigliarsi** *vpr*: **meravigliarsi (di)** to marvel (at); (*stupirsi*) to be amazed (at), be astonished (at); **meravigli'oso, -a** *ag* wonderful, marvellous (*BRIT*), marvelous (*US*)
mer'cante *sm* merchant; **~ d'arte** art dealer
merca'tino *sm* (*rionale*) local street market; (*Econ*) unofficial stock market
mer'cato *sm* market; **~ dei cambi** exchange market; **~ nero** black market
'merce ['mɛrtʃe] *sf* goods *pl*, merchandise
mercé [mer'tʃe] *sf* mercy
merce'ria [mertʃe'ria] *sf* (*articoli*) haberdashery (*BRIT*), notions *pl* (*US*); (*bottega*) haberdasher's shop (*BRIT*), notions store (*US*)
mercoledì *sm inv* Wednesday; **di** *o* **il ~** on Wednesdays; **~ delle Ceneri** Ash Wednesday
mer'curio *sm* mercury
'merda *sf* (*fam!*) shit (*!*)
me'renda *sf* afternoon snack
meren'dina *sf* snack
meridi'ano, -a *ag* (*di mezzogiorno*) midday *cpd*, noonday ▷ *sm* meridian ▷ *sf* (*orologio*) sundial
meridi'onale *ag* southern ▷ *smf* southerner
meridi'one *sm* south
me'ringa, -ghe *sf* (*Cuc*) meringue
meri'tare /72/ *vt* to deserve, merit ▷ *vb impers*: **merita andare** it's worth going
meri'tevole *ag* worthy
'merito *sm* merit; (*valore*) worth; **dare ~ a qn di** to give sb credit for; **finire a pari ~** to finish joint first (*o second ecc*); to tie; **in ~ a** as regards, with regard to
mer'letto *sm* lace
'merlo *sm* (*Zool*) blackbird; (*Archit*) battlement
mer'luzzo [mer'luttso] *sm* (*Zool*) cod
mes'chino, -a [mes'kino] *ag* wretched; (*scarso*) scanty, poor; (*persona: gretta*) mean; (: *limitata*) narrow-minded, petty
mesco'lare /72/ *vt* to mix; (*vini, colori*) to blend; (*mettere in disordine*) to mix up, muddle up; (*carte*) to shuffle
'mese *sm* month
'messa *sf* (*Rel*) mass; **~ in moto** starting; **~ in piega** set; **~ a punto** (*Tecn*) adjustment; (*Aut*) tuning; (*fig*) clarification; **~ in scena = messinscena**
messag'gero [messad'dʒero] *sm* messenger
messaggi'arsi [messad'dʒarsi] /72/ *vpr* to text; **messaggiamoci** we'll text each other
messag'gino [messad'dʒino] *sm* (*di telefonino*) text (message)
mes'saggio [mes'saddʒo] *sm* message

messag'gistica [messad'dʒistica] *sf*: ~ **immediata** (*Inform*) instant messaging; **programma di ~ immediata** instant messenger

mes'sale *sm* (*Rel*) missal

messi'cano, -a *ag*, *sm/f* Mexican

'Messico *sm*: **il ~** Mexico

messin'scena [messin'ʃena] *sf* (*Teat*) production

'messo, -a *pp di* **mettere** ▷ *sm* messenger

mesti'ere *sm* (*professione*) job; (: *manuale*) trade; (: *artigianale*) craft; (*fig*: *abilità nel lavoro*) skill, technique; **essere del ~** to know the tricks of the trade

'mestolo *sm* (*Cuc*) ladle

mestruazi'one [mestruat'tsjone] *sf* menstruation

'meta *sf* destination; (*fig*) aim, goal

metà *sf inv* half; (*punto di mezzo*) middle; **dividere qc a** *o* **per ~** to divide sth in half, halve sth; **fare a ~ (di qc con qn)** to go halves (with sb in sth); **a ~ prezzo** at half price; **a ~ strada** halfway

meta'done *sm* methadone

me'tafora *sf* metaphor

me'tallico, -a, -ci, -che *ag* (*di metallo*) metal *cpd*; (*splendore, rumore ecc*) metallic

me'tallo *sm* metal

metalmec'canico, -a, -ci, -che *ag* engineering *cpd* ▷ *sm* engineering worker

me'tano *sm* methane

meteoro'logico, -a, -ci, -che [meteoro'lɔdʒiko] *ag* meteorological, weather *cpd*

me'ticcio, -a, -ci, -ce [me'tittʃo] *sm/f* half-caste (!), half-breed (!)

micidi'ale [mitʃi'djale] *ag* fatal; (*dannosissimo*) deadly

me'todico, -a, -ci, -che *ag* methodical

'metodo *sm* method

'metro *sm* metre; (*nastro*) tape measure; (*asta*) (metre) rule

metropoli'tano, -a *ag* metropolitan ▷ *sf* underground (BRIT), subway (US)

metroses'suale *ag* metrosexual

'mettere /63/ *vt* to put; (*abito*) to put on; (: *portare*) to wear; (*installare*: *telefono*) to put in; (*fig*: *provocare*): **~ fame/allegria a qn** to make sb hungry/happy; (*supporre*): **mettiamo che ...** let's suppose *o* say that ...; **mettersi** *vpr* (*persona*) to put o.s.; (*oggetto*) to go; (*disporsi*: *faccenda*) to turn out; **mettersi a** (*cominciare*) to begin to, start to; **mettersi a sedere** to sit down; **mettersi al lavoro** to set to work; **mettersi a letto** to get into bed; (*per malattia*) to take to one's bed; **mettersi il cappello** to put on one's hat; **mettersi con qn** (*in società*) to team up with sb; (*in coppia*) to start going out with sb; **metterci**: **metterci molta cura/molto tempo** to take a lot of care/a lot of time; **mettercela tutta** to do one's best; **~ a tacere qn/qc** to keep sb/sth quiet; **~ su casa** to set up house; **~ su un negozio** to start a shop; **~ via** to put away

mezza'notte [meddza'nɔtte] *sf* midnight

'mezzo, -a ['meddzo] *ag* half; **un ~ litro/panino** half a litre/roll ▷ *av* half-; **~ morto** half-dead ▷ *sm* (*metà*) half; (*parte centrale*: *di strada ecc*) middle; (*per raggiungere un fine*) means *sg*; (*veicolo*) vehicle; (*nell'indicare l'ora*): **le nove e ~** half past nine; **mezzogiorno e ~** half past twelve; **mezzi** *smpl* (*possibilità economiche*) means; **di mezza età** middle-aged; **un soprabito di mezza stagione** a spring (*o* autumn) coat; **di ~** middle, in the middle; **andarci di ~** (*patir danno*) to suffer; **levarsi** *o* **togliersi di ~** to get out of the way; **in ~ a** in the middle of; **per** *o* **a ~ di** by means of; **mezzi di comunicazione di massa** mass media *pl*; **mezzi pubblici** public transport *sg*; **mezzi di trasporto** means of transport

mezzogi'orno [meddzo'dʒorno] *sm* midday, noon; **a ~** at 12 (o'clock) *o* midday *o* noon; **il ~ d'Italia** southern Italy

mi *pron* (*dav lo, la, li, le, ne diventa* **me**: *oggetto*) me; (*complemento di termine*) (to) me; (*riflessivo*) myself ▷ *sm* (*Mus*) E; (: *solfeggiando la scala*) mi

miago'lare /72/ *vi* to miaow, mew

'mica *av* (*fam*): **non ... ~** not ... at all; **non sono ~ stanco** I'm not a bit tired; **non sarà ~ partito?** he wouldn't have left, would he?; **~ male** not bad

'miccia, -ce ['mittʃa] *sf* fuse

micro'fibra *sf* microfibre

mi'crofono *sm* microphone

micros'copio *sm* microscope

mi'dollo (*pl f* **midolla**) *sm* (*Anat*) marrow; **~ osseo** bone marrow

mi'ele *sm* honey

'miglia ['miʎʎa] *sfpl di* **miglio¹**

migli'aio [miʎ'ʎajo] (*pl f* **migliaia**) *sm* thousand; **un ~ (di)** about a thousand; **a migliaia** by the thousand, in thousands

'miglio¹ ['miʎʎo] (*pl f* **miglia**) *sm* (*unità di misura*) mile; **~ marino** *o* **nautico** nautical mile

'miglio² ['miʎʎo] *sm* (*Bot*) millet

migliora'mento [miʎʎora'mento] *sm* improvement

miglio'rare [miʎʎo'rare] /72/ *vt, vi* to improve

migli'ore [miʎ'ʎore] *ag* (*comparativo*) better; (*superlativo*) best ▷ *sm*: **il ~** the best (thing) ▷ *smf*: **il (la) ~** the best (person); **il miglior vino di questa regione** the best wine in this area

'mignolo ['miɲɲolo] *sm* (Anat) little finger, pinkie; (: *dito del piede*) little toe

Mi'lano *sf* Milan

miliar'dario, -a *sm/f* millionaire

mili'ardo *sm* thousand million, billion (US)

mili'one *sm* million

mili'tante *ag*, *smf* militant

mili'tare /72/ *vi* (Mil) to be a soldier, serve; (fig: *in un partito*) to be a militant ▷ *ag* military ▷ *sm* serviceman; **fare il ~** to do one's military service

'mille (*pl* **mila**) *num* a o one thousand; **diecimila** ten thousand; **~ euro** one thousand euros

mil'lennio *sm* millennium

millepi'edi *sm inv* centipede

mil'lesimo, -a *ag*, *sm* thousandth

milli'grammo *sm* milligram(me)

mil'limetro *sm* millimetre

'milza ['miltsa] *sf* (Anat) spleen

mimetiz'zare [mimetid'dzare] /72/ *vt* to camouflage; **mimetizzarsi** *vpr* to camouflage o.s.

'mimo *sm* (*attore, componimento*) mime

mi'mosa *sf* mimosa

min. *abbr* (= *minuto, minimo*) min

'mina *sf* (*esplosiva*) mine; (*di matita*) lead

mi'naccia, -ce [mi'nattʃa] *sf* threat; **minacci'are** /14/ *vt* to threaten; **minacciare qn di morte** to threaten to kill sb; **minacciare di fare qc** to threaten to do sth

mi'nare /72/ *vt* (Mil) to mine; (fig) to undermine

mina'tore *sm* miner

mine'rale *ag*, *sm* mineral

mine'rario, -a *ag* (*delle miniere*) mining; (*dei minerali*) ore *cpd*

mi'nestra *sf* soup; **~ in brodo** noodle soup; **~ di verdura** vegetable soup

minia'tura *sf* miniature

mini'bar *sm inv* minibar

mini'era *sf* mine

mini'gonna *sf* miniskirt

'minimo, -a *ag* minimum, least, slightest; (*piccolissimo*) very small, slight; (*il più basso*) lowest, minimum ▷ *sm* minimum; **al ~** at least; **girare al ~** (Aut) to idle

minis'tero *sm* (Pol, Rel) ministry; (*governo*) government; **M~ delle Finanze** Ministry of Finance, ≈ Treasury

mi'nistro *sm* (Pol, Rel) minister

mino'ranza [mino'rantsa] *sf* minority

mi'nore *ag* (*comparativo*) less; (*più piccolo*) smaller; (*numero*) lower; (*inferiore*) lower, inferior; (*meno importante*) minor; (*più giovane*) younger; (*superlativo*) least; smallest; lowest, least important, youngest ▷ *smf* = **minorenne**

mino'renne *ag* under age ▷ *smf* minor, person under age

mi'nuscolo, -a *ag* (*scrittura, carattere*) small; (*piccolissimo*) tiny ▷ *sf* small letter

mi'nuto, -a *ag* tiny, minute; (*pioggia*) fine; (*corporatura*) delicate, fine ▷ *sm* (*unità di misura*) minute; **al ~** (Comm) retail

'mio (*f* **'mia**, *pl* **mi'ei** o **'mie**) *det*: **il ~, la mia** *ecc* my ▷ *pron*: **il ~, la mia** *ecc* mine; **i miei** my family; **un ~ amico** a friend of mine

'miope *ag* short-sighted

'mira *sf* (*anche fig*) aim; **prendere la ~** to take aim; **prendere di ~ qn** (fig) to pick on sb

mi'racolo *sm* miracle

mi'raggio [mi'raddʒo] *sm* mirage

mi'rare /72/ *vi*: **~ a** to aim at; **mi'rato, -a** *ag* targetted

mi'rino *sm* (Tecn) sight; (Fot) viewer, viewfinder

mir'tillo *sm* bilberry (BRIT), blueberry (US), whortleberry

mi'scela [miʃʃela] *sf* mixture; (*di caffè*) blend

'mischia ['miskja] *sf* scuffle; (Rugby) scrum, scrummage

mis'cuglio [mis'kuʎʎo] *sm* mixture, hotchpotch, jumble

'mise *vb vedi* **mettere**

mise'rabile *ag* (*infelice*) miserable, wretched; (*povero*) poverty-stricken; (*di scarso valore*) miserable

mi'seria *sf* extreme poverty; (*infelicità*) misery

miseri'cordia *sf* mercy, pity

'misero, -a *ag* miserable, wretched; (*povero*) poverty-stricken; (*insufficiente*) miserable

'misi *vb vedi* **mettere**

mi'sogino [mi'zɔdʒino] *sm* misogynist

'missile *sm* missile

missio'nario, -a *ag*, *smf* missionary

missi'one *sf* mission

misteri'oso, -a *ag* mysterious

mis'tero *sm* mystery

'misto, -a *ag* mixed; (*scuola*) mixed, coeducational ▷ *sm* mixture

mis'tura *sf* mixture

mi'sura *sf* measure; (*misurazione, dimensione*) measurement; (*taglia*) size; (*provvedimento*) measure, step; (*moderazione*) moderation; (Mus) time; (: *divisione*) bar; (fig: *limite*) bounds *pl*, limit; **nella ~ in cui** inasmuch as, insofar as; **su ~** made to measure

misu'rare /72/ *vt* (*ambiente, stoffa*) to measure; (*terreno*) to survey; (*abito*) to try on; (*pesare*) to weigh; (fig: *parole ecc*) to weigh up; (: *spese, cibo*) to limit ▷ *vi* to measure; **misurarsi** *vpr*: **misurarsi con qn** to have a confrontation with sb; (*competere*) to compete with sb

'mite *ag* mild

'mitico, -a, -ci, -che *ag* mythical

'mito *sm* myth; **mitolo'gia, -'gie** *sf* mythology

'mitra *sf* (*Rel*) mitre ▷ *sm inv* (*arma*) sub-machine gun

mit'tente *smf* sender

mm *abbr* (= *millimetro*) mm

'mobile *ag* mobile; (*parte di macchina*) moving; (*Dir: bene*) movable, personal ▷ *sm* (*arredamento*) piece of furniture; **mobili** *smpl* (*mobilia*) furniture *sg*

mocas'sino *sm* moccasin

'moda *sf* fashion; **alla ~, di ~** fashionable, in fashion

modalità *sf inv* formality

mo'della *sf* model

mo'dello *sm* model; (*stampo*) mould ▷ *ag inv* model *cpd*

'modem *sm inv* modem

modera'tore, -'trice *sm/f* moderator

mo'derno, -a *ag* modern

mo'desto, -a *ag* modest

'modico, -a, -ci, -che *ag* reasonable, moderate

mo'difica, -che *sf* modification

modifi'care /20/ *vt* to modify, alter

'modo *sm* way, manner; (*mezzo*) means, way; (*occasione*) opportunity; (*Ling*) mood; (*Mus*) mode; **modi** *smpl* (*maniere*) manners; **a suo ~, a ~ suo** in his own way; **ad o in ogni ~** anyway; **di o in ~ che** so that; **in ~ da** so as to; **in tutti i modi** at all costs; (*comunque sia*) anyway; (*in ogni caso*) in any case; **in qualche ~** somehow or other; **~ di dire** turn of phrase; **per ~ di dire** so to speak

'modulo *sm* (*modello*) form; (*Archit: lunare, di comando*) module

mo'gano *sm* mahogany

'mogio, -a, -gi, -gie ['mɔdʒo] *ag* down in the dumps, dejected

'moglie ['mɔʎʎe] *sf* wife

mo'ine *sfpl* cajolery *sg*; (*leziosità*) affectation *sg*

mo'lare /72/ *sm* (*dente*) molar

'mole *sf* mass; (*dimensioni*) size; (*edificio grandioso*) massive structure

moles'tare /72/ *vt* to bother, annoy; **mo'lestia** *sf* annoyance, bother; **recar molestia a qn** to bother sb; **molestie sessuali** sexual harassment *sg*

'molla *sf* spring; **molle** *sfpl* (*per camino*) tongs

mol'lare /72/ *vt* to release, let go; (*Naut*) to ease; (*fig: ceffone*) to give ▷ *vi* (*cedere*) to give in

'molle *ag* soft; (*muscoli*) flabby

mol'letta *sf* (*per capelli*) hairgrip; (*per panni stesi*) clothes peg (BRIT) o pin (US)

mol'lica, -che *sf* crumb, soft part

mol'lusco, -schi *sm* mollusc

'molo *sm* breakwater; jetty

moltipli'care /20/ *vt* to multiply; **moltiplicarsi** *vpr* to multiply; (*richieste*) to increase in number; **moltiplicazi'one** *sf* multiplication

 PAROLA CHIAVE

'molto, -a *det* (*quantità*) a lot of, much; (*numero*) a lot of, many; **molto pane/ carbone** a lot of bread/coal; **molta gente** a lot of people, many people; **molti libri** a lot of books, many books; **non ho molto tempo** I haven't got much time; **per molto (tempo)** for a long time

▶ *av* **1** a lot, (very) much; **viaggia molto** he travels a lot; **non viaggia molto** he doesn't travel much o a lot

2 (*intensivo: con aggettivi, avverbi*) very; (: *con participio passato*) (very) much; **molto buono** very good; **molto migliore, molto meglio** much o a lot better

▶ *pron* much, a lot

momentanea'mente *av* at the moment, at present

momen'taneo, -a *ag* momentary, fleeting

mo'mento *sm* moment; **da un ~ all'altro** at any moment; (*all'improvviso*) suddenly; **al ~ di fare** just as I was (o you were o he was *ecc*) doing; **a momenti** (*da un mo'mento all'altro*) any time o moment now; (*quasi*) nearly; **per il ~** for the time being; **dal ~ che** ever since; (*dato che*) since

'monaca, -che *sf* nun

'Monaco *sf* Monaco; **~ (di Baviera)** Munich

'monaco, -ci *sm* monk

monar'chia *sf* monarchy

monas'tero *sm* (*di monaci*) monastery; (*di monache*) convent

mon'dano, -a *ag* (*anche fig*) worldly; (*dell'alta società*) society *cpd*; fashionable

mondi'ale *ag* (*campionato, popolazione*) world *cpd*; (*influenza*) world-wide

'mondo *sm* world; (*grande quantità*) **un ~ di** lots of, a host of; **il gran o bel ~** high society

mo'nello, -a *sm/f* street urchin; (*ragazzo vivace*) scamp, imp

mo'neta *sf* coin; (*Econ: valuta*) currency; (*denaro spicciolo*) (small) change; **~ estera** foreign currency; **~ legale** legal tender

mongol'fiera *sf* hot-air balloon

'monitor *sm inv* (*Tecn, TV*) monitor

monolo'cale *sm* ≈ studio flat

mono'polio *sm* monopoly

mo'notono, -a *ag* monotonous

monovo'lume *sf inv* (*anche:* **automobile ~**) people carrier, MPV

mon'sone sm monsoon

monta'carichi [monta'kariki] sm inv hoist, goods lift

mon'taggio [mon'taddʒo] sm (Tecn) assembly; (Cine) editing

mon'tagna [mon'taɲɲa] sf mountain; (zona montuosa): **la ~** the mountains pl; **andare in ~** to go to the mountains; **montagne russe** roller coaster sg, big dipper sg (BRIT)

monta'naro, -a ag mountain cpd ⊳ sm/f mountain dweller

mon'tano, -a ag mountain cpd; alpine

mon'tare /72/ vt to go (o come) up; (cavallo) to ride; (apparecchiatura) to set up, assemble; (Cuc) to whip; (Zool) to cover; (incastonare) to mount, set; (Cine) to edit; (Fot) to mount ⊳ vi to go (o come) up; (aumentare di livello, volume) to rise; (a cavallo): **~ bene/male** to ride well/badly

monta'tura sf assembling no pl; (di occhiali) frames pl; (di gioiello) mounting, setting; (fig): **~ pubblicitaria** publicity stunt

'monte sm mountain; **a ~** upstream; **mandare a ~ qc** to upset sth, cause sth to fail; **il M~ Bianco** Mont Blanc; **~ di pietà** pawnshop; **~ premi** prize

mon'tone sm (Zool) ram; **carne di ~** mutton

montu'oso, -a ag mountainous

monu'mento sm monument

mo'quette [mɔ'kɛt] sf fitted carpet

'mora sf (del rovo) blackberry; (del gelso) mulberry; (Dir) delay; (: somma) arrears pl

mo'rale ag moral ⊳ sf (scienza) ethics sg, moral philosophy; (complesso di norme) moral standards pl, morality; (condotta) morals pl; (insegnamento morale) moral ⊳ sm morale; **essere giù di ~** to be feeling down

'morbido, -a ag soft; (pelle) soft, smooth
> Attenzione! In inglese esiste la parola morbid, che però significa morboso.

mor'billo sm (Med) measles sg

'morbo sm disease

mor'boso, -a ag (fig) morbid

'mordere /64/ vt to bite; (addentare) to bite into

mor'fina sf morphine

mori'bondo, -a ag dying, moribund

mo'rire /65/ vi to die; (abitudine, civiltà) to die out; **~ di fame** to die of hunger; (fig) to be starving; **~ di noia/paura** to be bored/scared to death; **fa un caldo da ~** it's terribly hot

mormo'rare /72/ vi to murmur; (brontolare) to grumble

'moro, -a ag dark(-haired), dark(-complexioned)

'morsa sf (Tecn) vice; (fig: stretta) grip

morsi'care /20/ vt to nibble (at), gnaw (at); (insetto) to bite

'morso, -a pp di **mordere** ⊳ sm bite; (di insetto) sting; (parte della briglia) bit; **i morsi della fame** pangs of hunger

morta'della sf (Cuc) mortadella (type of salted pork meat)

mor'taio sm mortar

mor'tale ag, sm mortal

'morte sf death

'morto, -a pp di **morire** ⊳ ag dead ⊳ sm/f dead man/woman; **i morti** the dead; **fare il ~ (nell'acqua)** to float on one's back; **il Mar M~** the Dead Sea

mo'saico, -ci sm mosaic

'Mosca sf Moscow

'mosca, -sche sf fly; **~ cieca** blind-man's buff

mosce'rino [moʃʃe'rino] sm midge, gnat

mos'chea [mos'kɛa] sf mosque

'moscio, -a, -sci, -sce ['moʃʃo] ag (fig) lifeless

mos'cone sm (Zool) bluebottle; (barca) pedalo; (: a remi) kind of pedalo with oars

'mossa sf movement; (nel gioco) move

'mossi ecc vb vedi **muovere**

'mosso, -a pp di **muovere** ⊳ ag (mare) rough; (capelli) wavy; (Fot) blurred

mos'tarda sf mustard; **~ di Cremona** pickled fruit with mustard

'mostra sf exhibition, show; (ostentazione) show; **in ~** on show; **far ~ di (fingere)** to pretend; **far ~ di sé** to show off

mos'trare /72/ vt to show

'mostro sm monster; **mostru'oso, -a** ag monstrous

mo'tel sm inv motel

moti'vare /72/ vt (causare) to cause; (giustificare) to justify, account for

mo'tivo sm (causa) reason, cause; (movente) motive; (letterario) (central) theme; (disegno) motif, design, pattern; (Mus) motif; **per quale ~?** why?, for what reason?

'moto sm (anche Fisica) motion; (movimento, gesto) movement; (esercizio fisico) exercise; (sommossa) rising, revolt; (commozione) feeling, impulse ⊳ sf inv (motocicletta) motorbike; **mettere in ~** to set in motion; (Aut) to start up

motoci'cletta sf motorcycle

motoci'clista, -i, -e smf motorcyclist

mo'tore, -'trice ag motor; (Tecn) driving ⊳ sm engine, motor; **a ~** motor cpd, power-driven; **~ a combustione interna/a reazione** internal combustion/jet engine; **~ di ricerca** (Inform) search engine; **moto'rino** sm moped; **motorino di avviamento** (Aut) starter

motos'cafo sm motorboat

'motto *sm* (*battuta scherzosa*) witty remark; (*frase emblematica*) motto, maxim

'mouse ['maus] *sm inv* (*Inform*) mouse

mo'vente *sm* motive

movi'mento *sm* movement; (*fig*) activity, hustle and bustle; (*Mus*) tempo, movement

mozi'one [mot'tsjone] *sf* (*Pol*) motion

mozza'rella [mottsa'rella] *sf* mozzarella

mozzi'cone [mottsi'kone] *sm* stub, butt, end; (*anche*: **~ di sigaretta**) cigarette end

'mucca, -che *sf* cow; **~ pazza**; mad cow disease

'mucchio ['mukkjo] *sm* pile, heap; (*fig*): **un ~ di** lots of, heaps of

'muco, -chi *sm* mucus

'muffa *sf* mould , mildew

mug'gire [mud'dʒire] /55/ *vi* (*vacca*) to low, moo; (*toro*) to bellow; (*fig*) to roar

mu'ghetto [mu'getto] *sm* lily of the valley

mu'lino *sm* mill; **~ a vento** windmill

'mulo *sm* mule

'multa *sf* fine

multi'etnico, -a, -ci, -che *ag* multiethnic

multiraz'ziale [multirat'tsjale] *ag* multiracial

multi'sala *ag inv* multiscreen

multivitami'nico, -a, -ci, -che *ag*: **complesso ~** multivitamin

'mummia *sf* mummy

'mungere ['mundʒere] /5/ *vt* (*anche fig*) to milk

munici'pale [munitʃi'pale] *ag* municipal; town *cpd*

muni'cipio [muni'tʃipjo] *sm* town council, corporation; (*edificio*) town hall

munizi'oni [munit'tsjoni] *sfpl* (*Mil*) ammunition *sg*

'munsi *ecc vb vedi* **mungere**

mu'oio *ecc vb vedi* **morire**

mu'overe /66/ *vt* to move; (*ruota, macchina*) to drive; (*sollevare: questione, obiezione*) to raise, bring up; (: *accusa*) to make, bring forward; **muoversi** *vpr* to move; **muoviti!** hurry up!, get a move on!

'mura *sfpl vedi* **muro**

mu'rale *ag* wall *cpd*; mural

mura'tore *sm* mason; (*con mattoni*) bricklayer

'muro *sm* wall

'muschio ['muskjo] *sm* (*Zool*) musk; (*Bot*) moss

musco'lare *ag* muscular, muscle *cpd*

'muscolo *sm* (*Anat*) muscle

mu'seo *sm* museum

museru'ola *sf* muzzle

'musica *sf* music; **~ da ballo/camera** dance/chamber music; **musi'cale** *ag* musical; **musi'cista, -i, -e** *smf* musician

'müsli ['mysli] *sm* muesli

'muso *sm* muzzle; (*di auto, aereo*) nose; **tenere il ~** to sulk

mus(s)ul'mano, -a *ag, sm/f* Muslim, Moslem

'muta *sf* (*di animali*) moulting; (*di serpenti*) sloughing; (*per immersioni subacquee*) diving suit; (*gruppo di cani*) pack

mu'tande *sfpl* (*da uomo*) (under)pants

'muto, -a *ag* (*emozione, dolore: Cine*) silent; (*Ling*) silent, mute; (*carta geografica*) blank; **~ per lo stupore** *ecc* speechless with amazement *etc*

'mutuo, -a *ag* (*reciproco*) mutual ▷ *sm* (*Econ*) (long-term) loan

n

N *abbr* (= *nord*) N

n *abbr* (= *numero*) no.

'nafta *sf* naphtha; (*per motori diesel*) diesel oil

nafta'lina *sf* (*Chim*) naphthalene; (*tarmicida*) mothballs *pl*

'naia *sf* (*Mil*) slang term for national service

na'if [na'if] *ag inv* naïve

'nanna *sf* (*linguaggio infantile*): **andare a ~** to go to beddy-byes

'nano, -a *ag, sm/f* dwarf (!)

napole'tano, -a *ag, sm/f* Neapolitan

'Napoli *sf* Naples

nar'ciso [nar'tʃizo] *sm* narcissus

nar'cotico, -ci *sm* narcotic

na'rice [na'ritʃe] *sf* nostril

nar'rare /72/ *vt* to tell the story of, recount

narra'tivo, -a *ag* narrative ▷ *sf* (*branca*) fiction

na'sale *ag* nasal

'nascere ['naʃʃere] /67/ *vi* (*bambino*) to be born; (*pianta*) to come o spring up; (*fiume*) to rise, have its source; (*sole*) to rise; (*dente*) to come through; (*fig: derivare, conseguire*): **~ da** to arise from, be born out of; **è nata nel 1952** she was born in 1952; **'nascita** *sf* birth

nas'condere /68/ *vt* to hide, conceal; **nascondersi** *vpr* to hide; **nascon'diglio** *sm* hiding place; **nascon'dino** *sm* (*gioco*) hide-and-seek; **nas'cosi** *ecc vb vedi* **nascondere**; **nas'costo, -a** *pp di* **nascondere** ▷ *ag* hidden; **di nascosto** secretly

na'sello *sm* (*Zool*) hake

'naso *sm* nose

'nastro *sm* ribbon; (*magnetico, isolante: Sport*) tape; **~ adesivo** adhesive tape; **~ trasportatore** conveyor belt

nas'turzio [nas'turtsjo] *sm* nasturtium

na'tale *ag* of one's birth ▷ *sm* (*Rel*): **N~** Christmas; (*giorno della nascita*) birthday; **nata'lizio, -a** *ag* (*del Natale*) Christmas *cpd*

'natica, -che *sf* (*Anat*) buttock

'nato, -a *pp di* **nascere** ▷ *ag*: **un attore ~** a born actor; **nata Pieri** née Pieri

na'tura *sf* nature; **pagare in ~** to pay in kind; **~ morta** still life

natu'rale *ag* natural

natural'mente *av* naturally; (*certamente, sì*) of course

natu'rista, -i, -e *ag, sm/f* naturist, nudist

naufra'gare /80/ *vi* (*nave*) to be wrecked; (*persona*) to be shipwrecked; (*fig*) to fall through; **'naufrago, -ghi** *sm* castaway, shipwreck victim

'nausea *sf* nausea; **nause'ante** *ag* (*odore*) nauseating; (*sapore*) disgusting; (*fig*) sickening

'nautico, -a, -ci, -che *ag* nautical

na'vale *ag* naval

na'vata *sf* (*anche*: **~ centrale**) nave; (*anche*: **~ laterale**) aisle

'nave *sf* ship, vessel; **~ cisterna** tanker; **~ da guerra** warship; **~ passeggeri** passenger ship

na'vetta *sf* shuttle; (*servizio di collegamento*) shuttle (service)

navi'cella [navi'tʃella] *sf* (*di aerostato*) gondola; **~ spaziale** spaceship

navi'gare /80/ *vi* to sail; **~ in Internet** to surf the Net; **naviga'tore** *sm*: **navigatore satellitare** satnav; **navigazi'one** *sf* navigation

nazio'nale [nattsjo'nale] *ag* national ▷ *sf* (*Sport*) national team; **nazionalità** *sf inv* nationality

nazi'one [nat'tsjone] *sf* nation

naziskin ['nɑːtsiskin] *sm inv* Nazi skinhead

NB *abbr* (= *nota bene*) NB

○ **PAROLA CHIAVE**

ne *pron* **1** (*di lui, lei, loro*) of him/her/them; about him/her/them; **ne riconosco la voce** I recognize his (o her) voice

2 (*di questa, quella cosa*) of it; about it; **ne voglio ancora** I want some more (of it o them); **non parliamone più!** let's not talk about it any more!

3 (*con valore partitivo*): **hai dei libri? — sì, ne ho** have you any books? — yes, I have (some); **hai del pane? — no, non ne ho** have you any bread? — no, I haven't any; **quanti anni hai? — ne ho 17** how old are you? — I'm 17

▷ *av* (*moto da luogo, da lì*) from there; **ne vengo ora** I've just come from there

né *cong*: **né ... né** neither ... nor; **né l'uno né l'altro lo vuole** neither of them wants it; **non parla né l'italiano né il tedesco**

he speaks neither Italian nor German, he doesn't speak either Italian or German; **non piove né nevica** it isn't raining or snowing

ne'anche [ne'anke] *av, cong* not even; **non ... ~** not even; **~ se volesse potrebbe venire** he couldn't come even if he wanted to; **non l'ho visto — neanch'io** I didn't see him — neither did I o I didn't either; **~ per idea** o **sogno!** not on your life!

'nebbia *sf* fog; *(foschia)* mist

necessaria'mente *av* necessarily

neces'sario, -a [netʃes'sarjo] *ag* necessary

necessità [netʃessi'ta] *sf inv* necessity; *(povertà)* need, poverty

necro'logio [nekro'lɔdʒo] *sm* obituary notice

ne'gare /80/ *vt* to deny; *(rifiutare)* to deny, refuse; **~ di aver fatto/che** to deny having done/that; **nega'tivo, -a** *ag, sf, sm* negative

negherò *ecc* [nege'rɔ] *vb vedi* **negare**

negli'gente [negli'dʒɛnte] *ag* negligent, careless

negozi'ante [negot'tsjante] *smf* trader, dealer; *(bottegaio)* shopkeeper (BRIT), storekeeper (US)

negozi'are [negot'tsjare] /19/ *vt* to negotiate ▷ *vi*: **~ in** to trade o deal in; **negozi'ato** *sm* negotiation

ne'gozio [ne'gɔttsjo] *sm (locale)* shop (BRIT), store (US)

ne'mico, -a, -ci, -che *ag* hostile; *(Mil)* enemy *cpd* ▷ *sm/f* enemy; **essere ~ di** to be strongly averse o opposed to

nem'meno *av, cong* = **neanche**

'neo *sm* mole; *(fig)* (slight) flaw

'neon *sm (Chim)* neon

neo'nato, -a *ag* newborn ▷ *sm/f* newborn baby

neozelan'dese [neoddzelan'dese] *ag* New Zealand *cpd* ▷ *smf* New Zealander

Ne'pal *sm*: **il ~** Nepal

nep'pure *av, cong* = **neanche**

'nero, -a *ag* black; *(scuro)* dark ▷ *sm* black; **il Mar N~** the Black Sea

'nervo *sm (Anat)* nerve; *(Bot)* vein; **avere i nervi** to be on edge; **dare sui nervi a qn** to get on sb's nerves; **ner'voso, -a** *ag* nervous; *(irritabile)* irritable ▷ *sm (fam)*: **far venire il nervoso a qn** to get on sb's nerves

'nespola *sf (Bot)* medlar; *(fig)* blow, punch

'nesso *sm* connection, link

PAROLA CHIAVE

nes'suno, -a *(det: dav sm* **nessun** + C, V, **nessuno** + *s impura, gn, pn, ps, x, z; dav sf* **nessuna** + C, **nessun'** + V) *det* **1** *(non uno)*

no; *(: espressione negativa)* + any; **non c'è nessun libro** there isn't any book, there is no book; **nessun altro** no one else, nobody else; **nessun'altra cosa** nothing else; **in nessun luogo** nowhere

2 *(qualche)* any; **hai nessuna obiezione?** do you have any objections?

▷ *pron* **1** *(non uno)* no one, nobody; *(espressione negativa)* + any(one); **nessuno è venuto, non è venuto nessuno** nobody came

2 *(cosa: espressione negativa)* none; *(: espressione negativa)* + any

3 *(qualcuno)* anyone, anybody; **ha telefonato nessuno?** did anyone phone?

net'tare *vt* to clean

net'tezza [net'tettsa] *sf* cleanness, cleanliness; **~ urbana** cleansing department

'netto, -a *ag (pulito)* clean; *(chiaro)* clear, clear-cut; *(deciso)* definite; *(Econ)* net

nettur'bino *sm* dustman (BRIT), garbage collector (US)

neu'trale *ag* neutral

'neutro, -a *ag* neutral; *(Ling)* neuter ▷ *sm (Ling)* neuter

'neve *sf* snow; **nevi'care** /20/ *vb impers* to snow; **nevi'cata** *sf* snowfall

ne'vischio [ne'viskjo] *sm* sleet

ne'voso, -a *ag* snowy; snow-covered

nevral'gia [nevral'dʒia] *sf* neuralgia

nevras'tenico, -a, -ci, -che *ag (Med)* neurasthenic; *(fig)* hot-tempered

ne'vrosi *sf inv* neurosis

ne'vrotico, -a, -ci, -che *ag, sm/f (anche fig)* neurotic

'nicchia ['nikkja] *sf* niche; *(naturale)* cavity, hollow; **~ di mercato** (Comm) niche market

nicchi'are [nik'kjare] /19/ *vi* to shilly-shally, hesitate

'nichel ['nikel] *sm* nickel

nico'tina *sf* nicotine

'nido *sm* nest; **a ~ d'ape** *(tessuto ecc)* honeycomb *cpd*

PAROLA CHIAVE

ni'ente *pron* **1** *(nessuna cosa)* nothing; **niente può fermarlo** nothing can stop him; **niente di niente** absolutely nothing; **grazie! — di niente!** thank you! — not at all!; **nient'altro** nothing else; **nient'altro che** nothing but, just, only; **niente affatto** not at all, not in the least; **come se niente fosse** as if nothing had happened; **cose da niente** trivial matters; **per niente** *(gratis, invano)* for nothing

2 *(qualcosa)*: **hai bisogno di niente?** do you need anything?

3: non ... niente nothing; (*espressione negativa*) + anything; **non ho visto niente** I saw nothing, I didn't see anything; **non ho niente da dire** I have nothing *o* haven't anything to say
▶ *sm* nothing; **un bel niente** absolutely nothing; **basta un niente per farla piangere** the slightest thing is enough to make her cry
▶ *av* (*in nessuna misura*): **non ... niente** not ... at all; **non è (per) niente buono** it isn't good at all

Ni'geria [ni'dʒɛrja] *sf*: **la ~** Nigeria
'ninfa *sf* nymph
nin'fea *sf* water lily
ninna'nanna *sf* lullaby
'ninnolo *sm* (*gingillo*) knick-knack
ni'pote *smf* (*di zii*) nephew (niece); (*di nonni*) grandson(-daughter), grandchild
'nitido, -a *ag* clear; (*specchio*) bright
ni'trire /55/ *vi* to neigh
ni'trito *sm* (*di cavallo*) neighing *no pl*; neigh; (*Chim*) nitrite
nitroglice'rina [nitroglitʃe'rina] *sf* nitroglycerine
no *av* (*risposta*) no; **vieni o no?** are you coming or not?; **perché no?** why not?; **lo conosciamo? — tu no ma io sì** do we know him? — you don't but I do; **verrai, no?** you'll come, won't you?
'nobile *ag* noble ▷ *smf* noble, nobleman/woman
'nocca, -che *sf* (*Anat*) knuckle
'noccio *ecc* ['nɔttʃo] *vb vedi* **nuocere**
nocci'ola [not'tʃɔla] *sf* hazelnut ▷ *ag inv* (*anche*: **color ~**) hazel, light brown
noccio'lina [nottʃo'lina] *sf* (*anche*: **~ americana**) peanut
'nocciolo ['nɔttʃolo] *sm* (*di frutto*) stone; (*fig*) heart, core
'noce ['nɔtʃe] *sm* (*albero*) walnut tree ▷ *sf* (*frutto*) walnut; **~ di cocco** coconut; **~ moscata** nutmeg
no'cevo *ecc* [no'tʃevo] *vb vedi* **nuocere**
no'civo, -a [no'tʃivo] *ag* harmful, noxious
'nocqui *ecc* *vb vedi* **nuocere**
'nodo *sm* (*di cravatta, legname, Naut*) knot; (*Aut, Ferr*) junction; (*Med, Astr, Bot*) node; (*fig: legame*) bond, tie; (: *punto centrale*) heart, crux; **avere un ~ alla gola** to have a lump in one's throat
no-'global [no-'global] *smf inv* anti-globalization protester ▷ *ag inv* (*movimento, manifestante*) anti-globalization
'noi *pron* (*soggetto*) we; (*oggetto: per dare rilievo, con preposizione*) us; **~ stessi(e)** we ourselves; (*oggetto*) ourselves
'noia *sf* boredom; (*disturbo, impaccio*) bother *no pl*, trouble *no pl*; **avere qn/qc a ~** not to

like sb/sth; **mi è venuto a ~** I'm tired of it; **dare ~ a** to annoy; **avere delle noie con qn** to have trouble with sb
noi'oso, -a *ag* boring; (*fastidioso*) annoying, troublesome

▌ Attenzione! In inglese esiste la parola *noisy*, che però significa *rumoroso*.

noleggi'are [noled'dʒare] /62/ *vt* (*prendere a noleggio*) to hire (BRIT), rent; (*dare a noleggio*) to hire out (BRIT), rent out; (*aereo, nave*) to charter; **no'leggio** *sm* hire (BRIT), rental; charter
'nomade *ag* nomadic ▷ *smf* nomad
'nome *sm* name; (*Ling*) noun; **in o a ~ di** in the name of; **di o per ~** (*chiamato*) called, named; **conoscere qn di ~** to know sb by name; **~ d'arte** stage name; **~ di battesimo** Christian name; **~ di famiglia** surname; **~ utente** login, username
no'mignolo [no'miɲɲolo] *sm* nickname
'nomina *sf* appointment
nomi'nale *ag* nominal; (*Ling*) noun *cpd*
nomi'nare /72/ *vt* to name; (*eleggere*) to appoint; (*citare*) to mention
nomina'tivo, -a *ag* (*intestato*) registered; (*Ling*) nominative ▷ *sm* (*Amm*) name; (*Ling*) nominative
non *av* not ▷ *prefisso* non-; **grazie — non c'è di che** thank you — don't mention it; *vedi anche* **affatto, appena** *ecc*
nonché [non'ke] *cong* (*tanto più, tanto meno*) let alone; (*e inoltre*) as well as
noncu'rante *ag*: **~ (di)** careless (of), indifferent (to)
'nonno, -a *sm/f* grandfather/mother; (*in senso più familiare*) grandma/grandpa; **nonni** *smpl* grandparents
non'nulla *sm inv*: **un ~** nothing, a trifle
'nono, -a *num* ninth
nonos'tante *prep* in spite of, notwithstanding ▷ *cong* although, even though
nontiscordardimé *sm inv* (*Bot*) forget-me-not
nord *sm* north ▷ *ag inv* north; northern; **il Mare del N~** the North Sea; **nor'dest** *sm* north-east; **nor'dovest** *sm* north-west
'norma *sf* (*principio*) norm; (*regola*) regulation, rule; (*consuetudine*) custom, rule; **a ~ di legge** according to law, as laid down by law; **norme di sicurezza** safety regulations; **norme per l'uso** instructions for use
nor'male *ag* normal; standard *cpd*
normal'mente *av* normally
norve'gese [norve'dʒese] *ag, sm/f, sm* Norwegian
Nor'vegia *sf*: **la ~** Norway
nostal'gia [nostal'dʒia] *sf* (*di casa, paese*) homesickness; (*del passato*) nostalgia

nos'trano, -a *ag* local; national; (*pianta, frutta*) home-produced

'nostro, -a *det*: **il (la) ~(a)** *ecc* our ▷ *pron*: **il (la) ~(a)** *ecc* ours ▷ *sm*: **il ~** our money; our belongings; **i nostri** our family; our own people; **è dei nostri** he's one of us

'nota *sf*(*segno*) mark; (*comunicazione scritta: Mus*) note; (*fattura*) bill; (*elenco*) list; **degno di ~** noteworthy, worthy of note

no'taio *sm* notary

no'tare /72/ *vt* (*segnare: errori*) to mark; (*registrare*) to note (down), write down; (*rilevare, osservare*) to note, notice; **farsi ~** to get o.s. noticed

no'tevole *ag* (*talento*) notable, remarkable; (*peso*) considerable

no'tifica, -che *sf* notification

no'tizia [no'tittsja] *sf* (piece of) news *sg*; (*informazione*) piece of information; **notizi'ario** *sm* (*Radio, TV, Stampa*) news *sg*

'noto, -a *ag* (well-)known

notorietà *sf* fame; notoriety

no'torio, -a *ag* well-known; (*peg*) notorious

not'tambulo, -a *sm/f* night-bird (*fig*)

not'tata *sf* night

'notte *sf* night; **di ~** at night; (*durante la notte*) in the night, during the night; **~ bianca** sleepless night

not'turno, -a *ag* nocturnal; (*servizio, guardiano*) night *cpd*

no'vanta *num* ninety; **novan'tesimo, -a** *num* ninetieth

'nove *num* nine

nove'cento [nove'tʃɛnto] *num* nine hundred ▷ *sm*: **il N~** the twentieth century

no'vella *sf* (*Letteratura*) short story

no'vello, -a *ag* (*piante, patate*) new; (*insalata, verdura*) early; (*sposo*) newly-married

no'vembre *sm* November

novità *sf inv* novelty; (*innovazione*) innovation; (*cosa originale, insolita*) something new; (*notizia*) (piece of) news *sg*; **le ~ della moda** the latest fashions

nozi'one [not'tsjone] *sf* notion, idea

'nozze ['nɔttse] *sfpl* wedding *sg*, marriage *sg*; **~ d'argento/d'oro** silver/golden wedding *sg*

'nubile *ag* (*donna*) unmarried, single

'nuca, -che *sf* nape of the neck

nucle'are *ag* nuclear

'nucleo *sm* nucleus; (*gruppo*) team, unit, group; (*Mil, Polizia*) squad; **il ~ familiare** the family unit

nu'dista, -i, -e *smf* nudist

'nudo, -a *ag* (*persona*) bare, naked, nude; (*membra*) bare, naked; (*montagna*) bare ▷ *sm* (*Arte*) nude

'nulla *pron, av* = **niente** ▷ *sm*: **il ~** nothing

nullità *sf inv* nullity; (*persona*) nonentity

'nullo, -a *ag* useless, worthless; (*Dir*) null (and void); (*Sport*): **incontro ~** draw

nume'rale *ag, sm* numeral

nume'rare /72/ *vt* to number

nu'merico, -a, -ci, -che *ag* numerical

'numero *sm* number; (*romano, arabo*) numeral; (*di spettacolo*) act, turn; **~ civico** house number; **~ di scarpe** shoe size; **~ di telefono** telephone number; **nume'roso, -a** *ag* numerous, many; (*folla, famiglia*) large

nu'occio *ecc* vedi **nuocere**

nu'ocere ['nwɔtʃere] /69/ *vi*: **~ a** to harm, damage

nu'ora *sf* daughter-in-law

nuo'tare /72/ *vi* to swim; (*galleggiare: oggetti*) to float; **nuota'tore, -'trice** *sm/f* swimmer; **nu'oto** *sm* swimming

nu'ova *sf* vedi **nuovo**

nuova'mente *av* again

Nu'ova Ze'landa [-dze'landa] *sf*: **la ~** New Zealand

nu'ovo, -a *ag* new ▷ *sf* (*notizia*) (piece of) news *sg*; **di ~** again; **~ fiammante** *o* **di zecca** brand-new

nutri'ente *ag* nutritious, nourishing

nutri'mento *sm* food, nourishment

nu'trire /45/ *vt* to feed; (*fig: sentimenti*) to harbour (*BRIT*), harbor (*US*), nurse; **nutrirsi** *vpr*: **nutrirsi di** to feed on, to eat

'nuvolo, -a *ag* cloudy ▷ *sf* cloud; **nuvo'loso, -a** *ag* cloudy

nuzi'ale [nut'tsjale] *ag* nuptial; wedding *cpd*

'nylon ['nailən] *sm* nylon

O

o cong (dav V spesso **od**) or; **o ... o** either ... or; **o l'uno o l'altro** either (of them)

O. abbr (= ovest) W

'oasi sf inv oasis

obbedi'ente ecc vedi **ubbidiente** ecc

obbli'gare /80/ vt (Dir) to bind; (costringere): **~ qn a fare** to force o oblige sb to do; **obbliga'torio, -a** ag compulsory, obligatory; **'obbligo, -ghi** sm obligation; (dovere) duty; **avere l'obbligo di fare** to be obliged to do; **essere d'obbligo** (discorso, applauso) to be called for

o'beso, -a ag obese

obiet'tare /72/ vt: **~ che** to object that; **~ su qc** to object to sth, raise objections concerning sth

obiet'tivo, -a ag objective ▷ sm (Ottica, Fot) lens sg, objective; (Mil, fig) objective

obiet'tore sm objector; **~ di coscienza** conscientious objector

obiezi'one [objet'tsjone] sf objection

obi'torio sm morgue

o'bliquo, -a ag oblique; (inclinato) slanting; (fig) devious, underhand

oblite'rare /72/ vt (francobollo) to cancel; (biglietto) to stamp

oblò sm inv porthole

'oboe sm (Mus) oboe

'oca (pl **oche**) sf goose

occasi'one sf (caso favorevole) opportunity; (causa, motivo, circostanza) occasion; (Comm) bargain; **d'~** (a buon prezzo) bargain cpd; (usato) secondhand

occhi'aia [ok'kjaja] sf eye socket; **avere le occhiaie** to have shadows under one's eyes

occhi'ali [ok'kjali] smpl glasses, spectacles; **~ da sole/da vista** sunglasses/ (prescription) glasses

occhi'ata [ok'kjata] sf look, glance; **dare un'~ a** to have a look at

occhi'ello [ok'kjɛllo] sm buttonhole; (asola) eyelet

'occhio ['ɔkkjo] sm eye; **~!** careful!, watch out!; **a ~ nudo** with the naked eye; **a quattr'occhi** privately, tête-à-tête; **dare all'~ o nell'~ a qn** to catch sb's eye; **fare l'~ a qc** to get used to sth; **tenere d'~ qn** to keep an eye on sb; **vedere di buon/mal ~ qc** to look favourably/unfavourably on sth

occhio'lino [okkjo'lino] sm: **fare l'~ a qn** to wink at sb

occiden'tale [ottʃiden'tale] ag western ▷ smf Westerner

occi'dente [ottʃi'dɛnte] sm west; (Pol): **l'O~** the West; **a ~** in the west

occor'rente ag necessary ▷ sm all that is necessary

occor'renza [okkor'rɛntsa] sf necessity, need; **all'~** in case of need

oc'correre /28/ vi to be needed, be required ▷ vb impers: **occorre farlo** it must be done; **occorre che tu parta** you must leave, you'll have to leave; **mi occorrono i soldi** I need the money

> ⚠ Attenzione! In inglese esiste il verbo to occur, che però significa succedere.

oc'culto, -a ag hidden, concealed; (scienze, forze) occult

occu'pare /72/ vt to occupy; (manodopera) to employ; (ingombrare) to occupy, take up; **occuparsi** vpr to occupy o.s., keep o.s. busy; (impiegarsi) to get a job; **occuparsi di** (interessarsi) to take an interest in; (prendersi cura di) to look after, take care of; **occu'pato, -a** ag (Mil, Pol) occupied; (persona: affaccendato) busy; (posto, sedia) taken; (toilette, Tel) engaged; **la linea è occupata** the line's engaged; **occupazi'one** sf occupation; (impiego, lavoro) job; (Econ) employment

o'ceano sm ocean

'ocra sf ochre

'OCSE sigla f (= Organizzazione per la Cooperazione e lo Sviluppo Economico) OECD

ocu'lare ag ocular, eye cpd; **testimone ~** eye witness

ocu'lato, -a ag (attento) cautious, prudent; (accorto) shrewd

ocu'lista, -i, -e smf eye specialist, oculist

odi'are /19/ vt to hate, detest

odi'erno, -a ag today's, of today; (attuale) present

'odio sm hatred; **avere in ~ qc/qn** to hate o detest sth/sb; **odi'oso, -a** ag hateful, odious

'odo ecc vb vedi **udire**

odo'rare /72/ vt (annusare) to smell; (profumare) to perfume, scent ▷ vi: **~ (di)** to smell (of)

o'dore *sm* smell; **gli odori** (*Cuc*) (aromatic) herbs

offendere /36/ *vt* to offend; (*violare*) to break, violate; (*insultare*) to insult; (*ferire*) to hurt; **offendersi** *vpr* (*con senso reciproco*) to insult one another; (*risentirsi*): **offendersi (di)** to take offence (at), be offended (by)

offe'rente *sm* (*in aste*): **al migliore ~** to the highest bidder

offerto, -a *pp di* **offrire** ▷ *sf* offer; (*donazione: anche Rel*) offering; (*in gara d'appalto*) offering; (*Econ*) supply; **fare un'offerta** to make an offer; (*per appalto*) to tender; (*ad un'asta*) to bid; **"offerte d'impiego"** "situations vacant"; **offerta speciale** special offer

offeso, -a *pp di* **offendere** ▷ *ag* offended; (*fisicamente*) hurt, injured ▷ *sm/f* offended party ▷ *sf* insult, affront; (*Mil*) attack; (*Dir*) offence

offi'cina [offi'tʃina] *sf* workshop

offrire /7o/ *vt* to offer; **offrirsi** *vpr* (*proporsi*) to offer (o.s.), volunteer; (*occasione*) to present itself; (*esporsi*): **offrirsi a** to expose o.s. to; **ti offro da bere** I'll buy you a drink

offus'care /2o/ *vt* to obscure, darken; (*fig: intelletto*) to dim, cloud; (: *fama*) to obscure, overshadow; **offuscarsi** *vpr* to grow dark; to cloud, grow dim; to be obscured

ogget'tivo, -a [oddʒet'tivo] *ag* objective

og'getto [od'dʒetto] *sm* object; (*materia, argomento*) subject (matter); **oggetti smarriti** lost property *sg*

'oggi ['ɔddʒi] *av, sm* today; **~ a otto** a week today; **oggigi'orno** *av* nowadays

OGM [odʒi'emme] *sigla mpl* (= *organismi geneticamente modificati*) GMO

'ogni ['oɲɲi] *det* every, each; (*tutti*) all; (*con valore distributivo*) every; **~ uomo è mortale** all men are mortal; **viene ~ due giorni** he comes every two days; **~ cosa** everything; **ad ~ costo** at all costs, at any price; **in ~ luogo** everywhere; **~ tanto** every so often; **~ volta che** every time that

Ognis'santi [oɲɲis'santi] *sm* All Saints' Day

o'gnuno [oɲ'ɲuno] *pron* everyone, everybody

O'landa *sf*: **l'~** Holland; **olan'dese** *ag* Dutch ▷ *sm* (*Ling*) Dutch ▷ *smf* Dutchman/woman; **gli Olandesi** the Dutch

ole'andro *sm* oleander

oleo'dotto *sm* oil pipeline

ole'oso, -a *ag* oily; (*che contiene olio*) oil-yielding

ol'fatto *sm* sense of smell

oli'are /19/ *vt* to oil

oli'era *sf* oil cruet

Olim'piadi *sfpl* Olympic Games®; **o'limpico, -a, -ci, -che** *ag* Olympic®

'olio *sm* oil; **sott'~** (*Cuc*) in oil; **~ di fegato di merluzzo** cod liver oil; **~ d'oliva** olive oil; **~ di semi** vegetable oil; **oli essenziali** essential oils

o'liva *sf* olive; **o'livo** *sm* olive tree

'olmo *sm* elm

OLP *sigla f* (= *Organizzazione per la Liberazione della Palestina*) PLO

ol'traggio [ol'traddʒo] *sm* outrage; offence , insult; (*Dir*): **~ a pubblico ufficiale** insulting a public official; (*Dir*): **~ al pudore** indecent behaviour (BRIT) o behavior (US)

ol'tranza [ol'trantsa] *sf*: **a ~** to the last, to the bitter end

'oltre *av* (*più in là*) further; (*di più: aspettare*) longer, more ▷ *prep* (*di là da*) beyond, over, on the other side of; (*più di*) more than, over; (*in aggiunta a*) besides; (*eccetto*): **~ a** except, apart from; **oltrepas'sare** /72/ *vt* to go beyond, exceed

o'maggio [o'maddʒo] *sm* (*dono*) gift; (*segno di rispetto*) homage, tribute; **omaggi** *smpl* (*complimenti*) respects; **in ~** (*copia, biglietto*) complimentary; **rendere ~ a** to pay homage o tribute to

ombe'lico, -chi *sm* navel

'ombra *sf* (*zona non assolata, fantasma*) shade; (*sagoma scura*) shadow; **sedere all'~** to sit in the shade; **restare nell'~** (*fig*) to remain in obscurity

om'brello *sm* umbrella; **ombrel'lone** *sm* beach umbrella

om'bretto *sm* eyeshadow

O.M.C. *sigla f* (= *Organizzazione Mondiale del Commercio*) WTO

ome'lette [ɔmə'lɛt] *sf inv* omelet(te)

ome'lia *sf* (*Rel*) homily, sermon

omeopa'tia *sf* hom(o)eopathy

omertà *sf* conspiracy of silence

o'mettere /63/ *vt* to omit, leave out; **~ di fare** to omit o fail to do

omi'cida, -i, -e [omi'tʃida] *ag* homicidal, murderous ▷ *smf* murderer/murderess

omi'cidio [omi'tʃidjo] *sm* murder; **~ colposo** culpable homicide

o'misi *ecc vb vedi* **omettere**

omissi'one *sf* omission; **~ di soccorso** (*Dir*) failure to stop and give assistance

omogeneiz'zato [omodʒeneid'dzato] *sm* baby food

omo'geneo, -a [omo'dʒɛneo] *ag* homogeneous

o'monimo, -a *sm/f* namesake ▷ *sm* (*Ling*) homonym

omosessu'ale *ag, smf* homosexual

O.M.S. *sigla f* = **Organizzazione Mondiale della Sanità**

On. *abbr* (*Pol*); = **onorevole**

'**onda** sf wave; **mettere** o **mandare in ~** (Radio, TV) to broadcast; **andare in ~** (Radio, TV) to go on the air; **onde corte/medie/ lunghe** short/medium/long wave sg

'**onere** sm burden; **oneri fiscali** taxes

onestà sf honesty

o'**nesto, -a** ag (probo, retto) honest; (giusto) fair; (casto) chaste, virtuous

ONG sigla f inv (= Organizzazione Non Governativa) NGO

onnipo'tente ag omnipotent

ono'**mastico, -ci** sm name day

ono'**rare** /72/ vt to honour (BRIT), honor (US); (far onore a) to do credit to

ono'**rario, -a** ag honorary ▷ sm fee

o'**nore** sm honour (BRIT), honor (US); **in ~ di** in honour of; **fare gli onori di casa** to play host (o hostess); **fare ~ a** to honour; (pranzo) to do justice to; (famiglia) to be a credit to; **farsi ~** to distinguish o.s.; **ono'revole** ag honourable (BRIT), honorable (US) ▷ smf (Pol) ≈ Member of Parliament (BRIT), ≈ Congressman/ woman (US)

on'**tano** sm (Bot) alder

'**O.N.U.** sigla f (= Organizzazione delle Nazioni Unite) UN, UNO

o'**paco, -a, -chi, -che** ag (vetro) opaque; (metallo) dull, matt

o'**pale** sm o f opal

'**opera** sf work; (azione rilevante) action, deed, work; (Mus) work; opus; (: melodramma) opera; (: teatro) opera house; (ente) institution, organization; **~ d'arte** work of art; **~ lirica** (grand) opera; **opere pubbliche (OO.PP.)** public works

ope'**raio, -a** ag working-class; workers' ▷ sm/f worker; **classe operaia** working class

ope'**rare** /72/ vt to carry out, make; (Med) to operate on ▷ vi to operate, work; (rimedio) to act, work; (Med) to operate; **operarsi** vpr (Med) to have an operation; **operarsi d'appendicite** to have one's appendix out; **operazi'one** sf operation

ope'**retta** sf (Mus) operetta, light opera

opini'**one** sf opinion; **l'~ pubblica** public opinion

'**oppio** sm opium

op'**pongo** ecc vb vedi **opporre**

op'**porre** /77/ vt to oppose; **opporsi** vpr: **opporsi (a qc)** to oppose (sth); to object (to sth); **~ resistenza/un rifiuto** to offer resistance/to refuse

opportu'**nista, -i, -e** smf opportunist

opportu'**nità** sf inv opportunity; (convenienza) opportuneness, timeliness

oppor'**tuno, -a** ag timely, opportune

op'**posi** ecc vb vedi **opporre**

opposizi'**one** [oppozit'tsjone] sf opposition; (Dir) objection

op'**posto, -a** pp di **opporre** ▷ ag opposite; (opinioni) conflicting ▷ sm opposite, contrary; **all'~** on the contrary

oppressi'**one** sf oppression

oppri'**mente** ag (caldo, noia) oppressive; (persona) tiresome; (deprimente) depressing

op'**primere** /50/ vt (premere, gravare) to weigh down; (estenuare: caldo) to suffocate, oppress; (tiranneggiare: popolo) to oppress

op'**pure** cong or (else)

op'**tare** /72/ vi: **~ per** to opt for

o'**puscolo** sm booklet, pamphlet

opzi'**one** [op'tsjone] sf option

'**ora** sf (60 minuti) hour; (momento) time; **che ~ è?, che ore sono?** what time is it?; **non veder l'~ di fare** to long to do, look forward to doing; **di buon'~** early; **alla buon'~!** at last!; **~ legale** o **estiva** summer time (BRIT), daylight saving time (US); **~ di cena** dinner time; **~ locale** local time; **~ di pranzo** lunchtime; **~ di punta** (Aut) rush hour

o'**racolo** sm oracle

o'**rale** ag, sm oral

o'**rario, -a** ag hourly; (fuso, segnale) time cpd; (velocità) per hour ▷ sm timetable, schedule; (di ufficio, visite ecc) hours pl; time(s); **in ~** on time

o'**rata** sf (Zool) sea bream

ora'**tore, -'trice** sm/f speaker; orator

'**orbita** sf (Astr, Fisica) orbit; (Anat) (eye-) socket

or'**chestra** [or'kɛstra] sf orchestra

orchi'**dea** [orki'dɛa] sf orchid

or'**digno** [or'diɲno] sm: **~ esplosivo** explosive device

ordi'**nale** ag, sm ordinal

ordi'**nare** /72/ vt (mettere in ordine) to arrange, organize; (Comm) to order; (prescrivere: medicina) to prescribe; (comandare): **~ a qn di fare qc** to order o command sb to do sth; (Rel) to ordain

ordi'**nario, -a** ag (comune) ordinary; everyday; standard; (grossolano) coarse, common ▷ sm ordinary; (Ins: di università) full professor

ordi'**nato, -a** ag tidy, orderly

ordinazi'**one** [ordinat'tsjone] sf (Comm) order; (Rel) ordination; **eseguire qc su ~** to make sth to order

'**ordine** sm order; (carattere): **d'~ pratico** of a practical nature; **all'~** (Comm: assegno) to order; **di prim'~** first-class; **fino a nuovo ~** until further notice; **essere in ~** (documenti) to be in order; (persona, stanza) to be tidy; **mettere in ~** to put in order, tidy (up); **~ del giorno** (di seduta) agenda; (Mil) order of the day; **~ di pagamento** (Comm) order for payment; **l'~ pubblico** law and order; **ordini (sacri)** (Rel) holy orders

orec'chino [orek'kino] sm earring

o'recchio [o'rekkjo] (pl f **orecchie**) sm (Anat) ear

orecchi'oni [orek'kjoni] smpl (Med) mumps sg

o'refice [o'refitfe] sm goldsmith; jeweller; **orefice'ria** sf (arte) goldsmith's art; (negozio) jeweller's (shop)

'orfano, -a ag orphan(ed) ▷ sm/f orphan; **~ di padre/madre** fatherless/motherless

orga'netto sm barrel organ; (fam: armonica a bocca) mouth organ; (: fisarmonica) accordion

or'ganico, -a, -ci, -che ag organic ▷ sm personnel, staff

organi'gramma, -i sm organization chart

orga'nismo sm (Biol) organism; (Anat, Amm) body, organism

organiz'zare [organid'dzare] /72/ vt to organize; **organizzarsi** vpr to get organized; **organizzazi'one** sf organization

'organo sm organ; (di congegno) part; (portavoce) spokesman/woman, mouthpiece

'orgia, -e ['ɔrdʒa] sf orgy

or'goglio [or'goʎʎo] sm pride; **orgogli'oso, -a** ag proud

orien'tale ag (paese, regione) eastern; (tappeti, lingua, civiltà) oriental; east

orienta'mento sm positioning; orientation; direction; **senso di ~** sense of direction; **perdere l'~** to lose one's bearings; **~ professionale** careers guidance

orien'tare /72/ vt (situare) to position; **orientarsi** vpr to find one's bearings; (fig: tendere) to tend, lean; (indirizzarsi): **orientarsi verso** to take up, go in for

ori'ente sm east; **l'O~** the East, the Orient; **a ~** in the east

o'rigano sm oregano

origi'nale [oridʒi'nale] ag original; (bizzarro) eccentric ▷ sm original

origi'nario, -a [oridʒi'narjo] ag original; **essere ~ di** to be a native of; (provenire da) to originate from; (animale, pianta) to be native to

o'rigine [o'ridʒine] sf origin; **all'~** originally; **d'~ inglese** of English origin; **dare ~ a** to give rise to

origli'are [oriʎ'ʎare] /27/ vi: **~ (a)** to eavesdrop (on)

o'rina sf urine

ori'nare /72/ vi to urinate ▷ vt to pass

orizzon'tale [oriddzon'tale] ag horizontal

oriz'zonte [orid'dzonte] sm horizon

'orlo sm edge, border; (di recipiente) rim, brim; (di vestito ecc) hem

'orma sf (di persona) footprint; (di animale) track; (impronta, traccia) mark, trace

or'mai av by now, by this time; (adesso) now; (quasi) almost, nearly

ormeggi'are [ormed'dʒare] /62/ vt (Naut) to moor

or'mone sm hormone

ornamen'tale ag ornamental, decorative

or'nare /72/ vt to adorn, decorate; **ornarsi** vpr: **ornarsi (di)** to deck o.s. (out) (with)

ornitolo'gia [ornitolo'dʒia] sf ornithology

'oro sm gold; **d'~, in ~** gold cpd; **d'~** (colore, occasione) golden; (persona) marvellous

oro'logio [oro'lɔdʒo] sm clock; (da tasca, da polso) watch; **~ da polso** wristwatch; **~ al quarzo** quartz watch

o'roscopo sm horoscope

or'rendo, -a ag (spaventoso) horrible, awful; (bruttissimo) hideous

or'ribile ag horrible

or'rore sm horror; **avere in ~ qn/qc** to loathe o detest sb/sth; **mi fanno ~** I loathe o detest them

orsacchi'otto [orsak'kjɔtto] sm teddy bear

'orso sm bear; **~ bruno/bianco** brown/ polar bear

or'taggio [or'taddʒo] sm vegetable

or'tensia sf hydrangea

or'tica, -che sf (stinging) nettle

orti'caria sf nettle rash

'orto sm vegetable garden, kitchen garden; (Agr) market garden (BRIT), truck farm (US); **~ botanico** botanical garden(s)

orto'dosso, -a ag orthodox

ortogra'fia sf spelling

orto'pedico, -a, -ci, -che ag orthopaedic ▷ sm orthopaedic specialist

orzai'olo [ordza'jɔlo] sm (Med) stye

'orzo ['ɔrdzo] sm barley

o'sare /72/ vt, vi to dare; **~ fare** to dare (to) do

oscenità [oʃʃeni'ta] sf inv obscenity

o'sceno, -a [oʃ'ʃɛno] ag obscene; (ripugnante) ghastly

oscil'lare [oʃʃil'lare] /72/ vi (pendolo) to swing; (dondolare: al vento ecc) to rock; (variare) to fluctuate; (Tecn) to oscillate; (fig): **~ fra** to waver o hesitate between

oscu'rare /72/ vt to darken, obscure; (fig) to obscure; **oscurarsi** vpr to darken, cloud over; (persona): **si oscurò in volto** his face clouded over

oscurità sf (vedi ag) darkness; obscurity

os'curo, -a ag dark; (fig) obscure; (vita, natali) humble, lowly ▷ sm: **all'~** in the dark; **tenere qn all'~ di qc** to keep sb in the dark about sth

ospe'dale _sm_ hospital

ospi'tale _ag_ hospitable

ospi'tare /72/ _vt_ to give hospitality to; (_albergo_) to accommodate

'ospite _smf_ (_persona che ospita_) host/hostess; (_persona ospitata_) guest

os'pizio [os'pittsjo] _sm_ (_per vecchi ecc_) home

osser'vare /72/ _vt_ to observe, watch; (_esaminare_) to examine; (_notare, rilevare_) to notice, observe; (_Dir: la legge_) to observe, respect; (_mantenere: silenzio_) to keep, observe; **far ~ qc a qn** to point sth out to sb; **osservazi'one** _sf_ observation; (_di legge ecc_) observance; (_considerazione critica_) observation, remark; (_rimprovero_) reproof; **in osservazione** under observation

ossessio'nare /72/ _vt_ to obsess, haunt; (_tormentare_) to torment, harass

ossessi'one _sf_ obsession

os'sia _cong_ that is, to be precise

'ossido _sm_ oxide; **~ di carbonio** carbon monoxide

ossige'nare [ossidʒe'nare] /72/ _vt_ to oxygenate; (_decolorare_) to bleach; **acqua ossigenata** hydrogen peroxide

os'sigeno _sm_ oxygen

'osso (_pl f_ **ossa**) _sm_ (_Anat_) bone; **d'~** (_bottone ecc_) of bone, bone _cpd_; **~ di seppia** cuttlebone

ostaco'lare /72/ _vt_ to block, obstruct

os'tacolo _sm_ obstacle; (_Equitazione_) hurdle, jump

os'taggio [os'taddʒo] _sm_ hostage

os'tello _sm_ hostel; **~ della gioventù** youth hostel

osten'tare /72/ _vt_ to make a show of, flaunt

oste'ria _sf_ inn

os'tetrico, -a, -ci, -che _ag_ obstetric ▷ _sm_ obstetrician

'ostia _sf_ (_Rel_) host; (_per medicinali_) wafer

'ostico, -a, -ci, -che _ag_ (_fig_) harsh; difficult, tough; unpleasant

os'tile _ag_ hostile

osti'narsi /72/ _vpr_ to insist, dig one's heels in; **~ a fare** to persist (obstinately) in doing; **osti'nato, -a** _ag_ (_caparbio_) obstinate; (_tenace_) persistent, determined

'ostrica, -che _sf_ oyster

> ▌ Attenzione! In inglese esiste la parola ostrich, che però significa _struzzo_.

ostru'ire /55/ _vt_ to obstruct, block

o'tite _sf_ ear infection

ot'tanta _num_ eighty

ot'tavo, -a _num_ eighth

otte'nere /121/ _vt_ to obtain, get; (_risultato_) to achieve, obtain

'ottico, -a, -ci, -che _ag_ (_della vista: nervo_) optic; (_dell'ottica_) optical ▷ _sm_ optician

▷ _sf_ (_scienza_) optics _sg_; (_Fot: lenti, prismi ecc_) optics _pl_

ottima'mente _av_ excellently, very well

otti'mismo _sm_ optimism; **otti'mista, -i, -e** _smf_ optimist

'ottimo, -a _ag_ excellent, very good

'otto _num_ eight

ot'tobre _sm_ October

otto'cento [otto'tʃɛnto] _num_ eight hundred ▷ _sm_: **l'O~** the nineteenth century

ot'tone _sm_ brass; **gli ottoni** (_Mus_) the brass

ottu'rare /72/ _vt_ to close (up); (_dente_) to fill; **otturarsi** _vpr_ to become o get blocked up; **otturazi'one** _sf_ closing (up); (_dentaria_) filling

ot'tuso, -a _ag_ (_Mat, fig_) obtuse; (_suono_) dull

o'vaia _sf_ (_Anat_) ovary

o'vale _ag, sm_ oval

o'vatta _sf_ cotton wool; (_per imbottire_) padding, wadding

'ovest _sm_ west

o'vile _sm_ pen, enclosure

ovulazi'one [ovulat'tsjone] _sf_ ovulation

'ovulo _sm_ (_Fisiol_) ovum

o'vunque _av_ = **dovunque**

ovvi'are /19/ _vi_: **~ a** to obviate

'ovvio, -a _ag_ obvious

ozi'are [ot'tsjare] /19/ _vi_ to laze around, idle

'ozio ['ɔttsjo] _sm_ idleness; (_tempo libero_) leisure; **ore d'~** leisure time; **stare in ~** to be idle

o'zono [od'dzɔno] _sm_ ozone

P

P *abbr* (= *parcheggio*) P; (*Aut*: = *principiante*) L

p. *abbr* (= *pagina*) p

pac'chetto [pak'ketto] *sm* packet; **~ azionario** (*Finanza*) shareholding

pacco, -chi *sm* parcel; (*involto*) bundle; **~ postale** parcel

pace ['patʃe] *sf* peace; **darsi ~** to resign o.s.; **fare (la) ~ con qn** to make it up with sb

pa'cifico, -a, -ci, -che [pa'tʃifiko] *ag* (*persona*) peaceable; (*vita*) peaceful; (*fig: indiscusso*) indisputable; (*: ovvio*) obvious, clear ▷ *sm*: **il P~, l'Oceano P~** the Pacific (Ocean)

paci'fista, -i, -e [patʃi'fista] *smf* pacifist

pa'della *sf* frying pan; (*per infermi*) bedpan

padigli'one [padiʎ'ʎone] *sm* pavilion

'Padova *sf* Padua

'padre *sm* father

pa'drino *sm* godfather

padro'nanza [padro'nantsa] *sf* command, mastery

pa'drone, -a *sm/f* master/mistress; (*proprietario*) owner; (*datore di lavoro*) employer; **essere ~ di sé** to be in control of o.s.; **~/padrona di casa** master/mistress of the house; (*per gli inquilini*) landlord/lady

pae'saggio [pae'zaddʒo] *sm* landscape

pa'ese *sm* (*nazione*) country, nation; (*terra*) country, land; (*villaggio*) village; **~ di provenienza** country of origin; **i Paesi Bassi** the Netherlands

'paga, -ghe *sf* pay, wages *pl*

paga'mento *sm* payment

pa'gare /80/ *vt* to pay; (*acquisto, fig, colpa*) to pay for; (*contraccambiare*) to repay, pay back ▷ *vi* to pay; **quanto l'ha pagato?** how much did you pay for it?; **~ con carta di credito** to pay by credit card; **~ in contanti** to pay cash

pa'gella [pa'dʒɛlla] *sf* (*Ins*) report card

paghe'rò [page'rɔ] *sm inv* acknowledgement of a debt, IOU

'pagina ['padʒina] *sf* page; **Pagine bianche** phone book, telephone directory; **Pagine Gialle®** Yellow Pages®

'paglia ['paʎʎa] *sf* straw

pagli'accio [paʎ'ʎattʃo] *sm* clown

pagli'etta [paʎ'ʎetta] *sf* (*cappello per uomo*) (straw) boater; (*per tegami ecc*) steel wool

pa'gnotta [paɲ'ɲɔtta] *sf* round loaf

'Pakistan *sm*: **il ~** Pakistan

'pala *sf* shovel; (*di remo, ventilatore, elica*) blade; (*di ruota*) paddle

pa'lato *sm* palate

pa'lazzo [pa'lattso] *sm* (*reggia*) palace; (*edificio*) building; **~ di giustizia** courthouse; **~ dello sport** sports stadium

'palco, -chi *sm* (*Teat*) box; (*tavolato*) platform, stand; (*ripiano*) layer

palco'scenico, -ci [palkoʃ'ʃeniko] *sm* (*Teat*) stage

pa'lese *ag* clear, evident

Pales'tina *sf*: **la ~** Palestine

palesti'nese *ag, smf* Palestinian

pa'lestra *sf* gymnasium; (*esercizio atletico*) exercise, training; (*fig*) training ground, school

pa'letta *sf* spade; (*per il focolare*) shovel; (*del capostazione*) signalling disc

pa'letto *sm* stake, peg; (*spranga*) bolt

'palio *sm* (*gara*): **il P~** horse race run at Siena; **mettere qc in ~** to offer sth as a prize

---

PALIO

The *Palio* is a horse race which takes place in a number of Italian towns, the most famous being the 'Palio di Siena'. The Tuscan race dates back to the thirteenth century; nowadays it is usually held twice a year, on 2 July and 16 August, in the Piazza del Campo. 10 of the 17 city districts or 'contrade' take part; the winner is the first horse to complete the course, whether or not it still has its rider. The race is preceded by a procession of 'contrada' members in historical dress.

'palla *sf* ball; (*pallottola*) bullet; **~ di neve** snowball; **~ ovale** rugby ball; **pallaca'nestro** *sf* basketball; **pallamano** [palla'mano] *sf* handball; **pallanu'oto** *sf* water polo; **palla'volo** *sf* volleyball

palleggi'are [palled'dʒare] /62/ *vi* (*Calcio*) to practise (BRIT) o practice (US) with the ball; (*Tennis*) to knock up

pallia'tivo *sm* palliative; (*fig*) stopgap measure

'pallido, -a *ag* pale

pal'lina sf (bilia) marble

pallon'cino [pallon'tʃino] sm balloon; (lampioncino) Chinese lantern

pal'lone sm (palla) ball; (Calcio) football; (aerostato) balloon; **gioco del ~** football

pal'lottola sf pellet; (proiettile) bullet

'palma sf (Anat) = **palmo**; (Bot, simbolo) palm; **~ da datteri** date palm

'palmo sm (Anat) palm; **restare con un ~ di naso** to be badly disappointed

'palo sm (legno appuntito) stake; (sostegno) pole; **fare da o il ~** (fig) to act as look-out

palom'baro sm diver

pal'pare /72/ vt to feel, finger

'palpebra sf eyelid

pa'lude sf marsh, swamp

pancarrè sm sliced bread

pan'cetta [pan'tʃetta] sf (Cuc) bacon

pan'china [pan'kina] sf garden seat; (di giardino pubblico) (park) bench

'pancia, -ce ['pantʃa] sf belly, stomach; **mettere o fare ~** to be getting a paunch; **avere mal di ~** to have stomach ache o a sore stomach

panci'otto [pan'tʃɔtto] sm waistcoat

'pancreas sm inv pancreas

'panda sm inv panda

pande'mia sf pandemic

'pane sm bread; (pagnotta) loaf (of bread); (forma): **un ~ di burro/cera** ecc a pat of butter/bar of wax etc; **guadagnarsi il ~** to earn one's living; **~ a cassetta** sliced bread; **~ integrale** wholemeal bread; **~ di Spagna** sponge cake; **~ tostato** toast

panette'ria sf (forno) bakery; (negozio) baker's (shop), bakery

panetti'ere, -a sm/f baker

panet'tone sm a kind of spiced brioche with sultanas (eaten at Christmas)

pangrat'tato sm breadcrumbs pl

'panico, -a, -ci, -che ag, sm panic

pani'ere sm basket

pani'ficio [pani'fitʃo] sm (forno) bakery; (negozio) baker's (shop), bakery

pa'nino sm roll; **~ caldo** toasted sandwich; **~ imbottito** filled roll; sandwich

panino'teca, -che sf sandwich bar

'panna sf (Cuc) cream; (Aut) = **panne**; **~ da cucina** cooking cream; **~ montata** whipped cream

'panne [pan] sf inv (Aut): **essere in ~** to have broken down

pan'nello sm panel; **~ solare** solar panel

'panno sm cloth; **panni** smpl (abiti) clothes; **mettiti nei miei panni** (fig) put yourself in my shoes

pan'nocchia [pan'nɔkkja] sf (di mais ecc) ear

panno'lino sm (per bambini) nappy (BRIT), diaper (US)

panno'lone sm incontinence pad

pano'rama, -i sm panorama

panta'loni smpl trousers (BRIT), pants (US), **pair** sg **of trousers** o **pants**

pan'tano sm bog

pan'tera sf panther

pan'tofola sf slipper

'papa, -i sm pope

papà sm inv dad(dy)

pa'pavero sm poppy

'pappa sf baby cereal; **~ reale** royal jelly

pappa'gallo sm parrot; (fig: uomo) Romeo, wolf

pa'rabola sf (Mat) parabola; (Rel) parable

para'bolico, -a, -ci, -che ag (Mat) parabolic; vedi anche **antenna**

para'brezza [para'breddza] sm inv (Aut) windscreen (BRIT), windshield (US)

paraca'dute sm inv parachute

para'diso sm paradise

parados'sale ag paradoxical

para'fulmine sm lightning conductor

pa'raggi [pa'raddʒi] smpl: **nei ~** in the vicinity, in the neighbourhood (BRIT) o neighborhood (US)

parago'nare /72/ vt: **~ con/a** to compare with/to

para'gone sm comparison; (esempio analogo) analogy, parallel; **reggere al ~** to stand comparison

pa'ragrafo sm paragraph

pa'ralisi sf inv paralysis

paral'lelo, -a ag parallel ▷ sm (Geo) parallel; (comparazione): **fare un ~ tra** to draw a parallel between

para'lume sm lampshade

pa'rametro sm parameter

para'noia sf paranoia; **para'noico, -a, -ci, -che** ag, sm/f paranoid

para'occhi [para'ɔkki] smpl blinkers

paraolim'piadi sfpl paralympics

para'petto sm parapet

pa'rare /72/ vt (addobbare) to adorn, deck; (proteggere) to shield, protect; (scansare: colpo) to parry; (Calcio) to save ▷ vi: **dove vuole andare a ~?** what are you driving at?

pa'rata sf (Sport) save; (Mil) review, parade

para'urti sm inv (Aut) bumper

para'vento sm folding screen; **fare da ~ a qn** (fig) to shield sb

par'cella [par'tʃɛlla] sf account, fee (of lawyer etc)

parcheggi'are [parked'dʒare] /62/ vt to park; **parcheggia'tore, -'trice** [parkedd'dʒa'tore] sm/f parking attendant

par'cheggio sm parking no pl; (luogo) car park; (singolo posto) parking space

par'chimetro [par'kimetro] sm parking meter

'parco, -chi sm park; (spazio per deposito) depot; (complesso di veicoli) fleet

par'cometro sm (Pay and Display) ticket machine

pa'recchio, -a [pa'rekkjo] det quite a lot of; (tempo) quite a lot of, a long

pareggi'are [pared'dʒare] /62/ vt to make equal; (terreno) to level, make level; (bilancio, conti) to balance ▷ vi (Sport) to draw; **pa'reggio** sm (Econ) balance; (Sport) draw

pa'rente smf relative, relation

🔺 Attenzione! In inglese esiste la parola parent, che però significa genitore.

paren'tela sf (vincolo di sangue, fig) relationship

pa'rentesi sf (segno grafico) bracket, parenthesis; (frase incisa) parenthesis; (digressione) parenthesis, digression

pa'rere /71/ sm (opinione) opinion; (consiglio) advice, opinion; **a mio ~** in my opinion ▷ vi to seem, appear ▷ vb impers: **pare che** it seems o appears that, they say that; **mi pare che** it seems to me that; **mi pare di sì/no** I think so/don't think so; **fai come ti pare** do as you like; **che ti pare del mio libro?** what do you think of my book?

pa'rete sf wall

'pari ag inv (uguale) equal, same; (in giochi) equal, drawn, tied; (Mat) even ▷ sm inv (Pol: di Gran Bretagna) peer ▷ smf inv peer, equal; **copiato ~ ~** copied word for word; **alla ~** on the same level; **ragazza alla ~** au pair (girl); **mettersi alla ~ con** to place o.s. on the same level as; **mettersi in ~ con** to catch up with; **andare di ~ passo con qn** to keep pace with sb

Pa'rigi [pa'ridʒi] sf Paris

pari'gino, -a [pari'dʒino] ag, sm/f Parisian

parità sf parity, equality; (Sport) draw, tie

parlamen'tare /72/ ag parliamentary ▷ smf ≈ Member of Parliament (BRIT), ≈ Congressman/woman (US) ▷ vi to negotiate, parley

parla'mento sm parliament

PARLAMENTO

The Italian constitution, which came into force on 1 January 1948, states that the Parlamento has legislative power. It is made up of two chambers, the 'Camera dei deputati' and the 'Senato'. Parliamentary elections are held every 5 years.

parlan'tina sf (fam) talkativeness; **avere ~** to have the gift of the gab

par'lare /72/ vi to speak, talk; (confidare cose segrete) to talk ▷ vt to speak; **~ (a qn) di** to speak o talk (to sb) about

parmigi'ano, -a [parmi'dʒano] sm (grana) Parmesan (cheese)

pa'rola sf word; (facoltà) speech; **parole** sfpl (chiacchiere) talk sg; **chiedere la ~** to ask permission to speak; **prendere la ~** to take the floor; **~ d'onore** word of honour; **~ d'ordine** (Mil) password; **parole incrociate** crossword (puzzle) sg; **paro'laccia, -ce** sf bad word, swearword

parrò ecc vb vedi **parere**

par'rocchia [par'rɔkkja] sf parish; (chiesa) parish church

par'rucca, -che sf wig

parrucchi'ere, -a [parruk'kjɛre] sm/f hairdresser ▷ sm barber

'parte sf part; (lato) side; (quota spettante a ciascuno) share; (direzione) direction; (Pol) party; faction; (Dir) party; **a ~** ag separate ▷ av separately; **scherzi a ~** joking aside; **a ~ ciò** apart from that; **da ~** (in disparte) to one side, aside; **mettere/prendere da ~** to put/take aside; **d'altra ~** on the other hand; **da ~ di** (per conto di) on behalf of; **da ~ mia** as far as I'm concerned, as for me; **da ~ a ~** right through; **da nessuna ~** nowhere; **da questa ~** (in questa direzione) this way; **da ogni ~** on all sides, everywhere; (moto da luogo) from all sides; **prendere ~ a qc** to take part in sth; **mettere qn a ~ di qc** to inform sb of sth

parteci'pare [partetʃi'pare] /72/ vi: **~ a** to take part in, participate in; (utili ecc) to share in; (spese ecc) to contribute to; (dolore, successo di qn) to share (in)

parteggi'are [parted'dʒare] /62/ vi: **~ per** to side with, be on the side of

par'tenza [par'tɛntsa] sf departure; (Sport) start; **essere in ~** to be about to leave, be leaving

parti'cipio [parti'tʃipjo] sm participle

partico'lare ag (specifico) particular; (proprio) personal, private; (speciale) special, particular; (caratteristico) distinctive, characteristic; (fuori dal comune) peculiar ▷ sm detail, particular; **in ~** in particular, particularly

par'tire /45/ vi to go, leave; (allontanarsi) to go o drive ecc) away o off; (petardo, colpo) to go off; (fig: avere inizio, Sport) to start; **sono partita da Roma alle 7** I left Rome at 7; **il volo parte da Ciampino** the flight leaves from Ciampino; **a ~ da** from

par'tita sf (Comm) lot, consignment; (Econ: registrazione) entry, item; (Carte, Sport: gioco) game; (: competizione) match, game; **~ di caccia** hunting party; **numero di ~ IVA** VAT registration number

par'tito sm (Pol) party; (decisione) decision, resolution; (persona da maritare) match

'**parto** sm (Med) labour (BRIT), labor (US), delivery, (child)birth

'**parvi** ecc vb vedi **parere**

parzi'ale ag (limitato) partial; (non obiettivo) biased, partial

pasco'lare /72/ vt, vi to graze

'**pascolo** sm pasture

'**Pasqua** sf Easter

Pasqu'etta sf Easter Monday

pas'sabile ag fairly good, passable

pas'saggio [pas'saddʒo] sm passing no pl, passage; (traversata) crossing no pl, passage; (luogo, prezzo della traversata, brano di libro ecc) passage; (su veicolo altrui) lift (BRIT), ride; (Sport) pass; **di ~** (persona) passing through; **~ pedonale/a livello** pedestrian/level (BRIT) o grade (US) crossing

passamon'tagna [passamon'taɲɲa] sm inv balaclava

pas'sante smf passer-by ▷ sm loop

passa'porto sm passport

pas'sare /72/ vi (andare) to go; (veicolo, pedone) to pass (by), to go by; (fare una breve sosta: postino ecc) to come, call; (: amico: per fare una visita) to call o drop in; (sole, aria, luce) to get through; (trascorrere: giorni, tempo) to pass, go by; (fig: proposta di legge) to be passed; (: dolore) to pass, go away; (Carte) to pass ▷ vt (attraversare) to cross; (trasmettere: messaggio): **~ qc a qn** to pass sth on to sb; (dare): **~ qc a qn** to pass sth to sb, give sb sth; (trascorrere: tempo) to spend; (superare: esame) to pass; (triturare: verdura) to strain; (approvare) to pass, approve; (oltrepassare, sorpassare: anche fig) to go beyond, pass; (fig: subire) to go through; **~ da ... a** to pass from ... to; **~ di padre in figlio** to be handed down o to pass from father to son; **~ per** (anche fig) to go through; **~ per stupido/un genio** to be taken for a fool/a genius; **~ sopra** (anche fig) to pass over; **~ attraverso** (anche fig) to go through; **~ alla storia** to pass into history; **~ a un esame** to go up (to the next class) after an exam; **~ inosservato** to go unnoticed; **~ di moda** to go out of fashion; **le passo il Signor X** (al telefono) here is Mr X; I'm putting you through to Mr X; **lasciar ~ qn/qc** to let sb/sth through; **come te la passi?** how are you getting on o along?

passa'tempo sm pastime, hobby

pas'sato, -a ag past; (sfiorito) faded ▷ sm past; (Ling) past (tense); **~ prossimo** (Ling) present perfect; **~ remoto** (Ling) past historic; **~ di verdura** (Cuc) vegetable purée

passeg'gero, -a [passed'dʒɛro] ag passing ▷ sm/f passenger

passeggi'are [passed'dʒare] /62/ vi to go for a walk, stroll; (in veicolo) to go for a drive; **passeggi'ata** sf walk; drive; (luogo) promenade; **fare una passeggiata** to go for a walk o drive); **passeg'gino** [passed'dʒino] sm pushchair (BRIT), stroller (US)

passe'rella sf footbridge; (di nave, aereo) gangway; (pedana) catwalk

'**passero** sm sparrow

passi'one sf passion

pas'sivo, -a ag passive ▷ sm (Ling) passive; (Econ) debit; (complesso dei debiti) liabilities pl

'**passo** sm step; (andatura) pace; (rumore) (foot)step; (orma) footprint; (passaggio, fig: brano) passage; (valico) pass; **a ~ d'uomo** at walking pace; **~ (a)** ~ step by step; **fare due** o **quattro passi** to go for a walk o a stroll; **di questo ~** at this rate; **"~ carraio"** "vehicle entrance — keep clear"

'**pasta** sf (Cuc) dough; (: impasto per dolce) pastry; (anche: **~ alimentare**) pasta; (massa molle di materia) paste; (fig: indole) nature; **paste** sfpl (pasticcini) pastries; **~ in brodo** noodle soup; **~ sfoglia** puff pastry o paste (US)

pastasci'utta [pastaʃ'ʃutta] sf pasta

pas'tella sf batter

pas'tello sm pastel

pas'ticca, -che sf = **pastiglia**

pasticce'ria [pastittʃe'ria] sf (pasticcini) pastries pl, cakes pl; (negozio) cake shop; (arte) confectionery

pasticci'ere, -a [pastit'tʃɛre] sm/f pastrycook; confectioner

pastic'cino [pastit'tʃino] sm petit four

pas'ticcio [pas'tittʃo] sm (Cuc) pie; (lavoro disordinato, imbroglio) mess; **trovarsi nei pasticci** to get into trouble

pas'tiglia [pas'tiλλa] sf pastille, lozenge

pas'tina sf small pasta shapes used in soup

'**pasto** sm meal

pas'tore sm shepherd; (Rel) pastor, minister; (anche: **cane ~**) sheepdog; **~ tedesco** (Zool) Alsatian (dog) (BRIT) German shepherd (dog)

pa'tata sf potato; **patate fritte** chips (BRIT), French fries; **pata'tine** sfpl (potato) crisps (BRIT) o chips (US); **patatine fritte** chips

pâté [pa'te] sm inv pâté

pa'tente sf licence; (anche: **~ di guida**) driving licence (BRIT), driver's license (US); **~ a punti** driving licence with penalty points

Attenzione! In inglese esiste la parola **patent**, che però significa **brevetto**.

paternità sf paternity, fatherhood

pa'tetico, -a, -ci, -che ag pathetic; (commovente) moving, touching

pa'tibolo sm gallows sg, scaffold

'**patina** sf (su rame ecc) patina; (sulla lingua) fur, coating

pa'tire /55/ vt, vi to suffer

pa'tito, -a sm/f enthusiast, fan, lover

patolo'gia [patolo'dʒia] sf pathology

'**patria** sf homeland

pa'trigno [pa'triɲɲo] sm stepfather

patri'monio sm estate, property; (fig) heritage

pa'trono sm (Rel) patron saint; (socio di patronato) patron; (Dir) counsel

patteggi'are [patted'dʒare] /62/ vt, vi to negotiate; (Dir) to plea-bargain

patti'naggio [patti'naddʒo] sm skating; ~ **a rotelle/sul ghiaccio** roller-/ice-skating

patti'nare /72/ vi to skate; ~ **sul ghiaccio** to ice-skate; **pattina'tore, -'trice** sm/f skater

'**pattino** sm skate; (di slitta) runner; (Aer) skid; (Tecn) sliding block; **pattini (da ghiaccio)** (ice) skates; **pattini in linea** rollerblades®; **pattini a rotelle** roller skates

'**patto** sm (accordo) pact, agreement; (condizione) term, condition; **a ~ che** on condition that

pat'tuglia [pat'tuʎʎa] sf (Mil) patrol

pattu'ire /55/ vt to reach an agreement on

pattumi'era sf (dust)bin (BRIT), ashcan (US)

pa'ura sf fear; **aver ~ di/di fare/che** to be frightened o afraid of/of doing/that; **far ~ a** to frighten; **per ~ di/che** for fear of/that; **pau'roso, -a** ag (che fa paura) frightening; (che ha paura) fearful, timorous

'**pausa** sf (sosta) break; (nel parlare, Mus) pause

pavi'mento sm floor

> ▌ Attenzione! In inglese esiste la parola pavement, che però significa marciapiede.

pa'vone sm peacock

pazien'tare [pattsjen'tare] /72/ vi to be patient

pazi'ente [pat'tsjɛnte] ag, smf patient; **pazi'enza** sf patience

paz'zesco, -a, -schi, -sche [pat'tsesko] ag mad, crazy

paz'zia [pat'tsia] sf (Med) madness, insanity; (di azione, decisione) madness, folly

'**pazzo, -a** ['pattso] ag (Med) mad, insane; (strano) wild, mad ▷ sm/f madman/woman; ~ **di** (gioia, amore ecc) mad o crazy with; ~ **per qc/qn** mad o crazy about sth/sb

PC sigla m inv (= personal computer) PC; **PC portatile** laptop

pec'care /20/ vi to sin; (fig) to err

pec'cato sm sin; **è un ~ che** it's a pity that; **che ~!** what a shame o pity!

pecche'rò ecc [pekke'rɔ] vb vedi **peccare**

'**pece** ['petʃe] sf pitch

Pe'chino [pe'kino] sf Beijing

'**pecora** sf sheep; **peco'rino** sm sheep's milk cheese

pe'daggio [pe'daddʒo] sm toll

pedago'gia [pedago'dʒia] sf pedagogy, educational methods pl

peda'lare /72/ vi to pedal; (andare in bicicletta) to cycle

pe'dale sm pedal

pe'dana sf footboard; (Sport: nel salto) springboard; (: nella scherma) piste

pe'dante ag pedantic ▷ smf pedant

pe'data sf (impronta) footprint; (colpo) kick; **prendere a pedate qn/qc** to kick sb/sth

pedi'atra, -i, -e smf paediatrician

pedi'cure sm inv, f inv chiropodist

pe'dina sf (della dama) draughtsman (BRIT), draftsman (US); (fig) pawn

pedi'nare /72/ vt to shadow, tail

pe'dofilo, -a ag, sm/f paedophile

pedo'nale ag pedestrian

pe'done, -a sm/f pedestrian ▷ sm (Scacchi) pawn

'**peggio** ['pɛddʒo] av, ag inv worse ▷ sm o f: **il o la ~** the worst; **alla ~** at worst, if the worst comes to the worst; **peggio'rare** /72/ vt to make worse, worsen ▷ vi to grow worse, worsen; **peggi'ore** ag (comparativo) worse; (superlativo) worst ▷ smf: **il (la) peggiore** the worst (person)

'**pegno** ['peɲɲo] sm (Dir) security, pledge; (nei giochi di società) forfeit; (fig) pledge, token; **dare in ~ qc** to pawn sth

pe'lare /72/ vt (spennare) to pluck; (spellare) to skin; (sbucciare) to peel; (fig) to make pay through the nose

pe'lato, -a ag peeled; **(pomodori) pelati** peeled tomatoes

'**pelle** sf skin; (di animale) skin, hide; (cuoio) leather; **avere la ~ d'oca** to have goose pimples o goose flesh

pellegri'naggio [pellegri'naddʒo] sm pilgrimage

pelle'rossa (pl **pellirosse**) smf (peg) Red Indian (!)

pelli'cano sm pelican

pel'liccia, -ce [pel'littʃa] sf (mantello di animale) coat, fur; (indumento) fur coat; ~ **ecologica** fake fur

pel'licola sf (membrana sottile) film, layer; (Fot, Cine) film

'**pelo** sm hair; (pelame) coat, hair; (pelliccia) fur; (di tappeto) pile; (di liquido) surface; **per un ~: per un ~ non ho perduto il treno:** I very nearly missed the train; **c'è mancato un ~ che affogasse** he narrowly escaped drowning; **pe'loso, -a** ag hairy

'peltro sm pewter

pe'luche [pə'lyʃ] sm plush; **giocattoli di ~** soft toys

pe'luria sf down

'pena sf (Dir) sentence; (punizione) punishment; (sofferenza) sadness no pl, sorrow; (fatica) trouble no pl, effort; (difficoltà) difficulty; **far ~** to be pitiful; **fai ~** I feel sorry for you; **prendersi o darsi la ~ di fare** to go to the trouble of doing; **~ di morte** death sentence; **~ pecuniaria** fine; **pe'nale** ag penal

pen'dente ag hanging; leaning ▷ sm (ciondolo) pendant; (orecchino) drop earring

'pendere /8/ vi (essere appeso): **~ da** to hang from; (essere inclinato) to lean; (fig: incombere): **~ su** to hang over

pen'dio, -ii sm slope, slant; (luogo in pendenza) slope

'pendola sf pendulum clock

pendo'lare smf commuter

pendo'lino sm high-speed train

pene'trante ag piercing, penetrating

pene'trare /72/ vi to come o get in ▷ vt to penetrate; **~ in** to enter; (proiettile) to penetrate; (acqua, aria) to go o come into

penicil'lina [penitʃil'lina] sf penicillin

pe'nisola sf peninsula

penitenzi'ario [peniten'tsjarjo] sm prison

'penna sf (di uccello) feather; (per scrivere) pen; **penne** sfpl (Cuc) quills (type of pasta); **~ a feltro/stilografica/a sfera** felt-tip/fountain/ballpoint pen

penna'rello sm felt(-tip) pen

pen'nello sm brush; (per dipingere) (paint) brush; **a ~** (perfettamente) to perfection, perfectly; **~ per la barba** shaving brush

pen'netta sf (Inform) dongle; **~ USB** memory stick

pe'nombra sf half-light, dim light

pen'sare /72/ vt, vi to think; (inventare, escogitare) to think out; **~ a** to think of; (amico, vacanze) to think of o about; (problema) to think about; **~ di fare qc** to think of doing sth; **ci penso io** I'll see to o take care of it

pensi'ero sm thought; (modo di pensare, dottrina) thinking no pl; (preoccupazione) worry, care, trouble; **stare in ~ per qn** to be worried about sb; **pensie'roso, -a** ag thoughtful

'pensile ag hanging ▷ sm (in cucina) wall cupboard

pensio'nato, -a sm/f pensioner

pensi'one sf (al prestatore di lavoro) pension; (vitto e alloggio) board and lodging; (albergo) boarding house; **andare in ~** to retire; **mezza ~** half board; **~ completa** full board

pen'tirsi /45/ vpr: **~ di** to repent of; (rammaricarsi) to regret, be sorry for

'pentola sf pot; **~ a pressione** pressure cooker

pe'nultimo, -a ag last but one (BRIT), next to last, penultimate

penzo'lare [pendzo'lare] /72/ vi to dangle, hang loosely

'pepe sm pepper; **~ macinato/in grani/nero** ground/whole/black pepper

peperon'cino [peperon'tʃino] sm chilli pepper

pepe'rone sm: **~ (rosso)** red pepper, capsicum; (piccante) chili

pe'pita sf nugget

⬤ **PAROLA CHIAVE**

per prep **1** (moto attraverso luogo) through; **i ladri sono passati per la finestra** the thieves got in (o out) through the window; **l'ho cercato per tutta la casa** I've searched the whole house o all over the house for it

2 (moto a luogo) for, to; **partire per la Germania/il mare** to leave for Germany/the sea; **il treno per Roma** the Rome train, the train for o to Rome

3 (stato in luogo): **seduto/sdraiato per terra** sitting/lying on the ground

4 (tempo) for; **per anni/lungo tempo** for years/a long time; **per tutta l'estate** throughout the summer, all summer long; **lo rividi per Natale** I saw him again at Christmas; **lo faccio per lunedì** I'll do it for Monday

5 (mezzo, maniera) by; **per lettera/ferrovia/via aerea** by letter/rail/airmail; **prendere qn per un braccio** to take sb by the arm

6 (causa, scopo) for; **assente per malattia** absent because of o through o owing to illness; **ottimo per il mal di gola** excellent for sore throats

7 (limitazione) for; **è troppo difficile per lui** it's too difficult for him; **per quel che mi riguarda** as far as I'm concerned; **per poco che sia** however little it may be; **per questa volta ti perdono** I'll forgive you this time

8 (prezzo, misura) for; (: distributivo) a, per; **venduto per 3 milioni** sold for 3 million; **15 euro per persona** 15 euros a o per person; **uno per volta** one at a time; **uno per uno** one by one; **5 per cento** 5 per cent; **3 per 4 fa 12** 3 times 4 equals 12; **dividere/moltiplicare 12 per 4** to divide/multiply 12 by 4

9 (in qualità di) as; (al posto di) for; **avere qn per professore** to have sb as a teacher; **ti ho preso per Mario** I mistook you for Mario, I thought you were Mario; **dare per**

morto qn to give sb up for dead
10 (*seguito da vb: finale*): **per fare qc** (so as) to do sth, in order to do sth; (: *causale*): **per aver fatto qc** for having done sth; (: *consecutivo*): **è abbastanza grande per andarci da solo** he's big enough to go on his own

'**pera** *sf* pear
per'bene *ag inv* respectable, decent ▷ *av* (*con cura*) properly, well
percentu'ale [pert∫entu'ale] *sf* percentage
perce'pire [pert∫e'pire] /55/ *vt* (*sentire*) to perceive; (*ricevere*) to receive

 PAROLA CHIAVE

perché [per'ke] *av* why; **perché no?** why not?; **perché non vuoi andarci?** why don't you want to go?; **spiegami perché l'hai fatto** tell me why you did it
▶ *cong* **1** (*causale*) because; **non posso uscire perché ho da fare** I can't go out because *o* as I've a lot to do
2 (*finale*) in order that, so that; **te lo do perché tu lo legga** I'm giving it to you so (that) you can read it
3 (*consecutivo*): **è troppo forte perché si possa batterlo** he's too strong to be beaten
▶ *sm inv* reason; **il perché di** the reason for

perciò [per't∫ɔ] *cong* so, for this *o* that reason
per'correre /28/ *vt* (*luogo*) to go all over; (: *paese*) to travel up and down, go all over; (*distanza*) to cover
per'corso, -a *pp di* **percorrere** ▷ *sm* (*tragitto*) journey; (*tratto*) route
percu'otere /106/ *vt* to hit, strike
percussi'one *sf* percussion; **strumenti a ~** (*Mus*) percussion instruments
'**perdere** /73/ *vt* to lose; (*lasciarsi sfuggire*) to miss; (*sprecare: tempo, denaro*) to waste ▷ *vi* to lose; (*serbatoio ecc*) to leak; **perdersi** *vpr* (*smarrirsi*) to get lost; (*svanire*) to disappear, vanish; **saper ~** to be a good loser; **lascia ~!** forget it!, never mind!
perdigi'orno [perdi'dʒorno] *sm inv, f inv* idler, waster
'**perdita** *sf* loss; (*spreco*) waste; (*fuoriuscita*) leak; **siamo in ~** (*Comm*) we are running at a loss; **a ~ d'occhio** as far as the eye can see
perdo'nare /72/ *vt* to pardon, forgive; (*scusare*) to excuse, pardon
per'dono *sm* forgiveness; (*Dir*) pardon
perduta'mente *av* desperately, passionately
pe'renne *ag* eternal, perpetual, perennial; (*Bot*) perennial

perfetta'mente *av* perfectly; **sai ~ che ...** you know perfectly well that ...
per'fetto, -a *ag* perfect ▷ *sm* (*Ling*) perfect (tense)
perfeziona'mento [perfettsjona'mento] *sm*: **~ (di)** improvement (in), perfection (of); **corso di ~** proficiency course
perfezio'nare [perfettsjo'nare] /72/ *vt* to improve, perfect; **perfezionarsi** *vpr* to improve
perfezi'one [perfet'tsjone] *sf* perfection
per'fino *av* even
perfo'rare /72/ *vt* to perforate, to punch a hole (*o* holes) in; (*banda, schede*) to punch; (*trivellare*) to drill
perga'mena *sf* parchment
perico'lante *ag* precarious
pe'ricolo *sm* danger; **mettere in ~** to endanger, put in danger; **perico'loso, -a** *ag* dangerous
perife'ria *sf* (*di città*) outskirts *pl*
pe'rifrasi *sf inv* circumlocution
pe'rimetro *sm* perimeter
peri'odico, -a, -ci, -che *ag* periodic(al); (*Mat*) recurring ▷ *sm* periodical
pe'riodo *sm* period
peripe'zie [peripet'tsie] *sfpl* ups and downs, vicissitudes
pe'rito, -a *ag* expert, skilled ▷ *sm/f* expert; (*agronomo, navale*) surveyor; **un ~ chimico** a qualified chemist
peri'zoma, -i [peri'dzɔma] *sm* G-string
'**perla** *sf* pearl; **per'lina** *sf* bead
perlus'trare /72/ *vt* to patrol
perma'loso, -a *ag* touchy
perma'nente *ag* permanent ▷ *sf* permanent wave, perm; **perma'nenza** *sf* permanence; (*soggiorno*) stay
perme'are /72/ *vt* to permeate
per'messo, -a *pp di* **permettere** ▷ *sm* (*autorizzazione*) permission, leave; (*dato a militare, impiegato*) leave; (*licenza*) licence, permit; (*Mil: foglio*) pass; **~?, è ~?** (*posso entrare?*) may I come in?; (*posso passare?*) excuse me; **~ di lavoro/pesca** work/ fishing permit; **~ di soggiorno** residence permit
per'mettere /63/ *vt* to allow, permit; **~ a qn qc/di fare qc** to allow sb sth/to do sth; **permettersi** *vpr*: **permettersi qc/di fare qc** to allow o.s. sth/to do sth; (*avere la possibilità*) to afford sth/to do sth
per'misi *ecc vb vedi* **permettere**
per'nacchia [per'nakkja] *sf* (*fam*): **fare una ~** to blow a raspberry
per'nice [per'nit∫e] *sf* partridge
'**perno** *sm* pivot
pernot'tare /72/ *vi* to spend the night, stay overnight

'pero sm pear tree

però cong (ma) but; (tuttavia) however, nevertheless

perpendico'lare ag, sf perpendicular

per'plesso, -a ag perplexed, puzzled; uncertain

perqui'sire /55/ vt to search; **perquisizi'one** sf (police) search

'perse ecc vb vedi **perdere**

persecuzi'one [persekut'tsjone] sf persecution

persegui'tare /72/ vt to persecute

perseve'rante ag persevering

'persi ecc vb vedi **perdere**

persi'ano, -a ag Persian ▷ sf shutter; **persiana avvolgibile** roller blind

per'sino av = **perfino**

persis'tente ag persistent

'perso, -a pp di **perdere**

per'sona sf person; (qualcuno): **una ~** someone, somebody; (espressione) anyone o anybody

perso'naggio [perso'naddʒo] sm (persona ragguardevole) personality, figure; (tipo) character, individual; (Letteratura) character

perso'nale ag personal ▷ sm staff; personnel; (figura fisica) build

personalità sf inv personality

perspi'cace [perspi'katʃe] ag shrewd, discerning

persu'adere /88/ vt: **~ qn (di qc/a fare)** to persuade sb (of sth/to do)

per'tanto cong (quindi) so, therefore

'pertica, -che sf pole

perti'nente ag: **~ (a)** relevant (to), pertinent (to)

per'tosse sf whooping cough

perturbazi'one [perturbat'tsjone] sf disruption; disturbance; **~ atmosferica** atmospheric disturbance

per'vadere /52/ vt to pervade

per'verso, -a ag perverted; perverse

perver'tito, -a sm/f pervert

p.es. abbr (= per esempio) e.g.

pe'sante ag heavy

pe'sare /72/ vt to weigh ▷ vi (avere un peso) to weigh; (essere pesante) to be heavy; (fig) to carry weight; **~ su** (fig) to lie heavy on; to influence; to hang over; **tutta la responsabilità pesa su di lui** all the responsibility rests on his shoulders; **è una situazione che mi pesa** it's a difficult situation for me; **il suo parere pesa molto** his opinion counts for a lot

'pesca (pl **pesche**) sf (frutto) peach; (il pescare) fishing; **andare a ~** to go fishing; **~ di beneficenza** (lotteria) lucky dip; **~ con la lenza** angling

pes'care /20/ vt (pesce) to fish for; to catch; (qc nell'acqua) to fish out; (fig: trovare) to get hold of, find

pesca'tore sm fisherman; (con lenza) angler

'pesce ['peʃʃe] sm fish (gen inv); **Pesci** (dello zodiaco) Pisces; **~ d'aprile!** April Fool!; **~ rosso** goldfish; **~ spada** swordfish; **pesce'cane** sm shark

pesche'reccio [peske'rettʃo] sm fishing boat

pesche'ria [peske'ria] sf fishmonger's (shop) (BRIT), fish store (US)

pescherò ecc [peske'rɔ] vb vedi **pescare**

'peso sm weight; (Sport) shot; **essere di ~ a qn** (fig) to be a burden to sb; **rubare sul ~** to give short weight; **~ lordo/netto** gross/net weight; **~ piuma/mosca/gallo/medio/ massimo** (Pugilato) feather/fly/bantam/ middle/heavyweight

pessi'mismo sm pessimism; **pessi'mista, -i, -e** ag pessimistic ▷ smf pessimist

'pessimo, -a ag very bad, awful

pes'tare /72/ vt to tread on, trample on; (sale, pepe) to grind; (uva, aglio) to crush; (fig: picchiare): **~ qn** to beat sb up

'peste sf plague; (persona) nuisance, pest

pes'tello sm pestle

'petalo sm (Bot) petal

pe'tardo sm firecracker, banger (BRIT)

petizi'one [petit'tsjone] sf petition

petroli'era sf (nave) oil tanker

pe'trolio sm oil, petroleum; (per lampada, fornello) paraffin

Attenzione! In inglese esiste la parola petrol, che però significa benzina.

pettego'lare /72/ vi to gossip

pettego'lezzo [pettego'leddzo] sm gossip no pl; **fare pettegolezzi** to gossip

pet'tegolo, -a ag gossipy ▷ sm/f gossip

petti'nare /72/ vt to comb (the hair of); **pettinarsi** vpr to comb one's hair; **pettina'tura** sf (acconciatura) hairstyle

'pettine sm comb; (Zool) scallop

petti'rosso sm robin

'petto sm chest; (seno) breast, bust; (Cuc: di carne bovina) brisket; (di pollo ecc) breast; **a doppio ~** (abito) double-breasted

petu'lante ag insolent

'pezza ['pɛttsa] sf piece of cloth; (toppa) patch; (cencio) rag, cloth

pez'zente [pet'tsɛnte] smf beggar

'pezzo ['pɛttso] sm (gen) piece; (brandello, frammento) piece, bit; (di macchina, arnese ecc) part; (Stampa) article; **aspettare un ~** to wait quite a while o some time; **in** o **a pezzi** in pieces; **andare a pezzi** to break into pieces; **un bel ~ d'uomo** a fine figure of a man; **abito a due pezzi** two-piece suit;

~ di cronaca (*Stampa*) report; **~ grosso** (*fig*) bigwig; **~ di ricambio** spare part

pi'accio *ecc* ['pjattʃo] *vb vedi* **piacere**

pia'cente [pja'tʃɛnte] *ag* attractive

pia'cere [pja'tʃere] /74/ *vi* to please ▷ *sm* pleasure; (*favore*) favour (BRIT), favor (US); **una ragazza che piace** a likeable girl; (*attraente*) an attractive girl; **mi piace** I like it; **quei ragazzi non mi piacciono** I don't like those boys; **gli piacerebbe andare al cinema** he would like to go to the cinema; **il suo discorso è piaciuto molto** his speech was well received; **"~!"** (*nelle presentazioni*) "pleased to meet you!"; **~ (di conoscerla)** nice to meet you; **con ~** certainly, with pleasure; **per ~** please; **fare un ~ a qn** to do sb a favour; **pia'cevole** *ag* pleasant, agreeable

pi'acqui *ecc vb vedi* **piacere**

pi'aga, -ghe *sf* (*lesione*) sore; (*ferita: anche fig*) wound; (*fig: flagello*) scourge, curse; (: *persona*) pest, nuisance

piagnuco'lare [pjaɲɲuko'lare] /72/ *vi* to whimper

pianeggi'ante [pjaned'dʒante] *ag* flat, level

piane'rottolo *sm* landing

pia'neta *sm* (*Astr*) planet

pi'angere [pjandʒere] /75/ *vi* to cry, weep; (*occhi*) to water ▷ *vt* to cry, weep; (*lamentare*) to bewail, lament; **~ la morte di qn** to mourn sb's death

pianifi'care /20/ *vt* to plan

pia'nista, -i, -e *smf* pianist

pi'ano, -a *ag* (*piatto*) flat, level; (*Mat*) plane; (*chiaro*) clear ▷ *av* (*adagio*) slowly; (*a bassa voce*) softly; (*con cautela*) slowly, carefully ▷ *sm* (*Mat*) plane; (*Geo*) plain; (*livello*) level, plane; (*di edificio*) floor; (*programma*) plan; (*Mus*) piano; **pian ~** very slowly; (*poco a poco*) little by little; **al ~ terra** on the ground floor; **in primo/secondo ~** in the foreground/background; **di primo ~** (*fig*) prominent, high-ranking

piano'forte *sm* piano, pianoforte

piano'terra *sm inv* = **piano terra**

pi'ansi *ecc vb vedi* **piangere**

pi'anta *sf* (*Bot*) plant; (*Anat: anche*: **~ del piede**) sole (of the foot); (*grafico*) plan; (*cartina topografica*) map; **in ~ stabile** on the permanent staff; **pian'tare** /72/ *vt* to plant; (*conficcare*) to drive *o* hammer in; (*tenda*) to put up, pitch; (*fig: lasciare*) to leave, desert; **piantarsi** *vpr*: **piantarsi davanti a qn** to plant o.s. in front of sb; **piantala!** (*fam*) cut it out!

pianter'reno *sm* ground floor

pian'tina *sf* (*di edificio, città*) (small) map; (*Bot*) (small) plant

pia'nura *sf* plain

pi'astra *sf* plate; (*di pietra*) slab; (*di fornello*) hotplate; **panino alla ~ ≈** toasted sandwich; **~ di registrazione** tape deck

pias'trella *sf* tile

pias'trina *sf* (*Mil*) identity disc (BRIT) *o* tag (US)

piatta'forma *sf* (*anche fig*) platform

piat'tino *sm* saucer

pi'atto, -a *ag* flat; (*fig: scialbo*) dull ▷ *sm* (*recipiente, vivanda*) dish; (*portata*) course; (*parte piana*) flat (part); **piatti** *smpl* (*Mus*) cymbals; **~ fondo** soup dish; **~ forte** main course; **~ del giorno** dish of the day, plat du jour; **~ del giradischi** turntable; **~ piano** dinner plate

pi'azza ['pjattsa] *sf* square; (*Comm*) market; **far ~ pulita** to make a clean sweep; **~ d'armi** (*Mil*) parade ground; **piaz'zale** *sm* (large) square

piaz'zola [pjat'tsɔla] *sf* (*Aut*) lay-by; (*di tenda*) pitch

pic'cante *ag* hot, pungent; (*fig*) racy; biting

pic'chetto [pik'ketto] *sm* (*Mil, di scioperanti*) picket; (*di tenda*) peg

picchi'are [pik'kjare] /19/ *vt* (*persona: colpire*) to hit, strike; (: *prendere a botte*) to beat (up); (*battere*) to beat; (*sbattere*) to bang ▷ *vi* (*bussare*) to knock; (: *con forza*) to bang; (*colpire*) to hit, strike; (*sole*) to beat down; **picchi'ata** *sf* (*Aer*) dive

'picchio ['pikkjo] *sm* woodpecker

pic'cino, -a [pit'tʃino] *ag* tiny, very small

picci'one [pit'tʃone] *sm* pigeon

'picco, -chi *sm* peak; **a ~** vertically

'piccolo, -a *ag* small; (*oggetto, mano, di età: bambino*) small, little; (*dav sostantivo: di breve durata, viaggio*) short; (*fig*) mean, petty ▷ *sm/f* child, little one

pic'cone *sm* pick(-axe)

pic'cozza [pik'kɔttsa] *sf* ice-axe

pic'nic *sm inv* picnic

pi'docchio [pi'dɔkkjo] *sm* louse

pi'ede *sm* foot; (*di mobile*) leg; **in piedi** standing; **a piedi** on foot; **a piedi nudi** barefoot; **su due piedi** (*fig*) at once; **prendere ~** (*fig*) to gain ground, catch on; **sul ~ di guerra** (*Mil*) ready for action; **~ di porco** crowbar

pi'ega, -ghe *sf* (*piegatura, Geo*) fold; (*di gonna*) pleat; (*di pantaloni*) crease; (*grinza*) wrinkle, crease; **prendere una brutta** *o* **cattiva ~** (*fig*) to take a turn for the worse

pie'gare /80/ *vt* to fold; (*braccia, gambe, testa*) to bend ▷ *vi* to bend; **piegarsi** *vpr* to bend; (*fig*): **piegarsi (a)** to yield (to), submit (to)

piegherò *ecc* [pjege'rɔ] *vb vedi* **piegare**

pie'ghevole *ag* pliable, flexible; (*porta*) folding

Pie'monte sm: **il ~** Piedmont

pi'ena sf vedi **pieno**

pi'eno, -a ag full; (muro, mattone) solid ▷ sm (colmo) height, peak; (carico) full load ▷ sf (di fiume) flood, spate; **~ di** full of; **in ~ giorno** in broad daylight; **fare il ~ (di benzina)** to fill up (with petrol)

'piercing ['pirsing] sm: **farsi il ~ all'ombelico** to have one's navel pierced

pietà sf pity, (Rel) piety; **senza ~** pitiless, ruthless; **avere ~ di** (compassione) to pity, feel sorry for; (misericordia) to have pity o mercy on

pie'tanza [pje'tantsa] sf dish, course

pie'toso, -a ag (compassionevole) pitying, compassionate; (che desta pietà) pitiful

pi'etra sf stone; **~ preziosa** precious stone, gem

'piffero sm (Mus) pipe

pigi'ama [pi'dʒama] sm pyjamas pl

pigli'are [piʎ'ʎare] /27/ vt to take, grab; (afferrare) to catch

'pigna ['pinna] sf pine cone

pi'gnolo, -a [pin'nɔlo] ag pernickety

pi'grizia [pi'grittsja] sf laziness

'pigro, -a ag lazy

PIL sigla m (= prodotto interno lordo) GDP

'pila sf (catasta, di ponte) pile; (Elettr) battery; (torcia) torch, flashlight

pi'lastro sm pillar

'pile ['pail] sm inv fleece

'pillola sf pill; **prendere la ~** to be on the pill

pi'lone sm (di ponte) pier; (di linea elettrica) pylon

pi'lota, -i, -e smf pilot; (Aut) driver ▷ ag inv pilot cpd; **~ automatico** automatic pilot

pinaco'teca, -che sf art gallery

pi'neta sf pinewood

ping-'pong [piŋ'pɔŋ] sm table tennis

pingu'ino sm (Zool) penguin

'pinna sf fin; (di cetaceo, per nuotare) flipper

'pino sm pine (tree); **pi'nolo** sm pine kernel

'pinza ['pintsa] sf pliers pl; (Med) forceps pl; (Zool) pincer

pin'zette [pin'tsette] sfpl tweezers

pi'oggia, -ge ['pjɔddʒa] sf rain; **~ acida** acid rain

pi'olo sm peg; (di scala) rung

piom'bare /72/ vi to fall heavily; (gettarsi con impeto): **~ su** to fall upon, assail ▷ vt (dente) to fill; **piomba'tura** sf (di dente) filling

piom'bino sm (sigillo) (lead) seal; (del filo a piombo) plummet; (Pesca) sinker

pi'ombo sm (Chim) lead; **a ~** (cadere) straight down; **senza ~** (benzina) unleaded

pioni'ere, -a sm/f pioneer

pi'oppo sm poplar

pi'overe /76/ vb impers to rain ▷ vi (fig: scendere dall'alto) to rain down; (affluire in gran numero): **~ in** to pour into; **pioviggi'nare** /72/ vb impers to drizzle; **pio'voso, -a** ag rainy

pi'ovra sf octopus

pi'ovve ecc vb vedi **piovere**

'pipa sf pipe

pipì sf (fam): **fare ~** to have a wee (wee)

pipis'trello sm (Zool) bat

pi'ramide sf pyramid

pi'rata, -i sm pirate; **~ informatico** hacker; **~ della strada** hit-and-run driver

Pire'nei smpl: **i ~** the Pyrenees

pi'romane smf pyromaniac; arsonist

pi'roscafo sm steamer, steamship

pisci'are [piʃʃare] /14/ vi (fam!) to piss (!), pee (!)

pi'scina [piʃʃina] sf (swimming) pool

pi'sello sm pea

piso'lino sm nap

'pista sf (traccia) track, trail; (di stadio) track; (di pattinaggio) rink; (da sci) run; (Aer) runway; (di circo) ring; **~ da ballo** dance floor

pis'tacchio [pis'takkjo] sm pistachio (tree); pistachio (nut)

pis'tola sf pistol, gun

pis'tone sm piston

pi'tone sm python

pit'tore, -'trice sm/f painter; **pitto'resco, -a, -schi, -sche** ag picturesque

pit'tura sf painting; **pittu'rare** /72/ vt to paint

⊙ **PAROLA CHIAVE**

più av **1** (in maggiore quantità) more; **più del solito** more than usual; **in più, di più** more; **ne voglio di più** I want some more; **ci sono 3 persone in o di più** there are 3 more o extra people; **più o meno** more or less; **per di più** (inoltre) what's more, moreover

2 (comparativo) more; (: se monosillabo, spesso) + ...er; **più ... di/che** more ... than; **lavoro più di te/di Paola** I work harder than you/than Paola; **è più intelligente che ricco** he's more intelligent than rich

3 (superlativo) most; (: se monosillabico, spesso) + ...est; **il più grande/intelligente** the biggest/most intelligent; **è quello che compro più spesso** that's the one I buy most often; **al più presto** as soon as possible; **al più tardi** at the latest

4 (negazione): **non ... più** no more, no longer; **non ho più soldi** I've got no more money, I don't have any more money; **non lavoro più** I'm no longer working, I don't work any more; **a più non posso** (gridare) at the top of one's voice; (correre) as fast as one can

5 (*Mat*) plus; **4 più 5 fa 9** 4 plus 5 equals 9; **più 5 gradi** 5 degrees above freezing, plus 5
▶ *prep* plus
▶ *ag inv* **1** : **più ... (di)** more ... (than); **più denaro/tempo** more money/time; **più persone di quante ci aspettassimo** more people than we expected
2 (*numerosi, diversi*) several; **l'aspettai per più giorni** I waited for it for several days
▶ *sm* **1** (*la maggior parte*): **il più è fatto** most of it is done
2 (*Mat*) plus (sign)
3 : **i più** the majority

pi'uma *sf* feather; **piu'mino** *sm* (eider) down; (*per letto*) eiderdown; (: *tipo danese*) duvet, continental quilt; (*giacca*) quilted jacket (*with goose-feather padding*); (*per cipria*) powder puff; (*per spolverare*) feather duster

piut'tosto *av* rather; **~ che** (*anziché*) rather than

'pizza ['pittsa] *sf* pizza; **pizze'ria** *sf* place where pizzas are made, sold or eaten

pizzi'care [pittsi'kare] /20/ *vt* (*stringere*) to nip, pinch; (*pungere*) to sting; to bite; (*Mus*) to pluck ▷ *vi* (*prudere*) to itch, be itchy; (*cibo*) to be hot o spicy

'pizzico ['pittsiko] *sm* (*pizzicotto*) pinch, nip; (*piccola quantità*) pinch, dash; (*d'insetto*) sting; bite

pizzi'cotto [pittsi'kɔtto] *sm* pinch, nip

'pizzo ['pittso] *sm* (*merletto*) lace; (*barbetta*) goatee beard

plagi'are [pla'dʒare] /62/ *vt* (*copiare*) to plagiarize

plaid [plɛd] *sm inv* (travelling) rug (BRIT), lap robe (US)

pla'nare /72/ *vi* (*Aer*) to glide

'plasma *sm* plasma

plas'mare /72/ *vt* to mould , shape

'plastico, -a, -ci, -che *ag* plastic ▷ *sf* (*arte*) plastic arts *pl*; (*Med*) plastic surgery; (*sostanza*) plastic; **plastica facciale** face lift

'platano *sm* plane tree

pla'tea *sf* (*Teat*) stalls *pl*

'platino *sm* platinum

plau'sibile *ag* plausible

pleni'lunio *sm* full moon

'plettro *sm* plectrum

pleu'rite *sf* pleurisy

'plico, -chi *sm* (*pacco*) parcel; **in ~ a parte** (*Comm*) under separate cover

plo'tone *sm* (*Mil*) platoon; **~ d'esecuzione** firing squad

plu'rale *ag, sm* plural

P.M. *abbr* (*Pol*) = **Pubblico Ministero**; (= **Polizia Militare**) MP

PMI *sigla fpl* (= *Piccole e Medie Imprese*) SME

pneu'matico, -a, -ci, -che *ag* inflatable; (*Tecn*) pneumatic ▷ *sm* (*Aut*) tyre (BRIT), tire (US)

po' *av, sm vedi* **poco**

 PAROLA CHIAVE

'poco, -a, -chi, -che *ag* (*quantità*) little, not much; (*numero*) few, not many; **poco pane/ denaro/spazio** little o not much bread/ money/space; **poche persone/idee** few o not many people/ideas; **ci vediamo tra poco** (*sottinteso: tempo*) see you soon
▶ *av* **1** (*in piccola quantità*) little, not much; (: *numero limitato*) few, not many; **guadagna poco** he doesn't earn much, he earns little
2 (*con ag, av*) (a) little, not very; **è poco più vecchia di lui** she's a little o slightly older than him; **sta poco bene** he isn't very well
3 (*tempo*): **poco dopo/prima** shortly afterwards/before; **il film dura poco** the film doesn't last very long; **ci vediamo molto poco** we don't see each other very often, we hardly ever see each other
4 : **un po'** a little, a bit; **è un po' corto** it's a little o a bit short; **arriverà fra un po'** he'll arrive shortly o in a little while
5 : **a dir poco** to say the least; **a poco a poco** little by little; **per poco non cadevo** I nearly fell; **è una cosa da poco** it's nothing, it's of no importance; **una persona da poco** a worthless person
▶ *pron* (a) little

podcast ['pɔdkast] *sm* podcast

po'dere *sm* (*Agr*) farm

'podio *sm* dais, platform; (*Mus*) podium

po'dismo *sm* (*Sport: marcia*) walking; (: *corsa*) running

poe'sia *sf* (*arte*) poetry; (*componimento*) poem

po'eta, -'essa *sm/f* poet/poetess

poggi'are [pod'dʒare] /62/ *vt* to lean, rest; (*posare*) to lay, place; **poggia'testa** *sm inv* (*Aut*) headrest

'poggio ['pɔddʒo] *sm* hillock, knoll

'poi *av* then; (*alla fine*) finally, at last; **e ~** (*inoltre*) and besides; **questa ~ - (è bella)!** (*ironico*) that's a good one!

poiché [poi'ke] *cong* since, as

'poker *sm* poker

po'lacco, -a, -chi, -che *ag* Polish ▷ *sm/f* Pole

po'lare *ag* polar

po'lemico, -a, -ci, -che *ag* polemical, controversial ▷ *sf* controversy

po'lenta *sf* (*Cuc*) sort of thick porridge made with maize flour

'polipo sm polyp

polisti'rolo sm polystyrene

po'litica, -che sf vedi **politico**; **politica'mente** av politically; **politicamente corretto** politically correct

po'litico, -a, -ci, -che ag political ▷ sm/f politician ▷ sf politics sg; (linea di condotta) policy

poli'zia [polit'tsia] sf police; ~ **giudiziaria** ≈ Criminal Investigation Department (CID) (BRIT), Federal Bureau of Investigation (FBI) (US); **polizi'esco, -a, -schi, -sche** ag police cpd; (film, romanzo) detective cpd; **polizi'otto** sm police officer; **cane poliziotto** police dog; **donna poliziotto** police officer; **poliziotto di quartiere** local police officer

- **POLIZIA DI STATO**

  - The remit of the polizia di stato is to
  - maintain public order, to uphold the law,
  - and to prevent and investigate crime.
  - This is a civilian branch of the police force;
  - male and female officers perform similar
  - duties. The polizia di stato reports to the
  - Minister of the Interior.

polizza ['polittsa] sf (Comm) bill; ~ **di assicurazione** insurance policy; ~ **di carico** bill of lading

pol'laio sm henhouse

'pollice ['pollitʃe] sm thumb

'polline sm pollen

'pollo sm chicken

pol'mone sm lung; ~ **d'acciaio** (Med) iron lung; **polmo'nite** sf pneumonia; **polmonite atipica** SARS

'polo sm (Geo, Fisica) pole; (gioco) polo; **il ~ sud/nord** the South/North Pole

Po'lonia sf: **la ~** Poland

'polpa sf flesh, pulp; (carne) lean meat

pol'paccio [pol'pattʃo] sm (Anat) calf

polpas'trello sm fingertip

pol'petta sf (Cuc) meatball

'polpo sm octopus

pol'sino sm cuff

'polso sm (Anat) wrist; (pulsazione) pulse; (fig: forza) drive, vigour

pol'trire /55/ vi to laze about

pol'trona sf armchair; (Teat: posto) seat in the front stalls (BRIT) o the orchestra (US)

'polvere sf dust; (sostanza ridotta minutissima) powder, dust; **caffè in ~** instant coffee; **latte in ~** dried o powdered milk; **sapone in ~** soap powder; ~ **pirica** o **da sparo** gunpowder

po'mata sf ointment, cream

po'mello sm knob

pome'riggio [pome'riddʒo] sm afternoon

'pomice ['pomitʃe] sf pumice

'pomo sm (mela) apple; (ornamentale) knob; (di sella) pommel; ~ **d'Adamo** (Anat) Adam's apple

pomo'doro sm tomato; **pomodori pelati** skinned tomatoes

'pompa sf pump; (sfarzo) pomp (and ceremony); ~ **antincendio** fire hose; ~ **di benzina** (BRIT) o gas (US) pump; (distributore) filling o gas (US) station; **impresa di pompe funebri** funeral parlour sg (BRIT), undertaker's sg; **pom'pare** /72/ vt to pump; (trarre) to pump out; (gonfiare d'aria) to pump up

pom'pelmo sm grapefruit

pompi'ere sm firefighter

po'nente sm west

'pongo vb vedi **porre**

'poni vb vedi **porre**

'ponte sm bridge; (di nave) deck; (anche: ~ **di comando**) bridge; (impalcatura) scaffold; **fare il ~** (fig) to take the extra day off; (between 2 public holidays): **governo ~** interim government; ~ **aereo** airlift; ~ **levatoio** drawbridge; ~ **sospeso** suspension bridge

pon'tefice sm (Rel) pontiff

'popcorn ['pɔpkɔːn] sm inv popcorn

popo'lare /72/ ag popular; (quartiere, clientela) working-class ▷ vt (rendere abitato) to populate; **popolarsi** vpr to fill with people, get crowded; **popolazi'one** sf population

'popolo sm people

'poppa sf (di nave) stern; (fam: mammella) breast

porcel'lana [portʃel'lana] sf porcelain, china; (oggetto) piece of porcelain

porcel'lino, -a [portʃel'lino] sm/f piglet; ~ **d'India** guinea pig

porche'ria [porke'ria] sf filth, muck; (fig: oscenità) obscenity; (: azione disonesta) dirty trick; (: cosa mal fatta) rubbish

por'cile [por'tʃile] sm pigsty

por'cino, -a [por'tʃino] ag of pigs, pork cpd ▷ sm (fungo) type of edible mushroom

'porco, -ci sm pig; (carne) pork

porcos'pino sm porcupine

'porgere ['pɔrdʒere] /115/ vt to hand, give; (tendere) to hold out

porno'grafia sf pornography; **porno'grafico, -a, -ci, -che** ag pornographic

'poro sm pore

'porpora sf purple

'porre /77/ vt (mettere) to put; (collocare) to place; (posare) to lay (down), put (down); (fig: supporre): **poniamo (il caso) che ...** let's suppose that ...

'porro sm (Bot) leek; (Med) wart
'porsi ecc vb vedi **porgere**
'porta sf door; (Sport) goal
porta...: portaba'gagli sm inv (facchino)
porter; (Aut, Ferr) luggage rack; **porta-
'CD** sm inv (mobile) CD rack; (astuccio) CD
holder; **porta'cenere** sm inv ashtray;
portachi'avi sm inv keyring; **porta'erei** sf
inv (nave) aircraft carrier; **portafi'nestra**
(pl **portefinestre**) sf French window;
porta'foglio sm wallet; (Pol, Borsa)
portfolio; **portafor'tuna** sm inv lucky
charm; mascot
por'tale sm (di chiesa, Inform) portal
porta'mento sm carriage, bearing
portamo'nete sm inv purse
por'tante ag (muro ecc) supporting, load-
bearing
portan'tina sf sedan chair; (per ammalati)
stretcher
portaom'brelli sm inv umbrella stand
porta'pacchi [porta'pakki] sm inv (di moto,
bicicletta) luggage rack
porta'penne [porta'penne] sm inv pen
holder; (astuccio) pencil case
por'tare /72/ vt (sostenere, sorreggere: peso,
bambino, pacco) to carry; (indossare: abito,
occhiali) to wear; (: capelli lunghi) to have;
(avere: nome, titolo) to have, bear; (recare):
~ **qc a qn** to take (o bring) sth to sb; (fig:
sentimenti) to bear
portasiga'rette sm inv cigarette case
por'tata sf (vivanda) course; (Aut) carrying
(o loading) capacity; (di arma) range;
(volume d'acqua) (rate of) flow; (fig: limite)
scope, capability; (: importanza) impact,
import; **alla ~ di tutti** (conoscenza) within
everybody's capabilities; (prezzo) within
everybody's means; **a/fuori ~ (di)** within/
out of reach (of); **a ~ di mano** within
(arm's) reach
por'tatile ag portable
por'tato, -a ag (incline): ~ **a** inclined o apt to
portau'ovo sm inv eggcup
porta'voce [porta'votʃe] smf inv
spokesman/woman
por'tento sm wonder, marvel
porti'era sf (Aut) door
porti'ere sm (portinaio) concierge,
caretaker; (di hotel) porter; (nel calcio)
goalkeeper
porti'naio, -a sm/f concierge, caretaker
portine'ria sf caretaker's lodge
'porto, -a pp di **porgere** ▷ sm (Naut)
harbour, port ▷ sm inv port (wine);
~ **d'armi** gun licence (BRIT) o license (US)
Porto'gallo sm: **il ~** Portugal; **porto'ghese**
ag, smf, sm Portuguese inv
por'tone sm main entrance, main door

portu'ale ag harbour cpd, port cpd ▷ sm
dock worker
porzi'one [por'tsjone] sf portion, share;
(di cibo) portion, helping
'posa sf (Fot) exposure; (atteggiamento, di
modello) pose
po'sare /72/ vt to put (down), lay (down)
▷ vi (ponte, edificio, teoria): ~ **su** to rest on;
(Fot: atteggiarsi) to pose; **al più tardi**: **posarsi** vpr (ape,
aereo) to land; (uccello) to alight; (sguardo)
to settle
po'sata sf piece of cutlery
pos'critto sm postscript
'posi ecc vb vedi **porre**
posi'tivo, -a ag positive
posizi'one [pozit'tsjone] sf position;
prendere ~ (fig) to take a stand; **luci di ~**
(Aut) sidelights
pos'porre /77/ vt to place after; (differire) to
postpone, defer
posse'dere /107/ vt to own, possess;
(qualità, virtù) to have, possess
posses'sivo, -a ag possessive
pos'sesso sm ownership no pl; possession
posses'sore sm owner
pos'sibile ag possible ▷ sm: **fare tutto il
~** to do everything possible; **nei limiti del
~** as far as possible; **al più tardi**: **al più tardi** as late
as possible; **possibilità** sf inv possibility
▷ sf pl (mezzi) means; **aver la possibilità di
fare** to be in a position to do; to have the
opportunity to do
possi'dente smf landowner
possi'edo ecc vb vedi **possedere**
'posso ecc vb vedi **potere**
'posta sf (servizio) post, postal service;
(corrispondenza) post, mail; (ufficio postale)
post office; (nei giochi d'azzardo) stake;
poste sf pl (amministrazione) post office;
~ **aerea** airmail; ~ **elettronica** E-mail,
e-mail, electronic mail; ~ **ordinaria**
≈ second-class mail; ~ **prioritaria** first
class (post); **ministro delle Poste e
Telecomunicazioni** Postmaster General;
pos'tale ag postal, post office cpd
posteggi'are [posted'dʒare] /62/ vt, vi
to park; **pos'teggio** sm car park (BRIT),
parking lot (US); (di taxi) rank (BRIT), stand
(US)
'poster sm inv poster
posteri'ore ag (dietro) back; (dopo) later
▷ sm (fam: sedere) behind
postici'pare [postitʃi'pare] /72/ vt to defer,
postpone
pos'tino sm postman (BRIT), mailman (US)
'posto, -a pp di **porre** ▷ sm (sito, posizione)
place; (impiego) job; (spazio libero) room,
space; (di parcheggio) space; (sedile: al teatro,
in treno ecc) seat; (Mil) post; **a ~** (in ordine) in

place, tidy; (*fig*) settled; (*persona*) reliable;
mettere a ~ to tidy (up), put in order;
(*faccende*) to straighten out; **al ~ di** in place
of; **sul ~ on** the spot; **~ di blocco** roadblock;
~ di lavoro job; **~ di polizia** police station;
posti in piedi (*Teat, in autobus*) standing
room

po'tabile *ag* drinkable; **acqua ~** drinking
water

po'tare /72/ *vt* to prune

po'tassio *sm* potassium

po'tente *ag* (*nazione*) strong, powerful;
(*veleno, farmaco*) potent, strong; **po'tenza**
sf power; (*forza*) strength

 PAROLA CHIAVE

po'tere /78/ *sm* power; **al potere** (*partito
ecc*) in power; **potere d'acquisto**
purchasing power

▶ *vb aus* **1** (*essere in grado di*) can, be able
to; **non ha potuto ripararlo** he couldn't *o*
he wasn't able to repair it; **non è potuto
venire** he couldn't *o* he wasn't able to come;
spiacente di non poter aiutare sorry not
to be able to help

2 (*avere il permesso*) can, may, be allowed to;
posso entrare? can *o* may I come in?; **posso
chiederti, dove sei stato?** where, may I
ask, have you been?

3 (*eventualità*) may, might, could; **potrebbe
essere vero** it might *o* could be true; **può
aver avuto un incidente** he may *o* might
o could have had an accident; **può darsi**
perhaps; **può darsi o può essere che non
venga** he may *o* might not come

4 (*augurio*): **potessi almeno parlargli!** if
only I could speak to him!

5 (*suggerimento*): **potresti almeno scusarti!**
you could at least apologize!

▶ *vt* can, be able to; **può molto per noi** he
can do a lot for us; **non ne posso più** (*per
stanchezza*) I'm exhausted; (*per rabbia*) I can't
take any more

potrò *ecc vb vedi* **potere**

'povero, -a *ag* poor; (*disadorno*) plain,
bare ▷ *sm/f* poor man/woman; **i poveri**
the poor; **~ di** lacking in, having little;
povertà *sf* poverty; **povertà energetica**
fuel poverty

poz'zanghera [pot'tsangera] *sf* puddle

'pozzo ['pottso] *sm* well; (*cava: di carbone*)
pit; (*di miniera*) shaft; **~ petrolifero** oil well

P.R.A. [pra] *sigla m* (= *Pubblico Registro
Automobilistico*) ≈ DVLA

pran'zare [pran'dzare] /72/ *vi* to dine, have
dinner, to lunch, have lunch

'pranzo ['prandzo] *sm* dinner; (*a mezzogiorno*)
lunch

'prassi *sf* usual procedure

'pratica, -che *sf* practice; (*esperienza*)
experience; (*conoscenza*) knowledge,
familiarity; (*tirocinio*) training, practice;
(*Amm: affare*) matter, case; (*: incartamento*)
file, dossier; **in ~** (*praticamente*) in practice;
mettere in ~ to put into practice

prati'cabile *ag* (*progetto*) practicable,
feasible; (*luogo*) passable, practicable

pratica'mente *av* (*in modo pratico*)
in a practical way, practically; (*quasi*)
practically, almost

prati'care /20/ *vt* to practise; (*Sport: tennis
ecc*) to play; (*: nuoto, scherma ecc*) to go in
for; (*eseguire: apertura, buco*) to make; **~ uno
sconto** to give a discount

'pratico, -a, -ci, -che *ag* practical; **~ di**
(*esperto*) experienced *o* skilled in; (*familiare*)
familiar with

'prato *sm* meadow; (*di giardino*) lawn

preav'viso *sm* notice; **telefonata con ~**
personal *o* person to person call

pre'cario, -a *ag* precarious; (*Ins*) temporary

precauzi'one [prekaut'tsjone] *sf* caution,
care; (*misura*) precaution

prece'dente [pretʃe'dɛnte] *ag* previous
▷ *sm* precedent; **il discorso/film ~** the
previous *o* preceding speech/film; **senza
precedenti** unprecedented; **precedenti
penali** criminal record *sg*; **prece'denza** *sf*
priority, precedence; (*Aut*) right of way

pre'cedere [pre'tʃɛdere] /29/ *vt* to precede,
go *o* (come) before

precipi'tare [pretʃipi'tare] /72/ *vi* (*cadere*)
to fall headlong; (*fig: situazione*) to get
out of control ▷ *vt* (*gettare dall'alto in
basso*) to hurl, fling; (*fig: affrettare*) to rush;
precipitarsi *vpr* (*gettarsi*) to hurl *o* fling
o.s.; (*affrettarsi*) to rush; **precipi'toso, -a** *ag*
(*caduta, fuga*) headlong; (*fig: avventato*) rash,
reckless; (*: affrettato*) hasty, rushed

preci'pizio [pretʃi'pittsjo] *sm* precipice;
a ~ (*fig: correre*) headlong

precisa'mente [pretʃiza'mente] *av* (*gen*)
precisely; (*con esattezza*) exactly

preci'sare [pretʃi'zare] /72/ *vt* to state,
specify; (*spiegare*) to explain (in detail)

precisi'one [pretʃi'zjone] *sf* precision;
accuracy

pre'ciso, -a [pre'tʃizo] *ag* (*esatto*) precise;
(*accurato*) accurate, precise; (*deciso: idea*)
precise, definite; (*uguale*): **2 vestiti precisi** 2
dresses exactly the same; **sono le 9 precise**
it's exactly 9 o'clock

pre'cludere /3/ *vt* to block, obstruct

pre'coce [pre'kɔtʃe] *ag* early; (*bambino*)
precocious; (*vecchiaia*) premature

precon'cetto, -a [prekon'tʃɛtto] *sm* preconceived idea, prejudice

precur'sore *sm* forerunner, precursor

'preda *sf (bottino)* booty; *(animale, fig)* prey; **essere ~ di** to fall prey to; **essere in ~ a** to be prey to

'predica, -che *sf* sermon; *(fig)* lecture, talking-to

predi'care /20/ *vt, vi* to preach

predi'cato *sm (Ling)* predicate

predi'letto, -a *pp di* **prediligere** ▷ *ag, sm/f* favourite

predi'ligere [predi'lidʒere] /117/ *vt* to prefer, have a preference for

pre'dire /38/ *vt* to foretell, predict

predis'porre /77/ *vt* to get ready, prepare; **~ qn a qc** to predispose sb to sth

predizi'one [predit'tsjone] *sf* prediction

prefazi'one [prefat'tsjone] *sf* preface, foreword

prefe'renza [prefe'rɛntsa] *sf* preference

prefe'rire /55/ *vt* to prefer, like better; **~ il caffè al tè** to prefer coffee to tea, like coffee better than tea

pre'figgersi [pre'fiddʒersi] /79/ *vpr*: **~ uno scopo** to set o.s. a goal

pre'fisso, -a *pp di* **prefiggersi** ▷ *sm (Ling)* prefix; *(Tel)* dialling (BRIT) o dial (US) code

pre'gare /80/ *vi* to pray ▷ *vt (Rel)* to pray to; *(implorare)* to beg; *(chiedere)*: **~ qn di fare** to ask sb to do; **farsi ~** to need coaxing o persuading

pre'gevole [pre'dʒevole] *ag* valuable

pregherò *ecc* [prege'rɔ] *vb vedi* **pregare**

preghi'era [pre'gjɛra] *sf (Rel)* prayer; *(domanda)* request

pregi'ato, -a [pre'dʒato] *ag (opera)* valuable; **vino ~** vintage wine

'pregio ['prɛdʒo] *sm (stima)* esteem, regard; *(qualità)* (good) quality, merit; *(valore)* value, worth

pregiudi'care [predʒudi'kare] /20/ *vt* to prejudice, harm, be detrimental to

pregiu'dizio [predʒu'dittsjo] *sm (idea errata)* prejudice; *(danno)* harm *no pl*

'prego *escl (a chi ringrazia)* don't mention it!; *(invitando qn ad accomodarsi)* please sit down!; *(invitando qn ad andare prima)* after you!

pregus'tare /72/ *vt* to look forward to

prele'vare /72/ *vt (denaro)* to withdraw; *(campione)* to take; *(polizia)* to take, capture

preli'evo *sm (Banca)* withdrawal; *(Med)*: **fare un ~ (di)** to take a sample (of); **fare un ~ di sangue** to take a blood sample

prelimi'nare *ag* preliminary

'premere /29/ *vt* to press ▷ *vi*: **~ su** to press down on; *(fig)* to put pressure on; **~ a** *(fig: importare)* to matter to

pre'mettere /63/ *vt* to put before; *(dire prima)* to start by saying, state first

premi'are /19/ *vt* to give a prize to; *(fig: merito, onestà)* to reward

premiazi'one [premjat'tsjone] *sf* prize giving

'premio *sm* prize; *(ricompensa)* reward; *(Comm)* premium; *(Amm: indennità)* bonus

pre'misi *ecc vb vedi* **premettere**

premu'nirsi /55/ *vpr*: **~ di** to provide o.s. with; **~ contro** to protect o.s. from, guard o.s. against

pre'mura *sf (fretta)* haste, hurry; *(riguardo)* attention, care; **premure** *sfpl (attenzioni, cure)* care *sg*; **aver ~ to** be in a hurry; **far ~ a qn** to hurry sb; **usare ogni ~ nei riguardi di qn** to be very attentive to sb; **premu'roso, -a** *ag* thoughtful, considerate

'prendere /81/ *vt* to take; *(andare a prendere)* to get, fetch; *(ottenere)* to get; *(guadagnare)* to get, earn; *(catturare: ladro, pesce)* to catch; *(collaboratore, dipendente)* to take on; *(passeggero)* to pick up; *(chiedere: somma, prezzo)* to charge, ask; *(trattare: persona)* to handle ▷ *vi (colla, cemento)* to set; *(pianta)* to take; *(fuoco: nel camino)* to catch; *(voltare)*: **~ a destra** to turn (to the) right; **prendersi** *vpr (azzuffarsi)*: **prendersi a pugni** to come to blows; **prende qualcosa?** *(da bere, da mangiare)* would you like something to eat *(o* drink)?; **prendo un caffè** I'll have a coffee; **~ qn/qc per** *(scambiare)* to take sb/sth for; **~ fuoco** to catch fire; **~ parte a** to take part in; **prendersi cura di qn/qc** to look after sb/sth; **prendersela** *(adirarsi)* to get annoyed; *(preoccuparsi)* to get upset, worry

preno'tare /72/ *vt* to book, reserve; **prenotazi'one** [prenotat'tsjone] *sf* booking, reservation

preoccu'pare /72/ *vt* to worry; to preoccupy; **preoccuparsi** *vpr*: **preoccuparsi di qn/qc** to worry about sb/ sth; **preoccuparsi per qn** to be anxious for sb; **preoccupazi'one** *sf* worry, anxiety

prepa'rare /72/ *vt* to prepare; *(esame, concorso)* to prepare for; **prepararsi** *vpr (vestirsi)* to get ready; **prepararsi a qc/a fare** to get ready o prepare (o.s.) for sth/ to do; **~ da mangiare** to prepare a meal; **prepara'tivi** *smpl* preparations

preposizi'one [prepozit'tsjone] *sf (Ling)* preposition

prepo'tente *ag (persona)* domineering, arrogant; *(bisogno, desiderio)* overwhelming, pressing ▷ *smf* bully

'presa *sf* taking *no pl*; catching *no pl*; *(di città)* capture; *(indurimento: di cemento)* setting; *(appiglio, Sport)* hold; *(di acqua, gas)* (supply) point; *(piccola quantità: di sale ecc)* pinch;

(*Carte*) trick; **~ (di corrente)** socket; (*al muro*) point; **far ~ (colla)** to set; **ha fatto ~ sul pubblico** (*fig*) it caught the public's imagination; **essere alle prese con qc** (*fig*) to be struggling with sth; **~ d'aria** air inlet

pre'sagio [pre'zadʒo] *sm* omen

'presbite *ag* long-sighted

pres'crivere /105/ *vt* to prescribe

'prese *ecc vb vedi* **prendere**

presen'tare /72/ *vt* to present; (*Amm: inoltrare*) to submit; (*far conoscere*): **~ qn (a)** to introduce sb (to); **presentarsi** *vpr* (*recarsi, farsi vedere*) to present o.s., appear; (*farsi conoscere*) to introduce o.s.; (*occasione*) to arise; **presentarsi come candidato** (*Pol*) to stand (*BRIT*) *o* run (*US*) as a candidate; **presentarsi bene/male** to have a good/ poor appearance

pre'sente *ag* present; (*questo*) this ▷ *sm* present; **i presenti** those present; **aver ~ qc/qn** to remember sth/sb; **tener ~ qn/qc** to keep sb/sth in mind

presenti'mento *sm* premonition

pre'senza [pre'zɛntsa] *sf* presence; (*aspetto esteriore*) appearance; **~ di spirito** presence of mind

pre'sepe, pre'sepio *sm* crib

preser'vare /72/ *vt* to protect; to save; **preserva'tivo** *sm* sheath, condom

'presi *ecc vb vedi* **prendere**

'preside *smf* (*Ins*) head (teacher) (*BRIT*), principal (*US*); (*di facoltà universitaria*) dean; **~ di facoltà** (*Università*) dean of faculty

presi'dente *sm* (*Pol*) president; (*di assemblea, Comm*) chairman; **P~ del Consiglio (dei Ministri)** ≈ Prime Minister

presi'edere /29/ *vt* to preside over ▷ *vi*: **~ a** to direct, be in charge of

pressap'poco *av* about, roughly

pres'sare /72/ *vt* to press

pressi'one *sf* pressure; **far ~ su qn** to put pressure on sb; **~ sanguigna** blood pressure; **~ atmosferica** atmospheric pressure

'presso *av* (*vicino*) nearby, close at hand ▷ *prep* (*vicino a*) near; (*accanto a*) beside, next to; (*in casa di*): **~ qn** at sb's home; (*nelle lettere*) care of, c/o; (*alle dipendenze di*): **lavora ~ di noi** he works for *o* with us ▷ *smpl*: **nei pressi di** near, in the vicinity of

pres'tante *ag* good-looking

pres'tare /72/ *vt*: **~ (qc a qn)** to lend (sb sth *o* sth to sb); **prestarsi** *vpr* (*offrirsi*): **prestarsi a fare** to offer to do; (*essere adatto*): **prestarsi a** to lend itself to, be suitable for; **~ aiuto** to lend a hand; **~ ascolto** *o* **orecchio** to listen; **~ attenzione** to pay attention; **~ fede a qc/qn** to give credence to sth/sb; **prestazi'one** *sf* (*Tecn, Sport*) performance

prestigia'tore, -'trice [prestidʒa'tore] *sm/f* conjurer

pres'tigio [pres'tidʒo] *sm* (*potere*) prestige; (*illusione*): **gioco di ~** conjuring trick

'prestito *sm* lending *no pl*; loan; **dar in ~** to lend; **prendere in ~** to borrow

'presto *av* (*tra poco*) soon; (*in fretta*) quickly; (*di buon'ora*) early; **a ~** see you soon; **fare ~ a fare qc** to hurry up and do sth; (*non costare fatica*) to have no trouble doing sth; **si fa ~ a criticare** it's easy to criticize

pre'sumere /12/ *vt* to presume, assume

pre'sunsi *ecc vb vedi* **presumere**

presuntu'oso, -a *ag* presumptuous

presunzi'one [prezun'tsjone] *sf* presumption

'prete *sm* priest

preten'dente *smf* pretender ▷ *sm* (*corteggiatore*) suitor

pre'tendere /120/ *vt* (*esigere*) to demand, require; (*sostenere*): **~ che** to claim that; **pretende di aver sempre ragione** he thinks he's always right

▌ Attenzione! In inglese esiste il verbo *to pretend*, che però significa *far finta*.

pre'teso, -a *pp di* **pretendere** ▷ *sf* (*esigenza*) claim, demand; (*presunzione, sfarzo*) pretentiousness; **senza pretese** unpretentious

pre'testo *sm* pretext, excuse

preva'lere /126/ *vi* to prevail

pre'vedere /82/ *vt* (*indovinare*) to foresee; (*presagire*) to foretell; (*considerare*) to make provision for

preve'nire /128/ *vt* (*anticipare*) to forestall; (*: domanda*) to anticipate; (*evitare*) to avoid, prevent

preven'tivo, -a *ag* preventive ▷ *sm* (*Comm*) estimate

prevenzi'one [preven'tsjone] *sf* prevention; (*preconcetto*) prejudice

previ'dente *ag* showing foresight, prudent; **previ'denza** *sf* foresight; **istituto di previdenza** provident institution; **previdenza sociale** social security (*BRIT*), welfare (*US*)

pre'vidi *ecc vb vedi* **prevedere**

previsi'one *sf* forecast, prediction; **previsioni meteorologiche** *o* **del tempo** weather forecast *sg*

pre'visto, -a *pp di* **prevedere** ▷ *sm*: **piú/ meno del ~** more/less than expected

prezi'oso, -a [pret'tsjoso] *ag* precious; (*aiuto, consiglio*) invaluable ▷ *sm* jewel; valuable

prez'zemolo [pret'tsemolo] *sm* parsley

'prezzo ['prɛttso] *sm* price; **~ d'acquisto/di vendita** purchase/selling price

prigi'one [pri'dʒone] *sf* prison; **prigioni'ero, -a** *ag* captive ▷ *sm/f* prisoner

'**prima** sf vedi **primo** ▷ av before; (in anticipo) in advance, beforehand; (per l'addietro) at one time, formerly; (più presto) sooner, earlier; (in primo luogo) first ▷ cong: ~ **di fare/che parta** before doing/he leaves; ~ **di** before; ~ **o poi** sooner or later

pri'**mario, -a** ag primary; (principale) chief, leading, primary ▷ sm/f (medico) chief physician

prima'**tista, -i, -e** smf (Sport) record holder

pri'**mato** sm supremacy; (Sport) record

prima'**vera** sf spring

primi'**tivo, -a** ag primitive; (significato) original

pri'**mizie** [pri'mittsje] sfpl early produce sg

'**primo, -a** ag first; (fig) initial; basic; prime ▷ sm/f first (one) ▷ sm (Cuc) first course; (in date): **il ~ luglio** the first of July ▷ sf (Teat) first night; (Cine) première; (Aut) first (gear); **le prime ore del mattino** the early hours of the morning; **ai primi di maggio** at the beginning of May; **viaggiare in prima** to travel first-class; **in ~ luogo** first of all, in the first place; **di prim'ordine** o **prima qualità** first-class, first-rate; **in un ~ tempo** o **momento** at first; **prima donna** leading lady; (di opera lirica) prima donna

primordi'**ale** ag primordial

'**primula** sf primrose

princi'**pale** [printʃi'pale] ag main, principal ▷ sm manager, boss

principal'**mente** [printʃipal'mente] av mainly, principally

'**principe** ['printʃipe] sm prince; ~ **ereditario** crown prince; **princi'pessa** sf princess

principi'**ante** [printʃi'pjante] smf beginner

prin'**cipio** [prin'tʃipjo] sm (inizio) beginning, start; (origine) origin, cause; (concetto, norma) principle; **principi** smpl (concetti fondamentali) principles; **al** o **in ~** at first; **per ~** on principle; **una questione di ~** a matter of principle

priorità sf priority

priori'**tario, -a** ag of utmost importance; (interesse) overriding

pri'**vare** /72/ vt: ~ **qn di** to deprive sb of; **privarsi** vpr: **privarsi di** to go o do without

pri'**vato, -a** ag private ▷ sm/f private citizen; **in ~** in private

privilegi'**are** [privile'dʒare] /62/ vt to grant a privilege to

privilegi'**ato, -a** [privile'dʒato] ag (individuo, classe) privileged; (trattamento, Comm: credito) preferential; **azioni privilegiate** preference shares (BRIT), preferred stock (US)

privi'**legio** [privi'lɛdʒo] sm privilege

'**privo, -a** ag: ~ **di** without, lacking

pro prep for, on behalf of ▷ sm inv (utilità) advantage, benefit; **a che ~?** what's the use?; **il ~ e il contro** the pros and cons

pro'**babile** ag probable, likely; **probabilità** sf inv probability

probabil'**mente** av probably

pro'**blema** sm problem

pro'**boscide** [pro'bɔʃʃide] sf (di elefante) trunk

pro'**cedere** [pro'tʃedere] /29/ vi to proceed; (comportarsi) to behave; (iniziare): ~ **a** to start; ~ **contro** (Dir) to start legal proceedings against; **proce'dura** sf (Dir) procedure

proces'**sare** [protʃes'sare] /72/ vt (Dir) to try

processi'**one** [protʃes'sjone] sf procession

pro'**cesso** [pro'tʃɛsso] sm (Dir) trial; proceedings pl; (metodo) process

pro'**cinto** [pro'tʃinto] sm: **in ~ di fare** about to do, on the point of doing

procla'**mare** /72/ vt to proclaim

procre'**are** /72/ vt to procreate

procu'**rare** /72/ vt: ~ **qc a qn** (fornire) to get o obtain sth for sb; (causare: noie ecc) to bring o give sb sth

pro'**digio** [pro'didʒo] sm marvel, wonder; (persona) prodigy

pro'**dotto, -a** pp di **produrre** ▷ sm product; **prodotti agricoli** farm produce sg

pro'**duco** ecc vb vedi **produrre**

pro'**durre** /90/ vt to produce

pro'**dussi** ecc vb vedi **produrre**

produzi'**one** sf production; (rendimento) output

Prof. abbr (= professore) Prof

profa'**nare** /72/ vt to desecrate

profes'**sare** /72/ vt to profess; (medicina ecc) to practise

professio'**nale** ag professional

professi'**one** sf profession; **professio'nista, -i, -e** smf professional

profes'**sore, -'essa** sm/f (Ins) teacher; (: di università) lecturer; (: titolare di cattedra) professor

pro'**filo** sm profile; (breve descrizione) sketch, outline; **di ~** in profile

pro'**fitto** sm advantage, profit, benefit; (fig: progresso) progress; (Comm) profit

profondità sf inv depth

pro'**fondo, -a** ag deep; (rancore, meditazione) profound ▷ sm depth(s), bottom; ~ **8 metri** 8 metres deep

'**profugo, -a, -ghi, -ghe** sm/f refugee

profu'**mare** /72/ vt to perfume ▷ vi to be fragrant; **profumarsi** vpr to put on perfume o scent

profu'mato, -a *ag (fiore, aria)* fragrant; *(fazzoletto, saponetta)* scented; *(pelle)* sweet-smelling; *(persona)* with perfume on

profume'ria *sf* perfumery; *(negozio)* perfume shop

pro'fumo *sm (prodotto)* perfume, scent; *(fragranza)* scent, fragrance

proget'tare [prodʒet'tare] /72/ *vt* to plan; *(edificio)* to plan, design; **pro'getto** *sm* plan; *(idea)* plan, project; **progetto di legge** bill

pro'gramma, -i *sm* programme; *(TV, Radio)* programmes *pl*; *(Ins)* syllabus, curriculum; *(Inform)* program; **program'mare** /72/ *vt* *(TV, Radio)* to put on; *(Inform)* to program; *(Econ)* to plan; **programma'tore, -'trice** *sm/f* *(Inform)* computer programmer (BRIT) *o* programer (US)

progre'dire /55/ *vi* to progress, make progress

pro'gresso *sm* progress *no pl;* **fare progressi** to make progress

proi'bire /55/ *vt* to forbid, prohibit

proiet'tare /72/ *vt (gen, Geom, Cine)* to project; *(: presentare)* to show, screen; *(luce, ombra)* to throw, cast, project; **proi'ettile** *sm* projectile, bullet, shell *etc;* **proiet'tore** *sm (Cine)* projector; *(Aut)* headlamp; *(Mil)* searchlight; **proiezi'one** *sf (Cine)* projection; showing

prolife'rare /72/ *vi (fig)* to proliferate

pro'lunga, -ghe *sf (di cavo elettrico ecc)* extension

prolun'gare /80/ *vt (discorso, attesa)* to prolong; *(linea, termine)* to extend

prome'moria *sm inv* memorandum

pro'messa *sf* promise

pro'mettere /63/ *vt* to promise ▷ *vi* to be *o* look promising; **~ a qn di fare** to promise sb that one will do

promi'nente *ag* prominent

pro'misi *ecc vb vedi* **promettere**

promon'torio *sm* promontory, headland

promozi'one [promot'tsjone] *sf* promotion

promu'overe /66/ *vt* to promote

proni'pote *smf (di nonni)* great-grandchild, great-grandson/granddaughter; *(di zii)* great-nephew/niece

pro'nome *sm (Ling)* pronoun

pron'tezza [pron'tettsa] *sf* readiness, quickness, promptness

'pronto, -a *ag* ready; *(rapido)* fast, quick, prompt; **~!** *(Tel)* hello!; **~ all'ira** quick-tempered; **~ soccorso** *(trattamento)* first aid; *(reparto)* A&E (BRIT), ER (US)

prontu'ario *sm* manual, handbook

pro'nuncia [pro'nuntʃa] *sf* pronunciation

pronunci'are [pronun'tʃare] /14/ *vt (parola, sentenza)* to pronounce; *(dire)* to utter; *(discorso)* to deliver

propa'ganda *sf* propaganda

pro'pendere /8/ *vi:* **~ per** to favour, lean towards

propi'nare /72/ *vt* to administer

pro'porre /77/ *vt (suggerire):* **~ qc (a qn)** to suggest sth (to sb); *(candidato)* to put forward; *(legge, brindisi)* to propose; **~ di fare** to suggest *o* propose doing; **proporsi di fare** to propose *o* intend to do; **proporsi una meta** to set o.s. a goal

proporzio'nale [proportsjo'nale] *ag* proportional

proporzi'one [propor'tsjone] *sf* proportion; **in ~ a** in proportion to; **proporzioni** *sfpl (dimensioni)* proportions; **di vaste proporzioni** huge

pro'posito *sm (intenzione)* intention, aim; *(argomento)* subject, matter; **a ~ di** regarding, with regard to; **di ~** *(apposta)* deliberately, on purpose; **a ~** by the way; **capitare a ~** *(cosa, persona)* to turn up at the right time

proposizi'one [propozit'tsjone] *sf (Ling)* clause; *(: periodo)* sentence

pro'posto, -a *pp di* **proporre** ▷ *sf* proposal; *(suggerimento)* suggestion; **proposta di legge** bill

proprietà *sf inv (ciò che si possiede)* property, estate; *(caratteristica)* property; *(correttezza)* correctness; **~ privata** private property; **proprie'tario, -a** *sm/f* owner; *(di albergo ecc)* proprietor, owner; *(per l'inquilino)* landlord/lady

'proprio, -a *ag (possessivo)* own; *(: impersonale)* one's; *(esatto)* exact, correct, proper; *(senso, significato)* literal; *(Ling: nome)* proper; *(particolare):* **~ di** characteristic of, peculiar to ▷ *av (precisamente)* just, exactly; *(davvero)* really; *(affatto):* **non ... ~** not ... at all; **l'ha visto con i (suoi) propri occhi** he saw it with his own eyes

proro'gare /80/ *vt* to extend; *(differire)* to postpone, defer

'prosa *sf* prose

pro'sciogliere [proʃ'ʃɔʎʎere] /103/ *vt* to release; *(Dir)* to acquit

prosciu'gare [proʃʃu'gare] /80/ *vt (terreni)* to drain, reclaim; **prosciugarsi** *vpr* to dry up

prosci'utto [proʃ'ʃutto] *sm* ham; **~ cotto/crudo** cooked/cured ham

prosegui'mento *sm* continuation; **buon ~!** all the best!; *(a chi viaggia)* enjoy the rest of your journey!

prosegu'ire /45/ *vt* to carry on with, continue ▷ *vi* to carry on, go on

prospe'rare /72/ *vi* to thrive

prospet'tare /72/ *vt (esporre)* to point out, show; **prospettarsi** *vpr* to look, appear

prospet'tiva sf (Arte) perspective; (veduta) view; (fig: previsione, possibilità) prospect

pros'petto sm (Disegno) elevation; (veduta) view, prospect; (facciata) façade, front; (tabella) table; (sommario) summary

prossimità sf nearness, proximity; **in ~ di** near (to), close to

'prossimo, -a ag (che viene subito dopo) next; (parente) close; (vicino): **~ a** near (to), close to ▷ sm neighbour, fellow man

prostitu'irsi /55/ vr to prostitute o.s.

prosti'tuta sf prostitute

protago'nista, -i, -e smf protagonist

pro'teggere [pro'tɛddʒere] /83/ vt to protect

prote'ina sf protein

pro'tendere /120/ vt to stretch out

pro'testa sf protest

protes'tante ag, smf Protestant

protes'tare /72/ vt, vi to protest

pro'tetto, -a pp di **proteggere**

protezi'one [protet'tsjone] sf protection; (patrocinio) patronage

pro'totipo sm prototype

pro'trarre /123/ vt (prolungare) to prolong; **protrarsi** vpr to go on, continue

protube'ranza [protube'rantsa] sf protuberance, bulge

'prova sf (esperimento, cimento) test, trial; (tentativo) attempt, try; (Mat) proof no pl; (Dir) evidence no pl, proof no pl; (Ins) exam, test; (Teat) rehearsal; (di abito) fitting; **a ~ di** (in testimonianza di) as proof of; **a ~ di fuoco** fireproof; **mettere alla ~** to put to the test; **giro di ~** test o trial run; **fino a ~ contraria** until (it's) proved otherwise; **~ generale** (Teat) dress rehearsal

pro'vare /72/ vt (sperimentare) to test; (tentare) to try, attempt; (assaggiare) to try, taste; (sperimentare in sé) to experience; (sentire) to feel; (cimentare) to put to the test; (dimostrare) to prove; (abito) to try on; **~ a fare** to try o attempt to do

proveni'enza [prove'njɛntsa] sf origin, source

prove'nire /128/ vi: **~ da** to come from

pro'venti smpl revenue sg

pro'verbio sm proverb

pro'vetta sf test tube; **bambino in ~** test-tube baby

pro'vider [pro'vaider] sm inv (Inform) service provider

pro'vincia [pro'vintʃa], **-ce** o **-cie** sf province

pro'vino sm (Cine) screen test; (campione) specimen

provo'cante ag (attraente) provocative

provo'care /20/ vt (causare) to cause, bring about; (eccitare: riso, pietà) to arouse; (irritare, sfidare) to provoke; **provocazi'one** sf provocation

provve'dere /82/ vi (prendere un provvedimento) to take steps, act; (disporre): **~ (a)** to provide (for); **provvedi'mento** sm measure; (di previdenza) precaution

provvi'denza [provvi'dɛntsa] sf: **la ~** providence

provvigi'one [provvi'dʒone] sf (Comm) commission

provvi'sorio, -a ag temporary

prov'vista sf supply

'prua sf (Naut) bow(s), prow

pru'dente ag cautious, prudent; (assennato) sensible, wise; **pru'denza** sf prudence, caution; wisdom

prudere /29/ vi to itch, be itchy

'prugna ['pruɲɲa] sf plum; **~ secca** prune

pru'rito sm itchiness no pl; itch

P.S. abbr (= postscriptum) PS ▷ sigla f (Polizia) = **Pubblica Sicurezza**

pseu'donimo sm pseudonym

psica'nalisi sf psychoanalysis

psicana'lista, -i, -e smf psychoanalyst

'psiche ['psike] sf (Psic) psyche

psichi'atra, -i, -e [psi'kjatra] smf psychiatrist; **psichi'atrico, -a, -ci, -che** ag psychiatric

psicolo'gia [psikolo'dʒia] sf psychology; **psico'logico, -a, -ci, -che** ag psychological; **psi'cologo, -a, -gi, -ghe** sm/f psychologist

psico'patico, -a, -ci, -che ag psychopathic ▷ sm/f psychopath

pubbli'care /20/ vt to publish

pubblicazi'one [pubblikat'tsjone] sf publication

pubblicità [pubblitʃi'ta] sf (diffusione) publicity; (attività) advertising; (annunci nei giornali) advertisements pl

'pubblico, -a, -ci, -che ag public; (statale, scuola ecc) state cpd ▷ sm public; (spettatori) audience; **in ~** in public; **~ funzionario** civil servant; **P~ Ministero** Public Prosecutor's Office; **la Pubblica Sicurezza** the police

'pube sm (Anat) pubis

pubertà sf puberty

'pudico, -a, -ci, -che ag modest

pu'dore sm modesty

pue'rile ag childish

pugi'lato [pudʒi'lato] sm boxing

'pugile ['pudʒile] sm boxer

pugna'lare [puɲɲa'lare] /72/ vt to stab

pu'gnale [puɲ'ɲale] sm dagger

'pugno ['puɲɲo] sm fist; (colpo) punch; (quantità) fistful

'pulce ['pultʃe] sf flea

pul'cino [pul'tʃino] sm chick

pu'lire /55/ vt to clean; (lucidare) to polish; **pu'lito, -a** ag (anche fig) clean; (ordinato) neat, tidy; **puli'tura** *sf* cleaning; **pulitura a secco** dry-cleaning; **puli'zia** *sf* cleaning; *(condizione)* cleanness; **fare le pulizie** to do the cleaning, do the housework; **pulizia etnica** ethnic cleansing

'**pullman** *sm inv* coach

pul'lover *sm inv* pullover, jumper

pullu'lare /72/ *vi* to swarm, teem

pul'mino *sm* minibus

'**pulpito** *sm* pulpit

pul'sante *sm* (push-)button

pul'sare /72/ *vi* to pulsate, beat

pul'viscolo *sm* fine dust; **~ atmosferico** specks *pl* of dust

'**puma** *sm inv* puma

pun'gente [pun'dʒɛnte] *ag* prickly; stinging; *(anche fig)* biting

'**pungere** ['pundʒere] /84/ *vt* to prick; *(insetto, ortica)* to sting; *(freddo)* to bite

pungigli'one [pundʒiʎ'ʎone] *sm* sting

pu'nire /55/ *vt* to punish; **punizi'one** *sf* punishment; *(Sport)* penalty

'**punsi** *ecc vb vedi* **pungere**

'**punta** *sf* point; *(parte terminale)* tip, end; *(di monte)* peak; *(di costa)* promontory; *(minima parte)* touch, trace; **in ~ di piedi** on tiptoe; **ore di ~** peak hours; **uomo di ~** front-rank *o* leading man

pun'tare /72/ *vt (piedi a terra, gomiti sul tavolo)* to plant; *(dirigere: pistola)* to point; *(scommettere):* **~ su** to bet on ▷ *vi (mirare):* **~ a** to aim at; *(avviarsi):* **~ su** to head o make for; *(fig: contare):* **~ su** to count o rely on

pun'tata *sf (gita)* short trip; *(scommessa)* bet; *(parte di opera)* instalment; **romanzo a puntate** serial

punteggia'tura [punted(d)ʒa'tura] *sf (Ling)* punctuation

pun'teggio [pun'tedd(d)ʒo] *sm* score

puntel'lare /72/ *vt* to support

pun'tello *sm* prop, support

pun'tina *sf:* **~ da disegno** drawing pin

pun'tino *sm* dot; **fare qc a ~** to do sth properly

'**punto, -a** *pp di* **pungere** ▷ *sm* point; *(segno, macchiolina)* dot; *(Ling)* full stop; *(di indirizzo e-mail)* dot; *(posto)* spot; *(a scuola)* mark; *(nel cucire, nella maglia, Med)* stitch ▷ *av:* **non ... ~** not ... at all; **~ cardinale** point of the compass, cardinal point; **~ debole** weak point; **~ esclamativo/ interrogativo** exclamation/question mark; **~ nero** *(comedone)* blackhead; **~ di partenza** *(anche fig)* starting point; **~ di riferimento** landmark; *(fig)* point of reference; **~ di vendita** retail outlet; **~ e virgola** semicolon; **~ di vista** *(fig)* point of view

puntu'ale *ag* punctual

pun'tura *sf (di ago)* prick; *(di insetto)* sting, bite; *(Med)* puncture; *(: iniezione)* injection; *(dolore)* sharp pain

▌ Attenzione! In inglese esiste la parola *puncture*, che si usa per indicare la foratura di una gomma.

punzecchi'are [puntsek'kjare] /19/ *vt* to prick; *(fig)* to tease

può *vb vedi* **potere**

pu'pazzo [pu'pattso] *sm* puppet

pu'pillo, -a *sm/f (Dir)* ward ▷ *sf (Anat)* pupil

purché [pur'ke] *cong* provided that, on condition that

'**pure** *cong (tuttavia)* and yet, nevertheless; *(anche se)* even if ▷ *av (anche)* too, also; **pur di** *(al fine di)* just to; **faccia ~!** go ahead!, please do!

purè *sm*, **pu'rea** *sf (Cuc)* purée; *(di patate)* mashed potatoes *pl*

pu'rezza [pu'rettsa] *sf* purity

pur'gante *sm (Med)* purgative, purge

purga'torio *sm* purgatory

purifi'care /20/ *vt* to purify; *(metallo)* to refine

'**puro, -a** *ag* pure; *(acqua)* clear, limpid; *(vino)* undiluted; **puro'sangue** *sm inv, f inv* thoroughbred

pur'troppo *av* unfortunately

pus *sm* pus

'**pustola** *sf* pimple

puti'ferio *sm* rumpus, row

put'tana *sf (fam!)* whore (!)

puz'zare [put'tsare] /72/ *vi* to stink

'**puzzo** ['puttso] *sm* stink, foul smell

puzzola ['puttsola] *sf* polecat

puzzo'lente [puttso'lɛnte] *ag* stinking

P.V.C. [pivi'tʃi] *sigla m* (= *polyvinyl chloride*) PVC

q

q *abbr* (= *quintale*) q

qua *av* here; **in ~** (*verso questa parte*) this way; **da un anno in ~** for a year now; **da quando in ~?** since when?; **per di ~** (*passare*) this way; **al di ~ di** (*fiume, strada*) on this side of; **~ dentro/fuori** *ecc* in/out here *ecc*; *vedi anche* **questo**

qua'derno *sm* notebook; (*per scuola*) exercise book

qua'drante *sm* quadrant; (*di orologio*) face

qua'drare /72/ *vi* (*bilancio*) to balance, tally; **~ (con)** to correspond (with) ▷ *vt* (*Mat*) to square; **non mi quadra** I don't like it; **qua'drato, -a** *ag* square; (*fig: equilibrato*) level-headed, sensible; (*: peg*) square ▷ *sm* (*Mat*) square; (*Pugilato*) ring; **5 al quadrato** 5 squared

quadri'foglio [kwadri'fɔʎʎo] *sm* four-leaf clover

quadri'mestre *sm* (*periodo*) four-month period; (*Ins*) term

'quadro *sm* (*pittura*) painting, picture; (*quadrato*) square; (*tabella*) table, chart; (*Tecn*) board, panel; (*Teat*) scene; (*fig: scena, spettacolo*) sight; (*: descrizione*) outline, description; **quadri** *smpl* (*Pol*) party organizers; (*Comm*) managerial staff; (*Mil*) cadres; (*Carte*) diamonds

'quadruplo, -a *ag, sm* quadruple

quaggiù [kwad'dʒu] *av* down here

'quaglia ['kwaʎʎa] *sf* quail

'qualche ['kwalke] *det* **1** some, a few; (*in interrogative*) any; **ho comprato qualche libro** I've bought some *o* a few books; **qualche volta** sometimes; **hai qualche sigaretta?** have you any cigarettes?
2 (*uno*): **c'è qualche medico?** is there a

doctor?; **in qualche modo** somehow
3 (*un certo, parecchio*) some; **un personaggio di qualche rilievo** a figure of some importance
4: **qualche cosa = qualcosa**

qual'cosa *pron* something; (*in espressioni interrogative*) anything; **qualcos'altro** something else; anything else; **~ di nuovo** something new; anything new; **~ da mangiare** something to eat; anything to eat; **c'è ~ che non va?** is there something *o* anything wrong?

qual'cuno *pron* (*persona*) someone, somebody; (*: in espressioni interrogative*) anyone, anybody; (*alcuni*) some; **~ è favorevole a noi** some are on our side; **qualcun altro** someone *o* somebody else; anyone *o* anybody else

'quale (*spesso troncato in* **qual**) *det*
1 (*interrogativo*) what; (*: scegliendo tra due o più cose o persone*) which; **quale uomo/ denaro?** what man/money?; which man/ money?; **quali sono i tuoi programmi?** what are your plans?; **quale stanza preferisci?** which room do you prefer?
2 (*relativo, come*): **il risultato fu quale ci si aspettava** the result was as expected
3 (*in elenchi*) such as, like; **piante quali l'edera** plants such as *o* like ivy
4 (*esclamativo*) what; **quale disgrazia!** what bad luck!
▶ *pron* **1** (*interrogativo*) which; **quale dei due scegli?** which of the two do you want?
2 (*relativo*): **il (la) quale** (*persona: soggetto*) who; (*: oggetto, con preposizione*) whom; (*cosa*) which; (*possessivo*) whose; **suo padre, il quale è avvocato, ...** his father, who is a lawyer, ...; **il signore con il quale parlavo** the gentleman to whom I was speaking; **l'albergo al quale ci siamo fermati** the hotel where we stayed *o* which we stayed at; **la signora della quale ammiriamo la bellezza** the lady whose beauty we admire
▶ *av* as; **quale sindaco di questa città** as mayor of this town

qua'lifica, -che *sf* qualification; (*titolo*) title

qualifi'cato, -a *ag* (*dotato di qualifica*) qualified; (*esperto, abile*) skilled; **non mi ritengo ~ per questo lavoro** I don't think I'm qualified for this job; **è un medico molto ~** he is a very distinguished doctor

qualificazi'one *sf*: **gara di ~** (*Sport*) qualifying event

qualità *sf inv* quality; **in ~ di** in one's capacity as

qua'lora *cong* in case, if

qual'siasi, qua'lunque *det (inv)* any; (*quale che sia*) whatever; (*discriminativo*) whichever; (*posposto, mediocre*) poor, indifferent; ordinary; **mettiti un vestito ~** put on any old dress; **~ cosa** anything; **~ cosa accada** whatever happens; **a ~ costo** at any cost, whatever the cost; **l'uomo ~** the man in the street; **~ persona** anyone, anybody

'quando *cong, av* when; **~ sarò ricco** when I'm rich; **da ~ (dacché)** since; (*interrogativo*): **da ~ sei qui?** how long have you been here?; **quand'anche** even if

quantità *sf inv* quantity; **una ~ di** (*gran numero*) a great deal of; a lot of; **in grande ~** in large quantities

 PAROLA CHIAVE

'quanto, -a *det* **1** (*interrogativo: quantità*) how much; (*: numero*) how many; **quanto pane/denaro?** how much bread/money?; **quanti libri/ragazzi?** how many books/boys?; **quanto tempo?** how long?; **quanti anni hai?** how old are you?

2 (*esclamativo*): **quante storie!** what a lot of nonsense!; **quanto tempo sprecato!** what a waste of time!

3 (*relativo: quantità*) as much ... as; (*: numero*) as many ... as; **ho quanto denaro mi occorre** I have as much money as I need; **prendi quanti libri vuoi** take as many books as you like

▶ *pron* **1** (*interrogativo: quantità*) how much; (*: numero*) how many; (*: tempo*) how long; **quanto mi dai?** how much will you give me?; **quanti me ne hai portati?** how many did you bring me?; **da quanto sei qui?** how long have you been here?; **quanti ne abbiamo oggi?** what's the date today?

2 (*relativo: quantità*) as much as; (*: numero*) as many as; **farò quanto posso** I'll do as much as I can; **possono venire quanti sono stati invitati** all those who have been invited can come

▶ *av* **1** (*interrogativo: con ag, av*) how; (*: con vb*) how much; **quanto stanco ti sembrava?** how tired did he seem to you?; **quanto corre la tua moto?** how fast can your motorbike go?; **quanto costa?** how much does it cost?; **quant'è?** how much is it?

2 (*esclamativo: con ag, av*) how; (*: con vb*) how much; **quanto sono felice!** how happy I am!; **sapessi quanto abbiamo camminato!** if you knew how far we've

walked!; **studierò quanto posso** I'll study as much as o all I can; **quanto prima** as soon as possible

3: **in quanto** (*in qualità di*) as; (*perché, per il fatto che*) as, since; **(in) quanto a** (*per ciò che riguarda*) as for, as regards

4: **per quanto** (*nonostante, anche se*) however; **per quanto si sforzi, non ce la farà** try as he may, he won't manage it; **per quanto sia brava, fa degli errori** however good she may be, she makes mistakes

qua'ranta *num* forty

quaran'tena *sf* quarantine

quaran'tesimo, -a *num* fortieth

quaran'tina *sf*: **una ~ (di)** about forty

'quarta *sf vedi* **quarto**

quar'tetto *sm* quartet(te)

quarti'ere *sm* district, area; (*Mil*) quarters *pl*; **~ generale** headquarters *pl*

'quarto, -a *ag* fourth ▷ *sm* fourth; (*quarta parte*) quarter ▷ *sf* (*Aut*) fourth (gear); **le 6 e un ~** a quarter past (BRIT) o after (US) 6; **~ d'ora** quarter of an hour; **quarti di finale** quarter finals

'quarzo ['kwartso] *sm* quartz

'quasi *av* almost, nearly ▷ *cong* (*anche*: **~ che**) as if; **(non) ... ~ mai** hardly ever; **~ ~ me ne andrei** I've half a mind to leave

quassù *av* up here

quat'tordici [kwat'torditʃi] *num* fourteen

quat'trini *smpl* money *sg*, cash *sg*

'quattro *num* four; **in ~ e quattr'otto** in less than no time; **quattro'cento** *num* four hundred ▷ *sm*: **il Quattrocento** the fifteenth century

 PAROLA CHIAVE

'quello, -a (*dav sm* **quel** + C, **quell'** + V, **quello** + *s impura, gn, pn, ps, x, z; pl* **quei** + C, **quegli** + V o *s impura, gn, pn, ps, x, z; dav sf* **quella** + C, **quell'** + V; *pl* **quelle**) *det* that; (*pl*) those; **quella casa** that house; **quegli uomini** those men; **voglio quella camicia (lì o là)** I want that shirt

▶ *pron* **1** (*dimostrativo*) that one; (*: pl*) those ones; (*: ciò*) that; **conosci quella?** do you know her?; **prendo quello bianco** I'll take the white one; **chi è quello?** who's that?; **prendiamo quello (lì o là)** let's take that one (there)

2 (*relativo*): **quello(a) che** (*persona*) the one (who); (*cosa*) the one (which), the one (that); **quelli(e) che** (*persone*) those who; (*cose*) those which; **è lui quello che non voleva venire** he's the one who didn't want to come; **ho fatto quello che potevo** I did what I could

'quercia, -ce ['kwɛrtʃa] *sf* oak (tree); *(legno)* oak

que'rela *sf (Dir)* (legal) action

que'sito *sm* question, query; problem

questio'nario *sm* questionnaire

questi'one *sf* problem, question; *(controversia)* issue; *(litigio)* quarrel; **in ~** in question; **è ~ di tempo** it's a matter o question of time

 PAROLA CHIAVE

'questo, -a *det* **1** *(dimostrativo)* this; *(: pl)* these; **questo libro (qui** o **qua)** this book; **io prendo questo cappotto, tu quello** I'll take this coat, you take that one; **quest'oggi** today; **questa sera** this evening **2** *(enfatico):* **non fatemi più prendere di queste paure** don't frighten me like that again

▶ *pron (dimostrativo)* this (one); *(: pl)* these (ones); *(: ciò)* this; **prendo questo (qui** o **qua)** I'll take this one; **preferisci questi o quelli?** do you prefer these (ones) or those (ones)?; **questo intendevo io** this is what I meant; **vengono Paolo e Luca: questo da Roma, quello da Palermo** Paolo and Luca are coming: the former from Palermo, the latter from Rome

ques'tura *sf* police headquarters *pl*

qui *av* here; **da** o **di ~** from here; **di ~ in avanti** from now on; **di ~ a poco/una settimana** in a little while/a week's time; **~ dentro/sopra/vicino** in/up/near here; *vedi anche* **questo**

quie'tanza [kwje'tantsa] *sf* receipt

qui'ete *sf* quiet, quietness; calmness; stillness; peace

qui'eto, -a *ag* quiet; *(notte)* calm, still; *(mare)* calm

'quindi *av* then ▷ *cong* therefore, so

'quindici ['kwinditʃi] *num* fifteen; **~ giorni** a fortnight (BRIT), two weeks

quindi'cina [kwindi'tʃina] *sf (serie):* **una ~ (di)** about fifteen; **fra una ~ di giorni** in a fortnight (BRIT) o two weeks

quinta *sf vedi* **quinto**

quin'tale *sm* quintal *(100 kg)*

'quinto, -a *num* fifth ▷ *sf (Aut)* fifth (gear)

quiz [kwidz] *sm inv (domanda)* question; *(anche:* **gioco a ~)** quiz game

'quota *sf (parte)* quota, share; *(Aer)* height, altitude; *(Ippica)* odds *pl;* **prendere/ perdere ~** *(Aer)* to gain/lose height o altitude; **~ d'iscrizione** enrolment fee; *(ad un club)* membership fee

quotidi'ano, -a *ag* daily; *(banale)* everyday ▷ *sm (giornale)* daily (paper)

quozi'ente [kwot'tsjɛnte] *sm (Mat)* quotient; **~ d'intelligenza** intelligence quotient, IQ

R, r ['ɛrre] *sm o f (lettera)* R, r; **R come Roma** ≈ R for Robert (*BRIT*), R for Roger (*US*)

'rabbia *sf (ira)* anger, rage; *(accanimento, furia)* fury; *(Med: idrofobia)* rabies *sg*

rab'bino *sm* rabbi

rabbi'oso, -a *ag* angry, furious; *(facile all'ira)* quick-tempered; *(forze, acqua ecc)* furious, raging; *(Med)* rabid, mad

rabbo'nire /55/ *vt* to calm down

rabbrivi'dire /55/ *vi* to shudder, shiver

raccapez'zarsi [rakkapet'tsarsi] /72/ *vpr*: **non ~** to be at a loss

raccapricci'ante [rakkaprit'tʃante] *ag* horrifying

raccatta'palle *sm inv (Sport)* ballboy

raccat'tare /72/ *vt* to pick up

rac'chetta [rak'ketta] *sf (per tennis)* racket; *(per ping-pong)* bat; **~ da neve** snowshoe; **~ da sci** ski stick

racchi'udere [rak'kjudere] /22/ *vt* to contain

rac'cogliere [rak'kɔʎʎere] /23/ *vt* to collect; *(raccattare)* to pick up; *(frutti, fiori)* to pick, pluck; *(Agr)* to harvest; *(approvazione, voti)* to win

raccogli'tore [rakkoʎʎi'tore] *sm (cartella)* folder, binder

rac'colta *sf vedi* **raccolto**

rac'colto, -a *pp di* **raccogliere** ▷ *ag (persona: pensoso)* thoughtful; *(luogo: appartato)* secluded, quiet ▷ *sm (Agr)* crop, harvest ▷ *sf* collecting *no pl*; collection; *(Agr)* harvesting *no pl*, gathering *no pl*; harvest, crop; *(adunata)* gathering; **raccolta differenziata** *(dei rifiuti)* separate collection of different kinds of household waste

raccoman'dabile *ag (highly)* commendable; **è un tipo poco ~** he is not to be trusted

raccoman'dare /72/ *vt* to recommend; *(affidare)* to entrust; **~ a qn di fare qc** to recommend that sb does sth

raccoman'dato, -a *ag (lettera, pacco)* recorded-delivery ▷ *sf (anche:* **lettera raccomandata**) recorded-delivery letter

raccon'tare /72/ *vt*: **~ (a qn)** *(dire)* to tell (sb); *(narrare)* to relate (to sb), tell (sb) about; **rac'conto** *sm* telling *no pl*, relating *no pl*; *(fatto raccontato)* story, tale; **racconti per bambini** children's stories

rac'cordo *sm (Tecn: giunzione)* connection, joint; **~ anulare** *(Aut)* ring road (*BRIT*), beltway (*US*); **~ autostradale** slip road (*BRIT*), entrance *(o exit)* ramp (*US*); **~ ferroviario** siding; **~ stradale** link road

racimo'lare [ratʃimo'lare] /72/ *vt (fig)* to scrape together, glean

'rada *sf (natural)* harbour (*BRIT*) *o* harbor (*US*)

'radar *sm inv* radar

raddoppi'are /19/ *vt, vi* to double

raddriz'zare [raddrit'tsare] /72/ *vt* to straighten; *(fig: correggere)* to put straight, correct

'radere /85/ *vt (barba)* to shave off; *(mento)* to shave; *(fig: rasentare)* to graze; to skim; **radersi** *vpr* to shave (o.s.); **~ al suolo** to raze to the ground

radi'are /19/ *vt* to strike off

radia'tore *sm* radiator

radiazi'one [radjat'tsjone] *sf (Fisica)* radiation; *(cancellazione)* striking off

radi'cale *ag* radical ▷ *sm (Ling)* root; **radicali liberi** free radicals

ra'dicchio [ra'dikkjo] *sm variety of chicory*

ra'dice [ra'ditʃe] *sf* root

'radio *sf inv radio* ▷ *sm (Chim)* radium; **radioat'tivo, -a** *ag* radioactive; **radio'cronaca, -che** *sf* radio commentary; **radiogra'fia** *sf* radiography; *(foto)* X-ray photograph

radi'oso, -a *ag* radiant

radios'veglia [radjoz'veʎʎa] *sf* radio alarm

'rado, -a *ag (capelli)* sparse, thin; *(visite)* infrequent; **di ~** rarely

radu'nare /72/ *vt,* **radu'narsi** *vpr* to gather, assemble

ra'dura *sf* clearing

raf'fermo, -a *ag* stale

'raffica, -che *sf (Meteor)* gust (of wind); **~ di colpi** *(di fucile)* burst of gunfire

raffigu'rare /72/ *vt* to represent

raffi'nato, -a *ag* refined

raffor'zare [raffor'tsare] /72/ *vt* to reinforce

raffredda'mento *sm* cooling

raffred'dare /72/ *vt* to cool; *(fig)* to dampen, have a cooling effect on; **raffreddarsi** *vpr* to grow cool *o* cold; *(prendere un raffreddore)* to catch a cold; *(fig)* to cool (off)

raffred'dato, -a *ag* (*Med*): **essere ~** to have a cold

raffred'dore *sm* (*Med*) cold

raf'fronto *sm* comparison

'rafia *sf* (*fibra*) raffia

'rafting ['rafting] *sm* white-water rafting

ra'gazzo, -a [ra'gattso] *sm/f* boy/girl; (*fam: fidanzato*) boyfriend/girlfriend; **ragazzi** *smpl* (*figli*) kids; **ragazza madre** unmarried mother; **ciao ragazzi!** (*gruppo*) hi guys!

raggi'ante [rad'dʒante] *ag* radiant, shining

'raggio ['raddʒo] *sm* (*di sole ecc*) ray; (*Mat, distanza*) radius; (*di ruota ecc*) spoke; **~ d'azione** range; **raggi X** X-rays

raggi'rare [raddʒi'rare] /72/ *vt* to take in, trick

raggi'ungere [rad'dʒundʒere] /5/ *vt* to reach; (*persona: riprendere*) to catch up (with); (*bersaglio*) to hit; (*fig: meta*) to achieve

raggomito'larsi /72/ *vpr* to curl up

raggranel'lare /72/ *vt* to scrape together

raggrup'pare /72/ *vt* to group (together)

ragiona'mento [radʒona'mento] *sm* reasoning *no pl*; arguing *no pl*; argument

ragio'nare [radʒo'nare] /72/ *vi* to reason; (*discorrere*): **~ (di)** to argue (about)

ragi'one [ra'dʒone] *sf* reason; (*dimostrazione, prova*) argument, reason; (*diritto*) right; **aver ~** to be right; **aver ~ di qn** to get the better of sb; **dare ~ a qn** (*persona*) to side with sb; (*fatto*) to prove sb right; **in ~ di** at the rate of; to the amount of; according to; **a o con ~** rightly, justly; **perdere la ~** to become insane; (*fig*) to take leave of one's senses; **a ragion veduta** after due consideration; **~ sociale** (*Comm*) corporate name

ragione'ria [radʒone'ria] *sf* accountancy; (*ufficio*) accounts department

ragio'nevole [radʒo'nevole] *ag* reasonable

ragioni'ere, -a [radʒo'njere] *sm/f* accountant

ragli'are [raʎ'ʎare] /27/ *vi* to bray

ragna'tela [raɲɲa'tela] *sf* cobweb, spider's web

'ragno ['raɲɲo] *sm* spider

ragù *sm inv* (*Cuc*) meat sauce (*for pasta*); stew

RAI-TV [raiti'vu] *sigla f* (= *Radio televisione italiana*) Italian Broadcasting Company

ralle'grare /72/ *vt* to cheer up; **rallegrarsi** *vpr* to cheer up; (*provare allegrezza*) to rejoice; **rallegrarsi con qn** to congratulate sb

rallen'tare /72/ *vt* to slow down; (*fig*) to lessen, slacken ▷ *vi* to slow down

rallenta'tore *sm* (*Cine*) slow-motion camera; **al ~** (*anche fig*) in slow motion

raman'zina [raman'dzina] *sf* lecture, telling-off

'rame *sm* (*Chim*) copper

rammari'carsi /20/ *vpr*: **~ (di)** (*rincrescersi*) to be sorry (about), regret; (*lamentarsi*) to complain (about)

rammen'dare /72/ *vt* to mend; (*calza*) to darn

'ramo *sm* branch

ramo'scello [ramoʃ'ʃello] *sm* twig

'rampa *sf* flight (of stairs); **~ di lancio** launching pad

rampi'cante *ag* (*Bot*) climbing

'rana *sf* frog

'rancido, -a ['rantʃido] *ag* rancid

ran'core *sm* rancour, resentment

ran'dagio, -a, -gi, -gie o -ge [ran'dadʒo] *ag* (*gatto, cane*) stray

ran'dello *sm* club, cudgel

'rango, -ghi *sm* (*grado*) rank; (*condizione sociale*) station

rannicchi'arsi [rannik'kjarsi] /19/ *vpr* to crouch, huddle

rannuvo'larsi /72/ *vpr* to cloud over, become overcast

'rapa *sf* (*Bot*) turnip

ra'pace [ra'patʃe] *ag* (*animale*) predatory; (*fig*) rapacious, grasping ▷ *sm* bird of prey

ra'pare /72/ *vt* (*capelli*) to crop, cut very short

rapida'mente *av* quickly, rapidly

rapidità *sf* speed

'rapido, -a *ag* fast; (*esame, occhiata*) quick, rapid ▷ *sm* (*Ferr*) express (train)

rapi'mento *sm* kidnapping; (*fig*) rapture

ra'pina *sf* robbery; **~ in banca** bank robbery; **~ a mano armata** armed robbery; **rapi'nare** /72/ *vt* to rob; **rapina'tore, -'trice** *sm/f* robber

ra'pire /55/ *vt* (*cose*) to steal; (*persone*) to kidnap; (*fig*) to enrapture, delight; **rapi'tore, -'trice** *sm/f* kidnapper

rap'porto *sm* (*resoconto*) report; (*legame*) relationship; (*Mat, Tecn*) ratio; **rapporti sessuali** sexual intercourse *sg*

rappre'saglia [rappre'saʎʎa] *sf* reprisal, retaliation

rappresen'tante *smf* representative

rappresen'tare /72/ *vt* to represent; (*Teat*) to perform; **rappresentazi'one** *sf* representation; performing *no pl*; (*spettacolo*) performance

rara'mente *av* seldom, rarely

rare'fatto, -a *ag* rarefied

'raro, -a *ag* rare

ra'sare /72/ *vt* (*barba ecc*) to shave off; (*siepi, erba*) to trim, cut; **rasarsi** *vpr* to shave (o.s.)

raschi'are [ras'kjare] /19/ *vt* to scrape; (*macchia, fango*) to scrape off ▷ *vi* to clear one's throat

ra'sente prep: ~ (a) close to, very near

'raso, -a pp di **radere** ▷ ag (barba) shaved; (capelli) cropped; (con misure di capacità) level; (pieno: bicchiere) full to the brim ▷ sm (tessuto) satin; ~ **terra** close to the ground; **un cucchiaio** ~ a level spoonful

ra'soio sm razor; ~ **elettrico** electric shaver o razor

ras'segna [ras'seɲɲa] sf (Mil) inspection, review; (esame) inspection; (resoconto) review, survey; (pubblicazione letteraria ecc) review; (mostra) exhibition, show; **passare in** ~ (Mil: fig) to review

rasse'gnare [rasseɲ'ɲare] /15/ vt: ~ **le dimissioni** to resign; **rassegnarsi** vpr (accettare): **rassegnarsi (a qc/a fare)** to resign o.s. (to sth/to doing)

rassicu'rare /72/ vt to reassure

rasso'dare /72/ vt to harden, stiffen; **rassodarsi** vpr to harden, to strengthen

rassomigli'anza [rassomiʎ'ʎantsa] sf resemblance

rassomigli'are [rassomiʎ'ʎare] /27/ vi: ~ **a** to resemble, look like

rastrel'lare /72/ vt to rake; (fig: perlustrare) to comb

ras'trello sm rake

'rata sf (quota) instalment; **pagare a rate** to pay by instal(l)ments o on hire purchase (BRIT)

ratifi'care /20/ vt (Dir) to ratify

'ratto sm (Dir) abduction; (Zool) rat

rattop'pare /72/ vt to patch

rattris'tare /72/ vt to sadden; **rattristarsi** vpr to become sad

'rauco, -a, -chi, -che ag hoarse

rava'nello sm radish

ravi'oli smpl ravioli sg

ravvi'vare /72/ vt to revive; (fig) to brighten up, enliven

razio'nale [rattsjo'nale] ag rational

razio'nare [rattsjo'nare] /72/ vt to ration

razi'one [rat'tsjone] sf ration; (porzione) portion, share

'razza ['rattsa] sf race; (Zool) breed; (discendenza, stirpe) stock, race; (sorta) sort, kind

razzi'ale [rat'tsjale] ag racial

raz'zismo [rat'tsizmo] sm racism, racialism

raz'zista, -i, -e [rat'tsista] ag, smf racist, racialist

'razzo ['raddzo] sm rocket

RC sigla = **Reggio Calabria**; (= partito della Rifondazione Comunista) left-wing Italian political party

re sm inv king; (Mus) D; (: solfeggiando la scala) re; **i Re Magi** the Three Wise Men, the Magi

rea'gire [rea'dʒire] /55/ vi to react

re'ale ag real; (di, da re) royal ▷ sm: **il** ~ reality

reality [ri'aliti] sm inv reality show

realiz'zare [realid'dzare] /72/ vt (progetto ecc) to realize, carry out; (sogno, desiderio) to realize, fulfil; (scopo) to achieve; (Comm: titoli ecc) to realize; (Calcio: ecc) to score; **realizzarsi** vpr to be realized

real'mente av really, actually

realtà sf inv reality

re'ato sm offence

reat'tore sm (Fisica) reactor; (Aer: aereo) jet; (: motore) jet engine

reazio'nario, -a [reattsjo'narjo] ag (Pol) reactionary

reazi'one [reat'tsjone] sf reaction

'rebus sm inv rebus; (fig) puzzle; enigma

recapi'tare /72/ vt to deliver

re'capito sm (indirizzo) address; (consegna) delivery; ~ **telefonico** phone number; ~ **a domicilio** home delivery (service)

re'care /20/ vt (portare) to bring; **recarsi** vpr: **recarsi in città/a scuola** to go into town/to school

re'cedere [re'tʃedere] /29/ vi to withdraw

recensi'one [retʃen'sjone] sf review

re'cente [re'tʃente] ag recent; **di** ~ recently; **recente'mente** av recently

re'cidere [re'tʃidere] /34/ vt to cut off, chop off

recin'tare [retʃin'tare] /72/ vt to enclose, fence off

re'cinto [re'tʃinto] sm enclosure; (ciò che recinge) fence; surrounding wall

recipi'ente [retʃi'pjɛnte] sm container

re'ciproco, -a, -ci, -che [re'tʃiproko] ag reciprocal

'recita ['rɛtʃita] sf performance

reci'tare [retʃi'tare] /72/ vt (poesia, lezione) to recite; (dramma) to perform; (ruolo) to play o act (the part of)

recla'mare /72/ vi to complain ▷ vt (richiedere) to demand

re'clamo sm complaint

recli'nabile ag (sedile) reclining

reclusi'one sf (Dir) imprisonment

'recluta sf recruit

re'condito, -a ag secluded; (fig) secret, hidden

'record ag inv record cpd ▷ sm inv record; **in tempo** ~, **a tempo di** ~ in record time; **detenere il** ~ **di** to hold the record for; ~ **mondiale** world record

recriminazi'one [rekriminat'tsjone] sf recrimination

recupe'rare ecc = **ricuperare** ecc

redargu'ire /55/ vt to rebuke

re'dassi ecc vb vedi **redigere**

reddi'tizio, -a [reddi'tittsjo] ag profitable

'reddito sm income; (dello Stato) revenue; (di un capitale) yield

re'densi ecc vb vedi **redimere**

re'dento, -a pp di **redimere**

re'digere [re'didʒere] /47/ vt to write; (contratto) to draw up

re'dimere /86/ vt to deliver; (Rel) to redeem

redini sfpl reins

reduce ['redutʃe] ag: ~ **da** returning from, back from ▷ smf survivor

refe'rendum sm inv referendum

refe'renza [refe'rentsa] sf reference

re'ferto sm medical report

rega'lare /72/ vt to give (as a present), make a present of

re'galo sm gift, present

re'gata sf regatta

reggere ['rɛddʒere] /87/ vt (tenere) to hold; (sostenere) to support, bear, hold up; (portare) to carry, bear; (resistere) to withstand; (dirigere: impresa) to manage, run; (governare) to rule, govern; (Ling) to take, be followed by ▷ vi (resistere): ~ **a** to stand up to, hold out against; (sopportare): ~ **a** to stand; (durare) to last; (fig: teoria ecc) to hold water; **reggersi** vpr (stare ritto) to stand

reggia, -ge ['rɛddʒa] sf royal palace

reggi'calze [rɛddʒi'kaltse] sm inv suspender belt

reggi'mento [rɛddʒi'mento] sm (Mil) regiment

reggi'seno [rɛddʒi'seno] sm bra

re'gia, -'gie [re'dʒia] sf (TV, Cine: ecc) direction

re'gime [re'dʒime] sm (Pol) regime; (Dir: aureo, patrimoniale ecc) system; (Med) diet; (Tecn) (engine) speed

re'gina [re'dʒina] sf queen

regio'nale [redʒo'nale] ag regional ▷ sm local train (stopping frequently)

regi'one [re'dʒone] sf (gen) region; (territorio) region, district, area

re'gista, -i, -e [re'dʒista] smf (TV, Cine ecc) director

regis'trare [redʒis'trare] /72/ vt (Amm) to register; (Comm) to enter; (notare) to report, note; (canzone, conversazione: strumento di misura) to record; (mettere a punto) to adjust, regulate; ~ **i bagagli** to check in one's luggage; **registra'tore** sm (strumento) recorder, register; (magnetofono) tape recorder; **registratore di cassa** cash register; **registratore a cassette** cassette recorder

re'gistro [re'dʒistro] sm register; (Dir) registry; (Comm): ~ **(di cassa)** ledger; ~ **di bordo** logbook

re'gnare [reɲ'ɲare] /15/ vi to reign, rule

regno ['reɲɲo] sm kingdom; (periodo) reign; (fig) realm; **il R~ animale/vegetale** the animal/vegetable kingdom; **il R~ Unito** the United Kingdom

regola sf rule; a ~ **d'arte** duly; perfectly; **avere le carte in** ~ to have one's papers in order

rego'labile ag adjustable

regola'mento sm (complesso di norme) regulations pl; (di debito) settlement; ~ **di conti** (fig) settling of scores

rego'lare /72/ ag regular; (in regola: documento) in order ▷ vt to regulate, control; (apparecchio) to adjust, regulate; (questione, conto, debito) to settle; **regolarsi** vpr (comportarsi) to behave, act; **regolarsi nel bere/nello spendere** (moderarsi) to control one's drinking/spending

rela'tivo, -a ag relative

relazi'one [relat'tsjone] sf (fra cose, persone) relation(ship); (resoconto) report, account

rele'gare /80/ vt to banish; (fig) to relegate

religi'one [reli'dʒone] sf religion

religi'oso, -a [reli'dʒoso] ag religious

re'liquia sf relic

re'litto sm wreck; (fig) down-and-out

re'mare /72/ vi to row

remini'scenze [reminiʃ'ʃentse] sfpl reminiscences

remis'sivo, -a ag submissive, compliant

remo sm oar

re'moto, -a ag remote

rendere /88/ vt (ridare) to return, give back; (: saluto ecc) to return; (produrre) to yield, bring in; (esprimere, tradurre) to render; ~ **qc possibile** to make sth possible; ~ **grazie a qn** to thank sb; ~ **omaggio a qn** to honour sb; ~ **un servizio a qn** to do sb a service; ~ **una testimonianza** to give evidence; ~ **la visita** to pay a return visit; **non so se rendo l'idea** I don't know whether I'm making myself clear

rendi'mento sm (reddito) yield; (di manodopera, Tecn) efficiency; (capacità) output; (di studenti) performance

rendita sf (di individuo) private o unearned income; (Comm) revenue; ~ **annua** annuity

rene sm kidney

renna sf reindeer inv

re'parto sm department, section; (Mil) detachment

repel'lente ag repulsive

repen'taglio [repen'taʎʎo] sm: **mettere a** ~ to jeopardize, risk

repen'tino, -a ag sudden, unexpected

reper'torio sm (Teat) repertory; (elenco) index, (alphabetical) list

replica, -che sf repetition; reply, answer; (obiezione) objection; (Teat, Cine) repeat performance; (copia) replica

repli'care /20/ vt (ripetere) to repeat; (rispondere) to answer, reply

repressi'one sf repression

re'presso, -a pp di **reprimere**

re'primere /50/ vt to suppress, repress

re'pubblica, -che sf republic

reputazi'one [reputat'tsjone] sf reputation

requi'sire /55/ vt to requisition

requi'sito sm requirement

'resa sf (l'arrendersi) surrender; (restituzione, rendimento) return; **~ dei conti** rendering of accounts; (fig) day of reckoning

'resi ecc vb vedi **rendere**

resi'dente ag resident; **residenzi'ale** ag residential

re'siduo, -a ag residual, remaining ▷ sm remainder; (Chim) residue

'resina sf resin

resis'tente ag (che resiste): **~ a** resistant to; (forte) strong; (duraturo) long-lasting, durable; **~ al caldo** heat-resistant; **resis'tenza** sf resistance; (di persona: fisica) stamina, endurance; (: mentale) endurance, resistance

● **RESISTENZA**
●
● The Italian Resistenza fought against
● both the Nazis and the Fascists during
● the Second World War. It was particularly
● active after the fall of the Fascist
● government on 25 July 1943, throughout
● the German occupation and during the
● period of Mussolini's Republic of Salò
● in northern Italy. Resistance members
● spanned the whole political spectrum
● and played a vital role in the Liberation
● and in the formation of the new
● democratic government.

re'sistere /11/ vi to resist; **~ a** (assalto, tentazioni) to resist; (dolore) to withstand; (non patir danno) to be resistant to

reso'conto sm report, account

res'pingere [res'pindʒere] /114/ vt to drive back, repel; (rifiutare) to reject; (Ins: bocciare) to fail

respi'rare /72/ vi to breathe; (fig) to get one's breath; to breathe again ▷ vt to breathe (in), inhale; **respirazi'one** sf breathing; **respirazione artificiale** artificial respiration; **res'piro** sm breathing no pl; (singolo atto) breath; (fig) respite, rest; **mandare un respiro di sollievo** to give a sigh of relief

respon'sabile ag responsible ▷ smf person responsible; (capo) person in charge; **~ di** responsible for; (Dir) liable for;

responsabilità sf inv responsibility; (legale) liability

res'ponso sm answer

'ressa sf crowd, throng

'ressi ecc vb vedi **reggere**

res'tare /72/ vi (rimanere) to remain, stay; (avanzare) to be left, remain; **~ orfano/cieco** to become o be left an orphan/become blind; **~ d'accordo** to agree; **non resta più niente** there's nothing left; **restano pochi giorni** there are only a few days left

restau'rare /72/ vt to restore

res'tio, -a, -'tii, -'tie ag: **~ a** reluctant to

restitu'ire /55/ vt to return, give back; (energie, forze) to restore

'resto sm remainder, rest; (denaro) change; (Mat) remainder; **resti** smpl leftovers; (di città) remains; **del ~** moreover, besides; **tenga pure il ~** keep the change; **resti mortali** (mortal) remains

res'tringere [res'trindʒere] /117/ vt to reduce; (vestito) to take in; (stoffa) to shrink; (fig) to restrict, limit; **restringersi** vpr (strada) to narrow; (stoffa) to shrink

'rete sf net; (di recinzione) netting; (Aut, Ferr, di spionaggio ecc) network; (fig) trap, snare; **segnare una ~** (Calcio) to score a goal; **~ ferroviaria/stradale/di distribuzione** railway/road/distribution network; **~ del letto** (sprung) bed base; **~ sociale** social network; **~ (televisiva)** (sistema) network; (canale) channel; **la R~** the web

reti'cente [reti'tʃɛnte] ag reticent

retico'lato sm grid; (rete metallica) wire netting; (di filo spinato) barbed wire fence

'retina sf (Anat) retina

re'torico, -a, -ci, -che ag rhetorical

retribu'ire /55/ vt to pay

'retro sm inv back ▷ av (dietro): **vedi ~** see over(leaf)

retro'cedere [retro'tʃɛdere] /29/ vi to withdraw ▷ vt (Calcio) to relegate; (Mil) to degrade

re'trogrado, -a ag (fig) reactionary, backward-looking

retro'marcia [retro'martʃa] sf (Aut) reverse; (: dispositivo) reverse gear

retro'scena [retroʃ'ʃɛna] sf inv (Teat) backstage ▷ sm inv: **i ~** (fig) the behind-the-scenes activities

retrovi'sore sm (Aut) (rear-view) mirror

'retta sf (Mat) straight line; (di convitto) charge for bed and board; (fig: ascolto): **dar ~ a** to listen to, pay attention to

rettango'lare ag rectangular

ret'tangolo, -a ag right-angled ▷ sm rectangle

ret'tifica, -che sf rectification, correction

'**rettile** sm reptile

retti'lineo, -a ag rectilinear

'**retto, -a** pp di **reggere** ▷ ag straight; (onesto) honest, upright; (giusto, esatto) correct, proper, right; **angolo ~** (Mat) right angle

ret'tore sm (Rel) rector; (di università) ≈ chancellor

retwit'tare /72/ vt (su Twitter) to retweet

reuma'tismo sm rheumatism

revisi'one sf auditing no pl; audit; servicing no pl; overhaul; review; revision; **~ contabile interna** internal audit

revi'sore sm: **~ di conti/bozze** auditor/proofreader

re'vival [ri'vaivəl] sm inv revival

'**revoca** sf revocation

revo'care /20/ vt to revoke

re'volver sm inv revolver

ri'abbia ecc vb vedi **riavere**

riabili'tare /72/ vt to rehabilitate

riabilitazi'one [riabilitat'tsjone] sf rehabilitation

rianimazi'one [rianimat'tsjone] sf (Med) resuscitation; **centro di ~** intensive care unit

ria'prire /9/ vt, **ria'prirsi** vpr to reopen, open again

ri'armo sm (Mil) rearmament

rias'sumere /12/ vt (riprendere) to resume; (impiegare di nuovo) to re-employ; (sintetizzare) to summarize; **rias'sunto, -a** pp di **riassumere** ▷ sm summary

riattac'care /20/ vt (attaccare di nuovo): **~ (a)** (manifesto, francobollo) to stick back (on); (bottone) to sew back (on); (quadro, chiavi) to hang back up (on); **~ (il telefono o il ricevitore)** to hang up (the receiver)

ria'vere /13/ vt to have again; (avere indietro) to get back; (riacquistare) to recover; **riaversi** vpr to recover

riba'dire /55/ vt (fig) to confirm

ri'balta sf flap; (Teat: proscenio) front of the stage; **luci della ~** footlights pl; (fig) limelight

ribal'tabile ag (sedile) tip-up

ribal'tare /72/ vt, vi (anche: **ribaltarsi**) to turn over, tip over

ribas'sare /72/ vt to lower, bring down ▷ vi to come down, fall

ri'battere /1/ vt to return, hit back; (confutare) to refute; **~ che** to retort that

ribel'larsi /72/ vpr: **~ (a)** to rebel (against); **ri'belle** ag (soldati) rebel; (ragazzo) rebellious ▷ smf rebel

'**ribes** sm inv currant; **~ nero** blackcurrant; **~ rosso** redcurrant

ri'brezzo [ri'breddzo] sm disgust, loathing; **far ~ a** to disgust

ribut'tante ag disgusting, revolting

rica'dere /18/ vi to fall again; (scendere a terra: fig: nel peccato ecc) to fall back; (vestiti, capelli ecc) to hang (down); (riversarsi: fatiche, colpe): **~ su** to fall on; **rica'duta** sf (Med) relapse

rica'mare /72/ vt to embroider

ricambi'are /19/ vt to change again; (contraccambiare) to return, repay; **ri'cambio** sm exchange, return; (Fisiol) metabolism

ri'camo sm embroidery

ricapito'lare /72/ vt to recapitulate, sum up

ricari'care /20/ vt (arma, macchina fotografica) to reload; (penna, pipa) to refill; (orologio, giocattolo) to rewind; (Elettr) to recharge

ricat'tare /72/ vt to blackmail; **ri'catto** sm blackmail

rica'vare /72/ vt (estrarre) to draw out, extract; (ottenere) to obtain, gain

ric'chezza [rik'kettsa] sf wealth; (fig) richness

'**riccio, -a, -ci, -ce** ['rittʃo] ag curly ▷ sm (Zool) hedgehog; (anche: **~ di mare**) sea urchin; '**ricciolo** sm curl

'**ricco, -a, -chi, -che** ag rich; (persona, paese) rich, wealthy ▷ sm/f rich man/woman; **i ricchi** the rich; **~ di** full of; (risorse, fauna ecc) rich in

ri'cerca, -che [ri'tʃerka] sf search; (indagine) investigation, inquiry; (studio): **la ~** research; **una ~** a piece of research; **~ di mercato** market research

ricer'care [ritʃer'kare] /20/ vt (motivi, cause) to look for, try to determine; (successo, piacere) to pursue; (onore, gloria) to seek; **ricer'cato, -a** ag (apprezzato) much sought-after; (affettato) studied, affected ▷ sm/f (Polizia) wanted man/woman

ricerca'tore, -'trice [ritʃerka'tore] sm/f (Ins) researcher

ri'cetta [ri'tʃetta] sf (Med) prescription; (Cuc) recipe

ricettazi'one [ritʃettat'tsjone] sf (Dir) receiving (stolen goods)

ri'cevere [ri'tʃevere] /29/ vt to receive; (stipendio, lettera) to get, receive; (accogliere: ospite) to welcome; (vedere: cliente, rappresentante ecc) to see; **ricevi'mento** sm receiving no pl; (trattenimento) reception; **ricevi'tore** sm (Tecn) receiver; **rice'vuta** sf receipt; **accusare ricevuta di qc** (Comm) to acknowledge receipt of sth; **ricevuta fiscale** official receipt (for tax purposes); **ricevuta di ritorno** (Posta) advice of receipt

richia'mare [rikja'mare] /72/ vt (chiamare indietro, ritelefonare) to call back; (*ambasciatore, truppe*) to recall; (*rimproverare*) to reprimand; (*attirare*) to attract, draw; **richiamarsi** *vpr*: **richiamarsi a** (*riferirsi a*) to refer to

richi'edere [ri'kjedere] /21/ *vt* to ask again for; (*chiedere: per sapere*) to ask; (: *per avere*) to ask for; (*Amm: documenti*) to apply for; (*esigere*) to need, require; (*chiedere indietro*): **~ qc** to ask for sth back

richi'esto, -a [ri'kjɛsto] *pp di* **richiedere** ▷ *sf* (*domanda*) request; (*Amm*) application, request; (*esigenza*) demand, request; **a richiesta** on request

rici'claggio [ritʃi'kladdʒo] *sm* recycling

rici'clare [ritʃi'klare] /72/ *vt* to recycle

'ricino ['ritʃino] *sm*: **olio di ~** castor oil

ricognizi'one [rikoɲɲit'tsjone] *sf* (*Mil*) reconnaissance; (*Dir*) recognition, acknowledgement

ricominci'are [rikomin'tʃare] /14/ *vt, vi* to start again, begin again

ricom'pensa *sf* reward

ricompen'sare /72/ *vt* to reward

riconcili'are [rikontʃi'ljare] /19/ *vt* to reconcile; **riconciliarsi** *vpr* to be reconciled

ricono'scente [rikonoʃʃente] *ag* grateful

rico'noscere [riko'noʃʃere] /26/ *vt* to recognize; (*Dir: figlio, debito*) to acknowledge; (*ammettere: errore*) to admit, acknowledge

rico'perto, -a *pp di* **ricoprire**

ricopi'are /19/ *vt* to copy

rico'prire /9/ *vt* (*coprire*) to cover; (*occupare: carica*) to hold

ricor'dare /72/ *vt* to remember, recall; (*richiamare alla memoria*): **~ qc a qn** to remind sb of sth; **ricordarsi** *vpr*: **ricordarsi (di)** to remember; **ricordarsi di qc/di aver fatto** to remember sth/having done

ri'cordo *sm* memory; (*regalo*) keepsake, souvenir; (*di viaggio*) souvenir

ricor'rente *ag* recurrent, recurring; **ricor'renza** *sf* recurrence; (*festività*) anniversary

ri'correre /28/ *vi* (*ripetersi*) to recur; **~ a** (*rivolgersi*) to turn to; (*Dir*) to appeal to; (*servirsi di*) to have recourse to

ricostitu'ente *ag* (*Med*): **cura ~** tonic

ricostru'ire /55/ *vt* (*casa*) to rebuild; (*fatti*) to reconstruct

ri'cotta *sf soft white unsalted cheese made from sheep's milk*

ricove'rare /72/ *vt* to give shelter to; **~ qn in ospedale** to admit sb to hospital

ri'covero *sm* shelter, refuge; (*Mil*) shelter; (*Med*) admission to hospital

ricreazi'one [rikreat'tsjone] *sf* recreation, entertainment; (*Ins*) break

ri'credersi /29/ *vpr* to change one's mind

ricupe'rare /72/ *vt* (*rientrare in possesso di*) to recover, get back; (*tempo perduto*) to make up for; (*Naut*) to salvage; (: *naufraghi*) to rescue; (*delinquente*) to rehabilitate; **~ lo svantaggio** (*Sport*) to close the gap

ridacchi'are [ridak'kjare] /19/ *vi* to snigger

ri'dare /33/ *vt* to return, give back

'ridere /89/ *vi* to laugh; (*deridere, beffare*): **~ di** to laugh at, make fun of

ri'dicolo, -a *ag* ridiculous, absurd

ridimensio'nare /72/ *vt* to reorganize; (*fig*) to see in the right perspective

ri'dire /38/ *vt* to repeat; (*criticare*) to find fault with; to object to; **trova sempre qualcosa da ~** he always manages to find fault

ridon'dante *ag* redundant

ri'dotto, -a *pp di* **ridurre** ▷ *ag* (*biglietto*) reduced; (*formato*) small

ri'duco *ecc vb vedi* **ridurre**

ri'durre /90/ *vt* (*anche Chim, Mat*) to reduce; (*prezzo, spese*) to cut, reduce; (*accorciare: opera letteraria*) to abridge; (: *Radio, TV*) to adapt; **ridursi** *vpr* (*diminuirsi*) to be reduced, shrink; **ridursi a** to be reduced to; **ridursi a pelle e ossa** to be reduced to skin and bone; **ri'dussi** *ecc vb vedi* **ridurre**; **ridut'tore** *sm* (*Tecn, Chim*) reducer; (*Elettr*) adaptor; **riduzi'one** *sf* reduction; abridgement; adaptation

ri'ebbi *ecc vb vedi* **riavere**

riem'pire /91/ *vt* to fill (up); (*modulo*) to fill in *o* out; **riempirsi** *vpr* to fill (up); **~ qc di** to fill sth (up) with

rien'tranza [rien'trantsa] *sf* recess; indentation

rien'trare /72/ *vi* (*entrare di nuovo*) to go (*o* come) back in; (*tornare*) to return; (*fare una rientranza*) to go in, curve inwards; to be indented; (*riguardare*): **~ in** to be included among, form part of

riepilo'gare /80/ *vt* to summarize ▷ *vi* to recapitulate

ri'esco *ecc vb vedi* **riuscire**

ri'fare /53/ *vt* to do again; (*ricostruire*) to make again; (*nodo*) to tie again, do up again; (*imitare*) to imitate, copy; **rifarsi** *vpr* (*risarcirsi*): **rifarsi di** to make up for; (*vendicarsi*): **rifarsi di qc su qn** to get one's own back on sb for sth; (*riferirsi*): **rifarsi a** to go back to; to follow; **~ il letto** to make the bed; **rifarsi una vita** to make a new life for o.s.

riferi'mento *sm* reference; **in** *o* **con ~ a** with reference to

rife'rire /55/ *vt* (*riportare*) to report ▷ *vi* to do a report; **riferirsi** *vpr*: **riferirsi a** to refer to

rifi'nire /55/ *vt* to finish off, put the finishing touches to

rifiu'tare /72/ vt to refuse; ~ **di fare** to refuse to do; **rifi'uto** sm refusal; **rifiuti** smpl (spazzatura) rubbish sg, refuse sg

riflessi'one sf (Fisica, meditazione) reflection; (il pensare) thought, reflection; (osservazione) remark

rifles'sivo, -a ag (persona) thoughtful, reflective; (Ling) reflexive

ri'flesso, -a pp di **riflettere** ▷ sm (di luce, allo specchio) reflection; (Fisiol) reflex; **di** o **per ~** indirectly

riflessolo'gia [riflessolo'dʒia] sf: reflexology

ri'flettere /92/ vt to reflect ▷ vi to think; **riflettersi** vpr to be reflected; ~ **su** to think over

riflet'tore sm reflector; (proiettore) floodlight; (Mil) searchlight

ri'flusso sm flowing back; (della marea) ebb; **un'epoca di ~** an era of nostalgia

ri'forma sf reform; **la R~** (Rel) the Reformation

riforma'torio sm (Dir) community home (BRIT), reformatory (US)

riforni'mento sm supplying, providing; restocking; (di carburante) refuelling; **rifornimenti** smpl (provviste) supplies, provisions

rifor'nire /55/ vt (fornire di nuovo: casa ecc) to restock; (provvedere): ~ **di** to supply o provide with; **rifornirsi** vpr: **rifornirsi di qc** to stock up on sth

rifugi'arsi [rifu'dʒarsi] /62/ vpr to take refuge; **rifugi'ato, -a** sm/f refugee

ri'fugio [ri'fudʒo] sm refuge, shelter; (in montagna) shelter; ~ **antiaereo** air-raid shelter

'riga, -ghe sf line; (striscia) stripe; (di persone, cose) line, row; (regolo) ruler; (scriminatura) parting; **mettersi in ~** to line up; **a righe** (foglio) lined; (vestito) striped

ri'gare /80/ vt (foglio) to rule ▷ vi: ~ **diritto** (fig) to toe the line

rigatti'ere sm junk dealer

ri'ghello [ri'gello] sm ruler

righerò ecc [rige'rɔ] vb vedi **rigare**

'rigido, -a ['ridʒido] ag rigid, stiff; (membra ecc, indurite) stiff; (Meteor) harsh, severe; (fig) strict

rigogli'oso, -a [rigoʎ'ʎoso] ag (pianta) luxuriant; (fig: commercio, sviluppo) thriving

ri'gore sm (Meteor) harshness, rigours pl; (fig) severity, strictness; (anche: **calcio di ~**) penalty; **di ~** compulsory; **a rigor di termini** strictly speaking

riguar'dare /72/ vt to look at again; (considerare) to regard; (concernere) to regard, concern; **riguardarsi** vpr (aver cura di sé) to look after o.s.

rigu'ardo sm (attenzione) care; (considerazione) regard, respect; ~ **a** concerning, with regard to; **non aver riguardi nell'agire/nel parlare** to act/ speak freely

rilasci'are [rilaʃ'ʃare] /14/ vt (rimettere in libertà) to release; (Amm: documenti) to issue

rilas'sare /72/ vt to relax; **rilassarsi** vpr to relax; (fig: disciplina) to become slack

rile'gare /80/ vt (libro) to bind

ri'leggere [ri'leddʒere] /61/ vt to reread, read again; (rivedere) to read over

ri'lento: a ~ av slowly

rile'vante ag considerable; important

rile'vare /72/ vt (ricavare) to find; (notare) to notice; (mettere in evidenza) to point out; (venire a conoscere: notizia) to learn; (raccogliere: dati) to gather, collect; (Topografia) to survey; (Mil) to relieve; (Comm) to take over

rili'evo sm (Arte, Geo) relief; (fig: rilevanza) importance; (osservazione) point, remark; (Topografia) survey; **dar ~ a** o **mettere in ~ qc** (fig) to bring sth out, highlight sth

rilut'tante ag reluctant

'rima sf rhyme; (verso) verse; **far ~ con** to rhyme with; **rispondere a qn per le rime** to give sb tit for tat

riman'dare /72/ vt to send again; (restituire, rinviare) to send back, return; ~ **qc (a)** (differire) to postpone sth o put sth off (till); ~ **qn a** (fare riferimento) to refer sb to; **essere rimandato** (Ins) to have to resit one's exams

ri'mando sm (rinvio) return; (dilazione) postponement; (riferimento) cross-reference

rima'nente ag remaining ▷ sm rest, remainder; **i rimanenti** (persone) the rest of them, the others

rima'nere /93/ vi (restare) to remain, stay; (avanzare) to be left, remain; (restare stupito) to be amazed; **rimangono poche settimane a Pasqua** there are only a few weeks left till Easter; ~ **vedovo** to be left a widower; ~ **confuso/sorpreso** to be confused/surprised; **rimane da vedere se** it remains to be seen whether

rimangi'are [riman'dʒare] /62/ vt to eat again; **rimangiarsi la parola/una promessa** (fig) to go back on one's word/ one's promise

ri'mango ecc vb vedi **rimanere**

rimargi'nare [rimardʒi'nare] /72/ vt, vi: **rimarginarsi** vpr to heal

rimbal'zare [rimbal'tsare] /72/ vi to bounce back, rebound; (proiettile) to ricochet

rimbam'bito, -a ag senile, in one's dotage

rimboc'care /20/ vt (*coperta*) to tuck in; (*maniche, pantaloni*) to turn o roll up

rimbom'bare /72/ vi to resound

rimbor'sare /72/ vt to pay back, repay

rimedi'are /19/ vi: ~ a to remedy ▷ vt (*fam: procurarsi*) to get o scrape together

ri'medio sm (*medicina*) medicine; (*cura, fig*) remedy, cure

ri'mettere /63/ vt (*mettere di nuovo*) to put back; (*Comm: merci*) to deliver; (: *denaro*) to remit; (*vomitare*) to bring up; (*perdere: anche:* **rimetterci**) to lose; (*indossare di nuovo*): ~ **qc** to put sth back on, put sth on again; (*affidare*) to entrust; (*decisione*) to refer; (*condonare*) to remit; **rimettersi al bello** (*tempo*) to clear up; **rimettersi in salute** to get better, recover one's health

ri'misi ecc vb vedi **rimettere**

'rimmel® sm inv mascara

rimoder'nare /72/ vt to modernize

rimorchi'are [rimor'kjare] /19/ vt to tow; (*fig: ragazza*) to pick up

ri'morchio [ri'mɔrkjo] sm tow; (*veicolo*) trailer

ri'morso sm remorse

rimozi'one [rimot'tsjone] sf removal; (*da un impiego*) dismissal; (*Psic*) repression

rimpatri'are /19/ vi to return home ▷ vt to repatriate

rimpi'angere [rim'pjandʒere] /75/ vt to regret; (*persona*) to miss; **rimpi'anto, -a** pp di **rimpiangere** ▷ sm regret

rimpiaz'zare [rimpjat'tsare] /72/ vt to replace

rimpiccio'lire [rimpittʃo'lire] /55/ vt to make smaller ▷ vi (*anche:* **rimpicciolirsi**) to become smaller

rimpin'zare [rimpin'tsare] /72/ vt: ~ **di** to cram o stuff with; **rimpinzarsi** vpr: **rimpinzarsi (di qc)** to stuff o.s. (with sth)

rimprove'rare /72/ vt to rebuke, reprimand

rimu'overe /66/ vt to remove; (*destituire*) to dismiss

Rinasci'mento [rinaʃʃi'mento] sm: **il ~ the** Renaissance

ri'nascita [ri'naʃʃita] sf rebirth, revival

rinca'rare /72/ vt to increase the price of ▷ vi to go up, become more expensive

rinca'sare /72/ vi to go home

rinchi'udere [rin'kjudere] /22/ vt to shut (o lock) up; **rinchiudersi** vpr: **rinchiudersi in** to shut o.s. up in; **rinchiudersi in se stesso** to withdraw into o.s.

rin'correre /28/ vt to chase, run after

rin'corso, -a pp di **rincorrere** ▷ sf short run

rin'crescere [rin'kreʃʃere] /30/ vb impers: **mi rincresce che/di non poter fare** I'm sorry that/I can't do, I regret that/being unable to do

rinfacci'are [rinfat'tʃare] /14/ vt (*fig*): ~ **qc a qn** to throw sth in sb's face

rinfor'zare [rinfor'tsare] /72/ vt to reinforce, strengthen ▷ vi (*anche:* **rinforzarsi**) to grow stronger

rinfres'care /20/ vt (*atmosfera, temperatura*) to cool (down); (*abito, pareti*) to freshen up ▷ vi (*tempo*) to grow cooler; **rinfrescarsi** vpr (*ristorarsi*) to refresh o.s.; (*lavarsi*) to freshen up; **rin'fresco, -schi** sm (*festa*) party; **rinfreschi** smpl refreshments

rin'fusa sf: **alla ~** in confusion, higgledy-piggledy

ringhi'are [rin'gjare] /19/ vi to growl, snarl

ringhi'era [rin'gjɛra] sf railing; (*delle scale*) banister(s)

ringiova'nire [rindʒova'nire] /55/ vt: ~ **qn** (*vestito, acconciatura ecc*) to make sb look younger; (*vacanze ecc*) to rejuvenate sb ▷ vi (*anche:* **ringiovanirsi**) to become (o look) younger

ringrazia'mento [ringrattsja'mento] sm thanks pl

ringrazi'are [ringrat'tsjare] /19/ vt to thank; ~ **qn di qc** to thank sb for sth

rinne'gare /80/ vt (*fede*) to renounce; (*figlio*) to disown, repudiate

rinno'vabile ag (*contratto, energia*) renewable

rinnova'mento sm renewal; (*economico*) revival

rinno'vare /72/ vt to renew; (*ripetere*) to repeat, renew

rinoce'ronte [rinotʃe'ronte] sm rhinoceros

rino'mato, -a ag renowned, celebrated

rintracci'are [rintrat'tʃare] /14/ vt to track down

rintro'nare /72/ vi to boom, roar ▷ vt (*assordare*) to deafen; (*stordire*) to stun

rinunci'are [rinun'tʃare] /14/ vi: ~ **a** to give up, renounce; ~ **a fare qc** to give up doing sth

rinvi'are /60/ vt (*rimandare indietro*) to send back, return; ~ **qc (a)** (*differire*) to postpone sth o put sth off (till); (*seduta*) to adjourn sth (till); ~ **qn a** (*fare un rimando*) to refer sb to

rin'vio, -'vii sm (*rimando*) return; (*differimento*) postponement; (: *di seduta*) adjournment; (*in un testo*) cross-reference; ~ **a giudizio** (*Dir*) indictment

riò ecc vb vedi **riavere**

ri'one sm district, quarter

riordi'nare /72/ vt (*rimettere in ordine*) to tidy; (*riorganizzare*) to reorganize

riorganiz'zare [riorganid'dzare] /72/ vt to reorganize

ripa'gare /80/ vt to repay

ripa'rare /72/ vt (*proteggere*) to protect, defend; (*correggere: male, torto*) to make up for; (: *errore*) to put right; (*aggiustare*) to repair ▷ *vi* (*mettere rimedio*): **~ a** to make up for; **ripararsi** *vpr* (*rifugiarsi*) to take refuge *o* shelter; **riparazi'one** *sf* (*di un torto*) reparation; (*di guasto, scarpe*) repairing *no pl*; repair; (*risarcimento*) compensation

ri'paro *sm* (*protezione*) shelter, protection; (*rimedio*) remedy

ripar'tire /45/ *vt* (*dividere*) to divide up; (*distribuire*) to share out ▷ *vi* to set off again; to leave again

ripas'sare /72/ *vi* to come (*o* go) back ▷ *vt* (*scritto, lezione*) to go over (again)

ripen'sare /72/ *vi* to think; (*cambiare idea*) to change one's mind; (*tornare col pensiero*): **~ a** to recall

ripercu'otersi /106/ *vpr*: **~ su** (*fig*) to have repercussions on

ripercussi'one *sf* (*fig*): **avere una ~** *o* **delle ripercussioni su** to have repercussions on

ripes'care /20/ *vt* (*pesce*) to catch again; (*persona, cosa*) to fish out; (*fig*: *ritrovare*) to dig out

ri'petere /1/ *vt* to repeat; (*ripassare*) to go over; **ripetizi'one** *sf* repetition; (*di lezione*) revision; **ripetizioni** *sfpl* (*Ins*) private tutoring *o* coaching *sg*

ripi'ano *sm* (*di mobile*) shelf

ri'picca *sf*: **per ~** out of spite

'ripido, -a *ag* steep

ripie'gare /80/ *vt* to refold; (*piegare più volte*) to fold (up) ▷ *vi* (*Mil*) to retreat, fall back; (*fig*: *accontentarsi*): **~ su** to make do with

ripi'eno, -a *ag* full; (*Cuc*) stuffed; (: *panino*) filled ▷ *sm* (*Cuc*) stuffing

ri'pone *vb vedi* **riporre**

ri'pongo *ecc vb vedi* **riporre**

ri'porre /77/ *vt* (*porre al suo posto*) to put back, replace; (*mettere via*) to put away; (*fiducia, speranza*): **~ qc in qn** to place *o* put sth in sb

ripor'tare /72/ *vt* (*portare indietro*) to bring (*o* take) back; (*riferire*) to report; (*citare*) to quote; (*vittoria*) to gain; (*successo*) to have; (*Mat*) to carry; **riportarsi** *vpr*: **riportarsi a** (*anche fig*) to go back to; (*riferirsi a*) to refer to; **~ danni** to suffer damage

ripo'sare /72/ *vt* to rest ▷ *vi* to rest; **riposarsi** *vpr* to rest

ri'posi *ecc vb vedi* **riporre**

ri'poso *sm* rest; (*Mil*): **~!** at ease!; **a ~** (*in pensione*) retired; **giorno di ~** day off

ripos'tiglio [ripos'tiλλo] *sm* lumber room

ri'prendere /81/ *vt* (*prigioniero, fortezza*) to recapture; (*prendere indietro*) to take back; (*ricominciare*: *lavoro*) to resume; (*andare a prendere*) to fetch, come back for; (*assumere di nuovo*: *impiegati*) to take on again, re-employ; (*rimproverare*) to tell off; (*restringere*: *abito*) to take in; (*Cine*) to shoot; **riprendersi** *vpr* to recover; (*correggersi*) to correct o.s.

ri'preso, -a *pp di* **riprendere** ▷ *sf* recapture; resumption; (*economica, da malattia, emozione*) recovery; (*Aut*) acceleration *no pl*; (*Teat, Cine*) rerun; (*Cine*: *presa*) shooting *no pl*; shot; (*Sport*) second half; (*Pugilato*) round; **a più riprese** on several occasions, several times; **ripresa cinematografica** shot

ripristi'nare /72/ *vt* to restore

ripro'durre /90/ *vt* to reproduce; **riprodursi** *vpr* (*Biol*) to reproduce; (*riformarsi*) to form again

ripro'vare /72/ *vt* (*provare di nuovo*: *gen*) to try again; (: *vestito*) to try on again; (: *sensazione*) to experience again ▷ *vi* (*tentare*): **~ (a fare qc)** to try (to do sth) again; **riproverò più tardi** I'll try again later

ripudi'are /19/ *vt* to repudiate, disown

ripu'gnante [ripuɲ'ɲante] *ag* disgusting, repulsive

ri'quadro *sm* square; (*Archit*) panel

ri'saia *sf* paddy field

risa'lire /98/ *vi* (*ritornare in su*) to go back up; **~ a** (*ritornare con la mente*) to go back to; (*datare da*) to date back to, go back to

risal'tare /72/ *vi* (*fig*: *distinguersi*) to stand out; (*Archit*) to project, jut out

risa'puto, -a *ag*: **è ~ che ...** everyone knows that ..., it's common knowledge that ...

risarci'mento [risartʃi'mento] *sm*: **~ (di)** compensation (for); **aver diritto al ~ dei danni** to be entitled to damages

risar'cire [risar'tʃire] /55/ *vt* (*cose*) to pay compensation for; (*persona*): **~ qn di qc** to compensate sb for sth

ri'sata *sf* laugh

riscalda'mento *sm* heating; **~ centrale** central heating

riscal'dare /72/ *vt* (*scaldare*) to heat; (: *mani, persona*) to warm; (*minestra*) to reheat; **riscaldarsi** *vpr* to warm up

ris'catto *sm* ransom; redemption

rischia'rare [riskja'rare] /72/ *vt* (*illuminare*) to light up; (*colore*) to make lighter; **rischiararsi** *vpr* (*tempo*) to clear up; (*cielo*) to clear; (*fig*: *volto*) to brighten up; **rischiararsi la voce** to clear one's throat

rischi'are [ris'kjare] /19/ *vt* to risk ▷ *vi*: **~ di fare qc** to run the risk of doing sth

'rischio ['riskjo] *sm* risk; **rischi'oso, -a** *ag* risky, dangerous

risciac'quare /72/ *vt* to rinse

riscon'trare /72/ *vt* (*rilevare*) to find

riscri'vibile *ag* (*CD, DVD*) rewritable

riscu'otere /106/ *vt* (*ritirare una somma dovuta*) to collect; (: *stipendio*) to draw, collect; (*assegno*) to cash; (*fig: successo ecc*) to win, earn

'**rise** *ecc vb vedi* **ridere**

risenti'mento *sm* resentment

risen'tire /45/ *vt* to hear again; (*provare*) to feel ▷ *vi*: ~ **di** to feel (*o show*) the effects of; **risentirsi** *vpr*: **risentirsi di** *o* **per** to take offence (BRIT) *o* offense (US) at, resent; **risen'tito, -a** *ag* resentful

ri'serbo *sm* reserve

ri'serva *sf* reserve; (*di caccia, pesca*) preserve; (*restrizione, di indigeni*) reservation; **tenere di** ~ to keep in reserve

riser'vare /72/ *vt* (*tenere in serbo*) to keep, put aside; (*prenotare*) to book, reserve; **riser'vato, -a** *ag* (*prenotato: fig: persona*) reserved; (*confidenziale*) confidential

'**risi** *ecc vb vedi* **ridere**

risi'edere /29/ *vi*: ~ **a** *o* **in** to reside in

'risma *sf* (*di carta*) ream; (*fig*) kind, sort

'riso¹, -a *pp di* **ridere** ▷ *sm* (*il ridere*): **un** ~ a laugh; **il** ~ laughter

'riso² *sm* (*pianta*) rice

riso'lino *sm* snigger

ri'solsi *ecc vb vedi* **risolvere**

ri'solto, -a *pp di* **risolvere**

riso'luto, -a *ag* determined, resolute

risoluzi'one [risolut'tsjone] *sf* solving *no pl*; (*Mat*) solution; (*decisione, di schermo, immagine*) resolution

ri'solvere /94/ *vt* (*difficoltà, controversia*) to resolve; (*problema*) to solve; (*decidere*): ~ **di fare** to resolve to do; **risolversi** *vpr* (*decidersi*): **risolversi a fare** to make up one's mind to do; (*andare a finire*): **risolversi in** to end up, turn out; **risolversi in nulla** to come to nothing

riso'nanza [riso'nantsa] *sf* resonance; **aver vasta** ~ (*fig: fatto ecc*) to be known far and wide

ri'sorgere [ri'sordʒere] /109/ *vi* to rise again; **risorgi'mento** *sm* revival; **il Risorgimento** (*Storia*) the Risorgimento

RISORGIMENTO

- The *Risorgimento*, the period stretching
- from the early nineteenth century to 1861
- and the proclamation of the Kingdom
- of Italy, saw considerable upheaval and
- change. Political and personal freedom
- took on new importance as the events
- of the French Revolution unfolded.
- The *Risorgimento* paved the way for the
- unification of Italy in 1871.

ri'sorsa *sf* expedient, resort; **risorse umane** human resources

ri'sorsi *ecc vb vedi* **risorgere**

ri'sotto *sm* (*Cuc*) risotto

risparmi'are /19/ *vt* to save; (*non uccidere*) to spare ▷ *vi* to save; ~ **qc a qn** to spare sb sth

ris'parmio *sm* saving *no pl*; (*denaro*) savings *pl*; **risparmi** *smpl* (*denaro*) savings

rispecchi'are [rispek'kjare] /19/ *vt* to reflect

rispet'tabile *ag* respectable

rispet'tare /72/ *vt* to respect; **farsi** ~ to command respect

rispet'tivo, -a *ag* respective

ris'petto *sm* respect; **rispetti** *smpl* (*saluti*) respects, regards; ~ **a** (*in paragone a*) compared to; (*in relazione a*) as regards, as for

ris'pondere /95/ *vi* to answer, reply; (*freni*) to respond; ~ **a** (*domanda*) to answer, reply to; (*persona*) to answer; (*invito*) to reply to; (*provocazione, veicolo, apparecchio*) to respond to; (*corrispondere a*) to correspond to; (*speranze, bisogno*) to answer; ~ **a qn di qc** (*essere responsabile*) to be answerable to sb for sth

ris'posto, -a *pp di* **rispondere** ▷ *sf* answer, reply; **in risposta a** in reply to

'rissa *sf* brawl

ris'tampa *sf* reprinting *no pl*; reprint

risto'rante *sm* restaurant

ris'tretto, -a *pp di* **restringere** ▷ *ag* (*racchiuso*) enclosed, hemmed in; (*angusto*) narrow; (*Cuc: brodo*) thick; (: *caffè*) extra strong; ~ **(a)** (*limitato*) restricted *o* limited (to)

ristruttu'rare /72/ *vt* (*azienda*) to reorganize; (*edificio*) to restore; (*appartamento*) to alter; (*crema, balsamo*) to repair

risucchi'are [risuk'kjare] /19/ *vt* to suck in

risul'tare /72/ *vi* (*dimostrarsi*) to prove (to be), turn out (to be); (*riuscire*): ~ **vincitore** to emerge as the winner; ~ **da** (*provenire*) to result from, be the result of; **mi risulta che …** I understand that …; **non mi risulta** not as far as I know; **risul'tato** *sm* result

risuo'nare /72/ *vi* (*rimbombare*) to resound

risurrezi'one [risurret'tsjone] *sf* (*Rel*) resurrection

risusci'tare [risuʃʃi'tare] /72/ *vt* to resuscitate, restore to life; (*fig*) to revive, bring back ▷ *vi* to rise (from the dead)

ris'veglio [riz've??o] *sm* waking up; (*fig*) revival

ris'volto *sm* (*di giacca*) lapel; (*di pantaloni*) turn-up; (*di manica*) cuff; (*di tasca*) flap; (*di libro*) inside flap; (*fig*) implication

ritagli'are [rita??'?are] /27/ *vt* (*tagliar via*) to cut out

ritar'dare /72/ *vi* (*persona, treno*) to be late;

(orologio) to be slow ▷ *vt (rallentare)* to slow down; *(impedire)* to delay, hold up; *(differire)* to postpone, delay

ri'tardo *sm* delay; *(di persona aspettata)* lateness *no pl*; *(fig: mentale)* learning difficulty; **in ~** late

ri'tegno [ri'teɲɲo] *sm* restraint

rite'nere /121/ *vt (trattenere)* to hold back; *(: somma)* to deduct; *(giudicare)* to consider, believe

ri'tengo *vb vedi* **ritenere**

ri'tenni *ecc vb vedi* **ritenere**

riterrò *ecc vb vedi* **ritenere**

ritiene *ecc vb vedi* **ritenere**

riti'rare /72/ *vt* to withdraw; *(Pol: richiamare)* to recall; *(andare a prendere: pacco ecc)* to collect, pick up; **ritirarsi** *vpr* to withdraw; *(da un'attività)* to retire; *(stoffa)* to shrink; *(marea)* to recede

'ritmo *sm* rhythm; *(fig)* rate; *(: della vita)* pace, tempo

'rito *sm* rite; **di ~** usual, customary

ritoc'care /20/ *vt (disegno, fotografia)* to touch up; *(testo)* to alter

ritor'nare /72/ *vi* to return, go *(o come)* back, get back; *(ripresentarsi)* to recur; *(ridiventare)*: **~ ricco** to become rich again ▷ *vt (restituire)* to return, give back

ritor'nello *sm* refrain

ri'torno *sm* return; **essere di ~** to be back; **avere un ~ di fiamma** *(Aut)* to backfire; *(fig: persona)* to be back in love again

ri'trarre /123/ *vt (trarre indietro, via)* to withdraw; *(distogliere: sguardo)* to turn away; *(rappresentare)* to portray, depict; *(ricavare)* to get, obtain

ritrat'tare /72/ *vt (disdire)* to retract, take back; *(trattare nuovamente)* to deal with again

ri'tratto, -a *pp di* **ritrarre** ▷ *sm* portrait

ritro'vare /72/ *vt* to find; *(salute)* to regain; *(persona)* to find; to meet again; **ritrovarsi** *vpr (essere, capitare)* to find o.s.; *(raccapezzarsi)* to find one's way; *(con senso reciproco)* to meet (again)

'ritto, -a *ag (in piedi)* standing, on one's feet; *(levato in alto)* erect, raised; *(: capelli)* standing on end; *(posto verticalmente)* upright

ritu'ale *ag, sm* ritual

riuni'one *sf (adunanza)* meeting; *(riconciliazione)* reunion

riu'nire /55/ *vt (ricongiungere)* to join (together); *(riconciliare)* to reunite, bring together (again); **riunirsi** *vpr (adunarsi)* to meet; *(tornare a stare insieme)* to be reunited

riu'scire [riuʃˈʃire] /125/ *vi (uscire di nuovo)* to go out again, go back out; *(aver esito: fatti, azioni)* to go, turn out; *(aver successo)*

to succeed, be successful; *(essere, apparire)* to be, prove; *(raggiungere il fine)* to manage, succeed; **~ a fare qc** to manage *o* be able to do sth

'riva *sf (di fiume)* bank; *(di lago, mare)* shore

ri'vale *smf* rival; **rivalità** *sf* rivalry

rivalu'tare /72/ *vt (Econ)* to revalue

rive'dere /127/ *vt* to see again; *(ripassare)* to revise; *(verificare)* to check

rivedrò *ecc vb vedi* **rivedere**

rive'lare /72/ *vt* to reveal; *(divulgare)* to reveal, disclose; *(dare indizio)* to reveal, show; **rivelarsi** *vpr (manifestarsi)* to be revealed; **rivelarsi onesto** *ecc* to prove to be honest *etc*; **rivelazi'one** *sf* revelation

rivendi'care /20/ *vt* to claim, demand

rivendi'tore, -'trice *smf* retailer; **~ autorizzato** *(Comm)* authorized dealer

ri'verbero *sm (di luce, calore)* reflection; *(di suono)* reverberation

rivesti'mento *sm* covering; coating

rives'tire /45/ *vt* to dress again; *(ricoprire)* to cover; *(con vernice)* to coat; *(fig: carica)* to hold

ri'vidi *ecc vb vedi* **rivedere**

ri'vincita [ri'vintʃita] *sf (Sport)* return match; *(fig)* revenge

ri'vista *sf* review; *(periodico)* magazine, review; *(Teat)* revue; variety show

ri'volgere [ri'voldʒere] /96/ *vt (attenzione, sguardo)* to turn, direct; *(parole)* to address; **rivolgersi** *vpr* to turn round; **rivolgersi a** *(fig: dirigersi per informazioni)* to go and see, go and speak to; *(ufficio)* to enquire at

ri'volsi *ecc vb vedi* **rivolgere**

ri'volta *sf* revolt, rebellion

rivol'tella *sf* revolver

rivoluzio'nare [rivoluttsjoˈnare] /72/ *vt* to revolutionize

rivoluzio'nario, -a [rivoluttsjoˈnarjo] *ag, sm/f* revolutionary

rivoluzi'one [rivolutˈtsjone] *sf* revolution

riz'zare [ritˈtsare] /72/ *vt* to raise, erect; **rizzarsi** *vpr* to stand up; *(capelli)* to stand on end

'roba *sf* stuff, things *pl*; *(possessi, beni)* belongings *pl*, things *pl*, possessions *pl*; **~ da mangiare** things to eat, food; **~ da matti!** it's sheer madness *o* lunacy!

'robot *sm inv* robot

ro'busto, -a *ag* robust, sturdy; *(solido: catena)* strong

roc'chetto [rokˈketto] *sm* reel, spool

'roccia, -ce ['rottʃa] *sf* rock; **fare ~** *(Sport)* to go rock climbing

'roco, -a, -chi, -che *ag* hoarse

ro'daggio [roˈdaddʒo] *sm* running *(BRIT) o* breaking *(US)* in; **in ~** running *o* breaking in

rodi'tore *sm (Zool)* rodent

rodo'dendro sm rhododendron

ro'gnone [roɲ'ɲone] sm (Cuc) kidney

'rogo, -ghi sm (per cadaveri) (funeral) pyre; (supplizio): **il ~** the stake

rol'lio sm roll(ing)

'Roma sf Rome

Roma'nia sf: **la ~** Romania

ro'manico, -a, -ci, -che ag Romanesque

ro'mano, -a ag, sm/f Roman

ro'mantico, -a, -ci, -che ag romantic

romanzi'ere [roman'dzjɛre] sm novelist

ro'manzo, -a [ro'mandzo] ag (Ling) romance cpd ▷ sm novel; **~ d'appendice** serial (story); **~ poliziesco, ~ giallo** detective story; **~ rosa** romantic novel

'rombo sm rumble, thunder, roar; (Mat) rhombus; (Zool) turbot; brill

'rompere /97/ vt to break; (conversazione, fidanzamento) to break off ▷ vi to break; **rompersi** vpr to break; **mi rompe le scatole** (fam) he (o she) is a pain in the neck; **rompersi un braccio** to break an arm; **rompis'catole** smf inv (fam) pest, pain in the neck

'rondine sf (Zool) swallow

ron'zare [ron'dzare] /72/ vi to buzz, hum

ron'zio, -ii [ron'dzio] sm buzzing

'rosa sf rose ▷ ag inv, sm pink; **ro'sato, -a** ag pink, rosy ▷ sm (vino) rosé (wine)

rosicchi'are [rosik'kjare] /19/ vt to gnaw (at); (mangiucchiare) to nibble (at)

rosma'rino sm rosemary

roso'lare /72/ vt (Cuc) to brown

roso'lia sf (Med) German measles sg, rubella

ro'sone sm rosette; (vetrata) rose window

'rospo sm (Zool) toad

ros'setto sm (per labbra) lipstick

'rosso, -a ag, sm, sm/f red; **il mar R~** the Red Sea; **~ d'uovo** egg yolk

rosticce'ria [rostittʃe'ria] sf shop selling roast meat and other cooked food

ro'taia sf rut, track; (Ferr) rail

ro'tella sf small wheel; (di mobile) castor

roto'lare /72/ vt, vi to roll; **rotolarsi** vpr to roll (about)

'rotolo sm roll; **andare a rotoli** (fig) to go to rack and ruin

ro'tondo, -a ag round

'rotta sf (Aer, Naut) course, route; (Mil) rout; **a ~ di collo** at breakneck speed; **essere in ~ con qn** to be on bad terms with sb

rotta'mare /72/ vt to scrap old vehicles in return for incentives

rottama'zione [rottamat'tsjone] sf (come incentivo) the scrapping of old vehicles in return for incentives

rot'tame sm fragment, scrap, broken bit; **rottami** smpl (di nave aereo ecc) wreckage sg

'rotto, -a pp di **rompere** ▷ ag broken; (calzoni) torn, split ▷ sm: **per il ~ della cuffia** by the skin of one's teeth

rot'tura sf breaking no pl; break; (di rapporti) breaking off; (Med) fracture, break

rou'lotte [ru'lɔt] sf inv caravan

ro'vente ag red-hot

'rovere sm oak

ro'vescia [ro'veʃʃa] sf: **alla ~** upside-down; inside-out; **oggi mi va tutto alla ~** everything is going wrong (for me) today

rovesci'are [roveʃʃare] /14/ vt (versare in giù) to pour; (: accidentalmente) to spill; (capovolgere) to turn upside down; (gettare a terra) to knock down; (fig: governo) to overthrow; (piegare all'indietro: testa) to throw back; **rovesciarsi** vpr (sedia, macchina) to overturn; (barca) to capsize; (liquido) to spill; (fig: situazione) to be reversed

ro'vescio [ro'veʃʃo] sm other side, wrong side; (della mano) back; (di moneta) reverse; (pioggia) sudden downpour; (fig) setback; (Maglia: anche: **punto ~**) purl (stitch); (Tennis) backhand (stroke); **a ~** upside-down; inside-out; **(con l'esterno all'interno)** to misunderstand sth

ro'vina sf ruin; **rovine** sfpl (ruderi) ruins; **andare in ~** (andare a pezzi) to collapse; (fig) to go to rack and ruin; **mandare qc/qn in ~** to ruin sth/sb

rovi'nare /72/ vi to collapse, fall down ▷ vt (danneggiare: fig) to ruin; **rovinarsi** vpr (persona) to ruin o.s.; (oggetto, vestito) to be ruined

rovis'tare /72/ vt (casa) to ransack; (tasche) to rummage in (o through)

'rovo sm (Bot) blackberry o bramble bush

'rozzo, -a ['roddzo] ag rough, coarse

ru'bare /72/ vt to steal; **~ qc a qn** to steal sth from sb

rubi'netto sm tap, faucet (us)

ru'bino sm ruby

ru'brica, -che sf (di giornale) column; (quadernetto) index book; address book; **~ d'indirizzi** address book; **~ telefonica** list of telephone numbers

'rudere sm (rovina) ruins pl

rudimen'tale ag rudimentary, basic

rudi'menti smpl rudiments; basic principles; basic knowledge sg

ruffi'ano sm pimp

'ruga, -ghe sf wrinkle

'ruggine ['ruddʒine] sf rust

rug'gire [rud'dʒire] /55/ vi to roar

rugi'ada [ru'dʒada] sf dew

ru'goso, -a ag wrinkled

rul'lino sm (Fot) (roll of) film, spool

'rullo *sm* (*di tamburi*) roll; (*arnese cilindrico*, *Tip*) roller; **~ compressore** steam roller; **~ di pellicola** roll of film

rum *sm* rum

ru'meno, -a *ag*, *sm/f*, *sm* Romanian

rumi'nare /72/ *vt* (*Zool*) to ruminate

ru'more *sm*: **un ~** a noise, a sound; **il ~** noise; **rumo'roso, -a** *ag* noisy

> ![!] Attenzione! In inglese esiste la parola *rumour*, che però significa *voce* nel senso *diceria*.

ru'olo *sm* (*Teat*, *fig*) role, part; (*elenco*) roll, register, list; **di ~** permanent, on the permanent staff

ru'ota *sf* wheel; **~ anteriore/posteriore** front/back wheel; **~ di scorta** spare wheel

ruo'tare /72/ *vt*, *vi* to rotate

'rupe *sf* cliff

'ruppi *ecc* *vb vedi* **rompere**

ru'rale *ag* rural, country *cpd*

ru'scello [ruʃʃɛllo] *sm* stream

'ruspa *sf* excavator

rus'sare /72/ *vi* to snore

'Russia *sf*: **la ~** Russia; **'russo, -a** *ag*, *sm/f*, *sm* Russian

'rustico, -a, -ci, -che *ag* rustic; (*fig*) rough, unrefined

rut'tare /72/ *vi* to belch; **'rutto** *sm* belch

'ruvido, -a *ag* rough, coarse

S

S. *abbr* (= *sud*) S; (= *santo*) St

sa *vb vedi* **sapere**

'sabato *sm* Saturday; **di** *o* **il ~** on Saturdays

'sabbia *sf* sand; **sabbie mobili** quicksand(s *pl*); **sabbi'oso, -a** *ag* sandy

'sacca, -che *sf* bag; (*bisaccia*) haversack; **~ da viaggio** travelling bag

sacca'rina *sf* saccharin(e)

saccheggi'are [sakked'dʒare] /62/ *vt* to sack, plunder

sac'chetto [sak'ketto] *sm* (small) bag; (small) sack; **~ di carta/di plastica** paper/plastic bag

'sacco, -chi *sm* bag; (*per carbone ecc*) sack; (*Anat*, *Biol*) sac; (*tela*) sacking; (*saccheggio*) sack(ing); (*fig*: *grande quantità*) **un ~ di** lots of, heaps of; **~ a pelo** sleeping bag; **~ per i rifiuti** bin bag

sacer'dote [satʃer'dɔte] *sm* priest

sacrifi'care /20/ *vt* to sacrifice; **sacrificarsi** *vpr* to sacrifice o.s.; (*privarsi di qc*) to make sacrifices

sacri'ficio [sakri'fitʃo] *sm* sacrifice

'sacro, -a *ag* sacred

'sadico, -a, -ci, -che *ag* sadistic ▷ *sm/f* sadist

sa'etta *sf* arrow; (*fulmine*) thunderbolt; flash of lightning

sa'fari *sm inv* safari

sag'gezza [sad'dʒettsa] *sf* wisdom

'saggio, -a, -gi, -ge ['sadd'ʒo] *ag* wise ▷ *sm* (*persona*) sage; (*operazione sperimentale*) test; (*fig*: *prova*) proof; (*campione indicativo*) sample; (*scritto*) essay

Sagit'tario [sadʒit'tarjo] *sm* Sagittarius

'sagoma *sf* (*profilo*) outline, profile; (*forma*) form, shape; (*Tecn*) template; (*bersaglio*) target; (*fig*: *persona*) character

'sagra *sf* festival

sagres'tano *sm* sacristan; sexton

sagres'tia *sf* sacristy

Sa'hara [sa'ara] *sm*: **il (Deserto del)** ~ the Sahara (Desert)

'sai *vb vedi* **sapere**

'sala *sf* hall; (*stanza*) room; (*Cine: di proiezione*) cinema; ~ **d'aspetto** waiting room; ~ **da ballo** ballroom; ~ **per concerti** concert hall; ~ **giochi** amusement arcade; ~ **operatoria** operating theatre (BRIT) o room (US); ~ **da pranzo** dining room

sa'lame *sm* salami *no pl*, salami sausage

sala'moia *sf* (*Cuc*) brine

sa'lato, -a *ag* (*sapore*) salty; (*Cuc*) salted, salt *cpd*; (*fig: prezzi*) steep, stiff

sal'dare /72/ *vt* (*congiungere*) to join, bind; (*parti metalliche*) to solder; (: *con saldatura autogena*) to weld; (*conto*) to settle, pay

'saldo, -a *ag* (*resistente, forte*) strong, firm; (*fermo*) firm, steady, stable; (*fig*) firm, steadfast ▷ *sm* (*svendita*) sale; (*di conto*) settlement; (*Econ*) balance; **saldi** *smpl* (*Comm*) sales; **essere ~ nella propria fede** (*fig*) to stick to one's guns

'sale *sm* salt; **ha poco ~ in zucca** he doesn't have much sense; ~ **grosso** cooking salt; ~ **fino** table salt

'salgo *ecc vb vedi* **salire**

'salice ['salitʃe] *sm* willow; ~ **piangente** weeping willow

sali'ente *ag* (*fig*) salient, main

sali'era *sf* salt cellar

sa'lire /98/ *vi* to go (o come) up; (*aereo ecc*) to climb, go up; (*passeggero*) to get on; (*sentiero, prezzi, livello*) to go up, rise ▷ *vt* (*scale, gradini*) to go (o come) up; ~ **su** to climb (up); ~ **sul treno/sull'autobus** to board the train/the bus; ~ **in macchina** to get into the car; **sa'lita** *sf* climb, ascent; (*erta*) hill, slope; **in salita** *ag, av* uphill

sa'liva *sf* saliva

'salma *sf* corpse

'salmo *sm* psalm

sal'mone *sm* salmon

sa'lone *sm* (*stanza*) sitting room, lounge; (*in albergo*) lounge; (*su nave*) lounge, saloon; (*mostra*) show, exhibition; ~ **di bellezza** beauty salon

sa'lotto *sm* lounge, sitting room; (*mobilio*) lounge suite

sal'pare /72/ *vi* (*Naut*) to set sail; (*anche*: ~ **l'ancora**) to weigh anchor

'salsa *sf* (*Cuc*) sauce; ~ **di pomodoro** tomato sauce

sal'siccia, -ce [sal'sittʃa] *sf* pork sausage

sal'tare /72/ *vi* to jump, leap; (*esplodere*) to blow up, explode; (: *valvola*) to blow; (*venir via*) to pop off; (*non aver luogo: corso ecc*) to be cancelled ▷ *vt* to jump (over), leap (over); (*fig: pranzo, capitolo*) to skip, miss (out); (*Cuc*) to sauté; **far** ~ to blow up; to burst open; ~ **fuori** to turn up

saltel'lare /72/ *vi* to skip; to hop

'salto *sm* jump; (*Sport*) jumping; **fare un** ~ to jump, leap; **fare un** ~ **da qn** to pop over to sb's (place); ~ **in alto/lungo** high/long jump; ~ **con l'asta** pole vaulting; ~ **mortale** somersault

saltu'ario, -a *ag* occasional, irregular

sa'lubre *ag* healthy, salubrious

sa'lume *sm* (*Cuc*) cured pork; **salumi** *smpl* cured pork meats

salume'ria *sf* delicatessen

salu'tare /72/ *ag* healthy; (*fig*) salutary, beneficial ▷ *vt* (*per dire buon giorno, fig*) to greet; (*per dire addio*) to say goodbye to; (*Mil*) to salute

sa'lute *sf* health; ~! (*a chi starnutisce*) bless you!; (*nei brindisi*) cheers!; **bere alla ~ di qn** to drink (to) sb's health

sa'luto *sm* (*gesto*) wave; (*parola*) greeting; (*Mil*) salute

salvada'naio *sm* moneybox, piggy bank

salva'gente [salva'dʒɛnte] *sm* (*Naut*) lifebuoy; (*stradale: pl inv*) traffic island; ~ **a ciambella** lifebelt; ~ **a giubbotto** lifejacket (BRIT), life preserver (US)

salvaguar'dare /72/ *vt* to safeguard

sal'vare /72/ *vt* to save; (*trarre da un pericolo*) to rescue; (*proteggere*) to protect; **salvarsi** *vpr* to save o.s.; to escape; **salvas'chermo** *sm* (*Inform*) screen saver; **salva'slip** *sm inv* panty liner; **salva'taggio** *sm* rescue

'salve *escl* (*fam*) hi!

'salvia *sf* (*Bot*) sage

salvi'etta *sf* napkin; ~ **umidificata** baby wipe

'salvo, -a *ag* safe, unhurt, unharmed; (*fuori pericolo*) safe, out of danger ▷ *sm*: **in ~** safe ▷ *prep* (*eccetto*) except; ~ **che** (*a meno che*) unless; (*eccetto che*) except (that); **mettere qc in ~** to put sth in a safe place; ~ **imprevisti** barring accidents

sam'buco *sm* elder (tree)

'sandalo *sm* (*Bot*) sandalwood; (*calzatura*) sandal

'sangue *sm* blood; **farsi cattivo ~** to fret, get worked up; ~ **freddo** (*fig*) sang-froid, calm; **a ~ freddo** in cold blood; **sangui'nare** /72/ *vi* to bleed

sa'nità *sf* health; (*salubrità*) healthiness; **Ministero della S~** Department of Health; ~ **mentale** sanity

sani'tario, -a *ag* health *cpd*; (*condizioni*) sanitary ▷ *sm* (*Amm*) doctor; **sanitari** (*impianti*) bathroom o sanitary fittings

'sanno *vb vedi* **sapere**

'sano, -a *ag* healthy; (*denti, costituzione*) healthy, sound; (*integro*) whole, unbroken;

(fig: politica, consigli) sound; **~ di mente** sane; **di sana pianta** completely, entirely; **~ e salvo** safe and sound

San Silvestro [san sil'vestro] *sm (giorno)* New Year's Eve

'**santo, -a** *ag* holy; *(fig)* saintly; *(seguito da nome proprio: dav sm* **san** + C, **sant'** + V, **santo** + *s impura, gn, pn, ps, x, z; dav sf* **santa** + C, **sant'** + V) saint ▷ *sm/f* saint; **la Santa Sede** the Holy See

santu'ario *sm* sanctuary

sanzi'one [san'tsjone] *sf* sanction; *(penale, civile)* sanction, penalty

sa'pere /99/ *vt* to know; *(essere capace di):* **so nuotare** I know how to swim, I can swim ▷ *vi:* **~ di** *(aver sapore)* to taste of; *(aver odore)* to smell of ▷ *sm* knowledge; **far ~ qc a qn** to inform sb about sth, let sb know sth; **mi sa che non sia vero** I don't think that's true; **non lo so** I don't know; **non so l'inglese** I don't speak English

sa'pone *sm* soap; **~ da bucato** washing soap

sa'pore *sm* taste, flavour; **sapo'rito, -a** *ag* tasty

sappi'amo *vb vedi* **sapere**

saprò *ecc vb vedi* **sapere**

sarà *ecc vb vedi* **essere**

saraci'nesca, -sche [saratʃi'neska] *sf (serranda)* rolling shutter

sar'castico, -a, -ci, -che *ag* sarcastic

Sar'degna [sar'deɲɲa] *sf:* **la ~** Sardinia

sar'dina *sf* sardine

'**sardo, -a** *ag, sm/f* Sardinian

sa'rei *ecc vb vedi* **essere**

SARS *sf (= severe acute respiratory syndrome)* SARS

'**sarta** *sf vedi* **sarto**

'**sarto, -a** *sm/f* tailor/dressmaker

'**sasso** *sm* stone; *(ciottolo)* pebble; *(masso)* rock

sas'sofono *sm* saxophone

sas'soso, -a *ag* stony; pebbly

'**Satana** *sm* Satan

satelli'tare *ag* satellite *cpd*

sa'tellite *sm, ag* satellite

'**satira** *sf* satire

'**sauna** *sf* sauna

sazi'are /19/ *vt* to satisfy, satiate; **saziarsi** *vpr:* **saziarsi (di)** to eat one's fill (of); *(fig):* **saziarsi di** to grow tired o weary of

'**sazio, -a** ['sattsjo] *ag:* **~ (di)** sated (with), full (of); *(fig: stufo)* fed up (with), sick (of); **sono ~** I'm full (up)

sba'dato, -a *ag* careless, inattentive

sbadigli'are [zbadiʎ'ʎare] /27/ *vi* to yawn; **sba'diglio** *sm* yawn

sbagli'are [zbaʎ'ʎare] /27/ *vt* to make a mistake in, get wrong ▷ *vi* to make

a mistake *(o mistakes)*, be mistaken; *(ingannarsi)* to be wrong; *(operare in modo non giusto)* to err; **sbagliarsi** *vpr* to make a mistake, be mistaken, be wrong; **~ la mira/strada** to miss one's target/take the wrong road

sbagli'ato, -a [zbaʎ'ʎato] *ag (gen)* wrong; *(compito)* full of mistakes; *(conclusione)* erroneous

'**sbaglio** *sm* mistake, error; *(morale)* error; **fare uno ~** to make a mistake

sbalor'dire /55/ *vt* to stun, amaze ▷ *vi* to be stunned, be amazed

sbal'zare [zbal'tsare] /72/ *vt* to throw, hurl ▷ *vi (balzare)* to bounce; *(saltare)* to leap, bound

sban'dare /72/ *vi (Naut)* to list; *(Aut)* to skid; *(Aer)* to bank

sba'raglio [zba'raʎʎo] *sm* rout; defeat; **gettarsi allo ~** to risk everything

sbaraz'zarsi [zbarat'tsarsi] /72/ *vpr:* **~ di** to get rid of, rid o.s. of

sbar'care /20/ *vt (passeggeri)* to disembark; *(merci)* to unload ▷ *vi* to disembark

'**sbarra** *sf* bar; *(di passaggio a livello)* barrier; *(Dir):* **mettere/presentarsi alla ~** to bring/ appear before the court

sbar'rare /72/ *vt (strada ecc)* to block, bar; *(assegno)* to cross; **~ il passo** to bar the way; **~ gli occhi** to open one's eyes wide

'**sbattere** /1/ *vt (porta)* to bang, slam; *(tappeti, ali, Cuc)* to beat; *(urtare)* to knock, hit ▷ *vi (porta, finestra)* to bang; *(agitarsi: ali, vele ecc)* to flap; **me ne sbatto!** *(fam)* I don't give a damn!

sba'vare /72/ *vi* to dribble; *(colore)* to smear, smudge

'**sberla** *sf* slap

sbia'dire /55/ *vi* to fade ▷ *vt* to fade; **sbia'dito, -a** *ag* faded; *(fig)* colourless, dull

sbian'care /20/ *vt* to whiten; *(tessuto)* to bleach ▷ *vi (impallidire)* to grow pale o white

sbirci'ata [zbir'tʃata] *sf:* **dare una ~ a qc** to glance at sth, have a look at sth

sbloc'care /20/ *vt* to unblock, free; *(freno)* to release; *(prezzi, affitti)* to free from controls; **sbloccarsi** *vpr (gen)* to become unblocked; *(passaggio, strada)* to clear, become unblocked

sboc'care /20/ *vi:* **~ in** *(fiume)* to flow into; *(strada)* to lead into; *(persona)* to come (out) into; *(fig: concludersi)* to end (up) in

sboc'cato, -a *ag (persona)* foul-mouthed; *(linguaggio)* foul

sbocci'are [zbot'tʃare] /14/ *vi (fiore)* to bloom, open (out)

sbol'lire /55/ *vi (fig)* to cool down, calm down

'**sbornia** *sf (fam):* **prendersi una ~** to get plastered

sbor'sare /72/ vt (denaro) to pay out

sbot'tare /72/ vi: ~ **in una risata/per la collera** to burst out laughing/explode with anger

sbotto'nare /72/ vt to unbutton, undo

sbrai'tare /72/ vi to yell, bawl

sbra'nare /72/ vt to tear to pieces

sbricio'lare [zbritʃo'lare] /72/ vt, **sbricio'larsi** vpr to crumble

sbri'gare /80/ vt to deal with; **sbrigarsi** vpr to hurry (up)

'sbronza ['zbrontsa] (fam) sf (ubriaco): **prendersi una ~** to get plastered

sbron'zarsi [zbron'tsarsi] /72/ vpr (fam) to get plastered

'sbronzo, -a ['zbrontso] ag (fam) plastered

sbruffone, -a sm/f boaster

sbu'care /20/ vi to come out, emerge; (improvvisamente) to pop out (o up)

sbucci'are [zbut'tʃare] /14/ vt (arancia, patata) to peel; (piselli) to shell; **sbucciarsi un ginocchio** to graze one's knee

sbucherò ecc [zbuke'rɔ] vb vedi **sbucare**

sbuf'fare /72/ vi (persona, cavallo) to snort; (: ansimare) to puff, pant; (treno) to puff

sca'broso, -a ag (fig: difficile) difficult, thorny; (: imbarazzante) embarrassing; (: sconcio) indecent

scacchi'era [skak'kjɛra] sf chessboard

scacci'are [skat'tʃare] /14/ vt to chase away o out, drive away o out

'scaddi ecc vb vedi **scadere**

sca'dente ag shoddy, of poor quality

sca'denza [ska'dɛntsa] sf (di cambiale, contratto) maturity; (di passaporto) expiry date; **a breve/lunga ~** short-/long-term; **data di ~** expiry date

sca'dere /18/ vi (contratto ecc) to expire; (debito) to fall due; (valore, forze, peso) to decline, go down

sca'fandro sm (di palombaro) diving suit; (di astronauta) spacesuit

scaf'fale sm shelf; (mobile) set of shelves

'scafo sm (Naut, Aer) hull

scagio'nare [skadʒo'nare] /72/ vt to exonerate, free from blame

'scaglia ['skaʎʎa] sf (Zool) scale; (scheggia) chip, flake

scagli'are [skaʎ'ʎare] /27/ vt (lanciare: anche fig) to hurl, fling; **scagliarsi** vpr: **scagliarsi su** o **contro** to hurl o fling o.s. at; (fig) to rail at

'scala sf (a gradini ecc) staircase, stairs pl; (a pioli, di corda) ladder; (Mus, Geo, di colori, valori, fig) scale; **scale** sfpl (scalinata) stairs; **su larga** o **vasta ~** on a large scale; **su ~ ridotta** on a small scale; **~ a libretto** stepladder; **~ mobile** escalator; (Econ) sliding scale; **~ mobile (dei salari)** index-linked pay scale

sca'lare /72/ vt (Alpinismo, muro) to climb, scale; (debito) to scale down, reduce

scalda'bagno [skalda'baɲɲo] sm water heater

scal'dare /72/ vt to heat; **scaldarsi** vpr to warm up, heat up; (al fuoco, al sole) to warm o.s.; (fig) to get excited

scal'fire /55/ vt to scratch

scali'nata sf staircase

sca'lino sm (anche fig) step; (di scala a pioli) rung

'scalo sm (Naut) slipway; (: porto d'approdo) port of call; (Aer) stopover; **fare ~ (a)** (Naut) to call (at), put in (at); (Aer) to land (at), make a stop (at); **~ merci** (Ferr) goods (BRIT) o freight yard

scalop'pina sf (Cuc) escalope

scal'pello sm chisel

scal'pore sm noise, row; **far ~** (notizia) to cause a sensation o a stir

'scaltro, -a ag cunning, shrewd

'scalzo, -a ['skaltso] ag barefoot

scambi'are /72/ vt to exchange; (confondere): **~ qn/qc per** to take o mistake sb/sth for; **mi hanno scambiato il cappello** they've given me the wrong hat; **scambiarsi** vpr (auguri, confidenze, visite) to exchange

'scambio sm exchange; (Ferr) points pl; **fare (uno) ~** to make a swap

scampa'gnata [skampaɲ'ɲata] sf trip to the country

scam'pare /72/ vt (salvare) to rescue, save; (evitare: morte, prigione) to escape ▷ vi: **~ (a qc)** to survive (sth), escape (sth); **scamparla bella** to have a narrow escape

'scampo sm (salvezza) escape; (Zool) prawn; **cercare ~ nella fuga** to seek safety in flight

'scampolo sm remnant

scanala'tura sf (incavo) channel, groove

scandagli'are [skandaʎ'ʎare] /27/ vt (Naut) to sound; (fig) to sound out; to probe

scandaliz'zare [skandalid'dzare] /72/ vt to shock, scandalize; **scandalizzarsi** vpr to be shocked

'scandalo sm scandal

Scandi'navia sf: **la ~** Scandinavia; **scandi'navo, -a** ag, sm/f Scandinavian

'scanner ['skanner] sm inv scanner

scansafa'tiche [skansafa'tike] smf inv idler, loafer

scan'sare /72/ vt (rimuovere) to move (aside), shift; (schivare: schiaffo) to dodge; (sfuggire) to avoid; **scansarsi** vpr to move aside

scan'sia sf shelves pl; (per libri) bookcase

'scanso sm: **a ~ di** in order to avoid, as a precaution against

scanti'nato *sm* basement

scapacci'one [skapat'tʃone] *sm* clout

scapes'trato, -a *ag* dissolute

'scapola *sf* shoulder blade

'scapolo *sm* bachelor

scappa'mento *sm* (*Aut*) exhaust

scap'pare /72/ *vi* (*fuggire*) to escape; (*andare via in fretta*) to rush off; **~ di prigione** to escape from prison; **~ di mano** (*oggetto*) to slip out of one's hands; **~ di mente a qn** to slip sb's mind; **lasciarsi ~** (*occasione, affare*) to let go by; **mi scappò detto** I let it slip; **scappa'toia** *sf* way out

scara'beo *sm* beetle

scarabocchi'are [skarabok'kjare] /19/ *vt* to scribble, scrawl; **scara'bocchio** *sm* scribble, scrawl

scara'faggio [skara'faddʒo] *sm* cockroach

scaraman'zia [skaraman'tsia] *sf*: **per ~** for luck

scaraven'tare /72/ *vt* to fling, hurl; **scaraventarsi** *vpr* to fling o.s.

scarce'rare [skartʃe'rare] /72/ *vt* to release (from prison)

scardi'nare /72/ *vt*: **~ una porta** to take a door off its hinges

scari'care /20/ *vt* (*merci, camion ecc*) to unload; (*passeggeri*) to set down, put off; (*da Internet*) to download; (*arma*) to unload; (: *sparare, anche Elettr*) to discharge; (*corso d'acqua*) to empty, pour; (*fig: liberare da un peso*) to unburden, relieve; **scaricarsi** *vpr* (*orologio*) to run o wind down; (*batteria, accumulatore*) to go flat o dead; (*fig: rilassarsi*) to unwind; (: *sfogarsi*) to let off steam

'scarico, -a, -chi, -che *ag* unloaded; (*orologio*) run down; (*batteria, accumulatore*) dead, flat ▷ *sm* (*di merci, materiali*) unloading; (*di immondizie*) dumping, tipping (*BRIT*); (*Tecn: deflusso*) draining; (: *dispositivo*) drain; (*Aut*) exhaust

scarlat'tina *sf* scarlet fever

scar'latto, -a *ag* scarlet

'scarpa *sf* shoe; **scarpe da ginnastica** gym shoes; **scarpe da tennis** tennis shoes

scar'pata *sf* escarpment

scarpi'era *sf* shoe rack

scar'pone *sm* boot; **scarponi da montagna** climbing boots; **scarponi da sci** ski-boots

scarseggi'are [skarsed'dʒare] /62/ *vi* to be scarce; **~ di** to be short of, lack

'scarso, -a *ag* (*insufficiente*) insufficient, meagre; (*povero: annata*) poor, lean; (*Ins: voto*) poor; **~ di** lacking in; **3 chili scarsi** just under 3 kilos, barely 3 kilos

scar'tare /72/ *vt* (*pacco*) to unwrap; (*idea*) to reject; (*Mil*) to declare unfit for military service; (*carte da gioco*) to discard; (*Calcio*) to dodge (past) ▷ *vi* to swerve

'scarto *sm* (*cosa scartata, anche Comm*) reject; (*di veicolo*) swerve; (*differenza*) gap, difference

scassi'nare /72/ *vt* to break, force

scate'nare /72/ *vt* (*fig*) to incite, stir up; **scatenarsi** *vpr* (*temporale*) to break; (*rivolta*) to break out; (*persona: infuriarsi*) to rage

'scatola *sf* box; (*di latta*) tin (*BRIT*), can; **cibi in ~** tinned (*BRIT*) o canned foods; **~ cranica** cranium; **scato'lone** *sm* (big) box

scat'tare /72/ *vt* (*fotografia*) to take ▷ *vi* (*congegno, molla ecc*) to be released; (*balzare*) to spring up; (*Sport*) to put on a spurt; (*fig: per l'ira*) to fly into a rage; **~ in piedi** to spring to one's feet

'scatto *sm* (*dispositivo*) release; (: *di arma da fuoco*) trigger mechanism; (*rumore*) click; (*balzo*) jump, start; (*Sport*) spurt; (*fig: di ira ecc*) fit; (: *di stipendio*) increment; **di ~** suddenly

scaval'care /20/ *vt* (*ostacolo*) to pass (o climb) over; (*fig*) to get ahead of, overtake

sca'vare /72/ *vt* (*terreno*) to dig; (*legno*) to hollow out; (*pozzo, galleria*) to bore; (*città sepolta ecc*) to excavate

'scavo *sm* excavating *no pl*; excavation

'scegliere ['ʃeʎʎere] /100/ *vt* to choose, select

sce'icco, -chi [ʃe'ikko] *sm* sheik

'scelgo *ecc* ['ʃelgo] *vb vedi* **scegliere**

scel'lino [ʃel'lino] *sm* shilling

'scelto, -a ['ʃelto] *pp di* **scegliere** ▷ *ag* (*gruppo*) carefully selected; (*frutta, verdura*) choice, top quality; (*Mil: specializzato*) crack *cpd*, highly skilled ▷ *sf* choice; (*selezione*) selection, choice; **frutta o formaggi a scelta** choice of fruit or cheese; **di prima scelta** top grade o quality

'scemo, -a ['ʃemo] *ag* stupid, silly

'scena ['ʃena] *sf* (*gen*) scene; (*palcoscenico*) stage; **le scene** (*fig: teatro*) the stage; **andare in ~** to be staged o put on o performed; **mettere in ~** to stage; **fare una ~** to make a scene

sce'nario [ʃe'narjo] *sm* scenery; (*di film*) scenario

sce'nata [ʃe'nata] *sf* row, scene

'scendere ['ʃendere] /101/ *vi* to go (o come) down; (*strada, sole*) to go down; (*notte*) to fall; (*passeggero: fermarsi*) to get out, alight; (*fig: temperatura, prezzi*) to fall, drop ▷ *vt* (*scale, pendio*) to go (o come) down; **~ dalle scale** to go (o come) down the stairs; **~ dal treno** to get off o out of the train; **~ dalla macchina** to get out of the car; **~ da cavallo** to dismount, get off one's horse

sceneggi'ato [ʃened'dʒato] *sm* television drama

'scettico, -a, -ci, -che [ˈʃettiko] *ag* sceptical

'scettro [ˈʃettro] *sm* sceptre

'scheda [ˈskɛda] *sf* (index) card; **~ elettorale** ballot paper; **~ di memoria** (*Inform*) memory card; **~ ricaricabile** (*Tel*) top-up card; **~ telefonica** phone card; **sche'dario** *sm* file; (*mobile*) filing cabinet

sche'dina [skeˈdina] *sf* ≈ pools coupon (BRIT)

'scheggia, -ge [ˈskeddʒa] *sf* splinter, sliver

'scheletro [ˈskɛletro] *sm* skeleton

'schema, -i [ˈskɛma] *sm* (*diagramma*) diagram, sketch; (*progetto, abbozzo*) outline, plan

'scherma [ˈskerma] *sf* fencing

scher'maglia [skerˈmaʎʎa] *sf* (*fig*) skirmish

'schermo [ˈskermo] *sm* shield, screen; (*Cine, TV*) screen; **a ~ panoramico** (*TV*) widescreen

scher'nire [skerˈnire] /55/ *vt* to mock, sneer at

scher'zare [skerˈtsare] /72/ *vi* to joke

'scherzo [ˈskertso] *sm* joke; (*tiro*) trick; (*Mus*) scherzo; **è uno ~!** (*una cosa facile*) it's child's play!, it's easy!; **per ~** in jest; for a joke *o* a laugh; **fare un brutto ~ a qn** to play a nasty trick on sb

schiaccia'noci [skjattʃaˈnotʃi] *sm inv* nutcracker

schiacci'are [skjatˈtʃare] /14/ *vt* (*dito*) to crush; (*noci*) to crack; **~ un pisolino** to have a nap; **schiacciarsi** *vpr* (*appiattirsi*) to get squashed; (*frantumarsi*) to get crushed

schiaffeggi'are [skjaffedˈdʒare] /62/ *vt* to slap

schi'affo [ˈskjaffo] *sm* slap

schian'tare [skjanˈtare] /72/ *vt* to break; **schiantarsi** *vpr* to break (up), shatter

schia'rire [skjaˈrire] /55/ *vt* to lighten, make lighter ▷ *vi* (*anche*: **schiarirsi**) to grow lighter; (*tornar sereno*) to clear, brighten up; **schiarirsi la voce** to clear one's throat

schiavitù [skjaviˈtu] *sf* slavery

schi'avo, -a [ˈskjavo] *sm/f* slave

schi'ena [ˈskjɛna] *sf* (*Anat*) back; **schie'nale** *sm* (*di sedia*) back

schi'era [ˈskjɛra] *sf* (*Mil*) rank; (*gruppo*) group, band

schiera'mento [skjeraˈmento] *sm* (*Mil, Sport*) formation; (*fig*) alliance

schie'rare [skjeˈrare] /72/ *vt* (*esercito*) to line up, draw up, marshal; **schierarsi** *vpr* to line up; (*fig*): **schierarsi con** *o* **dalla parte di/contro qn** to side with/oppose sb

'schifo [ˈskifo] *sm* disgust; **fare ~** (*essere fatto male, dare pessimi risultati*) to be awful; **mi fa ~** it makes me sick, it's disgusting; **quel libro è uno ~** that book's rotten;

schi'foso, -a *ag* disgusting, revolting; (*molto scadente*) rotten, lousy

schioc'care /20/ *vt* (*frusta*) to crack; (*dita*) to snap; (*lingua*) to click; **~ le labbra** to smack one's lips

schi'udere [ˈskjudere] /22/ *vt*, **schi'udersi** *vpr* to open

schi'uma [ˈskjuma] *sf* foam; (*di sapone*) lather; (*di latte*) froth; (*fig: feccia*) scum

schi'vare [skiˈvare] /72/ *vt* to dodge, avoid

'schivo, -a [ˈskivo] *ag* (*ritroso*) stand-offish, reserved; (*timido*) shy

schiz'zare [skitˈtsare] /72/ *vt* (*spruzzare*) to spurt, squirt; (*sporcare*) to splash, spatter; (*fig: abbozzare*) to sketch ▷ *vi* to spurt, squirt; (*saltar fuori*) to dart up (*o* off *ecc*)

schizzi'noso, -a [skittsiˈnoso] *ag* fussy, finicky

'schizzo [ˈskittso] *sm* (*di liquido*) spurt, splash, spatter; (*abbozzo*) sketch

sci [ʃi] *sm inv* (*attrezzo*) ski; (*attività*) skiing; **~ di fondo** cross-country skiing, ski touring (US); **~ d'acqua** *o* **nautico** water-skiing

'scia [ˈʃia] (*pl* **scie**) *sf* (*di imbarcazione*) wake; (*di profumo*) trail

scià [ʃa] *sm inv* shah

sci'abola [ˈʃabola] *sf* sabre

scia'callo [ʃaˈkallo] *sm* jackal

sciac'quare [ʃakˈkware] /72/ *vt* to rinse

scia'gura [ʃaˈgura] *sf* disaster, calamity; misfortune

scialac'quare [ʃalakˈkware] /72/ *vt* to squander

sci'albo, -a [ˈʃalbo] *ag* pale, dull; (*fig*) dull, colourless

sci'alle [ˈʃalle] *sm* shawl

scia'luppa [ʃaˈluppa] *sf* (*anche*: **~ di salvataggio**) lifeboat

sci'ame [ˈʃame] *sm* swarm

sci'are [ʃiˈare] /60/ *vi* to ski

sci'arpa [ˈʃarpa] *sf* scarf; (*fascia*) sash

scia'tore, -'trice [ʃiaˈtore] *sm/f* skier

sci'atto, -a [ˈʃatto] *ag* (*persona*) slovenly, unkempt

scien'tifico, -a, -ci, -che [ʃenˈtifiko] *ag* scientific

sci'enza [ˈʃentsa] *sf* science; (*sapere*) knowledge; **scienze** *sfpl* (*Ins*) science *sg*; **scienze naturali** natural sciences; **scienzi'ato, -a** *sm/f* scientist

'scimmia [ˈʃimmja] *sf* monkey

scimpan'zé [ʃimpanˈtse] *sm inv* chimpanzee

'scindere [ˈʃindere] /102/, **'scindersi** *vpr* to split (up)

scin'tilla [ʃinˈtilla] *sf* spark; **scintil'lare** /72/ *vi* to spark; (*acqua, occhi*) to sparkle

scioc'chezza [ʃokˈkettsa] *sf* stupidity *no pl*; stupid *o* foolish thing; **dire sciocchezze** to talk nonsense

sci'occo, -a, -chi, -che ['ʃɔkko] *ag* stupid, foolish

sci'ogliere ['ʃɔʎʎere] /103/ *vt* (*nodo*) to untie; (*capelli*) to loosen; (*persona, animale*) to untie, release; (*nell'acqua: zucchero ecc*) to dissolve; (*fig: mistero*) to solve; (*porre fine a: contratto*) to cancel; (: *società, matrimonio*) to dissolve; (: *riunione*) to bring to an end; (*fig: persona*): ~ **da** to release from; (*neve*) to melt; **sciogliersi** *vpr* to loosen, come untied; to melt; to dissolve; (*assemblea, corteo, duo*) to break up; ~ **i muscoli** to limber up; **scioglilingua** [ʃɔʎʎi'lingwa] *sm inv* tongue-twister

sci'olgo *ecc* [ʃolgo] *vb vedi* **sciogliere**

sci'olto, -a ['ʃolto] *pp di* **sciogliere** ⊳ *ag* loose; (*agile*) agile, nimble; supple; (*disinvolto*) free and easy; **versi sciolti** (*Poesia*) blank verse

sciope'rare [ʃope'rare] /72/ *vi* to strike, go on strike

sci'opero ['ʃopero] *sm* strike; **fare** ~ **to** strike; ~ **bianco** work-to-rule (BRIT), slowdown (US); ~ **selvaggio** wildcat strike; ~ **a singhiozzo** on-off strike

scio'via [ʃio'via] *sf* ski lift

scip'pare [ʃip'pare] /72/ *vt*: ~ **qn** to snatch sb's bag

sci'rocco [ʃi'rɔkko] *sm* sirocco

sci'roppo [ʃi'rɔppo] *sm* syrup

'scisma, -i ['ʃizma] *sm* (Rel) schism

scissi'one [ʃis'sjone] *sf* (*anche fig*) split, division; (*Fisica*) fission

'scisso, -a ['ʃisso] *pp di* **scindere**

sciu'pare [ʃu'pare] /72/ *vt* (*abito, libro, appetito*) to spoil, ruin; (*tempo, denaro*) to waste

scivo'lare [ʃivo'lare] /72/ *vi* to slide *o* glide along; (*involontariamente*) to slip, slide; **'scivolo** *sm* slide; (*Tecn*) chute; **scivo'loso, -a** *ag* slippery

scle'rosi *sf* sclerosis

scoc'care /20/ *vt* (*freccia*) to shoot ⊳ *vi* (*guizzare*) to shoot up; (*battere: ora*) to strike

scoccherò *ecc* [skokke'rɔ] *vb vedi* **scoccare**

scocci'are [skot'tʃare] /14/ *vt* to bother, annoy; **scocciarsi** *vpr* to be bothered *o* annoyed

sco'della *sf* bowl

scodinzo'lare [skodintso'lare] /72/ *vi* to wag its tail

scogli'era [skoʎ'ʎera] *sf* reef; (*rupe*) cliff

'scoglio ['skɔʎʎo] *sm* (*al mare*) rock

scoi'attolo *sm* squirrel

scola'pasta *sm inv* colander

scolapi'atti *sm inv* drainer (*for plates*)

sco'lare /72/ *ag*: **età** ~ school age ⊳ *vt* to drain ⊳ *vi* to drip

scola'resca *sf* schoolchildren *pl*, pupils *pl*

sco'laro, -a *sm/f* pupil, schoolboy/girl

> ⚠ Attenzione! In inglese esiste la parola *scholar*, che però significa *studioso*.

sco'lastico, -a, -ci, -che *ag* (*gen*) scholastic; (*libro, anno, divisa*) school *cpd*

scol'lato, -a *ag* (*vestito*) low-cut, low-necked; (*donna*) wearing a low-cut dress (*o blouse ecc*)

scolla'tura *sf* neckline

scolle'gare /80/ *vt* (*fili, apparecchi*) to disconnect; **scollegarsi** *vpr* (*da Internet*) to disconnect; (*da chat-line*) to log off

'scolo *sm* drainage

scolo'rire /55/ *vt* to fade; to discolour (BRIT), discolor (US) ⊳ *vi* (*anche*: **scolorirsi**) to fade; to become discoloured; (*impallidire*) to turn pale

scol'pire /55/ *vt* to carve, sculpt

scombusso'lare /72/ *vt* to upset

scom'messo, -a *pp di* **scommettere** ⊳ *sf* bet, wager

scom'mettere /63/ *vt, vi* to bet

scomo'dare /72/ *vt* to trouble, bother, disturb; **scomodarsi** *vpr* to put o.s. out; **scomodarsi a fare** to go to the bother *o* trouble of doing

'scomodo, -a *ag* uncomfortable; (*sistemazione, posto*) awkward, inconvenient

scompa'rire /7/ *vi* (*sparire*) to disappear, vanish; (*fig*) to be insignificant

scomparti'mento *sm* compartment

scompigli'are [skompiʎ'ʎare] /27/ *vt* (*cassetto, capelli*) to mess up, disarrange; (*fig: piani*) to upset

scomuni'care /20/ *vt* to excommunicate

'sconcio, -a, -ci, -ce ['skontʃo] *ag* (*osceno*) indecent, obscene ⊳ *sm* disgrace

scon'figgere [skon'fiddʒere] /104/ *vt* to defeat, overcome

sconfi'nare /72/ *vi* to cross the border; (*in proprietà privata*) to trespass; (*fig*): ~ **da** to stray *o* digress from

scon'fitto, -a *pp di* **sconfiggere** ⊳ *sf* defeat

scon'forto *sm* despondency

sconge'lare [skondʒe'lare] /72/ *vt* to defrost

scongiu'rare [skondʒu'rare] /72/ *vt* (*implorare*) to beseech, entreat, implore; (*eludere: pericolo*) to ward off, avert; **scongi'uro** *sm* (*esorcismo*) exorcism; **fare gli scongiuri** to touch wood (BRIT), knock on wood (US)

scon'nesso, -a *ag* incoherent

sconosci'uto, -a [skonoʃ'ʃuto] *ag* unknown; new, strange ⊳ *sm/f* stranger; unknown person

sconsigli'are [skonsiʎ'ʎare] /27/ *vt*: ~ **qc a qn** to advise sb against sth; ~ **qn dal fare qc** to advise sb not to do *o* against doing sth

sconso'lato, -a *ag* inconsolable; desolate

scon'tare /72/ *vt* (*Comm: detrarre*) to deduct; (*: debito*) to pay off; (*: cambiale*) to discount; (*pena*) to serve; (*colpa, errori*) to pay for, suffer for

scon'tato, -a *ag* (*previsto*) foreseen, taken for granted; **dare per ~ che** to take it for granted that

scon'tento, -a *ag*: **~ (di)** discontented *o* dissatisfied (with) ▷ *sm* dissatisfaction

'sconto *sm* discount; **fare** *o* **concedere uno ~** to give a discount; **uno ~ del 10%** a 10% discount

scon'trarsi /72/ *vpr* (*treni ecc*) to crash, collide; (*venire ad uno scontro: fig*) to clash; **~ con** to crash into, collide with

scon'trino *sm* ticket; (*di cassa*) receipt

'scontro *sm* clash, encounter; (*di veicoli*) crash, collision

scon'troso, -a *ag* sullen, surly; (*permaloso*) touchy

sconveni'ente *ag* unseemly, improper

scon'volgere [skon'vɔldʒere] /96/ *vt* to throw into confusion, upset; (*turbare*) to shake, disturb, upset; **scon'volto, -a** *pp di* **sconvolgere**

'scooter ['skuter] *sm inv* scooter

'scopa *sf* broom; (*Carte*) Italian card game; **sco'pare** /72/ *vt* to sweep

sco'perto, -a *pp di* **scoprire** ▷ *ag* uncovered; (*capo*) uncovered, bare; (*macchina*) open; (*Mil*) exposed, without cover; (*conto*) overdrawn ▷ *sf* discovery

'scopo *sm* aim, purpose; **a che ~?** what for?

scoppi'are /19/ *vi* (*spaccarsi*) to burst; (*esplodere*) to explode; (*fig*) to break out; **~ in pianto** *o* **a piangere** to burst out crying; **~ dalle risa** *o* **dal ridere** to split one's sides laughing

scoppiet'tare /72/ *vi* to crackle

'scoppio *sm* explosion; (*di tuono, arma ecc*) crash, bang; (*fig: di risa, ira*) fit; (*di pneumatico*) bang; (*fig: di guerra*) outbreak; **a ~ ritardato** delayed-action

sco'prire /9/ *vt* to discover; (*: liberare da ciò che copre*) to uncover; (*: monumento*) to unveil; **scoprirsi** *vpr* to put on lighter clothes; (*fig*) to give o.s. away

scoraggi'are [skorad'dʒare] /62/ *vt* to discourage; **scoraggiarsi** *vpr* to become discouraged, lose heart

scorcia'toia [skortʃa'toja] *sf* short cut

'scorcio ['skortʃo] *sm* (*Arte*) foreshortening; (*di secolo, periodo*) end, close; **~ panoramico** vista

scor'dare /72/ *vt* to forget; **scordarsi** *vpr*: **scordarsi di qc/di fare** to forget sth/to do

'scorgere ['skɔrdʒere] /59/ *vt* to make out, distinguish, see

scorpacci'ata [skorpat'tʃata] *sf*: **fare una ~ (di)** to stuff o.s. (with), eat one's fill (of)

scorpi'one *sm* scorpion; **S~** Scorpio

'scorrere /28/ *vt* (*giornale, lettera*) to run *o* skim through ▷ *vi* (*liquido, fiume*) to run, flow; (*fune*) to run; (*cassetto, porta*) to slide easily; (*tempo*) to pass (by)

scor'retto, -a *ag* incorrect; (*sgarbato*) impolite; (*sconveniente*) improper

scor'revole *ag* (*porta*) sliding; (*fig: stile*) fluent, flowing

'scorsi *ecc vb vedi* **scorgere**

'scorso, -a *pp di* **scorrere** ▷ *ag* last

scor'soio, -a *ag*: **nodo ~** noose

'scorta *sf* (*di personalità, convoglio*) escort; (*provvista*) supply, stock

scor'tese *ag* discourteous, rude

'scorza ['skɔrdza] *sf* (*di albero*) bark; (*di agrumi*) peel, skin

sco'sceso, -a [skoʃ'ʃeso] *ag* steep

scosso, -a *pp di* **scuotere** ▷ *ag* (*turbato*) shaken, upset ▷ *sf* jerk, jolt, shake; (*Elettr, fig*) shock; **scossa di terremoto** earth tremor

scos'tante *ag* (*fig*) off-putting (*BRIT*), unpleasant

scotch [skɔtʃ] *sm inv* (*whisky*) Scotch®; (*nastro adesivo*) Scotch tape®, Sellotape®

scot'tare /72/ *vt* (*ustionare*) to burn; (*: con liquido bollente*) to scald ▷ *vi* to burn; (*caffè*) to be too hot; **scottarsi** *vpr* to burn/ scald o.s.; (*fig*) to have one's fingers burnt; **scotta'tura** *sf* burn; scald

'scotto, -a *ag* overcooked ▷ *sm* (*fig*): **pagare lo ~ (di)** to pay the penalty (for)

sco'vare /72/ *vt* to drive out, flush out; (*fig*) to discover

'Scozia ['skɔttsja] *sf*: **la ~** Scotland; **scoz'zese** *ag* Scottish ▷ *smf* Scot

scredi'tare /72/ *vt* to discredit

'screen saver ['skriːn'seɪvər] *sm inv* (*Inform*) screen saver

scre'mato, -a *ag* skimmed; **parzialmente ~** semi-skimmed

screpo'lato, -a *ag* (*labbra*) chapped; (*muro*) cracked

'screzio ['skrettsjo] *sm* disagreement

scricchio'lare [skrikkjo'lare] /72/ *vi* to creak, squeak

'scrigno ['skriɲɲo] *sm* casket

scrimina'tura *sf* parting

'scrissi *ecc vb vedi* **scrivere**

'scritto, -a *pp di* **scrivere** ▷ *ag* written ▷ *sm* writing; (*lettera*) letter, note ▷ *sf* inscription

scrit'toio *sm* writing desk

scrit'tore, -'trice *sm/f* writer

scrit'tura *sf* writing; (*Comm*) entry; (*contratto*) contract; (*Rel*): **la Sacra S~** the Scriptures *pl*

scrittu'rare /72/ vt (Teat, Cine) to sign up, engage; (Comm) to enter

scriva'nia sf desk

'scrivere /72/ vt to write; **come si scrive?** how is it spelt?, how do you write it?

scroc'cone, -a sm/f scrounger

'scrofa sf (Zool) sow

scrol'lare /72/ vt to shake; **scrollarsi** vpr (anche fig) to give o.s. a shake; **~ le spalle/ il capo** to shrug one's shoulders/shake one's head

'scrupolo sm scruple; (meticolosità) care, conscientiousness

scrupo'loso, -a ag scrupulous; conscientious

scru'tare /72/ vt to scrutinize; (intenzioni, causa) to examine, scrutinize

scu'cire [sku'tʃire] /31/ vt (orlo ecc) to unpick, undo; **scucirsi** vpr to come unstitched

scude'ria sf stable

scu'detto sm (Sport) (championship) shield; (distintivo) badge

'scudo sm shield

sculacci'are [skulat'tʃare] /14/ vt to spank

scul'tore, -'trice sm/f sculptor

scul'tura sf sculpture

scu'ola sf school; **~ elementare** o **primaria** primary (BRIT) o grade (US) school (for children from 6 to 11 years of age); **~ guida** driving school; **~ imposta** (window) shutter; (fig) to drop dead; **~ media** secondary (BRIT) o high (US) school; **~ dell'obbligo** compulsory education; **scuole serali** evening classes, night school sg; **~ tecnica** technical college

scu'otere /106/ vt to shake

'scure sf axe

'scuro, -a ag dark; (fig: espressione) grim ▷ sm darkness; dark colour (BRIT) o color (US); (imposta) (window) shutter; **verde/ rosso** ecc **~** dark green/red etc

'scusa sf excuse; **scuse** sfpl apology sg, apologies; **chiedere ~ a qn (per)** to apologize to sb (for); **chiedo ~** I'm sorry; (disturbando ecc) excuse me

scu'sare /72/ vt to excuse; **scusarsi** vpr: **scusarsi (di)** to apologize (for); **(mi) scusi** I'm sorry; (per richiamare l'attenzione) excuse me

sde'gnato, -a [zdeɲ'ɲato] ag indignant, angry

'sdegno ['zdeɲɲo] sm scorn, disdain

sdolci'nato, -a [zdoltʃi'nato] ag mawkish, oversentimental

sdrai'arsi /19/ vpr to stretch out, lie down

'sdraio sm: **sedia a ~** deck chair

sdruccio'levole [zdruttʃo'levole] ag slippery

PAROLA CHIAVE

se pron vedi **si**
▸ cong 1 (condizionale, ipotetica) if; **se nevica non vengo** I won't come if it snows; **sarei rimasto se me l'avessero chiesto** I would have stayed if they'd asked me; **non puoi fare altro se non telefonare** all you can do is phone; **se mai** if, if ever; **siamo noi che le siamo grati** it is we who should be grateful to you; **se no** (altrimenti) or (else), otherwise
2 (in frasi dubitative, interrogative indirette) if, whether; **non so se scrivere o telefonare** I don't know whether to write o if I should write o phone

sé pron (gen) oneself; (esso, essa, lui, lei, loro) itself; himself; herself; themselves; **sé stesso(a)** pron oneself; itself; himself; herself

seb'bene cong although, though

sec. abbr (= secolo) c.

'secca sf vedi **secco**

sec'care /20/ vt to dry; (prosciugare) to dry up; (fig: importunare) to annoy, bother ▷ vi to dry; to dry up; **seccarsi** vpr to dry; to dry up; (fig) to grow annoyed

sec'cato, -a ag (fig: infastidito) bothered, annoyed; (: stufo) fed up

secca'tura sf (fig) bother no pl, trouble no pl

seccherò ecc [sekke'rɔ] vb vedi **seccare**

secchi'ello sm bucket; **~ del ghiaccio** ice bucket

'secchio ['sekkjo] sm bucket, pail

'secco, -a, -chi, -che ag dry; (fichi, pesce) dried; (foglie, ramo) withered; (magro: persona) thin, skinny; (fig: risposta, modo di fare) curt, abrupt; (: colpo) clean, sharp ▷ sm (siccità) drought ▷ sf (del mare) shallows pl; **restarci ~** (morire sul colpo) to drop dead; **tirare a ~** (barca) to beach; **rimanere a ~** (fig) to be left in the lurch

seco'lare ag age-old, centuries-old; (laico, mondano) secular

'secolo sm century; (epoca) age

se'conda sf vedi **secondo**

secon'dario, -a ag secondary

se'condo, -a ag second ▷ sm second; (di pranzo) main course ▷ sf (Aut) second (gear) ▷ prep according to; (nel modo prescritto) in accordance with; **seconda classe** second-class; **di seconda mano** second-hand; **viaggiare in seconda** to travel second-class; **a seconda di** according to; in accordance with; **~ me** in my opinion, to my mind

'sedano sm celery

seda'tivo, -a ag, sm sedative

'sede *sf* (*di ditta: principale*) head office; (*di organizzazione*) headquarters *pl*; ~ **centrale** head office; ~ **sociale** registered office

seden'tario, -a *ag* sedentary

se'dere /107/ *vi* to sit, be seated

'sedia *sf* chair; ~ **elettrica** electric chair; ~ **a rotelle** wheelchair

'sedici ['seditʃi] *num* sixteen

se'dile *sm* seat; (*panchina*) bench

sedu'cente [sedu'tʃɛnte] *ag* seductive; (*proposta*) very attractive

se'durre /90/ *vt* to seduce

se'duta *sf* session, sitting; (*riunione*) meeting; ~ **stante** (*fig*) immediately; ~ **spiritica** seance

seduzi'one [sedut'tsjone] *sf* seduction; (*fascino*) charm, appeal

SEeO *abbr* (= *salvo errori e omissioni*) E & OE

'sega, -ghe *sf* saw

'segale *sf* rye

se'gare /80/ *vt* to saw; (*recidere*) to saw off

'seggio ['sɛddʒo] *sm* seat; ~ **elettorale** polling station

seggi'ola ['sɛddʒola] *sf* chair; **seggio'lone** *sm* (*per bambini*) highchair

seggio'via [sɛddʒo'via] *sf* chairlift

segherò *ecc* [sege'rɔ] *vb vedi* **segare**

segna'lare [seɲɲa'lare] /72/ *vt* (*avvertire*) to signal; (*menzionare*) to indicate; (: *fatto, risultato, aumento*) to report; (: *errore, dettaglio*) to point out; (*persona*) to single out

se'gnale [seɲ'ɲale] *sm* signal; (*cartello*): ~ **stradale** road sign; ~ **acustico** acoustic *o* sound signal; ~ **d'allarme** alarm; (*Ferr*) communication cord; ~ **orario** (*Radio*) time signal

segna'libro [seɲɲa'libro] *sm* (*anche Inform*) bookmark

se'gnare [seɲ'ɲare] /15/ *vt* to mark; (*prendere nota*) to note; (*indicare*) to indicate, mark; (*Sport: goal*) to score

'segno ['seɲɲo] *sm* sign; (*impronta, contrassegno*) mark; (*limite*) limit, bounds *pl*; (*bersaglio*) target; **fare** ~ **di sì/no** to nod (one's head)/shake one's head; **fare** ~ **a qn di fermarsi** to motion (to) sb to stop; **cogliere** *o* **colpire nel** ~ (*fig*) to hit the mark; ~ **zodiacale** star sign

segre'tario, -a *sm/f* secretary; ~ **comunale** town clerk; **S**~ **di Stato** Secretary of State

segrete'ria *sf* (*di ditta, scuola*) (secretary's) office; (*d'organizzazione internazionale*) secretariat; (*Pol: ecc: carica*) office of Secretary; ~ **telefonica** answering machine

se'greto, -a *ag* secret ▷ *sm* secret; secrecy *no pl* ▷ *sf* dungeon; **in** ~ in secret, secretly

segu'ace [se'gwatʃe] *smf* follower, disciple

segu'ente *ag* following, next

segu'ire /45/ *vt* (*anche su Twitter*) to follow; (*frequentare: corso*) to attend ▷ *vi* to follow; (*continuare: testo*) to continue

segui'tare /72/ *vt* to continue, carry on with ▷ *vi* to continue, carry on

'seguito *sm* (*scorta*) suite, retinue; (*discepoli*) followers *pl*; (*favore*) following; (*continuazione*) continuation; (*conseguenza*) result; **di** ~ at a stretch, on end; **in** ~ later on; **in** ~ **a, a** ~ **di** following; (*a causa di*) as a result of, owing to

'sei *vb vedi* **essere** ▷ *num* six

sei'cento [sei'tʃɛnto] *num* six hundred ▷ *sm*: **il S**~ the seventeenth century

selci'ato [sel'tʃato] *sm* cobbled surface

selezio'nare [selettsjo'nare] /72/ *vt* to select

selezi'one [selet'tsjone] *sf* selection

'sella *sf* saddle

sel'lino *sm* saddle

selvag'gina [selvad'dʒina] *sf* (*animali*) game

sel'vaggio, -a, -gi, -ge [sel'vaddʒo] *ag* wild; (*tribù*) savage, uncivilized; (*fig*) savage, brutal ▷ *sm/f* savage

sel'vatico, -a, -ci, -che *ag* wild

se'maforo *sm* (*Aut*) traffic lights *pl*

sem'brare /72/ *vi* to seem ▷ *vb impers*: **sembra che** it seems that; **mi sembra che** it seems to me that; I think (that); ~ **di essere** to seem to be

'seme *sm* seed; (*sperma*) semen; (*Carte*) suit

se'mestre *sm* half-year, six-month period

semifi'nale *sf* semifinal

semi'freddo *sm* ice-cream dessert

semi'nare /72/ *vt* to sow

semi'nario *sm* seminar; (*Rel*) seminary

seminter'rato *sm* basement; (*appartamento*) basement flat (BRIT) *o* apartment (US)

'semola *sf*: ~ **di grano duro** durum wheat

semo'lino *sm* semolina

'semplice ['semplitʃe] *ag* simple; (*di un solo elemento*) single

'sempre *av* always; (*ancora*) still; **posso** ~ **tentare** I can always *o* still try; **da** ~ always; **per** ~ forever; **una volta per** ~ once and for all; ~ **che** provided (that); ~ **più** more and more; ~ **meno** less and less

sempre'verde *ag, sm o f* (*Bot*) evergreen

'senape *sf* (*Cuc*) mustard

se'nato *sm* senate; **sena'tore, -'trice** *sm/f* senator

'senno *sm* judgment, (*common*) sense; **col** ~ **di poi** with hindsight

'seno *sm* (*Anat: petto, mammella*) breast; (: *grembo, anche fig*) womb; (: *cavità*) sinus

sen'sato, -a *ag* sensible

sensazio'nale [sensattsjo'nale] *ag* sensational

sensazi'one [sensat'tsjone] *sf* feeling, sensation; **fare ~** to cause a sensation, create a stir; **avere la ~ che** to have a feeling that

sen'sibile *ag* sensitive; *(ai sensi)* perceptible; *(rilevante, notevole)* appreciable, noticeable; **~ a** sensitive to

▎ Attenzione! In inglese esiste la parola *sensible*, che però significa *ragionevole*.

sensibiliz'zare [sensibilid'dzare] /72/ *vt* *(fig)* to make aware, awaken

'senso *sm (Fisiol, istinto)* sense; *(impressione, sensazione)* feeling, sensation; *(significato)* meaning, sense; *(direzione)* direction; **sensi** *smpl (coscienza)* consciousness *sg*; *(sensualità)* senses; **fare ~ a** *(ripugnare)* to disgust, repel; **ciò non ha ~** that doesn't make sense; **~ comune** common sense; **in ~ orario/antiorario** clockwise/anticlockwise; **~ di colpa** sense of guilt; **a ~ unico** one-way; **"~ vietato"** *(Aut)* "no entry"

sensu'ale *ag* sensual; sensuous

sen'tenza [sen'tentsa] *sf (Dir)* sentence; *(massima)* maxim

senti'ero *sm* path

sentimen'tale *ag* sentimental; *(vita, avventura)* love *cpd*

senti'mento *sm* feeling

senti'nella *sf* sentry

sen'tire /45/ *vt (percepire al tatto, fig)* to feel; *(udire)* to hear; *(ascoltare)* to listen to; *(odore)* to smell; *(avvertire con il gusto, assaggiare)* to taste ▷ *vi*: **~ di** *(avere sapore)* to taste of; *(avere odore)* to smell of; **sentirsi** *vpr (uso reciproco)* to be in touch; **sentirsi bene/male** to feel well/unwell o ill; **sentirsi di fare qc** *(essere disposto)* to feel like doing sth

sen'tito, -a *ag (sincero)* sincere, warm; **per ~ dire** by hearsay

'senza ['sentsa] *prep, cong* without; **~ dir nulla** without saying a word; **fare ~ qc** to do without sth; **~ di me** without me; **~ che io lo sapessi** without me o my knowing; **~ amici** friendless; **senz'altro** of course, certainly; **~ dubbio** no doubt; **~ scrupoli** unscrupulous

sepa'rare /72/ *vt* to separate; *(dividere)* to divide; *(tenere distinto)* to distinguish; **separarsi** *vpr (coniugi)* to separate, part; *(amici)* to part, leave each other; **separarsi da** *(coniuge)* to separate o part from; *(amico, socio)* to part company with; *(oggetto)* to part with; **sepa'rato, -a** *ag (letti, conto ecc)* separate; *(coniugi)* separated

seppel'lire /55/ *vt* to bury

'seppi *ecc vb vedi* **sapere**

'seppia *sf* cuttlefish ▷ *ag inv* sepia

se'quenza [se'kwentsa] *sf* sequence

seques'trare /72/ *vt (Dir)* to impound; *(rapire)* to kidnap; **se'questro** *sm (Dir)* impoundment; **sequestro di persona** kidnapping

'sera *sf* evening; **di ~** in the evening; **domani ~** tomorrow evening, tomorrow night; **se'rale** *ag* evening *cpd*; **se'rata** *sf* evening; *(ricevimento)* party

ser'bare /72/ *vt* to keep; *(mettere da parte)* to put aside; **~ rancore/odio verso qn** to bear sb a grudge/hate sb

serba'toio *sm* tank; *(cisterna)* cistern

'Serbia *sf*: **la ~** Serbia

'serbo, -a *ag* Serbian ▷ *sm/f* Serbian, Serb ▷ *sm (Ling)* Serbian; *(il serbare)*: **mettere/tenere** o **avere in ~ qc** to put/keep sth aside

se'reno, -a *ag (tempo, cielo)* clear; *(fig)* serene, calm

ser'gente [ser'dʒɛnte] *sm (Mil)* sergeant

'serie *sf inv (successione)* series *inv*; *(gruppo, collezione di chiavi ecc)* set; *(Sport)* division; league; *(Comm)*: **modello di ~/fuori ~** standard/custom-built model; **in ~** in quick succession; *(Comm)* mass *cpd*

serietà *sf* seriousness; reliability

'serio, -a *ag* serious; *(impiegato)* responsible, reliable; *(ditta, cliente)* reliable, dependable; **sul ~** *(davvero)* really, truly; *(seriamente)* seriously, in earnest

ser'pente *sm* snake; **~ a sonagli** rattlesnake

'serra *sf* greenhouse; hothouse

ser'randa *sf* roller shutter

serra'tura *sf* lock

'server ['server] *sm inv (Inform)* server

ser'vire /45/ *vt* to serve; *(clienti: al ristorante)* to wait on; *(: al negozio)* to serve, attend to; *(fig: giovare)* to aid, help; *(Carte)* to deal ▷ *vi* *(Tennis)* to serve; *(essere utile)*: **~ a qn** to be of use to sb; **servirsi** *vpr (usare)*: **servirsi di** to use; *(prendere: cibo)*: **servirsi (di)** to help o.s. (to); *(essere cliente abituale)*: **servirsi da** to be a regular customer at, go to; **~ a qc/a fare** *(utensile ecc)* to be used for sth/for doing; **~ (a qn) da** to serve as (for sb); **serviti pure!** help yourself!

servi'zievole [servit'tsjevole] *ag* obliging, willing to help

ser'vizio [ser'vittsjo] *sm* service; *(al ristorante, sul conto)* service (charge); *(Stampa, TV, Radio)* report; *(da tè, caffè ecc)* set, service; **servizi** *smpl (di casa)* kitchen and bathroom; *(Econ)* services; **essere di ~** to be on duty; **fuori ~** *(telefono ecc)* out of order; **~ compreso/escluso** service included/not included; **~ assistenza clienti** customer service; **~ di posate** set of cutlery; **~ militare** military service; **servizi segreti** secret service *sg*

ses'santa num sixty; **sessan'tesimo, -a** num sixtieth
sessi'one sf session
'sesso sm sex; **sessu'ale** ag sexual, sex cpd
ses'tante sm sextant
'sesto, -a num sixth
'seta sf silk
'sete sf thirst; **avere ~** to be thirsty
'setola sf bristle
'setta sf sect
set'tanta num seventy; **settan'tesimo, -a** num seventieth
set'tare /72/ vt (Inform) to set up
'sette num seven
sette'cento [sette'tʃɛnto] num seven hundred ▷ sm: **il S~** the eighteenth century
set'tembre sm September
settentrio'nale ag northern
settentri'one sm north
setti'mana sf week; **settima'nale** ag, sm weekly

* **SETTIMANA BIANCA**
*
* Settimana bianca is the name given to a
* week-long winter-sports holiday taken
* by many Italians some time in the skiing
* season.

'settimo, -a num seventh
set'tore sm sector
severità sf severity
se'vero, -a ag severe
sevizi'are [sevit'tsjare] /19/ vt to torture
sezio'nare [settsjo'nare] /72/ vt to divide into sections; (Med) to dissect
sezi'one [set'tsjone] sf section
sfacchi'nata [sfakki'nata] sf (fam) chore, drudgery no pl
sfacci'ato, -a [sfat'tʃato] ag (maleducato) cheeky, impudent; (vistoso) gaudy
sfa'mare /72/ vt to feed; (cibo) to fill; **sfamarsi** vpr to satisfy one's hunger, fill o.s. up
sfasci'are [sfaʃ'ʃare] /14/ vt (ferita) to unbandage; (distruggere) to smash, shatter; **sfasciarsi** vpr (rompersi) to smash, shatter
sfavo'revole ag unfavourable
'sfera sf sphere
sfer'rare /72/ vt (fig: colpo) to land, deal; (: attacco) to launch
'sfida sf challenge
sfi'dare /72/ vt to challenge; (fig) to defy, brave
sfi'ducia [sfi'dutʃa] sf distrust, mistrust
sfi'gato, -a (fam) ag: **essere ~** (sfortunato) to be unlucky
sfigu'rare /72/ vt (persona) to disfigure; (quadro, statua) to deface ▷ vi (far cattiva figura) to make a bad impression

sfi'lare /72/ vt (ago) to unthread; (abito, scarpe) to slip off ▷ vi (truppe) to march past, parade; (atleti) to parade; **sfilarsi** vpr (perle ecc) to come unstrung; (orlo, tessuto) to fray; (calza) to run, ladder; **sfi'lata** sf (Mil) parade; (di manifestanti) march; **sfilata di moda** fashion show
'sfinge ['sfindʒe] sf sphinx
sfi'nito, -a ag exhausted
sfio'rare /72/ vt to brush (against); (argomento) to touch upon
sfio'rire /55/ vi to wither, fade
sfo'cato, -a ag (Fot) out of focus
sfoci'are [sfo'tʃare] /14/ vi: **~ in** to flow into; (fig: malcontento) to develop into
sfode'rato, -a ag (vestito) unlined
sfo'gare /80/ vt to vent; **sfogarsi** vpr (sfogare la propria rabbia) to give vent to one's anger; (confidarsi): **sfogarsi (con)** to pour out one's feelings (to); **non sfogarti su di me!** don't take your bad temper out on me!
sfoggi'are [sfod'dʒare] /62/ vt, vi to show off
'sfoglia sf sheet of pasta dough; **pasta ~** (Cuc) puff pastry
sfogli'are /27/ vt (libro) to leaf through
'sfogo, -ghi sm (eruzione cutanea) rash; (fig) outburst; **dare ~ a** (fig) to give vent to
sfon'dare /72/ vt (porta) to break down; (scarpe) to wear a hole in; (cesto, scatola) to burst, knock the bottom out of; (Mil) to break through ▷ vi (riuscire) to make a name for o.s.
'sfondo sm background
sfor'mato sm (Cuc) type of soufflé
sfor'tuna sf misfortune, ill luck no pl; **avere ~** to be unlucky; **sfortu'nato, -a** ag unlucky; (impresa, film) unsuccessful
sfor'zare [sfor'tsare] /72/ vt to force; **sforzarsi** vpr: **sforzarsi di o a o per fare** to try hard to do
'sforzo ['sfortso] sm effort; (tensione eccessiva, Tecn) strain; **fare uno ~** to make an effort
sfrat'tare /72/ vt to evict; **'sfratto** sm eviction
sfrecci'are [sfret'tʃare] /14/ vi to shoot o flash past
sfre'gare /80/ vt (strofinare) to rub; (graffiare) to scratch; **sfregarsi le mani** to rub one's hands; **~ un fiammifero** to strike a match
sfregi'are [sfre'dʒare] /62/ vt to slash, gash; (persona) to disfigure; (quadro) to deface
sfre'nato, -a ag (fig) unrestrained, unbridled
sfron'tato, -a ag shameless

sfrutta'mento sm exploitation

sfrut'tare /72/ vt (terreno) to overwork, exhaust; (miniera) to exploit, work; (fig: operai, occasione, potere) to exploit

sfug'gire [sfud'dʒire] /31/ vi to escape; ~ **a** (custode) to escape (from); (morte) to escape; ~ **a qn** (dettaglio, nome) to escape sb; ~ **di mano a qn** to slip out of sb's hand (o hands)

sfu'mare /72/ vt (colori, contorni) to soften, shade off ▷ vi to shade (off), fade; (fig: svanire) to vanish, disappear; (: speranze) to come to nothing

sfuma'tura sf shading off no pl; (tonalità) shade, tone; (fig) touch, hint

sfuri'ata sf (scatto di collera) fit of anger; (rimprovero) sharp rebuke

sga'bello sm stool

sgabuz'zino [zgabud'dzino] sm lumber room

sgambet'tare /72/ vi to kick one's legs about

sgam'betto sm: **far lo ~ a qn** to trip sb up; (fig) to oust sb

sganci'are [zgan'tʃare] /14/ vt to unhook; (Ferr) to uncouple; (bombe: da aereo) to release, drop; (fig: fam: soldi) to fork out; **sganciarsi** vpr (fig): **sganciarsi (da)** to get away (from)

sganghe'rato, -a [zgange'rato] ag (porta) off its hinges; (auto) ramshackle; (riso) wild, boisterous

sgar'bato, -a ag rude, impolite

'sgarbo sm: **fare uno ~ a qn** to be rude to sb

sgargi'ante [zgar'dʒante] ag gaudy, showy

sgattaio'lare /72/ vi to sneak away o off

sge'lare [zdʒe'lare] /72/ vi, vt to thaw

sghignaz'zare [zgiɲɲat'tsare] /72/ vi to laugh scornfully

sgob'bare /72/ vi (scolaro) to swot; (operaio) to slog

sgombe'rare /72/, **sgomb'rare** vt (tavolo, stanza) to clear; (evacuare: piazza, città) to evacuate ▷ vi to move

'sgombro, -a ag: ~ **(di)** clear (of), free (from) ▷ sm (Zool) mackerel; (anche: **sgombero**) clearing; vacating; evacuation; (trasloco) removal

sgonfi'are /19/ vt to let down, deflate; **sgonfiarsi** vpr to go down

'sgonfio, -a ag (pneumatico, pallone) flat

'sgorbio sm blot; scribble

sgra'devole ag unpleasant, disagreeable

sgra'dito, -a ag unpleasant, unwelcome

sgra'nare /72/ vt (piselli) to shell; ~ **gli occhi** to open one's eyes wide

sgran'chire [zgran'kire] /55/ vt, **sgranchirsi** [zgran'kirsi] vpr to stretch; **sgranchirsi le gambe** to stretch one's legs

sgranocchi'are [zgranok'kjare] /19/ vt to munch

'sgravio sm: ~ **fiscale** o **contributivo** tax relief

sgrazi'ato, -a [zgrat'tsjato] ag clumsy, ungainly

sgri'dare /72/ vt to scold

sgual'cire [zgwal'tʃire] /55/ vt to crumple (up), crease

sgual'drina sf (peg) slut (!)

sgu'ardo sm (occhiata) look, glance; (espressione) look (in one's eye)

sguaz'zare [zgwat'tsare] /72/ vi (nell'acqua) to splash about; (nella melma) to wallow; ~ **nell'oro** to be rolling in money

sguinzagli'are [zgwintsaʎ'ʎare] /27/ vt to let off the leash; (fig: persona): ~ **qn dietro a qn** to set sb on sb

sgusci'are [zguʃ'ʃare] /14/ vt to shell ▷ vi (sfuggire di mano) to slip; ~ **via** to slip o slink away

'shampoo ['ʃampo] sm inv shampoo

'shiatzu ['tʃjatsu] sm inv shiatsu

shock [ʃɔk] sm inv shock

PAROLA CHIAVE

si (dav lo, la, li, le, ne diventa **se**) pron

1 (riflessivo: maschile) himself; (: femminile) herself; (: neutro) itself; (: impersonale) oneself; (: pl) themselves; **lavarsi** to wash (oneself); **si è tagliato** he has cut himself; **si credono importanti** they think a lot of themselves

2 (riflessivo, con complemento oggetto): **lavarsi le mani** to wash one's hands; **si sta lavando i capelli** he (o she) is washing his (o her) hair

3 (reciproco) one another, each other; **si amano** they love one another o each other

4 (passivo): **si ripara facilmente** it is easily repaired

5 (impersonale): **si dice che ...** they o people say that ...; **si vede che è vecchio** one o you can see that it's old

6 (noi) we; **tra poco si parte** we're leaving soon

sì av yes; **un giorno sì e uno no** every other day

'sia ecc vb vedi **essere**

si'amo vb vedi **essere**

si'cario sm hired killer

sicché [sik'ke] cong (perciò) so (that), therefore; (e quindi) (and) so

siccità [sittʃi'ta] sf drought

sic'come cong since, as

Si'cilia [si'tʃilja] sf: **la ~** Sicily; **sicili'ano, -a** [sitʃi'ljano] ag, sm/f Sicilian

si'cura sf safety catch; (Aut) safety lock

sicu'rezza [siku'rettsa] *sf* safety; security; confidence; certainty; **di ~** safety *cpd*; **la ~ stradale** road safety

si'curo, -a *ag* safe; (*ben difeso*) secure; (*fiducioso*) confident; (*certo*) sure, certain; (*notizia, amico*) reliable; (*esperto*) skilled ▷ *av* (*anche:* **di ~**) certainly; **essere/mettere al ~** to be safe/put in a safe place; **~ di sé** self-confident, sure of o.s.; **sentirsi ~** to feel safe *o* secure

si'edo *ecc vb vedi* **sedere**

si'epe *sf* hedge

si'ero *sm* (*Med*) serum; **sieronega'tivo, -a** *ag* HIV-negative; **sieroposi'tivo, -a** *ag* HIV-positive

si'ete *vb vedi* **essere**

si'filide *sf* syphilis

Sig. *abbr* (= *signore*) Mr

siga'retta *sf* cigarette; **~ elettronica** e-cigarette

'sigaro *sm* cigar

Sigg. *abbr* (= *signori*) Messrs

sigil'lare [sidʒil'lare] /72/ *vt* to seal

si'gillo [si'dʒillo] *sm* seal

'sigla *sf* initials *pl*; (*abbreviazione*) acronym, abbreviation; **~ automobilistica** *abbreviation of province on vehicle number plate*; **~ musicale** signature tune

Sig.na *abbr* (= *signorina*) Miss

signifi'care [siɲɲifi'kare] /20/ *vt* to mean; **signifi'cato** *sm* meaning

si'gnora [siɲ'ɲora] *sf* lady; **la ~ X** Mrs X; **buon giorno S~/Signore/Signorina** good morning; (*deferente*) good morning Madam/Sir/Madam; (*quando si conosce il nome*) good morning Mrs/Mr/Miss X; **Gentile S~/Signore/Signorina** (*in una lettera*) Dear Madam/Sir/Madam; **il signor Rossi e ~** Mr Rossi and his wife; **signore e signori** ladies and gentlemen

si'gnore [siɲ'ɲore] *sm* gentleman; (*padrone*) lord, master; (*Rel*): **il S~** the Lord; **il signor X** Mr X; **i signori Bianchi** (*coniugi*) Mr and Mrs Bianchi; *vedi anche* **signora**

signo'rile [siɲɲo'rile] *ag* refined

signo'rina [siɲɲo'rina] *sf* young lady; **la ~ X** Miss X; *vedi anche* **signora**

Sig.ra *abbr* (= *signora*) Mrs

silenzia'tore [silentsja'tore] *sm* silencer

si'lenzio [si'lentsjo] *sm* silence; **fare ~** to be quiet, stop talking; **silenzi'oso, -a** *ag* silent, quiet

si'licio [si'litʃo] *sm* silicon

sili'cone *sm* silicone

'sillaba *sf* syllable

si'luro *sm* torpedo

SIM [sim] *sigla f inv* (*Tel*): **~ card** SIM card

simboleggi'are [simboled'dʒare] /62/ *vt* to symbolize

'simbolo *sm* symbol

'simile *ag* (*analogo*) similar; (*di questo tipo*): **un uomo ~** such a man, a man like this; **libri simili** such books; **~ a** similar to; **i suoi simili** one's fellow men; one's peers

simme'tria *sf* symmetry

simpa'tia *sf* (*qualità*) pleasantness; (*inclinazione*) liking; **avere ~ per qn** to like sb, have a liking for sb; **sim'patico, -a, -ci, -che** *ag* (*persona*) nice, pleasant, likeable; (*casa, albergo ecc*) nice, pleasant

> Attenzione! In inglese esiste la parola *sympathetic*, che però significa *comprensivo*.

simpatiz'zare [simpatid'dzare] /72/ *vi*: **~ con** to take a liking to

simu'lare /72/ *vt* to sham, simulate; (*Tecn*) to simulate

simul'taneo, -a *ag* simultaneous

sina'goga, -ghe *sf* synagogue

sincerità [sintʃeri'ta] *sf* sincerity

sin'cero, -a [sin'tʃero] *ag* sincere; (*onesto*) genuine; heartfelt

sinda'cale *ag* (trade-)union *cpd*

sinda'cato *sm* (*di lavoratori*) (trade) union; (*Amm, Econ, Dir*) syndicate, trust, pool

'sindaco, -ci *sm* mayor

sinfo'nia *sf* (*Mus*) symphony

singhioz'zare [singjot'tsare] /72/ *vi* to sob; to hiccup

singhi'ozzo [sin'gjottso] *sm* sob; (*Med*) hiccup; **avere il ~** to have the hiccups; **a ~** (*fig*) by fits and starts

'single ['singol] *ag inv*, *smf inv* single

singo'lare *ag* (*insolito*) remarkable, singular; (*Ling*) singular ▷ *sm* (*Ling*) singular; (*Tennis*): **~ maschile/femminile** men's/women's singles

'singolo, -a *ag* single, individual ▷ *sm* (*persona*) individual; (*Tennis*) = **singolare**

si'nistro, -a *ag* left, left-hand; (*fig*) sinister ▷ *sm* (*incidente*) accident ▷ *sf* (*Pol*) left (wing); **a sinistra** on the left; (*direzione*) to the left

si'nonimo *sm* synonym; **~ di** synonymous with

sin'tassi *sf* syntax

'sintesi *sf* synthesis; (*riassunto*) summary, résumé

sin'tetico, -a, -ci, -che *ag* synthetic

sintetiz'zare [sintetid'dzare] /72/ *vt* to synthesize; (*riassumere*) to summarize

sinto'matico, -a, -ci, -che *ag* symptomatic

'sintomo *sm* symptom

sintoniz'zare [sintonid'dzare] /72/ *vt* to tune (in); **sintonizzarsi** *vpr*: **sintonizzarsi su** to tune in to

si'pario *sm* (*Teat*) curtain

si'rena sf (apparecchio) siren; (nella mitologia, fig) siren, mermaid

'Siria sf: **la ~** Syria

si'ringa, -ghe sf syringe

'sismico, -a, -ci, -che ag seismic

sis'tema, -i sm system; (metodo) method, way; **~ nervoso** nervous system; **~ operativo** (Inform) operating system; **~ solare** solar system

siste'mare /72/ vt (mettere a posto) to tidy, put in order; (risolvere: questione) to sort out, settle; (procurare un lavoro a) to find a job for; (dare un alloggio a) to settle, find accommodation (BRIT) o accommodations (US) for; **sistemarsi** vpr (problema) to be settled; (persona: trovare alloggio) to find accommodation(s); (: trovarsi un lavoro) to get fixed up with a job; **ti sistemo io!** I'll soon sort you out!

siste'matico, -a, -ci, -che ag systematic

sistemazi'one [sistemat'tsjone] sf arrangement, order; settlement; employment; accommodation (BRIT), accommodations (US)

'sito sm: **~ Internet** website

situ'ato, -a ag: **~ a/su** situated at/on

situazi'one [situat'tsjone] sf situation

ski-lift [ski'lift] sm inv ski tow

slacci'are [zlat'tʃare] /14/ vt to undo, unfasten

slanci'ato, -a [zlan'tʃato] ag slender

'slancio sm dash, leap; (fig) surge; **di ~** impetuously

'slavo, -a ag Slav(onic), Slavic

sle'ale ag disloyal; (concorrenza ecc) unfair

sle'gare /80/ vt to untie

slip [zlip] sm inv briefs pl

'slitta sf sledge; (trainata) sleigh

slit'tare /72/ vi to slip, slide; (Aut) to skid

s.l.m. abbr (= sul livello del mare) a.s.l.

slo'gare /80/ vt (Med) to dislocate

sloggi'are [zlod'dʒare] /62/ vt (inquilino) to turn out ▷ vi to move out

Slo'vacchia [zlo'vakkja] sf Slovakia

slo'vacco, -a, -ci, -che ag, sm/f Slovak

Slo'venia sf Slovenia

slo'veno, -a ag, sm/f Slovene, Slovenian ▷ sm (Ling) Slovene

smacchi'are [zmak'kjare] /19/ vt to remove stains from; **smacchia'tore** sm stain remover

'smacco, -chi sm humiliating defeat

smagli'ante [zmaʎ'ʎante] ag brilliant, dazzling

smaglia'tura [zmaʎʎa'tura] sf (su maglia, calza) ladder; (sulla pelle) stretch mark

smalizi'ato, -a [smalit'tsjato] ag shrewd, cunning

smalti'mento sm (di rifiuti) disposal

smal'tire /55/ vt (merce) to sell off; (rifiuti) to dispose of; (cibo) to digest; (peso) to lose; (rabbia) to get over; **~ la sbornia** to sober up

'smalto sm (anche di denti) enamel; (per ceramica) glaze; **~ per unghie** nail varnish

smantel'lare /72/ vt to dismantle

smarri'mento sm loss; (fig) bewilderment; dismay

smar'rire /55/ vt to lose; (non riuscire a trovare) to mislay; **smarrirsi** vpr (perdersi) to lose one's way, get lost; (: oggetto) to go astray

'smartphone ['zmartfon] sm inv smartphone

smasche'rare [zmaske'rare] /72/ vt to unmask

SME abbr = **Stato Maggiore Esercito** ▷ sigla m (= Sistema Monetario Europeo) EMS

smen'tire /55/ vt (negare) to deny; (testimonianza) to refute; **smentirsi** vpr to be inconsistent

sme'raldo sm emerald

'smesso, -a pp di **smettere**

'smettere /63/ vt to stop; (vestiti) to stop wearing ▷ vi to stop, cease; **~ di fare** to stop doing

'smilzo, -a ['zmiltso] ag thin, lean

sminu'ire /72/ vt to diminish, lessen; (fig) to belittle

sminuz'zare [zminut'tsare] /72/ vt to break into small pieces; to crumble

'smisi ecc vb vedi **smettere**

smis'tare /72/ vt (pacchi ecc) to sort; (Ferr) to shunt

smisu'rato, -a ag boundless, immeasurable; (grandissimo) immense, enormous

'smoking ['zmoukiŋ] sm inv dinner jacket

smon'tare /72/ vt (mobile, macchina ecc) to take to pieces, dismantle; (fig: scoraggiare) to dishearten ▷ vi (scendere: da cavallo) to dismount; (: da treno) to get off; (terminare il lavoro) to stop (work); **smontarsi** vpr to lose heart; to lose one's enthusiasm

'smorfia sf grimace; (atteggiamento lezioso) simpering; **fare smorfie** to make faces; to simper

'smorto, -a ag (viso) pale, wan; (colore) dull

smor'zare [zmor'tsare] /72/ vt (suoni) to deaden; (colori) to tone down; (luce) to dim; (sete) to quench; (entusiasmo) to dampen; **smorzarsi** vpr (suono, luce) to fade; (entusiasmo) to dampen

sms ['ɛsse'ɛmme'ɛsse] sm inv text (message)

smu'overe /66/ vt to move, shift; (fig: commuovere) to move; (: dall'inerzia) to rouse, stir

snatu'rato, -a ag inhuman, heartless

'snello, -a ag (agile) agile; (svelto) slender, slim

sner'vante ag (attesa, lavoro) exasperating

sniffare [znif'fare] /72/ vt (fam: cocaina) to snort

snob'bare /72/ vt to snub

sno'dare /72/ vt (rendere agile, mobile) to loosen; **snodarsi** vpr to come loose; (articolarsi) to bend; (strada, fiume) to wind

sno'dato, -a ag (articolazione, persona) flexible; (fune ecc) undone

so vb vedi **sapere**

sobbar'carsi /20/ vpr: **~ a** to take on, undertake

'sobrio, -a ag sober

socchi'udere [sok'kjudere] /22/ vt (porta) to leave ajar; (occhi) to half-close; **socchi'uso, -a** pp di **socchiudere**

soc'correre /28/ vt to help, assist

soccorri'tore, -'trice sm/f rescuer

soc'corso, -a pp di **soccorrere** ▷ sm help, aid, assistance; **~ stradale** breakdown service

soci'ale [so'tʃale] ag social; (di associazione) club cpd, association cpd

socia'lismo [sotʃa'lizmo] sm socialism; **socia'lista, -i, -e** ag, smf socialist; **socializ'zare** [sotʃalid'dzare] /72/ vi to socialize

società [sotʃe'ta] sf inv society; (sportiva) club; (Comm) company; **~ per azioni** joint-stock company; **~ a responsabilità limitata** type of limited liability company

soci'evole [so'tʃevole] ag sociable

'socio [ˈsɔtʃo] sm (Dir, Comm) partner; (membro di associazione) member

'soda sf (Chim) soda; (acqua gassata) soda (water)

soddisfa'cente [soddisfa'tʃɛnte] ag satisfactory

soddis'fare /41/ vt, vi: **~ (a)** to satisfy; (impegno) to fulfil; (debito) to pay off; (richiesta) to meet, comply with; **soddis'fatto, -a** pp di **soddisfare** ▷ ag satisfied; **essere soddisfatto di** to be satisfied o pleased with; **soddisfazi'one** sf satisfaction

'sodo, -a ag firm, hard; (uovo) hard-boiled ▷ av (picchiare, lavorare) hard; **dormire ~** to sleep soundly

sofà sm inv sofa

soffe'renza [soffe'rɛntsa] sf suffering

soff'erto, -a pp di **soffrire**

soffi'are /19/ vt to blow; (notizia, segreto) to whisper ▷ vi to blow; (sbuffare) to puff (and blow); **soffiarsi il naso** to blow one's nose; **~ qc/qn a qn** (fig) to pinch o steal sth/sb from sb; **~ via qc** to blow sth away

soffi'ata sf (fam) tip-off; **fare una ~ alla polizia** to tip off the police

'soffice [ˈsɔffitʃe] ag soft

'soffio sm (di vento) breath; (Med) murmur

soff'itta sf attic

soff'itto sm ceiling

soffo'cante ag suffocating, stifling

soffo'care /20/ vi (anche: **soffocarsi**) to suffocate, choke ▷ vt to suffocate, choke; (fig) to stifle, suppress

soff'rire /70/ vt to suffer, endure; (sopportare) to bear, stand ▷ vi to suffer; to be in pain; **~ (di) qc** (Med) to suffer from sth

soff'ritto, -a pp di **soffriggere** ▷ sm (Cuc) fried mixture of herbs, bacon and onions

sofisti'cato, -a ag sophisticated; (vino) adulterated

'software [ˈsɔftwɛa] sm: **~ applicativo** applications package

sogget'tivo, -a [soddʒet'tivo] ag subjective

sog'getto, -a [sod'dʒetto] ag: **~ a** (sottomesso) subject to; (esposto: a variazioni, danni ecc) subject o liable to ▷ sm subject

soggezi'one [soddʒet'tsjone] sf subjection; (timidezza) awe; **avere ~ di qn** to stand in awe of sb; to be ill at ease in sb's presence

sogg'iorno [sod'dʒorno] sm (permanenza) stay; (stanza) living room

'soglia [ˈsɔʎʎa] sf doorstep; (anche fig) threshold

sogli'ola [ˈsɔʎʎola] sf (Zool) sole

so'gnare [son'nare] /15/ vt, vi to dream; **~ a occhi aperti** to daydream

'sogno [ˈsonno] sm dream

'soia sf (Bot) soya

sol sm (Mus) G; (: solfeggiando la scala) so(h)

so'laio sm (soffitta) attic

sola'mente av only, just

so'lare ag solar, sun cpd

'solco, -chi sm (scavo, fig: ruga) furrow; (incavo) rut, track; (di disco) groove

sol'dato sm soldier; **~ semplice** private

'soldo sm (fig): **non vale un ~** it's not worth a penny; **soldi** smpl (denaro) money sg; **non ho soldi** I haven't got any money

'sole sm sun; (luce) sun(light); (tempo assolato) sun(shine); **prendere il ~** to sunbathe

soleggi'ato, -a [soled'dʒato] ag sunny

so'lenne ag solemn

so'lere /108/ vb impers: **come suole accadere** as is usually the case, as usually happens

soli'dale ag: **essere ~ con qn** to be in agreement with sb

solidarietà sf solidarity

'solido, -a ag solid; (forte, robusto) sturdy, solid; (fig: ditta) sound, solid ▷ sm (Mat) solid

so'lista, -i, -e *ag* solo ▷ *smf* soloist

solita'mente *av* usually, as a rule

soli'tario, -a *ag* (*senza compagnia*) solitary, lonely; (*solo, isolato*) solitary, lone; (*deserto*) lonely ▷ *sm* (*gioiello, gioco*) solitaire

'solito, -a *ag* usual; **essere ~ fare** to be in the habit of doing; **di ~** usually; **più tardi del ~** later than usual; **come al ~** as usual

soli'tudine *sf* solitude

sol'letico *sm* tickling; **soffrire il ~** to be ticklish

solleva'mento *sm* raising; lifting; (*ribellione*) revolt; **~ pesi** (*Sport*) weight-lifting

solle'vare /72/ *vt* to lift, raise; (*fig: persona: alleggerire*): **~ (da)** to relieve (of); (: *dar conforto*) to comfort, relieve; (: *questione*) to raise; (: *far insorgere*) to stir (to revolt); **sollevarsi** *vpr* to rise; (*fig: riprendersi*) to recover; (: *ribellarsi*) to rise up

solli'evo *sm* relief; (*conforto*) comfort

'solo, -a *ag* alone; (*in senso spirituale: isolato*) lonely; (*unico*) **un ~ libro** only one book, a single book; (*con ag numerale*): **veniamo noi tre soli** just *o* only the three of us are coming ▷ *av* (*soltanto*) only, just; **non ~ ... ma anche** not only ... but also; **fare qc da ~** to do sth (all) by oneself

sol'tanto *av* only

so'lubile *ag* (*sostanza*) soluble

soluzi'one [soluttsjone] *sf* solution

sol'vente *ag*, *sm* solvent

so'maro *sm* ass, donkey

somigli'anza [somiʎʎantsa] *sf* resemblance

somigli'are [somiʎʎare] /27/ *vi*: **~ a** to be like, resemble; (*nell'aspetto fisico*) to look like; **somigliarsi** *vpr* to be (*o* look) alike

'somma *sf* (*Mat*) sum; (*di denaro*) sum (of money)

som'mare /72/ *vt* to add up; (*aggiungere*) to add; **tutto sommato** all things considered

som'mario, -a *ag* (*racconto, indagine*) brief; (*giustizia*) summary ▷ *sm* summary

sommer'gibile [sommer'dʒibile] *sm* submarine

som'merso, -a *pp di* **sommergere**

sommità *sf inv* summit, top; (*fig*) height

som'mossa *sf* uprising

'sonda *sf* (*Med, Meteor, Aer*) probe; (*Mineralogia*) drill ▷ *ag inv*: **pallone m ~** weather balloon

son'daggio [son'daddʒo] *sm* sounding; probe; boring, drilling; (*indagine*) survey; **~ d'opinioni** opinion poll

son'dare /72/ *vt* (*Naut*) to sound; (*atmosfera, piaga*) to probe; (*Mineralogia*) to bore, drill; (*fig: opinione ecc*) to survey, poll

so'netto *sm* sonnet

son'nambulo, -a *sm/f* sleepwalker

sonnel'lino *sm* nap

son'nifero *sm* sleeping drug (*o* pill)

'sonno *sm* sleep; **aver ~** to be sleepy; **prendere ~** to fall asleep

'sono *vb vedi* **essere**

so'noro, -a *ag* (*ambiente*) resonant; (*voce*) sonorous, ringing; (*onde: Cine*) sound *cpd*

sontu'oso, -a *ag* sumptuous; lavish

sop'palco, -chi *sm* mezzanine

soppor'tare /72/ *vt* (*subire: perdita, spese*) to bear, sustain; (*soffrire: dolore*) to bear, endure; (*cosa: freddo*) to withstand; (*persona: freddo, vino*) to take; (*tollerare*) to put up with, tolerate

> Attenzione! In inglese esiste il verbo *to support*, che però non significa *sopportare*.

sop'primere /50/ *vt* (*carica, privilegi ecc*) to do away with; (*pubblicazione*) to suppress; (*parola, frase*) to delete

'sopra *prep* (*gen*) on; (*al di sopra di, più in alto di*) above; over; (*riguardo a*) on, about ▷ *av* on top; (*attaccato, scritto*) on it; (*al di sopra*) above; (*al piano superiore*) upstairs; **donne ~ i 30 anni** women over 30 (years of age); **abito di ~** I live upstairs; **dormirci ~** (*fig*) to sleep on it

so'prabito *sm* overcoat

soprac'ciglio [soprat'tʃiʎʎo] (*pl f* **sopracciglia**) *sm* eyebrow

sopraffare /41/ *vt* to overcome, overwhelm

soprallu'ogo, -ghi *sm* (*di esperti*) inspection; (*di polizia*) on-the-spot investigation

sopram'mobile *sm* ornament

soprannatu'rale *ag* supernatural

sopran'nome *sm* nickname

so'prano, -a *sm/f* (*persona*) soprano ▷ *sm* (*voce*) soprano

soprappensi'ero *av* lost in thought

sopras'salto *sm*: **di ~** with a start; suddenly

soprasse'dere /107/ *vi*: **~ a** to delay, put off

soprat'tutto *av* (*anzitutto*) above all; (*specialmente*) especially

sopravvalu'tare /72/ *vt* to overestimate

soprav'vento *sm*: **avere/prendere il ~ su qn** to have/get the upper hand over sb

sopravvis'suto, -a *pp di* **sopravvivere**

soprav'vivere /130/ *vi* to survive; (*continuare a vivere*): **~ (in)** to live on (in); **~ a** (*incidente ecc*) to survive; (*persona*) to outlive

so'pruso *sm* abuse of power; **subire un ~** to be abused

soq'quadro *sm*: **mettere a ~** to turn upside-down

sor'betto *sm* sorbet, water ice

sor'dina *sf*: **in ~** softly; (*fig*) on the sly

'**sordo, -a** *ag* deaf; (*rumore*) muffled; (*dolore*) dull; (*odio, rancore*) veiled ▷ *sm/f* deaf person; **sordo'muto, -a** *ag* hearing- and speech-impaired ▷ *sm/f* person with a hearing- and speech-impairment

so'**rella** *sf* sister; **sorel'lastra** *sf* stepsister; (*con genitore in comune*) half sister

sor'**gente** [sor'dʒɛnte] *sf* (*acqua che sgorga*) spring; (*di fiume, Fisica, fig*) source

'**sorgere** ['sordʒere] /109/ *vi* to rise; (*scaturire*) to spring, rise; (*fig: difficoltà*) to arise

sorni'**one, -a** *ag* sly

sorpas'**sare** /72/ *vt* (*Aut*) to overtake; (*fig*) to surpass; (: *eccedere*) to exceed, go beyond; **~ in altezza** to be higher than; (*persona*) to be taller than

sorpren'**dente** *ag* surprising

sor'**prendere** /81/ *vt* (*cogliere: in flagrante ecc*) to catch; (*stupire*) to surprise; **sorprendersi** *vpr*: **sorprendersi (di)** to be surprised (at); **sor'preso, -a** *pp di* **sorprendere** ▷ *sf* surprise; **fare una sorpresa a qn** to give sb a surprise

sor'**reggere** [sor'rɛddʒere] /87/ *vt* to support, hold up; (*fig*) to sustain; **sorreggersi** *vpr* (*tenersi ritto*) to stay upright

sor'**ridere** /89/ *vi* to smile; **sor'riso, -a** *pp di* **sorridere** ▷ *sm* smile

'**sorsi** *ecc vb vedi* **sorgere**

'**sorso** *sm* sip

'**sorta** *sf* sort, kind; **di ~** whatever, of any kind at all

'**sorte** *sf* (*fato*) fate, destiny; (*evento fortuito*) chance; **tirare a ~** to draw lots

sor'**teggio** [sor'tɛddʒo] *sm* draw

sorvegli'**ante** [sorveʎ'ʎante] *smf* (*di carcere*) guard, warder (BRIT); (*di fabbrica ecc*) supervisor

sorvegli'**anza** [sorveʎ'ʎantsa] *sf* watch; supervision; (*Polizia, Mil*) surveillance

sorvegli'**are** [sorveʎ'ʎare] /27/ *vt* (*bambino, bagagli, prigioniero*) to watch, keep an eye on; (*malato*) to watch over; (*territorio, casa*) to watch o keep watch over; (*lavori*) to supervise

sorvo'**lare** /72/ *vt* (*territorio*) to fly over ▷ *vi*: **~ su** (*fig*) to skim over

S.O.S. *sigla m* mayday, SOS

'**sosia** *sm inv* double

sos'**pendere** /8/ *vt* (*appendere*) to hang (up); (*interrompere, privare di una carica*) to suspend; (*rimandare*) to defer; (*appendere*) to hang

sospet'**tare** /72/ *vt* to suspect ▷ *vi*: **~ di** to suspect; (*diffidare*) to be suspicious of

sos'**petto, -a** *ag* suspicious ▷ *sm* suspicion; **sospet'toso, -a** *ag* suspicious

sospi'**rare** /72/ *vi* to sigh ▷ *vt* to long for, yearn for; **sos'piro** *sm* sigh

'**sosta** *sf* (*fermata*) stop, halt; (*pausa*) pause, break; **senza ~** non-stop, without a break

sostan'**tivo** *sm* noun, substantive

sos'**tanza** [sos'tantsa] *sf* substance; **sostanze** *sfpl* (*ricchezze*) wealth *sg*, possessions; **in ~** in short, to sum up

sos'**tare** /72/ *vi* (*fermarsi*) to stop (for a while), stay; (*fare una pausa*) to take a break

sos'**tegno** [sos'teɲɲo] *sm* support

soste'**nere** /121/ *vt* to support; (*prendere su di sé*) to take on, bear; (*resistere*) to withstand, stand up to; (*affermare*): **~ che** to maintain that; **sostenersi** *vpr* to hold o.s. up, support o.s.; (*fig*) to keep up one's strength; **~ gli esami** to sit exams

sostenta'**mento** *sm* maintenance, support

sostitu'**ire** /55/ *vt* (*mettere al posto di*): **~ qn/ qc a** to substitute sb/sth for; (*prendere il posto di*) to replace, take the place of

sosti'**tuto, -a** *sm/f* substitute

sostituzi'**one** [sostitut'tsjone] *sf* substitution; **in ~ di** as a substitute for, in place of

sotta'**ceti** [sotta'tʃeti] *smpl* pickles

sot'**tana** *sf* (*sottoveste*) underskirt; (*gonna*) skirt; (*Rel*) soutane, cassock

sotter'**fugio** [sotter'fudʒo] *sm* subterfuge

sotter'**raneo, -a** *ag* underground ▷ *sm* cellar

sotter'**rare** /72/ *vt* to bury

sot'**tile** *ag* thin; (*figura, caviglia*) thin, slim, slender; (*fine: polvere, capelli*) fine; (*fig: leggero*) light; (: *vista*) sharp, keen; (: *olfatto*) fine, discriminating; (: *mente*) subtle; shrewd ▷ *sm*: **non andare per il ~** not to mince matters

sottin'**teso, -a** *pp di* **sottintendere** ▷ *sm* allusion; **parlare senza sottintesi** to speak plainly

'**sotto** *prep* (*gen*) under; (*più in basso di*) below ▷ *av* underneath, beneath; below; **(al piano) di ~** downstairs; **~ il monte** at the foot of the mountain; **~ la pioggia/ il sole** in the rain/sun(shine); **siamo ~ Natale/Pasqua** it's nearly Christmas/ Easter; **~ forma di** in the form of; **~ terra** underground; **chiuso ~ vuoto** vacuum packed

sotto'**fondo** *sm* background; **~ musicale** background music

sottoline'**are** /72/ *vt* to underline; (*fig*) to emphasize, stress

sottoma'**rino, -a** *ag* (*flora*) submarine; (*cavo, navigazione*) underwater ▷ *sm* (*Naut*) submarine

sottopas'**saggio** [sottopas'saddʒo] *sm* (*Aut*) underpass; (*pedonale*) subway, underpass

sotto'porre /77/ vt (costringere) to subject; (fig: presentare) to submit; **sottoporsi** vpr to submit; **sottoporsi a** (subire) to undergo

sotto'sopra av upside-down

sotto'terra av underground

sotto'titolo sm subtitle

sottovalu'tare /72/ vt to underestimate

sotto'veste sf underskirt

sotto'voce [sotto'votʃe] av in a low voice

sottovu'oto av: **confezionare ~** to vacuum-pack ▷ ag: **confezione** f **~** vacuum pack

sot'trarre /123/ vt (Mat) to subtract, take away; **sottrarsi** vpr: **sottrarsi a** (sfuggire) to escape; (evitare) to avoid; **~ qn/qc a** (togliere) to remove sb/sth from; (salvare) to save o rescue sb/sth from; **~ qc a qn** (rubare) to steal sth from sb; **sottrazi'one** sf subtraction; (furto) removal

souve'nir [suv(ə)'nir] sm inv souvenir

sovi'etico, -a, -ci, -che ag Soviet ▷ sm/f Soviet citizen

sovrac'carico, -a, -chi, -che ag: **~ (di)** overloaded (with) ▷ sm excess load; **~ di lavoro** extra work

sovraffol'lato, -a ag overcrowded

sovrannatu'rale ag = **soprannaturale**

so'vrano, -a ag sovereign; (fig: sommo) supreme ▷ sm/f sovereign, monarch

sovrap'porre /77/ vt to place on top of, put on top of

sovvenzi'one [sovven'tsjone] sf subsidy, grant

'sozzo, -a ['sottso] ag filthy, dirty

S.p.A. abbr vedi **società per azioni**

spac'care /20/ vt to split, break; (legna) to chop; **spaccarsi** vpr to split, break; **spacca'tura** sf split

spaccherò ecc [spakke'rɔ] vb vedi **spaccare**

spacci'are /14/ vt (vendere) to sell (off); (mettere in circolazione) to circulate; (droga) to peddle, push; **spacciarsi** vpr: **spacciarsi per** (farsi credere) to pass o.s. off as, pretend to be; **spaccia'tore, -'trice** [spattʃa'tore] sm/f (di droga) pusher; (di denaro falso) dealer; **spaccio** sm: **spaccio (di)** (di merce rubata, droga) trafficking (in); (di denaro falso) passing (of); (vendita) sale; (bottega) shop

'spacco, -chi sm (fenditura) split, crack; (strappo) tear; (di gonna) slit

spac'cone smf boaster, braggart

'spada sf sword

spae'sato, -a ag disorientated, lost

spa'ghetti [spa'getti] smpl (Cuc) spaghetti sg

'Spagna ['spaɲɲa] sf: **la ~** Spain; **spa'gnolo, -a** ag Spanish ▷ sm/f Spaniard ▷ sm (Ling) Spanish; **gli Spagnoli** the Spanish

'spago, -ghi sm string, twine

spai'ato, -a ag (calza, guanto) odd

spalan'care /20/ vt, **spalan'carsi** vpr to open wide

spa'lare /72/ vt to shovel

'spalla sf shoulder; (fig: Teat) stooge; **spalle** sfpl (dorso) back

spalli'era sf (di sedia ecc) back; (di letto: da capo) head(board); (: da piedi) foot(board); (Ginnastica) wall bars pl

spal'lina sf (di sottoveste, maglietta) strap; (imbottitura) shoulder pad

spal'mare /72/ vt to spread

'spalti smpl (di stadio) terraces

spamming ['spammin] sm (Internet) spamming

'spandere /110/ vt to spread; (versare) to pour (out)

spa'rare /72/ vt to fire ▷ vi (far fuoco) to fire; (tirare) to shoot; **spara'toria** sf exchange of shots

sparecchi'are [sparek'kjare] /19/ vt: **~ (la tavola)** to clear the table

spa'reggio [spa'reddʒo] sm (Sport) play-off

'spargere ['spardʒere] /111/ vt (sparpagliare) to scatter; (versare: vino) to spill; (: lacrime, sangue) to shed; (diffondere) to spread; (emanare) to give off (o out); **spargersi** vpr to spread

spa'rire /112/ vi to disappear, vanish

spar'lare /72/ vi: **~ di** to run down, speak ill of

'sparo sm shot

spar'tire /55/ vt (eredità, bottino) to share out; (avversari) to separate

spar'tito sm (Mus) score

sparti'traffico sm inv (Aut) central reservation (BRIT), median (strip) (US)

spar'viero sm (Zool) sparrowhawk

spasi'mante sm suitor

spassio'nato, -a ag dispassionate, impartial

'spasso sm (divertimento) amusement, enjoyment; **andare a ~** to go out for a walk; **essere a ~** (fig) to be out of work; **mandare qn a ~** (fig) to give sb the sack

'spatola sf spatula; (di muratore) trowel

spa'valdo, -a ag arrogant, bold

spaventa'passeri sm inv scarecrow

spaven'tare /72/ vt to frighten, scare; **spaventarsi** vpr to become frightened, become scared; to get a fright; **spa'vento** sm fear, fright; **far spavento a qn** to give sb a fright; **spaven'toso, -a** ag frightening, terrible; (fig: fam) tremendous, fantastic

spazien'tirsi [spattsjen'tirsi] /55/ vpr to lose one's patience

'spazio ['spattsjo] sm space; **~ aereo** airspace; **spazi'oso, -a** ag spacious

spazzaca'mino [spattsaka'mino] *sm* chimney sweep

spazza'neve [spattsa'neve] *sm inv* snowplough

spaz'zare [spat'tsare] /72/ *vt* to sweep; (*foglie ecc*) to sweep up; (*cacciare*) to sweep away; **spazza'tura** *sf* sweepings *pl*; (*immondizia*) rubbish; **spaz'zino** *sm* street sweeper

'spazzola ['spattsola] *sf* brush; ~ **per abiti** clothesbrush; ~ **da capelli** hairbrush; **spazzo'lare** /72/ *vt* to brush; **spazzo'lino** *sm* (small) brush; **spazzolino da denti** toothbrush

specchi'arsi [spek'kjarsi] /19/ *vpr* to look at o.s. in a mirror; (*riflettersi*) to be mirrored, be reflected

specchi'etto [spek'kjetto] *sm* (*tabella*) table, chart; ~ **da borsetta** pocket mirror; ~ **retrovisore** (*Aut*) rear-view mirror

'specchio ['spɛkkjo] *sm* mirror

speci'ale [spe'tʃale] *ag* special; **specia'lista, -i, -e** *smf* specialist; **specialità** *sf inv* speciality; (*branca di studio*) special field, speciality; **specializzazi'one** *sf* specialization; **special'mente** *av* especially, particularly

'specie ['spɛtʃe] *sf inv* (*Biol, Bot, Zool*) species *inv*; (*tipo*) kind, sort ▷ *av* especially, particularly; **una ~ di** a kind of; **fare ~ a qn** to surprise sb; **la ~ umana** mankind

specifi'care [spetʃifi'kare] /20/ *vt* to specify, state

spe'cifico, -a, -ci, -che [spe'tʃifiko] *ag* specific

specu'lare /72/ *vi*: ~ **su** (*Comm*) to speculate in; (*sfruttare*) to exploit; (*meditare*) to speculate on; **speculazi'one** *sf* speculation

spe'dire /55/ *vt* to send

'spegnere ['spɛɲɲere] /113/ *vt* (*fuoco, sigaretta*) to put out, extinguish; (*apparecchio elettrico*) to turn o switch off; (*gas*) to turn off; (*fig: suoni, passioni*) to stifle; (*debito*) to cancel; **spegnersi** *vpr* to go out; to go off; (*morire*) to pass away; **puoi ~ la luce?** could you switch off the light?

spel'lare /72/ *vt* (*scuoiare*) to skin; **spellarsi** *vpr* to peel

'spendere /8/ *vt* to spend

'spengo *ecc vb vedi* **spegnere**

'spensi *ecc vb vedi* **spegnere**

spensie'rato, -a *ag* carefree

'spento, -a *pp di* **spegnere** ▷ *ag* (*suono*) muffled; (*colore*) dull; (*sigaretta*) out; (*civiltà, vulcano*) extinct

spe'ranza [spe'rantsa] *sf* hope

spe'rare /72/ *vt* to hope for ▷ *vi*: ~ **in** to trust in; ~ **che/di fare** to hope that/to do; **lo spero, spero di sì** I hope so

sper'duto, -a *ag* (*isolato*) out-of-the-way; (*persona: smarrita, a disagio*) lost

sperimen'tale *ag* experimental

sperimen'tare /72/ *vt* to experiment with, test; (*fig*) to test, put to the test

'sperma, -i *sm* sperm

spe'rone *sm* spur

sperpe'rare /72/ *vt* to squander

'spesa *sf* (*soldi spesi*) expense; (*costo*) cost; (*acquisto*) purchase; (*fam: acquisto del cibo quotidiano*) shopping; **spese postali** postage *sg*; **spese di viaggio** travelling (*BRIT*) o traveling (*US*) expenses

'spesso, -a *ag* (*fitto*) thick; (*frequente*) frequent ▷ *av* often; **spesse volte** frequently, often

spes'sore *sm* thickness

Spett. *abbr vedi* **spettabile**

spet'tabile *ag* (*in lettere, abbr Spett.*): ~ **ditta X** Messrs X and Co

spet'tacolo *sm* (*rappresentazione*) performance, show; (*vista, scena*) sight; **dare ~ di sé** to make an exhibition o a spectacle of o.s.

spet'tare /72/ *vi*: ~ **a** (*decisione*) to be up to; (*stipendio*) to be due to; **spetta a lei decidere** it's up to you to decide

spetta'tore, -'trice *sm/f* (*Cine, Teat*) member of the audience; (*di avvenimento*) onlooker, witness

spettego'lare /72/ *vi* to gossip

spetti'nato, -a *ag* dishevelled

'spettro *sm* (*fantasma*) spectre; (*Fisica*) spectrum

'spezie ['spɛttsje] *sfpl* (*Cuc*) spices

spez'zare [spet'tsare] /72/ *vt* (*rompere*) to break; (*fig: interrompere*) to break up; **spezzarsi** *vpr* to break

spezza'tino [spettsa'tino] *sm* (*Cuc*) stew

spezzet'tare [spettset'tare] /72/ *vt* to break up (o chop) into small pieces

'spia *sf* spy; (*confidente della polizia*) informer; (*Elettr*) indicating light; warning light; (*fessura*) peephole; (*fig: sintomo*) sign, indication

spia'cente [spja'tʃɛnte] *ag* sorry; **essere ~ di qc/di fare qc** to be sorry about sth/for doing sth

spia'cevole [spja'tʃevole] *ag* unpleasant, disagreeable

spi'aggia, -ge ['spjaddʒa] *sf* beach; ~ **libera** public beach

spia'nare /72/ *vt* (*terreno*) to level, make level; (*edificio*) to raze to the ground; (*pasta*) to roll out; (*rendere liscio*) to smooth (out)

spi'are /60/ *vt* to spy on

spi'azzo ['spjattso] *sm* open space; (*radura*) clearing

'spicchio ['spikkjo] *sm* (*di agrumi*) segment; (*di aglio*) clove; (*parte*) piece, slice

spicci'are [spit'tʃare] /14/ vt to finish off; **spicciarsi** vpr to hurry up

'spicciolo, -a ['spittʃolo] ag: **moneta spicciola** (small) change; **spiccioli** smpl (small) change

'spicco, -chi sm: **fare ~** to stand out; **di ~** outstanding; (tema) main, principal

spie'dino sm (utensile) skewer; (cibo) kebab

spi'edo sm (Cuc) spit

spie'gare /80/ vt (far capire) to explain; (tovaglia) to unfold; (vele) to unfurl; **spiegarsi** vpr to explain o.s., make o.s. clear; **~ qc a qn** to explain sth to sb; **spiegazi'one** sf explanation

spiegherò [spjege'rɔ] vb vedi **spiegare**

spie'tato, -a ag ruthless, pitiless

spiffe'rare /72/ vt (fam) to blurt out, blab

'spiffero sm draught (BRIT), draft (US)

'spiga, -ghe (Bot) ear

spigli'ato, -a [spiʎ'ʎato] ag self-possessed, self-confident

'spigolo sm corner; (Geom) edge

'spilla sf brooch; (da cravatta, cappello) pin; **~ di sicurezza o da balia** safety pin

'spillo sm pin; **~ di sicurezza o da balia** safety pin; **~ di sicurezza** (Mil) (safety) pin

spi'lorcio, -a, -ci, -ce [spi'lortʃo] ag mean, stingy

'spina sf (Bot) thorn; (Zool) spine, prickle; (di pesce) bone; (Elettr) plug; (di botte) bunghole; **birra alla ~** draught beer; **~ dorsale** (Anat) backbone

spi'nacio [spi'natʃo] sm spinach no pl; (Cuc): **spinaci** spinach sg

spi'nello sm (Droga: gergo) joint

'spingere ['spindʒere] /114/ vt to push; (condurre: anche fig) to drive; (stimolare): **~ qn a fare** to urge o press sb to do

spi'noso, -a ag thorny, prickly

'spinsi ecc vb vedi **spingere**

'spinto, -a pp di **spingere** ▷ sf (urto) push; (Fisica) thrust; (fig: stimolo) incentive, spur; (: appoggio) string-pulling no pl; **dare una spinta a qn** (fig) to pull strings for sb

spio'naggio [spio'naddʒo] sm espionage, spying

spion'cino [spion'tʃino] sm peephole

spi'raglio [spi'raʎʎo] sm (fessura) chink, narrow opening; (raggio di luce, fig) glimmer, gleam

spi'rale sf spiral; (contraccettivo) coil; **a ~** spiral(-shaped)

spiri'tato, -a ag possessed; (fig: persona, espressione) wild

spiri'tismo sm spiritualism

'spirito sm (Rel, Chim, disposizione d'animo, di legge ecc, fantasma) spirit; (pensieri, intelletto) mind; (arguzia) wit; (umorismo) humour, wit; **lo S~ Santo** the Holy Spirit o Ghost

spirito'saggine [spirito'saddʒine] sf witticism; (peg) wisecrack

spiri'toso, -a ag witty

spiritu'ale ag spiritual

'splendere /29/ vi to shine

'splendido, -a ag splendid; (splendente) shining; (sfarzoso) magnificent, splendid

splen'dore sm splendour; (luce intensa) brilliance, brightness

spogli'are [spoʎ'ʎare] /27/ vt (svestire) to undress; (privare, fig: depredare): **~ qn di qc** to deprive sb of sth; (togliere ornamenti: anche fig): **~ qn/qc di** to strip sb/sth of; **spogliarsi** vpr to undress, strip; **spogliarsi di** (ricchezze ecc) to deprive o.s. of, give up; (pregiudizi) to rid o.s. of; **spoglia'rello** sm striptease; **spoglia'toio** sm dressing room; (di scuola ecc) cloakroom; (Sport) changing room

'spola sf (bobina) spool; **fare la ~ (fra)** to go to and fro o shuttle (between)

spolve'rare /72/ vt (anche Cuc) to dust; (con spazzola) to brush; (con battipanni) to beat; (fig) to polish off ▷ vi to dust

spon'taneo, -a ag spontaneous; (persona) unaffected, natural

spor'care /20/ vt to dirty, make dirty; (fig) to sully, soil; **sporcarsi** vpr to get dirty

spor'cizia [spor'tʃittsja] sf (stato) dirtiness; (sudiciume) dirt, filth; (cosa sporca) dirt no pl, something dirty

'sporco, -a, -chi, -che ag dirty, filthy

spor'genza [spor'dʒentsa] sf projection

'sporgere ['spɔrdʒere] /115/ vt to put out, stretch out ▷ vi (venire in fuori) to stick out; **sporgersi** vpr to lean out; **~ querela contro qn** (Dir) to take legal action against sb

'sporsi ecc vb vedi **sporgere**

sport sm inv sport

spor'tello sm (di treno, auto ecc) door; (di banca, ufficio) window, counter; **~ automatico** (Banca) cash dispenser, automated telling machine

spor'tivo, -a ag (gara, giornale) sports cpd; (persona) sporty; (abito) casual; (spirito, atteggiamento) sporting

'sposa sf bride; (moglie) wife

sposa'lizio [spoza'littsjo] sm wedding

spo'sare /72/ vt to marry; (fig: idea, fede) to espouse; **sposarsi** vpr to get married, marry; **sposarsi con qn** to marry sb, get married to sb; **spo'sato, -a** ag married

'sposo sm (bride)groom; (marito) husband

spos'sato, -a ag exhausted, weary

spos'tare /72/ vt to move, shift; (cambiare: orario) to change; **spostarsi** vpr to move

'spranga, -ghe sf (sbarra) bar

spre'care /20/ vt to waste

spre'gevole [spre'dʒevole] ag contemptible, despicable

'**spremere** /62/ *vt* to squeeze

spremia'grumi *sm inv* lemon squeezer

spre'muta *sf* fresh fruit juice; **~ d'arancia** fresh orange juice

sprez'zante [spret'tsante] *ag* scornful, contemptuous

sprofon'dare /72/ *vi* to sink; (*casa*) to collapse; (*suolo*) to give way, subside

spro'nare /72/ *vt* to spur (on)

sproporzio'nato, -a [sproportsjo'nato] *ag* disproportionate, out of all proportion

sproporzi'one [spropor'tsjone] *sf* disproportion

spro'posito *sm* blunder; **a ~** at the wrong time; (*rispondere, parlare*) irrelevantly

sprovve'duto, -a *ag* inexperienced, naïve

sprov'visto, -a *ag* (*mancante*): **~ di** lacking in, without; (*alla*) **sprovvista** unawares

spruz'zare [sprut'tsare] /72/ *vt* (*a nebulizzazione*) to spray; (*aspergere*) to sprinkle; (*inzaccherare*) to splash

'**spugna** ['spuɲɲa] *sf* (*Zool*) sponge; (*tessuto*) towelling

'**spuma** *sf* (*schiuma*) foam; (*bibita*) fizzy drink

spu'mante *sm* sparkling wine

spun'tare /72/ *vt* (*coltello*) to break the point of; (*capelli*) to trim ▷ *vi* (*uscire: germogli*) to sprout; (: *capelli*) to begin to grow; (: *denti*) to come through; (*apparire*) to appear (suddenly)

spun'tino *sm* snack

'**spunto** *sm* (*Teat, Mus*) cue; (*fig*) starting point; **dare lo ~ a** (*fig*) to give rise to

spu'tare /72/ *vt* to spit out; (*fig*) to belch (out) ▷ *vi* to spit

'**squadra** *sf* (*strumento*) (set) square; (*gruppo*) team, squad; (*di operai*) gang, squad; (*Mil*) squadron; (: *Aer, Naut*) squadron; (*Sport*) team; **lavoro a squadre** teamwork

squagli'arsi [skwaʎ'ʎarsi] /27/ *vpr* to melt; (*fig*) to sneak off

squa'lifica, -che *sf* disqualification

squalifi'care /20/ *vt* to disqualify

'**squallido, -a** *ag* wretched, bleak

'**squalo** *sm* shark

'**squama** *sf* scale

squarcia'gola [skwartʃa'gola]: **a ~** *av* at the top of one's voice

squattri'nato, -a *ag* penniless

squili'brato, -a *ag* (*Psic*) unbalanced

squil'lante *ag* shrill, sharp

squil'lare /72/ *vi* (*campanello, telefono*) to ring (out); (*tromba*) to blare; '**squillo** *sm* ring, ringing *no pl*; blare ▷ *sf inv* (*anche:* **ragazza squillo**) call girl

squi'sito, -a *ag* exquisite; (*cibo*) delicious; (*persona*) delightful

squit'tire /55/ *vi* (*uccello*) to squawk; (*topo*) to squeak

sradi'care /20/ *vt* to uproot; (*fig*) to eradicate

srego'lato, -a *ag* (*senza ordine: vita*) disorderly; (*smodato*) immoderate; (*dissoluto*) dissolute

S.r.l. *abbr vedi* **società a responsabilità limitata**

sroto'lare /72/ *vt*, **sroto'larsi** *vpr* to unroll

SS *sigla* = **Sassari**

S.S.N. *abbr* (= *Servizio Sanitario Nazionale*) ≈ NHS

sta *ecc vb vedi* **stare**

'**stabile** *ag* stable, steady; (*tempo: non variabile*) settled; (*Teat: compagnia*) resident ▷ *sm* (*edificio*) building

stabili'mento *sm* (*edificio*) establishment; (*fabbrica*) plant, factory

stabi'lire /55/ *vt* to establish; (*fissare: prezzi, data*) to fix; (*decidere*) to decide; **stabilirsi** *vpr* (*prendere dimora*) to settle

stac'care /20/ *vt* (*levare*) to detach, remove; (*separare: anche fig*) to separate, divide; (*strappare*) to tear off (o out); (*scandire: parole*) to pronounce clearly; (*Sport*) to leave behind; **staccarsi** *vpr* (*bottone ecc*) to come off; (*scostarsi*) **staccarsi (da)** to move away (from); (*fig: separarsi*) **staccarsi da** to leave; **non ~ gli occhi da qn** not to take one's eyes off sb

'**stadio** *sm* (*Sport*) stadium; (*periodo, fase*) phase, stage

'**staffa** *sf* (*di sella, Tecn*) stirrup; **perdere le staffe** (*fig*) to fly off the handle

staf'fetta *sf* (*messo*) dispatch rider; (*Sport*) relay race

stagio'nale [stadʒo'nale] *ag* seasonal

stagio'nato, -a [stadʒo'nato] *ag* seasoned; matured; (*scherzoso: attempato*) getting on in years

stagi'one [sta'dʒone] *sf* season; **alta/ bassa ~** high/low season

sta'gista, -i, -e [sta'dʒista] *smf* trainee, intern (*us*)

'**stagno, -a** ['staɲɲo] *ag* watertight; (*a tenuta d'aria*) airtight ▷ *sm* (*acquitrino*) pond; (*Chim*) tin

sta'gnola [staɲ'ɲɔla] *sf* tinfoil

'**stalla** *sf* (*per bovini*) cowshed; (*per cavalli*) stable

stal'lone *sm* stallion

stamat'tina *av* this morning

stam'becco, -chi *sm* ibex

stami'nale *ag*: **cellula ~** stem cell

'**stampa** *sf* (*Tip, Fot: tecnica*) printing; (*impressione, copia fotografica*) print; (*insieme di quotidiani, giornalisti ecc*): **la ~** the press

stam'pante *sf* (*Inform*) printer

stam'pare /72/ *vt* to print; (*pubblicare*) to publish; (*coniare*) to strike, coin; (*imprimere: anche fig*) to impress

stampa'tello *sm* block letters *pl*

stam'pella *sf* crutch

'**stampo** *sm* mould; (*fig: indole*) type, kind, sort

sta'nare /72/ *vt* to drive out

stan'care /20/ *vt* to tire, make tired; (*annoiare*) to bore; (*infastidire*) to annoy; **stancarsi** *vpr* to get tired, tire o.s. out; **stancarsi (di)** to grow weary (of), grow tired (of)

stan'chezza [stan'kettsa] *sf* tiredness, fatigue

'**stanco, -a, -chi, -che** *ag* tired; ~ **di** tired of, fed up with

stan'ghetta [stan'getta] *sf* (*di occhiali*) leg; (*Mus, di scrittura*) bar

'**stanno** *vb vedi* **stare**

sta'notte *av* tonight; (*notte passata*) last night

'**stante** *prep*: **a sé** ~ (*appartamento, casa*) independent, separate

stan'tio, -a, -'tii, -'tie *ag* stale; (*burro*) rancid; (*fig*) old

stan'tuffo *sm* piston

'**stanza** ['stantsa] *sf* room; (*Poesia*) stanza; ~ **da bagno** bathroom; ~ **da letto** bedroom

stap'pare /72/ *vt* to uncork; (*tappo a corona*) to uncap

'**stare** /116/ *vi* (*restare in un luogo*) to stay, remain; (*abitare*) to stay, live; (*essere situato*) to be, be situated; (*anche:* ~ **in piedi**) to stand; (*essere, trovarsi*) to be; (*seguito da gerundio*) **sta studiando** he's studying; **se stesse in me** if it were up to me, if it depended on me; ~ **per fare qc** to be about to do sth; **starci** (*esserci spazio*): **nel baule non ci sta più niente** there's no more room in the boot; (*accettare*) to accept; **ci stai?** is that okay with you?; ~ **a** (*attenersi a*) to follow, stick to; (*seguito dall'infinito*): **stiamo a discutere** we're talking; (*toccare a*): **sta a te giocare** it's your turn to play; ~ **a qn** (*abiti ecc*) to fit sb; **queste scarpe mi stanno strette** these shoes are tight for me; **il rosso ti sta bene** red suits you; **come sta?** how are you?; **io sto bene/male** I'm very well/not very well

starnu'tire /55/ *vi* to sneeze; **star'nuto** *sm* sneeze

sta'sera *av* this evening, tonight

sta'tale *ag* state *cpd*, government *cpd* ⊳ *smf* state employee, local authority employee; (*nell'amministrazione*) ≈ civil servant; **strada** ~ ≈ trunk (BRIT) *o* main road

sta'tista, -i *sm* statesman

sta'tistico, -a, -ci, -che *ag* statistical ⊳ *sf* statistics *sg*

'**stato, -a** *pp di* **essere**; **stare** ⊳ *sm* (*condizione*) state, condition; (*Pol*) state;

(*Dir*) status; **essere in** ~ **d'accusa** (*Dir*) to be committed for trial; ~ **d'assedio/ d'emergenza** state of siege/emergency; ~ **civile** (*Amm*) marital status; ~ **d'animo** mood; ~ **maggiore** (*Mil*) general staff; **gli Stati Uniti (d'America)** the United States (of America)

'**statua** *sf* statue

statuni'tense *ag* United States *cpd*, of the United States

sta'tura *sf* (*Anat*) height, stature; (*fig*) stature

sta'tuto *sm* (*Dir*) statute; constitution

sta'volta *av* this time

stazio'nario, -a [stattsjo'narjo] *ag* stationary; (*fig*) unchanged

stazi'one [stat'tsjone] *sf* station; (*balneare, invernale ecc*) resort; ~ **degli autobus** bus station; ~ **balneare** seaside resort; ~ **ferroviaria** railway (BRIT) *o* railroad (US) station; ~ **invernale** winter sports resort; ~ **di polizia** police station (*in small town*); ~ **di servizio** service *o* petrol (BRIT) *o* filling station

stecca, -che *sf* stick; (*di ombrello*) rib; (*di sigarette*) carton; (*Med*) splint; (*stonatura*): **fare una** ~ to sing (*o* play) a wrong note

stec'cato *sm* fence

'**stella** *sf* star; ~ **alpina** (*Bot*) edelweiss; ~ **cadente** *o* **filante** shooting star; ~ **di mare** (*Zool*) starfish

'**stelo** *sm* stem; (*asta*) rod; **lampada a** ~ standard lamp

'**stemma, -i** *sm* coat of arms

'**stemmo** *vb vedi* **stare**

stempi'ato, -a *ag* with a receding hairline

'**stendere** /120/ *vt* (*braccia, gambe*) to stretch (out); (*tovaglia*) to spread (out); (*bucato*) to hang out; (*mettere a giacere*) to lay (down); (*spalmare: colore*) to spread; (*mettere per iscritto*) to draw up; **stendersi** *vpr* (*coricarsi*) to stretch out, lie down; (*estendersi*) to extend, stretch

stenogra'fia *sf* shorthand

sten'tare /72/ *vi*: ~ **a fare** to find it hard to do, have difficulty doing

'**stento** *sm* (*fatica*) difficulty; **stenti** *smpl* (*privazioni*) hardship *sg*, privation *sg*: **a** ~ with difficulty, barely

'**sterco** *sm* dung

'**stereo** *ag inv* stereo ⊳ *sm inv* (*impianto*) stereo

'**sterile** *ag* sterile; (*terra*) barren; (*fig*) futile, fruitless

steriliz'zare [sterilid'dzare] /72/ *vt* to sterilize

ster'lina *sf* pound (sterling)

stermi'nare /72/ *vt* to exterminate, wipe out

stermi'nato, -a ag immense; endless

ster'minio sm extermination, destruction

'sterno sm (Anat) breastbone

ste'roide sm steroid

ster'zare [ster'tsare] /72/ vt, vi (Aut) to steer; **'sterzo** sm steering; (volante) steering wheel

'stessi ecc vb vedi **stare**

'stesso, -a ag same; (rafforzativo: in persona, proprio): **il re ~** the king himself o in person ▷ pron: **lo(la) ~(a)** the same (one); **i suoi stessi avversari lo ammirano** even his enemies admire him; **fa lo ~** it doesn't matter; **per me è lo ~** it's all the same to me, it doesn't matter to me; vedi **io; tu** ecc

ste'sura sf drafting no pl, drawing up no pl; (documento) draft

'stetti ecc vb vedi **stare**

'stia ecc vb vedi **stare**

sti'lare /72/ vt to draw up, draft

'stile sm style; **~ libero** freestyle; **sti'lista, -i, -e** smf designer

stilo'grafica, -che sf (anche: **penna ~**) fountain pen

'stima sf esteem; valuation; assessment, estimate

sti'mare /72/ vt (persona) to esteem, hold in high regard; (terreno, casa ecc) to value; (stabilire in misura approssimativa) to estimate, assess; (ritenere): **~ che** to consider that; **stimarsi fortunato** to consider o.s. (to be) lucky

stimo'lare /72/ vt to stimulate; (incitare): **~ qn (a fare)** to spur sb on (to do)

'stimolo sm (anche fig) stimulus

'stingere ['stindʒere] /37/ vt, vi (anche: **stingersi**) to fade; **'stinto, -a** pp di **stingere**

sti'pare /72/ vt to cram, pack; **stiparsi** vpr (accalcarsi) to crowd, throng

sti'pendio sm salary

'stipite sm (di porta, finestra) jamb

stipu'lare /72/ vt (redigere) to draw up

sti'rare /72/ vt (abito) to iron; (distendere) to stretch; (strappare: muscolo) to strain; **stirarsi** vpr to stretch (o.s.)

stiti'chezza [stiti'kettsa] sf constipation

'stitico, -a, -ci, -che ag constipated

'stiva sf (di nave) hold

sti'vale sm boot

'stizza ['stittsa] sf anger, vexation

'stoffa sf material, fabric; (fig): **aver la ~ di** to have the makings of

'stomaco, -chi sm stomach; **dare di ~ to** vomit, be sick

sto'nato, -a ag (persona) off-key; (strumento) off-key, out of tune

stop sm inv (Telegrafia) stop; (Aut: cartello) stop sign; (: fanalino d'arresto) brake-light

'storcere ['stɔrtʃere] /106/ vt to twist; **storcersi** vpr to writhe, twist; **~ il naso** (fig) to turn up one's nose; **storcersi la caviglia** to twist one's ankle

stor'dire /55/ vt (intontire) to stun, daze; **stor'dito, -a** ag stunned

'storia sf (scienza, avvenimenti) history; (racconto, bugia) story; (faccenda, questione) business no pl; (pretesto) excuse, pretext; **storie** sfpl (smancerie) fuss sg;
'storico, -a, -ci, -che ag historic(al) ▷ sm/f historian

stori'one sm (Zool) sturgeon

'stormo sm (di uccelli) flock

'storpio, -a ag crippled, maimed

'storsi ecc vb vedi **storcere**

'storto, -a pp di **storcere** ▷ ag (chiodo) twisted, bent; (gamba, quadro) crooked ▷ sf (distorsione) sprain, twist

sto'viglie [sto'viʎʎe] sfpl dishes pl, crockery sg

'strabico, -a, -ci, -che ag squint-eyed; (occhi) squint

strac'chino [strak'kino] sm type of soft cheese

stracci'are [strat'tʃare] /14/ vt to tear; **stracciarsi** vpr to tear

'straccio, -a, -ci, -ce ['strattʃo] ag: **carta straccia** waste paper ▷ sm (per pulire) cloth, duster; **stracci** smpl (indumenti) rags; **si è ridotto a uno ~** he's worn himself out; **non ha uno ~ di lavoro** he's not got a job of any sort

'strada sf road; (di città) street; (cammino, via, fig) way; **~ facendo** on the way; **essere fuori ~** (fig) to be on the wrong track; **fare o farsi ~** (fig) to get on in life; **~ senza uscita** dead end; **stra'dale** ag road cpd

strafalci'one [strafal'tʃone] sm blunder, howler

stra'fare /53/ vi to overdo it

strafot'tente ag: **è ~** he doesn't give a damn, he couldn't care less

'strage ['stradʒe] sf massacre, slaughter

stralu'nato, -a ag (occhi) rolling; (persona) beside o.s., very upset

'strambo, -a ag strange, queer

strampa'lato, -a ag odd, eccentric

stra'nezza [stra'nettsa] sf strangeness

strango'lare /72/ vt to strangle

strani'ero, -a ag foreign ▷ sm/f foreigner

    Attenzione! In inglese esiste la parola *stranger*, che però significa *sconosciuto* oppure *estraneo*.

'strano, -a ag strange, odd

straordi'nario, -a ag extraordinary; (treno ecc) special ▷ sm (lavoro) overtime

strapi'ombo sm overhanging rock; **a ~** overhanging

strap'pare /72/ vt (gen) to tear, rip; (pagina ecc) to tear off, tear out; (sradicare) to pull up; (fig) to wrest sth from sb; (togliere): ~ **qc a qn** to snatch sth from sb; **strapparsi** vpr (lacerarsi) to rip, tear; (rompersi) to break; **strapparsi un muscolo** to tear a muscle; **'strappo** sm pull, tug; (lacerazione) tear, rip; **fare uno strappo alla regola** to make an exception to the rule; **strappo muscolare** torn muscle

strari'pare /72/ vi to overflow

'strascico, -chi ['straʃʃiko] sm (di abito) train; (conseguenza) after-effect

strata'gemma, -i [strata'dʒɛmma] sm stratagem

strate'gia, -'gie [strate'dʒia] sf strategy; **stra'tegico, -a, -ci, -che** ag strategic

'strato sm layer; (rivestimento) coat, coating; (Geo, fig) stratum; (Meteor) stratus; ~ **d'ozono** ozone layer

strat'tone sm tug, jerk; **dare uno** ~ **a qc** to tug o jerk sth, give sth a tug o jerk

strava'gante ag odd, eccentric

'strazio ['strattsjo] sm torture; (fig: cosa fatta male): **essere uno** ~ to be appalling

'strega, -ghe sf witch

stre'gare /80/ vt to bewitch

stre'gone sm (mago) wizard; (di tribù) witch doctor

strepi'toso, -a ag clamorous, deafening; (fig: successo) resounding

stres'sante ag stressful

stres'sato, -a ag under stress

stretch [stretʃ] ag inv stretch

'stretta sf vedi **stretto**

stretta'mente av tightly; (rigorosamente) strictly

'stretto, -a pp di **stringere** ▷ ag (corridoio, limiti) narrow; (gonna, scarpe, nodo, curva) tight; (intimo: parente, amico) close; (rigoroso: osservanza) strict; (preciso: significato) precise, exact ▷ sm (braccio di mare) strait ▷ sf (di mano) grasp; (finanziaria) squeeze; (fig: dolore, turbamento) pang; **a denti stretti** with clenched teeth; **lo** ~ **necessario** the bare minimum; **una stretta di mano** a handshake; **essere alle strette** to have one's back to the wall; **stret'toia** sf bottleneck; (fig) tricky situation

stri'ato, -a ag streaked

'stridulo, -a ag shrill

stril'lare /72/ vt, vi to scream, shriek; **'strillo** sm scream, shriek

strimin'zito, -a [strimin'tsito] ag (misero) shabby; (molto magro) skinny

strimpel'lare /72/ vt (Mus) to strum

'stringa, -ghe sf lace

strin'gato, -a ag (fig) concise

'stringere ['strindʒere] /117/ vt (avvicinare due cose) to press (together), squeeze (together); (tenere stretto) to hold tight, clasp, clutch; (pugno, mascella, denti) to clench; (labbra) to compress; (avvitare) to tighten; (abito) to take in; (scarpe) to pinch, be tight for; (fig: concludere: patto) to make; (: accelerare: passo) to quicken ▷ vi (essere stretto) to be tight; (tempo: incalzare) to be pressing

'strinsi ecc vb vedi **stringere**

'striscia, -sce ['striʃʃa] sf (di carta, tessuto ecc) strip; (riga) stripe; **strisce (pedonali)** zebra crossing sg

strisci'are [striʃʃare] /14/ vt (piedi) to drag; (muro, macchina) to graze ▷ vi to crawl, creep

'striscio ['striʃʃo] sm graze; (Med) smear; **colpire di** ~ to graze

strisci'one [striʃʃone] sm banner

strito'lare /72/ vt to grind

striz'zare [strit'tsare] /72/ vt (panni) to wring (out); ~ **l'occhio** to wink

'strofa sf strophe

strofi'naccio [strofi'nattʃo] sm duster, cloth; (per piatti) dishcloth; (per pavimenti) floorcloth

strofi'nare /72/ vt to rub

stron'care /20/ vt to break off; (fig: ribellione) to suppress, put down; (: film, libro) to tear to pieces

'stronzo ['strontso] sm (sterco) turd; (fam!: persona) shit (!)

stroz'zare [strot'tsare] /72/ vt (soffocare) to choke, strangle

struc'care /20/ vt to remove make-up from; **struccarsi** vpr to remove one's make-up

strumen'tale ag (Mus) instrumental

strumentaliz'zare [strumentalid'dzare] /72/ vt to exploit, use to one's own ends

stru'mento sm (arnese, fig) instrument, tool; (Mus) instrument; ~ **a corda** o **ad arco/a fiato** string(ed)/wind instrument

'strutto sm lard

strut'tura sf structure

'struzzo ['struttso] sm ostrich

stuc'care /20/ vt (muro) to plaster; (vetro) to putty; (decorare con stucchi) to stucco

'stucco, -chi sm plaster; (da vetri) putty; (ornamentale) stucco; **rimanere di** ~ (fig) to be dumbfounded

stu'dente, -'essa sm/f student; (scolaro) pupil, schoolboy/girl

studi'are /19/ vt to study

'studio sm studying; (ricerca, saggio, stanza) study; (di professionista) office; (di artista, Cine, TV, Radio) studio; (di medico) surgery (BRIT), office (US); **studi** smpl (Ins) studies

studi'oso, -a ag studious, hardworking ▷ sm/f scholar

'stufa sf stove; **~ elettrica** electric fire o heater

stu'fare /72/ vt (Cuc) to stew; (fig: fam) to bore; **stufarsi** vpr (fam): **stufarsi (di)** (fig) to get fed up (with); **'stufo, -a** ag (fam): **essere stufo di** to be fed up with, be sick and tired of

stu'oia sf mat

stupefa'cente [stupefa'tʃɛnte] ag stunning, astounding ▷ sm drug, narcotic

stu'pendo, -a ag marvellous, wonderful

stupi'daggine [stupi'daddʒine] sf stupid thing (to do o say)

stupidità sf stupidity

'stupido, -a ag stupid

stu'pire /55/ vt to amaze, stun ▷ vi (anche: **stupirsi**): **~ (di)** to be amazed (at), be stunned (by)

stu'pore sm amazement, astonishment

stu'prare /72/ vt to rape

'stupro sm rape

stu'rare /72/ vt (lavandino) to clear

stuzzica'denti [stuttsika'dɛnti] sm toothpick

stuzzi'care [stuttsi'kare] /20/ vt (ferita ecc) to poke (at), prod (at); (fig) to tease; (: appetito) to whet; (: curiosità) to stimulate; **~ i denti** to pick one's teeth

 PAROLA CHIAVE

su (su + il = **sul**, su + lo = **sullo**, su + l' = **sull'**, su + la = **sulla**, su + i = **sui**, su + gli = **sugli**, su + le = **sulle**) prep 1 (gen) on; (moto) on(to); (in cima a) on (top of); **mettilo sul tavolo** put it on the table; **un paesino sul mare** a village by the sea

2 (argomento) about, on; **un libro su Cesare** a book on o about Caesar

3 (circa) about; **costerà sui 3 milioni** it will cost about 3 million; **una ragazza sui 17 anni** a girl of about 17 (years of age)

4: su misura made to measure; **su richiesta** on request; **3 casi su dieci** 3 cases out of 10

▶ av 1 (in alto, verso l'alto) up; **vieni su** come on up; **guarda su** look up; **su le mani!** hands up!; **in su** (verso l'alto) up(wards); (in poi) onwards; **dai 20 anni in su** from the age of 20 onwards

2 (addosso) on; **cos'hai su?** what have you got on?

▶ escl come on!; **su coraggio!** come on, cheer up!

su'bacqueo, -a ag underwater ▷ sm skin-diver

sub'buglio [sub'buʎʎo] sm confusion, turmoil

'subdolo, -a ag underhand, sneaky

suben'trare /72/ vi: **~ a qn in qc** to take over sth from sb

su'bire /55/ vt to suffer, endure

'subito av immediately, at once, straight away

subodo'rare /72/ vt (insidia ecc) to smell, suspect

subordi'nato, -a ag subordinate; (dipendente): **~ a** dependent on, subject to

suc'cedere [sut'tʃedere] /118/ vi (accadere) to happen; **~ a** (prendere il posto di) to succeed; (venire dopo) to follow; **cos'è successo?** what happened?; **succes'sivo, -a** ag successive; **suc'cesso, -a** pp di **succedere** ▷ sm (esito) outcome; (buona riuscita) success; **di successo** (libro, personaggio) successful

succhi'are [suk'kjare] /19/ vt to suck (up)

succhi'otto [suk'kjɔtto] sm dummy (BRIT), pacifier (US), comforter (US)

suc'cinto, -a [sut'tʃinto] ag (discorso) succinct; (abito) brief

'succo, -chi sm juice; (fig) essence, gist; **~ di frutta/pomodoro** fruit/tomato juice

succur'sale sf branch (office)

sud sm south ▷ ag inv south; (regione) southern

Su'dafrica sm: **il ~** South Africa; **sudafri'cano, -a** ag, sm/f South African

Suda'merica sm: **il ~** South America

su'dare /72/ vi to perspire, sweat; **~ freddo** to come out in a cold sweat

su'dato, -a ag (persona, mani) sweaty; (fig: denaro) hard-earned ▷ sf (anche fig) sweat; **una vittoria sudata** a hard-won victory; **ho fatto una bella sudata per finirlo in tempo** it was a real sweat to get it finished in time

suddi'videre /43/ vt to subdivide

su'dest sm south-east

'sudicio, -a, -ci, -ce ['suditʃo] ag dirty, filthy

su'doku sm inv sudoku

su'dore sm perspiration, sweat

su'dovest sm south-west

suffici'ente [suffi'tʃɛnte] ag enough, sufficient; (borioso) self-important; (Ins) satisfactory; **sufficienza** sf self-importance; (Ins) pass mark; **a sufficienza** enough; **ne ho avuto a sufficienza!** I've had enough of this!

suf'fisso sm (Ling) suffix

suggeri'mento [suddʒeri'mento] sm suggestion; (consiglio) piece of advice, advice no pl

sugge'rire [suddʒe'rire] /55/ vt (risposta) to tell; (consigliare) to advise; (proporre) to suggest; (Teat) to prompt

suggestio'nare [suddʒestjo'nare] /72/ vt
to influence

sugges'tivo, -a [suddʒes'tivo] ag
(*paesaggio*) evocative; (*teoria*) interesting,
attractive

'sughero ['sugero] sm cork

'sugo, -ghi sm (*succo*) juice; (*di carne*) gravy;
(*condimento*) sauce; (*fig*) gist, essence

sui'cida, -i, -e [sui'tʃida] ag suicidal ▷ smf
suicide

suici'darsi [suitʃi'darsi] /72/ vpr to commit
suicide

sui'cidio [sui'tʃidjo] sm suicide

su'ino, -a ag: **carne suina** pork ▷ sm pig

sul'tano, -a sm/f sultan (sultana)

'suo (f **'sua**, pl **'sue**, **su'oi**) det: **il ~, la sua** ecc
(*di lui*) his; (*di lei*) her; (*di esso*) its; (*con valore
indefinito*) one's, his/her; (*forma di cortesia*:
anche: **S~**) your ▷ pron: **il ~, la sua** ecc his;
hers; yours; **i ~i** his (*o* her ecc) family

su'ocero, -a ['swɔtʃero] sm/f father/
mother-in-law

su'ola sf (*di scarpa*) sole

su'olo sm (*terreno*) ground; (*terra*) soil

suo'nare /72/ vt (*Mus*) to play; (*campana*)
to ring; (*ore*) to strike; (*clacson, allarme*) to
sound ▷ vi to play; (*telefono, campana*) to
ring; (*ore*) to strike; (*clacson, fig: parole*) to
sound

suone'ria sf alarm

su'ono sm sound

su'ora sf (*Rel*) nun; **Suor Maria** Sister Maria

'super ag inv: (*benzina*) **~** ≈ four-star
(petrol) (BRIT), ≈ premium (US)

supe'rare /72/ vt (*oltrepassare: limite*) to
exceed, surpass; (*percorrere*) to cover;
(*attraversare: fiume*) to cross; (*sorpassare:
veicolo*) to overtake; (*fig: essere più bravo di*)
to surpass, outdo; (: *difficoltà*) to overcome;
(: *esame*) to get through; **~ qn in altezza/
peso** to be taller/heavier than sb; **ha
superato la cinquantina** he's over fifty
(years of age)

su'perbia sf pride; **su'perbo, -a** ag proud;
(*fig*) magnificent, superb

superfici'ale [superfi'tʃale] ag superficial

super'ficie, -ci [super'fitʃe] sf surface

su'perfluo, -a ag superfluous

superi'ore ag (*piano, arto, classi*) upper; (*più
elevato: temperatura, livello*): **~ (a)** higher
(than); (*migliore*): **~ (a)** superior (to)

superla'tivo, -a ag, sm superlative

supermer'cato sm supermarket

su'perstite ag surviving ▷ smf survivor

superstizi'one [superstit'tsjone] sf
superstition; **superstizi'oso, -a** ag
superstitious

super'strada sf ≈ expressway

su'pino, -a ag supine

supplemen'tare ag extra; (*treno*) relief cpd;
(*entrate*) additional

supple'mento sm supplement

sup'plente smf temporary member of staff;
supply (*o* substitute) teacher

'supplica, -che sf (*preghiera*) plea; (*domanda
scritta*) petition, request

suppli'care /20/ vt to implore, beseech

sup'plizio [sup'plittsjo] sm torture

sup'pongo, sup'poni ecc vb vedi **supporre**

sup'porre /77/ vt to suppose; **supponiamo
che ...** let's o just suppose that ...

sup'porto sm (*sostegno*) support

sup'posta sf (*Med*) suppository

su'premo, -a ag supreme

surge'lare [surdʒe'lare] /72/ vt to (deep-)
freeze

surge'lato, -a [surdʒe'lato] ag (deep-)
frozen ▷ smpl: **i surgelati** frozen food sg

sur'plus sm inv (*Econ*) surplus

surriscal'dare /72/ vt to overheat

suscet'tibile [suʃʃet'tibile] ag (*sensibile*)
touchy, sensitive

susci'tare [suʃʃi'tare] /72/ vt to provoke,
arouse

su'sina sf plum

sussegu'ire /45/ vt to follow; **susseguirsi**
vpr to follow one another

sus'sidio sm subsidy; **sussidi didattici/
audiovisivi** teaching/audiovisual aids

sussul'tare /72/ vi to shudder

sussur'rare /72/ vt, vi to whisper, murmur;
sus'surro sm whisper, murmur

sva'gare /80/ vt (*divertire*) to amuse;
svagarsi vpr to amuse o.s.

'svago, -ghi sm (*riposo*) relaxation; (*ricreazione*)
amusement; (*passatempo*) pastime

svaligi'are [zvali'dʒare] /62/ vt to rob,
burgle (BRIT), burglarize (US)

svalu'tare /72/ vt (*Econ*) to devalue;
svalutarsi vpr (*Econ*) to be devalued

svalutazi'one sf devaluation

sva'nire /55/ vi to disappear, vanish

svantaggi'ato, -a [zvantad'dʒato] ag at a
disadvantage

svan'taggio [zvan'taddʒo] sm
disadvantage; (*inconveniente*) drawback,
disadvantage

svari'ato, -a ag varied; (*numeroso*) various

'svastica, -che sf swastika

sve'dese ag Swedish ▷ smf Swede ▷ sm
(*Ling*) Swedish

'sveglia ['zveʎʎa] sf waking up; (*orologio*)
alarm (clock); **~ telefonica** alarm call

svegli'are [zveʎ'ʎare] /27/ vt to wake up;
(*fig*) to awaken, arouse; **svegliarsi** vpr to
wake up; (*fig*) to be revived, reawaken

'sveglio, -a ['zveʎʎo] ag awake; (*fig*) quick-
witted

sve'lare /72/ vt to reveal

'svelto, -a ag (passo) quick; (mente) quick, alert; **alla svelta** quickly

'svendere /29/ vt to sell off, clear

'svendita sf (Comm) (clearance) sale

'svengo ecc vb vedi **svenire**

sveni'mento sm fainting fit, faint

sve'nire /128/ vi to faint

sven'tare /72/ vt to foil, thwart

sven'tato, -a ag (distratto) scatterbrained; (imprudente) rash

svento'lare /72/ vt, vi to wave, flutter

sven'tura sf misfortune

sverrò ecc vb vedi **svenire**

sves'tire /45/ vt to undress; **svestirsi** vpr to get undressed

'Svezia ['zvɛttsja] sf: **la ~** Sweden

svi'are /60/ vt to divert; (fig) to lead astray

svi'gnarsela [zviɲ'ɲarsela] /72/ vpr to slip away, sneak off

svilup'pare /72/ vt, **svilup'parsi** vpr to develop

sviluppa'tore, -trice sm/f (Inform) developer

svi'luppo sm development

'svincolo sm (stradale) motorway (BRIT) o expressway (US) intersection

'svista sf oversight

svi'tare /72/ vt to unscrew

'Svizzera ['zvittsera] sf: **la ~** Switzerland; **'svizzero, -a** ['zvittsero] ag, sm/f Swiss

svogli'ato, -a [zvoʎ'ʎato] ag listless; (pigro) lazy

'svolgere ['zvɔldʒere] /96/ vt to unwind; (srotolare) to unroll; (fig: argomento) to develop; (: piano, programma) to carry out; **svolgersi** vpr to unwind; to unroll; (fig: aver luogo) to take place; (: procedere) to go on

'svolsi ecc vb vedi **svolgere**

'svolta sf (atto) turning no pl; (curva) turn, bend; (fig) turning-point

svol'tare /72/ vi to turn

svuo'tare /72/ vt to empty (out)

T, t [ti] sf o m inv (lettera) T, t; **T come Taranto** ≈ T for Tommy

t abbr = **tonnellata**

tabacche'ria [tabakke'ria] sf tobacconist's (shop)

ta'bacco, -chi sm tobacco

ta'bella sf (tavola) table; (elenco) list

tabel'lone sm (per pubblicità) billboard; (in stazione) timetable board

'tablet ['tablet] sm inv (Inform) tablet

TAC sigla f (Med: = Tomografia Assiale Computerizzata) CAT

tac'chino [tak'kino] sm turkey

'tacco, -chi sm heel; **tacchi a spillo** stiletto heels

taccu'ino sm notebook

ta'cere [ta'tʃere] /119/ vi to be silent o quiet; (smettere di parlare) to fall silent ▷ vt to keep to oneself, say nothing about; **far ~ qn** to make sb be quiet; (fig) to silence sb

ta'chimetro [ta'kimetro] sm speedometer

'tacqui ecc vb vedi **tacere**

ta'fano sm horsefly

'taglia ['taʎʎa] sf (statura) height; (misura) size; (riscatto) ransom; (ricompensa) reward; **taglie forti** (Abbigliamento) outsize

taglia'carte [taʎʎa'karte] sm inv paperknife

tagli'ando [taʎ'ʎando] sm coupon

tagli'are [taʎ'ʎare] /27/ vt to cut; (recidere, interrompere) to cut off; (intersecare) to cut across, intersect; (carne) to carve; (vini) to blend ▷ vi to cut; (prendere una scorciatoia) to take a short-cut; **tagliarsi** vpr to cut o.s.; **~ la strada a qn** to cut across in front of sb; **~ corto** (fig) to cut short; **~ la corda** (fig) to sneak off; **~ i ponti (con)** (fig) to break off relations (with); **mi sono tagliato** I've cut myself

taglia'telle [taʎʎa'tɛlle] sfpl tagliatelle pl

taglia'unghie [taʎʎa'ungje] *sm inv* nail clippers *pl*
tagli'ente [taʎ'ʎɛnte] *ag* sharp
'taglio ['taʎʎo] *sm* (*anche fig*) cut; cutting *no pl*; (*parte tagliente*) cutting edge; (*di abito*) cut, style; (*di stoffa*) length; (*di vini*) blending; **di ~** on edge, edgeways; **banconote di piccolo/grosso ~** notes of small/large denomination; **~ cesareo** Caesarean section
tailan'dese *ag, smf, sm* Thai
Tai'landia *sf*: **la ~** Thailand
'talco *sm* talcum powder

 PAROLA CHIAVE

'tale *det* **1** (*simile, così grande*) such; **un(a) tale ...** such a ...; **non accetto tali discorsi** I won't allow such talk; **è di una tale arroganza** he is so arrogant; **fa una tale confusione!** he makes such a mess!
2 (*persona o cosa indeterminata*) such-and-such; **il giorno tale all'ora tale** on such-and-such a day at such-and-such a time; **la tal persona** that person; **ha telefonato una tale Giovanna** somebody called Giovanna phoned
3 (*nelle similitudini*): **tale ... tale** like ... like; **tale padre tale figlio** like father, like son; **hai il vestito tale quale il mio** your dress is just *o* exactly like mine
▶ *pron* (*indefinito, persona*): **un(a) tale** someone; **quel** (*o* **quella**) **tale** that person, that man (*o* wòman); **il tal dei tali** what's-his-name

tale'bano *sm* Taliban
ta'lento *sm* talent
talis'mano *sm* talisman
tallon'cino [tallon'tʃino] *sm* counterfoil
tal'lone *sm* heel
tal'mente *av* so
'talpa *sf* (*Zool*: *anche fig*) mole
tal'volta *av* sometimes, at times
tambu'rello *sm* tambourine
tam'buro *sm* drum
Ta'migi [ta'midʒi] *sm*: **il ~** the Thames
tampo'nare /72/ *vt* (*otturare*) to plug; (*urtare: macchina*) to crash *o* ram into
tam'pone *sm* (*Med*) wad, pad; (*per timbri*) ink-pad; (*respingente*) buffer; **~ assorbente** tampon
'tana *sf* lair, den
'tanga *sm inv* G-string
tan'gente [tan'dʒɛnte] *ag* (*Mat*): **~ a** tangential to ▶ *sf* tangent; (*quota*) share
tangenzi'ale [tandʒen'tsjale] *sf* (*strada*) bypass
'tanica *sf* (*contenitore*) jerry can

'tanto, -a *det* **1** (*molto: quantità*) a lot of, much; (: *numero*) a lot of, many; **tanto tempo** a lot of time, a long time; **tanti auguri!** all the best!; **tante grazie** many thanks; **tante volte** many times, often; **ogni tanti chilometri** every so many kilometres
2 (*così tanto: quantità*) so much, such a lot of; (: *numero*) so many, such a lot of; **ho aspettato per tanto tempo** I waited so long *o* for such a long time
3: **tanto ... quanto** (*quantità*) as much ... as; (*numero*) as many ... as; **ho tanta pazienza quanta ne hai tu** I have as much patience as you have *o* as you; **ha tanti amici quanti nemici** he has as many friends as he has enemies
▶ *pron* **1** (*molto*) much, a lot; (*così tanto*) so much, such a lot; **tanti, -e** many, a lot; so many; such a lot; **credevo ce ne fosse tanto** I thought there was (such) a lot, I thought there was plenty
2: **tanto quanto** (*denaro*) as much as; (*cioccolatini*) as many as; **ne ho tanto quanto basta** I have as much as I need; **due volte tanto** twice as much
3 (*indeterminato*) so much; **tanto per l'affitto, tanto per il gas** so much for the rent, so much for the gas; **costa un tanto al metro** it costs so much per metre; **di tanto in tanto, ogni tanto** every so often; **tanto vale che ...** I (*o* we *ecc*) may as well ...; **tanto meglio!** so much the better!; **tanto peggio per lui!** so much the worse for him!
▶ *av* **1** (*molto*) very; **vengo tanto volentieri** I'd be very glad to come; **non ci vuole tanto a capirlo** it doesn't take much to understand it
2 (*così tanto: con ag, av*) so; (: *con vb*) so much, such a lot; **è tanto bella!** she's so beautiful!; **non urlare tanto** (*forte*) don't shout so much; **sto tanto meglio adesso** I'm so much better now; **tanto ... che** so ... (that); **tanto ... da** so ... as
3: **tanto ... quanto** as ... as; **conosco tanto Carlo quanto suo padre** I know both Carlo and his father; **non è poi tanto complicato quanto sembra** it's not as difficult as it seems; **tanto più insisti, tanto più non mollerà** the more you insist, the more stubborn he'll be; **quanto più ... tanto meno** the more ... the less
4 (*solamente*) just; **tanto per cambiare/scherzare** just for a change/a joke; **una volta tanto** for once
5 (*a lungo*) (for) long
▶ *cong* after all

'tappa sf (luogo di sosta, fermata) stop, halt; (parte di un percorso) stage, leg; (Sport) lap; **a tappe** in stages

tap'pare /72/ vt to plug, stop up; (bottiglia) to cork; **tapparsi** vpr: **tapparsi in casa** to shut o.s. up at home; **tapparsi la bocca** to shut up; **tapparsi le orecchie** to turn a deaf ear

tappa'rella sf rolling shutter

tappe'tino sm (per auto) car mat; **~ antiscivolo** (da bagno) non-slip mat; **~ del mouse** mouse mat

tap'peto sm carpet; (anche: **tappetino**) rug; (Sport): **andare al ~** to go down for the count; **mettere sul ~** (fig) to bring up for discussion

tappez'zare [tappet'tsare] /72/ vt (con carta) to paper; (rivestire): **~ qc (di)** to cover sth (with); **tappezze'ria** sf (tessuto) tapestry; (carta da parati) wallpaper; (arte) upholstery; **far da tappezzeria** (fig) to be a wallflower

'tappo sm stopper; (in sughero) cork

tar'dare /72/ vi to be late ▷ vt to delay; **~ a fare** to delay doing

'tardi av late; **più ~** later (on); **al più ~** at the latest; **sul ~** (verso sera) late in the day; **far ~** to be late; (restare alzato) to stay up late; **è troppo ~** it's too late

'targa, -ghe sf plate; (Aut) number (BRIT) o license (US) plate; **targ'hetta** sf (con nome: su porta) nameplate; (: su bagaglio) name tag

ta'riffa sf (gen) rate, tariff; (di trasporti) fare; (elenco) price list; tariff

'tarlo sm woodworm

'tarma sf moth

ta'rocco, -chi sm tarot card; **tarocchi** smpl (gioco) tarot sg

tarta'ruga, -ghe sf tortoise; (di mare) turtle; (materiale) tortoiseshell

tar'tina sf canapé

tar'tufo sm (Bot) truffle

'tasca, -sche sf pocket; **tas'cabile** ag (libro) pocket cpd

'tassa sf (imposta) tax; (doganale) duty; (per iscrizione, a scuola ecc) fee; **~ di circolazione/di soggiorno** road/tourist tax

tas'sare /72/ vt to tax; to levy a duty on

tas'sello sm plug; (assaggio) wedge

tassì sm inv = **taxi**; **tas'sista, -i, -e** smf taxi driver

'tasso sm (di natalità, d'interesse ecc) rate; (Bot) yew; (Zool) badger; **~ di cambio/ d'interesse** rate of exchange/interest

tas'tare /72/ vt to feel; **~ il terreno** (fig) to see how the land lies

tasti'era sf keyboard

tastie'rino sm keypad

'tasto sm key; (tatto) touch, feel

tas'toni av: **procedere (a) ~** to grope one's way forward

'tatto sm (senso) touch; (fig) tact; **duro al ~** hard to the touch; **aver ~** to be tactful, have tact

tatu'aggio [tatu'addʒo] sm tattooing; (disegno) tattoo

tatu'are /72/ vt to tattoo

TAV [tav] sigla m (inv), sigla f (inv) (= treno alta velocità) high-speed train; (sistema) high-speed rail system

'tavola sf table; (asse) plank, board; (lastra) tablet; (quadro) panel (painting); (illustrazione) plate; **~ calda** snack bar; **~ rotonda** (fig) round table; **~ a vela** windsurfer

tavo'letta sf tablet, bar; **a ~** (Aut) flat out

tavo'lino sm small table; (scrivania) desk

'tavolo sm table

'taxi sm inv taxi

'tazza ['tattsa] sf cup; **~ da caffè/tè** coffee/ tea cup; **una ~ di caffè/tè** a cup of coffee/ tea

TBC abbr f (= tubercolosi) TB

te pron (soggetto: in forme comparative, oggetto) you

tè sm inv tea; (trattenimento) tea party

tea'trale ag theatrical

te'atro sm theatre

techno ['tɛkno] ag inv (musica) techno

'tecnico, -a, -ci, -che ag technical ▷ sm/f technician ▷ sf technique; (tecnologia) technology

tecnolo'gia [teknolo'dʒia] sf technology

te'desco, -a, -schi, -sche ag, sm/f, sm German

te'game sm (Cuc) pan

'tegola sf tile

tei'era sf teapot

tel. abbr (= telefono) tel.

'tela sf (tessuto) cloth; (per vele, quadri) canvas; (dipinto) canvas, painting; **di ~** (calzoni) (heavy) cotton cpd; (scarpe, borsa) canvas cpd; **~ cerata** oilcloth

te'laio sm (apparecchio) loom; (struttura) frame

tele'camera sf television camera

teleco'mando sm remote control

tele'cronaca, -che sf television report

telefo'nare /72/ vi to telephone, ring; (fare una chiamata) to make a phone call ▷ vt to telephone; **~ a qn** to phone o ring o call sb (up)

telefo'nata sf (telephone) call; **~ a carico del destinatario** reverse charge (BRIT) o collect (US) call

tele'fonico, -a, -ci, -che ag (tele)phone cpd

telefo'nino sm mobile phone
te'lefono sm telephone; **~ a gettoni** ≈ pay phone; **~ fisso** landline
telegior'nale [teledʒor'nale] sm television news (programme)
tele'gramma, -i sm telegram
telela'voro sm teleworking
teleno'vela sf soap opera
Tele'pass® sm inv automatic payment card for use on Italian motorways
telepa'tia sf telepathy
teles'copio sm telescope
teleselezi'one [teleselet'tsjone] sf direct dialling
telespetta'tore, -'trice sm/f (television) viewer
tele'vendita sf teleshopping
televisi'one sf television
televi'sore sm television set
'tema, -i sm theme; (Ins) essay, composition
te'mere /29/ vt to fear, be afraid of; (essere sensibile a: freddo, calore) to be sensitive to ▷ vi to be afraid; (essere preoccupato): **~ per** to worry about, fear for; **~ di/che** to be afraid of/that
temperama'tite sm inv pencil sharpener
tempera'mento sm temperament
tempera'tura sf temperature
tempe'rino sm penknife
tem'pesta sf storm; **~ di sabbia/neve** sand/snowstorm
'tempia sf (Anat) temple
'tempio sm (edificio) temple
'tempo sm (Meteor) weather; (cronologico) time; (epoca) time, times pl; (di film, gioco: parte) part; (Mus) time; (: battuta) beat; (Ling) tense; **che ~ fa?** what's the weather like?; **un ~** once; **~ fa** some time ago; **al ~ stesso** o **a un ~** at the same time; **per ~** early; **aver fatto il proprio ~** to have had its (o his ecc) day; **primo/secondo ~** (Teat) first/second part; (Sport) first/second half; **in ~ utile** in due time o course; **a ~ pieno** full-time; **~ libero** free time
tempo'rale ag temporal ▷ sm (Meteor) (thunder)storm
tempo'raneo, -a ag temporary
te'nace [te'natʃe] ag strong, tough; (fig) tenacious
te'naglie [te'naʎʎe] sfpl pincers pl
'tenda sf (riparo) awning; (di finestra) curtain; (per campeggio ecc) tent
ten'denza [ten'dɛntsa] sf tendency; (orientamento) trend; **avere ~ a** o **per qc** to have a bent for sth
'tendere /120/ vt (allungare al massimo) to stretch, draw tight; (porgere: mano) to hold out; (fig: trappola) to lay, set ▷ vi: **~**

a qc/a fare to tend towards sth/to do; **~ l'orecchio** to prick up one's ears; **il tempo tende al caldo** the weather is getting hot; **un blu che tende al verde** a greenish blue
'tendine sm tendon, sinew
ten'done sm (da circo) big top
'tenebre sfpl darkness sg
te'nente sm lieutenant
te'nere /121/ vt to hold; (conservare, mantenere) to keep; (ritenere, considerare) to consider; (occupare: spazio) to take up, occupy; (seguire: strada) to keep to ▷ vi to hold; (colori) to be fast; (dare importanza): **~ a** to care about; **~ a fare** to want to do, be keen to do; **tenersi** vpr (stare in una determinata posizione) to stand; (stimarsi) to consider o.s.; (aggrapparsi): **tenersi a** to hold on to; (attenersi): **tenersi a** to stick to; **~ una conferenza** to give a lecture; **~ conto di qc** to take sth into consideration; **~ presente qc** to bear sth in mind
'tenero, -a ag tender; (pietra, cera, colore) soft; (fig) tender, loving
'tengo ecc vb vedi **tenere**
'tenni ecc vb vedi **tenere**
'tennis sm tennis
ten'nista, -i, -e sm/f tennis player
te'nore sm (tono) tone; (Mus) tenor; **~ di vita** (livello) standard of living
tensi'one sf tension
ten'tare /72/ vt (indurre) to tempt; (provare): **~ qc/di fare** to attempt o try sth/to do; **tenta'tivo** sm attempt; **tentazi'one** sf temptation
tenten'nare /72/ vi to shake, be unsteady; (fig) to hesitate, waver
ten'toni av: **andare a ~** (anche fig) to grope one's way
'tenue ag (sottile) fine; (colore) soft; (fig) slender, slight
te'nuta sf (capacità) capacity; (divisa) uniform; (abito) dress; (Agr) estate; **a ~ d'aria** airtight; **~ di strada** roadholding power
teolo'gia [teolo'dʒia] sf theology
teo'ria sf theory
te'pore sm warmth
tep'pista, -i sm hooligan
tera'pia sf therapy; **~ intensiva** intensive care
tergicris'tallo [terdʒikris'tallo] sm windscreen (BRIT) o windshield (US) wiper
tergiver'sare [terdʒiver'sare] /72/ vi to shilly-shally
ter'male ag thermal; **stazione** sf **~** spa
'terme sfpl thermal baths
termi'nale ag, sm terminal
termi'nare /72/ vt to end; (lavoro) to finish ▷ vi to end

'termine sm term; (fine, estremità) end; (di territorio) boundary, limit; **contratto a ~** (Comm) forward contract; **a breve/lungo ~** short-/long-term; **parlare senza mezzi termini** to talk frankly, not to mince one's words

ter'mometro sm thermometer

'termos sm inv = **thermos**

termosi'fone sm radiator

ter'mostato sm thermostat

'terra sf (gen, Elettr) earth; (sostanza) soil, earth; (opposto al mare) land no pl; (regione, paese) land; (argilla) clay; **terre** sfpl (possedimento) lands, land sg; **a o per ~** (stato) on the ground (o floor); (moto) to the ground, down; **mettere a ~** to earth

terra'cotta sf terracotta; **vasellame** sm **di ~** earthenware

terra'ferma sf dry land, terra firma; (continente) mainland

ter'razza [ter'rattsa] sf, **ter'razzo** [ter'rattso] sm terrace

terre'moto sm earthquake

ter'reno, -a ag (vita, beni) earthly ▷ sm (suolo, fig) ground; (Comm) land no pl, plot (of land); site; (Sport, Mil) field

ter'restre ag (superficie) of the earth, earth's; (di terra: battaglia, animale) land cpd; (Rel) earthly, worldly

ter'ribile ag terrible, dreadful

terrifi'cante ag terrifying

ter'rina sf tureen

territori'ale ag territorial

terri'torio sm territory

ter'rore sm terror; **terro'rismo** sm terrorism; **terro'rista, -i, -e** smf terrorist

terroriz'zare [terrorid'dzare] /72/ vt to terrorize

'terza ['tɛrtsa] sf vedi **terzo**

ter'zino [ter'tsino] sm (Calcio) fullback, back

'terzo, -a ['tɛrtso] ag third ▷ sm (frazione) third; (Dir) third party ▷ sf (Aut) third (gear); (Ins: elementare) third year at primary school; (: media) third year at secondary school; (: superiore) sixth year at secondary school; **terzi** smpl (altri) others, other people; **la terza pagina** (Stampa) the Arts page

'teschio ['tɛskjo] sm skull

'tesi ecc vb vedi **tendere**

'teso, -a pp di **tendere** ▷ ag (tirato) taut, tight; (fig) tense

te'soro sm treasure; **il Ministero del T~** the Treasury

'tessera sf (documento) card

tes'suto sm fabric, material; (Biol) tissue

'test ['tɛst] sm inv test

'testa sf head; (di cose: estremità, parte anteriore) head, front; **di ~** (vettura ecc) front; **fare di ~ propria** to go one's own way; **in ~** (Sport) in the lead; **tenere ~ a qn** (nemico ecc) to stand up to sb; **una ~ d'aglio** a bulb of garlic; **~ o croce?** heads or tails?; **avere la ~ dura** to be stubborn; **~ di serie** (Tennis) seed, seeded player

testa'mento sm (atto) will; **l'Antico/il Nuovo T~** (Rel) the Old/New Testament

tes'tardo, -a ag stubborn, pig-headed

tes'tata sf (parte anteriore) head; (intestazione) heading

tes'ticolo sm testicle

testi'mone smf (Dir) witness; **~ oculare** eyewitness

testimoni'are /19/ vt to testify; (fig) to bear witness to, testify to ▷ vi to give evidence, testify

'testo sm text; **fare ~** (opera, autore) to be authoritative; **questo libro non fa ~** this book is not essential reading

tes'tuggine [tes'tuddʒine] sf tortoise; (di mare) turtle

'tetano sm (Med) tetanus

'tetto sm roof; **tet'toia** sf roofing; canopy

tet'tuccio [tet'tuttʃo] sm: **~ apribile** (Aut) sunroof

Tevere sm: **il ~** the Tiber

TG [tid'dʒi], **tg** abbr m (= telegiornale) TV news sg

'thermos® ['tɛrmos] sm inv vacuum o Thermos® flask

ti pron (dav lo, la, li, le, ne diventa **te**, oggetto) you; (complemento di termine) (to) you; (riflessivo) yourself

Tibet sm: **il ~** Tibet

'tibia sf tibia, shinbone

tic sm inv tic, (nervous) twitch; (fig) mannerism

ticchet'tio [tikket'tio] sm (di macchina da scrivere) clatter; (di orologio) ticking; (della pioggia) patter

'ticket sm inv (Med) prescription charge (BRIT)

ti'ene ecc vb vedi **tenere**

ti'epido, -a ag lukewarm, tepid

'tifo sm (Med) typhus; (fig): **fare il ~ per** to be a fan of

ti'fone sm typhoon

ti'foso, -a sm/f (Sport: ecc) fan

tigì [ti'dʒi] sm inv TV news

'tiglio ['tiʎʎo] sm lime (tree), linden (tree)

'tigre sf tiger

tim'brare /72/ vt to stamp; (annullare: francobolli) to postmark; **~ il cartellino** to clock in

'timbro sm stamp; (Mus) timbre, tone

'timido, -a ag shy; timid

'timo sm thyme

ti'mone sm (Naut) rudder

ti'more *sm (paura)* fear; *(rispetto)* awe

'timpano *sm (Anat)* eardrum

'tingere ['tindʒere] /37/ *vt* to dye

'tinsi *ecc vb vedi* **tingere**

'tinta *sf (materia colorante)* dye; *(colore)* shade

tintin'nare /72/ *vi* to tinkle

tinto'ria *sf (lavasecco)* dry cleaner's *(shop)*

tin'tura *sf (operazione)* dyeing; *(colorante)* dye; **~ di iodio** tincture of iodine

'tipico, -a, -ci, -che *ag* typical

'tipo *sm* type; *(genere)* kind, type; *(fam)* chap, fellow; **che ~ di …?** what kind of …?

tipogra'fia *sf* typography; *(procedimento)* letterpress *(printing)*; *(officina)* printing house

T.I.R. *sigla m* (= Transports Internationaux Routiers) International Heavy Goods Vehicle

ti'rare /72/ *vt (gen)* to pull; *(chiudere: tenda ecc)* to draw, pull; *(tracciare, disegnare)* to draw, trace; *(lanciare: sasso, palla)* to throw; *(stampare)* to print; *(pistola, freccia)* to fire; *(estrarre)*: **~ qc da** to take *o* pull sth out of; to get sth out of; to extract sth from ▷ *vi (pipa, camino)* to draw; *(vento)* to blow; *(abito)* to be tight; *(fare fuoco)* to fire; *(fare del tiro, Calcio)* to shoot; **~ a indovinare** to take a guess; **~ sul prezzo** to bargain; **~ avanti** to struggle on; *vt* to keep going; **~ fuori** *(estrarre)* to take out, pull out; **~ giù** *(abbassare)* to bring down, to lower; *(da scaffale ecc)* to take down; **~ su** to pull up; *(capelli)* to put up; *(fig: bambino)* to bring up; **tirar dritto** to keep right on going; **~ via** *(togliere)* to take off; **tirarsi indietro** to move back; *(fig)* to back out; **tirati su!** cheer up!

tira'tura *sf (azione)* printing; *(di libro) (print)* run; *(di giornale)* circulation

'tirchio, -a ['tirkjo] *ag* mean, stingy

'tiro *sm* shooting *no pl*, firing *no pl*; *(colpo, sparo)* shot; *(di palla: lancio)* throwing *no pl*; *(fig)* trick; **cavallo da ~** draught (BRIT) *o* draft (US) horse; **~ a segno** target shooting; *(luogo)* shooting range; **~ con l'arco** archery

tiro'cinio [tiro'tʃinjo] *sm* apprenticeship; *(professionale)* training

ti'roide *sf* thyroid *(gland)*

Tir'reno *sm*: **il (mar) ~** the Tyrrhenian Sea

ti'sana *sf* herb tea

tito'lare *smf* incumbent; *(proprietario)* owner; *(Calcio)* regular player

'titolo *sm* title; *(di giornale)* headline; *(diploma)* qualification; *(Comm)* security; *(: azione)* share; **a che ~?** for what reason?; **a ~ di amicizia** out of friendship; **a ~ di premio** as a prize; **~ di credito** share; **titoli di stato** government securities; **titoli di testa** *(Cine)* credits

titu'bante *ag* hesitant, irresolute

toast [toust] *sm inv* toasted sandwich *(generally with ham and cheese)*

toc'cante *ag* touching

toc'care /20/ *vt* to touch; *(tastare)* to feel; *(fig: riguardare)* to concern; *(: commuovere)* to touch, move; *(: pungere)* to hurt, wound; *(: far cenno a: argomento)* to touch on, mention ▷ *vi*: **~ a** *(accadere)* to happen to; *(spettare)* to be up to; **tocca a te difenderci** it's up to you to defend us; **a chi tocca?** whose turn is it?; **mi toccò pagare** I had to pay; **~ il fondo** *(in acqua)* to touch the bottom

toccherò *ecc* [tokke'rɔ] *vb vedi* **toccare**

'togliere ['tɔʎʎere] /122/ *vt (rimuovere)* to take away *(o off)*, remove; *(riprendere, non concedere più)* to take away, remove; *(Mat)* to take away, subtract; **~ qc a qn** to take sth *(away)* from sb; **ciò non toglie che …** nevertheless …, be that as it may …; **togliersi il cappello** to take off one's hat

toilette [twa'lɛt] *sf inv* toilet; *(mobile)* dressing table

'Tokyo *sf* Tokyo

'tolgo *ecc vb vedi* **togliere**

tolle'rare /72/ *vt* to tolerate

'tolsi *ecc vb vedi* **togliere**

'tomba *sf* tomb

tom'bino *sm* manhole cover

'tombola *sf (gioco)* tombola; *(ruzzolone)* tumble

'tondo, -a *ag* round

'tonfo *sm* splash; *(rumore sordo)* thud; *(caduta)*: **fare un ~** to take a tumble

tonifi'care /20/ *vt (muscoli, pelle)* to tone up; *(irrobustire)* to invigorate, brace

tonnel'lata *sf* ton

'tonno *sm* tuna *(fish)*

'tono *sm (gen, Mus)* tone; *(di pezzo)* key; *(di colore)* shade, tone

ton'silla *sf* tonsil

'tonto, -a *ag* dull, stupid

to'pazio [to'pattsjo] *sm* topaz

'topo *sm* mouse

'toppa *sf (serratura)* keyhole; *(pezza)* patch

to'race [to'ratʃe] *sm* chest

'torba *sf* peat

'torcere ['tɔrtʃere] /106/ *vt* to twist; **torcersi** *vpr* to twist, writhe

'torcia, -ce ['tɔrtʃa] *sf* torch; **~ elettrica** torch (BRIT), flashlight (US)

torci'collo [tortʃi'kɔllo] *sm* stiff neck

'tordo *sm* thrush

To'rino *sf* Turin

tor'menta *sf* snowstorm

tormen'tare /72/ *vt* to torment; **tormentarsi** *vpr* to fret, worry o.s.

tor'nado *sm* tornado

tor'nante *sm* hairpin bend (BRIT) *o* curve (US)

tor'nare /72/ *vi* to return, go (*o* come) back; (*ridiventare: anche fig*) to become (again); (*riuscire giusto, esatto: conto*) to work out; (*risultare*) to turn out (to be), prove (to be); **~ a casa** to go (*o* come) home; **~ utile** to prove *o* turn out (to be) useful; **torno a casa martedì** I'm going home on Tuesday

tor'neo *sm* tournament

'tornio *sm* lathe

'toro *sm* bull; **T~** Taurus

'torre *sf* tower; (*Scacchi*) rook, castle; **~ di controllo** (*Aer*) control tower

tor'rente *sm* torrent

torri'one *sm* keep

tor'rone *sm* nougat

'torsi *ecc vb vedi* **torcere**

torsi'one *sf* twisting; (*Tecn*) torsion

'torso *sm* torso, trunk; (*Arte*) torso

'torsolo *sm* (*di cavolo ecc*) stump; (*di frutta*) core

'torta *sf* cake

tortel'lini *smpl* (*Cuc*) tortellini

'torto, -a *pp di* **torcere** ▷ *ag* (*ritorto*) twisted; (*storto*) twisted, crooked ▷ *sm* (*ingiustizia*) wrong; (*colpa*) fault; **a ~** wrongly; **aver ~** to be wrong

'tortora *sf* turtle dove

tor'tura *sf* torture; **tortu'rare** /72/ *vt* to torture

to'sare /72/ *vt* (*pecora*) to shear; (*siepe*) to clip

Tos'cana *sf*: **la ~** Tuscany

'tosse *sf* cough; **ho la ~** I've got a cough

'tossico, -a, -ci, -che *ag* toxic; (*Econ*): **titolo ~** toxic asset

tossicodipen'dente *smf* drug addict

tos'sire /55/ *vi* to cough

'tosta'pane *sm inv* toaster

to'tale *ag, sm* total

toto'calcio [toto'kaltʃo] *sm* gambling pool betting on football results ≈ (football) pools *pl* (BRIT)

to'vaglia [to'vaʎʎa] *sf* tablecloth; **tovagli'olo** *sm* napkin

tra *prep* (*di due persone, cose*) between; (*di più persone, cose*) among(st); (*tempo: entro*) within, in; **litigano ~ (di) loro** they're fighting amongst themselves; **~ 5 giorni** in 5 days' time; **~ breve** *o* **poco** soon; **~ sé e sé** (*parlare ecc*) to oneself; **sia detto ~ noi ...** between you and me ...

trabocchare /20/ *vi* to overflow

trabocchetto [trabok'ketto] *sm* (*fig*) trap

'traccia, -ce ['trattʃa] *sf* (*segno, striscia*) trail, track; (*orma*) tracks *pl*; (*residuo, testimonianza*) trace, sign; (*abbozzo*) outline

tracci'are [trat'tʃare] /14/ *vt* to trace, mark (out); (*disegnare*) to draw; (*fig: abbozzare*) to outline

tra'chea [tra'kɛa] *sf* windpipe, trachea

tra'colla *sf* shoulder strap; **borsa a ~** shoulder bag

tradi'mento *sm* betrayal; (*Dir, Mil*) treason

tra'dire /55/ *vt* to betray; (*coniuge*) to be unfaithful to; (*doveri: mancare*) to fail in; (*rivelare*) to give away, reveal

tradizio'nale [tradittsjo'nale] *ag* traditional

tradizi'one [tradit'tsjone] *sf* tradition

tra'durre /90/ *vt* to translate; (*spiegare*) to render, convey; **tradut'tore, -'trice** *sm/f* translator; **traduzi'one** *sf* translation

'trae *vb vedi* **trarre**

traffi'cante *smf* dealer; (*peg*) trafficker

traffi'care /20/ *vi* (*affaccendarsi*) to busy o.s.; (*commerciare*): **~ (in)** to trade (in), deal (in) ▷ *vt* (*peg*) to traffic in

'traffico, -ci *sm* traffic; (*commercio*) trade, traffic; **~ di armi/droga** arms/drug trafficking

tra'gedia [tra'dʒɛdja] *sf* tragedy

'traggo *ecc vb vedi* **trarre**

tra'ghetto [tra'getto] *sm* ferry(boat)

'tragico, -a, -ci, -che *ag* tragic

tra'gitto [tra'dʒitto] *sm* (*passaggio*) crossing; (*viaggio*) journey

tragu'ardo *sm* (*Sport*) finishing line; (*fig*) goal, aim

'trai *ecc vb vedi* **trarre**

traiet'toria *sf* trajectory

trai'nare /72/ *vt* to drag, haul; (*rimorchiare*) to tow

tralasci'are [tralaʃʃare] /14/ *vt* (*studi*) to neglect; (*dettagli*) to leave out, omit

tra'liccio [tra'littʃo] *sm* (*Elettr*) pylon

tram *sm inv* tram

'trama *sf* (*filo*) weft, woof; (*fig: argomento, maneggio*) plot

traman'dare /72/ *vt* to pass on, hand down

tram'busto *sm* turmoil

tramez'zino [tramed'dzino] *sm* sandwich

'tramite *prep* through

tramon'tare /72/ *vi* to set, go down; **tra'monto** *sm* setting; (*del sole*) sunset

trampo'lino *sm* (*per tuffi*) springboard, diving board; (*per lo sci*) ski-jump

tra'nello *sm* trap

'tranne *prep* except (for), but (for); **~ che** unless

tranquil'lante *sm* (*Med*) tranquillizer

tranquillità *sf* calm, stillness; quietness; peace of mind

tranquilliz'zare [trankwillid'dzare] /72/ *vt* to reassure

> Attenzione! In inglese esiste il verbo *to tranquillize*, che però significa "calmare con un tranquillante".

tran'quillo, -a *ag* calm, quiet; *(bambino, scolaro)* quiet; *(sereno)* with one's mind at rest; **sta' ~** don't worry

transazi'one [transat'tsjone] *sf* compromise; *(Dir)* settlement; *(Comm)* transaction, deal

tran'senna *sf* barrier

trans'genico, -a, -ci, -che [trans'dʒɛniko] *ag* genetically modified

tran'sigere [tran'sidʒere] /47/ *vi (venire a patti)* to compromise, come to an agreement

transi'tabile *ag* passable

transi'tare /72/ *vi* to pass

transi'tivo, -a *ag* transitive

'transito *sm* transit; **di ~** *(merci)* in transit; *(stazione)* transit *cpd*; **"divieto di ~"** "no entry"

'trapano *sm (utensile)* drill; *(Med)* trepan

trape'lare /72/ *vi* to leak, drip; *(fig)* to leak out

tra'pezio [tra'pɛttsjo] *sm (Mat)* trapezium; *(attrezzo ginnico)* trapeze

trapian'tare /72/ *vt* to transplant; **trapi'anto** *sm* transplanting; *(Med)* transplant; **trapianto cardiaco** heart transplant

'trappola *sf* trap

tra'punta *sf* quilt

'trarre /123/ *vt* to draw, pull; *(portare)* to take; *(prendere, tirare fuori)* to take (out), draw; *(derivare)* to obtain; **~ origine da qc** to have its origins o originate in sth

trasa'lire /55/ *vi* to start, jump

trasan'dato, -a *ag* shabby

trasci'nare [traʃʃi'nare] /72/ *vt* to drag; **trascinarsi** *vpr* to drag o.s. along; *(fig)* to drag on

tras'correre /28/ *vt (tempo)* to spend, pass ▷ *vi* to pass

tras'crivere /105/ *vt* to transcribe

trascu'rare /72/ *vt* to neglect; *(non considerare)* to disregard

trasferi'mento *sm* transfer; *(trasloco)* removal, move; **~ di chiamata** *(Tel)* call forwarding

trasfe'rire /55/ *vt* to transfer; **trasferirsi** *vpr* to move; **tras'ferta** *sf* transfer; *(indennità)* travelling expenses *pl*; *(Sport)* away game

trasfor'mare /72/ *vt* to transform, change; **trasformarsi** *vpr* to be transformed; **trasformarsi in qc** to turn into sth; **trasforma'tore** *sm (Elettr)* transformer

trasfusi'one *sf (Med)* transfusion

trasgre'dire /55/ *vt* to disobey, contravene

traslo'care /20/ *vt* to move, transfer; **tras'loco, -chi** *sm* removal

tras'mettere /63/ *vt (passare)*: **~ qc a qn** to pass sth on to sb; *(mandare)* to send; *(Tecn, Tel, Med)* to transmit; *(TV, Radio)* to broadcast; **trasmissi'one** *sf (gen, Fisica, Tecn)* transmission; *(passaggio)* transmission, passing on; *(TV, Radio)* broadcast

traspa'rente *ag* transparent

traspor'tare /72/ *vt* to carry, move; *(merce)* to transport, convey; **lasciarsi ~ (da qc)** *(fig)* to let o.s. be carried away (by sth); **tras'porto** *sm* transport

'trassi *ecc vb vedi* **trarre**

trasver'sale *ag* cross(-); *(retta)* transverse; running at right angles

'tratta *sf (Econ)* draft; **la ~ delle bianche** the white slave trade

tratta'mento *sm* treatment; *(servizio)* service

trat'tare /72/ *vt (gen)* to treat; *(commerciare)* to deal in; *(svolgere: argomento)* to discuss, deal with; *(negoziare)* to negotiate ▷ *vi*: **~ di** to deal with; **~ con** *(persona)* to deal with; **si tratta di …** it's about …

tratte'nere /121/ *vt (far rimanere: persona)* to detain; *(intrattenere: ospiti)* to entertain; *(tenere, frenare, reprimere)* to hold back, keep back; *(astenersi dal consegnare)* to hold, keep; *(detrarre: somma)* to deduct; **trattenersi** *vpr (astenersi)* to restrain o.s., stop o.s.; *(soffermarsi)* to stay, remain

trat'tino *sm* dash; *(in parole composte)* hyphen

'tratto, -a *pp di* **trarre** ▷ *sm (di penna, matita)* stroke; *(parte)* part, piece; *(di strada)* stretch; *(di mare, cielo)* expanse; *(di tempo)* period (of time)

trat'tore *sm* tractor

tratto'ria *sf* (small) restaurant

'trauma, -i *sm* trauma

tra'vaglio [tra'vaʎʎo] *sm (angoscia)* pain, suffering; *(Med)* pains *pl*

trava'sare /72/ *vt* to decant

tra'versa *sf (trave)* crosspiece; *(via)* sidestreet; *(Ferr)* sleeper (BRIT), (railroad) tie (US); *(Calcio)* crossbar

traver'sata *sf* crossing; *(Aer)* flight, trip

traver'sie *sfpl* mishaps, misfortunes

tra'verso, -a *ag* oblique; **di ~** *ag* askew ▷ *av* sideways; **andare di ~** *(cibo)* to go down the wrong way; **guardare di ~** to look askance at

travesti'mento *sm* disguise

traves'tire /45/ *vt* to disguise; **travestirsi** *vpr* to disguise o.s.

tra'volgere [tra'vɔldʒere] /96/ *vt* to sweep away, carry away; *(fig)* to overwhelm

tre *num* three

'treccia, -ce ['trettʃa] *sf* plait, braid

tre'cento [tre'tʃɛnto] *num* three hundred
▷ *sm*: **il T~** the fourteenth century
tredici ['tredɪtʃi] *num* thirteen
tregua *sf* truce; *(fig)* respite
tre'mare /72/ *vi*: **~ di** *(freddo ecc)* to shiver
o tremble with; *(paura, rabbia)* to shake o
tremble with
tre'mendo, -a *ag* terrible, awful

> Attenzione! In inglese esiste la parola
> *tremendous*, che però significa *enorme*
> oppure *fantastico, strepitoso*.

tremito *sm* trembling *no pl*; shaking *no pl*;
shivering *no pl*
treno *sm* train;**~ di gomme** set of tyres o
(BRIT) o tires *(US)*; **~ merci** goods *(BRIT)* o
freight train; **~ viaggiatori** passenger train

trenta *num* thirty; **tren'tesimo, -a** *num*
thirtieth; **tren'tina** *sf*: **una trentina (di)**
thirty or so, about thirty
trepi'dante *ag* anxious
triango'lare *ag* triangular
tri'angolo *sm* triangle
tribù *sf inv* tribe
tri'buna *sf* *(podio)* platform; *(in aule ecc)*
gallery; *(di stadio)* stand
tribu'nale *sm* court
tri'ciclo [tri'tʃiklo] *sm* tricycle
tri'foglio [tri'fɔʎʎo] *sm* clover
triglia ['triʎʎa] *sf* red mullet
tri'mestre *sm* period of three months; *(Ins)*
term, quarter *(US)*; *(Comm)* quarter
trin'cea [trin'tʃea] *sf* trench
trion'fare /72/ *vi* to triumph, win; **~ su**
to triumph over, overcome; **tri'onfo** *sm*
triumph
tripli'care /20/ *vt* to triple
triplo, -a *ag* triple; treble ▷ *sm*: **il ~ (di)**
three times as much (as); **la spesa è tripla**
it costs three times as much

trippa *sf (Cuc)* tripe
triste *ag* sad; *(luogo)* dreary, gloomy
tri'tare /72/ *vt* to mince, grind *(US)*
trivi'ale *ag* vulgar, low
tro'feo *sm* trophy
tromba *sf (Mus)* trumpet; *(Aut)* horn; **~ d'aria**
whirlwind; **~ delle scale** stairwell
trom'bone *sm* trombone
trom'bosi *sf* thrombosis
tron'care /20/ *vt* to cut off; *(spezzare)* to
break off
tronco, -a, -chi, -che *ag* cut off; broken
off; *(Ling)* truncated; *(fig)* cut short ▷ *sm*
(Bot, Anat) trunk; *(fig: tratto)* section;
licenziare qn in ~ to fire sb on the spot
trono *sm* throne
tropi'cale *ag* tropical

 PAROLA CHIAVE

troppo, -a *det (in eccesso: quantità)* too
much; *(: numero)* too many; **c'era troppa
gente** there were too many people; **fa
troppo caldo** it's too hot
▷ *pron (in eccesso: quantità)* too much;
(: numero) too many; **ne hai messo troppo**
you've put in too much; **meglio troppi che
pochi** better too many than too few
▷ *av (eccessivamente)* too; *(con ag, av)* too;
(: con vb) too much; **troppo amaro/tardi** too bitter/
late; **lavora troppo** he works too much;
costa troppo it costs too much; **di troppo**
too much; too many; **qualche tazza di
troppo** a few cups too many; **5 euro di
troppo** 5 euros too much; **essere di troppo**
to be in the way

trota *sf* trout
trottola *sf* spinning top
tro'vare /72/ *vt* to find; *(giudicare)*: **trovo
che** I find o think that; **trovarsi** *vpr*
(reciproco: incontrarsi) to meet; *(essere, stare)*
to be; *(arrivare, capitare)* to find o.s.; **andare
a ~ qn** to go and see sb; **~ qn colpevole** to
find sb guilty; **trovarsi bene/male** *(in un
luogo, con qn)* to get on well/badly
truc'care /20/ *vt (falsare)* to fake; *(attore ecc)*
to make up; *(travestire)* to disguise; *(Sport)*
to fix; *(Aut)* to soup up; **truccarsi** *vpr* to
make up (one's face)
trucco, -chi *sm* trick; *(cosmesi)* make-up
truffa *sf* fraud, swindle; **truf'fare** /72/ *vt* to
swindle, cheat
truffa'tore, -'trice *sm/f* swindler, cheat
truppa *sf* troop
tu *pron* you; **tu stesso(a)** you yourself; **dare
del tu a qn** to address sb as "tu"
tubo *sm* tube; *(per conduttore)* pipe;
~ digerente *(Anat)* alimentary canal,

digestive tract; **~ di scappamento** (Aut) exhaust pipe

tuf'fare /72/ vt to plunge; **tuffarsi** vpr to plunge, dive

'tuffo sm dive; (breve bagno) dip

tuli'pano sm tulip

tu'more sm (Med) tumour

Tuni'sia sf: **la ~** Tunisia

'tuo (f'tua, pl 'tuoi, 'tue) det: **il ~, la tua** ecc your ▷ pron: **il ~, la tua** ecc yours

tuo'nare /72/ vi to thunder; **tuona** it is thundering, there's some thunder

tu'ono sm thunder

tu'orlo sm yolk

tur'bante sm turban

tur'bare /72/ vt to disturb, trouble

tur'bato, -a ag upset; (preoccupato, ansioso) anxious

turbo'lenza [turbo'lentsa] sf turbulence

tur'chese [tur'kese] sf turquoise

Tur'chia [tur'kia] sf: **la ~** Turkey

'turco, -a, -chi, -che ag Turkish ▷ sm/f Turk (Turkish woman) ▷ sm (Ling) Turkish; **parlare ~** (fig) to talk double Dutch

tu'rismo sm tourism; tourist industry; **~ sessuale** sex tourism; **tu'rista, -i, -e** smf tourist; **tu'ristico, -a, -ci, -che** ag tourist cpd

'turno sm turn; (di lavoro) shift; **di ~** (soldato, medico, custode) on duty; **a ~** (rispondere) in turn; (lavorare) in shifts; **fare a ~ a fare qc** to take turns to do sth; **è il suo ~** it's your (o his ecc) turn

'turpe ag filthy, vile

'tuta sf overalls pl; (Sport) tracksuit

tu'tela sf (Dir: di minore) guardianship; (: protezione) protection; (difesa) defence

tutor ['tiutor] sm inv (Aut) speed monitoring system

tutta'via cong nevertheless, yet

🔵 **PAROLA CHIAVE**

'tutto, -a det **1** (intero) all; **tutto il latte** all the milk; **tutta la notte** all night, the whole night; **tutto il libro** the whole book; **tutta una bottiglia** a whole bottle

2 (pl, collettivo) all; every; **tutti i libri** all the books; **tutte le notti** every night; **tutti i venerdì** every Friday; **tutti gli uomini** all the men; (collettivo) all men; **tutto l'anno** all year long; **tutti e due** both o each of us (o them o you); **tutti e cinque** all five of us (o them o you)

3 (completamente): **era tutta sporca** she was all dirty; **tremava tutto** he was trembling all over; **è tutta sua madre** she's just o exactly like her mother

4: a tutt'oggi so far, up till now; **a tutta**

velocità at full o top speed

▶ pron **1** (ogni cosa) everything, all; (qualsiasi cosa) anything; **ha mangiato tutto** he's eaten everything; **tutto considerato** all things considered; **100 euro in tutto** 100 euros in all; **in tutto eravamo 50** there were 50 of us in all

2: tutti, e (ognuno) all, everybody; **vengono tutti** they are all coming, everybody's coming; **tutti quanti** all and sundry

▶ av (completamente) entirely, quite; **è tutto il contrario** it's quite o exactly the opposite; **tutt'al più: saranno stati tutt'al più una cinquantina** there were about fifty of them at (the very) most; **tutt'al più possiamo prendere un treno** if the worst comes to the worst we can take a train; **tutt'altro** on the contrary; **è tutt'altro che felice** he's anything but happy; **tutt'a un tratto** suddenly

▶ sm: **il tutto** the whole lot, all of it

tutt'tora av still

TV [ti'vu] sf inv (= televisione) TV ▷ sigla = **Treviso**

twit'tare /72/ vt (su Twitter) to tweet

u

ubbidi'ente *ag* obedient
ubbi'dire /55/ *vi* to obey; **~ a** to obey; (*veicolo, macchina*) to respond to
ubria'care /20/ *vt*: **~ qn** to get sb drunk; (*alcool*) to make sb drunk; (*fig*) to make sb's head spin o reel; **ubriacarsi** *vpr* to get drunk; **ubriacarsi di** (*fig*) to become intoxicated with
ubri'aco, -a, -chi, -che *ag*, *sm/f* drunk
uc'cello [ut'tʃɛllo] *sm* bird
uc'cidere [ut'tʃidere] /34/ *vt* to kill; **uccidersi** *vpr* (*suicidarsi*) to kill o.s.; (*perdere la vita*) to be killed
u'dire /124/ *vt* to hear
u'dito *sm* (sense of) hearing
UE *sigla f* (= *Unione Europea*) EU
UEM *sigla f* (= *Unione economica e monetaria*) EMU
'uffa *escl* tut!
uffici'ale [uffi'tʃale] *ag* official ▷ *sm* (*Amm*) official, officer; (*Mil*) officer; **~ di stato civile** registrar
uf'ficio [uf'fitʃo] *sm* (*gen*) office; (*dovere*) duty; (*mansione*) task, function, job; (*agenzia*) agency, bureau; (*Rel*) service; **d'~** *ag* office *cpd*; official ▷ *av* officially; **~ di collocamento** employment office; **~ informazioni** information bureau; **~ oggetti smarriti** lost property office (*BRIT*), lost and found (*US*); **~ postale** post office; **~ vendite/del personale** sales/ personnel department
uffici'oso, -a [uffi'tʃoso] *ag* unofficial
uguagli'anza [ugwaʎ'ʎantsa] *sf* equality
uguagli'are [ugwaʎ'ʎare] /27/ *vt* to make equal; (*essere uguale*) to equal, be equal to; (*livellare*) to level; **uguagliarsi** *vpr*: **uguagliarsi a** *o* **con qn** (*paragonarsi*) to compare o.s. to sb

ugu'ale *ag* equal; (*identico*) identical, the same; (*uniforme*) level, even ▷ *av*: **costano ~** they cost the same; **sono bravi ~** they're equally good
UIL *sigla f* (= *Unione Italiana del Lavoro*) trade union federation
'ulcera ['ultʃera] *sf* ulcer
U'livo *sm* (*Pol*) centre-left coalition
ulteri'ore *ag* further
ultima'mente *av* lately, of late
ulti'mare /72/ *vt* to finish, complete
'ultimo, -a *ag* (*finale*) last; (*estremo*) farthest, utmost; (*recente: notizia, moda*) latest; (*fig: sommo, fondamentale*) ultimate ▷ *sm/f* last (one); **fino all'~** to the last, until the end; **da ~, in ~** in the end; **per ~** (*entrare, arrivare*) last; **abitare all'~ piano** to live on the top floor
ultravio'letto, -a *ag* ultraviolet
ulu'lare /72/ *vi* to howl
umanità *sf* humanity
u'mano, -a *ag* human; (*comprensivo*) humane
umidità *sf* dampness; humidity
'umido, -a *ag* damp; (*mano, occhi*) moist; (*clima*) humid ▷ *sm* dampness, damp; **carne in ~** stew
'umile *ag* humble
umili'are /19/ *vt* to humiliate; **umiliarsi** *vpr* to humble o.s.
u'more *sm* (*disposizione d'animo*) mood; (*carattere*) temper; **di buon/cattivo ~** in a good/bad mood
umo'rismo *sm* humour (*BRIT*), humor (*US*); **avere il senso dell'~** to have a sense of humour; **umo'ristico, -a, -ci, -che** *ag* humorous, funny
u'nanime *ag* unanimous
unci'netto [untʃi'netto] *sm* crochet hook
un'cino [un'tʃino] *sm* hook
undi'cenne [undi'tʃɛnne] *ag*, *smf* eleven- year-old
undi'cesimo, -a [undi'tʃɛzimo] *ag* eleventh
'undici ['unditʃi] *num* eleven
'ungere ['undʒere] /5/ *vt* to grease, oil; (*Rel*) to anoint; (*fig*) to flatter, butter up
unghe'rese [unge'rese] *ag*, *smf*, *sm* Hungarian
Unghe'ria [unge'ria] *sf*: **l'~** Hungary
'unghia ['ungja] *sf* (*Anat*) nail; (*di animale*) claw; (*di rapace*) talon; (*di cavallo*) hoof
ungu'ento *sm* ointment
'unico, -a, -ci, -che *ag* (*solo*) only; (*ineguagliabile*) unique; (*singolo: binario*) single; **è figlio ~** he's an only child
unifi'care /20/ *vt* to unite, unify; (*sistemi*) to standardize; **unificazi'one** *sf* uniting; unification; standardization

uni'forme *ag* uniform; (*superficie*) even ▷ *sf* (*divisa*) uniform

uni'one *sf* union; (*fig: concordia*) unity, harmony; **U~ Europea** European Union; **ex U~ Sovietica** former Soviet Union

u'nire /55/ *vt* to unite; (*congiungere*) to join, connect; (: *ingredienti, colori*) to combine; (*in matrimonio*) to unite, join together; **unirsi** *vpr* to unite; (*in matrimonio*) to be joined together; **~ qc a** to unite sth with; to join o connect sth with; to combine sth with; **unirsi a** (*gruppo, società*) to join

unità *sf inv* (*unione, concordia*) unity; (*Mat, Mil, Comm, di misura*) unit; **~ di misura** unit of measurement

u'nito, -a *ag* (*paese*) united; (*amici, famiglia*) close; **in tinta unita** plain, self-coloured

univer'sale *ag* universal; general

università *sf inv* university

uni'verso *sm* universe

🔵 **PAROLA CHIAVE**

'uno, -a (*dav sm* **un** + C, V, **uno** + *s impura, gn, pn, ps, x, z; dav sf* **un'** + V, **una** + C) *det* **1** a; (*dav vocale*) an; **un bambino** a child; **una strada** a street; **uno zingaro** a gypsy
2 (*intensivo*): **ho avuto una paura!** I got such a fright!
▶ *pron* **1** one; **prendine uno** take one (of them); **l'uno o l'altro** either (of them); **l'uno e l'altro** both (of them); **aiutarsi l'un l'altro** to help one another o each other; **sono entrati l'uno dopo l'altro** they came in one after the other
2 (*un tale*) someone, somebody
3 (*con valore impersonale*) one, you; **se uno vuole** if one wants, if you want
▶ *num* one; **una mela e due pere** one apple and two pears; **uno più uno fa due** one plus one equals two, one and one are two
▶ *sf*: **è l'una** it's one (o'clock)

'unsi *ecc vb vedi* **ungere**

'unto, -a *pp di* **ungere** ▷ *ag* greasy, oily ▷ *sm* grease

u'omo (*pl* **uomini**) *sm* man; **da ~** (*abito, scarpe*) men's, for men; **~ d'affari** businessman; **~ di paglia** stooge; **~ politico** politician; **~ rana** frogman

u'ovo (*pl f* **uova**) *sm* egg; **~ affogato** o **in camicia** poached egg; **~ bazzotto/sodo** soft-/hard-boiled egg; **~ alla coque** boiled egg; **~ di Pasqua** Easter egg; **~ al tegame** o **all'occhio di bue** fried egg; **uova strapazzate** scrambled eggs

ura'gano *sm* hurricane

urba'nistica *sf* town planning

ur'bano, -a *ag* urban, city *cpd*, town *cpd*; (*Tel: chiamata*) local; (*fig*) urbane

ur'gente [ur'dʒɛnte] *ag* urgent; **ur'genza** *sf* urgency; **in caso d'urgenza** in (case of) an emergency; **d'urgenza** *ag* emergency; *av* urgently, as a matter of urgency

ur'lare /72/ *vi* (*persona*) to scream, yell; (*animale, vento*) to howl ▷ *vt* to scream, yell

'urlo (*pl m* **urli** o *pl f* **urla**) *sm* scream, yell; howl

URP *sigla m* (= *Ufficio Relazioni con il Pubblico*) PR Office

urrà *escl* hurrah!

U.R.S.S. *sigla f* = **Unione delle Repubbliche Socialiste Sovietiche**; **l'~** the USSR

ur'tare /72/ *vt* to bump into, knock against, crash into; (*fig: irritare*) to annoy ▷ *vi*: **~ contro** o **in** to bump into, knock against; (*fig: imbattersi*) to come up against; **urtarsi** *vpr* (*reciproco: scontrarsi*) to collide; (: *fig*) to clash; (*irritarsi*) to get annoyed

'USA *smpl*: **gli ~** the USA

u'sanza [u'zantsa] *sf* custom; (*moda*) fashion

u'sare /72/ *vt* to use, employ ▷ *vi* (*essere di moda*) to be fashionable; (*servirsi*): **~ di** to use; (*diritto*) to exercise; (*essere solito*): **~ fare** to be in the habit of doing, be accustomed to doing ▷ *vb impers*: **qui usa così** it's the custom round here; **u'sato, -a** *ag* used; (*consumato*) worn; (*di seconda mano*) used, second-hand ▷ *sm* second-hand goods *pl*

u'scire [uʃʃire] /125/ *vi* (*gen*) to come out; (*partire, andare a passeggio, a uno spettacolo ecc*) to go out; (*essere sorteggiato: numero*) to come up; **~ da** (*gen*) to leave; (*posto*) to go o (*come out*) of, leave; (*solco, vasca ecc*) to come out of; (*muro*) to stick out of; (*competenza ecc*) to be outside; (*infanzia, adolescenza*) to leave behind; (*famiglia nobile ecc*) to come from; **~ da** o **di casa** to go out; (*fig*) to leave home; **~ in automobile** to go out in the car, go for a drive; **~ di strada** (*Aut*) to go off o leave the road

u'scita [uʃʃita] *sf* (*passaggio, varco*) exit, way out; (*per divertimento*) outing; (*Econ: somma*) expenditure; (*Teat*) entrance; (*fig: battuta*) witty remark; **~ di sicurezza** emergency exit

usi'gnolo [uziɲ'ɲɔlo] *sm* nightingale

'uso *sm* (*utilizzazione*) use; (*esercizio*) practice; (*abitudine*) custom; **a ~ di** for (the use of); **d'~** (*corrente*) in use; **fuori ~** out of use; **per ~ esterno** for external use only

usti'one *sf* burn

usu'ale *ag* common, everyday

u'sura *sf* usury; (*logoramento*) wear (and tear)

uten'sile *sm* tool, implement; **utensili da cucina** kitchen utensils

u'tente *smf* user

'utero *sm* uterus

'utile *ag* useful ▷ *sm* (*vantaggio*) advantage, benefit; (*Econ: profitto*) profit

utiliz'zare [utilid'dzare] /72/ *vt* to use, make use of, utilize

UVA *abbr* (= *ultravioletto prossimo*) UVA

'uva *sf* grapes *pl*; **~ passa** raisins *pl*; **~ spina** gooseberry

UVB *abbr* (= *ultravioletto lontano*) UVB

v. *abbr* (= *vedi*) v.

va, va' *vb vedi* **andare**

va'cante *ag* vacant

va'canza [va'kantsa] *sf* (*riposo, ferie*) holiday(s *pl*) (BRIT), vacation (US); (*giorno di permesso*) day off, holiday; **vacanze** *sfpl* (*periodo di ferie*) holidays, vacation *sg*; **essere/andare in ~** to be/go on holiday *o* vacation; **vacanze estive** summer holiday(s) *o* vacation; **vacanze natalizie** Christmas holidays *o* vacation

> Attenzione! In inglese esiste la parola *vacancy* che però indica un posto vacante o una camera disponibile.

'vacca, -che *sf* cow

vacci'nare [vattʃi'nare] /72/ *vt* to vaccinate

vac'cino [vat'tʃino] *sm* (*Med*) vaccine

vacil'lare [vatʃil'lare] /72/ *vi* to sway, wobble; (*fiamma, luce*) to flicker; (*fig: memoria, coraggio*) to be failing, falter

'vacuo, -a *ag* (*fig*) empty, vacuous

'vado *ecc vb vedi* **andare**

vaga'bondo, -a *sm/f* tramp, vagrant

va'gare /80/ *vi* to wander

vagherò *ecc* [vage'rɔ] *vb vedi* **vagare**

va'gina [va'dʒina] *sf* vagina

'vaglia ['vaʎʎa] *sm inv* money order; **~ postale** postal order

vagli'are [vaʎ'ʎare] /27/ *vt* to sift; (*fig*) to weigh up

'vago, -a, -ghi, -ghe *ag* vague

va'gone *sm* (*Ferr: per passeggeri*) coach; (: *per merci*) truck, wagon; **~ letto** sleeper, sleeping car; **~ ristorante** dining *o* restaurant car

'vai *vb vedi* **andare**

vai'olo *sm* smallpox

va'langa, -ghe *sf* avalanche

va'lere /126/ *vi* (*avere forza, potenza*) to have influence; (*essere valido*) to be valid; (*avere* *vigore, autorità*) to hold, apply; (*essere capace: poeta, studente*) to be good, be able ▷ *vt* (*prezzo, sforzo*) to be worth; (*corrispondere*) to correspond to; (*procurare*) **~ qc a qn** to earn sb sth; **valersi** *vpr*: **valersi di** to make use of, take advantage of; **far ~** (*autorità ecc*) to assert; **vale a dire** that is to say; **~ la pena** to be worth the effort *o* worth it

'valgo *ecc vb vedi* **valere**

vali'care /20/ *vt* to cross

'valico, -chi *sm* (*passo*) pass

'valido, -a *ag* valid; (*rimedio*) effective; (*aiuto*) real; (*persona*) worthwhile

vali'getta *sf* briefcase; **~ ventiquattrore** overnight bag *o* case

va'ligia, -gie *o* **-ge** [va'lidʒa] *sf* (suit)case; **fare le valigie** to pack (up)

'valle *sf* valley; **a ~** (*di fiume*) downstream; **scendere a ~** to go downhill

va'lore *sm* (*gen*) value; (*merito*) merit, worth; (*coraggio*) valour , courage; (*Finanza: titolo*) security; **valori** *smpl* (*oggetti preziosi*) valuables

valoriz'zare [valorid'dzare] /72/ *vt* (*terreno*) to develop; (*fig*) to make the most of

va'luta *sf* currency, money; (*Banca*): **~ 15 gennaio** interest to run from January 15th

valu'tare /72/ *vt* (*casa, gioiello, fig*) to value; (*stabilire: peso, entrate, fig*) to estimate

'valvola *sf* (*Tecn, Anat*) valve; (*Elettr*) fuse

'valzer ['valtser] *sm inv* waltz

vam'pata *sf* (*di fiamma*) blaze; (*di calore*) blast; (: *al viso*) flush

vam'piro *sm* vampire

vanda'lismo *sm* vandalism

'vandalo *sm* vandal

vaneggi'are [vaned'dʒare] /62/ *vi* to rave

'vanga, -ghe *sf* spade

van'gelo [van'dʒelo] *sm* gospel

va'niglia [va'niʎʎa] *sf* vanilla

vanità *sf* vanity; (*di promessa*) emptiness; (*di sforzo*) futility; **vani'toso, -a** *ag* vain, conceited

'vanno *vb vedi* **andare**

'vano, -a *ag* vain ▷ *sm* (*spazio*) space; (*apertura*) opening; (*stanza*) room

van'taggio [van'taddʒo] *sm* advantage; **essere/portarsi in ~** (*Sport*) to be in/ take the lead; **vantaggi'oso, -a** *ag* advantageous, favourable

van'tare /72/ *vt* to praise, speak highly of; **vantarsi** *vpr*: **vantarsi (di/di aver fatto)** to boast *o* brag (about/about having done)

'vanvera *sf*: **a ~** haphazardly; **parlare a ~** to talk nonsense

va'pore *sm* vapour; (*anche*: **~ acqueo**) steam; (*nave*) steamer; **a ~** (*turbina ecc*) steam *cpd*; **al ~** (*Cuc*) steamed

va'rare /72/ *vt* (*Naut, fig*) to launch; (*Dir*) to pass

var'care /20/ *vt* to cross

'varco, -chi *sm* passage; **aprirsi un ~ tra la folla** to push one's way through the crowd

vare'china [vare'kina] *sf* bleach

vari'abile *ag* variable; (*tempo, umore*) changeable, variable ▷ *sf* (*Mat*) variable

vari'cella [vari'tʃɛlla] *sf* chickenpox

vari'coso, -a *ag* varicose

varietà *sf inv* variety ▷ *sm inv* variety show

'vario, -a *ag* varied; (*parecchi: col sostantivo al pl*) various; (*mutevole: umore*) changeable

'varo *sm* (*Naut, fig*) launch; (*di leggi*) passing

varrò *ecc vb vedi* **valere**

Var'savia *sf* Warsaw

va'saio *sm* potter

'vasca, -sche *sf* basin; (*anche*: **~ da bagno**) bathtub, bath

vas'chetta [vas'ketta] *sf* (*per gelato*) tub; (*per sviluppare fotografie*) dish

vase'lina *sf* vaseline

'vaso *sm* (*recipiente*) pot; (: *barattolo*) jar; (: *decorativo*) vase; (*Anat*) vessel; **~ da fiori** vase; (*per piante*) flowerpot

vas'soio *sm* tray

'vasto, -a *ag* vast, immense

Vati'cano *sm*: **il ~** the Vatican

ve *pron, av vedi* **vi**

vecchi'aia [vek'kjaja] *sf* old age

'vecchio, -a ['vɛkkjo] *ag* old ▷ *sm/f* old man/woman; **i vecchi** the old

ve'dere /127/ *vt, vi* to see; **vedersi** *vpr* to meet, see one another; **avere a che ~ con** to have to do with; **far ~ qc a qn** to show sb sth; **farsi ~** to show o.s.; (*farsi vivo*) to show one's face; **vedi di non farlo** make sure *o* see you don't do it; **non (ci) si vede** (*è buio ecc*) you can't see a thing; **non lo posso ~** (*fig*) I can't stand him

ve'detta *sf* (*sentinella, posto*) look-out; (*Naut*) patrol boat

'vedovo, -a *sm/f* widower (widow)

vedrò *ecc vb vedi* **vedere**

ve'duta *sf* view; **vedute** *sfpl* (*fig: opinioni*) views; **di larghe** *o* **ampie vedute** broad-minded; **di vedute limitate** narrow-minded

vege'tale [vedʒe'tale] *ag, sm* vegetable

vegetari'ano, -a [vedʒeta'rjano] *ag, sm/f* vegetarian

vegetazi'one [vedʒetat'tsjone] *sf* vegetation

'vegeto, -a ['vɛdʒeto] *ag* (*pianta*) thriving; (*persona*) strong, vigorous

'veglia ['veʎʎa] *sf* wakefulness; (*sorveglianza*) watch; (*trattenimento*) evening gathering; **fare la ~ a un malato** to watch over a sick person

vegli'one [veʎˈʎone] *sm* ball, dance; **~ di Capodanno** New Year's Eve party

ve'icolo *sm* vehicle

'vela *sf* (*Naut: tela*) sail; (*: sport*) sailing

ve'leno *sm* poison; **vele'noso, -a** *ag* poisonous

veli'ero *sm* sailing ship

vel'luto *sm* velvet; **~ a coste** cord

'velo *sm* veil; (*tessuto*) voile

ve'loce [ve'lotʃe] *ag* fast, quick ▷ *av* fast, quickly; **velocità** *sf* speed; **a forte velocità** at high speed; **velocità di crociera** cruising speed

'vena *sf* (*gen*) vein; (*filone*) vein, seam; (*fig: ispirazione*) inspiration; (*: umore*) mood; **essere in ~ di qc** to be in the mood for sth

ve'nale *ag* (*prezzo, valore*) market *cpd*; (*fig*) venal; mercenary

ven'demmia *sf* (*raccolta*) grape harvest; (*quantità d'uva*) grape crop, grapes *pl*; (*vino ottenuto*) vintage

'vendere /29/ *vt* to sell; **"vendesi"** "for sale"

ven'detta *sf* revenge

vendi'care /20/ *vt* to avenge; **vendicarsi** *vpr*: **vendicarsi (di)** to avenge o.s. (for); (*per rancore*) to take one's revenge (for); **vendicarsi su qn** to revenge o.s. on sb

'vendita *sf* sale; **la ~** (*attività*) selling; (*smercio*) sales *pl*; **in ~** on sale; **~ all'asta** sale by auction; **~ per telefono** telesales *sg*

vene'rare /72/ *vt* to venerate

venerdì *sm inv* Friday; **di o il ~** on Fridays; **V~ Santo** Good Friday

ve'nereo, -a *ag* venereal

Ve'nezia [ve'nɛttsja] *sf* Venice

'vengo *ecc vb vedi* **venire**

veni'ale *ag* venial

ve'nire /128/ *vi* to come; (*riuscire: dolce, fotografia*) to turn out; (*come ausiliare: essere*): **viene ammirato da tutti** he is admired by everyone; **~ da** to come from; **quanto viene?** how much does it cost?; **far ~** (*mandare a chiamare*) to send for; **~ giù** to come down; **~ meno** (*svenire*) to faint; **~ meno a qc** not to fulfil sth; **~ su** to come up; **~ via** to come away; **~ a trovare qn** to come and see sb

'venni *ecc vb vedi* **venire**

ven'taglio [ven'taʎʎo] *sm* fan

ven'tata *sf* gust (of wind)

ven'tenne *ag*: **una ragazza ~** a twenty-year-old girl, a girl of twenty

ven'tesimo, -a *num* twentieth

'venti *num* twenty

venti'lare /72/ *vt* (*stanza*) to air, ventilate; (*fig: idea, proposta*) to air; **ventila'tore** *sm* ventilator, fan

ven'tina *sf*: **una ~ (di)** around twenty, twenty or so

'vento *sm* wind

'ventola *sf* (*Aut, Tecn*) fan

ven'tosa *sf* (*Zool*) sucker; (*di gomma*) suction pad

ven'toso, -a *ag* windy

'ventre *sm* stomach

'vera *sf* wedding ring

vera'mente *av* really

ve'randa(h)

ver'bale *ag* verbal ▷ *sm* (*di riunione*) minutes *pl*

'verbo *sm* (*Ling*) verb; (*parola*) word; (*Rel*): **il V~** the Word

'verde *ag, sm* green; **~ bottiglia/oliva** bottle/olive green; **essere al ~** to be broke

ver'detto *sm* verdict

ver'dura *sf* vegetables *pl*

'vergine ['verdʒine] *sf* virgin; **V~** Virgo ▷ *ag* virgin; (*ragazza*): **essere ~** to be a virgin

ver'gogna [ver'goɲɲa] *sf* shame; (*timidezza*) shyness, embarrassment; **vergo'gnarsi (di)** to be *o* feel ashamed (of); to be shy (about); embarrassed (about); **vergo'gnoso, -a** *ag* ashamed; (*timido*) shy, embarrassed; (*causa di vergogna: azione*) shameful

ve'rifica, -che *sf* checking *no pl*; check

verifi'care /20/ *vt* (*controllare*) to check; (*confermare*) to confirm, bear out

verità *sf inv* truth

'verme *sm* worm

ver'miglio [ver'miʎʎo] *sm* vermilion, scarlet

ver'nice [ver'nitʃe] *sf* (*colorazione*) paint; (*trasparente*) varnish; (*pelle*) patent leather; **"~ fresca"** "wet paint"; **vernici'are** /14/ *vt* to paint; to varnish

'vero, -a *ag* (*veridico: fatti, testimonianza*) true; (*autentico*) real ▷ *sm* (*verità*) truth; (*realtà*) (real) life; **un ~ e proprio delinquente** a real criminal, an out and out criminal

vero'simile *ag* likely, probable

verrò *ecc vb vedi* **venire**

ver'ruca, -che *sf* wart

versa'mento *sm* (*pagamento*) payment; (*deposito di denaro*) deposit

ver'sante *sm* slopes *pl*, side

ver'sare /72/ *vt* (*fare uscire: vino, farina*) to pour (out); (*spargere: lacrime, sangue*) to shed; (*rovesciare*) to spill; (*Econ*) to pay; (*: depositare*) to deposit, pay in

versa'tile *ag* versatile

versi'one *sf* version; (*traduzione*) translation

'verso *sm* (*di poesia*) verse, line; (*di animale, uccello, venditore ambulante*) cry; (*direzione*) direction; (*modo*) way; (*di foglio di carta*) verso; (*di moneta*) reverse; **versi** *smpl* (*poesia*) verse *sg* ▷ *prep* (*in direzione di*) toward(s); (*nei pressi di*) near, around (about); (*in senso temporale*) about, around; (*nei confronti di*) for; **non c'è ~ di persuaderlo** there's no way of persuading him, he can't be persuaded; **~ di me** towards me; **~ sera** towards evening

'vertebra *sf* vertebra

verte'brale *ag* vertebral; **colonna ~** spinal column, spine

verti'cale *ag, sf* vertical

'vertice ['vɛrtitʃe] *sm* summit, top; (*Mat*) vertex; **conferenza al ~** (*Pol*) summit conference

ver'tigine [ver'tidʒine] *sf* dizziness *no pl*; dizzy spell; (*Med*) vertigo; **avere le vertigini** to feel dizzy

ve'scica [veʃʃika] *sf* (*Anat*) bladder; (*Med*) blister

'vescovo *sm* bishop

'vespa *sf* wasp

ves'taglia [ves'taʎʎa] *sf* dressing gown

ves'tire /45/ *vt* (*bambino, malato*) to dress; (*avere indosso*) to have on, wear; **vestirsi** *vpr* to dress, get dressed; **ves'tito, -a** *ag* dressed ▷ *sm* garment; (*da donna*) dress; (*da uomo*) suit; **vestiti** *smpl* (*indumenti*) clothes; **vestito di bianco** dressed in white

veteri'nario, -a *ag* veterinary ▷ *sm* veterinary surgeon (*BRIT*), veterinarian (*US*), vet

'veto *sm inv* veto

ve'traio *sm* glassmaker; (*per finestre*) glazier

ve'trato, -a *ag* (*porta, finestra*) glazed; (*che contiene vetro*) glass *cpd* ▷ *sf* glass door (*o* window); (*di chiesa*) stained glass window; **carta vetrata** sandpaper

ve'trina *sf* (*di negozio*) (shop) window; (*armadio*) display cabinet; **vetri'nista, -i, -e** *smf* window dresser

'vetro *sm* glass; (*per finestra, porta*) pane (of glass)

'vetta *sf* peak, summit, top

vet'tura *sf* (*carrozza*) carriage; (*Ferr*) carriage (*BRIT*), car (*US*); (*auto*) car (*BRIT*), automobile (*US*)

vezzeggia'tivo [vettseddʒa'tivo] *sm* (*Ling*) term of endearment

vi (*dav lo, la, li, le, ne diventa* **ve**) *pron* (*oggetto*) you; (*complemento di termine*) (to) you; (*riflessivo*) yourselves; (*reciproco*) each other ▷ *av* (*lì*) here; (*qui*) here; (*per questo/quel luogo*) through here/there; **vi è/sono** there is/are

'via *sf* (*gen*) way; (*strada*) street; (*sentiero, pista*) path, track; (*Amm: procedimento*) channels *pl* ▷ *prep* (*passando per*) via, by way of ▷ *av* away ▷ *escl* go away!; (*suvvia*) come on!; (*Sport*) go! ▷ *sm* (*Sport*) starting signal;

per ~ di (*a causa di*) because of, on account of; **in** *o* **per ~** on the way; **in ~ di guarigione** on the road to recovery; **per ~ aerea** by air; (*lettere*) by airmail; **andare/essere ~** to go/be away; **~ ~** (*a mano a mano*) as; **dare il ~** (*Sport*) to give the starting signal; **dare il ~ a** (*fig*) to start; **in ~ provvisoria** provisionally; **V~ lattea** (*Astr*) Milky Way; **~ di mezzo** middle course; **non c'è ~ di scampo** *o* **d'uscita** there's no way out

via'dotto *sm* viaduct

viaggi'are [viad'dʒare] /62/ *vi* to travel; **viaggia'tore, -'trice** *ag* travelling ▷ *sm* traveller, passenger

vi'aggio *sm* travel(ling); (*tragitto*) journey, trip; **buon ~!** I have a good trip!; **~ di nozze** honeymoon

vi'ale *sm* avenue

via'vai *sm* coming and going, bustle

vi'brare /72/ *vi* to vibrate

'vice ['vitʃe] *sm/f* deputy

vi'cenda [vi'tʃɛnda] *sf* event; **a ~** in turn

vice'versa [vitʃe'vɛrsa] *av* vice versa; **da Roma a Pisa e ~** from Rome to Pisa and back

vici'nanza [vitʃi'nantsa] *sf* nearness, closeness

vi'cino, -a [vi'tʃino] *ag* (*gen*) near; (*nello spazio*) near, nearby; (*accanto*) next; (*nel tempo*) near, close at hand ▷ *sm/f* neighbour (*BRIT*), neighbor (*US*) ▷ *av* near, close; **da ~** (*guardare*) close up; (*esaminare, seguire*) closely; (*conoscere*) well, intimately; **~ a** near (to), close to; (*accanto a*) beside; **~ di casa** neighbour

'vicolo *sm* alley; **~ cieco** blind alley

'video *sm inv* (*TV: schermo*) screen; **video'camera** *sf* camcorder; **videocas'setta** *sf* videocassette

videochia'mare [videokja'mare] /72/ *vt* to video call

video: video'clip [video'klip] *sm inv* videoclip; **videogi'oco, -chi** [video'dʒɔko] *sm* video game; **videoregistra'tore** *sm* video (recorder); **videote'lefono** *sm* videophone

'vidi *ecc vb vedi* **vedere**

vie'tare /72/ *vt* to forbid; (*Amm*) to prohibit; **~ a qn di fare** to forbid sb to do; to prohibit sb from doing

vie'tato, -a *ag* (*vedi vb*) forbidden; prohibited; banned; **"~ fumare/l'ingresso"** "no smoking/admittance"; **~ ai minori di 14/18 anni** prohibited to children under 14/18; **"senso ~"** (*Aut*) "no entry"; **"sosta vietata"** (*Aut*) "no parking"

Viet'nam *sm*: **il ~** Vietnam; **vietna'mita, -i, -e** *ag, smf, sm* Vietnamese *inv*

vi'gente [vi'dʒɛnte] *ag* in force

'vigile ['vidʒile] *ag* watchful ▷ *sm* (*anche*: **~ urbano**) police officer (*in towns*); **~ del fuoco** firefighter

vi'gilia [vi'dʒilja] *sf* (*giorno antecedente*) eve; **la ~ di Natale** Christmas Eve

vigli'acco, -a, -chi, -che [viʎ'ʎakko] *ag* cowardly ▷ *sm/f* coward

'vigna ['viɲɲa] *sf*, **vi'gneto** [viɲ'ɲeto] *sm* vineyard

vi'gnetta [viɲ'ɲetta] *sf* cartoon; (*Aut: anche*: **~ autostradale**: *tassa*) car tax (*for motorways*); (: *adesivo*) sticker showing that this tax has been paid

vi'gore *sm* vigour; (*Dir*): **essere/entrare in ~** to be in/come into force

'vile *ag* (*spregevole*) low, mean, base; (*codardo*) cowardly

'villa *sf* villa

vil'laggio [vil'laddʒo] *sm* village; **~ turistico** holiday village

vil'lano, -a *ag* rude, ill-mannered

villeggia'tura [villeddʒa'tura] *sf* holiday(s *pl*) (BRIT), vacation (US)

vil'letta *sf*, **vil'lino** *sm* small house (with a garden), cottage

'vimini *smpl* wicker; **mobili di ~** wicker furniture *sg*

'vincere ['vintʃere] /129/ *vt* (*in guerra, al gioco, a una gara*) to defeat, beat; (*premio, guerra, partita*) to win; (*fig*) to overcome, conquer ▷ *vi* to win; **~ qn in** (*abilità, bellezza*) to surpass sb in; **vinci'tore, -'trice** *sm/f* winner; (*Mil*) victor

vi'nicolo, -a *ag* wine *cpd*

'vino *sm* wine; **~ bianco/rosato/rosso** white/rosé/red wine; **~ da pasto** table wine

'vinsi *ecc vb vedi* **vincere**

vi'ola *sf* (*Bot*) violet; (*Mus*) viola ▷ *ag, sm inv* (*colore*) purple

vio'lare /72/ *vt* (*chiesa*) to desecrate, violate; (*giuramento, legge*) to violate

violen'tare /72/ *vt* to use violence on; (*donna*) to rape

vio'lento, -a *ag* violent; **vio'lenza** *sf* violence; **violenza carnale** rape

vio'letto, -a *ag, sm* (*colore*) violet ▷ *sf* (*Bot*) violet

violi'nista, -i, -e *smf* violinist

vio'lino *sm* violin

violon'cello [violon'tʃello] *sm* cello

vi'ottolo *sm* path, track

VIP [vip] *sm inv, f inv* (= *Very Important Person*) VIP

'vipera *sf* viper, adder

vi'rale *ag* (*Inform*) viral

vi'rare /72/ *vi* (*Naut, Aer*) to turn; (*Fot*) to tone; **~ di bordo** to change course; (*Naut*) to tack

'virgola *sf* (*Ling*) comma; (*Mat*) point; **virgo'lette** *sfpl* inverted commas, quotation marks

vi'rile *ag* (*proprio dell'uomo*) masculine; (*non puerile, da uomo*) manly, virile

virtù *sf inv* virtue; **in o per ~ di** by virtue of, by

virtu'ale *ag* virtual

'virus *sm inv* (*anche Inform*) virus

'viscere ['viʃʃere] *sfpl* (*di animale*) entrails *pl*; (*fig*) bowels *pl*

'vischio ['viskjo] *sm* (*Bot*) mistletoe; (*pania*) birdlime

'viscido, -a ['viʃʃido] *ag* slimy

vi'sibile *ag* visible

visibilità *sf* visibility

visi'era *sf* (*di elmo*) visor; (*di berretto*) peak

visi'one *sf* vision; **prendere ~ di qc** to examine sth, look sth over; **prima/seconda ~** (*Cine*) first/second showing

'visita *sf* visit; (*Med*) visit, call; (: *esame*) examination; **~ medica** medical examination; **~ guidata** guided tour; **visi'tare** /72/ *vt* to visit; (*Med*) to visit, call on; (: *esaminare*) to examine; **visita'tore, -'trice** *sm/f* visitor

vi'sivo, -a *ag* visual

'viso *sm* face

vi'sone *sm* mink

'vispo, -a *ag* quick, lively

'vissi *ecc vb vedi* **vivere**

'vista *sf* (*facoltà*) (eye)sight; (*veduta*) view; (*fatto di vedere*): **la ~ di** the sight of; **sparare a ~** to shoot on sight; **in ~** in sight; **perdere qn di ~** to lose sight of sb; (*fig*) to lose touch with sb; **far ~ di fare** to pretend to do; **a ~ d'occhio** as far as the eye can see; (*fig*) before one's very eyes

'visto, -a *pp di* **vedere** ▷ *sm* visa; **~ che** seeing (that)

vis'toso, -a *ag* gaudy, garish; (*ingente*) considerable

visu'ale *ag* visual

'vita *sf* life; (*Anat*) waist; **a ~** for life

vi'tale *ag* vital

vita'mina *sf* vitamin

'vite *sf* (*Bot*) vine; (*Tecn*) screw

vi'tello *sm* (*Zool*) calf; (*carne*) veal; (*pelle*) calfskin

'vittima *sf* victim

'vitto *sm* food; (*in un albergo ecc*) board; **~ e alloggio** board and lodging

vit'toria *sf* victory

'viva *escl*: **~ il re!** long live the king!

vi'vace [vi'vatʃe] *ag* (*vivo, animato*) lively; (: *mente*) lively, sharp; (*colore*) bright

vi'vaio *sm* (*di pesci*) hatchery; (*Agr*) nursery

viva'voce [viva'votʃe] *sm inv* (*dispositivo*) loudspeaker; **mettere in ~** to switch on the loudspeaker

vi'vente *ag* living, alive; **i viventi** the living
'vivere /130/ *vi* to live ▷ *vt* to live; (*passare: brutto momento*) to live through, go through; (*sentire: gioie, pene di qn*) to share ▷ *sm* life; (*anche*: **modo di ~**) way of life; **viveri** *smpl* (*cibo*) food *sg*, provisions; **~ di** to live on
'vivido, -a *ag* (*colore*) vivid, bright
vivisezi'one [vivisɛt'tsjone] *sf* vivisection
'vivo, -a *ag* (*vivente*) alive, living; (: *animale*) live; (*fig*) lively; (: *colore*) bright, brilliant; **i vivi** the living; **~ e vegeto** hale and hearty; **farsi ~** to show one's face; to keep in touch; **ritrarre dal ~** to paint from life; **pungere qn nel ~** (*fig*) to cut sb to the quick
vivrò *ecc vb vedi* **vivere**
vizi'are [vit'tsjare] /19/ *vt* (*bambino*) to spoil; (*corrompere moralmente*) to corrupt; **vizi'ato, -a** *ag* spoilt; (*aria, acqua*) polluted
'vizio ['vittsjo] *sm* (*morale*) vice; (*cattiva abitudine*) bad habit; (*imperfezione*) flaw, defect; (*errore*) fault, mistake
V.le *abbr* = **viale**
vocabo'lario *sm* (*dizionario*) dictionary; (*lessico*) vocabulary
vo'cabolo *sm* word
vo'cale *ag* vocal ▷ *sf* vowel
vocazi'one [vokat'tsjone] *sf* vocation; (*fig*) natural bent
'voce ['votʃe] *sf* voice; (*diceria*) rumour; (*di un elenco: in bilancio*) item; **aver ~ in capitolo** (*fig*) to have a say in the matter
'voga *sf* (*Naut*) rowing; (*usanza*): **essere in ~** to be in fashion *o* in vogue
vo'gare /80/ *vi* to row
vogherò *ecc* [voge'rɔ] *vb vedi* **vogare**
'voglia ['vɔʎʎa] *sf* desire, wish; (*macchia*) birthmark; **aver ~ di qc/di fare** to feel like sth/like doing; (*più forte*) to want sth/to do
'voglio *ecc* ['vɔʎʎo] *vb vedi* **volere**
'voi *pron* you; **voi'altri** *pron* you
vo'lante *ag* flying ▷ *sm* (steering) wheel
volan'tino *sm* leaflet
vo'lare /72/ *vi* (*uccello, aereo, fig*) to fly; (*cappello*) to blow away *o* off, fly away *o* off; **~ via** to fly away *o* off
vo'latile *ag* (*Chim*) volatile ▷ *sm* (*Zool*) bird
volente'roso, -a *ag* willing
volenti'eri *av* willingly; **"~"** "with pleasure", "I'd be glad to"

○ **PAROLA CHIAVE**

vo'lere /131/ *sm* will, wish(es); **contro il volere di** against the wishes of; **per volere di qn** in obedience to sb's will *o* wishes
▶ *vt* **1** (*esigere, desiderare*) to want; **volere fare qc** to want to do sth; **volere che qn faccia qc** to want sb to do sth; **vorrei**

questo/fare I would *o* I'd like this/to do; **come vuoi** as you like; **vuoi un caffè?** would you like a coffee?; **senza volere** (*inavvertitamente*) without meaning to, unintentionally

2 (*consentire*): **vogliate attendere, per piacere** please wait; **vogliamo andare?** shall we go?; **vuole essere così gentile da …?** would you be so kind as to …?; **non ha voluto ricevermi** he wouldn't see me

3: **volerci** (*essere necessario*) (*materiale, attenzione*) to be needed; (*tempo*) to take; **quanta farina ci vuole per questa torta?** how much flour do you need for this cake?; **ci vuole un'ora per arrivare a Venezia** it takes an hour to get to Venice

4: **voler bene a qn** (*amore*) to love sb; (*affetto*) to be fond of sb, like sb very much; **voler male a qn** to dislike sb; **volerne a qn** to bear sb a grudge; **voler dire** to mean

vol'gare *ag* vulgar
voli'era *sf* aviary
voli'tivo, -a *ag* strong-willed
'volli *ecc vb vedi* **volere**
'volo *sm* flight; **colpire qc al ~** to hit sth as it flies past; **capire al ~** to understand straight away; **~ charter** charter flight; **~ di linea** scheduled flight
volontà *sf inv* will; **a ~** (*mangiare, bere*) as much as one likes; **buona/cattiva ~** goodwill/lack of goodwill
volontari'ato *sm* (*lavoro*) voluntary work
volon'tario, -a *ag* voluntary ▷ *sm* (*Mil*) volunteer
'volpe *sf* fox
'volta *sf* (*momento, circostanza*) time; (*turno, giro*) turn; (*curva*) turn, bend; (*Archit*) vault; (*direzione*): **partire alla ~ di** to set off for; **a mia** (*o tua ecc*) **~** in turn; **una ~** once; **una ~ sola** only once; **due volte** twice; **una cosa per ~** one thing at a time; **una ~ per tutte** once and for all; **a volte** at times, sometimes; **una ~ che** (*temporale*) once; (*causale*) since; **3 volte 4** 3 times 4
volta'faccia [volta'fattʃa] *sm inv* (*fig*) volte-face
vol'taggio [vol'taddʒo] *sm* (*Elettr*) voltage
vol'tare /72/ *vt* to turn; (*girare: moneta*) to turn over; (*rigirare*) to turn round ▷ *vi* to turn; **voltarsi** *vpr* to turn; to turn over; to turn round
voltas'tomaco *sm* nausea; (*fig*) disgust
'volto, -a *pp di* **volgere** ▷ *sm* face
vo'lubile *ag* changeable, fickle
vo'lume *sm* volume
vomi'tare /72/ *vt, vi* to vomit; **'vomito** *sm* vomiting *no pl*; vomit
'vongola *sf* clam

vo'race [voˈratʃe] *ag* voracious, greedy

vo'ragine [voˈradʒine] *sf* abyss, chasm

vorrò *ecc vb vedi* **volere**

'vortice [ˈvortitʃe] *sm* whirlwind; whirlpool; (*fig*) whirl

'vostro, -a *det*: **il (la) ~(a)** *ecc* your ▷ *pron*: **il (la) ~(a)** *ecc* yours

vo'tante *smf* voter

vo'tare /72/ *vi* to vote ▷ *vt* (*sottoporre a votazione*) to take a vote on; (*approvare*) to vote for; (*Rel*): **~ qc a** to dedicate sth to

'voto *sm* (*Pol*) vote; (*Ins*) mark (BRIT), grade (US); (*Rel*) vow; (: *offerta*) votive offering; **aver voti belli/brutti** (*Ins*) to get good/bad marks *o* grades

vs. *abbr* (= *vostro*) yr

vul'cano *sm* volcano

vulne'rabile *ag* vulnerable

vu'oi, vu'ole *vb vedi* **volere**

vuo'tare /72/ *vt*, **vuo'tarsi** *vpr* to empty

vu'oto, -a *ag* empty; (*fig: privo*): **~ di** (*senso ecc*) devoid of ▷ *sm* empty space, gap; (*spazio in bianco*) blank; (*Fisica*) vacuum; (*fig: mancanza*) gap, void; **a mani vuote** empty-handed; **~ d'aria** air pocket; **"~ a rendere"** "returnable bottle"

'wafer [ˈvafer] *sm inv* (*Cuc, Elettr*) wafer

'water [ˈwɔːtəʳ] *sm inv* toilet

watt [vat] *sm inv* watt

WC *sm inv* WC

web [ueb] *sm*: **il ~** the web ▷ *ag inv*: **pagina ~** webpage; **cercare nel ~** to search the web; **webcam** [webˈkam] *sf inv* (*Inform*) webcam

'weekend [ˈwiːkend] *sm inv* weekend

'western [ˈwɛstern] *ag* (*Cine*) cowboy *cpd* ▷ *sm inv* western, cowboy film; **~ all'italiana** spaghetti western

'whisky [ˈwiski] *sm inv* whisky

Wi-Fi [uaiˈfai] (*Inform*) *sm* Wi-Fi ▷ *ag inv* Wi-Fi

'windsurf [ˈwindsəːf] *sm inv* (*tavola*) windsurfer; (*sport*) windsurfing

'würstel [ˈvyrstəl] *sm inv* frankfurter

x y

xe'nofobo, -a [kseˈnɔfobo] *ag* xenophobic
▷ *sm/f* xenophobe

xi'lofono [ksiˈlɔfono] *sm* xylophone

yacht [jɔt] *sm inv* yacht

'yoga [ˈjɔga] *ag inv*, *sm* yoga (*cpd*)

yogurt [ˈjɔgurt] *sm inv* yog(h)urt

Z

zabai'one [dzaba'jone] *sm dessert made of egg yolks, sugar and marsala*
zaf'fata [tsaf'fata] *sf (tanfo)* stench
zaffe'rano [dzaffe'rano] *sm* saffron
zaf'firo [dzaf'firo] *sm* sapphire
zai'netto [dzai'netto] *sm (small)* rucksack
'zaino ['dzaino] *sm* rucksack
'zampa ['tsampa] *sf (di animale: gamba)* leg; (: *piede)* paw; **a quattro zampe** on all fours
zampil'lare [tsampil'lare] /72/ *vi* to gush, spurt
zan'zara [dzan'dzara] *sf* mosquito; **zanzari'era** *sf* mosquito net
'zappa ['tsappa] *sf* hoe
'zapping ['tsapɪŋ] *sm (TV)* channel-hopping
zar, za'rina [tsar, tsa'rina] *sm/f* tsar (tsarina)
'zattera ['dzattera] *sf* raft
'zebra ['dzebra] *sf* zebra; **zebre** *sfpl (Aut)* zebra crossing *sg (BRIT)*, crosswalk *sg (US)*
'zecca, -che ['tsekka] *sf (Zool)* tick; (*officina di monete)* mint
'zelo ['dzelo] *sm* zeal
zen'zero ['dzendzero] *sm* ginger
'zeppa ['tseppa] *sf* wedge
'zeppo, -a ['tseppo] *ag:* ~ **di** crammed *o* packed with
zer'bino [dzer'bino] *sm* doormat
'zero ['dzɛro] *sm* zero, nought; **vincere per tre a** ~ *(Sport)* to win three-nil
'zia ['tsia] *sf* aunt
zibel'lino [dzibel'lino] *sm* sable
'zigomo ['dzigomo] *sm* cheekbone
zig'zag [dzig'dzag] *sm inv* zigzag; **andare a** ~ to zigzag
Zim'babwe [tsim'babwe] *sm:* **lo** ~ Zimbabwe
'zinco ['dzinko] *sm* zinc
'zingaro, -a ['dzingaro] *sm/f* gipsy
'zio ['tsio] (*pl* **zii**) *sm* uncle

zip'pare /72/ *vt (Inform: file)* to zip
zi'tella [dzi'tɛlla] *sf* spinster; (*peg)* old maid
'zitto, -a ['tsitto] *ag* quiet, silent; **sta'** ~! be quiet!
'zoccolo ['tsɔkkolo] *sm (calzatura)* clog; (*di cavallo ecc)* hoof; (*Archit)* plinth; (*di armadio)* base
zodia'cale [dzodia'kale] *ag* zodiac *cpd;* **segno** ~ sign of the zodiac
zo'diaco [dzo'diako] *sm* zodiac
'zolfo ['tsolfo] *sm* sulphur
'zolla ['dzolla] *sf* clod (of earth)
zol'letta [dzol'letta] *sf* sugar lump
'zona ['dzɔna] *sf* zone, area; ~ **di depressione** *(Meteor)* trough of low pressure; ~ **disco** *(Aut)* ≈ meter zone; ~ **industriale** industrial estate; ~ **pedonale** pedestrian precinct; ~ **verde** (*di abitato)* green area
'zonzo ['dzondzo]: **a** ~ *av* **andare a** ~ to wander about, stroll about
'zoo ['dzɔo] *sm inv* zoo
zoolo'gia [dzoolo'dʒia] *sf* zoology
zoppi'care [tsoppi'kare] /20/ *vi* to limp; (*fig: mobile)* to be shaky, rickety
'zoppo, -a ['tsɔppo] *ag* lame; (*fig: mobile)* shaky, rickety
ZTL *sigla f (= Zona a Traffico Limitato)* controlled traffic zone
'zucca, -che ['tsukka] *sf (Bot)* marrow; pumpkin
zucche'rare [tsukke'rare] /72/ *vt* to put sugar in; **zucche'rato, -a** *ag* sweet, sweetened
zuccheri'era [tsukke'rjera] *sf* sugar bowl
'zucchero ['tsukkero] *sm* sugar; ~ **di canna** cane sugar; ~ **filato** candy floss, cotton candy *(US)*
zuc'china [tsuk'kina] *sf* courgette *(BRIT)*, zucchini *(US)*
'zuffa ['tsuffa] *sf* brawl
'zuppa ['tsuppa] *sf* soup; (*fig)* mixture, muddle; ~ **inglese** *(Cuc)* dessert made with sponge cake, custard and chocolate, ≈ trifle *(BRIT)*
'zuppo, -a ['tsuppo] *ag:* ~ **(di)** drenched (with), soaked (with)

Italian Grammar

1 Nouns

1.1 The Gender of Nouns

In Italian, all nouns are either masculine or feminine, whether they denote people, animals or things.

The gender of a noun is often indicated by its final letter. Here are some guidelines to help you determine which gender a noun is:

• Nearly all nouns ending in **-o** are masculine, e.g.

il treno	*the train*
l'uomo	*the man*

• Very many nouns ending in **-a** are feminine, e.g.

la casa	*the house*
una donna	*a woman*

There are, however, numerous exceptions, e.g.

il problema	*the problem*

A few nouns ending in **-a** are feminine, but can refer to a man or a woman, e.g.

una persona	*a person* (male or female)

• Nearly all words ending in **-à**, **-sione** and **-zione** are feminine, e.g.

una difficoltà	*a difficulty*
una conversazione	*a conversation*

• Nouns ending in a consonant are nearly always masculine, e.g.

un film	a film

• Nouns ending in **-e** or **-i** can be masculine or feminine, e.g.

un mese	*a month*
una crisi	*a crisis*

• The names of languages, and all months, are masculine, whether they end in **-o** or **-e**, e.g.

il prossimo dicembre	*next December*

• Some words have different meanings depending on their gender, e.g.

il fine	*the objective*	**la fine**	*the end*
un modo	*a way*	**la moda**	*the fashion*
un mostro	*a monster*	**una mostra**	*an exhibition*

1.2 The Formation of Feminines

As in English, male and female are sometimes differentiated by the use of quite different words, e.g.

un fratello	*a brother*
una sorella	*a sister*

More often, however, words in Italian show gender by their ending:

- Many Italian nouns ending in **-o** can be made feminine by changing the ending to **-a**

uno zio	*an uncle*
una zia	*an aunt*

- Some nouns ending in **-e** also change the ending to **-a** for the feminine

un signore	*a gentleman*
una signora	*a lady*

- Some nouns ending in **-a** or **-e** have no change of ending for the feminine

un collega	*a (male)* colleague
una collega	*a (female)* colleague

- Nouns ending in **-ese** that describe nationality are the same for masculine and feminine

uno scozzese	*a Scotsman*
una scozzese	*a Scotswoman*

1.3 The Formation of Plurals

Masculine nouns, whether they end in **-o, -a** or **-e,** nearly always take the ending **-i** in the plural, e.g.

un anno	*one year*
due anni	*two years*

Feminine nouns ending in **-a** take the ending **-e** in the plural, e.g.

una ragazza	*one girl*
due ragazze	*two girls*

Feminine nouns ending in **-e** take the ending **-i** in the plural, e.g.

un'inglese	*an Englishwoman*
due inglesi	*two Englishwomen*

However, some nouns have no change of ending in the plural:

- Nouns ending in an accented vowel, e.g.

la città	*the city*
le città	*the cities*

- Nouns ending in **-i** and **-ie**, e.g.

una serie	*a series*
due serie	*two series*

- Words ending with a consonant, e.g.

il film	*the film*
i film	*the films*

2 Articles

2.1 The Definite Article

The form of the Italian article depends on the gender and number of the noun it accompanies. It also depends on the letter the noun starts with.

	Masculine	Feminine
Singular	il/lo/l'	la/l'
Plural	i/gli	le

- **il** is used with masculine nouns starting with most consonants, except for **z**, **gn**, **pn**, **ps**, **x**, **y** and impure **s** (this means **s** + another consonant); **lo** is used with these. **l'** is used before vowels.

il ragazzo	*the boy*
lo zio	*the uncle*
l'ospedale	*the hospital*

- **i** is used with masculine plural nouns starting with most consonants; **gli** is used before vowels and **z**, **gn**, **pn**, **ps**, **x**, **y** and impure **s**.

i fratelli	*the brothers*
gli studenti	*the students*
gli amici	*the friends*

- **la** is used before feminine singular nouns beginning with a consonant, and **l'** is used before a vowel.

la macchina	*the car*
l'arancia	*the orange*

- **le** is used with all feminine plural nouns.

le ragazze	*the girls*

- If the article is separated from the noun by an adjective, the first letter of the adjective determines the choice of article.

l'amico	*the friend*
il migliore amico	*the best friend*

The prepositions **a**, **da**, **di**, **in**, **su** and **con** combine with the article to form one word. Some examples of this are:

a + il = al	a + la = alla	da + l' = dall'
di + i = dei	in + le = nelle	su + gli = sugli

2.2 The Partitive Article

The partitive article has the sense of 'some' or 'any', although the Italian is not always translated in English.

Forms of the partitive

	With masculine noun	With feminine noun
Singular	del/dell'/dello	della/dell'
Plural	dei/degli	delle

Hanno rotto dei bicchieri.	*They broke some glasses.*
Mi ha fatto vedere delle foto.	*He showed me some photos.*
Ci vuole del sale.	*It needs (some) salt.*

2.3 The Indefinite Article

With masculine noun	With feminine noun
un	una
uno	un'

The form of the indefinite article depends on the gender of the noun it accompanies. It also depends on the letter the noun starts with:

- **un** is used with masculine nouns starting with vowels and most consonants, except for **z**, **gn**, **pn**, **ps**, **x**, **y** and impure **s**

  un uomo   *a man*

- **uno** is used with masculine nouns starting with **z**, **gn**, **pn**, **ps**, **x**, **y** and impure **s**

  uno studente   *a student*
  uno zio   *an uncle*

- **una** is used before feminine nouns beginning with a consonant, and **un'** is used before a vowel

  una ragazza   *a girl*
  un'ora   *an hour*

If the article is separated from the noun by an adjective, the first letter of the adjective determines the choice of article.

  uno splendido albergo   *a magnificent hotel*
  È medico.   *He's a doctor.*
  Fa l'avvocato.   *She's a lawyer.*

3 Adjectives

3.1 The Formation of Feminines and Plurals

Most adjectives agree in number and gender with the noun or pronoun. The feminine and plural forms of adjectives are formed as follows:

- If the masculine singular form of the adjective ends in **-o**, the feminine ends in **-a**

  un ragazzo alto   *a tall boy*
  una ragazza alta   *a tall girl*

- If the adjective ends in **-e**, the ending does not change for the feminine

  un libro inglese   *an English book*
  una famiglia inglese   *an English family*

- If the masculine singular of the adjective ends in **-o**, the ending changes to **-i** for the masculine plural, and to **-e** for the feminine plural

un fiore rosso	*a red flower*
dei fiori rossi	*red flowers*
una moto nera	*a black motorbike*
delle moto nere	*black motorbikes*

- If the adjective ends in **-e**, the ending changes to **-i** for both masculine and feminine plural

delle storie tristi	*sad stories*
degli esercizi difficili	*difficult exercises*

3.2 Demonstrative Adjectives

To say *this*, use **questo**, which has four forms, like any other adjective ending in **-o**.

	Masculine	Feminine	
Singular	questo	questa	this
Plural	questi	queste	these

questa gonna	*this skirt*
queste scarpe	*these shoes*

quello has different forms, depending on the gender of the following noun, and the letter it starts with.

	Masculine	Feminine	
Singular	quel/quello/quell'	quella/quell'	that
Plural	quei/quegli	quelle	those

quel ragazzo	*that boy*
quei cani	*those dogs*

3.3 Possessive Adjectives

In Italian, possessive adjectives agree in number and gender with the noun they describe, not with the owner. You usually put the definite article (**il**, **la**, **i**, **le**) in front of the possessive adjective.

With singular noun		
Masculine	**Feminine**	
il mio	la mia	my
il tuo	la tua	your
il suo	la sua	his; her; its; your
il nostro	la nostra	our
il vostro	la vostra	your
il loro	la loro	their

With plural noun		
Masculine	**Feminine**	
i miei	**le mie**	my
i tuoi	**le tue**	your
i suoi	**le sue**	his; her; its; your
i nostri	**le nostre**	our
i vostri	**le vostre**	your
i loro	**le loro**	their

3.4 Position of Adjectives

Italian adjectives usually follow the noun, e.g.

un gesto spontaneo   *a spontaneous gesture*

As in English, demonstrative, possessive, numerical and interrogative adjectives precede the noun, e.g.

questo cellulare   *this mobile phone*
la mia mamma   *my mum*

3.5 Interrogative Adjectives

In Italian, the interrogative adjectives are **che** (meaning *what?*), **quale** (meaning *which?*) and **quanto** (meaning *how much/many?*):

• **che** does not change in the masculine, feminine or plural

Che ore sono?   *What time is it?*

• **quale** is used with masculine or feminine singular nouns; **quali** is used with masculine or feminine plural nouns

Quale tipo vuoi?   *What kind do you want?*

• **quanto** changes according to number and gender, as shown in the table below

	Masculine		Feminine	
Singular	**quanto**	how much?	**quanta**	how much?
Plural	**quanti**	how many?	**quante**	how many?

Quanto pane hai comprato?   *How much bread did you buy?*

Interrogative adjectives are often preceded by prepositions

Di che colore è?   *What colour is it?*

4 Pronouns

4.1 Personal Pronouns

These are the Italian subject pronouns:

Subject Pronouns			
Singular		**Plural**	
io	I	**noi**	we
tu	you	**voi**	you
lui **lei** **lei/Lei**	he she you (*used as polite* 'you')	**loro**	they

Italian verbs are frequently used without subject pronouns.

Italian has both unstressed and stressed object pronouns.

Unstressed direct object pronouns generally come before the verb. They come after the verb:

- in imperatives, with the pronoun joined onto the verb, e.g.

    Aiutami! *Help me!*

- in infinitive constructions, when the final **-e** of the infinitive is dropped, and replaced by the pronoun e.g.

    Non posso aiutarvi. *I can't help you.*

Unstressed Direct Object Pronouns		
	Singular	**Plural**
1st person	**mi**	**ci**
2nd person	**ti**	**vi**
3rd person (*masculine*)	**lo (l')**	**li**
(*feminine*)	**la (l')**	**le**
(*used as polite* 'you')	**la/La (l')**	**le**

- Stressed direct object pronouns are used for emphasis or contrast, after prepositions and in comparisons e.g.

    Vengo con te. *I'll come with you.*

Stressed Direct Object Pronouns		
	Singular	**Plural**
1st person	**me**	**noi**
2nd person	**te**	**voi**
3rd person (*masculine*)	**lui**	**loro**
(*feminine*)	**lei**	**loro**
(*used as polite* 'you')	**lei/Lei**	**loro**

Unstressed indirect object pronouns generally come before the verb. They come after the verb:

• in imperatives, with the pronoun joined onto the verb e.g.

    Mandami un SMS.   *Send me a text.*

• in infinitive constructions. The final **-e** of the infinitive is dropped, and replaced by the pronoun e.g.

    Dovresti scriverle.   *You ought to write to her.*

Unstressed Indirect Object Pronouns		
	Singular	Plural
1st person	mi	ci
2nd person	ti	vi
3rd person (*masculine*)	gli	gli *or* loro
(*feminine*)	le	gli *or* loro
(*used as polite 'you'*)	le	loro

The pronouns in the above table replace the preposition **a** + *noun*, where the noun is a person or an animal:

    Ho detto la verità a Paola   *I told Paola the truth.*
    Le ho detto la verità   *I told her the truth.*

• Stressed indirect object pronouns are used for special emphasis, either before or after the verb e.g.

    A me piace, ma Luca preferisce l'altro.
    I like it, but Luca would rather have the other one.

Stressed Indirect Object Pronouns		
	Singular	Plural
1st person	a me	a noi
2nd person	a te	a voi
3rd person (*masculine*)	a lui	a loro
(*feminine*)	a lei	a loro
(*used as polite 'you'*)	a lei/Lei	a loro

4.2 Possessive Pronouns

Possessive pronouns in Italian are formed in exactly the same way as the strong forms of possessive adjectives (see page 6).

4.3 Interrogative Pronouns

Interrogative pronouns are used in direct questions. The following interrogative pronouns do not change their form for gender or number:

    chi? *who? whom?*
    che? *what?*
    cosa? *what?*
    che cosa? *what?*

The interrogative pronouns **quale?** (meaning *which one?*), **quanto?** (meaning *how much?*) and **quanti?** (meaning *how many?*) change form in the same way as interrogative adjectives (see page 7).

Prepositions come before the interrogative pronoun, and never at the end of the question.

> **Con chi parlavi?** *Who were you talking to?*
> **Ho rotto dei bicchieri. — Quali?**
> *I broke some glasses. —Which ones?*
> **Farina? Quanta ce ne vuole?** *Flour? How much is needed?*
>
> **Quante di loro passano la sera a leggere?**
> *How many of them spend the evening reading?*

5 Verbs

5.1 Simple Tenses: Formation

In Italian the simple tenses are formed by adding endings to a verb stem. The endings show the number and person of the subject of the verb.

There are three regular verb patterns (called conjugations), each identifiable by the ending of the infinitive:

- First conjugation verbs end in **-are** e.g. **parlare** *to speak*
- Second conjugation verbs end in **-ere** e.g. **credere** *to believe*
- Third conjugation verbs end in **-ire** e.g. **finire** *to finish*; **dormire** *to sleep*

The stem is formed by taking the **-are**, **-ere**, or **-ire** ending off the infinitive of each of the verbs.

The stem and endings of regular verbs are totally predictable. The following sections show all the patterns for regular verbs.

Simple Tenses

The following tables show how to form the simple tenses of each of the first, second and third conjugations:

- For first conjugation verbs (like **parlare**), add the following endings to the stem (**parl-**):

		Present	Imperfect	Future
singular	1st person	-o	-avo	-erò
	2nd person	-i	-avi	-erai
	3rd person	-a	-ava	-erà
plural	1st person	-iamo	-avamo	-eremo
	2nd person	-ate	-avate	-erete
	3rd person	-ano	-avano	-eranno

		Present conditional	Past historic
	1st person	-erei	-ai
singular	2nd person	-eresti	-asti
	3rd person	-erebbe	-ò
	1st person	-eremmo	-ammo
plural	2nd person	-ereste	-aste
	3rd person	-erebbero	-arono

		Present subjunctive	Imperfect subjunctive
	1st person	-i	-assi
singular	2nd person	-i	-assi
	3rd person	-i	-asse
	1st person	-iamo	-assimmo
plural	2nd person	-iate	-aste
	3rd person	-ino	-assero

• For second conjugation verbs (e.g. **credere**), add the following endings to the stem (**cred-**):

		Present	Imperfect	Future
	1st person	-o	-evo	-erò
singular	2nd person	-i	-evi	-erai
	3rd person	-e	-eva	-erà
	1st person	-iamo	-evamo	-eremo
plural	2nd person	-ete	-evate	-erete
	3rd person	-ono	-evano	-eranno

		Present conditional	Past historic
	1st person	-erei	-ei or -etti
singular	2nd person	-eresti	-esti
	3rd person	-erebbe	-ette
	1st person	-eremmo	-emmo
plural	2nd person	-ereste	-este
	3rd person	-erebbero	-ettero

		Present subjunctive	Imperfect subjunctive
	1st person	-a	-essi
singular	2nd person	-a	-essi
	3rd person	-a	-essè
	1st person	-iamo	-essimmo
plural	2nd person	-iate	-este
	3rd person	-ano	-essero

- Generally, the stem of third conjugation verbs in Italian is formed by taking the **-ire** ending off the infinitive, for example, the stem of **finire** is **fin-**. In addition, in the present tense and present subjunctive of most verbs, **-isc-** is added to the basic stem (except for the 1st and 2nd person plural). There are some exceptions where **-isc-** is not added, for example **dormire** to sleep, **sentire** to feel, **partire** to leave.

The present tense of **finire** and **dormire** are shown below:

		finire	dormire
singular	1st person	finisco	dormo
	2nd person	finisci	dormi
	3rd person	finisce	dorme
plural	1st person	finiamo	dormiamo
	2nd person	finite	dormite
	3rd person	finiscono	dormono

For other tenses of third conjugation verbs (e.g. **finire** and **dormire**), add the following endings to the stem (**fin-**, **dorm-**):

		Imperfect	Future
singular	1st person	-ivo	-irò
	2nd person	-ivi	-irai
	3rd person	-iva	-irà
plural	1st person	-ivamo	-iremo
	2nd person	-ivate	-irete
	3rd person	-ivano	-iranno

		Present conditional	Past historic
singular	1st person	-irei	-i
	2nd person	-iresti	-isti
	3rd person	-irebbe	-ì
plural	1st person	-iremmo	-immo
	2nd person	-ireste	-iste
	3rd person	-irebbero	-irono

		Present subjunctive		Imperfect subjunctive	
		finire	dormire	finire	dormire
singular	1st person	finisca	dorma	finiscissi	dormissi
	2nd person	finisca	dorma	finiscissi	dormissi
	3rd person	finisca	dorma	finiscissi	dormissi
plural	1st person	finiamo	dormiamo	finissimmo	dormissimmo
	2nd person	finitiate	dormiate	finitiste	dormiste
	3rd person	finiscano	dormano	finiscissero	dormissero

5.2 Reflexive Verbs

A reflexive verb is one accompanied by a reflexive pronoun, e.g. **divertirsi** (meaning *to enjoy oneself*); **annoiarsi** (meaning *to get bored*).

The reflexive pronouns in Italian are:

	Singular	Plural
1st person	mi	ci
2nd person	ti	vi
3rd person	si	si

The Italian reflexive pronoun is often not translated in English e.g.

| **Mi annoio.** | *I'm getting bored.* |
| **Ti fidi di lui?** | *Do you trust him?* |

5.3 When to use the Subjunctive

The subjunctive follows the conjunction **che**:

• when used with verbs expressing belief or hope, such as **credere**, **pensare** e.g.

| **Penso che sia giusto.** | *I think it's fair.* |

• when used with verbs and expressions expressing uncertainty e.g.

Non so se sia la risposta giusta.
I don't know if it's the right answer.

• when it is used with **volere** e.g.

Voglio che i miei ragazzi siano felici.
I want my children to be happy.

• after impersonal constructions which express necessity, possibility:

| **è meglio che** | *it's better (that)* |
| **è possibile che** | *it's possible (that)* |

5.4 essere and stare

In Italian there are two irregular verbs, **essere** and **stare**, that both mean *to be*. In the present tense they follow the patterns shown below:

Pronoun	essere	stare	Meaning: to be
(io)	sono	sto	I am
(tu)	sei	stai	you are
(lui/lei) (Lei)	è	sta	he/she/it is you are
(noi)	siamo	stiamo	we are
(voi)	siete	state	you are
(loro)	sono	stanno	they are

essere is the verb generally used to translate *to be*:

| **Cosa sono?** | *What are they?* |
| **È italiana.** | *She's Italian.* |

However, **stare** is used for *to be* in some common contexts:

- to say or ask how someone or something is

   Come stai?   *How are you?*

- to say where someone is

   Luigi sta a casa.   *Luigi's at home.*
   La casa sta sulla collina.   *The house is on the hill.*

- to make continuous tenses

   Sta studiando.   *He's studying.*

5.5 Compound Tenses

Compound tenses, such as the perfect tense (*I have arrived; she has eaten*), consist of the past participle and an auxiliary verb. Most verbs take the auxiliary **avere**, but some take **essere**. You do not use **avere** to make the perfect tense of reflexive verbs, or verbs that do not take a direct object, for example, **andare** (meaning *to go*), **venire** (meaning *to come*) and **diventare** (meaning *to become*).

The past participle of regular verbs is formed as follows:

- First conjugation: replace the **-are** of the infinitive with **-ato**, e.g.

   parlare *to speak* → **parlato** *spoken*

- Second conjugation: replace the **-ere** of the infinitive with **-uto**, e.g.

   credere *to believe* → **creduto** *believed*

- Third conjugation: replace the **-ire** of the infinitive with **-ito**, e.g.

   finire *to finish* → **finito** *finished*

When you make the perfect tense with **avere**, the past participle does not change its form, unless the object pronouns **lo**, **la**, **li** or **le** come before the verb. When you make the perfect tense with **essere**, the ending of the participle agrees with the subject.

   Hai visto Lucia? – Non l'ho vista.
   Have you seen Lucia? – No, I haven't seen her.

	with **avere**		with **essere**	
Perfect	**ho parlato**	I spoke, have spoken	**sono andato**	I went, have gone
Pluperfect	**avevo parlato**	I had spoken	**ero andato**	I had gone
Future Perfect	**avrò parlato**	I will have spoken	**sarò andato**	I will have gone
Perfect Conditional	**avrei parlato**	I would have spoken	**sarei andato**	I would have gone
Past Anterior	**ebbi parlato**	I had spoken	**fui andato**	I had gone
Perfect Subjunctive	**abbia parlato**	I spoke, have spoken	**sia andato**	I went, have gone
Pluperfect Subjunctive	**avessi parlato**	I had spoken	**fossi andato**	I had gone

The Gerund

To conjugate the gerund replace the **-are** of the infinitive with **-ando**, or the **-ere** or **-ire** of the infinitive by **-endo**.

parlare *to speak*	→	**parlando** *speaking*
andare *to go*	→	**andando** *going*
credere *to believe*	→	**credendo** *believing*
essere *to be*	→	**essendo** *being*
finire *to finish*	→	**finendo** *finishing*
dormire *to sleep*	→	**dormendo** *sleeping*

The gerund is used:

• with the present tense of **stare** to make the present continuous tense

Sto lavorando. *I'm working.*

• with the imperfect tense of **stare** to make the past continuous tense

Il bambino stava piangendo. *The little boy was crying.*

• adverbially, to indicate when or why something happens

Sentendomi male, sono andato a letto.
Because I felt ill, I went to bed.

Pronouns are usually joined onto the end of the gerund.

Sta vestendosi. *He's getting dressed.*

6 Sentence Structure

6.1 Word Order

Word order in Italian is very flexible, but:

• unstressed object pronouns always come before the verb, except when attached to the end of an infinitive or an imperative, e.g.

Li vedo! *I can see them!*
Me l'ha dato. *He gave it to me.*

• most adjectives come after the noun, e.g.

un vino rosso *a red wine*

• adverbs of frequency accompanying verbs in a simple tense usually follow the verb, and those used with a compound tense follow the auxiliary verb, e.g.

Ci vado spesso. *I often go there.*
Non ci sono mai stato. *I've never been there.*

Unlike in English, the word order in questions in Italian is no different from those in statements. In Italian, questions differ from statements only in intonation, or the use of a question mark in writing, e.g.

Basta	*That's enough*
Basta?	*Is that enough?*
Sono di qui.	*They're from here.*
Sono di qui?	*Are they from here?*

6.2 Negatives

In Italian, sentences are generally made negative by adding **non** before the verb, e.g.

Non posso venire.	*I can't come.*

o no is used to mean 'or not', e.g.

Vieni o no?	*Are you coming or not?*

no is used when making a distinction between people or things, e.g.

Invito lui, lei no.	*I'm going to invite him, but not her.*
Prendo un dolce, il caffè no.	*I'll have a sweet, but not a coffee.*

More than one negative word can follow a negative verb, e.g.

Non fanno mai niente.	*They never do anything.*

7 Stress

Most words are stressed on the next to the last syllable, e.g. **fi|ne|stra**.
In addition:

- Two-syllable words always stress the first vowel, unless the final vowel has an accent

ca|sa	*house*
gior|no	*day*

- Words with three or more syllables generally have the stress on the next to the last vowel

gen|ti|le	*nice*
set|ti|ma|na	*week*

- There are a number of nouns in Italian that have the stress on the final syllable and are spelled with an accent. They sometimes correspond to English nouns that end with *ty*, such as *university* and *faculty*.

u|ni|ver|si|tà	*university*
fa|col|tà	*faculty*

- Some words have the stress on a syllable which is neither the last, nor the next to the last.

u|ti|le	*useful*
dif|fi|ci|le	*difficult*

- In a few cases one word has two pronunciations, depending on its meaning. The following are some examples:

an|co|ra	*again*
an|co|ra	*anchor*
me|tro	*metre*
me|trò	*metro*

Grammatica inglese

1 Verbi

1.1 Tipi di verbi

I verbi possono esser divisi in due categorie a seconda della loro funzione. Alcuni, detti lessicali, descrivono l'azione e lo stato.

Correvamo nel campo di calcio.
*We were **running** across the football field.*

Le sono sempre piaciute le barche e la vela.
*She always **liked** boats and sailing.*

Altri sono gli ausiliari **be** e **have**, usati per formare i tempi composti di altri verbi. Di questa categoria fanno parte anche i verbi modali, che indicano certezza, volontà, potere ecc.

Sto lavorando.   *I **am** working.*

Amanda aveva già mangiato quando siamo arrivati.
*Amanda **had** already eaten when we arrived.*

Charlie andrà a casa venerdì.
*Charlie **will** go home on Friday.*

1.2 Presente semplice

Il tempo presente dell'indicativo in inglese si chiama presente semplice per distinguersi dal *present continous*. Viene usato per indicare:

• azioni abituali e gusti

    A colazione mi piace il caffè.   *I **like** coffee for breakfast.*

• un fatto, come ad esempio una dichiarazione scientifica o uno stato permanente

    D'inverno gli uccelli migrano a sud.
    *Birds **fly** south in the winter.*

• affermazioni che descrivono l'opinione del parlante o qualcosa in cui crede

    Penso sia un ottimo insegnante.
    *I **think** he's a very good teacher.*

Il presente semplice del verbo **do** accompagna gli ausiliari per:

• fare una domanda

    Ci conosciamo?   ***Do** I know you?*

• una frase negativa che usa **not**

    Lei non ti conosce.   *She **does not** know you.*

• sostituire un verbo nelle risposte brevi

    Prendi solo un caffè a colazione? – Sì.
    ***Do** you just have coffee for breakfast? – Yes, I **do**.*

Il presente semplice esprime anche un'azione che avverrà in un preciso momento, come ad esempio orari e viaggi.

    Il treno parte alle 10.40   *The train **leaves** at 10.40 a.m.*

Il presente semplice dei verbi regolari ha la stessa forma dell'infinito ad eccezione della 3ª persona singolare che alla fine prende la **-s**.

    *I **walk** to the park.*   *She **walks** to the park.*

Quando la forma dell'infinito del verbo termina in **-o**, **-ch**, **-sh**, **-ss**, **-x** o **-zz**, la 3ª persona singolare prende **-es** invece che la sola **-s**:

   catch → catch**es**   miss → miss**es**   push → push**es**

Quando l'infinito termina in **-y**, nella 3ª persona singolare la **-y** diventa **-i** seguita da **-es**:

   carry → carr**ies**   worry → worr**ies**   fly → fl**ies**

Il presente semplice di alcuni verbi è irregolare:

	to have	to be	to do	to go
I	have	am	do	go
you	have	are	do	go
he/she/it	has	is	does	goes
we	have	are	do	go
you *(pl)*	have	are	do	go
they	have	are	do	go

1.3 Presente progressivo

Il presente progressivo (in inglese *present continuous*) è formato dal presente dell'ausiliare **be** seguito dalla forma in **-ing** del verbo principale. Si usa per:

- qualcosa che sta accadendo nel momento in cui se ne parla

   Sta cantando.   *She is singing*.

- un'attività temporanea che avviene non solo nel momento in cui se ne parla

   Studia tedesco all'università.
   He is studying German at university.

- una situazione che è temporanea e non permanente

   Fiona lavora alle stalle durante le vacanze.
   Fiona is working in the stables over the holidays.

- uno stato o una situazione che sta cambiando

   Il mal di testa sta passando.   *My headache is getting better.*

Il presente progressivo si usa anche per riferirsi a qualcosa che avverrà in futuro con un avverbio o un'espressione temporale.

   Vado a New York la settimana prossima.
   I am flying to New York next week.

Il presente progressivo di verbi regolari corrisponde alla forma dell'infinito seguita da **-ing**, ad esempio:

   walk → walk**ing**   help → help**ing**   laugh → laugh**ing**

Quando il verbo termina in **-e**, la **-e** cade prima dell'aggiunta di **-ing**:

   live → liv**ing**   smile → smil**ing**   bake → bak**ing**

Alcuni dei verbi che terminano in consonante la raddoppiano e poi aggiungono **-ing**, ad esempio:

   get → ge**tting**   hop → ho**pping**   run → ru**nning**
   sob → so**bbing**   travel → trave**lling**

1.4 Passato semplice

Il passato semplice non ha bisogno dell'ausiliare. Si usa per:

- singole azioni avvenute nel passato

> **Chiuse a chiave la porta di casa e se ne andò.**
> He **locked** the door and **left** the house.

- azioni abituali del passato, spesso accompagnate da **always**, **never**, o **often**

> **Andavo spesso a Glasgow per lavoro.**
> I often **visited** Glasgow on business.

- azioni avvenute nel passato e finite, spesso accompagnate da parole come **ago** o **last month** per indicare un periodo preciso

> **Vidi Roger tempo fa.**   I **saw** Roger a little while back.

- il momento di un'azione finita del passato, accompagnata da una frase al presente progressivo

> **Stavamo uscendo di casa quando squillò il telefono.**
> We were leaving the house when the phone **rang**.

Per le forme interrogative, negative e le risposte brevi, anziché gli ausiliari **have** e **be**, si usa **did**, il passato dell'ausiliare **do**.

L'ho conosciuto?	**Did** I meet him?
Non ci andò.	He **did** not go there.
Penny ti telefonò? – Sì.	**Did** Penny phone you? – Yes, she **did**.

Il passato semplice dei verbi regolari si forma aggiungendo **–ed** alla forma dell'infinito:

> walk → walk**ed**   help → help**ed**   laugh → laugh**ed**

Se l'infinito termina in **-e**, si aggiunge solo la consonante **-d**:

> live → live**d**   smile → smile**d**   bake → bake**d**

Alcuni dei verbi che terminano in consonante la raddoppiano e poi aggiungono **-ed**:

> hop → hop**ped**   sob → sob**bed**   travel → travel**led**

Alcuni verbi hanno la forma irregolare:

> go → went   have → had   do → did
> swim → swam   think → thought   eat → ate

La forma irregolare del passato semplice del verbo **be** è la seguente:

to be	
I	was
you	were
he/she/it	was
we	were
you (pl)	were
they	were

1.5 Passato progressivo

Il passato progressivo (in inglese *past continuous*) è composto dal passato dell'ausiliare *be* seguito dalla forma in *-ing* del verbo principale. Viene usato per indicare:

- un'azione, lunga o breve, andata in corso in un momento o periodo del passato, con un inizio e una fine

  Ero alla fermata dell'autobus. *I was standing at the bus stop.*

- un'azione in corso nel passato che viene interrotta e la frase di ciò che interrompe è al passato semplice

  Eravamo seduti ai nostri posti quando squillò il telefono.
  We were sitting in our places when the telephone rang.

- un'azione breve, accaduta mentre un'altra più lunga stava già accadendo

  Mentre stavo aspettando l'autobus mi cadde il portafoglio.
  While I was waiting for the bus I dropped my purse.

1.6 Passato composto

Il passato composto (in inglese *present perfect*) è formato dal presente dell'ausiliare *have* seguito dal participio passato del verbo principale. Viene spesso confuso con il passato prossimo italiano, ma ha una funzione differente: indica un'azione avvenuta in passato con importanza nel presente.

Hanno comprato i biglietti e prenotato i posti.
They have bought their tickets and booked their seats.

Se nella frase c'è la parola *just* significa che l'azione o l'avvenimento sono stati completati da poco.

Ha appena finito i compiti. *He has just finished his homework.*

Il passato composto è spesso usato per rispondere alla domanda *How long...?* Se la risposta indica il periodo di durata dell'azione si usa *for*, se invece indica il momento o periodo in cui è iniziata si usa *since*.

Ho vissuto a Edimburgo per 15 anni.
I have lived in Edinburgh for 15 years.

Abbiamo questa macchina dal 2015.
We've had this car since 2015.

Present perfect continuous

Il *present perfect continuous* è formato dal passato composto (*present perfect*) dell'ausiliare *have* (cioè *have/has been*) e la forma in *-ing* del verbo principale. Esso indica:

- azioni iniziate in passato e non ancora terminate, o appena terminate

  Mia madre mi aiuta. *My mother has been helping me.*

- un'azione abituale

  Compro la rivista tutti i mesi.
  I've been getting this magazine every month.

Anche il verbo *used to* indica uno stato o una azione abituali del passato; viene anche usato quando qualcosa che era vero non lo è più.

Gerry andava sempre a correre prima di colazione.
Gerry always used to go for a run before breakfast.

Come sempre, **for** descrive la durata dell'azione e **since** il momento dell'inizio.

Studio l'inglese da tre anni.
I have been studying English for three years.

1.7 Trapassato

Il trapassato (in inglese *past perfect*) è composto dal passato semplice dell'ausiliare **have** (cioè **had**) e il participio passato del verbo principale. Indica ciò che è avvenuto in passato prima di qualcos'altro avvenuto anch'esso in passato.

Era in ritardo perché aveva perso il treno.
She was late because she had missed her train.

Il *past perfect* si usa spesso con parole che indicano un periodo di tempo, come ad esempio **always** e **for several days**.

Avevamo sempre desiderato visitare il Canada e l'anno scorso ci siamo decisi ad andare.
We had always wanted to visit Canada, so last year we decided to go.

Past perfect continuous

Il *past perfect continuous* si forma con il trapassato dell'ausiliare **have** (cioè **had been**) seguito dalla forma in **-ing** del verbo principale. Viene usato per:

• un'azione del passato cominciata prima di un'altra avvenuta nel passato

Aveva lavorato in Italia quell'estate e decise di rimanere un altro po'.
He had been working in Italy that summer, and decided to stay a bit longer.

• un'azione iniziata nel passato che continua a ripetersi

Aveva provato a telefonare alla madre tutto il giorno.
She had been trying to phone her mother all day.

1.8 Futuro

Il futuro viene espresso generalmente dall'infinito del verbo principale preceduto dal verbo modale **will**. Questo tipo di futuro semplice si usa per:

• parlare di fatti futuri

Pranzeremo alle 12.   *We will have lunch at 12 o'clock.*

• promettere o rassicurare

Sarò a casa per cena.   *I'll be home in time for tea.*

• esprimere la forma negativa o il rifiuto; in questi casi si usa **won't**, la forma negativa di **will**

Non ci tornerò, il servizio era pessimo.
I won't go there again – the service was terrible.

Altri modi per esprimere il futuro sono:

Be going to che indica una previsione o un'intenzione.

Sembra stia per piovere.   *It looks like it's going to rain.*

Be about to che indica qualcosa che sta per compiersi.

Non posso mettermi a chiacchierare, sto per andare a lavoro.
I can't stop and chat; I'm about to leave for work.

Talvolta si usano altri tempi verbali:

- il presente semplice accompagnato da un avverbio temporale e usato per esprimere un orario o qualcosa programmato per il futuro

    Partiamo domani pomeriggio alle quattro.
    We leave at 4pm tomorrow.

- il presente progressivo (il presente dell'ausiliare *be* seguito dalla forma in *-ing* del verbo principale) accompagnato da un avverbio temporale per esprimere eventi e azioni del futuro prossimo

    Venerdì vado a Glasgow in aereo.
    I am flying to Glasgow on Friday.

- il *future perfect*, che corrisponde al futuro anteriore italiano, formato da *will have* seguito dal participio passato del verbo principale

    Papà avrà preparato la cena quando torniamo.
    Dad will have made dinner by the time we get back.

- il futuro progressivo, che è un modo informale per suggerire che qualcosa sta per accadere o accadrà in un momento non precisato

    Non vedremo lo zio Jim quando saremo a Londra.
    We won't be seeing Uncle Jim while we are in London.

1.9 Verbi frasali

I verbi frasali sono formati da un verbo seguito da un avverbio, da una preposizione oppure da un avverbio e preposizione. I verbi frasali hanno molto spesso un significato diverso dal singolo verbo e dal singolo avverbio o preposizione.

L'aereo partì in orario.	*The plane took off on time.*

Quando un verbo frasale ha un complemento oggetto questo può andare tra il verbo e la preposizione o avverbio, oppure dopo la preposizione o avverbio.

Ripose gli abiti.	*She tidied away her clothes.*
Spense la candela.	*She blew the candle out.*

1.10 Verbi modali

I verbi modali sono un tipo di ausiliari e reggono l'infinito del verbo principale; a seconda di quale venga usato, il significato del verbo che accompagnano viene modificato, esprimendo ad esempio la possibiltà, il dovere, la volontà ecc. I principali verbi modali sono:

can, could, may , might, shall, should , will, would, must, ought

A seconda del tipo, tempo e modo, i modali si usano per:

- esprimere diversi gradi di dubbio e possibilità

    Potrei non essere capace di farlo.
    I may not be able to do it.

    Potresti avermi attaccato tu il raffreddore.
    I think I might have caught your cold.

- esprimere un diverso grado di probabilità nel futuro

La vedrai venerdì.	*You **will** be seeing her on Friday night.*
Forse li porto con me.	*I **might** bring them with me.*

- chiedere o dare un'autorizzazione

Puoi prendere in prestito la mia macchina se vuoi.
*You **can** borrow my car if you like.*

- esprimere una supposizione

Fa un tempo talmente brutto che il volo potrebbe essere in ritardo.
*The weather's so bad the flight **could** be late.*

- esprimere un obbligo o un dovere

Devi consegnare il tema per casa domani.
*You **must** hand in your essay tomorrow.*

- fare con gentilezza una richiesta

Potrebbe chiudere la porta?   ***Would** you please close the door?*

I verbi modali non hanno l'infinito, il gerundio né le forme composte. Non prendono la –s alla 3ª persona singolare, e con il verbo che li segue non si usa il **to** (a parte **ought to**). Vengono sostituiti da un altro verbo nei tempi e modi verbali che non hanno. Ad esempio **had** to sostituisce **must**:

Devo andare a trovare mia zia May oggi pomeriggio.
*I **must** visit my Aunt May this afternoon.*

Sono dovuto andare a trovare mia zia May ieri.
*I **had** to visit Aunt May yesterday.*

Can/could/may

Can e **could** si usano per indicare:

- abilità e capacità di fare qualcosa

So andare a cavallo.   *I **can** ride a horse.*

- permesso o richiesta; in questo caso si usano spesso **could** e **may**, più formali

Potrei prendere in prestito la macchina?
***Could** I borrow the car, please?*

Potrei usare il suo telefono per cortesia?
***May** I use your phone?*

Must/should

Must e **should** si usano per esprimere:

- obbligo o proibizione

Tutti gli alunni devono portare a scuola una matita.
*All pupils **must** bring a pencil to school.*

Dovrebbe segnalarlo alla polizia.
*You **should** report the matter to the police.*

- ordini o suggerimenti

Ora devi andare a letto.	*You **must** go to sleep now.*
Dovresti fare cosa ti dice il dottore.	*You **should** do what the doctor says.*

- consigli e raccomandazioni

Questo film devi vederlo, è stupendo!
*You **must** see this film, it's great!*

Dovrebbe prima svitare le viti in alto.
*He **should** undo the top screws first.*

Quando **should** è seguito dal *present perfect* del verbo principale esprime il rimpianto per aver o non aver fatto qualcosa. In questi casi si può usare anche **ought to**, che però è meno comune.

Avresti dovuto dirmi che eri in ritardo.
*You **should have told** me you were running late.*

1.11 Forme contratte

Gli ausiliari alla forma negativa sono spesso usati in forma contratta, costituita dall'ausiliare più **-n't**.

Full forms		Contracted forms
do not, does not, did not	→	**don't, doesn't, didn't**
will not	→	**won't**
is not, are not, was not, were not	→	**isn't, aren't, wasn't, weren't**
have not, has not, had not	→	**haven't, hasn't, hadn't**
cannot	→	**can't**
I am	→	**I'm**
he is, she is, it is	→	**he's, she's, it's**
you are, we are, they are	→	**you're, we're, they're**
I have, you have, they have, we have	→	**I've, you've, they've, we've**
he has, she has, it has	→	**he's, she's, it's**
I had, he had, she had, *ecc*	→	**I'd, he'd, she'd,** *etc*
I would, he would, she would, *ecc*	→	**I'd, he'd, she'd,** *etc*
I will, he will, she will, *ecc*	→	**I'll, he'll, she'll,** *etc*

1.12 infinito con il *to* e forma in *-ing*

Alcuni verbi seguiti da altre frasi verbali reggono l'infinito preceduto dal **to**, altri la forma in **-ing**. I verbi seguiti dall'infinito con il **to**, che può essere preceduto da un complemento, includono **agree**, **choose**, **decide**, **force**, **help**, **hope**, **invite**, **learn**, **offer**, **see**, **tell**, **want**.

Spero di rivederti presto.   *I **hope to see** you again soon.*
Ama ballare.   *He **loves to dance**.*

I verbi che reggono la forma in -ing includono **avoid**, **dislike**, **finish**, **imagine**.

Hai finito di leggere quel libro?   *Have you **finished reading** that book?*

Esistono verbi che reggono sia l'infinito con il **to** che la forma in **-ing**, senza particolari differenze di significato. Tra questi ci sono **begin**, **continue**, **like**, **love**, **hate**, **prefer**.

Le piace nuotare in mare.
*She **likes to swim/likes swimming** in the sea.*

2 Nomi

2.1 Tipi di nomi

In inglese i nomi propri, come ad esempio, quelli di una persona, un giornale, una città, hanno di solito la lettera iniziale maiuscola.

John Lennon   *Spain*   *Easter*   *The Times*   *Mr Brown*

Anche i nomi dei giorni della settimana, dei mesi, delle lingue e delle nazionalità hanno, a differenza dell'italiano, la maiuscola.

Thursday   *June*   *English*

I nomi comuni sono quelli che designano categorie di persone, cose, ecc.

Mio fratello e mia sorella sono andati a trovare nostra madre.
My **brother** and **sister** visited my **mother**.

La rabbia che John provava era travolgente.
The **anger** that John felt was overwhelming.

I nomi collettivi designano un gruppo di persone o animali.

*a **herd** of cows*   *a **swarm** of bees*

I numerabili designano i nomi che hanno sia il singolare che il plurale: *one cat*, *two cats*, *seventeen cats*, ecc. Il plurale di solito si forma aggiungendo –s al singolare. La forma singolare dei numerabili viene preceduta da un determinante:

Prendi una sedia per Maddy.   Fetch **a chair** for Maddy, will you?
Abbiamo comprato sei nuove sedie.
We've bought **six new chairs**.

In genere i non numerabili, come ad esempio i nomi astratti, sono usati soltanto al singolare, e il verbo è pertanto coniugato al singolare. I nomi non numerabili di solito non sono accompagnati dall'articolo indefinito (l'indeterminativo italiano).

John mi ha chiesto un consiglio.   John asked me for some **advice**.
Trevor ha testimoniato al processo.
Trevor gave **evidence** at the trial.

In certi casi un nome è numerabile in alcune frasi e non numerabile in altre, e generalmente il significato è diverso.

Il tempo passò lentamente.   **Time** passed slowly.
Lo fece quattro volte.   She did it four **times**.

In inglese il termine nome composto indica un nome formato dall'unione di due o più elementi, talvolta separati da uno spazio o da un trattino. Il suo significato è spesso diverso da quello dei singoli nomi, e la parte dominante della parola è per lo più l'ultimo elemento.

*tea**pot***   *head**ache***   *washing **machine***

L'uso di più nomi non genera sempre un nome composto; ad esempio il primo o i primi due nomi possono fare da modificatori per l'ultimo, senza formare un nome composto.

*a **concrete** slab*   *old **oak** beams*

2.2 Numero dei nomi

In inglese la forma plurale regolare di un nome termina generalmente in **-s**.

cat → *cats*   *paper* → *papers*   *thought* → *thoughts*

Qui sotto alcuni esempi di forme irregolari:

nome singolare che finisce in:	nome plurale che finisce in:
-s, -ss, -ch, -x, -zz focus, princess, church, box, buzz	**-es** focuses, princesses, churches, boxes, buzzes
-o hero, piano, potato	**-s** o **-es** heroes, pianos, potatoes
consonante + **y** baby, hobby	**-ies** babies, hobbies
vocale + **y** key, ray	**-s** keys, rays
-f hoof, dwarf, thief, roof	**-s** o **-ves** hoofs o hooves, dwarf o dwarves, thieves, roofs
-fe knife, life	**-ves** knives, lives

Alcuni nomi hanno la stessa forma per il singolare e il plurale.

a sheep → *ten sheep*   *a goldfish* → *several goldfish*

Alcuni cambiano la vocale o il suono vocalico nella forma plurale.

man → *men*   *woman* → *women*   *child* → *children*

I nomi di oggetti formati da due parti identiche, come ad esempio **trousers**, **binoculars**, e **tongs** sono considerati nomi plurali e quindi accompagnati dal verbo al plurale.

Le forbici sono sul tavolo.   *The scissors **are** on the table.*

Il plurale di nomi stranieri entrati in uso è talvolta diverso da quello che ha nella lingua originaria e riflette la comune forma inglese:

a pizza → *two pizzas*   *one cappuccino* → *three cappuccinos*

In altri casi, ad esempio per parole del greco e del latino, viene conservata la forma plurale originale e ne esiste anche una variante inglese:

a crisis → *two crises*   *a formula* → *some formulae (or formulas)*

3 Determinanti

3.1 Tipi di determinanti

In inglese i determinanti sono gli articoli e alcuni gruppi di aggettivi che 'determinano' a cosa si riferisce un nome:

- l'articolo indefinito (corrispondente all'indeterminativo italiano) *a* o *an*

  Un uomo entrò in negozio.   ***A** man came into the shop.*

- l'articolo definito (corrispondente al determinativo italiano) **the**

  Il cane rincorse il coniglio.   *The dog chased the rabbit.*

- gli aggettivi dimostrativi **this**, **that**, **these**, **those**

  Questo libro è meglio di quello.   *This book is better than that one.*

- gli aggettivi possessivi **my**, **your**, **his**, **her**, **its**, **our**, **their**

  Sean ha trovato il mio libro nella sua macchina.
  Sean found my book in his car.

- gli aggettivi quantitativi, come **some**, **any** e **all**

  Ho del caffè ma non ho zucchero.
  I've got some coffee but I haven't got any sugar.

- i numerali cardinali e ordinali

  I due ragazzi sono cresciuti insieme.
  The two boys grew up together.

  Il loro secondo figlio nascerà a ottobre.
  Their second child is due in October.

- gli aggettivi indefiniti, come ad esempio, **each** e **every**

  Ciascun bambino ha ricevuto un libro.
  Each child received a book.

- gli esclamativi **what** e **such**

  Che peccato!   *What a shame!*

3.2   Articoli indefiniti e definiti

L'articolo indefinito è usato con il singolare dei nomi numerabili, cioè quelli che hanno anche il plurale.

Un uomo è stato visto allontanarsi con una macchina nera.
A man was seen driving away in a black car.

La forma **an** viene usata quando il nome inizia con una vocale o l'**h** muta.

un'esperienza unica   **un terribile errore**
a unique experience   *an awful mistake*

L'articolo definito è usato con i nomi singolari e plurali, e con quelli numerabili e non numerabili.

Hai acceso il riscaldamento?   *Did you switch the heating on?*
Portiamo i bambini in piscina.   *Let's take the children to the pool.*

I nomi numerabili e non numerabili vengono usati senza l'articolo se riferiti al senso generale della parola.

La verdura fa bene.   *Vegetables are good for you.*

3.3   Dimostrativi

Gli aggettivi dimostrativi indicano la distanza nel tempo o nello spazio rispetto a chi parla. I dimostrativi sono: **this**, **that**, **these**, **those**.

This e **these** indicano qualcuno o qualcosa vicino a chi parla.

Queste mele arrivano dall'Australia.
These apples come from Australia.

That e *those* indicano qualcuno o qualcosa lontano da chi parla.

Vedi quell'uomo sulla collina?
*Can you see **that man** up on the hill?*

This e *that* vengono usati davanti ai nomi non numerabili e alla forma singolare di quelli numerabili.

Questo libro è mio.   ***This** book is mine.*

Quegli uomini stanno riparando il tetto.
***Those** men are mending the roof.*

3.4 Possessivi

A differenza dell'italiano in inglese gli aggettivi possessivi prendono forme diverse a seconda del numero e del genere della persona o cosa che possiede:

persona	singolare	plurale
1ª	**my**	**our**
2ª	**your**	**your**
3ª maschile	**his**	**their**
3ª femminile	**hers**	**their**
3ª neutra	**its**	**their**

Le tue scarpe sono sotto il tuo letto.   ***Your** shoes are under **your** bed.*

Talvolta il possesso non è indicato dal determinante, ma dal nome di persona o cosa seguito da **-'s** se al singolare o soltanto dall'apostrofo se il plurale termina in **-s**.

*Robert**'s** mother*   *the children**'s** toys*

4 Aggettivi qualificativi

4.1 Forma invariabile

Come gli aggettivi nella categoria dei determinanti (*my*, *this*, *each* ecc.), in inglese anche gli aggettivi che descrivono una qualità sono invariabili, non hanno cioè forme diverse per genere e numero.

a young girl   *my old friends*   *that beautiful garden*

4.2 Posizione

Quando gli aggettivi caratterizzano un nome in genere lo precedono.

a tall girl   *green grass*   *four well-behaved little boys*

Quando seguono un verbo che li collega a un nome, come *be* o *seem*, la posizione è simile all'italiano.

Le rose sono gialle.   *The roses are **yellow**.*

La maggior parte degli aggettivi possono venir usati in entrambi i modi. Alcuni invece hanno un'unica funzione e seguono sempre il verbo. Molti degli aggettivi di questo tipo iniziano con la lettera a-: *afloat, afraid, alike, alive, alone, ashamed, asleep, awake*.

Le ragazze dormivano.   *The girls were **asleep**.*

4.3 Ordine di più aggettivi

Nel caso ci sia più di un aggettivo qualificativo l'ordine è di solito il seguente:

- aggettivi che descrivono emozioni e qualità

    pleasant childhood memories

- aggettivi che indicano misura, età e temperatura

    a *lovely big* smile

- aggettivi che indicano il colore

    her beautiful *blue* eyes

- aggettivi di nazionalità e di origine

    an elegant *French* woman

- aggettivi che indicano la sostanza e il materiale di un oggetto

    a large *wooden* door

Come dimostrano gli esempi, quando due o più aggettivi precedono un nome di solito non sono separati da *and*. Lo sono invece quando tutti indicano un colore.

    a *red and blue* flag

4.4 Comparativi e superlativi

In genere per gli aggettivi di una sola sillaba si aggiunge *–er* per avere la forma comparativa e *–est* per la superlativa. Se l'aggettivo termina in *–e*, la *–e* rimane; quando invece termina in *–y*, questa viene sostituita da *–i*.

	comparativo	superlativo
wise	**wiser**	the **wisest**
pretty	**prettier**	the **prettiest**
weary	**wearier**	the **weariest**

Gli aggettivi di tre o più sillabe vengono invece preceduti dalla parola *more* per la forma comparativa e *most* per la superlativa.

> **Questi sono i fiori più belli che abbia mai ricevuto.**
> These are the *most beautiful* flowers I have ever received.

Alcuni aggettivi si definiscono irregolari perché prendono una forma diversa sia per il comparativo che superlativo.

	comparativo	superlativo
good	**better**	the **best**
bad	**worse**	the **worst**
far	**further**	the **furthest**

5 Pronomi

5.1 Tipi di pronomi

Ci sono vari tipi di pronomi:

- pronomi personali

    Le dette una scatola di cioccolatini.
    He gave her a box of chocolates.

30

- pronomi riflessivi

   Mi sono tagliato con un pezzo di vetro.
   I've cut **myself** on a piece of glass.

- pronomi possessivi

   Ridammelo, è mio.   Give it back, it's **mine**.

- pronomi dimostrativi

   Queste sono carine. Dove le hai trovate?
   These are nice. Where did you find them?

- pronomi relativi

   Non so cosa tu voglia dire.   I don't know **what** you mean.

- pronomi interrogativi

   Chi è stato il responsabile?   **Who** was responsible?

- pronomi indefiniti

   Tutti avevano bussola.   **Everyone** had a compass.

5.2 Pronomi personali

I pronomi personali sono i seguenti:

persona	soggetto	complemento	soggetto plurale	complemento plurale
1ª	I	me	we	us
2ª	you	you	you	you
3ª maschile	he	him	they	them
3ª femminile	she	her	they	them
3ª neutra	it	it	they	them

Quando due pronomi o un nome personale e un pronome sono il soggetto del verbo, va usata la forma soggetto del pronome.

   Lui e io andiamo al cinema.   **He and I** are going to the cinema.

Quando invece sono il complemento oggetto del verbo, quello di termine o dopo una preposizione, si usa la forma complemento del pronome. Questa viene usata, anche quando il pronome è preceduto dalla parola **than** del comparativo.

   Hanno deciso di aiutare Jane e me.
   They decided to help **Jane and me**.

   John è più giovane di me.   John is younger than **me**.

5.3 Pronomi possessivi

In inglese i pronomi possessivi si accordano con il possessore e non con la cosa posseduta come in italiano. Hanno forme diverse al singolare e plurale, ad eccezione della 2ª persona. La 3ª persona singolare ha tre forme differenti a seconda del genere del possessore. In inglese i pronomi possessivi sono diversi dagli aggettivi, a parte la 3ª persona singolare maschile (**his**).

pronomi possessivi	aggettivi possessivi
mine	my
yours	your (*singolare*)
his	his
hers	her
(*nessuna forma*)	its
ours	our
yours	your (*plurale*)
theirs	their

Ricorda di non scrivere queste parole con l'apostrofo, in particolare *its*: la forma apostrofata, *it's*, è la contrazione di *it is*.

5.4 Pronomi relativi

I pronomi relativi sono *who*, *whom*, *which* e *that* e collegano la proposizione principale alla secondaria.

>**Potrebbe perdere il lavoro, il che sarebbe disastroso.**
>*He might lose his job, **which** would be disastrous.*

Who e *whom* vengono usati quando il soggetto o il complemento è una persona, mentre *which* per cose, animali e concetti astratti.

>**Mi ha presentato all'amico che era appena tornato dalla Cina.**
>*He introduced me to his friend, **who** had just returned from China.*

>**Quella è la macchina che ha appena comprato.**
>*That is the car **which** she has just bought.*

Whom è molto formale e nell'uso viene spesso sostituito da *who*.

>**Ho scoperto chi è andato a trovare.**
>*I discovered **who** he was visiting.*

5.5 Pronomi interrogativi

I pronomi interrogativi *who*, *whom* e *whose* si usano soltanto in riferimento a persone, per le cose si usano invece *which* e *what*.

>**Chi sta ballando con Lucy?**   *Who is dancing with Lucy?*

>**Quale di questi libri raccomanderebbe?**
>*Which of these books would you recommend?*

Whose è la forma possessiva del pronome interrogativo.

>**Di chi è la macchina qui fuori?**   *Whose is that car outside?*

Whom è molto formale e, quando è possibile, nella comunicazione informale viene molto spesso sostituito da *who*.

>**Con chi stavi parlando?**   *Who were you speaking to?*

Quando il pronome interrogativo è seguito da una preposizione si usa la forma del complemento oggetto. Nella lingua di tutti i giorni la preposizione va alla fine della frase.

>**Di chi è questo?**   *Who does this belong to?*

Inglese – Italiano

English – Italian

a

A [eɪ] *n* (*Mus*) la *m*; **A road** *n* (*BRIT Aut*) ≈ strada statale; **A to Z®** *n* stradario

 KEYWORD

a [ə] (*before vowel or silent h: an*) *indef art* **1** un, uno (+ *s impure, gn, pn, ps, x, z*), una *f*, un' + *vowel*; **a book** un libro; **a mirror** uno specchio; **an apple** una mela; **she's a doctor** è medico **2** (*instead of the number "one"*) un(o), una *f*; **a year ago** un anno fa; **a hundred/thousand pounds** cento/mille sterline **3** (*in expressing ratios, prices etc*) a, per; **3 a day/week** 3 al giorno/alla settimana; **10 km an hour** 10 km all'ora; **£5 a person** 5 sterline a persona *or* per persona

A2 *n abbr* (*BRIT Scol*) seconda parte del diploma di studi superiori chiamato "A level"
AA *n abbr* (*BRIT*: = *Automobile Association*) ≈ A.C.I. *m*; (= *Alcoholics Anonymous*) A.A. *f*
AAA *n abbr* (= *American Automobile Association*) ≈ A.C.I. *m*
aback [ə'bæk] *adv*: **to be taken ~** essere sbalordito/a
abandon [ə'bændən] *vt* abbandonare ▷ *n* abbandono; **with ~** sfrenatamente, spensieratamente
abattoir ['æbətwɑː'] *n* (*BRIT*) mattatoio
abbey ['æbɪ] *n* abbazia, badia
abbreviation [əbriːvɪ'eɪʃən] *n* abbreviazione *f*
abdomen ['æbdəmən] *n* addome *m*
abduct [æb'dʌkt] *vt* rapire
abide [ə'baɪd] *vt* sopportare; **I can't ~ it/ him** non lo posso soffrire *or* sopportare; **abide by** *vt fus* conformarsi a
ability [ə'bɪlɪtɪ] *n* abilità *f inv*
able ['eɪbl] *adj* capace; **to be ~ to do sth** essere capace di fare qc, poter fare qc

abnormal [æb'nɔːməl] *adj* anormale
aboard [ə'bɔːd] *adv* a bordo ▷ *prep* a bordo di
abolish [ə'bɔlɪʃ] *vt* abolire
abolition [æbəu'lɪʃən] *n* abolizione *f*
abort [ə'bɔːt] *vt* abortire; **abortion** [ə'bɔːʃən] *n* aborto; **to have an abortion** abortire

 KEYWORD

about [ə'baut] *adv* **1** (*approximately*) circa, quasi; **about a hundred/thousand** un centinaio/migliaio, circa cento/mille; **it takes about 10 hours** ci vogliono circa 10 ore; **at about 2 o'clock** verso le 2; **I've just about finished** ho quasi finito **2** (*referring to place*) qua e là, in giro; **to leave things lying about** lasciare delle cose in giro; **to run about** correre qua e là; **to walk about** camminare **3**: **to be about to do sth** stare per fare qc ▷ *prep* **1** (*relating to*) su, di; **a book about London** un libro su Londra; **what is it about?** di che si tratta?; (*book, film etc*) di cosa tratta?; **we talked about it** ne abbiamo parlato; **what** *or* **how about doing this?** che ne dici di fare questo? **2** (*referring to place*): **to walk about the town** camminare per la città; **her clothes were scattered about the room** i suoi vestiti erano sparsi *or* in giro per tutta la stanza

above [ə'bʌv] *adv*, *prep* sopra; **mentioned ~** suddetto; **~ all** soprattutto
abroad [ə'brɔːd] *adv* all'estero
abrupt [ə'brʌpt] *adj* (*sudden*) improvviso/a; (*gruff, blunt*) brusco/a
abscess ['æbsɪs] *n* ascesso
absence ['æbsəns] *n* assenza
absent ['æbsənt] *adj* assente; **absent-minded** *adj* distratto/a
absolute ['æbsəluːt] *adj* assoluto/a; **absolutely** [-'luːtlɪ] *adv* assolutamente
absorb [əb'sɔːb] *vt* assorbire; **to be ~ed in a book** essere immerso in un libro; **absorbent cotton** [əb'zɔːbənt-] *n* (*US*) cotone *m* idrofilo; **absorbing** *adj* avvincente, molto interessante
abstain [əb'steɪn] *vi*: **to ~ (from)** astenersi (da)
abstract ['æbstrækt] *adj* astratto/a
absurd [əb'səːd] *adj* assurdo/a
abundance [ə'bʌndəns] *n* abbondanza
abundant [ə'bʌndənt] *adj* abbondante
abuse *n* [ə'bjuːs] abuso; (*insults*) ingiurie *fpl* ▷ *vt* [ə'bjuːz] abusare di; **abusive** *adj* ingiurioso/a

abysmal [ə'bɪzməl] *adj* spaventoso/a
academic [ækə'dɛmɪk] *adj* accademico/a;
(*pej: issue*) puramente formale ▷ *n*
universitario/a; **academic year** *n* anno
accademico
academy [ə'kædəmɪ] *n* (*learned body*)
accademia; (*school*) scuola privata; **~ of
music** conservatorio
accelerate [æk'sɛləreɪt] *vt*, *vi* accelerare;
acceleration *n* accelerazione *f*;
accelerator *n* acceleratore *m*
accent ['æksɛnt] *n* accento
accept [ək'sɛpt] *vt* accettare; **acceptable** *adj*
accettabile; **acceptance** *n* accettazione *f*
access ['æksɛs] *n* accesso; **accessible**
[æk'sɛsəbl] *adj* accessibile
accessory [æk'sɛsərɪ] *n* accessorio; (*Law*):
~ complice *m/f* di
accident ['æksɪdənt] *n* incidente *m*;
(*chance*) caso; **I've had an ~** ho avuto
un incidente; **by ~** per caso; **accidental**
[-'dɛntl] *adj* accidentale; **accidentally**
[-'dɛntəlɪ] *adv* per caso; **Accident and
Emergency Department** *n* (*BRIT*)
pronto soccorso; **accident insurance** *n*
assicurazione *f* contro gli infortuni
acclaim [ə'kleɪm] *n* acclamazione *f*
accommodate [ə'kɔmədeɪt] *vt* alloggiare;
(*oblige, help*) favorire
accommodation [əkɔmə'deɪʃən] *n*, (*us*)
accommodations *n pl* alloggio
accompaniment [ə'kʌmpənɪmənt] *n*
accompagnamento
accompany [ə'kʌmpənɪ] *vt*
accompagnare
accomplice [ə'kʌmplɪs] *n* complice *m/f*
accomplish [ə'kʌmplɪʃ] *vt* compiere;
(*goal*) raggiungere; **accomplishment** *n*
compimento; realizzazione *f*
accord [ə'kɔːd] *n* accordo ▷ *vt* accordare; **of
his own ~** di propria iniziativa; **accordance**
n: **in accordance with** in conformità con;
according: **according to** *prep* secondo;
accordingly *adv* in conformità
account [ə'kaunt] *n* (*Comm*) conto; (*report*)
descrizione *f*; **accounts** *npl* (*Comm*) conti
mpl; **of little ~** di poca importanza; **on ~** in
acconto; **on no ~** per nessun motivo; **on
~ of** a causa di; **to take into ~, take ~ of**
tener conto di; **account for** *vt fus* (*explain*)
spiegare; giustificare; **accountable** *adj*:
accountable (to) responsabile (verso);
accountant [ə'kauntənt] *n* ragioniere/a;
account number *n* numero di conto
accumulate [ə'kjuːmjuleɪt] *vt*
accumulare ▷ *vi* accumularsi
accuracy ['ækjurəsɪ] *n* precisione *f*
accurate ['ækjurɪt] *adj* preciso/a;
accurately *adv* precisamente

accusation [ækjuˈzeɪʃən] *n* accusa
accuse [ə'kjuːz] *vt* accusare; **accused** *n*
accusato/a
accustomed [ə'kʌstəmd] *adj*: **~ to**
abituato/a a
ace [eɪs] *n* asso
ache [eɪk] *n* male *m*, dolore *m* ▷ *vi* (*be sore*)
far male, dolere; **my head ~s** mi fa male
la testa
achieve [ə'tʃiːv] *vt* (*aim*) raggiungere;
(*victory, success*) ottenere; **achievement** *n*
compimento; successo
acid ['æsɪd] *adj* acido/a ▷ *n* acido
acknowledge [ək'nɔlɪdʒ] *vt* (*fact*)
riconoscere; (*letter: also*: **~ receipt of**)
accusare ricevuta di; **acknowledgement** *n*
riconoscimento; (*of letter*) conferma
acne ['æknɪ] *n* acne *f*
acorn ['eɪkɔːn] *n* ghianda
acoustic [ə'kuːstɪk] *adj* acustico/a
acquaintance [ə'kweɪntəns] *n*
conoscenza; (*person*) conoscente *m/f*
acquire [ə'kwaɪəʳ] *vt* acquistare;
acquisition [ækwɪ'zɪʃən] *n* acquisto
acquit [ə'kwɪt] *vt* assolvere; **to ~ o.s. well**
comportarsi bene
acre ['eɪkəʳ] *n* acro (= 4047 m²)
acronym ['ækrənɪm] *n* acronimo
across [ə'krɔs] *prep* (*on the other side*)
dall'altra parte di; (*crosswise*) attraverso
▷ *adv* dall'altra parte; in larghezza; **to run/
swim ~** attraversare di corsa/a nuoto;
~ from di fronte a
acrylic [ə'krɪlɪk] *adj* acrilico/a
act [ækt] *n* atto; (*in music-hall etc*) numero;
(*Law*) decreto ▷ *vi* agire; (*Theat*) recitare;
(*pretend*) fingere ▷ *vt* (*part*) recitare; **to
~ as** agire da; **act up** (*col*) *vi* (*person*)
comportarsi male; (*knee, back, injury*) fare
male; (*machine*) non funzionare; **acting** *adj*
che fa le funzioni di ▷ *n* (*of actor*) recitazione
f; **to do some acting** fare del teatro (*or* del
cinema)
action ['ækʃən] *n* azione *f*; (*Mil*)
combattimento; (*Law*) processo ▷ *vt*
(*Comm: request*) evadere; (*tasks*) portare
a termine; **to take ~** agire; **out of ~**
fuori combattimento; (*machine etc*) fuori
servizio; **action replay** *n* (*TV*) replay *m inv*
activate ['æktɪveɪt] *vt* (*mechanism*) fare
funzionare, attivare
active ['æktɪv] *adj* attivo/a; **actively** *adv*
(*participate*) attivamente; (*discourage,
dislike*) vivamente
activist ['æktɪvɪst] *n* attivista *m/f*
activity [æk'tɪvɪtɪ] *n* attività *f inv*; **activity
holiday** *n* vacanza attiva (*in bici, a cavallo,
in barca, a vela ecc.*)
actor ['æktəʳ] *n* attore *m*

actress ['æktrɪs] n attrice f

actual ['æktjuəl] adj reale, vero/a

> ▌ Be careful not to translate *actual* by the Italian word *attuale*.

actually ['æktjuəlɪ] adv veramente; (*even*) addirittura

> ▌ Be careful not to translate *actually* by the Italian word *attualmente*.

acupuncture ['ækjupʌnktʃər] n agopuntura

acute [ə'kjuːt] adj acuto/a; (*mind, person*) perspicace

AD adv abbr (= *Anno Domini*) d. C.

ad [æd] n abbr = **advertisement**

adamant ['ædəmənt] adj irremovibile

adapt [ə'dæpt] vt adattare ▷ vi: **to ~ (to)** adattarsi (a); **adapter, adaptor** n (*Elec*) adattatore m

add [æd] vt aggiungere ▷ vi: **to ~ to** (*increase*) aumentare ▷ n (*Internet*): **thanks for the ~** grazie per avermi aggiunto (come amico); **add up** vt (*figures*) addizionare ▷ vi (*fig*): **it doesn't ~ up** non ha senso; **it doesn't ~ up to much** non è un granché

addict ['ædɪkt] n tossicomane m/f; (*fig*) fanatico/a; **addicted** [ə'dɪktɪd] adj: **to be addicted to** (*drink etc*) essere dedito/a a; (*fig: football etc*) essere tifoso/a di; **addiction** [ə'dɪkʃən] n (*Med*) tossicodipendenza; **addictive** [ə'dɪktɪv] adj che dà assuefazione

addition [ə'dɪʃən] n addizione f; (*thing added*) aggiunta; **in ~** inoltre; **in ~ to** oltre; **additional** adj supplementare

additive ['ædɪtɪv] n additivo

address [ə'drɛs] n indirizzo; (*talk*) discorso ▷ vt indirizzare; (*speak to*) fare un discorso a; (*issue*) affrontare; **my ~ is ...** il mio indirizzo è ...; **address book** n rubrica

adequate ['ædɪkwɪt] adj adeguato/a; sufficiente

adhere [əd'hɪər] vi: **to ~ to** aderire a; (*fig: rule, decision*) seguire

adhesive [əd'hiːzɪv] n adesivo; **~ tape** (BRIT: *for parcels etc*) nastro adesivo; (US *Med*) cerotto adesivo

adjacent [ə'dʒeɪsənt] adj adiacente; **~ to** accanto a

adjective ['ædʒɛktɪv] n aggettivo

adjoining [ə'dʒɔɪnɪŋ] adj accanto inv, adiacente

adjourn [ə'dʒəːn] vt rimandare ▷ vi essere aggiornato/a

adjust [ə'dʒʌst] vt aggiustare; (*Comm: change*) rettificare ▷ vi: **to ~ (to)** adattarsi (a); **adjustable** adj regolabile; **adjustment** n (*Psych*) adattamento; (*of machine*) regolazione f; (*of prices, wages*) aggiustamento

administer [əd'mɪnɪstər] vt amministrare; (*justice*) somministrare; **administration** [ədmɪnɪs'treɪʃən] n amministrazione f; **administrative** [əd'mɪnɪstrətɪv] adj amministrativo/a

administrator [əd'mɪnɪstreɪtər] n amministratore/trice

admiral ['ædmərəl] n ammiraglio

admiration [ædmə'reɪʃən] n ammirazione f

admire [əd'maɪər] vt ammirare; **admirer** n ammiratore/trice

admission [əd'mɪʃən] n ammissione f; (*to exhibition, nightclub etc*) ingresso; (*confession*) confessione f

admit [əd'mɪt] vt ammettere; far entrare; (*agree*) riconoscere; **admit to** vt fus riconoscere; **admittance** n ingresso; **admittedly** adv bisogna pur riconoscere (che)

adolescent [ædəu'lɛsnt] adj, n adolescente m/f

adopt [ə'dɔpt] vt adottare; **adopted** adj adottivo/a; **adoption** [ə'dɔpʃən] n adozione f

adore [ə'dɔːr] vt adorare

adorn [ə'dɔːn] vt ornare

Adriatic [eɪdrɪ'ætɪk] n: **the ~ (Sea)** il mare Adriatico, l'Adriatico

adrift [ə'drɪft] adv alla deriva

ADSL n abbr (= *asymmetric digital subscriber line*) ADSL m

adult ['ædʌlt] n adulto/a ▷ adj adulto/a; (*work, education*) per adulti; **adult education** n scuola per adulti

adultery [ə'dʌltərɪ] n adulterio

advance [əd'vaːns] n avanzamento; (*money*) anticipo ▷ adj (*booking etc*) in anticipo ▷ vt (*date, money*) anticipare ▷ vi avanzare; **in ~** in anticipo; **do I need to book in ~?** occorre che prenoti in anticipo?; **advanced** adj avanzato/a; (*Scol: studies*) superiore

advantage [əd'vaːntɪdʒ] n (*also Tennis*) vantaggio; **to take ~ of** approfittarsi di

advent ['ædvənt] n avvento; **A~** (*Rel*) Avvento

adventure [əd'vɛntʃər] n avventura; **adventurous** [əd'vɛntʃərəs] adj avventuroso/a

adverb ['ædvəːb] n avverbio

adversary ['ædvəsərɪ] n avversario/a

adverse ['ædvəːs] adj avverso/a

advert ['ædvəːt] n abbr (BRIT) = **advertisement**

advertise ['ædvətaɪz] vi, vt fare pubblicità or réclame (a), fare un'inserzione (per vendere); **to ~ for** (*staff*) cercare tramite annuncio; **advertisement** [əd'vəːtɪsmənt] n

(*Comm*) réclame *f inv*, pubblicità *f inv*; (*in classified ads*) inserzione *f*; **advertiser** *n* azienda che reclamizza un prodotto; (*in newspaper*) inserzionista *m/f*; **advertising** ['ædvətaızıŋ] *n* pubblicità

advice [əd'vaıs] *n* consigli *mpl*; **piece of ~** consiglio; **to take legal ~** consultare un avvocato

advisable [əd'vaızəbl] *adj* consigliabile

advise [əd'vaız] *vt* consigliare; **to ~ sb of sth** informare qn di qc; **to ~ sb against sth/against doing sth** sconsigliare qc a qn/a qn di fare qc; **adviser** *n* consigliere/a; (*in business*) consulente *m/f*, consigliere/a; **advisory** [-ərı] *adj* consultivo/a

advocate *n* ['ædvəkɪt] (*upholder*) sostenitore/trice; (*Law*) avvocato (difensore) ▷ *vt* ['ædvəkeɪt] propugnare

Aegean (Sea) [i:'dʒi:ən-] *n* (mare *m*) Egeo

aerial ['ɛərɪəl] *n* antenna ▷ *adj* aereo/a

aerobics [ɛə'rəubıks] *n* aerobica

aeroplane ['ɛərəpleɪn] (*BRIT*) *n* aeroplano

aerosol ['ɛərəsɔl] (*BRIT*) *n* aerosol *m inv*

affair [ə'fɛər] *n* affare *m*; (*also*: **love ~**) relazione *f* amorosa; **affairs** (*business*) affari

affect [ə'fɛkt] *vt* toccare; (*influence*) influire su, incidere su; (*feign*) fingere; **affected** *adj* affettato/a; **affection** [ə'fɛkʃən] *n* affetto; **affectionate** *adj* affettuoso/a

afflict [ə'flıkt] *vt* affliggere

affluent ['æfluənt] *adj* ricco/a; **the ~ society** la società del benessere

afford [ə'fɔːd] *vt* permettersi; (*provide*) fornire; **affordable** *adj* (che ha un prezzo) abbordabile

Afghanistan [æf'gænıstɑːn] *n* Afganistan *m*

afraid [ə'freıd] *adj* impaurito/a; **to be ~ of** aver paura di; **to be ~ of doing** *or* **to do** aver paura di fare; **to be ~ that** aver paura che; **I'm ~ so!** ho paura di sì!; **I'm ~ not** no, mi dispiace

Africa ['æfrıkə] *n* Africa; **African** *adj*, *n* africano/a; **African-American** *adj*, *n* afroamericano/a

after ['ɑːftər] *prep*, *adv* dopo ▷ *conj* dopo che; **what/who are you ~?** che/chi cerca?; **~ he left/having done** dopo che se ne fu andato/dopo aver fatto; **to name sb ~ sb** dare a qn il nome di qn; **it's twenty ~ eight** (*us*) sono le otto e venti; **to ask ~ sb** chiedere di qn; **~ you!** dopo di lei!; **~ all** dopo tutto; **after-effects** *npl* conseguenze *fpl*; (*of illness*) postumi *mpl*; **aftermath** *n* conseguenze *fpl*; **in the aftermath of** nel periodo dopo; **afternoon** *n* pomeriggio; **after-shave (lotion)** ['ɑːftʃəʃeɪv-] *n* dopobarba *m inv*; **aftersun** ['ɑːftəsʌn] *adj*: **aftersun (lotion/cream)** (lozione *f*/

crema) doposole *m inv*; **afterwards,** (*us*) **afterward** *adv* dopo

again [ə'gɛn] *adv* di nuovo; **to begin/see ~** ricominciare/rivedere; **not ... ~** non ... più; **~ and ~** ripetutamente

against [ə'gɛnst] *prep* contro

age [eıdʒ] *n* età *f inv* ▷ *vt*, *vi* invecchiare; **he is 20 years of ~** ha 20 anni; **~d 10** di 10 anni; **to come of ~** diventare maggiorenne; **it's been ages since ...** sono secoli che ...; **age group** *n* generazione *f*; **age limit** *n* limite *m* d'età

agency ['eɪdʒənsı] *n* agenzia

agenda [ə'dʒɛndə] *n* ordine *m* del giorno

agent ['eɪdʒənt] *n* agente *m*

aggravate ['ægrəveɪt] *vt* aggravare; (*annoy*) esasperare

aggression [ə'grɛʃən] *n* aggressione *f*

aggressive [ə'grɛsıv] *adj* aggressivo/a

agile ['ædʒaıl] *adj* agile

agitated ['ædʒıteɪtıd] *adj* agitato/a, turbato/a

AGM *n abbr* = **annual general meeting**

ago [ə'gəu] *adv*: **2 days ~** 2 giorni fa; **not long ~** poco tempo fa; **how long ~?** quanto tempo fa?

agony ['ægənı] *n* dolore *m* atroce; **I was in ~** avevo dei dolori atroci

agree [ə'griː] *vt* (*price*) pattuire ▷ *vi*: **to ~ (with)** essere d'accordo (con); (*Ling*) concordare (con); **to ~ to sth/to do sth** accettare qc/di fare qc; **to ~ that** (*admit*) ammettere che; **to ~ on sth** accordarsi su qc; **garlic doesn't ~ with me** l'aglio non mi va; **agreeable** *adj* gradevole; (*willing*) disposto/a; **agreed** *adj* (*time, place*) stabilito/a; **agreement** *n* accordo; **in agreement** d'accordo

agricultural [ægrı'kʌltʃərəl] *adj* agricolo/a

agriculture ['ægrıkʌltʃər] *n* agricoltura

ahead [ə'hɛd] *adv* avanti; davanti; **~ of** davanti a; (*fig: schedule etc*) in anticipo su; **~ of time** in anticipo; **go right** *or* **straight ~** tiri diritto

aid [eıd] *n* aiuto ▷ *vt* aiutare; **in ~ of** a favore di

aide [eıd] *n* (*person*) aiutante *m/f*

AIDS [eıdz] *n abbr* (= *acquired immune deficiency* or *immunodeficiency syndrome*) AIDS *f*

ailing ['eılıŋ] *adj* sofferente; (*fig: economy, industry etc*) in difficoltà

ailment ['eılmənt] *n* indisposizione *f*

aim [eım] *vt*: **to ~ sth at** (*gun*) mirare qc a, puntare qc a; (*camera, remark*) rivolgere qc a; (*missile*) lanciare qc contro ▷ *vi* (*also*: **take ~**) prendere la mira ▷ *n* mira; **to ~ at** mirare; **to ~ to do** aver l'intenzione di fare

ain't [eɪnt] (col) = **am not; aren't; isn't**

air [ɛəʳ] n aria ▷ vt (room, bed) arieggiare; (clothes) far prendere aria a; (idea, grievance) esprimere pubblicamente ▷ cpd (currents) d'aria; (attack) aereo/a; **to throw sth into the ~** lanciare qc in aria; **by ~** (travel) in aereo; **to be on the ~** (Radio, TV: programme) essere in onda; **airbag** n airbag m inv; **airbed** n (BRIT) materassino; **airborne** ['ɛəbɔːn] adj (plane) in volo; (troops) aerotrasportato/a; **as soon as the plane was airborne** appena l'aereo ebbe decollato; **air-conditioned** adj con or ad aria condizionata; **air conditioning** n condizionamento d'aria; **aircraft** n (pl inv) apparecchio; **airfield** n campo d'aviazione; **Air Force** n aviazione f militare; **air hostess** n (BRIT) hostess f inv; **airing cupboard** ['ɛərɪŋ-] n armadio riscaldato per asciugare panni; **airlift** n ponte m aereo; **airline** n linea aerea; **airliner** n aereo di linea; **airmail** n posta aerea; **by airmail** per via or posta aerea; **airplane** n (US) aeroplano; **airport** n aeroporto; **air raid** n incursione f aerea; **airsick** adj: **to be airsick** soffrire di mal d'aereo; **airspace** n spazio aereo; **airstrip** n pista d'atterraggio; **air terminal** n air-terminal m inv; **airtight** adj ermetico/a; **air traffic controller** n controllore m del traffico aereo; **airy** adj arioso/a; (manners) noncurante

aisle [aɪl] n (of church) navata laterale; navata centrale; (of plane) corridoio; **aisle seat** n (on plane) posto sul corridoio

ajar [ə'dʒɑːʳ] adj socchiuso/a

à la carte [ɑːlɑːˈkɑːt] adv alla carta

alarm [ə'lɑːm] n allarme m ▷ vt allarmare; **alarm call** n (in hotel etc) could I have an alarm call at 7 am, please? vorrei essere svegliato alle 7, per favore; **alarm clock** n sveglia; **alarmed** adj (person) allarmato/a; (house, car etc) dotato/a di allarme; **alarming** adj allarmante, preoccupante

Albania [æl'beɪnɪə] n Albania

albeit [ɔːl'biːɪt] conj sebbene + sub, benché + sub

album ['ælbəm] n album m inv

alcohol ['ælkəhɔl] n alcool m; **alcohol-free** adj analcolico/a; **alcoholic** [-'hɔlɪk] adj alcolico/a ▷ n alcolizzato/a

alcove ['ælkəuv] n alcova

ale [eɪl] n birra

alert [ə'lə:t] adj vigile ▷ n allarme m ▷ vt: **to ~ sb (to sth)** avvertire qn (di qc); **to ~ sb to the dangers of sth** mettere qn in guardia contro qc

algebra ['ældʒɪbrə] n algebra

Algeria [æl'dʒɪərɪə] n Algeria

alias ['eɪlɪəs] adv alias ▷ n pseudonimo, falso nome m

alibi ['ælɪbaɪ] n alibi m inv

alien ['eɪlɪən] n straniero/a; (extraterrestrial) alieno/a ▷ adj: **~ (to)** estraneo/a (a); **alienate** vt alienare

alight [ə'laɪt] adj acceso/a ▷ vi scendere; (bird) posarsi

align [ə'laɪn] vt allineare

alike [ə'laɪk] adj simile ▷ adv allo stesso modo; **to look ~** assomigliarsi

alive [ə'laɪv] adj vivo/a; (active) attivo/a

KEYWORD

all [ɔːl] adj tutto/a; **all day** tutto il giorno; **all night** tutta la notte; **all men** tutti gli uomini; **all five came** sono venuti tutti e cinque; **all the books** tutti i libri; **all the food** tutto il cibo; **all the time** tutto il tempo; (always) sempre; **all his life** tutta la vita

▷ pron **1** tutto/a; **I ate it all, I ate all of it** l'ho mangiato tutto; **all of us went** siamo andati; **all of the boys went** tutti i ragazzi sono andati

2 (in phrases): **above all** soprattutto; **after all** dopotutto; **at all: not at all** (in answer to question) niente affatto; (in answer to thanks) prego!, di niente!, s'immagini!; **I'm not at all tired** non sono affatto stanco; **anything at all will do** andrà bene qualsiasi cosa; **all in all** tutto sommato

▷ adv: **all alone** tutto/a solo/a; **it's not as hard as all that** non è poi così difficile; **all the more/the better** tanto più/meglio; **all but** quasi; **the score is two all** il punteggio è di due a due or è due pari

Allah ['ælə] n Allah m

allegation [ælɪ'geɪʃən] n asserzione f

alleged [ə'lɛdʒd] adj presunto/a; **allegedly** [ə'lɛdʒɪdlɪ] adv secondo quanto si asserisce

allegiance [ə'liːdʒəns] n fedeltà

allergic [ə'lə:dʒɪk] adj: **~ to** allergico/a a

allergy ['ælədʒɪ] n allergia

alleviate [ə'liːvɪeɪt] vt sollevare

alley ['ælɪ] n vicolo

alliance [ə'laɪəns] n alleanza

allied ['ælaɪd] adj alleato/a

alligator ['ælɪgeɪtəʳ] n alligatore m

all-in ['ɔːlɪn] adj, adv (BRIT: charge) tutto compreso

allocate ['æləkeɪt] vt: **to ~ sth to** assegnare qc a

allot [ə'lɔt] vt: **to ~ sth to** (duties) assegnare qc a

all-out ['ɔːlaut] adj (effort etc) totale ▷ adv: **to go all out for** mettercela tutta per

allow [ə'lau] vt (practice, behaviour) permettere; (sum to spend etc) accordare; (sum, time estimated) dare; (concede): **to ~ that** ammettere che; **to ~ sb to do** permettere a qn di fare; **he is ~ed to (do it)** lo può fare; **allow for** vt fus tener conto di; **allowance** n (money received) assegno; (for travelling, accommodation) indennità f inv; (Tax) detrazione f di imposta; **to make allowance(s) for** tener conto di

all right adv (feel, work) bene; (as answer) va bene

ally n ['ælaɪ] alleato

almighty [ɔ:l'maɪtɪ] adj onnipotente; (row etc) colossale

almond ['ɑ:mənd] n mandorla

almost ['ɔ:lməust] adv quasi

alone [ə'ləun] adj, adv solo/a; **to leave sb ~** lasciare qn in pace; **to leave sth ~** lasciare stare qc; **let ~ ...** figuriamoci poi ..., tanto meno ...

along [ə'lɔŋ] prep lungo ▷ adv: **is he coming ~?** viene con noi?; **he was hopping/limping ~** veniva saltellando/zoppicando; **~ with** insieme con; **all ~** (all the time) sempre, fin dall'inizio; **alongside** prep accanto a; lungo ▷ adv accanto

aloof [ə'lu:f] adj distaccato/a ▷ adv a distanza, in disparte; **to stand ~** tenersi a distanza or in disparte

aloud [ə'laud] adv ad alta voce

alphabet ['ælfəbɛt] n alfabeto

Alps [ælps] npl: **the ~** le Alpi

already [ɔ:l'rɛdɪ] adv già

alright [ɔ:l'raɪt] adv (BRIT) = **all right**

also ['ɔ:lsəu] adv anche

altar ['ɔltə²] n altare m

alter ['ɔltə²] vt, vi alterare; **alteration** [ɔltə'reɪʃən] n modificazione f, alterazione f; **alterations** (Sewing, Archit) modifiche fpl; **timetable subject to alteration** orario soggetto a variazioni

alternate adj [ɔl'tə:nɪt] alterno/a; (US: plan etc) alternativo/a ▷ vi ['ɔltə:neɪt]: **to ~ (with)** alternarsi (a); **on ~ days** ogni due giorni

alternative [ɔl'tə:nətɪv] adj alternativo/a ▷ n (choice) alternativa; **alternatively** adv come alternativa

although [ɔ:l'ðəu] conj benché + sub, sebbene + sub

altitude ['æltɪtju:d] n altitudine f

altogether [ɔ:ltə'gɛðə²] adv del tutto, completamente; (on the whole) tutto considerato; (in all) in tutto

aluminium [ælju'mɪnɪəm], (US) **aluminum** [ə'lu:mɪnəm] n alluminio

always ['ɔ:lweɪz] adv sempre

Alzheimer's ['æltshaɪməz] n (also: **~ disease**) morbo di Alzheimer

am [æm] vb see **be**

amalgamate [ə'mælgəmeɪt] vt amalgamare ▷ vi amalgamarsi

amass [ə'mæs] vt ammassare

amateur ['æmətə²] n dilettante m/f ▷ adj (Sport) dilettante

amaze [ə'meɪz] vt stupire; **amazed** adj sbalordito/a; **to be amazed (at)** essere sbalordito/a (da); **amazement** n stupore m; **amazing** adj sorprendente, sbalorditivo/a

Amazon ['æməzən] n (Mythology) Amazzone f; **the ~** il Rio delle Amazzoni ▷ cpd (basin, jungle) amazzonico/a

ambassador [æm'bæsədə²] n ambasciatore/trice

amber ['æmbə²] n ambra; **at ~** (BRIT Aut) giallo

ambiguous [æm'bɪgjuəs] adj ambiguo/a

ambition [æm'bɪʃən] n ambizione f; **ambitious** [æm'bɪʃəs] adj ambizioso/a

ambulance ['æmbjuləns] n ambulanza

ambush ['æmbuʃ] n imboscata

amen ['ɑ:'mɛn] excl così sia, amen

amend [ə'mɛnd] vt (law) emendare; (text) correggere; **to make ~s** fare ammenda; **amendment** n emendamento; correzione f

amenities [ə'mi:nɪtɪz] npl attrezzature fpl ricreative e culturali

America [ə'mɛrɪkə] n America; **American** adj, n americano/a; **American football** n (BRIT) football m americano

amicable ['æmɪkəbl] adj amichevole

amid(st) [ə'mɪd(st)] prep in mezzo a

ammunition [æmju'nɪʃən] n munizioni fpl

amnesty ['æmnɪstɪ] n amnistia; **to grant an ~ to** concedere l'amnistia a, amnistiare

among(st) [ə'mʌŋ(st)] prep fra, tra, in mezzo a

amount [ə'maunt] n somma; ammontare m; (quantity) quantità f inv ▷ vi: **to ~ to** (total) ammontare a; (be same as) essere come

amp(ère) ['æmp(ɛə²)] n ampere m inv

ample ['æmpl] adj ampio/a; spazioso/a; (enough): **this is ~** questo è più che sufficiente

amplifier ['æmplɪfaɪə²] n amplificatore m

amputate ['æmpjuteɪt] vt amputare

Amtrak ['æmtræk] (US) n società ferroviaria americana

amuse [ə'mju:z] vt divertire; **amusement** n divertimento; **amusement arcade** n sala giochi; **amusement park** n luna park m inv

amusing [ə'mju:zɪŋ] adj divertente

an [æn, ən, n] indef art see **a**

anaemia [ə'ni:mɪə] n anemia

anaemic [ə'ni:mɪk] adj anemico/a

anaesthetic [ænɪs'θɛtɪk] *adj* anestetico/a
▷ *n* anestetico

analog(ue) ['ænəlɔg] *adj* (*watch, computer*)
analogico/a

analogy [ə'nælədʒɪ] *n* analogia; **to draw
an ~ between** fare un'analogia tra

analyse, (us) **analyze** ['ænəlaɪz] *vt*
analizzare; **analysis** (*pl* **analyses**)
[ə'næləsɪs, -siːz] *n* analisi *f inv*; **analyst**
['ænəlɪst] *n* (*political analyst etc*) analista
m/f; (us) (psic)analista *m/f*

analyze ['ænəlaɪz] *vt* (us) = **analyse**

anarchy ['ænəkɪ] *n* anarchia

anatomy [ə'nætəmɪ] *n* anatomia

ancestor ['ænsɪstər] *n* antenato/a

anchor ['æŋkər] *n* ancora ▷ *vi* (*also:* **to
drop ~**) gettare l'ancora ▷ *vt* ancorare; **to
weigh ~** salpare or levare l'ancora

anchovy ['æntʃəvɪ] *n* acciuga

ancient ['eɪnʃənt] *adj* antico/a; (*person, car*)
vecchissimo/a

and [ænd] *conj* e (*often 'ed' before vowel*);
~ so on e così via; **try ~ come** cerca di
venire; **he talked ~ talked** non la finiva di
parlare; **better ~ better** sempre meglio

Andes ['ændiːz] *npl*: **the ~** le Ande

anemia *etc* [ə'niːmɪə] (us) = **anaemia** *etc*

anesthetic [ænɪs'θɛtɪk] (us)
= **anaesthetic**

angel ['eɪndʒəl] *n* angelo

anger ['æŋgər] *n* rabbia

angina [æn'dʒaɪnə] *n* angina pectoris

angle ['æŋgl] *n* angolo; **from their ~** dal
loro punto di vista

angler ['æŋglər] *n* pescatore *m* con la lenza

Anglican ['æŋglɪkən] *adj, n* anglicano/a

angling ['æŋglɪŋ] *n* pesca con la lenza

angrily ['æŋgrɪlɪ] *adv* con rabbia

angry ['æŋgrɪ] *adj* arrabbiato/a, furioso/a;
(*wound*) infiammato/a; **to be ~ with sb/at
sth** essere in collera con qn/per qc; **to get ~**
arrabbiarsi; **to make sb ~** fare arrabbiare qn

anguish ['æŋgwɪʃ] *n* angoscia

animal ['ænɪməl] *adj* animale ▷ *n*
animale *m*

animated ['ænɪmeɪtɪd] *adj* animato/a

animation [ænɪ'meɪʃən] *n* animazione *f*

aniseed ['ænɪsiːd] *n* semi *mpl* di anice

ankle ['æŋkl] *n* caviglia

annex *n* ['ænɛks] (brit: *also:* **~e**) edificio
annesso ▷ *vt* [ə'nɛks] annettere

anniversary [ænɪ'vəːsərɪ] *n* anniversario

announce [ə'naʊns] *vt* annunciare;
announcement *n* annuncio; (*letter, card*)
partecipazione *f*; **announcer** *n* (*Radio, TV:
between programmes*) annunciatore/trice;
(: *in a programme*) presentatore/trice

annoy [ə'nɔɪ] *vt* dare fastidio a; **don't get
~ed!** non irritarti!; **annoying** *adj* irritante

annual ['ænjuəl] *adj* annuale ▷ *n* (*Bot*)
pianta annua; (*book*) annuario; **annually**
adv annualmente

anonymous [ə'nɔnɪməs] *adj* anonimo/a

anorak ['ænəræk] *n* giacca a vento

anorexia [ænə'rɛksɪə] *n* (*Med: also:*
~ nervosa) anoressia

anorexic [ænə'rɛksɪk] *adj, n* anoressico/a

another [ə'nʌðər] *adj*: **~ book** (*one more*)
un altro libro, ancora un libro; (*a different
one*) un altro libro ▷ *pron* un altro (un'altra),
ancora uno/a; *see also* **one**

answer ['ɑːnsər] *n* risposta; soluzione *f*
▷ *vi* rispondere ▷ *vt* (*reply to*) rispondere a;
(*problem*) risolvere; (*prayer*) esaudire; **in ~
to your letter** in risposta alla sua lettera;
to ~ the phone rispondere (al telefono);
to ~ the bell rispondere al campanello; **to
~ the door** aprire la porta; **answer back**
vi ribattere; **answerphone** *n* (*esp brit*)
segreteria telefonica

ant [ænt] *n* formica

Antarctic [ænt'ɑːktɪk] *n*: **the ~**
l'Antartide *f*

antelope ['æntɪləʊp] *n* antilope *f*

antenatal ['æntɪ'neɪtl] *adj* prenatale

antenna (*pl* **antennae**) [æn'tɛnə, -niː] *n*
antenna

anthem ['ænθəm] *n*: **national ~** inno
nazionale

anthology [æn'θɔlədʒɪ] *n* antologia

anthrax ['ænθræks] *n* antrace *m*

anthropology [ænθrə'pɔlədʒɪ] *n*
antropologia

anti- ['æntɪ] *prefix* anti...; **antibiotic**
['æntɪbaɪ'ɔtɪk] *n* antibiotico; **antibody**
['æntɪbɔdɪ] *n* anticorpo

anticipate [æn'tɪsɪpeɪt] *vt* prevedere;
pregustare; (*wishes, request*) prevenire;
anticipation [æntɪsɪ'peɪʃən] *n*
anticipazione *f*; (*expectation*) aspettative *fpl*

anticlimax ['æntɪ'klaɪmæks] *n*: **it was
an ~** fu una completa delusione

anticlockwise ['æntɪ'klɔkwaɪz] *adj, adv* in
senso antiorario

antics ['æntɪks] *npl* buffonerie *fpl*

anti: antidote ['æntɪdəʊt] *n*
antidoto; **antifreeze** ['æntɪfriːz] *n*
anticongelante *m*; **anti-globalization**
[æntɪgləʊbəlaɪ'zeɪʃən] *n*
antiglobalizzazione *f*; **antihistamine**
[æntɪ'hɪstəmɪn] *n* antistaminico;
antiperspirant ['æntɪ'pəːspərənt] *adj*
antitraspirante

antique [æn'tiːk] *n* antichità *f inv* ▷ *adj*
antico/a; **antique shop** *n* negozio
d'antichità

antiseptic [æntɪ'sɛptɪk] *n* antisettico

antisocial ['æntɪ'səʊʃəl] *adj* asociale

antiviral [ænti'vaiərəl] adj (Med) antivirale
antivirus [ænti'vaiərəs] adj (Comput)
antivirus inv; **antivirus software** n
antivirus m inv
antlers ['æntləz] npl palchi mpl
anxiety [æŋ'zaiəti] n ansia; (keenness): ~ to
do smania di fare
anxious ['æŋkʃəs] adj ansioso/a,
inquieto/a; (worrying) angoscioso/a; (keen):
~ to do/that impaziente di fare/che + sub

🄚 KEYWORD

any ['ɛni] adj 1 (in questions etc): **have
you any butter?** hai del burro?, hai un po'
di burro?; **have you any children?** hai
bambini?; **if there are any tickets left** se
ci sono ancora (dei) biglietti, se c'è ancora
qualche biglietto
2 (with negative): **I haven't any money/
books** non ho soldi/libri
3 (no matter which) qualsiasi, qualunque;
choose any book you like scegli un libro
qualsiasi
4 (in phrases): **in any case** in ogni caso;
any day now da un giorno all'altro; **at
any moment** in qualsiasi momento, da
un momento all'altro; **at any rate** ad ogni
modo
▶ pron 1 (in questions, with negative): **have
you got any?** ne hai?; **can any of you sing?**
qualcuno di voi sa cantare?; **I haven't any
(of them)** non ne ho
2 (no matter which one(s)): **take any of those
books (you like)** prendi uno qualsiasi di
quei libri
▶ adv 1 (in questions etc): **do you want any
more soup/sandwiches?** vuoi ancora un
po' di minestra/degli altri panini?; **are you
feeling any better?** ti senti meglio?
2 (with negative): **I can't hear him any more**
non lo sento più; **don't wait any longer**
non aspettare più

anybody ['ɛnibɒdi] pron (in interrogative
sentences) qualcuno; (in negative sentences)
nessuno; (no matter who) chiunque; **can
you see ~?** vedi qualcuno or nessuno?; **if ~
should phone ...** se telefona qualcuno ...;
I don't see ~ non vedo nessuno; **~ could do
it** chiunque potrebbe farlo
anyhow ['ɛnihau] adv (at any rate) ad ogni
modo, comunque; (haphazard): **do it ~ you
like** fallo come ti pare; **I shall go ~** ci andrò
lo stesso or comunque; **she leaves things
just ~** lascia tutto come capita
anyone ['ɛniwʌn] pron = **anybody**
anything ['ɛniθiŋ] pron (in interrogative
sentences) qualcosa, niente; (with negative)

niente; **you can say ~ you like** (no matter
what) puoi dire quello che ti pare; **can
you see ~?** vedi niente or qualcosa?; **if ~
happens to me ...** se mi dovesse succedere
qualcosa ...; **I can't see ~** non vedo niente;
~ will do va bene qualsiasi cosa or tutto;
~ else? (in shop) basta (così)?; **it can cost
~ between £15 and £20** può costare
qualcosa come 15 o 20 sterline
anytime ['ɛnitaim] adv in qualunque
momento; quando vuole
anyway ['ɛniwei] adv (at any rate) ad ogni
modo, comunque; (besides) ad ogni modo
anywhere ['ɛniwɛər] adv (in interrogative
sentences) da qualche parte; (with negative)
da nessuna parte; (no matter where) da
qualsiasi or qualunque parte, dovunque;
can you see him ~? lo vedi da qualche
parte?; **I don't see him ~** non lo vedo da
nessuna parte; **~ in the world** dovunque
nel mondo
apart [ə'pɑːt] adv (to one side) a parte;
(separately) separatamente; **with one's
legs ~** con le gambe divaricate; **10 miles/a
long way ~** a 10 miglia di distanza/molto
lontani l'uno dall'altro; **to take ~** smontare;
~ from a parte, eccetto
apartment [ə'pɑːtmənt] n (US)
appartamento; (room) locale m;
apartment building n (US) stabile m,
caseggiato
apathy ['æpəθi] n apatia
ape [eip] n scimmia ▷ vt scimmiottare
aperitif [ə'pɛritiːf] n aperitivo
aperture ['æpətʃjuər] n apertura
APEX n abbr (= advance purchase excursion)
APEX m inv
apologize [ə'pɒlədʒaiz] vi: **to ~ (for sth to
sb)** scusarsi (di qc a qn), chiedere scusa (a
qn per qc)
apology [ə'pɒlədʒi] n scuse fpl
apostrophe [ə'pɒstrəfi] n (sign)
apostrofo
app n abbr (col: Comput) = **application**
applicazione f
appal, (US) **appall** [ə'pɔːl] vt atterrire;
sconvolgere; **appalling** adj spaventoso/a
apparatus [æpə'reitəs] n apparato; (in
gymnasium) attrezzatura
apparent [ə'pærənt] adj evidente;
apparently adv evidentemente
appeal [ə'piːl] vi (Law) appellarsi alla
legge ▷ n (Law) appello; (request) richiesta;
(charm) attrattiva; **to ~ for** chiedere (con
insistenza); **to ~ to** (person) appellarsi a;
(thing) piacere a; **it doesn't ~ to me** mi dice
poco; **appealing** adj (attractive) attraente
appear [ə'piər] vi apparire; (Law) comparire;
(publication) essere pubblicato/a; (seem)

sembrare; **it would ~ that** sembra che;
appearance n apparizione f; apparenza;
(look, aspect) aspetto
appendicitis [əpendɪˈsaɪtɪs] n
appendicite f
appendix (pl **appendices**) [əˈpɛndɪks, -siːz]
n appendice f
appetite [ˈæpɪtaɪt] n appetito
appetizer [ˈæpɪtaɪzəʳ] n stuzzichino
applaud [əˈplɔːd] vt, vi applaudire
applause [əˈplɔːz] n applauso
apple [ˈæpl] n mela; **apple pie** n torta di
mele
appliance [əˈplaɪəns] n apparecchio
applicable [əˈplɪkəbl] adj applicabile;
to be ~ to essere valido per; **the law is ~
from January** la legge entrerà in vigore in
gennaio
applicant [ˈæplɪkənt] n candidato/a
application [æplɪˈkeɪʃən] n applicazione
f; (for a job, a grant etc) domanda; (Comput)
applicazione f; **application form** n modulo
per la domanda
apply [əˈplaɪ] vt: **to ~ (to)** (paint, ointment)
dare (a); (theory, technique) applicare (a)
▷ vi: **to ~ to** (ask) rivolgersi a; (be suitable for,
relevant to) riguardare, riferirsi a; **to ~ (for)**
(permit, grant, job) fare domanda (per); **to ~
o.s. to** dedicarsi a
appoint [əˈpɔɪnt] vt nominare;
appointment n nomina; (arrangement
to meet) appuntamento; **to make
an appointment with sb** prendere
un appuntamento con qn; **I have
an appointment (with)** ... ho un
appuntamento (con) ...
appraisal [əˈpreɪzl] n valutazione f
appreciate [əˈpriːʃɪeɪt] vt (like) apprezzare;
(be grateful for) essere riconoscente di; (be
aware of) rendersi conto di ▷ vi (Comm)
aumentare; **I'd ~ your help** ti sono grato
per l'aiuto; **appreciation** [əpriːʃɪˈeɪʃən]
n apprezzamento; (Finance) aumento del
valore
apprehension [æprɪˈhɛnʃən] n (fear)
inquietudine f
apprehensive [æprɪˈhɛnsɪv] adj
apprensivo/a
apprentice [əˈprɛntɪs] n apprendista m/f
approach [əˈprəʊtʃ] vi avvicinarsi ▷ vt
(come near) avvicinarsi a; (ask, apply to)
rivolgersi a; (subject, passer-by) avvicinare
▷ n approccio; accesso; (to problem) modo
di affrontare
appropriate vt [əˈprəʊprieɪt] (take)
appropriarsi di ▷ adj [əˈprəʊpriɪt]
appropriato/a, adatto/a
approval [əˈpruːvəl] n approvazione f; **on ~**
(Comm) in prova, in esame

approve [əˈpruːv] vt, vi approvare;
approve of vt fus approvare
approximate adj [əˈprɒksɪmɪt]
approssimativo/a; **approximately** adv
circa
Apr. abbr (= April) apr.
apricot [ˈeɪprɪkɔt] n albicocca
April [ˈeɪprəl] n aprile m; **~ fool!** pesce
d'aprile!; **April Fools' Day** n vedi nota **"April
Fools' Day"**

<hr>

* **APRIL FOOLS' DAY**
*
* April Fools' Day è il primo aprile, il giorno
* degli scherzi e delle burle. Il nome deriva
* dal fatto che, se una persona cade nella
* trappola che gli è stata tesa, fa la figura
* del fool, cioè dello sciocco. Di recente gli
* scherzi stanno diventando sempre più
* elaborati, e persino i giornalisti a volte
* inventano vicende incredibili per burlarsi
* dei lettori.

apron [ˈeɪprən] n grembiule m
apt [æpt] adj (suitable) adatto/a; (able)
capace; (likely): **to be ~ to do** avere
tendenza a fare
aquarium [əˈkwɛərɪəm] n acquario
Aquarius [əˈkwɛərɪəs] n Acquario
Arab [ˈærəb] adj, n arabo/a
Arabia [əˈreɪbɪə] n Arabia; **Arabian**
[əˈreɪbɪən] adj arabo/a; **Arabic** [ˈærəbɪk]
adj arabico/a, arabo/a ▷ n arabo;
Arabic numerals npl numeri mpl arabi,
numerazione f araba
arbitrary [ˈɑːbɪtrərɪ] adj arbitrario/a
arbitration [ɑːbɪˈtreɪʃən] n (Law) arbitrato;
(Industry) arbitraggio
arc [ɑːk] n arco
arcade [ɑːˈkeɪd] n portico; (passage with
shops) galleria
arch [ɑːtʃ] n arco; (of foot) arco plantare ▷ vt
inarcare
archaeology [ɑːkɪˈɔlədʒɪ] n archeologia
archbishop [ɑːtʃˈbɪʃəp] n arcivescovo
archeology [ɑːkɪˈɔlədʒɪ] = **archaeology**
architect [ˈɑːkɪtɛkt] n architetto;
architectural [ɑːkɪˈtɛktʃərəl] adj
architettonico/a; **architecture**
[ˈɑːkɪtɛktʃəʳ] n architettura
archive [ˈɑːkaɪv] n (also Comput) archivio;
archives npl archivi mpl
Arctic [ˈɑːktɪk] adj artico/a ▷ n: **the ~**
l'Artico
are [ɑːʳ] vb see **be**
area [ˈɛərɪə] n (Geom) area; (zone) zona;
(: smaller) settore m; **area code** n (us Tel)
prefisso
arena [əˈriːnə] n arena

aren't [ɑ:nt] = **are not**

Argentina [ɑ:dʒən'ti:nə] n Argentina; **Argentinian** [-'tɪnɪən] adj, n argentino/a

arguably ['ɑ:gjuəblɪ] adv: **it is ~ ...** si può sostenere che sia ...

argue ['ɑ:gju:] vi (quarrel) litigare; (reason) ragionare; **to ~ that** sostenere che

argument ['ɑ:gjumənt] n (reasons) argomento; (quarrel) lite f

Aries ['ɛərɪz] n Ariete m

arise (pt **arose**, pp **arisen**) [ə'raɪz, ə'rəuz, ə'rɪzn] vi (opportunity, problem) presentarsi

arithmetic [ə'rɪθmətɪk] n aritmetica

arm [ɑ:m] n braccio ▷ vt armare; **~ in ~** a braccetto; see also **arms**; **armchair** n poltrona

armed [ɑ:md] adj armato/a; **armed robbery** n rapina a mano armata

armour, (US) **armor** ['ɑ:məʳ] n armatura; (Mil: tanks) mezzi mpl blindati

armpit ['ɑ:mpɪt] n ascella

armrest ['ɑ:mrest] n bracciolo

arms [ɑ:mz] npl (weapons) armi fpl

army ['ɑ:mɪ] n esercito

aroma [ə'rəumə] n aroma; **aromatherapy** n aromaterapia

arose [ə'rəuz] pt of **arise**

around [ə'raund] adv attorno, intorno ▷ prep intorno a; (fig: about): **~ £5/3 o'clock** circa 5 sterline/le 3; **is he ~?** è in giro?

arouse [ə'rauz] vt (sleeper) svegliare; (curiosity, passions) suscitare

arrange [ə'reɪndʒ] vt sistemare; (programme) preparare; **to ~ to do sth** mettersi d'accordo per fare qc; **arrangement** n sistemazione f; (agreement) accordo; **arrangements** npl (plans etc) progetti mpl, piani mpl

array [ə'reɪ] n: **~ of** fila di

arrears [ə'rɪəz] npl arretrati mpl; **to be in ~ with one's rent** essere in arretrato con l'affitto

arrest [ə'rest] vt arrestare; (sb's attention) attirare ▷ n arresto; **under ~** in arresto

arrival [ə'raɪvəl] n arrivo; (person) arrivato/a; **a new ~** un nuovo venuto; (baby) un neonato

arrive [ə'raɪv] vi arrivare; **arrive at** vt fus arrivare a

arrogance ['ærəgəns] n arroganza

arrogant ['ærəgənt] adj arrogante

arrow ['ærəu] n freccia

arse [ɑ:s] n (col!) culo (!)

arson ['ɑ:sn] n incendio doloso

art [ɑ:t] n arte f; (craft) mestiere m; see also **arts**; **art college** n scuola di belle arti

artery ['ɑ:tərɪ] n arteria

art gallery n galleria d'arte

arthritis [ɑ:'θraɪtɪs] n artrite f

artichoke ['ɑ:tɪtʃəuk] n carciofo; **Jerusalem ~** topinambur m inv

article ['ɑ:tɪkl] n articolo; **articles** npl (BRIT Law: training) contratto di tirocinio; **~s of clothing** indumenti mpl

articulate adj [ɑ:'tɪkjulɪt] (person) che si esprime forbitamente; (speech) articolato/a ▷ vi [ɑ:'tɪkjuleɪt] articolare

artificial [ɑ:tɪ'fɪʃəl] adj artificiale

artist ['ɑ:tɪst] n artista m/f; **artistic** [ɑ:'tɪstɪk] adj artistico/a

arts [ɑ:ts] npl (Scol) lettere fpl

art school n scuola d'arte

KEYWORD

as [æz] conj **1** (referring to time) mentre; **as the years went by** col passare degli anni; **he came in as I was leaving** arrivò mentre stavo uscendo; **as from tomorrow** da domani

2 (in comparisons): **as big as** grande come; **twice as big as** due volte più grande di; **as much/many as** tanto quanto/tanti quanti; **as soon as possible** prima possibile

3 (since, because) dal momento che, siccome

4 (referring to manner, way) come; **do as you wish** fa' come vuoi; **as she said** come ha detto lei

5 (concerning): **as for** or **to that** per quanto riguarda or quanto a quello

6: **as if** or **though** come se; **he looked as if he was ill** sembrava stare male; see also **long; such; well**

▶ prep: **he works as a driver** fa l'autista; **as chairman of the company, he ...** come presidente della compagnia, lui ...; **he gave me it as a present** me lo ha regalato

a.s.a.p. abbr (= as soon as possible) prima possibile

asbestos [æz'bestəs] n asbesto, amianto

ASBO n abbr (BRIT: = antisocial behaviour order) provvedimento restrittivo per comportamento antisociale

ascent [ə'sent] n salita

ash [æʃ] n (dust) cenere f; **~ (tree)** frassino

ashamed [ə'ʃeɪmd] adj vergognoso/a; **to be ~** vergognarsi di

ashore [ə'ʃɔ:ʳ] adv a terra

ashtray ['æʃtreɪ] n portacenere m

Ash Wednesday n Mercoledì m inv delle Ceneri

Asia ['eɪʃə] n Asia; **Asian** adj, n asiatico/a

aside [ə'saɪd] adv da parte ▷ n a parte m

ask [ɑ:sk] vt (question) domandare; (invite) invitare; **to ~ sb sth/sb to do sth** chiedere qc a qn/a qn di fare qc; **to ~ sb about sth** chiedere a qn di qc; **to ~ (sb) a question**

fare una domanda (a qn); **to ~ sb out to dinner** invitare qn a mangiare fuori; **ask for** vt fus chiedere; **it's just ~ing for trouble** or **for it** è proprio (come) andarsele a cercare

asleep [ə'sli:p] adj addormentato/a; **to be ~** dormire; **to fall ~** addormentarsi

AS level n abbr (= Advanced Subsidiary level) prima parte del diploma di studi superiori chiamato "A level"

asparagus [əs'pærəgəs] n asparagi mpl

aspect ['æspekt] n aspetto

aspiration [æspə'reɪʃən] n aspirazione f; **aspirations** npl aspirazioni fpl

aspire [əs'paɪə'] vi: **to ~** aspirare a

aspirin ['æsprɪn] n aspirina

ass [æs] n asino; (col) scemo/a; (us col!) culo (!)

assassin [ə'sæsɪn] n assassino; **assassinate** [ə'sæsɪneɪt] vt assassinare

assault [ə'sɔ:lt] n (Mil) assalto; (gen: attack) aggressione f ▷ vt assaltare; aggredire; (sexually) violentare

assemble [ə'sɛmbl] vt riunire; (Tech) montare ▷ vi riunirsi

assembly [ə'sɛmblɪ] n (meeting) assemblea; (construction) montaggio

assert [ə'sə:t] vt asserire; (insist on) far valere; **assertion** [ə'sə:ʃən] n asserzione f

assess [ə'sɛs] vt valutare; **assessment** n valutazione f

asset ['æsɛt] n vantaggio; **assets** npl (Comm: of individual) beni mpl; (: of company) attivo

assign [ə'saɪn] vt: **to ~ (to)** (task) assegnare (a); (resources) riservare (a); (cause, meaning) attribuire (a); **to ~ a date to sth** fissare la data di qc; **assignment** n compito

assist [ə'sɪst] vt assistere, aiutare; **assistance** n assistenza, aiuto; **assistant** n assistente m/f; (BRIT: also: **shop assistant**) commesso/a

associate adj [ə'səʊʃɪɪt] associato/a; (member) aggiunto/a ▷ n [ə'səʊʃɪɪt] collega m/f ▷ vt [ə'səʊʃɪeɪt] associare ▷ vi [ə'səʊʃɪeɪt]: **to ~ with sb** frequentare qn

association [əsəʊsɪ'eɪʃən] n associazione f

assorted [ə'sɔ:tɪd] adj assortito/a

assortment [ə'sɔ:tmənt] n assortimento

assume [ə'sju:m] vt supporre; (responsibilities etc) assumere; (attitude, name) prendere

assumption [ə'sʌmpʃən] n supposizione f, ipotesi f inv; (of power) assunzione f

assurance [ə'ʃuərəns] n assicurazione f; (self-confidence) fiducia in se stesso

assure [ə'ʃuə'] vt assicurare

asterisk ['æstərɪsk] n asterisco

asthma ['æsmə] n asma

astonish [ə'stɒnɪʃ] vt stupire; **astonished** adj stupito/a, sorpreso/a; **to be astonished (at)** essere stupito/a (da); **astonishing** adj sorprendente, stupefacente; **I find it astonishing that …** mi stupisce che …; **astonishment** n stupore m

astound [ə'staund] vt sbalordire

astray [ə'streɪ] adv: **to go ~** smarrirsi; **to lead ~** portare sulla cattiva strada

astrology [əs'trɒlədʒɪ] n astrologia

astronaut ['æstrənɔ:t] n astronauta m/f

astronomer [əs'trɒnəmə'] n astronomo/a

astronomical [æstrə'nɒmɪkl] adj astronomico/a

astronomy [əs'trɒnəmɪ] n astronomia

astute [əs'tju:t] adj astuto/a

asylum [ə'saɪləm] n asilo; (lunatic asylum) manicomio

KEYWORD

at [æt] prep **1** (referring to position, direction) a; **at the top** in cima; **at the desk** al banco, alla scrivania; **at home/school** a casa/scuola; **at the baker's** dal panettiere; **to look at sth** guardare qc; **to throw sth at sb** lanciare qc a qn

2 (referring to time) a; **at 4 o'clock** alle 4; **at night** di notte; **at Christmas** a Natale; **at times** a volte

3 (referring to rates, speed etc) a; **at £1 a kilo** a 1 sterlina al chilo; **two at a time** due alla volta, due per volta; **at 50 km/h** a 50 km/h

4 (referring to manner): **at a stroke** d'un solo colpo; **at peace** in pace

5 (referring to activity): **to be at work** essere al lavoro; **to play at cowboys** giocare ai cowboy; **to be good at sth/doing sth** essere bravo in qc/a fare qc

6 (referring to cause): **shocked/surprised/annoyed at sth** colpito da/sorpreso da/arrabbiato per qc; **I went at his suggestion** ci sono andato dietro suo consiglio n

▶ n (@ symbol) chiocciola

ate [eɪt] pt of **eat**

atheist ['eɪθɪɪst] n ateo/a

Athens ['æθɪnz] n Atene f

athlete ['æθli:t] n atleta m/f

athletic [æθ'lɛtɪk] adj atletico/a; **athletics** n atletica

Atlantic [ət'læntɪk] adj atlantico/a ▷ n: **the ~ (Ocean)** l'Atlantico, l'Oceano Atlantico

atlas ['ætləs] n atlante m

ATM abbr (= automated telling machine) (sportello) Bancomat® m inv

atmosphere ['ætməsfɪə'] n atmosfera

atom ['ætəm] n atomo; **atomic** [ə'tɒmɪk] adj atomico/a; **atom(ic) bomb** n bomba atomica

atrocity [ə'trɒsɪtɪ] n atrocità f inv

attach [ə'tætʃ] vt attaccare; (document, letter) allegare; (importance etc) attribuire; **to be ~ed to sb/sth** (to like) essere affezionato/a a qn/qc; **attachment** [ə'tætʃmənt] n (tool) accessorio; (love): **attachment (to)** affetto (per)

attack [ə'tæk] vt attaccare; (person) aggredire; (task etc) iniziare; (problem) affrontare ▷ n attacco; (also: **heart ~**) infarto; **attacker** n aggressore m

attain [ə'teɪn] vt (also: **~ to**) arrivare a, raggiungere

attempt [ə'tɛmpt] n tentativo ▷ vt tentare; **to make an ~ on sb's life** attentare alla vita di qn

attend [ə'tɛnd] vt frequentare; (meeting, talk) andare a; (patient) assistere; **attend to** vt fus (needs, affairs etc) prendersi cura di; (customer) occuparsi di; **attendance** n (being present) presenza; (people present) gente f presente; **attendant** n custode m/f; persona di servizio ▷ adj concomitante

> ▌ Be careful not to translate attend by the Italian word attendere.

attention [ə'tɛnʃən] n attenzione f; (Mil) attenti!; **for the ~ of** (Admin) per l'attenzione di

attic ['ætɪk] n soffitta

attitude ['ætɪtjuːd] n atteggiamento; (posture) posa

attorney [ə'tɜːnɪ] n (lawyer) avvocato; (having proxy) mandatario; **Attorney General** n (BRIT) Procuratore m Generale; (US) Ministro della Giustizia

attract [ə'trækt] vt attirare; **attraction** [ə'trækʃən] n (gen pl: pleasant things) attrattiva; (Physics, fig: towards sth) attrazione f; **attractive** adj attraente

attribute n ['ætrɪbjuːt] attributo ▷ vt [ə'trɪbjuːt]: **to ~ sth to** attribuire qc a

aubergine ['əʊbəʒiːn] n melanzana

auburn ['ɔːbən] adj tizianesco/a

auction ['ɔːkʃən] n (also: **sale by ~**) asta ▷ vt (also: **sell by ~**) vendere all'asta; (also: **put up for ~**) mettere all'asta

audible ['ɔːdɪbl] adj udibile

audience ['ɔːdɪəns] n (people) pubblico; spettatori mpl; ascoltatori mpl; (interview) udienza

audit ['ɔːdɪt] vt rivedere, verificare

audition [ɔː'dɪʃən] n audizione f

auditor ['ɔːdɪtəʳ] n revisore m

auditorium [ɔːdɪ'tɔːrɪəm] n sala, auditorio

Aug. abbr (= August) ago., ag.

August ['ɔːgəst] n agosto

aunt [ɑːnt] n zia; **auntie, aunty** ['ɑːntɪ] n zietta

au pair ['əʊ'pɛəʳ] n (also: **~ girl**) (ragazza f) alla pari inv

aura ['ɔːrə] n aura

austerity [ɒs'tɛrɪtɪ] n austerità f inv

Australia [ɒs'treɪlɪə] n Australia; **Australian** adj, n australiano/a

Austria ['ɒstrɪə] n Austria; **Austrian** adj, n austriaco/a

authentic [ɔː'θɛntɪk] adj autentico/a

author ['ɔːθəʳ] n autore/trice

authority [ɔː'θɒrɪtɪ] n autorità f inv; (permission) autorizzazione f; **the authorities** npl (government etc) le autorità

authorize ['ɔːθəraɪz] vt autorizzare

auto ['ɔːtəʊ] n (US) auto f inv; **autobiography** [ɔːtəbaɪ'ɒgrəfɪ] n autobiografia; **autograph** ['ɔːtəgrɑːf] n autografo ▷ vt firmare; **automatic** [ɔːtə'mætɪk] adj automatico/a ▷ n (gun) arma automatica; (car) automobile f con cambio automatico; (washing machine) lavatrice f automatica; **automatically** adv automaticamente; **automobile** ['ɔːtəməbiːl] n (US) automobile f; **autonomous** [ɔː'tɒnəməs] adj autonomo/a; **autonomy** [ɔː'tɒnəmɪ] n autonomia

autumn ['ɔːtəm] n autunno

auxiliary [ɔːg'zɪlɪərɪ] adj ausiliario/a ▷ n ausiliare m/f

avail [ə'veɪl] vt: **to ~ o.s. of** servirsi di; approfittarsi di ▷ n: **to no ~** inutilmente

availability [əveɪlə'bɪlɪtɪ] n disponibilità

available [ə'veɪləbl] adj disponibile

avalanche ['ævəlɑːnʃ] n valanga

Ave. abbr = **avenue**

avenue ['ævənjuː] n viale m; (fig) strada, via

average ['ævərɪdʒ] n media ▷ adj medio/a ▷ vt (also: **~ out at**) essere in media di; **on ~** in media

avert [ə'vɜːt] vt evitare, prevenire; (one's eyes) distogliere

avid ['ævɪd] adj (supporter etc) accanito/a

avocado [ævə'kɑːdəʊ] n (BRIT: also: **~ pear**) avocado m inv

avoid [ə'vɔɪd] vt evitare

await [ə'weɪt] vt aspettare

awake [ə'weɪk] (pt **awoke**, pp **awoken** or **awaked**) vt svegliare ▷ vi svegliarsi ▷ adj sveglio/a

award [ə'wɔːd] n premio; (Law) decreto; (sum) risarcimento ▷ vt assegnare; (Law: damages) decretare

aware [ə'wɛəʳ] adj: **~ of** (conscious) conscio/a di; (informed) informato/a di; **to become ~ of** accorgersi di; **awareness** n consapevolezza

away [ə'weɪ] *adj, adv* via; lontano/a; **two kilometres ~** a due chilometri di distanza; **two hours ~ by car** a due ore di distanza in macchina; **the holiday was two weeks ~** mancavano due settimane alle vacanze; **he's ~ for a week** è andato via per una settimana; **to take ~** portare via; **he was working/pedalling ~** lavorava/pedalava più che poteva; **to fade ~** scomparire

awe [ɔː] *n* timore *m*

awe-inspiring ['ɔːɪnspaɪərɪŋ], **awesome** ['ɔːsəm] *adj* imponente

awful ['ɔːfəl] *adj* terribile; **an ~ lot of** (*people, cars, dogs*) un numero incredibile di; (*jam, flowers*) una quantità incredibile di; **awfully** *adv* (*very*) terribilmente

awkward ['ɔːkwəd] *adj* (*clumsy*) goffo/a; (*inconvenient*) scomodo/a; (*embarrassing*) imbarazzante

awoke [ə'wəuk] *pt of* **awake**

awoken [ə'wəukən] *pp of* **awake**

axe, (*us*) **ax** [æks] *n* scure *f* ▷ *vt* (*project etc*) abolire; (*jobs*) sopprimere

axle ['æksl] *n* (*also*: **~-tree**) asse *m*

ay(e) [aɪ] *excl* (*yes*) sì

azalea [ə'zeɪlɪə] *n* azalea

b

B [biː] *n* (*Mus*) si *m*; **B road** *n* (*BRIT Aut*) ≈ strada secondaria

BA *n abbr* = **Bachelor of Arts**

baby ['beɪbɪ] *n* bambino/a; **baby carriage** *n* (*US*) carrozzina; **baby-sit** *vi* fare il (*or* la) babysitter; **baby-sitter** *n* baby-sitter *mf inv*; **baby wipe** *n* salvietta umidificata

bachelor ['bætʃələ*ʳ*] *n* scapolo; **B~ of Arts/Science (BA/BSc)** ≈ laureato/a in lettere/scienze

back [bæk] *n* (*of person, horse*) dorso, schiena; (*as opposed to front*) dietro; (*of hand*) dorso; (*of train*) coda; (*of chair*) schienale *m*; (*of page*) rovescio; (*of book*) retro; (*Football*) difensore *m* ▷ *vt* (*candidate*) appoggiare; (*horse: at races*) puntare su; (*car*) guidare a marcia indietro ▷ *vi* indietreggiare; (*car etc*) fare marcia indietro ▷ *adj* (*in compounds*) posteriore, di dietro ▷ *adv* (*not forward*) indietro; (*returned*): **he's ~** è tornato; **he ran ~** tornò indietro di corsa; **throw the ball ~** (*restitution*) ritira la palla; **can I have it ~?** posso riaverlo?; **he called ~** (*again*) ha richiamato; **~ seats/wheels** (*Aut*) sedili *mpl*/ruote *fpl* posteriori; **back down** *vi* (*fig*) fare marcia indietro; **back out** *vi* (*of promise*) tirarsi indietro; **back up** *vt* (*support*) appoggiare, sostenere; (*Comput*) fare una copia di riserva di; **backache** ['bækeɪk] *n* mal *m* di schiena; **backbencher** *n* (*BRIT*) parlamentare che non ha incarichi né al governo né all'opposizione; **backbone** *n* spina dorsale; **back door** *n* porta sul retro; **backfire** *vi* (*Aut*) dar ritorni di fiamma; (*plans*) fallire; **backgammon** *n* tavola reale; **background** *n* sfondo; (*of events*) background *m inv*; (*basic knowledge*) base *f*; (*experience*) esperienza; **family background** ambiente *m* familiare; **backing** *n* (*fig*) appoggio; **backlog** *n*:

backlog of work lavoro arretrato; **backpack** n zaino; **backpacker** n chi viaggia con zaino e sacco a pelo; **backslash** n backslash m inv, barra obliqua inversa; **backstage** adv nel retroscena; **backstroke** n nuoto sul dorso; **backup** adj (train, plane) supplementare; (Comput) di riserva ▷ n (support) appoggio, sostegno; (also: **backup file**) file m inv di riserva; **backward** adj (movement) indietro inv; (person) tardivo/a; (country) arretrato/a; **backwards** adv indietro; (fall, walk) all'indietro; **back yard** n cortile m sul retro

bacon ['beɪkən] n pancetta

bacteria [bæk'tɪərɪə] npl batteri mpl

bad [bæd] adj cattivo/a; (child) cattivello/a; (meat, food) andato/a a male; **his ~ leg** la sua gamba malata; **to go ~** andare a male

badge [bædʒ] n insegna; (of police officer) stemma m

badger ['bædʒəʳ] n tasso

badly ['bædlɪ] adv (work, dress etc) male; **~ wounded** gravemente ferito; **he needs it ~** ne ha gran bisogno

bad-mannered [bæd'mænəd] adj maleducato/a, sgarbato/a

badminton ['bædmɪntən] n badminton m

bad-tempered [bæd'tempəd] adj irritabile; (in bad mood) di malumore

bag [bæg] n sacco m; (handbag etc) borsa; **~s of** (col: lots of) un sacco di

baggage n bagagli mpl; **baggage allowance** n peso bagaglio consentito; **baggage claim, baggage reclaim** n ritiro m bagaglio inv

baggy adj largo/a, sformato/a

bagpipes npl cornamusa

bail [beɪl] n cauzione f ▷ vt (prisoner: also: **grant ~ to**) concedere la libertà provvisoria su cauzione a; (Naut: also: **~ out**) aggottare; **on ~** in libertà provvisoria su cauzione

bait [beɪt] n esca ▷ vt (hook) innescare; (trap) munire di esca; (fig) tormentare

bake [beɪk] vt cuocere al forno ▷ vi cuocersi al forno; **baked beans** [-biːnz] npl fagioli mpl in salsa di pomodoro; **baked potato** n patata (con la buccia) cotta al forno; **baker** n fornaio/a, panettiere/a; **bakery** n panetteria; **baking** n cottura (al forno); **baking powder** n lievito in polvere

balance ['bæləns] n equilibrio; (Comm: sum) bilancio; (remainder) resto; (scales) bilancia ▷ vt tenere in equilibrio; (budget) far quadrare; (account) pareggiare; (compensate) contrappesare; **~ of trade/ payments** bilancia commerciale/dei pagamenti; **balanced** adj (personality, diet) equilibrato/a; **balance sheet** n bilancio

balcony ['bælkənɪ] n balcone m; (in theatre) balconata

bald [bɔːld] adj calvo/a; (tyre) liscio/a

Balearics [bælɪ'ærɪks], **Balearic Islands** npl: **the ~** le Baleari fpl

ball [bɔːl] n palla; (football) pallone m; (for golf) pallina; (of wool, string) gomitolo; (dance) ballo; **to play ~ (with sb)** (fig) stare al gioco (di qn)

ballerina [bælə'riːnə] n ballerina

ballet ['bæleɪ] n balletto; **ballet dancer** n ballerino/a classico/a

balloon [bə'luːn] n pallone m

ballot ['bælət] n scrutinio

ball-point pen ['bɔːlpɔɪnt-] n penna a sfera

ballroom ['bɔːlrum] n sala da ballo

Baltic ['bɔːltɪk] adj, n: **the ~ Sea** il (mar) Baltico

bamboo [bæm'buː] n bambù m

ban [bæn] n interdizione f ▷ vt interdire

banana [bə'nɑːnə] n banana

band [bænd] n banda; (at a dance) orchestra; (Mil) fanfara

bandage ['bændɪdʒ] n benda, fascia

Band-Aid® ['bændeɪd] n (us) cerotto

B & B n abbr = **bed and breakfast**

bandit ['bændɪt] n bandito

bang [bæŋ] n (of door) lo sbattere; (blow) colpo ▷ vt battere (violentemente); (door) sbattere ▷ vi scoppiare; sbattere

Bangladesh [bɑːŋglə'deʃ] n Bangladesh m

bangle ['bæŋgl] n braccialetto

bangs [bæŋz] npl (us: fringe) frangia, frangetta

banish ['bænɪʃ] vt bandire

banister(s) ['bænɪstə(z)] n(pl) ringhiera

banjo ['bændʒəu] n (pl **banjoes** or **banjos**) banjo m inv

bank [bæŋk] n banca, banco; (of river, lake) riva, sponda; (of earth) banco ▷ vi (Aviat) inclinarsi in virata; **bank on** vt fus contare su; **bank account** n conto in banca; **bank balance** n saldo; **a healthy bank balance** un solido conto in banca; **bank card** n carta f assegni inv; **bank charges** npl (BRIT) spese fpl bancarie; **banker** n banchiere m; **bank holiday** n (BRIT) giorno di festa; vedi nota **"bank holiday"**; **banking** n attività bancaria; professione f di banchiere; **bank manager** n direttore m di banca; **banknote** n banconota

* **BANK HOLIDAY**

* Una bank holiday, in Gran Bretagna, è una
* giornata in cui le banche e molti negozi
* sono chiusi. Generalmente le bank holiday
* cadono di lunedì e molti ne approfittano
* per fare una breve vacanza fuori città.
* Di conseguenza, durante questi fine
* settimana lunghi ("bank holiday weekend")

* si verifica un notevole aumento del
* traffico sulle strade, negli aeroporti e
* nelle stazioni e molte località turistiche
* registrano il tutto esaurito.

bankrupt ['bæŋkrʌpt] *adj* fallito/a; **to go ~** fallire; **bankruptcy** *n* fallimento

bank statement *n* estratto conto

banner ['bænə'] *n* striscione *m*

bannister(s) ['bænɪstə(z)] *n(pl) see* **banister(s)**

banquet ['bæŋkwɪt] *n* banchetto

baptism ['bæptɪzəm] *n* battesimo

baptize [bæp'taɪz] *vt* battezzare

bar [bɑː'] *n (rod)* barra; *(of window etc)* sbarra; *(of chocolate)* tavoletta; *(fig)* ostacolo; restrizione *f*; *(pub)* bar *m inv*; *(counter)* banco; *(Mus)* battuta ▷ *vt (road, window)* sbarrare; *(person)* escludere; *(activity)* interdire; **~ of soap** saponetta; **the B~** *(Law)* l'Ordine *m* degli avvocati; **behind ~s** *(prisoner)* dietro le sbarre; **~ none** senza eccezione

barbaric [bɑː'bærɪk] *adj* barbarico/a

barbecue ['bɑːbɪkjuː] *n* barbecue *m inv*

barbed wire ['bɑːbd-] *n* filo spinato

barber ['bɑːbə'] *n* barbiere *m*; **barber's (shop)**, *(us)* **barber shop** *n* barbiere *m*

bar code *n* codice *m* a barre

bare [bɛə'] *adj* nudo/a ▷ *vt* scoprire, denudare; *(teeth)* mostrare; **the ~ essentials, the ~ necessities** lo stretto necessario; **barefoot** *adj, adv* scalzo/a; **barely** *adv* appena

bargain ['bɑːgɪn] *n (transaction)* contratto; *(good buy)* affare *m* ▷ *vi* contrattare; **into the ~** per giunta; **bargain for** *vt fus (col)*: **to ~ for sth** aspettarsi qc; **he got more than he ~ed for** gli è andata peggio di quel che si aspettasse

barge [bɑːdʒ] *n* chiatta; **barge in** *vi (walk in)* piombare dentro; *(interrupt talk)* intromettersi a sproposito

bark [bɑːk] *n (of tree)* corteccia; *(of dog)* abbaio ▷ *vi* abbaiare

barley ['bɑːlɪ] *n* orzo

barmaid ['bɑːmeɪd] *n* cameriera al banco

barman ['bɑːmən] *n (irreg)* barista *m*

barn [bɑːn] *n* granaio

barometer [bə'rɔmɪtə'] *n* barometro

baron ['bærən] *n* barone *m*; **baroness** *n* baronessa

barracks ['bærəks] *npl* caserma

barrage ['bærɑːʒ] *n (Mil, dam)* sbarramento; *(fig)* fiume *m*

barrel ['bærəl] *n* barile *m*; *(of gun)* canna

barren ['bærən] *adj* sterile; *(soil)* arido/a

barrette [bə'rɛt] *n (us)* fermaglio per capelli

barricade [bærɪ'keɪd] *n* barricata

barrier ['bærɪə'] *n* barriera

barring ['bɑːrɪŋ] *prep* salvo

barrister ['bærɪstə'] *n (brit)* avvocato/essa

barrow ['bærəu] *n (cart)* carriola

bartender ['bɑːtendə'] *n (us)* barista *m*

base [beɪs] *n* base *f* ▷ *adj* vile ▷ *vt*: **to ~ sth on** basare qc su

baseball ['beɪsbɔːl] *n* baseball *m*; **baseball cap** *n* berretto da baseball

basement ['beɪsmənt] *n* seminterrato; *(of shop)* piano interrato

bases ['beɪsiːz] *npl of* **basis**

bash [bæʃ] *vt (col)* picchiare

basic ['beɪsɪk] *adj (principles, precautions, rules)* elementare; **basically** ['beɪsɪklɪ] *adv* fondamentalmente, sostanzialmente; **basics** *npl*: **the basics** l'essenziale *m*

basil ['bæzl] *n* basilico

basin ['beɪsn] *n (vessel, also Geo)* bacino; *(also:* **wash~**) lavabo

basis *(pl* **bases)** ['beɪsɪs, -siːz] *n* base *f*; **on a part-time ~** part-time; **on a trial ~** in prova

basket ['bɑːskɪt] *n* cesta; *(smaller)* cestino; *(with handle)* paniere *m*; **basketball** *n* pallacanestro *f*

bass [beɪs] *n (Mus)* basso

bastard ['bɑːstəd] *n* bastardo/a; *(col!)* stronzo *(!)*

bat [bæt] *n* pipistrello; *(for baseball etc)* mazza; *(brit: for table tennis)* racchetta ▷ *vt*: **he didn't ~ an eyelid** non battè ciglio

batch [bætʃ] *n (of bread)* infornata; *(of papers)* cumulo

bath *(pl* **baths)** [bɑːθ, bɑːðz] *n* bagno; *(bathtub)* vasca da bagno ▷ *vt* far fare il bagno a; **to have a ~** fare un bagno; *see also* **baths**

bathe [beɪð] *vi* fare il bagno ▷ *vt (wound etc)* lavare

bathing ['beɪðɪŋ] *n* bagni *mpl*; **bathing costume**, *(us)* **bathing suit** *n* costume *m* da bagno

bath: bathrobe ['bɑːθrəub] *n* accappatoio; **bathroom** ['bɑːθrum] *n* stanza da bagno; **baths** [bɑːðz] *npl* bagni *mpl* pubblici; **bath towel** *n* asciugamano da bagno; **bathtub** *n* (vasca da) bagno

baton ['bætən] *n (Mus)* bacchetta; *(Athletics)* testimone *m*; *(club)* manganello

batter ['bætə'] *vt* battere ▷ *n* pastetta; **battered** *adj (hat)* sformato/a; *(pan)* ammaccato/a

battery ['bætərɪ] *n* batteria; *(of torch)* pila; **battery farming** *n* allevamento in batteria

battle ['bætl] *n* battaglia ▷ *vi* battagliare, lottare; **battlefield** *n* campo di battaglia

bay [beɪ] *n (of sea)* baia; **to hold sb at ~** tenere qn a bada

bazaar [bə'zɑːʳ] n bazar m inv; vendita di beneficenza

BBC n abbr = **British Broadcasting Corporation**

● **BBC**

● La BBC è l'azienda statale che fornisce il
● servizio radiofonico e televisivo in Gran
● Bretagna. Pur dovendo rispondere al
● Parlamento del proprio operato, la BBC
● non è soggetta al controllo dello stato
● per scelte e programmi, anche perché si
● autofinanzia con il ricavato dei canoni
● d'abbonamento. La BBC ha canali
● televisivi digitali e terrestri, oltre a diverse
● emittenti radiofoniche nazionali e locali.
● Fornisce un servizio di informazione
● internazionale, il "BBC World Service",
● trasmesso in tutto il mondo.

BC adv abbr (= before Christ) a.C.

 KEYWORD

be [biː] (pt **was**, **were**, pp **been**) aux vb
1 (with present participle, forming continuous tenses): **what are you doing?** che fai?, che stai facendo?; **they're coming tomorrow** vengono domani; **I've been waiting for her for hours** sono ore che l'aspetto
2 (with pp, forming passives) essere; **to be killed** essere or venire ucciso/a; **the box had been opened** la scatola era stata aperta; **the thief was nowhere to be seen** il ladro non si trovava da nessuna parte
3 (in tag questions): **it was fun, wasn't it?** è stato divertente, no?; **he's good-looking, isn't he?** è un bell'uomo, vero?; **she's back, is she?** così è tornata, eh?
4 (+ to + infinitive): **the house is to be sold** abbiamo (or hanno etc) intenzione di vendere casa; **you're to be congratulated for all your work** dovremo farvi i complimenti per tutto il vostro lavoro; **he's not to open it** non deve aprirlo
▶ vb + complement **1** (gen) essere; **I'm English** sono inglese; **I'm tired** sono stanco/a; **I'm hot/cold** ho caldo/freddo; **he's a doctor** è medico; **2 and 2 are 4** 2 più 2 fa 4; **be careful!** sta attento/a!; **be good** sii buono/a
2 (of health) stare; **how are you?** come sta?; **he's very ill** sta molto male
3 (of age): **how old are you?** quanti anni hai?; **I'm sixteen (years old)** ho sedici anni
4 (cost) costare; **how much was the meal?** quant'era or quanto costava il pranzo?;

that'll be £5, please (sono) 5 sterline, per favore
▶ vi **1** (exist, occur etc) essere, esistere; **the best singer that ever was** il migliore cantante mai esistito or di tutti tempi; **be that as it may** comunque sia, sia come sia; **so be it** sia pure, e sia
2 (referring to place) essere, trovarsi; **I won't be here tomorrow** non ci sarò domani; **Edinburgh is in Scotland** Edimburgo si trova in Scozia
3 (referring to movement): **where have you been?** dove sei stato?; **I've been to China** sono stato in Cina
▶ impers vb **1** (referring to time, distance) essere; **it's 5 o'clock** sono le 5; **it's the 28th of April** è il 28 aprile; **it's 10 km to the village** di qui al paese sono 10 km
2 (referring to the weather) fare; **it's too hot/cold** fa troppo caldo/freddo; **it's windy** c'è vento
3 (emphatic): **it's me** sono io; **it was Maria who paid the bill** è stata Maria che ha pagato il conto

beach [biːtʃ] n spiaggia ▷ vt tirare in secco
beacon ['biːkən] n (lighthouse) faro; (marker) segnale m
bead [biːd] n perlina; **beads** npl (necklace) collana
beak [biːk] n becco
beam [biːm] n trave f; (of light) raggio ▷ vi brillare
bean [biːn] n fagiolo; (coffee bean) chicco; **runner ~** fagiolino; **beansprouts** npl germogli mpl di soia
bear [bɛəʳ] (pt **bore**, pp **borne**) n orso ▷ vt portare; (produce) generare; (endure) sopportare ▷ vi: **to ~ right/left** piegare a destra/sinistra
beard [biəd] n barba
bearer ['bɛərəʳ] n portatore m
bearing ['bɛərɪŋ] n portamento; (connection) rapporto; **bearings** npl (also: **ball ~s**) cuscinetti mpl a sfere; **to take a ~** fare un rilevamento; **to find one's ~s** orientarsi
beast [biːst] n bestia
beat [biːt] n colpo; (of heart) battito; (Mus) tempo, battuta; (of police officer) giro ▷ vt (pt **beat**, pp **beaten**) battere; (eggs, cream) sbattere; **off the ~en track** fuori mano; **~ it!** (col) fila!, fuori dai piedi!; **beat up** vt (col: person) picchiare; (eggs) sbattere; **beating** n botte fpl
beautiful ['bjuːtɪful] adj bello/a; **beautifully** adv splendidamente
beauty ['bjuːtɪ] n bellezza; **beauty parlour** [-'pɑːləʳ], (US) **beauty parlor** n salone

m di bellezza; **beauty salon** *n* istituto di bellezza; **beauty spot** *n* (BRIT Tourism) luogo pittoresco

beaver ['bi:vəʳ] *n* castoro

became [bɪ'keɪm] *pt of* **become**

because [bɪ'kɒz] *conj* perché; **~ of** a causa di

beckon ['bɛkən] *vt* (also: **~ to**) chiamare con un cenno

become [bɪ'kʌm] *vt* (irreg: like **come**) diventare; **to ~ fat/thin** ingrassarsi/dimagrire

bed [bɛd] *n* letto; (of flowers) aiuola; (of coal, clay) strato; **bed and breakfast** *n* (terms) camera con colazione; (place) ≈ pensione *f* familiare; vedi nota **"bed and breakfast (B & B)"**; **bedclothes** ['bɛdkləʊðz] *npl* coperte *fpl* e lenzuola *fpl*; **bedding** *n* coperte e lenzuola *fpl*; **bed linen** *n* biancheria da letto; **bedroom** *n* camera da letto; **bedside** *n*: **at sb's bedside** al capezzale di qn; **bedside lamp** *n* lampada da comodino; **bedside table** *n* comodino; **bedsit(ter)** ['bɛdsɪt(əʳ)] *n* (BRIT) monolocale *m*; **bedspread** *n* copriletto; **bedtime** *n*: **it's bedtime** è ora di andare a letto

BED AND BREAKFAST (B & B)

I bed and breakfasts, anche B & Bs, sono piccole pensioni a conduzione familiare, in case private o fattorie, dove si affittano camere e viene servita al mattino la tradizionale colazione all'inglese. Queste pensioni offrono un servizio di camera con prima colazione, appunto bed and breakfast, a prezzi più contenuti rispetto agli alberghi.

bee [bi:] *n* ape *f*

beech [bi:tʃ] *n* faggio

beef [bi:f] *n* manzo; **roast ~** arrosto di manzo; **beefburger** *n* hamburger *m inv*; **Beefeater** *n* guardia della Torre di Londra

been [bi:n] *pp of* **be**

beer [bɪəʳ] *n* birra; **beer garden** *n* (BRIT) giardino (di pub)

beet [bi:t] *n* (US) (also: **red ~**) barbabietola rossa

beetle ['bi:tl] *n* scarafaggio; coleottero

beetroot ['bi:tru:t] *n* (BRIT) barbabietola

before [bɪ'fɔːʳ] *prep* (in time) prima di; (in space) davanti a ▷ *conj* prima che + sub; prima di ▷ *adv* prima; **~ going** prima di andare; **~ she goes** prima che vada; **the week ~** la settimana prima; **I've seen it ~** l'ho già visto; **I've never seen it ~** è la prima volta che lo vedo; **beforehand** *adv* in anticipo

beg [bɛg] *vi* chiedere l'elemosina ▷ *vt* (also: **~ for**) chiedere in elemosina; (favour) chiedere; **to ~ sb to do** pregare qn di fare

began [bɪ'gæn] *pt of* **begin**

beggar ['bɛgəʳ] *n* mendicante *m/f*

begin (*pt* **began**, *pp* **begun**) [bɪ'gɪn, bɪ'gæn, bɪ'gʌn] *vt*, *vi* cominciare; **to ~ doing** or **to do sth** incominciare or iniziare a fare qc; **beginner** *n* principiante *m/f*; **beginning** *n* inizio, principio

begun [bɪ'gʌn] *pp of* **begin**

behalf [bɪ'hɑːf] *n*: **on ~ of** per conto di; a nome di

behave [bɪ'heɪv] *vi* comportarsi; (well: also: **~ o.s.**) comportarsi bene; **behaviour**, (US) **behavior** [bɪ'heɪvjəʳ] *n* comportamento, condotta

behind [bɪ'haɪnd] *prep* dietro; (followed by pronoun) dietro di; (time) in ritardo con ▷ *adv* dietro; (leave, stay) indietro ▷ *n* didietro; **~ the scenes** dietro le quinte; **to be ~ (schedule) with sth** essere indietro con qc

beige [beɪʒ] *adj* beige *inv*

Beijing [beɪ'dʒɪŋ] *n* Pechino *f*

being ['bi:ɪŋ] *n* essere *m*

belated [bɪ'leɪtɪd] *adj* tardo/a

belch [bɛltʃ] *vi* ruttare ▷ *vt* (gen: also: **~ out**: smoke etc) eruttare

Belgian ['bɛldʒən] *adj*, *n* belga *m/f*

Belgium ['bɛldʒəm] *n* Belgio

belief [bɪ'li:f] *n* (opinion) opinione *f*, convinzione *f*; (trust, faith) fede *f*

believe [bɪ'li:v] *vt*, *vi* credere; **to ~ in** (God) credere in; (ghosts) credere a; (method) avere fiducia in; **believer** *n* (Rel) credente *m/f*; (in idea, activity): **to be a believer in** credere in

bell [bɛl] *n* campana; (small, on door, electric) campanello

bellboy ['bɛlbɔɪ], (US) **bellhop** ['bɛlhɒp] *n* ragazzo d'albergo, fattorino d'albergo

bellow ['bɛləʊ] *vi* muggire

bell pepper (esp US) *n* peperone *m*

belly ['bɛlɪ] *n* pancia; **bellybutton** *n* ombelico

belong [bɪ'lɒŋ] *vi*: **to ~ to** appartenere a; (club etc) essere socio di; **this book ~s here** questo libro va qui; **belongings** *npl* cose *fpl*, roba

beloved [bɪ'lʌvɪd] *adj* adorato/a

below [bɪ'ləʊ] *prep* sotto, al di sotto di ▷ *adv* sotto, di sotto; giù; **see ~** vedi sotto or oltre

belt [bɛlt] *n* cintura; (Tech) cinghia ▷ *vt* (thrash) picchiare ▷ *vi* (col) filarsela; **beltway** *n* (US: Aut: ring road) circonvallazione *f*; (: motorway) autostrada

bemused [bɪ'mju:zd] *adj* perplesso/a, stupito/a

bench [bɛntʃ] *n* panca; (in workshop, Pol) banco; **the B~** (Law) la Corte

bend [bɛnd] (pt, pp **bent**) vt curvare; (leg, arm) piegare ▷ vi curvarsi; piegarsi ▷ n (in road) curva; (in pipe, river) gomito; **bend down** vi chinarsi; **bend over** vi piegarsi

beneath [bɪˈniːθ] prep sotto, al di sotto di; (unworthy of) indegno/a di ▷ adv sotto, di sotto

beneficial [bɛnɪˈfɪʃəl] adj che fa bene; vantaggioso/a

benefit ['bɛnɪfɪt] n beneficio, vantaggio; (allowance of money) indennità f inv ▷ vt far bene a ▷ vi: **he'll ~ from it** ne trarrà beneficio or profitto

benign [bɪˈnaɪn] adj (person, smile) benevolo/a; (Med) benigno/a

bent [bɛnt] pt, pp of **bend** ▷ n inclinazione f ▷ adj (col: dishonest) losco/a; **to be ~ on** essere deciso/a a

bereaved [bɪˈriːvd] npl: **the ~** i familiari in lutto

beret ['bɛreɪ] n berretto

Berlin [bɜːˈlɪn] n Berlino f

Bermuda [bɜːˈmjuːdə] n le Bermude

berry ['bɛrɪ] n bacca

berth [bɜːθ] n (bed) cuccetta; (for ship) ormeggio ▷ vi (in harbour) entrare in porto; (at anchor) gettare l'ancora

beside [bɪˈsaɪd] prep accanto a; **to be ~ o.s. (with anger)** essere fuori di sé; **that's ~ the point** non c'entra; **besides** [bɪˈsaɪdz] adv inoltre, per di più ▷ prep oltre a; (except) a parte

best [bɛst] adj migliore ▷ adv meglio; **the ~ part of** (quantity) la maggior parte di; **at ~** tutt'al più; **to make the ~ of sth** cavare il meglio possibile da qc; **to do one's ~** fare del proprio meglio; **to the ~ of my knowledge** per quel che ne so; **to the ~ of my ability** al massimo delle mie capacità; **best-before date** n (Comm): **"best-before date: ..."** da consumarsi preferibilmente entro il...; **best man** n (irreg) testimone m dello sposo; **bestseller** n bestseller m inv

bet [bɛt] n scommessa ▷ vt, vi (pt, pp **bet** or **betted**) scommettere; **to ~ sb sth** scommettere qc con qn

betray [bɪˈtreɪ] vt tradire

better ['bɛtə*] adj migliore ▷ adv meglio ▷ vt migliorare ▷ n: **to get the ~ of** avere la meglio su; **you had ~ do it** è meglio che lo faccia; **he thought ~ of it** cambiò idea; **to get ~** migliorare

betting ['bɛtɪŋ] n scommesse fpl; **betting shop** n (BRIT) ufficio dell'allibratore

between [bɪˈtwiːn] prep tra ▷ adv in mezzo, nel mezzo

beverage ['bɛvərɪdʒ] n bevanda

beware [bɪˈwɛə*] vt, vi: **to ~ (of)** stare attento/a (a); **"~ of the dog"** "attenti al cane"

bewildered [bɪˈwɪldəd] adj sconcertato/a, confuso/a

beyond [bɪˈjɔnd] prep (in space) oltre; (exceeding) al di sopra di ▷ adv di là; **~ doubt** senza dubbio; **~ repair** irreparabile

bias ['baɪəs] n (prejudice) pregiudizio; (preference) preferenza; **bias(s)ed** adj parziale

bib [bɪb] n bavaglino

Bible ['baɪbl] n Bibbia

bicarbonate of soda [baɪˈkɑːbənɪt-] n bicarbonato (di sodio)

biceps ['baɪsɛps] n bicipite m

bicycle ['baɪsɪkl] n bicicletta; **bicycle pump** n pompa della bicicletta

bid [bɪd] (pt **bade** or **bid**, pp **bidden** or **bid**) n offerta; (attempt) tentativo ▷ vi fare un'offerta ▷ vt fare un'offerta di; **to ~ sb good day** dire buon giorno a qn; **bidder** n: **the highest bidder** il maggior offerente

bidet ['biːdeɪ] n bidè m inv

big [bɪg] adj grande; grosso/a; **Big Apple** n vedi nota **"Big Apple"**; **bigheaded** ['bɪgˈhɛdɪd] adj presuntuoso/a; **big toe** n alluce m

⬤ BIG APPLE

⬤ Tutti sanno che The Big Apple, la Grande
⬤ Mela, è New York ("apple" in gergo
⬤ significa grande città), ma sicuramente
⬤ i soprannomi di altre città americane
⬤ non sono così conosciuti. Chicago è
⬤ soprannominata "theWindy City" perché
⬤ è ventosa, New Orleans si chiama "the
⬤ Big Easy" per il modo di vivere tranquillo
⬤ e rilassato dei suoi abitanti, e l'industria
⬤ automobilistica ha fatto sì che Detroit
⬤ fosse soprannominata "Motown".

bike [baɪk] n bici f inv; **bike lane** n pista ciclabile

bikini [bɪˈkiːnɪ] n bikini m inv

bilateral [baɪˈlætərl] adj bilaterale

bilingual [baɪˈlɪŋgwəl] adj bilingue

bill [bɪl] n conto; (Pol) atto; (us: banknote) banconota; (of bird) becco; (of show) locandina; **may I have the ~ please?** posso avere il conto per piacere?; **"stick or post no ~s"** "divieto di affissione"; **to fit or fill the ~** (fig) fare al caso; **billboard** n tabellone m; **billfold** ['bɪlfəʊld] n (us) portafoglio

billiards ['bɪljədz] n biliardo

billion ['bɪljən] n (BRIT) bilione m; (us) miliardo

bin [bɪn] n (for coal, rubbish) bidone m; (for bread) cassetta; (BRIT: also: **dust~**) pattumiera; (: also: **litter ~**) cestino

bind (*pt, pp* **bound**) [baɪnd, baund] *vt* legare; (*oblige*) obbligare ▷ *n* (*col*) scocciatura

binge [bɪndʒ] *n* (*col*): **to go on a ~** fare baldoria; **binge drinker** *n* persona che di norma beve troppo

bingo ['bɪŋgəu] *n* gioco simile alla tombola

binoculars [bɪ'nɔkjuləz] *npl* binocolo

bio... [baɪə...] *prefix* bio; **biochemistry** [baɪəu'kemɪstrɪ] *n* biochimica; **biodegradable** ['baɪəudɪ'greɪdəbl] *adj* biodegradabile; **biofuel** ['baɪəufjuəl] *n* biocarburante; **biography** [baɪ'ɔgrəfɪ] *n* biografia; **biological** *adj* biologico/a; **biology** [baɪ'ɔlədʒɪ] *n* biologia; **biometric** [baɪəu'mɛtrɪk] *adj* biometrico/a

bipolar [baɪ'pəulə^r] *adj* bipolare

birch [bə:tʃ] *n* betulla

bird [bə:d] *n* uccello; (BRIT *col: girl*) bambola; **bird flu** *n* influenza aviaria; **bird of prey** *n* (uccello) rapace *m*; **birdwatching** *n* birdwatching *m*

Biro® ['baɪrəu] *n* biro® *f inv*

birth [bə:θ] *n* nascita; **to give ~ to** dare alla luce, partorire; **birth certificate** *n* certificato di nascita; **birth control** *n* controllo delle nascite; contraccezione *f*; **birthday** *n* compleanno ▷ *cpd* di compleanno; **birthmark** *n* voglia; **birthplace** *n* luogo di nascita

biscuit ['bɪskɪt] *n* (BRIT) biscotto

bishop ['bɪʃəp] *n* vescovo

bistro ['bi:strəu] *n* bistrò *m inv*

bit [bɪt] *pt of* **bite** ▷ *n* pezzo; (*of horse*) morso; (*Comput*) bit *m inv*; **a ~ of** un po' di; **a ~ mad/dangerous** un po' matto/ pericoloso; **~ by ~** a poco a poco

bitch [bɪtʃ] *n* (*dog*) cagna; (*col!*) puttana (!)

bite [baɪt] *vt, vi* (*pt* **bit**, *pp* **bitten**) mordere; (*insect*) pungere ▷ *n* morso; (*insect bite*) puntura; (*mouthful*) boccone *m*; **let's have a ~ to eat** mangiamo un boccone; **to ~ one's nails** mangiarsi le unghie

bitten ['bɪtn] *pp of* **bite**

bitter ['bɪtə^r] *adj* amaro/a; (*wind, criticism*) pungente ▷ *n* (BRIT: *beer*) birra amara

bizarre [bɪ'zɑ:^r] *adj* bizzarro/a

black [blæk] *adj* nero/a ▷ *n* nero ▷ *vt* (BRIT *Industry*) boicottare; **~ coffee** caffè *m inv* nero; **to give sb a ~ eye** fare un occhio nero a qn; **in the ~** (*in credit*) in attivo; **black out** *vi* (*faint*) svenire; **blackberry** *n* mora; **blackbird** *n* merlo; **blackboard** *n* lavagna; **blackcurrant** *n* ribes *m inv*; **black ice** *n* strato trasparente di ghiaccio; **blackmail** *n* ricatto ▷ *vt* ricattare; **black market** *n* mercato nero; **blackout** *n* oscuramento; (*fainting*) svenimento; (*TV*) interruzione *f* delle trasmissioni; **black pepper** *n* pepe *m*

nero; **black pudding** *n* sanguinaccio; **Black Sea** *n*: **the Black Sea** il mar Nero

bladder ['blædə^r] *n* vescica

blade [bleɪd] *n* lama; (*of oar*) pala; **~ of grass** filo d'erba

blame [bleɪm] *n* colpa ▷ *vt*: **to ~ sb/sth for sth** dare la colpa di qc a qn/qc; **who's to ~?** chi è colpevole?

bland [blænd] *adj* mite; (*taste*) blando/a

blank [blæŋk] *adj* bianco/a; (*look*) distratto/a ▷ *n* spazio vuoto; (*cartridge*) cartuccia a salve

blanket ['blæŋkɪt] *n* coperta

blast [blɑ:st] *n* (*of wind*) raffica; (*bomb blast*) esplosione *f* ▷ *vt* far saltare

blatant ['bleɪtənt] *adj* flagrante

blaze [bleɪz] *n* (*fire*) incendio; (*fig*) vampata; splendore *m* ▷ *vi* (*fire*) ardere, fiammeggiare; (*guns*) sparare senza sosta; (*fig: eyes*) ardere ▷ *vt*: **to ~ a trail** (*fig*) tracciare una via nuova; **in a ~ of publicity** circondato da grande pubblicità

blazer ['bleɪzə^r] *n* blazer *m inv*

bleach [bli:tʃ] *n* (*also*: **household ~**) varechina ▷ *vt* (*material*) candeggiare; **bleachers** *npl* (US *Sport*) posti *mpl* di gradinata

bleak [bli:k] *adj* tetro/a

bled [blɛd] *pt, pp of* **bleed**

bleed (*pt, pp* **bled**) [bli:d, blɛd] *vi* sanguinare; **my nose is ~ing** mi viene fuori sangue dal naso

blemish ['blɛmɪʃ] *n* macchia

blend [blɛnd] *n* miscela ▷ *vt* mescolare ▷ *vi* (*colours etc: also*: **~ in**) armonizzare; **blender** *n* (*Culin*) frullatore *m*

bless (*pt, pp* **blessed** *or* **blest**) [blɛs, blɛst] *vt* benedire; **~ you!** (*sneezing*) salute!; **blessing** *n* benedizione *f*; fortuna

blew [blu:] *pt of* **blow**

blight [blaɪt] *vt* (*hopes etc*) deludere; (*life*) rovinare

blind [blaɪnd] *adj* cieco/a ▷ *n* (*for window*) avvolgibile *m*; (*Venetian blind*) veneziana ▷ *vt* accecare; **~ people** i ciechi; **blind alley** *n* vicolo cieco; **blindfold** *n* benda ▷ *adj, adv* bendato/a ▷ *vt* bendare gli occhi a

blink [blɪŋk] *vi* battere gli occhi; (*light*) lampeggiare

bliss [blɪs] *n* estasi *f*

blister ['blɪstə^r] *n* (*on skin*) vescica; (*on paintwork*) bolla ▷ *vi* (*paint*) coprirsi di bolle

blizzard ['blɪzəd] *n* bufera di neve

bloated ['bləutɪd] *adj* gonfio/a

blob [blɔb] *n* (*drop*) goccia; (*stain, spot*) macchia

block [blɔk] *n* blocco; (*in pipes*) ingombro; (*toy*) cubo; (*of buildings*) isolato ▷ *vt* bloccare; **the sink is ~ed** il lavandino è otturato; **block up** vt bloccare; (pipe) ingorgare, intasare; **blockade** [blɔ'keɪd] n blocco; **blockage** n ostacolo; **blockbuster** n grande successo; **block capitals** npl stampatello; **block letters** npl stampatello

blog [blɒg] n blog m inv ▷ vi scrivere blog, bloggare

blogger [blɒgəʳ] n (Comput) blogger mf inv

blogging [ˈblɒgɪŋ] n blogging m ▷ adj: ~ **website** sito di blogging

blogosphere [ˈblɒgəsfɪəʳ] n blogosfera

bloke [bləuk] n (BRIT col) tizio

blond(e) [blɒnd] n ▷ adj biondo/a

blood [blʌd] n sangue m; **blood donor** n donatore/trice di sangue; **blood group** n gruppo sanguigno; **blood poisoning** n setticemia; **blood pressure** n pressione f sanguigna; **bloodshed** n spargimento di sangue; **bloodshot** adj: bloodshot eyes occhi iniettati di sangue; **bloodstream** n flusso del sangue; **blood test** n analisi f inv del sangue; **blood transfusion** n trasfusione f di sangue; **blood type** n gruppo sanguigno; **blood vessel** n vaso sanguigno; **bloody** adj (fight) sanguinoso/a; (nose) sanguinante; (BRIT col!): this bloody ... questo maledetto ...; **bloody awful/good** (col!) veramente terribile/buono; **a bloody awful day** (col!) una giornata di merda (!)

bloom [bluːm] n fiore m ▷ vi essere in fiore

blossom [ˈblɒsəm] n fiore m; (with pl sense) fiori mpl ▷ vi essere in fiore

blot [blɒt] n macchia ▷ vt macchiare

blouse [blauz] n camicetta

blow [bləu] (pt blew, pp blown) n colpo ▷ vi soffiare ▷ vt (fuse) far saltare; (wind) spingere; (instrument) suonare; **to ~ one's nose** soffiarsi il naso; **to ~ a whistle** fischiare; **blow away** ▷ n volare via ▷ vt portare via; **blow out** vi scoppiare; **blow up** vi saltare in aria ▷ vt far saltare in aria; (tyre) gonfiare; (Phot) ingrandire; **blow-dry** n messa in piega a föhn

blown [bləun] pp of **blow**

blue [bluː] adj azzurro/a; (depressed) giù inv; (joke) film/barzelletta pornografico(a); **out of the ~** (fig) all'improvviso; **bluebell** n giacinto di bosco; **blueberry** n mirtillo; **blue cheese** n formaggio tipo gorgonzola; **blues** npl: **the blues** (Mus) il blues; **to have the blues** (col: feeling) essere a terra; **bluetit** n cinciarella

bluff [blʌf] vi bluffare ▷ n bluff m inv ▷ adj (person) brusco/a; **to call sb's ~** mettere alla prova il bluff di qn

blunder [ˈblʌndəʳ] n abbaglio ▷ vi prendere un abbaglio

blunt [blʌnt] adj smussato/a; (point) spuntato/a; (person) brusco/a

blur [bləːʳ] n forma indistinta ▷ vt offuscare; **blurred** adj (photo) mosso/a; (TV) sfuocato/a

blush [blʌʃ] vi arrossire ▷ n rossore m; **blusher** n fard m inv

board [bɔːd] n tavola; (on wall) tabellone m; (committee) consiglio, comitato; (in firm) consiglio d'amministrazione; (Naut, Aviat) **on ~** a bordo ▷ vt (ship) salire a bordo di; (train) salire su; **full ~** (BRIT) pensione f completa; **half ~** (BRIT) mezza pensione; **~ and lodging** vitto e alloggio; **to go by the ~** venir messo/a da parte; **board game** n gioco da tavolo; **boarding card** n (Aviat, Naut) carta d'imbarco; **boarding pass** n (BRIT) = **boarding card**; **boarding school** n collegio; **board room** n sala del consiglio

boast [bəust] vi: **to ~ (about or of)** vantarsi (di)

boat [bəut] n nave f; (small) barca

bob [bɒb] vi (boat, cork on water: also: ~ **up and down**) andare su e giù

bobby pin [ˈbɒbɪ-] (US) n fermaglio per capelli

body [ˈbɒdɪ] n corpo; (of car) carrozzeria; (of plane) fusoliera; (fig: group) gruppo; (: organization) associazione f, organizzazione f; (quantity) quantità f inv; **body-building** n culturismo; **bodyguard** n guardia del corpo; **bodywork** n carrozzeria

bog [bɒg] n palude f ▷ vt: **to get ~ged down** (fig) impantanarsi

bogus [ˈbəugəs] adj falso/a; finto/a

boil [bɔɪl] vt, vi bollire ▷ n (Med) foruncolo; **to come to the** or (US) **a ~** raggiungere l'ebollizione; **~ed egg** uovo alla coque; **~ed potatoes** patate fpl bollite or lesse; **boil over** vi traboccare (bollendo); **boiler** n caldaia; **boiling** adj bollente; **I'm boiling (hot)** (col) sto morendo di caldo; **boiling point** n punto di ebollizione

bold [bəuld] adj audace; (child) impudente; (colour) deciso/a

Bolivia [bəˈlɪvɪə] n Bolivia

Bolivian [bəˈlɪvɪən] adj, n boliviano/a

bollard [ˈbɒləd] n (Aut) colonnina luminosa

Bollywood [ˈbɒlɪwud] n Bollywood f

bolt [bəult] n chiavistello; (with nut) bullone m ▷ adv: **~ upright** diritto/a come un fuso ▷ vt serrare; (also: ~ **together**) imbullonare; (food) mangiare in fretta ▷ vi scappare via

bomb [bɒm] n bomba ▷ vt bombardare; **bombard** [bɒmˈbɑːd] vt bombardare; **bomber** n (Aviat) bombardiere m; (terrorist) dinamitardo/a; **bomb scare** n stato di allarme (per sospetta presenza di una bomba)

bond [bɔnd] n legame m; (binding promise, Finance) obbligazione f; (Comm): **in ~** in attesa di sdoganamento

bone [bəʊn] n osso; (of fish) spina, lisca ▷ vt disossare; togliere le spine a

bonfire ['bɔnfaɪəʳ] n falò m inv

bonnet ['bɔnɪt] n cuffia; (BRIT: of car) cofano

bonus ['bəʊnəs] n premio; (fig) sovrappiù m inv

boo [buː] excl ba! ▷ vt fischiare

book [buk] n libro; (of stamps etc) blocchetto ▷ vt (ticket, seat, room) prenotare; (driver) multare; (football player) ammonire; **books** npl (Comm) conti mpl; **book in** vi (BRIT: at hotel) prendere una camera; **book up** vt riservare, prenotare; **the hotel is ~ed up** l'albergo è al completo; **all seats are ~ed up** è tutto esaurito; **bookcase** n libreria; **booking** n (BRIT) prenotazione f; **booking office** n (BRIT: Rail) biglietteria; (Theat) botteghino; **book-keeping** n contabilità; **booklet** n opuscolo, libriccino; **bookmaker** n allibratore m; **bookmark** n segnalibro ▷ vt (Comput) mettere un segnalibro a; (Internet) aggiungere a "Preferiti"; **bookseller** n libraio; **bookshelf** n mensola (per libri); **bookshop** n libreria

boom [buːm] n (noise) rimbombo; (busy period) boom m inv ▷ vi rimbombare; andare a gonfie vele

boost [buːst] n spinta ▷ vt spingere

boot [buːt] n stivale m; (for hiking) scarpone m da montagna; (for football etc) scarpa; (BRIT: of car) portabagagli m inv ▷ vt (Comput) inizializzare; **to ~** (in addition) per giunta, in più

booth [buːð] n (at fair) baraccone m; (of cinema, telephone etc) cabina

booze [buːz] (col) n alcool m

border ['bɔːdəʳ] n orlo; margine m; (of a country) frontiera; (for flowers) aiuola (laterale) ▷ vt (road) costeggiare; **the B~s** la zona di confine tra l'Inghilterra e la Scozia; **border on** vt fus confinare con; **borderline** n: **on the borderline** incerto/a

bore [bɔːʳ] pt of **bear** ▷ vt (hole) scavare; (person) annoiare ▷ n (person) seccatore/trice; (of gun) calibro; **bored** adj annoiato/a; **to be bored** annoiarsi; **he's bored to tears** or **bored to death** or **bored stiff** è annoiato a morte; **boredom** n noia

boring ['bɔːrɪŋ] adj noioso/a

born [bɔːn] adj: **to be ~** nascere; **I was ~ in 1960** sono nato nel 1960

borne [bɔːn] pp of **bear**

borough ['bʌrə] n comune m

borrow ['bɔrəʊ] vt: **to ~ sth (from sb)** prendere in prestito qc (da qn)

Bosnia-Herzegovina ['bɔznɪəhɛrtsə'gəʊviːnə] n Bosnia-Erzegovina; **Bosnian** ['bɔznɪən] adj, n bosniaco/a

bosom ['buːzəm] n petto; (fig) seno

boss [bɔs] n capo ▷ vt (also: **~ about** or **around**) comandare a bacchetta; **bossy** adj prepotente

both [bəʊθ] adj entrambi/e, tutt'e due ▷ pron: **~ of them** entrambi/e ▷ adv: **they sell ~ meat and poultry** vendono insieme la carne ed il pollame; **~ of us went, we ~ went** ci siamo andati tutt'e due

bother ['bɔðəʳ] vt (worry) preoccupare; (annoy) infastidire ▷ vi (also: **~ o.s.**) preoccuparsi ▷ n: **it is a ~ to have to do** è una seccatura dover fare; **it was no ~** non c'era problema; **to ~ doing sth** darsi la pena di fare qc

bottle ['bɔtl] n bottiglia; (baby's) biberon m inv ▷ vt imbottigliare; **bottle bank** n contenitore m per la raccolta del vetro; **bottle-opener** n apribottiglie m inv

bottom ['bɔtəm] n fondo; (buttocks) sedere m ▷ adj più basso/a, ultimo/a; **at the ~ of** in fondo a

bought [bɔːt] pt, pp of **buy**

boulder ['bəʊldəʳ] n masso (tondeggiante)

bounce [baʊns] vi (ball) rimbalzare; (cheque) essere restituito/a ▷ vt far rimbalzare ▷ n (rebound) rimbalzo; **bouncer** (col) n buttafuori m inv

bound [baʊnd] pt, pp of **bind** ▷ n (gen pl) limite m; (leap) salto ▷ vi saltare ▷ vt (limit) delimitare ▷ adj: **~ by law** obbligato/a per legge; **to be ~ to do sth** (obliged) essere costretto/a a fare qc; **he's ~ to fail** (likely) fallirà di certo; **~ for** diretto/a a; **out of ~s** il cui accesso è vietato

boundary ['baʊndrɪ] n confine m

bouquet ['bʊkeɪ] n bouquet m inv

bourbon ['bʊəbən] n (US: also: **~ whiskey**) bourbon m inv

bout [baʊt] n periodo; (of malaria etc) attacco; (Boxing etc) incontro

boutique [buː'tiːk] n boutique f inv

bow¹ [bəʊ] n nodo; (weapon) arco; (Mus) archetto

bow² [baʊ] n (with body) inchino; (Naut: also: **~s**) prua ▷ vi inchinarsi; (yield): **to ~ to** or **before** sottomettersi a

bowels [baʊəlz] npl intestini mpl; (fig) viscere fpl

bowl [bəʊl] n (for eating) scodella; (for washing) bacino; (ball) boccia ▷ vi (Cricket) servire (la palla); **bowler** n (Cricket) lanciatore m; (BRIT: also: **bowler hat**) bombetta; **bowling** ['bəʊlɪŋ] n (game) gioco delle bocce; **bowling alley** n pista da

bowling; **bowling green** n campo di bocce; **bowls** [bəʊlz] n gioco delle bocce
bow tie n cravatta a farfalla
box [bɒks] n scatola; (also: **cardboard ~**) (scatola di) cartone m; (Theat) palco ▷ vt fare pugilato ▷ vt mettere in (una) scatola, inscatolare; **boxer** n (person) pugile m; **boxer shorts** ['bɒksəfɔ:ts] npl boxer; **a pair of boxer shorts** un paio di boxer; **boxing** n (Sport) pugilato; **Boxing Day** n (BRIT) ≈ Santo Stefano; vedi nota "**Boxing Day**"; **boxing gloves** npl guantoni mpl da pugile; **boxing ring** n ring m inv; **box office** n biglietteria

- **BOXING DAY**
-
- Il Boxing Day è un giorno di festa e cade
- in genere il 26 dicembre. Prende il nome
- dall'usanza di donare pacchi regalo
- natalizi, un tempo chiamati "Christmas
- boxes", a fornitori e dipendenti.

boy [bɔɪ] n ragazzo
boycott ['bɔɪkɒt] n boicottaggio ▷ vt boicottare
boyfriend ['bɔɪfrɛnd] n ragazzo
bra [brɑ:] n reggipetto, reggiseno
brace [breɪs] n (on teeth) apparecchio correttore; (tool) trapano ▷ vt rinforzare, sostenere; **to ~ o.s.** (fig) farsi coraggio; see also **braces**
bracelet ['breɪslɪt] n braccialetto
braces ['breɪsɪz] npl (BRIT) bretelle fpl
bracket ['brækɪt] n (Tech) mensola; (group) gruppo; (Typ) parentesi f inv ▷ vt mettere fra parentesi
brag [bræg] vi vantarsi
braid [breɪd] n (trimming) passamano; (of hair) treccia
brain [breɪn] n cervello; **brains** npl (intelligence) cervella fpl; **he's got ~s** è intelligente
braise [breɪz] vt brasare
brake [breɪk] n (on vehicle) freno ▷ vi frenare; **brake light** n (fanalino dello) stop m inv
bran [bræn] n crusca
branch [brɑ:ntʃ] n ramo; (Comm) succursale f; **branch off** vi diramarsi; **branch out** vi: **to ~ out into** intraprendere una nuova attività nel ramo di
brand [brænd] n marca; (fig) tipo ▷ vt (cattle) marcare (a ferro rovente); **brand name** n marca; **brand-new** adj nuovo/a di zecca
brandy ['brændɪ] n brandy m inv
brash [bræʃ] adj sfacciato/a
brass [brɑ:s] n ottone m; **the ~** (Mus) gli ottoni; **brass band** n fanfara

brat [bræt] n (pej) marmocchio, monello/a
brave [breɪv] adj coraggioso/a ▷ vt affrontare; **bravery** n coraggio
brawl [brɔ:l] n rissa
Brazil [brə'zɪl] n Brasile m; **Brazilian** adj, n brasiliano/a
breach [bri:tʃ] vt aprire una breccia in ▷ n (gap) breccia, varco; (breaking): **~ of contract** rottura di contratto; **~ of the peace** violazione f dell'ordine pubblico
bread [brɛd] n pane m; **breadbin** n cassetta f portapane inv; **breadbox** n (US) cassetta f portapane inv; **breadcrumbs** npl briciole fpl; (Culin) pangrattato
breadth [brɛtθ] n larghezza; (fig: of knowledge etc) ampiezza
break [breɪk] (pt **broke**, pp **broken**) vt rompere; (law) violare ▷ vi rompersi; (storm) scoppiare; (weather) cambiare; (dawn) spuntare; (news) saltare fuori ▷ n (gap) breccia; (fracture) rottura; (rest, also Scol) intervallo; (: short) pausa; (chance) possibilità f inv; **to ~ one's leg etc** rompersi la gamba etc; **to ~ a record** battere un primato; **to ~ the news to sb** comunicare per primo la notizia a qn; **to ~ even** coprire le spese; **to ~ free** or **loose** liberarsi; **break down** vt (figures, data) analizzare; (door etc) buttare giù, abbattere; (resistance) stroncare ▷ vi crollare; (Med) avere un esaurimento (nervoso); (Aut) guastarsi; **break in** vt (horse etc) domare ▷ vi (burglar) fare irruzione; **break into** vt fus (house) fare irruzione in; **break off** vi (speaker) interrompersi; (branch) troncarsi ▷ vt (talks, engagement) rompere; **break out** vi evadere; **to ~ out in spots** coprirsi di macchie; **break up** vi (partnership) sciogliersi; (friends) separarsi; **the line's** or **you're ~ing up** la linea è disturbata ▷ vt fare in pezzi, spaccare; (fight etc) interrompere, far cessare; (marriage) finire; **breakdown** n (Aut) guasto; (in communications) interruzione f; (of marriage) rottura; (Med: also: **nervous breakdown**) esaurimento nervoso; (of payments, statistics etc) resoconto; **breakdown truck, breakdown van** n carro m attrezzi inv
breakfast ['brɛkfəst] n colazione f
break: break-in n irruzione f; **breakthrough** n (fig) passo avanti
breast [brɛst] n (of woman) seno; (chest, Culin) petto; **breast-feed** vt, vi (irreg: like **feed**) allattare (al seno); **breast-stroke** n nuoto a rana
breath [brɛθ] n respiro; **out of ~** senza fiato
Breathalyser® ['brɛθəlaɪzər] (BRIT) n alcoltest m inv

breathe [briːð] vt, vi respirare; **breathe in** vi inspirare ▷ vt respirare; **breathe out** vt, vi espirare; **breathing** n respiro, respirazione f

breath: breathless ['brɛθlɪs] adj senza fiato; **breathtaking** ['brɛθteɪkɪŋ] adj mozzafiato inv; **breath test** n ≈ prova del palloncino

bred [brɛd] pt, pp of **breed**

breed [briːd] (pt, pp **bred**) vt allevare ▷ vi riprodursi ▷ n razza; (type, class) varietà f inv

breeze [briːz] n brezza

breezy ['briːzɪ] adj allegro/a

brew [bruː] vt (tea) fare un infuso di; (beer) fare ▷ vi (storm, fig: trouble etc) prepararsi; **brewery** n fabbrica di birra

bribe [braɪb] n bustarella ▷ vt comprare; **bribery** n corruzione f

bric-a-brac ['brɪkəbræk] n bric-a-brac m

brick [brɪk] n mattone m; **bricklayer** n muratore m

bride [braɪd] n sposa; **bridegroom** n sposo; **bridesmaid** n damigella d'onore

bridge [brɪdʒ] n ponte m; (Naut) ponte di comando; (of nose) dorso; (Cards, Dentistry) bridge m inv ▷ vt (fig: gap) colmare

bridle ['braɪdl] n briglia

brief [briːf] adj breve ▷ n (Law) comparsa; (gen) istruzioni fpl ▷ vt: **to ~ sb (about sth)** mettere qn al corrente (di qc); see also **briefs**; **briefcase** n cartella; **briefing** n istruzioni fpl, briefing m inv; **briefly** adv (speak, visit, explain, say) brevemente; (glimpse, glance) di sfuggita

brigadier [brɪɡə'dɪəʳ] n generale m di brigata

bright [braɪt] adj luminoso/a; (person) sveglio/a; (colour) vivace

brilliant ['brɪljənt] adj brillante; (light, smile) radioso/a; (col) splendido/a

brim [brɪm] n orlo

brine [braɪn] n (Culin) salamoia

bring (pt, pp **brought**) [brɪŋ, brɔːt] vt portare; **bring about** vt causare; **bring back** vt riportare; **bring down** vt (lower) far scendere; (shoot down) abbattere; (government) far cadere; **bring in** vt (person) fare entrare; (object) portare; (Pol: bill) presentare; (: legislation) introdurre; (Law: verdict) emettere; (produce: income) rendere; **bring on** vt (illness, attack) causare, provocare; (player, substitute) far scendere in campo; **bring out** vt (meaning) mettere in evidenza; (new product) lanciare; (book) pubblicare, fare uscire; **bring up** vt allevare; (question) introdurre

brink [brɪŋk] n orlo

brisk [brɪsk] adj (person, tone) spiccio/a; (trade etc) vivace; (pace) svelto/a

bristle ['brɪsl] n setola ▷ vi rizzarsi; **bristling with** irto/a di

Brit [brɪt] n abbr (col: = British person) britannico/a

Britain ['brɪtən] n (also: **Great ~**) Gran Bretagna

British ['brɪtɪʃ] adj britannico/a; **the ~ Isles** n pl le Isole Britanniche

Briton ['brɪtən] n britannico/a

brittle ['brɪtl] adj fragile

broad [brɔːd] adj largo/a; (distinction) generale; (accent) spiccato/a; **in ~ daylight** in pieno giorno; **broadband** adj (Comput) a banda larga, ADSL ▷ n banda larga, ADSL m inv; **broad bean** n fava; **broadcast** (pt, pp **broadcast**) n trasmissione f ▷ vt trasmettere per radio (or per televisione) ▷ vi fare una trasmissione; **broaden** vt allargare ▷ vi allargarsi; **broadly** adv (fig) in generale; **broad-minded** adj di mente aperta

broccoli ['brɔkəlɪ] n broccoli mpl

brochure ['brəʊʃjʊəʳ] n dépliant m inv

broil [brɔɪl] vt cuocere a fuoco vivo; **broiler** ['brɔɪləʳ] (us) n (grill) griglia

broke [brəʊk] pt of **break** ▷ adj (col) squattrinato/a

broken ['brəʊkən] pp of **break** ▷ adj rotto/a; **a ~ leg** una gamba rotta; **in ~ French/English** in un francese/inglese stentato

broker ['brəʊkəʳ] n agente m

bronchitis [brɔn'kaɪtɪs] n bronchite f

bronze [brɔnz] n bronzo

brooch [brəʊtʃ] n spilla

brood [bruːd] n covata ▷ vi (person) rimuginare

broom [brum] n scopa; (Bot) ginestra

Bros. abbr (= brothers) F.lli

broth [brɔθ] n brodo

brothel ['brɔθl] n bordello

brother ['brʌðəʳ] n fratello; **brother-in-law** n cognato

brought [brɔːt] pt, pp of **bring**

brow [braʊ] n fronte f; (rare, gen: also: **eye~**) sopracciglio; (of hill) cima

brown [braʊn] adj bruno/a, marrone; (tanned) abbronzato/a ▷ n (colour) color m bruno or marrone ▷ vt (Culin) rosolare; **brown bread** n pane m integrale, pane nero

Brownie ['braʊnɪ] n giovane esploratrice f

brown rice n riso greggio

brown sugar n zucchero greggio

browse [braʊz] vi (in bookshop etc) curiosare; **to ~ through a book** sfogliare un libro; **browser** n (Comput) browser m inv

bruise [bruːz] n (on person) livido ▷ vt farsi un livido a

brunette [bruː'nɛt] n bruna
brush [brʌʃ] n spazzola; (for painting, shaving) pennello; (quarrel) schermaglia ▷ vt spazzolare; (also: ~ **past**, ~ **against**) sfiorare
Brussels ['brʌslz] n Bruxelles f; **Brussels sprout** [spraut] n cavolo di Bruxelles
brutal ['bruːtl] adj brutale
BSc n abbr (Univ) = **Bachelor of Science**
BSE n abbr (= bovine spongiform encephalopathy) encefalite f bovina spongiforme
bubble ['bʌbl] n bolla ▷ vi ribollire; (sparkle, fig) essere effervescente; **bubble bath** n bagno m schiuma inv; **bubble gum** n gomma americana
buck [bʌk] n maschio (di camoscio, caprone, coniglio ecc); (us col) dollaro ▷ vi sgroppare; **to pass the ~ (to sb)** scaricare (su di qn) la propria responsabilità
bucket ['bʌkɪt] n secchio; **bucket list** n elenco di cose da fare prima di morire
buckle ['bʌkl] n fibbia ▷ vt allacciare ▷ vi (wheel etc) piegarsi
bud [bʌd] n gemma; (of flower) bocciolo ▷ vi germogliare; (flower) sbocciare
Buddhism ['budɪzəm] n buddismo
Buddhist ['budɪst] adj, n buddista (m/f)
buddy ['bʌdɪ] n (us) compagno
budge [bʌdʒ] vt scostare; (fig) smuovere ▷ vi spostarsi; smuoversi
budgerigar ['bʌdʒərɪgɑːʳ] n pappagallino
budget ['bʌdʒɪt] n bilancio preventivo ▷ vi: **to ~ for sth** fare il bilancio per qc
budgie ['bʌdʒɪ] n = **budgerigar**
buff [bʌf] adj color camoscio inv ▷ n (col: enthusiast) appassionato/a
buffalo ['bʌfələu] (pl **buffalo** or **buffaloes**) n bufalo; (us) bisonte m
buffer ['bʌfəʳ] n respingente m; (Comput) memoria tampone, buffer m inv ▷ vi (Comput) fare il buffering, trasferire nella memoria tampone; **buffering** n buffering m inv, trasferimento nella memoria tampone
buffet n ['bufeɪ] (food, BRIT: bar) buffet m inv ▷ vt ['bʌfɪt] sferzare; **buffet car** n (BRIT Rail) ≈ servizio ristoro
bug [bʌg] n (insect) insetto; (fig: germ) virus m inv; (spy device) microfono spia; (Comput) bug m inv ▷ vt mettere sotto controllo; (annoy) scocciare
buggy ['bʌgɪ] n (baby buggy) passeggino
build [bɪld] n (of person) corporatura ▷ vt (pt, pp **built**) costruire; **build up** vt (reputation) consolidare; (increase) incrementare; **builder** n costruttore m; **building** n costruzione f; edificio; (also: **building trade**) edilizia; **building site** n

cantiere m di costruzione; **building society** n società immobiliare e finanziaria
built [bɪlt] pt, pp of **build**; **built-in** adj (cupboard) a muro; (device) incorporato/a; **built-up area** ['bɪltʌp-] n abitato
bulb [bʌlb] n (Bot) bulbo; (Elec) lampadina
Bulgaria [bʌl'gɛərɪə] n Bulgaria; **Bulgarian** adj bulgaro/a ▷ n bulgaro/a; (Ling) bulgaro
bulge [bʌldʒ] n rigonfiamento ▷ vi essere protuberante or rigonfio/a; **to be bulging with** essere pieno/a or zeppo/a di
bulimia [bə'lɪmɪə] n bulimia
bulimic [bjuː'lɪmɪk] adj, n bulimico/a
bulk [bʌlk] n massa, volume m; **the ~ of** il grosso di; **(to buy) in ~** (comprare) in grande quantità; (Comm) (comprare) all'ingrosso; **bulky** adj grosso/a; voluminoso/a
bull [bul] n toro; (male elephant, whale) maschio
bulldozer ['buldəuzəʳ] n bulldozer m inv
bullet ['bulɪt] n pallottola
bulletin ['bulɪtɪn] n bollettino; **bulletin board** n (Comput) bulletin board m inv
bullfight ['bulfaɪt] n corrida; **bullfighter** n torero; **bullfighting** n tauromachia
bully ['bulɪ] n prepotente m ▷ vt angariare; (frighten) intimidire
bum [bʌm] n (col: backside) culo; (tramp) vagabondo/a
bumblebee ['bʌmblbiː] n bombo
bump [bʌmp] n (in car) piccolo tamponamento; (jolt) scossa; (on road etc) protuberanza; (on head) bernoccolo ▷ vt battere; **bump into** vt fus scontrarsi con; (meet) imbattersi in; **bumper** n paraurti m inv ▷ adj: **bumper harvest** raccolto eccezionale; **bumpy** ['bʌmpɪ] adj (road) dissestato/a
bun [bʌn] n focaccia; (of hair) crocchia
bunch [bʌntʃ] n (of flowers, keys) mazzo; (of bananas) casco; (of people) gruppo; **~ of grapes** grappolo d'uva; **bunches** npl (in hair) codine fpl
bundle ['bʌndl] n fascio ▷ vt (also: ~ **up**) legare in un fascio; (put): **to ~ sth/sb into** spingere qc/qn in
bungalow ['bʌŋgələu] n bungalow m inv
bungee jumping ['bʌndʒiː'dʒʌmpɪŋ] n salto nel vuoto da ponti, grattacieli ecc con un cavo fissato alla caviglia
bunion ['bʌnjən] n callo (al piede)
bunk [bʌŋk] n cuccetta; **bunk beds** npl letti mpl a castello
bunker ['bʌŋkəʳ] n (coal store) ripostiglio per il carbone; (Mil, Golf) bunker m inv
bunny ['bʌnɪ] n (also: ~ **rabbit**) coniglietto
buoy [bɔɪ] n boa; **buoyant** adj galleggiante; (fig) vivace

burden [ˈbəːdn] n carico, fardello ▷ vt caricare; **to ~ sb with** caricare qn di

bureau (pl **bureaux**) [ˈbjuərəu, -z] n (BRIT: writing desk) scrivania; (US: chest of drawers) cassettone m; (office) ufficio, agenzia

bureaucracy [bjuəˈrɔkrəsɪ] n burocrazia

bureaucrat [ˈbjuərəkræt] n burocrate m/f

bureau de change [-dəˈʃɑːʒ] (pl **bureaux de change**) n cambiavalute m inv

bureaux [bjuəˈrəuz] npl of **bureau**

burger [ˈbəːgəʳ] n hamburger m inv

burglar [ˈbəːgləʳ] n scassinatore m; **burglar alarm** n (allarme m) antifurto m inv; **burglary** n furto con scasso

burial [ˈbɛrɪəl] n sepoltura

burn [bəːn] vt, vi (pt, pp **burned** or **burnt**) bruciare ▷ n bruciatura, scottatura; **burn down** vt distruggere col fuoco; **burn out** vt (writer etc): **to ~ o.s. out** esaurirsi; **burning** adj in fiamme; (sand) che scotta; (ambition) bruciante

Burns Night n vedi nota "Burns Night"

burnt [bəːnt] pt, pp of **burn**

burp [bəːp] (col) n rutto ▷ vi ruttare

burrow [ˈbʌrəu] n tana ▷ vt scavare

burst [bəːst] (pt, pp **burst**) vt far scoppiare or esplodere ▷ vi esplodere; (tyre) scoppiare ▷ n scoppio; (also: **~ pipe**) rottura nel tubo, perdita; **a ~ of speed** uno scatto (di velocità); **to ~ into flames/tears** scoppiare in fiamme/lacrime; **to be ~ing with** essere pronto a scoppiare di; **to ~ out laughing** scoppiare a ridere; **burst into** vt fus (room etc) irrompere in

bury [ˈbɛrɪ] vt seppellire

bus [bʌs] (pl **buses**) n autobus m inv; **bus conductor** n autista m/f (dell'autobus)

bush [buʃ] n cespuglio; (scrub land) macchia; **to beat about the ~** menare il cane per l'aia

business [ˈbɪznɪs] n (matter) affare m; (trading) affari mpl; (firm) azienda; (job, duty) lavoro; **to be away on ~** essere andato via per affari; **it's none of my ~** questo non mi riguarda; **he means ~** non scherza; **business class** n (Aviat) business class f;

businesslike adj serio/a; efficiente;

businessman n (irreg) uomo d'affari;

business trip n viaggio d'affari;

businesswoman n (irreg) donna d'affari

busker [ˈbʌskəʳ] n (BRIT) suonatore/trice ambulante

bus: bus pass n tessera dell'autobus; **bus shelter** n pensilina (alla fermata dell'autobus); **bus station** n stazione f delle corriere, autostazione f; **bus stop** n fermata d'autobus

bust [bʌst] n busto; (Anat) seno ▷ adj (col: broken) rotto/a; **to go ~** fallire

bustling [ˈbʌslɪŋ] adj animato/a

busy [ˈbɪzɪ] adj occupato/a; (shop, street) molto frequentato/a ▷ vt: **to ~ o.s.** darsi da fare; **busy signal** n (US Tel) segnale m di occupato

 KEYWORD

but [bʌt] conj ma; **I'd love to come, but I'm busy** vorrei tanto venire, ma ho da fare
▶ prep (apart from, except) eccetto, tranne, meno; **he was nothing but trouble** non dava altro che guai; **no-one but him can do it** nessuno può farlo tranne lui; **but for you/your help** se non fosse per te/per il tuo aiuto; **anything but that** tutto ma non questo
▶ adv (just, only) solo, soltanto; **she's but a child** è solo una bambina; **had I but known** se solo avessi saputo; **I can but try** tentar non nuoce; **all but finished** quasi finito

butcher [ˈbutʃəʳ] n macellaio ▷ vt macellare; **~'s (shop)** n macelleria

butler [ˈbʌtləʳ] n maggiordomo

butt [bʌt] n (cask) grossa botte f; (of gun) calcio; (of cigarette) mozzicone m; (BRIT fig: target) oggetto ▷ vt cozzare

butter [ˈbʌtəʳ] n burro ▷ vt imburrare; **buttercup** n ranuncolo

butterfly [ˈbʌtəflaɪ] n farfalla; (Swimming: also: **~ stroke**) (nuoto a) farfalla

buttocks [ˈbʌtəks] npl natiche fpl

button [ˈbʌtn] n bottone m; (US: badge) distintivo ▷ vt (also: **~ up**) abbottonare ▷ vi abbottonarsi

buy [baɪ] vt (pt, pp **bought**) comprare ▷ n acquisto; **to ~ sb sth/sth from sb** comprare qc per qn/qc da qn; **to ~ sb a drink** offrire da bere a qn; **buy out** vt (business) rilevare; **buy up** vt accaparrare; **buyer** n compratore/trice

buzz [bʌz] n ronzio; (col: phone call) colpo di telefono ▷ vi ronzare; **buzzer** [ˈbʌzəʳ] n cicalino

by [baɪ] prep 1 (referring to cause, agent) da; **killed by lightning** ucciso da un fulmine; **surrounded by a fence** circondato da uno steccato; **a painting by Picasso** un quadro di Picasso

2 (referring to method, manner, means): **by bus/car/train** in autobus/macchina/treno, con l'autobus/la macchina/il treno; **to pay by cheque** pagare con (un) assegno; **by moonlight** al chiaro di luna; **by saving hard, he …** risparmiando molto, lui …

3 (via, through) per; **we came by Dover** siamo venuti via Dover

4 (close to, past) accanto a; **the house by the river** la casa sul fiume; **a holiday by the sea** una vacanza al mare; **she sat by his bed** si sedette accanto al suo letto; **she rushed by me** mi è passata accanto correndo; **I go by the post office every day** passo davanti all'ufficio postale ogni giorno

5 (not later than) per, entro; **by 4 o'clock** per o entro le 4; **by this time tomorrow** domani a quest'ora; **by the time I got here it was too late** quando sono arrivato era ormai troppo tardi

6 (during): **by day/night** di giorno/notte

7 (amount) a; **by the kilo** a chili; **paid by the hour** pagato all'ora; **one by one** uno per uno; **little by little** a poco a poco

8 (Math: measure): **to divide/multiply by 3** dividere/moltiplicare per 3; **it's broader by a metre** è un metro più largo, è più largo di un metro

9 (according to) per; **to play by the rules** attenersi alle regole; **it's all right by me** per me va bene

10: **(all) by oneself** (tutto/a) solo/a; **he did it (all) by himself** lo ha fatto (tutto) da solo

11: **by the way** a proposito; **this wasn't my idea by the way** tra l'altro l'idea non è stata mia

▶ adv 1 see **go; pass** etc

2: **by and by** (in past) poco dopo; (in future) fra breve; **by and large** nel complesso

bye(-bye) ['baɪ('baɪ)] excl ciao!, arrivederci!
by-election ['baɪɪlɛkʃən] n (BRIT) elezione f straordinaria
bypass ['baɪpɑːs] n circonvallazione f; (Med) by-pass m inv ▷ vt fare una deviazione intorno a
byte [baɪt] n (Comput) byte m inv, bicarattere m

C [siː] n (Mus) do
cab [kæb] n taxi m inv; (of train, truck) cabina
cabaret ['kæbəreɪ] n cabaret m inv
cabbage ['kæbɪdʒ] n cavolo
cabin ['kæbɪn] n capanna; (on ship) cabina; **cabin crew** n equipaggio
cabinet ['kæbɪnɪt] n (Pol) consiglio dei ministri; (furniture) armadietto; (also: **display ~**) vetrinetta; **cabinet minister** n ministro (membro del Consiglio)
cable ['keɪbl] n cavo; fune f; (Tel) cablogramma m ▷ vt telegrafare; **cable-car** n funivia; **cable television** n televisione f via cavo
cactus (pl **cacti**) ['kæktəs, -taɪ] n cactus m inv
café ['kæfeɪ] n caffè m inv
cafeteria [kæfɪ'tɪərɪə] n self-service m inv
caffein(e) ['kæfiːn] n caffeina
cage [keɪdʒ] n gabbia
cagoule [kə'guːl] n K-way® m inv
cake [keɪk] n (large) torta; (small) pasticcino; **~ of soap** saponetta
calcium ['kælsɪəm] n calcio
calculate ['kælkjuleɪt] vt calcolare; **calculation** [kælkju'leɪʃən] n calcolo; **calculator** n calcolatrice f
calendar ['kæləndəʳ] n calendario
calf (pl **calves**) [kɑːf, kɑːvz] n (of cow) vitello; (of other animals) piccolo; (also: **~skin**) (pelle f di) vitello; (Anat) polpaccio
calibre (US) **caliber** ['kælɪbəʳ] n calibro
call [kɔːl] vt (gen, also Tel) chiamare; (meeting, strike) indire ▷ vi chiamare; (visit: also: **~ in, ~ round**) passare ▷ n (shout) grido, urlo; (also: **telephone ~**) telefonata; **to be ~ed** (person, object) chiamarsi; **to be on ~** essere a disposizione; **call back** vi (return) ritornare; (Tel) ritelefonare,

richiamare; **can you ~ back later?** può richiamare più tardi?; **call for** *vt fus* richiedere; (*collect*) passare a prendere; **call in** *vt* (*doctor, expert, police*) chiamare, far venire; **call off** *vt* disdire; **call on** *vt fus* (*visit*) passare da; (*request*): **to ~ on sb to do** chiedere a qn di fare; **call out** *vi* (*in pain*) urlare; (*to person*) chiamare; **call up** *vt* (*Mil*) chiamare; (*Tel*) telefonare a; **callbox** *n* (BRIT) cabina telefonica; **call centre**, (US) **call center** *n* centro informazioni telefoniche; **caller** *n* persona che chiama; visitatore/trice

callous ['kæləs] *adj* indurito/a, insensibile

calm [kɑːm] *adj* calmo/a ▷ *n* calma ▷ *vt* calmare; **calm down** *vi* calmarsi ▷ *vt* calmare; **calmly** *adv* con calma

Calor gas® ['kælɔːˀ-] *n* butano

calorie ['kælərɪ] *n* caloria

calves [kɑːvz] *npl of* **calf**

camcorder ['kæmkɔːdəˀ] *n* videocamera

came [keɪm] *pt of* **come**

camel ['kæməl] *n* cammello

camera ['kæmərə] *n* macchina fotografica; (*Cine, TV*) cinepresa; **in ~** a porte chiuse; **cameraman** *n* (*irreg*) cameraman *m inv*; **camera phone** *n* telefono cellulare con fotocamera integrata

camouflage ['kæməflɑːʒ] *n* (*Mil, Zool*) mimetizzazione *f* ▷ *vt* mimetizzare

camp [kæmp] *n* campeggio; (*Mil*) campo ▷ *vi* accamparsi ▷ *adj* effeminato/a

campaign [kæm'peɪn] *n* (*Mil, Pol etc*) campagna ▷ *vi*: **to ~ (for/against)** (*also fig*) fare una campagna (per/contro); **campaigner** *n*: **campaigner for** fautore/trice di; **campaigner against** oppositore/trice di

camp: campbed *n* (BRIT) brandina; **camper** ['kæmpəˀ] *n* campeggiatore/trice; (*vehicle*) camper *m inv*; **campground** *n* (US) campeggio; **camping** ['kæmpɪŋ] *n* campeggio; **to go camping** andare in campeggio; **camp site** ['kæmpsaɪt] *n* campeggio

campus ['kæmpəs] *n* campus *m inv*

can¹ [kæn] *n* (*of milk*) scatola; (*of oil*) bidone *m*; (*of water*) tanica; (*tin*) scatola ▷ *vt* mettere in scatola

 KEYWORD

can² [kæn] (*negative* **cannot, can't**, *conditional, pt* **could**) *aux vb* **1** (*be able to*) potere; **I can't go any further** non posso andare oltre; **you can do it if you try** sei in grado di farlo - basta provarci; **I'll help you all I can** ti aiuterò come potrò; **I can't see you** non ti vedo

2 (*know how to*) sapere, essere capace di; **I can swim** so nuotare; **can you speak French?** parla francese?

3 (*may*) potere; **could I have a word with you?** posso parlarle un momento?

4 (*expressing disbelief, puzzlement etc*): **it can't be true!** non può essere vero!; **what CAN he want?** cosa può mai volere?

5 (*expressing possibility, suggestion etc*): **he could be in the library** può darsi che sia in biblioteca; **she could have been delayed** può aver avuto un contrattempo

Canada ['kænədə] *n* Canada *m*; **Canadian** [kə'neɪdɪən] *adj, n* canadese (*m/f*)

canal [kə'næl] *n* canale *m*

canary [kə'nɛərɪ] *n* canarino

Canary Islands, Canaries [kə'nɛərɪz] *npl*: **the ~** le (isole) Canarie

cancel ['kænsəl] *vt* annullare; (*train*) sopprimere; (*cross out*) cancellare; **cancellation** [kænsə'leɪʃən] *n* annullamento; soppressione *f*; cancellazione *f*; (*Tourism*) prenotazione *f* annullata

cancer ['kænsəˀ] *n* cancro; **C~** (*sign*) Cancro

candidate ['kændɪdeɪt] *n* candidato/a

candle ['kændl] *n* candela; (*in church*) cero; **candlestick** *n* bugia; (*bigger, ornate*) candeliere *m*

candy ['kændɪ] *n* zucchero candito; (US) caramella; caramelle *fpl*; **candy bar** (US) *n* lungo biscotto, in genere ricoperto di cioccolata; **candy-floss** ['kændɪflɔs] *n* (BRIT) zucchero filato

cane [keɪn] *n* canna; (*for baskets, chairs etc*) bambù *m*; (*Scol*) verga ▷ *vt* (BRIT *Scol*) punire a colpi di verga

canister ['kænɪstəˀ] *n* scatola metallica

cannabis ['kænəbɪs] *n* canapa indiana

canned [kænd] *adj* (*food*) in scatola

cannon ['kænən] (*pl* **cannon** *or* **cannons**) *n* (*gun*) cannone *m*

cannot ['kænɔt] = **can not**

canoe [kə'nuː] *n* canoa; **canoeing** *n* canottaggio

canon ['kænən] *n* (*clergyman*) canonico; (*standard*) canone *m*

can opener [-əupnəˀ] *n* apriscatole *m inv*

can't [kænt] = **can not**

canteen [kæn'tiːn] *n* mensa; (BRIT: *of cutlery*) portaposate *m inv*

　　Be careful not to translate *canteen* by the Italian word *cantina*.

canter ['kæntəˀ] *vi* andare al piccolo galoppo

canvas ['kænvəs] *n* tela

canvass ['kænvəs] vi (Pol): **to ~ for** raccogliere voti per ▷ vt fare un sondaggio di
canyon ['kænjən] n canyon m inv
cap [kæp] n (also BRIT Football: hat) berretto; (of pen) coperchio; (of bottle) tappo; (contraceptive) diaframma m ▷ vt (outdo) superare; (limit) fissare un tetto (a)
capability [keɪpə'bɪlɪtɪ] n capacità f inv, abilità f inv
capable ['keɪpəbl] adj capace
capacity [kə'pæsɪtɪ] n capacità f inv; (of lift etc) capienza
cape [keɪp] n (garment) cappa; (Geo) capo
caper ['keɪpəʳ] n (Culin) cappero; (prank) scherzetto
capital ['kæpɪtl] n (also: ~ city) capitale f; (money) capitale m; (also: ~ letter) (lettera) maiuscola; **capitalism** n capitalismo; **capitalist** adj, n capitalista (m/f); **capital punishment** n pena capitale
Capitol ['kæpɪtl] n: **the ~** il Campidoglio
Capricorn ['kæprɪkɔːn] n Capricorno
capsize [kæp'saɪz] vt capovolgere ▷ vi capovolgersi
capsule ['kæpsjuːl] n capsula
captain ['kæptɪn] n capitano
caption ['kæpʃən] n leggenda
captivity [kæp'tɪvɪtɪ] n prigionia
capture ['kæptʃəʳ] vt catturare; (Comput) registrare ▷ n cattura; (data capture) registrazione f o rilevazione f di dati
car [kɑːʳ] n macchina, automobile f; (Rail) vagone m
carafe [kə'ræf] n caraffa
caramel ['kærəməl] n caramello
carat ['kærət] n carato; **18 ~ gold** oro a 18 carati
caravan ['kærəvæn] n (BRIT) roulotte f inv; (of camels) carovana; **caravan site** n (BRIT) campeggio per roulotte
carbohydrate [kɑːbəʊ'haɪdreɪt] n carboidrato
carbon ['kɑːbən] n carbonio; **carbon copy** n copia f carbone inv; **carbon dioxide** [-daɪ'ɔksaɪd] n diossido di carbonio; **carbon footprint** n impronta di carbonio; **carbon monoxide** [-mɔ'nɔksaɪd] n monossido di carbonio; **carbon-neutral** adj carbon neutral, ad emissioni zero CO_2
car boot sale n vedi nota "car boot sale"

● **CAR BOOT SALE**

● Il car boot sale è un mercatino dell'usato
● molto popolare in Gran Bretagna.
● Normalmente ha luogo in un parcheggio
● o in un grande spiazzo, e la merce viene in
● genere esposta nei bagagliai, in inglese
● appunto "boots", aperti delle macchine.

carburettor, (US) **carburetor** [kɑː'bjuːrɛtəʳ] n carburatore m
card [kɑːd] n carta; (visiting card etc) biglietto; (Christmas card etc) cartolina; **cardboard** n cartone m; **card game** n gioco di carte
cardigan ['kɑːdɪgən] n cardigan m inv
cardinal ['kɑːdɪnl] adj, n cardinale (m)
cardphone ['kɑːdfəʊn] n telefono a scheda (magnetica)
care [kɛəʳ] n cura, attenzione f; (worry) preoccupazione f ▷ vi: **to ~** (about) curarsi di; (thing, idea) interessarsi di; **in sb's ~** alle cure di qn; **to take ~** fare attenzione; **to take ~ of** curarsi di; (details, arrangements, bill, problem) occuparsi di; **I don't ~** non me ne importa; **I couldn't ~ less** non me ne importa un bel niente; **~ of** (c/o) presso; **care for** vt fus aver cura di; (like) voler bene a
career [kə'rɪəʳ] n carriera ▷ vi (also: ~ along) andare di (gran) carriera
care: carefree ['kɛəfriː] adj sgombro/a di preoccupazioni; **careful** ['kɛəful] adj attento/a; (cautious) cauto/a; **(be) careful!** attenzione!; **carefully** adv con cura, cautamente; **caregiver** (US) n (professional) badante m/f; (unpaid) persona che si prende cura di un parente malato o anziano; **careless** ['kɛəlɪs] adj negligente; (heedless) spensierato/a; **carelessness** n negligenza; mancanza di tatto; **carer** ['kɛərəʳ] n chi si occupa di un familiare anziano o invalido; **caretaker** ['kɛəteɪkəʳ] n custode m
car-ferry ['kɑːfɛrɪ] n traghetto
cargo ['kɑːgəʊ] (pl **cargoes**) n carico
car hire n autonoleggio
Caribbean [kærɪ'biːən] adj: **the ~ (Sea)** il Mar dei Caraibi
caring ['kɛərɪŋ] adj (person) premuroso/a; (society, organization) umanitario/a
carnation [kɑː'neɪʃən] n garofano
carnival ['kɑːnɪvəl] n (public celebration) carnevale m; (US: funfair) luna park m inv
carol ['kærəl] n: **(Christmas) ~** canto di Natale
carousel [kærə'sɛl] n (US) giostra
car park n (BRIT) parcheggio
carpenter ['kɑːpɪntəʳ] n carpentiere m
carpet ['kɑːpɪt] n tappeto ▷ vt coprire con tappeto
car rental n (US) autonoleggio
carriage ['kærɪdʒ] n vettura; (of goods) trasporto; **carriageway** n (BRIT: part of road) carreggiata
carrier ['kærɪəʳ] n (of disease) portatore/trice; (Comm) impresa di trasporti; **carrier bag** n (BRIT) sacchetto
carrot ['kærət] n carota

carry ['kærɪ] vt (person) portare; (vehicle) trasportare; (involve: responsibilities etc) comportare; (Med) essere portatore/trice di ▷ vi (sound) farsi sentire; **to be** or **get carried away** (fig) farsi trascinare; **carry on** vi: **to ~ on with sth/doing** continuare qc/a fare ▷ vt mandare avanti; **carry out** vt (orders) eseguire; (investigation) svolgere

cart [kɑːt] n carro ▷ vt (col) trascinare

carton ['kɑːtən] n (box) scatola di cartone; (of yogurt) cartone m; (of cigarettes) stecca

cartoon [kɑː'tuːn] n (in newspaper etc) vignetta; (comic strip) fumetto; (Cine, TV) cartone m animato

cartridge ['kɑːtrɪdʒ] n (for gun, pen) cartuccia; (music tape) cassetta

carve [kɑːv] vt (meat) trinciare; (wood, stone) intagliare; **carving** n (in wood etc) scultura

car wash n lavaggio auto

case [keɪs] n caso; (Law) causa, processo; (box) scatola; (BRIT: also: **suit~**) valigia; **in ~ of** in caso di; **in ~ he** caso mai lui; **in any ~** in ogni caso; **just in ~** in caso di bisogno

cash [kæʃ] n (coins, notes) soldi mpl, denaro ▷ vt incassare; **I haven't got any ~** non ho contanti; **to pay (in) ~** pagare in contanti; **~ with order/on delivery (COD)** pagamento all'ordinazione/alla consegna; **cashback** n (discount) sconto; (at supermarket etc) anticipo di contanti ottenuto presso la cassa di un negozio tramite una carta di debito; **cash card** n (BRIT) carta per prelievi automatici; **cash desk** n (BRIT) cassa; **cash dispenser** n (BRIT) sportello automatico

cashew [kæ'ʃuː] n (also: **~ nut**) anacardio

cashier [kæ'ʃɪə'] n cassiere/a

cashmere ['kæʃmɪə'] n cachemire m

cash point n sportello bancario automatico, Bancomat® m inv

cash register n registratore m di cassa

casino [kə'siːnəu] n casinò m inv

casket ['kɑːskɪt] n cofanetto; (us: coffin) bara

casserole ['kæsərəul] n casseruola; **chicken ~** pollo in casseruola

cassette [kæ'sɛt] n cassetta; **cassette player** n riproduttore m a cassette

cast [kɑːst] vt (pt, pp **cast**) (throw) gettare; (metal) gettare, fondere; (Theat): **to ~ sb as Hamlet** scegliere qn per la parte di Amleto ▷ n (Theat) cast m inv; (also: **plaster ~**) ingessatura; **to ~ one's vote** votare, dare il voto; **cast off** vi (Naut) salpare

castanets [kæstə'nɛts] npl castagnette fpl

caster sugar ['kɑːstə-] n (BRIT) zucchero semolato

cast iron n ghisa ▷ adj: **cast-iron** (lit) di ghisa; (fig: will, alibi) di ferro

castle ['kɑːsl] n castello

casual ['kæʒjul] adj (chance) casuale, fortuito/a; (irregular: work etc) avventizio/a; (unconcerned) noncurante, indifferente; **~ wear** casual m

casualty ['kæʒjultɪ] n ferito/a; (dead) morto/a, vittima; (Med: department) pronto soccorso

cat [kæt] n gatto

catalogue, (us) **catalog** ['kætələg] n catalogo ▷ vt catalogare

catalytic converter [kætə'lɪtɪk kən'vəːtə'] n marmitta catalitica, catalizzatore m

cataract ['kætərækt] n (also Med) cateratta

catarrh [kə'tɑː'] n catarro

catastrophe [kə'tæstrəfɪ] n catastrofe f

catch [kætʃ] (pt, pp **caught**) vt prendere; (ball) afferrare; (person: by surprise) sorprendere; (attention) attirare; (comment, whisper) cogliere; (person) raggiungere ▷ vi (fire) prendere ▷ n (fish etc caught) retata; (of ball) presa; (trick) inganno; (Tech) gancio; (game) catch m inv; **to ~ fire** prendere fuoco; **to ~ sight of** scorgere; **catch up** vi mettersi in pari ▷ vt (also: **~ up with**) raggiungere; **catching** ['kætʃɪŋ] adj (Med) contagioso/a

category ['kætɪgərɪ] n categoria

cater ['keɪtə']: **cater for** vt fus (BRIT: needs) provvedere a; (: readers, consumers) incontrare i gusti di; (Comm: provide food) provvedere alla ristorazione di

caterpillar ['kætəpɪlə'] n bruco

cathedral [kə'θiːdrəl] n cattedrale f, duomo

Catholic ['kæθəlɪk] adj, n (Rel) cattolico/a

Catseye® ['kæts'aɪ] n (BRIT Aut) catarifrangente m

cattle ['kætl] npl bestiame m, bestie fpl

catwalk ['kætwɔːk] n passerella

caught [kɔːt] pt, pp of **catch**

cauliflower ['kɔlɪflauə'] n cavolfiore m

cause [kɔːz] n causa ▷ vt causare

caution ['kɔːʃən] n prudenza; (warning) avvertimento ▷ vt avvertire; ammonire; **cautious** ['kɔːʃəs] adj cauto/a, prudente

cave [keɪv] n caverna, grotta; **cave in** vi (roof etc) crollare

caviar(e) ['kævɪɑː'] n caviale m

cavity ['kævɪtɪ] n cavità f inv

cc abbr (= cubic centimetre) cc; (on letter etc) = **carbon copy**

CCTV n abbr (= closed-circuit television) televisione f a circuito chiuso

CD n abbr (= compact disk) CD m inv; (player) lettore m CD inv; **CD burner** n masterizzatore m (di) CD; **CD player** n lettore *m* CD; **CD-ROM** ['si:'di:'rɔm] *n abbr* (= *compact disc read-only memory*) CD-ROM *m inv*

cease [si:s] *vt, vi* cessare; **ceasefire** *n* cessate il fuoco *m inv*

cedar ['si:dəʳ] *n* cedro

ceilidh ['keɪlɪ] *n* festa con musiche e danze popolari scozzesi o irlandesi

ceiling ['si:lɪŋ] *n* soffitto; (*fig: upper limit*) tetto

celebrate ['sɛlɪbreɪt] *vt, vi* celebrare; **celebration** [sɛlɪ'breɪʃən] *n* celebrazione *f*

celebrity [sɪ'lɛbrɪtɪ] *n* celebrità *f inv*

celery ['sɛlərɪ] *n* sedano

cell [sɛl] *n* cella; (*of revolutionaries, Biol*) cellula; (*Elec*) elemento (di batteria)

cellar ['sɛləʳ] *n* sottosuolo; cantina

cello ['tʃɛləu] *n* violoncello

cellophane® ['sɛləfeɪn] *n* cellophane® *m*

cellphone ['sɛlfəun] *n* cellulare *m*

Celsius ['sɛlsɪəs] *adj* Celsius *inv*

Celtic ['kɛltɪk, 'sɛltɪk] *adj* celtico/a

cement [sə'mɛnt] *n* cemento

cemetery ['sɛmɪtrɪ] *n* cimitero

censor ['sɛnsəʳ] *n* censore *m* ▷ *vt* censurare; **censorship** *n* censura

census ['sɛnsəs] *n* censimento

cent [sɛnt] *n* (*of dollar, euro*) centesimo; *see also* **per cent**

centenary [sɛn'ti:nərɪ], (US) **centennial** [sɛn'tɛnɪəl] *n* centenario

center ['sɛntəʳ] *n*, *vt* (US) = **centre**

centi...: **centigrade** ['sɛntɪɡreɪd] *adj* centigrado/a; **centimetre**, (US) **centimeter** ['sɛntɪmi:təʳ] *n* centimetro; **centipede** ['sɛntɪpi:d] *n* centopiedi *m inv*

central ['sɛntrəl] *adj* centrale; **Central America** *n* America centrale; **central heating** *n* riscaldamento centrale; **central reservation** (BRIT Aut) banchina *f* spartitraffico *inv*

centre, (US) **center** ['sɛntəʳ] *n* centro ▷ *vt* centrare; (*concentrate*): **to ~ (on)** concentrare (su); **centre-forward** *n* (*Sport*) centroavanti *m inv*; **centre-half** *n* (*Sport*) centromediano

century ['sɛntjurɪ] *n* secolo; **in the twentieth ~** nel ventesimo secolo

CEO *n abbr* = **chief executive officer**

ceramic [sɪ'ræmɪk] *adj* ceramico/a

cereal ['si:rɪəl] *n* cereale *m*

ceremony ['sɛrɪmənɪ] *n* cerimonia; **to stand on ~** fare complimenti

certain ['sə:tən] *adj* certo/a; **to make ~ of** assicurarsi di; **for ~** per certo, di sicuro; **certainly** *adv* certamente, certo; **certainty** *n* certezza

certificate [sə'tɪfɪkɪt] *n* certificato; diploma *m*

certify ['sə:tɪfaɪ] *vt* certificare; (*award diploma to*) conferire un diploma a; (*declare insane*) dichiarare pazzo/a

cf. *abbr* (= *compare*) cfr

CFC *n abbr* (= *chlorofluorocarbon*) CFC *m inv*

chain [tʃeɪn] *n* catena ▷ *vt* (*also:* **~ up**) incatenare; **chain-smoke** *vi* fumare una sigaretta dopo l'altra

chair [tʃɛəʳ] *n* sedia; (*armchair*) poltrona; (*of university*) cattedra; (*of meeting*) presidenza ▷ *vt* (*meeting*) presiedere; **chairlift** *n* seggiovia; **chairman** *n* (*irreg*) presidente *m*; **chairperson** *n* presidente/essa; **chairwoman** *n* (*irreg*) presidentessa

chalet ['ʃæleɪ] *n* chalet *m inv*

chalk [tʃɔ:k] *n* gesso; **chalkboard** (US) *n* lavagna

challenge ['tʃælɪndʒ] *n* sfida ▷ *vt* sfidare; (*statement, right*) mettere in dubbio; **to ~ sb to do** sfidare qn a fare; **challenging** *adj* (*task*) impegnativo/a; (*remark*) provocatorio/a; (*look*) di sfida

chamber ['tʃeɪmbəʳ] *n* camera; **chambermaid** *n* cameriera

champagne [ʃæm'peɪn] *n* champagne *m inv*

champion ['tʃæmpɪən] *n* campione/essa; **championship** *n* campionato

chance [tʃɑ:ns] *n* caso; (*opportunity*) occasione *f*; (*likelihood*) possibilità *f inv* ▷ *vt*: **to ~ it** rischiare, provarci ▷ *adj* fortuito/a; **to take a ~** rischiare; **by ~** per caso

chancellor ['tʃɑ:nsələʳ] *n* cancelliere *m*; **C~ of the Exchequer** (BRIT) Cancelliere *m* dello Scacchiere

chandelier [ʃændə'lɪəʳ] *n* lampadario

change [tʃeɪndʒ] *vt* cambiare; (*transform*): **to ~ sb into** trasformare qn in ▷ *vi* cambiare; (*change one's clothes*) cambiarsi; (*be transformed*): **to ~ into** trasformarsi in ▷ *n* cambiamento; (*money*) resto; **to ~ one's mind** cambiare idea; **a ~ of clothes** un cambio (di vestiti); **for a ~** tanto per cambiare; **small ~** spiccioli *mpl*; **keep the ~** tenga il resto; **sorry, I don't have any ~** mi dispiace, non ho spiccioli; **change over** *vi* (*from sth to sth*) passare; (*players etc*) scambiarsi (*di posto o di campo*) ▷ *vt* cambiare; **changeable** *adj* (*weather*) variabile; **change machine** *n* distributore *m* automatico di monete; **changing room** *n* (BRIT: *in shop*) camerino; (*Sport*) spogliatoio

channel ['tʃænl] *n* canale *m*; (*of river, sea*) alveo ▷ *vt* canalizzare; **Channel Tunnel** *n*: **the Channel Tunnel** il tunnel sotto la Manica

chant [tʃɑːnt] n canto; salmodia ▷ vt
cantare; salmodiare

chaos ['keɪɒs] n caos m

chaotic [keɪ'ɒtɪk] adj caotico/a

chap [tʃæp] n (BRIT col: man) tipo

chapel ['tʃæpl] n cappella

chapped [tʃæpt] adj (skin, lips)
screpolato/a

chapter ['tʃæptə'] n capitolo

character ['kærɪktə'] n carattere m; (in
novel, film) personaggio; **characteristic**
['kærɪktə'rɪstɪk] adj caratteristico/a ▷ n
caratteristica; **characterize**
['kærɪktəraɪz] vt caratterizzare;
(describe): **to characterize (as)** descrivere
(come)

charcoal ['tʃɑːkəul] n carbone m di legna

charge [tʃɑːdʒ] n accusa; (cost) prezzo;
(responsibility) responsabilità ▷ vt (gun,
battery, Mil: enemy) caricare; (customer)
fare pagare a; (sum) fare pagare; (Law): **to
~ sb (with)** accusare qn (di) ▷ vi (gen with,
up, along etc) lanciarsi; **charges** npl: **bank
~s** commissioni fpl bancarie; **to reverse
the ~s** (Tel) fare una telefonata a carico
del destinatario; **to take ~ of** incaricarsi
di; **to be in ~ of** essere responsabile per;
how much do you ~ for this repair?
quanto chiede per la riparazione?; **to ~ an
expense (up) to sb** addebitare una spesa
a qn; **charge card** n (of shop) carta f clienti
inv; **charger** n (also: **battery charger**)
caricabatterie m inv; (old: warhorse)
destriero

charismatic [kærɪz'mætɪk] adj
carismatico/a

charity ['tʃærɪtɪ] n carità; (organization)
opera pia; **charity shop** n (BRIT) negozi che
vendono articoli di seconda mano e devolvono il
ricavato in beneficenza

charm [tʃɑːm] n fascino; (on bracelet)
ciondolo ▷ vt affascinare, incantare;
charming adj affascinante

chart [tʃɑːt] n tabella; grafico; (map) carta
nautica ▷ vt fare una carta nautica di;
charts npl (Mus) hit parade f

charter ['tʃɑːtə'] vt (plane) noleggiare ▷ n
(document) carta; **chartered accountant**
['tʃɑːtəd-] n (BRIT) ragioniere/a
professionista; **charter flight** n volo m
charter inv

chase [tʃeɪs] vt inseguire; (also: **~ away**)
cacciare ▷ n caccia

chat [tʃæt] vi (also: **have a ~**) chiacchierare;
(on the internet) chattare ▷ n chiacchierata;
(on the internet) chat f inv; **chat up** vt (BRIT
col: girl, boy) abbordare; **chat room** n
(Internet) chat f inv; **chat show** n (BRIT) talk
show m inv

chatter ['tʃætə'] vi (person) ciarlare; (bird)
cinguettare; (teeth) battere ▷ n ciarle fpl;
cinguettio

chauffeur ['ʃəufə'] n autista m

chauvinist ['ʃəuvɪnɪst] n (also: **male ~**)
maschilista m; (nationalist) sciovinista m/f

cheap [tʃiːp] adj a buon mercato,
economico/a; (joke) grossolano/a; (poor
quality) di cattiva qualità ▷ adv a buon
mercato; **cheap day return** n biglietto
ridotto di andata e ritorno valido in giornata;
cheaply adv a buon prezzo, a buon
mercato

cheat [tʃiːt] vi imbrogliare; (at school)
copiare ▷ vt ingannare ▷ n imbroglione
m; **to ~ sb out of sth** defraudare qn di qc;
cheat on vt fus (husband, wife) tradire

Chechnya [tʃɪtʃ'njaː] n Cecenia

check [tʃɛk] vt verificare; (passport, ticket)
controllare; (halt) fermare; (restrain)
contenere ▷ n verifica; controllo; (curb)
freno; (us: bill) conto; (pattern: gen pl)
quadretti mpl; (us) = **cheque** ▷ adj (pattern,
cloth) a quadretti; **check in** vi (in hotel)
registrare; (at airport) presentarsi
all'accettazione ▷ vt (luggage) depositare;
check off vt segnare; **check out** vi (from
hotel) saldare il conto; **check up** vi: **to ~ up
(on sth)** investigare (qc); **to ~ up on sb**
informarsi sul conto di qn; **checkbook** n
(us) = **chequebook**; **checkers** n (us)
dama; **check-in** n (also: **check-in desk**)
(at airport) check-in m inv, accettazione f
(bagagli inv); **checking account** n (us)
conto corrente; **checklist** n lista di
controllo; **checkmate** n scaccomatto;
checkout n (in supermarket) cassa;
checkpoint n posto di blocco; **checkroom**
n (us) deposito m bagagli inv; **checkup** n
(Med) controllo medico

cheddar ['tʃɛdə'] n formaggio duro di latte di
mucca di colore bianco o arancione

cheek [tʃiːk] n guancia; (impudence) faccia
tosta; **cheekbone** n zigomo; **cheeky** adj
sfacciato/a

cheer [tʃɪə'] vt applaudire; (gladden)
rallegrare ▷ vi applaudire ▷ n grido (di
incoraggiamento); **cheers** npl (of approval,
encouragement) applausi mpl; evviva mpl; **~s!**
salute!; **cheer up** vi rallegrarsi, farsi animo
▷ vt rallegrare; **cheerful** adj allegro/a

cheerio ['tʃɪərɪ'əu] excl (BRIT) ciao!

cheerleader ['tʃɪəliːdə'] n cheerleader f inv

cheese [tʃiːz] n formaggio; **cheeseburger**
n cheeseburger m inv; **cheesecake** n specie
di torta di ricotta, a volte con frutta

chef [ʃɛf] n capocuoco

chemical ['kɛmɪkl] adj chimico/a ▷ n
prodotto chimico

chemist ['kɛmɪst] n (BRIT: pharmacist) farmacista m/f; (scientist) chimico/a; **~'s shop** n (BRIT) farmacia; **chemistry** n chimica

cheque, (US) **check** [tʃɛk] n assegno; **chequebook** n libretto degli assegni; **cheque card** n carta f assegni inv

cherry ['tʃɛrɪ] n ciliegia; (also: ~ **tree**) ciliegio

chess [tʃɛs] n scacchi mpl

chest [tʃɛst] n petto; (box) cassa

chestnut ['tʃɛsnʌt] n castagna; (also: ~ **tree**) castagno

chest of drawers n cassettone m

chew [tʃuː] vt masticare; **chewing gum** n chewing gum m

chic [ʃiːk] adj elegante

chick [tʃɪk] n pulcino; (col) pollastrella

chicken ['tʃɪkɪn] n pollo; (col: coward) coniglio; **chicken out** vi (col) avere fifa; **chickenpox** n varicella

chickpea ['tʃɪkpiː] n cece m

chief [tʃiːf] n capo ▷ adj principale; **chief executive**, (US) **chief executive officer** n direttore m generale; **chiefly** adv per lo più, soprattutto

child (pl **children**) [tʃaɪld, 'tʃɪldrən] n bambino/a; (offspring) figlio/a; **children** minori; **child benefit** n (BRIT) ≈ assegni mpl familiari; **childbirth** n parto; **childcare** n il badare ai bambini; **childhood** n infanzia; **childish** adj puerile; **child minder** [-'maɪndə(r)] n (BRIT) bambinaia; **children** ['tʃɪldrən] npl of **child**

Chile ['tʃɪlɪ] n Cile m

Chilean ['tʃɪlɪən] adj, n cileno/a

chill [tʃɪl] n freddo; (Med) infreddatura ▷ vt raffreddare; **chill out** vi (esp US col) darsi una calmata

chilli, (US) **chili** ['tʃɪlɪ] n peperoncino

chilly ['tʃɪlɪ] adj freddo/a, fresco/a; **to feel ~** sentirsi infreddolito/a

chimney ['tʃɪmnɪ] n camino

chimpanzee [tʃɪmpæn'ziː] n scimpanzé m inv

chin [tʃɪn] n mento

China ['tʃaɪnə] n Cina

china ['tʃaɪnə] n porcellana

Chinese [tʃaɪ'niːz] adj cinese ▷ n (pl inv) cinese m/f; (Ling) cinese m

chip [tʃɪp] n (gen pl: Culin) patatina fritta; (: US: also: **potato ~**) patatina; (of wood, glass, stone) scheggia; (microchip) chip m inv ▷ vt (cup, plate) scheggiare; **chip and PIN** n sistema m chip e PIN; **chip and PIN machine** lettore m di carte chip e PIN; **chip and PIN card** carta chip e PIN; **chip shop** n (BRIT) vedi nota **"chip shop"**

chiropodist [kɪ'rɔpədɪst] n (BRIT) pedicure m f inv

chisel ['tʃɪzl] n cesello

chives [tʃaɪvz] npl erba cipollina

chlorine ['klɔːriːn] n cloro

choc-ice ['tʃɔkaɪs] n (BRIT) gelato ricoperto al cioccolato

chocolate ['tʃɔklɪt] n (substance) cioccolato, cioccolata; (drink) cioccolata; (a sweet) cioccolatino

choice [tʃɔɪs] n scelta ▷ adj scelto/a

choir ['kwaɪə(r)] n coro

choke [tʃəuk] vi soffocare ▷ vt soffocare; (block) ingombrare ▷ n (Aut) valvola dell'aria; **to be ~d with** essere intasato/a

cholesterol [kə'lɛstərɔl] n colesterolo

chook [tʃuk] n (AUST, NZ col) gallina

choose (pt **chose**, pp **chosen**) [tʃuːz, tʃəuz, 'tʃəuzn] vt scegliere; **to ~ to do** decidere di fare; preferire fare

chop [tʃɔp] vt (wood) spaccare; (Culin: also: ~ **up**) tritare ▷ n (Culin) costoletta; **chop down** vt (tree) abbattere; **chop off** vt tagliare; **chopsticks** ['tʃɔpstɪks] npl bastoncini mpl cinesi

chord [kɔːd] n (Mus) accordo

chore [tʃɔː(r)] n faccenda; **household ~s** faccende fpl domestiche

chorus ['kɔːrəs] n coro; (repeated part of song, also fig) ritornello

chose [tʃəuz] pt of **choose**

chosen ['tʃəuzn] pp of **choose**

Christ [kraɪst] n Cristo

christen ['krɪsn] vt battezzare; **christening** n battesimo

Christian ['krɪstɪən] adj, n cristiano/a; **Christianity** [krɪstɪ'ænɪtɪ] n cristianesimo; **Christian name** n nome m di battesimo

Christmas ['krɪsməs] n Natale m; **happy** or **merry ~!** Buon Natale!; **Christmas card** n cartolina di Natale; **Christmas carol** n canto natalizio; **Christmas Day** n il giorno di Natale; **Christmas Eve** n la vigilia di Natale; **Christmas pudding** n (esp BRIT) specie di budino con frutta secca, spezie e brandy; **Christmas tree** n albero di Natale

chrome [krəum] n cromo

chronic ['krɔnɪk] adj cronico/a

chrysanthemum [krɪˈsænθəməm] *n* crisantemo

chubby [ˈtʃʌbɪ] *adj* paffuto/a

chuck [tʃʌk] *vt* buttare, gettare; **to ~ (up** *or* **in)** (BRIT) piantare; **chuck out** *vt* buttar fuori

chuckle [ˈtʃʌkl] *vi* ridere sommessamente

chum [tʃʌm] *n* compagno/a

chunk [tʃʌŋk] *n* pezzo

church [tʃəːtʃ] *n* chiesa; **churchyard** *n* sagrato

churn [tʃəːn] *n* (*for butter*) zangola; (*also:* **milk ~**) bidone *m*

chute [ʃuːt] *n* (*also:* **rubbish ~**) canale *m* di scarico; (BRIT: *children's slide*) scivolo

chutney [ˈtʃʌtnɪ] *n* salsa piccante (di frutta, zucchero e spezie)

CIA *n abbr* (US: = *Central Intelligence Agency*) C.I.A. *f*

CID *n abbr* (BRIT: = *Criminal Investigation Department*) ≈ polizia giudiziaria

cider [ˈsaɪdəʳ] *n* sidro

cigar [sɪˈɡɑːʳ] *n* sigaro

cigarette [sɪɡəˈret] *n* sigaretta; **cigarette lighter** *n* accendino

cinema [ˈsɪnəmə] *n* cinema *m inv*

cinnamon [ˈsɪnəmən] *n* cannella

circle [ˈsəːkl] *n* cerchio; (*of friends etc*) circolo; (*in cinema*) galleria ▷ *vi* girare in circolo ▷ *vt* (*surround*) circondare; (*move round*) girare intorno a

circuit [ˈsəːkɪt] *n* circuito

circular [ˈsəːkjuləʳ] *adj* circolare ▷ *n* circolare *f*

circulate [ˈsəːkjuleɪt] *vi* circolare ▷ *vt* far circolare; **circulation** [səːkjuˈleɪʃən] *n* circolazione *f*; (*of newspaper*) tiratura

circumstances [ˈsəːkəmstənsɪz] *npl* circostanze *fpl*; (*financial condition*) condizioni *fpl* finanziarie

circus [ˈsəːkəs] *n* circo

cite [saɪt] *vt* citare

citizen [ˈsɪtɪzn] *n* (*of country*) cittadino/a; (*of town*) abitante *m/f*; **citizenship** *n* cittadinanza

citrus fruit [ˈsɪtrəs-] *n* agrume *m*

city [ˈsɪtɪ] *n* città *f inv*; **the C~** la Città di Londra (*centro commerciale*); **city centre** *n* centro della città; **City Technology College** *n* (BRIT) istituto tecnico superiore (*finanziato dall'industria*)

civic [ˈsɪvɪk] *adj* civico/a

civil [ˈsɪvɪl] *adj* civile; **civilian** [sɪˈvɪlɪən] *adj*, *n* borghese (*m/f*)

civilization [sɪvɪlaɪˈzeɪʃən] *n* civiltà *f inv*

civilized [ˈsɪvɪlaɪzd] *adj* civilizzato/a; (*fig*) cortese

civil: civil law *n* codice *m* civile; (*study*) diritto civile; **civil rights** *npl* diritti *mpl* civili;

civil servant *n* impiegato/a statale; **Civil Service** *n* amministrazione *f* statale; **civil war** *n* guerra civile

CJD *n abbr* (= *Creutzfeld-Jakob disease*) malattia di Creutzfeldt-Jakob

claim [kleɪm] *vt* (*rights etc*) rivendicare; (*damages*) richiedere; (*assert*) sostenere ▷ *vi* (*for insurance*) fare una domanda d'indennizzo ▷ *n* rivendicazione *f*; pretesa; richiesta; **claim form** *n* (*gen*) modulo di richiesta; (*for expenses*) modulo di rimborso spese

clam [klæm] *n* vongola

clamp [klæmp] *n* pinza; morsa ▷ *vt* stringere con una morsa; (*Aut: wheel*) applicare le ganasce a

clan [klæn] *n* clan *m inv*

clap [klæp] *vi* applaudire

claret [ˈklærət] *n* vino di Bordeaux

clarify [ˈklærɪfaɪ] *vt* chiarificare, chiarire

clarinet [klærɪˈnet] *n* clarinetto

clarity [ˈklærɪtɪ] *n* chiarezza

clash [klæʃ] *n* frastuono; (*fig*) scontro ▷ *vi* scontrarsi; cozzare

clasp [klɑːsp] *n* (*hold*) stretta; (*of necklace, bag*) fermaglio, fibbia ▷ *vt* stringere

class [klɑːs] *n* classe *f* ▷ *vt* classificare

classic [ˈklæsɪk] *adj* classico/a ▷ *n* classico; **classical** *adj* classico/a

classification [klæsɪfɪˈkeɪʃən] *n* classificazione *f*

classify [ˈklæsɪfaɪ] *vt* classificare

classmate [ˈklɑːsmeɪt] *n* compagno/a di classe

classroom [ˈklɑːsrum] *n* aula

classy [ˈklɑːsɪ] *adj* (*col*) chic *inv*, elegante

clatter [ˈklætəʳ] *n* tintinnio; scalpitio ▷ *vi* tintinnare; scalpitare

clause [klɔːz] *n* clausola; (*Ling*) proposizione *f*

claustrophobic [klɔːstrəˈfəubɪk] *adj* claustrofobico/a

claw [klɔː] *n* (*of bird of prey*) artiglio; (*of lobster*) pinza

clay [kleɪ] *n* argilla

clean [kliːn] *adj* pulito/a; (*outline, break, movement*) netto/a ▷ *vt* pulire; **clean up** *vt* (*also fig*) ripulire; **cleaner** *n* (*person*) uomo (donna) delle pulizie; **cleaner's** *n* (*also:* **dry cleaner's**) tintoria; **cleaning** *n* pulizia

cleanser [ˈklenzəʳ] *n* detergente *m*

clear [klɪəʳ] *adj* chiaro/a; (*glass etc*) trasparente; (*road, way*) libero/a; (*conscience*) pulito/a ▷ *vt* sgombrare; liberare; (*table*) sparecchiare; (*Law: suspect*) discolpare; (*obstacle*) superare; (*cheque*) fare la compensazione di ▷ *vi* (*weather*) rasserenarsi; (*fog*) andarsene ▷ *adv*: **~ of** distante da; **clear away** *vt* (*things, clothes,* *etc*) mettere a posto; **to ~ away the dishes** sparecchiare la tavola; **clear up** *vt* mettere in ordine; (*mystery*) risolvere; **clearance** *n* (*removal*) sgombro; (*permission*) autorizzazione *f*, permesso; **clear-cut** *adj* ben delineato/a, distinto/a; **clearing** *n* radura; **clearly** *adv* chiaramente; **clearway** *n* (BRIT) strada con divieto di sosta

clench [klɛntʃ] *vt* stringere

clergy ['klɜːdʒɪ] *n* clero

clerk [klɑːk, US klɜːrk] *n* (BRIT) impiegato/a; (US) commesso/a

clever ['klɛvər] *adj* (*mentally*) intelligente; (*deft, skilful*) abile; (*device, arrangement*) ingegnoso/a

cliché ['kliːʃeɪ] *n* cliché *m inv*

click [klɪk] *vi* scattare; (*Comput*) cliccare ⊳ *vt*: **to ~ one's tongue** schioccare la lingua; **to ~ one's heels** battere i tacchi

client ['klaɪənt] *n* cliente *m/f*

cliff [klɪf] *n* scogliera scoscesa, rupe *f*

climate ['klaɪmɪt] *n* clima *m*; **climate change** *n* cambiamenti *mpl* climatici

climax ['klaɪmæks] *n* culmine *m*; (*sexual*) orgasmo

climb [klaɪm] *vi* salire; (*clamber*) arrampicarsi ⊳ *vt* salire; (*Climbing*) scalare ⊳ *n* salita; arrampicata; scalata; **climb down** *vi* scendere; (BRIT *fig*) far marcia indietro; **climber** *n* rocciatore/trice; alpinista *m/f*; **climbing** *n* alpinismo

clinch [klɪntʃ] *vt* (*deal*) concludere

cling (*pt, pp* **clung**) [klɪŋ, klʌŋ] *vi*: **to ~ (to)** tenersi stretto/a (a), aggrapparsi (a); (*clothes*) aderire strettamente (a)

clingfilm® ['klɪŋfɪlm] *n* pellicola trasparente (*per alimenti*)

clinic ['klɪnɪk] *n* clinica

clip [klɪp] *n* (*for hair*) forcina; (*also*: **paper ~**) graffetta; (*TV, Cine*) sequenza ⊳ *vt* attaccare insieme; (*hair, nails*) tagliare; (*hedge*) tosare; **clipping** *n* (*from newspaper*) ritaglio

cloak [kləʊk] *n* mantello ⊳ *vt* avvolgere; **cloakroom** *n* (*for coats etc*) guardaroba *m inv*; (BRIT: *W.C.*) gabinetti *mpl*

clock [klɒk] *n* orologio; **clock in, clock on** *vi* timbrare il cartellino (all'entrata); **clock off, clock out** *vi* timbrare il cartellino (all'uscita); **clockwise** *adv* in senso orario; **clockwork** *n* movimento *or* meccanismo a orologeria ⊳ *adj* a molla

clog [klɒg] *n* zoccolo ⊳ *vt* intasare ⊳ *vi* (*also*: **~ up**) intasarsi, bloccarsi

clone [kləʊn] *n* clone *m*

close¹ [kləʊs] *adj* vicino/a; (*watch*) stretto/a; (*examination*) attento/a; (*contest*) combattuto/a; (*weather*) afoso/a ⊳ *adv* vicino, dappresso; **~ to** vicino a; **~ by, ~ at**

hand qui (*or* lì) vicino; **a ~ friend** un amico intimo; **to have a ~ shave** (*fig*) scamparla bella

close² [kləʊz] *vt* chiudere ⊳ *vi* (*shop etc*) chiudere; (*lid, door etc*) chiudersi; (*end*) finire ⊳ *n* (*end*) fine *f*; **close down** *vi* cessare (definitivamente); **closed** *adj* chiuso/a

closely ['kləʊslɪ] *adv* (*examine, watch*) da vicino; **we are ~ related** siamo parenti stretti

closet ['klɒzɪt] *n* (*cupboard*) armadio

close-up ['kləʊsʌp] *n* primo piano

closing time *n* orario di chiusura

closure ['kləʊʒər] *n* chiusura

clot [klɒt] *n* (*also*: **blood ~**) coagulo; (*col: idiot*) scemo/a ⊳ *vi* coagularsi

cloth [klɒθ] *n* (*material*) tessuto, stoffa; (BRIT: *also*: **tea~**) strofinaccio

clothes [kləʊðz] *npl* abiti *mpl*, vestiti *mpl*; **clothes line** *n* corda (per stendere il bucato); **clothes peg**, (US) **clothes pin** *n* molletta

clothing ['kləʊðɪŋ] *n* = **clothes**

cloud [klaʊd] *n* nuvola; **cloud over** *vi* rannuvolarsi; (*fig*) offuscarsi; **cloudy** *adj* nuvoloso/a; (*liquid*) torbido/a

clove [kləʊv] *n* chiodo di garofano; **clove of garlic** *n* spicchio d'aglio

clown [klaʊn] *n* pagliaccio ⊳ *vi* (*also*: **~ about, ~ around**) fare il pagliaccio

club [klʌb] *n* (*society*) club *m inv*, circolo; (*weapon, Golf*) mazza ⊳ *vt* bastonare ⊳ *vi*: **to ~ together** associarsi; **clubs** *npl* (*Cards*) fiori *mpl*; **club class** *n* (*Aviat*) classe *f* club *inv*

clue [kluː] *n* indizio; (*in crosswords*) definizione *f*; **I haven't a ~** non ho la minima idea

clump [klʌmp] *n* (*of flowers, trees*) gruppo; (*of grass*) ciuffo

clumsy ['klʌmzɪ] *adj* goffo/a

clung [klʌŋ] *pt, pp of* **cling**

cluster ['klʌstər] *n* gruppo ⊳ *vi* raggrupparsi

clutch [klʌtʃ] *n* (*grip, grasp*) presa, stretta; (*Aut*) frizione *f* ⊳ *vt* afferrare, stringere forte

cm *abbr* (= *centimetre*) cm

Co. *abbr* = *county*; (= *company*) C., C.ia

c/o *abbr* (= *care of*) presso

coach [kəʊtʃ] *n* (*bus*) pullman *m inv*; (*horse-drawn, of train*) carrozza; (*Sport*) allenatore/ trice; (*tutor*) chi dà ripetizioni a ⊳ *vt* allenare; dare ripetizioni a; **coach station** (BRIT) *n* stazione *f* delle corriere; **coach trip** *n* viaggio in pullman

coal [kəʊl] *n* carbone *m*

coalition [kəʊə'lɪʃən] *n* coalizione *f*

coarse [kɔːs] *adj* (*salt, sand etc*) grosso/a; (*cloth, person*) rozzo/a

coast [kəust] n costa ▷ vi (with cycle etc) scendere a ruota libera; **coastal** adj costiero/a; **coastguard** n guardia costiera; **coastline** n linea costiera

coat [kəut] n cappotto; (of animal) pelo; (of paint) mano f ▷ vt coprire; **coat hanger** n attaccapanni m inv; **coating** n rivestimento

coax [kəuks] vt indurre (con moine)

cob [kɔb] n see **corn**

cobbled ['kɔbld] adj: ~ **street** strada pavimentata a ciottoli

cobweb ['kɔbwɛb] n ragnatela

cocaine [kə'keɪn] n cocaina

cock [kɔk] n (rooster) gallo; (male bird) maschio ▷ vt (gun) armare; **cockerel** n galletto

cockney ['kɔknɪ] n cockney mf inv (abitante dei quartieri popolari dell'East End di Londra)

cockpit ['kɔkpɪt] n abitacolo

cockroach ['kɔkrəutʃ] n blatta

cocktail ['kɔkteɪl] n cocktail m inv

cocoa ['kəukəu] n cacao

coconut ['kəukənʌt] n noce f di cocco

cod [kɔd] n merluzzo

C.O.D. abbr = **cash on delivery**

code [kəud] n codice m

coeducational ['kəuɛdju'keɪʃənl] adj misto/a

coffee ['kɔfɪ] n caffè m inv; **coffee bar** n (BRIT) caffè m inv; **coffee bean** n grano or chicco di caffè; **coffee break** n pausa per il caffè; **coffee maker** n bollitore m per il caffè; **coffeepot** n caffettiera; **coffee shop** n ≈ caffè m inv; **coffee table** n tavolino

coffin ['kɔfɪn] n bara

cog [kɔg] n dente m

cognac ['kɔnjæk] n cognac m inv

coherent [kəu'hɪərənt] adj coerente

coil [kɔɪl] n rotolo; (Aut, Elec) bobina; (contraceptive) spirale f ▷ vt avvolgere

coin [kɔɪn] n moneta ▷ vt (word) coniare

coincide [kəun'saɪd] vi coincidere; **coincidence** [kəu'ɪnsɪdəns] n combinazione f

Coke® [kəuk] n coca f inv

coke [kəuk] n coke m

colander ['kɔləndər] n colino

cold [kəuld] adj freddo/a ▷ n freddo; (Med) raffreddore m; it's ~ fa freddo; **to be** ~ (person) aver freddo; (object) essere freddo/a; **to catch** ~ prendere freddo; **to catch a** ~ prendere un raffreddore; **in** ~ **blood** a sangue freddo; **cold sore** n erpete m

coleslaw ['kəulslɔː] n insalata di cavolo bianco

colic ['kɔlɪk] n colica

collaborate [kə'læbəreɪt] vi collaborare

collapse [kə'læps] vi crollare ▷ n crollo; (Med) collasso

collar ['kɔlər] n (of coat, shirt) colletto; (for dog) collare m; **collarbone** n clavicola

colleague ['kɔliːg] n collega m/f

collect [kə'lɛkt] vt (gen) raccogliere; (as a hobby) fare collezione di; (BRIT: call for) prendere; (money owed, pension) riscuotere; (donations, subscriptions) fare una colletta di ▷ vi adunarsi, riunirsi; (rubbish etc) ammucchiarsi ▷ (US Tel): **to call** ~ fare una chiamata a carico del destinatario; **collection** [kə'lɛkʃən] n collezione f; raccolta; (for money) colletta; **collective** adj collettivo/a ▷ n collettivo; **collector** [kə'lɛktər] n collezionista m/f

college ['kɔlɪdʒ] n college m inv; (of technology, agriculture etc) istituto superiore

collide [kə'laɪd] vi: **to** ~ (**with**) scontrarsi (con)

collision [kə'lɪʒən] n collisione f, scontro

cologne [kə'ləun] n (also: **eau de ~**) acqua di colonia

Colombia [kə'lɔmbɪə] n Colombia; **Colombian** adj, n colombiano/a

colon ['kəulən] n (sign) due punti mpl; (Med) colon m inv

colonel ['kəːnl] n colonnello

colonial [kə'ləunɪəl] adj coloniale

colony ['kɔlənɪ] n colonia

colour, (US) **color** ['kʌlər] n colore m ▷ vt colorare; (tint, dye) tingere; (fig: affect) influenzare ▷ vi (blush) arrossire; **colour in** vt colorare; **colour-blind** adj daltonico/a; **coloured** adj (photo) a colori; **colour film** n (for camera) pellicola a colori; **colourful** adj pieno/a di colore, a vivaci colori; (personality) colorato/a; **colouring** n (substance) colorante m; (complexion) colorito; **colour television** n televisione f a colori

column ['kɔləm] n colonna

coma ['kəumə] n coma m inv

comb [kəum] n pettine m ▷ vt (hair) pettinare; (area) battere a tappeto

combat ['kɔmbæt] n combattimento ▷ vt combattere, lottare contro

combination [kɔmbɪ'neɪʃən] n combinazione f

combine vt [kəm'baɪn]: **to** ~ (**with**) combinare (con); (one quality with another): **to** ~ **sth with sth** unire qc a qc ▷ vi unirsi; (Chem) combinarsi ▷ n ['kɔmbaɪn] (Econ) associazione f

come (pt **came**, pp **come**) [kʌm, keɪm] vi venire; arrivare; **to** ~ **to** (decision etc) raggiungere; **I've** ~ **to like him** ha cominciato a piacermi; **to** ~ **undone/loose** slacciarsi/allentarsi; **come across** vt fus trovare per caso; **come along** vi (pupil, work) fare progressi; ~ **along!** avanti!, andiamo!, forza!; **come back** vi ritornare; **come down** vi scendere; (*prices*) calare; (*buildings*) essere demolito/a; **come from** vt fus venire da; provenire da; **come in** vi entrare; **come off** vi (*button*) staccarsi; (*stain*) andar via; (*attempt*) riuscire; **come on** vi (*lights*) accendersi; (*electricity*) entrare in funzione; (*pupil, undertaking*) fare progressi; **~ on!** avanti!, andiamo!, forza!; **come out** vi uscire; (*stain*) andare via; **come round** n (*after faint, operation*) riprendere conoscenza, rinvenire; **come to** vi rinvenire; **come up** vi (*sun*) salire; (*problem*) sorgere; (*event*) essere in arrivo; (*in conversation*) saltar fuori; **come up with** vt fus: **he came up with an idea** venne fuori con un'idea

comeback ['kʌmbæk] n (*Theat etc*) ritorno

comedian [kə'miːdɪən] n comico

comedy ['kɔmɪdɪ] n commedia

comet ['kɔmɪt] n cometa

comfort ['kʌmfət] n comodità f inv, benessere m; (*relief*) consolazione f, conforto ▷ vt consolare, confortare; **comfortable** adj comodo/a; (*financially*) agiato/a; **comfort station** n (*us*) gabinetti mpl

comic ['kɔmɪk] adj (*also*: **~al**) comico/a ▷ n comico; (*BRIT: magazine*) giornaletto; **comic book** n (*us*) giornalino (a fumetti); **comic strip** n fumetto

comma ['kɔmə] n virgola

command [kə'mɑːnd] n ordine m, comando; (*Mil: authority*) comando; (*mastery*) padronanza ▷ vt comandare; **to ~ sb to do** ordinare a qn di fare; **commander** n capo; (*Mil*) comandante m

commemorate [kə'mɛmərent] vt commemorare

commence [kə'mɛns] vt, vi cominciare; **commencement** n (*us Univ*) cerimonia di consegna dei diplomi

commend [kə'mɛnd] vt lodare; raccomandare

comment ['kɔmɛnt] n commento ▷ vi: **to ~ (on)** fare commenti (su); **commentary** ['kɔməntərɪ] n commentario; (*Sport*) radiocronaca; telecronaca; **commentator** ['kɔmənteɪtəˀ] n commentatore/trice; (*Sport*) radiocronista m/f; telecronista m/f

commerce ['kɔməːs] n commercio

commercial [kə'məːʃəl] adj commerciale ▷ n (*TV, Radio*) pubblicità f inv; **commercial break** n intervallo pubblicitario

commission [kə'mɪʃən] n commissione f ▷ vt (*work of art*) commissionare; **out of ~** (*Naut*) in disarmo; **commissioner** n (*Police*) questore m

commit [kə'mɪt] vt (*act*) commettere; (*to sb's care*) affidare; **to ~ o.s. (to do)** impegnarsi (a fare); **to ~ suicide** suicidarsi; **commitment** n impegno; promessa

committee [kə'mɪtɪ] n comitato, commissione f

commodity [kə'mɔdɪtɪ] n prodotto, articolo

common ['kɔmən] adj comune; (*pej*) volgare; (*usual*) normale ▷ n terreno comune; **in ~** in comune; *see also* **Commons**; **commonly** adv comunemente, usualmente; **commonplace** adj banale, ordinario/a; **Commons** npl (*BRIT Pol*): **the (House of) Commons** la Camera dei Comuni; **common sense** n buon senso; **Commonwealth** n: **the Commonwealth** il Commonwealth

◦ **COMMONWEALTH**
◦
◦ Il *Commonwealth* è un'associazione di stati
◦ sovrani indipendenti e di alcuni territori
◦ annessi che facevano parte dell'antico
◦ Impero Britannico. Ancora oggi molti
◦ stati del *Commonwealth* riconoscono
◦ simbolicamente il sovrano britannico
◦ come capo di stato, e i loro rappresentanti
◦ si riuniscono per discutere questioni di
◦ comune interesse.

communal ['kɔmjuːnl] adj (*for common use*) pubblico/a

commune n ['kɔmjuːn] (*group*) comune f ▷ vi [kə'mjuːn]: **to ~ with** mettersi in comunione con

communicate [kə'mjuːnɪkeɪt] vt comunicare, trasmettere ▷ vi: **to ~ (with)** comunicare (con)

communication [kəmjuːnɪ'keɪʃən] n comunicazione f

communion [kə'mjuːnɪən] n (*also*: **Holy C~**) comunione f

communism ['kɔmjunɪzəm] n comunismo; **communist** adj, n comunista (m/f)

community [kə'mjuːnɪtɪ] n comunità f inv; **community centre**, (*us*) **community center** n circolo ricreativo; **community service** n (*BRIT*) ≈ lavoro sostitutivo

commute [kə'mjuːt] vi fare il pendolare ▷ vt (*Law*) commutare; **commuter** n pendolare m/f

compact adj [kəm'pækt] compatto/a ▷ n ['kɔmpækt] (*also*: **powder ~**) portacipria m inv; **compact disc** n compact disc m inv; **compact disc player** n lettore m CD inv

companion [kəm'pænjən] n compagno/a

company ['kʌmpəni] n (also Comm, Mil, Theat) compagnia; **to keep sb ~** tenere compagnia a qn; **company car** n macchina (di proprietà) della ditta; **company director** n amministratore m, consigliere m di amministrazione

comparable ['kɔmpərəbl] adj simile; **~ to** or **with** paragonabile a

comparative [kəm'pærətɪv] adj relativo/a; (adjective, adverb etc) comparativo/a; **comparatively** adv relativamente

compare [kəm'pɛəʳ] vt: **to ~ sth/sb with/to** confrontare qc/qn con/a ▷ vi: **to ~ (with)** reggere il confronto (con); **comparison** [kəm'pærɪsn] n confronto; **in comparison with** confronto a

compartment [kəm'paːtmənt] n compartimento; (Rail) scompartimento

compass ['kʌmpəs] n bussola; **(a pair of) ~es** (Math) compasso; **within the ~ of** entro i limiti di

compassion [kəm'pæʃən] n compassione f

compatible [kəm'pætɪbl] adj compatibile

compel [kəm'pɛl] vt costringere, obbligare; **compelling** adj (fig: argument) irresistibile

compensate ['kɔmpənseɪt] vt risarcire ▷ vi: **to ~ for** compensare; **compensation** [kɔmpən'seɪʃən] n compensazione f; (money) risarcimento

compete [kəm'piːt] vi (take part) concorrere; (vie): **to ~ (with)** fare concorrenza (a)

competent ['kɔmpɪtənt] adj competente

competition [kɔmpɪ'tɪʃən] n gara; concorso; (Econ) concorrenza

competitive [kəm'petɪtɪv] adj (sports) agonistico/a; (person) che ha spirito di competizione; che ha spirito agonistico; (Econ) concorrenziale

competitor [kəm'petɪtəʳ] n concorrente m/f

complacent [kəm'pleɪsnt] adj compiaciuto/a di sé

complain [kəm'pleɪn] vi lagnarsi, lamentarsi; **complaint** n lamento; (in shop etc) reclamo; (Med) malattia

complement n ['kɔmplɪmənt] complemento; (especially of ship's crew etc) effettivo ▷ vt ['kɔmplɪmɛnt] (enhance) accompagnarsi bene a; **complementary** [kɔmplɪ'mɛntərɪ] adj complementare

complete [kəm'pliːt] adj completo/a ▷ vt completare; (form) riempire; **completely** adv completamente; **completion** n completamento

complex ['kɔmplɛks] adj complesso/a ▷ n (Psych, buildings etc) complesso

complexion [kəm'plɛkʃən] n (of face) carnagione f

compliance [kəm'plaɪəns] n acquiescenza; **in ~ with** (orders, wishes etc) in conformità con

complicate ['kɔmplɪkeɪt] vt complicare; **complicated** adj complicato/a; **complication** [kɔmplɪ'keɪʃən] n complicazione f

compliment n ['kɔmplɪmənt] complimento ▷ vt ['kɔmplɪmɛnt] fare un complimento a; **complimentary** [kɔmplɪ'mɛntərɪ] adj complimentoso/a, elogiativo/a; (free) in omaggio

comply [kəm'plaɪ] vi: **to ~ with** assentire a; conformarsi a

component [kəm'pəunənt] adj, n componente (m)

compose [kəm'pəuz] vt (music, poem etc) comporre; **to ~ o.s.** ricomporsi; **~d of** composto/a di; **composer** n (Mus) compositore/trice; **composition** [kɔmpə'zɪʃən] n composizione f

composure [kəm'pəuʒəʳ] n calma

compound ['kɔmpaund] n (Chem, Ling) composto; (enclosure) recinto ▷ adj composto/a

comprehension [kɔmprɪ'hɛnʃən] n comprensione f

comprehensive [kɔmprɪ'hɛnsɪv] adj completo/a; **comprehensive (school)** n (BRIT) scuola secondaria aperta a tutti

> Be careful not to translate comprehensive by the Italian word comprensivo.

compress vt [kəm'prɛs] comprimere ▷ n ['kɔmprɛs] (Med) compressa

comprise [kəm'praɪz] vt (also: **be ~d of**) comprendere

compromise ['kɔmprəmaɪz] n compromesso ▷ vt compromettere ▷ vi venire a un compromesso

compulsive [kəm'pʌlsɪv] adj (liar, gambler) che non riesce a controllarsi; (viewing, reading) cui non si può fare a meno

compulsory [kəm'pʌlsərɪ] adj obbligatorio/a

computer [kəm'pjuːtəʳ] n computer m inv, elaboratore m elettronico; **computer game** n gioco per computer; **computer-generated** adj realizzato/a al computer; **computerize** vt computerizzare; **computer programmer** n programmatore/trice; **computer programming** n programmazione f di computer; **computer science** n informatica; **computer studies** npl informatica; **computing** n informatica

con [kɔn] vt (col) truffare ▷ n truffa

conceal [kən'siːl] vt nascondere
concede [kən'siːd] vt concedere; (*admit*) ammettere
conceited [kən'siːtɪd] adj presuntuoso/a, vanitoso/a
conceive [kən'siːv] vt concepire ▷ vi concepire un bambino
concentrate ['kɔnsəntreɪt] vi concentrarsi ▷ vt concentrare
concentration [kɔnsən'treɪʃən] n concentrazione f
concept ['kɔnsɛpt] n concetto
concern [kən'səːn] n affare m; (*Comm*) azienda, ditta; (*anxiety*) preoccupazione f ▷ vt riguardare; **to be ~ed (about)** preoccuparsi (di); **concerning** prep riguardo a, circa
concert ['kɔnsət] n concerto; **concert hall** n sala da concerti
concerto [kən'tʃəːtəu] n concerto
concession [kən'sɛʃən] n concessione f
concise [kən'saɪs] adj conciso/a
conclude [kən'kluːd] vt concludere; **conclusion** [kən'kluːʒən] n conclusione f
concrete ['kɔŋkriːt] n calcestruzzo ▷ adj concreto/a; di calcestruzzo
concussion [kən'kʌʃən] n commozione f cerebrale
condemn [kən'dɛm] vt condannare; (*building*) dichiarare pericoloso/a
condensation [kɔndɛn'seɪʃən] n condensazione f
condense [kən'dɛns] vi condensarsi ▷ vt condensare
condition [kən'dɪʃən] n condizione f; (*disease*) malattia ▷ vt condizionare; **on ~ that** a condizione che + sub, a condizione di; **conditional** adj condizionale; **to be conditional upon** dipendere da; **conditioner** n (*for hair*) balsamo; (*for fabrics*) ammorbidente m
condo ['kɔndəu] n abbr (*US col*) = **condominium**
condom ['kɔndəm] n preservativo
condominium [kɔndə'mɪnɪəm] n (*US*) condominio
condone [kən'dəun] vt condonare
conduct n ['kɔndʌkt] condotta ▷ vt [kən'dʌkt] condurre; (*manage*) dirigere; amministrare; (*Mus*) dirigere; **to ~ o.s.** comportarsi; **conducted tour** [kən'dʌktɪd-] n gita accompagnata; **conductor** n (*of orchestra*) direttore m d'orchestra; (*on bus*) bigliettaio; (*US Rail*) controllore m; (*Elec*) conduttore m
cone [kəun] n cono; (*Bot*) pigna; (*traffic cone*) birillo
confectionery [kən'fɛkʃənərɪ] n dolciumi mpl

confer [kən'fəːʳ] vt: **to ~ sth on** conferire qc a ▷ vi conferire
conference ['kɔnfərns] n congresso
confess [kən'fɛs] vt confessare, ammettere ▷ vi confessarsi; **confession** [kən'fɛʃən] n confessione f
confide [kən'faɪd] vi: **to ~ in** confidarsi con
confidence ['kɔnfɪdns] n confidenza; (*trust*) fiducia; (*also:* **self-~**) sicurezza di sé; **in ~** (*speak, write*) in confidenza, confidenzialmente; **confident** adj sicuro/a; sicuro/a di sé; **confidential** [kɔnfɪ'dɛnʃəl] adj riservato/a, confidenziale
confine [kən'faɪn] vt limitare; (*shut up*) rinchiudere; **confined** adj (*space*) ristretto/a
confirm [kən'fəːm] vt confermare; **confirmation** [kɔnfə'meɪʃən] n conferma; (*Rel*) cresima
confiscate ['kɔnfɪskeɪt] vt confiscare
conflict n ['kɔnflɪkt] conflitto ▷ vi [kən'flɪkt] essere in conflitto
conform [kən'fɔːm] vi: **to ~ (to)** conformarsi (a)
confront [kən'frʌnt] vt (*enemy, danger*) affrontare; **confrontation** [kɔnfrən'teɪʃən] n scontro
confuse [kən'fjuːz] vt (*one thing with another*) confondere; **confused** adj confuso/a; **confusing** adj che fa confondere; **confusion** [kən'fjuːʒən] n confusione f
congestion [kən'dʒɛstʃən] n congestione f
congratulate [kən'grætjuleɪt] vt: **to ~ sb (on)** congratularsi con qn (per *or* di); **congratulations** [kəngrætju'leɪʃənz] npl auguri mpl; (*on success*) complimenti mpl; **congratulations (on)** congratulazioni fpl (per)
congregation [kɔŋgrɪ'geɪʃən] n congregazione f
congress ['kɔŋgrɛs] n congresso; **congressman** ['kɔŋgrɛsmən] n (*irreg: US*) membro del Congresso; **congresswoman** ['kɔŋgrɛswumən] n (*irreg: US*) (donna) membro del Congresso
conifer ['kɔnɪfəʳ] n conifero
conjugate ['kɔndʒugeɪt] vt coniugare
conjugation [kɔndʒə'geɪʃən] n coniugazione f
conjunction [kən'dʒʌŋkʃən] n congiunzione f
conjure ['kʌndʒəʳ] vi fare giochi di prestigio
connect [kə'nɛkt] vt connettere, collegare; (*Elec*) collegare; (*fig*) associare ▷ vi (*train*): **to ~ with** essere in coincidenza con; **to be ~ed with** (*associated*) aver rapporti con; **connecting flight** n volo in coincidenza;

connection [kəˈnɛkʃən] n relazione f, rapporto; (Elec) connessione f; (Tel) collegamento; (train, plane etc) coincidenza

conquer [ˈkɒŋkəʳ] vt conquistare; (feelings) vincere

conquest [ˈkɒŋkwɛst] n conquista

cons [kɒnz] npl see **pro**; **convenience**

conscience [ˈkɒnʃəns] n coscienza

conscientious [kɒnʃɪˈɛnʃəs] adj coscienzioso/a

conscious [ˈkɒnʃəs] adj consapevole; (Med) cosciente; **consciousness** n consapevolezza; (Med) coscienza

consecutive [kənˈsɛkjutɪv] adj consecutivo/a; **on 3 ~ occasions** 3 volte di fila

consensus [kənˈsɛnsəs] n consenso; **the ~ of opinion** l'opinione f unanime or comune

consent [kənˈsɛnt] n consenso ▷ vi: **to ~ (to)** acconsentire (a)

consequence [ˈkɒnsɪkwəns] n conseguenza, risultato; importanza

consequently [ˈkɒnsɪkwəntlɪ] adv di conseguenza, dunque

conservation [kɒnsəˈveɪʃən] n conservazione f

conservative [kənˈsəːvətɪv] adj, n conservatore/trice; (cautious) cauto/a; **C~** adj, n (BRIT Pol) conservatore/trice

conservatory [kənˈsəːvətrɪ] n (greenhouse) serra; (Mus) conservatorio

consider [kənˈsɪdəʳ] vt considerare; (take into account) tener conto di; **to ~ doing sth** considerare la possibilità di fare qc; **considerable** [kənˈsɪdərəbl] adj considerevole, notevole; **considerably** adv notevolmente, decisamente; **considerate** [kənˈsɪdərɪt] adj premuroso/a; **consideration** [kənsɪdəˈreɪʃən] n considerazione f; **considering** [kənˈsɪdərɪŋ] prep in considerazione di

consignment [kənˈsaɪnmənt] n (of goods) consegna; spedizione f

consist [kənˈsɪst] vi: **to ~ of** constare di, essere composto/a di

consistency [kənˈsɪstənsɪ] n consistenza; (fig) coerenza

consistent [kənˈsɪstənt] adj coerente

consolation [kɒnsəˈleɪʃən] n consolazione f

console vt [kənˈsəul] consolare ▷ n [ˈkɒnsəul] quadro di comando

consonant [ˈkɒnsənənt] n consonante f

conspicuous [kənˈspɪkjuəs] adj cospicuo/a

conspiracy [kənˈspɪrəsɪ] n congiura, cospirazione f

constable [ˈkʌnstəbl] n (BRIT) ≈ poliziotto, agente m di polizia; **chief ~** ≈ questore m

constant [ˈkɒnstənt] adj costante; continuo/a; **constantly** adv costantemente; continuamente

constipated [ˈkɒnstɪpeɪtɪd] adj stitico/a; **constipation** [kɒnstɪˈpeɪʃən] n stitichezza

constituency [kənˈstɪtjuənsɪ] n collegio elettorale

constitute [ˈkɒnstɪtjuːt] vt costituire

constitution [kɒnstɪˈtjuːʃən] n costituzione f

constraint [kənˈstreɪnt] n costrizione f

construct [kənˈstrʌkt] vt costruire; **construction** [kənˈstrʌkʃən] n costruzione f; **constructive** adj costruttivo/a

consul [ˈkɒnsl] n console m; **consulate** [ˈkɒnsjulɪt] n consolato

consult [kənˈsʌlt] vt: **to ~ sb (about sth)** consultare qn (su or riguardo a qc); **consultant** n (Med) consulente m medico; (other specialist) consulente; **consultation** [kɒnsəlˈteɪʃən] n (discussion) consultazione f; (Med, Law) consulto; **consulting room** [kənˈsʌltɪŋ-] n (BRIT) ambulatorio

consume [kənˈsjuːm] vt consumare; **consumer** n consumatore/trice

consumption [kənˈsʌmpʃən] n consumo

cont. abbr (= continued) segue

contact [ˈkɒntækt] n contatto; (person) conoscenza ▷ vt mettersi in contatto con; **contact lenses** npl lenti fpl a contatto

contagious [kənˈteɪdʒəs] adj (also fig) contagioso/a

contain [kənˈteɪn] vt contenere; **to ~ o.s.** contenersi; **container** n recipiente m; (for shipping etc) container m inv

contaminate [kənˈtæmɪneɪt] vt contaminare

cont'd abbr (= continued) segue

contemplate [ˈkɒntəmpleɪt] vt contemplare; (consider) pensare a (or di)

contemporary [kənˈtɛmpərərɪ] adj, n contemporaneo/a

contempt [kənˈtɛmpt] n disprezzo; **~ of court** (Law) oltraggio alla Corte

contend [kənˈtɛnd] vt: **to ~ that** sostenere che ▷ vi: **to ~ with** lottare contro

content¹ [ˈkɒntɛnt] n contenuto; **contents** npl (of box, case etc) contenuto; **(table of) ~s** indice m

content² [kənˈtɛnt] adj contento/a, soddisfatto/a ▷ vt contentare, soddisfare; **contented** [kənˈtɛntɪd] adj contento/a, soddisfatto/a

contest n [ˈkɒntɛst] lotta; (competition) gara, concorso ▷ vt [kənˈtɛst] contestare; (Law) impugnare; (compete for) contendersi; **contestant** [kənˈtɛstənt] n concorrente m/f; (in fight) avversario/a

context ['kɒntekst] n contesto

continent ['kɒntɪnənt] n continente m; **the C~** (BRIT) l'Europa continentale; **continental** [kɒntɪ'nentl] adj continentale; **continental breakfast** n colazione f all'europea (senza piatti caldi); **continental quilt** n (BRIT) piumino

continual [kən'tɪnjuəl] adj continuo/a; **continually** adv di continuo

continue [kən'tɪnju:] vi continuare ▷ vt continuare; (start again) riprendere

continuity [kɒntɪ'nju:ɪtɪ] n continuità; (Cine) (ordine m della) sceneggiatura

continuous [kən'tɪnjuəs] adj continuo/a, ininterrotto/a; **continuous assessment** n (BRIT) valutazione f continua; **continuously** adv (repeatedly) continuamente; (uninterruptedly) ininterrottamente

contour ['kɒntuər] n contorno, profilo; (also: **~ line**) curva di livello

contraception [kɒntrə'sepʃən] n contraccezione f

contraceptive [kɒntrə'septɪv] adj contraccettivo/a ▷ n contraccettivo

contract n ['kɒntrækt] contratto ▷ vi [kən'trækt] (become smaller) contrarsi; (Comm): **to ~ to do sth** fare un contratto per fare qc ▷ vt [kən'trækt] (illness) contrarre; **contractor** n imprenditore m

contradict [kɒntrə'dɪkt] vt contraddire; **contradiction** [kɒntrə'dɪkʃən] n contraddizione f; **to be in contradiction with** discordare con

contrary¹ ['kɒntrərɪ] adj contrario/a; (unfavourable) avverso/a, contrario/a ▷ n contrario; **on the ~** al contrario; **unless you hear to the ~** salvo contrordine

contrary² [kən'trɛərɪ] adj (perverse) bisbetico/a

contrast n ['kɒntrɑ:st] contrasto ▷ vt [kən'trɑ:st] mettere in contrasto; **in ~ to or with** contrariamente a

contribute [kən'trɪbju:t] vi contribuire ▷ vt: **to ~ £10/an article to** dare 10 sterline/un articolo a; **to ~ to** contribuire a; (newspaper) scrivere per; **contribution** [kɒntrɪ'bju:ʃən] n contributo; **contributor** [kən'trɪbjutər] n (to newspaper) collaboratore/trice

control [kən'trəul] vt (firm, operation etc) dirigere; (check) controllare ▷ n controllo; **controls** npl (of vehicle etc) comandi mpl; **to be in ~ of** avere il controllo di; **to go out of ~** (car) non rispondere ai comandi; (situation) sfuggire di mano; **control tower** n (Aviat) torre f di controllo

controversial [kɒntrə'və:ʃl] adj controverso/a, polemico/a

controversy ['kɒntrəvə:sɪ] n controversia, polemica

convenience [kən'vi:nɪəns] n comodità f inv; **at your ~** a suo comodo; **all modern ~s**, (BRIT) **all mod cons** tutte le comodità moderne

convenient [kən'vi:nɪənt] adj comodo/a

⬛ Be careful not to translate convenient by the Italian word conveniente.

convent ['kɒnvənt] n convento

convention [kən'venʃən] n convenzione f; (meeting) convegno; **conventional** adj convenzionale

conversation [kɒnvə'seɪʃən] n conversazione f

conversely [kɒn'və:slɪ] adv al contrario, per contro

conversion [kən'və:ʃən] n conversione f; (BRIT: of house) trasformazione f, rimodernamento

convert vt [kən'və:t] (Rel, Comm) convertire; (alter) trasformare ▷ n ['kɒnvə:t] convertito/a; **convertible** n macchina decappottabile

convey [kən'veɪ] vt trasportare; (thanks) comunicare; (idea) dare; **conveyor belt** [kən'veɪər-] n nastro trasportatore

convict vt [kən'vɪkt] dichiarare colpevole ▷ n ['kɒnvɪkt] carcerato/a; **conviction** [kən'vɪkʃən] n condanna; (belief) convinzione f

convince [kən'vɪns] vt: **to ~ sb (of sth/ that)** convincere qn (di qc/che), persuadere qn (di qc/che); **convinced** adj: **convinced of/that** convinto/a di/che; **convincing** adj convincente

convoy ['kɒnvɔɪ] n convoglio

cook [kuk] vt cucinare, cuocere ▷ vi cuocere; (person) cucinare ▷ n cuoco/a; **cookbook** ['kukbuk] n = **cookery book**; **cooker** n fornello, cucina; **cookery** n cucina; **cookery book** n (BRIT) libro di cucina; **cookie** n (US) biscotto; (Comput) cookie m inv; **cooking** n cucina

cool [ku:l] adj fresco/a; (not afraid) calmo/a; (unfriendly) freddo/a ▷ vt raffreddare; (room) rinfrescare ▷ vi (water) raffreddarsi; (air) rinfrescarsi; **cool down** vi raffreddarsi; (fig: person, situation) calmarsi; **cool off** vi (become calmer) calmarsi; (lose enthusiasm) perdere interesse

cop [kɒp] n (col) sbirro

cope [kəup] vi: **to ~ with** (problems) far fronte a

copper ['kɒpər] n rame m; (col: police officer) sbirro

copy ['kɒpɪ] n copia ▷ vt copiare; **copyright** n diritto d'autore

coral ['kɒrəl] n corallo

cord [kɔːd] n corda; (Elec) filo; **cords** npl (trousers) calzoni mpl (di velluto) a coste; **cordless** adj senza cavo

corduroy ['kɔːdərɔɪ] n fustagno

core [kɔːr] n (of fruit) torsolo; (of organization etc) cuore m ▷ vt estrarre il torsolo da

coriander [kɔrɪ'ændər] n coriandolo

cork [kɔːk] n sughero; (of bottle) tappo; **corkscrew** n cavatappi m inv

corn [kɔːn] n (BRIT: wheat) grano; (US: maize) granturco; (on foot) callo; **~ on the cob** (Culin) pannocchia cotta

corned beef ['kɔːnd-] n carne f di manzo in scatola

corner ['kɔːnər] n angolo; (Aut) curva ▷ vt intrappolare; mettere con le spalle al muro; (Comm: market) accaparrare ▷ vi prendere una curva

corner shop n (BRIT) piccolo negozio di generi alimentari

cornflakes ['kɔːnfleɪks] npl fiocchi mpl di granturco

cornflour ['kɔːnflauər] n (BRIT) farina finissima di granturco

cornstarch ['kɔːnstɑːtʃ] n (US) = **cornflour**

Cornwall ['kɔːnwəl] n Cornovaglia

coronary ['kɔrənərɪ] n: **~ (thrombosis)** trombosi f coronaria

coronation [kɔrə'neɪʃən] n incoronazione f

coroner ['kɔrənər] n magistrato incaricato di indagare la causa di morte in circostanze sospette

corporal ['kɔːprəl] n caporalmaggiore m ▷ adj: **~ punishment** pena corporale

corporate ['kɔːpərɪt] adj comune; (Comm) costituito/a (in corporazione)

corporation [kɔːpə'reɪʃən] n (of town) consiglio comunale; (Comm) ente m

corps (pl **corps**) [kɔːr, kɔːz] n corpo

corpse [kɔːps] n cadavere m

correct [kə'rɛkt] adj (accurate) corretto/a, esatto/a; (proper) corretto/a ▷ vt correggere; **correction** [kə'rɛkʃən] n correzione f

correspond [kɔrɪs'pɔnd] vi corrispondere; **correspondence** n corrispondenza; **correspondent** n corrispondente m/f; **corresponding** adj corrispondente

corridor ['kɔrɪdɔːr] n corridoio

corrode [kə'rəud] vt corrodere ▷ vi corrodersi

corrupt [kə'rʌpt] adj corrotto/a; (Comput) alterato/a ▷ vt corrompere; **corruption** n corruzione f

Corsica ['kɔːsɪkə] n Corsica

cosmetic [kɔz'mɛtɪk] n cosmetico; **cosmetic surgery** n chirurgia plastica

cosmopolitan [kɔzmə'pɔlɪtn] adj cosmopolita

cost [kɔst] (pt, pp **cost**) n costo ▷ vi costare ▷ vt stabilire il prezzo di; **costs** npl (Law) spese fpl; **how much does it ~?** quanto costa?

co-star ['kəustɑːr] n attore/trice della stessa importanza del protagonista

Costa Rica ['kɔstə'riːkə] n Costa Rica

costly ['kɔstlɪ] adj costoso/a, caro/a

cost-of-living ['kɔstəv'lɪvɪŋ] adj: **~ allowance** indennità f inv di contingenza

costume ['kɔstjuːm] n costume m; (lady's suit) tailleur m inv; (BRIT: also: **swimming ~**) costume da bagno

cosy, (US) **cozy** ['kəuzɪ] adj intimo/a; **I'm very ~ here** sto proprio bene qui

cot [kɔt] n (BRIT: child's) lettino; (US: folding bed) brandina

cottage ['kɔtɪdʒ] n cottage m inv; **cottage cheese** n fiocchi mpl di latte magro

cotton ['kɔtn] n cotone m; **~ dress** etc vestito etc di cotone; **cotton on** vi (col): to **~ on (to sth)** afferrare (qc); **cotton bud** n (BRIT) cotton fioc® m inv; **cotton candy** (US) n zucchero filato; **cotton wool** n (BRIT) cotone m idrofilo

couch [kautʃ] n sofà m inv

cough [kɔf] vi tossire ▷ n tosse f; **I've got a ~** ho la tosse; **cough mixture, cough syrup** n sciroppo per la tosse

could [kud] pt of **can²**

couldn't ['kudnt] = **could not**

council ['kaunsl] n consiglio; **city** or **town ~** consiglio comunale; **council estate** n (BRIT) quartiere m di case popolari; **council house** n (BRIT) casa popolare; **councillor** n consigliere/a; **council tax** n (BRIT) tassa comunale sulla proprietà

counsel ['kaunsl] n avvocato; consultazione f ▷ vt: to **~ sth/sb to do sth** consigliare qc/a qn di fare qc; **counselling**, (US) **counseling** n (Psych) assistenza psicologica; **counsellor**, (US) **counselor** n consigliere/a; (US) avvocato

count [kaunt] vt, vi contare ▷ n conto; (nobleman) conte m; **count in** vt (col) includere; **~ me in** ci sto anch'io; **count on** vt fus contare su; **countdown** n conto alla rovescia

counter ['kauntər] n banco ▷ vt opporsi a ▷ adv: **~ to** contro; in opposizione a; **counter-clockwise** ['kauntə'klɔkwaɪz] (US) adv in senso antiorario

counterfeit ['kauntəfɪt] n contraffazione f, falso ▷ vt contraffare, falsificare ▷ adj falso/a

counterpart ['kauntəpɑːt] n (of document etc) copia; (of person) corrispondente m/f

counterterrorism ['kauntə'terərızəm] n antiterrorismo

countess ['kauntıs] n contessa

countless ['kauntlıs] adj innumerevole

country ['kʌntrı] n paese m; (native land) patria; (as opposed to town) campagna; (region) regione f; **country and western (music)** n musica country e western, country m; **country house** n villa in campagna; **countryside** n campagna

county ['kauntı] n contea

coup (pl **coups**) [ku:, ku:z] n colpo; (also: **~ d'état**) colpo di Stato

couple ['kʌpl] n coppia; **a ~ of** un paio di

coupon ['ku:pɔn] n buono; (Comm) coupon m inv

courage ['kʌrıdʒ] n coraggio; **courageous** adj coraggioso/a

courgette [kuə'ʒet] n (BRIT) zucchina

courier ['kurıəʳ] n corriere m; (for tourists) guida

course [kɔ:s] n corso; (of ship) rotta; (for golf) campo; (part of meal) piatto; **of ~** senz'altro, naturalmente; **~ (of action)** modo d'agire; **a ~ of treatment** (Med) una cura

court [kɔ:t] n corte f; (Tennis) campo ▷ vt (woman) fare la corte a; **to take to ~** citare in tribunale

courtesy ['kə:təsı] n cortesia; **by ~ of** per gentile concessione di; **courtesy bus, courtesy coach** n navetta gratuita (di hotel, aeroporto)

court: court-house n (US) palazzo di giustizia; **courtroom** n ['kɔ:trum] n tribunale m; **courtyard** ['kɔ:tjɑ:d] n cortile m

cousin ['kʌzn] n cugino/a; **first ~** cugino di primo grado

cover ['kʌvəʳ] vt coprire; (book, table) rivestire; (include) comprendere; (Press) fare un servizio su ▷ n (of pan) coperchio; (over furniture) fodera; (of bed) copriletto; (of book) copertina; (shelter) riparo; (Comm, Insurance, of spy) copertura; **covers** npl (on bed) lenzuola fpl e coperte fpl; **to take ~** mettersi al riparo; **under ~** al riparo; **under ~ of darkness** protetto dall'oscurità; **under separate ~** (Comm) a parte, in plico separato; **cover up** vi: **to ~ up for sb** (fig) coprire qn; **coverage** n (Press, TV, Radio): **to give full coverage to** fare un ampio servizio su; **cover charge** n coperto; **cover-up** n occultamento (di informazioni)

cow [kau] n vacca ▷ vt (person) intimidire

coward ['kauəd] n vigliacco/a; **cowardly** adj vigliacco/a

cowboy ['kaubɔı] n cow-boy m inv

cozy ['kəuzı] adj (US) = **cosy**

crab [kræb] n granchio

crack [kræk] n fessura, crepa; incrinatura; (noise) schiocco; (: of gun) scoppio; (Drugs) crack m inv ▷ vt spaccare; incrinare; (whip) schioccare; (nut) schiacciare; (solve: problem, case) risolvere; (: code) decifrare ▷ cpd (troops) fuori classe; **to ~ jokes** dire battute, scherzare; **to get ~ing** (col) darsi una mossa; **crack down on** vt fus prendere serie misure contro, porre freno a; **cracked** adj (col) matto/a; **cracker** ['krækəʳ] n cracker m inv; (firework) petardo

crackle ['krækl] vi crepitare

cradle ['kreıdl] n culla

craft [krɑ:ft] n mestiere m; (cunning) astuzia; (boat) naviglio; **craftsman** n artigiano; **craftsmanship** n abilità

cram [kræm] vi (for exams) prepararsi (in gran fretta) ▷ vt (fill): **to ~ sth with** riempire qc di; (put): **to ~ sth into** stipare qc in

cramp [kræmp] n crampo; **I've got ~ in my leg** ho un crampo alla gamba; **cramped** adj ristretto/a

cranberry ['krænbərı] n mirtillo

crane [kreın] n gru f inv

crap [kræp] n (col!) fesserie fpl; **to have a ~** cacare (!)

crash [kræʃ] n fragore m; (of car) incidente m; (of plane) caduta; (Stock Exchange) crollo ▷ vt fracassare ▷ vi (plane) fracassarsi; (car) avere un incidente; (two cars) scontrarsi; (business etc) fallire, andare in rovina; **crash course** n corso intensivo; **crash helmet** n casco

crate [kreıt] n cassa

crave [kreıv] vt, vi: **to ~ (for)** desiderare ardentemente

crawl [krɔ:l] vi strisciare carponi; (vehicle) avanzare lentamente ▷ n (Swimming) crawl m

crayfish ['kreıfıʃ] n inv (freshwater) gambero (d'acqua dolce); (saltwater) gambero

crayon ['kreıən] n matita colorata

craze [kreız] n mania

crazy ['kreızı] adj matto/a; (col: keen): **to be ~ about sb** essere pazzo di qn; **to be ~ about sth** andare matto per qc

creak [kri:k] vi cigolare, scricchiolare

cream [kri:m] n crema; (fresh) panna ▷ adj (colour) color crema inv; **cream cheese** n formaggio fresco; **creamy** adj cremoso/a

crease [kri:s] n grinza; (deliberate) piega ▷ vt sgualcire ▷ vi sgualcirsi

create [kri:'eıt] vt creare; **creation** [kri:'eıʃən] n creazione f; **creative** adj creativo/a; **creator** n creatore/trice

creature ['kri:tʃəʳ] n creatura

crèche [krɛʃ] n asilo infantile

credentials [krɪ'dɛnʃlz] *npl* credenziali *fpl*

credibility [krɛdɪ'bɪlɪtɪ] *n* credibilità

credible ['krɛdɪbl] *adj* credibile; (*witness, source*) attendibile

credit ['krɛdɪt] *n* credito; onore *m* ▷ *vt* (*Comm*) accreditare; (*believe: also:* **give ~ to**) credere, prestar fede a; **to ~ sb with sth** (*fig*) attribuire qc a qn; **to be in ~** (*person*) essere creditore/trice; (*bank account*) essere coperto/a; *see also* **credits**; **credit card** *n* carta di credito; **credit crunch** *n* improvvisa stretta di credito

credits ['krɛdɪts] *npl* (*Cine*) titoli *mpl*

creek [kriːk] *n* insenatura; (*us*) piccolo fiume *m*

creep (*pt, pp* **crept**) [kriːp, krɛpt] *vi* avanzare furtivamente (*o pian piano*)

cremate [krɪ'meɪt] *vt* cremare

crematorium (*pl* **crematoria**) [krɛmə'tɔːrɪəm, -'tɔːrɪə] *n* forno crematorio

crept [krɛpt] *pt, pp of* **creep**

crescent ['krɛsnt] *n* (*shape*) mezzaluna; (*street*) strada semicircolare

cress [krɛs] *n* crescione *m*

crest [krɛst] *n* cresta; (*of coat of arms*) cimiero

crew [kruː] *n* equipaggio; **crew-neck** *n* girocollo

crib [krɪb] *n* culla ▷ *vt* (*col*) copiare

cricket ['krɪkɪt] *n* (*insect*) grillo; (*game*) cricket *m*; **cricketer** *n* giocatore *m* di cricket

crime [kraɪm] *n* crimine *m*; **criminal** ['krɪmɪnl] *adj, n* criminale (*m/f*)

crimson ['krɪmzn] *adj* color cremisi *inv*

cringe [krɪndʒ] *vi* acquattarsi; (*in embarrassment*) sentirsi sprofondare

cripple ['krɪpl] *vt* azzoppare

crisis (*pl* **crises**) ['kraɪsɪs, -siːz] *n* crisi *f inv*

crisp [krɪsp] *adj* croccante; (*fig*) frizzante; vivace; deciso/a; **crispy** *adj* croccante

criterion (*pl* **criteria**) [kraɪ'tɪərɪən, -'tɪərɪə] *n* criterio

critic ['krɪtɪk] *n* critico/a; **critical** *adj* critico/a; **criticism** ['krɪtɪsɪzəm] *n* critica; **criticize** ['krɪtɪsaɪz] *vt* criticare

Croat ['krəuæt] *adj, n* = **Croatian**

Croatia [krəu'eɪʃə] *n* Croazia; **Croatian** *adj* croato/a ▷ *n* croato/a; (*Ling*) croato

crockery ['krɔkərɪ] *n* vasellame *m*

crocodile ['krɔkədaɪl] *n* coccodrillo

crocus ['krəukəs] *n* croco

croissant ['krwasã] *n* brioche *f inv*, croissant *m inv*

crook [kruk] *n* (*col*) truffatore *m*; (*of shepherd*) bastone *m*; **crooked** ['krukɪd] *adj* curvo/a, storto/a; (*person, action*) disonesto/a

crop [krɔp] *n* (*produce*) coltivazione *f*; (*amount produced*) raccolto; (*riding crop*) frustino ▷ *vt* (*hair*) rapare; **crop up** *vi* presentarsi

cross [krɔs] *n* croce *f*; (*Biol*) incrocio ▷ *vt* (*street etc*) attraversare; (*arms, legs, Biol*) incrociare; (*cheque*) sbarrare ▷ *adj* di cattivo umore; **cross off** *vt* cancellare (*tirando una riga con la penna*); **cross out** *vt* cancellare; **cross over** *vi* attraversare; **cross-Channel ferry** ['krɔs'tʃænl-] *n* traghetto che attraversa la Manica; **crosscountry (race)** *n* cross-country *m inv*; **crossing** *n* incrocio; (*sea-passage*) traversata; (*also:* **pedestrian crossing**) passaggio pedonale; **crossing guard** (*us*) *n dipendente comunale che aiuta i bambini ad attraversare la strada*; **crossroads** *n* incrocio; **crosswalk** *n* (*us*) strisce *fpl* pedonali, passaggio pedonale; **crossword** *n* cruciverba *m inv*

crotch [krɔtʃ] *n* (*Anat*) inforcatura; (*of garment*) pattina

crouch [krautʃ] *vi* acquattarsi; rannicchiarsi

crouton ['kruːton] *n* crostino

crow [krəu] *n* (*bird*) cornacchia; (*of cock*) canto del gallo ▷ *vi* (*cock*) cantare

crowd [kraud] *n* folla ▷ *vt* affollare, stipare ▷ *vi*: **to ~ round/in** affollarsi intorno a/in; **crowded** *adj* affollato/a; **crowded with** stipato/a di

crown [kraun] *n* corona; (*of head*) calotta cranica; (*of hat*) cocuzzolo; (*of hill*) cima ▷ *vt* incoronare; (*fig: career*) coronare; **crown jewels** *npl* gioielli *mpl* della Corona

crucial ['kruːʃl] *adj* cruciale, decisivo/a

crucifix ['kruːsɪfɪks] *n* crocifisso

crude [kruːd] *adj* (*materials*) greggio/a; non raffinato/a; (*fig: basic*) crudo/a, primitivo/a; (*: vulgar*) rozzo/a, grossolano/a ▷ *n* (*also:* **~ oil**) (petrolio) greggio

cruel ['kruəl] *adj* crudele; **cruelty** *n* crudeltà *f inv*

cruise [kruːz] *n* crociera ▷ *vi* andare a velocità di crociera; (*taxi*) circolare

crumb [krʌm] *n* briciola

crumble ['krʌmbl] *vt* sbriciolare ▷ *vi* sbriciolarsi; (*plaster etc*) sgretolarsi; (*land, earth*) franare; (*building, fig*) crollare

crumpet ['krʌmpɪt] *n specie di frittella*

crumple ['krʌmpl] *vt* raggrinzare, spiegazzare

crunch [krʌntʃ] *vt* sgranocchiare; (*underfoot*) scricchiolare ▷ *n* (*fig*) punto o momento cruciale; **crunchy** *adj* croccante

crush [krʌʃ] *n* folla; (*love*): **to have a ~ on sb** avere una cotta per qn; (*drink*): **lemon ~** spremuta di limone ▷ *vt* schiacciare; (*crumple*) sgualcire

crust [krʌst] n crosta; **crusty** adj (bread) croccante; (person) brontolone/a; (remark) brusco/a

crutch [krʌtʃ] n gruccia

cry [kraɪ] vi piangere; (shout) urlare ▷ n urlo, grido; **cry out** vi, vt gridare

crystal ['krɪstl] n cristallo

cub [kʌb] n cucciolo; (also: ~ **scout**) lupetto

Cuba ['kjuːbə] n Cuba

Cuban ['kjuːbən] adj, n cubano/a

cube [kjuːb] n cubo ▷ vt (Math) elevare al cubo; **cubic** adj cubico/a; **cubic metre** etc metro etc cubo

cubicle ['kjuːbɪkl] n scompartimento separato; cabina

cuckoo ['kuːkuː] n cucù m inv

cucumber ['kjuːkʌmbər] n cetriolo

cuddle ['kʌdl] vt abbracciare, coccolare ▷ vi abbracciarsi

cue [kjuː] n stecca; (Theat etc) segnale m

cuff [kʌf] n (BRIT: of shirt, coat etc) polsino; (US: on trousers) risvolto; **off the ~** improvvisando; **cufflink** ['kʌflɪŋk] n gemello

cuisine [kwɪ'ziːn] n cucina

cul-de-sac ['kʌldəsæk] n vicolo cieco

cull [kʌl] vt (ideas etc) scegliere ▷ n (of animals) abbattimento selettivo

culminate ['kʌlmɪneɪt] vi: **to ~ in** culminare con

culprit ['kʌlprɪt] n colpevole m/f

cult [kʌlt] n culto

cultivate ['kʌltɪveɪt] vt (also fig) coltivare

cultural ['kʌltʃərəl] adj culturale

culture ['kʌltʃər] n (also fig) cultura

cumin ['kʌmɪn] n (spice) cumino

cunning ['kʌnɪŋ] n astuzia, furberia ▷ adj astuto/a, furbo/a

cup [kʌp] n tazza; (prize, of bra) coppa

cupboard ['kʌbəd] n armadio

cup final n (BRIT Football) finale f di coppa

curator [kjuə'reɪtər] n direttore m (di museo ecc)

curb [kəːb] vt tenere a freno ▷ n freno; (US) bordo del marciapiede

curdle ['kəːdl] vi cagliare

cure [kjuər] vt guarire; (Culin) trattare; affumicare; essiccare ▷ n rimedio

curfew ['kəːfjuː] n coprifuoco

curiosity [kjuərɪ'ɔsɪtɪ] n curiosità

curious ['kjuərɪəs] adj curioso/a

curl [kəːl] n riccio ▷ vt ondulare; (tightly) arricciare ▷ vi arricciarsi; **curl up** vi rannicchiarsi; **curler** n bigodino; **curly** ['kəːlɪ] adj ricciuto/a

currant ['kʌrnt] n (dried) uvetta; (bush, fruit) ribes m inv

currency ['kʌrnsɪ] n moneta; **to gain ~** (fig) acquistare larga diffusione

current ['kʌrnt] adj corrente ▷ n corrente f; **current account** n (BRIT) conto corrente; **current affairs** npl attualità fpl; **currently** adv attualmente

curriculum (pl **curriculums** or **curricula**) [kə'rɪkjuləm, -lə] n curriculum m inv; **curriculum vitae** [-'viːtaɪ] n curriculum vitae m inv

curry ['kʌrɪ] n curry m inv ▷ vt: **to ~ favour with** cercare di attirarsi i favori di; **curry powder** n curry m

curse [kəːs] vt maledire ▷ vi bestemmiare ▷ n maledizione f; bestemmia

cursor ['kəːsər] n (Comput) cursore m

curt [kəːt] adj secco/a

curtain ['kəːtn] n tenda; (Theat) sipario

curve [kəːv] n curva ▷ vi curvarsi; **curved** adj curvo/a

cushion ['kuʃən] n cuscino ▷ vt (shock) fare da cuscinetto a

custard ['kʌstəd] n (for pouring) crema

custody ['kʌstədɪ] n (of child) custodia; **to take sb into ~** mettere qn in detenzione preventiva

custom ['kʌstəm] n costume m; consuetudine f; (Comm) clientela

customer ['kʌstəmər] n cliente m/f

customized ['kʌstəmaɪzd] adj (car) fuoriserie inv

customs ['kʌstəmz] npl dogana; **customs officer** n doganiere m

cut [kʌt] (pt, pp **cut**) vt tagliare; (shape, make) intagliare; (reduce) ridurre ▷ vi tagliare ▷ n taglio; (in salary etc) riduzione f; **I've ~ myself** mi sono tagliato; **to ~ a tooth** mettere un dente; **cut back** vt (plants) tagliare; (production, expenditure) ridurre; **cut down** vt (tree) abbattere; **cut down on** vt fus ridurre; **cut off** vt tagliare; (fig) isolare; **cut out** vt tagliare; eliminare; (picture) ritagliare; **cut up** vt tagliare a pezzi; **cutback** n riduzione f

cute [kjuːt] adj carino/a

cutlery ['kʌtlərɪ] n posate fpl

cutlet ['kʌtlɪt] n costoletta; (nut cutlet) cotoletta vegetariana

cut: cut-price, (US) **cut-rate** adj a prezzo ridotto; **cutting** ['kʌtɪŋ] adj tagliente ▷ n (Press) ritaglio (di giornale); (from plant) talea

CV n abbr = **curriculum vitae**

cwt. abbr = **hundredweight**

cyberbullying ['saɪbəbulɪɪŋ] n bullismo informatico

cybercafé ['saɪbəkæfeɪ] n cybercaffè m inv

cybercrime ['saɪbəkraɪm] n delinquenza informatica

cyberspace ['saɪbəspeɪs] n ciberspazio

cycle ['saɪkl] n ciclo; (bicycle) bicicletta ▷ vi andare in bicicletta; **cycle hire** n

noleggio m biciclette inv; **cycle lane** n
pista ciclabile; **cycle path** n pista ciclabile;
cycling ['saɪklɪŋ] n ciclismo; **to go on a
cycling holiday** (BRIT) fare una vacanza in
bicicletta; **cyclist** ['saɪklɪst] n ciclista m/f
cyclone ['saɪkləun] n ciclone m
cylinder ['sɪlɪndə^r] n cilindro
cymbals ['sɪmblz] npl piatti mpl
cynical ['sɪnɪkl] adj cinico/a
Cypriot ['sɪprɪət] adj, n cipriota (m/f)
Cyprus ['saɪprəs] n Cipro
cyst [sɪst] n cisti f inv; **cystitis** [sɪ'staɪtɪs]
n cistite f
czar [zɑ:^r] n zar m inv
Czech [tʃɛk] adj ceco/a ▷ n ceco/a; (Ling)
ceco; **Czech Republic** n: **the Czech
Republic** la Repubblica Ceca

D [di:] n (Mus) re m
dab [dæb] vt (eyes, wound) tamponare;
(paint, cream) applicare (con leggeri
colpetti)
dad [dæd], **daddy** ['dædɪ] n babbo, papà
m inv
daffodil ['dæfədɪl] n trombone m,
giunchiglia
daft [dɑ:ft] adj sciocco/a
dagger ['dægə^r] n pugnale m
daily ['deɪlɪ] adj quotidiano/a, giornaliero/a
▷ n quotidiano ▷ adv tutti i giorni
dairy ['dɛərɪ] n (shop) latteria; (on farm)
caseificio ▷ cpd caseario/a; **dairy produce**
n latticini mpl
daisy ['deɪzɪ] n margherita
dam [dæm] n diga ▷ vt sbarrare; costruire
dighe su
damage ['dæmɪdʒ] n danno, danni mpl;
(fig) danno ▷ vt danneggiare; **damages** npl
(Law) danni mpl
damn [dæm] vt condannare; (curse)
maledire ▷ n (col): **I don't give a ~** non
me ne frega niente ▷ adj (col: also: **~ed**):
this ~ ... questo maledetto ...; **~ (it)!**
accidenti!
damp [dæmp] adj umido/a ▷ n umidità,
umido ▷ vt (also: **~en**: cloth, rag) inumidire,
bagnare; (: enthusiasm etc) spegnere
dance [dɑ:ns] n danza, ballo; (ball) ballo
▷ vi ballare; **dance floor** n pista da ballo;
dancer n danzatore/trice; (professional)
ballerino/a; **dancing** ['dɑ:nsɪŋ] n danza,
ballo
dandelion ['dændɪlaɪən] n dente m di
leone
dandruff ['dændrəf] n forfora
Dane [deɪn] n danese m/f
danger ['deɪndʒə^r] n pericolo; **there is
a ~ of fire** c'è pericolo di incendio; **in ~** in

pericolo; **he was in ~ of falling** rischiava di cadere; **dangerous** adj pericoloso/a

dangle ['dæŋgl] vt dondolare; (fig) far balenare ▷ vi pendolare

Danish ['deɪnɪʃ] adj danese ▷ n (Ling) danese m

dare [dɛəʳ] vt: **to ~ sb to do** sfidare qn a fare ▷ vi: **to ~ (to) do sth** osare fare qc; **I ~ say** (I suppose) immagino (che); **daring** adj audace, ardito/a ▷ n audacia

dark [dɑːk] adj (night, room) buio/a, scuro/a; (colour, complexion) scuro/a; (fig) cupo/a, tetro/a, nero/a ▷ n: **in the ~** al buio; **in the ~ about** (fig) all'oscuro di; **after ~** a notte fatta; **darken** vt (colour) scurire ▷ vi (sky, room) oscurarsi; **darkness** n oscurità, buio; **darkroom** n camera oscura

darling ['dɑːlɪŋ] adj caro/a ▷ n tesoro

dart [dɑːt] n freccetta; (Sewing) pince f inv ▷ vi: **to ~ towards** precipitarsi verso; **to ~ along** passare come un razzo; **to ~ away/ along** sfrecciare via/lungo; **dartboard** n bersaglio (per freccette); **darts** n tiro al bersaglio (con freccette)

dash [dæʃ] n (sign) lineetta; (small quantity: of liquid) goccio, goccino ▷ vt (missile) gettare; (hopes) infrangere ▷ vi: **to ~ towards** precipitarsi verso

dashboard ['dæʃbɔːd] n (Aut) cruscotto

data ['deɪtə] npl dati mpl; **database** n database m inv, base f di dati; **data processing** n elaborazione f (elettronica) dei dati

date [deɪt] n data; (appointment) appuntamento; (fruit) dattero ▷ vt datare; (person) uscire con; **what's the ~ today?** quanti ne abbiamo oggi?; **~ of birth** data di nascita; **to ~** (until now) fino a oggi; **dated** adj passato/a di moda

daughter ['dɔːtəʳ] n figlia; **daughter-in-law** n nuora

daunting ['dɔːntɪŋ] adj non invidiabile

dawn [dɔːn] n alba ▷ vi (day) spuntare; **it ~ed on him that ...** gli è venuto in mente che ...

day [deɪ] n giorno; (as duration) giornata; (period of time, age) tempo, epoca; **the ~ before** il giorno avanti or prima; **the ~ after, the following ~** il giorno dopo, il giorno seguente; **the ~ before yesterday** l'altroieri; **the ~ after tomorrow** dopodomani; **by ~** di giorno; **day care centre** n scuola materna; **daydream** vi sognare a occhi aperti; **daylight** n luce f del giorno; **day return** n (BRIT) biglietto giornaliero di andata e ritorno; **daytime** n giorno; **day-to-day** adj (routine, life, organization) quotidiano/a; **day trip** n gita (di un giorno)

dazed [deɪzd] adj stordito/a

dazzle ['dæzl] vt abbagliare; **dazzling** adj (light) abbagliante; (colour) violento/a; (smile) smagliante

DC abbr (= direct current) c.c.

dead [dɛd] adj morto/a; (numb) intirizzito/a; (telephone) muto/a; (battery) scarico/a ▷ adv assolutamente, perfettamente; **the dead** npl i morti; **he was shot ~** fu colpito a morte; **~ tired** stanco/a morto/a; **to stop ~** fermarsi di colpo; **dead end** n vicolo cieco; **deadline** n scadenza; **deadly** adj mortale; (weapon, poison) micidiale; **Dead Sea** n: **the Dead Sea** il mar Morto

deaf [dɛf] adj sordo/a; **deafen** vt assordare; **deafening** adj fragoroso/a, assordante

deal [diːl] n accordo; (business deal) affare m ▷ vt (pt, pp **dealt** [dɛlt]) (blow, cards) dare; **a great ~ of** molto/a; **deal with** vt fus (Comm) fare affari con, trattare con; (handle) occuparsi di; (be about: book etc) trattare di; **dealer** n commerciante m/f; **dealings** npl (Comm) relazioni fpl; (relations) rapporti mpl

dealt [dɛlt] pt, pp of **deal**

dean [diːn] n (Rel) decano; (Scol) preside m di facoltà (or di collegio)

dear [dɪəʳ] adj caro/a ▷ n: **my ~** caro mio/ cara mia ▷ excl: **~ me!** Dio mio!; **D~ Sir/ Madam** (in letter) Egregio Signore/Egregia Signora; **D~ Mr/Mrs X** Gentile Signor/ Signora X; **dearly** adv (love) moltissimo; (pay) a caro prezzo

death [dɛθ] n morte f; (Admin) decesso; **death penalty** n pena di morte; **death sentence** n condanna a morte

debate [dɪ'beɪt] n dibattito ▷ vt dibattere; discutere

debit ['dɛbɪt] n debito ▷ vt: **to ~ a sum to sb** or **to sb's account** addebitare una somma a qn; **debit card** n carta di debito

debris ['dɛbriː] n detriti mpl

debt [dɛt] n debito; **to be in ~** essere indebitato/a

debug [diː'bʌg] vt (Comput) localizzare e rimuovere errori in

debut ['deɪbjuː] n debutto

Dec. abbr (= December) dic.

decade ['dɛkeɪd] n decennio

decaffeinated [dɪ'kæfɪneɪtɪd] adj decaffeinato/a

decay [dɪ'keɪ] n decadimento; (also: **tooth ~**) carie f ▷ vi (rot) imputridire

deceased [dɪ'siːst] n: **the ~** il (la) defunto(a)

deceit [dɪ'siːt] n inganno; **deceive** [dɪ'siːv] vt ingannare

December [dɪ'sɛmbəʳ] n dicembre m

decency ['diːsənsɪ] n decenza

decent ['di:sənt] *adj* decente; (*respectable*) per bene; (*kind*) gentile

deception [dɪ'sɛpʃən] *n* inganno

deceptive [dɪ'sɛptɪv] *adj* ingannevole

decide [dɪ'saɪd] *vt* (*person*) far prendere una decisione a; (*question, argument*) risolvere, decidere ▷ *vi* decidere, decidersi; **to ~ to do/that** decidere di fare/che; **to ~ on** decidere per

decimal ['dɛsɪməl] *adj, n* decimale (*m*)

decision [dɪ'sɪʒən] *n* decisione *f*

decisive [dɪ'saɪsɪv] *adj* decisivo/a; (*manner, person*) deciso/a

deck [dɛk] *n* (*Naut*) ponte *m*; **top~** imperiale *m*; **record ~** piatto (giradischi); (*of cards*) mazzo; **deckchair** *n* sedia a sdraio

declaration [dɛklə'reɪʃən] *n* dichiarazione *f*

declare [dɪ'klɛə'] *vt* dichiarare

decline [dɪ'klaɪn] *n* (*decay*) declino; (*lessening*) ribasso ▷ *vt* declinare; rifiutare ▷ *vi* declinare; diminuire

decorate ['dɛkəreɪt] *vt* (*adorn, give a medal to*) decorare; (*paint and paper*) tinteggiare e tappezzare; **decoration** [dɛkə'reɪʃən] *n* (*medal etc, adornment*) decorazione *f*; **decorator** *n* decoratore/trice

decrease *n* ['di:kri:s] diminuzione *f* ▷ *vt, vi* [di:'kri:s] diminuire

decree [dɪ'kri:] *n* decreto

dedicate ['dɛdɪkeɪt] *vt* consacrare; (*book etc*) dedicare; **dedicated** *adj* coscienzioso/a; (*Comput*) specializzato/a, dedicato/a; **dedication** [dɛdɪ'keɪʃən] *n* (*devotion*) dedizione *f*; (*in book*) dedica

deduce [dɪ'dju:s] *vt* dedurre

deduct [dɪ'dʌkt] *vt*: **to ~ sth (from)** dedurre qc (da); **deduction** [dɪ'dʌkʃən] *n* deduzione *f*

deed [di:d] *n* azione *f*, atto; (*Law*) atto

deem [di:m] *vt* (*frml*) giudicare, ritenere; **to ~ it wise to do** ritenere prudente fare

deep [di:p] *adj* profondo/a ▷ *adv*: **spectators stood 20 ~** c'erano 20 file di spettatori; **4 metres ~** profondo(a) 4 metri; **how ~ is the water?** quanto è profonda l'acqua?; **deep-fry** *vt* friggere in olio abbondante; **deeply** *adv* profondamente

deer [dɪə'] *n* (*pl inv*): **the ~** i cervidi (*Zool*); **(red) ~** cervo; **(fallow) ~** daino; **(roe) ~** capriolo

default [dɪ'fɔ:lt] *n* (*Comput: also:* **~ value**) default *m inv*; **by ~** (*Sport*) per abbandono

defeat [dɪ'fi:t] *n* sconfitta ▷ *vt* (*team, opponents*) sconfiggere

defect *n* ['di:fɛkt] difetto ▷ *vi* [dɪ'fɛkt]: **to ~ to the enemy/the West** passare al nemico/all'Ovest; **defective** [dɪ'fɛktɪv] *adj* difettoso/a

defence, (*us*) **defense** [dɪ'fɛns] *n* difesa

defend [dɪ'fɛnd] *vt* difendere; **defendant** *n* imputato/a; **defender** *n* difensore/a

defense [dɪ'fɛns] *n* (*us*) = **defence**

defensive [dɪ'fɛnsɪv] *adj* difensivo/a ▷ *n*: **on the ~** sulla difensiva

defer [dɪ'fə:'] *vt* (*postpone*) differire, rinviare

defiance [dɪ'faɪəns] *n* sfida; **in ~ of** a dispetto di; **defiant** [dɪ'faɪənt] *adj* (*attitude*) di sfida; (*person*) ribelle

deficiency [dɪ'fɪʃənsɪ] *n* deficienza; carenza; **deficient** *adj* deficiente; insufficiente; **to be deficient in** mancare di

deficit ['dɛfɪsɪt] *n* disavanzo, deficit *m inv*

define [dɪ'faɪn] *vt* definire

definite ['dɛfɪnɪt] *adj* (*fixed*) definito/a, preciso/a; (*clear, obvious*) ben definito/a, esatto/a; (*Ling*) determinativo/a; **he was ~ about it** ne era sicuro; **definitely** *adv* indubbiamente

definition [dɛfɪ'nɪʃən] *n* definizione *f*

deflate [di:'fleɪt] *vt* sgonfiare

deflect [dɪ'flɛkt] *vt* deflettere, deviare

defraud [dɪ'frɔ:d] *vt*: **to ~ (of)** defraudare (di)

defriend [di:'frɛnd] *vt* (*Internet*) cancellare dagli amici

defrost [di:'frɔst] *vt* (*fridge*) disgelare

defuse [di:'fju:z] *vt* disinnescare; (*fig*) distendere

defy [dɪ'faɪ] *vt* sfidare; (*efforts etc*) resistere a; **it defies description** supera ogni descrizione

degree [dɪ'gri:] *n* grado; (*Scol*) laurea (universitaria); **a (first) ~ in maths** una laurea in matematica; **by ~s** (*gradually*) gradualmente, a poco a poco; **to some ~** fino a un certo punto, in certa misura

dehydrated [di:haɪ'dreɪtɪd] *adj* disidratato/a; (*milk, eggs*) in polvere

de-icer ['di:aɪsə'] *n* sbrinatore *m*

delay [dɪ'leɪ] *vt* ritardare ▷ *vi*: **to ~ (in doing sth)** ritardare (a fare qc) ▷ *n* ritardo; **to be ~ed** subire un ritardo; (*person*) essere trattenuto/a

delegate *n* ['dɛlɪgɪt] delegato/a ▷ *vt* ['dɛlɪgeɪt] delegare

delete [dɪ'li:t] *vt* cancellare

deli ['dɛlɪ] *n* = **delicatessen**

deliberate *adj* [dɪ'lɪbərɪt] (*intentional*) intenzionale; (*slow*) misurato/a ▷ *vi* [dɪ'lɪbəreɪt] deliberare, riflettere; **deliberately** *adv* (*on purpose*) deliberatamente

delicacy ['dɛlɪkəsɪ] *n* delicatezza

delicate ['dɛlɪkɪt] *adj* delicato/a

delicatessen [dɛlɪkə'tɛsn] *n* = salumeria

delicious [dɪ'lɪʃəs] *adj* delizioso/a, squisito/a

delight [dɪ'laɪt] n delizia, gran piacere m ▷ vt dilettare; **to take ~ in** divertirsi a; **delighted** adj: **delighted (at** or **with sth)** contentissimo/a (di qc), felice (di qc); **to be delighted to do sth/that** essere felice di fare qc/che + sub; **delightful** adj delizioso/a; incantevole

delinquent [dɪ'lɪŋkwənt] adj, n delinquente (m/f)

deliver [dɪ'lɪvəʳ] vt (mail) distribuire; (goods) consegnare; (speech) pronunciare; (Med) far partorire; **delivery** n distribuzione f; consegna; (of speaker) dizione f; (Med) parto

delusion [dɪ'luːʒən] n illusione f

de luxe [də'lʌks] adj di lusso

delve [dɛlv] vi: **to ~ into** frugare in; (subject) far ricerche in

demand [dɪ'mɑːnd] vt richiedere; (rights) rivendicare ▷ n richiesta; (claim) rivendicazione f; **in ~** ricercato/a, richiesto/a; **on ~** a richiesta; **demanding** adj (boss) esigente; (work) impegnativo/a

demise [dɪ'maɪz] n decesso

demo ['dɛməʊ] n abbr (col: = demonstration) manifestazione f

democracy [dɪ'mɔkrəsɪ] n democrazia; **democrat** ['dɛməkræt] n democratico/a; **democratic** [dɛmə'krætɪk] adj democratico/a

demolish [dɪ'mɔlɪʃ] vt demolire

demolition [dɛmə'lɪʃən] n demolizione f

demon ['diːmən] n (also fig) demonio ▷ cpd: **a ~ squash player** un mago dello squash; **a ~ driver** un guidatore folle

demonstrate ['dɛmənstreɪt] vt dimostrare, provare ▷ vi: **to ~ (for/against)** dimostrare (per/contro), manifestare (per/contro); **demonstration** [dɛmən'streɪʃən] n dimostrazione f; (Pol) manifestazione f, dimostrazione; **demonstrator** n (Pol) dimostrante m/f; (Comm) dimostratore/trice

demote [dɪ'məʊt] vt far retrocedere

den [dɛn] n tana, covo; (room) buco

denial [dɪ'naɪəl] n diniego; rifiuto

denim ['dɛnɪm] n tessuto di cotone ritorto; see also **denims**

denims ['dɛnɪmz] npl blue jeans mpl

Denmark ['dɛnmɑːk] n Danimarca

denomination [dɪnɔmɪ'neɪʃən] n (of money) valore m; (Rel) confessione f

denounce [dɪ'naʊns] vt denunciare

dense [dɛns] adj fitto/a; (smoke) denso/a; (col: stupid) ottuso/a, duro/a

density ['dɛnsɪtɪ] n densità f inv

dent [dɛnt] n ammaccatura ▷ vt (also: **make a ~ in**) ammaccare

dental ['dɛntl] adj dentale; **dental floss** [-flɔs] n filo interdentale; **dental surgery** n studio dentistico

dentist ['dɛntɪst] n dentista m/f

denture(s) ['dɛntʃə(z)] n(pl) dentiera

deny [dɪ'naɪ] vt negare; (refuse) rifiutare

deodorant [diː'əʊdərənt] n deodorante m

depart [dɪ'pɑːt] vi partire; **to ~ from** (fig) deviare da

department [dɪ'pɑːtmənt] n (Comm) reparto; (Scol) sezione f, dipartimento; (Pol) ministero; **department store** n grande magazzino

departure [dɪ'pɑːtʃəʳ] n partenza; (fig): **~ from** deviazione f da; **a new ~** una svolta (decisiva); **departure lounge** n sala d'attesa

depend [dɪ'pɛnd] vi: **to ~ (up)on** dipendere da; (rely on) contare su; **it ~s** dipende; **~ing on the result ...** a seconda del risultato ...; **dependant** n persona a carico; **dependent** adj: **to be dependent (on)** dipendere (da); (child, relative) essere a carico (di) ▷ n = **dependant**

depict [dɪ'pɪkt] vt (in picture) dipingere; (in words) descrivere

deport [dɪ'pɔːt] vt deportare; espellere

deposit [dɪ'pɔzɪt] n (Comm, Geo) deposito; (of ore, oil) giacimento; (Chem) sedimento; (part payment) acconto; (for hired goods etc) cauzione f ▷ vt depositare; dare in acconto; (luggage etc) mettere o lasciare in deposito; **deposit account** n conto vincolato

depot ['dɛpəʊ] n deposito; (US) stazione f ferroviaria

depreciate [dɪ'priːʃɪeɪt] vi svalutarsi

depress [dɪ'prɛs] vt deprimere; (price, wages) abbassare; (press down) premere; **depressed** adj (person) depresso/a, abbattuto/a; (market, trade) in ribasso; (industry) in crisi; **depressing** adj deprimente; **depression** [dɪ'prɛʃən] n depressione f

deprive [dɪ'praɪv] vt: **to ~ sb of** privare qn di; **deprived** adj disgraziato/a

dept. abbr = **department**

depth [dɛpθ] n profondità f inv; **in the ~s of** nel profondo di; nel cuore di; **to be out of one's ~** (BRIT: swimmer) essere dove non si tocca; (fig) non sentirsi all'altezza della situazione

deputy ['dɛpjʊtɪ] n (second in command) vice m/f; (US: also: **~ sheriff**) vice-sceriffo ▷ cpd: **~ head** (BRIT: Scol) vicepreside m/f

derail [dɪ'reɪl] vt: **to be ~ed** deragliare

derelict ['dɛrɪlɪkt] adj abbandonato/a

derive [dɪ'raɪv] vt: **to ~ sth from** derivare qc da; trarre qc da ▷ vi: **to ~ from** derivare da

descend [dɪ'sɛnd] vt, vi discendere, scendere; **to ~ from** discendere da; **to ~ to** (lying, begging) abbassarsi a; **descendant** n discendente m/f; **descent** [dɪ'sɛnt] n discesa; (origin) discendenza, famiglia

describe [dɪs'kraɪb] vt descrivere; **description** [dɪs'krɪpʃən] n descrizione f; (sort) genere m, specie f

desert n ['dɛzət] deserto ▷ vt [dɪ'zə:t] lasciare, abbandonare ▷ vi [dɪ'zə:t] (Mil) disertare; **deserted** [dɪ'zə:tɪd] adj deserto/a

deserve [dɪ'zə:v] vt meritare

design [dɪ'zaɪn] n (sketch) disegno; (layout, shape) linea; (pattern) fantasia; (intention) intenzione f ▷ vt disegnare; progettare; **design and technology** n (BRIT Scol) progettazione e tecnologie fpl

designate vt ['dɛzɪgneɪt] designare ▷ adj ['dɛzɪgnɪt] designato/a

designer [dɪ'zaɪnəʳ] n (Tech) disegnatore/trice; (fashion designer) disegnatore/trice di moda

desirable [dɪ'zaɪərəbl] adj desiderabile; **it is ~ that** è opportuno che + sub

desire [dɪ'zaɪəʳ] n desiderio, voglia ▷ vt desiderare, volere

desk [dɛsk] n (in office) scrivania; (for pupil) banco; (BRIT: in shop, restaurant) cassa; (in hotel) ricevimento; (at airport) accettazione f; **desktop** n desktop m inv; **desktop publishing** n desktop publishing m

despair [dɪs'pɛəʳ] n disperazione f ▷ vi: **to ~ of** disperare di

despatch [dɪs'pætʃ] n, vt = **dispatch**

desperate ['dɛspərɪt] adj disperato/a; (fugitive) capace di tutto; **to be ~ for sth/to do** volere disperatamente qc/fare; **desperately** adv disperatamente; (very) terribilmente, estremamente; **desperation** [dɛspə'reɪʃən] n disperazione f

despise [dɪs'paɪz] vt disprezzare, sdegnare

despite [dɪs'paɪt] prep malgrado, a dispetto di, nonostante

dessert [dɪ'zə:t] n dolce m; frutta; **dessertspoon** n cucchiaio da dolci

destination [dɛstɪ'neɪʃən] n destinazione f

destined ['dɛstɪnd] adj: **to be ~ to do sth** essere destinato(a) a fare qc; **~ for London** diretto a Londra

destiny ['dɛstɪnɪ] n destino

destroy [dɪs'trɔɪ] vt distruggere

destruction [dɪs'trʌkʃən] n distruzione f

destructive [dɪs'trʌktɪv] adj distruttivo/a

detach [dɪ'tætʃ] vt staccare, distaccare; **detached** adj (attitude) distante; **detached house** n villa

detail ['di:teɪl] n particolare m, dettaglio ▷ vt dettagliare, particolareggiare; **in ~** nei particolari; **detailed** adj particolareggiato/a

detain [dɪ'teɪn] vt trattenere; (in captivity) detenere

detect [dɪ'tɛkt] vt scoprire, scorgere; (Med, Police, Radar etc) individuare; **detection** [dɪ'tɛkʃən] n scoperta; individuazione f; **detective** n investigatore/trice; **detective story** n giallo

detention [dɪ'tɛnʃən] n detenzione f; (Scol) permanenza forzata per punizione

deter [dɪ'tə:ʳ] vt dissuadere

detergent [dɪ'tə:dʒənt] n detersivo

deteriorate [dɪ'tɪərɪəreɪt] vi deteriorarsi

determination [dɪtə:mɪ'neɪʃən] n determinazione f

determine [dɪ'tə:mɪn] vt determinare; **determined** adj (person) risoluto/a, deciso/a; **to be determined to do sth** essere determinato or deciso a fare qc

deterrent [dɪ'tɛrənt] n deterrente m; **to act as a ~** fungere da deterrente

detest [dɪ'tɛst] vt detestare

detour ['di:tuəʳ] n deviazione f

detox ['di:tɔks] n disintossicazione f

detract [dɪ'trækt] vi: **to ~ from** detrarre da

detrimental [dɛtrɪ'mɛntl] adj: **~ to** dannoso/a a, nocivo/a a

devastating ['dɛvəsteɪtɪŋ] adj devastatore/trice, sconvolgente

develop [dɪ'vɛləp] vt sviluppare; (habit) prendere (gradualmente) ▷ vi svilupparsi; (facts, symptoms: appear) manifestarsi, rivelarsi; **developing country** n paese m in via di sviluppo; **development** n sviluppo

device [dɪ'vaɪs] n (apparatus) congegno

devil ['dɛvl] n diavolo; demonio

devious ['di:vɪəs] adj (person) subdolo/a

devise [dɪ'vaɪz] vt escogitare, concepire

devote [dɪ'vəut] vt: **to ~ sth to** dedicare qc a; **devoted** adj devoto/a; **to be devoted to** essere molto affezionato/a a; **devotion** [dɪ'vəuʃən] n devozione f, attaccamento; (Rel) atto di devozione, preghiera

devour [dɪ'vauəʳ] vt divorare

devout [dɪ'vaut] adj pio/a, devoto/a

dew [dju:] n rugiada

diabetes [daɪə'bi:ti:z] n diabete m

diabetic [daɪə'bɛtɪk] adj, n diabetico/a

diagnose [daɪəg'nəuz] vt diagnosticare

diagnosis (pl **diagnoses**) [daɪəg'nəusɪs, -si:z] n diagnosi f inv

diagonal [daɪ'ægənl] adj, n diagonale (f)

diagram ['daɪəgræm] n diagramma m

dial ['daɪəl] n quadrante m; (on radio) lancetta; (on telephone) disco combinatore ▷ vt (number) fare

dialect ['daɪəlɛkt] n dialetto

dialling code ['daɪəlɪŋ-], (US) **area code** n prefisso

dialling tone ['daɪəlɪŋ-], (US) **dial tone** n segnale m di linea libera

dialogue ['daɪəlɔg], (US) **dialog** n dialogo

diameter [daɪ'æmɪtə^r] n diametro

diamond ['daɪəmənd] n diamante m; (shape) rombo; **diamonds** npl (Cards) quadri mpl

diaper ['daɪəpə^r] n (US) pannolino

diarrhoea, (US) **diarrhea** [daɪə'riːə] n diarrea

diary ['daɪərɪ] n (daily account) diario; (book) agenda

dice [daɪs] n (pl inv) dado ▷ vt (Culin) tagliare a dadini

dictate vt [dɪk'teɪt] dettare; **dictation** [dɪk'teɪʃən] n (to secretary etc) dettatura; (Scol) dettato

dictator [dɪk'teɪtə^r] n dittatore m

dictionary ['dɪkʃənrɪ] n dizionario

did [dɪd] pt of **do**

didn't ['dɪdnt] = **did not**

die [daɪ] vi morire; **to be dying for sth/ to do sth** morire dalla voglia di qc/di fare qc; **die down** vi abbassarsi; **die out** vi estinguersi

diesel ['diːzl] n (vehicle) diesel m inv

diet ['daɪət] n alimentazione f; (restricted food) dieta ▷ vi (also: **be on a ~**) stare a dieta

differ ['dɪfə^r] vi: **to ~ from sth** differire da qc; essere diverso/a da qc; **to ~ from sb over sth** essere in disaccordo con qn su qc; **difference** n differenza; (quarrel) screzio; **different** adj diverso/a; **differentiate** [dɪfə'rɛnʃɪeɪt] vi differenziarsi; **to differentiate between** discriminare fra, fare differenza fra; **differently** adv diversamente

difficult ['dɪfɪkəlt] adj difficile; **difficulty** n difficoltà f inv

dig [dɪg] (pt, pp **dug**) vt (hole) scavare; (garden) vangare ▷ n (prod) gomitata; (fig) frecciata; (Archaeology) scavo; **dig up** vt (tree etc) sradicare; (information) scavare fuori

digest vt [daɪ'dʒɛst] digerire ▷ n ['daɪdʒɛst] compendio; **digestion** [dɪ'dʒɛstʃən] n digestione f

digit ['dɪdʒɪt] n cifra; (finger) dito; **digital** adj digitale; **digital camera** n fotocamera digitale; **digital TV** n televisione f digitale

dignified ['dɪgnɪfaɪd] adj dignitoso/a

dignity ['dɪgnɪtɪ] n dignità

digs [dɪgz] npl (BRIT col) camera ammobiliata

dilemma [daɪ'lɛmə] n dilemma m

dill [dɪl] n aneto

dilute [daɪ'luːt] vt diluire; (with water) annacquare

dim [dɪm] adj (light, eyesight) debole; (memory, outline) vago/a; (room) in penombra; (col: stupid) ottuso/a, tonto/a ▷ vt (light) abbassare

dime [daɪm] n (US) = **10 cents**

dimension [dɪ'mɛnʃən] n dimensione f

diminish [dɪ'mɪnɪʃ] vt, vi diminuire

din [dɪn] n chiasso, fracasso

dine [daɪn] vi pranzare; **diner** n (person) cliente m/f; (US: eating place) tavola calda

dinghy ['dɪŋgɪ] n gommone m; (also: **sailing ~**) dinghy m inv

dingy ['dɪndʒɪ] adj grigio/a

dining car ['daɪnɪŋ-] (BRIT) n vagone m ristorante

dining room n sala da pranzo

dining table n tavolo da pranzo

dinkum ['dɪŋkʌm] adj (AUST, NZ col) genuino/a

dinner ['dɪnə^r] n (lunch) pranzo; (evening meal) cena; (public) banchetto; **dinner jacket** n smoking m inv; **dinner party** n cena; **dinner time** n ora di pranzo (or cena)

dinosaur ['daɪnəsɔː^r] n dinosauro

dip [dɪp] n discesa; (in sea) bagno; (Culin) salsetta ▷ vt immergere; bagnare; (BRIT Aut: lights) abbassare ▷ vi abbassarsi

diploma [dɪ'pləumə] n diploma m

diplomacy [dɪ'pləuməsɪ] n diplomazia

diplomat ['dɪpləmæt] n diplomatico; **diplomatic** [dɪplə'mætɪk] adj diplomatico/a

dipstick ['dɪpstɪk] n (Aut) indicatore m di livello dell'olio

dire [daɪə^r] adj terribile; estremo/a

direct [daɪ'rɛkt] adj diretto/a ▷ vt dirigere; (order): **to ~ sb to do sth** dare direttive a qn di fare qc ▷ adv direttamente; **can you ~ me to ...?** mi può indicare la strada per ...?; **direct debit** n (Banking) addebito effettuato per ordine di un cliente di banca

direction [dɪ'rɛkʃən] n direzione f; **directions** npl (advice) chiarimenti mpl; **~s for use** istruzioni fpl; **sense of ~** senso dell'orientamento

directly [dɪ'rɛktlɪ] adv (in straight line) direttamente; (at once) subito

director [dɪ'rɛktə^r] n direttore/trice, amministratore/trice; (Theat, Cine, TV) regista m/f

directory [dɪ'rɛktərɪ] n elenco; **directory enquiries**, (US) **directory assistance** n (Tel) informazioni fpl elenco abbonati

dirt [dəːt] n sporcizia; immondizia; (earth) terra; **dirty** adj sporco/a ▷ vt sporcare

disability [dɪsə'bɪlɪtɪ] n invalidità f inv; (Law) incapacità f inv

disabled [dɪsˈeɪbld] *adj* disabile
disadvantage [dɪsədˈvɑːntɪdʒ] *n* svantaggio
disagree [dɪsəˈgriː] *vi* (*differ*) discordare; (*be against, think otherwise*): **to ~ (with)** essere in disaccordo (con), dissentire (da); (*quarrel*) dissapore *m*; **disagreeable** *adj* sgradevole; (*person*) antipatico/a; **disagreement** *n* disaccordo;
disappear [dɪsəˈpɪəʳ] *vi* scomparire; **disappearance** *n* scomparsa
disappoint [dɪsəˈpɔɪnt] *vt* deludere; **disappointed** *adj* deluso/a; **disappointing** *adj* deludente; **disappointment** *n* delusione *f*
disapproval [dɪsəˈpruːvəl] *n* disapprovazione *f*
disapprove [dɪsəˈpruːv] *vi*: **to ~ of** disapprovare
disarm [dɪsˈɑːm] *vt* disarmare; **disarmament** *n* disarmo
disaster [dɪˈzɑːstəʳ] *n* disastro; **disastrous** [dɪˈzɑːstrəs] *adj* disastroso/a
disbelief [ˈdɪsbəˈliːf] *n* incredulità
disc [dɪsk] *n* disco; (*Comput*) = **disk**
discard [dɪsˈkɑːd] *vt* (*old things*) scartare; (*fig*) abbandonare
discharge *vt* [dɪsˈtʃɑːdʒ] (*duties*) compiere; (*Elec, waste etc*) scaricare; (*Med*) emettere; (*patient*) dimettere; (*employee*) licenziare; (*soldier*) congedare; (*defendant*) liberare ▷ *n* [ˈdɪstʃɑːdʒ] (*Elec*) scarica; (*Med*) emissione *f*; licenziamento; congedo; liberazione *f*
discipline [ˈdɪsɪplɪn] *n* disciplina ▷ *vt* disciplinare; (*punish*) punire
disc jockey *n* disc jockey *m inv*
disclose [dɪsˈkləʊz] *vt* rivelare, svelare
disco [ˈdɪskəʊ] *n abbr* discoteca
discoloured, (*us*) **discolored** [dɪsˈkʌləd] *adj* scolorito/a, ingiallito/a
discomfort [dɪsˈkʌmfət] *n* disagio; (*lack of comfort*) scomodità *f inv*
disconnect [dɪskəˈnɛkt] *vt* sconnettere, staccare; (*Elec, Radio*) staccare; (*gas, water*) chiudere
discontent [dɪskənˈtɛnt] *n* scontentezza
discontinue [dɪskənˈtɪnjuː] *vt* smettere, cessare; "**~d**" (*Comm*) "fuori produzione"
discount *n* [ˈdɪskaʊnt] sconto ▷ *vt* [dɪsˈkaʊnt] scontare; (*report, idea etc*) non badare a
discourage [dɪsˈkʌrɪdʒ] *vt* scoraggiare
discover [dɪsˈkʌvəʳ] *vt* scoprire; **discovery** *n* scoperta
discredit [dɪsˈkrɛdɪt] *vt* screditare; mettere in dubbio
discreet [dɪˈskriːt] *adj* discreto/a
discrepancy [dɪˈskrɛpənsɪ] *n* discrepanza

discretion [dɪˈskrɛʃən] *n* discrezione *f*; **use your own ~** giudichi lei
discriminate [dɪsˈkrɪmɪneɪt] *vi*: **to ~ between** distinguere tra; **to ~ against** discriminare contro; **discrimination** [dɪskrɪmɪˈneɪʃən] *n* discriminazione *f*; (*judgement*) discernimento
discuss [dɪsˈkʌs] *vt* discutere; (*debate*) dibattere; **discussion** [dɪsˈkʌʃən] *n* discussione *f*; **discussion forum** *n* (*Comput*) forum *m inv* di discussione
disease [dɪˈziːz] *n* malattia
disembark [dɪsɪmˈbɑːk] *vt*, *vi* sbarcare
disgrace [dɪsˈgreɪs] *n* vergogna; (*disfavour*) disgrazia ▷ *vt* disonorare, far cadere in disgrazia; **disgraceful** *adj* scandaloso/a, vergognoso/a
disgruntled [dɪsˈgrʌntld] *adj* scontento/a, di cattivo umore
disguise [dɪsˈgaɪz] *n* travestimento ▷ *vt*: **to ~ o.s. as** travestirsi da; **in ~** travestito/a
disgust [dɪsˈgʌst] *n* disgusto, nausea ▷ *vt* disgustare, far schifo a; **disgusted** [dɪsˈgʌstɪd] *adj* indignato/a; **disgusting** [dɪsˈgʌstɪŋ] *adj* disgustoso/a, ripugnante
dish [dɪʃ] *n* piatto; **to do** *or* **wash the ~es** fare i piatti; **dishcloth** *n* strofinaccio dei piatti
dishonest [dɪsˈɔnɪst] *adj* disonesto/a
dishtowel [ˈdɪʃtaʊəl] *n* strofinaccio dei piatti
dishwasher [ˈdɪʃwɔʃəʳ] *n* lavastoviglie *f inv*
disillusion [dɪsɪˈluːʒən] *vt* disilludere, disingannare
disinfectant [dɪsɪnˈfɛktənt] *n* disinfettante *m*
disintegrate [dɪsˈɪntɪgreɪt] *vi* disintegrarsi
disk [dɪsk] *n* (*Comput*) disco; **double-sided ~** disco a doppia faccia; **disk drive** *n* disk drive *m inv*; **diskette** *n* (*Comput*) dischetto
dislike [dɪsˈlaɪk] *n* antipatia, avversione *f*; (*gen pl*) cosa che non piace ▷ *vt*: **he ~s it** non gli piace
dislocate [ˈdɪsləkeɪt] *vt* slogare
disloyal [dɪsˈlɔɪəl] *adj* sleale
dismal [ˈdɪzml] *adj* triste, cupo/a
dismantle [dɪsˈmæntl] *vt* (*machine*) smontare
dismay [dɪsˈmeɪ] *n* costernazione *f* ▷ *vt* sgomentare
dismiss [dɪsˈmɪs] *vt* congedare; (*employee*) licenziare; (*idea*) scacciare; (*Law*) respingere; **dismissal** *n* congedo; licenziamento
disobedient [dɪsəˈbiːdɪənt] *adj* disubbidiente
disobey [dɪsəˈbeɪ] *vt* disubbidire a
disorder [dɪsˈɔːdəʳ] *n* disordine *m*; (*rioting*) tumulto; (*Med*) disturbo

disorganized [dɪs'ɔːgənaɪzd] adj (person, life) disorganizzato/a; (system, meeting) male organizzato/a

disown [dɪs'əʊn] vt rinnegare, disconoscere

dispatch [dɪs'pætʃ] vt spedire, inviare ▷ n spedizione f, invio; (Mil, Press) dispaccio

dispel [dɪs'pɛl] vt dissipare, scacciare

dispense [dɪs'pɛns] vt distribuire, amministrare; **dispenser** n (container) distributore m

disperse [dɪs'pəːs] vt disperdere; (knowledge) disseminare ▷ vi disperdersi

display [dɪs'pleɪ] n esposizione f; (of feeling etc) manifestazione f; (screen) schermo ▷ vt mostrare; (goods) esporre; (pej) ostentare

displease [dɪs'pliːz] vt dispiacere a, scontentare; **~d with** scontento/a di

disposable [dɪs'pəʊzəbl] adj (pack etc) a perdere; (income) disponibile

disposal [dɪs'pəʊzl] n (of rubbish) smaltimento; (of property etc) cessione f; **at one's ~** alla sua disposizione

dispose [dɪs'pəʊz] vt disporre; **dispose of** vt fus sbarazzarsi di; **disposition** [dɪspə'zɪʃən] n disposizione f; (temperament) carattere m

disproportionate [dɪsprə'pɔːʃənət] adj sproporzionato/a

dispute [dɪs'pjuːt] n disputa; (also: **industrial ~**) controversia (sindacale) ▷ vt contestare; (matter) discutere; (victory) disputare

disqualify [dɪs'kwɒlɪfaɪ] vt (Sport) squalificare; **to ~ sb from sth/from doing** rendere qn incapace a qc/a fare; **to ~ sb from driving** ritirare la patente a qn

disregard [dɪsrɪ'gɑːd] vt non far caso a, non badare a

disrupt [dɪs'rʌpt] vt disturbare; (public transport) creare scompiglio in; **disruption** [dɪs'rʌpʃən] n disordine m; interruzione f

dissatisfaction [dɪssætɪs'fækʃən] n scontentezza, insoddisfazione f

dissatisfied [dɪs'sætɪsfaɪd] adj: **~ (with)** scontento/a o insoddisfatto/a (di)

dissect [dɪ'sɛkt] vt sezionare

dissent [dɪ'sɛnt] n dissenso

dissertation [dɪsə'teɪʃən] n tesi f inv, dissertazione f

dissolve [dɪ'zɒlv] vt dissolvere, sciogliere; (Comm, Pol, marriage) sciogliere ▷ vi dissolversi, sciogliersi

distance ['dɪstns] n distanza; **in the ~** in lontananza

distant ['dɪstnt] adj lontano/a, distante; (manner) riservato/a, freddo/a

distil, (US) **distill** [dɪs'tɪl] vt distillare; **distillery** n distilleria

distinct [dɪs'tɪŋkt] adj distinto/a; **as ~ from** a differenza di; **distinction** [dɪs'tɪŋkʃən] n distinzione f; (in exam) lode f; **distinctive** adj distintivo/a

distinguish [dɪs'tɪŋgwɪʃ] vt distinguere; discernere; **distinguished** adj (eminent) eminente

distort [dɪs'tɔːt] vt distorcere; (Tech) deformare

distract [dɪs'trækt] vt distrarre; **distracted** adj distratto/a; **distraction** [dɪs'trækʃən] n distrazione f

distraught [dɪs'trɔːt] adj stravolto/a

distress [dɪs'trɛs] n angoscia ▷ vt affliggere; **distressing** adj doloroso/a

distribute [dɪs'trɪbjuːt] vt distribuire; **distribution** [dɪstrɪ'bjuːʃən] n distribuzione f; **distributor** n distributore m

district ['dɪstrɪkt] n (of country) regione f; (of town) quartiere m; (Admin) distretto; **district attorney** n (US) ≈ sostituto procuratore m della Repubblica

distrust [dɪs'trʌst] n diffidenza, sfiducia ▷ vt non aver fiducia in

disturb [dɪs'təːb] vt disturbare; **disturbance** n disturbo; (by drunks etc) disordini mpl; **disturbed** adj (worried, upset) turbato/a; **to be emotionally disturbed** avere turbe emotive; **disturbing** adj sconvolgente

ditch [dɪtʃ] n fossa ▷ vt (col) piantare in asso

ditto ['dɪtəʊ] adv idem

dive [daɪv] n tuffo; (of submarine) immersione f ▷ vi tuffarsi; immergersi; **diver** n tuffatore/trice; palombaro

diverse [daɪ'vəːs] adj vario/a

diversion [daɪ'vəːʃən] n (BRIT Aut) deviazione f; (distraction) divertimento

diversity [daɪ'vəːsɪti] n diversità f inv, varietà f inv

divert [daɪ'vəːt] vt deviare

divide [dɪ'vaɪd] vt dividere; (separate) separare ▷ vi dividersi; **divided highway** n (US) strada a doppia carreggiata

divine [dɪ'vaɪn] adj divino/a

diving ['daɪvɪŋ] n tuffo; **diving board** n trampolino

division [dɪ'vɪʒən] n divisione f; separazione f; (Football) serie f inv

divorce [dɪ'vɔːs] n divorzio ▷ vt divorziare da; (dissociate) separare; **divorced** adj divorziato/a; **divorcee** [dɪvɔː'siː] n divorziato/a

D.I.Y. n abbr (BRIT) = **do-it-yourself**

dizzy ['dɪzɪ] adj: **to feel ~** avere il capogiro

DJ n abbr = **disc jockey**

DNA n abbr (= deoxyribonucleic acid) DNA m; **DNA test** n test m inv del DNA

○ **KEYWORD**

do [duː] (pt **did**, pp **done**) aux vb **1** (in negative constructions) non tradotto; **I don't understand** non capisco

2 (to form questions) non tradotto; **didn't you know?** non lo sapevi?; **why didn't you come?** perché non sei venuto?

3 (for emphasis, in polite expressions): **she does seem rather late** sembra essere piuttosto in ritardo; **do sit down** si accomodi la prego, prego si sieda; **do take care!** mi raccomando, stai attento!

4 (used to avoid repeating vb): **she swims better than I do** lei nuota meglio di me; **do you agree? — yes, I do/no, I don't** sei d'accordo? — sì/no; **she lives in Glasgow — so do I** lei vive a Glasgow — anch'io; **he asked me to help him and I did** mi ha chiesto di aiutarlo ed io l'ho fatto

5 (in question tags): **you like him, don't you?** ti piace, vero?; **I don't know him, do I?** non lo conosco, vero?

▶ vt (gen: carry out, perform etc) fare; **what are you doing tonight?** che fai stasera?; **to do the cooking** cucinare; **to do the washing-up** fare i piatti; **to do one's teeth** lavarsi i denti; **to do one's hair/nails** farsi i capelli/le unghie; **the car was doing 100** la macchina faceva i 100 all'ora

▶ vi **1** (act, behave) fare; **do as I do** faccia come me, faccia come faccio io

2 (get on, fare) andare; **he's doing well/badly at school** va bene/male a scuola; **how do you do?** piacere!

3 (suit) andare bene; **this room will do** questa stanza va bene

4 (be sufficient) bastare; **will £10 do?** basteranno 10 sterline?; **that'll do** basta così; **that'll do!** (in annoyance) ora basta!; **to make do (with)** arrangiarsi (con)

▶ n (col: party etc) festa; **it was rather a grand do** è stato un ricevimento piuttosto importante

do away with vt fus (col: kill) far fuori; (abolish) abolire

do up vt (laces) allacciare; (dress, buttons) abbottonare; (renovate: room, house) rimettere a nuovo, rifare

do with vt fus (need) aver bisogno di; (be connected): **what has it got to do with you?** e tu che c'entri?; **I won't have anything to do with it** non voglio avere niente a che farci; **it has to do with money** si tratta di soldi

do without vi fare senza ▶ vt fus fare a meno di

dock [dɔk] n (Naut) bacino; (Law) banco degli imputati ▶ vi entrare in bacino; (Space) agganciarsi; **docks** npl (Naut) dock m inv

doctor ['dɔktəʳ] n medico/a; (PhD etc) dottore/essa ▶ vt (food, drink) adulterare; **Doctor of Philosophy, PhD** n dottorato di ricerca; (person) titolare m/f di un dottorato di ricerca

document n ['dɔkjumənt] documento; **documentary** [dɔkju'mɛntəri] adj (evidence) documentato/a ▶ n documentario; **documentation** [dɔkjumən'teɪʃən] n documentazione f

dodge [dɔdʒ] n trucco; schivata ▶ vt schivare, eludere

dodgy ['dɔdʒi] adj (BRIT col: uncertain) rischioso/a; (untrustworthy) sospetto/a

does [dʌz] see **do**

doesn't ['dʌznt] = **does not**

dog [dɔg] n cane m ▶ vt (follow closely) pedinare; (fig: memory etc) perseguitare; **doggy bag** n sacchetto per gli avanzi (da portare a casa)

do-it-yourself ['duːɪtjɔː'sɛlf] n il far da sé

dole [dəul] n (BRIT) sussidio di disoccupazione; **to be on the ~** vivere del sussidio

doll [dɔl] n bambola

dollar ['dɔləʳ] n dollaro

dolphin ['dɔlfin] n delfino

dome [dəum] n cupola

domestic [də'mɛstik] adj (duty, happiness, animal) domestico/a; (policy, affairs, flights) nazionale; **domestic appliance** n elettrodomestico

dominant ['dɔminənt] adj dominante

dominate ['dɔmineit] vt dominare

domino ['dɔminəu] (pl **dominoes**) n domino; **dominoes** npl (game) gioco del domino

donate [də'neit] vt donare; **donation** [də'neiʃən] n donazione f

done [dʌn] pp of **do**

dongle ['dɔngl] n (Comput) chiavetta, pennetta

donkey ['dɔnki] n asino

donor ['dəunəʳ] n donatore/trice; **donor card** n tessera di donatore di organi

don't [dəunt] = **do not**

donut ['dəunʌt] n (US) = **doughnut**

doodle ['duːdl] vi scarabocchiare

doom [duːm] n destino; rovina ▶ vt: **to be ~ed (to failure)** essere predestinato/a (a fallire)

door [dɔːʳ] n porta; **doorbell** n campanello; **door handle** n maniglia; **doorknob** ['dɔːnɔb] n pomello, maniglia; **doorstep** n gradino della porta; **doorway** n porta

dope [dəup] n (col: drugs) roba ▶ vt (horse etc) drogare

dormitory ['dɔːmɪtrɪ] n dormitorio; (US) casa dello studente

DOS [dɔs] n abbr (= disk operating system) DOS m

dosage ['dəʊsɪdʒ] n posologia

dose [dəʊs] n dose f; (bout) attacco

dot [dɔt] n punto; macchiolina ▷ vt: ~ted with punteggiato(a) di; on the ~ in punto; **dotcom** [dɔt'kɔm] n azienda che opera in Internet; **dotted line** ['dɔtɪd-] n linea punteggiata

double ['dʌbl] adj doppio/a ▷ adv (twice): to cost ~ sth costare il doppio (di qc) ▷ n sosia m inv ▷ vt raddoppiare; (fold) piegare doppio or in due ▷ vi raddoppiarsi; on the ~, (BRIT) at the ~ a passo di corsa; **double back** vi (person) tornare sui propri passi; **double bass** n contrabbasso; **double bed** n letto matrimoniale; **double-check** vt, vi ricontrollare; **double-click** vi (Comput) fare doppio click; **double-cross** ['dʌbl'krɔs] vt fare il doppio gioco con; **doubledecker** n autobus m inv a due piani; **double glazing** n (BRIT) doppi vetri mpl; **double room** n camera matrimoniale; **doubles** n (Tennis) doppio; **double yellow lines** npl (BRIT Aut) linea gialla doppia continua che segnala il divieto di sosta

doubt [daʊt] n dubbio ▷ vt dubitare di; to ~ that dubitare che + sub; **doubtful** adj dubbioso/a, incerto/a; (person) equivoco/a; **doubtless** adv indubbiamente

dough [dəʊ] n pasta, impasto; **doughnut**, (US) **donut** n bombolone m

dove [dʌv] n colombo/a

down [daʊn] n piumino ▷ adv giù, di sotto ▷ prep giù per ▷ vt (col: drink) scolarsi; ~ with X! abbasso X!; **down-and-out** n barbone m; **downfall** n caduta; rovina; **downhill** adv: to go downhill andare in discesa; (business) lasciarsi andare; andare a rotoli

Downing Street ['daʊnɪŋ-] n: 10 ~ residenza del primo ministro inglese

○ **DOWNING STREET**
○
○ Downing Street è la via di Westminster che
○ porta da Whitehall al parco di St James
○ dove, al numero 10, si trova la residenza
○ del primo ministro inglese. Nella stessa
○ via, al numero 11, si trova la residenza del
○ Cancelliere dello Scacchiere. Spesso si
○ usa Downing Street per indicare il governo
○ britannico.

down: download vt (Comput) scaricare; **downloadable** adj (Comput) scaricabile; **downright** adj franco/a; (refusal) assoluto/a

Down's syndrome n sindrome f di Down

down: downstairs adv di sotto; al piano inferiore; **down-to-earth** adj pratico/a; **downtown** adv in città; **down under** adv (Australia etc) agli antipodi; **downward** adj, adv in giù, in discesa; **downwards** ['daʊnwədz] adv in giù, in discesa

doz. abbr = **dozen**

doze [dəʊz] vi sonnecchiare

dozen ['dʌzn] n dozzina; a ~ books una dozzina di libri; 80p a ~ 80 pence la dozzina; ~s of times centinaia or migliaia di volte

Dr, Dr. abbr (= doctor) Dr, Dott./Dott.ssa; (in street names) = **drive**

drab [dræb] adj tetro/a, grigio/a

draft [drɑːft] n abbozzo; (Pol) bozza; (Comm) tratta; (US Mil: call-up) leva ▷ vt abbozzare; see also **draught**

drag [dræg] vt trascinare; (river) dragare ▷ vi trascinarsi ▷ n (col) noioso/a; (: task) noia; (women's clothing): in ~ travestito (da donna)

dragon ['drægən] n drago

dragonfly ['drægənflaɪ] n libellula

drain [dreɪn] n (for sewage) fogna; (on resources) salasso ▷ vt (land, marshes) prosciugare; (vegetables) scolare ▷ vi (water) defluire; **drainage** n prosciugamento; fognatura; **drainpipe** n tubo di scarico

drama ['drɑːmə] n (art) dramma m, teatro; (play) commedia; (event) dramma; **dramatic** [drə'mætɪk] adj drammatico/a

drank [dræŋk] pt of **drink**

drape [dreɪp] vt drappeggiare; see also **drapes**; **drapes** [dreɪps] npl (US: curtains) tende fpl

drastic ['dræstɪk] adj drastico/a

draught, (US) **draft** [drɑːft] n corrente f d'aria; (Naut) pescaggio; on ~ (beer) alla spina; **draught beer** n birra alla spina; **draughts** n (BRIT) (gioco della) dama

draw [drɔː] (pt **drew**, pp **drawn**) vt tirare; (take out) estrarre; (attract) attirare; (picture) disegnare; (line, circle) tracciare; (money) ritirare ▷ vi (Sport) pareggiare ▷ n pareggio; (in lottery) estrazione f; to ~ near avvicinarsi; **draw out** vi (lengthen) allungarsi ▷ vt (money) ritirare; **draw up** vi (stop) arrestarsi, fermarsi ▷ vt (chair) avvicinare; (document) compilare; **drawback** n svantaggio, inconveniente m

drawer [drɔːʳ] n cassetto

drawing ['drɔːɪŋ] n disegno; **drawing pin** n (BRIT) puntina da disegno; **drawing room** n salotto

drawn [drɔːn] pp of **draw**

dread [drɛd] n terrore m ▷ vt tremare all'idea di; **dreadful** adj terribile

dream [driːm] n sogno ▷ vt, vi (pt, pp **dreamed** or **dreamt** [drɛmt]) sognare; **dreamer** n sognatore/trice

dreamt [drɛmt] pt, pp of **dream**

dreary ['drɪərɪ] adj tetro/a; monotono/a

drench [drɛntʃ] vt inzuppare

dress [drɛs] n vestito; (no pl: clothing) abbigliamento ▷ vt vestire; (wound) fasciare ▷ vi vestirsi; **to get ~ed** vestirsi; **dress up** vi vestirsi a festa; (in fancy dress) vestirsi in costume; **dress circle** (BRIT) n prima galleria; **dresser** n (furniture) credenza; (US) cassettone m; **dressing** n (Med) benda; (Culin) condimento; **dressing gown** n (BRIT) vestaglia; **dressing room** n (Theat) camerino; (Sport) spogliatoio; **dressing table** n toilette f inv; **dressmaker** n sarta

drew [druː] pt of **draw**

dribble ['drɪbl] vi (baby) sbavare ▷ vt (ball) dribblare

dried [draɪd] adj (fruit, beans) secco/a; (eggs, milk) in polvere

drier ['draɪəʳ] n = **dryer**

drift [drɪft] n (of current etc) direzione f; forza; (of sand, snow) cumulo; turbine m; (general meaning) senso ▷ vi (boat) essere trasportato/a dalla corrente; (sand, snow) ammucchiarsi

drill [drɪl] n trapano; (Mil) esercitazione f ▷ vt trapanare; (soldiers) addestrare ▷ vi (for oil) fare trivellazioni

drink [drɪŋk] n bevanda, bibita; (alcoholic drink) bicchierino; (sip) sorso ▷ vt, vi (pt **drank**, pp **drunk**) bere; **to have a ~** bere qualcosa; **a ~ of water** un po' d'acqua; **drink-driving** n guida in stato di ebbrezza; **drinker** n bevitore/trice; **drinking water** n acqua potabile

drip [drɪp] n goccia; (dripping) sgocciolio; (Med) fleboclisi f inv ▷ vi gocciolare; (washing, tap) sgocciolare

drive (pt **drove**, pp **driven**) [draɪv, drəʊv, 'drɪvn] n passeggiata or giro in macchina; (also: **~way**) viale m d'accesso; (energy) energia; (campaign) campagna; (also: **disk ~**) disk drive m inv ▷ vt guidare; (nail) piantare; (push) cacciare, spingere; (Tech: motor) azionare; far funzionare ▷ vi (Aut: at controls) guidare; (: travel) andare in macchina; **left-/right-hand ~** guida a sinistra/destra; **to ~ sb mad** far impazzire qn; **drive out** vt (force out) cacciare, mandare via; **drive-in** adj, n (esp US) drive-in (m inv)

driven ['drɪvn] pp of **drive**

driver ['draɪvəʳ] n conducente m/f; (of taxi) tassista m; (chauffeur: of bus) autista m/f; **driver's license** n (US) patente f di guida

driveway ['draɪvweɪ] n viale m d'accesso

driving ['draɪvɪŋ] n guida; **driving instructor** n istruttore/trice di scuola guida; **driving lesson** n lezione f di guida; **driving licence** n (BRIT) patente f di guida; **driving test** n esame m di guida

drizzle ['drɪzl] n pioggerella

droop [druːp] vi (flower) appassire; (head, shoulders) chinarsi

drop [drɔp] n (of water) goccia; (lessening) diminuzione f; (fall) caduta ▷ vt lasciar cadere; (name from list) lasciare fuori ▷ vi cascare; (wind, temperature, price) calare, abbassarsi; (voice) abbassarsi; **drops** npl (Med) gocce fpl; **drop in** vi (col: visit): **to ~ in (on)** fare un salto (da), passare (da); **drop off** vi (sleep) addormentarsi ▷ vt: **to ~ sb off** far scendere qn; **drop out** vi (withdraw) ritirarsi; (student etc) smettere di studiare

drought [draʊt] n siccità f inv

drove [drəʊv] pt of **drive**

drown [draʊn] vt affogare; (fig: noise) soffocare

drowsy ['draʊzɪ] adj sonnolento/a, assonnato/a

drug [drʌg] n farmaco; (narcotic) droga ▷ vt drogare; **to be on ~s** drogarsi; (Med) prendere medicinali; **hard/soft ~s** droghe pesanti/leggere; **drug addict** n tossicomane m/f; **drug dealer** n trafficante m/f di droga; **druggist** n (US) farmacista m/f; **drugstore** n ['drʌgstɔːʳ] n (US) negozio di generi vari e di articoli di farmacia con un bar

drum [drʌm] n tamburo; (for oil, petrol) fusto ▷ vi tamburellare; **drums** npl (set of drums) batteria; **drummer** n batterista m/f

drunk [drʌŋk] pp of **drink** ▷ adj ubriaco/a, ebbro/a ▷ n ubriacone/a; **drunken** adj ubriaco/a, da ubriaco

dry [draɪ] adj secco/a; (day, clothes) asciutto/a ▷ vt seccare; (clothes, hair, hands) asciugare ▷ vi asciugarsi; **dry off** vi asciugarsi ▷ vt asciugare; **dry up** vi seccarsi; **dry-cleaner's** n lavasecco m inv; **dry-cleaning** n pulitura a secco; **dryer** n (for hair) föhn m inv, asciugacapelli m inv; (for clothes) asciugabiancheria m inv; (US: spin-dryer) centrifuga

DSS n abbr (BRIT: = Department of Social Security) ministero della Previdenza sociale

DTP n abbr (= desk-top publishing) desktop publishing m inv

dual ['djuəl] adj doppio/a; **dual carriageway** n (BRIT) strada a doppia carreggiata

dubious ['djuːbɪəs] adj dubbio/a

Dublin ['dʌblɪn] n Dublino f

duck [dʌk] n anatra ▷ vi abbassare la testa

due [djuː] adj dovuto/a; (expected) atteso/a; (fitting) giusto/a ▷ n dovuto ▷ adv: **~ north** diritto verso nord

duel [ˈdjuəl] n duello

duet [djuːˈɛt] n duetto

dug [dʌg] pt, pp of **dig**

duke [djuːk] n duca m

dull [dʌl] adj (light) debole; (boring) noioso/a; (slow-witted) ottuso/a; (sound, pain) sordo/a; (weather, day) fosco/a, scuro/a ▷ vt (pain, grief) attutire; (mind, senses) intorpidire

dumb [dʌm] adj (stupid) stupido/a

dummy [ˈdʌmɪ] n (tailor's model) manichino; (Tech, Comm) riproduzione f; (BRIT: for baby) tettarella ▷ adj falso/a, finto/a

dump [dʌmp] n (also: **rubbish ~**) mucchio di rifiuti (place) discarica ▷ vt (put down) scaricare; mettere giù; (get rid of) buttar via

dumpling [ˈdʌmplɪŋ] n specie di gnocco

dune [djuːn] n duna

dungarees [dʌŋgəˈriːz] npl tuta

dungeon [ˈdʌndʒən] n prigione f sotterranea

duplex [ˈdjuːplɛks] n (US: house) casa con muro divisorio in comune con un'altra; (: also: **~ apartment**) appartamento su due piani

duplicate n [ˈdjuːplɪkət] doppio ▷ vt [ˈdjuːplɪkeɪt] duplicare; **in ~** in duplice copia

durable [ˈdjuərəbl] adj durevole; (clothes, metal) resistente

duration [djuəˈreɪʃən] n durata

during [ˈdjuərɪŋ] prep durante, nel corso di

dusk [dʌsk] n crepuscolo

dust [dʌst] n polvere f ▷ vt (furniture) spolverare; (cake etc): **to ~ with** cospargere con; **dustbin** n (BRIT) pattumiera; **duster** n straccio per la polvere; **dustman** n (irreg: BRIT) netturbino; **dustpan** n pattumiera; **dusty** adj polveroso/a

Dutch [dʌtʃ] adj olandese ▷ n (Ling) olandese m ▷ adv: **to go ~** or **d~** (col) fare alla romana; **the ~** gli Olandesi; **Dutchman, Dutchwoman** n (irreg) olandese m/f

duty [ˈdjuːtɪ] n dovere m; (tax) dazio, tassa; **on ~** di servizio; **off ~** libero(a), fuori servizio; **duty-free** adj esente da dazio

duvet [ˈduːveɪ] (BRIT) n piumino, piumone m

DVD n abbr (= digital versatile or video disc) DVD m inv; **DVD burner** n masterizzatore m (di) DVD; **DVD player** n lettore m DVD **DVD writer** n masterizzatore m (di) DVD

dwarf [dwɔːf] n (coll) nano/a ▷ vt far apparire piccolo

dwell (pt, pp **dwelt**) [dwɛl, dwɛlt] vi dimorare; **dwell on** vt fus indugiare su

dwelt [dwɛlt] pt, pp of **dwell**

dwindle [ˈdwɪndl] vi diminuire

dye [daɪ] n tintura ▷ vt tingere

dying [ˈdaɪɪŋ] adj morente, moribondo/a

dynamic [daɪˈnæmɪk] adj dinamico/a

dynamite [ˈdaɪnəmaɪt] n dinamite f

dyslexia [dɪsˈlɛksɪə] n dislessia

dyslexic [dɪsˈlɛksɪk] adj, n dislessico/a

e

E [i:] n (Mus) mi m

E111 n abbr (formerly) E111 (modulo UE per rimborso spese mediche)

each [i:tʃ] adj ogni, ciascuno/a ▷ pron ciascuno/a, ognuno/a; ~ **one** ognuno(a); ~ **other** si (or ci etc); **they hate** ~ **other** si odiano (l'un l'altro); **you are jealous of** ~ **other** siete gelosi l'uno dell'altro; **they have 2 books** ~ hanno 2 libri ciascuno

eager ['i:gə'] adj impaziente; desideroso/a; ardente; **to be** ~ **for** essere desideroso di, aver gran voglia di

eagle ['i:gl] n aquila

ear [ɪə'] n orecchio; (of corn) pannocchia; **earache** n mal m d'orecchi; **eardrum** n timpano

earl [ə:l] (BRIT) n conte m

earlier ['ə:lɪə'] adj precedente ▷ adv prima

early ['ə:lɪ] adv presto, di buon'ora; (ahead of time) in anticipo ▷ adj primo/a; (quick: reply) veloce; **at an** ~ **hour** di buon'ora; **have an** ~ **night/start** vada a letto/parta presto; **in the** ~ **or** ~ **in the spring/19th century** all'inizio della primavera/dell'Ottocento; **early retirement** n prepensionamento

earmark ['ɪəmɑ:k] vt: **to** ~ **sth for** destinare qc a

earn [ə:n] vt guadagnare; (rest, reward) meritare

earnest ['ə:nɪst] adj serio/a; **in** ~ sul serio

earnings ['ə:nɪŋz] npl guadagni mpl; (salary) stipendio

ear: earphones ['ɪəfəunz] npl cuffia; **earplugs** npl tappi mpl per le orecchie; **earring** n orecchino

earth [ə:θ] n terra ▷ vt (BRIT Elec) mettere a terra; **earthquake** n terremoto

ease [i:z] n agio, comodo ▷ vt (soothe) calmare; (loosen) allentare; **at** ~ a proprio agio; (Mil) a riposo; **to** ~ **sth out/in** tirare fuori/infilare qc con delicatezza; facilitare l'uscita/l'entrata di qc

easily ['i:zɪlɪ] adv facilmente

east [i:st] n est m ▷ adj dell'est ▷ adv a oriente; **the E~** l'Oriente m; (Pol) i Paesi dell'Est; **eastbound** ['i:stbaund] adj (traffic) diretto/a a est; (carriageway) che porta a est

Easter ['i:stə'] n Pasqua; **Easter egg** n uovo di Pasqua

eastern ['i:stən] adj orientale, d'oriente; (Pol) dell'est

Easter Sunday n domenica di Pasqua

easy ['i:zɪ] adj facile; (manner) disinvolto/a ▷ adv: **to take it** or **things** ~ prendersela con calma; **easy-going** adj accomodante

eat (pt **ate**, pp **eaten**) [i:t, eɪt, 'i:tn] vt mangiare; **eat out** vi mangiare fuori

eavesdrop ['i:vzdrɔp] vi: **to** ~ **(on a conversation)** origliare (una conversazione)

e-book ['i:buk] n libro elettronico

e-business ['i:bɪznɪs] n (company) azienda che opera in Internet; (commerce) commercio elettronico

EC n abbr (= European Community) CE f

eccentric [ɪk'sɛntrɪk] adj, n eccentrico/a

echo ['ɛkəu] (pl **echoes**) n eco m or f ▷ vt ripetere; fare eco a ▷ vi echeggiare; dare un eco

e-cigarette ['i:sɪgərɛt] n sigaretta elettronica

eclipse [ɪ'klɪps] n eclissi f inv

eco-friendly [i:kəu'frɛndlɪ] adj ecologico/a

ecological [i:kə'lɔdʒɪkəl] adj ecologico/a

ecology [ɪ'kɔlədʒɪ] n ecologia

e-commerce [i:'kɔmə:s] n commercio elettronico

economic [i:kə'nɔmɪk] adj economico/a; **economical** adj economico/a; (person) economo/a; **economics** n economia ▷ npl (financial aspect) lato finanziario

economist [ɪ'kɔnəmɪst] n economista m/f

economize [ɪ'kɔnəmaɪz] vi risparmiare, fare economia

economy [ɪ'kɔnəmɪ] n economia; **economy class** n (Aviat etc) classe f turistica; **economy class syndrome** n sindrome f della classe economica

ecstasy ['ɛkstəsɪ] n estasi f inv; **ecstatic** [ɛks'tætɪk] adj estatico/a, in estasi

eczema ['ɛksɪmə] n eczema m

edge [ɛdʒ] n margine m; (of table, plate, cup) orlo; (of knife etc) taglio ▷ vt bordare; **on** ~ (fig) = **edgy**; **to** ~ **away from** sgattaiolare da

edgy ['ɛdʒɪ] adj nervoso/a

edible ['ɛdɪbl] adj commestibile; (meal) mangiabile

Edinburgh ['ɛdɪnbərə] n Edimburgo f

edit ['ɛdɪt] vt curare; **edition** [ɪ'dɪʃən] n edizione f; **editor** n (in newspaper) redattore/trice; redattore/trice capo; (of sb's work) curatore/trice; **editorial** [ɛdɪ'tɔːrɪəl] adj redazionale, editoriale ▷ n editoriale m

> Be careful not to translate editor by the Italian word editore.

educate ['ɛdjukeɪt] vt istruire; educare; **educated** adj istruito/a

education [ɛdju'keɪʃən] n (teaching) insegnamento; (schooling) istruzione f; **educational** adj pedagogico/a; scolastico/a; istruttivo/a

eel [iːl] n anguilla

eerie ['ɪərɪ] adj che fa accapponare la pelle

effect [ɪ'fɛkt] n effetto ▷ vt effettuare; **to take ~** (law) entrare in vigore; (drug) fare effetto; **in ~** effettivamente; **effective** adj efficace; (actual) effettivo/a; **effectively** adv efficacemente; effettivamente; **effects** npl (Theat) effetti mpl scenici; (property) effetti mpl

efficiency [ɪ'fɪʃənsɪ] n efficienza; rendimento effettivo

efficient [ɪ'fɪʃənt] adj efficiente; **efficiently** adv efficientemente; efficacemente

effort ['ɛfət] n sforzo; **effortless** adj senza sforzo, facile

e.g. adv abbr (= exempli gratia) per esempio, p.es.

egg [ɛg] n uovo; **hard-boiled/soft-boiled ~** uovo sodo/alla coque; **eggcup** n portauovo m inv; **eggplant** n (esp us) melanzana; **eggshell** n guscio d'uovo; **egg white** n albume m, bianco d'uovo; **egg yolk** n tuorlo, rosso (d'uovo)

ego ['iːgəu] n ego m inv

Egypt ['iːdʒɪpt] n Egitto; **Egyptian** [ɪ'dʒɪpʃən] adj, n egiziano/a

eight [eɪt] num otto; **eighteen** num diciotto; **eighteenth** num diciottesimo/a; **eighth** [eɪtθ] num ottavo/a; **eightieth** ['eɪtɪɪθ] num ottantesimo/a; **eighty** num ottanta

Eire ['ɛərə] n Repubblica d'Irlanda

either ['aɪðə'] adj l'uno o l'altro/a; (both, each) ciascuno/a; **on ~ side** su ciascun lato ▷ pron: **~ (of them)** (o) l'uno o l'altro/a; **I don't like ~** non mi piace né l'uno né l'altro ▷ adv neanche; **no, I don't ~** no, neanch'io ▷ conj: **~ good or bad** o buono o cattivo

eject [ɪ'dʒɛkt] vt espellere; lanciare

elaborate adj [ɪ'læbərɪt] elaborato/a, minuzioso/a ▷ vt [ɪ'læbəreɪt] elaborare ▷ vi [ɪ'læbəreɪt] fornire i dettagli

elastic [ɪ'læstɪk] adj elastico/a ▷ n elastico; **elastic band** n (BRIT) elastico

elbow ['ɛlbəu] n gomito

elder ['ɛldə'] adj maggiore, più vecchio/a ▷ n (tree) sambuco; **one's ~s** i più anziani; **elderly** adj anziano/a

eldest ['ɛldɪst] adj, n: **the ~ (child)** il (la) maggiore (dei bambini)

elect [ɪ'lɛkt] vt eleggere; **to ~ to do** decidere di fare ▷ adj: **the president ~** il presidente designato; **election** [ɪ'lɛkʃən] n elezione f; **electoral** [ɪ'lɛktərəl] adj elettorale; **electorate** n elettorato

electric [ɪ'lɛktrɪk] adj elettrico/a; **electrical** adj elettrico/a; **electric blanket** n coperta elettrica; **electric fire** n stufa elettrica; **electrician** [ɪlɛk'trɪʃən] n elettricista m; **electricity** [ɪlɛk'trɪsɪtɪ] n elettricità; **electric shock** n scossa (elettrica); **electrify** [ɪ'lɛktrɪfaɪ] vt (Rail) elettrificare; (audience) elettrizzare

electronic [ɪlɛk'trɔnɪk] adj elettronico/a; **electronic mail** n posta elettronica; **electronics** n elettronica

elegance ['ɛlɪgəns] n eleganza

elegant ['ɛlɪgənt] adj elegante

element ['ɛlɪmənt] n elemento; (of heater, kettle etc) resistenza

elementary [ɛlɪ'mɛntərɪ] adj elementare; **elementary school** n (us) scuola elementare

elephant ['ɛlɪfənt] n elefante/essa

elevate ['ɛlɪveɪt] vt elevare

elevator ['ɛlɪveɪtə'] n elevatore m; (us: lift) ascensore m

eleven [ɪ'lɛvn] num undici; **eleventh** adj undicesimo/a

eligible ['ɛlɪdʒəbl] adj eleggibile; (for membership) che ha i requisiti

eliminate [ɪ'lɪmɪneɪt] vt eliminare

elm [ɛlm] n olmo

eloquent ['ɛləkwənt] adj eloquente

else [ɛls] adv altro; **something ~** qualcos'altro; **somewhere ~** altrove; **everywhere ~** in qualsiasi altro luogo; **nobody ~** nessun altro; **where ~?** in quale altro luogo?; **little ~** poco altro; **elsewhere** adv altrove

elusive [ɪ'luːsɪv] adj elusivo/a

email [iː'meɪl] n abbr (= electronic mail) posta elettronica, e-mail m or f inv ▷ vt mandare un messaggio di posta elettronica or un e-mail a; **email address** n indirizzo di posta elettronica

embankment [ɪm'bæŋkmənt] n (of road, railway) massicciata

embargo [ɪm'bɑːgəu] n (pl **embargoes**) (Comm, Naut) embargo ▷ vt mettere l'embargo su; **to put an ~ on sth** mettere l'embargo su qc

embark [ɪmˈbɑːk] vi: **to ~ (on)** imbarcarsi (su) ▷ vt imbarcare; **to ~ on** (fig) imbarcarsi in

embarrass [ɪmˈbærəs] vt imbarazzare; **embarrassed** adj imbarazzato/a; **embarrassing** adj imbarazzante; **embarrassment** n imbarazzo

embassy [ˈɛmbəsɪ] n ambasciata

embrace [ɪmˈbreɪs] vt abbracciare ▷ vi abbracciarsi ▷ n abbraccio

embroider [ɪmˈbrɔɪdəʳ] vt ricamare; **embroidery** n ricamo

embryo [ˈɛmbrɪəʊ] n embrione m

emerald [ˈɛmərəld] n smeraldo

emerge [ɪˈməːdʒ] vi emergere

emergency [ɪˈməːdʒənsɪ] n emergenza; **in an ~** in caso di emergenza; **emergency brake** (us) n freno a mano; **emergency exit** n uscita di sicurezza; **emergency landing** n atterraggio forzato; **emergency room** (us Med) n pronto soccorso

emergency service n servizio di pronto intervento

emigrate [ˈɛmɪɡreɪt] vi emigrare; **emigration** [ɛmɪˈɡreɪʃən] n emigrazione f

eminent [ˈɛmɪnənt] adj eminente

emission [ɪˈmɪʃən] n (of gas, radiation) emissione f

emit [ɪˈmɪt] vt emettere

emoticon [ɪˈməʊtɪkən] n (Comput) faccina

emotion [ɪˈməʊʃən] n emozione f; **emotional** adj (person) emotivo/a; (scene) commovente; (tone, speech) carico/a d'emozione

emperor [ˈɛmpərəʳ] n imperatore m

emphasis (pl **emphases**) [ˈɛmfəsɪs, -siːz] n enfasi f inv; importanza

emphasize [ˈɛmfəsaɪz] vt (word, point) sottolineare; (feature) mettere in evidenza

empire [ˈɛmpaɪəʳ] n impero

employ [ɪmˈplɔɪ] vt impiegare; **employee** [ɪmplɔɪˈiː] n impiegato/a; **employer** n principale m/f, datore m di lavoro; **employment** n impiego; **employment agency** n agenzia di collocamento

empower [ɪmˈpaʊəʳ] vt: **to ~ sb to do** concedere autorità a qn di fare

empress [ˈɛmprɪs] n imperatrice f

emptiness [ˈɛmptɪnɪs] n vuoto

empty [ˈɛmptɪ] adj vuoto/a; (threat, promise) vano/a ▷ vt vuotare ▷ vi vuotarsi; (liquid) scaricarsi; **empty-handed** adj a mani vuote

EMU n abbr (= economic and monetary union) UEM f

emulsion [ɪˈmʌlʃən] n emulsione f

enable [ɪˈneɪbl] vt: **to ~ sb to do** permettere a qn di fare

enamel [ɪˈnæməl] n smalto; **enamel paint** n vernice f a smalto

enchanting [ɪnˈtʃɑːntɪŋ] adj incantevole, affascinante

encl. abbr (on letters etc: = enclosed, enclosure) all., alleg.

enclose [ɪnˈkləʊz] vt (land) circondare, recingere; (letter etc): **to ~ (with)** allegare (con); **please find ~d** trovi qui accluso

enclosure [ɪnˈkləʊʒəʳ] n recinto

encore [ɔŋˈkɔːʳ] excl, n bis (m inv)

encounter [ɪnˈkaʊntəʳ] n incontro ▷ vt incontrare

encourage [ɪnˈkʌrɪdʒ] vt incoraggiare; **encouragement** n incoraggiamento

encouraging [ɪnˈkʌrɪdʒɪŋ] adj incoraggiante

encyclop(a)edia [ɛnsaɪkləʊˈpiːdɪə] n enciclopedia

end [ɛnd] n fine f; (aim) fine m; (of table) bordo estremo; (of pointed object) punta ▷ vt finire; (also: **bring to an ~, put an ~ to**) mettere fine a ▷ vi finire; **in the ~** alla fine; **on ~** (object) ritto(a); **to stand on ~** (hair) rizzarsi; **for hours on ~** per ore e ore; **end up** vi: **to ~ up in** finire in

endanger [ɪnˈdeɪndʒəʳ] vt mettere in pericolo

endearing [ɪnˈdɪərɪŋ] adj accattivante

endeavour, (us) **endeavor** [ɪnˈdɛvəʳ] n sforzo, tentativo ▷ vi: **to ~ to do** cercare or sforzarsi di fare

ending [ˈɛndɪŋ] n fine f, conclusione f; (Ling) desinenza

endless [ˈɛndlɪs] adj senza fine

endorse [ɪnˈdɔːs] vt (cheque) girare; (approve) approvare, appoggiare; **endorsement** n approvazione f; (on driving licence) contravvenzione registrata sulla patente

endurance [ɪnˈdjʊərəns] n resistenza; pazienza

endure [ɪnˈdjʊəʳ] vt sopportare, resistere a ▷ vi durare

enemy [ˈɛnəmɪ] adj, n nemico/a

energetic [ɛnəˈdʒɛtɪk] adj energico/a, attivo/a

energy [ˈɛnədʒɪ] n energia

enforce [ɪnˈfɔːs] vt (Law) applicare, far osservare

engaged [ɪnˈɡeɪdʒd] adj (brit: busy, in use) occupato/a; (betrothed) fidanzato/a; **the line's ~** (brit) la linea è occupata; **to get ~** fidanzarsi; **engaged tone** n (brit Tel) segnale m di occupato

engagement [ɪnˈɡeɪdʒmənt] n impegno, obbligo; appuntamento; (to marry) fidanzamento; **engagement ring** n anello di fidanzamento

engaging [ɪnˈɡeɪdʒɪŋ] adj attraente

engine [ˈɛndʒɪn] n (Aut) motore m; (Rail) locomotiva

engineer [ɛndʒɪˈnɪəʳ] n ingegnere m; (BRIT: for domestic appliances) tecnico; (us Rail) macchinista m; **engineering** n ingegneria

England [ˈɪŋɡlənd] n Inghilterra

English [ˈɪŋɡlɪʃ] adj inglese ▷ n (Ling) inglese m; **the English** npl gli Inglesi; **English Channel** n: **the English Channel** il Canale della Manica; **Englishman** n (irreg) inglese m; **Englishwoman** n (irreg) inglese f

engrave [ɪnˈɡreɪv] vt incidere

engraving [ɪnˈɡreɪvɪŋ] n incisione f

enhance [ɪnˈhɑːns] vt accrescere

enjoy [ɪnˈdʒɔɪ] vt godere; (have: success, fortune) avere; **to ~ o.s.** godersela, divertirsi; **enjoyable** adj piacevole; **enjoyment** n piacere m, godimento

enlarge [ɪnˈlɑːdʒ] vt ingrandire ▷ vi: **to ~ on** (subject) dilungarsi su; **enlargement** n (Phot) ingrandimento

enlist [ɪnˈlɪst] vt arruolare; (support) procurare ▷ vi arruolarsi

enormous [ɪˈnɔːməs] adj enorme

enough [ɪˈnʌf] adj, n: **~ time/books** assai tempo/libri; **have you got ~?** ne ha abbastanza or a sufficienza? ▷ adv: **big ~** abbastanza grande; **he has not worked ~** non ha lavorato abbastanza; **~!** basta!; **that's ~, thanks** basta così, grazie; **I've had ~ of him** ne ho abbastanza di lui; **... which, funnily ~** ... che, strano a dirsi

enquire [ɪnˈkwaɪəʳ] vt, vi (esp BRIT) = **inquire**

enquiry [ɪnˈkwaɪərɪ] n (esp BRIT) = **inquiry**

enrage [ɪnˈreɪdʒ] vt fare arrabbiare

enrich [ɪnˈrɪtʃ] vt arricchire

enrol, (us) **enroll** [ɪnˈrəul] vt iscrivere ▷ vi iscriversi; **enrolment**, (us) **enrollment** n iscrizione f

en route [ɔnˈruːt] adv: **~ for/from/to** in viaggio per/da/a

en suite [ɔnˈswiːt] adj: **room with ~ bathroom** camera con bagno

ensure [ɪnˈʃuəʳ] vt assicurare; garantire

entail [ɪnˈteɪl] vt comportare

enter [ˈɛntəʳ] vt entrare in; (army) arruolarsi in; (competition) partecipare a; (sb for a competition) iscrivere; (write down) registrare; (Comput) inserire ▷ vi entrare

enterprise [ˈɛntəpraɪz] n (undertaking, company) impresa; (spirit) iniziativa; **free ~** liberalismo economico; **private ~** iniziativa privata; **enterprising** [ˈɛntəpraɪzɪŋ] adj intraprendente

entertain [ɛntəˈteɪn] vt divertire; (invite) ricevere; (idea, plan) nutrire; **entertainer** n comico/a; **entertaining** adj divertente; **entertainment** n (amusement) divertimento; (show) spettacolo

enthusiasm [ɪnˈθuːzɪæzəm] n entusiasmo

enthusiast [ɪnˈθuːzɪæst] n entusiasta m/f; **enthusiastic** [ɪnθuːzɪˈæstɪk] adj entusiasta, entusiastico/a; **to be enthusiastic about sth/sb** essere appassionato di qc/entusiasta di qn

entire [ɪnˈtaɪəʳ] adj intero/a; **entirely** adv completamente, interamente

entitle [ɪnˈtaɪtl] vt (give right): **to ~ sb to sth/to do** dare diritto a qn a qc/a fare; **entitled** adj (book) che si intitola; **to be entitled to sth** avere diritto a qc; **to be entitled to do sth** avere il diritto di fare qc

entrance n [ˈɛntrns] entrata, ingresso; (of person) entrata ▷ vt [ɪnˈtrɑːns] incantare, rapire; **to gain ~ to** (university etc) essere ammesso a; **entrance examination** n esame m di ammissione; **entrance fee** n tassa d'iscrizione; (to museum etc) prezzo d'ingresso; **entrance ramp** n (us Aut) rampa di accesso; **entrant** [ˈɛntrnt] n partecipante m/f; concorrente m/f

entrepreneur [ˈɔntrəprəˈnəːʳ] n imprenditore m

entrust [ɪnˈtrʌst] vt: **to ~ sth to** affidare qc a

entry [ˈɛntrɪ] n entrata; (way in) entrata, ingresso; (item: on list) iscrizione f; (in dictionary) vóce f; **"no ~"** "vietato l'ingresso"; (Aut) "divieto di accesso"; **entry phone** n citofono

envelope [ˈɛnvələup] n busta

envious [ˈɛnvɪəs] adj invidioso/a

environment [ɪnˈvaɪərənmənt] n ambiente m; **environmental** [ɪnvaɪərənˈmɛntl] adj ecologico/a; ambientale; **environmentally** [ɪnvaɪərənˈmɛntəlɪ] adv: **environmentally sound/friendly** che rispetta l'ambiente

envisage [ɪnˈvɪzɪdʒ] vt immaginare; prevedere

envoy [ˈɛnvɔɪ] n inviato/a

envy [ˈɛnvɪ] n invidia ▷ vt invidiare; **to ~ sb sth** invidiare qn per qc

epic [ˈɛpɪk] n poema m epico ▷ adj epico/a

epidemic [ɛpɪˈdɛmɪk] n epidemia

epilepsy [ˈɛpɪlɛpsɪ] n epilessia

epileptic [ɛpɪˈlɛptɪk] adj, n epilettico/a; **epileptic fit** n attacco epilettico

episode [ˈɛpɪsəud] n episodio

equal [ˈiːkwl] adj, n pari (m/f) ▷ vt uguagliare; **~ to** (task) all'altezza di; **equality** [iːˈkwɔlɪtɪ] n uguaglianza;

equalize vi pareggiare; **equally** adv ugualmente

equation [ɪ'kweɪʃən] n (Math) equazione f

equator [ɪ'kweɪtə'] n equatore m

equip [ɪ'kwɪp] vt equipaggiare, attrezzare; **to ~ sb/sth with** fornire qn/qc di; **to be well ~ped** (office etc) essere ben attrezzato/a; **he is well ~ped for the job** ha i requisiti necessari per quel lavoro; **equipment** n attrezzatura; (electrical etc) apparecchiatura

equivalent [ɪ'kwɪvələnt] adj, n equivalente (m); **to be ~ to** equivalere a

ER abbr (BRIT) = **Elizabeth Regina**; (US Med) = **emergency room**

era ['ɪərə] n era, età f inv

erase [ɪ'reɪz] vt cancellare; **eraser** n gomma

e-reader ['iːriːdə'] n e-reader m inv, lettore m di libri digitali

erect [ɪ'rɛkt] adj eretto/a ▷ vt costruire; (assemble) montare; **erection** [ɪ'rɛkʃən] n (also Physiol) erezione f; (of building) costruzione f; (of machinery) montaggio

ERM n abbr (= Exchange Rate Mechanism) ERM m, meccanismo dei tassi di cambio

erode [ɪ'rəud] vt erodere; (metal) corrodere

erosion [ɪ'rəuʒən] n erosione f

erotic [ɪ'rɔtɪk] adj erotico/a

errand ['ɛrənd] n commissione f

erratic [ɪ'rætɪk] adj imprevedibile; (person, mood) incostante

error ['ɛrə'] n errore m

erupt [ɪ'rʌpt] vi (volcano) mettersi (or essere) in eruzione; (war, crisis) scoppiare; **eruption** [ɪ'rʌpʃən] n eruzione f; scoppio

escalate ['ɛskəleɪt] vi intensificarsi

escalator ['ɛskəleɪtə'] n scala mobile

escape [ɪ'skeɪp] n evasione f; fuga; (of gas etc) fuga, fuoriuscita ▷ vi fuggire; (from jail) evadere, scappare; (leak) uscire ▷ vt sfuggire a; **to ~ from** (place) fuggire da; (person) sfuggire a

escort n ['ɛskɔːt] scorta; (to a dance etc): **her ~** il suo cavaliere ▷ vt [ɪ'skɔːt] scortare; accompagnare

especially [ɪ'spɛʃlɪ] adv specialmente; (above all) soprattutto; (specifically) espressamente

espionage ['ɛspɪənɑːʒ] n spionaggio

essay ['ɛseɪ] n (Scol) composizione f; (Literature) saggio

essence ['ɛsns] n essenza

essential [ɪ'sɛnʃəl] adj essenziale ▷ n elemento essenziale; **essentially** adv essenzialmente; **essentials** npl: **the essentials** l'essenziale msg

establish [ɪ'stæblɪʃ] vt stabilire; (business) mettere su; (one's power etc) affermare;

establishment n stabilimento; **the Establishment** la classe dirigente; l'establishment m

estate [ɪ'steɪt] n proprietà f inv; (Law) beni mpl, patrimonio; (BRIT: also: **housing ~**) complesso edilizio; **estate agent** n (BRIT) agente m immobiliare; **estate car** n (BRIT) giardiniera

estimate n ['ɛstɪmət] stima; (Comm) preventivo ▷ vt ['ɛstɪmeɪt] stimare, valutare

etc. abbr (= et cetera) ecc., etc.

eternal [ɪ'təːnl] adj eterno/a

eternity [ɪ'təːnɪtɪ] n eternità

ethical ['ɛθɪkl] adj etico/a, morale; **ethics** ['ɛθɪks] n etica ▷ npl morale f

Ethiopia [iːθɪ'əupɪə] n Etiopia

ethnic ['ɛθnɪk] adj etnico/a; **ethnic minority** n minoranza etnica

e-ticket ['iːtɪkɪt] n biglietto elettronico

etiquette ['ɛtɪkɛt] n etichetta

EU n abbr (= European Union) UE f

euro ['juərəu] n (currency) euro m inv

Europe ['juərəp] n Europa; **European** [juərə'piːən] adj, n europeo/a; **European Community** n Comunità Europea; **European Union** n Unione f europea

Eurostar® ['juərəustɑː'] n Eurostar® m inv

evacuate [ɪ'vækjueɪt] vt evacuare

evade [ɪ'veɪd] vt (tax) evadere; (duties etc) sottrarsi a; (person) schivare

evaluate [ɪ'væljueɪt] vt valutare

evaporate [ɪ'væpəreɪt] vi evaporare

eve [iːv] n: **on the ~ of** alla vigilia di

even ['iːvn] adj regolare; (number) pari inv ▷ adv anche, perfino; **~ if, ~ though** anche se; **~ more** ancora di più; **~ so** ciò nonostante; **not ~ ...** nemmeno ...; **to get ~ with sb** dare la pari a qn

evening ['iːvnɪŋ] n sera; (as duration, event) serata; **in the ~** la sera; **evening class** n corso serale; **evening dress** n (woman's) abito da sera; **in evening dress** (man) in abito scuro; (woman) in abito lungo

event [ɪ'vɛnt] n avvenimento; (Sport) gara; **in the ~ of** in caso di; **eventful** adj denso/a di eventi

eventual [ɪ'vɛntʃuəl] adj finale

Be careful not to translate eventual by the Italian word eventuale.

eventually [ɪ'vɛntʃuəlɪ] adv alla fine

Be careful not to translate eventually by the Italian word eventualmente.

ever ['ɛvə'] adv mai; (at all times) sempre; **the best ~** il migliore che ci sia mai stato; **have you ~ seen it?** l'ha mai visto?; **~ so pretty** così bello(a); **~ since** adv da allora; conj sin da quando; **evergreen** n sempreverde m

every ['ɛvrɪ] adj ogni; ~ **day** tutti i giorni, ogni giorno; ~ **other/third day** ogni due/tre giorni; ~ **other car** una macchina su due; ~ **now and then** ogni tanto, di quando in quando; **everybody** pron ognuno, tutti pl; **everyday** adj quotidiano/a; di ogni giorno; **everyone** ['ɛvrɪwʌn] = **everybody**; **everything** pron tutto, ogni cosa; **everywhere** adv dappertutto; (wherever) ovunque

evict [ɪ'vɪkt] vt sfrattare

evidence ['ɛvɪdəns] n (proof) prova; (of witness) testimonianza; **to show ~ of** (sign) dare segni di; **to give ~** deporre

evident ['ɛvɪdənt] adj evidente; **evidently** adv evidentemente

evil ['iːvl] adj cattivo/a, maligno/a ▷ n male m

evoke [ɪ'vəʊk] vt evocare

evolution [iːvə'luːʃən] n evoluzione f

evolve [ɪ'vɒlv] vt elaborare ▷ vi svilupparsi, evolversi

ewe [juː] n pecora

ex (col) [ɛks] n: **my ex** il (la) mio/a ex

ex- [ɛks] prefix ex

exact [ɪg'zækt] adj esatto/a ▷ vt: **to ~ sth (from)** estorcere qc (da); esigere qc (da); **exactly** adv esattamente

exaggerate [ɪg'zædʒəreɪt] vt, vi esagerare; **exaggeration** [ɪgzædʒə'reɪʃən] n esagerazione f

exam [ɪg'zæm] n abbr (Scol) = **examination**

examination [ɪgzæmɪ'neɪʃən] n (Scol) esame m; (Med) controllo

examine [ɪg'zæmɪn] vt esaminare; **examiner** n esaminatore/trice

example [ɪg'zaːmpl] n esempio; **for ~** ad or per esempio

exasperated [ɪg'zaːspəreɪtɪd] adj esasperato/a

excavate ['ɛkskəveɪt] vt scavare

exceed [ɪk'siːd] vt superare; (one's powers, time limit) oltrepassare; **exceedingly** adv eccessivamente

excel [ɪk'sɛl] vi eccellere ▷ vt sorpassare; **to ~ o.s.** (BRIT) superare se stesso

excellence ['ɛksələns] n eccellenza

excellent ['ɛksələnt] adj eccellente

except [ɪk'sɛpt] prep (also: ~ **for**, ~**ing**) salvo, all'infuori di, eccetto ▷ vt escludere; ~ **if/when** salvo se/quando; ~ **that** salvo che; **exception** [ɪk'sɛpʃən] n eccezione f; **to take exception to** trovare a ridire su; **exceptional** [ɪk'sɛpʃənl] adj eccezionale; **exceptionally** [ɪk'sɛpʃənəlɪ] adv eccezionalmente

excerpt ['ɛksəːpt] n estratto

excess [ɪk'sɛs] n eccesso; **excess baggage** n bagaglio in eccedenza; **excessive** adj eccessivo/a

exchange [ɪks'tʃeɪndʒ] n scambio; (also: **telephone ~**) centralino ▷ vt: **to ~ (for)** scambiare (con); **exchange rate** n tasso di cambio

excite [ɪk'saɪt] vt eccitare; **to get ~d** eccitarsi; **excited** adj: **to get excited** essere elettrizzato/a; **excitement** n eccitazione f; agitazione f; **exciting** adj avventuroso/a; (film, book) appassionante

exclaim [ɪk'skleɪm] vi esclamare; **exclamation** [ɛksklə'meɪʃən] n esclamazione f; **exclamation mark**, (US) **exclamation point** n punto esclamativo

exclude [ɪk'skluːd] vt escludere

excluding [ɪk'skluːdɪŋ] prep: ~ **VAT** IVA esclusa

exclusion [ɪk'skluːʒən] n esclusione f; **to the ~ of** escludendo

exclusive [ɪk'skluːsɪv] adj esclusivo/a; ~ **of VAT** IVA esclusa; **exclusively** adv esclusivamente

excruciating [ɪk'skruːʃɪeɪtɪŋ] adj straziante, atroce

excursion [ɪk'skəːʃən] n escursione f, gita

excuse n [ɪk'skjuːs] scusa ▷ vt [ɪk'skjuːz] scusare; **to ~ sb from** (activity) dispensare qn da; ~ **me!** mi scusi!; **now if you will ~ me, ...** ora, mi scusi ma ...

ex-directory ['ɛksdɪ'rɛktərɪ] adj (BRIT): **to be ~** non essere sull'elenco

execute ['ɛksɪkjuːt] vt (prisoner) giustiziare; (plan etc) eseguire; **execution** [ɛksɪ'kjuːʃən] n esecuzione f

executive [ɪg'zɛkjutɪv] n (Comm) dirigente m; (Pol) esecutivo ▷ adj esecutivo/a

exempt [ɪg'zɛmpt] adj: ~ **(from)** esentato/a (da) ▷ vt: **to ~ sb from** esentare qn da

exercise ['ɛksəsaɪz] n (keep fit) moto; (Scol, Mil etc) esercizio ▷ vt esercitare; (patience) usare; (dog) portar fuori ▷ vi (also: **take ~**) fare il movimento or moto; **exercise book** n quaderno

exert [ɪg'zəːt] vt esercitare; **to ~ o.s.** sforzarsi; **exertion** [ɪg'zəːʃən] n sforzo

exhale [ɛks'heɪl] vt, vi espirare

exhaust [ɪg'zɔːst] n (also: ~ **fumes**) scappamento; (also: ~ **pipe**) tubo di scappamento ▷ vt esaurire; **exhausted** adj esaurito/a; **exhaustion** [ɪg'zɔːstʃən] n esaurimento; **nervous exhaustion** sovraffaticamento mentale

exhibit [ɪg'zɪbɪt] n (Art) oggetto esposto; (Law) documento or oggetto esibito ▷ vt esporre; (courage, skill) dimostrare; **exhibition** [ɛksɪ'bɪʃən] n mostra, esposizione f

exhilarating [ɪg'zɪləreɪtɪŋ] adj esilarante; stimolante

exile ['ɛksaɪl] n esilio; (person) esiliato/a ▷ vt esiliare

exist [ɪg'zɪst] vi esistere; **existence** n esistenza; **existing** adj esistente; attuale

exit ['ɛksɪt] n uscita ▷ vi (Comput, Theat) uscire; **exit ramp** n (us Aut) rampa di uscita

exotic [ɪg'zɔtɪk] adj esotico/a

expand [ɪk'spænd] vt espandere; (influence) estendere; (horizons) allargare ▷ vi (gas) espandersi; (metal) dilatarsi

expansion [ɪk'spænʃən] n (gen) espansione f; (of town, economy) sviluppo; (of metal) dilatazione f

expect [ɪk'spɛkt] vt (anticipate) prevedere, aspettarsi, prevedere or aspettarsi che + sub; (require) richiedere, esigere; (suppose) supporre; (await, also baby) aspettare ▷ vi: **to be ~ing** essere in stato interessante; **to ~ sb to do** aspettarsi che qn faccia; **expectation** [ɛkspɛk'teɪʃən] n aspettativa; speranza

expedition [ɛkspə'dɪʃən] n spedizione f

expel [ɪk'spɛl] vt espellere

expenditure [ɪk'spɛndɪtʃəʳ] n spesa

expense [ɪk'spɛns] n spesa; (high cost) costo; **expenses** npl (Comm) spese fpl, indennità fpl; **at the ~ of** a spese di; **expense account** n conto m spese inv

expensive [ɪk'spɛnsɪv] adj caro/a, costoso/a

experience [ɪk'spɪərɪəns] n esperienza ▷ vt (pleasure) provare; (hardship) soffrire; **experienced** adj esperto/a

experiment n [ɪk'spɛrɪmənt] esperimento, esperienza ▷ vi [ɪk'spɛrɪmɛnt] fare esperimenti; **experimental** [ɪkspɛrɪ'mɛntl] adj sperimentale; **at the experimental stage** in via di sperimentazione

expert ['ɛkspəːt] adj, n esperto/a; **expertise** [ɛkspəː'tiːz] n competenza

expire [ɪk'spaɪəʳ] vi (period of time, licence) scadere; **expiry** n scadenza; **expiry date** n (of medicine, food item) data di scadenza

explain [ɪk'spleɪn] vt spiegare; **explanation** [ɛksplə'neɪʃən] n spiegazione f

explicit [ɪk'splɪsɪt] adj esplicito/a

explode [ɪk'spləud] vi esplodere

exploit n ['ɛksplɔɪt] impresa ▷ vt [ɪk'splɔɪt] sfruttare; **exploitation** [ɛksplɔɪ'teɪʃən] n sfruttamento

explore [ɪk'splɔːʳ] vt esplorare; (possibilities) esaminare; **explorer** n esploratore/trice

explosion [ɪk'spləuʒən] n esplosione f; **explosive** [ɪk'spləusɪv] adj esplosivo/a ▷ n esplosivo

export vt [ɛk'spɔːt] esportare ▷ n ['ɛkspɔːt] esportazione f; articolo di esportazione ▷ cpd d'esportazione; **exporter** n esportatore m

expose [ɪk'spəuz] vt esporre; (unmask) smascherare; **exposed** adj (land, house) esposto/a; **exposure** [ɪk'spəuʒəʳ] n esposizione f; (Phot) posa; (Med) assideramento

express [ɪk'sprɛs] adj (definite) chiaro/a, espresso/a; (BRIT: letter etc) espresso inv ▷ n (train) espresso ▷ vt esprimere; **expression** [ɪk'sprɛʃən] n espressione f; **expressway** n (us: urban motorway) autostrada che attraversa la città

exquisite [ɛk'skwɪzɪt] adj squisito/a

extend [ɪk'stɛnd] vt (visit) protrarre; (road, deadline) prolungare; (building) ampliare; (offer) offrire, porgere ▷ vi (land) estendersi; **extension** [ɪk'stɛnʃən] n (of road, term) prolungamento; (of contract, deadline) proroga; (building) annesso; (to wire, table) prolunga; (telephone) interno; (: in private house) apparecchio supplementare; **extension cable** or **lead** n (Elec) prolunga

extensive [ɪk'stɛnsɪv] adj esteso/a, ampio/a; (damage) su larga scala; (inquiries, coverage, discussion) esauriente; (use) grande

extent [ɪk'stɛnt] n estensione f; **to some ~** fino a un certo punto; **to what ~?** fino a che punto?; **to such an ~ that ...** a tal punto che ...; **to the ~ of ...** fino al punto di ...

exterior [ɛk'stɪərɪəʳ] adj esteriore, esterno/a ▷ n esteriore m, esterno; aspetto (esteriore)

external [ɛk'stəːnl] adj esterno/a, esteriore

extinct [ɪk'stɪŋkt] adj estinto/a; **extinction** [ɪk'stɪŋkʃən] n estinzione f

extinguish [ɪk'stɪŋgwɪʃ] vt estinguere

extra ['ɛkstrə] adj extra inv, supplementare ▷ adv (in addition) di più ▷ n extra m inv; (surcharge) supplemento; (Theat) comparso

extract vt [ɪk'strækt] estrarre; (money, promise) strappare ▷ n ['ɛkstrækt] estratto; (passage) brano

extradite ['ɛkstrədaɪt] vt estradare

extraordinary [ɪk'strɔːdnrɪ] adj straordinario/a

extravagance [ɪk'strævəgəns] n sperpero; (thing bought) stravaganza

extravagant [ɪk'strævəgənt] adj (in spending) prodigo/a; (: tastes) dispendioso/a; esagerato/a

> Be careful not to translate extravagant by the Italian word stravagante.

extreme [ɪk'striːm] adj estremo/a ▷ n estremo; **extremely** adv estremamente

extremist [ɪk'striːmɪst] *adj, n* estremista (*m/f*)

extrovert ['ɛkstrəvəːt] *n* estroverso/a

eye [aɪ] *n* occhio; (*of needle*) cruna ▷ *vt* osservare; **to keep an ~ on** tenere d'occhio; **eyeball** *n* globo dell'occhio; **eyebrow** *n* sopracciglio; **eyedrops** *npl* gocce *fpl* oculari, collirio; **eyelash** *n* ciglio; **eyelid** *n* palpebra; **eyeliner** *n* eye-liner *m inv*; **eyeshadow** *n* ombretto; **eyesight** *n* vista; **eye witness** *n* testimone *m/f* oculare

F [ɛf] *n* (*Mus*) fa *m*

fabric ['fæbrɪk] *n* stoffa, tessuto

fabulous ['fæbjuləs] *adj* favoloso/a; (*super*) favoloso/a, fantastico/a

face [feɪs] *n* faccia, viso, volto; (*expression*) faccia; (*of clock*) quadrante *m*; (*of building*) facciata ▷ *vt* fronteggiare; (*fig*) affrontare; **~ down** (*person*) bocconi; (*object*) a faccia in giù; **to pull a ~** fare una smorfia; **in the ~ of** (*difficulties etc*) di fronte a; **on the ~ of it** a prima vista; **~ to ~** faccia a faccia; **face up to** *vt fus* affrontare, far fronte a; **face cloth** *n* (*BRIT*) guanto di spugna; **face pack** *n* (*BRIT*) maschera di bellezza

facial ['feɪʃəl] *adj* facciale, del viso ▷ *n* trattamento del viso

facilitate [fə'sɪlɪteɪt] *vt* facilitare

facility [fə'sɪlɪtɪ] *n* facilità; **facilities** *npl* attrezzature *fpl*; **credit facilities** facilitazioni *fpl* di credito

fact [fækt] *n* fatto; **in ~** in effetti

faction ['fækʃən] *n* fazione *f*

factor ['fæktəʳ] *n* fattore *m*

factory ['fæktərɪ] *n* fabbrica, stabilimento
▮ Be careful not to translate *factory* by the Italian word *fattoria*.

factual ['fæktjuəl] *adj* che si attiene ai fatti

faculty ['fækəltɪ] *n* facoltà *f inv*; (*US*) corpo insegnante

fad [fæd] *n* mania; capriccio

fade [feɪd] *vi* sbiadire, sbiadirsi; (*light, sound, hope*) attenuarsi, affievolirsi; (*flower*) appassire; **fade away** *vi* (*sound*) affievolirsi

fag [fæg] *n* (*BRIT: col: cigarette*) cicca

Fahrenheit ['fɑːrənhaɪt] *n* Fahrenheit *m inv*

fail [feɪl] *vt* (*exam*) non superare; (*candidate*) bocciare; (*courage, memory*) mancare a ▷ *vi* fallire; (*student*) essere respinto/a; (*eyesight, health, light*) venire a mancare; **to ~ to do**

sth (neglect) mancare di fare qc; (be unable)
non riuscire a fare qc; **without ~** senza
fallo; certamente; **failing** n difetto ▷ prep in
mancanza di; **failure** ['feɪljəʳ] n fallimento;
(person) fallito/a; (mechanical etc) guasto

faint [feɪnt] adj debole; (recollection)
vago/a; (mark) indistinto/a ▷ n (Med)
svenimento ▷ vi svenire; **to feel ~** sentirsi
svenire; **faintest** adj: **I haven't the
faintest idea** non ho la più pallida idea;
faintly adv debolmente; vagamente

fair [fɛəʳ] adj (person, decision) giusto/a,
equo/a; (quite large, quite good) discreto/a;
(hair etc) biondo/a; (skin, complexion)
chiaro/a; (weather) bello/a, clemente ▷ adv:
to play ~ giocare correttamente ▷ n fiera;
(BRIT: funfair) luna park m inv; **fairground** n
luna park m inv; **fair-haired** [fɛəˈhɛəd] adj
(person) biondo/a; **fairly** adv equamente;
(quite) abbastanza; **fair trade** n commercio
equo e solidale; **fairway** n (Golf) fairway
m inv

fairy ['fɛərɪ] n fata; **fairy tale** n fiaba

faith [feɪθ] n fede f; (trust) fiducia; (sect)
religione f, fede f; **faithful** adj fedele;
faithfully adv fedelmente; **yours
faithfully** (BRIT: in letters) distinti saluti

fake [feɪk] n imitazione f; (picture) falso;
(person) impostore/a ▷ adj falso/a ▷ vt
(accounts) falsificare; (illness) fingere;
(painting) contraffare

falcon ['fɔːlkən] n falco, falcone m

fall [fɔːl] n caduta; (in temperature)
abbassamento; (in price) ribasso; (us:
autumn) autunno ▷ vi (pt **fell**, pp **fallen**)
cadere; (temperature, price) scendere; **to ~
flat** (on one's face) cadere bocconi; (joke) fare
cilecca; (plan) fallire; **fall apart** vi cadere
a pezzi; **fall down** vi (person) cadere;
(building, hopes) crollare; **fall for** vt fus
(person) prendere una cotta per; **to ~ for
a trick** (or a story etc) cascarci; **fall off** vi
cadere; (diminish) diminuire, abbassarsi;
fall out vi (hair, teeth) cadere; (friends etc)
litigare; **fall through** vi (plan, project) fallire

fallen ['fɔːlən] pp of **fall**

fallout ['fɔːlaut] n fall-out m

falls npl (waterfall) cascate fpl

false [fɔːls] adj falso/a; **under ~ pretences**
con l'inganno; **false alarm** n falso allarme
m; **false teeth** npl (BRIT) denti mpl finti

fame [feɪm] n fama, celebrità

familiar [fəˈmɪlɪəʳ] adj familiare; (close)
intimo/a; **to be ~ with** conoscere;
familiarize [fəˈmɪlɪəraɪz] vt: **to
familiarize o.s. with** familiarizzare con

family ['fæmɪlɪ] n famiglia; **family doctor**
n medico di famiglia; **family planning** n
pianificazione f familiare

famine ['fæmɪn] n carestia

famous ['feɪməs] adj famoso/a

fan [fæn] n (folding) ventaglio; (machine)
ventilatore m; (person) ammiratore/trice;
tifoso/a ▷ vt far vento a; (fire, quarrel)
alimentare

fanatic [fəˈnætɪk] n fanatico/a

fan belt n cinghia del ventilatore

fan club n fan club m inv

fancy ['fænsɪ] n immaginazione f, fantasia;
(whim) capriccio ▷ adj (hat) stravagante;
(hotel, food) speciale ▷ vt (feel like, want) aver
voglia di; (imagine) immaginare; **to take a ~
to** incapricciarsi di; **he fancies her** gli piace;
fancy dress n costume m (per maschera)

fan heater n (BRIT) stufa ad aria calda

fantasize ['fæntəsaɪz] vi fantasticare,
sognare

fantastic [fænˈtæstɪk] adj fantastico/a

fantasy ['fæntəsɪ] n fantasia,
immaginazione f; fantasticheria; chimera

fanzine ['fænziːn] n rivista specialistica
(per appassionati)

FAQ abbr (= frequently asked question(s)) FAQ

far [fɑːʳ] adj lontano/a ▷ adv (much,
greatly) molto; **is it ~ from here?** è molto
lontano da qui?; **how ~?** quanto lontano?;
(referring to activity etc) fino a dove?; **how ~
is the town centre?** quanto dista il centro
da qui?; **~ away, ~ off** lontano, distante;
~ better assai migliore; **~ from** lontano
da; **by ~** di gran lunga; **go as ~ as the farm**
vada fino alla fattoria; **as ~ as I know** per
quel che so

farce [fɑːs] n farsa

fare [fɛəʳ] n (on trains, buses) tariffa; (in taxi)
prezzo della corsa; (food) vitto, cibo; **half ~**
metà tariffa; **full ~** tariffa intera

Far East n: **the ~** l'Estremo Oriente m

farewell [fɛəˈwɛl] excl, n addio

farm [fɑːm] n fattoria, podere m ▷ vt
coltivare; **farmer** n coltivatore/trice,
agricoltore/trice; **farmhouse** n fattoria;
farming n (gen) agricoltura; (of crops)
coltivazione f; (of animals) allevamento;
farmyard n aia

far-reaching ['fɑːˈriːtʃɪŋ] adj di vasta portata

fart [fɑːt] (col!) n scoreggia (!) ▷ vi
scoreggiare (!)

farther ['fɑːðəʳ] adv più lontano ▷ adj più
lontano/a

farthest ['fɑːðɪst] adv superlative of **far**

fascinate ['fæsɪneɪt] vt affascinare;
fascinated adj affascinato/a; **fascinating**
adj affascinante; **fascination** [fæsɪˈneɪʃən]
n fascino

fascist ['fæʃɪst] adj, n fascista (m/f)

fashion ['fæʃən] n moda; (manner) maniera,
modo ▷ vt foggiare, formare; **in ~** alla

moda; **out of ~** passato/a di moda;
fashionable *adj* alla moda, di moda;
fashionista [fæʃəˈnɪstə] *n* fashionista *m/f*,
maniaco/a della moda; **fashion show** *n*
sfilata di moda
fast [fɑːst] *adj* rapido/a, svelto/a, veloce;
(*clock*): **to be ~** andare avanti; (*dye, colour*)
solido/a ▷ *adv* rapidamente; (*stuck, held*)
saldamente ▷ *n* digiuno ▷ *vi* digiunare;
~ asleep profondamente addormentato
fasten [ˈfɑːsn] *vt* chiudere, fissare; (*coat*)
abbottonare, allacciare ▷ *vi* chiudersi,
fissarsi; abbottonarsi, allacciarsi
fast food *n* fast food *m inv*
fat [fæt] *adj* grasso/a; (*book, profit etc*)
grosso/a ▷ *n* grasso
fatal [ˈfeɪtl] *adj* fatale; mortale; disastroso/a;
fatality [fəˈtælɪtɪ] *n* (*road death etc*)
morto/a, vittima; **fatally** *adv* a morte
fate [feɪt] *n* destino; (*of person*) sorte *f*
father [ˈfɑːðəʳ] *n* padre *m*; **Father
Christmas** *n* Babbo Natale; **father-in-law**
n suocero
fatigue [fəˈtiːg] *n* stanchezza
fattening [ˈfætnɪŋ] *adj* (*food*) che fa
ingrassare
fatty [ˈfætɪ] *adj* (*food*) grasso/a ▷ *n* (*col*)
ciccione/a
faucet [ˈfɔːsɪt] *n* (*us*) rubinetto
fault [fɔːlt] *n* colpa; (*Tennis*) fallo; (*defect*)
difetto; (*Geo*) faglia ▷ *vt* criticare; **it's my ~**
è colpa mia; **to find ~ with** trovare da ridire
su; **at ~** in fallo; **faulty** *adj* difettoso/a
fauna [ˈfɔːnə] *n* fauna
favour, (*us*) **favor** [ˈfeɪvəʳ] *n* favore *m* ▷ *vt*
(*proposition*) favorire, essere favorevole a;
(*pupil etc*) favorire; (*team, horse*) dare per
vincente; **to do sb a ~** fare un favore *or* una
cortesia a qn; **in ~ of** in favore di; **to find ~
with sb** (*person*) entrare nelle buone grazie
di qn; (*suggestion*) avere l'approvazione di
qn; **favourable** *adj* favorevole; **favourite**
[ˈfeɪvrɪt] *adj, n* favorito/a
fawn [fɔːn] *n* daino ▷ *adj* (*also:* **~-coloured**)
marrone chiaro *inv* ▷ *vi*: **to ~ (up)on**
adulare servilmente
fax [fæks] *n* (*document, machine*) facsimile *m*
inv, telecopia; (*machine*) telecopiatrice *f* ▷ *vt*
teletrasmettere, spedire via fax
FBI *n abbr* (*us*: = *Federal Bureau of
Investigation*) FBI *f*
fear [fɪəʳ] *n* paura, timore *m* ▷ *vt* aver paura
di, temere; **for ~ of** per paura di; **fearful**
adj pauroso/a; (*sight, noise*) terribile,
spaventoso/a; **fearless** *adj* intrepido/a,
senza paura
feasible [ˈfiːzəbl] *adj* fattibile, realizzabile
feast [fiːst] *n* festa, banchetto; (*Rel: also:*
~ day) festa ▷ *vi* banchettare

feat [fiːt] *n* impresa, fatto insigne
feather [ˈfeðəʳ] *n* penna
feature [ˈfiːtʃəʳ] *n* caratteristica;
(*article*) articolo ▷ *vt* (*film*) avere come
protagonista ▷ *vi* figurare; **features** *npl* (*of
face*) fisionomia; **feature film** *n* film *m inv*
principale
Feb. [fɛb] *abbr* (= *February*) feb.
February [ˈfebruərɪ] *n* febbraio
fed [fɛd] *pt, pp of* **feed**
federal [ˈfedərəl] *adj* federale
federation [fedəˈreɪʃən] *n* federazione *f*
fed up *adj*: **to be ~** essere stufo/a
fee [fiː] *n* pagamento; (*of doctor, lawyer*)
onorario; (*for examination*) tassa d'esame;
school ~s tasse *fpl* scolastiche
feeble [ˈfiːbl] *adj* debole
feed [fiːd] *n* (*of baby*) pappa; (*of animal*)
mangime *m*; (*on printer*) meccanismo di
alimentazione ▷ *vt* (*pt, pp* **fed**) nutrire;
(*baby*) allattare; (*horse etc*) dare da mangiare
a; (*fire, machine*) alimentare ▷ *vi* (*baby,
animal*) mangiare; **to ~ data/information
into sth** inserire dati/informazioni in qc;
feedback *n* feed-back *m*
feel [fiːl] *n* (*sense of touch*) tatto; (*of
substance*) consistenza ▷ *vt* (*pt, pp* **felt**)
toccare; palpare; tastare; (*cold, pain, anger*)
sentire; (*think, believe*): **to ~ that** pensare
che; **to ~ hungry/cold** aver fame/freddo;
to ~ lonely/better sentirsi solo/meglio;
I don't ~ well non mi sento bene; **it ~s soft**
è morbido al tatto; **to ~ like** (*want*) aver
voglia di; **to ~ about** *or* **around for** cercare
a tastoni; **feeling** *n* sensazione *f*; (*emotion*)
sentimento
feet [fiːt] *npl of* **foot**
fell [fɛl] *pt of* **fall** ▷ *vt* (*tree*) abbattere
fellow [ˈfeləu] *n* individuo, tipo; (*comrade*)
compagno; (*of learned society*) membro *cpd*;
fellow citizen *n* concittadino/a; **fellow
countryman** *n* (*irreg*) compatriota *m*;
fellow men *npl* simili *mpl*; **fellowship** *n*
associazione *f*; compagnia; (*Scol*) specie di
borsa di studio universitaria
felony [ˈfelənɪ] *n* reato, crimine *m*
felt [fɛlt] *pt, pp of* **feel** ▷ *n* feltro
female [ˈfiːmeɪl] *n* (*Zool*) femmina; (*pej:
woman*) donna, femmina ▷ *adj* (*sex,
character*) femminile; (*Biol, Elec*) femmina
inv; (*vote etc*) di donne
feminine [ˈfemɪnɪn] *adj, n* femminile (*m*)
feminist [ˈfemɪnɪst] *n* femminista *m/f*
fence [fens] *n* recinto ▷ *vt* (*also:* **~ in**)
recingere ▷ *vi*: (*Sport*) tirare di scherma;
fencing *n* (*Sport*) scherma
fend [fend] *vi*: **to ~ for o.s.** arrangiarsi;
fend off *vt* (*attack, attacker*) respingere,
difendersi da

fender ['fɛndə^r] n parafuoco; (on boat) parabordo; (us) parafango; paraurti m inv

fennel ['fɛnl] n finocchio

ferment vi [fə'mɛnt] fermentare ▷ n ['fə:mɛnt] (fig) agitazione f, eccitazione f

fern [fə:n] n felce f

ferocious [fə'rəuʃəs] adj feroce

ferret ['fɛrɪt] n furetto

ferry ['fɛrɪ] n (small) traghetto; (large: also: ~boat) nave f traghetto inv ▷ vt traghettare

fertile ['fə:taɪl] adj fertile; (Biol) fecondo/a; **fertilize** ['fə:tɪlaɪz] vt fertilizzare; fecondare; **fertilizer** ['fə:tɪlaɪzə^r] n fertilizzante m

festival ['fɛstɪvəl] n (Rel) festa; (Art, Mus) festival m inv

festive ['fɛstɪv] adj di festa; **the ~ season** (BRIT: Christmas) il periodo delle feste

fetch [fɛtʃ] vt andare a prendere; (sell for) essere venduto/a per

fête [feɪt] n festa

fetus ['fi:təs] n (US) = **foetus**

feud [fju:d] n contesa, lotta

fever ['fi:və^r] n febbre f; **feverish** adj febbrile

few [fju:] adj pochi/e ▷ pron alcuni/e; **a ~ ...** qualche ...; **fewer** adj meno inv; meno numerosi/e; **fewest** adj il minor numero di

fiancé [fɪ'ɑ̃:nseɪ] n fidanzato; **fiancée** n fidanzata

fiasco [fɪ'æskəu] n fiasco

fib [fɪb] n piccola bugia

fibre, (us) **fiber** ['faɪbə^r] n fibra; **fibreglass,** (us) **fiberglass** n fibra di vetro

fickle ['fɪkl] adj incostante, capriccioso/a

fiction ['fɪkʃən] n narrativa, romanzi mpl; (sth made up) finzione f; **fictional** adj immaginario/a

fiddle ['fɪdl] n (Mus) violino; (cheating) imbroglio; truffa ▷ vt (BRIT: accounts) falsificare, falsare; **fiddle with** vt fus gingillarsi con

fidelity [fɪ'dɛlɪtɪ] n fedeltà; (accuracy) esattezza

field [fi:ld] n campo; **field marshal** n feldmaresciallo

fierce [fɪəs] adj (look) fiero/a; (fighting) accanito/a; (wind) furioso/a; (heat) intenso/a; (animal, person, attack) feroce

fifteen [fɪf'ti:n] num quindici; **fifteenth** [fɪf'ti:nθ] num quindicesimo/a

fifth [fɪfθ] num quinto/a

fiftieth ['fɪftɪɪθ] num cinquantesimo/a

fifty ['fɪftɪ] num cinquanta; **fifty-fifty** adj: **a fifty-fifty chance** una possibilità su due ▷ adv: **to go fifty-fifty with sb** fare a metà con qn

fig [fɪg] n fico

fight (pt, pp **fought**) [faɪt, fɔ:t] n zuffa, rissa; (Mil) battaglia, combattimento; (against cancer etc) lotta ▷ vt (person) azzuffarsi con; (enemy: also Mil) combattere; (cancer, alcoholism, emotion) lottare contro, combattere; (election) partecipare a ▷ vi combattere; **fight off** vt (attack, attacker) respingere; (disease, sleep, urge) lottare contro; **fighting** n combattimento

figure ['fɪgə^r] n figura; (number, cipher) cifra ▷ vt (think: esp US) pensare ▷ vi (appear) figurare; **figure out** vt riuscire a capire; calcolare

file [faɪl] n (tool) lima; (dossier) incartamento; (folder) cartellina; (row) fila; (Comput) archivio ▷ vt (nails, wood) limare; (papers) archiviare; (Law: claim) passare agli atti; **filing cabinet** ['faɪlɪŋ-] n casellario

Filipino [fɪlɪ'pi:nəu] n filippino/a; (Ling) tagal m

fill [fɪl] vt riempire; (job) coprire ▷ n: **to eat one's ~** mangiare a sazietà; **fill in** vt (hole) riempire; (form) compilare; **fill out** vt (form, receipt) riempire; **fill up** vt riempire; **~ it up, please** (Aut) il pieno, per favore

fillet ['fɪlɪt] n filetto; **fillet steak** n bistecca di filetto

filling ['fɪlɪŋ] n (Culin) impasto, ripieno; (for tooth) otturazione f; **filling station** n stazione f di rifornimento

film [fɪlm] n (Cine) film m inv; (Phot) pellicola, rullino; (of powder, liquid) sottile strato ▷ vt (scene) filmare ▷ vi girare; **film star** n divo/a dello schermo

filter ['fɪltə^r] n filtro ▷ vt filtrare; **filter lane** n (BRIT Aut) corsia di svincolo

filth [fɪlθ] n sporcizia; **filthy** adj lordo/a, sozzo/a; (language) osceno/a

fin [fɪn] n (of fish) pinna

final ['faɪnl] adj finale, ultimo/a; definitivo/a ▷ n (Sport) finale f; **finals** npl (Scol) esami mpl finali; **finale** [fɪ'nɑ:lɪ] n finale m; **finalist** ['faɪnəlɪst] n (Sport) finalista m/f; **finalize** ['faɪnəlaɪz] vt mettere a punto; **finally** ['faɪnəlɪ] adv (lastly) alla fine; (eventually) finalmente

finance [faɪ'næns] n finanza; (capital) capitale m ▷ vt finanziare; **finances** npl (funds) finanze fpl; **financial** [faɪ'nænʃəl] adj finanziario/a; **financial year** n anno finanziario, esercizio finanziario

find [faɪnd] vt (pt, pp **found**) trovare; (lost object) ritrovare ▷ n trovata, scoperta; **to ~ sb guilty** (Law) giudicare qn colpevole; **find out** vt (truth, secret) scoprire; (person) cogliere in fallo ▷ vi: **to ~ out about** informarsi su; (by chance) venire a sapere;

findings npl (Law) sentenza, conclusioni fpl; (of report) conclusioni

fine [faɪn] adj bello/a; ottimo/a; (thin, subtle) fine ▷ adv (well) molto bene ▷ n (Law) multa ▷ vt (Law) multare; **to be ~** (person) stare bene; (weather) far bello; **fine arts** npl belle arti fpl

finger ['fɪŋgə'] n dito ▷ vt toccare, tastare; **little/index ~** mignolo (dito) indice m; **fingernail** n unghia; **fingerprint** n impronta digitale; **fingertip** n punta del dito

finish ['fɪnɪʃ] n fine f; (polish etc) finitura ▷ vt, vi finire; **to ~ doing sth** finire di fare qc; **to ~ first/second** arrivare primo/secondo; **finish off** vt compiere; (kill) uccidere; **finish up** vi, vt finire

Finland ['fɪnlənd] n Finlandia; **Finn** [fɪn] n finlandese m/f; **Finnish** adj finlandese ▷ n (Ling) finlandese m

fir [fə:'] n abete m

fire [faɪə'] n fuoco; (destructive) incendio; (gas fire, electric fire) stufa ▷ vt (discharge): **to ~ a gun** fare fuoco; (arrow) sparare; (fig) infiammare; (dismiss) licenziare ▷ vi sparare, far fuoco; **~!** al fuoco!; **on ~** in fiamme; **fire alarm** n allarme m d'incendio; **firearm** n arma da fuoco; **fire brigade** [-brɪˈgeɪd], (US) **fire department** n (corpo dei) pompieri mpl; **fire engine** n autopompa; **fire escape** n scala di sicurezza; **fire exit** n uscita di sicurezza; **fire extinguisher** [-ɪkˈstɪŋgwɪʃə'] n estintore m; **firefighter** n pompiere m; **fireplace** n focolare m; **fire station** n caserma dei pompieri; **firetruck** (US) n = **fire engine**; **firewall** n (Internet) firewall m inv; **firewood** ['faɪəwud] n legna; **fireworks** npl fuochi mpl d'artificio

firm [fə:m] adj fermo/a ▷ n ditta, azienda; **firmly** adv fermamente

first [fə:st] adj primo/a ▷ adv (before others) il primo, la prima; (before other things) per primo; (when listing reasons etc) per prima cosa ▷ n (person: in race) primo/a; (BRIT Scol) laurea con lode; (Aut) prima; **at ~** dapprima, all'inizio; **~ of all** prima di tutto; **first aid** n pronto soccorso; **first-aid kit** n cassetta pronto soccorso; **first-class** adj di prima classe; **first-hand** adj di prima mano; **first lady** n (US) moglie f del presidente; **firstly** adv in primo luogo; **first name** n prenome m; **first-rate** adj di prima qualità, ottimo/a

fiscal ['fɪskəl] adj fiscale; **~ year** anno fiscale

fish [fɪʃ] n pesce m ▷ vt (river, area) pescare in ▷ vi pescare; **to go ~ing** andare a pesca; **fish-and-chip shop** [fɪʃənˈtʃɪp-] n ≈ friggitoria; see **chip shop**; **fisherman** n

(irreg) pescatore m; **fish fingers** npl (BRIT) bastoncini mpl di pesce (surgelati); **fishing** n pesca; **fishing boat** n barca da pesca; **fishing line** n lenza; **fishmonger** n pescivendolo; **fishmonger's (shop)** n pescheria; **fish sticks** npl (US) = **fish fingers**; **fishy** ['fɪʃɪ] adj (tale, story) sospetto/a

fist [fɪst] n pugno

fit [fɪt] adj (Med, Sport) in forma; (proper) adatto/a, appropriato/a; conveniente ▷ vt (clothes) stare bene a; (put in, attach) installare; (equip) fornire, equipaggiare ▷ vi (clothes) stare bene; (parts) andare bene, adattarsi; (in space, gap) entrare ▷ n (Med) accesso, attacco; **~ to** in grado di; **~ for** adatto(a) a; degno(a) di; **this dress is a tight/good ~** questo vestito è stretto/sta bene; **~ of anger/enthusiasm** accesso d'ira/d'entusiasmo; **fit in** vi accordarsi; adattarsi; **fitness** n (Med) forma fisica; **fitted** adj: **fitted carpet** moquette f inv; **fitted cupboards** armadi mpl a muro; **fitted kitchen** (BRIT) cucina componibile; **fitting** adj appropriato/a ▷ n (of dress) prova; (of piece of equipment) montaggio, aggiustaggio; **fitting room** n (in shop) camerino; **fittings** ['fɪtɪŋz] npl (in building) impianti mpl

five [faɪv] num cinque; **fiver** n (col: BRIT) biglietto da cinque sterline; (: US) biglietto da cinque dollari

fix [fɪks] vt fissare; (mend) riparare; (meal, drink) preparare ▷ n: **to be in a ~** essere nei guai; **fix up** vt (date, meeting) fissare; **to ~ sb up with sth** procurare qc a qn; **fixed** [fɪkst] adj (prices etc) fisso/a; **fixture** ['fɪkstʃə'] n impianto (fisso); (Sport) incontro (del calendario sportivo)

fizzy ['fɪzɪ] adj frizzante; gassato/a

flag [flæg] n bandiera; (also: **~stone**) pietra da lastricare ▷ vi stancarsi; affievolirsi; **flagpole** ['flægpəul] n albero

flair [flɛə'] n (for business etc) fiuto; (for languages etc) facilità; (style) stile m

flak [flæk] n (Mil) fuoco d'artiglieria; (col: criticism) critiche fpl

flake [fleɪk] n (of rust, paint) scaglia; (of snow, soap powder) fiocco ▷ vi (also: **~ off**) sfaldarsi

flamboyant [flæmˈbɔɪənt] adj sgargiante

flame [fleɪm] n fiamma

flamingo [fləˈmɪŋgəu] n fenicottero, fiammingo

flammable ['flæməbl] adj infiammabile

flan [flæn] n (BRIT) flan m inv

flank [flæŋk] n fianco ▷ vt fiancheggiare

flannel ['flænl] n (BRIT: also: **face ~**) guanto di spugna; (fabric) flanella

flap [flæp] n (of pocket) patta; (of envelope) lembo ▷ vt (wings) battere ▷ vi (sail, flag) sbattere; (col: also: **be in a ~**) essere in agitazione

flare [flɛəʳ] n razzo; (in skirt etc) svasatura; **flares** (trousers) pantaloni mpl a zampa d'elefante; **flare up** vi andare in fiamme; (fig: person) infiammarsi di rabbia; (: revolt) scoppiare

flash [flæʃ] n vampata; (also: **news ~**) notizia f lampo inv; (Phot) flash m inv ▷ vt accendere e spegnere; (send: message) trasmettere; (: look, smile) lanciare ▷ vi brillare; (light on ambulance, eyes etc) lampeggiare; **in a ~** in un lampo; **to ~ one's headlights** lampeggiare; **he ~ed by** or **past** ci passò davanti come un lampo; **flashback** n flashback m inv; **flashbulb** n cubo m flash inv; **flashlight** n lampadina tascabile

flask [flɑ:sk] n fiasco; (also: **vacuum ~**) thermos® m inv

flat [flæt] adj piatto/a; (tyre) sgonfio/a, a terra; (battery) scarico/a; (beer) svampito/a; (denial) netto/a; (Mus) bemolle inv; (: voice) stonato/a ▷ n (BRIT: rooms) appartamento; (Mus) bemolle m; (Aut) pneumatico sgonfio ▷ adv: **(to work) ~ out** (lavorare) a più non posso; **~ rate of pay** tariffa unica di pagamento; **flatten** vt (also: **flatten out**) appiattire; (house, city) abbattere

flatter ['flætəʳ] vt lusingare; **flattering** adj lusinghiero/a; (clothes etc) che dona

flaunt [flɔ:nt] vt fare mostra di

flavour (US) **flavor** ['fleɪvəʳ] n gusto ▷ vt insaporire, aggiungere sapore a; **what ~s do you have?** che gusti avete?; **vanilla-~ed** al gusto di vaniglia; **flavouring** n essenza (artificiale)

flaw [flɔ:] n difetto; **flawless** adj senza difetti

flea [fli:] n pulce f; **flea market** n mercato delle pulci

flee (pt, pp **fled**) [fli:, flɛd] vt fuggire da ▷ vi fuggire, scappare

fleece [fli:s] n vello ▷ vt (col) pelare

fleet [fli:t] n flotta; (of lorries etc) convoglio; (of cars) parco

fleeting ['fli:tɪŋ] adj fugace, fuggitivo/a; (visit) volante

Flemish ['flɛmɪʃ] adj fiammingo/a

flesh [flɛʃ] n carne f; (of fruit) polpa

flew [flu:] pt of **fly**

flex [flɛks] n filo (flessibile) ▷ vt flettere; (muscles) contrarre; **flexibility** n flessibilità; **flexible** adj flessibile; **flexitime** ['flɛksɪtaɪm] n orario flessibile

flick [flɪk] n colpetto; scarto ▷ vt dare un colpetto a; **flick through** vt fus sfogliare

flicker ['flɪkəʳ] vi tremolare

flies [flaɪz] npl of **fly**

flight [flaɪt] n volo; (escape) fuga; (also: **~ of steps**) scalinata; **flight attendant** n (US) steward m, hostess f inv

flimsy ['flɪmzɪ] adj (fabric) leggero/a; (building) poco solido/a; (excuse) debole

flinch [flɪntʃ] vi ritirarsi; **to ~ from** tirarsi indietro di fronte a

fling (pt, pp **flung**) [flɪŋ, flʌŋ] vt lanciare, gettare

flint [flɪnt] n selce f; (in lighter) pietrina

flip [flɪp] vt (switch) far scattare; (coin) lanciare in aria

flip-flops ['flɪpflɔps] npl (esp BRIT: sandals) infradito mpl

flipper ['flɪpəʳ] n pinna

flirt [flə:t] vi flirtare ▷ n civetta

float [fləut] n galleggiante m; (in procession) carro; (sum of money) somma ▷ vi galleggiare

flock [flɔk] n (of sheep, Rel) gregge m; (of birds) stormo ▷ vi: **to ~ to** accorrere in massa a

flood [flʌd] n alluvione f; (of letters etc) marea ▷ vt allagare; (people) invadere ▷ vi (place) allagarsi; (people): **to ~ into** riversarsi in; **flooding** n inondazione f; **floodlight** n riflettore m ▷ vt illuminare a giorno

floor [flɔ:ʳ] n pavimento; (storey) piano; (of sea, valley) fondo ▷ vt (knock down) atterrare; (silence) far tacere; **on the ~** sul pavimento, per terra; **ground ~**, (US) **first ~** pianterreno; **first ~**, (US) **second ~** primo piano; **floorboard** n tavellone m di legno; **flooring** n (floor) pavimento; (material) materiale m per pavimentazioni; **floor show** n spettacolo di varietà

flop [flɔp] n fiasco ▷ vi far fiasco; (fall) lasciarsi cadere; **floppy** ['flɔpɪ] adj floscio/a, molle

flora ['flɔ:rə] n flora

floral ['flɔ:rl] adj floreale

Florence ['flɔrəns] n Firenze f

Florentine ['flɔrəntaɪn] adj fiorentino/a

florist ['flɔrɪst] n fioraio/a; **florist's (shop)** n fioraio/a

flotation [fləu'teɪʃən] n (Comm) lancio

flour ['flauəʳ] n farina

flourish ['flʌrɪʃ] vi fiorire ▷ n (bold gesture): **with a ~** con ostentazione

flow [fləu] n flusso; circolazione f ▷ vi fluire; (traffic, blood in veins) circolare; (hair) scendere

flower ['flauəʳ] n fiore m ▷ vi fiorire; **flower bed** n aiuola; **flowerpot** n vaso da fiori

flown [fləun] pp of **fly**

fl. oz. abbr = **fluid ounce**

flu [flu:] n influenza

fluctuate ['flʌktjueɪt] vi fluttuare, oscillare

fluent ['fluːənt] *adj* (*speech*) facile, sciolto/a; corrente; **he speaks ~ Italian, he's ~ in Italian** parla l'italiano correntemente

fluff [flʌf] *n* lanugine *f*; **fluffy** *adj* lanuginoso/a; (*toy*) di peluche

fluid ['fluːɪd] *adj* fluido/a ▷ *n* fluido; **fluid ounce** *n* (BRIT) = 0.028 l; 0.05 pints

fluke [fluːk] *n* (*col*) colpo di fortuna

flung [flʌŋ] *pt, pp of* **fling**

fluorescent [fluə'rɛsnt] *adj* fluorescente

fluoride ['fluəraɪd] *n* fluoruro

flurry ['flʌrɪ] *n* (*of snow*) tempesta; **a ~ of activity/excitement** un'intensa attività/un'improvvisae agitazione

flush [flʌʃ] *n* rossore *m*; (*fig: of youth, beauty etc*) rigoglio, pieno vigore ▷ *vt* ripulire con un getto d'acqua ▷ *vi* arrossire ▷ *adj*: **~ with** a livello di, pari a; **to ~ the toilet** tirare l'acqua

flute [fluːt] *n* flauto

flutter ['flʌtə'] *n* agitazione *f*; (*of wings*) battito ▷ *vi* (*bird*) battere le ali

fly (*pt* **flew**, *pp* **flown**) [flaɪ, fluː, fləʊn] *n* (*insect*) mosca; (*on trousers: also*: **flies**) patta ▷ *vt* pilotare; (*passengers, cargo*) trasportare (in aereo); (*distances*) percorrere ▷ *vi* volare; (*passengers*) andare in aereo; (*escape*) fuggire; (*flag*) sventolare; **fly away** *vi* volar via; **fly-drive** *n*: **fly-drive holiday** fly and drive *m inv*; **flying** *n* (*activity*) aviazione *f*; (*action*) volo ▷ *adj*: **flying visit** visita volante; **with flying colours** con risultati brillanti; **flying saucer** *n* disco volante; **flyover** *n* (BRIT: *bridge*) cavalcavia *m inv*

FM *abbr* = **frequency modulation**

foal [fəʊl] *n* puledro

foam [fəʊm] *n* schiuma; (*also*: **~ rubber**) gommapiuma® ▷ *vi* schiumare; (*soapy water*) fare la schiuma

focus ['fəʊkəs] *n* (*pl* **focuses**) fuoco; (*of interest*) centro ▷ *vt* (*field glasses etc*) mettere a fuoco ▷ *vi*: **to ~ on** (*with camera*) mettere a fuoco; (*person*) fissare lo sguardo su; **in ~** a fuoco; **out of ~** sfocato/a

foetus, (US) **fetus** ['fiːtəs] *n* feto

fog [fɒg] *n* nebbia; **foggy** *adj*: **it's foggy** c'è nebbia; **fog lamp**, (US) **fog light** *n* (Aut) faro *m* antinebbia *inv*

foil [fɔɪl] *vt* confondere, frustrare ▷ *n* lamina di metallo; (*also*: **kitchen ~**) foglio di alluminio; (*Fencing*) fioretto; **to act as a ~ to** (*fig*) far risaltare

fold [fəʊld] *n* (*bend, crease*) piega; (*Agr*) ovile *m*; (*fig*) gregge *m* ▷ *vt* piegare; **to ~ one's arms** incrociare le braccia; **fold up** *vi* (*map etc*) piegarsi; (*business*) crollare ▷ *vt* (*map etc*) piegare, ripiegare; **folder** *n* (*for papers*) cartella; cartellina; **folding** *adj* (*chair, bed*) pieghevole

foliage ['fəʊlɪɪdʒ] *n* fogliame *m*

folk [fəʊk] *npl* gente *f* ▷ *cpd* popolare; **folks** *npl*: **my ~s** i miei; **folklore** ['fəʊklɔː'] *n* folclore *m*; **folk music** *n* musica folk *inv*; **folksong** *n* canto popolare

follow ['fɒləʊ] *vt* (*also on Twitter*) seguire ▷ *vi* seguire; (*result*) conseguire, risultare; **he ~ed suit** lui ha fatto lo stesso; **follow up** *vt* (*letter, offer*) fare seguito a; (*case*) seguire; **follower** *n* seguace *m/f*; **following** *adj* seguente ▷ *n* seguito, discepoli *mpl*; **follow-up** *n* seguito

fond [fɒnd] *adj* (*memory, look*) tenero/a, affettuoso/a; **to be ~ of** volere bene a; **she's ~ of swimming** le piace nuotare

food [fuːd] *n* cibo; **food mixer** *n* frullatore *m*; **food poisoning** *n* intossicazione *f* alimentare; **food processor** ['prəʊsɛsə] *n* tritatutto *m inv* elettrico; **food stamp** *n* (US) buono alimentare dato agli indigenti

fool [fuːl] *n* sciocco/a; (*Culin*) frullato ▷ *vt* ingannare ▷ *vi* (*gen*): **~ around** fare lo sciocco; **fool about, fool around** *vi* (*waste time*) perdere tempo; **foolish** *adj* scemo/a, stupido/a; imprudente; **foolproof** *adj* (*plan etc*) sicurissimo/a

foot [fut] *n* (*pl* **feet** [fiːt]) piede *m*; (*measure*) piede (= 304 mm; = 12 inches); (*of animal*) zampa ▷ *vt* (*bill*) pagare; **on ~** a piedi; **footage** *n* (Cine: *length*) ≈ metraggio; (: *material*) sequenza; **foot and mouth (disease)** *n* afta epizootica; **football** *n* pallone *m*; (*sport*: BRIT) calcio; (: US) football *m* americano; **footballer** *n* (BRIT) = **football player**; **football match** *n* (BRIT) partita di calcio; **football player** *n* (BRIT: *also*: **footballer**) calciatore *m*; (US) giocatore *m* di football americano; **footbridge** *n* passerella; **foothills** *npl* contrafforti *fpl*; **foothold** *n* punto d'appoggio; **footing** *n* (*fig*) posizione *f*; **to lose one's footing** mettere un piede in fallo; **footnote** *n* nota (a piè di pagina); **footpath** *n* sentiero; (*in street*) marciapiede *m*; **footprint** *n* orma, impronta; **footstep** *n* passo; **footwear** *n* calzatura

O **KEYWORD**

for [fɔː'] *prep* **1** (*indicating destination, intention, purpose*) per; **the train for London** il treno per Londra; **he went for the paper** è andato a prendere il giornale; **it's time for lunch** è ora di pranzo; **what's it for?** a che serve?; **what for?** (*why*) perché? **2** (*on behalf of, representing*) per; **to work for sb/sth** lavorare per qn/qc; **I'll ask him for you** glielo chiederò a nome tuo; **G for George** ≈ G come George

3 (*because of*) per, a causa di; **for this reason** per questo motivo
4 (*with regard to*) per; **it's cold for July** è freddo per luglio; **for everyone who voted yes, 50 voted no** per ogni voto a favore ce n'erano 50 contro
5 (*in exchange for*) per; **I sold it for £5** l'ho venduto per 5 sterline
6 (*in favour of*) per, a favore di; **are you for or against us?** sei con noi o contro di noi?; **I'm all for it** sono completamente a favore
7 (*referring to distance, time*) per; **there are roadworks for 5 km** ci sono lavori in corso per 5 km; **he was away for 2 years** è stato via per 2 anni; **she will be away for a month** starà via un mese; **it hasn't rained for 3 weeks** non piove da 3 settimane; **can you do it for tomorrow?** può farlo per domani?
8 (*with infinitive clauses*): **it is not for me to decide** non sta a me decidere; **it would be best for you to leave** sarebbe meglio che lei se ne andasse; **there is still time for you to do it** ha ancora tempo per farlo; **for this to be possible …** perché ciò sia possibile …
9 (*in spite of*) nonostante; **for all his complaints, he's very fond of her** nonostante tutte le sue lamentele, le vuole molto bene
▶ *conj* (*since, as: formal*) dal momento che, poiché

forbid (*pt* **forbad(e)**, *pp* **forbidden**) [fə'bɪd, -'bæd, -'bɪdn] *vt* vietare, interdire; **to ~ sb to do sth** proibire a qn di fare qc; **forbidden** *pt of* **forbid** ▷ *adj* (*food*) proibito/a; (*area, territory*) vietato/a; (*word, subject*) tabù *inv*
force [fɔːs] *n* forza ▷ *vt* forzare; **forced** *adj* forzato/a; **forceful** *adj* forte, vigoroso/a
ford [fɔːd] *n* guado
fore [fɔːʳ] *n*: **to come to the ~** mettersi in evidenza; **forearm** ['fɔːrɑːm] *n* avambraccio; **forecast** ['fɔːkɑːst] *n* (*irreg: like* **cast**) previsione *f* ▷ *vt* prevedere; **forecourt** ['fɔːkɔːt] *n* (*of garage*) corte *f* esterna; **forefinger** ['fɔːfɪŋɡəʳ] *n* (*dito*) indice *m*; **forefront** ['fɔːfrʌnt] *n*: **in the forefront of** all'avanguardia di; **foreground** ['fɔːɡraʊnd] *n* primo piano; **forehead** ['fɔrɪd] *n* fronte *f*
foreign ['fɔrən] *adj* straniero/a; (*trade*) estero/a; (*object, matter*) estraneo/a; **foreign currency** *n* valuta estera; **foreigner** *n* straniero/a; **foreign exchange** *n* cambio di valuta; (*currency*) valuta estera; **Foreign Office** *n* (BRIT) Ministero degli Esteri; **foreign secretary** *n* (BRIT) ministro degli Affari esteri
fore: foreman ['fɔːmən] *n* (*irreg*) caposquadra *m*; **foremost** ['fɔːməust]

adj principale; più in vista ▷ *adv*: **first and foremost** innanzitutto; **forename** *n* nome *m* di battesimo
forensic [fə'rɛnsɪk] *adj*: **~ medicine** medicina legale
foresee [fɔː'siː] *vt* (*irreg: like* **see**) prevedere; **foreseeable** *adj* prevedibile
forest ['fɔrɪst] *n* foresta; **forestry** ['fɔrɪstrɪ] *n* silvicoltura
forever [fə'rɛvəʳ] *adv* per sempre; (*endlessly*) sempre, di continuo
foreword ['fɔːwəd] *n* prefazione *f*
forfeit ['fɔːfɪt] *vt* perdere; (*one's happiness, health*) giocarsi
forgave [fə'ɡeɪv] *pt of* **forgive**
forge [fɔːdʒ] *n* fucina ▷ *vt* (*signature*) contraffare, falsificare; (*wrought iron*) fucinare, foggiare; **forger** *n* contraffattore *m*; **forgery** *n* falso; (*activity*) contraffazione *f*
forget (*pt* **forgot**, *pp* **forgotten**) [fə'ɡɛt, -'ɡɔt, -'ɡɔtn] *vt*, *vi* dimenticare; **forgetful** *adj* di corta memoria; **forgetful of** dimentico(a) di
forgive (*pt* **forgave**, *pp* **forgiven**) [fə'ɡɪv, -'ɡeɪv, -'ɡɪvn] *vt* perdonare; **to ~ sb for sth/ for doing sth** perdonare qc a qn/a qn di aver fatto qc
forgot [fə'ɡɔt] *pt of* **forget**
forgotten [fə'ɡɔtn] *pp of* **forget**
fork [fɔːk] *n* (*for eating*) forchetta; (*for gardening*) forca; (*of roads, railways*) bivio, biforcazione *f* ▷ *vi* (*road*) biforcarsi
forlorn [fə'lɔːn] *adj* (*person*) sconsolato/a; (*cottage*) abbandonato/a; (*attempt*) disperato/a; (*hope*) vano/a
form [fɔːm] *n* forma; (*Scol*) classe *f*; (*questionnaire*) modulo ▷ *vt* formare; **in top ~** in gran forma
formal ['fɔːməl] *adj* formale; (*gardens*) simmetrico/a, regolare; **formality** [fɔː'mælɪtɪ] *n* formalità *f inv*
format ['fɔːmæt] *n* formato ▷ *vt* (*Comput*) formattare
formation [fɔː'meɪʃən] *n* formazione *f*
former ['fɔːməʳ] *adj* vecchio/a (*before n*), ex *inv* (*before n*); **the ~ … the latter** quello … questo; **formerly** *adv* in passato
formidable ['fɔːmɪdəbl] *adj* formidabile
formula ['fɔːmjulə] *n* formula
fort [fɔːt] *n* forte *m*
forthcoming [fɔːθ'kʌmɪŋ] *adj* (*event*) prossimo/a; (*help*) disponibile; (*character*) aperto/a, comunicativo/a
fortieth ['fɔːtɪɪθ] *num* quarantesimo/a
fortify ['fɔːtɪfaɪ] *vt* (*city*) fortificare; (*person*) armare
fortnight ['fɔːtnaɪt] *n* (BRIT) quindici giorni *mpl*, due settimane *fpl*; **fortnightly** *adj* bimensile ▷ *adv* ogni quindici giorni

fortress ['fɔːtrɪs] n fortezza, rocca
fortunate ['fɔːtʃənɪt] adj fortunato/a; **it is ~ that** è una fortuna che + sub; **fortunately** adv fortunatamente
fortune ['fɔːtʃən] n fortuna; **fortune-teller** ['fɔːtʃəntɛləʳ] n indovino/a
forty ['fɔːtɪ] num quaranta
forum ['fɔːrəm] n foro
forward ['fɔːwəd] adj (ahead of schedule) in anticipo; (movement, position) in avanti; (not shy) sfacciato/a ▷ n (Sport) avanti m inv ▷ vt (letter) inoltrare; (parcel, goods) spedire; (career, plans) promuovere, appoggiare; **to move ~** avanzare; **forwarding address** n nuovo recapito cui spedire la posta; **forwards** adv avanti; **forward slash** n barra obliqua
fossick ['fɔsɪk] vi (AUST, NZ col) cercare; **to ~ in a drawer** rovistare in un cassetto
fossil ['fɔsl] adj, n fossile (m)
foster ['fɔstəʳ] vt incoraggiare, nutrire; (child) avere in affidamento; **foster child** n bambino/a preso/a in affidamento; **foster mother** n madre f affidataria
fought [fɔːt] pt, pp of **fight**
foul [faul] adj (smell, food) cattivo/a; (weather) brutto/a; (language) osceno/a ▷ n (Football) fallo ▷ vt sporcare; **foul play** n: **foul play is not suspected** si è scartata l'ipotesi dell'atto criminale
found [faund] pt, pp of **find** ▷ vt (establish) fondare; **foundation** [faun'deɪʃən] n (act) fondazione f; (base) base f; (also: **foundation cream**) fondo tinta; **foundations** npl (of building) fondamenta fpl
founder ['faundəʳ] n fondatore/trice ▷ vi affondare
fountain ['fauntɪn] n fontana; **fountain pen** n penna stilografica
four [fɔːʳ] num quattro; **on all ~s** a carponi; **four-letter word** n parolaccia; **four-poster** n (also: **four-poster bed**) letto a quattro colonne; **fourteen** num quattordici; **fourteenth** num quattordicesimo/a; **fourth** num quarto/a; **four-wheel drive** ['fɔːwiːl-] n (Aut): **with four-wheel drive** con quattro ruote motrici
fowl [faul] n pollame m; volatile m
fox [fɔks] n volpe f ▷ vt confondere
foyer ['fɔɪeɪ] n atrio; (Theat) ridotto
fracking ['frækɪŋ] n fracking m inv
fraction ['frækʃən] n frazione f
fracture ['fræktʃəʳ] n frattura
fragile ['frædʒaɪl] adj fragile
fragment ['frægmənt] n frammento
fragrance ['freɪgrəns] n fragranza, profumo
frail [freɪl] adj debole, delicato/a
frame [freɪm] n (of building) armatura; (of human, animal) ossatura, corpo; (of picture) cornice f; (of door, window) telaio; (of

spectacles: also: **~s**) montatura ▷ vt (picture) incorniciare; **framework** n struttura
France [frɑːns] n Francia
franchise ['fræntʃaɪz] n (Pol) diritto di voto; (Comm) concessione f
frank [fræŋk] adj franco/a, aperto/a ▷ vt (letter) affrancare; **frankly** adv francamente, sinceramente
frantic ['fræntɪk] adj frenetico/a
fraud [frɔːd] n truffa; (Law) frode f; (person) impostore/a
fraught [frɔːt] adj: **~ with** pieno(a) di, intriso(a) da
fray [freɪ] vt logorare ▷ vi logorarsi
freak [friːk] n fenomeno, mostro
freckle ['frɛkl] n lentiggine f
free [friː] adj libero/a; (gratis) gratuito/a ▷ vt (prisoner, jammed person) liberare; (jammed object) districare; **~ (of charge)** gratuitamente; **freedom** ['friːdəm] n libertà; **Freefone®** n = numero verde; **free gift** n regalo, omaggio; **free kick** n calcio libero; **freelance** adj indipendente; **freely** adv liberamente, (liberally) liberalmente; **Freepost®** n affrancatura a carica del destinatario; **free-range** adj (hen) ruspante; (eggs) di gallina ruspante; **freeway** n (US) superstrada; **free will** n libero arbitrio; **of one's own free will** di spontanea volontà
freeze (pt **froze**, pp **frozen**) [friːz, frəuz, 'frəuzn] vi gelare ▷ vt gelare; (food) congelare; (prices, salaries) bloccare ▷ n gelo; blocco; **freezer** n congelatore m; **freezing** ['friːzɪŋ] adj (wind, weather) gelido/a ▷ n (also: **freezing point**) punto di congelamento; **3 degrees below freezing** 3 gradi sotto zero
freight [freɪt] n (goods) merce f, merci fpl; (money charged) spese fpl di trasporto; **freight train** n (US) treno m merci inv
French [frɛntʃ] adj francese ▷ n (Ling) francese m; **the French** npl i Francesi; **French bean** n fagiolino; **French bread** n baguette f inv; **French dressing** n (Culin) condimento per insalata; **French fried potatoes**, (US) **French fries** npl patate fpl fritte; **Frenchman** n (irreg) francese m; **French stick** n baguette f inv; **French window** n portafinestra; **Frenchwoman** n (irreg) francese f
frenzy ['frɛnzɪ] n frenesia
frequency ['friːkwənsɪ] n frequenza
frequent adj ['friːkwənt] frequente ▷ vt [frɪ'kwɛnt] frequentare; **frequently** adv frequentemente, spesso
fresh [frɛʃ] adj fresco/a; (new) nuovo/a; (cheeky) sfacciato/a; **freshen** vi (wind, air) rinfrescare; **freshen up** vi rinfrescarsi;

fresher n (BRIT Scol: col) = **freshman**; **freshly** adv di recente, di fresco; **freshman** n (irreg: Scol) matricola; **freshwater** adj (fish) d'acqua dolce

fret [frɛt] vi agitarsi, affliggersi

Fri. abbr (= Friday) ven.

friction ['frɪkʃən] n frizione f, attrito

Friday ['fraɪdɪ] n venerdì m inv

fridge [frɪdʒ] n (BRIT) frigo, frigorifero

fried [fraɪd] pt, pp of **fry** ▷ adj fritto/a

friend [frɛnd] n amico/a ▷ vt (Internet) aggiungere tra gli amici; **friendly** adj amichevole; **friendship** n amicizia

fries [fraɪz] npl (esp US) patate fpl fritte

frigate ['frɪɡɪt] n (Naut: modern) fregata

fright [fraɪt] n paura, spavento; **to take ~** spaventarsi; **frighten** vt spaventare, far paura a; **frightened** adj spaventato/a; **frightening** adj spaventoso/a, pauroso/a; **frightful** adj orribile

frill [frɪl] n balza

fringe [frɪndʒ] n (BRIT: of hair) frangia; (edge: of forest etc) margine m

Frisbee® ['frɪzbɪ] n frisbee® m inv

fritter ['frɪtər] n frittella

frivolous ['frɪvələs] adj frivolo/a

fro [frəu] adv: **to and ~** avanti e indietro

frock [frɔk] n vestito

frog [frɔɡ] n rana; **frogman** ['frɔɡmən] n (irreg) uomo m rana inv

KEYWORD

from [frɔm] prep **1** (indicating starting place, origin etc) da; **where do you come from?**, **where are you from?** da dove viene?, di dov'è?; **from London to Glasgow** da Londra a Glasgow; **a letter from my sister** una lettera da mia sorella; **tell him from me that ...** gli dica da parte mia che ...

2 (indicating time) da; **from one o'clock to** or **until** or **till two** dall'una alle due; **from January (on)** da gennaio, a partire da gennaio

3 (indicating distance) da; **the hotel is 1 km from the beach** l'albergo è a 1 km dalla spiaggia

4 (indicating price, number etc) da; **prices range from £10 to £50** i prezzi vanno dalle 10 alle 50 sterline

5 (indicating difference) da; **he can't tell red from green** non sa distinguere il rosso dal verde

6 (because of, on the basis of): **from what he says** da quanto dice lui; **weak from hunger** debole per la fame

front [frʌnt] n (of house, dress) davanti m inv; (of train) testa; (of book) copertina; (promenade: also: **sea ~**) lungomare m; (Mil, Pol, Meteor) fronte m; (fig: appearances) fronte f ▷ adj primo/a; anteriore, davanti inv; **in ~ (of)** davanti (a); **front door** n porta d'entrata; (of car) sportello anteriore; **frontier** ['frʌntɪər] n frontiera; **front page** n prima pagina; **front-wheel drive** ['frʌntwiːl-] n trasmissione f anteriore

frost [frɔst] n gelo; (also: **hoar~**) brina; **frostbite** n congelamento; **frosting** n (US: on cake) glassa; **frosty** adj (weather, look, welcome) gelido/a

froth ['frɔθ] n spuma; schiuma

frown [fraun] vi accigliarsi

froze [frəuz] pt of **freeze**

frozen ['frəuzn] pp of **freeze**

fruit [fruːt] n (pl inv) frutto; (collectively) frutta; **fruit juice** n succo di frutta; **fruit machine** n (BRIT) macchina f mangiasoldi inv; **fruit salad** n macedonia

frustrate [frʌs'treɪt] vt frustrare; **frustrated** adj frustrato/a

fry (pt, pp **fried**) [fraɪ, -d] vt friggere ▷ npl: **the small ~** i pesci piccoli; **frying pan** n padella

ft. abbr = **foot**; **feet**

fudge [fʌdʒ] n (Culin) specie di caramella a base di latte, burro e zucchero

fuel [fjuəl] n (for heating) combustibile m; (for propelling) carburante m; **fuel poverty** n povertà energetica; **fuel tank** n deposito m nafta inv; (on vehicle) serbatoio (della benzina)

fulfil [ful'fɪl] vt (function) compiere; (order) eseguire; (wish, desire) soddisfare, appagare

full [ful] adj pieno/a; (details, skirt) ampio/a ▷ adv: **to know ~ well that** sapere benissimo che; **I'm ~ (up)** sono sazio; **a ~ two hours** due ore intere; **at ~ speed** a tutta velocità; **in ~** per intero; **full-length** adj (portrait) in piedi; (film) a lungometraggio; (coat, novel) lungo/a; **full moon** n luna piena; **full-scale** adj (plan, model) in grandezza naturale; (attack, search, retreat) su vasta scala; **full stop** n punto; **full-time** adj, adv (work) a tempo pieno; **fully** adv interamente, pienamente, completamente

fumble ['fʌmbl] vi brancolare; **fumble with** vt fus trafficare con

fume [fjuːm] vi essere furioso/a; **fumes** npl esalazioni fpl, vapori mpl

fun [fʌn] n divertimento, spasso; **to have ~** divertirsi; **for ~** per scherzo; **to make ~ of** prendersi gioco di

function ['fʌŋkʃən] n funzione f; cerimonia, ricevimento ▷ vi funzionare

fund [fʌnd] n fondo, cassa; (source) fondo; (store) riserva; **funds** npl (money) fondi mpl

fundamental [fʌndə'mɛntl] *adj* fondamentale

funeral ['fju:nərəl] *n* funerale *m*; **funeral director** *n* impresario di pompe funebri; **funeral parlour** [-'pɑ:lər] *n* impresa di pompe funebri

fun fair ['fʌnfɛər] *n* luna park *m inv*

fungus (*pl* **fungi**) ['fʌŋgəs, -gaɪ] *n* fungo; (*mould*) muffa

funnel ['fʌnl] *n* imbuto; (*of ship*) ciminiera

funny ['fʌnɪ] *adj* divertente, buffo/a; (*strange*) strano/a, bizzarro/a

fur [fə:r] *n* pelo; pelliccia; (*BRIT: in kettle etc*) deposito calcare; **fur coat** *n* pelliccia

furious ['fjuərɪəs] *adj* furioso/a; (*effort*) accanito/a

furnish ['fə:nɪʃ] *vt* ammobiliare; (*supply*) fornire; **furnishings** *npl* mobili *mpl*, mobilia

furniture ['fə:nɪtʃər] *n* mobili *mpl*; **piece of ~** mobile *m*

furry ['fə:rɪ] *adj* (*animal*) peloso/a

further ['fə:ðər] *adj* supplementare, altro/a; nuovo/a; più lontano/a ▷ *adv* più lontano; (*more*) di più; (*moreover*) inoltre ▷ *vt* favorire, promuovere; **further education** *n* ≈ corsi *mpl* di formazione; **college of further education** istituto statale con corsi specializzati (*di formazione professionale, aggiornamento professionale ecc*); **furthermore** [fə:ðə'mɔ:r] *adv* inoltre, per di più

furthest ['fə:ðɪst] *adv superlative of* **far**

fury ['fjuərɪ] *n* furore *m*

fuse, (*US*) **fuze** [fju:z] *n* fusibile *m*; (*for bomb etc*) miccia, spoletta ▷ *vt* fondere; (*Elec*): **to ~ the lights** far saltare i fusibili ▷ *vi* fondersi; **fuse box** *n* cassetta dei fusibili

fusion ['fju:ʒən] *n* fusione *f*

fuss [fʌs] *n* agitazione *f*; (*complaining*) storie *fpl*; **to make a ~** fare delle storie; **fussy** *adj* (*person*) puntiglioso/a, esigente; che fa le storie; (*dress*) carico/a di fronzoli; (*style*) elaborato/a

future ['fju:tʃər] *adj* futuro/a ▷ *n* futuro, avvenire *m*; (*Ling*) futuro; **futures** *npl* (*Comm*) operazioni *fpl* a termine; **in ~** in futuro

fuze [fju:z] *n*, *vt*, *vi* (*US*) = **fuse**

fuzzy ['fʌzɪ] *adj* (*Phot*) indistinto/a, sfocato/a; (*hair*) crespo/a

g

G [dʒi:] *n* (*Mus*) sol *m*

g *abbr* (= *gram, gravity*) g

G8 *n abbr* (*Pol: = Group of Eight*) G8 *m*

G20 *n abbr* (*Pol: = Group of Twenty*) G20 *m*

gadget ['gædʒɪt] *n* aggeggio

Gaelic ['geɪlɪk] *adj* gaelico/a ▷ *n* (*language*) gaelico

gag [gæg] *n* bavaglio; (*joke*) facezia, scherzo ▷ *vt* imbavagliare

gain [geɪn] *n* guadagno, profitto ▷ *vt* guadagnare ▷ *vi* (*watch*) andare avanti; (*benefit*): **to ~ (from)** trarre beneficio (da); **to ~ 3lbs (in weight)** aumentare di 3 libbre; **gain (up)on** *vt fus* guadagnare terreno su

gal. *abbr* = **gallon**

gala ['gɑ:lə] *n* gala; **swimming ~** manifestazione *f* di nuoto

galaxy ['gæləksɪ] *n* galassia

gale [geɪl] *n* vento forte; burrasca

gall bladder ['gɔ:l-] *n* cistifellea

gallery ['gælərɪ] *n* galleria

gallon ['gælən] *n* gallone *m* (*Brit = 4.543 l; 8 pints; US = 3.785 l*)

gallop ['gæləp] *n* galoppo ▷ *vi* galoppare

gallstone ['gɔ:lstəun] *n* calcolo biliare

gamble ['gæmbl] *n* azzardo, rischio calcolato ▷ *vt, vi* giocare; **to ~ on** (*fig*) giocare su; **gambler** *n* giocatore/trice d'azzardo; **gambling** ['gæmblɪŋ] *n* gioco d'azzardo

game [geɪm] *n* gioco; (*event*) partita; (*Tennis*) game *m inv*; (*Hunting, Culin*) selvaggina ▷ *adj* (*ready*): **to be ~ (for sth/to do)** essere pronto/a (a qc/a fare); **games** *npl* (*Scol*) attività *fpl* sportive; **big ~** selvaggina grossa; **gamer** ['geɪmər] *n* chi gioca con i videogame; **games console** *n* console *f inv* dei videogame; **gameshow** ['geɪmʃəu] *n* gioco a premi; **gaming** ['geɪmɪŋ] *n* (*Comput*) il giocare con i videogame

gammon ['gæmən] n (bacon) quarto di maiale; (ham) prosciutto affumicato

gang [gæŋ] n banda, squadra ▷ vi: **to ~ up on sb** far combutta contro qn

gangster ['gæŋstə'] n gangster m inv

gap [gæp] n (space) buco; (in time) intervallo; (difference): **~ (between)** divario (tra)

gape [geɪp] vi (person) restare a bocca aperta; (shirt, hole) essere spalancato/a

gap year n (Scol) anno di pausa preso prima di iniziare l'università, per lavorare o viaggiare

garage ['gærɑːʒ] n garage m inv; **garage sale** n vendita di oggetti usati nel garage di un privato

garbage ['gɑːbɪdʒ] (US) n immondizie fpl, rifiuti mpl; (col) sciocchezze fpl; **garbage can** n (US) bidone m della spazzatura; **garbage collector** n (US) spazzino/a

garden ['gɑːdn] n giardino; **gardens** npl (public) giardini pubblici; **garden centre** n vivaio; **gardener** n giardiniere/a; **gardening** n giardinaggio

garlic ['gɑːlɪk] n aglio

garment ['gɑːmənt] n indumento

garnish ['gɑːnɪʃ] vt (food) guarnire

garrison ['gærɪsn] n guarnigione f ▷ vt guarnire

gas [gæs] n gas m inv; (US: gasoline) benzina ▷ vt asfissiare con il gas; **gas cooker** n (BRIT) cucina a gas; **gas cylinder** n bombola del gas; **gas fire** n (BRIT) radiatore m a gas

gasket ['gæskɪt] n (Aut) guarnizione f

gasoline ['gæsəliːn] n (US) benzina

gasp [gɑːsp] n respiro affannoso, ansito ▷ vi ansimare, boccheggiare; (in surprise) restare senza fiato

gas: gas pedal (esp US) n pedale m dell'acceleratore; **gas station** n (US) distributore m di benzina; **gas tank** n (US Aut) serbatoio (di benzina)

gate [geɪt] n cancello; (at airport) uscita

gâteau (pl **gâteaux**) ['gætəu, -z] n torta

gatecrash ['geɪtkræʃ] (BRIT) vt partecipare senza invito a

gateway ['geɪtweɪ] n porta

gather ['gæðə'] vt (flowers, fruit) cogliere; (pick up) raccogliere; (assemble) radunare; raccogliere; (understand) capire; (Sewing) increspare ▷ vi (assemble) radunarsi; **to ~ speed** acquistare velocità; **gathering** n adunanza

gauge [geɪdʒ] n (instrument) indicatore m ▷ vt misurare; (fig) valutare

gave [geɪv] pt of **give**

gay [geɪ] adj (homosexual) omosessuale; (cheerful) gaio/a, allegro/a; (colour) vivace, vivo/a

gaze [geɪz] n sguardo fisso ▷ vi: **to ~ at** guardare fisso

GB abbr (= Great Britain) GB

GCSE n abbr (BRIT: = General Certificate of Secondary Education) diploma di istruzione secondaria conseguito a 16 anni in Inghilterra e Galles

gear [gɪə'] n attrezzi mpl, equipaggiamento; (Tech) ingranaggio; (Aut) marcia ▷ vt (fig: adapt): **to ~ sth to** adattare qc a; **top** or **high/low/bottom ~** (US) quinta (or sesta)/seconda/prima; **in ~** in marcia; **gear up** vi: **to ~ up (to do)** prepararsi (a fare); **gear box** n scatola del cambio; **gear lever**, (US) **gear shift** n leva del cambio

geese [giːs] npl of **goose**

gel [dʒɛl] n gel m inv

gem [dʒɛm] n gemma

Gemini ['dʒɛmɪnaɪ] n Gemelli mpl

gender ['dʒɛndə'] n genere m

gene [dʒiːn] n (Biol) gene m

general ['dʒɛnərl] n generale m ▷ adj generale; **in ~** in genere; **general anaesthetic**, (US) **general anesthetic** n anestesia totale; **general election** n elezioni fpl generali; **generalize** vi generalizzare; **generally** adv generalmente; **general practitioner** n medico generico; **general store** n emporio

generate ['dʒɛnəreɪt] vt generare

generation [dʒɛnə'reɪʃən] n generazione f

generator ['dʒɛnəreɪtə'] n generatore m

generosity [dʒɛnə'rɔsɪtɪ] n generosità

generous ['dʒɛnərəs] adj generoso/a; (copious) abbondante

genetic [dʒɪ'nɛtɪk] adj genetico/a; **~ engineering** ingegneria genetica; **genetically modified** adj geneticamente modificato/a, transgenico/a; **genetics** [dʒɪ'nɛtɪks] n genetica

Geneva [dʒɪ'niːvə] n Ginevra

genitals ['dʒɛnɪtlz] npl genitali mpl

genius ['dʒiːnɪəs] n genio

Genoa ['dʒɛnəuə] n Genova

genome ['giːnəum] n genoma m inv

gent [dʒɛnt] n abbr = **gentleman**

gentle ['dʒɛntl] adj delicato/a; (person) dolce

▎ Be careful not to translate gentle by the Italian word gentile.

gentleman ['dʒɛntlmən] n (irreg) signore m; (well-bred man) gentiluomo

gently ['dʒɛntlɪ] adv delicatamente

gents [dʒɛnts] n W.C. m (per signori)

genuine ['dʒɛnjuɪn] adj autentico/a; sincero/a; **genuinely** adv genuinamente

geographic(al) [dʒɪə'græfɪk(l)] adj geografico/a

geography [dʒɪˈɒgrəfɪ] n geografia
geology [dʒɪˈɒlədʒɪ] n geologia
geometry [dʒɪˈɒmətrɪ] n geometria
geranium [dʒɪˈreɪnɪəm] n geranio
geriatric [dʒɛrɪˈætrɪk] adj geriatrico/a
germ [dʒɜːm] n (Med) microbo; (Biol, fig)
germe m
German [ˈdʒɜːmən] adj tedesco/a ▷ n
tedesco/a; (Ling) tedesco; **German
measles** (BRIT) n rosolia
Germany [ˈdʒɜːmənɪ] n Germania
gesture [ˈdʒɛstjəʳ] n gesto

KEYWORD

get [gɛt] (pt, pp **got**, (US) pp **gotten**) vi
1 (become, be) diventare, farsi; **to get drunk**
ubriacarsi; **to get killed** venire or rimanere
ucciso/a; **it's getting late** si sta facendo
tardi; **to get old** invecchiare; **when do I
get paid?** quando mi pagate?; **to get tired**
stancarsi
2 (go): **to get to/from** andare a/da; **to get
home** arrivare or tornare a casa; **how did
you get here?** come sei venuto?
3 (begin) mettersi a, cominciare a; **to get to
know sb** incominciare a conoscere qn; **let's
get going** or **started** muoviamoci
4 (modal aux vb): **you've got to do it** devi
farlo
▶ vt **1**: **to get sth done** (do) fare qc; (have
done) far fare qc; **to get one's hair cut**
tagliarsi or farsi tagliare i capelli; **to get sb
to do sth** far fare qc a qn
2 (obtain: money, permission, results)
ottenere; (find: job, flat) trovare; (fetch:
person, doctor) chiamare; (object) prendere;
get me Mr Jones, please (Tel) mi passi il
signor Jones, per favore; **to get sth for sb**
prendere or procurare qc a qn; **can I get
you a drink?** le posso offrire da bere?
3 (receive: present, letter, prize) ricevere;
(acquire: reputation) farsi; **how much did
you get for the painting?** quanto le hanno
dato per il quadro?
4 (catch) prendere; **to get sb by the arm/
throat** afferrare qn per un braccio/alla
gola; **get him!** prendetelo!
5 (hit: target etc) colpire
6 (take, move) portare; **to get sth to sb** far
avere qc a qn; **do you think we'll get it
through the door?** pensi che riusciremo a
farlo passare per la porta?
7 (catch, take: plane, bus etc) prendere;
where do we get the ferry to …? dove si
prende il traghetto per …?
8 (understand) afferrare; **I've got it!** ci sono
arrivato!, ci sono!
9 (hear) sentire; **I'm sorry, I didn't get your
name** scusi, non ho capito (or sentito) come
si chiama
10 (have, possess): **to have got** avere; **how
many have you got?** quanti ne ha?

get along vi (agree) andare d'accordo;
(depart) andarsene; (manage) = **get by**
get at vt fus (attack) prendersela con;
(reach) raggiungere, arrivare a
get away vi partire, andarsene; (escape)
scappare
get away with vt fus cavarsela; farla franca
get back vi (return) ritornare, tornare
▷ vt riottenere, riavere; **when do we get
back?** quando ritorniamo?
get by vi (pass) passare; (manage) farcela
get down vi, vt fus scendere ▷ vt far
scendere; (depress) buttare giù
get down to vt fus (work) mettersi a (fare)
get in vi entrare; (train) arrivare; (arrive
home) ritornare, tornare
get into vt fus entrare in; **to get into a
rage** incavolarsi
get off vi (from train etc) scendere; (depart:
person, car) andare via; (escape) cavarsela
▷ vt (remove: clothes, stain) levare ▷ vt fus
(train, bus) scendere da
get on vi: **how did you get on?** com'è
andata?; **to get on (with sb)** andare
d'accordo (con qn) ▷ vt fus montare in;
(horse) montare su
get out vi uscire; (of vehicle) scendere
▷ vt tirar fuori, far uscire
get out of vt fus uscire da; (duty etc) evitare
get over vt fus (illness) riaversi da
get round vt fus aggirare; (fig: person)
rigirare
get through vi (Tel) avere la linea
get through to vt fus (Tel) parlare a
get together vi riunirsi ▷ vt raccogliere;
(people) adunare
get up vi (rise) alzarsi ▷ vt fus salire su per
get up to vt fus (reach) raggiungere; (prank
etc) fare

getaway [ˈgɛtəweɪ] n fuga
Ghana [ˈgɑːnə] n Ghana m
ghastly [ˈgɑːstlɪ] adj orribile, orrendo/a;
(pale) spettrale
ghetto [ˈgɛtəu] n ghetto
ghost [gəust] n fantasma m, spettro
giant [ˈdʒaɪənt] n gigante/essa ▷ adj
gigantesco/a, enorme
gift [gɪft] n regalo; (donation, ability) dono;
gifted adj dotato/a; **gift shop**, (US) **gift
store** n negozio di souvenir; **gift token,
gift voucher** n buono (acquisto)
gig [gɪg] n (col: of musician) serata
gigabyte [ˈgiːgəbaɪt] n gigabyte m inv
gigantic [dʒaɪˈgæntɪk] adj gigantesco/a

giggle ['gɪgl] vi ridere sciocamente

gills [gɪlz] npl (of fish) branchie fpl

gilt [gɪlt] n doratura ▷ adj dorato/a

gimmick ['gɪmɪk] n trucco

gin [dʒɪn] n (liquor) gin m inv

ginger ['dʒɪndʒəʳ] n zenzero

gipsy ['dʒɪpsɪ] n zingaro/a

giraffe [dʒɪ'rɑːf] n giraffa

girl [gəːl] n ragazza; (young unmarried woman) signorina; (daughter) figlia, figliola; **girlfriend** n (of girl) amica; (of boy) ragazza; **Girl Scout** n (US) Giovane Esploratrice f

gist [dʒɪst] n succo

give [gɪv] (pt **gave**, pp **given**) vt dare ▷ vi cedere; **to ~ sb sth, ~ sth to sb** dare qc a qn; **I'll ~ you £5 for it** te lo pago 5 sterline; **to ~ a cry/sigh** emettere un grido/sospiro; **to ~ a speech** fare un discorso; **give away** vt dare via; (disclose) rivelare; (bride) condurre all'altare; **give back** vt rendere; **give in** vi cedere ▷ vt consegnare; **give out** vt distribuire; annunciare; **give up** vi rinunciare ▷ vt rinunciare a; **to ~ up smoking** smettere di fumare; **to ~ o.s. up** arrendersi

given ['gɪvn] pp of **give** ▷ adj (fixed: time, amount) dato/a, determinato/a ▷ conj: **~ (that)** ... dato che ...; **~ the circumstances** ... date le circostanze ...

glacier ['glæsɪəʳ] n ghiacciaio

glad [glæd] adj lieto/a, contento/a; **gladly** ['glædlɪ] adv volentieri

glamorous ['glæmərəs] adj affascinante, seducente

glamour, (US) **glamor** ['glæməʳ] n fascino

glance [glɑːns] n occhiata, sguardo ▷ vi: **to ~** dare un'occhiata a; **glance off** vt fus (bullet) rimbalzare su

gland [glænd] n ghiandola

glare [glɛəʳ] n (of anger) sguardo furioso; (of light) riverbero, luce f abbagliante; (of publicity) chiasso ▷ vi abbagliare; **to ~ at** guardare male; **glaring** adj (mistake) madornale

glass [glɑːs] n (substance) vetro; (tumbler) bicchiere m; **glasses** ['glɑːsɪz] npl (spectacles) occhiali mpl

glaze [gleɪz] vt (door) fornire di vetri; (pottery) smaltare ▷ n smalto

gleam [gliːm] vi luccicare

glen [glɛn] n valletta

glide [glaɪd] vi scivolare; (Aviat, birds) planare; **glider** n (Aviat) aliante m

glimmer ['glɪməʳ] n barlume m

glimpse [glɪmps] n impressione f fugace ▷ vt vedere di sfuggita

glint [glɪnt] vi luccicare

glisten ['glɪsn] vi luccicare

glitter ['glɪtəʳ] vi scintillare

global ['gləubl] adj globale; **globalization** [gləubəlaɪ'zeɪʃən] n globalizzazione f; **global warming** n riscaldamento globale

globe [gləub] n globo, sfera

gloom [gluːm] n oscurità, buio; (sadness) tristezza, malinconia; **gloomy** adj scuro/a, fosco/a, triste

glorious ['glɔːrɪəs] adj glorioso/a, magnifico/a

glory ['glɔːrɪ] n gloria; splendore m

gloss [glɔs] n (shine) lucentezza; (also: **~ paint**) vernice f a olio

glossary ['glɔsərɪ] n glossario

glossy ['glɔsɪ] adj lucente

glove [glʌv] n guanto; **glove compartment** n (Aut) vano portaoggetti

glow [gləu] vi ardere; (face) essere luminoso/a

glucose ['gluːkəus] n glucosio

glue [gluː] n colla ▷ vt incollare

GM adj abbr (= genetically modified) geneticamente modificato/a; **GM crop** n cultura GM

gm abbr = **gram**

GM-free [dʒiːɛm'friː] adj privo/a di OGM

GMO n abbr (= genetically modified organism) OGM m inv

GMT abbr (= Greenwich Mean Time) T.M.G.

gnaw [nɔː] vt rodere

go [gəu] vi (pt **went**, pp **gone**) andare; (depart) partire, andarsene; (work) funzionare; (time) passare; (break etc) cedere; (be sold): **to go for £10** essere venduto per 10 sterline; (fit, suit): **to go with** andare bene con; (become): **to go pale** diventare pallido/a; **to go mouldy** ammuffire ▷ n (pl **goes**): **to have a go (at)** provare; **to be on the go** essere in moto; **whose go is it?** a chi tocca?; **he's going to do** sta per fare; **to go for a walk** andare a fare una passeggiata; **to go dancing/ shopping** andare a ballare/fare la spesa; **just then the bell went** proprio allora suonò il campanello; **how did it go?** com'è andato?; **to go round the back/by the shop** passare da dietro/davanti al negozio; **go ahead** vi andare avanti; **go away** vi partire, andarsene; **go back** vi tornare, ritornare; **go by** vi (years, time) scorrere ▷ vt fus attenersi a, seguire (alla lettera); prestar fede a; **go down** vi scendere; (ship) affondare; (sun) tramontare ▷ vt fus scendere; **go for** vt fus (fetch) andare a prendere; (like) andar matto/a per; (attack) attaccare; saltare addosso a; **go in** vi entrare; **go into** vt fus entrare in; (investigate) indagare, esaminare; (embark on) lanciarsi in; **go off** vi partire, andar via; (food) guastarsi; (explode) esplodere, scoppiare; (*event*) passare ▷ *vt fus*: **I've gone off chocolate** la cioccolata non mi piace più; **the gun went off** il fucile si scaricò; **go on** *vi* continuare; (*happen*) succedere; **to go on doing** continuare a fare; **go out** *vi* uscire; (*fire, light*) spegnersi; **they went out for 3 years** (*couple*) sono stati insieme per 3 anni; **go over** *vi* (*ship*) ribaltarsi ▷ *vt fus* (*check*) esaminare; **go past** *vi* passare ▷ *vt fus* passare davanti a; **go round** *vi* (*circulate: news, rumour*) circolare; (*revolve*) girare; (*suffice*) bastare (per tutti); **to go round (to sb's)** (*visit*) passare (da qn); **to go round (by)** (*make a detour*) passare (per); **go through** *vt fus* (*town etc*) attraversare; (*files, papers*) vagliare attentamente; (*examine: list, book*) leggere da cima a fondo; **go up** *vi* salire; **go with** *vt fus* (*accompany*) accompagnare; **go without** *vt fus* fare a meno di

go-ahead ['gəʊəhɛd] *adj* intraprendente ▷ *n*: **to give sb/sth the ~** dare il via libera a qn/qc

goal [gəʊl] *n* (*Sport*) gol *m*, rete *f*; (: *place*) porta; (*fig: aim*) fine *m*, scopo; **goalkeeper** *n* portiere *m*; **goalpost** ['gəʊlpəʊst] *n* palo (della porta)

goat [gəʊt] *n* capra

gobble ['gɔbl] *vt* (*also*: **~ down, ~ up**) ingoiare

god [gɔd] *n* dio; **G~** Dio; **godchild** *n* figlioccio/a; **goddaughter** *n* figlioccia; **goddess** *n* dea; **godfather** *n* padrino; **godmother** *n* madrina; **godson** *n* figlioccio

goggles ['gɔglz] *npl* occhiali *mpl* (di protezione)

going ['gəʊɪŋ] *n* (*conditions*) andare *m*, stato del terreno ▷ *adj*: **the ~ rate** la tariffa in vigore

gold [gəʊld] *n* oro ▷ *adj* d'oro; **golden** *adj* (*made of gold*) d'oro; (*gold in colour*) dorato/a; **goldfish** *n* pesce *m* dorato *or* rosso; **goldmine** *n* (*also fig*) miniera d'oro; **gold-plated** *adj* placcato/a oro inv

golf [gɔlf] *n* golf *m*; **golf ball** *n* (*for game*) pallina da golf; (*on typewriter*) pallina; **golf club** *n* circolo di golf; (*stick*) bastone *m* or mazza da golf; **golf course** *n* campo di golf; **golfer** *n* giocatore/trice di golf

gone [gɔn] *pp of* **go** ▷ *adj* partito/a

gong [gɔŋ] *n* gong *m* inv

good [gud] *adj* buono/a; (*kind*) buono/a, gentile; (*child*) bravo/a ▷ *n* bene *m*; **~!** bene!, ottimo!; **to be ~ at** essere bravo/a in; **to be ~ for** andare bene per; **it's ~ for you** fa bene; **to make ~** (*loss, damage*) compensare; **it's no ~ complaining** brontolare non serve a niente; **for ~** per sempre, definitivamente;

would you be ~ enough to …? avrebbe la gentilezza di …?; **a ~ deal (of)** molto/a, una buona quantità (di); **a ~ many** molti/e; **~ morning!** buon giorno!; **~ afternoon/evening!** buona sera!; **~ night!** buona notte!; **goodbye** *excl* arrivederci!; **Good Friday** *n* Venerdì Santo; **good-looking** *adj* bello/a; **good-natured** *adj* affabile; **goodness** *n* (*of person*) bontà; **for goodness sake!** per amor di Dio!; **goodness gracious!** santo cielo!, mamma mia!; **goods** *npl* (*Comm etc*) merci *fpl*, articoli *mpl*; **goods train** *n* (BRIT) treno *m* merci *inv*; **goodwill** *n* amicizia, benevolenza

google ['guːgl] *vt, vi* cercare con Google®

goose (*pl* **geese**) [guːs, giːs] *n* oca

gooseberry ['guzbərɪ] *n* uva spina; **to play ~** (BRIT) tenere la candela

goose bumps ['guːsbʌmpz] *n*, **gooseflesh** ['guːsflɛʃ] *n*, **goosepimples** ['guːspɪmplz] *npl* pelle *f* d'oca

gorge [gɔːdʒ] *n* gola ▷ *vt*: **to ~ o.s. (on)** ingozzarsi (di)

gorgeous ['gɔːdʒəs] *adj* magnifico/a

gorilla [gə'rɪlə] *n* gorilla *m* inv

gosh [gɔʃ] *excl* (*col*) perdinci!

gospel ['gɔspl] *n* vangelo

gossip ['gɔsɪp] *n* chiacchiere *fpl*; pettegolezzi *mpl*; (*person*) pettegolo/a ▷ *vi* chiacchierare; **gossip column** *n* cronaca mondana

got [gɔt] *pt, pp of* **get**

gotten ['gɔtn] (US) *pp of* **get**

gourmet ['guəmeɪ] *n* buongustaio/a

govern ['gʌvən] *vt* governare; **government** *n* governo; **governor** ['gʌvənəʳ] *n* (*of state, bank*) governatore *m*; (*of school, hospital*) amministratore *m*; (BRIT: *of prison*) direttore/trice

gown [gaun] *n* vestito lungo; (*of teacher, judge*: BRIT) toga

GP *n abbr* = **general practitioner**

GPS *n abbr* (= *global positioning system*) GPS *m*

grab [græb] *vt* afferrare, arraffare; (*property, power*) impadronirsi di ▷ *vi*: **to ~ at** cercare di afferrare

grace [greɪs] *n* grazia ▷ *vt* onorare; **5 days' ~** dilazione *f* di 5 giorni; **graceful** *adj* elegante, aggraziato/a; **gracious** ['greɪʃəs] *adj* grazioso/a, misericordioso/a

grade [greɪd] *n* (*Comm*) qualità *f* inv; classe *f*; categoria; (*in hierarchy*) grado; (US Scol: *mark*) voto; (: *school class*) classe ▷ *vt* classificare; ordinare; graduare; **grade crossing** *n* (US) passaggio a livello; **grade school** *n* (US) scuola elementare *or* primaria

gradient ['greɪdɪənt] *n* pendenza, inclinazione *m*

gradual ['grædjuəl] *adj* graduale;
gradually *adv* man mano, a poco a poco
graduate *n* ['grædjuɪt] laureato/a;
(*us Scol*) diplomato/a ▷ *vi* ['grædjueɪt]
laurearsi; diplomarsi; **graduation**
[grædju'eɪʃən] *n* cerimonia del
conferimento della laurea
graffiti [grə'fi:tɪ] *npl* graffiti *mpl*
graft [grɑːft] *n* (*Agr, Med*) innesto; (*col:
bribery*) corruzione *f* ▷ *vt* innestare; **it's
hard ~** (*BRIT col*) è un lavoraccio
grain [greɪn] *n* grano; (*of sand*) granello; (*of
wood*) venatura
gram [græm] *n* grammo
grammar ['græmə'] *n* grammatica;
grammar school (*BRIT*) ≈ liceo
gramme [græm] *n* = **gram**
gran (*col*) [græn] *n* (*BRIT col*) nonna
grand [grænd] *adj* grande, magnifico/a;
grandioso/a; **grandad** (*col*) *n* = **granddad**;
grandchild (*pl* **-children**) *n* nipote *m*;
granddad (*col*) nonno; **granddaughter**
n nipote *f*; **grandfather** *n* nonno;
grandma (*col*) nonna; **grandmother**
n nonna; **grandpa** (*col*); = **granddad**;
grandparent *n* nonno/a; **grand piano** *n*
pianoforte *m* a coda; **Grand Prix** ['grɑ̃:'pri:]
n (*Aut*) Gran Premio, Grand Prix *m inv*;
grandson *n* nipote *m*
granite ['grænɪt] *n* granito
granny ['grænɪ] *n* (*col*) nonna
grant [grɑːnt] *vt* accordare; (*a request*)
accogliere; (*admit*) ammettere, concedere
▷ *n* (*Scol*) borsa; (*Admin*) sussidio,
sovvenzione *f*; **to take sth for ~ed** dare qc
per scontato; **to take sb for ~ed** dare per
scontata la presenza di qn
grape [greɪp] *n* chicco d'uva, acino
grapefruit ['greɪpfru:t] *n* pompelmo
graph [grɑːf] *n* grafico; **graphic** *adj*
grafico/a; (*vivid*) vivido/a; **graphics** *n* (*art,
process*) grafica ▷ *npl* illustrazioni *fpl*
grasp [grɑːsp] *vt* afferrare ▷ *n* (*grip*) presa;
(*fig*) potere *m*; comprensione *f*
grass [grɑːs] *n* erba; **grasshopper** *n*
cavalletta
grate [greɪt] *n* graticola (del focolare) ▷ *vi*
cigolare, stridere ▷ *vt* (*Culin*) grattugiare
grateful ['greɪtful] *adj* grato/a,
riconoscente
grater ['greɪtə'] *n* grattugia
gratitude ['grætɪtjuːd] *n* gratitudine *f*
grave [greɪv] *n* tomba ▷ *adj* grave, serio/a
gravel ['grævl] *n* ghiaia
gravestone ['greɪvstəun] *n* pietra tombale
graveyard ['greɪvjɑːd] *n* cimitero
gravity ['grævɪtɪ] *n* (*Physics*) gravità;
pesantezza; (*seriousness*) gravità, serietà
gravy ['greɪvɪ] *n* intingolo della carne; salsa

gray [greɪ] *adj* (*us*) = **grey**
graze [greɪz] *vi* pascolare, pascere ▷ *vt*
(*touch lightly*) sfiorare; (*scrape*) escoriare ▷ *n*
(*Med*) escoriazione *f*
grease [griːs] *n* (*fat*) grasso; (*lubricant*)
lubrificante *m* ▷ *vt* ingrassare; lubrificare;
greasy *adj* grasso/a, untuoso/a
great [greɪt] *adj* grande; (*col*) magnifico/a,
meraviglioso/a; **Great Britain** *n* Gran
Bretagna; **great-grandfather** *n* bisnonno;
great-grandmother *n* bisnonna; **greatly**
adv molto
Greece [griːs] *n* Grecia
greed [griːd] *n* (*also*: **~iness**) avarizia; (*for
food*) golosità, ghiottoneria; **greedy** *adj*
avido/a; goloso/a, ghiotto/a
Greek [griːk] *adj* greco/a ▷ *n* greco/a; (*Ling*)
greco
green [griːn] *adj* verde; (*inexperienced*)
inesperto/a, ingenuo/a ▷ *n* verde *m*;
(*stretch of grass*) prato; (*of golf course*) green
m inv; **greens** *npl* (*vegetables*) verdura;
green card *n* (*BRIT Aut*) carta verde; (*us
Admin*) permesso di soggiorno e di lavoro;
greengage ['griːngeɪdʒ] *n* susina Regina
Claudia; **greengrocer** *n* (*BRIT*)
fruttivendolo/a, erbivendolo/a;
greenhouse *n* serra; **greenhouse effect**
n: **the greenhouse effect** l'effetto serra;
green tax *n* tassa verde
Greenland ['griːnlənd] *n* Groenlandia
green salad *n* insalata verde
greet [griːt] *vt* salutare; **greeting** *n* saluto;
greeting(s) card *n* cartolina d'auguri
grew [gruː] *pt of* **grow**
grey, (*us*) **gray** [greɪ] *adj* grigio/a; **grey-
haired** *adj* dai capelli grigi; **greyhound** *n*
levriere *m*
grid [grɪd] *n* grata; (*Elec*) rete *f*; **gridlock**
['grɪdlɔk] *n* (*traffic jam*) paralisi *f inv* del
traffico; **gridlocked** *adj* paralizzato/a dal
traffico; (*talks etc*) in fase di stallo
grief [griːf] *n* dolore *m*
grievance ['griːvəns] *n* lagnanza
grieve [griːv] *vi* affliggersi ▷ *vt* addolorare;
to ~ for sb (*dead person*) piangere qn
grill [grɪl] *n* (*on cooker*) griglia; (*also*:
mixed ~) grigliata mista ▷ *vt* (*BRIT*) cuocere
ai ferri; (*col: question*) interrogare senza
sosta
grille [grɪl] *n* grata; (*Aut*) griglia
grim [grɪm] *adj* sinistro/a, brutto/a
grime [graɪm] *n* sudiciume *m*
grin [grɪn] *n* sorriso smagliante ▷ *vi*: **to ~
(at)** fare un gran sorriso (a)
grind [graɪnd] (*pt, pp* **ground**) *vt* macinare;
(*make sharp*) arrotare ▷ *n* (*work*) sgobbata
grip [grɪp] *n* impugnatura; presa; (*holdall*)
borsa da viaggio ▷ *vt* (*object*) afferrare;

(*attention*) catturare; **to come to ~s with** affrontare; cercare di risolvere; **gripping** ['grɪpɪŋ] *adj* avvincente

grit [grɪt] *n* ghiaia; (*courage*) fegato ▷ *vt* (*road*) coprire di sabbia; **to ~ one's teeth** stringere i denti

grits [grɪts] *npl* (*US*) macinato grosso (di avena *etc*)

groan [grəʊn] *n* gemito ▷ *vi* gemere

grocer ['grəʊsəʳ] *n* negoziante *m* di generi alimentari; **~'s (shop)** negozio di alimentari; **grocery** ['grəʊsərɪ] *n* (*shop*) (negozio di) alimentari; **groceries** *npl* provviste *fpl*

groin [grɔɪn] *n* inguine *m*

groom [gruːm] *n* palafreniere *m*; (*also*: **bride~**) sposo ▷ *vt* (*horse*) strigliare; (*fig*): **to ~ sb for** avviare qn a; **well-~ed** (*person*) curato/a

groove [gruːv] *n* scanalatura, solco

grope [grəʊp] *vi*: **to ~ for sth** cercare qc a tastoni

gross [grəʊs] *adj* grossolano/a; (*Comm*) lordo/a; **grossly** *adv* (*greatly*) molto

grotesque [grəʊˈtɛsk] *adj* grottesco/a

ground [graʊnd] *pt*, *pp of* **grind** ▷ *n* suolo, terra; (*land*) terreno; (*Sport*) campo; (*reason*: *gen pl*) ragione *f*; (*US*: *also*: **~ wire**) (presa a) terra ▷ *vt* (*plane*) tenere a terra; (*US Elec*) mettere la presa a terra a; **grounds** *npl* (*of coffee etc*) fondi *mpl*; (*gardens etc*) terreno, giardini *mpl*; **on/to the ~** per/a terra; **to gain/lose ~** guadagnare/perdere terreno; **ground floor** *n* pianterreno; **groundsheet** *n* (*BRIT*) telone *m* impermeabile; **groundwork** *n* preparazione *f*

group [gruːp] *n* gruppo ▷ *vt* (*also*: **~ together**) raggruppare ▷ *vi* (*also*: **~ together**) raggrupparsi

grouse [graʊs] *n* (*pl inv*: *bird*) tetraone *m* ▷ *vi* (*complain*) brontolare

grovel ['grɔvl] *vi* (*fig*): **to ~ (before)** strisciare (di fronte a)

grow (*pt* **grew**, *pp* **grown**) [grəʊ, gruː, grəʊn] *vi* crescere; (*increase*) aumentare; (*develop*) svilupparsi; (*become*): **to ~ rich/ weak** arricchirsi/indebolirsi ▷ *vt* coltivare, far crescere; **grow on** *vt fus*: **that painting is ~ing on me** quel quadro più lo guardo più mi piace; **grow up** *vi* farsi grande, crescere

growl [graʊl] *vi* ringhiare

grown [grəʊn] *pp of* **grow**; **grown-up** *n* adulto/a, grande *m/f*

growth [grəʊθ] *n* crescita, sviluppo; (*what has grown*) crescita; (*Med*) escrescenza, tumore *m*

grub [grʌb] *n* larva; (*col*: *food*) roba (da mangiare)

grubby ['grʌbɪ] *adj* sporco/a

grudge [grʌdʒ] *n* rancore *m* ▷ *vt*: **to ~ sb sth** dare qc a qn di malavoglia; invidiare qc a qn; **to bear sb a ~ (for)** serbar rancore a qn (per)

gruelling, (*US*) **grueling** ['gruəlɪŋ] *adj* estenuante

gruesome ['gruːsəm] *adj* orribile

grumble ['grʌmbl] *vi* brontolare, lagnarsi

grumpy ['grʌmpɪ] *adj* scorbutico/a

grunt [grʌnt] *vi* grugnire

guarantee [gærənˈtiː] *n* garanzia ▷ *vt* garantire

guard [gɑːd] *n* guardia; (*one man*) guardia, sentinella; (*BRIT Rail*) capotreno; (*on machine*) schermo protettivo; (*also*: **fire ~**) parafuoco ▷ *vt* fare la guardia a; **to ~ (against or from)** proteggere (da); **to be on one's ~** stare in guardia; **guardian** *n* custode *m*; (*of minor*) tutore/trice

guerrilla [gəˈrɪlə] *n* guerrigliero

guess [gɛs] *vi* indovinare ▷ *vt* indovinare; (*US*) credere, pensare ▷ *n* congettura; **to take or have a ~** provare a indovinare

guest [gɛst] *n* ospite *m/f*; (*in hotel*) cliente *m/f*; **guest-house** *n* pensione *f*; **guest room** *n* camera degli ospiti

guidance ['gaɪdəns] *n* guida, direzione *f*

guide [gaɪd] *n* guida; (*BRIT*: *also*: **girl ~**) giovane esploratrice *f* ▷ *vt* guidare; **guidebook** *n* guida; **guide dog** *n* cane *m* guida *inv*; **guided tour** *n* visita guidata; **what time does the guided tour start?** a che ora comincia la visita guidata?; **guidelines** *npl* (*fig*) indicazioni *fpl*, linee *fpl* direttive

guild [gɪld] *n* arte *f*, corporazione *f*; associazione *f*

guilt [gɪlt] *n* colpevolezza; **guilty** *adj* colpevole

guinea pig ['gɪnɪ-] *n* cavia

guitar [gɪˈtɑːʳ] *n* chitarra; **guitarist** *n* chitarrista *m/f*

gulf [gʌlf] *n* golfo; (*abyss*) abisso

gull [gʌl] *n* gabbiano

gulp [gʌlp] *vi* deglutire; (*from emotion*) avere il nodo in gola ▷ *vt* (*also*: **~ down**) tracannare, inghiottire

gum [gʌm] *n* (*Anat*) gengiva; (*glue*) colla; (*sweet*) caramella gommosa; (*also*: **chewing-~**) chewing-gum *m* ▷ *vt* incollare

gun [gʌn] *n* fucile *m*; (*small*) pistola, rivoltella; (*rifle*) carabina; (*shotgun*) fucile da caccia; (*cannon*) cannone *m*; **gunfire** *n* spari *mpl*; **gunman** *n* (*irreg*) bandito armato; **gunpoint** *n*: **at gunpoint** sotto minaccia di fucile; **gunpowder** *n* polvere *f* da sparo; **gunshot** *n* sparo

gush [gʌʃ] *vi* sgorgare; (*fig*) abbandonarsi ad effusioni

gust [gʌst] n (of wind) raffica; (of smoke) buffata

gut [gʌt] n intestino, budello; **guts** npl (of animals) interiora fpl; (courage) fegato

gutter ['gʌtər] n (of roof) grondaia; (in street) cunetta

guy [gaɪ] n (also: **~rope**) cavo or corda di fissaggio; (col: man) tipo, elemento; (figure) effigie di Guy Fawkes

Guy Fawkes Night [-'fɔːks-] n (BRIT) vedi nota "Guy Fawkes Night"

gym [dʒɪm] n (also: **gymnasium**) palestra; (also: **gymnastics**) ginnastica; **gymnasium** [dʒɪm'neɪzɪəm] n palestra; **gymnast** ['dʒɪmnæst] n ginnasta m/f; **gymnastics** [dʒɪm'næstɪks] n, npl ginnastica; **gym shoes** npl scarpe fpl da ginnastica

gynaecologist, (US) **gynecologist** [gaɪnɪ'kɔlədʒɪst] n ginecologo/a

gypsy ['dʒɪpsɪ] n = **gipsy**

haberdashery ['hæbədæʃərɪ] (BRIT) n merceria

habit ['hæbɪt] n abitudine f; (costume) abito; (Rel) tonaca

habitat ['hæbɪtæt] n habitat m inv

hack [hæk] vt tagliare, fare a pezzi ▷ n (pej: writer) scribacchino/a; **hacker** ['hækər] n (Comput) pirata m informatico

had [hæd] pt, pp of **have**

haddock ['hædək] (pl **haddock** or **haddocks**) n eglefino

hadn't ['hædnt] = **had not**

haemorrhage, (US) **hemorrhage** ['hɛmərɪdʒ] n emorragia

haemorrhoids, (US) **hemorrhoids** ['hɛmərɔɪdz] npl emorroidi fpl

haggle ['hægl] vi mercanteggiare

Hague [heɪg] n: **The ~** L'Aia

hail [heɪl] n grandine f; (of criticism etc) pioggia ▷ vt (call) chiamare; (flag down: taxi) fermare; (greet) salutare ▷ vi grandinare; **hailstone** n chicco di grandine

hair [hɛər] n capelli mpl; (single hair: on head) capello; (: on body) pelo; **to do one's ~** pettinarsi; **hairband** ['hɛəbænd] n (elastic) fascia per i capelli; (rigid) cerchietto; **hairbrush** n spazzola per capelli; **haircut** n taglio di capelli; **hairdo** ['hɛəduː] n acconciatura, pettinatura; **hairdresser** n parrucchiere/a; **hairdresser's** n parrucchiere/a; **hair-dryer** ['hɛədraɪər] n asciugacapelli m inv; **hair gel** n gel m inv per capelli; **hair spray** n lacca per capelli; **hairstyle** n pettinatura, acconciatura; **hairy** adj irsuto/a; peloso/a; (col: frightening) spaventoso/a

haka ['hɑːkə] n (NZ) danza eseguita dai giocatori prima di una partita

hake [heɪk] (pl **hake** or **hakes**) n nasello

half [hɑːf] n (pl **halves**) mezzo, metà f inv
▷ adj mezzo/a ▷ adv a mezzo, a metà;
~ **an hour** mezz'ora; ~ **a dozen** mezza
dozzina; ~ **a pound** mezza libbra; **two and
a** ~ due e mezzo; **a week and a** ~ una
settimana e mezza; ~ **(of it)** la metà; ~ **(of)**
la metà di; **to cut sth in** ~ tagliare qc in due;
~ **asleep** mezzo/a addormentato/a; **half
board** (BRIT) n mezza pensione;
half-brother n fratellastro; **half day** n
mezza giornata; **half fare** n tariffa a metà
prezzo; **half-hearted** adj tiepido/a;
half-hour n mezz'ora; **half-price** adj, adv a
metà prezzo; **half term** n (BRIT Scol)
vacanza a or di metà trimestre; **half-time** n
(Sport) intervallo; **halfway** adv a metà
strada

hall [hɔːl] n sala, salone m; (entrance way)
entrata; ~ **of residence** n (BRIT) casa dello
studente

hallmark ['hɔːlmɑːk] n marchio di
garanzia; (fig) caratteristica

hallo [hə'ləʊ] excl = **hello**

hall of residence (BRIT) n casa dello
studente

Halloween ['hæləʊ'iːn] n vigilia
d'Ognissanti

- **HALLOWEEN**
-
- Secondo la tradizione anglosassone,
- durante la notte di Halloween, il 31 di
- ottobre, è possibile vedere le streghe
- e i fantasmi. I bambini, travestiti da
- fantasmi, streghe, mostri o simili, vanno
- di porta in porta e raccolgono dolci e
- piccoli doni.

hallucination [həluːsɪ'neɪʃən] n
allucinazione f

hallway ['hɔːlweɪ] n ingresso; corridoio

halo ['heɪləʊ] n (of saint etc) aureola

halt [hɔːlt] n fermata ▷ vt fermare ▷ vi
fermarsi

halve [hɑːv] vt (apple etc) dividere a metà;
(expense) ridurre di metà

halves [hɑːvz] npl of **half**

ham [hæm] n prosciutto

hamburger ['hæmbɜːgəʳ] n hamburger
m inv

hamlet ['hæmlɪt] n paesetto

hammer ['hæməʳ] n martello ▷ vt
martellare ▷ vi: **to** ~ **on** or **at the door**
picchiare alla porta

hammock ['hæmək] n amaca

hamper ['hæmpəʳ] vt impedire ▷ n cesta

hamster ['hæmstəʳ] n criceto

hamstring ['hæmstrɪŋ] n (Anat) tendine m
del ginocchio

hand [hænd] n mano f; (of clock) lancetta;
(handwriting) scrittura; (at cards) mano;
(: game) partita; (worker) operaio/a ▷ vt
dare, passare; **to give sb a** ~ dare una
mano a qn; **at** ~ a portata di mano; **in** ~
a disposizione; (work) in corso; **to be on** ~
(person) essere disponibile; (emergency
services) essere pronto/a a intervenire;
to ~ (information etc) a portata di mano;
on the one ~ ..., **on the other** ~ da un
lato ..., dall'altro; **hand down** vt passare
giù; (tradition, heirloom) tramandare;
(US: sentence, verdict) emettere; **hand in** vt
consegnare; **hand out** vt distribuire;
hand over vt passare; cedere;
handbag n borsetta; **hand baggage** n
bagaglio a mano; **handbook** n
manuale m; **handbrake** n freno a mano;
handcuffs npl manette fpl; **handful** n
manciata, pugno

handicap ['hændɪkæp] n handicap m inv
▷ vt handicappare

handkerchief ['hæŋkətʃɪf] n fazzoletto

handle ['hændl] n (of door etc) maniglia; (of
cup etc) ansa; (of knife etc) impugnatura; (of
saucepan) manico; (for winding) manovella
▷ vt toccare, maneggiare; (deal with)
occuparsi di; (treat: people) trattare; **"~ with
care"** "fragile"; **to fly off the** ~ (fig) perdere
le staffe, uscire dai gangheri

handlebar(s) ['hændlbɑː(z)] n(pl)
manubrio

hand: hand luggage ['hændlʌgɪdʒ] n
bagagli mpl a mano; **handmade** adj
fatto/a a mano; **handout** n (money, food)
elemosina; (leaflet) volantino; (at lecture)
prospetto; **hands-free** n, adj (telephone)
con auricolare; (microphone) vivavoce inv

handsome ['hænsəm] adj bello/a; (profit,
fortune) considerevole

handwriting ['hændraɪtɪŋ] n scrittura

handy ['hændɪ] adj (person) bravo/a; (close
at hand) a portata di mano; (convenient)
comodo/a

hang (pt, pp **hung**) [hæŋ, hʌŋ] vt
appendere; (criminal) impiccare ▷ vi
(painting) essere appeso/a; (hair) scendere;
(drapery) cadere; **to get the** ~ **of (doing)
sth** (col) cominciare a capire (come) si fa qc;
hang about vi bighellonare, ciondolare;
hang down vi ricadere; **hang on** vi (wait)
aspettare; **hang out** vt (washing) stendere
(fuori); (col: live) stare ▷ vi penzolare,
pendere; **hang round** vi = **hang around**;
hang up vi (Tel) riattaccare ▷ vt
appendere

hanger ['hæŋəʳ] n gruccia

hang-gliding ['hæŋglaɪdɪŋ] n volo col
deltaplano

hangover ['hæŋəʊvə'] n (after drinking) postumi mpl di sbornia

hankie ['hæŋkɪ] n abbr = **handkerchief**

happen ['hæpən] vi accadere, succedere; **to ~ to do sth** fare qc per caso; **as it ~s** guarda caso; **what's ~ing?** cosa succede?

happily ['hæpɪlɪ] adv felicemente; fortunatamente

happiness ['hæpɪnɪs] n felicità, contentezza

happy ['hæpɪ] adj felice, contento/a; **~ with** (arrangements etc) soddisfatto/a di; **to be ~ to do** (willing) fare volentieri; **~ birthday!** buon compleanno!

harass ['hærəs] vt molestare; **harassment** n molestia

harbour, (US) **harbor** ['hɑːbə'] n porto ▷ vt (hope) nutrire; (fear) avere; (grudge) covare; (criminal) dare rifugio a

hard [hɑːd] adj duro/a ▷ adv (work) sodo; (think, try) bene; **to look ~ at** guardare fissamente; esaminare attentamente; **no ~ feelings!** senza rancore!; **to be ~ of hearing** essere duro/a d'orecchio; **to be ~ done by** essere trattato/a ingiustamente; **hardback** n libro rilegato; **hardboard** n legno precompresso; **hard disk** n (Comput) disco rigido; **harden** vt indurire

hardly ['hɑːdlɪ] adv (scarcely) appena; **it's ~ the case** non è proprio il caso; **~ anyone/ anywhere** quasi nessuno/da nessuna parte; **~ ever** quasi mai

hard: hardship ['hɑːdʃɪp] n avversità f inv; privazioni fpl; **hard shoulder** n (BRIT Aut) corsia d'emergenza; **hard-up** adj (col) al verde; **hardware** ['hɑːdwɛə'] n ferramenta fpl; (Comput) hardware m; (Mil) armamenti mpl; **hardware shop**, (US) **hardware store** n (negozio di) ferramenta fpl; **hardworking** [hɑːd'wəːkɪŋ] adj lavoratore/ trice

hardy ['hɑːdɪ] adj robusto/a; (plant) resistente al gelo

hare [hɛə'] n lepre f

harm [hɑːm] n male m; (wrong) danno ▷ vt (person) fare male a; (thing) danneggiare; **out of ~'s way** al sicuro; **harmful** adj dannoso/a; **harmless** adj innocuo/a; inoffensivo/a

harmony ['hɑːmənɪ] n armonia

harness ['hɑːnɪs] n (for horse) bardatura, finimenti mpl; (for child) briglie fpl; (safety harness) imbracatura ▷ vt (horse) bardare; (resources) sfruttare

harp [hɑːp] n arpa ▷ vi: **to ~ on about** insistere tediosamente su

harsh [hɑːʃ] adj (life, winter) duro/a; (judge, criticism) severo/a; (sound) rauco/a; (colour) chiassoso/a; (light) violento/a

harvest ['hɑːvɪst] n raccolto m; (of grapes) vendemmia ▷ vt fare il raccolto di, raccogliere; vendemmiare

has [hæz] see **have**

hashtag ['hæʃtæg] n (on Twitter) hashtag m inv

hasn't ['hæznt] = **has not**

hassle ['hæsl] n (col) sacco di problemi

haste [heɪst] n fretta; precipitazione f; **hasten** ['heɪsn] vt affrettare ▷ vi: **to hasten (to)** affrettarsi (a); **hastily** adv in fretta, precipitosamente; **hasty** adj affrettato/a, precipitoso/a

hat [hæt] n cappello

hatch [hætʃ] n (Naut: also: **~way**) boccaporto; (also: **service ~**) portello di servizio ▷ vi (bird) uscire dal guscio; (egg) schiudersi

hatchback ['hætʃbæk] n (Aut) tre (or cinque) porte f inv

hate [heɪt] vt odiare, detestare ▷ n odio; **hater** ['heɪtə'] n: **cop-~** persona che odia i poliziotti; **woman-~** misogino/a; **hatred** ['heɪtrɪd] n odio

haul [hɔːl] vt trascinare, tirare ▷ n (of fish) pescata; (of stolen goods etc) bottino

haunt [hɔːnt] vt (fear) pervadere; (person) frequentare ▷ n rifugio; **this house is ~ed** questa casa è abitata da un fantasma; **haunted** adj (castle etc) abitato/a dai fantasmi or dagli spiriti; (look) ossessionato/a, tormentato/a

KEYWORD

have [hæv] (pt, pp **had**) aux vb **1** (gen) avere; essere; **to have arrived/gone** essere arrivato/a/andato/a; **to have eaten/slept** avere mangiato/dormito; **he has been kind/promoted** è stato gentile/promosso; **having finished** or **when he had finished, he left** dopo aver finito, se n'è andato

2 (in tag questions): **you've done it, haven't you?** l'hai fatto, (non è) vero?; **he hasn't done it, has he?** non l'ha fatto, vero?

3 (in short answers and questions): **you've made a mistake — no I haven't/so I have** ha fatto un errore — ma no, niente affatto/ sì, è vero; **we haven't paid — yes we have!** non abbiamo pagato — ma sì che abbiamo pagato!; **I've been there before, have you?** ci sono già stato, e lei?

▶ modal aux vb (be obliged): **to have (got) to do sth** dover fare qc; **I haven't got** or **I don't have to wear glasses** non ho bisogno di portare gli occhiali

▶ vt **1** (possess, obtain) avere; **he has (got) blue eyes/dark hair** ha gli occhi azzurri/i capelli scuri; **have you got** or **do you have**

a car/phone? ha la macchina/il telefono?;
may I have your address? potrebbe darmi
il suo indirizzo?; **you can have it for £5** te lo
do per 5 sterline
2 (+ noun: take, hold etc): **to have
breakfast/a swim/a bath** fare colazione/
una nuotata/un bagno; **to have a
cigarette** fumare una sigaretta; **to have
dinner** cenare; **to have a drink** bere
qualcosa; **to have lunch** pranzare
3: **to have sth done** far fare qc; **to have
one's hair cut** tagliarsi or farsi tagliare i
capelli; **to have sb do sth** far fare qc a qn
4 (experience, suffer) avere; **to have a cold/
flu** avere il raffreddore/l'influenza; **she had
her bag stolen** le hanno rubato la borsa
5 (phrases: col): **you've been had!** ci sei
cascato!
have out vt: **to have it out with sb** (settle a
problem etc) mettere le cose in chiaro con qn

haven ['heɪvn] n porto; (fig) rifugio
haven't ['hævnt] = **have not**
havoc ['hævək] n gran subbuglio; **to play ~
with sth** scombussolare qc
Hawaii [həˈwaɪː] n le Hawaii
hawk [hɔːk] n falco
hawthorn ['hɔːθɔːn] n biancospino
hay [heɪ] n fieno; **hay fever** n febbre f da
fieno; **haystack** n pagliaio
hazard ['hæzəd] n azzardo, ventura;
(risk) pericolo, rischio ▷ vt (guess, remark)
azzardare; **hazardous** adj pericoloso/a;
hazard warning lights npl (Aut) luci fpl di
emergenza
haze [heɪz] n foschia
hazel ['heɪzl] n (tree) nocciolo ▷ adj (eyes)
(color) nocciola inv; **hazelnut** ['heɪzlnʌt]
n nocciola
hazy ['heɪzɪ] adj fosco/a; (idea) vago/a
HD abbr (= high definition) HD, alta
definizione
HDTV n abbr (= high definition television)
televisore m HD, TV f inv ad alta definizione
he [hiː] pron lui, egli; **it is he who ...** è lui
che ...
head [hɛd] n testa; (leader) capo; (of school)
preside m/f ▷ vt (list) essere in testa a;
(group) essere a capo di; **~s (or tails)** testa
(o croce), pari (o dispari); **~ first** a capofitto,
di testa; **~ over heels in love** pazzamente
innamorato/a; **to ~ the ball** dare di testa
alla palla; **head for** vt fus dirigersi verso;
head off vt (threat, danger) sventare;
headache n mal m di testa; **heading**
n titolo; intestazione f; **headlamp**
['hɛdlæmp] n (BRIT) = **headlight**;
headlight n fanale m; **headline** n
titolo; **head office** n sede f (centrale);

headphones npl cuffia; **headquarters** npl
ufficio centrale; (Mil) quartiere m generale;
headroom n (in car) altezza dell'abitacolo;
(under bridge) altezza limite; **headscarf** n
foulard m inv; **headset** n = **headphones**;
headteacher n (of primary school)
direttore/trice; (of secondary school) preside
m/f; **head waiter** n capocameriere m
heal [hiːl] vt, vi guarire
health [hɛlθ] n salute f; **health care** n
assistenza sanitaria; **health centre** n
(BRIT) poliambulatorio; **health food** n
alimenti mpl macrobiotici; **Health Service**
n: **the Health Service** (BRIT) ≈ il Servizio
Sanitario Statale; **healthy** adj (person)
sano/a, in buona salute; (climate) salubre;
(appetite, attitude etc) sano/a; (economy)
florido/a; (bank balance) solido/a
heap [hiːp] n mucchio ▷ vt (stones, sand):
to ~ (up) ammucchiare; **~s (of)** (col: = lots)
un mucchio (di)
hear (pt, pp heard) [hɪər, hɜːd] vt sentire;
(news) ascoltare ▷ vi sentire; **to ~ about**
avere notizie di; sentire parlare di
hearing ['hɪərɪŋ] n (sense) udito; (of
witnesses) audizione f; (of a case) udienza;
hearing aid n apparecchio acustico
hearse [hɜːs] n carro funebre
heart [hɑːt] n cuore m; **hearts** npl (Cards)
cuori mpl; **at ~** in fondo; **by ~** (learn, know)
a memoria; **to take ~** farsi coraggio
or animo; **to lose ~** perdere coraggio,
scoraggiarsi; **heart attack** n attacco di
cuore; **heartbeat** n battito del cuore;
heartbroken adj: **to be heartbroken**
avere il cuore spezzato; **heartburn** n
bruciore m di stomaco; **heart disease** n
malattia di cuore
hearth [hɑːθ] n focolare m
heartless ['hɑːtlɪs] adj senza cuore
hearty ['hɑːtɪ] adj caloroso/a; robusto/a,
sano/a; vigoroso/a
heat [hiːt] n calore m; (fig) ardore m;
fuoco; (Sport: also: **qualifying ~**) prova
eliminatoria ▷ vt scaldare; **heat up** vi
(liquids) scaldarsi; (room) riscaldarsi ▷ vt
riscaldare; **heated** adj riscaldato/a;
(argument) acceso/a; **heater** n radiatore m;
(stove) stufa
heather ['hɛðər] n erica
heating ['hiːtɪŋ] n riscaldamento
heatwave ['hiːtweɪv] n ondata di caldo
heaven ['hɛvn] n paradiso, cielo; **heavenly**
adj divino/a, celeste
heavily ['hɛvɪlɪ] adv pesantemente; (drink,
smoke) molto
heavy ['hɛvɪ] adj pesante; (sea) grosso/a;
(rain) forte; (weather) afoso/a; (drinker,
smoker) gran (before noun)

Hebrew ['hi:bru:] *adj* ebreo/a ▷ *n* (*Ling*) ebraico

hectare ['hɛktɑ:'] *n* (BRIT) ettaro

hectic ['hɛktɪk] *adj* movimentato/a

he'd [hi:d] = **he would; he had**

hedge [hɛdʒ] *n* siepe *f* ▷ *vi* essere elusivo/a; **to ~ one's bets** (*fig*) coprirsi dai rischi

hedgehog ['hɛdʒhɔg] *n* riccio

heed [hi:d] *vt* (*also*: **take ~ of**) badare a, far conto di

heel [hi:l] *n* (*Anat*) calcagno; (*of shoe*) tacco ▷ *vt* (*shoe*) rifare i tacchi a

hefty ['hɛftɪ] *adj* (*person*) solido/a; (*parcel*) pesante; (*piece, price, profit*) grosso/a

height [haɪt] *n* altezza; (*high ground*) altura; (*fig: of glory*) apice *m*; (: *of stupidity*) colmo; **heighten** *vt* (*fig*) accrescere

heir [ɛə'] *n* erede *m*; **heiress** *n* erede *f*

held [hɛld] *pt, pp of* **hold**

helicopter ['hɛlɪkɔptə'] *n* elicottero

hell [hɛl] *n* inferno; **oh ~!** (*col*) porca miseria!, accidenti!

he'll [hi:l] = **he will; he shall**

hello [hə'ləu] *excl* buon giorno!; ciao! (*to sb one addresses as "tu"*); (*surprise*) ma guarda!

helmet ['hɛlmɪt] *n* casco

help [hɛlp] *n* aiuto; (*charwoman*) donna di servizio ▷ *vt* aiutare; **~!** aiuto!; **can you ~ me?** può aiutarmi?; **~ yourself (to bread)** si serva (del pane); **he can't ~ it** non ci può far niente; **help out** *vi* aiutare ▷ *vt*: **to ~ sb out** aiutare qn; **helper** *n* aiutante *m/f*, assistente *m/f*; **helpful** *adj* di grande aiuto; (*useful*) utile; **helping** *n* porzione *f*; **helpless** *adj* impotente; debole; **helpline** *n* ≈ telefono amico; (*Comm*) servizio *m* informazioni *inv* (*a pagamento*)

hem [hɛm] *n* orlo ▷ *vt* fare l'orlo a

hemisphere ['hɛmɪsfɪə'] *n* emisfero

hemorrhage ['hɛmərɪdʒ] *n* (US) = **haemorrhage**

hemorrhoids ['hɛmərɔɪdz] *npl* (US) = **haemorrhoids**

hen [hɛn] *n* gallina; (*female bird*) femmina

hence [hɛns] *adv* (*therefore*) dunque; **2 years ~** di qui a 2 anni

hen night *n* (*col*) addio al nubilato

hepatitis [hɛpə'taɪtɪs] *n* epatite *f*

her [hə:'] *pron* (*direct*) la, l' + *vowel*; (*indirect*) le; (*stressed, after prep*) lei ▷ *adj* il (la) suo/a, i (le) suoi (sue); *see also* **me; my**

herb [hə:b] *n* erba; **herbal** *adj* di erbe; **herbal tea** tisana

herd [hə:d] *n* mandria

here [hɪə'] *adv* qui, qua ▷ *excl* ehi!; **~!** (*at roll call*) presente!; **~ is, ~ are** ecco; **~ he/she is** eccolo/eccola

hereditary [hɪ'rɛdɪtrɪ] *adj* ereditario/a

heritage ['hɛrɪtɪdʒ] *n* eredità; (*of country, nation*) retaggio

hernia ['hə:nɪə] *n* ernia

hero ['hɪərəu] (*pl* **heroes**) *n* eroe *m*; **heroic** [hɪ'rəuɪk] *adj* eroico/a

heroin ['hɛrəuɪn] *n* eroina (*droga*)

heroine ['hɛrəuɪn] *n* eroina (*donna*)

heron ['hɛrən] *n* airone *m*

herring ['hɛrɪŋ] *n* aringa

hers [hə:z] *pron* il (la) suo/a, i (le) suoi (sue); *see also* **mine¹**

herself [hə:'sɛlf] *pron* (*reflexive*) si; (*emphatic*) lei stessa; (*after prep*) se stessa, sé; *see also* **oneself**

he's [hi:z] = **he is; he has**

hesitant ['hɛzɪtənt] *adj* esitante, indeciso/a

hesitate ['hɛzɪteɪt] *vi*: **to ~ (about/to do)** esitare (su/a fare); **hesitation** [hɛzɪ'teɪʃən] *n* esitazione *f*

heterosexual [hɛtərəu'sɛksjuəl] *adj, n* eterosessuale (*m/f*)

hexagon ['hɛksəgən] *n* esagono

hey [heɪ] *excl* ehi!

heyday ['heɪdeɪ] *n*: **the ~ of** i bei giorni di, l'età d'oro di

HGV *n abbr* = **heavy goods vehicle**

hi [haɪ] *excl* ciao!

hibernate ['haɪbəneɪt] *vi* ibernare

hiccough, hiccup ['hɪkʌp] *vi* singhiozzare

hid [hɪd] *pt of* **hide**

hidden ['hɪdn] *pp of* **hide**

hide [haɪd] (*pt* **hid**, *pp* **hidden**) *n* (*skin*) pelle *f* ▷ *vt*: **to ~ sth (from sb)** nascondere qc (a qn) ▷ *vi*: **to ~ (from sb)** nascondersi (da qn)

hideous ['hɪdɪəs] *adj* laido/a; orribile

hiding ['haɪdɪŋ] *n* (*beating*) bastonata; **to be in ~** (*concealed*) tenersi nascosto/a

hi-fi ['haɪ'faɪ] *adj, n abbr* (= **high fidelity**) hi-fi (*m*) *inv*

high [haɪ] *adj* alto/a; (*speed, respect, number*) grande; (*wind*) forte; (*voice*) acuto/a ▷ *adv* alto, in alto; **20m ~** alto/a 20m; **highchair** *n* seggiolone *m*; **high-class** *adj* (*neighbourhood*) elegante; (*hotel*) di prim'ordine; (*person*) di gran classe; (*food*) raffinato/a; **higher education** *n* istruzione *f* superiore *or* universitaria; **high heels** *npl* (*heels*) tacchi *mpl* alti; (*shoes*) scarpe *fpl* con i tacchi alti; **high jump** *n* (*Sport*) salto in alto; **highlands** *npl* zona montuosa; **the Highlands** le Highlands scozzesi; **highlight** *n* (*fig: of event*) momento culminante; (*in hair*) colpo di sole ▷ *vt* mettere in evidenza; **highlights** *npl* (*in hair*) colpi *mpl* di sole; **highlighter** *n* (*pen*) evidenziatore *m*; **highly** *adv* molto; **to speak highly of** parlare molto bene di; **highness** *n*: **Her Highness** Sua Altezza;

high-rise n (also: **high-rise block, high-rise building**) palazzone m; **high school** n scuola secondaria; (us) istituto d'istruzione secondaria; **high season** n (BRIT) alta stagione; **high street** n (BRIT) strada principale; **high-tech** (col) adj high-tech inv; **highway** ['haɪweɪ] n strada maestra; **Highway Code** n (BRIT) codice m della strada

hijack ['haɪdʒæk] vt dirottare; **hijacker** n dirottatore/trice

hike [haɪk] vi fare un'escursione a piedi ▷ n escursione f a piedi; **hiker** n escursionista m/f; **hiking** n escursioni fpl a piedi

hilarious [hɪ'lɛərɪəs] adj (behaviour, event) spassosissimo/a

hill [hɪl] n collina, colle m; (fairly high) montagna; (on road) salita; **hillside** n fianco della collina; **hill walking** n escursioni fpl in collina; **hilly** ['hɪlɪ] adj collinoso/a

him [hɪm] pron (direct) lo, l' + vowel; (indirect) gli; (stressed, after prep) lui; **himself** pron (reflexive) si; (emphatic) lui stesso; (after prep) se stesso, sé; see also **oneself**

hind [haɪnd] adj posteriore ▷ n cerva

hinder ['hɪndəʳ] vt ostacolare

hindsight ['haɪndsaɪt] n: with (the benefit of) ~ con il senno di poi

Hindu ['hɪnduː] n indù mf inv; **Hinduism** n (Rel) induismo

hinge [hɪndʒ] n cardine m ▷ vi (fig): to ~ on dipendere da

hint [hɪnt] n (suggestion) allusione f; (advice) consiglio; (sign) accenno ▷ vt: to ~ that lasciar capire che ▷ vi: to ~ at accennare a, alludere a

hip [hɪp] n anca, fianco

hippie ['hɪpɪ] n hippy mf inv

hippo ['hɪpəu] (pl hippos) n ippopotamo

hippopotamus (pl **hippopotamuses** or **hippopotami**) [hɪpə'pɔtəməs, -'pɔtəmaɪ] n ippopotamo

hippy ['hɪpɪ] n = **hippie**

hire ['haɪəʳ] vt (BRIT: car, equipment) noleggiare; (worker) assumere, dare lavoro a ▷ n nolo, noleggio; **for** ~ da nolo; (taxi) libero/a; **hire(d) car** n (BRIT) macchina a nolo; **hire purchase** n (BRIT) acquisto (or vendita) rateale

his [hɪz] adj, pron il (la) suo (sua), i (le) suoi (sue); see also **my; mine¹**

Hispanic [hɪs'pænɪk] adj ispanico/a

hiss [hɪs] vi fischiare; (cat, snake) sibilare

historian [hɪ'stɔːrɪən] n storico/a

historic(al) [hɪ'stɔrɪk(l)] adj storico/a

history ['hɪstərɪ] n storia

hit [hɪt] vt (pt, pp **hit**) colpire, picchiare; (knock against) battere; (reach: target) raggiungere; (collide with: car) urtare contro; (fig: affect) colpire; (find: problem) incontrare ▷ n colpo; (success, song) successo; **to ~ it off with sb** andare molto d'accordo con qn; **hit back** vi: to ~ back at sb restituire il colpo a qn

hitch [hɪtʃ] vt (fasten) attaccare; (also: ~ up) tirare su ▷ n (difficulty) intoppo, difficoltà f inv; to ~ a lift fare l'autostop; **hitch-hike** vi fare l'autostop; **hitch-hiker** n autostoppista m/f; **hitch-hiking** n autostop m

hi-tech ['haɪ'tɛk] adj high-tech inv

hitman ['hɪtmæn] n (col) sicario

HIV n abbr: **~-negative/-positive** adj sieronegativo/a/sieropositivo/a

hive [haɪv] n alveare m

hoard [hɔːd] n (of food) provviste fpl; (of money) gruzzolo ▷ vt ammassare

hoarse [hɔːs] adj rauco/a

hoax [həuks] n scherzo; falso allarme

hob [hɔb] n piastra (con fornelli)

hobble ['hɔbl] vi zoppicare

hobby ['hɔbɪ] n hobby m inv, passatempo

hobo ['həubəu] n (us) vagabondo

hockey ['hɔkɪ] n hockey m; **hockey stick** n bastone m da hockey

hog [hɔg] n maiale m ▷ vt (fig) arraffare; to **go the whole** ~ farlo fino in fondo

Hogmanay [hɔgmə'neɪ] n (SCOTTISH) ≈ San Silvestro

hoist [hɔɪst] n paranco ▷ vt issare

hold [həuld] (pt, pp **held**) vt tenere; (contain) contenere; (keep back) trattenere; (believe) mantenere; considerare; (possess) avere, possedere; detenere ▷ vi (withstand pressure) tenere; (be valid) essere valido/a ▷ n presa; (control): **to have a ~ over** avere controllo su; (Naut) stiva; **~ the line!** (Tel) resti in linea!; **to ~ one's own** (fig) difendersi bene; **to catch** or **get (a) ~ of** afferrare; **hold back** vt trattenere; (secret) tenere celato/a; **hold on** vi tener fermo; (wait) aspettare; **~ on!** (Tel) resti in linea!; **hold out** vt offrire ▷ vi (resist): **to ~ out (against)** resistere a; **hold up** vt (raise) alzare; (support) sostenere; (delay) ritardare; (rob) assaltare; **holdall** n (BRIT) borsone m; **holder** n (container) contenitore m; (of ticket, title) possessore (posseditrice); (of office etc) incaricato/a; (of record) detentore/trice

hole [həul] n buco, buca

holiday ['hɔlədɪ] n vacanza; (day off) giorno di vacanza; (public) giorno festivo; **to be on** ~ essere in vacanza; **holiday camp** n (BRIT) (also: **holiday centre**) ≈ villaggio (di vacanze); **holiday home** n seconda casa (per le vacanze); **holiday job** n (BRIT) ≈ lavoro estivo; **holiday-maker** n

(BRIT) villeggiante m/f; **holiday resort** n luogo di villeggiatura

Holland ['hɔlənd] n Olanda

hollow ['hɔləu] adj cavo/a; (container, claim) vuoto/a; (laugh) forzato/a; (sound) cavernoso/a ▷ n cavità f inv; (in land) valletta, depressione f; **hollow out** vt scavare

holly ['hɔlɪ] n agrifoglio

Hollywood ['hɔlɪwud] n Hollywood f

holocaust ['hɔləkɔːst] n olocausto

holy ['həulɪ] adj santo/a; (bread) benedetto/a, consacrato/a

home [həum] n casa; (country) patria; (institution) casa, ricovero ▷ cpd familiare; (cooking etc) casalingo/a; (Econ, Pol) nazionale, interno/a; (Sport) di casa ▷ adv a casa; in patria; (right in: nail etc) fino in fondo; **at ~** a casa; (in situation) a proprio agio; **to go** (or come) **~** tornare a casa (or in patria); **make yourself at ~** si metta a suo agio; **home address** n indirizzo di casa; **homeland** n patria; **homeless** adj senza tetto; spatriato/a; **homely** ['həumlɪ] adj semplice, alla buona; accogliente; **home-made** adj casalingo/a; **home match** n partita in casa; **Home Office** n (BRIT) ministero degli Interni; **home owner** n proprietario/a di casa; **home page** n (Comput) home page f inv; **Home Secretary** n (BRIT) ministro degli Interni; **homesick** adj: **to be homesick** avere la nostalgia; **home town** n città f inv natale; **homework** n compiti mpl (per casa)

homicide ['hɔmɪsaɪd] n (US) omicidio

homoeopathic, (US) **homeopathic** ['həumɪəu'pæθɪk] adj omeopatico/a

homoeopathy, (US) **homeopathy** [həumɪ'ɔpəθɪ] n omeopatia

homosexual [hɔməu'sɛksjuəl] adj, n omosessuale (m/f)

honest ['ɔnɪst] adj onesto/a; sincero/a; **honestly** adv onestamente; sinceramente; **honesty** n onestà

honey ['hʌnɪ] n miele m; **honeymoon** n luna di miele, viaggio di nozze; **honeysuckle** ['hʌnɪsʌkl] n (Bot) caprifoglio

Hong Kong ['hɔŋ'kɔŋ] n Hong Kong f

honorary ['ɔnərərɪ] adj onorario/a; (duty, title) onorifico/a

honour, (US) **honor** ['ɔnəʳ] vt onorare ▷ n onore m; **honourable**, (US) **honorable** adj onorevole; **honours degree** n (Scol) laurea (con corso di studi di 4 o 5 anni)

hood [hud] n cappuccio; (on cooker) cappa; (BRIT Aut) capote f; (US Aut) cofano

hoof (pl **hoofs** or **hooves**) [huːf, huːvz] n zoccolo

hook [huk] n gancio; (for fishing) amo ▷ vt uncinare; (dress) agganciare

hooligan ['huːlɪgən] n giovinastro, teppista m

hoop [huːp] n cerchio

hooray [huː'reɪ] excl = **hurrah**

hoot [huːt] vi (Aut) suonare il clacson; (siren) ululare; (owl) gufare

Hoover® ['huːvəʳ] n (BRIT) aspirapolvere m inv ▷ vt pulire con l'aspirapolvere

hooves [huːvz] npl of **hoof**

hop [hɔp] vi saltellare, saltare; (on one foot) saltare su una gamba

hope [həup] vt: **to ~ that/to do** sperare che/di fare ▷ vi sperare ▷ n speranza; **I ~ so/ not** spero di sì/no; **hopeful** adj (person) pieno/a di speranza; (situation) promettente; **hopefully** adv con speranza; **hopefully he will recover** speriamo che si riprenda; **hopeless** adj senza speranza, disperato/a; (useless) inutile

hops [hɔps] npl luppoli mpl

horizon [hə'raɪzn] n orizzonte m; **horizontal** [hɔrɪ'zɔntl] adj orizzontale

hormone ['hɔːməun] n ormone m

horn [hɔːn] n (Zool, Mus) corno; (Aut) clacson m inv

horoscope ['hɔrəskəup] n oroscopo

horrendous [hɔ'rɛndəs] adj orrendo/a

horrible ['hɔrɪbl] adj orribile, tremendo/a

horrid ['hɔrɪd] adj orrido/a; (person) odioso/a

horrific [hɔ'rɪfɪk] adj (accident) spaventoso/a; (film) orripilante

horrifying ['hɔrɪfaɪɪŋ] adj terrificante

horror ['hɔrəʳ] n orrore m; **horror film** n film m inv dell'orrore

hors d'œuvre [ɔː'dəːvrə] n antipasto

horse [hɔːs] n cavallo; **horseback: on horseback** adj, adv a cavallo; **horse chestnut** n ippocastano; **horsepower** n cavallo (vapore); **horse-racing** n ippica; **horseradish** n rafano; **horse riding** n (BRIT) equitazione f

hose [həuz] n (also: **~pipe**) tubo; (also: **garden ~**) tubo per annaffiare

hospital ['hɔspɪtl] n ospedale m

hospitality [hɔspɪ'tælɪtɪ] n ospitalità

host [həust] n ospite m; (Rel) ostia; (large number): **a ~ of** una schiera di

hostage ['hɔstɪdʒ] n ostaggio/a

hostel ['hɔstl] n ostello; (also: **youth ~**) ostello della gioventù

hostess ['həustɪs] n ospite f; (BRIT Aviat) hostess f inv

hostile ['hɔstaɪl] adj ostile

hostility [hɔ'stɪlɪtɪ] n ostilità f inv

hot [hɔt] adj caldo/a; (as opposed to only warm) molto caldo/a; (spicy) piccante; (fig) accanito/a; ardente; violento/a, focoso/a; **to be ~** (person) aver caldo; (thing) essere caldo/a; (Meteor) far caldo; **hot dog** n hot dog m inv

hotel [həʊˈtɛl] n albergo

hotspot [ˈhɒtspɒt] n (Comput: also: **wireless ~**) hotspot m inv Wi-Fi

hot-water bottle [hɔtˈwɔːtə-] n borsa dell'acqua calda

hound [haʊnd] vt perseguitare ⊳ n segugio

hour [ˈaʊəʳ] n ora; **hourly** adj (ad) ogni ora

house n [haʊs, ˈhaʊzɪz] casa; (Pol) camera; (Theat) sala; pubblico; spettacolo ⊳ vt [haʊz] (person) ospitare, alloggiare; **on the ~** (fig) offerto/a dalla casa; **household** n famiglia; casa; **householder** n padrone/a di casa; (head of house) capofamiglia m/f; **housekeeper** n governante f; **housekeeping** n (work) governo della casa; (also: **housekeeping money**) soldi mpl per le spese di casa; **housewife** n (irreg) massaia, casalinga; **house wine** n vino della casa; **housework** n faccende fpl domestiche

housing [ˈhaʊzɪŋ] n alloggio; **housing development**, (BRIT) **housing estate** n zona residenziale con case popolari e/o private

hover [ˈhɒvəʳ] vi (bird) librarsi; **hovercraft** n hovercraft m inv

how [haʊ] adv come; **~ are you?** come sta?; **~ do you do?** piacere!; **~ far is it to …?** quanto è lontano …?; **~ long have you been here?** da quanto tempo è qui?; **~ lovely!** che bello!; **~ many?** quanti/e?; **~ much?** quanto/a?; **~ many people/much milk?** quante persone/quanto latte?; **~ old are you?** quanti anni ha?

however [haʊˈɛvəʳ] adv in qualsiasi modo or maniera che; (+ adjective) per quanto + sub; (in questions) come ⊳ conj comunque, però

howl [haʊl] vi ululare; (baby, person) urlare

HP n abbr (BRIT) = **hire purchase**

hp abbr (Aut) = **horsepower**

HQ n abbr (= headquarters) Q.G.

hr abbr (= hour) h

hrs abbr (= hours) h

HTML n abbr (= hypertext markup language) HTML m inv

hubcap [ˈhʌbkæp] n coprimozzo

huddle [ˈhʌdl] vi: **~ together** rannicchiarsi l'uno contro l'altro

huff [hʌf] n: **in a ~** stizzito/a

hug [hʌg] vt abbracciare; (shore, kerb) stringere

huge [hjuːdʒ] adj enorme, immenso/a

hull [hʌl] n (of ship) scafo

hum [hʌm] vt (tune) canticchiare ⊳ vi canticchiare; (insect, plane, tool) ronzare

human [ˈhjuːmən] adj (irreg) umano/a ⊳ n essere m umano

humane [hjuːˈmeɪn] adj umanitario/a

humanitarian [hjuːmænɪˈtɛərɪən] adj umanitario/a

humanity [hjuːˈmænɪtɪ] n umanità

human rights npl diritti mpl dell'uomo

humble [ˈhʌmbl] adj umile, modesto/a ⊳ vt umiliare

humid [ˈhjuːmɪd] adj umido/a; **humidity** [hjuːˈmɪdɪtɪ] n umidità

humiliate [hjuːˈmɪlɪeɪt] vt umiliare; **humiliating** adj umiliante; **humiliation** [hjuːmɪlɪˈeɪʃən] n umiliazione f

hummus [ˈhuməs] n purè di ceci

humorous [ˈhjuːmərəs] adj umoristico/a; (person) buffo/a

humour, (US) **humor** [ˈhjuːməʳ] n umore m ⊳ vt assecondare

hump [hʌmp] n gobba

hunch [hʌntʃ] n (premonition) intuizione f

hundred [ˈhʌndrəd] num cento; **~s of people** centinaia fpl di persone; **hundredth** [-ɪdθ] num centesimo/a

hung [hʌŋ] pt, pp of **hang**

Hungarian [hʌŋˈgɛərɪən] adj ungherese ⊳ n ungherese m/f; (Ling) ungherese m

Hungary [ˈhʌŋgərɪ] n Ungheria

hunger [ˈhʌŋgəʳ] n fame f ⊳ vi: **to ~ for** desiderare ardentemente

hungry [ˈhʌŋgrɪ] adj affamato/a; **to be ~** aver fame

hunt [hʌnt] vt (seek) cercare; (Sport) cacciare ⊳ vi: **to ~ (for)** andare a caccia (di) ⊳ n caccia; **hunter** n cacciatore m; **hunting** n caccia

hurdle [ˈhəːdl] n (Sport, fig) ostacolo

hurl [həːl] vt lanciare con violenza

hurrah [huˈrɑː], **hurray** [huˈreɪ] excl urra!, evviva!

hurricane [ˈhʌrɪkən] n uragano

hurry [ˈhʌrɪ] n fretta ⊳ vi (also: **~ up**) affrettarsi ⊳ vt (also: **~ up**: person) affrettare; (: work) far in fretta; **to be in a ~** aver fretta; **hurry up** vi sbrigarsi

hurt [həːt] (pt, pp **hurt**) vt (cause pain to) far male a; (injure, fig) ferire ⊳ vi far male

husband [ˈhʌzbənd] n marito

hush [hʌʃ] n silenzio, calma ⊳ vt zittire

husky [ˈhʌskɪ] adj roco/a ⊳ n cane m eschimese

hut [hʌt] n rifugio; (shed) ripostiglio

hyacinth [ˈhaɪəsɪnθ] n giacinto

hydrangea [haɪˈdreɪndʒə] n ortensia

hydrofoil [ˈhaɪdrəfɔɪl] n aliscafo

hydrogen [ˈhaɪdrədʒən] n idrogeno

hygiene [ˈhaɪdʒiːn] n igiene f; **hygienic** [haɪˈdʒiːnɪk] adj igienico/a

hymn [hɪm] n inno; cantica

hype [haɪp] *n* (col) battage *m inv*
  pubblicitario
hyperlink ['haɪpəlɪŋk] *n* link *m inv*
  ipertestuale
hyphen ['haɪfn] *n* trattino
hypnotize ['hɪpnətaɪz] *vt* ipnotizzare
hypocrite ['hɪpəkrɪt] *n* ipocrita *m/f*
hypocritical [hɪpə'krɪtɪkl] *adj* ipocrita
hypothesis (*pl* **hypotheses**) [haɪ'pɔθɪsɪs,
  -siːz] *n* ipotesi *f inv*
hysterical [hɪ'stɛrɪkl] *adj* isterico/a
hysterics [hɪ'stɛrɪks] *npl* accesso di isteria;
  (*laughter*) attacco di riso

I [aɪ] *pron* io
ice [aɪs] *n* ghiaccio; (*on road*) gelo ▷ *vt* (*cake*)
  glassare ▷ *vi* (*also*: ~ **over**) ghiacciare;
  (*also*: ~ **up**) gelare; **iceberg** *n* iceberg *m inv*;
  ice cream *n* gelato; **ice cube** *n* cubetto
  di ghiaccio; **ice hockey** *n* hockey *m* su
  ghiaccio
Iceland ['aɪslənd] *n* Islanda; **Icelander** *n*
  islandese *m/f*; **Icelandic** [aɪs'lændɪk] *adj*
  islandese ▷ *n* (*Ling*) islandese *m*
ice: ice lolly *n* (BRIT) ghiacciolo; **ice rink**
  n pista di pattinaggio; **ice skating** *n*
  pattinaggio sul ghiaccio
icing ['aɪsɪŋ] *n* (*Culin*) glassa; **icing sugar**
  (BRIT) *n* zucchero a velo
icon ['aɪkɔn] *n* icona
icy ['aɪsɪ] *adj* ghiacciato/a; (*weather,
  temperature*) gelido/a
I'd [aɪd] = **I would; I had**
ID card *n* = **identity card**
idea [aɪ'dɪə] *n* idea
ideal [aɪ'dɪəl] *adj, n* ideale (*m*);
  ideally [aɪ'dɪəlɪ] *adv* perfettamente,
  assolutamente; **ideally the book
  should have ...** l'ideale sarebbe che il libro
  avesse ...
identical [aɪ'dɛntɪkl] *adj* identico/a
identification [aɪdɛntɪfɪ'keɪʃən] *n*
  identificazione *f*; **means of ~** carta
  d'identità
identify [aɪ'dɛntɪfaɪ] *vt* identificare
identity [aɪ'dɛntɪtɪ] *n* identità *f inv*;
  identity card *n* carta d'identità; **identity
  theft** *n* furto d'identità
ideology [aɪdɪ'ɔlədʒɪ] *n* ideologia
idiom ['ɪdɪəm] *n* idioma *m*; (*phrase*)
  espressione *f* idiomatica
idiot ['ɪdɪət] *n* idiota *m/f*
idle ['aɪdl] *adj* inattivo/a; (*lazy*) pigro/a,
  ozioso/a; (*unemployed*) disoccupato/a;

(*question, pleasures*) ozioso/a ▷ *vi* (*engine*) girare al minimo

idol ['aɪdl] *n* idolo

idyllic [ɪ'dɪlɪk] *adj* idillico/a

i.e. *abbr* (*that is*) cioè

if [ɪf] *conj* se; **if I were you ...** se fossi in te ..., io al tuo posto ...; **if so** se è così; **if not** se no; **if only** se solo *or* soltanto

ignite [ɪg'naɪt] *vt* accendere ▷ *vi* accendersi

ignition [ɪg'nɪʃən] *n* (*Aut*) accensione *f*; **to switch on/off the ~** accendere/spegnere il motore

ignorance ['ɪgnərəns] *n* ignoranza; **to keep sb in ~ of sth** tenere qn all'oscuro di qc

ignorant ['ɪgnərənt] *adj* ignorante; **to be ~ of** (*subject*) essere ignorante in; (*events*) essere ignaro/a di

ignore [ɪg'nɔ:ʳ] *vt* non tener conto di; (*person, fact*) ignorare

ill [ɪl] *adj* (*sick*) malato/a; (*bad*) cattivo/a ▷ *n* male *m*; **to take** *or* **be taken ~** ammalarsi; **to speak/think ~ of sb** parlar/pensar male di qn

I'll [aɪl] = **I will; I shall**

illegal [ɪ'li:gl] *adj* illegale

illegible [ɪ'lɛdʒɪbl] *adj* illeggibile

illegitimate [ɪlɪ'dʒɪtɪmət] *adj* illegittimo/a

ill health *n* problemi *mpl* di salute

illiterate [ɪ'lɪtərət] *adj* analfabeta, illetterato/a; (*letter*) scorretto/a

illness ['ɪlnɪs] *n* malattia

illuminate [ɪ'lu:mɪneɪt] *vt* illuminare

illusion [ɪ'lu:ʒən] *n* illusione *f*

illustrate ['ɪləstreɪt] *vt* illustrare

illustration [ɪlə'streɪʃən] *n* illustrazione *f*

IM *n* (= *instant messaging*) messaggeria istantanea

I'm [aɪm] = **I am**

image ['ɪmɪdʒ] *n* immagine *f*; (*public face*) immagine (pubblica)

imaginary [ɪ'mædʒɪnərɪ] *adj* immaginario/a

imagination [ɪmædʒɪ'neɪʃən] *n* immaginazione *f*, fantasia

imaginative [ɪ'mædʒɪnətɪv] *adj* immaginoso/a

imagine [ɪ'mædʒɪn] *vt* immaginare

imam [ɪ'mɑ:m] *n* imam *m inv*

imbalance [ɪm'bæləns] *n* squilibrio

imitate ['ɪmɪteɪt] *vt* imitare; **imitation** [ɪmɪ'teɪʃən] *n* imitazione *f*

immaculate [ɪ'mækjulət] *adj* immacolato/a; (*dress, appearance*) impeccabile

immature [ɪmə'tjuəʳ] *adj* immaturo/a

immediate [ɪ'mi:dɪət] *adj* immediato/a; **immediately** *adv* (*at once*) subito, immediatamente; **immediately next to** proprio accanto a

immense [ɪ'mɛns] *adj* immenso/a; enorme; **immensely** *adv* immensamente

immerse [ɪ'mə:s] *vt* immergere

immigrant ['ɪmɪgrənt] *n* immigrante *m/f*; (*already established*) immigrato/a; **immigration** [ɪmɪ'greɪʃən] *n* immigrazione *f*

imminent ['ɪmɪnənt] *adj* imminente

immoral [ɪ'mɔrl] *adj* immorale

immortal [ɪ'mɔ:tl] *adj, n* immortale (*m/f*)

immune [ɪ'mju:n] *adj*: **~ (to)** immune (da); **immune system** *n* sistema *m* immunitario

immunize ['ɪmjunaɪz] *vt* immunizzare

impact ['ɪmpækt] *n* impatto

impair [ɪm'pɛəʳ] *vt* danneggiare

impartial [ɪm'pɑ:ʃl] *adj* imparziale

impatience [ɪm'peɪʃəns] *n* impazienza

impatient [ɪm'peɪʃənt] *adj* impaziente; **to get** *or* **grow ~** perdere la pazienza

impeccable [ɪm'pɛkəbl] *adj* impeccabile

impending [ɪm'pɛndɪŋ] *adj* imminente

imperative [ɪm'pɛrətɪv] *adj* imperativo/a; necessario/a, urgente; (*voice*) imperioso/a

imperfect [ɪm'pə:fɪkt] *adj* imperfetto/a; (*goods etc*) difettoso/a ▷ *n* (*Ling: also*: **~ tense**) imperfetto

imperial [ɪm'pɪərɪəl] *adj* imperiale; (*measure*) legale

impersonal [ɪm'pə:sənl] *adj* impersonale

impersonate [ɪm'pə:səneɪt] *vt* spacciarsi per, fingersi; (*Theat*) imitare

impetus ['ɪmpɪtəs] *n* impeto

implant [ɪm'plɑ:nt] *vt* (*Med*) innestare; (*fig: idea, principle*) inculcare

implement *n* ['ɪmplɪmənt] attrezzo; (*for cooking*) utensile *m* ▷ *vt* ['ɪmplɪmɛnt] effettuare

implicate ['ɪmplɪkeɪt] *vt* implicare

implication [ɪmplɪ'keɪʃən] *n* implicazione *f*; **by ~** implicitamente

implicit [ɪm'plɪsɪt] *adj* implicito/a; (*complete*) completo/a

imply [ɪm'plaɪ] *vt* insinuare; suggerire

impolite [ɪmpə'laɪt] *adj* scortese

import *vt* [ɪm'pɔ:t] importare ▷ *n* ['ɪmpɔ:t] (*Comm*) importazione *f*

importance [ɪm'pɔ:tns] *n* importanza

important [ɪm'pɔ:tnt] *adj* importante; **it's not ~** non ha importanza

importer [ɪm'pɔ:təʳ] *n* importatore/trice

impose [ɪm'pəuz] *vt* imporre ▷ *vi*: **to ~ on sb** sfruttare la bontà di qn; **imposing** [ɪm'pəuzɪŋ] *adj* imponente

impossible [ɪm'pɔsɪbl] *adj* impossibile

impotent ['ɪmpətnt] *adj* impotente

impoverished [ɪm'pɔvərɪʃt] *adj* impoverito/a

impractical [ɪm'præktɪkl] *adj* non pratico/a

impress [ɪm'prɛs] vt impressionare; (*mark*) imprimere, stampare; **to ~ sth on sb** far capire qc a qn

impression [ɪm'prɛʃən] n impressione f; **to be under the ~ that** avere l'impressione che

impressive [ɪm'prɛsɪv] adj notevole

imprison [ɪm'prɪzn] vt imprigionare; **imprisonment** n imprigionamento

improbable [ɪm'prɔbəbl] adj improbabile; (*excuse*) inverosimile

improper [ɪm'prɔpər] adj scorretto/a; (*unsuitable*) inadatto/a, improprio/a; sconveniente, indecente

improve [ɪm'pruːv] vt migliorare ▷ vi migliorare; (*pupil etc*) fare progressi; **improvement** n miglioramento; progresso

improvise ['ɪmprəvaɪz] vt, vi improvvisare

impulse ['ɪmpʌls] n impulso; **to act on ~** agire d'impulso o impulsivamente; **impulsive** [ɪm'pʌlsɪv] adj impulsivo/a

🅞 **KEYWORD**

in [ɪn] prep **1** (*indicating place, position*) in; **in the house/garden** in casa/giardino; **in the box** nella scatola; **in the fridge** nel frigorifero; **I have it in my hand** ce l'ho in mano; **in town/the country** in città/ campagna; **in school** a scuola; **in here/ there** qui/lì dentro
2 (*with place names, of town, region, country*): **in London** a Londra; **in England** in Inghilterra; **in the United States** negli Stati Uniti; **in Yorkshire** nello Yorkshire
3 (*indicating time: during, in the space of*) in; **in spring/summer** in primavera/estate; **in 1988** nel 1988; **in May** in o a maggio; **I'll see you in July** ci vediamo a luglio; **in the afternoon** nel pomeriggio; **at 4 o'clock in the afternoon** alle 4 del pomeriggio; **I did it in 3 hours/days** l'ho fatto in 3 ore/giorni; **I'll see you in 2 weeks** or **in 2 weeks' time** ci vediamo tra 2 settimane
4 (*indicating manner etc*) a; **in a loud/soft voice** a voce alta/bassa; **in pencil** a matita; **in English/French** in inglese/francese; **the boy in the blue shirt** il ragazzo con la camicia blu
5 (*indicating circumstances*): **in the sun** al sole; **in the shade** all'ombra; **in the rain** sotto la pioggia; **a rise in prices** un aumento dei prezzi
6 (*indicating mood, state*): **in tears** in lacrime; **in anger** per la rabbia; **in despair** disperato/a; **in good condition** in buono stato, in buone condizioni; **to live in luxury** vivere nel lusso

7 (*with ratios, numbers*): **1 in 10** 1 su 10; **20 pence in the pound** 20 pence per sterlina; **they lined up in twos** si misero in fila per due
8 (*referring to people, works*) in; **the disease is common in children** la malattia è comune nei bambini; **in (the works of) Dickens** in Dickens
9 (*indicating profession etc*) in; **to be in teaching** fare l'insegnante, insegnare; **to be in publishing** lavorare nell'editoria
10 (*after superlative*) di; **the best in the class** il migliore della classe
11 (*with present participle*): **in saying this** dicendo questo, nel dire questo
▷ adv: **to be in** (*person: at home, work*) esserci; (*train, ship, plane*) essere arrivato/a; (*in fashion*) essere di moda; **to ask sb in** invitare qn ad entrare; **to run/limp** etc **in** entrare di corsa/zoppicando etc
▷ n: **the ins and outs of the problem** tutti gli aspetti del problema

inability [ɪnə'bɪlɪtɪ] n incapacità

inaccurate [ɪn'ækjurət] adj inesatto/a; impreciso/a

inadequate [ɪn'ædɪkwət] adj insufficiente

inadvertently [ɪnəd'vəːtntlɪ] adv senza volerlo

inappropriate [ɪnə'prəuprɪət] adj non adatto/a; (*word, expression*) improprio/a

inaugurate [ɪ'nɔːgjureɪt] vt inaugurare; (*president, official*) insediare

Inc. abbr (us: = incorporated) S.A.

incapable [ɪn'keɪpəbl] adj: **~ (of doing sth)** incapace (di fare qc)

incense n ['ɪnsɛns] incenso ▷ vt [ɪn'sɛns] (*anger*) infuriare

incentive [ɪn'sɛntɪv] n incentivo

inch [ɪntʃ] n pollice m (= 25 mm; 12 in a foot); **within an ~ of** a un pelo da; **he wouldn't give an ~** (fig) non ha ceduto di un millimetro

incidence ['ɪnsɪdns] n (of crime, disease) incidenza

incident ['ɪnsɪdnt] n incidente m; (in book) episodio

incidentally [ɪnsɪ'dɛntəlɪ] adv (by the way) a proposito

inclination [ɪnklɪ'neɪʃən] n inclinazione f

incline n ['ɪnklaɪn] pendenza, pendio ▷ vt [ɪn'klaɪn] inclinare ▷ vi (*surface*) essere inclinato/a; **to be ~d to do** tendere a fare; essere propenso/a a fare

include [ɪn'kluːd] vt includere, comprendere; **including** prep compreso/a, incluso/a; **inclusion** [ɪn'kluːʒən] n inclusione f; **inclusive** [ɪn'kluːsɪv] adj incluso/a, compreso/a; **inclusive of tax** etc tasse etc comprese

income ['ɪnkʌm] n reddito; **income support** n (BRIT) sussidio di indigenza or povertà; **income tax** n imposta sul reddito

incoming ['ɪnkʌmɪŋ] adj (passengers, flight, mail) in arrivo; (government, tenant) subentrante; **~ tide** marea montante

incompatible [ɪnkəm'pætɪbl] adj incompatibile

incompetence [ɪn'kɔmpɪtns] n incompetenza, incapacità

incompetent [ɪn'kɔmpɪtnt] adj incompetente, incapace

incomplete [ɪnkəm'pli:t] adj incompleto/a

inconsistent [ɪnkən'sɪstnt] adj incoerente; **~ with** in contraddizione con

inconvenience [ɪnkən'vi:njəns] n inconveniente m; (trouble) disturbo ▷ vt disturbare

inconvenient [ɪnkən'vi:njənt] adj scomodo/a

incorporate [ɪn'kɔːpəreɪt] vt incorporare; (contain) contenere

incorrect [ɪnkə'rɛkt] adj scorretto/a; (statement) inesatto/a

increase n ['ɪnkriːs] aumento ▷ vi [ɪn'kriːs] aumentare; **increasingly** adv sempre più

incredible [ɪn'krɛdɪbl] adj incredibile; **incredibly** adv incredibilmente

incur [ɪn'kəːʳ] vt (expenses) incorrere; (debt) contrarre; (loss) subire; (anger, risk) esporsi a

indecent [ɪn'diːsnt] adj indecente

indeed [ɪn'diːd] adv infatti; veramente; **yes ~!** certamente!

indefinitely [ɪn'dɛfɪnɪtlɪ] adv (wait) indefinitamente

independence [ɪndɪ'pɛndns] n indipendenza; **Independence Day** n (US) vedi nota **"Independence Day"**

independent [ɪndɪ'pɛndnt] adj indipendente; **independent school** n (BRIT) istituto scolastico indipendente che si autofinanzia

index ['ɪndɛks] n (pl **indexes**: in book) indice m; (: in library etc) catalogo; (pl **indices**: ratio, sign) indice m

India ['ɪndɪə] n India; **Indian** adj, n indiano/a

indicate ['ɪndɪkeɪt] vt indicare; **indication** [ɪndɪ'keɪʃən] n indicazione f, segno; **indicative** [ɪn'dɪkətɪv] adj: **indicative of** indicativo/a di ▷ n (Ling) indicativo; **to be indicative of sth** essere indicativo/a or un indice di qc; **indicator** ['ɪndɪkeɪtəʳ] n (Aut) indicatore m di direzione, freccia

indices ['ɪndɪsiːz] npl of **index**

indict [ɪn'daɪt] vt accusare; **indictment** [ɪn'daɪtmənt] n accusa

indifference [ɪn'dɪfrəns] n indifferenza

indifferent [ɪn'dɪfrənt] adj indifferente; (poor) mediocre

indigenous [ɪn'dɪdʒɪnəs] adj indigeno/a

indigestion [ɪndɪ'dʒɛstʃən] n indigestione f

indignant [ɪn'dɪgnənt] adj: **~ (at sth/with sb)** indignato/a (per qc/contro qn)

indirect [ɪndɪ'rɛkt] adj indiretto/a

indispensable [ɪndɪ'spɛnsəbl] adj indispensabile

individual [ɪndɪ'vɪdjuəl] n individuo ▷ adj individuale; (characteristic) particolare, originale; **individually** adv singolarmente, uno/a per uno/a

Indonesia [ɪndəu'niːzɪə] n Indonesia

indoor ['ɪndɔːʳ] adj da interno; (plant) d'appartamento; (swimming pool) coperto/a; (sport, games) fatto/a al coperto; **indoors** [ɪn'dɔːz] adv all'interno

induce [ɪn'djuːs] vt persuadere; (bring about, Med) provocare

indulge [ɪn'dʌldʒ] vt (whim) compiacere, soddisfare; (child) viziare ▷ vi: **to ~ in sth** concedersi qc; abbandonarsi a qc; **indulgent** adj indulgente

industrial [ɪn'dʌstrɪəl] adj industriale; (injury) sul lavoro; **industrial estate** (BRIT) n zona industriale; **industrialist** [ɪn'dʌstrɪəlɪst] n industriale m; **industrial park** n (US) zona industriale

industry ['ɪndəstrɪ] n industria; (diligence) operosità

inefficient [ɪnɪ'fɪʃənt] adj inefficiente

inequality [ɪnɪ'kwɔlɪtɪ] n ineguaglianza

inevitable [ɪn'ɛvɪtəbl] adj inevitabile; **inevitably** adv inevitabilmente

inexpensive [ɪnɪk'spɛnsɪv] adj poco costoso/a

inexperienced [ɪnɪk'spɪərɪənst] adj inesperto/a, senza esperienza

inexplicable [ɪnɪk'splɪkəbl] adj inesplicabile

infamous ['ɪnfəməs] adj infame

infant ['ɪnfənt] n bambino/a
infantry ['ɪnfəntrɪ] n fanteria
infant school n (BRIT) scuola elementare (per bambini dall'età di 5 a 7 anni)
infect [ɪn'fɛkt] vt infettare; **infection** [ɪn'fɛkʃən] n infezione f; **infectious** [ɪn'fɛkʃəs] adj (disease) infettivo/a, contagioso/a; (person, laughter, enthusiasm) contagioso/a
infer [ɪn'fəːʳ] vt: to ~ (from) dedurre (da), concludere (da)
inferior [ɪn'fɪərɪəʳ] adj inferiore; (goods) di qualità scadente ▷ n inferiore m/f; (in rank) subalterno/a
infertile [ɪn'fəːtaɪl] adj sterile
infertility [ɪnfəː'tɪlɪtɪ] n sterilità
infested [ɪn'fɛstɪd] adj: ~ (with) infestato/a (di)
infinite ['ɪnfɪnɪt] adj infinito/a; **infinitely** adv infinitamente
infirmary [ɪn'fəːmərɪ] n ospedale m; (in school, factory) infermeria
inflamed [ɪn'fleɪmd] adj infiammato/a
inflammation [ɪnflə'meɪʃən] n infiammazione f
inflatable [ɪn'fleɪtəbl] adj gonfiabile
inflate [ɪn'fleɪt] vt (tyre, balloon) gonfiare; (fig) esagerare; gonfiare; **inflation** [ɪn'fleɪʃən] n (Econ) inflazione f
inflexible [ɪn'flɛksɪbl] adj inflessibile, rigido/a
inflict [ɪn'flɪkt] vt: to ~ on infliggere a
influence ['ɪnfluəns] n influenza ▷ vt influenzare; **under the ~ of alcohol** sotto l'influenza or l'effetto dell'alcool; **influential** [ɪnflu'ɛnʃl] adj influente
influx ['ɪnflʌks] n afflusso
info ['ɪnfəu] n (col) = **information**
inform [ɪn'fɔːm] vt: to ~ sb (of) informare qn (di) ▷ vi: to ~ on sb denunciare qn
informal [ɪn'fɔːml] adj informale; (announcement, invitation) non ufficiale
information [ɪnfə'meɪʃən] n informazioni fpl; particolari mpl; **a piece of ~** un'informazione; **information office** n ufficio m informazioni inv; **information technology** n informatica
informative [ɪn'fɔːmətɪv] adj istruttivo/a
infra-red [ɪnfrə'rɛd] adj infrarosso/a
infrastructure ['ɪnfrəstrʌktʃəʳ] n infrastruttura
infrequent [ɪn'friːkwənt] adj infrequente, raro/a
infuriate [ɪn'fjuərɪeɪt] vt rendere furioso/a
infuriating [ɪn'fjuərɪeɪtɪŋ] adj molto irritante
ingenious [ɪn'dʒiːnjəs] adj ingegnoso/a
ingredient [ɪn'griːdɪənt] n ingrediente m; elemento

inhabit [ɪn'hæbɪt] vt abitare; **inhabitant** [ɪn'hæbɪtnt] n abitante m/f
inhale [ɪn'heɪl] vt inalare ▷ vi (in smoking) aspirare; **inhaler** n inalatore m
inherent [ɪn'hɪərənt] adj: ~ (in or to) inerente (a)
inherit [ɪn'hɛrɪt] vt ereditare; **inheritance** n eredità
inhibit [ɪn'hɪbɪt] vt (Psych) inibire; **inhibition** [ɪnhɪ'bɪʃən] n inibizione f
initial [ɪ'nɪʃl] adj iniziale ▷ n iniziale f ▷ vt siglare; **initials** npl (of name) iniziali fpl; (as signature) sigla; **initially** adv inizialmente, all'inizio
initiate [ɪ'nɪʃɪeɪt] vt (start) avviare; intraprendere; iniziare; (person) iniziare; **to ~ sb into a secret** mettere qn a parte di un segreto; **to ~ proceedings against sb** (Law) intentare causa a or contro qn
initiative [ɪ'nɪʃətɪv] n iniziativa
inject [ɪn'dʒɛkt] vt (liquid) iniettare; (person) fare un'iniezione a; (money): **to ~ sb with sth** fare a qn un'iniezione di qc; **to ~ into** immettere in; **injection** [ɪn'dʒɛkʃən] n iniezione f, puntura
injure ['ɪndʒəʳ] vt ferire; (damage: reputation etc) nuocere a; **injured** adj ferito/a; **injury** ['ɪndʒərɪ] n ferita
injustice [ɪn'dʒʌstɪs] n ingiustizia
ink [ɪŋk] n inchiostro; **ink-jet printer** ['ɪŋkdʒɛt-] n stampante f a getto d'inchiostro
inland adj ['ɪnlənd] interno/a ▷ adv [ɪn'lænd] all'interno; **Inland Revenue** n (BRIT) Fisco
in-laws ['ɪnlɔːz] npl suoceri mpl; famiglia del marito (or della moglie)
inmate ['ɪnmeɪt] n (in prison) carcerato/a; (in asylum) ricoverato/a
inn [ɪn] n locanda
inner ['ɪnəʳ] adj interno/a, interiore; **inner city** n centro di una zona urbana
inning ['ɪnɪŋ] n (US Baseball) ripresa; **~s** (Cricket) turno di battuta
innocence ['ɪnəsns] n innocenza
innocent ['ɪnəsnt] adj innocente
innovation [ɪnəu'veɪʃən] n innovazione f
innovative ['ɪnəu'veɪtɪv] adj innovativo/a
in-patient ['ɪnpeɪʃənt] n ricoverato/a
input ['ɪnput] n input m
inquest ['ɪnkwɛst] n inchiesta
inquire [ɪn'kwaɪəʳ] vi informarsi ▷ vt domandare, informarsi di or su; **inquiry** n domanda; (Law) indagine f, investigazione f; **"inquiries"** "informazioni"
ins. abbr = **inches**
insane [ɪn'seɪn] adj matto/a, pazzo/a; (Med) alienato/a

insanity [ɪn'sænɪtɪ] n follia; (Med) alienazione f mentale

insect ['ɪnsɛkt] n insetto; **insect repellent** n insettifugo

insecure [ɪnsɪ'kjuəʳ] adj malsicuro/a; (person) insicuro/a

insecurity [ɪnsɪ'kjuərɪtɪ] n mancanza di sicurezza

insensitive [ɪn'sɛnsɪtɪv] adj insensibile

insert [ɪn'sə:t] vt inserire, introdurre

inside ['ɪn'saɪd] n interno, parte f interiore ▷ adj interno/a, interiore ▷ adv dentro, all'interno ▷ prep dentro, all'interno di; (of time): ~ 10 minutes entro 10 minuti; **insides** npl (col) ventre m; ~ **out** adv alla rovescia; **to turn sth ~ out** rivoltare qc; **to know sth ~ out** conoscere qc a fondo; **inside lane** n (Aut) corsia di marcia

insight ['ɪnsaɪt] n acume m, perspicacia; (glimpse, idea) percezione f

insignificant [ɪnsɪg'nɪfɪknt] adj insignificante

insincere [ɪnsɪn'sɪəʳ] adj insincero/a

insist [ɪn'sɪst] vi insistere; **to ~ on doing** insistere per fare; **to ~ that** insistere perché + sub; (claim) sostenere che; **insistent** adj insistente

insomnia [ɪn'sɔmnɪə] n insonnia

inspect [ɪn'spɛkt] vt ispezionare; (BRIT: ticket) controllare; **inspection** [ɪn'spɛkʃən] n ispezione f, controllo; **inspector** n ispettore/trice; (BRIT: on buses, trains) controllore m

inspiration [ɪnspə'reɪʃən] n ispirazione f; **inspire** [ɪn'spaɪəʳ] vt ispirare; **inspiring** adj stimolante

instability [ɪnstə'bɪlɪtɪ] n instabilità

install [ɪn'stɔ:l], (us) **instal** vt installare; **installation** [ɪnstə'leɪʃən] n installazione f

instalment, (us) **installment** [ɪn'stɔ:lmənt] n rata; (of TV serial etc) puntata; **in ~s** (pay) a rate; (receive) una parte per volta; (publication) a fascicoli

instance ['ɪnstəns] n esempio, caso; **for ~** per or ad esempio; **in the first ~** in primo luogo

instant ['ɪnstənt] n istante m, attimo ▷ adj immediato/a; urgente; (coffee, food) in polvere; **instantly** adv immediatamente, subito; **instant messaging** n messaggeria istantanea

instead [ɪn'stɛd] adv invece; ~ **of** invece di

instinct ['ɪnstɪŋkt] n istinto; **instinctive** adj istintivo/a

institute ['ɪnstɪtju:t] n istituto ▷ vt istituire, stabilire; (inquiry) avviare; (proceedings) iniziare

institution [ɪnstɪ'tju:ʃən] n istituzione f; istituto (d'istruzione); istituto (psichiatrico)

instruct [ɪn'strʌkt] vt: **to ~ sb in sth** insegnare qc a qn; **to ~ sb to do** dare ordini a qn di fare; **instruction** [ɪn'strʌkʃən] n istruzione f; **instructions (for use)** istruzioni per l'uso; **instructor** n istruttore/trice; (for skiing) maestro/a

instrument ['ɪnstrumənt] n strumento; **instrumental** [ɪnstru'mɛntl] adj (Mus) strumentale; **to be instrumental in sth/ in doing sth** contribuire fattivamente a qc/a fare qc

insufficient [ɪnsə'fɪʃənt] adj insufficiente

insulate ['ɪnsjuleɪt] vt isolare; **insulation** [ɪnsju'leɪʃən] n isolamento

insulin ['ɪnsjulɪn] n insulina

insult n ['ɪnsʌlt] insulto, affronto ▷ vt [ɪn'sʌlt] insultare; **insulting** adj offensivo/a, ingiurioso/a

insurance [ɪn'ʃuərəns] n assicurazione f; **fire/life ~** assicurazione contro gli incendi/ sulla vita; **insurance company** n società di assicurazioni; **insurance policy** n polizza d'assicurazione

insure [ɪn'ʃuəʳ] vt assicurare

intact [ɪn'tækt] adj intatto/a

intake ['ɪnteɪk] n (Tech) immissione f; (of food) consumo; (BRIT: of pupils etc) afflusso

integral ['ɪntɪgrəl] adj integrale; (part) integrante

integrate ['ɪntɪgreɪt] vt integrare ▷ vi integrarsi

integrity [ɪn'tɛgrɪtɪ] n integrità

intellect ['ɪntəlɛkt] n intelletto; **intellectual** [ɪntə'lɛktjuəl] adj, n intellettuale (m/f)

intelligence [ɪn'tɛlɪdʒəns] n intelligenza; (Mil etc) informazioni fpl

intelligent [ɪn'tɛlɪdʒənt] adj intelligente

intend [ɪn'tɛnd] vt (gift etc): **to ~ sth for** destinare qc a; **to ~ to do** aver l'intenzione di fare

intense [ɪn'tɛns] adj intenso/a; (person) di forti sentimenti

intensify [ɪn'tɛnsɪfaɪ] vt intensificare

intensity [ɪn'tɛnsɪtɪ] n intensità

intensive [ɪn'tɛnsɪv] adj intensivo/a; **intensive care** n terapia intensiva; **intensive care unit** n reparto terapia intensiva

intent [ɪn'tɛnt] n intenzione f ▷ adj: ~ **(on)** intento/a (a), immerso/a (in); **to all ~s and purposes** a tutti gli effetti; **to be ~ on doing sth** essere deciso a fare qc

intention [ɪn'tɛnʃən] n intenzione f; **intentional** adj intenzionale, deliberato/a

interact [ɪntər'ækt] vi interagire; **interaction** [ɪntər'ækʃən] n azione f reciproca, interazione f; **interactive** adj (Comput) interattivo/a

intercept [ɪntə'sɛpt] vt intercettare; (person) fermare

interchange n ['ɪntətʃeɪndʒ] (exchange) scambio; (on motorway) incrocio pluridirezionale

intercourse ['ɪntəkɔːs] n rapporti mpl

interest ['ɪntrɪst] n interesse m; (Comm: stake, share) interessi mpl ▷ vt interessare; **interested** adj interessato/a; **to be interested in** interessarsi di; **interesting** adj interessante; **interest rate** n tasso di interesse

interface ['ɪntəfeɪs] n (Comput) interfaccia

interfere [ɪntə'fɪər] vi: **to ~ (in)** (quarrel, other people's business) immischiarsi (in); **to ~ with** (object) toccare; (plans, duty) interferire con; **interference** [ɪntə'fɪərəns] n interferenza

interim ['ɪntərɪm] adj provvisorio/a ▷ n: **in the ~** nel frattempo

interior [ɪn'tɪərɪər] n interno; (of country) entroterra ▷ adj interno/a; (minister) degli Interni; **interior design** n architettura d'interni

intermediate [ɪntə'miːdɪət] adj intermedio/a

intermission [ɪntə'mɪʃən] n pausa; (Theat, Cine) intermissione f, intervallo

intern vt [ɪn'təːn] internare ▷ n ['ɪntəːn] (US) medico interno

internal [ɪn'təːnl] adj interno/a; **Internal Revenue, Internal Revenue Service** n (US) Fisco

international [ɪntə'næʃənl] adj internazionale ▷ n (BRIT Sport) incontro internazionale

Internet ['ɪntənɛt] n: **the ~** Internet f; **Internet café** n cybercaffè m inv; **Internet Service Provider** n Provider m inv; **Internet user** n utente m/f Internet

interpret [ɪn'təːprɪt] vt interpretare ▷ vi fare da interprete; **interpretation** [ɪntəːprɪ'teɪʃən] n interpretazione f; **interpreter** n interprete m/f

interrogate [ɪn'tɛrəugeɪt] vt interrogare; **interrogation** [ɪntɛrəu'geɪʃən] n interrogazione f; (of suspect etc) interrogatorio

interrogative [ɪntə'rɔgətɪv] adj interrogativo/a ▷ n (Ling) interrogativo

interrupt [ɪntə'rʌpt] vt, vi interrompere; **interruption** [ɪntə'rʌpʃən] n interruzione f

intersection [ɪntə'sɛkʃən] n intersezione f; (of roads) incrocio

interstate ['ɪntərsteɪt] (US) n fra stati

interval ['ɪntəvl] n intervallo; **at ~s** a intervalli

intervene [ɪntə'viːn] vi (time) intercorrere; (event, person) intervenire

interview ['ɪntəvjuː] n (Radio, TV etc) intervista; (for job) colloquio ▷ vt intervistare; avere un colloquio con; **interviewer** n intervistatore/trice

intimate adj ['ɪntɪmət] intimo/a; (knowledge) profondo/a ▷ vt ['ɪntɪmeɪt] lasciar capire

intimidate [ɪn'tɪmɪdeɪt] vt intimidire, intimorire

intimidating [ɪn'tɪmɪdeɪtɪŋ] adj (sight) spaventoso/a; (appearance, figure) minaccioso/a

into ['ɪntu] prep dentro, in; **come ~ the house** entra in casa; **he worked late ~ the night** lavorò fino a tarda notte; **~ Italian** in italiano

intolerant [ɪn'tɔlərnt] adj: **~ (of)** intollerante (di)

intranet ['ɪntrənɛt] n Intranet f

intransitive [ɪn'trænsɪtɪv] adj intransitivo/a

intricate ['ɪntrɪkət] adj intricato/a, complicato/a

intrigue [ɪn'triːg] n intrigo ▷ vt affascinare; **intriguing** adj affascinante

introduce [ɪntrə'djuːs] vt introdurre; **to ~ sb (to sb)** presentare qn (a qn); **to ~ sb to** (pastime, technique) iniziare qn a; **introduction** [ɪntrə'dʌkʃən] n introduzione f; (of person) presentazione f; (to new experience) iniziazione f; **introductory** adj introduttivo/a

intrude [ɪn'truːd] vi (person) intromettersi; **to ~ on**; intromettersi in; **intruder** n intruso/a

intuition [ɪntjuː'ɪʃən] n intuizione f

inundate ['ɪnʌndeɪt] vt: **to ~ with** inondare di

invade [ɪn'veɪd] vt invadere

invalid n ['ɪnvəlɪd] malato/a; (with disability) invalido/a ▷ adj [ɪn'vælɪd] (not valid) invalido/a, non valido/a

invaluable [ɪn'væljuəbl] adj prezioso/a; inestimabile

invariably [ɪn'vɛərɪəblɪ] adv invariabilmente; sempre

invasion [ɪn'veɪʒən] n invasione f

invent [ɪn'vɛnt] vt inventare; **invention** [ɪn'vɛnʃən] n invenzione f; **inventor** n inventore m

inventory ['ɪnvəntrɪ] n inventario

inverted commas [ɪn'vəːtɪd-] npl (BRIT) virgolette fpl

invest [ɪn'vɛst] vt investire ▷ vi: **to ~ in** investire in

investigate [ɪn'vɛstɪgeɪt] vt investigare, indagare; (crime) fare indagini su; **investigation** [ɪnvɛstɪ'geɪʃən] n investigazione f; (of crime) indagine f

investigator [ɪnˈvɛstɪɡeɪtəʳ] n investigatore/trice; **a private ~** un investigatore privato, un detective

investment [ɪnˈvɛstmənt] n investimento

investor [ɪnˈvɛstəʳ] n investitore/trice; (shareholder) azionista m/f

invisible [ɪnˈvɪzɪbl] adj invisibile

invitation [ɪnvɪˈteɪʃən] n invito

invite [ɪnˈvaɪt] vt invitare; (opinions etc) sollecitare; **inviting** adj invitante, attraente

invoice [ˈɪnvɔɪs] n fattura ▷ vt fatturare

involve [ɪnˈvɔlv] vt (entail) richiedere, comportare; (associate): **to ~ sb (in)** implicare qn (in); coinvolgere qn (in); **involved** adj involuto/a, complesso/a; **to be involved in** essere coinvolto/a in; **involvement** n implicazione f; coinvolgimento

inward [ˈɪnwəd] adj (movement) verso l'interno; (thought, feeling) interiore, intimo/a ▷ adv verso l'interno

iPod® [ˈaɪpɔd] n iPod® m inv

IQ n abbr (= intelligence quotient) quoziente m d'intelligenza

IRA n abbr (= Irish Republican Army) I.R.A. f

Iran [ɪˈrɑːn] n Iran m; **Iranian** [ɪˈreɪnɪən] adj, n iraniano/a

Iraq [ɪˈrɑːk] n Iraq m; **Iraqi** adj, n iracheno/a

Ireland [ˈaɪələnd] n Irlanda

iris [ˈaɪrɪs, -ɪz] n (pl **irises**) iride f; (Bot) giaggiolo, iride

Irish [ˈaɪrɪʃ] adj irlandese ▷ npl: **the ~** gli Irlandesi; **Irishman** n (irreg) irlandese m; **Irish Sea** n: **the Irish Sea** il mar d'Irlanda; **Irishwoman** n (irreg) irlandese f

iron [ˈaɪən] n ferro; (for clothes) ferro da stiro ▷ adj di or in ferro ▷ vt (clothes) stirare

ironic(al) [aɪˈrɔnɪk(l)] adj ironico/a; **ironically** adv ironicamente

ironing [ˈaɪənɪŋ] n (act) stirare m; (clothes) roba da stirare; **ironing board** n asse f da stiro

irony [ˈaɪrənɪ] n ironia

irrational [ɪˈræʃənl] adj irrazionale

irregular [ɪˈrɛɡjuləʳ] adj irregolare

irrelevant [ɪˈrɛləvənt] adj non pertinente

irresistible [ɪrɪˈzɪstɪbl] adj irresistibile

irresponsible [ɪrɪˈspɔnsɪbl] adj irresponsabile

irrigation [ɪrɪˈɡeɪʃən] n irrigazione f

irritable [ˈɪrɪtəbl] adj irritabile

irritate [ˈɪrɪteɪt] vt irritare; **irritating** adj (person, sound etc) irritante; **irritation** [ɪrɪˈteɪʃən] n irritazione f

IRS n abbr (US) = **Internal Revenue Service**

is [ɪz] vb see **be**

ISDN n abbr (= Integrated Services Digital Network) ISDN f

Islam [ˈɪzlɑːm] n Islam m; **Islamic** [ɪzˈlæmɪk] adj islamico/a

island [ˈaɪlənd] n isola; **islander** n isolano/a

isle [aɪl] n isola

isn't [ˈɪznt] = **is not**

isolated [ˈaɪsəleɪtɪd] adj isolato/a

isolation [aɪsəˈleɪʃən] n isolamento

ISP n abbr (Comput: = internet service provider) provider m inv

Israel [ˈɪzreɪl] n Israele m; **Israeli** [ɪzˈreɪlɪ] adj, n israeliano/a

issue [ˈɪʃjuː] n questione f, problema m; (of banknotes etc) emissione f; (of newspaper etc) numero ▷ vt (statement) rilasciare; (rations, equipment) distribuire; (book) pubblicare; (banknotes, cheques, stamps) emettere; **at ~** in gioco, in discussione; **to take ~ with sb (over sth)** prendere posizione contro qn (riguardo a qc); **to make an ~ of sth** fare un problema di qc

IT n abbr = **information technology**

KEYWORD

it [ɪt] pron **1** (specific: subject) esso/a; (: direct object) lo (la), l'; (: indirect object) gli (le); **where's my book? — it's on the table** dov'è il mio libro? — è sulla tavola; **I can't find it** non lo (or la) trovo; **give it to me** dammelo (or dammela); **about/from/ of it** ne; **I spoke to him about it** gliene ho parlato; **what did you learn from it?** quale insegnamento ne hai tratto?; **I'm proud of it** ne sono fiero; **put the book in it** mettici il libro; **did you go to it?** ci sei andato?

2 (impers): **it's raining** piove; **it's Friday tomorrow** domani è venerdì; **it's 6 o'clock** sono le 6; **who is it? — it's me** chi è? — sono io

Italian [ɪˈtæljən] adj italiano/a ▷ n italiano/a; (Ling) italiano; **the ~s** gli Italiani

italic [ɪˈtælɪk] adj corsivo/a; **italics** npl corsivo

Italy [ˈɪtəlɪ] n Italia

ITC n abbr (BRIT: = Independent Television Commission) organo di controllo sulle reti televisive

itch [ɪtʃ] n prurito ▷ vi (person) avere il prurito; (part of body) prudere; **to be ~ing to do** avere una gran voglia di fare; **itchy** adj che prude; **my back is itchy** ho prurito alla schiena

it'd [ˈɪtd] = **it would**; **it had**

item [ˈaɪtəm] n articolo; (on agenda) punto; (also: **news ~**) notizia

itinerary [aɪˈtɪnərərɪ] n itinerario

it'll [ˈɪtl] = **it will**; **it shall**

its [ɪts] *adj* il (la) suo/a, i (le) suoi (sue)
it's [ɪts] = **it is; it has**
itself [ɪt'sɛlf] *pron* (*emphatic*) esso/a
stesso/a; (*reflexive*) si
ITV *n abbr* (BRIT: = *Independent Television*) rete
televisiva indipendente
I've [aɪv] = **I have**
ivory ['aɪvərɪ] *n* avorio
ivy ['aɪvɪ] *n* edera

j

jab [dʒæb] *vt* dare colpetti a; **to ~ sth into**
affondare *or* piantare qc dentro ▷ *n* (*Med:
col*) puntura
jack [dʒæk] *n* (*Aut*) cricco; (*Cards*) fante *m*
jacket ['dʒækɪt] *n* giacca; (*of book*)
copertura; **jacket potato** *n* patata cotta al
forno con la buccia
jackpot ['dʒækpɔt] *n* primo premio (in
denaro)
Jacuzzi® [dʒə'kuːzɪ] *n* vasca per
idromassaggio Jacuzzi®
jagged ['dʒægɪd] *adj* seghettato/a; (*cliffs
etc*) frastagliato/a
jail [dʒeɪl] *n* prigione *f* ▷ *vt* mandare in
prigione; **jail sentence** *n* condanna al
carcere
jam [dʒæm] *n* marmellata; (*also*: **traffic ~**)
ingorgo; (*col*) pasticcio ▷ *vt* (*passage etc*)
ingombrare, ostacolare; (*mechanism, drawer
etc*) bloccare; (*Radio*) disturbare con
interferenze ▷ *vi* incepparsi; **to ~ sth into**
forzare qc dentro; infilare qc a forza dentro
Jamaica [dʒə'meɪkə] *n* Giamaica
jammed [dʒæmd] *adj* (*door*) bloccato/a;
(*rifle, printer*) inceppato/a
Jan. *abbr* (= *January*) gen., genn.
janitor ['dʒænɪtər] *n* (*caretaker*) portiere *m*;
(: *Scol*) bidello
January ['dʒænjuərɪ] *n* gennaio
Japan [dʒə'pæn] *n* Giappone *m*; **Japanese**
[dʒæpə'niːz] *adj* giapponese ▷ *n* (*pl inv*)
giapponese *m/f*; (*Ling*) giapponese *m*
jar [dʒɑː] *n* (*container*) barattolo, vasetto
▷ *vi* (*sound*) stridere; (*colours etc*) stonare
jargon ['dʒɑːgən] *n* gergo
javelin ['dʒævlɪn] *n* giavellotto
jaw [dʒɔː] *n* mascella
jazz [dʒæz] *n* jazz *m*
jealous ['dʒɛləs] *adj* geloso/a; **jealousy** *n*
gelosia

jeans [dʒiːnz] npl (blue-)jeans mpl
Jello® [ˈdʒɛləʊ] n (US) gelatina di frutta
jelly [ˈdʒɛlɪ] n gelatina; **jellyfish** n medusa
jeopardize [ˈdʒɛpədaɪz] vt mettere in pericolo
jerk [dʒəːk] n sobbalzo, scossa; sussulto; (col) povero/a scemo/a ⊳ vt dare una scossa a ⊳ vi (vehicles) sobbalzare
Jersey [ˈdʒəːzɪ] n Jersey m
jersey [ˈdʒəːzɪ] n maglia; (fabric) jersey m
Jesus [ˈdʒiːzəs] n Gesù m
jet [dʒɛt] n (of gas, liquid) getto; (Aviat) aviogetto; **jet lag** n (problemi mpl dovuti allo) sbalzo dei fusi orari; **jet-ski** vi acquascooter m inv
jetty [ˈdʒɛtɪ] n molo
Jew [dʒuː] n ebreo
jewel [ˈdʒuːəl] n gioiello; **jeweller**, (US) **jeweler** n orefice m, gioielliere/a; **jeweller's shop** oreficeria, gioielleria; **jewellery**, (US) **jewelry** n gioielli mpl; **jewelry store** (US) oreficeria, gioielleria
Jewish [ˈdʒuːɪʃ] adj ebreo/a, ebraico/a
jigsaw [ˈdʒɪɡsɔː] n (also: **~ puzzle**) puzzle m inv
job [dʒɔb] n lavoro; (employment) impiego, posto; **that's not my ~** non è compito mio; **it's a good ~ that …** meno male che …; **just the ~!** proprio quello che ci vuole!; **job centre** (BRIT) n ufficio di collocamento; **jobless** adj senza lavoro, disoccupato/a
jockey [ˈdʒɔkɪ] n fantino, jockey m inv ⊳ vi: **to ~ for position** manovrare per una posizione di vantaggio
jog [dʒɔɡ] vt urtare ⊳ vi (Sport) fare footing, fare jogging; **to ~ along** trottare; (fig) andare avanti pian piano; **to ~ sb's memory** rinfrescare la memoria di qn; **jogging** n footing m, jogging m
join [dʒɔɪn] vt unire, congiungere; (become member of) iscriversi a; (meet) raggiungere; riunirsi a ⊳ vi (roads, rivers) confluire ⊳ n giuntura; **join in** vt fus unirsi a ⊳ vi partecipare; **join up** vi incontrarsi; (Mil) arruolarsi
joiner [ˈdʒɔɪnəʳ] n (BRIT) falegname m
joint [dʒɔɪnt] n (Tech) giuntura; giunto; (Anat) articolazione f, giuntura; (BRIT Culin) arrosto; (col: place) locale m; (: of cannabis) spinello ⊳ adj comune; **joint account** n (at bank etc) conto comune; **jointly** adv in comune, insieme
joke [dʒəʊk] n scherzo; (funny story) barzelletta; (also: **practical ~**) beffa ⊳ vi scherzare; **to play a ~ on** fare uno scherzo a; **joker** n (Cards) matta, jolly m inv
jolly [ˈdʒɔlɪ] adj allegro/a, gioioso/a ⊳ adv (BRIT col) veramente, proprio
jolt [dʒəʊlt] n scossa, sobbalzo ⊳ vt urtare

Jordan [ˈdʒɔːdən] n (country) Giordania; (river) Giordano
journal [ˈdʒəːnl] n giornale m; (periodical) rivista; (diary) diario; **journalism** n giornalismo; **journalist** n giornalista m/f
journey [ˈdʒəːnɪ] n viaggio; (distance covered) tragitto; **how was your ~?** com'è andato il viaggio?; **the ~ takes two hours** il viaggio dura due ore
joy [dʒɔɪ] n gioia; **joyrider** [ˈdʒɔɪraɪdəʳ] n chi ruba una macchina per andare a farsi un giro; **joy stick** [ˈdʒɔɪstɪk] n (Aviat) barra di comando; (Comput) joystick m inv
Jr. abbr = **junior**
judge [dʒʌdʒ] n giudice m/f ⊳ vt giudicare
judo [ˈdʒuːdəʊ] n judo
jug [dʒʌɡ] n brocca, bricco
juggle [ˈdʒʌɡl] vi fare giochi di destrezza; **juggler** n giocoliere/a
juice [dʒuːs] n succo; **juicy** [ˈdʒuːsɪ] adj succoso/a
Jul. abbr (= July) lug., lu.
July [dʒuːˈlaɪ] n luglio
jumble [ˈdʒʌmbl] n miscuglio ⊳ vt (also: **~ up**, **~ together**) mischiare; **jumble sale** (BRIT) n ≈ vendita di beneficenza

jumbo [ˈdʒʌmbəʊ] adj: **~ jet** jumbo-jet m inv; **~ size** formato gigante
jump [dʒʌmp] vi saltare, balzare; (start) sobbalzare; (increase) rincarare ⊳ vt saltare ⊳ n salto, balzo; sobbalzo
jumper [ˈdʒʌmpəʳ] n (BRIT: pullover) maglione m; (US: pinafore dress) scamiciato
jump leads, (US) **jumper cables** npl cavi mpl per batteria
Jun. abbr = **junior**
junction [ˈdʒʌŋkʃən] n (BRIT: of roads) incrocio; (of rails) nodo ferroviario
June [dʒuːn] n giugno
jungle [ˈdʒʌŋɡl] n giungla
junior [ˈdʒuːnɪəʳ] adj, n: **he's ~ to me (by 2 years), he's my ~ (by 2 years)** è più giovane di me (di 2 anni); **he's ~ to me** (seniority) è al di sotto di me, ho più anzianità di lui; **junior high school** n (US) scuola media (da 12 a 15 anni); **junior school** n (BRIT) scuola elementare (da 8 a 11 anni)
junk [dʒʌŋk] n cianfrusaglie fpl; (cheap goods) robaccia; **junk food** n porcherie fpl

junkie ['dʒʌŋkɪ] n (col) drogato/a

junk mail n pubblicità f inv in cassetta

Jupiter ['dʒuːpɪtəʳ] n (planet) Giove m

jurisdiction [dʒuərɪs'dɪkʃən] n giurisdizione f; **it falls** or **comes within/outside our ~** è/non è di nostra competenza

jury ['dʒuərɪ] n giuria

just [dʒʌst] adj giusto/a ▷ adv: **he's ~ done it/left** lo ha appena fatto/è appena partito; **~ right** proprio giusto; **~ 2 o'clock** le 2 precise; **she's ~ as clever as you** è in gamba proprio quanto te; **~ as I arrived** proprio mentre arrivavo; **it was ~ before/enough/ here** era poco prima/appena assai/proprio qui; **it's ~ me** sono solo io; **~ missed/ caught** appena perso/preso; **~ listen to this!** senta un po' questo!; **it's ~ as well you didn't go** meno male che non ci sei andato

justice ['dʒʌstɪs] n giustizia

justification [dʒʌstɪfɪ'keɪʃən] n giustificazione f; (Typ) giustezza

justify ['dʒʌstɪfaɪ] vt giustificare

jut [dʒʌt] vi (also: **~ out**) sporgersi

juvenile ['dʒuːvənaɪl] adj giovane, giovanile; (court) dei minorenni; (books) per ragazzi ▷ n giovane m/f, minorenne m/f

K n abbr (= one thousand) mille ▷ abbr (= kilobyte) K

kangaroo [kæŋgə'ruː] n canguro

karaoke [kɑːrə'əʊkɪ] n karaoke m inv

karate [kə'rɑːtɪ] n karate m

kebab [kə'bæb] n spiedino

keel [kiːl] n chiglia; **on an even ~** (fig) in uno stato normale

keen [kiːn] adj (interest, desire) vivo/a; (eye, intelligence) acuto/a; (competition) serrato/a; (edge) affilato/a; (eager) entusiasta; **to be ~ to do** or **on doing sth** avere una gran voglia di fare qc; **to be ~ on sth** essere appassionato/a di qc; **to be ~ on sb** avere un debole per qn

keep (pt, pp **kept**) [kiːp, kɛpt] vt tenere; (hold back) trattenere; (feed: one's family etc) mantenere, sostentare; (a promise) mantenere; (chickens, bees, pigs etc) allevare ▷ vi (food) mantenersi; (remain: in a certain state or place) restare ▷ n (of castle) maschio; (food etc): **enough for his ~** abbastanza per vitto e alloggio; **to ~ doing sth** continuare a fare qc; fare qc di continuo; **to ~ sb from doing/sth from happening** impedire a qn di fare/che qc succeda; **to ~ sb busy/a place tidy** tenere qn occupato/a/un luogo in ordine; **to ~ sth to o.s.** tenere qc per sé; **to ~ sth (back) from sb** celare qc a qn; **to ~ time** (clock) andar bene; **keep away** vt: **to ~ sth/sb away from sb** tenere qc/qn lontano da qn ▷ vi: **to ~ away (from)** stare lontano (da); **keep back** vt (crowds, tears, money) trattenere ▷ vi tenersi indietro; **keep off** vt (dog, person) tenere lontano da ▷ vi stare alla larga; **~ your hands off!** non toccare!, giù le mani!; **"~ off the grass"** "non calpestare l'erba"; **keep on** vi: **to ~ on doing** continuare a fare; **to ~ on (about sth)** continuare a insistere (su qc); **keep out** vt tener fuori; **"~ out"** "vietato l'accesso"; **keep up** vt continuare, mantenere ▷ vi: **to ~ up with** tener dietro a, andare di pari passo con; (work etc) farcela a seguire; **keeper** n custode m/f, guardiano/a; **keeping** n (care) custodia; **in keeping with** in armonia con; in accordo con; **keeps** n: **for keeps** (col) per sempre

kennel ['kɛnl] n canile m; **kennels** npl canile m; **to put a dog in ~s** mettere un cane al canile

Kenya ['kɛnjə] n Kenia m

kept [kɛpt] pt, pp of **keep**

kerb [kə:b] n (BRIT) orlo del marciapiede

kerosene ['kɛrəsi:n] n cherosene m

ketchup ['kɛtʃəp] n ketchup m inv

kettle ['kɛtl] n bollitore m

key [ki:] n (gen, Mus) chiave f; (of piano, typewriter) tasto ▷ cpd chiave inv; **key in** vt (text) digitare; **keyboard** n tastiera; **keyhole** n buco della serratura; **keypad** n tastierino; **key ring** n portachiavi m inv

kg abbr (= kilogram) Kg

khaki ['kɑ:kɪ] adj, n cachi (m)

kick [kɪk] vt calciare, dare calci a; (col: habit etc) liberarsi di ▷ vi (horse) tirar calci ▷ n calcio; (col: thrill): **he does it for ~s** lo fa giusto per il piacere di farlo; **kick off** vi (Sport) dare il primo calcio; **kick-off** n (Sport) calcio d'inizio

kid [kɪd] n (col: child) ragazzino/a; (animal, leather) capretto ▷ vi (col) scherzare

kidnap ['kɪdnæp] vt rapire, sequestrare; **kidnapping** n sequestro (di persona)

kidney ['kɪdnɪ] n (Anat) rene m; (Culin) rognone m; **kidney bean** n fagiolo borlotto

kill [kɪl] vt uccidere, ammazzare ▷ n uccisione f; **killer** n uccisore m, killer m inv; assassino/a; **killing** n assassinio; (col): **to make a killing** fare un bel colpo

kiln [kɪln] n forno

kilo ['ki:ləu] n abbr chilo; **kilobyte** n (Comput) kilobyte m inv; **kilogram(me)** ['kɪləugræm] n chilogrammo; **kilometre**, (US) **kilometer** ['kɪləmi:tər] n chilometro; **kilowatt** ['kɪləuwɔt] n chilowatt m inv

kilt [kɪlt] n gonnellino scozzese

kin [kɪn] n see **next of kin**

kind [kaɪnd] adj gentile, buono/a ▷ n sorta, specie f; (species) genere m; **what ~ of ...?** che tipo di ...?; **to be two of a ~** essere molto simili; **in ~** (Comm) in natura

kindergarten ['kɪndəgɑ:tn] n giardino d'infanzia

kindly ['kaɪndlɪ] adj pieno/a di bontà, benevolo/a ▷ adv con bontà, gentilmente; **will you ~ ...** vuole ... per favore

kindness ['kaɪndnɪs] n bontà, gentilezza

king [kɪŋ] n re m inv; **kingdom** n regno, reame m; **kingfisher** n martin m inv pescatore

king-size(d) ['kɪŋsaɪz(d)] adj super inv; **king-size(d) bed** n letto king-size

kiosk ['ki:ɔsk] n edicola, chiosco; (BRIT: also: **telephone ~**) cabina (telefonica)

kipper ['kɪpər] n aringa affumicata

kiss [kɪs] n bacio ▷ vt baciare; **to ~ (each other)** baciarsi; **~ of life** respirazione f bocca a bocca

kit [kɪt] n equipaggiamento, corredo; (set of tools etc) attrezzi mpl; (for assembly) scatola di montaggio

kitchen ['kɪtʃɪn] n cucina

kite [kaɪt] n (toy) aquilone m

kitten ['kɪtn] n gattino/a, micino/a

kiwi ['ki:wi:], **kiwi fruit** n kiwi m inv

km abbr (= kilometre) km

km/h abbr (= kilometres per hour) km/h

knack [næk] n: **to have the ~ of** avere l'abilità di

knee [ni:] n ginocchio; **kneecap** n rotula

kneel [ni:l] vi (pt, pp knelt [nɛlt]) (also: **~ down**) inginocchiarsi

knelt [nɛlt] pt, pp of **kneel**

knew [nju:] pt of **know**

knickers ['nɪkəz] npl (BRIT) mutandine fpl

knife [naɪf] n (pl **knives**) coltello ▷ vt accoltellare, dare una coltellata a

knight [naɪt] n cavaliere m; (Chess) cavallo

knit [nɪt] vt fare a maglia ▷ vi lavorare a maglia; (broken bones) saldarsi; **to ~ one's brows** aggrottare le sopracciglia; **knitting** n lavoro a maglia; **knitting needle** n ferro (da calza); **knitwear** n maglieria

knives [naɪvz] npl of **knife**

knob [nɔb] n bottone m; manopola

knock [nɔk] vt colpire, urtare; (fig: col) criticare ▷ vi (at door etc): **to ~ at/on** bussare a ▷ n bussata; colpo, botta; **knock down** vt abbattere; **knock off** vi (col: finish) smettere (di lavorare) ▷ vt (from price) far abbassare; (col: steal) sgraffignare; **knock out** vt stendere; (Boxing) mettere K.O.; (defeat) battere; **knock over** vt (object) far cadere; (pedestrian) investire; **knockout** n (Boxing) knock out m inv ▷ cpd a eliminazione

knot [nɔt] n nodo ▷ vt annodare

know [nəu] vt (pt knew [nju:], pp known [nəun]) sapere; (person, author, place) conoscere; **to ~ how to do** sapere fare; **I don't ~** non lo so; **to ~ about** or **of sth/sb** conoscere qc/qn; **know-all** n sapientone/a; **know-how** n tecnica; pratica; **knowing** adj (look etc) d'intesa; **knowingly** adv (purposely)

consapevolmente; (*smile, look*) con aria d'intesa; **know-it-all** *n* (*US*) = **know-all**
knowledge ['nɔlɪdʒ] *n* consapevolezza; (*learning*) conoscenza, sapere *m*;
   knowledgeable *adj* ben informato/a
known [nəun] *pp of* **know**
knuckle ['nʌkl] *n* nocca
koala [kəu'ɑːlə] *n* (*also*: ~ **bear**) koala *m inv*
Koran [kɔ'rɑːn] *n* Corano
Korea [kə'riːə] *n* Corea; **Korean** *adj, n* coreano/a
kosher ['kəuʃəʳ] *adj* kasher *inv*
Kosovar, Kosovan ['kɔsəvaʳ, 'kɔsəvən] *adj* kosovaro/a
Kosovo ['kusəvəu] *n* Kosovo
Kremlin ['krɛmlɪn] *n*: **the ~** il Cremlino
Kuwait [ku'weɪt] *n* Kuwait *m*

L *abbr* (*BRIT*) = **learner**
l *abbr* (= *litre*) l
lab [læb] *n abbr* (= *laboratory*) laboratorio
label ['leɪbl] *n* etichetta, cartellino; (*brand: of record*) casa ▷ *vt* etichettare
labor *etc* ['leɪbəʳ] (*US*) = **labour** *etc*
laboratory [lə'bɔrətərɪ] *n* laboratorio
Labor Day *n* (*US*) festa del lavoro

  ◦ **LABOR DAY**
  ◦
  ◦ Negli Stati Uniti e nel Canada il *Labor Day*,
  ◦ la festa del lavoro, cade il primo lunedì
  ◦ di settembre, contrariamente a quanto
  ◦ accade nella maggior parte dei paesi
  ◦ europei dove tale celebrazione ha luogo il
  ◦ primo maggio.

labor union *n* (*US*) sindacato
Labour ['leɪbəʳ] *n* (*BRIT Pol: also:* **the ~ Party**) il partito laburista, i laburisti
labour, (*US*) **labor** ['leɪbəʳ] *n* (*task*) lavoro; (*workmen*) manodopera ▷ *vi*: **to ~ (at)** lavorare duro(a); **to be in ~** (*Med*) avere le doglie; **hard ~** lavori *mpl* forzati; **labourer,** (*US*) **laborer** ['leɪbərəʳ] *n* manovale *m*; **farm labourer** lavoratore *m* agricolo
lace [leɪs] *n* merletto, pizzo; (*of shoe etc*) laccio ▷ *vt* (*shoe: also:* **~ up**) allacciare
lack [læk] *n* mancanza ▷ *vt* mancare di; **through** *or* **for ~ of** per mancanza di; **to be ~ing** mancare; **to be ~ing in** mancare di
lacquer ['lækəʳ] *n* lacca
lacy ['leɪsɪ] *adj* (*like lace*) che sembra un pizzo
lad [læd] *n* ragazzo, giovanotto
ladder ['lædəʳ] *n* scala; (*BRIT: in tights*) smagliatura
ladle ['leɪdl] *n* mestolo

lady ['leɪdɪ] n signora; dama; **L~ Smith** lady Smith; **the ladies' (toilets)** i gabinetti per signore; **ladybird** ['leɪdɪbəːd], (US) **ladybug** ['leɪdɪbʌg] n coccinella

lag [læg] n (of time) lasso, intervallo ▷ vi (also: **~ behind**) trascinarsi ▷ vt (pipes) rivestire di materiale isolante

lager ['lɑːgəʳ] n lager m inv

lagoon [ləˈguːn] n laguna

laid [leɪd] pt, pp of **lay**

laid-back [leɪd'bæk] adj (col) rilassato/a, tranquillo/a

lain [leɪn] pp of **lie**

lake [leɪk] n lago

lamb [læm] n agnello

lame [leɪm] adj zoppo/a; (excuse etc) zoppicante

lament [ləˈmɛnt] n lamento ▷ vt lamentare, piangere

lamp [læmp] n lampada; **lamppost** ['læmppəust] (BRIT) n lampione m; **lampshade** ['læmpʃeɪd] n paralume m

land [lænd] n (as opposed to sea) terra (ferma); (country) paese m; (soil) terreno; suolo; (estate) terreni mpl, terre fpl ▷ vi (from ship) sbarcare; (Aviat) atterrare; (fig: fall) cadere ▷ vt (passengers) sbarcare; (goods) scaricare; **to ~ sb with sth** affibbiare qc a qn; **landing** n atterraggio; (of staircase) pianerottolo; **landing card** n carta di sbarco; **landlady** n padrona or proprietaria di casa; **landline** n telefono fisso; **landlord** n padrone m or proprietario di casa; (of pub etc) padrone m; **landmark** n punto di riferimento; (fig) pietra miliare; **landowner** ['lændəunəʳ] n proprietario/a terriero/a; **landscape** n paesaggio; **landslide** n (Geo) frana; (fig: Pol) valanga

lane [leɪn] n (in town) stradina; (Aut, in race) corsia; **"get in ~"** "immettersi in corsia"

language ['læŋgwɪdʒ] n lingua; (way one speaks) linguaggio; **bad ~** linguaggio volgare; **language laboratory** n laboratorio linguistico

lantern ['læntn] n lanterna

lap [læp] n (of track) giro; (of body) in or on one's **~** in grembo ▷ vt (also: **~ up**) papparsi, leccare ▷ vi (waves) sciabordare

lapel [ləˈpɛl] n risvolto

lapse [læps] n lapsus m inv; (longer) caduta ▷ vi (law, act) cadere; (ticket, passport, membership, contract) scadere; **to ~ into bad habits** pigliare cattive abitudini; **~ of time** spazio di tempo

laptop ['læptɔp] n (also: **~ computer**) laptop m inv

lard [lɑːd] n lardo

larder ['lɑːdəʳ] n dispensa

large [lɑːdʒ] adj grande; (person, animal) grosso/a; **at ~** (free) in libertà; (generally) in generale; nell'insieme; **largely** adv in gran parte; **large-scale** adj (map, drawing etc) in grande scala; (reforms, business activities) su vasta scala

lark [lɑːk] n (bird) allodola; (joke) scherzo, gioco

larrikin ['lærɪkɪn] n (AUST, NZ col) furfante m/f

laryngitis [lærɪn'dʒaɪtɪs] n laringite f

lasagne [ləˈzænjə] n lasagne fpl

laser ['leɪzəʳ] n laser m; **laser printer** n stampante f laser inv

lash [læʃ] n frustata; (also: **eye~**) ciglio ▷ vt frustare; (tie) legare; **to ~ to/ together** legare a insieme; **lash out** vi: **to ~ out (at** or **against sb/sth)** attaccare violentemente (qn/qc)

lass [læs] n ragazza

last [lɑːst] adj ultimo/a; (week, month, year) scorso/a, passato/a ▷ adv per ultimo ▷ vi durare; **~ week** la settimana scorsa; **~ night** ieri sera, la notte scorsa; **at ~** finalmente, alla fine; **~ but one** penultimo/a; **lastly** adv infine, per finire; **last-minute** adj fatto/a (or preso/a etc) all'ultimo momento

latch [lætʃ] n chiavistello; (automatic lock) serratura a scatto; **latch on to** vt fus (cling to: person) attaccarsi a, appiccicarsi a; (: idea) afferrare, capire

late [leɪt] adj (not on time) in ritardo; (far on in day etc) tardi inv; (former) ex; (dead) defunto/a ▷ adv tardi; (behind time, schedule) in ritardo; **sorry I'm ~** scusi il ritardo; **the flight is two hours ~** il volo ha due ore di ritardo; **it's too ~** è troppo tardi; **of ~** di recente; **in the ~ afternoon** nel tardo pomeriggio; **in ~ May** verso la fine di maggio; **latecomer** n ritardatario/a; **lately** adv recentemente; **later** ['leɪtəʳ] adj (date etc) posteriore; (version etc) successivo/a ▷ adv più tardi; **later on today** oggi più tardi; **latest** ['leɪtɪst] adj ultimo/a, più recente; **at the latest** al più tardi

lather ['lɑːðəʳ] n schiuma di sapone ▷ vt insaponare

Latin ['lætɪn] n latino ▷ adj latino/a; **Latin America** n America Latina; **Latin American** adj sudamericano/a

latitude ['lætɪtjuːd] n latitudine f; (fig) libertà d'azione

latter ['lætəʳ] adj secondo/a; più recente ▷ n: **the ~** quest'ultimo, il secondo

laugh [lɑːf] n risata ▷ vi ridere; **laugh at** vt fus (misfortune etc) ridere di; **laughter** n riso; risate fpl

launch [lɔːntʃ] n (of rocket, product etc) lancio; (of new ship) varo; (also: **motor ~**) lancia ▷ vt (rocket, product) lanciare; (ship, plan) varare; **launch into** vt fus lanciarsi in

launder [ˈlɔːndəʳ] vt lavare e stirare

Launderette® [lɔːnˈdrɛt], (US) **Laundromat®** [ˈlɔːndrəmæt] n lavanderia (automatica)

laundry [ˈlɔːndrɪ] n lavanderia; (clothes) biancheria; (: dirty) panni mpl da lavare

lava [ˈlɑːvə] n lava

lavatory [ˈlævətərɪ] n gabinetto

lavender [ˈlævəndəʳ] n lavanda

lavish [ˈlævɪʃ] adj copioso/a, abbondante; (giving freely): **~ with** prodigo/a di, largo/a in ▷ vt: **to ~ sth on sb/sth** colmare qn/qc di qc

law [lɔː] n legge f; **civil/criminal ~** diritto civile/penale; **lawful** adj legale, lecito/a; **lawless** adj senza legge

lawn [lɔːn] n tappeto erboso; **lawnmower** n tosaerba m inv or f inv

lawsuit [ˈlɔːsuːt] n processo, causa

lawyer [ˈlɔːjəʳ] n (for sales, wills etc) ≈ notaio; (partner, in court) ≈ avvocato/essa

lax [læks] adj rilassato/a; negligente

laxative [ˈlæksətɪv] n lassativo

lay [leɪ] pt of **lie** ▷ adj (not expert) profano/a ▷ vt (pt, pp **laid** [leɪd]) posare, mettere; (eggs) fare; (trap) tendere; (plans) fare, elaborare; **to ~ the table** apparecchiare la tavola; **lay down** vt mettere giù; (rules etc) formulare, fissare; **to ~ down the law** dettar legge; **to ~ down one's life** dare la propria vita; **lay off** vt (workers) licenziare; **lay on** vt (provide) fornire; **lay out** vt (display) presentare; **lay-by** n (BRIT) piazzola (di sosta)

layer [ˈleɪəʳ] n strato

layman [ˈleɪmən] n (irreg) laico; profano

layout [ˈleɪaʊt] n lay-out m inv, disposizione f; (Press) impaginazione f

lazy [ˈleɪzɪ] adj pigro/a

lb. abbr (= pound (weight)) lb.

lead¹ [pt, pp **led**] [liːd, lɛd] n (front position) posizione f di testa; (distance, time ahead) vantaggio; (clue) indizio; (Elec) filo (elettrico); (for dog) guinzaglio; (Theat) parte f principale ▷ vt guidare, condurre; (induce) indurre; (be leader of) essere a capo di ▷ vi condurre; (Sport) essere in testa; **in the ~** in testa; **to ~ the way** fare strada; **lead up to** vt fus portare a

lead² [lɛd] n (metal) piombo; (in pencil) mina

leader [ˈliːdəʳ] n capo; leader m inv; (in newspaper) articolo di fondo; (Sport) chi è in testa; **leadership** n direzione f; capacità di comando

lead-free [ˈlɛdfriː] adj senza piombo

leading [ˈliːdɪŋ] adj primo/a, principale

lead singer n cantante alla testa di un gruppo

leaf [liːf] n (pl **leaves**) foglia; **to turn over a new ~** cambiar vita; **leaf through** vt sfogliare

leaflet [ˈliːflɪt] n dépliant m inv; (Pol, Rel) volantino

league [liːg] n lega; (Football) campionato; **to be in ~ with** essere in lega con

leak [liːk] n (out) fuga; (in) infiltrazione f; (security leak) fuga d'informazioni ▷ vi (roof, bucket) perdere; (liquid) uscire; (shoes) lasciar passare l'acqua ▷ vt (information) divulgare

lean (pt, pp **leaned** or **leant**) [liːn, lɛnt] adj magro/a ▷ vt: **to ~ sth on** appoggiare qc su ▷ vi (slope) pendere; (rest): **to ~ against** appoggiarsi contro; essere appoggiato/a a; **to ~ on** appoggiarsi a; **lean forward** vi sporgersi in avanti; **lean over** vi inclinarsi; **leaning** n: **leaning (towards)** propensione f (per)

leant [lɛnt] pt, pp of **lean**

leap [liːp] n salto, balzo ▷ vi (pt, pp **leaped** or **leapt** [lɛpt]) saltare, balzare

leapt [lɛpt] pt, pp of **leap**

leap year n anno bisestile

learn (pt, pp **learned** or **learnt**) [ləːn, -t] vt, vi imparare; **to ~ (how) to do sth** imparare a fare qc; **to ~ about sth** (hear) apprendere qc; **learner** n principiante m/f; apprendista m/f; **he's a learner (driver)** (BRIT) sta imparando a guidare; **learning** n erudizione f, sapienza

learnt [ləːnt] pt, pp of **learn**

lease [liːs] n contratto d'affitto ▷ vt affittare

leash [liːʃ] n guinzaglio

least [liːst] adj: **the ~** (+ noun) il (la) più piccolo/a, il (la) minimo/a; (smallest amount of) il (la) meno ▷ adv (+ verb) meno; **the ~** (+ adjective): **the ~ beautiful girl** la ragazza meno bella; **the ~ possible effort** il minimo sforzo possibile; **I have the ~ money** ho meno denaro di tutti; **at ~** almeno; **not in the ~** affatto, per nulla

leather [ˈlɛðəʳ] n cuoio

leave (pt, pp **left**) [liːv, lɛft] vt lasciare; (go away from) partire da ▷ vi partire, andarsene; (bus, train) partire ▷ n (time off) congedo; (Mil, consent) licenza; **to be left** rimanere; **there's some milk left over** c'è rimasto del latte; **on ~** in congedo; **leave behind** vt (also fig) lasciare; (forget) dimenticare; **leave out** vt omettere, tralasciare

leaves [liːvz] npl of **leaf**

Lebanon [ˈlɛbənən] n Libano

lecture ['lɛktʃə^r] n conferenza; (Scol) lezione f ▷ vi fare conferenze; fare lezioni ▷ vt (scold): **to ~ sb on** or **about sth** rimproverare qn or fare una ramanzina a qn per qc; **to give a ~ (on)** fare una conferenza (su); **lecture hall** n aula magna; **lecturer** ['lɛktʃərə^r] n (BRIT: at university) professore/essa, docente m/f; **lecture theatre** n = **lecture hall**

led [lɛd] pt, pp of **lead¹**

ledge [lɛdʒ] n (of window) davanzale m; (on wall etc) sporgenza; (of mountain) cornice f, cengia

leek [liːk] n porro

left [lɛft] pt, pp of **leave** ▷ adj sinistro/a ▷ adv a sinistra ▷ n sinistra; **on the ~, to the ~** a sinistra; **the L~** (Pol) la sinistra; **left-hand** adj: **the left-hand side** il lato sinistro; **left-hand drive** adj guida a sinistra; **left-handed** adj mancino/a; **left-luggage locker** n armadietto per deposito bagagli; **left-luggage (office)** n deposito m bagagli inv; **left-overs** npl avanzi mpl, resti mpl; **left wing** n (Pol) sinistra ▷ adj: **left-wing** (Pol) di sinistra

leg [lɛg] n gamba; (of animal) zampa; (of furniture) piede m; (Culin: of chicken) coscia; (of journey) tappa; **1st/2nd ~** (Sport) partita di andata/ritorno

legacy ['lɛgəsɪ] n eredità f inv

legal ['liːgl] adj legale; **legal holiday** n (US) giorno festivo, festa nazionale; **legalize** vt legalizzare; **legally** adv legalmente; **legally binding** legalmente vincolante

legend ['lɛdʒənd] n leggenda; **legendary** ['lɛdʒəndərɪ] adj leggendario/a

leggings ['lɛgɪŋz] npl ghette fpl

legible ['lɛdʒəbl] adj leggibile

legislation [lɛdʒɪs'leɪʃən] n legislazione f

legislative ['lɛdʒɪslətɪv] adj legislativo/a

legitimate [lɪ'dʒɪtɪmət] adj legittimo/a

leisure ['lɛʒə^r] n agio, tempo libero; ricreazioni fpl; **at ~** con comodo; **leisure centre** n centro di ricreazione; **leisurely** adj tranquillo/a, fatto/a con comodo or senza fretta

lemon ['lɛmən] n limone m; **lemonade** [lɛmə'neɪd] n limonata; **lemon tea** n tè m inv al limone

lend (pt, pp **lent**) [lɛnd, lɛnt] vt: **to ~ sth (to sb)** prestare qc (a qn)

length [lɛŋθ] n lunghezza; (distance) distanza; (section: of road, pipe etc) pezzo, tratto; **~ of time** periodo (di tempo); **at ~** (at last) finalmente, alla fine; (lengthily) a lungo; **lengthen** vt allungare, prolungare ▷ vi allungarsi; **lengthways** adv per il lungo; **lengthy** adj molto lungo/a

lens [lɛnz] n lente f; (of camera) obiettivo

Lent [lɛnt] n Quaresima

lent [lɛnt] pt, pp of **lend**

lentil ['lɛntl] n lenticchia

Leo ['liːəu] n Leone m

leopard ['lɛpəd] n leopardo

leotard ['liːətɑːd] n calzamaglia

leprosy ['lɛprəsɪ] n lebbra

lesbian ['lɛzbɪən] n lesbica

less [lɛs] adj, pron, adv, prep meno; **~ tax/10% discount** meno tasse/il 10% di sconto; **~ than you/ever** meno di lei/che mai; **~ than half** meno della metà; **~ and ~** sempre meno; **the ~ he works ...** meno lavora ...; **lessen** ['lɛsn] vi diminuire, attenuarsi ▷ vt diminuire, ridurre; **lesser** ['lɛsə^r] adj minore, più piccolo/a; **to a lesser extent** or **degree** in grado or misura minore

lesson ['lɛsn] n lezione f; **to teach sb a ~** dare una lezione a qn

let (pt, pp **let**) [lɛt] vt lasciare; (BRIT: lease) dare in affitto; **to ~ sb do sth** lasciar fare qc a qn, lasciare che qn faccia qc; **to ~ sb know sth** far sapere qc a qn; **~'s go** andiamo; **~ him come** lo lasci venire; **"to ~"** "affittasi"; **let down** vt (lower) abbassare; (dress) allungare; (hair) sciogliere; (disappoint) deludere; (BRIT: tyre) sgonfiare; **let in** vt lasciare entrare; (visitor etc) far entrare; **let off** vt (allow to go) lasciare andare; (firework etc) far partire; **let out** vt lasciare uscire; (scream) emettere

lethal ['liːθl] adj letale, mortale

letter ['lɛtə^r] n lettera; **letterbox** (BRIT) n buca delle lettere

lettuce ['lɛtɪs] n lattuga, insalata

leukaemia, (US) **leukemia** [luː'kiːmɪə] n leucemia

level ['lɛvl] adj piatto/a, piano/a; orizzontale ▷ n livello ▷ vt livellare, spianare; **to be ~ with** essere alla pari di; **to draw ~ with** mettersi alla pari di; **level crossing** n (BRIT) passaggio a livello

lever ['liːvə^r] n leva; **leverage** n: **leverage (on** or **with)** forza (su); (fig) ascendente m (su)

levy ['lɛvɪ] n tassa, imposta ▷ vt imporre

liability [laɪə'bɪlətɪ] n responsabilità f inv; (handicap) peso

liable ['laɪəbl] adj (subject): **~ to** soggetto/a a; passibile di; (responsible): **~ (for)** responsabile (di); (likely): **~ to do** propenso/a a fare

liaise [liː'eɪz] vi: **to ~ (with)** mantenere i contatti (con)

liar ['laɪə^r] n bugiardo/a

liberal ['lɪbərl] adj liberale; (generous): **to be ~ with** distribuire liberalmente; **Liberal Democrat** n liberaldemocratico/a

liberate ['lɪbəreɪt] vt liberare
liberation [lɪbə'reɪʃən] n liberazione f
liberty ['lɪbətɪ] n libertà f inv; **at ~** (criminal) in libertà; **at ~ to do** libero/a di fare
Libra ['liːbrə] n Bilancia
librarian [laɪ'brɛərɪən] n bibliotecario/a
library ['laɪbrərɪ] n biblioteca
Libya ['lɪbɪə] n Libia
lice [laɪs] npl of **louse**
licence, (US) **license** ['laɪsns] n autorizzazione f, permesso; (Comm) licenza; (Radio, TV) canone m, abbonamento; (also: **driving ~**, (US) **driver's license**) patente f di guida; (excessive freedom) licenza
license ['laɪsns] n (US) = **licence** ▷ vt dare una licenza a; **licensed** adj (for alcohol) che ha la licenza di vendere bibite alcoliche; **license plate** n (esp US Aut) targa (automobilistica); **licensing hours** (BRIT) npl orario d'apertura (di un pub)
lick [lɪk] vt leccare; (col: defeat) stracciare; **to ~ one's lips** (fig) leccarsi i baffi
lid [lɪd] n coperchio; (eyelid) palpebra
lie [laɪ] n bugia, menzogna ▷ vi mentire, dire bugie; (rest) giacere, star disteso/a; (object: be situated) trovarsi, essere; **to tell ~s** raccontare o dire bugie; **to ~ low** (fig) latitare; **lie about, lie around** vi (things) essere in giro; (person) bighellonare; **lie down** vi stendersi, sdraiarsi
Liechtenstein ['lɪktənstaɪn] n Liechtenstein m
lie-in ['laɪɪn] n (BRIT): **to have a ~** rimanere a letto
lieutenant [lɛf'tɛnənt, US luː'tɛnənt] n tenente m
life [laɪf] n (pl **lives**) vita ▷ cpd di vita; della vita; a vita; **to come to ~** rianimarsi; **life assurance** n (BRIT) = **life insurance**; **lifeboat** n scialuppa di salvataggio; **lifeguard** n bagnino; **life insurance** n assicurazione f sulla vita; **life jacket** n giubbotto di salvataggio; **lifelike** adj che sembra vero/a; rassomigliante; **life preserver** [-prɪ'zəːvəʳ] n (US) salvagente m; giubbotto di salvataggio; **life sentence** n (condanna all')ergastolo; **life style** n stile m di vita; **lifetime** ['laɪftaɪm] n: **in his lifetime** durante la sua vita; **in a lifetime** nell'arco della vita; in tutta la vita; **the chance of a lifetime** un'occasione unica
lift [lɪft] vt sollevare; (ban, rule) levare ▷ vi (fog) alzarsi ▷ n (BRIT: elevator) ascensore m; **to give sb a ~** (BRIT) dare un passaggio a qn; **lift up** vt sollevare, alzare; **lift-off** n decollo
light (pt, pp **lighted**, pt, pp **lit**) [laɪt, lɪt] n luce f, lume m; (daylight) luce, giorno; (lamp) lampada; (Aut: rear light) luce f di posizione;

(: headlamp) fanale m; (for cigarette etc): **have you got a ~?** ha da accendere? ▷ vt (candle, cigarette, fire) accendere; (room) illuminare ▷ adj (room, colour) chiaro/a; (not heavy, also fig) leggero/a; **lights** npl (Aut: traffic lights) semaforo; **to come to ~** venire alla luce, emergere; **to be lit by** essere illuminato/a da; **light up** vi illuminarsi ▷ vt illuminare; **light bulb** n lampadina; **lighten** vt (make less heavy) alleggerire; **lighter** n (also: **cigarette lighter**) accendino; **light-hearted** adj gioioso/a, gaio/a; **lighthouse** n faro; **lighting** n illuminazione f; **lightly** ['laɪtlɪ] adv leggermente; **to get off lightly** cavarsela a buon mercato
lightning ['laɪtnɪŋ] n lampo, fulmine m
lightweight ['laɪtweɪt] adj (suit) leggero/a ▷ n (Boxing) peso leggero
like [laɪk] vt (person) volere bene a; (activity, object, food): **I ~ swimming/that book/ chocolate** mi piace nuotare/quel libro/il cioccolato ▷ prep come ▷ adj simile, uguale ▷ n: **the ~** uno/a uguale; **I would ~**, **I'd ~** mi piacerebbe, vorrei; **would you ~ a coffee?** gradirebbe un caffè?; **to be/look ~ sb/sth** somigliare a qn/qc; **what does it look/ taste ~?** che aspetto/gusto ha?; **what does it sound ~?** come fa?; **that's just ~ him** è proprio da lui; **do it ~ this** fallo così; **it is nothing ~ ...** non è affatto come ...; **his ~s and dislikes** i suoi gusti; **likeable** adj simpatico/a
likelihood ['laɪklɪhud] n probabilità
likely ['laɪklɪ] adj probabile; plausibile; **he's ~ to leave** probabilmente partirà, è probabile che parta; **not ~!** neanche per sogno!
likewise ['laɪkwaɪz] adv similmente, nello stesso modo
liking ['laɪkɪŋ] n: **~ (for)** debole m (per); **to be sb's ~** piacere a qn
lilac ['laɪlək] n lilla m inv
Lilo® ['laɪləu] n materasso gonfiabile
lily ['lɪlɪ] n giglio
limb [lɪm] n arto
limbo ['lɪmbəu] n: **to be in ~** (fig) essere lasciato/a nel dimenticatoio
lime [laɪm] n (tree) tiglio; (fruit) limetta; (Geo) calce f
limelight ['laɪmlaɪt] n: **in the ~** (fig) alla ribalta, in vista
limestone ['laɪmstəun] n pietra calcarea; (Geo) calcare m
limit ['lɪmɪt] n limite m ▷ vt limitare; **limited** adj limitato/a, ristretto/a; **to be limited to** limitarsi a
limousine ['lɪməziːn] n limousine f inv
limp [lɪmp] n: **to have a ~** zoppicare ▷ vi zoppicare ▷ adj floscio/a, flaccido/a

line [laɪn] *n* linea; (*rope*) corda; (*for fishing*) lenza; (*wire*) filo; (*of poem*) verso; (*row, series*) fila, riga; coda; (*on face*) ruga ▷ *vt* (*trees, crowd*) fiancheggiare; **to ~ (with)** (*clothes*) foderare (di); (*box*) rivestire *or* foderare (di); **in his ~ of business** nel suo ramo; **in ~ with** in linea con; **line up** *vi* allinearsi, mettersi in fila ▷ *vt* mettere in fila; (*event, celebration*) preparare

linear ['lɪnɪə'] *adj* lineare

linen ['lɪnɪn] *n* biancheria, panni *mpl*; (*cloth*) tela di lino

liner ['laɪnə'] *n* nave *f* di linea; **dustbin ~** sacchetto per la pattumiera

line-up ['laɪnʌp] *n* allineamento, fila; (*Sport*) formazione *f* di gioco

linger ['lɪŋgə'] *vi* attardarsi; indugiare; (*smell, tradition*) persistere

lingerie ['lænʒəri:] *n* biancheria intima (femminile)

linguist ['lɪŋgwɪst] *n* linguista *m/f*; poliglotta *m/f*; **linguistic** *adj* linguistico/a

lining ['laɪnɪŋ] *n* fodera

link [lɪŋk] *n* (*of a chain*) anello; (*relationship*) legame *m*; (*connection*) collegamento ▷ *vt* collegare, unire, congiungere; (*associate*): **to ~ with** *or* **to** collegare a; **link up** *vt* collegare, unire ▷ *vi* riunirsi; associarsi; **links** [lɪŋks] *npl* pista *or* terreno da golf

lion ['laɪən] *n* leone *m*; **lioness** *n* leonessa

lip [lɪp] *n* labbro; (*of cup etc*) orlo; **lipread** ['lɪpriːd] *vi* leggere sulle labbra; **lip salve** [-sælv] *n* burro di cacao; **lipstick** *n* rossetto

liqueur [lɪˈkjuə'] *n* liquore *m*

liquid ['lɪkwɪd] *n* liquido ▷ *adj* liquido/a; **liquidizer** *n* frullatore *m* (a brocca)

liquor ['lɪkə'] *n* alcool *m*; **liquor store** *n* (*US*) negozio di liquori

Lisbon ['lɪzbən] *n* Lisbona

lisp [lɪsp] *n* pronuncia blesa della "s"

list [lɪst] *n* lista, elenco ▷ *vt* (*write down*) mettere in lista; fare una lista di; (*enumerate*) elencare

listen ['lɪsn] *vi* ascoltare; **to ~ to** ascoltare; **listener** *n* ascoltatore/trice

lit [lɪt] *pt, pp of* **light**

liter ['liːtə'] *n* (*US*) = **litre**

literacy ['lɪtərəsɪ] *n* il sapere leggere e scrivere

literal ['lɪtərl] *adj* letterale; **literally** *adv* alla lettera, letteralmente

literary ['lɪtərərɪ] *adj* letterario/a

literate ['lɪtərɪt] *adj* che sa leggere e scrivere

literature ['lɪtərɪtʃə'] *n* letteratura; (*brochures etc*) materiale *m*

litre, (*US*) **liter** ['liːtə'] *n* litro

litter ['lɪtə'] *n* (*rubbish*) rifiuti *mpl*; (*young animals*) figliata; **litter bin** *n* (*BRIT*) cestino per rifiuti; **littered** *adj*: **littered with** coperto/a di

little ['lɪtl] *adj* (*small*) piccolo/a; (*not much*) poco/a ▷ *adv* poco; **a ~** un po' (di); **a ~ bit** un pochino; **~ by ~** a poco a poco; **little finger** *n* mignolo

live¹ [lɪv] *vi* vivere; (*reside*) vivere, abitare; **where do you ~?** dove abita?; **live together** *vi* vivere insieme, convivere; **live up to** *vt fus* tener fede a, non venir meno a

live² [laɪv] *adj* (*animal*) vivo/a; (*wire*) sotto tensione; (*broadcast*) diretto/a; (*ammunition*) inesploso/a; (*performance*) dal vivo

livelihood ['laɪvlɪhud] *n* mezzi *mpl* di sostentamento

lively ['laɪvlɪ] *adj* vivace, vivo/a

liven up ['laɪvn-] *vt* (*discussion, evening*) animare ▷ *vi* ravvivarsi

liver ['lɪvə'] *n* fegato

lives [laɪvz] *npl of* **life**

livestock ['laɪvstɔk] *n* bestiame *m*

living ['lɪvɪŋ] *adj* vivo/a, vivente ▷ *n*: **to earn** *or* **make a ~** guadagnarsi la vita; **living room** *n* soggiorno

lizard ['lɪzəd] *n* lucertola

load [ləud] *n* (*weight*) peso; (*thing carried*) carico ▷ *vt* (*also*: **~ up**): **to ~ (with)** (*lorry, ship*) caricare (di); (*gun, camera*) caricare (con); **a ~ of, ~s of** (*fig*) un sacco di; **to ~ a program** (*Comput*) caricare un programma; **loaded** *adj* (*question, word*) capzioso/a; (*col: rich*) pieno/a di soldi; **loaded (with)** (*vehicle*) carico/a (di)

loaf [ləuf] *n* (*pl* **loaves**) pane *m*, pagnotta

loan [ləun] *n* prestito ▷ *vt* dare in prestito; **on ~** in prestito

loathe [ləuð] *vt* detestare, aborrire

loaves [ləuvz] *npl of* **loaf**

lobby ['lɔbɪ] *n* atrio, vestibolo; (*Pol: pressure group*) gruppo di pressione ▷ *vt* fare pressione su

lobster ['lɔbstə'] *n* aragosta

local ['ləukl] *adj* locale ▷ *n* (*BRIT: pub*) ≈ bar *m inv* all'angolo; **the locals** *npl* la gente della zona; **local anaesthetic** *n* anestesia locale; **local authority** *n* ente *m* locale; **local government** *n* amministrazione *f* locale; **locally** ['ləukəlɪ] *adv* da queste parti; nel vicinato

locate [ləuˈkeɪt] *vt* (*find*) trovare; (*situate*) collocare; situare

location [ləuˈkeɪʃən] *n* posizione *f*; **on ~** (*Cine*) all'esterno

loch [lɔx] *n* lago

lock [lɔk] *n* (*of door, box*) serratura; (*of canal*) chiusa; (*of hair*) ciocca, riccio ▷ *vt* (*with key*) chiudere a chiave ▷ *vi* (*door etc*) chiudersi; (*wheels*) bloccarsi, incepparsi;

lock in vt chiudere dentro (a chiave); **lock out** vt chiudere fuori; **lock up** vt (criminal) rinchiudere; (house) chiudere (a chiave) ▷ vi chiudere tutto (a chiave)

locker ['lɔkəʳ] n armadietto; **locker-room** n (us Sport) spogliatoio

locksmith ['lɔksmiθ] n magnano

locomotive [ləukə'məutiv] n locomotiva

lodge [lɔdʒ] n casetta, portineria; (hunting lodge) casino di caccia ▷ vi (person): to ~ (with) essere a pensione (presso or da); (bullet etc) conficcarsi ▷ vt (appeal etc) presentare, fare; to ~ a complaint presentare un reclamo; **lodger** n affittuario/a; (with room and meals) pensionante m/f

lodging ['lɔdʒɪŋ] n alloggio; see also **board**

loft [lɔft] n solaio, soffitta

log [lɔg] n (of wood) ceppo; (also: ~book) (Naut, Aviat) diario di bordo; (Aut) libretto di circolazione ▷ vt registrare; **log in, log on** vi (Comput) aprire una sessione (con codice di riconoscimento); **log off, log out** vi (Comput) terminare una sessione

logic ['lɔdʒik] n logica; **logical** adj logico/a

login ['lɔgin] n (Comput) nome m utente inv

logo ['ləugəu] n logo m inv

lol abbr (Internet, Tel: = laugh out loud) lol (morto dal ridere)

lollipop ['lɔlipɔp] n lecca lecca m inv

lolly ['lɔli] n (col) lecca lecca m inv; (also: **ice ~**) ghiacciolo; (money) grana

London ['lʌndən] n Londra; **Londoner** n londinese m/f

lone [ləun] adj solitario/a

loneliness ['ləunlinis] n solitudine f, isolamento

lonely ['ləunli] adj solo/a; solitario/a; isolato/a

long [lɔŋ] adj lungo/a ▷ adv a lungo, per molto tempo ▷ vi: to ~ for sth/to do desiderare qc/di fare; non veder l'ora di aver qc/di fare; **how ~ is this river/course?** quanto è lungo questo fiume/corso?; **6 metres ~** lungo 6 metri; **6 months ~** che dura 6 mesi, di 6 mesi; **all night ~** tutta la notte; **he no longer comes** non viene più; **~ before** molto tempo prima; **before ~** (+ future) presto, fra poco; (+ past) poco tempo dopo; **don't be ~!** faccia presto!; **at ~ last** finalmente; **so or as ~ as** (while) finché; (provided that) sempre che + sub; **long-distance** adj (race) di fondo; (call) interurbano/a; **long-haul** ['lɔŋ,hɔ:l] adj (flight) a lunga percorrenza inv; **longing** n desiderio, voglia, brama

longitude ['lɔŋgitju:d] n longitudine f

long: long jump n salto in lungo; **long-life** adj (milk) a lunga conservazione; (batteries) di lunga durata; **long-sighted** adj presbite; **long-standing** adj di vecchia data; **long-term** adj a lungo termine

loo [lu:] n (BRIT col) W.C. m inv, cesso

look [luk] vi guardare; (seem) sembrare, parere; (building etc): to ~ south/on to the sea dare a sud/sul mare ▷ n sguardo; (appearance) aspetto, aria; **looks** npl (good looks) bellezza; **look after** vt fus occuparsi di, prendersi cura di; (keep an eye on) guardare, badare a; **look around** vi guardarsi intorno; **look at** vt fus guardare; **look back** vi: to ~ back on (event, period) ripensare a; **look down on** vt fus (fig) guardare dall'alto, disprezzare; **look for** vt fus cercare; **look forward to** vt fus non veder l'ora di; **~ing forward to hearing from you** (in letter) in attesa di una vostra gentile risposta; **look into** vt fus esaminare; **look out** vi (beware): to ~ out (for) stare in guardia (per); **look out for** vt fus cercare; **look round** vi (turn) girarsi, voltarsi; (in shops) dare un'occhiata; **look through** vt fus (papers, book) scorrere; (telescope) guardare attraverso; **look up** vi alzare gli occhi; (improve) migliorare ▷ vt (word) cercare; (friend) andare a trovare; **look up to** vt fus avere rispetto per; **lookout** n posto d'osservazione; guardia; **to be on the lookout (for)** stare in guardia (per)

loom [lu:m] n telaio ▷ vi sorgere; (fig) incombere

loony ['lu:ni] n (col!) pazzo/a

loop [lu:p] n cappio ▷ vt: to ~ sth round sth passare qc intorno a qc; **loophole** n via d'uscita; scappatoia

loose [lu:s] adj (knot) sciolto/a; (screw) allentato/a; (stone) cadente; (clothes) ampio/a, largo/a; (animal) in libertà, scappato/a; (life, morals) dissoluto/a ▷ n: **to be on the ~** essere in libertà; **loosely** adv senza stringere; approssimativamente; **loosen** ['lu:sn] vt sciogliere; (belt etc) allentare

loot [lu:t] n bottino ▷ vt saccheggiare

lop-sided ['lɔp'saidid] adj non equilibrato/a, asimmetrico/a

lord [lɔ:d] n signore m; **L~ Smith** lord Smith; **the L~** il Signore; **Good L~!** buon Dio!; **the (House of) L~s** (BRIT) la Camera dei Lord

lorry ['lɔri] n (BRIT) camion m inv; **lorry driver** n (BRIT) camionista m

lose (pt, pp **lost**) [lu:z, lɔst] vt perdere ▷ vi perdere; to ~ (time) (clock) ritardare; **lose out** vi rimetterci; **loser** n perdente m/f

loss [lɔs] n perdita; to be at a ~ essere perplesso/a

lost [lɔst] pt, pp of **lose** ▷ adj perduto/a; **lost property**, (us) **lost and found** n oggetti mpl smarriti

lot [lɔt] n (*at auctions*) lotto; (*destiny*) destino, sorte f; (*lot*) tutto/a quanto/a; tutti/e quanti/e; **a ~** molto; **a ~ of** una gran quantità di, un sacco di; **~s of** molto/a; **to draw ~s (for sth)** tirare a sorte (per qc)

lotion ['ləʊʃən] n lozione f

lottery ['lɔtərɪ] n lotteria

loud [laʊd] adj forte, alto/a; (*gaudy*) vistoso/a, sgargiante ▷ adv (*speak etc*) forte; **out ~** (*read etc*) ad alta voce; **loudly** adv fortemente, ad alta voce; **loudspeaker** n altoparlante m

lounge [laʊndʒ] n salotto, soggiorno; (*of airport*) sala d'attesa; (BRIT: *also*: **~ bar**) bar m inv con servizio a tavolino ▷ vi oziare

louse [laʊs] n (pl **lice**) pidocchio

lousy ['laʊzɪ] adj (col: fig) orrendo/a, schifoso/a; **to feel ~** stare da cani

love [lʌv] n amore m ▷ vt amare; voler bene a; **I ~ you** ti amo; **to ~ to do: I ~ to do** mi piace fare; **to be in ~ with** essere innamorato/a di; **to fall in ~ with** innamorarsi di; **to make ~** fare l'amore; **"15 ~"** (*Tennis*) "15 a zero"; **love affair** n relazione f; **love life** n vita sentimentale

lovely ['lʌvlɪ] adj bello/a; (*delicious: smell, meal*) buono/a

lover ['lʌvə'] n amante m/f; (*person in love*) innamorato/a; (*amateur*): **a ~ of** un (un') amante di; un (un')appassionato/a di

loving ['lʌvɪŋ] adj affettuoso/a

low [ləʊ] adj basso/a ▷ adv in basso ▷ n (*Meteor*) depressione f; **to be ~ on** (*supplies etc*) avere scarsità di; **to feel ~** sentirsi giù; **low-alcohol** adj a basso contenuto alcolico; **low-calorie** adj a basso contenuto calorico

lower ['ləʊə'] adj, adv comparative (*bottom: of 2 things*) più basso/a; (*less important*) meno importante ▷ vt calare; (*price, eyes, voice*) abbassare

low-fat ['ləʊ'fæt] adj magro/a

loyal ['lɔɪəl] adj fedele, leale; **loyalty** n fedeltà, lealtà; **loyalty card** n carta che offre sconti a clienti abituali

LP n abbr (= *long-playing record*) LP m

L-plate ['ɛlpleɪt] (BRIT) n ≈ contrassegno P principiante

Lt. abbr (= *lieutenant*) Ten.

Ltd abbr (= *limited*) ≈ S.r.l.

luck [lʌk] n fortuna, sorte f; **bad ~** sfortuna, mala sorte; **good ~** (buona) fortuna; **luckily** adv fortunatamente, per fortuna; **lucky** adj fortunato/a; (*number etc*) che porta fortuna

lucrative ['luːkrətɪv] adj lucrativo/a, lucroso/a, profittevole

ludicrous ['luːdɪkrəs] adj ridicolo/a

luggage ['lʌgɪdʒ] n bagagli mpl; **luggage rack** n portabagagli m inv

lukewarm ['luːkwɔːm] adj tiepido/a

lull [lʌl] n intervallo di calma ▷ vt: **to ~ sb to sleep** cullare qn finché si addormenta

lullaby ['lʌləbaɪ] n ninnananna

lumber ['lʌmbə'] n (*wood*) legname m; (*junk*) roba vecchia

luminous ['luːmɪnəs] adj luminoso/a

lump [lʌmp] n pezzo; (*in sauce*) grumo; (*swelling*) gonfiore m; (*also*: **sugar ~**) zolletta ▷ vt (*also*: **~ together**) riunire, mettere insieme; **lump sum** n somma globale; **lumpy** adj (*sauce*) pieno/a di grumi; (*bed*) bitorzoluto/a

lunatic ['luːnətɪk] adj pazzo/a, matto/a

lunch [lʌntʃ] n pranzo, colazione f; **lunch break** n intervallo del pranzo; **lunchtime** n ora di pranzo

lung [lʌŋ] n polmone m

lure [luə'] n richiamo; lusinga ▷ vt attirare (con l'inganno)

lurk [ləːk] vi stare in agguato

lush [lʌʃ] adj lussureggiante

lust [lʌst] n lussuria; cupidigia; desiderio; (*fig*): **~ for** sete f di

Luxembourg ['lʌksəmbəːg] n (*state*) Lussemburgo m; (*city*) Lussemburgo f

luxurious [lʌg'zjʊərɪəs] adj sontuoso/a, di lusso

luxury ['lʌkʃərɪ] n lusso ▷ cpd di lusso

▌ Be careful not to translate *luxury* by the Italian word *lussuria*.

Lycra® ['laɪkrə] n lycra® f inv

lying ['laɪɪŋ] n bugie fpl, menzogne fpl ▷ adj bugiardo/a

lyric ['lɪrɪk] adj lirico/a; **lyrics** npl (*of song*) parole fpl

m

m *abbr* (= *metre*) m; = **mile; million**

MA *n abbr* = **Master of Arts**

ma [mɑː] *n* (*col*) mamma

mac [mæk] *n* (*BRIT*) impermeabile *m*

macaroni [mækə'rəʊnɪ] *n* maccheroni *mpl*

Macedonia [mæsɪ'dəʊnɪə] *n* Macedonia; **Macedonian** [mæsɪ'dəʊnɪən] *adj* macedone ▷ *n* macedone *m/f*; (*Ling*) macedone *m*

machine [mə'ʃiːn] *n* macchina ▷ *vt* (*dress etc*) cucire a macchina; (*Tech*) lavorare (a macchina); **machine gun** *n* mitragliatrice *f*; **machinery** *n* macchinario, macchine *fpl*; (*fig*) macchina; **machine washable** *adj* lavabile in lavatrice

macho ['mætʃəʊ] *adj* macho *inv*

mackerel ['mækrəl] *n* (*pl inv*) sgombro

mackintosh ['mækɪntɔʃ] *n* (*BRIT*) impermeabile *m*

mad [mæd] *adj* matto/a, pazzo/a; (*foolish*) sciocco/a; (*angry*) furioso/a; **to be ~ (keen) about** *or* **on sth** (*col*) andar matto/a per qc

Madagascar [mædə'gæskə*r] *n* Madagascar *m*

madam ['mædəm] *n* signora

mad cow disease *n* encefalite *f* bovina spongiforme

made [meɪd] *pt, pp of* **make; made-to-measure** *adj* (*BRIT*) fatto/a su misura; **made-up** ['meɪdʌp] *adj* (*story*) inventato/a

madly ['mædlɪ] *adv* follemente

madman ['mædmən] *n* (*irreg*) pazzo, alienato

madness ['mædnɪs] *n* pazzia

Madrid [mə'drɪd] *n* Madrid *f*

Mafia ['mæfɪə] *n* mafia *f*

mag. [mæg] *n abbr* (*BRIT col: Press*); = **magazine**

magazine [mægə'ziːn] *n* (*Press*) rivista; (*Radio, TV*) rubrica

> Be careful not to translate *magazine* by the Italian word *magazzino*.

maggot ['mægət] *n* baco, verme *m*

magic ['mædʒɪk] *n* magia ▷ *adj* magico/a; **magical** *adj* magico/a; **magician** [mə'dʒɪʃən] *n* mago/a

magistrate ['mædʒɪstreɪt] *n* magistrato; giudice *m/f*

magnet ['mægnɪt] *n* magnete *m*, calamita; **magnetic** [mæg'nɛtɪk] *adj* magnetico/a

magnificent [mæg'nɪfɪsnt] *adj* magnifico/a

magnify ['mægnɪfaɪ] *vt* ingrandire; **magnifying glass** *n* lente *f* d'ingrandimento

magpie ['mægpaɪ] *n* gazza

mahogany [mə'hɔgənɪ] *n* mogano

maid [meɪd] *n* domestica; (*in hotel*) cameriera

maiden name ['meɪdn-] *n* nome da *m* nubile *or* da ragazza

mail [meɪl] *n* posta ▷ *vt* spedire (per posta); **mailbox** *n* (*US*) cassetta delle lettere; **mailing list** *n* elenco d'indirizzi; **mailman** *n* (*irreg*: *US*) portalettere *m inv*, postino; **mail-order** *n* vendita (*or* acquisto) per corrispondenza

main [meɪn] *adj* principale ▷ *n* (*pipe*) conduttura principale; **the ~s** (*Elec*) la linea principale; **in the ~** nel complesso, nell'insieme; **main course** *n* (*Culin*) piatto principale, piatto forte; **mainland** *n* continente *m*; **mainly** *adv* principalmente, soprattutto; **main road** *n* strada principale; **mainstream** *n* (*fig*) corrente *f* principale; **main street** *n* strada principale

maintain [meɪn'teɪn] *vt* mantenere; (*affirm*) sostenere; **maintenance** ['meɪntənəns] *n* manutenzione *f*; (*alimony*) alimenti *mpl*

maisonette [meɪzə'nɛt] *n* (*BRIT*) appartamento a due piani

maize [meɪz] *n* granturco, mais *m*

majesty ['mædʒɪstɪ] *n* maestà *f inv*

major ['meɪdʒə*r] *n* (*Mil*) maggiore *m* ▷ *adj* (*greater, Mus*) maggiore; (*in importance*) principale, importante

Majorca [mə'jɔːkə] *n* Maiorca

majority [mə'dʒɔrɪtɪ] *n* maggioranza

make [meɪk] *vt* (*pt, pp* **made**) fare; (*manufacture*) fare, fabbricare; (*cause to be*): **to ~ sb sad** *etc* rendere qn triste *etc*; (*force*): **to ~ sb do sth** costringere qn a fare qc, far fare qc a qn; (*equal*): **2 and 2 ~ 4** 2 più 2 fa 4 ▷ *n* fabbricazione *f*; (*brand*) marca; **to ~ a fool of sb** far fare a qn la figura dello scemo; **to ~ a profit** realizzare un profitto;

to ~ a loss subire una perdita; to ~ it (in time etc) arrivare; (succeed) farcela; what time do you ~ it? che ora fai?; to ~ do with arrangiarsi con; **make off** vi svignarsela; **make out** vt (write out) scrivere; (: cheque) emettere; (understand) capire; (see) distinguere; (: numbers) decifrare; **make up** vt (constitute) formare; (invent) inventare; (parcel) fare ▷ vi conciliarsi; (with cosmetics) truccarsi; **make up for** vt fus compensare; ricuperare; **makeover** ['meɪkəʊvər] n cambio di immagine; **to give sb a makeover** far cambiare immagine a qn; **maker** n (of programme etc) creatore/trice; (manufacturer) fabbricante m; **makeshift** adj improvvisato/a; **make-up** n trucco

making ['meɪkɪŋ] n (fig): **in the ~** in formazione; **he has the ~s of an actor** ha la stoffa dell'attore

malaria [mə'lɛərɪə] n malaria

Malaysia [mə'leɪzɪə] n Malaysia

male [meɪl] n (Biol, Elec) maschio ▷ adj maschile; (animal, child) maschio/a

malicious [mə'lɪʃəs] adj malevolo/a; (Law) doloso/a

malignant [mə'lɪgnənt] adj (Med) maligno/a

mall [mɔːl] n (also: **shopping ~**) centro commerciale

mallet ['mælɪt] n maglio

malnutrition [mælnjuː'trɪʃən] n denutrizione f

malpractice [mæl'præktɪs] n prevaricazione f; negligenza

malt [mɔːlt] n malto

Malta ['mɔːltə] n Malta; **Maltese** [mɔːl'tiːz] adj, n (pl inv) maltese (m/f); (Ling) maltese m

mammal ['mæml] n mammifero

mammoth ['mæməθ] adj enorme, gigantesco/a

man [mæn] n (pl men) uomo ▷ vt fornire d'uomini; stare a; **an old ~** un vecchio; **~ and wife** marito e moglie

manage ['mænɪdʒ] vi farcela ▷ vt (be in charge of) occuparsi di; (shop, restaurant) gestire; **to ~ to do sth** riuscire a far qc; **manageable** adj maneggevole; (task etc) fattibile; **management** n amministrazione f, direzione f; **manager** n direttore m; (of shop, restaurant) gerente m; (of artist, Sport) manager m inv; **manageress** [mænɪdʒə'rɛs] n direttrice f; gerente f; **managerial** [mænə'dʒɪərɪəl] adj dirigenziale; **managing director** ['mænɪdʒɪŋ-] n amministratore m delegato

mandarin ['mændərɪn] n (person, fruit) mandarino

mandate ['mændeɪt] n mandato

mandatory ['mændətərɪ] adj obbligatorio/a; ingiuntivo/a

mane [meɪn] n criniera

mangetout ['mɔ̃ʒ'tuː] n pisello dolce, taccola

mango ['mæŋgəʊ] (pl **mangoes**) n mango

man: manhole ['mænhəʊl] n botola stradale; **manhood** ['mænhud] n età virile; virilità

mania ['meɪnɪə] n mania; **maniac** ['meɪnɪæk] n maniaco/a

manic ['mænɪk] adj (behaviour, activity) maniacale

manicure ['mænɪkjʊər] n manicure f inv

manifest ['mænɪfɛst] vt manifestare ▷ adj manifesto/a, palese

manifesto [mænɪ'fɛstəʊ] n manifesto

manipulate [mə'nɪpjuleɪt] vt manipolare

man: mankind [mæn'kaɪnd] n umanità, genere m umano; **manly** ['mænlɪ] adj virile; coraggioso/a; **man-made** adj sintetico/a; artificiale

manner ['mænər] n maniera, modo; (behaviour) modo di fare; (type, sort): **all ~ of things** ogni genere di cosa; **manners** npl (conduct) maniere fpl; **bad ~s** maleducazione f; **all ~ of** ogni sorta di

manoeuvre, (us) **maneuver** [mə'nuːvər] vt manovrare ▷ vi far manovre ▷ n manovra

manpower ['mænpaʊər] n manodopera

mansion ['mænʃən] n casa signorile

manslaughter ['mænslɔːtər] n omicidio preterintenzionale

mantelpiece ['mæntlpiːs] n mensola del caminetto

manual ['mænjuəl] adj, n manuale (m)

manufacture [mænju'fæktʃər] vt fabbricare ▷ n fabbricazione f, manifattura; **manufacturer** n fabbricante m

manure [mə'njuər] n concime m

manuscript ['mænjuskrɪpt] n manoscritto

many ['mɛnɪ] adj molti/e ▷ pron molti/e; **a great ~** moltissimi/e, un gran numero (di); **~ a ...** molti/e ...

map [mæp] n carta (geografica); (of city) cartina

maple ['meɪpl] n acero

mar [mɑːr] vt sciupare

Mar. abbr (= March) mar.

marathon ['mærəθən] n maratona

marble ['mɑːbl] n marmo; (toy) pallina, bilia

March [mɑːtʃ] n marzo

march [mɑːtʃ] vi marciare; sfilare ▷ n marcia

mare [mɛər] n giumenta

margarine [mɑːdʒə'riːn] n margarina

margin ['mɑːdʒɪn] n margine m; **marginal**
adj marginale; **marginal seat** (Pol)
seggio elettorale ottenuto con una stretta
maggioranza; **marginally** adv (bigger, better)
lievemente, di poco; (different) un po'

marigold ['mærɪgəʊld] n calendola

marijuana [mærɪ'wɑːnə] n marijuana

marina [mə'riːnə] n marina

marinade n [mærɪ'neɪd] marinata ▷ vt
['mærɪneɪd] = **marinate**

marinate ['mærɪneɪt] vt marinare

marine [mə'riːn] adj (animal, plant)
marino/a; (forces, engineering) marittimo/a
▷ n (BRIT) fante m di marina; (US) marine
m inv

marital ['mærɪtl] adj maritale, coniugale;
~ **status** stato coniugale

maritime ['mærɪtaɪm] adj marittimo/a

marjoram ['mɑːdʒərəm] n maggiorana

mark [mɑːk] n segno; (stain) macchia; (of
skid etc) traccia; (BRIT Scol) voto; (Sport)
bersaglio; (currency) marco ▷ vt segnare;
(stain) macchiare; (indicate) indicare; (BRIT
Scol) dare un voto a; correggere; **to ~ time**
segnare il passo; **marked** adj spiccato/a,
chiaro/a; **marker** n (sign) segno; (bookmark)
segnalibro

market ['mɑːkɪt] n mercato ▷ vt (Comm)
mettere in vendita; **marketing** n
marketing m; **marketplace** n (piazza del)
mercato; (world of trade) piazza, mercato;
market research n indagine f or ricerca di
mercato

marmalade ['mɑːməleɪd] n marmellata
d'arance

maroon [mə'ruːn] vt (fig): **to be ~ed** (in
or at) essere abbandonato/a (in) ▷ adj
bordeaux inv

marquee [mɑː'kiː] n padiglione m

marriage ['mærɪdʒ] n matrimonio;
marriage certificate n certificato di
matrimonio

married ['mærɪd] adj sposato/a; (life, love)
coniugale, matrimoniale

marrow ['mærəʊ] n midollo; (vegetable)
zucca

marry ['mærɪ] vt sposare, sposarsi con;
(father, priest etc) dare in matrimonio ▷ vi
(also: **get married**) sposarsi

Mars [mɑːz] n (planet) Marte m

marsh [mɑːʃ] n palude f

marshal ['mɑːʃl] n maresciallo; (US: fire
marshal) capo; (: police marshal) capitano
▷ vt (thoughts, support) ordinare; (soldiers)
adunare

martyr ['mɑːtər] n martire m/f

marvel ['mɑːvl] n meraviglia ▷ vi: **to ~**
(at) meravigliarsi (di); **marvellous**, (US)
marvelous adj meraviglioso/a

Marxism ['mɑːksɪzəm] n marxismo

Marxist ['mɑːksɪst] adj, n marxista (m/f)

marzipan ['mɑːzɪpæn] n marzapane m

mascara [mæs'kɑːrə] n mascara m inv

mascot ['mæskət] n mascotte f inv

masculine ['mæskjulɪn] adj maschile;
(woman) mascolino/a

mash [mæʃ] vt passare, schiacciare

mashed [mæʃt] adj: ~ **potatoes** purè m
di patate

mask [mɑːsk] n maschera ▷ vt mascherare

mason ['meɪsn] n (also: **stone~**)
scalpellino; (also: **free~**) massone m;
masonry n muratura

mass [mæs] n moltitudine f, massa;
(Physics) massa; (Rel) messa ▷ cpd di massa
▷ vi ammassarsi; **the ~es** (ordinary people) le
masse; **~es of** (col) una montagna di

massacre ['mæsəkər] n massacro

massage ['mæsɑːʒ] n massaggio

massive ['mæsɪv] adj enorme, massiccio/a

mass media npl mass media mpl

mass-produce ['mæsprə'djuːs] vt
produrre in serie

mast [mɑːst] n albero

master ['mɑːstər] n padrone m; (teacher:
in primary school, Art etc) maestro; (: in
secondary school) professore m; (title for
boys): **M~ X** Signorino X ▷ vt domare; (learn)
imparare a fondo; (understand) conoscere
a fondo; **mastermind** n mente f superiore
▷ vt essere il cervello di; **Master of Arts/**
Science n Master m inv in lettere/scienze;
masterpiece n capolavoro

masturbate ['mæstəbeɪt] vi masturbare

mat [mæt] n stuoia; (also: **door~**) stoino,
zerbino; (also: **table ~**) sottopiatto ▷ adj
= **matt**

match [mætʃ] n fiammifero; (game) partita,
incontro; (fig) uguale m/f; matrimonio;
partito ▷ vt intonare; (go well with) andare
benissimo con; (equal) uguagliare; (correspond
to) corrispondere a; (pair: also: ~ **up**)
accoppiare ▷ vi intonarsi; **to be a good ~**
andare bene; **matchbox** n scatola per
fiammiferi; **matching** adj ben assortito/a

mate [meɪt] n compagno/a di lavoro; (col:
friend) amico/a; (animal) compagno/a; (in
merchant navy) secondo ▷ vi accoppiarsi

material [mə'tɪərɪəl] n (substance)
materiale m, materia; (cloth) stoffa ▷ adj
materiale; **materials** npl (equipment etc)
materiali mpl

materialize [mə'tɪərɪəlaɪz] vi
materializzarsi, realizzarsi

maternal [mə'təːnl] adj materno/a

maternity [mə'təːnɪtɪ] n maternità;
maternity hospital n ≈ clinica ostetrica;
maternity leave n congedo di maternità

math [mæθ] n abbr (US) = **mathematics**
mathematical [mæθə'mætɪkl] adj
matematico/a
mathematician [mæθəmə'tɪʃən] n
matematico/a
mathematics [mæθə'mætɪks] n
matematica
maths [mæθs] n abbr (BRIT)
= **mathematics**
matinée ['mætɪneɪ] n matinée f inv
matron ['meɪtrən] n (in hospital)
capoinfermiera; (in school) infermiera
matt [mæt] adj opaco/a
matter ['mætə'] n questione f; (Physics)
materia, sostanza; (content) contenuto;
(Med: pus) pus m ⊳ vi importare; **matters**
npl (affairs) questioni; **it doesn't ~** non
importa; (I don't mind) non fa niente;
what's the ~? che cosa c'è?; **no ~ what**
qualsiasi cosa accada; **as a ~ of course**
come cosa naturale; **as a ~ of fact** in verità
mattress ['mætrɪs] n materasso
mature [mə'tjuə'] adj maturo/a; (cheese)
stagionato/a ⊳ vi maturare; stagionare;
mature student n studente universitario che
ha più di 25 anni; **maturity** n maturità
maul [mɔːl] vt lacerare
mauve [məuv] adj malva inv
max. abbr = **maximum**
maximize ['mæksɪmaɪz] vt (profits etc)
massimizzare; (chances) aumentare al
massimo
maximum ['mæksɪməm] adj massimo/a
⊳ n (pl **maxima**) massimo
May [meɪ] n maggio
may [meɪ] vi (conditional **might**) (indicating
possibility): **he ~ come** può darsi che venga;
(be allowed to): **~ I smoke?** posso fumare?;
(wishes): **~ God bless you!** Dio la benedica!;
I might as well go potrei anche
andarmene
maybe ['meɪbiː] adv forse, può darsi; **~ he'll
...** può darsi che lui ... + sub, forse lui ...
May Day n il primo maggio
mayhem ['meɪhɛm] n cagnara
mayonnaise [meɪə'neɪz] n maionese f
mayor [mɛə'] n sindaco; **mayoress** n
sindaco (donna); moglie f del sindaco
maze [meɪz] n labirinto, dedalo
MD n abbr (= Doctor of Medicine) titolo di
studio; (Comm) = **managing director**
me [miː] pron mi, m' + vowel or silent "h";
(stressed, after prep) me; **he heard me** mi ha
or m'ha sentito; **give me a book** dammi (or
mi dia) un libro; **it's me** sono io; **with me**
con me; **without me** senza di me
meadow ['mɛdəu] n prato
meagre, (US) **meager** ['miːgə'] adj
magro/a

meal [miːl] n pasto; (flour) farina;
mealtime n l'ora di mangiare
mean [miːn] adj (with money) avaro/a,
gretto/a; (unkind) meschino/a, maligno/a;
(shabby) misero/a; (average) medio/a ⊳ vt
(pt, pp **meant**) (signify) significare, voler
dire; (intend): **to ~ to do** aver l'intenzione di
fare ⊳ n mezzo; (Math) media; **to be ~t for**
essere destinato/a a; **do you ~ it?** dice sul
serio?; **what do you ~?** che cosa vuol dire?;
see also **means**
meaning ['miːnɪŋ] n significato,
senso; **meaningful** adj significativo/a;
meaningless adj senza senso
means [miːnz] npl (way, money) mezzi mpl;
by means of per mezzo di; **by all means**
ma certo, prego
meant [mɛnt] pt, pp of **mean**
meantime ['miːntaɪm], **meanwhile**
['miːnwaɪl] adv (also: **in the ~**) nel
frattempo
measles ['miːzlz] n morbillo
measure ['mɛʒə'] vt, vi misurare ⊳ n
misura; (ruler) metro
measurement ['mɛʒəmənt] n (act)
misurazione f; (measure) misura; **chest/
hip ~** giro petto/fianchi; **to take sb's ~s**
prendere le misure di qn
meat [miːt] n carne f; **cold ~s** affettati mpl;
meatball n polpetta di carne
Mecca ['mɛkə] n La Mecca; (fig): **a ~ (for)** la
Mecca (di)
mechanic [mɪ'kænɪk] n meccanico;
mechanical adj meccanico/a
mechanism ['mɛkənɪzəm] n meccanismo
medal ['mɛdl] n medaglia; **medallist**, (US)
medalist n (Sport): **to be a gold medallist**
essere medaglia d'oro
meddle ['mɛdl] vi: **to ~ in** immischiarsi in,
mettere le mani in; **to ~ with** toccare
media ['miːdɪə] npl media mpl
mediaeval [mɛdɪ'iːvl] adj = **medieval**
mediate ['miːdɪeɪt] vi fare da mediatore/
trice
medical ['mɛdɪkl] adj medico/a; **~
(examination)** n visita medica; **medical
certificate** n certificato medico
medicated ['mɛdɪkeɪtɪd] adj medicato/a
medication [mɛdɪ'keɪʃən] n medicinali
mpl, farmaci mpl
medicine ['mɛdsɪn] n medicina
medieval [mɛdɪ'iːvl] adj medievale
mediocre [miːdɪ'əukə'] adj mediocre
meditate ['mɛdɪteɪt] vi: **to ~ (on)** meditare
(su)
meditation [mɛdɪ'teɪʃən] n meditazione f
Mediterranean [mɛdɪtə'reɪnɪən] adj
mediterraneo/a; **the ~ (Sea)** il (mare)
Mediterraneo

medium ['mi:dɪəm] adj medio/a ▷ n (pl **media**: means) mezzo; (pl **mediums**: person) medium m inv; **medium-sized** adj (tin etc) di grandezza media; (clothes) di taglia media; **medium wave** n onde fpl medie

meek [mi:k] adj dolce, umile

meet (pt, pp **met**) [mi:t, mɛt] vt incontrare; (for the first time) fare la conoscenza di; (go and fetch) andare a prendere; (fig) affrontare; soddisfare; raggiungere ▷ vi incontrarsi; (in session) riunirsi; (join: objects) unirsi ▷ n (BRIT Hunting) raduno (dei partecipanti alla caccia alla volpe); (US Sport) raduno (sportivo); **I'll ~ you at the station** verrò a prenderla alla stazione; **pleased to ~ you!** piacere (di conoscerla)!; **meet up** vi: **to ~ up with sb** incontrare qn; **meet with** vt fus incontrare; **meeting** n incontro; (session: of club etc) riunione f; (interview) intervista; **she's at a meeting** (Comm) è in riunione; **meeting place** n luogo d'incontro

megabyte ['mɛgəbaɪt] n (Comput) megabyte m inv

megaphone ['mɛgəfəʊn] n megafono

megapixel ['mɛgəpɪksl] n megapixel m inv

melancholy ['mɛlənkəlɪ] n malinconia ▷ adj malinconico/a

melody ['mɛlədɪ] n melodia

melon ['mɛlən] n melone m

melt [mɛlt] vi (gen) sciogliersi, struggersi; (metals) fondersi ▷ vt sciogliere, struggere; fondere

member ['mɛmbəʳ] n membro; **Member of Congress** (US) n membro del Congresso; **Member of Parliament** (BRIT) n deputato/a; **Member of the European Parliament** (BRIT) n eurodeputato/a; **Member of the House of Representatives** (US) n membro della Camera dei Rappresentanti; **Member of the Scottish Parliament** (BRIT) n deputato/a del Parlamento scozzese; **membership** n iscrizione f; (numero d') iscritti mpl, membri mpl; **membership card** n tessera (di iscrizione)

memento [mə'mɛntəʊ] n ricordo, souvenir m inv

memo ['mɛməʊ] n appunto; (Comm etc) comunicazione f di servizio

memorable ['mɛmərəbl] adj memorabile

memorandum (pl **memoranda**) [mɛmə'rændəm, -də] n appunto; (Comm etc) comunicazione f di servizio

memorial [mɪ'mɔ:rɪəl] n monumento commemorativo ▷ adj commemorativo/a

memorize ['mɛməraɪz] vt memorizzare

memory ['mɛmərɪ] n (gen, Comput) memoria; (recollection) ricordo; **memory stick** n (Comput) stick m inv di memoria

men [mɛn] npl of **man**

menace ['mɛnɪs] n minaccia ▷ vt minacciare

mend [mɛnd] vt aggiustare, riparare; (darn) rammendare ▷ n: **on the ~** in via di guarigione

meningitis [mɛnɪn'dʒaɪtɪs] n meningite f

menopause ['mɛnəʊpɔ:z] n menopausa

men's room n: **the ~** (esp US) la toilette degli uomini

menstruation [mɛnstru'eɪʃən] n mestruazione f

menswear ['mɛnzwɛəʳ] n abbigliamento maschile

mental ['mɛntl] adj mentale; **mental hospital** n (pej) ospedale m psichiatrico; **mentality** [mɛn'tælɪtɪ] n mentalità f inv; **mentally** adv: **to be mentally ill** essere malato di mente

menthol ['mɛnθəl] n mentolo

mention ['mɛnʃən] n menzione f ▷ vt menzionare, far menzione di; **don't ~ it!** non c'è di che!, prego!

menu ['mɛnju:] n (set menu, Comput) menù m inv; (printed) carta

MEP n abbr = **Member of the European Parliament**

mercenary ['mə:sɪnərɪ] adj venale ▷ n mercenario

merchandise ['mə:tʃəndaɪz] n merci fpl

merchant ['mə:tʃənt] n mercante m, commerciante m; **merchant navy**, (US) **merchant marine** n marina mercantile

merciless ['mə:sɪlɪs] adj spietato/a

mercury ['mə:kjʊrɪ] n mercurio

mercy ['mə:sɪ] n pietà; (Rel) misericordia; **at the ~ of** alla mercé di

mere [mɪəʳ] adj semplice; **by a ~ chance** per mero caso; **merely** adv semplicemente, non … che

merge [mə:dʒ] vt unire ▷ vi fondersi, unirsi; (Comm) fondersi; **merger** n (Comm) fusione f

meringue [mə'ræŋ] n meringa

merit ['mɛrɪt] n merito, valore m ▷ vt meritare

mermaid ['mə:meɪd] n sirena

merry ['mɛrɪ] adj gaio/a, allegro/a; **M~ Christmas!** Buon Natale!; **merry-go-round** n carosello

mesh [mɛʃ] n maglia; rete f

mess [mɛs] n confusione f, disordine m; (fig) pasticcio; (dirt) sporcizia; (Mil) mensa; **mess about**, **mess around** vi (col) trastullarsi; **mess with** vt fus (col: challenge, confront) litigare con; (: drugs, drinks) abusare di; **mess up** vt (col) sporcare; fare un pasticcio di; rovinare

message ['mɛsɪdʒ] n messaggio; **message board** n (Comput) bacheca elettronica

messenger ['mɛsɪndʒəʳ] n messaggero/a

Messrs, Messrs. ['mɛsəz] abbr (on letters: = messieurs) Spett.

messy ['mɛsɪ] adj sporco/a; disordinato/a

met [mɛt] pt, pp of **meet**

metabolism [mɛ'tæbəlɪzəm] n metabolismo

metal ['mɛtl] n metallo; **metallic** [mɛ'tælɪk] adj metallico/a

metaphor ['mɛtəfəʳ] n metafora

meteor ['miːtɪəʳ] n meteora; **meteorite** ['miːtɪəraɪt] n meteorite m

meteorology [miːtɪə'rɔlədʒɪ] n meteorologia

meter ['miːtəʳ] n (instrument) contatore m; (parking meter) parchimetro; (us: unit) = **metre**

method ['mɛθəd] n metodo; **methodical** [mɪ'θɔdɪkl] adj metodico/a

meths [mɛθs] (BRIT) n = **methylated spirits**

methylated spirits ['mɛθɪleɪtɪd-] n (BRIT: also: **meths**) alcool m denaturato

meticulous [mɛ'tɪkjuləs] adj meticoloso/a

metre, (us) **meter** ['miːtəʳ] n metro

metric ['mɛtrɪk] adj metrico/a

metro ['mɛtrəu] n metro m inv

metropolitan [mɛtrə'pɔlɪtən] adj metropolitano/a

Mexican ['mɛksɪkən] adj, n messicano/a

Mexico ['mɛksɪkəu] n Messico

mg abbr (= milligram) mg

mice [maɪs] npl of **mouse**

micro... ['maɪkrəu] prefix micro...; **microchip** n microcircuito integrato; **microphone** n microfono; **microscope** n microscopio; **microwave** n (also: **microwave oven**) forno a microonde

mid [mɪd] adj: **~ May** metà maggio; **~ afternoon** metà pomeriggio; **in ~ air** a mezz'aria; **midday** n mezzogiorno

middle ['mɪdl] n mezzo; centro; (waist) vita ▷ adj di mezzo; **in the ~ of the night** nel cuore della notte; **middle-aged** adj di mezza età; **Middle Ages** npl: **the Middle Ages** il Medioevo; **middle class** adj (also: **middle-class**) ≈ borghese; **Middle East** n: **the Middle East** il Medio Oriente; **middle name** n secondo nome m; **middle school** n (us) scuola media per ragazzi dagli 11 ai 14 anni; (BRIT) scuola media per ragazzi dagli 8 o 9 ai 12 o 13 anni

midge [mɪdʒ] n moscerino

midget ['mɪdʒɪt] n (col!) nano/a

midnight ['mɪdnaɪt] n mezzanotte f

midst [mɪdst] n: **in the ~ of** in mezzo a

midsummer [mɪd'sʌməʳ] n mezza or piena estate f

midway [mɪd'weɪ] adj, adv: **~ (between)** a mezza strada (fra); **~ (through)** a metà (di)

midweek [mɪd'wiːk] adv a metà settimana

midwife (pl **midwives**) ['mɪdwaɪf, -vz] n levatrice f

midwinter [mɪd'wɪntəʳ] n pieno inverno

might [maɪt] vb see **may** ▷ n potere m, forza; **mighty** adj forte, potente

migraine ['miːɡreɪn] n emicrania

migrant ['maɪɡrənt] adj (bird) migratore/trice; (worker) emigrato/a

migrate [maɪ'ɡreɪt] vi (bird) migrare; (person) emigrare

migration [maɪ'ɡreɪʃən] n migrazione f

mike [maɪk] n abbr (= microphone) microfono

Milan [mɪ'læn] n Milano f

mild [maɪld] adj mite; (person, voice) dolce; (flavour) delicato/a; (illness) leggero/a; (interest) blando/a ▷ n (beer) birra leggera; **mildly** ['maɪldlɪ] adv mitemente; dolcemente; delicatamente; leggermente; blandamente; **to put it mildly** a dire poco

mile [maɪl] n miglio; **mileage** n distanza in miglia, ≈ chilometraggio; **mileometer** [maɪ'lɔmɪtəʳ] n (BRIT) = **milometer**; **milestone** ['maɪlstəun] n pietra miliare

military ['mɪlɪtərɪ] adj militare

militia [mɪ'lɪʃə] n milizia

milk [mɪlk] n latte m ▷ vt (cow) mungere; (fig) sfruttare; **milk chocolate** n cioccolato al latte; **milkman** n (irreg) lattaio; **milky** adj lattiginoso/a; (colour) latteo/a

mill [mɪl] n mulino; (small, for coffee, pepper etc) macinino; (factory) fabbrica; (spinning mill) filatura ▷ vt macinare ▷ vi (also: **~ about**) brulicare

millennium (pl **millenniums** or **millennia**) [mɪ'lɛnɪəm, -'lɛnɪə] n millennio

milli... ['mɪlɪ] prefix milli...; **milligram(me)** n milligrammo; **millilitre**, (us) **milliliter** ['mɪlɪliːtəʳ] n millilitro; **millimetre**, (us) **millimeter** n millimetro

million ['mɪljən] num milione m; **millionaire** n milionario, ≈ miliardario; **millionth** num milionesimo/a

milometer [maɪ'lɔmɪtəʳ] n ≈ contachilometri m inv

mime [maɪm] n mimo ▷ vt, vi mimare

mimic ['mɪmɪk] n imitatore/trice ▷ vt imitare

min. abbr = **minute**; (= minimum) min.

mince [mɪns] vt tritare, macinare ▷ n (BRIT Culin) carne f tritata or macinata; **mincemeat** n frutta secca tritata per uso in pasticceria; (us) carne f tritata or macinata; **mince pie** n specie di torta con frutta secca

mind [maɪnd] n mente f ▷ vt (attend to, look after) badare a, occuparsi di; (be careful) fare attenzione a, stare attento/a a; (object to): **I don't ~ the noise** il rumore non mi dà alcun fastidio; **do you ~ if ...?** le dispiace se ...?; **I don't ~** non m'importa; **~ you, ... sì,** però va detto che ...; **never ~** non importa, non fa niente; (don't worry) non preoccuparti; **it is on my ~** mi preoccupa; **to my ~** secondo me, a mio parere; **to be out of one's ~** essere uscito/a di mente; **to keep sth in ~** non dimenticare qc; **to bear sth in ~** tener presente qc; **to make up one's ~** decidersi; "**~ the step**" "attenzione allo scalino"; **mindless** adj idiota

mine¹ [maɪn] pron il (la) mio/a; (pl) i (le) miei (mie); **this book is ~** questo libro è mio; **yours is red, ~ is green** il tuo è rosso, il mio è verde; **a friend of ~** un mio amico

mine² [maɪn] n miniera; (explosive) mina ▷ vt (coal) estrarre; (ship, beach) minare; **minefield** ['maɪnfiːld] n campo minato; **miner** ['maɪnə'] n minatore m

mineral ['mɪnərəl] adj minerale ▷ n minerale m; **mineral water** n acqua minerale

mingle ['mɪŋgl] vi: **to ~ with** mescolarsi a, mischiarsi con

miniature ['mɪnətʃə'] adj in miniatura ▷ n miniatura

minibar ['mɪnɪbɑː'] n minibar m inv

minibus ['mɪnɪbʌs] n minibus m inv

minicab ['mɪnɪkæb] n (BRIT) ≈ taxi m inv

minimal ['mɪnɪml] adj minimo/a

minimize ['mɪnɪmaɪz] vt minimizzare

minimum ['mɪnɪməm] n (pl **minima**) minimo ▷ adj minimo/a

mining ['maɪnɪŋ] n industria mineraria

miniskirt ['mɪnɪskəːt] n minigonna

minister ['mɪnɪstə'] n (BRIT Pol) ministro; (Rel) pastore m

ministry ['mɪnɪstrɪ] n ministero

minor ['maɪnə'] adj minore, di poca importanza; (Mus) minore ▷ n (Law) minorenne m/f

Minorca [mɪ'nɔːkə] n Minorca

minority [maɪ'nɔrɪtɪ] n minoranza

mint [mɪnt] n (plant) menta; (sweet) pasticca di menta ▷ vt (coins) battere; **the (Royal) M~** (BRIT), **the (US) M~** (US) la Zecca; **in ~ condition** come nuovo/a di zecca

minus ['maɪnəs] n (also: **~ sign**) segno meno ▷ prep meno

minute¹ ['mɪnɪt] n minuto; **minutes** npl (of meeting) verbale m

minute² [maɪ'njuːt] adj minuscolo/a; (detail) minuzioso/a

miracle ['mɪrəkl] n miracolo

miraculous [mɪ'rækjuləs] adj miracoloso/a

mirage ['mɪrɑːʒ] n miraggio

mirror ['mɪrə'] n specchio; (in car) specchietto

misbehave [mɪsbɪ'heɪv] vi comportarsi male

misc. abbr = **miscellaneous**

miscarriage ['mɪskærɪdʒ] n (Med) aborto spontaneo; **~ of justice** errore m giudiziario

miscellaneous [mɪsɪ'leɪnɪəs] adj (items) vario/a; (selection) misto/a

mischief ['mɪstʃɪf] n (naughtiness) birichineria; (maliciousness) malizia; **mischievous** adj birichino/a

misconception [mɪskən'sɛpʃən] n idea sbagliata

misconduct [mɪs'kɔndʌkt] n cattiva condotta; **professional ~** reato professionale

miser ['maɪzə'] n avaro

miserable ['mɪzərəbl] adj infelice; (wretched) miserabile; (weather) deprimente; (offer, failure) misero/a

misery ['mɪzərɪ] n (unhappiness) tristezza; (wretchedness) miseria

misfortune [mɪs'fɔːtʃən] n sfortuna

misgiving [mɪs'gɪvɪŋ] n dubbi mpl; **to have ~s about sth** essere diffidente or avere dei dubbi per quanto riguarda qc

misguided [mɪs'gaɪdɪd] adj sbagliato/a; poco giudizioso/a

mishap ['mɪshæp] n disgrazia

misinterpret [mɪsɪn'təːprɪt] vt interpretare male

misjudge [mɪs'dʒʌdʒ] vt giudicare male

mislay [mɪs'leɪ] vt (irreg) smarrire

mislead [mɪs'liːd] vt (irreg) sviare; **misleading** adj ingannevole

misplace [mɪs'pleɪs] vt smarrire

misprint ['mɪsprɪnt] n errore m di stampa

misrepresent [mɪsrɛprɪ'zɛnt] vt travisare

Miss [mɪs] n Signorina

miss [mɪs] vt (fail to get) perdere; (fail to hit) mancare; (fail to see): **you can't ~ it** non puoi non vederlo; (regret the absence of): **I ~ him/it** sento la sua mancanza ▷ vi mancare ▷ n (shot) colpo mancato; **we ~ed our train** abbiamo perso il treno; **miss out** vt (BRIT) omettere; **miss out on** vt fus (fun, party) perdersi; (chance, bargain) lasciarsi sfuggire

missile ['mɪsaɪl] n (Aviat) missile m; (object thrown) proiettile m

missing ['mɪsɪŋ] adj perso/a, smarrito/a; (removed) mancante; **~ person** scomparso/a, disperso/a; **~ in action** (Mil) disperso/a; **to be ~** mancare

mission ['mɪʃən] n missione f; **missionary** n missionario/a

misspell [mɪs'spɛl] vt (irreg: like **spell**)
sbagliare l'ortografia di

mist [mɪst] n nebbia, foschia ▷ vi (also:
~ over, ~ up) annebbiarsi; (BRIT: windows)
appannarsi

mistake [mɪs'teɪk] n sbaglio, errore m ▷ vt
(irreg: like **take**) sbagliarsi di; fraintendere;
to ~ for prendere per; **by ~** per sbaglio;
to make a ~ fare uno sbaglio or un errore,
sbagliare; **there must be some ~** ci
dev'essere un errore; **mistaken** pp of
mistake ▷ adj (idea etc) sbagliato/a; **to be
mistaken** sbagliarsi

mister ['mɪstəʳ] n (col) signore m; see **Mr**

mistletoe ['mɪsltəʊ] n vischio

mistook [mɪs'tʊk] pt of **mistake**

mistress ['mɪstrɪs] n padrona; (lover)
amante f; (BRIT Scol) insegnante f

mistrust [mɪs'trʌst] vt diffidare di

misty ['mɪstɪ] adj nebbioso/a, brumoso/a

misunderstand [mɪsʌndə'stænd]
vt, vi (irreg) capire male, fraintendere;
misunderstanding n malinteso, equivoco;
there's been a misunderstanding c'è stato
un malinteso

misunderstood [mɪsʌndə'stʊd] pt, pp of
misunderstand

misuse n [mɪs'juːs] cattivo uso; (of power)
abuso ▷ vt [mɪs'juːz] far cattivo uso di;
abusare di

mitt(en) ['mɪt(n)] n mezzo guanto;
manopola

mix [mɪks] vt mescolare ▷ vi (people): **to ~
with** avere a che fare con ▷ n mescolanza;
preparato; **mix up** vt mescolare; (confuse)
confondere; **mixed** adj misto/a; **mixed
grill** n (BRIT) misto alla griglia; **mixed
salad** n insalata mista; **mixed-up** adj
(confused) confuso/a; **mixer** n (for food:
electric) frullatore m; (: hand) frullino m; **he
is a good mixer** è molto socievole;
mixture n mescolanza; (blend: of tobacco
etc) miscela; (Med) sciroppo; **mix-up** n
confusione f

ml abbr (= millilitre(s)) ml

mm abbr (= millimetre) mm

moan [məʊn] n gemito ▷ vi (col: complain):
to ~ (about) lamentarsi (di)

moat [məʊt] n fossato

mob [mɔb] n calca ▷ vt accalcarsi intorno a

mobile ['məʊbaɪl] adj mobile ▷ n (phone)
telefonino, cellulare m; (Art) mobile m
inv; **mobile home** n grande roulotte f inv
(utilizzata come domicilio); **mobile phone** n
telefono portatile, telefonino

mobility [məʊ'bɪlɪtɪ] n mobilità; (of
applicant) disponibilità a viaggiare

mobilize ['məʊbɪlaɪz] vt mobilitare ▷ vi
mobilitarsi

mock [mɔk] vt deridere, burlarsi di
▷ adj falso/a; **mocks** npl (BRIT col: Scol)
simulazione f degli esami; **mockery** n
derisione f; **to make a mockery of** burlarsi
di; (exam) rendere una farsa

mod cons ['mɔd'kɔnz] npl abbr (BRIT)
= **modern conveniences**

mode [məʊd] n modo

model ['mɔdl] n modello; (person: for
fashion) indossatore/trice; (: for artist)
modello/a ▷ vt modellare ▷ vi fare
l'indossatore (or l'indossatrice) ▷ adj (small-
scale: railway etc) in miniatura; (child, factory)
modello inv; **to ~ clothes** presentare degli
abiti; **to ~ sb/sth on** modellare qn/qc su

modem ['məʊdɛm] n modem m inv

moderate adj ['mɔdərɪt] moderato/a
▷ vi ['mɔdəreɪt] moderarsi, placarsi ▷ vt
moderare

moderation [mɔdə'reɪʃən] n moderazione
f, misura; **in ~** in quantità moderata, con
moderazione

modern ['mɔdən] adj moderno/a;
~ conveniences comodità fpl moderne;
~ languages lingue fpl moderne;
modernize vt modernizzare

modest ['mɔdɪst] adj modesto/a;
modesty n modestia

modification [mɔdɪfɪ'keɪʃən] n
modificazione f; **to make ~s** fare or
apportare delle modifiche

modify ['mɔdɪfaɪ] vt modificare

module ['mɔdjuːl] n modulo

mohair ['məʊhɛəʳ] n mohair m

Mohammed [məʊ'hæmɪd] n Maometto

moist [mɔɪst] adj umido/a; **moisture**
['mɔɪstʃəʳ] n umidità; (on glass) goccioline
fpl di vapore; **moisturizer** ['mɔɪstʃəraɪzəʳ]
n idratante f

mold etc [məʊld] (US) = **mould** etc

mole [məʊl] n (animal, fig) talpa; (spot) neo

molecule ['mɔlɪkjuːl] n molecola

molest [məʊ'lɛst] vt molestare

molten ['məʊltən] adj fuso/a

mom [mɔm] n (US) = **mum**

moment ['məʊmənt] n momento,
istante m; **at that ~** in quel momento; **at
the ~** al momento, in questo momento;
momentarily ['məʊməntərɪlɪ] adv per un
momento; (US: very soon) da un momento
all'altro; **momentary** adj momentaneo/a,
passeggero/a; **momentous**
[məʊ'mɛntəs] adj di grande importanza

momentum [məʊ'mɛntəm] n (Physics)
momento; (fig) impeto; **to gather ~**
aumentare di velocità

mommy ['mɔmɪ] n (US) mamma

Mon. abbr (= Monday) lun.

Monaco ['mɔnəkəʊ] n Monaco f

monarch ['mɒnək] n monarca m;
monarchy n monarchia
monastery ['mɒnəstəri] n monastero
Monday ['mʌndɪ] n lunedì m inv
monetary ['mʌnɪtəri] adj monetario/a
money ['mʌnɪ] n denaro, soldi mpl; **money belt** n marsupio (per soldi); **money order** n vaglia m inv
mongrel ['mʌŋgrəl] n (dog) cane m bastardo
monitor ['mɒnɪtə*] n (TV, Comput) monitor m inv ▷ vt controllare
monk [mʌŋk] n monaco
monkey ['mʌŋkɪ] n scimmia
monologue ['mɒnəlɒg] n monologo
monopoly [mə'nɒpəlɪ] n monopolio
monosodium glutamate [mɒnə'səudɪəm'glu:təmeɪt] n glutammato di sodio
monotonous [mə'nɒtənəs] adj monotono/a
monsoon [mɒn'su:n] n monsone m
monster ['mɒnstə*] n mostro
month [mʌnθ] n mese m; **monthly** adj mensile ▷ adv al mese; ogni mese
monument ['mɒnjumənt] n monumento
mood [mu:d] n umore m; **to be in a good/ bad ~** essere di buon/cattivo umore; **moody** adj (variable) capriccioso/a, lunatico/a; (sullen) imbronciato/a
moon [mu:n] n luna; **moonlight** n chiaro di luna
moor [muə*] n brughiera ▷ vt (ship) ormeggiare ▷ vi ormeggiarsi
moose [mu:s] n (pl inv) alce m
mop [mɒp] n lavapavimenti m inv; (also: **~ of hair**) zazzera ▷ vt lavare con lo straccio; (face) asciugare; **mop up** vt asciugare con uno straccio
mope [məup] vi fare il broncio
moped ['məupɛd] n (BRIT) ciclomotore m
moral ['mɒrəl] adj morale ▷ n morale f; **morals** npl (principles) moralità
morale [mɒ'rɑ:l] n morale m
morality [mə'rælɪtɪ] n moralità
morbid ['mɔ:bɪd] adj morboso/a

KEYWORD

more [mɔ:*] adj 1 (greater in number etc) più; **more people/letters than we expected** più persone/lettere di quante ne aspettavamo; **I have more wine/money than you** ho più vino/soldi di te; **I have more wine than beer** ho più vino che birra
2 (additional) altro/a, ancora; **do you want (some) more tea?** vuole dell'altro tè?, vuole ancora del tè?; **I have no** or **I don't have any more money** non ho più soldi

▷ pron 1 (greater amount) più; **more than 10** più di 10; **it cost more than we expected** è costato più di quanto ci aspettassimo
2 (further or additional amount) ancora; **is there any more?** ce n'è ancora?; **there's no more** non ce n'è più; **a little more** ancora un po'; **many/much more** molti/e/ molto/a di più
▷ adv: **more dangerous/easily (than)** più pericoloso/facilmente (di); **more and more** sempre di più; **more and more difficult** sempre più difficile; **more or less** più o meno; **more than ever** più che mai

moreover [mɔ:'rəuvə*] adv inoltre, di più
morgue [mɔ:g] n obitorio
morning ['mɔ:nɪŋ] n mattina, mattino; (duration) mattinata ▷ cpd del mattino; **in the ~** la mattina; **7 o'clock in the ~** le 7 di or della mattina; **morning sickness** n nausee fpl mattutine
Moroccan [mə'rɒkən] adj, n marocchino/a
Morocco [mə'rɒkəu] n Marocco
moron ['mɔ:rɒn] n (col!) deficiente m/f
morphine ['mɔ:fi:n] n morfina
morris dancing ['mɒrɪs-] n vedi nota "morris dancing"

MORRIS DANCING

Il morris dancing è una danza folcloristica inglese tradizionalmente riservata agli uomini. Vestiti di bianco e con dei campanelli attaccati alle caviglie, i ballerini eseguono una danza tenendo in mano dei fazzoletti bianchi e lunghi bastoni. Questa danza è molto popolare nelle feste paesane.

Morse [mɔ:s] n (also: **~ code**) alfabeto Morse
mortal ['mɔ:tl] adj, n mortale (m)
mortar ['mɔ:tə*] n (Constr) malta; (dish) mortaio
mortgage ['mɔ:gɪdʒ] n ipoteca; (loan) prestito ipotecario ▷ vt ipotecare
mortician [mɔ:'tɪʃən] n (US) impresario di pompe funebri
mortified ['mɔ:tɪfaɪd] adj umiliato/a
mortuary ['mɔ:tjuərɪ] n camera mortuaria; obitorio
mosaic [məu'zeɪɪk] n mosaico
Moscow ['mɒskəu] n Mosca
Moslem ['mɒzləm] adj, n = **Muslim**
mosque [mɒsk] n moschea
mosquito [mɒs'ki:təu] (pl **mosquitoes**) n zanzara
moss [mɒs] n muschio

most [məʊst] adj (almost all) la maggior parte di; (largest, greatest): **who has (the) ~ money?** chi ha più soldi di tutti? ▷ pron la maggior parte ▷ adv più; (work, sleep etc) di più; (very) molto, estremamente; **the ~** (also + adjective) il (la) più; **~ of** la maggior parte di; **~ of them** quasi tutti; **I saw ~** ho visto più io; **at the (very) ~** al massimo; **to make the ~ of** trarre il massimo vantaggio da; **a ~ interesting book** un libro estremamente interessante; **mostly** adv per lo più

MOT n abbr (BRIT) = **Ministry of Transport**; **the ~ (test)** revisione obbligatoria degli autoveicoli

motel [məʊˈtɛl] n motel m inv

moth [mɔθ] n farfalla notturna; tarma

mother [ˈmʌðəʳ] n madre f ▷ vt (care for) fare da madre a; **motherhood** n maternità; **mother-in-law** n suocera; **mother-of-pearl** [mʌðərəvˈpəːl] n madreperla; **Mother's Day** n la festa della mamma; **mother-to-be** [mʌðətəˈbiː] n futura mamma; **mother tongue** n madrelingua

motif [məʊˈtiːf] n motivo

motion [ˈməʊʃən] n movimento, moto; (gesture) gesto; (at meeting) mozione f ▷ vt, vi: **to ~ (to) sb to do** fare cenno a qn di fare; **motionless** adj immobile; **motion picture** n film m inv

motivate [ˈməʊtɪveɪt] vt (act, decision) dare origine a, motivare; (person) spingere

motivation [məʊtɪˈveɪʃən] n motivazione f

motive [ˈməʊtɪv] n motivo

motor [ˈməʊtəʳ] n motore m; (BRIT col: vehicle) macchina ▷ adj (industry, accident) automobilistico/a; autoveicolo; **motorbike** n moto f inv; **motorboat** n motoscafo; **motorcar** n (BRIT) automobile f; **motorcycle** n motocicletta; **motorcyclist** n motociclista m/f; **motoring** n (BRIT) turismo automobilistico; **motorist** n automobilista m/f; **motor racing** n (BRIT) corse fpl automobilistiche; **motorway** n (BRIT) autostrada

motto [ˈmɔtəʊ] (pl **mottoes**) n motto

mould, (US) **mold** [məʊld] n forma, stampo; (mildew) muffa ▷ vt formare; (fig) foggiare; **mouldy**, (US) **moldy** adj ammuffito/a; (smell) di muffa

mound [maʊnd] n rialzo, collinetta; (heap) mucchio

mount [maʊnt] n (Geo) monte m ▷ vt montare; (horse) montare a ▷ vi salire; **mount up** vi (build up) accumularsi

mountain [ˈmaʊntɪn] n montagna ▷ cpd di montagna; **mountain bike** n mountain bike f inv; **mountaineer** [maʊntɪˈnɪəʳ] n alpinista m/f; **mountaineering** [maʊntɪˈnɪərɪŋ] n alpinismo; **mountainous** adj montagnoso/a; **mountain range** n catena montuosa

mourn [mɔːn] vt piangere, lamentare ▷ vi: **to ~ (for sb)** piangere (la morte di qn); **mourner** n parente m/f (o amico/a) del defunto; **mourning** n lutto; **in mourning** in lutto

mouse (pl **mice**) [maʊs, maɪs] n topo; (Comput) mouse m inv; **mouse mat, mouse pad** n (Comput) tappetino del mouse

moussaka [muˈsɑːkə] n moussaka

mousse [muːs] n mousse f inv

moustache [məsˈtɑːʃ], (US) **mustache** n baffi mpl

mouth [maʊθ] n bocca; (of river) bocca, foce f; (opening) orifizio; **mouthful** n boccata; **mouth organ** n armonica; **mouthpiece** n (Mus) imboccatura, bocchino; (person) portavoce mf inv; **mouthwash** n collutorio

move [muːv] n (movement) movimento; (in game) mossa; (: turn to play) turno; (change: of house) trasloco; (: of job) cambiamento ▷ vt muovere; (change position of) spostare; (emotionally) commuovere; (Pol: resolution etc) proporre ▷ vi (gen) muoversi, spostarsi; (also: **~ house**) cambiar casa, traslocare; **to ~ towards** andare verso; **to ~ sb to do sth** indurre o spingere qn a fare qc; **to get a ~ on** affrettarsi, sbrigarsi; **move back** vi (return) ritornare; **move in** vi (to a house) entrare (in una nuova casa); (police etc) intervenire; **move off** vi partire; **move on** vi riprendere la strada; **move out** vi (of house) sgombrare; **move over** vi spostarsi; **move up** vi avanzare; **movement** [ˈmuːvmənt] n (gen) movimento; (gesture) gesto; (of stars, water, physical) moto

movie [ˈmuːvɪ] n film m inv; **the ~s** il cinema; **movie theater** (US) n cinema m inv

moving [ˈmuːvɪŋ] adj mobile; (causing emotion) commovente

mow (pt **mowed**, pp **mowed** or **mown**) [məʊ, -n] vt (grass) tagliare; (corn) mietere; **mower** n (also: **lawn mower**) tagliaerba m inv

Mozambique [məʊzəmˈbiːk] n Mozambico

MP n abbr = **Member of Parliament**

MP3 n MP3 m inv; **MP3 player** n lettore m MP3

mpg n abbr = **miles per gallon**

mph n abbr = **miles per hour**

Mr, (US) **Mr.** [ˈmɪstəʳ] n: **Mr X** Signor X, Sig. X

Mrs, (US) **Mrs.** [ˈmɪsɪz] n: **~ X** Signora X, Sig.ra X

Ms, (US) **Ms.** [mɪz] n = **Miss**; **Mrs**; **Ms X** ≈ Signora X, ≈ Sig.ra X

- **MS**

- In inglese si usa Ms al posto di "Mrs" (Signora) o "Miss" (Signorina) per evitare
- la distinzione tradizionale tra le donne sposate e quelle nubili.

MSP n abbr = **Member of the Scottish Parliament**

Mt abbr (Geo: = mount) M

🔵 **KEYWORD**

much [mʌtʃ] adj, pron molto/a; **he's done so much work** ha lavorato così tanto; **I have as much money as you** ho tanti soldi quanti ne hai tu; **how much is it?** quant'è?; **it costs too much** costa troppo; **as much as you want** quanto vuoi
▶ adv **1** (greatly) molto, tanto; **thank you very much** molte grazie; **he's very much the gentleman** è il vero gentiluomo; **I read as much as I can** leggo quanto posso; **as much as you** tanto quanto te
2 (by far) molto; **it's much the biggest company in Europe** è di gran lunga la più grossa società in Europa
3 (almost) grossomodo, praticamente; **they're much the same** sono praticamente uguali

muck [mʌk] n (dirt) sporcizia; **muck up** vt (col: spoil) rovinare; **mucky** adj (dirty) sporco/a, lordo/a
mucus ['mju:kəs] n muco
mud [mʌd] n fango
muddle ['mʌdl] n confusione f, disordine m; pasticcio ▶ vt (also: ~ **up**) confondere
muddy ['mʌdɪ] adj fangoso/a
mudguard ['mʌdgɑːd] n parafango
muesli ['mju:zlɪ] n muesli m inv
muffin ['mʌfɪn] n specie di pasticcino soffice da tè
muffled ['mʌfld] adj smorzato/a, attutito/a
muffler ['mʌfləʳ] n (US: Aut) marmitta; (: on motorbike) silenziatore m
mug [mʌg] n (cup) tazzone m; (for beer) boccale m; (col: face) muso; (: fool) scemo/a ▶ vt (assault) assalire; **mugger** ['mʌgəʳ] n aggressore m; **mugging** n aggressione f (a scopo di rapina)
muggy ['mʌgɪ] adj afoso/a
mule [mju:l] n mulo
multicoloured, (US) **multicolored** ['mʌltɪkʌləd] adj multicolore, variopinto/a

multimedia ['mʌltɪ'miːdɪə] adj multimedia inv
multinational [mʌltɪ'næʃənl] adj, n multinazionale (f)
multiple ['mʌltɪpl] adj multiplo/a; molteplice ▶ n multiplo; **multiple choice (test)** n esercizi mpl a scelta multipla; **multiple sclerosis** [-sklɪ'rəusɪs] n sclerosi f a placche
multiplex ['mʌltɪpleks] n (also: ~ **cinema**) cinema m inv multisale inv
multiplication [mʌltɪplɪ'keɪʃən] n moltiplicazione f
multiply ['mʌltɪplaɪ] vt moltiplicare ▶ vi moltiplicarsi
multistorey ['mʌltɪ'stɔːrɪ] adj (BRIT: building, car park) a più piani
mum [mʌm] n (BRIT col) mamma ▶ adj: **to keep** ~ non aprire bocca
mumble ['mʌmbl] vt, vi borbottare
mummy ['mʌmɪ] n (BRIT: mother) mamma; (embalmed) mummia
mumps [mʌmps] n orecchioni mpl
munch [mʌntʃ] vt, vi sgranocchiare
municipal [mju:'nɪsɪpl] adj municipale
mural ['mjuərəl] n dipinto murale
murder ['məːdəʳ] n assassinio, omicidio ▶ vt assassinare; **to commit** ~ commettere un omicidio; **murderer** n omicida m, assassino
murky ['məːkɪ] adj tenebroso/a
murmur ['məːməʳ] n mormorio ▶ vt, vi mormorare
muscle ['mʌsl] n muscolo; (fig) forza; **muscular** ['mʌskjuləʳ] adj muscolare; (person, arm) muscoloso/a
museum [mju:'zɪəm] n museo
mushroom ['mʌʃrum] n fungo ▶ vi svilupparsi rapidamente
music ['mju:zɪk] n musica; **musical** adj musicale; (person) portato/a per la musica ▶ n (show) commedia musicale; **musical instrument** n strumento musicale.
musician [mju:'zɪʃən] n musicista m/f
Muslim ['mʌzlɪm] adj, n musulmano/a
muslin ['mʌzlɪn] n mussola
mussel ['mʌsl] n cozza
must [mʌst] aux vb (obligation): **I** ~ **do it** devo farlo; (probability): **he** ~ **be there by now** dovrebbe essere arrivato ormai; **I** ~ **have made a mistake** devo essermi sbagliato ▶ n: **this programme/trip is a** ~ è un programma/viaggio da non perdersi
mustache ['mʌstæʃ] n (US) = **moustache**
mustard ['mʌstəd] n senape f, mostarda
mustn't ['mʌsnt] = **must not**
mute [mju:t] adj muto/a
mutilate ['mju:tɪleɪt] vt mutilare
mutiny ['mju:tɪnɪ] n ammutinamento

mutter ['mʌtər] vt, vi borbottare, brontolare

mutton ['mʌtn] n carne f di montone

mutual ['mjuːtʃuəl] adj mutuo/a, reciproco/a

muzzle ['mʌzl] n muso; (protective device) museruola; (of gun) bocca ▷ vt mettere la museruola a

my [maɪ] adj il (la) mio/a; (pl) i (le) miei (mie); **my house** la mia casa; **my books** i miei libri; **my brother** mio fratello; **I've washed my hair/cut my finger** mi sono lavato i capelli/tagliato

myself [maɪ'sɛlf] pron (reflexive) mi; (emphatic) io stesso/a; (after prep) me; see also **oneself**

mysterious [mɪs'tɪərɪəs] adj misterioso/a

mystery ['mɪstərɪ] n mistero

mystical ['mɪstɪkəl] adj mistico/a

mystify ['mɪstɪfaɪ] vt mistificare; (puzzle) confondere

myth [mɪθ] n mito; **mythology** [mɪ'θɒlədʒɪ] n mitologia

n

n/a abbr (= not applicable) non pertinente

nag [næg] vt tormentare ▷ vi brontolare in continuazione

nail [neɪl] n (human) unghia; (metal) chiodo ▷ vt inchiodare; **to ~ sb down to a date/ price** costringere qn a un appuntamento/ ad accettare un prezzo; **nailbrush** n spazzolino da or per unghie; **nailfile** n lima da or per unghie; **nail polish** n smalto da or per unghie; **nail polish remover** n acetone m, solvente m; **nail scissors** npl forbici fpl da or per unghie; **nail varnish** n (BRIT) = **nail polish**

naïve [naɪ'iːv] adj ingenuo/a

naked ['neɪkɪd] adj nudo/a

name [neɪm] n nome m; (reputation) nome, reputazione f ▷ vt (baby etc) chiamare; (plant, illness) nominare; (person, object) identificare; (price, date) fissare; **by ~** di nome; **she knows them all by ~** li conosce tutti per nome; **what's your ~?** come si chiama?; **namely** adv cioè

nanny ['nænɪ] n bambinaia

nap [næp] n (sleep) pisolino; (of cloth) peluria ▷ vi: **to be caught ~ping** essere preso alla sprovvista

napkin ['næpkɪn] n tovagliolo

nappy ['næpɪ] n (BRIT) pannolino

narcotic [nɑː'kɒtɪk] n (Med) narcotico; **narcotics** npl (drugs) narcotici, stupefacenti mpl

narrative ['nærətɪv] n narrativa

narrator [nə'reɪtər] n narratore/trice

narrow ['nærəʊ] adj stretto/a; (resources, means) limitato/a, modesto/a ▷ vi restringersi; **to have a ~ escape** farcela per un pelo; **narrow down** vt (search, investigation, possibilities) restringere; (list) ridurre; **narrowly** adv per un pelo; (time) per poco; **narrow-minded** adj meschino/a

nasal ['neɪzl] *adj* nasale
nasty ['nɑːstɪ] *adj* (*unpleasant: person, remark*) cattivo/a; (*rude*) villano/a; (*smell, wound, situation*) brutto/a
nation ['neɪʃən] *n* nazione *f*
national ['næʃənl] *adj* nazionale ▷ *n* cittadino/a; **national anthem** *n* inno nazionale; **national dress** *n* costume *m* nazionale; **National Health Service** *n* (BRIT) ≈ Servizio sanitario nazionale; **National Insurance** *n* (BRIT) ≈ Previdenza Sociale; **nationalist** *adj, n* nazionalista (*m/f*); **nationality** [næʃə'nælɪtɪ] *n* nazionalità *f inv*; **nationalize** *vt* nazionalizzare; **national park** *n* parco nazionale; **National Trust** *n* sovrintendenza ai beni culturali e ambientali

○ **NATIONAL TRUST**

○ Fondato nel 1895, il *National Trust*
○ è un'organizzazione che si occupa
○ della tutela e salvaguardia di edifici e
○ monumenti di interesse storico e di
○ territori di interesse ambientale nel
○ Regno Unito.

nationwide ['neɪʃənwaɪd] *adj* diffuso/a in tutto il paese ▷ *adv* in tutto il paese
native ['neɪtɪv] *n* abitante *m/f* del paese ▷ *adj* indigeno/a; (*country*) natio/a; (*ability*) innato/a; **a ~ of Russia** un nativo della Russia; **a ~ speaker of French** una persona di madrelingua francese; **Native American** *n* discendente di tribù dell'America settentrionale
NATO ['neɪtəu] *n abbr* (= *North Atlantic Treaty Organization*) N.A.T.O. *f*
natural ['nætʃrəl] *adj* naturale; (*ability*) innato/a; (*manner*) semplice; **natural gas** *n* gas *m* metano; **natural history** *n* storia naturale; **naturally** *adv* naturalmente; (*by nature: gifted*) di natura; **natural resources** *npl* risorse *fpl* naturali
nature ['neɪtʃə'] *n* natura; (*character*) natura, indole *f*; **by ~** di natura; **nature reserve** *n* (BRIT) parco naturale
naughty ['nɔːtɪ] *adj* (*child*) birichino/a, cattivello/a; (*story, film*) spinto/a
nausea ['nɔːsɪə] *n* (Med) nausea; (*fig: disgust*) schifo
naval ['neɪvl] *adj* navale
navel ['neɪvl] *n* ombelico
navigate ['nævɪgeɪt] *vt* percorrere navigando ▷ *vi* navigare; (*Aut*) fare da navigatore; **navigation** [nævɪ'geɪʃən] *n* navigazione *f*
navy ['neɪvɪ] *n* marina

Nazi ['nɑːtsɪ] *n* nazista (*m/f*)
NB *abbr* (= *nota bene*) N.B.
near [nɪə'] *adj* vicino/a; (*relation*) prossimo/a ▷ *adv* vicino ▷ *prep* (*also:* **~ to**) vicino a, presso; (*in time*) verso ▷ *vt* avvicinarsi a; **nearby** [nɪə'baɪ] *adj* vicino/a ▷ *adv* vicino; **nearly** *adv* quasi; **I nearly lost it** per poco non lo perdevo; **near-sighted** [nɪə'saɪtɪd] *adj* miope
neat [niːt] *adj* (*person, room*) ordinato/a; (*work*) pulito/a; (*solution, plan*) ben indovinato/a, azzeccato/a; (*spirits*) liscio/a; **neatly** *adv* con ordine; (*skilfully*) abilmente
necessarily ['nɛsɪsrɪlɪ] *adv* necessariamente
necessary ['nɛsɪsrɪ] *adj* necessario/a
necessity [nɪ'sɛsɪtɪ] *n* necessità *f inv*
neck [nɛk] *n* collo; (*of garment*) colletto ▷ *vi* (*col*) pomiciare, sbaciucchiarsi; **~ and ~** testa a testa; **necklace** ['nɛklɪs] *n* collana; **necktie** ['nɛktaɪ] *n* cravatta
nectarine ['nɛktərɪn] *n* nocepesca
need [niːd] *n* bisogno ▷ *vt* aver bisogno di; **do you ~ anything?** ha bisogno di qualcosa?; **I ~ to do it** lo devo fare, bisogna che io lo faccia; **you don't ~ to go** non deve andare, non c'è bisogno che lei vada
needle ['niːdl] *n* ago; (*on record player*) puntina ▷ *vt* punzecchiare
needless ['niːdlɪs] *adj* inutile
needlework ['niːdlwəːk] *n* cucito
needn't ['niːdnt] = **need not**
needy ['niːdɪ] *adj* bisognoso/a
negative ['nɛgətɪv] *n* (Phot) negativo; (Ling) negazione *f* ▷ *adj* negativo/a
neglect [nɪ'glɛkt] *vt* trascurare ▷ *n* (*of person, duty*) negligenza; (*of child, house etc*) scarsa cura; **state of ~** stato di abbandono
negotiate [nɪ'gəuʃɪeɪt] *vi* negoziare ▷ *vt* (Comm) negoziare; (*obstacle*) superare; **negotiation** [nɪgəuʃɪ'eɪʃən] *n* trattativa; (Pol) negoziato
negotiator [nɪ'gəuʃɪeɪtə'] *n* negoziatore/ trice
neighbour, (US) **neighbor** ['neɪbə'] *n* vicino/a; **neighbourhood** *n* vicinato; **neighbouring** *adj* vicino/a
neither ['naɪðə'] *adj, pron* né l'uno/a né l'altro/a, nessuno/a dei (delle) due ▷ *conj* neanche, nemmeno, neppure ▷ *adv*: **~ good nor bad** né buono né cattivo; **I didn't move and ~ did Claude** io non mi mossi e nemmeno Claude; **... ~ did I refuse** ..., ma non ho nemmeno rifiutato
neon ['niːɔn] *n* neon *m*
Nepal [nɪ'pɔːl] *n* Nepal *m*
nephew ['nɛvjuː] *n* nipote *m*

nerve [nə:v] n nervo; (fig) coraggio; (impudence) faccia tosta; **he gets on my ~s** mi dà ai nervi; **a fit of ~s** una crisi di nervi

nervous ['nə:vəs] adj nervoso/a; (anxious) agitato/a, in apprensione; **nervous breakdown** n esaurimento nervoso

nest [nɛst] n nido ▷ vi fare il nido, nidificare

net [nɛt] n rete f ▷ adj netto/a ▷ vt (person, profit) ricavare un utile netto di; (fish etc) prendere con la rete; **the N~** (Internet) Internet f; **netball** n specie di pallacanestro

Netherlands ['nɛðələndz] npl: **the ~** i Paesi Bassi

netiquette ['nɛtɪkɛt] n netiquette f inv

nett [nɛt] adj = **net**

nettle ['nɛtl] n ortica

network ['nɛtwə:k] n rete f

neurotic [njuə'rɔtɪk] adj, n nevrotico/a

neuter ['nju:tər] adj neutro/a ▷ vt (cat etc) castrare

neutral ['nju:trəl] adj neutro/a; (person, nation) neutrale ▷ n (Aut): **in ~** in folle

never ['nɛvər] adv (non...) mai; **~ again** mai più; **I'll ~ go there again** non ci vado più; **~ in my life** mai in vita mia; see also **mind**; **never-ending** adj interminabile; **nevertheless** [nɛvəðə'lɛs] adv tuttavia, ciò nonostante, ciò nondimeno

new [nju:] adj nuovo/a; (brand new) nuovo/a di zecca; **New Age** n New Age f inv; **newbie** ['nju:bɪ] n (Comput, Tech) utilizzatore/trice inesperto/a; (to a job or group) nuovo/a arrivato/a; (to a hobby or experience) neofita m/f; **newborn** adj neonato/a; **newcomer** ['nju:kʌmər] n nuovo/a venuto/a; **newly** adv di recente

news [nju:z] n notizie fpl; (Radio) giornale m radio; (TV) telegiornale m; **a piece of ~** una notizia; **news agency** n agenzia di stampa; **newsagent** n (BRIT) giornalaio; **newscaster** n (Radio, TV) annunciatore/trice; **newsdealer** ['nju:zdi:lər] n (US) = **newsagent**; **newsletter** n bollettino; **newspaper** n giornale m; **newsreader** n = **newscaster**

newt [nju:t] n tritone m

New Year n Anno Nuovo; **New Year's Day** n il Capodanno; **New Year's Eve** n la vigilia di Capodanno

New York [-'jɔ:k] n New York f

New Zealand [-'zi:lənd] n Nuova Zelanda; **New Zealander** n neozelandese m/f

next [nɛkst] adj prossimo/a ▷ adv accanto; (in time) dopo; **~ to** accanto a; **~ to nothing** quasi niente; **~ please!** (avanti) il prossimo!; **~ time** la prossima volta; **the ~ day** il giorno dopo, l'indomani; **~ year** l'anno prossimo or venturo; **when do we meet ~?** quando ci rincontriamo?; **next door** adv, adj accanto inv; **next of kin** n parente m/f prossimo/a

NHS n abbr = **National Health Service**

nibble ['nɪbl] vt mordicchiare

nice [naɪs] adj (holiday, trip) piacevole; (flat, picture) bello/a; (person) simpatico/a, gentile; **nicely** adv bene

niche [ni:ʃ] n (Archit) nicchia

nick [nɪk] n taglietto; tacca ▷ vt (col) rubare; **in the ~ of time** appena in tempo

nickel ['nɪkl] n nichel m; (US) moneta da cinque centesimi di dollaro

nickname ['nɪkneɪm] n soprannome m

nicotine ['nɪkəti:n] n nicotina

niece [ni:s] n nipote f

Nigeria [naɪ'dʒɪərɪə] n Nigeria

night [naɪt] n notte f; (evening) sera; **at ~** la sera; **by ~** di notte; **the ~ before last** l'altro ieri notte; l'altro ieri sera; **night club** n locale m notturno; **nightdress** n camicia da notte; **nightie** ['naɪtɪ] n camicia da notte; **night life** ['naɪtlaɪf] n vita notturna; **nightly** ['naɪtlɪ] adj di ogni notte or sera; (by night) notturno/a ▷ adv ogni notte or sera; **nightmare** ['naɪtmɛər] n incubo; **night school** n scuola serale; **nightshift** ['naɪtʃɪft] n turno di notte; **night-time** n notte f

nil [nɪl] n nulla m; (BRIT Sport) zero

nine [naɪn] num nove; **nineteen** [naɪn'ti:n] num diciannove; **nineteenth** [naɪn'ti:nθ] num diciannovesimo/a; **ninetieth** ['naɪntɪθ] num novantesimo/a; **ninety** num novanta; **ninth** [naɪnθ] num nono/a

nip [nɪp] vt pizzicare; (bite) mordere

nipple ['nɪpl] n (Anat) capezzolo

nitrogen ['naɪtrədʒən] n azoto

 KEYWORD

no [nəu] adv (opposite of "yes") no; **are you coming? — no (I'm not)** viene? — no (non vengo); **would you like some more? — no thank you** ne vuole ancora un po'? — no, grazie

▶ adj (not any) nessuno/a; **I have no money/time/books** non ho soldi/tempo/libri; **no student would have done it** nessuno studente lo avrebbe fatto; **"no parking"** "divieto di sosta"; **"no smoking"** "vietato fumare"

▶ n (pl **noes**) no m inv

nobility [nəu'bɪlɪtɪ] n nobiltà

noble ['nəubl] adj nobile

nobody ['nəubədɪ] pron nessuno

nod [nɔd] vi accennare col capo, fare un cenno; (in agreement) annuire con un cenno del capo; (*sleep*) sonnecchiare ▷ *vt*: **to ~ one's head** fare di sì col capo ▷ *n* cenno; **nod off** *vi* assopirsi

noise [nɔɪz] *n* rumore *m*; (*din, racket*) chiasso; **noisy** *adj* (*street, car*) rumoroso/a; (*person*) chiassoso/a

nominal ['nɔmɪnl] *adj* nominale; (*rent*) simbolico/a

nominate ['nɔmɪneɪt] *vt* (*propose*) proporre come candidato; (*elect*) nominare; **nomination** [nɔmɪ'neɪʃən] *n* nomina; candidatura; **nominee** [nɔmɪ'niː] *n* persona nominata; candidato/a

none [nʌn] *pron* (*not one thing*) niente; (*not one person*) nessuno/a; **~ of you** nessuno di voi; **I have ~ left** non ne ho più; **he's the worse for it** non ne ha risentito

nonetheless ['nʌnðə'lɛs] *adv* nondimeno

non-fiction [nɔn'fɪkʃən] *n* saggistica

nonsense ['nɔnsəns] *n* sciocchezze *fpl*

non-: non-smoker *n* non fumatore/trice; **non-smoking** *adj* (*person*) che non fuma; (*area, section*) per non fumatori; **non-stick** *adj* antiaderente, antiadesivo/a

noodles ['nuːdlz] *npl* taglierini *mpl*

noon [nuːn] *n* mezzogiorno

no one ['nəuwʌn] *pron* = **nobody**

nor [nɔːr] *conj* = **neither** ▷ *adv see* **neither**

norm [nɔːm] *n* norma

normal ['nɔːml] *adj* normale; **normally** *adv* normalmente

north [nɔːθ] *n* nord *m*, settentrione *m* ▷ *adj* nord *inv*, del nord, settentrionale ▷ *adv* verso nord; **North America** *n* America del Nord; **North American** *adj, n* nordamericano/a; **northbound** ['nɔːθbaund] *adj* (*traffic*) diretto/a a nord; (*carriageway*) nord *inv*; **north-east** *n* nord-est *m*; **northeastern** *adj* nordorientale; **northern** ['nɔːðən] *adj* del nord, settentrionale; **Northern Ireland** *n* Irlanda del Nord; **North Korea** *n* Corea del Nord; **North Pole** *n*: **the North Pole** il Polo Nord; **North Sea** *n*: **the North Sea** il mare del Nord; **north-west** *n* nord-ovest *m*; **northwestern** *adj* nordoccidentale

Norway ['nɔːweɪ] *n* Norvegia; **Norwegian** [nɔː'wiːdʒən] *adj* norvegese ▷ *n* norvegese *m/f*; (*Ling*) norvegese *m*

nose [nəuz] *n* naso; (*of animal*) muso; **nose about** *vi* aggirarsi; **nosebleed** *n* emorragia nasale; **nosey** ['nəuzɪ] *adj* curioso/a

nostalgia [nɔs'tældʒɪə] *n* nostalgia

nostalgic [nɔs'tældʒɪk] *adj* nostalgico/a

nostril ['nɔstrɪl] *n* narice *f*; (*of horse*) frogia

nosy ['nəuzɪ] *adj* = **nosey**

not [nɔt] *adv* non; **you must ~ or mustn't do this** non deve fare questo; **it's too late, isn't it or is it ~?** è troppo tardi, vero?; **he is ~ or isn't here** non è qui, non c'è; **~ that I don't like him** non che (lui) non mi piaccia; **~ yet/now** non ancora/ora

notable ['nəutəbl] *adj* notevole; **notably** ['nəutəblɪ] *adv* notevolmente; (*in particular*) in particolare

notch [nɔtʃ] *n* tacca; (*in saw*) dente *m*

note [nəut] *n* nota; (*letter, banknote*) biglietto ▷ *vt*: **to take ~ of** prendere nota di; **to take ~s** prendere appunti; **notebook** *n* taccuino; **noted** ['nəutɪd] *adj* celebre; **notepad** *n* bloc-notes *m inv*; **notepaper** *n* carta da lettere

nothing ['nʌθɪŋ] *n* nulla *m*, niente *m*; (*zero*) zero; **he does ~ non** fa niente; **~ new** niente di nuovo; **for ~** per niente

notice ['nəutɪs] *n* avviso; (*of leaving*) preavviso ▷ *vt* notare, accorgersi di; **to take ~ of** fare attenzione a; **to bring sth to sb's ~** far notare qc a qn; **to hand in one's ~** licenziarsi; **at short ~** con un breve preavviso; **until further ~** fino a nuovo avviso; **noticeable** *adj* evidente

notify ['nəutɪfaɪ] *vt*: **to ~ sth to sb** notificare qc a qn; **to ~ sb of sth** avvisare qn di qc

notion ['nəuʃən] *n* idea; (*concept*) nozione *f*; **notions** ['nəuʃənz] *npl* (*US: haberdashery*) merceria

notorious [nəu'tɔːrɪəs] *adj* famigerato/a

notwithstanding [nɔtwɪθ'stændɪŋ] *adv* nondimeno ▷ *prep* nonostante, malgrado

nought [nɔːt] *n* zero

noun [naun] *n* nome *m*, sostantivo

nourish ['nʌrɪʃ] *vt* nutrire; **nourishment** *n* nutrimento

Nov. *abbr* (= *November*) nov.

novel ['nɔvl] *n* romanzo ▷ *adj* nuovo/a; **novelist** *n* romanziere/a; **novelty** *n* novità *f inv*

November [nəu'vɛmbər] *n* novembre *m*

novice ['nɔvɪs] *n* principiante *m/f*; (*Rel*) novizio/a

now [nau] *adv* ora, adesso ▷ *conj*: **~ (that)** adesso che, ora che; **right ~** subito; **by ~** ormai; **just ~** proprio ora; **that's the fashion just ~** è la moda del momento; **I saw her just ~** l'ho vista proprio adesso; **~ and then, ~ and again** ogni tanto; **from ~ on** da ora in poi; **nowadays** ['nauədeɪz] *adv* oggidì

nowhere ['nəuwɛər] *adv* in nessun luogo, da nessuna parte

nozzle ['nɔzl] *n* (*of hose etc*) boccaglio; (*of fire extinguisher*) lancia

nr *abbr* (*BRIT*) = **near**

nuclear ['njuːklɪər] *adj* nucleare

nucleus (*pl* **nuclei**) ['njuːklɪəs, 'njuːklɪaɪ] *n* nucleo

nude [njuːd] *adj* nudo/a ⊳ *n* (*Art*) nudo; **in the ~** tutto/a nudo/a

nudge [nʌdʒ] *vt* dare una gomitata a

nudist ['njuːdɪst] *n* nudista *m/f*

nudity ['njuːdɪtɪ] *n* nudità

nuisance ['njuːsns] *n*: **it's a ~** è una seccatura; **he's a ~** dà fastidio

numb [nʌm] *adj* intorpidito/a; **~ with** (*fear*, *grief*) paralizzato/a da; **~ with cold** intirizzito/a (dal freddo)

number ['nʌmbə^r] *n* numero ⊳ *vt* numerare; (*include*) contare; **a ~ of** un certo numero di; **to be ~ed among** venire annoverato/a tra; **they were 10 in ~** erano in tutto 10; **number plate** *n* (*BRIT Aut*) targa; **Number Ten** *n* (*BRIT* = 10 *Downing Street*) residenza del Primo Ministro del Regno Unito

numerical [njuː'mɛrɪkl] *adj* numerico/a

numerous ['njuːmərəs] *adj* numeroso/a

nun [nʌn] *n* suora, monaca

nurse [nəːs] *n* infermiere/a; (*also*: **~maid**) bambinaia ⊳ *vt* (*patient*, *cold*) curare; (*baby*: *BRIT*) cullare; (: *US*) allattare, dare il latte a

nursery ['nəːsərɪ] *n* (*room*) camera dei bambini; (*institution*) asilo; (*for plants*) vivaio; **nursery rhyme** *n* filastrocca; **nursery school** *n* scuola materna; **nursery slope** *n* (*BRIT Ski*) pista per principianti

nursing ['nəːsɪŋ] *n* (*profession*) professione *f* di infermiere (*or* di infermiera); (*care*) cura; **nursing home** *n* casa di cura

nurture ['nəːtʃə^r] *vt* allevare; nutrire

nut [nʌt] *n* (*of metal*) dado; (*fruit*) noce *f* (*or* nocciola *or* mandorla *etc*); **he's ~s** (*col*) è matto

nutmeg ['nʌtmɛg] *n* noce *f* moscata

nutrient ['njuːtrɪənt] *adj* nutriente ⊳ *n* sostanza nutritiva

nutrition [njuː'trɪʃən] *n* nutrizione *f*

nutritious [njuː'trɪʃəs] *adj* nutriente

NVQ *n abbr* (*BRIT*) = **National Vocational Qualification**

nylon ['naɪlɔn] *n* nailon *m* ⊳ *adj* di nailon

oak [əuk] *n* quercia ⊳ *cpd* di quercia

OAP *n abbr* (*BRIT*) = **old-age pensioner**

oar [ɔː^r] *n* remo

oasis (*pl* **oases**) [əu'eɪsɪs, əu'eɪsiːz] *n* oasi *f inv*

oath [əuθ] *n* giuramento; (*swear word*) bestemmia

oatmeal ['əutmiːl] *n* farina d'avena

oats [əuts] *npl* avena

obedience [ə'biːdɪəns] *n* ubbidienza

obedient [ə'biːdɪənt] *adj* ubbidiente

obese [əu'biːs] *adj* obeso/a

obesity [əu'biːsɪtɪ] *n* obesità

obey [ə'beɪ] *vt* ubbidire a; (*instructions*, *regulations*) osservare

obituary [ə'bɪtjuərɪ] *n* necrologia

object *n* ['ɔbdʒɪkt] oggetto; (*purpose*) scopo, intento; (*Ling*) complemento oggetto ⊳ *vi* [əb'dʒɛkt]: **to ~ to** (*attitude*) disapprovare; (*proposal*) protestare contro, sollevare delle obiezioni contro; **I ~!** mi oppongo!; **he ~ed that ...** obiettò che ...; **expense is no ~** non si bada a spese; **objection** [əb'dʒɛkʃən] *n* obiezione *f*; **objective** *n* obiettivo

obligation [ɔblɪ'geɪʃən] *n* obbligo, dovere *m*; **"without ~"** "senza impegno"

obligatory [ə'blɪgətərɪ] *adj* obbligatorio/a

oblige [ə'blaɪdʒ] *vt* (*do a favour*) fare una cortesia a; (*force*): **to ~ sb to do** costringere qn a fare; **to be ~d to sb for sth** essere grato a qn per qc

oblique [ə'bliːk] *adj* obliquo/a; (*allusion*) indiretto/a

obliterate [ə'blɪtəreɪt] *vt* cancellare

oblivious [ə'blɪvɪəs] *adj*: **~ of** incurante di; inconscio/a di

oblong ['ɔblɔŋ] *adj* oblungo/a ⊳ *n* rettangolo

obnoxious [əb'nɔkʃəs] *adj* odioso/a; (*smell*) disgustoso/a, ripugnante

oboe ['əubəu] *n* oboe *m*

obscene [əb'si:n] *adj* osceno/a

obscure [əb'skjuəʳ] *adj* oscuro/a ▷ *vt* oscurare; (*hide: sun*) nascondere

observant [əb'zə:vnt] *adj* attento/a

⬛ Be careful not to translate *observant* by the Italian word *osservante*.

observation [ɔbzə'veiʃən] *n* osservazione *f*; (*by police etc*) sorveglianza

observatory [əb'zə:vətri] *n* osservatorio

observe [əb'zə:v] *vt* osservare; (*remark*) fare osservare; **observer** *n* osservatore/trice

obsess [əb'sɛs] *vt* ossessionare; **obsession** [əb'sɛʃən] *n* ossessione *f*; **obsessive** *adj* ossessivo/a

obsolete ['ɔbsəli:t] *adj* obsoleto/a

obstacle ['ɔbstəkl] *n* ostacolo

obstinate ['ɔbstinit] *adj* ostinato/a

obstruct [əb'strʌkt] *vt* (*block*) ostruire, ostacolare; (*halt*) fermare; (*hinder*) impedire; **obstruction** [əb'strʌkʃən] *n* ostruzione *f*; ostacolo

obtain [əb'tein] *vt* ottenere

obvious ['ɔbviəs] *adj* ovvio/a, evidente; **obviously** *adv* ovviamente; **obviously!** certo!

occasion [ə'keiʒən] *n* occasione *f*; (*event*) avvenimento; **occasional** *adj* occasionale; **occasionally** *adv* ogni tanto

occult ['ɔkʌlt] *adj* occulto/a ▷ *n*: **the ~** l'occulto

occupant ['ɔkjupənt] *n* occupante *m/f*; (*of boat, car etc*) persona a bordo

occupation [ɔkju'peiʃən] *n* occupazione *f*; (*job*) mestiere *m*, professione *f*

occupy ['ɔkjupai] *vt* occupare; **to ~ o.s. by doing** occuparsi a fare

occur [ə'kə:ʳ] *vi* accadere; (*difficulty, opportunity*) capitare; **to ~ to sb** venire in mente a qn; **occurrence** *n* caso, fatto; presenza

⬛ Be careful not to translate *occur* by the Italian word *occorrere*.

ocean ['əuʃən] *n* oceano

o'clock [ə'klɔk] *adv*: **it is 5 ~** sono le 5

Oct. *abbr* (= October) ott.

October [ɔk'təubəʳ] *n* ottobre *m*

octopus ['ɔktəpəs] *n* polpo, piovra

odd [ɔd] *adj* (*strange*) strano/a, bizzarro/a; (*number*) dispari *inv*; (*not of a set*) spaiato/a; **60~~6o** 6o e oltre; **at ~ times** di tanto in tanto; **the ~ one out** l'eccezione *f*; **oddly** *adv* stranamente; **odds** *npl* (*in betting*) quota

odometer ['ɔ'dɔmitəʳ] *n* odometro

odour, (*US*) **odor** ['əudəʳ] *n* odore *m*; (*unpleasant*) cattivo odore

🔵 **KEYWORD**

of [ɔv, əv] *prep* **1** (*gen*) di; **a boy of 10** un ragazzo di 10 anni; **a friend of ours** un nostro amico; **that was kind of you** è stato molto gentile da parte sua

2 (*expressing quantity, amount, dates etc*) di; **a kilo of flour** un chilo di farina; **how much of this do you need?** quanto gliene serve?; **there were four of them** (*people*) erano in quattro; (*objects*) ce n'erano quattro; **three of us went** tre di noi sono andati; **the 5th of July** il 5 luglio

3 (*from, out of*) di, in; **made of wood** (fatto) di *or* in legno

🔵 **KEYWORD**

off [ɔf] *adv* **1** (*distance, time*): **it's a long way off** è lontano; **the game is 3 days off** la partita è tra 3 giorni

2 (*departure, removal*) via; **to go off to Paris** andarsene a Parigi; **I must be off** devo andare via; **to take off one's coat** togliersi il cappotto; **the button came off** il bottone è venuto via *or* si è staccato; **10% off** con lo sconto del 10%

3 (*not at work*): **to have a day off** avere un giorno libero; **to be off sick** essere assente per malattia

▷ *adj* (*engine*) spento/a; (*tap*) chiuso/a; (*cancelled*) sospeso/a; (BRIT: *food*) andato/a a male; **on the off chance** nel caso; **to have an off day** non essere in forma

▷ *prep* **1** (*motion, removal etc*) da; (*distant from*) a poca distanza da; **a street off the square** una strada che parte dalla piazza

2: **to be off meat** non mangiare più la carne

offence, (*US*) **offense** [ə'fɛns] *n* (*Law*) contravvenzione *f*; (: *more serious*) reato; **to take ~ at** offendersi per

offend [ə'fɛnd] *vt* (*person*) offendere; **offender** *n* delinquente *m/f*; (*against regulations*) contravventore/trice

offense [ə'fɛns] *n* (*US*) = **offence**

offensive [ə'fɛnsiv] *adj* offensivo/a; (*smell etc*) sgradevole, ripugnante ▷ *n* (*Mil*) offensiva

offer ['ɔfəʳ] *n* offerta, proposta ▷ *vt* offrire; **"on ~"** (*Comm*) "in offerta speciale"

offhand [ɔf'hænd] *adj* disinvolto/a, noncurante ▷ *adv*: **I can't tell you ~** non posso dirglielo su due piedi

office ['ɔfis] *n* (*place*) ufficio; (*position*) carica; **doctor's ~** (*US*) ambulatorio; **to take ~** entrare in carica; **office block**, (*US*) **office building** *n* complesso di uffici; **office hours** *npl* orario d'ufficio; (*US Med*) orario di visite

officer ['ɔfɪsəʳ] n (Mil etc) ufficiale m; (of organization) funzionario; (also: **police ~**) agente m di polizia
office worker n impiegato/a d'ufficio
official [ə'fɪʃl] adj (authorized) ufficiale ▷ n ufficiale m; (civil servant) impiegato/a statale; funzionario
off: **off-licence** n (BRIT) spaccio di bevande alcoliche; **off-line** adj, adv (Comput) off-line inv, non in linea; (: switched off) spento/a; **off-peak** adj (ticket etc) a tariffa ridotta; (time) non di punta; **off-putting** adj (BRIT) sgradevole; **off-season** adj, adv fuori stagione; **offset** ['ɔfsɛt] vt (irreg: counteract) controbilanciare, compensare; **offshore** [ɔf'ʃɔːʳ] adj (breeze) di terra; (island) vicino alla costa; (fishing) costiero/a; **offside** ['ɔf'saɪd] adj (Sport) fuori gioco; (Aut: with right-hand drive) destro/a; (: with left-hand drive) sinistro/a; **offspring** ['ɔfsprɪŋ] n prole f, discendenza
often ['ɔfn] adv spesso; **how ~ do you go?** quanto spesso ci va?
oh [əu] excl oh!
oil [ɔɪl] n olio; (petroleum) petrolio; (for central heating) nafta ▷ vt (machine) lubrificare; **oil filter** n (Aut) filtro dell'olio; **oil painting** n quadro a olio; **oil refinery** n raffineria di petrolio; **oil rig** n derrick m inv; (at sea) piattaforma per trivellazioni subacquee; **oil slick** n chiazza d'olio; **oil tanker** n (ship) petroliera; (truck) autocisterna per petrolio; **oil well** n pozzo petrolifero; **oily** adj unto/a, oleoso/a; (food) grasso/a
ointment ['ɔɪntmənt] n unguento
O.K. [əu'keɪ] excl d'accordo! ▷ vt approvare ▷ adj non male inv; **is it ~?, are you ~?** tutto bene?
old [əuld] adj vecchio/a; (ancient) antico/a, vecchio/a; (person) vecchio/a, anziano/a; **how ~ are you?** quanti anni ha?; **he's 10 years ~** ha 10 anni; **~er brother/sister** fratello/sorella maggiore; **old age** n vecchiaia; **old-age pension** ['əuldeɪdʒ-] n (BRIT) pensione f di vecchiaia; **old-age pensioner** n (BRIT) pensionato/a; **old-fashioned** adj antiquato/a, fuori moda; (person) all'antica; **old people's home** n ricovero per anziani
olive ['ɔlɪv] n (fruit) oliva; (tree) olivo ▷ adj (also: **~-green**) verde oliva inv; **olive oil** n olio d'oliva
Olympic® [əu'lɪmpɪk] adj olimpico/a; **the ~ Games®, the ~s®** i giochi olimpici, le Olimpiadi
omelet(te) ['ɔmlɪt] n omelette f inv
omen ['əumən] n presagio, augurio
ominous ['ɔmɪnəs] adj minaccioso/a; (event) di malaugurio
omit [əu'mɪt] vt omettere

KEYWORD

on [ɔn] prep **1** (indicating position) su; **on the wall** sulla parete; **on the left** a o sulla sinistra
2 (indicating means, method, condition etc): **on foot** a piedi; **on the train/plane** in treno/aereo; **on the telephone** al telefono; **on the radio/television** alla radio/ televisione; **to be on drugs** drogarsi; **on holiday** in vacanza
3 (referring to time): **on Friday** venerdì; **on Fridays** il o di venerdì; **on June 20th** il 20 giugno; **on Friday, June 20th** venerdì, 20 giugno; **a week on Friday** venerdì a otto; **on his arrival** al suo arrivo; **on seeing this** vedendo ciò
4 (about, concerning) su, di; **information on train services** informazioni sui collegamenti ferroviari; **a book on Goldoni/physics** un libro su Goldoni/di o sulla fisica
▶ adv **1** (referring to dress, covering): **to have one's coat on** avere indosso il cappotto; **to put one's coat on** mettersi il cappotto; **what's she got on?** cosa indossa?; **she put her boots/gloves/hat on** si mise gli stivali/i guanti/il cappello; **screw the lid on tightly** avvita bene il coperchio
2 (further, continuously): **to walk on, go on** etc continuare, proseguire; **to read on** continuare a leggere; **on and off** ogni tanto
▶ adj **1** (in operation: machine, TV, light) acceso/a; (tap) aperto/a; (brake) inserito/a; **is the meeting still on?** (in progress) la riunione è ancora in corso?; (not cancelled) è confermato l'incontro?; **there's a good film on at the cinema** danno un buon film al cinema
2 (col): **that's not on!** (not acceptable) non si fa così!; (not possible) non se ne parla neanche!

once [wʌns] adv una volta ▷ conj non appena, quando; **~ he had left/it was done** dopo che se n'era andato/fu fatto; **at ~** subito; (simultaneously) a un tempo; **~ a week** una volta alla settimana; **~ more** ancora una volta; **~ and for all** una volta per sempre; **~ upon a time there was ...** c'era una volta ...
oncoming ['ɔnkʌmɪŋ] adj (traffic) che viene in senso opposto

KEYWORD

one [wʌn] num uno/a; **one hundred and fifty** centocinquanta; **one day** un giorno
▶ adj **1** (sole) unico/a; **the one book which**

l'unico libro che; **the one man who** l'unico che

2 (*same*) stesso/a; **they came in the one car** sono venuti nella stessa macchina ▶ *pron* **1**: **this one** questo/a; **that one** quello/a; **I've already got one/a red one** ne ho già uno/uno rosso; **one by one** uno per uno

2: **one another** l'un l'altro; **to look at one another** guardarsi; **to help one another** aiutarsi l'un l'altro *or* a vicenda

3 (*impersonal*) si; **one never knows** non si sa mai; **to cut one's finger** tagliarsi un dito; **one needs to eat** bisogna mangiare; **one-off** (*BRIT col*) *n* fatto eccezionale

oneself [wʌn'sɛlf] *pron* (*reflexive*) si; (*after prep*) sé, se stesso/a; **to do sth (by)** ~ fare qc da sé; **to hurt** ~ farsi male; **to keep sth for** ~ tenere qc per sé; **to talk to** ~ parlare da solo

one: **one-shot** [wʌn'ʃɔt] *n* (*US*) = **one-off**; **one-sided** *adj* (*decision, view, argument*) unilaterale; **one-to-one** *adj* (*relationship*) univoco/a; **one-way** *adj* (*street, traffic*) a senso unico

ongoing ['ɔngəʊɪŋ] *adj* in corso; in attuazione

onion ['ʌnjən] *n* cipolla

on-line ['ɔnlaɪn] *adj*, *adv* (*Comput*) on-line *inv*

onlooker ['ɔnlʊkəʳ] *n* spettatore/trice

only ['əʊnlɪ] *adv* solo, soltanto ▷ *adj* solo/a, unico/a ▷ *conj* solo che, ma; **an** ~ **child** un figlio unico; **not** ~ non solo

on-screen [ɔn'skriːn] *adj* sullo schermo *inv*

onset ['ɔnsɛt] *n* inizio

onto ['ɔntu] *prep* su, sopra

onward(s) ['ɔnwəd(z)] *adv* (*move*) in avanti; **from this time onward(s)** d'ora in poi

oops [ups] *excl* ops! (*esprime rincrescimento per un piccolo contrattempo*); **~-a-daisy!** oplà!

ooze [uːz] *vi* stillare

opaque [əʊ'peɪk] *adj* opaco/a

open ['əʊpn] *adj* aperto/a; (*road*) libero/a; (*meeting*) pubblico/a ▷ *vt* aprire ▷ *vi* (*eyes, door, debate*) aprirsi; (*flower*) sbocciare; (*shop, bank, museum*) aprire; (*book etc*) *commence*) cominciare; **in the** ~ (**air**) all'aperto; **is it** ~ **to the public?** è aperto al pubblico?; **what time do you** ~? a che ora aprite?; **open up** *vt* aprire; (*blocked road*) sgombrare ▷ *vi* (*shop, business*) aprire; **open-air** *adj* all'aperto; **opening** *n* apertura; (*opportunity*) occasione *f*, opportunità *f inv*; sbocco ▷ *adj* (*speech*) di apertura; **opening hours** *npl* orario d'apertura; **open learning** *n* sistema educativo secondo il quale lo studente ha maggior controllo e gestione delle modalità di apprendimento; **openly** *adv* apertamente; **open-minded** *adj* che ha la mente aperta; **open-necked** *adj* col collo slacciato; **open-plan** *adj* senza pareti divisorie; **Open University** *n* (*BRIT*) *vedi nota* "Open University"

● **OPEN UNIVERSITY**
●
● La *Open University* (*OU*), fondata in
● Gran Bretagna nel 1969, organizza corsi
● universitari per corrispondenza o via
● Internet, basati anche su lezioni che
● vengono trasmesse dalla *BBC* per radio e
● per televisione e su corsi estivi.

opera ['ɔpərə] *n* opera; **opera house** *n* opera; **opera singer** *n* cantante *m/f* d'opera *or* lirico/a

operate ['ɔpəreɪt] *vt* (*machine*) azionare, far funzionare; (*system*) usare ▷ *vi* funzionare; (*drug, person*) agire; **to** ~ **on sb (for)** (*Med*) operare qn (di)

operating room *n* (*US*) = **operating theatre**

operating theatre *n* (*Med*) sala operatoria

operation [ɔpə'reɪʃən] *n* operazione *f*; **to be in** ~ (*machine*) essere in azione *or* funzionamento; (*system*) essere in vigore; **to have an** ~ (**for**) (*Med*) essere operato/a (di); **operational** *adj* d'esercizio; (*ready for use or action*) in funzione

operative ['ɔpərətɪv] *adj* (*measure*) operativo/a

operator ['ɔpəreɪtəʳ] *n* (*of machine*) operatore/trice; (*Tel*) centralinista *m/f*

opinion [ə'pɪnjən] *n* opinione *f*, parere *m*; **in my** ~ secondo me, a mio avviso; **opinion poll** *n* sondaggio di opinioni

opponent [ə'pəʊnənt] *n* avversario/a

opportunity [ɔpə'tjuːnɪtɪ] *n* opportunità *f inv*, occasione *f*; **to take the** ~ **to do** *or* **of doing** cogliere l'occasione per fare

oppose [ə'pəʊz] *vt* opporsi a; **~d to** contrario/a a; **as** ~**d to** in contrasto con

opposite ['ɔpəzɪt] *adj* opposto/a; (*house etc*) di fronte ▷ *adv* di fronte, dirimpetto ▷ *prep* di fronte a ▷ *n* opposto, contrario; **the** ~ **sex** l'altro sesso

opposition [ɔpə'zɪʃən] *n* opposizione *f*

oppress [ə'prɛs] *vt* opprimere

opt [ɔpt] *vi*: **to** ~ **for** optare per; **to** ~ **to do** scegliere di fare; **opt out** *vi*: **to** ~ **out of** ritirarsi da

optician [ɔp'tɪʃən] *n* ottico/a

optimism ['ɔptɪmɪzəm] *n* ottimismo

optimist ['ɔptɪmɪst] *n* ottimista *m/f*; **optimistic** [ɔptɪ'mɪstɪk] *adj* ottimistico/a

optimum ['ɔptɪməm] *adj* ottimale

option ['ɔpʃən] n scelta; (Scol) materia
facoltativa; (Comm) opzione f; **optional** adj
facoltativo/a; (Comm) a scelta

or [ɔːʳ] conj o, oppure; (with negative): **he
hasn't seen or heard anything** non ha
visto né sentito niente; **or else** se no,
altrimenti; oppure

oral ['ɔːrəl] adj orale ▷ n esame m orale

orange ['ɔrɪndʒ] n (fruit) arancia ▷ adj
arancione; **orange juice** n succo d'arancia;
orange squash n succo d'arancia (da
diluire con l'acqua)

orbit ['ɔːbɪt] n orbita ▷ vt orbitare intorno a

orchard ['ɔːtʃəd] n frutteto

orchestra ['ɔːkɪstrə] n orchestra; (us:
seating) platea

orchid ['ɔːkɪd] n orchidea

ordeal [ɔːˈdiːl] n prova, travaglio

order ['ɔːdəʳ] n ordine m; (Comm)
ordinazione f ▷ vt ordinare; **to ~ sb to
do** ordinare a qn di fare; **in ~** in ordine;
(document) in regola; **in ~ to do** per fare;
in ~ that affinché + sub; **a machine in
working ~** una macchina che funziona
bene; **out of ~** non in ordine; **to be out
of ~** (machine, toilets) essere guasto/a;
to be on ~ essere stato ordinato; **order
form** n modulo d'ordinazione; **orderly** n
(Mil) attendente m; (Med) inserviente m
▷ adj (room) in ordine; (mind) metodico/a;
(person) ordinato/a, metodico/a

ordinary ['ɔːdnrɪ] adj normale, comune;
(pej) mediocre ▷ n: **out of the ~** diverso dal
solito, fuori dell'ordinario

ore [ɔːʳ] n minerale m grezzo

oregano [ɔrɪˈgɑːnəu] n origano

organ ['ɔːgən] n organo; **organic**
[ɔːˈgænɪk] adj organico/a; (food, produce)
biologico/a; **organism** n organismo

organization [ˌɔːgənaɪˈzeɪʃən] n
organizzazione f

organize ['ɔːgənaɪz] vt organizzare;
to get ~d organizzarsi; **organized**
['ɔːgənaɪzd] adj organizzato/a; **organizer**
n organizzatore/trice

orgasm ['ɔːgæzəm] n orgasmo

orgy ['ɔːdʒɪ] n orgia

oriental [ɔːrɪˈɛntl] adj, n orientale (m/f)

orientation [ˌɔːrɪɛnˈteɪʃən] n
orientamento

origin ['ɔrɪdʒɪn] n origine f

original [əˈrɪdʒɪnl] adj originale; (earliest)
originario/a ▷ n originale m; **originally** adv
(at first) all'inizio

originate [əˈrɪdʒɪneɪt] vi: **to ~ from** essere
originario/a di; (suggestion) provenire da;
to ~ in avere origine in

Orkneys ['ɔːknɪz] npl: **the ~** (also: **the
Orkney Islands**) le (isole) Orcadi

ornament ['ɔːnəmənt] n ornamento;
(trinket) ninnolo; **ornamental**
[ɔːnəˈmɛntl] adj ornamentale

ornate [ɔːˈneɪt] adj molto ornato/a

orphan ['ɔːfn] n orfano/a

orthodox ['ɔːθədɔks] adj ortodosso/a

orthopaedic, (us) **orthopedic**
[ɔːθəˈpiːdɪk] adj ortopedico/a

osteopath ['ɔstɪəpæθ] n specialista m/f di
osteopatia

ostrich ['ɔstrɪtʃ] n struzzo

other ['ʌðəʳ] adj altro/a ▷ pron: **the ~**
l'altro/a; **the ~s** gli altri; **~ than** altro che;
a parte; **otherwise** adv, conj altrimenti

otter ['ɔtəʳ] n lontra

ouch [autʃ] excl ohi!, ahi!

ought [ɔːt] aux vb: **I ~ to do it** dovrei farlo;
this ~ to have been corrected questo
avrebbe dovuto essere corretto; **he ~ to
win** dovrebbe vincere

ounce [auns] n oncia (= 28.35 g; 16 in a
pound)

our [auəʳ] adj il (la) nostro/a; (pl) i (le)
nostri/e; **ours** pron il (la) nostro/a; (pl) i (le)
nostri/e; see also **mine¹**; **ourselves** pl pron
(reflexive) ci; (after preposition) noi; (emphatic)
noi stessi/e; see also **oneself**

oust [aust] vt cacciare, espellere

Ⓞ **KEYWORD**

out [aut] adv (gen) fuori; **out here/there**
qui/là fuori; **to speak out loud** parlare
forte; **to have a night out** uscire una sera;
the boat was 10 km out la barca era a 10
km dalla costa; **3 days out from Plymouth**
a 3 giorni da Plymouth
▶ prep: **out of** (outside, beyond) fuori di;
(because of) per; (from) su 10; **out of
petrol** senza benzina

out: outback ['autbæk] n (in Australia)
interno, entroterra; **outbound** adj:
outbound (for or from) in partenza (per
or da); **outbreak** n scoppio; epidemia;
outburst n scoppio; **outcast** ['autkɑːst]
n esule m/f; (socially) paria m inv;
outcome ['autkʌm] n esito, risultato;
outcry ['autkraɪ] n protesta, clamore m;
outdated [aut'deɪtɪd] adj (custom, clothes)
fuori moda; (idea) sorpassato/a; **outdoor**
[aut'dɔːʳ] adj all'aperto; **outdoors** adv
fuori; all'aria aperta

outer ['autəʳ] adj esteriore; **outer space** n
spazio cosmico

outfit ['autfɪt] n (clothes) completo; (: for
sport) tenuta

out: outgoing ['autgəuɪŋ] adj (character)
socievole; **outgoings** npl (BRIT: expenses)

spese *fpl*, uscite *fpl*; **outhouse** ['authaus] *n* costruzione *f* annessa

outing ['autɪŋ] *n* gita; escursione *f*

out: outlaw ['autlɔː] *n* fuorilegge *m/f* ▷ *vt* bandire; **outlay** ['autleɪ] *n* spese *fpl*; (*investment*) sborsa, spesa; **outlet** ['autlɛt] *n* (*for liquid etc*) sbocco, scarico; (*also:* **retail outlet**) punto di vendita; (*US Elec*) presa di corrente; **outline** ['autlaɪn] *n* contorno, profilo; (*summary*) abbozzo, grandi linee *fpl* ▷ *vt* (*fig*) descrivere a grandi linee; **outlook** ['autluk] *n* prospettiva, vista; **outnumber** [aut'nʌmbəʳ] *vt* superare in numero; **out-of-date** (*passport, ticket*) scaduto/a; (*clothes*) fuori moda *inv*; **out-of-doors** [autəv'dɔːz] *adv* all'aperto; **out-of-the-way** (*remote*) fuori mano; **out-of-town** [ˌautəv'taun] *adj* (*shopping centre etc*) *inv* uori città; **outpatient** ['autpeɪʃənt] *n* paziente *m/f* esterno/a; **outpost** ['autpəust] *n* avamposto; **output** ['autput] *n* produzione *f*; (*Comput*) output *m inv*

outrage ['autreɪdʒ] *n* oltraggio; scandalo ▷ *vt* oltraggiare; **outrageous** [aut'reɪdʒəs] *adj* oltraggioso/a; scandaloso/a

outright *adv* [aut'raɪt] completamente; schiettamente; apertamente; sul colpo ▷ *adj* ['autraɪt] completo/a; schietto/a e netto/a

outset ['autsɛt] *n* inizio

outside [aut'saɪd] *n* esterno, esteriore *m* ▷ *adj* esterno/a, esteriore ▷ *adv* fuori, all'esterno ▷ *prep* fuori di, all'esterno di; **at the ~** (*fig*) al massimo; **outside lane** *n* (*Aut*) corsia di sorpasso; **outside line** *n* (*Tel*) linea esterna; **outsider** *n* (*in race etc*) outsider *m inv*; (*stranger*) straniero/a

out: outsize ['autsaɪz] *adj* (*clothes*) per taglie forti; **outskirts** ['autskəːts] *npl* sobborghi *mpl*; **outspoken** [aut'spəukən] *adj* molto franco/a; **outstanding** [aut'stændɪŋ] *adj* eccezionale, di rilievo; (*unfinished*) non completo/a; non evaso/a; non regolato/a

outward ['autwəd] *adj* (*sign, appearances*) esteriore; (*journey*) d'andata; **outwards** ['autwədz] *adv* (*esp BRIT*) = **outward**

outweigh [aut'weɪ] *vt* avere maggior peso di

oval ['əuvl] *adj*, *n* ovale (*m*)

ovary ['əuvərɪ] *n* ovaia

oven ['ʌvn] *n* forno; **oven glove** *n* guanto da forno; **ovenproof** *adj* da forno; **oven-ready** *adj* pronto/a da infornare

over ['əuvəʳ] *adv* al di sopra ▷ *adj*, *adv* (*finished*) finito/a, terminato/a; (*too much*) troppo; (*remaining*) che avanza ▷ *prep* su; sopra; (*above*) al di sopra di; (*on the other side of*) di là di; (*more than*) più di; (*during*) durante; **~ here** qui; **~ there** là; **all ~** (*everywhere*) dappertutto; (*finished*) tutto/a finito/a; **~ and ~ (again)** più e più volte; **~ and above** oltre (a); **to ask ~** invitare qn (a passare)

overall *adj* ['əuvərɔːl] totale ▷ *n* ['əuvərɔːl] (*BRIT*) grembiule *m* ▷ *adv* [əuvər'ɔːl] nell'insieme, complessivamente; **overalls** *npl* tuta (da lavoro)

overboard ['əuvəbɔːd] *adv* (*Naut*) fuori bordo, in acqua

overcame [əuvə'keɪm] *pt of* **overcome**

overcast ['əuvəkɑːst] *adj* (*sky*) coperto/a

overcharge [əuvə'tʃɑːdʒ] *vt*: **to ~ sb for sth** far pagare troppo caro a qn per qc

overcoat ['əuvəkəut] *n* soprabito, cappotto

overcome [əuvə'kʌm] *vt* (*irreg*) superare; sopraffare

over: overcrowded [əuvə'kraudɪd] *adj* sovraffollato/a; **overdo** [əuvə'duː] *vt* (*irreg*) esagerare; (*overcook*) cuocere troppo; **overdone** [əuvə'dʌn] *adj* troppo cotto/a; **overdose** ['əuvədəus] *n* dose *f* eccessiva; **overdraft** ['əuvədrɑːft] *n* scoperto (di conto); **overdrawn** [əuvə'drɔːn] *adj* (*account*) scoperto/a; **overdue** [əuvə'djuː] *adj* in ritardo; **overestimate** [əuvər'ɛstɪmeɪt] *vt* sopravvalutare

overflow *vi* [əuvə'fləu] traboccare ▷ *n* ['əuvəfləu] (*also:* **~ pipe**) troppopieno

overgrown [əuvə'grəun] *adj* (*garden*) ricoperto/a di vegetazione

overhaul *vt* [əuvə'hɔːl] revisionare ▷ *n* ['əuvəhɔːl] revisione *f*

overhead *adv* [əuvə'hɛd] di sopra ▷ *adj* ['əuvəhɛd] aereo/a; (*lighting*) verticale ▷ *n* ['əuvəhɛd] (*US*) = **overheads**; **overhead projector** *n* lavagna luminosa; **overheads** *npl* spese *fpl* generali

over: overhear [əuvə'hɪəʳ] *vt* (*irreg*) sentire (per caso); **overheat** [əuvə'hiːt] *vi* surriscaldarsi; **overland** *adj*, *adv* per via di terra; **overlap** *vi* [əuvə'læp] sovrapporsi; **overleaf** [əuvə'liːf] *adv* a tergo; **overload** [əuvə'ləud] *vt* sovraccaricare; **overlook** [əuvə'luk] *vt* (*have view of*) dare su; (*miss*) trascurare; (*forgive*) passare sopra a

overnight *adv* [əuvə'naɪt] (*happen*) durante la notte; (*fig*) tutto ad un tratto ▷ *adj* ['əuvənaɪt] di notte; **he stayed there ~** ci ha passato la notte; **overnight bag** *n* borsa da viaggio

overpass ['əuvəpɑːs] *n* cavalcavia *m inv*

overpower [əuvə'pauəʳ] *vt* sopraffare; **overpowering** *adj* irresistibile; (*heat, stench*) soffocante

over: overreact [əuvəriː'ækt] *vi* reagire in modo esagerato; **overrule** [əuvə'ruːl] *vt* (*decision*) annullare; (*claim*) respingere; **overrun** [əuvə'rʌn] *vt* (*irreg: like* **run**) (*country etc*) invadere; (*time limit etc*) superare

overseas [əuvə'si:z] *adv* oltremare; (*abroad*) all'estero ▷ *adj* (*trade*) estero/a; (*visitor*) straniero/a

oversee [əuvə'si:] *vt* (*oversee*) sorvegliare

overshadow [əuvə'ʃædəu] *vt* far ombra su; (*fig*) eclissare

oversight ['əuvəsait] *n* omissione *f*, svista

oversleep [əuvə'sli:p] *vi* (*irreg*) dormire troppo a lungo

overspend [əuvə'spɛnd] *vi* (*irreg*) spendere troppo; **we have overspent by 5000 dollars** abbiamo speso 5000 dollari di troppo

overt [əu'və:t] *adj* palese

overtake [əuvə'teik] *vt* (*irreg*) sorpassare

over: overthrow [əuvə'θrəu] *vt* (*irreg: government*) rovesciare; **overtime** ['əuvətaim] *n* (lavoro) straordinario

overtook [əuvə'tuk] *pt of* **overtake**

over: overturn [əuvə'tə:n] *vt* rovesciare ▷ *vi* rovesciarsi; **overweight** [əuvə'weit] *adj* (*person*) troppo grasso/a; **overwhelm** [əuvə'wɛlm] *vt* sopraffare; sommergere; schiacciare; **overwhelming** *adj* (*victory, defeat*) schiacciante; (*heat, desire*) intenso/a

ow [au] *excl* ahi!

owe [əu] *vt*: **to ~ sb sth, to ~ sth to sb** dovere qc a qn; **owing to** *prep* a causa di

owl [aul] *n* gufo

own [əun] *adj* proprio/a ▷ *vt* possedere; **a room of my ~** la mia propria camera; **to get one's ~ back** vendicarsi; **on one's ~** tutto/a solo/a; **own up** *vi* confessare; **owner** *n* proprietario/a; **ownership** *n* possesso

ox (*pl* **oxen**) [ɔks, 'ɔksn] *n* bue *m*

Oxbridge ['ɔksbrɪdʒ] *n* le università di Oxford e/o Cambridge

oxen ['ɔksn] *npl of* **ox**

oxygen ['ɔksɪdʒən] *n* ossigeno

oyster ['ɔɪstəʳ] *n* ostrica

oz. *abbr* = **ounce**

ozone ['əuzəun] *n* ozono; **ozone-friendly** *adj* che non danneggia lo strato d'ozono; **ozone layer** *n* fascia d'ozono

p [pi:] *abbr* = **penny; pence**

PA *n abbr* = **personal assistant; public address system**

p.a. *abbr* = **per annum**

pace [peis] *n* passo; (*speed*) passo; velocità ▷ *vi*: **to ~ up and down** camminare su e giù; **to keep ~ with** camminare di pari passo a; (*events*) tenersi al corrente di; **pacemaker** *n* (*Med*) pacemaker *m inv*, stimolatore *m* cardiaco; (*Sport*) chi fa l'andatura

Pacific [pə'sɪfɪk] *n*: **the ~ (Ocean)** il Pacifico, l'Oceano Pacifico

pacifier ['pæsɪfaɪəʳ] *n* (*US: dummy*) succhiotto, ciuccio (*col*)

pack [pæk] *n* pacco; (*US: of cigarettes*) pacchetto; (*of hounds*) muta; (*of thieves etc*) banda; (*of cards*) mazzo ▷ *vt* (*in suitcase etc*) mettere; (*box*) riempire; (*cram*) stipare, pigiare ▷ *vi*: **to ~ one's bags** fare la valigia; **to send sb ~ing** spedire via qn; **pack in** (*BRIT col*) *vi* (*watch, car*) guastarsi ▷ *vt* mollare, piantare; **~ it in!** piantala!, dacci un taglio!; **pack off** *vt* (*person*) spedire; **to ~ sb off** spedire via qn; **pack up** *vi* (*BRIT col: machine*) guastarsi; (*person*) far fagotto ▷ *vt* (*belongings, clothes*) mettere in una valigia; (*goods, presents*) imballare

package ['pækɪdʒ] *n* pacco; balla; (*also: ~ deal*) pacchetto; forfait *m inv*; **package holiday** *n* vacanza organizzata; **package tour** *n* viaggio organizzato

packaging ['pækɪdʒɪŋ] *n* confezione *f*, imballo

packed [pækt] *adj* (*crowded*) affollato/a; **~ lunch** (*BRIT*) pranzo al sacco

packet ['pækɪt] *n* pacchetto

packing ['pækɪŋ] *n* imballaggio

pact [pækt] *n* patto, accordo; trattato

pad [pæd] n blocco; (to prevent friction) cuscinetto; (col: flat) appartamentino ▷ vt imbottire; **padded** adj imbottito/a

paddle ['pædl] n (oar) pagaia; (us: for table tennis) racchetta da ping-pong ▷ vi sguazzare ▷ vt (boat) fare andare a colpi di pagaia; **paddling pool** n (BRIT) piscina per bambini

paddock ['pædək] n prato recintato; (at racecourse) paddock m inv

padlock ['pædlɔk] n lucchetto

paedophile, (us) **pedophile** ['pi:dəufaɪl] adj, n pedofilo/a

page [peɪdʒ] n pagina; (also: ~ **boy**) paggio ▷ vt (in hotel etc) (far) chiamare

pager ['peɪdʒə'] n (Tel) cercapersone m inv

paid [peɪd] pt, pp of **pay** ▷ adj (work, official) rimunerato/a; **to put ~ to** (BRIT) mettere fine a

pain [peɪn] n dolore m; **to be in ~** soffrire, aver male; **to take ~s to do** mettercela tutta per fare; **painful** adj doloroso/a, che fa male; (difficult) difficile, penoso/a; **painkiller** n antalgico, antidolorifico; **painstaking** ['peɪnzteɪkɪŋ] adj (person) sollecito/a; (work) accurato/a

paint [peɪnt] n vernice f; colore m ▷ vt dipingere; (door etc) verniciare; **to ~ the door blue** verniciare la porta di azzurro; **paintbrush** n pennello; **painter** n (artist) pittore m; (decorator) imbianchino; **painting** n pittura; verniciatura; (picture) dipinto, quadro

pair [pɛə'] n (of shoes, gloves etc) paio; (of people) coppia; duo m inv; **a ~ of scissors/ trousers** un paio di forbici/pantaloni

pajamas [pə'dʒɑ:məz] npl (us) pigiama m

Pakistan [pɑ:kɪ'stɑ:n] n Pakistan m; **Pakistani** adj, n pakistano/a

pal [pæl] n (col) amico/a, compagno/a

palace ['pæləs] n palazzo

pale [peɪl] adj pallido/a ▷ n: **to be beyond the ~** aver oltrepassato ogni limite

Palestine ['pælɪstaɪn] n Palestina; **Palestinian** [pælɪs'tɪnɪən] adj, n palestinese (m/f)

palm [pɑ:m] n (Anat) palma, palmo; (also: ~ **tree**) palma ▷ vt: **to ~ sth off on sb** (col) rifilare qc a qn

pamper ['pæmpə'] vt viziare, coccolare

pamphlet ['pæmflət] n dépliant m inv

pan [pæn] n (also: **sauce~**) casseruola; (also: **frying ~**) padella

pancake ['pænkeɪk] n frittella

panda ['pændə] n panda m inv

pandemic [pæn'dɛmɪk] n pandemia

pane [peɪn] n vetro

panel ['pænl] n (of wood, cloth etc) pannello; (Radio, TV) giuria

panhandler ['pænhændlə'] n (us col) accattone/a

panic ['pænɪk] n panico ▷ vi perdere il sangue freddo

panorama [pænə'rɑ:mə] n panorama m

pansy ['pænzɪ] n (Bot) viola del pensiero, pensée f inv; (col!) femminuccia

pant [pænt] vi ansare

panther ['pænθə'] n pantera

panties ['pæntɪz] npl slip m, mutandine fpl

pantomime ['pæntəmaɪm] n (BRIT: at Christmas) spettacolo natalizio; (tecnica) pantomima

● **PANTOMIME**
●
● In Gran Bretagna la pantomime
● (abbreviata in panto) è una sorta di
● libera interpretazione delle favole più
● conosciute che vengono messe in scena
● nei teatri durante il periodo natalizio. Gli
● attori principali sono la dama, "dame",
● che è un uomo vestito da donna, il
● protagonista, "principal boy", che è una
● donna travestita da uomo, e il cattivo,
● "villain". È uno spettacolo per tutta la
● famiglia, che prevede la partecipazione
● del pubblico.

pants [pænts] npl mutande fpl, slip m; (us: trousers) pantaloni mpl

paper ['peɪpə'] n carta; (also: **wall~**) carta da parati, tappezzeria; (also: **news~**) giornale m; (study, article) saggio; (exam) prova scritta ▷ adj di carta ▷ vt tappezzare; see also **papers**; **paperback** n tascabile m; edizione f economica; **paper bag** n sacchetto di carta; **paper clip** n graffetta, clip f inv; **papers** npl (also: **identity papers**) carte fpl, documenti mpl; **paper shop** n (BRIT) giornalaio (negozio); **paperwork** n lavoro amministrativo

paprika ['pæprɪkə] n paprica

par [pɑ:'] n parità, pari f; (Golf) norma; **on a ~ with** alla pari con

paracetamol [pærə'si:təmɔl] n (BRIT) paracetamolo

parachute ['pærəʃu:t] n paracadute m inv

parade [pə'reɪd] n parata ▷ vt (fig) fare sfoggio di ▷ vi sfilare in parata

paradise ['pærədaɪs] n paradiso

paradox ['pærədɔks] n paradosso

paraffin ['pærəfɪn] n (BRIT): ~ (**oil**) paraffina

paragraph ['pærəgrɑ:f] n paragrafo

parallel ['pærəlɛl] adj parallelo/a; (fig) analogo/a ▷ n (line) parallela; (fig, Geo) parallelo

paralysed ['pærəlaɪzd] adj paralizzato/a

paralysis (pl **paralyses**) [pəˈrælɪsɪs, -siːz] n paralisi f inv

paramedic [ˌpærəˈmɛdɪk] n paramedico

paranoid [ˈpærənɔɪd] adj paranoico/a

parasite [ˈpærəsaɪt] n parassita m

parcel [ˈpɑːsl] n pacco, pacchetto ▷ vt (also: ~ **up**) impaccare

pardon [ˈpɑːdn] n perdono; grazia ▷ vt perdonare; (Law) graziare; ~ **me!** mi scusi!; **I beg your ~!** scusi!; (**I beg you**) ~**?**, (US) ~ **me?** prego?

parent [ˈpɛərənt] n padre m (or madre f); **parents** npl genitori mpl; **parental** [pəˈrɛntl] adj dei genitori

■ Be careful not to translate parent by the Italian word parente.

Paris [ˈpærɪs] n Parigi f

parish [ˈpærɪʃ] n parrocchia; (Brit: civil) ≈ municipio

Parisian [pəˈrɪzɪən] adj, n parigino/a

park [pɑːk] n parco ▷ vt, vi parcheggiare

parking [ˈpɑːkɪŋ] n parcheggio; "**no ~**" "sosta vietata"; **parking lot** n (US) posteggio, parcheggio; **parking meter** n parchimetro; **parking ticket** n multa per sosta vietata

parkway [ˈpɑːkweɪ] n (US) viale m

parliament [ˈpɑːləmənt] n parlamento; **parliamentary** [pɑːləˈmɛntərɪ] adj parlamentare

Parmesan [pɑːmɪˈzæn] n (also: ~ **cheese**) parmigiano

parole [pəˈrəʊl] n: **on ~** in libertà per buona condotta

parrot [ˈpærət] n pappagallo

parsley [ˈpɑːslɪ] n prezzemolo

parsnip [ˈpɑːsnɪp] n pastinaca

parson [ˈpɑːsn] n prete m; (Church of England) parroco

part [pɑːt] n parte f; (of machine) pezzo; (US: in hair) scriminatura ▷ adj in parte ▷ adv = **partly** ▷ vt separare ▷ vi (people) separarsi; **to take ~ in** prendere parte a; **to take sb's ~** parteggiare per qn, prendere le parti di qn; **for my ~** per parte mia; **for the most ~** in generale; nella maggior parte dei casi; **to take sth in good/bad ~** prendere bene/male qc; ~ **of speech** parte del discorso; **part with** vt fus separarsi da; rinunciare a

partial [ˈpɑːʃl] adj parziale; **to be ~ to** avere un debole per

participant [pɑːˈtɪsɪpənt] n: ~ (**in**) partecipante m/f (a)

participate [pɑːˈtɪsɪpeɪt] vi: **to ~ (in**) prendere parte (a), partecipare (a)

particle [ˈpɑːtɪkl] n particella

particular [pəˈtɪkjʊlər] adj particolare; speciale; (fussy) difficile; meticoloso/a;

particulars npl particolari mpl, dettagli mpl; (information) informazioni fpl; **in ~** in particolare, particolarmente; **particularly** adv particolarmente; in particolare

parting [ˈpɑːtɪŋ] n separazione f; (Brit: in hair) scriminatura ▷ adj d'addio

partition [pɑːˈtɪʃən] n (Pol) partizione f; (wall) tramezzo

partly [ˈpɑːtlɪ] adv parzialmente; in parte

partner [ˈpɑːtnər] n (Comm) socio/a; (wife, husband etc, Sport) compagno/a; (at dance) cavaliere (dama); **partnership** n associazione f; (Comm) società f inv

partridge [ˈpɑːtrɪdʒ] n pernice f

part-time [ˈpɑːtˈtaɪm] adj, adv a orario ridotto

party [ˈpɑːtɪ] n (Pol) partito; (team) squadra; (Law) parte f; (celebration) ricevimento; serata; festa ▷ adj (Pol) del partito, di partito

pass [pɑːs] vt (gen) passare; (place) passare davanti a; (exam) passare, superare; (candidate) promuovere; (overtake, surpass) sorpassare, superare; (approve) approvare ▷ vi passare ▷ n (permit) lasciapassare m inv; permesso; (in mountains) passo, gola; (Sport) passaggio; (Scol): **to get a ~** prendere la sufficienza; **could you ~ the vegetables round?** potrebbe far passare i contorni?; **to ~ sth through a hole** etc far passare qc attraverso un buco etc; **to make a ~ at sb** (col) fare delle proposte or delle avances a qn; **pass away** vi morire; **pass by** vi passare ▷ vt trascurare; **pass on** vt: **to ~ on (to)** passare (a); **pass out** vi svenire; **pass over** vi (die) spirare ▷ vt lasciare da parte; **pass up** vt (opportunity) lasciarsi sfuggire, perdere; **passable** adj (road) praticabile; (work) accettabile

passage [ˈpæsɪdʒ] n (gen) passaggio; (also: ~**way**) corridoio; (in book) brano, passo; (by boat) traversata

passenger [ˈpæsɪndʒər] n passeggero/a

passer-by [pɑːsəˈbaɪ] n passante m/f

passing place n (Aut) piazzola (di sosta)

passion [ˈpæʃən] n passione f; amore m; **passionate** adj appassionato/a; **passion fruit** n frutto della passione

passive [ˈpæsɪv] adj (also Ling) passivo/a

passport [ˈpɑːspɔːt] n passaporto; **passport control** n controllo m passaporti inv; **passport office** n ufficio m passaporti inv

password [ˈpɑːswəːd] n parola d'ordine

past [pɑːst] prep (further than) oltre, di là di; dopo; (later than) dopo ▷ adv: **to run ~** passare di corsa ▷ adj passato/a; (president etc) ex inv ▷ n passato; **he's ~ forty** ha più di quarant'anni; **ten ~ eight** le otto e dieci;

for the ~ few days da qualche giorno; in questi ultimi giorni

pasta ['pæstə] n pasta

paste [peɪst] n (glue) colla; (Culin) pâté m inv; pasta ▷ vt collare

pastel ['pæstl] adj pastello inv

pasteurized ['pæstəraɪzd] adj pastorizzato/a

pastime ['pɑ:staɪm] n passatempo

pastor ['pɑ:stə'] n pastore m

past participle [-'pɑ:tɪsɪpl] n (Ling) participio passato

pastry ['peɪstrɪ] n pasta

pasture ['pɑ:stʃə'] n pascolo

pasty¹ ['pæstɪ] n pasticcio di carne

pasty² ['peɪstɪ] adj (complexion) pallido/a, smorto/a

pat [pæt] vt accarezzare, dare un colpetto (affettuoso) a

patch [pætʃ] n (of material) toppa; (eye patch) benda; (spot) macchia ▷ vt rattoppare; **a bad ~** un brutto periodo; **patchy** adj irregolare

pâté ['pæteɪ] n pâté m inv

patent ['peɪtnt] n brevetto ▷ vt brevettare ▷ adj patente, manifesto/a

paternal [pə'tə:nl] adj paterno/a

paternity leave [pə'tə:nɪtɪ-] n congedo di paternità

path [pɑ:θ] n sentiero, viottolo; viale m; (fig) via, strada; (of planet, missile) traiettoria

pathetic [pə'θɛtɪk] adj (pitiful) patetico/a; (very bad) penoso/a

pathway ['pɑ:θweɪ] n sentiero

patience ['peɪʃns] n pazienza; (Brit Cards) solitario

patient ['peɪʃnt] n paziente m/f; malato/a ▷ adj paziente

patio ['pætɪəu] n terrazza

patriotic [pætrɪ'ɔtɪk] adj patriottico/a

patrol [pə'trəul] n pattuglia ▷ vt pattugliare; **patrol car** n autoradio f inv (della polizia)

patron ['peɪtrən] n (in shop) cliente m/f; (of charity) benefattore/trice; **~ of the arts** mecenate m/f

patronizing ['pætrənaɪzɪŋ] adj condiscendente

pattern ['pætən] n modello; (design) disegno, motivo; **patterned** adj a disegni, a motivi; (material) fantasia inv

pause [pɔ:z] n pausa ▷ vi fare una pausa, arrestarsi

pave [peɪv] vt pavimentare; **to ~ the way for** aprire la via a

pavement ['peɪvmənt] n (Brit) marciapiede m

> Be careful not to translate pavement by the Italian word pavimento.

pavilion [pə'vɪlɪən] n (Sport) edificio annesso ad un campo sportivo

paving ['peɪvɪŋ] n pavimentazione f

paw [pɔ:] n zampa

pawn [pɔ:n] n (Chess) pedone m; (fig) pedina ▷ vt dare in pegno; **pawnbroker** n prestatore m su pegno

pay [peɪ] (pt, pp **paid**) n stipendio; paga ▷ vt pagare ▷ vi (be profitable) rendere; **to ~ attention (to)** fare attenzione (a); **to ~ sb a visit** far visita a qn; **to ~ one's respects to sb** porgere i propri rispetti a qn; **pay back** vt rimborsare; **pay for** vt fus pagare; **pay in** vt versare; **pay off** vt (debts) saldare; (creditor) pagare; (workers) licenziare ▷ vi (scheme) funzionare; (patience) dare dei frutti; **pay out** vt (money) sborsare, tirar fuori; (rope) far allentare; **pay up** vt saldare; **payable** adj pagabile; **pay-as-you-go** ['peɪəzjə'gəu] adj (mobile phone) con scheda prepagata; **pay day** n giorno di paga; **pay envelope** n (US) busta f paga inv; **payment** n pagamento; versamento; saldo; **payout** n pagamento; (in competition) premio; **pay packet** n (Brit) busta f paga inv; **payphone** n cabina telefonica; **payroll** n ruolo (organico); **pay slip** n foglio m paga inv; **pay television** n televisione f a pagamento, pay-tv f inv

PC n abbr = **personal computer** ▷ adj abbr = **politically correct**

pc abbr = **per cent**

PDA n abbr (= personal digital assistant) PDA m inv

PE n abbr (= physical education) ed. fisica

pea [pi:] n pisello

peace [pi:s] n pace f; **peaceful** adj pacifico/a, calmo/a

peach [pi:tʃ] n pesca

peacock ['pi:kɔk] n pavone m

peak [pi:k] n (of mountain) cima, vetta; (mountain itself) picco; (of cap) visiera; (fig) apice m; **peak hours** npl ore fpl di punta

peanut ['pi:nʌt] n arachide f, nocciolina americana; **peanut butter** n burro di arachidi

pear [pɛə'] n pera

pearl [pə:l] n perla

peasant ['pɛznt] n contadino/a

peat [pi:t] n torba

pebble ['pɛbl] n ciottolo

peck [pɛk] vt (also: ~ **at**) beccare ▷ n colpo di becco; (kiss) bacetto; **peckish** adj (Brit col): **I feel peckish** ho un languorino

peculiar [pɪ'kju:lɪə'] adj strano/a, bizzarro/a; (particular) particolare; **~ to** tipico/a di

pedal ['pɛdl] n pedale m ▷ vi pedalare

pedalo ['pɛdələu] n pedalò m inv

pedestal ['pɛdəstl] n piedestallo
pedestrian [pɪ'dɛstrɪən] n pedone/a
▷ adj pedonale; (fig) prosaico/a,
pedestre; **pedestrian crossing** n (BRIT)
passaggio pedonale; **pedestrianized**
adj: **a pedestrianized street** una zona
pedonalizzata; **pedestrian precinct,** (US)
pedestrian zone n zona pedonale
pedigree ['pɛdɪgriː] n (of animal) pedigree
m inv; (fig) background m inv ▷ cpd (animal)
di razza
pedophile ['piːdəʊfaɪl] (US) n
= **paedophile**
pee [piː] vi (col) pisciare
peek [piːk] vi guardare furtivamente
peel [piːl] n buccia; (of orange, lemon) scorza
▷ vt sbucciare ▷ vi (paint etc) staccarsi
peep [piːp] n (look) sguardo furtivo,
sbirciata; (sound) pigolio ▷ vi guardare
furtivamente
peer [pɪər] vi: **to ~ at** scrutare ▷ n (noble)
pari m inv; (equal) pari m f inv, uguale m/f;
(contemporary) contemporaneo/a
peg [pɛg] n caviglia; (for coat etc)
attaccapanni m inv; (BRIT: also: **clothes ~**)
molletta
pelican ['pɛlɪkən] n pellicano; **pelican
crossing** n (BRIT Aut) attraversamento
pedonale con semaforo a controllo manuale
pelt [pɛlt] vt: **to ~ sb (with)** bombardare qn
(con) ▷ vi (rain) piovere a dirotto; (col: run)
filare ▷ n pelle f
pelvis ['pɛlvɪs] n pelvi f inv, bacino
pen [pɛn] n penna; (for sheep) recinto
penalty ['pɛnltɪ] n penalità f inv;
sanzione f penale; (fine) ammenda; (Sport)
penalizzazione f
pence [pɛns] npl (BRIT) of **penny**
pencil ['pɛnsl] n matita ▷ vt (also: **~ in**)
scrivere a matita; **pencil case** n astuccio
per matite; **pencil sharpener** n
temperamatite m inv
pendant ['pɛndnt] n pendaglio
pending ['pɛndɪŋ] prep in attesa di ▷ adj
in sospeso
penetrate ['pɛnɪtreɪt] vt penetrare
penfriend ['pɛnfrɛnd] n (BRIT)
corrispondente m/f
penguin ['pɛŋgwɪn] n pinguino
penicillin [pɛnɪ'sɪlɪn] n penicillina
peninsula [pə'nɪnsjulə] n penisola
penis ['piːnɪs] n pene m
penitentiary [pɛnɪ'tɛnʃərɪ] n (US)
carcere m
penknife ['pɛnnaɪf] n temperino
penniless ['pɛnɪlɪs] adj senza un soldo
penny (pl **pennies** or **pence**) ['pɛnɪ, 'pɛnɪz,
pɛns] n (BRIT) penny m; (US) centesimo
penpal ['pɛnpæl] n corrispondente m/f

pension ['pɛnʃən] n pensione f; **pensioner**
n (BRIT) pensionato/a
pentagon ['pɛntəgən] n pentagono; **the
P~** (US Pol) il Pentagono
penthouse ['pɛnthaus] n appartamento
(di lusso) nell'attico
penultimate [pɪ'nʌltɪmət] adj
penultimo/a
people ['piːpl] npl gente f; persone fpl;
(citizens) popolo ▷ n (nation, race) popolo;
4/several ~ came 4/parecchie persone
sono venute; **~ say that ...** si dice or la
gente dice che ...
pepper ['pɛpər] n pepe m; (vegetable)
peperone m ▷ vt (fig): **to ~ with** spruzzare
di; **peppermint** n (sweet) pasticca di menta
per [pɜːr] prep per; a; **~ hour** all'ora; **~ kilo**
etc il chilo etc; **~ day** al giorno
perceive [pə'siːv] vt percepire; (notice)
accorgersi di
per cent adv per cento
percentage [pə'sɛntɪdʒ] n percentuale f
perception [pə'sɛpʃən] n percezione f;
sensibilità; perspicacia
perch [pɜːtʃ] n (fish) pesce m persico; (for
bird) sostegno, ramo ▷ vi appollaiarsi
percussion [pə'kʌʃən] n percussione f;
(Mus) strumenti mpl a percussione
perfect ['pɜːfɪkt] adj perfetto/a ▷ n (also:
~ tense) perfetto, passato prossimo ▷ vt
[pə'fɛkt] perfezionare; mettere a punto;
perfection [pə'fɛkʃən] n perfezione
f; **perfectly** adv perfettamente, alla
perfezione
perform [pə'fɔːm] vt (carry out) eseguire,
fare; (symphony etc) suonare; (play, ballet)
dare; (opera) fare ▷ vi suonare; recitare;
performance n esecuzione f; (at theatre
etc) rappresentazione f, spettacolo; (of
an artist) interpretazione f; (of player etc)
performance f; (of car, engine) prestazione f;
performer n artista m/f
perfume ['pɜːfjuːm] n profumo
perhaps [pə'hæps] adv forse
perimeter [pə'rɪmɪtər] n perimetro
period ['pɪərɪəd] n periodo; (Hist)
epoca; (Scol) lezione f; (full stop)
punto; (Med) mestruazioni fpl ▷ adj
(costume, furniture) d'epoca; **periodical**
[pɪərɪ'ɔdɪkl] n periodico; **periodically** adv
periodicamente
perish ['pɛrɪʃ] vi perire, morire; (decay)
deteriorarsi
perjury ['pɜːdʒərɪ] n spergiuro
perk [pɜːk] n (col) vantaggio
perm [pɜːm] n (for hair) permanente f
permanent ['pɜːmənənt] adj permanente;
permanently adv definitivamente
permission [pə'mɪʃən] n permesso

permit n ['pə:mɪt] permesso ▷ vt [pə'mɪt] permettere; **to ~ sb to do** permettere a qn di fare

perplex [pə'plɛks] vt lasciare perplesso/a

persecute ['pə:sɪkju:t] vt perseguitare

persecution [pə:sɪ'kju:ʃən] n persecuzione f

persevere [pə:sɪ'vɪə'] vi perseverare

Persian ['pə:ʃən] adj persiano/a ▷ n (Ling) persiano; **the ~ Gulf** n il Golfo Persico

persist [pə'sɪst] vi: **to ~ (in doing)** persistere (nel fare); ostinarsi (a fare); **persistent** adj persistente; ostinato/a

person ['pə:sn] n persona; **in ~** di or in persona, personalmente; **personal** adj personale; individuale; **personal assistant** n segretaria personale; **personal computer** n personal computer m inv; **personality** [pə:sə'nælɪtɪ] n personalità f inv; **personally** adv personalmente; **to take sth personally** prendere qc come una critica personale; **personal organizer** n agenda; (electronic) agenda elettronica; **personal stereo** [pə'ɔ̃] n walkman® m inv

personnel [pə:sə'nɛl] n personale m

perspective [pə'spɛktɪv] n prospettiva

perspiration [pə:spɪ'reɪʃən] n traspirazione f, sudore m

persuade [pə'sweɪd] vt: **to ~ sb to do sth** persuadere qn a fare qc

persuasion [pə'sweɪʒən] n persuasione f; (creed) convinzione f, credo

persuasive [pə'sweɪsɪv] adj persuasivo/a

perverse [pə'və:s] adj perverso/a

pervert n ['pə:və:t] pervertito/a ▷ vt [pə'və:t] pervertire

pessimism ['pɛsɪmɪzəm] n pessimismo

pessimist ['pɛsɪmɪst] n pessimista m/f; **pessimistic** [pɛsɪ'mɪstɪk] adj pessimistico/a

pest [pɛst] n animale m (or insetto) pestifero; (fig) peste f

pester ['pɛstə'] vt tormentare, molestare

pesticide ['pɛstɪsaɪd] n pesticida m

pet [pɛt] n animale m domestico; (favourite) favorito/a ▷ vt accarezzare; **teacher's ~** favorito/a del maestro

petal ['pɛtl] n petalo

petite [pə'ti:t] adj piccolo/a e aggraziato/a

petition [pə'tɪʃən] n petizione f

petrified ['pɛtrɪfaɪd] adj (fig) morto/a di paura

petrol ['pɛtrəl] n (BRIT) benzina; **two/four-star ~** ≈ benzina normale/super

> Be careful not to translate petrol by the Italian word petrolio.

petroleum [pə'trəʊlɪəm] n petrolio

petrol: petrol pump n (BRIT: in car, at garage) pompa di benzina; **petrol station** n (BRIT) stazione f di rifornimento; **petrol tank** n (BRIT) serbatoio della benzina

petticoat ['pɛtɪkəʊt] n sottana

petty ['pɛtɪ] adj (mean) meschino/a; (unimportant) insignificante

pew [pju:] n panca (di chiesa)

pewter ['pju:tə'] n peltro

phantom ['fæntəm] n fantasma m

pharmacist ['fɑ:məsɪst] n farmacista m/f

pharmacy ['fɑ:məsɪ] n farmacia

phase [feɪz] n fase f, periodo; **phase in** vt introdurre gradualmente; **phase out** vt (machinery) eliminare gradualmente; (product) ritirare gradualmente; (job, subsidy) abolire gradualmente

PhD n abbr = **Doctor of Philosophy**

pheasant ['fɛznt] n fagiano

phenomena [fə'nɔmɪnə] npl of **phenomenon**

phenomenal [fɪ'nɔmɪnl] adj fenomenale

phenomenon (pl **phenomena**) [fə'nɔmɪnən, -nə] n fenomeno

Philippines ['fɪlɪpi:nz] npl: **the ~** le Filippine

philosopher [fɪ'lɔsəfə'] n filosofo/a

philosophical [fɪlə'sɔfɪkl] adj filosofico/a

philosophy [fɪ'lɔsəfɪ] n filosofia

phlegm [flɛm] n flemma

phobia ['fəʊbjə] n fobia

phone [fəʊn] n telefono ▷ vt telefonare a ▷ vi telefonare; **to be on the ~** avere il telefono; (be calling) essere al telefono; **phone back** vt, vi richiamare; **phone up** vt telefonare a ▷ vi telefonare; **phone book** n guida del telefono, elenco telefonico; **phone box**, (US) **phone booth** n cabina telefonica; **phone call** n telefonata; **phonecard** n scheda telefonica; **phone number** n numero di telefono

phonetics [fə'nɛtɪks] n fonetica

phoney ['fəʊnɪ] adj falso/a, fasullo/a

photo ['fəʊtəʊ] n foto f inv; **photo album** n (new) album m inv per fotografie; (containing photos) album m inv delle fotografie; **photocopier** n fotocopiatrice f; **photocopy** n fotocopia ▷ vt fotocopiare

photograph ['fəʊtəgræf] n fotografia ▷ vt fotografare; **photographer** [fə'tɔgrəfə'] n fotografo; **photography** [fə'tɔgrəfɪ] n fotografia

phrase [freɪz] n espressione f; (Ling) locuzione f; (Mus) frase f ▷ vt esprimere

phrasebook ['freɪzbuk] n vocabolarietto

physical ['fɪzɪkl] adj fisico/a; **~ education** educazione f fisica; **physically** adv fisicamente

physician [fɪ'zɪʃən] n medico

physicist ['fɪzɪsɪst] n fisico

physics ['fɪzɪks] n fisica

physiotherapist [fɪziəu'θerəpɪst] n
fisioterapista m/f
physiotherapy [fɪziəu'θerəpɪ] n
fisioterapia
physique [fɪ'ziːk] n fisico; costituzione f
pianist ['piːənɪst] n pianista m/f
piano [pɪ'ænəu] n pianoforte m
pick [pɪk] n (tool: also: **~-axe**) piccone m
▷ vt scegliere; (gather) cogliere; (remove)
togliere; (lock) far scattare; **take your ~**
scelga; **the ~ of** il fior fiore di; **to ~ one's
nose** mettersi le dita nel naso; **to ~ one's
teeth** pulirsi i denti con lo stuzzicadenti;
to ~ a fight/quarrel with sb attaccar
rissa/briga con qn; **pick on** vt fus (person)
avercela con; **pick out** vt scegliere;
(distinguish) distinguere; **pick up** vi
(improve) migliorarsi ▷ vt raccogliere;
(Police) prendere; (collect) passare a
prendere; (Aut: give lift to) far salire;
(person: for sexual encounter) rimorchiare;
(learn) imparare; (Radio, TV, Tel) ricevere;
to ~ o.s. up rialzarsi; **to ~ up speed**
acquistare velocità
pickle ['pɪkl] n (also: **~s**) (as condiment)
sottaceti mpl; (fig): **in a ~** nei pasticci ▷ vt
mettere sottaceto; mettere in salamoia
pickpocket ['pɪkpɔkɪt] n borsaiolo
pickup ['pɪkʌp] n (BRIT: on record player)
pick-up m inv; (small truck: also: **~ truck,
~ van**) camioncino
picnic ['pɪknɪk] n picnic m inv; **picnic area**
n area per il picnic
picture ['pɪktʃəʳ] n quadro; (painting)
pittura; (photograph) foto(grafia); (drawing)
disegno; (film) film m inv ▷ vt raffigurarsi;
the ~s (BRIT) il cinema; **to take a ~ of sb/
sth** fare una foto a qn/di qc; **picture frame**
n cornice m inv; **picture messaging** n
picture messaging m, invio di messaggini
con immagini
picturesque [pɪktʃə'rɛsk] adj pittoresco/a
pie [paɪ] n torta; (of meat) pasticcio
piece [piːs] n pezzo; (of land)
appezzamento; (item): **a ~ of furniture/
advice** un mobile/consiglio ▷ vt: **to ~
together** mettere insieme; **to take to ~s**
smontare
pie chart n grafico a torta
pier [pɪəʳ] n molo; (of bridge etc) pila
pierce [pɪəs] vt forare; (with arrow etc)
trafiggere; **pierced** adj: **I've got pierced
ears** ho i buchi per gli orecchini
pig [pɪg] n maiale m, porco
pigeon ['pɪdʒən] n piccione m
piggy bank ['pɪgɪ-] n salvadanaio
pigsty ['pɪgstaɪ] n porcile m
pigtail ['pɪgteɪl] n treccina
pike [paɪk] n (fish) luccio

pilchard ['pɪltʃəd] n specie di sardina
pile [paɪl] n (pillar, of books) pila; (heap)
mucchio; (of carpet) pelo; **to ~ into** (car)
stiparsi or ammucchiarsi in; **pile up** vt
ammucchiare; **piles** [paɪlz] npl emorroidi
fpl; **pileup** ['paɪlʌp] n (Aut) tamponamento
a catena
pilgrimage ['pɪlgrɪmɪdʒ] n
pellegrinaggio
pill [pɪl] n pillola; **to be on the ~** prendere
la pillola
pillar ['pɪləʳ] n colonna
pillow ['pɪləu] n guanciale m; **pillowcase**
n federa
pilot ['paɪlət] n pilota m/f ▷ cpd (scheme
etc) pilota inv ▷ vt pilotare; **pilot light** n
fiamma pilota
pimple ['pɪmpl] n foruncolo
PIN n abbr (= personal identification number)
codice m segreto, PIN m inv
pin [pɪn] n spillo; (Tech) perno ▷ vt attaccare
con uno spillo; **~s and needles** formicolio;
to ~ sth on sb (fig) addossare la colpa di
qc a qn; **pin down** vt (fig): **to ~ sb down**
obbligare qn a pronunciarsi
pinafore ['pɪnəfɔːʳ] n (also: **~ dress**)
scamiciato
pinch [pɪntʃ] n pizzicotto, pizzico ▷ vt
pizzicare; (col: steal) grattare; **at a ~** in caso
di bisogno
pine [paɪn] n (also: **~ tree**) pino ▷ vi: **to ~ for**
struggersi dal desiderio di
pineapple ['paɪnæpl] n ananas m inv
ping [pɪŋ] n (noise) tintinnio; **Ping-Pong®**
['pɪŋpɔŋ] n ping-pong® m
pink [pɪŋk] adj rosa inv ▷ n (colour) rosa m
inv; (Bot) garofano
pinpoint ['pɪnpɔɪnt] vt indicare con
precisione
pint [paɪnt] n pinta (Brit = 0.57 l; US = 0.47 l);
(BRIT col: of beer) ≈ birra grande
pioneer [paɪə'nɪəʳ] n pioniere/a
pious ['paɪəs] adj pio/a
pip [pɪp] n (seed) seme m; (BRIT: time signal on
radio) segnale m orario
pipe [paɪp] n tubo; (for smoking) pipa ▷ vt
portare per mezzo di tubazione; **pipeline**
n conduttura; (for oil) oleodotto; **piper** n
piffero; suonatore/trice di cornamusa
pirate ['paɪərət] n pirata m ▷ vt riprodurre
abusivamente
Pisces ['paɪsiːz] n Pesci mpl
piss [pɪs] vi (col!) pisciare; **pissed** adj (BRIT
col: drunk) ubriaco/a fradicio/a
pistol ['pɪstl] n pistola
piston ['pɪstən] n pistone m
pit [pɪt] n buca, fossa; (also: **coal ~**) miniera;
(quarry) cava ▷ vt: **to ~ sb against sb**
opporre qn a qn

pitch [pɪtʃ] n (Mus) tono; (fig) grado, punto; (BRIT Sport) campo; (tar) pece f ▷ vt (throw) lanciare ▷ vi (fall) cascare; **to ~ a tent** piantare una tenda; **pitch-black** adj nero/a come la pece

pitfall ['pɪtfɔːl] n trappola

pith [pɪθ] n (of plant) midollo; (of orange) parte interna della scorza; (fig) essenza, succo; vigore m

pitiful ['pɪtɪful] adj (touching) pietoso/a

pity ['pɪtɪ] n pietà ▷ vt aver pietà di; **what a ~!** che peccato!

pizza ['piːtsə] n pizza

placard ['plækɑːd] n affisso

place [pleɪs] n posto, luogo; (proper position, rank, seat) posto; (house) casa, alloggio; (home): **at/to his ~** a casa sua ▷ vt (object) posare, mettere; (identify) riconoscere; individuare; **to take ~** aver luogo; succedere; **out of ~** (not suitable) inopportuno/a; **in the first ~** in primo luogo; **to change ~s with sb** scambiare il posto con qn; **to ~ an order with sb (for)** fare un'ordinazione a qn (di); **to be ~d** (in race, exam) classificarsi; **place mat** n sottopiatto; (in linen etc) tovaglietta; **placement** n collocamento; (job) lavoro

placid ['plæsɪd] adj placido/a, calmo/a

plague [pleɪg] n peste f ▷ vt tormentare

plaice [pleɪs] n (pl inv) pianuzza

plain [pleɪn] adj (clear) chiaro/a, palese; (simple) semplice; (frank) franco/a, aperto/a; (not handsome) bruttino/a; (without seasoning etc) scondito/a; (in one colour) tinta unita inv ▷ adv francamente, chiaramente ▷ n pianura; **plain chocolate** n cioccolato fondente; **plainly** adv chiaramente; (frankly) francamente

plaintiff ['pleɪntɪf] n attore/trice

plait [plæt] n treccia

plan [plæn] n pianta; (scheme) progetto, piano ▷ vt (think in advance) progettare; (prepare) organizzare ▷ vi: **to ~ (for)** far piani or progetti (per); **to ~ to do** progettare di fare

plane [pleɪn] n (Aviat) aereo; (tree) platano; (tool) pialla; (Art, Math etc) piano ▷ adj piano/a, piatto/a ▷ vt (with tool) piallare

planet ['plænɪt] n pianeta m

plank [plæŋk] n tavola, asse f

planning ['plænɪŋ] n progettazione f; **family ~** pianificazione delle nascite

plant [plɑːnt] n pianta; (machinery) impianto; (factory) fabbrica ▷ vt piantare; (bomb) mettere

plantation [plænˈteɪʃən] n piantagione f

plaque [plæk] n placca

plaster ['plɑːstəʳ] n intonaco; (also: **~ of Paris**) gesso; (BRIT: also: **sticking ~**) cerotto ▷ vt intonacare; ingessare; (cover): **to ~ with** coprire di; **plaster cast** n (Med) ingessatura, gesso; (model, statue) modello in gesso

plastic ['plæstɪk] n plastica ▷ adj (made of plastic) di or in plastica; **plastic bag** n sacchetto di plastica; **plastic surgery** n chirurgia plastica

plate [pleɪt] n (dish) piatto; (in book) tavola; (dental plate) dentiera; **gold/silver ~** vasellame m d'oro/d'argento

plateau (pl **plateaus** or **plateaux**) ['plætəu, -z] n altipiano

platform ['plætfɔːm] n (stage, at meeting) palco; (BRIT: on bus) piattaforma; (Rail) marciapiede m; **the train leaves from ~ 7** il treno parte dal binario 7

platinum ['plætɪnəm] n platino

platoon [pləˈtuːn] n plotone m

platter ['plætəʳ] n piatto

plausible ['plɔːzɪbl] adj plausibile, credibile; (person) convincente

play [pleɪ] n (Theat) commedia ▷ vt (game) giocare a; (team, opponent) giocare contro; (instrument, piece of music) suonare; (record, tape) ascoltare; (play, part) interpretare ▷ vi giocare; suonare; recitare; **to ~ safe** giocare sul sicuro; **play back** vt riascoltare, risentire; **play up** vi (cause trouble) fare i capricci; **player** n giocatore/trice; (Theat) attore/trice; (Mus) musicista m/f; **playful** adj gioioso/a; **playground** n (in school) cortile m per la ricreazione; (in park) parco m giochi inv; **playgroup** n giardino d'infanzia; **playing card** n carta da gioco; **playing field** n campo sportivo; **playschool** n = **playgroup**; **playtime** n (Scol) ricreazione f; **playwright** n drammaturgo/a

plc abbr (BRIT: = public limited company) società per azioni a responsabilità limitata quotata in borsa

plea [pliː] n (request) preghiera, domanda; (Law) (argomento di) difesa

plead [pliːd] vt patrocinare; (give as excuse) addurre a pretesto ▷ vi (Law) perorare la causa; (beg): **to ~ with sb** implorare qn

pleasant ['plɛznt] adj piacevole, gradevole

please [pliːz] vt piacere a ▷ vi (think fit): **do as you ~** faccia come le pare; **~!** per piacere!, per favore!; (acceptance): **yes, ~** sì, grazie; **~ yourself!** come ti (or le) pare!; **pleased** adj: **pleased (with)** contento/a (di); **pleased to meet you!** piacere!

pleasure ['plɛʒəʳ] n piacere m; **"it's a ~"** "prego"

pleat [pliːt] n piega

pledge [plɛdʒ] n pegno; (*promise*) promessa ▷ vt impegnare; promettere

plentiful ['plɛntɪful] adj abbondante, copioso/a

plenty ['plɛntɪ] n: ~ **of** tanto/a, molto/a; un'abbondanza di

pliers ['plaɪəz] npl pinza

plight [plaɪt] n situazione f critica

plod [plɔd] vi camminare a stento; (*fig*) sgobbare

plonk [plɔŋk] (col) n (BRIT: *wine*) vino da poco ▷ vt: **to ~ sth down** buttare giù qc bruscamente

plot [plɔt] n congiura, cospirazione f; (*of story, opera*) trama; (*of land*) lotto ▷ vt (*mark out*) fare la pianta di; rilevare; (: *diagram etc*) tracciare; (*conspire*) congiurare, cospirare ▷ vi congiurare

plough, (US) **plow** [plau] n aratro ▷ vt (*earth*) arare; **to ~ money into** (*company etc*) investire danaro in; **ploughman**, (US) **plowman** ['plaumən] n (*irreg*) aratore m; **ploughman's lunch** n (BRIT) semplice pasto a base di pane e formaggio

plow etc [plau] (US) = **plough** etc

ploy [plɔɪ] n stratagemma m

pluck [plʌk] vt (*fruit*) cogliere; (*musical instrument*) pizzicare; (*bird*) spennare; (*hairs*) togliere ▷ n coraggio, fegato; **to ~ up courage** farsi coraggio

plug [plʌg] n tappo; (*Elec*) spina; (*Aut: also:* **spark(ing) ~**) candela ▷ vt (*hole*) tappare; (*col: advertise*) spingere; **plug in** (*Elec*) vt attaccare a una presa; **plughole** n (BRIT) scarico

plum [plʌm] n (*fruit*) susina

plumber ['plʌmə^r] n idraulico

plumbing ['plʌmɪŋ] n (*trade*) lavoro di idraulico; (*piping*) tubature fpl

plummet ['plʌmɪt] vi: **to ~ (down)** cadere a piombo

plump [plʌmp] adj grassoccio/a; **plump for** vt fus (col: *choose*) decidersi per

plunge [plʌndʒ] n tuffo; (*fig*) caduta ▷ vt immergere ▷ vi (*dive*) tuffarsi; (*fall*) cadere, precipitare; **to take the ~** saltare il fosso

plural ['pluərl] adj, n plurale (m)

plus [plʌs] n (also: **~ sign**) segno più ▷ prep più; **ten/twenty ~** più di dieci/venti

ply [plaɪ] n (*of wool*) capo ▷ vt (*a trade*) esercitare ▷ vi (*ship*) fare il servizio; **three ~ (wool)** lana a tre capi; **to ~ sb with drink** dare da bere continuamente a qn; **plywood** n legno compensato

PM n abbr = **prime minister**

p.m. adv abbr (= *post meridiem*) del pomeriggio

PMS n abbr (= *premenstrual syndrome*) sindrome f premestruale

PMT n abbr (= *premenstrual tension*) sindrome f premestruale

pneumatic [nju:'mætɪk] adj pneumatico/a; **~ drill** martello pneumatico

pneumonia [nju:'məunɪə] n polmonite f

poach [pəutʃ] vt (*cook: egg*) affogare; (: *fish*) cuocere in bianco; (*steal*) cacciare (or pescare) di frodo ▷ vi fare il bracconiere; **poached** adj (*egg*) affogato/a

PO box n abbr = **post office box**

pocket ['pɔkɪt] n tasca ▷ vt intascare; **to be out of ~** (BRIT) rimetterci; **pocketbook** n (US: *wallet*) portafoglio; **pocket money** n paghetta, settimana

pod [pɔd] n guscio

podcast ['pɔdkɑːst] n podcast m inv

podiatrist [pɔ'di:ətrɪst] n (US) callista m/f, pedicure m/f

podium ['pəudɪəm] n podio

poem ['pəuɪm] n poesia

poet ['pəuɪt] n poeta/essa; **poetic** [pəu'ɛtɪk] adj poetico/a; **poetry** n poesia

poignant ['pɔɪnjənt] adj struggente

point [pɔɪnt] n (*gen*) punto; (*tip: of needle etc*) punta; (*Elec*) presa (di corrente); (*in time*) punto, momento; (*Scol*) voto; (*main idea, important part*) nocciolo; (*also:* **decimal ~**): **2 ~ 3 (2.3)** 2 virgola 3 (2,3) ▷ vt (*show*) indicare; (*gun etc*): **to ~ sth at** puntare qc contro ▷ vi: **to ~** mostrare a dito; **points** npl (*Aut*) puntine fpl; (*Rail*) scambio; **to make a ~** fare un'osservazione; **to get/miss the ~** capire/non capire; **to come to the ~** venire al fatto; **to be on the ~ of doing sth** essere sul punto di or stare (proprio) per fare qc; **there's no ~ (in doing)** è inutile (fare); **~ of view** punto di vista; **point out** vt far notare; **point-blank** adv (also: **at point-blank range**) a bruciapelo; (*fig*) categoricamente; **pointed** adj (*shape*) aguzzo/a, appuntito/a; (*remark*) specifico/a; **pointer** n (*needle*) lancetta; (*clue*) indicazione f; (*advice*) consiglio; **pointless** adj inutile, vano/a

poison ['pɔɪzn] n veleno ▷ vt avvelenare; **poisonous** adj velenoso/a

poke [pəuk] vt (*fire*) attizzare; (*jab with finger, stick etc*) punzecchiare; (*put*): **to ~ sth in(to)** spingere qc dentro; **poke about, poke around** vi frugare; **poke out** vi (*stick out*) sporger fuori

poker ['pəukə^r] n attizzatoio; (*Cards*) poker m

Poland ['pəulənd] n Polonia

polar ['pəulə^r] adj polare; **polar bear** n orso bianco

Pole [pəul] n polacco/a

pole [pəul] n (of wood) palo; (Elec, Geo) polo; **pole bean** n (US: runner bean) fagiolino; **pole vault** n salto con l'asta

police [pə'li:s] n polizia ▷ vt mantenere l'ordine in; **police car** n macchina della polizia; **police constable** n (BRIT) agente m di polizia; **police force** n corpo di polizia, polizia; **policeman** n (irreg) poliziotto, agente m di polizia; **police officer** n = agente di polizia m, donna f poliziotto inv; **police station** n posto di polizia; **policewoman** n (irreg) donna f poliziotto inv

policy ['pɔlɪsɪ] n politica; (also: **insurance ~**) polizza (d'assicurazione)

polio ['pəulɪəu] n polio f

Polish ['pəulɪʃ] adj polacco/a ▷ n (Ling) polacco

polish ['pɔlɪʃ] n (for shoes) lucido; (for floor) cera; (for nails) smalto; (shine) lucentezza, lustro; (fig: refinement) raffinatezza ▷ vt lucidare; (fig: improve) raffinare; **polish off** vt (food) mangiarsi; **polished** adj (fig) raffinato/a

polite [pə'laɪt] adj cortese; **politeness** n cortesia

political [pə'lɪtɪkl] adj politico/a; **politically** adv politicamente; **politically correct** adj politicamente corretto/a

politician [pɔlɪ'tɪʃən] n politico

politics ['pɔlɪtɪks] n politica ▷ npl (views, policies) idee fpl politiche

poll [pəul] n scrutinio; (votes cast) voti mpl; (also: **opinion ~**) sondaggio (d'opinioni) ▷ vt ottenere

pollen ['pɔlən] n polline m

polling station ['pəulɪŋ-] n (BRIT) sezione f elettorale

pollute [pə'lu:t] vt inquinare

pollution [pə'lu:ʃən] n inquinamento

polo ['pəuləu] n polo; **polo neck** n collo alto; (also: **polo neck sweater**) dolcevita ▷ adj a collo alto; **polo shirt** n polo f inv

polyester [pɔlɪ'ɛstər] n poliestere m

polystyrene [pɔlɪ'staɪri:n] n polistirolo

polythene ['pɔlɪθi:n] n politene m; **polythene bag** n sacchetto di plastica

pomegranate ['pɔmɪgrænɪt] n melagrana

pompous ['pɔmpəs] adj pomposo/a

pond [pɔnd] n pozza; stagno

ponder ['pɔndər] vt ponderare, riflettere su

pony ['pəunɪ] n pony m inv; **ponytail** n coda di cavallo; **pony trekking** [-trɛkɪŋ] n (BRIT) escursione f a cavallo

poodle ['pu:dl] n barboncino, barbone m

pool [pu:l] n (of rain) pozza; (pond) stagno; (also: **swimming ~**) piscina; (fig: of light)

cerchio; (billiards) specie di biliardo a buca ▷ vt mettere in comune; **typing** ~ servizio comune di dattilografia; **to do the (football) ~s** ≈ giocare al totocalcio

poor [puər] adj povero/a; (mediocre) mediocre, cattivo/a ▷ npl: **the** ~ i poveri; ~ **in** povero/a di; **poorly** adv poveramente; (badly) male ▷ adj indisposto/a, malato/a

pop [pɔp] n (noise) schiocco; (Mus) musica pop; (US col: father) babbo; (col: drink) bevanda gasata ▷ vt (put) mettere (in fretta) ▷ vi scoppiare; (cork) schioccare; **pop in** vi passare; **pop out** vi fare un salto fuori; **popcorn** n pop-corn m

poplar ['pɔplər] n pioppo

popper ['pɔpər] n bottone m a pressione

poppy ['pɔpɪ] n papavero

Popsicle® ['pɔpsɪkl] n (US: ice lolly) ghiacciolo

pop star n pop star f inv

popular ['pɔpjulər] adj popolare; (fashionable) in voga; **popularity** [pɔpju'lærɪtɪ] n popolarità

population [pɔpju'leɪʃən] n popolazione f

pop-up adj (Comput: menu, window) a comparsa

porcelain ['pɔ:slɪn] n porcellana

porch [pɔ:tʃ] n veranda

pore [pɔ:r] n poro ▷ vi: **to ~ over** essere immerso/a in

pork [pɔ:k] n carne f di maiale; **pork chop** n braciola or costoletta di maiale; **pork pie** n (BRIT Culin) pasticcio di maiale in crosta

porn [pɔ:n] (col) n pornografia ▷ adj porno inv; **pornographic** [pɔ:nə'græfɪk] adj pornografico/a; **pornography** [pɔ:'nɔgrəfɪ] n pornografia

porridge ['pɔrɪdʒ] n porridge m

port¹ [pɔ:t] n porto; (Naut: left side) babordo; ~ **of call** (porto di) scalo

port² [pɔ:t] n (wine) porto

portable ['pɔ:təbl] adj portatile

porter ['pɔ:tər] n (for luggage) facchino, portabagagli m inv; (doorkeeper) portiere m, portinaio

portfolio [pɔ:t'fəulɪəu] n (case) cartella; (Pol, Econ) portafoglio; (of artist) raccolta dei propri lavori

portion ['pɔ:ʃən] n porzione f

portrait ['pɔ:treɪt] n ritratto

portray [pɔ:'treɪ] vt fare il ritratto di; (character on stage) rappresentare; (in writing) ritrarre

Portugal ['pɔ:tjugl] n Portogallo

Portuguese [pɔ:tju'gi:z] adj portoghese ▷ n (pl inv) portoghese m/f; (Ling) portoghese m

pose [pəuz] n posa ▷ vi posare; (pretend): **to ~ as** atteggiarsi a, posare a ▷ vt porre

posh [pɒʃ] *adj* (*col*) elegante; (*family*) per
bene

position [pə'zɪʃən] *n* posizione *f*; (*job*) posto
▷ *vt* sistemare

positive ['pɒzɪtɪv] *adj* positivo/a; (*certain*)
sicuro/a, certo/a; (*definite*) preciso/a;
definitivo/a; **positively** *adv* (*affirmatively,
enthusiastically*) positivamente; (*decisively*)
decisamente; (*really*) assolutamente

possess [pə'zɛs] *vt* possedere; **possession**
[pə'zɛʃən] *n* possesso; **possessions** *npl*
(*belongings*) beni *mpl*; **possessive** *adj*
possessivo/a

possibility [pɒsɪ'bɪlɪtɪ] *n* possibilità *f inv*

possible ['pɒsɪbl] *adj* possibile; **as big as ~**
il più grande possibile; **possibly** *adv*
(*perhaps*) forse; **if you possibly can** se le è
possibile; **I cannot possibly come** proprio
non posso venire

post [pəust] *n* (*BRIT*) posta; (*: collection*)
levata; (*job, situation*) posto; (*Mil*)
postazione *f*; (*pole*) palo; (*on blog, social
network*) post *m inv*, commento ▷ *vt* (*BRIT*:
send by post) impostare; (*Mil*) appostare;
(*notice*) affiggere; (*to internet: video*)
caricare; (*: comment*) mandare; (*BRIT*:
appoint): **to ~ to** assegnare a; **postage** *n*
affrancatura; **postal** *adj* postale; **postal
order** *n* vaglia *m inv* postale; **postbox**
(*BRIT*) *n* cassetta delle lettere; **postcard** *n*
cartolina; **postcode** *n* (*BRIT*) codice *m* (di
avviamento) postale

poster ['pəustə'] *n* manifesto, affisso

postgraduate ['pəust'grædjuət] *n*
laureato/a che continua gli studi

postman ['pəustmən] *n* (*irreg: BRIT*) postino

postmark ['pəustmɑːk] *n* bollo or timbro
postale

post-mortem [pəust'mɔːtəm] *n* autopsia

post office *n* (*building*) ufficio postale; **the
Post Office** ≈ le Poste e Telecomunicazioni

postpone [pəust'pəun] *vt* rinviare

posture ['pɒstʃə'] *n* portamento; (*pose*)
posa, atteggiamento

postwoman ['pəustwumən] (*irreg: BRIT*)
n postina

pot [pɒt] *n* (*for cooking*) pentola; casseruola;
(*teapot*) teiera; (*coffeepot*) caffettiera; (*for
plants, jam*) vaso; (*col: marijuana*) erba
▷ *vt* (*plant*) piantare in vaso; **a ~ of tea
for two** tè per due; **to go to ~** (*col: work,
performance*) andare in malora

potato [pə'teɪtəu] (*pl* **potatoes**) *n* patata;
potato peeler *n* sbucciapatate *m inv*

potent ['pəutnt] *adj* potente, forte

potential [pə'tɛnʃl] *adj* potenziale ▷ *n*
possibilità *fpl*

pothole ['pɒthəul] *n* (*in road*) buca; (*BRIT*:
underground) caverna

pot plant *n* pianta in vaso

potter ['pɒtə'] *n* vasaio ▷ *vi* (*BRIT*): **to ~
around, ~ about** lavoracchiare; **pottery**
n ceramiche *fpl*; (*factory*) fabbrica di
ceramiche

potty ['pɒtɪ] *adj* (*col: mad*) tocco/a ▷ *n*
(*child's*) vasino

pouch [pautʃ] *n* borsa; (*Zool*) marsupio

poultry ['pəultrɪ] *n* pollame *m*

pounce [pauns] *vi*: **to ~ (on)** piombare
(su)

pound [paund] *n* (*weight*) libbra; (*money*)
(lira) sterlina ▷ *vt* (*beat*) battere; (*crush*)
pestare, polverizzare ▷ *vi* (*beat*) battere,
martellare; **pound sterling** *n* sterlina

pour [pɔː'] *vt* versare ▷ *vi* riversarsi; (*rain*)
piovere a dirotto; **pour in** *vi* affluire
in gran quantità; **pour out** *vi* (*people*)
riversarsi fuori ▷ *vt* vuotare; versare; (*fig*)
sfogare; **pouring** *adj*: **pouring rain** pioggia
torrenziale

pout [paut] *vi* sporgere le labbra; fare il
broncio

poverty ['pɒvətɪ] *n* povertà, miseria

powder ['paudə'] *n* polvere *f* ▷ *vt*: **~ed
milk** latte *m* in polvere; **to ~ one's nose**
incipriarsi il naso

power ['pauə'] *n* (*strength*) potenza,
forza; (*ability, Pol: of party, leader*) potere
m; (*Elec*) corrente *f*; **to be in ~** essere al
potere; **power cut** *n* (*BRIT*) interruzione
f or mancanza *f* di corrente; **power
failure** *n* interruzione *f* della corrente
elettrica; **powerful** *adj* potente, forte;
powerless *adj* impotente; **powerless to
do** impossibilitato/a a fare; **power point** *n*
(*BRIT*) presa di corrente; **power station** *n*
centrale *f* elettrica

pp *abbr* (= *pages*) pp; (= *per procurationem*):
pp J. Smith per il Signor J. Smith

PR *n abbr* = **public relations**

practical ['præktɪkl] *adj* pratico/a;
practical joke *n* beffa; **practically** *adv*
praticamente

practice ['præktɪs] *n* pratica; (*of profession*)
esercizio; (*at football etc*) allenamento;
(*business*) gabinetto; clientela ▷ *vt, vi* (*US*)
= **practise**; **in ~** (*in reality*) in pratica; **out
of ~** fuori esercizio

practise, (*US*) **practice** ['præktɪs] *vt* (*work
at: piano, one's backhand etc*) esercitarsi a;
(*train for: skiing, running etc*) allenarsi a;
(*a sport, religion*) praticare; (*method*) usare;
(*profession*) esercitare ▷ *vi* esercitarsi;
(*train*) allenarsi; (*lawyer, doctor*) esercitare;
practising *adj* (*Christian etc*) praticante;
(*lawyer*) che esercita la professione

practitioner [præk'tɪʃənə'] *n*
professionista *m/f*

pragmatic [præg'mætɪk] *adj* pragmatico/a

prairie ['prɛərɪ] *n* prateria

praise [preɪz] *n* elogio, lode *f* ▷ *vt* elogiare, lodare

pram [præm] *n* (*BRIT*) carrozzina

prank [præŋk] *n* burla

prawn [prɔ:n] *n* gamberetto; **prawn cocktail** *n* cocktail *m inv* di gamberetti

pray [preɪ] *vi* pregare; **prayer** [prɛəʳ] *n* preghiera

preach [pri:tʃ] *vt, vi* predicare; **preacher** *n* predicatore/trice; (*US: minister*) pastore *m*

precarious [prɪ'kɛərɪəs] *adj* precario/a

precaution [prɪ'kɔ:ʃən] *n* precauzione *f*

precede [prɪ'si:d] *vt* precedere; **precedent** ['prɛsɪdənt] *n* precedente *m*; **preceding** [prɪ'si:dɪŋ] *adj* precedente

precinct ['pri:sɪŋkt] *n* (*US*) circoscrizione *f*

precious ['prɛʃəs] *adj* prezioso/a

precise [prɪ'saɪs] *adj* preciso/a; **precisely** *adv* precisamente

precision [prɪ'sɪʒən] *n* precisione *f*

predator ['prɛdətəʳ] *n* predatore *m*

predecessor ['pri:dɪsɛsəʳ] *n* predecessore/a

predicament [prɪ'dɪkəmənt] *n* situazione *f* difficile

predict [prɪ'dɪkt] *vt* predire; **predictable** *adj* prevedibile; **prediction** [prɪ'dɪkʃən] *n* predizione *f*

predominantly [prɪ'dɔmɪnəntlɪ] *adv* in maggior parte; soprattutto

preface ['prɛfəs] *n* prefazione *f*

prefect ['pri:fɛkt] *n* (*BRIT: in school*) studente/essa con funzioni disciplinari; (*Admin: in Italy*) prefetto

prefer [prɪ'fə:ʳ] *vt* preferire; **to ~ doing** or **to do** preferire fare; **preferable** ['prɛfrəbl] *adj* preferibile; **preferably** ['prɛfrəblɪ] *adv* preferibilmente; **preference** ['prɛfrəns] *n* preferenza

prefix ['pri:fɪks] *n* prefisso

pregnancy ['prɛgnənsɪ] *n* gravidanza

pregnant ['prɛgnənt] *adj* incinta *f adj*

prehistoric ['pri:hɪs'tɔrɪk] *adj* preistorico/a

prejudice ['prɛdʒudɪs] *n* pregiudizio; (*harm*) torto, danno; **prejudiced** *adj* (*view*) prevenuto/a; **to be prejudiced against sb/sth** essere prevenuto contro qn/qc; **prejudiced (in favour of)** ben disposto/a (verso)

preliminary [prɪ'lɪmɪnərɪ] *adj* preliminare

prelude ['prɛlju:d] *n* preludio

premature ['prɛmətʃuəʳ] *adj* prematuro/a

premier ['prɛmɪəʳ] *adj* primo/a ▷ *n* (*Pol*) primo ministro

première ['prɛmɪɛəʳ] *n* prima

Premier League *n* ≈ serie A

premises ['prɛmɪsɪz] *npl* locale *m*; **on the ~** sul posto; **business ~** locali commerciali

premium ['pri:mɪəm] *n* premio; **to be at a ~** essere ricercatissimo

premonition [prɛmə'nɪʃən] *n* premonizione *f*

preoccupied [pri:'ɔkjupaɪd] *adj* preoccupato/a

prepaid [pri:'peɪd] *adj* pagato/a in anticipo

preparation [prɛpə'reɪʃən] *n* preparazione *f*; **preparations** *npl* (*for trip, war*) preparativi *mpl*

preparatory school [prɪ'pærətərɪ-] *n* scuola elementare privata

prepare [prɪ'pɛəʳ] *vt* preparare ▷ *vi*: **to ~ for** prepararsi a; **prepared** *adj*: **prepared to** pronto/a a

preposition [prɛpə'zɪʃən] *n* preposizione *f*

prep school ['prɛp-] *n* = **preparatory school**

prerequisite [pri:'rɛkwɪzɪt] *n* requisito indispensabile

preschool ['pri:'sku:l] *adj* (*age*) prescolastico/a; (*child*) in età prescolastica

prescribe [prɪ'skraɪb] *vt* (*Med*) prescrivere

prescription [prɪ'skrɪpʃən] *n* prescrizione *f*; (*Med*) ricetta

presence ['prɛzns] *n* presenza; **~ of mind** presenza di spirito

present ['prɛznt] *adj* presente; (*wife, residence, job*) attuale ▷ *n* (*gift*) regalo; **the ~** il presente ▷ *vt* [prɪ'zɛnt] presentare; (*give*): **to ~ sb with sth** offrire qc a qn; **at ~** al momento; **to give sb a ~** fare un regalo a qn; **presentable** [prɪ'zɛntəbl] *adj* presentabile; **presentation** [prɛzn'teɪʃən] *n* presentazione *f*; (*ceremony*) consegna ufficiale; **present-day** *adj* attuale, d'oggigiorno; **presenter** *n* (*Radio, TV*) presentatore/trice; **presently** *adv* (*soon*) fra poco, presto; (*at present*) al momento; **present participle** *n* participio presente

preservation [prɛzə'veɪʃən] *n* preservazione *f*, conservazione *f*

preservative [prɪ'zə:vətɪv] *n* conservante *m*

preserve [prɪ'zə:v] *vt* (*keep safe*) preservare, proteggere; (*maintain*) conservare; (*food*) mettere in conserva ▷ *n* (*often pl: jam*) marmellata; (: *fruit*) frutta sciroppata

preside [prɪ'zaɪd] *vi*: **to ~ (over)** presiedere (a)

president ['prɛzɪdənt] *n* presidente *m*; **presidential** [prɛzɪ'dɛnʃl] *adj* presidenziale

press [prɛs] *n* (*tool, machine*) pressa; (*for wine*) torchio; (*newspapers*) stampa ▷ *vt* (*push*) premere, pigiare; (*squeeze*) spremere;

(: *hand*) stringere; (*clothes: iron*) stirare; (*pursue*) incalzare; (*insist*): **to ~ sth on sb** far accettare qc da qn ▷ *vi* premere; accalcare; **we are ~ed for time** ci manca il tempo; **to ~ for sth** insistere per avere qc; **press conference** *n* conferenza stampa; **pressing** *adj* urgente; **press stud** *n* (BRIT) bottone *m* a pressione; **press-up** *n* (BRIT) flessione *f* sulle braccia

pressure ['prɛʃə'] *n* pressione *f* ▷ *vt*: **to put ~ on sb (to do)** mettere qn sotto pressione (affinché faccia); **pressure cooker** *n* pentola di pressione; **pressure group** *n* gruppo di pressione

prestige [prɛs'tiːʒ] *n* prestigio

prestigious [prɛs'tɪdʒəs] *adj* prestigioso/a

presumably [prɪ'zjuːməblɪ] *adv* presumibilmente

presume [prɪ'zjuːm] *vt* supporre

pretence, (US) **pretense** [prɪ'tɛns] *n* (*claim*) pretesa; **to make a ~ of doing** far finta di fare; **under false ~s** con l'inganno

pretend [prɪ'tɛnd] *vt* (*feign*) fingere ▷ *vi* far finta; **to ~ to do** far finta di fare

pretense [prɪ'tɛns] *n* (US) = **pretence**

pretentious [prɪ'tɛnʃəs] *adj* pretenzioso/a

pretext ['priːtɛkst] *n* pretesto

pretty ['prɪtɪ] *adj* grazioso/a, carino/a ▷ *adv* abbastanza, assai

prevail [prɪ'veɪl] *vi* (*win, be usual*) prevalere; (*persuade*): **to ~ (up)on sb to do** persuadere qn a fare; **prevailing** *adj* dominante

prevalent ['prɛvələnt] *adj* (*belief*) predominante; (*customs*) diffuso/a; (*fashion*) corrente; (*disease*) comune

prevent [prɪ'vɛnt] *vt*: **to ~ sb from doing** impedire a qn di fare; **to ~ sth from happening** impedire che qc succeda; **prevention** [prɪ'vɛnʃən] *n* prevenzione *f*; **preventive** *adj* preventivo/a

preview ['priːvjuː] *n* (*of film*) anteprima

previous ['priːvɪəs] *adj* precedente; anteriore; **previously** *adv* prima

prey [preɪ] *n* preda ▷ *vi*: **to ~ on** far preda di; **it was ~ing on his mind** lo stava ossessionando

price [praɪs] *n* prezzo ▷ *vt* (*goods*) fissare il prezzo di; valutare; **priceless** *adj* di valore inestimabile; **price list** *n* listino (dei) prezzi

prick [prɪk] *n* puntura ▷ *vt* pungere; **to ~ up one's ears** drizzare gli orecchi

prickly ['prɪklɪ] *adj* spinoso/a

pride [praɪd] *n* orgoglio; superbia ▷ *vt*: **to ~ o.s. on** essere orgoglioso/a di; vantarsi di

priest [priːst] *n* prete *m*, sacerdote *m*

primarily ['praɪmərɪlɪ] *adv* principalmente, essenzialmente

primary ['praɪmərɪ] *adj* primario/a; (*first in importance*) primo/a ▷ *n* (US: *election*)

primarie *fpl*; **primary school** *n* (BRIT) scuola elementare

prime [praɪm] *adj* primario/a, fondamentale; (*excellent*) di prima qualità ▷ *n*: **in the ~ of life** nel fiore della vita ▷ *vt* (*wood*) preparare; (*fig*) mettere al corrente; **prime minister** *n* primo ministro

primitive ['prɪmɪtɪv] *adj* primitivo/a

primrose ['prɪmrəuz] *n* primavera

prince [prɪns] *n* principe *m*

princess [prɪn'sɛs] *n* principessa

principal ['prɪnsɪpl] *adj* principale ▷ *n* (*of school, college etc*) preside *m/f*; **principally** *adv* principalmente

principle ['prɪnsɪpl] *n* principio; **in ~** in linea di principio; **on ~** per principio

print [prɪnt] *n* (*mark*) impronta; (*letters*) caratteri *mpl*; (*fabric*) tessuto stampato; (*Art, Phot*) stampa ▷ *vt* imprimere; (*publish*) stampare, pubblicare; (*write in capitals*) scrivere in stampatello; **out of ~** esaurito/a; **print out** *vt* (*Comput*) stampare; **printer** *n* tipografo; (*machine*) stampante *f*; **print-out** *n* tabulato

prior ['praɪə'] *adj* precedente; (*claim etc*) più importante; **~ to doing** prima di fare

priority [praɪ'ɔrɪtɪ] *n* priorità *f inv*; precedenza

prison ['prɪzn] *n* prigione *f* ▷ *cpd* (*system*) carcerario/a; (*conditions, food*) nelle or delle prigioni; **prisoner** *n* prigioniero/a; **prisoner of war** *n* prigioniero/a di guerra

pristine ['prɪstiːn] *adj* originario/a

privacy ['prɪvəsɪ] *n* solitudine *f*, intimità

private ['praɪvɪt] *adj* privato/a, personale ▷ *n* soldato semplice; **"~"** (*on envelope*) "riservata"; (*on door*) "privato"; **in ~** in privato; **privately** *adv* in privato; (*within o.s.*) dentro di sé; **private property** *n* proprietà privata; **private school** *n* scuola privata

privatize ['praɪvɪtaɪz] *vt* privatizzare

privilege ['prɪvɪlɪdʒ] *n* privilegio

prize [praɪz] *n* premio ▷ *adj* (*example, idiot*) perfetto/a; (*bull, novel*) premiato/a ▷ *vt* apprezzare, pregiare; **prize giving** *n* premiazione *f*; **prizewinner** *n* premiato/a

pro [prəu] *n* (*Sport*) professionista *m/f* ▷ *prep* pro; **the ~s and cons** il pro e il contro

probability [prɔbə'bɪlɪtɪ] *n* probabilità *f inv*; **in all ~** con ogni probabilità

probable ['prɔbəbl] *adj* probabile

probably ['prɔbəblɪ] *adv* probabilmente

probation [prə'beɪʃən] *n*: **on ~** (*employee*) in prova; (*Law*) in libertà vigilata

probe [prəub] *n* (*Med, Space*) sonda; (*enquiry*) indagine *f*, investigazione *f* ▷ *vt* sondare, esplorare; indagare

problem ['prɔbləm] *n* problema *m*

procedure [prə'si:dʒəʳ] n (Admin, Law) procedura; (method) metodo, procedimento

proceed [prə'si:d] vi (go forward) avanzare, andare avanti; (go about it) procedere; (continue): **to ~ (with)** continuare; **to ~ to** andare a; passare a; **to ~ to do** mettersi a fare; **proceedings** npl misure fpl; (Law) procedimento; (meeting) riunione f; (records) rendiconti mpl; atti mpl; **proceeds** ['prəusi:dz] npl profitto, incasso

process n ['prəusɛs] n processo; (method) metodo, sistema m ▷ vt trattare; (information) elaborare

procession [prə'sɛʃən] n processione f, corteo; **funeral ~** corteo funebre

proclaim [prə'kleɪm] vt proclamare, dichiarare

prod [prɔd] vt dare un colpetto a; pungolare ▷ n colpetto

produce n ['prɔdju:s] (Agr) prodotto, prodotti mpl ▷ vt [prə'dju:s] produrre; (show) esibire, mostrare; (cause) cagionare, causare; **producer** n (Theat, Cine, Agr) produttore m

product ['prɔdʌkt] n prodotto; **production** [prə'dʌkʃən] n produzione f; **productive** [prə'dʌktɪv] adj produttivo/a; **productivity** [prɔdʌk'tɪvɪtɪ] n produttività

Prof. abbr (= professor) Prof.

profession [prə'fɛʃən] n professione f; **professional** n professionista m/f ▷ adj professionale; (work) da professionista

professor [prə'fɛsəʳ] n professore m (titolare di una cattedra); (us) professore/essa

profile ['prəufaɪl] n profilo

profit ['prɔfɪt] n profitto; beneficio ▷ vi: **to ~ (by or from)** approfittare (di); **profitable** adj redditizio/a

profound [prə'faund] adj profondo/a

programme, (us) **program** ['prəugræm] n programma m ▷ vt programmare; **programmer**, (us) **programer** n programmatore/trice; **programming**, (us) **programing** n programmazione f

progress n ['prəugrɛs] progresso ▷ vi [prə'grɛs] avanzare, procedere; (also: **make ~**) far progressi; **in ~** in corso; **progressive** [prə'grɛsɪv] adj progressivo/a; (person) progressista

prohibit [prə'hɪbɪt] vt proibire, vietare

project n ['prɔdʒɛkt] (plan) piano; (venture) progetto; (Scol) studio ▷ vt [prə'dʒɛkt] proiettare ▷ vi (stick out) sporgere; **projection** [prə'dʒɛkʃən] n proiezione f; sporgenza; **projector** [prə'dʒɛktəʳ] n proiettore m

prolific [prə'lɪfɪk] adj (artist etc) fecondo/a

prolong [prə'lɔŋ] vt prolungare

prom [prɔm] n abbr = **promenade**; **promenade concert**; (us: ball) ballo studentesco

promenade [prɔmə'nɑ:d] n (by sea) lungomare m

prominent ['prɔmɪnənt] adj (standing out) prominente; (important) importante

promiscuous [prə'mɪskjuəs] adj (sexually) di facili costumi

promise ['prɔmɪs] n promessa ▷ vt, vi promettere; **to ~ sb sth, to ~ sth to sb** promettere qc a qn; **to ~ (sb) that/to do sth** promettere (a qn) che/di fare qc; **promising** adj promettente

promote [prə'məut] vt promuovere; (venture, event) organizzare; **promotion** [prə'məuʃən] n promozione f

prompt [prɔmpt] adj rapido/a, svelto/a; puntuale; (reply) sollecito/a ▷ adv (punctually) in punto ▷ n (Comput) prompt m inv ▷ vt incitare; provocare; (Theat) suggerire a; **to ~ sb to do** spingere qn a fare; **promptly** adv prontamente; puntualmente

prone [prəun] adj (lying) prono/a; **~ to** propenso/a a, incline a

prong [prɔŋ] n rebbio, punta

pronoun ['prəunaun] n pronome m

pronounce [prə'nauns] vt pronunciare; **how do you ~ it?** come si pronuncia?

pronunciation [prənʌnsɪ'eɪʃən] n pronuncia

proof [pru:f] n prova; (of book) bozza; (Phot) provino ▷ adj: **~ against** a prova di

prop [prɔp] n sostegno, appoggio ▷ vt (also: **~ up**) sostenere, appoggiare; (lean): **to ~ sth against** appoggiare qc contro or a; **props** oggetti m inv di scena

propaganda [prɔpə'gændə] n propaganda

propeller [prə'pɛləʳ] n elica

proper ['prɔpəʳ] adj (suited, right) adatto/a, appropriato/a; (seemly) decente; (authentic) vero/a; (col: real) vero/a e proprio/a; **properly** ['prɔpəlɪ] adv (eat, study) bene;

(behave) come si deve; **proper noun** n nome m proprio

property ['prɒpəti] n (things owned) beni mpl; (land, building, Chem etc, quality) proprietà f inv

prophecy ['prɒfisi] n profezia

prophet ['prɒfit] n profeta m

proportion [prə'pɔ:ʃən] n proporzione f; (share) parte f; **proportions** npl (size) proporzioni fpl; **proportional** adj proporzionale

proposal [prə'pəuzl] n proposta; (plan) progetto; (of marriage) proposta di matrimonio

propose [prə'pəuz] vt proporre, suggerire ▷ vi fare una proposta di matrimonio; **to ~ to do** proporsi di fare, aver l'intenzione di fare

proposition [prɒpə'zɪʃən] n proposizione f; (proposal) proposta

proprietor [prə'praɪətə^r] n proprietario/a

prose [prəuz] n prosa

prosecute ['prɒsɪkju:t] vt (Law) perseguire; **prosecution** [prɒsɪ'kju:ʃən] n (accusing side) accusa; **prosecutor** n (also: **public prosecutor**) ≈ procuratore m della Repubblica

prospect n ['prɒspɛkt] prospettiva; (hope) speranza ▷ vt [prə'spɛkt] esplorare ▷ vi: **to ~ for gold** cercare l'oro; **prospective** [prə'spɛktɪv] adj (legislation, son-in-law) futuro/a; **prospects** ['prɒspɛkts] npl (for work etc) prospettive fpl

prospectus [prə'spɛktəs] n prospetto, programma m

prosper ['prɒspə^r] vi prosperare; **prosperity** [prɒ'spɛrɪtɪ] n prosperità; **prosperous** adj prospero/a

prostitute ['prɒstɪtju:t] n prostituta; **male ~** uomo che si prostituisce

protect [prə'tɛkt] vt proteggere, salvaguardare; **protection** n protezione f; **protective** adj protettivo/a

protein ['prəuti:n] n proteina

protest n ['prəutɛst] protesta ▷ vt, vi [prə'tɛst] protestare

Protestant ['prɒtɪstənt] adj, n protestante (m/f)

protester [prə'tɛstə^r] n dimostrante m/f

protractor [prə'træktə^r] n (Geom) goniometro

proud [praud] adj fiero/a, orgoglioso/a; (pej) superbo/a

prove [pru:v] vt provare, dimostrare ▷ vi: **to ~ (to be) correct** etc risultare vero/a etc; **to ~ o.s.** mostrare le proprie capacità

proverb ['prɒvə:b] n proverbio

provide [prə'vaɪd] vt fornire, provvedere; **to ~ sb with sth** fornire or provvedere qn di

qc; **provide for** vt fus provvedere a; (future event) prevedere; **provided** conj: **provided (that)** purché + sub, a condizione che + sub; **providing** [prə'vaɪdɪŋ] conj purché + sub, a condizione che + sub

province ['prɒvɪns] n provincia; **provincial** [prə'vɪnʃəl] adj provinciale

provision [prə'vɪʒən] n (supply) riserva; (supplying) provvista; rifornimento; (stipulation) condizione f; **provisions** npl (food) provviste fpl; **provisional** adj provvisorio/a

provocative [prə'vɒkətɪv] adj (aggressive) provocatorio/a; (thought-provoking) stimolante; (seductive) provocante

provoke [prə'vəuk] vt provocare; incitare

prowl [praul] vi (also: ~ about, ~ around) aggirarsi furtivamente ▷ n: **on the ~** in caccia

proximity [prɒk'sɪmɪtɪ] n prossimità

proxy ['prɒksɪ] n: **by ~** per procura

prudent ['pru:dnt] adj prudente

prune [pru:n] n prugna secca ▷ vt potare

pry [praɪ] vi: **to ~ into** ficcare il naso in

PS n abbr (= postscript) P.S.

pseudonym ['sju:dənɪm] n pseudonimo

psychiatric [saɪkɪ'ætrɪk] adj psichiatrico/a

psychiatrist [saɪ'kaɪətrɪst] n psichiatra m/f

psychic ['saɪkɪk] adj (also: ~al) psichico/a; (person) dotato/a di qualità telepatiche

psychoanalysis (pl -ses) [saɪkəuə'nælɪsɪs, -si:z] n psicanalisi f inv

psychological [saɪkə'lɒdʒɪkl] adj psicologico/a

psychologist [saɪ'kɒlədʒɪst] n psicologo/a

psychology [saɪ'kɒlədʒɪ] n psicologia

psychotherapy [saɪkəu'θɛrəpɪ] n psicoterapia

pt abbr = **pint**; (= point) pt

PTO abbr (= please turn over) v.r.

pub [pʌb] n abbr (= public house) pub m inv

puberty ['pju:bətɪ] n pubertà

public ['pʌblɪk] adj pubblico/a ▷ n pubblico; **in ~** in pubblico

publication [pʌblɪ'keɪʃən] n pubblicazione f

public: public company n ≈ società f inv per azioni (costituita tramite pubblica sottoscrizione); **public convenience** n (BRIT) gabinetti mpl; **public holiday** n (BRIT) giorno festivo, festa nazionale; **public house** n (BRIT) pub m inv

publicity [pʌb'lɪsɪtɪ] n pubblicità

publicize ['pʌblɪsaɪz] vt rendere pubblico/a

public: public limited company n ≈ società per azioni a responsabilità limitata (quotata in Borsa); **publicly** ['pʌblɪklɪ] adv pubblicamente; **public opinion** n opinione f pubblica; **public relations** n pubbliche relazioni fpl; **public school** n (BRIT) scuola privata; (US) scuola statale; **public transport** n mezzi mpl pubblici

publish ['pʌblɪʃ] vt pubblicare; **publisher** n editore m; **publishing** n (industry) editoria; (of a book) pubblicazione f

pub lunch n: **to go for a ~** andare a mangiare al pub

pudding ['pudɪŋ] n budino; (BRIT: dessert) dolce m; **black ~**, (US) **blood ~** sanguinaccio

puddle ['pʌdl] n pozza, pozzanghera

Puerto Rico ['pwɜː'təʊ'riː'kəʊ] n Portorico

puff [pʌf] n sbuffo ▷ vi (pant) ansare; **to ~ one's pipe** tirare sboccate di fumo; **puff pastry** n pasta sfoglia

pull [pul] n (tug) strattone m ▷ vt tirare; (muscle) strappare; (trigger) premere ▷ vi tirare; **to give sth a ~** tirare su qc; **to ~ to pieces** fare a pezzi; **to ~ one's punches** (Boxing) risparmiare l'avversario; **to ~ one's weight** dare il proprio contributo; **to ~ o.s. together** ricomporsi, riprendersi; **to ~ sb's leg** prendere in giro qn; **pull apart** vt (break) fare a pezzi; **pull away** vi (move off: vehicle) muoversi, partire; (: boat) staccarsi dal molo, salpare; (draw back: person) indietreggiare; **pull back** vt (lever etc) tirare indietro; (curtains) aprire ▷ vi (from confrontation etc) tirarsi indietro; (Mil: withdraw) ritirarsi; **pull down** vt (house) demolire; (tree) abbattere; **pull in** vi (Aut: at the kerb) accostarsi; (Rail) entrare in stazione; **pull off** vt (clothes) togliere; (deal etc) portare a compimento; **pull out** vi partire; (Aut: come out of line) spostarsi sulla mezzeria ▷ vt staccare; far uscire; (withdraw) ritirare; **pull over** vi (Aut) accostare; **pull up** vi (stop) fermarsi ▷ vt (uproot) sradicare; (raise) sollevare

pulley ['pulɪ] n puleggia, carrucola

pullover ['pulˈəʊvəʳ] n pullover m inv

pulp [pʌlp] n (of fruit) polpa

pulpit ['pulpɪt] n pulpito

pulse [pʌls] n polso; (Bot) legume m; **pulses** npl (Culin) legumi mpl

puma ['pjuːmə] n puma m inv

pump [pʌmp] n pompa; (shoe) scarpetta ▷ vt pompare; **pump up** vt gonfiare

pumpkin ['pʌmpkɪn] n zucca

pun [pʌn] n gioco di parole

punch [pʌntʃ] n (blow) pugno; (tool) punzone m; (drink) ponce m ▷ vt (hit): **to ~ sb/sth** dare un pugno a qn/qc; **punch-up** n (BRIT col) rissa

punctual ['pʌŋktjuəl] adj puntuale

punctuation [pʌŋktju'eɪʃən] n interpunzione f, punteggiatura

puncture ['pʌŋktʃəʳ] n foratura ▷ vt forare
▮ Be careful not to translate puncture by the Italian word puntura.

punish ['pʌnɪʃ] vt punire; **punishment** n punizione f

punk [pʌŋk] n (also: **~ rocker**) punk mf inv; (also: **~ rock**) musica punk, punk rock m; (US col: hoodlum) teppista m

pup [pʌp] n cucciolo/a

pupil ['pjuːpl] n allievo/a; (Anat) pupilla

puppet ['pʌpɪt] n burattino

puppy ['pʌpɪ] n cucciolo/a, cagnolino/a

purchase ['pɜːtʃɪs] n acquisto, compera ▷ vt comprare

pure [pjuəʳ] adj puro/a; **purely** ['pjuəlɪ] adv puramente

purify ['pjuərɪfaɪ] vt purificare

purity ['pjuərɪtɪ] n purezza

purple ['pɜːpl] adj di porpora; viola inv

purpose ['pɜːpəs] n intenzione f, scopo; **on ~** apposta

purr [pɜː'] vi fare le fusa

purse [pɜːs] n (BRIT) borsellino; (US) borsetta ▷ vt contrarre

pursue [pə'sjuː] vt inseguire; (fig: activity etc) continuare con; (: aim etc) perseguire

pursuit [pə'sjuːt] n inseguimento; (fig) ricerca; (pastime) passatempo

pus [pʌs] n pus m

push [puʃ] n spinta; (effort) grande sforzo; (drive) energia ▷ vt spingere; (button) premere; (fig) fare pubblicità a; (thrust): **to ~ sth (into)** ficcare qc (in) ▷ vi spingere; premere; **to ~ for** insistere per ottenere; **push in** vi introdursi a forza; **push off** vi (col) filare; **push on** vi (continue) continuare; **push over** vt far cadere; **push through** vi farsi largo spingendo ▷ vt (measure) far approvare; **pushchair** (BRIT) n passeggino; **pusher** n (also: **drug pusher**) spacciatore/trice (di droga); **push-up** n (US: press-up) flessione f sulle braccia

puss [pus], **pussy(-cat)** ['pusɪ-] n micio

put (pt, pp put) [put] vt mettere, porre; (say) dire, esprimere; (a question) fare; (estimate) stimare; **put aside** vt (lay down: book etc) mettere da una parte, posare; (save) mettere da parte; (in shop) mettere da parte; **put away** vt (return) mettere a posto; **put back** vt (replace) rimettere (a posto); (postpone) rinviare; (delay) ritardare; **put by** vt (money) mettere da parte; **put down** vt (parcel etc) posare, mettere giù; (pay) versare; (in writing) mettere per iscritto; (revolt etc) sopprimere; (attribute) attribuire; **put forward** vt (ideas) avanzare, proporre; **put in** vt (application, complaint) presentare; (time, effort) mettere; **put off** vt (postpone) rimandare, rinviare;

(*discourage*) dissuadere; **put on** *vt* (*clothes, lipstick etc*) mettere; (*light etc*) accendere; (*play etc*) mettere in scena; (*food, meal*) mettere su; (*brake*) mettere; **to ~ on weight** ingrassare; **to ~ on airs** darsi delle arie; **put out** *vt* mettere fuori; (*one's hand*) porgere; (*light etc*) spegnere; (*inconvenience: person*) scomodare; **put through** *vt* (*Tel: caller*) mettere in comunicazione; (: *call*) passare; (*plan*) far approvare; **put together** *vt* mettere insieme, riunire; (*assemble: furniture*) montare; (: *meal*) improvvisare; **put up** *vt* (*raise*) sollevare, alzare; (: *umbrella*) aprire; (: *tent*) montare; (*pin up*) affiggere; (*hang*) appendere; (*build*) costruire, erigere; (*increase*) aumentare; (*accommodate*) alloggiare; **put up with** *vt fus* sopportare

putt [pʌt] *n* colpo leggero; **putting green** *n* green *m inv*; campo da putting

puzzle ['pʌzl] *n* enigma *m*, mistero; (*jigsaw*) puzzle *m*; (*also*: **crossword ~**) parole *fpl* incrociate, cruciverba *m inv* ▷ *vt* confondere, rendere perplesso/a ▷ *vi* scervellarsi; **puzzled** *adj* perplesso/a; **puzzling** *adj* (*question*) poco chiaro/a; (*attitude, set of instructions*) incomprensibile

pyjamas (BRIT) [pə'dʒɑːməz] *npl* pigiama *m*

pylon ['paɪlən] *n* pilone *m*

pyramid ['pɪrəmɪd] *n* piramide *f*

Pyrenees [pɪrə'niːz] *npl*: **the ~** i Pirenei

q

quack [kwæk] *n* (*of duck*) qua qua *m inv*; (*pej: doctor*) ciarlatano/a

quadruple [kwɔ'drupl] *vt* quadruplicare ▷ *vi* quadruplicarsi

quail [kweɪl] *n* (*Zool*) quaglia ▷ *vi* (*person*): **to ~ at** *or* **before** perdersi d'animo davanti a

quaint [kweɪnt] *adj* bizzarro/a; (*old-fashioned*) antiquato/a e pittoresco/a

quake [kweɪk] *vi* tremare ▷ *n abbr* = **earthquake**

qualification [kwɔlɪfɪ'keɪʃən] *n* (*degree etc*) qualifica, titolo; (*ability*) competenza, qualificazione *f*; (*limitation*) riserva, restrizione *f*

qualified ['kwɔlɪfaɪd] *adj* qualificato/a; (*able*) competente, qualificato/a; (*limited*) condizionato/a; **~ for/to do** qualificato/a per/per fare

qualify ['kwɔlɪfaɪ] *vt* abilitare; (*limit: statement*) modificare, precisare ▷ *vi*: **to ~ (as)** qualificarsi (come); **to ~ (for)** acquistare i requisiti necessari (per); (*Sport*) qualificarsi (per *or* a)

quality ['kwɔlɪtɪ] *n* qualità *f inv*

qualm [kwɑːm] *n* dubbio; scrupolo

quantify ['kwɔntɪfaɪ] *vt* quantificare

quantity ['kwɔntɪtɪ] *n* quantità *f inv*

quarantine ['kwɔrntiːn] *n* quarantena

quarrel ['kwɔrl] *n* lite *f*, disputa ▷ *vi* litigare

quarry ['kwɔrɪ] *n* (*for stone*) cava; (*animal*) preda

quart [kwɔːt] *n* ≈ litro

quarter ['kwɔːtəʳ] *n* quarto; (*of year*) trimestre *m*; (*district*) quartiere *m*; (US: *25 cents*) quarto di dollaro ▷ *vt* dividere in quattro; (*Mil*) alloggiare; **quarters** *npl* (*living quarters*) alloggio; (*Mil*) alloggi *mpl*, quadrato; **a ~ of an hour** un quarto d'ora; **quarter final** *n* quarto di finale; **quarterly**

adj trimestrale ▷ *adv* trimestralmente ▷ *n* periodico trimestrale

quartet(te) [kwɔː'tɛt] *n* quartetto

quartz [kwɔːts] *n* quarzo

quay [kiː] *n* (*also*: **~side**) banchina

queasy ['kwiːzɪ] *adj* (*stomach*) delicato/a; **to feel ~** aver la nausea

queen [kwiːn] *n* (*gen*) regina; (*Cards etc*) regina, donna

queer [kwɪə^r] *adj* strano/a, curioso/a ▷ *n* (*col!*) finocchio

quench [kwɛntʃ] *vt*: **to ~ one's thirst** dissetarsi

query ['kwɪərɪ] *n* domanda, questione *f* ▷ *vt* mettere in questione

quest [kwɛst] *n* cerca, ricerca

question ['kwɛstʃən] *n* domanda, questione *f* ▷ *vt* (*person*) interrogare; (*plan, idea*) mettere in questione *or* in dubbio; **it's a ~ of doing** si tratta di fare; **beyond ~** fuori di dubbio; **out of the ~** fuori discussione, impossibile; **questionable** *adj* discutibile; **question mark** *n* punto interrogativo; **questionnaire** [kwɛstʃə'nɛə^r] *n* questionario

queue [kjuː] *n* (BRIT) coda, fila ▷ *vi* fare la coda

quiche [kiːʃ] *n* torta salata a base di uova, formaggio, prosciutto o altro

quick [kwɪk] *adj* rapido/a, veloce; (*reply*) pronto/a; (*mind*) pronto/a, acuto/a ▷ *n*: **cut to the ~** (*fig*) toccato/a sul vivo; **be ~!** fa presto!; **quickly** *adv* rapidamente, velocemente

quid [kwɪd] *n* (*pl inv*: BRIT col) sterlina

quiet ['kwaɪət] *adj* tranquillo/a, quieto/a; (*ceremony*) semplice ▷ *n* tranquillità, calma ▷ *vt*, *vi* (*US*) = **quieten**; **keep ~!** sta zitto!; **quieten** *vi* (*also*: **quieten down**) calmarsi, chetarsi ▷ *vt* calmare, chetare; **quietly** *adv* tranquillamente, calmamente; silenziosamente

quilt [kwɪlt] *n* trapunta; **continental ~** piumino

quirky ['kwəːkɪ] *adj* stravagante

quit [kwɪt] (*pt, pp* **quit** *or* **quitted**) *vt* mollare; (*premises*) lasciare, partire da ▷ *vi* (*give up*) mollare; (*resign*) dimettersi

quite [kwaɪt] *adv* (*rather*) assai; (*entirely*) completamente, del tutto; **I ~ understand** capisco perfettamente; **~ a few of them** non pochi di loro; **~ (so)!** esatto!; **that's not ~ right** non è proprio esatto

quits [kwɪts] *adj*: **~ (with)** pari (con); **let's call it ~** adesso siamo pari

quiver ['kwɪvə^r] *vi* tremare, fremere

quiz [kwɪz] *n* (*game*) quiz *m inv*; indovinello ▷ *vt* interrogare

quota ['kwəutə] *n* quota

quotation [kwəu'teɪʃən] *n* citazione *f*; (*of shares etc*) quotazione *f*; (*estimate*) preventivo; **quotation marks** *npl* virgolette *fpl*

quote [kwəut] *n* citazione *f* ▷ *vt* (*sentence*) citare; (*price*) dare, fissare; (*shares*) quotare ▷ *vi*: **to ~ from** citare; **quotes** *npl* = **quotation marks**

r

rabbi ['ræbaɪ] n rabbino
rabbit ['ræbɪt] n coniglio
rabies ['reɪbiːz] n rabbia
RAC n abbr (BRIT: = Royal Automobile Club) ≈ A.C.I. m
raccoon [rə'kuːn], **racoon** n procione m
race [reɪs] n razza; (competition, rush) corsa ▷ vt (horse) far correre ▷ vi correre; (engine) imballarsi; **race car** n (US) = **racing car**; **racecourse** n campo di corse, ippodromo; **racehorse** n cavallo da corsa; **racetrack** n pista
racial ['reɪʃl] adj razziale
racing ['reɪsɪŋ] n corsa; **racing car** n (BRIT) macchina da corsa; **racing driver** n (BRIT) corridore m automobilista
racism ['reɪsɪzəm] n razzismo; **racist** adj, n razzista m/f
rack [ræk] n rastrelliera; (also: **luggage ~**) rete f, portabagagli m inv; (also: **roof ~**) portabagagli; (dish rack) scolapiatti m inv ▷ vt: **to ~ one's brains** scervellarsi; **~ed by** torturato/a da
racket ['rækɪt] n (for tennis) racchetta; (noise) fracasso; baccano; (swindle) imbroglio, truffa; (organized crime) racket m inv
racquet ['rækɪt] n racchetta
radar ['reɪdɑːʳ] n radar m
radiation [reɪdɪ'eɪʃən] n irradiamento; (radioactive) radiazione f
radiator ['reɪdɪeɪtəʳ] n radiatore m
radical ['rædɪkl] adj radicale
radio ['reɪdɪəu] n radio f inv; **on the ~** alla radio; **radioactive** ['reɪdɪəu'æktɪv] adj radioattivo/a; **radio station** n stazione f radio inv
radish ['rædɪʃ] n ravanello
RAF n abbr = **Royal Air Force**
raffle ['ræfl] n lotteria

raft [rɑːft] n zattera; (also: **life ~**) zattera di salvataggio
rag [ræg] n straccio, cencio; (pej: newspaper) giornalaccio, bandiera; (for charity) iniziativa studentesca a scopo benefico; **rags** npl (torn clothes) stracci mpl, brandelli mpl
rage [reɪdʒ] n (fury) collera, furia ▷ vi (person) andare su tutte le furie; (storm) infuriare; **it's all the ~** fa furore
ragged ['rægɪd] adj (edge) irregolare; (cuff) logoro/a; (appearance) pezzente
raid [reɪd] n (Mil) incursione f; (criminal) rapina; (by police) irruzione f ▷ vt fare un'incursione in; rapinare; fare irruzione in
rail [reɪl] n (on stair) ringhiera; (on bridge, balcony) parapetto; (of ship) battagliola; **railcard** n (BRIT) tessera di riduzione ferroviaria; **railing(s)** n(pl) ringhiere fpl; **railroad** (US) n = **railway**; **railway** (BRIT) n ferrovia; **railway line** n (BRIT) linea ferroviaria; **railway station** n (BRIT) stazione f ferroviaria
rain [reɪn] n pioggia ▷ vi piovere; **in the ~** sotto la pioggia; **it's ~ing** piove; **rainbow** n arcobaleno; **raincoat** n impermeabile m; **raindrop** n goccia di pioggia; **rainfall** n pioggia; (measurement) piovosità; **rainforest** n foresta pluviale or equatoriale; **rainy** adj piovoso/a
raise [reɪz] n aumento ▷ vt (lift) alzare; sollevare; (increase) aumentare; (a protest, doubt, question) sollevare; (cattle, family) allevare; (crop) coltivare; (army, funds) raccogliere; (loan) ottenere; **to ~ one's voice** alzare la voce
raisin ['reɪzn] n uva secca
rake [reɪk] n (tool) rastrello ▷ vt (garden) rastrellare
rally ['rælɪ] n (Pol etc) riunione f; (Aut) rally m inv; (Tennis) scambio ▷ vt riunire, radunare ▷ vi (sick person, Stock Exchange) riprendersi
RAM [ræm] n abbr (Comput: = random access memory) RAM f
ram [ræm] n montone m, ariete m ▷ vt conficcare; (crash into) cozzare, sbattere contro; percuotere; speronare
Ramadan [ræmə'dæn] n Ramadan m inv
ramble ['ræmbl] n escursione f ▷ vi (pej: also: **~ on**) divagare; **rambler** n escursionista m/f; (Bot) rosa rampicante; **rambling** adj (speech) sconnesso/a; (Bot) rampicante; (house) tutto/a nicchie e corridoi
ramp [ræmp] n rampa; **on/off ~** (US Aut) raccordo di entrata/uscita
rampage [ræm'peɪdʒ] n: **to go on the ~** scatenarsi in modo violento

ran [ræn] *pt of* **run**

ranch [rɑːntʃ] *n* ranch *m inv*

random ['rændəm] *adj* fatto/aor detto/a per caso; (*Comput, Math*) casuale ▷ *n*: **at ~** a casaccio

rang [ræŋ] *pt of* **ring**

range [reɪndʒ] *n* (*of mountains*) catena; (*of missile, voice*) portata; (*of products*) gamma; (*Mil: also:* **shooting ~**) campo di tiro; (*also:* **kitchen ~**) fornello, cucina economica ▷ *vt* disporre ▷ *vi*: **to ~ over** coprire; **to ~ from ... to** andare da ... a

ranger ['reɪndʒəʳ] *n* guardia forestale

rank [ræŋk] *n* fila; (*status, Mil*) grado; (*BRIT: also:* **taxi ~**) posteggio di taxi ▷ *vi*: **to ~ among** essere tra ▷ *adj* puzzolente; (*hypocrisy, injustice*) vero/a e proprio/a; **the ~ and file** (*fig*) la gran massa

ransom ['rænsəm] *n* riscatto; **to hold sb to ~** (*fig*) esercitare pressione su qn

rant [rænt] *vi* vociare

rap [ræp] *n* (*music*) rap *m inv* ▷ *vt* dare dei colpetti a; bussare a

rape [reɪp] *n* violenza carnale, stupro; (*Bot*) ravizzone *m* ▷ *vt* violentare

rapid ['ræpɪd] *adj* rapido/a; **rapidly** *adv* rapidamente; **rapids** (*Geo*) rapida

rapist ['reɪpɪst] *n* violentatore *m*

rapport [ræ'pɔːt] *n* rapporto

rare [rɛəʳ] *adj* raro/a; (*Culin: steak*) al sangue; **rarely** ['rɛəlɪ] *adv* raramente

rash [ræʃ] *adj* imprudente, sconsiderato/a ▷ *n* (*Med*) eruzione *f*; (*of events etc*) scoppio

rasher ['ræʃəʳ] *n* fetta sottile (di lardo *or* prosciutto)

raspberry ['rɑːzbərɪ] *n* lampone *m*

rat [ræt] *n* ratto

rate [reɪt] *n* (*proportion*) tasso, percentuale *f*; (*speed*) velocità *f inv*; (*price*) tariffa ▷ *vt* valutare; stimare; **to ~ sb/sth as** valutare qn/qc come; **rates** *npl* (*BRIT: property tax*) imposte *fpl* comunali; (*fees*) tariffe *fpl*

rather ['rɑːðəʳ] *adv* piuttosto; **it's ~ expensive** è piuttosto caro; (*too much*) è un po' caro; **there's ~ a lot** ce n'è parecchio; **I would** *or* **I'd ~ go** preferirei andare

rating ['reɪtɪŋ] *n* (*assessment*) valutazione *f*; (*score*) punteggio di merito; **ratings** *npl* (*Radio, TV*) indice *m* di ascolto

ratio ['reɪʃɪəu] *n* proporzione *f*; **in the ~ of 2 to 1** in rapporto di 2 a 1

ration ['ræʃən] *n* razione *f* ▷ *vt* razionare; **rations** *npl* razioni *fpl*

rational ['ræʃənl] *adj* razionale, ragionevole; (*solution, reasoning*) logico/a

rattle ['rætl] *n* tintinnio; (*louder*) rumore *m* di ferraglia; (*of baby*) sonaglino ▷ *vi* risuonare, tintinnare; fare un rumore di ferraglia

rave [reɪv] *vi* (*in anger*) infuriarsi; (*with enthusiasm*) andare in estasi; (*Med*) delirare ▷ *n* (*BRIT*): **a ~ (party)** un rave

raven ['reɪvən] *n* corvo

ravine [rə'viːn] *n* burrone *m*

raw [rɔː] *adj* (*uncooked*) crudo/a; (*not processed*) greggio/a; (*sore*) vivo/a; (*inexperienced*) inesperto/a; (*weather, day*) gelido/a

ray [reɪ] *n* raggio; **a ~ of hope** un barlume di speranza

razor ['reɪzəʳ] *n* rasoio; **razor blade** *n* lama di rasoio

Rd *abbr* = **road**

RE *n abbr* (*BRIT Mil: = Royal Engineers*) ≈ G.M.; (*BRIT*) = **religious education**

re [riː] *prep* con riferimento a

reach [riːtʃ] *n* portata; (*of river etc*) tratto ▷ *vt* raggiungere; arrivare a ▷ *vi* stendersi; **out of/within ~** fuori/a portata di mano; **within easy ~ (of)** vicino (a); **reach out** *vt* (*hand*) allungare ▷ *vi*: **to ~ out for** stendere la mano per prendere

react [riː'ækt] *vi* reagire; **reaction** [riː'ækʃən] *n* reazione *f*; **reactor** [riː'æktəʳ] *n* reattore *m*

read (*pt, pp* **read**) [riːd, rɛd] *vi* leggere ▷ *vt* leggere; (*understand*) intendere, interpretare; (*study*) studiare; **read out** *vt* leggere ad alta voce; **reader** *n* lettore/trice; (*BRIT: at university*) professore con funzioni preminenti di ricerca

readily ['rɛdɪlɪ] *adv* volentieri; (*easily*) facilmente; (*quickly*) prontamente

reading ['riːdɪŋ] *n* lettura; (*understanding*) interpretazione *f*; (*on instrument*) indicazione *f*

ready ['rɛdɪ] *adj* pronto/a; (*willing*) pronto/a, disposto/a; (*available*) disponibile ▷ *n*: **at the ~** (*Mil*) pronto a sparare ▷ *vt* preparare; **to get ~** *vi* prepararsi; **ready-made** *adj* prefabbricato/a; (*clothes*) confezionato/a

real [rɪəl] *adj* reale; vero/a; **in ~ terms** in realtà; **real ale** *n* birra ad effervescenza naturale; **real estate** *n* beni *mpl* immobili; **realistic** [rɪə'lɪstɪk] *adj* realistico/a; **reality** [riː'ælɪtɪ] *n* realtà *f inv*; **reality TV** *n* reality TV *f*

realization [rɪəlaɪ'zeɪʃən] *n* presa di coscienza; (*of hopes, project etc*) realizzazione *f*

realize ['rɪəlaɪz] *vt* (*understand*) rendersi conto di

really ['rɪəlɪ] *adv* veramente, davvero; **~!** (*indicating annoyance*) oh, insomma!

realm [rɛlm] *n* reame *m*, regno

Realtor® ['rɪəltɔːʳ] *n* (*US*) agente *m* immobiliare

reappear [riːəˈpɪəʳ] vi ricomparire, riapparire

rear [rɪəʳ] adj di dietro; (Aut: wheel etc) posteriore ▷ n didietro, parte f posteriore ▷ vt (cattle, family) allevare ▷ vi (also: ~ up: animal) impennarsi

rearrange [riːəˈreɪndʒ] vt riordinare

rear: rear-view mirror [ˈrɪəvjuː-] n (Aut) specchio retrovisivo; **rear-wheel drive** n trazione fpl posteriore

reason [ˈriːzn] n ragione f; (cause, motive) ragione, motivo ▷ vi: **to ~ with sb** far ragionare qn; **it stands to ~ that** è ovvio che; **reasonable** adj ragionevole; (not bad) accettabile; **reasonably** adv ragionevolmente; **reasoning** n ragionamento

reassurance [riːəˈʃuərəns] n rassicurazione f

reassure [riːəˈʃuəʳ] vt rassicurare; **to ~ sb of** rassicurare qn di or su

rebate [ˈriːbeɪt] n (on tax etc) sgravio

rebel n [ˈrɛbl] ribelle m/f ▷ vi [rɪˈbɛl] ribellarsi; **rebellion** n ribellione f; **rebellious** adj ribelle

rebuild [riːˈbɪld] vt (irreg) ricostruire

recall vt [rɪˈkɔːl] richiamare; (remember) ricordare, richiamare alla mente ▷ n [ˈriːkɔːl] richiamo

recd. abbr = **received**

receipt [rɪˈsiːt] n (document) ricevuta; (act of receiving) ricevimento; **receipts** npl (Comm) introiti mpl

receive [rɪˈsiːv] vt ricevere; (guest) ricevere, accogliere; **receiver** [rɪˈsiːvəʳ] n (Tel) ricevitore m; (Radio) apparecchio ricevente; (of stolen goods) ricettatore/trice; (Law, Comm) curatore m fallimentare

recent [ˈriːsnt] adj recente; **recently** adv recentemente

reception [rɪˈsɛpʃən] n ricevimento; (welcome) accoglienza; (TV etc) ricezione f; **reception desk** n (in hotel) reception f inv; (in hospital, at doctor's) accettazione f; (in large building, offices) portineria; **receptionist** n receptionist mf inv

recession [rɪˈsɛʃən] n recessione f; **recessionista** [rɪsɛʃəˈnɪstə] n recessionista m/f

recharge [riːˈtʃɑːdʒ] vt (battery) ricaricare

recipe [ˈrɛsɪpɪ] n ricetta

recipient [rɪˈsɪpɪənt] n beneficiario/a; (of letter) destinatario/a

recital [rɪˈsaɪtl] n recital m inv

recite [rɪˈsaɪt] vt (poem) recitare

reckless [ˈrɛkləs] adj (driver etc) spericolato/a; (spending) folle

reckon [ˈrɛkən] vt (count) calcolare; (think): **I ~ that ...** penso che ..

reclaim [rɪˈkleɪm] vt (land) bonificare; (demand back) richiedere, reclamare; (materials) recuperare

recline [rɪˈklaɪn] vi stare sdraiato/a

recognition [rɛkəɡˈnɪʃən] n riconoscimento; **transformed beyond ~** irriconoscibile

recognize [ˈrɛkəɡnaɪz] vt: **to ~ (by/as)** riconoscere (a or da/come)

recollection [rɛkəˈlɛkʃən] n ricordo

recommend [rɛkəˈmɛnd] vt raccomandare; (advise) consigliare; **recommendation** [rɛkəmɛnˈdeɪʃən] n raccomandazione f; consiglio

reconcile [ˈrɛkənsaɪl] vt (two people) riconciliare; (two facts) conciliare, quadrare; **to ~ o.s. to** rassegnarsi a

reconsider [riːkənˈsɪdəʳ] vt riconsiderare

reconstruct [riːkənˈstrʌkt] vt ricostruire

record n [ˈrɛkɔːd] ricordo, documento; (of meeting etc) nota, verbale m; (register) registro; (file) pratica, dossier m inv; (Comput) record m inv; (also: **police ~**) fedina penale sporca; (Mus: disc) disco; (Sport) record m inv, primato ▷ vt [rɪˈkɔːd] (set down) prendere nota di, registrare; (Comput, Mus: song etc) registrare; **off the ~** adj ufficioso/a; adv ufficiosamente; **in ~ time** a tempo di record; **recorded delivery letter** n (BRIT Post) lettera raccomandata; **recorder** n (Mus) flauto diritto; **recording** n (Mus) registrazione f; **record player** n giradischi m inv

recount [rɪˈkaunt] vt raccontare, narrare

recover [rɪˈkʌvəʳ] vt ricuperare ▷ vi: **to ~ (from)** riprendersi (da); **recovery** [rɪˈkʌvərɪ] n ricupero; ristabilimento; ripresa

⃞ Be careful not to translate *recover* by the Italian word *ricoverare*.

recreate [riːkrɪˈeɪt] vt ricreare

recreation [rɛkrɪˈeɪʃən] n ricreazione f; svago; **recreational drug** [rɛkrɪˈeɪʃənl-] n droga usata saltuariamente; **recreational vehicle** n (US) camper m inv

recruit [rɪˈkruːt] n recluta; (in company) nuovo/a assunto/a ▷ vt reclutare; **recruitment** n reclutamento

rectangle [ˈrɛktæŋgl] n rettangolo; **rectangular** [rɛkˈtæŋgjuləʳ] adj rettangolare

rectify [ˈrɛktɪfaɪ] vt (error) rettificare; (omission) riparare

rector [ˈrɛktəʳ] n (Rel) parroco (anglicano)

recur [rɪˈkəːʳ] vi riaccadere; (symptoms) ripresentarsi; **recurring** adj (Math) periodico/a

recyclable [riːˈsaɪkləbl] *adj* riciclabile

recycle [riːˈsaɪkl] *vt* riciclare

recycling [riːˈsaɪklɪŋ] *n* riciclaggio

red [red] *n* rosso; (*Pol: pej*) rosso/a ▷ *adj* rosso/a; **in the ~** (*account*) scoperto; (*business*) in deficit; **Red Cross** *n* Croce *f* Rossa; **redcurrant** *n* ribes *m inv*

redeem [rɪˈdiːm] *vt* (*debt*) riscattare; (*sth in pawn*) ritirare; (*fig, also Rel*) redimere

red: red-haired [-ˈhɛəd] *adj* dai capelli rossi; **redhead** [ˈrɛdhɛd] *n* rosso/a; **red-hot** *adj* arroventato/a; **red light** *n*: **to go through a red light** (*Aut*) passare col rosso; **red-light district** [rɛdˈlaɪt-] *n* quartiere *m* a luci rosse; **red meat** *n* carne *f* rossa

reduce [rɪˈdjuːs] *vt* ridurre; (*lower*) ridurre, abbassare; **"~ speed now"** (*Aut*) "rallentare"; **at a ~d price** scontato/a; **reduced** *adj* (*decreased*) ridotto/a; **at a reduced price** a prezzo ribassato *or* ridotto; **"greatly reduced prices"** "grandi ribassi"; **reduction** [rɪˈdʌkʃən] *n* riduzione *f*; (*of price*) ribasso; (*discount*) sconto

redundancy [rɪˈdʌndənsɪ] *n*; licenziamento

redundant [rɪˈdʌndnt] *adj* (*worker*) licenziato/a; (*detail, object*) superfluo/a; **to be made ~** (*BRIT*) essere licenziato (per eccesso di personale)

reed [riːd] *n* (*Bot*) canna; (*Mus: of clarinet etc*) ancia

reef [riːf] *n* (*at sea*) scogliera

reel [riːl] *n* bobina, rocchetto; (*Fishing*) mulinello; (*Cine*) rotolo; (*dance*) danza veloce scozzese ▷ *vi* (*sway*) barcollare

ref [rɛf] *n abbr* (*col: = referee*) arbitro

refectory [rɪˈfɛktərɪ] *n* refettorio

refer [rɪˈfəːʳ] *vt*: **to ~ sth to** (*dispute, decision*) deferire qc a; **to ~ sb to** (*inquirer, Med: patient*) indirizzare qn a; (*reader: to text*) rimandare qn a; **refer to** *vt fus* (*allude to*) accennare a; (*consult*) rivolgersi a

referee [rɛfəˈriː] *n* arbitro; (*BRIT: for job application*) referenza ▷ *vt* arbitrare

reference [ˈrɛfrəns] *n* riferimento; (*mention*) menzione *f*, allusione *f*; (*for job application*) referenza; **with ~ to** (*Comm: in letter*) in *or* con riferimento a; **reference number** *n* numero di riferimento

refill *vt* [riːˈfɪl] riempire di nuovo; (*pen, lighter etc*) ricaricare ▷ *n* [ˈriːfɪl] (*for pen etc*) ricambio

refine [rɪˈfaɪn] *vt* raffinare; **refined** *adj* (*person, taste*) raffinato/a; **refinery** *n* raffineria

reflect [rɪˈflɛkt] *vt* (*light, image*) riflettere; (*fig*) rispecchiare ▷ *vi* (*think*) riflettere, considerare; **it ~s badly/well on him** si ripercuote su di lui in senso negativo/

positivo; **reflection** [rɪˈflɛkʃən] *n* riflessione *f*; (*image*) riflesso; (*criticism*): **reflection on** giudizio su; attacco a; **on reflection** pensandoci sopra

reflex [ˈriːflɛks] *adj* riflesso/a ▷ *n* riflesso

reform [rɪˈfɔːm] *n* (*of sinner etc*) correzione *f*; (*of law etc*) riforma ▷ *vt* correggere; riformare

refrain [rɪˈfreɪn] *vi*: **to ~ from doing** trattenersi dal fare ▷ *n* ritornello

refresh [rɪˈfrɛʃ] *vt* rinfrescare; (*food, sleep*) ristorare; **refreshing** *adj* (*drink*) rinfrescante; (*sleep*) riposante, ristoratore/ trice

refreshment *n* ristoro; **~(s)** rinfreschi *mpl*

refrigerator [rɪˈfrɪdʒəreɪtəʳ] *n* frigorifero

refuel [riːˈfjuəl] *vi* far rifornimento (di carburante)

refuge [ˈrɛfjuːdʒ] *n* rifugio; **to take ~ in** rifugiarsi in; **refugee** [rɛfjuˈdʒiː] *n* rifugiato/a, profugo/a

refund *n* [ˈriːfʌnd] rimborso ▷ *vt* [rɪˈfʌnd] rimborsare

refurbish [riːˈfəːbɪʃ] *vt* rimettere a nuovo

refusal [rɪˈfjuːzəl] *n* rifiuto; **to have first ~ on sth** avere il diritto d'opzione su qc

refuse¹ [ˈrɛfjuːs] *n* rifiuti *mpl*

refuse² [rɪˈfjuːz] *vt, vi* rifiutare; **to ~ to do sth** rifiutare *or* rifiutarsi di fare qc

regain [rɪˈɡeɪn] *vt* riguadagnare; riacquistare, ricuperare

regard [rɪˈɡɑːd] *n* riguardo, stima ▷ *vt* considerare, stimare; **to give one's ~s to** porgere i suoi saluti a; **(kind) ~s** cordiali saluti; **regarding** *prep* riguardo a, per quanto riguarda; **regardless** *adv* lo stesso; **regardless of** a dispetto di, nonostante

regenerate [rɪˈdʒɛnəreɪt] *vt* rigenerare

reggae [ˈrɛɡeɪ] *n* reggae *m*

regiment *n* [ˈrɛdʒɪmənt] reggimento

region [ˈriːdʒən] *n* regione *f*; **in the ~ of** (*fig*) all'incirca di; **regional** *adj* regionale

register [ˈrɛdʒɪstəʳ] *n* registro; (*also*: **electoral ~**) lista elettorale ▷ *vt* registrare; (*vehicle*) immatricolare; (*letter*) assicurare; (*instrument*) segnare ▷ *vi* iscriversi; (*at hotel*) firmare il registro; (*make impression*) entrare in testa; **registered** *adj* (*BRIT: letter*) assicurato/a

registrar [ˈrɛdʒɪstrɑːʳ] *n* ufficiale *m* di stato civile; segretario

registration [rɛdʒɪsˈtreɪʃən] *n* (*act*) registrazione *f*; iscrizione *f*; (*Aut: also*: **~ number**) numero di targa

registry office *n* (*BRIT*) anagrafe *f*; **to get married in a ~** ≈ sposarsi in municipio

regret [rɪˈɡrɛt] *n* rimpianto, rincrescimento ▷ *vt* rimpiangere; **regrettable** *adj* deplorevole

regular ['rɛgjʊlə^r] adj regolare; (usual) abituale, normale; (soldier) dell'esercito regolare ▷ n (client etc) cliente m/f abituale; **regularly** adv regolarmente

regulate ['rɛgjʊleɪt] vt regolare; **regulation** [rɛgjʊ'leɪʃən] n (rule) regola, regolamento; (adjustment) regolazione f

rehabilitation ['riːəbɪlɪ'teɪʃən] n (of offender) riabilitazione f; (of disabled person) riadattamento

rehearsal [rɪ'həːsəl] n prova

rehearse [rɪ'həːs] vt provare

reign [reɪn] n regno ▷ vi regnare

reimburse [riːɪm'bəːs] vt rimborsare

rein [reɪn] n (for horse) briglia

reincarnation [riːɪnkɑː'neɪʃən] n reincarnazione f

reindeer ['reɪndɪə^r] n (pl inv) renna

reinforce [riːɪn'fɔːs] vt rinforzare

reinforcement n rinforzamento; **reinforcements** npl (Mil) rinforzi mpl

reinstate [riːɪn'steɪt] vt reintegrare

reject n ['riːdʒɛkt] (Comm) scarto ▷ vt [rɪ'dʒɛkt] rifiutare, respingere; (Comm: goods) scartare; **rejection** [rɪ'dʒɛkʃən] n rifiuto

rejoice [rɪ'dʒɔɪs] vi: **to ~ (at or over)** provare diletto (in)

relate [rɪ'leɪt] vt (tell) raccontare; (connect) collegare ▷ vi: **to ~ to** (refer to) riferirsi a; (get on with) stabilire un rapporto con; **relating to** che riguarda, rispetto a; **related** adj: **related to** imparentato/a con

relation [rɪ'leɪʃən] n (person) parente m/f; (link) rapporto, relazione f; **relations** npl (relatives) parenti mpl; **relationship** n rapporto; (personal ties) rapporti mpl, relazioni fpl; (also: **family relationship**) legami mpl di parentela

relative ['rɛlətɪv] n parente m/f ▷ adj relativo/a; (respective) rispettivo/a; **relatively** adv relativamente; (fairly, rather) abbastanza

relax [rɪ'læks] vi rilasciarsi; (person: unwind) rilassarsi ▷ vt rilasciare; (mind, person) rilassare; **relaxation** [riːlæk'seɪʃən] n rilasciamento; rilassamento; (entertainment) ricreazione f, svago; **relaxed** adj rilassato/a; **relaxing** adj rilassante

relay ['riːleɪ] n (Sport) corsa a staffetta ▷ vt (message) trasmettere

release [rɪ'liːs] n (from prison) rilascio; (from obligation) liberazione f; (of gas etc) emissione f; (of film etc) distribuzione f; (record) disco; (device) disinnesto ▷ vt (prisoner) rilasciare; (from obligation, wreckage etc) liberare; (book, film) fare

uscire; (news) rendere pubblico/a; (gas etc) emettere; (Tech: catch, spring etc) disinnestare

relegate ['rɛləgeɪt] vt relegare; (BRIT Sport): **to be ~d** essere retrocesso/a

relent [rɪ'lɛnt] vi cedere; **relentless** adj implacabile

relevant ['rɛləvənt] adj pertinente; (chapter) in questione; **~ to** pertinente a
▌ Be careful not to translate relevant by the Italian word rilevante.

reliable [rɪ'laɪəbl] adj (person, firm) fidato/a, che dà affidamento; (method) sicuro/a; (machine) affidabile

relic ['rɛlɪk] n (Rel) reliquia; (of the past) resto

relief [rɪ'liːf] n (from pain, anxiety) sollievo; (help, supplies) soccorsi mpl; (Art, Geo) rilievo

relieve [rɪ'liːv] vt (pain, patient) sollevare; (bring help) soccorrere; (take over from: gen) sostituire; (: guard) rilevare; **to ~ sb of sth** (load) alleggerire qn di qc; **to ~ o.s.** fare i propri bisogni; **relieved** adj sollevato/a; **to be relieved that ...** essere sollevato/a (dal fatto) che ...; **I'm relieved to hear it** mi hai tolto un peso con questa notizia

religion [rɪ'lɪdʒən] n religione f

religious [rɪ'lɪdʒəs] adj religioso/a; **religious education** n religione f

relish ['rɛlɪʃ] n (Culin) condimento; (enjoyment) gran piacere m ▷ vt (food etc) godere; **to ~ doing** adorare fare

relocate [riːləu'keɪt] vt trasferire ▷ vi trasferirsi

reluctance [rɪ'lʌktəns] n riluttanza

reluctant [rɪ'lʌktənt] adj riluttante, mal disposto/a; **reluctantly** adv di mala voglia, a malincuore

rely [rɪ'laɪ]: **to ~ on** vt fus contare su; (be dependent) dipendere da

remain [rɪ'meɪn] vi restare, rimanere; **remainder** n resto; (Comm) rimanenza; **remaining** adj che rimane; **remains** npl resti mpl

remand [rɪ'mɑːnd] n: **on ~** in detenzione preventiva ▷ vt: **to ~ in custody** rinviare in carcere; trattenere a disposizione della legge

remark [rɪ'mɑːk] n osservazione f ▷ vt osservare, dire; **remarkable** adj notevole; eccezionale

remarry [riː'mærɪ] vi risposarsi

remedy ['rɛmədɪ] n: **~ (for)** rimedio (per) ▷ vt rimediare a

remember [rɪ'mɛmbə^r] vt ricordare, ricordarsi di; **~ me to your wife and children!** saluti sua moglie e i bambini da parte mia!

Remembrance Day (BRIT),
Remembrance Sunday n vedi nota
"Remembrance Day"

* **REMEMBRANCE DAY**
*
* Nel Regno Unito, la domenica più
* vicina all'11 di novembre, data in cui fu
* firmato l'armistizio con la Germania
* nel 1918, ricorre il *Remembrance Day*
* o *Remembrance Sunday*, giorno in cui
* vengono commemorati i caduti in guerra.
* In questa occasione molti portano un
* papavero di carta appuntato al petto in
* segno di rispetto.

remind [rɪ'maɪnd] vt: **to ~ sb of sth**
ricordare qc a qn; **to ~ sb to do** ricordare a
qn di fare; **reminder** n richiamo; (note etc)
promemoria m inv

reminiscent [rɛmɪ'nɪsnt] adj: **~ of** che fa
pensare a, che richiama

remnant ['rɛmnənt] n resto, avanzo

remorse [rɪ'mɔːs] n rimorso

remote [rɪ'məut] adj remoto/a,
lontano/a; (person) distaccato/a; **remote
control** n telecomando; **remotely** adv
remotamente; (slightly) vagamente

removal [rɪ'muːvəl] n (taking away)
rimozione f; soppressione f; (BRIT: from
house) trasloco; (from office: sacking)
destituzione f; (Med) ablazione f; **removal
man** n (irreg: BRIT) addetto ai traslochi;
removal van n (BRIT) furgone m per
traslochi

remove [rɪ'muːv] vt togliere, rimuovere;
(employee) destituire; (stain) far sparire;
(doubt, abuse) sopprimere, eliminare

Renaissance [rə'neɪsəns] n: **the ~** il
Rinascimento

rename [riː'neɪm] vt ribattezzare

render ['rɛndər] vt rendere

rendez-vous ['rɒndɪvuː] n appuntamento;
(place) luogo d'incontro; (meeting) incontro

renew [rɪ'njuː] vt rinnovare; (negotiations)
riprendere; **renewable** adj riutilizzabile;
(contract) rinnovabile; **renewable energy,
renewables** fonti mpl di energia rinnovabile

renovate ['rɛnəveɪt] vt rinnovare; (art
work) restaurare

renowned [rɪ'naund] adj rinomato/a

rent [rɛnt] n affitto ▷ vt (take for rent)
prendere in affitto; (also: **~ out**) dare in
affitto; **rental** n (cost: on TV, telephone)
abbonamento; (: on car) noleggio

reorganize [riː'ɔːgənaɪz] vt riorganizzare

rep [rɛp] n abbr (Comm: = representative)
rappresentante m/f; (Theat: = repertory)
teatro di repertorio

repair [rɪ'pɛər] n riparazione f ▷ vt riparare;
in good/bad ~ in buono/cattivo stato;
repair kit n kit m inv per riparazioni

repay [riː'peɪ] vt (irreg: money, creditor)
rimborsare, ripagare; (sb's efforts)
ricompensare; (favour) ricambiare;
repayment n rimborso

repeat [rɪ'piːt] n (Radio, TV) replica ▷ vt
ripetere; (pattern) riprodurre; (promise,
attack, also Comm: order) rinnovare ▷ vi
ripetere; **repeatedly** adv ripetutamente,
spesso; **repeat prescription** n (BRIT)
ricetta ripetibile

repellent [rɪ'pɛlənt] adj repellente ▷ n:
insect ~ prodotto m anti-insetti inv

repercussion [riːpə'kʌʃən] n
ripercussione f

repetition [rɛpɪ'tɪʃən] n ripetizione f

repetitive [rɪ'pɛtɪtɪv] adj (movement) che
si ripete; (work) monotono/a; (speech)
pieno/a di ripetizioni

replace [rɪ'pleɪs] vt (put back) rimettere
a posto; (take the place of) sostituire;
replacement n rimessa; sostituzione f;
(person) sostituto/a

replay ['riːpleɪ] n (of match) partita
ripetuta; (of tape, film) replay m inv

replica ['rɛplɪkə] n replica, copia

reply [rɪ'plaɪ] n risposta ▷ vi rispondere

report [rɪ'pɔːt] n rapporto; (Press etc)
cronaca; (BRIT: also: **school ~**) pagella; (of
gun) sparo ▷ vt riportare; (Press etc) fare
una cronaca su; (bring to notice: occurrence)
segnalare; (: person) denunciare ▷ vi (make
a report) fare un rapporto (or una cronaca);
(present o.s.): **to ~ (to sb)** presentarsi (a
qn); **report card** n (US, SCOTTISH) pagella;
reportedly adv stando a quanto si dice; **he
reportedly told them to …** avrebbe detto
loro di …; **reporter** n reporter m inv

represent [rɛprɪ'zɛnt] vt rappresentare;
representation [rɛprɪzɛn'teɪʃən]
n rappresentazione f; (petition)
rappresentanza; **representative** n
rappresentante m (di commercio); (US Pol)
deputato/a ▷ adj: **representative (of)**
rappresentativo/a (di)

repress [rɪ'prɛs] vt reprimere; **repression**
[rɪ'prɛʃən] n repressione f

reprimand ['rɛprɪmɑːnd] n rimprovero
▷ vt rimproverare

reproduce [riːprə'djuːs] vt riprodurre ▷ vi
riprodursi; **reproduction** [riːprə'dʌkʃən] n
riproduzione f

reptile ['rɛptaɪl] n rettile m

republic [rɪ'pʌblɪk] n repubblica;
republican adj, n repubblicano/a

reputable ['rɛpjutəbl] adj di buona
reputazione; (occupation) rispettabile

reputation [rɛpjʊˈteɪʃən] n reputazione f
request [rɪˈkwɛst] n domanda; (formal)
richiesta ▷ vt: **to ~ (of** or **from sb)** chiedere
(a qn); **request stop** n (BRIT: for bus)
fermata facoltativa or a richiesta
require [rɪˈkwaɪəʳ] vt (need: person) aver
bisogno di; (: thing, situation) richiedere;
(want) volere; esigere; **to ~ sb to do sth/
sth of sb** esigere che qn faccia qc/qc da
qn; **requirement** n esigenza; bisogno;
(condition) requisito
resat [riːˈsæt] pt, pp of **resit**
rescue [ˈrɛskjuː] n salvataggio; (help)
soccorso ▷ vt salvare
research [rɪˈsɜːtʃ] n ricerca, ricerche fpl ▷ vt
fare ricerche su
resemblance [rɪˈzɛmbləns] n
somiglianza
resemble [rɪˈzɛmbl] vt assomigliare a
resent [rɪˈzɛnt] vt risentirsi di; **resentful**
adj pieno/a di risentimento; **resentment** n
risentimento
reservation [rɛzəˈveɪʃən] n (booking)
prenotazione f; (doubt) dubbio; (protected
area) riserva; (BRIT Aut: also: **central ~**)
spartitraffico m inv; **reservation desk** n
(US: in hotel) reception f inv
reserve [rɪˈzɜːv] n riserva ▷ vt (seats etc)
prenotare; **reserved** adj (shy) riservato/a
reservoir [ˈrɛzəvwɑːʳ] n serbatoio
residence [ˈrɛzɪdəns] n residenza;
residence permit n (BRIT) permesso di
soggiorno
resident [ˈrɛzɪdənt] n residente m/f; (in
hotel) cliente m/f fisso/a ▷ adj residente;
(doctor) fisso/a; (course, college) a tempo
pieno con pernottamento; **residential**
[rɛzɪˈdɛnʃəl] adj di residenza; (area)
residenziale
residue [ˈrɛzɪdjuː] n resto; (Chem, Physics)
residuo
resign [rɪˈzaɪn] vt (one's post) dimettersi da
▷ vi: **to ~ (from)** dimettersi (da); **to ~ o.s. to**
rassegnarsi a; **resignation** [rɛzɪɡˈneɪʃən] n
dimissioni fpl; rassegnazione f
resin [ˈrɛzɪn] n resina
resist [rɪˈzɪst] vt resistere a; **resistance** n
resistenza
resit [ˈriːsɪt] (pt, pp **resat**) (BRIT) vt (exam)
ripresentarsi a; (subject) ridare l'esame di
▷ n: **he's got his French ~ on Friday** deve
ridare l'esame di francese venerdì
resolution [rɛzəˈluːʃən] n risoluzione f
resolve [rɪˈzɔlv] n risoluzione f ▷ vi (decide):
to ~ to do decidere di fare ▷ vt (problem)
risolvere
resort [rɪˈzɔːt] n (town) stazione f; (recourse)
ricorso ▷ vi: **to ~ to** far ricorso a; **as a last ~**
come ultima risorsa

resource [rɪˈsɔːs] n risorsa; **resourceful** adj
pieno/a di risorse, intraprendente
respect [rɪsˈpɛkt] n rispetto ▷ vt rispettare;
respectable adj rispettabile; **respectful**
adj rispettoso/a; **respective** [rɪsˈpɛktɪv]
adj rispettivo/a; **respectively** adv
rispettivamente
respite [ˈrɛspaɪt] n respiro, tregua
respond [rɪsˈpɔnd] vi rispondere;
response [rɪsˈpɔns] n risposta
responsibility [rɪspɔnsɪˈbɪlɪtɪ] n
responsabilità f inv
responsible [rɪsˈpɔnsɪbl] adj: **~ (for)**
responsabile (di); (trustworthy) fidato/a;
(job) di (grande) responsabilità;
responsibly adv responsabilmente
responsive [rɪsˈpɔnsɪv] adj che reagisce
rest [rɛst] n riposo; (stop) sosta, pausa;
(Mus) pausa; (support) appoggio, sostegno;
(remainder) resto, avanzi mpl ▷ vi riposarsi;
(remain) rimanere, restare; (be supported):
to ~ on appoggiarsi su ▷ vt (far) riposare;
(lean): **to ~ sth on/against** appoggiare
qc su/contro; **the ~ of them** gli altri; **it ~s
with him to decide** sta a lui decidere
restaurant [ˈrɛstərɔŋ] n ristorante
m; **restaurant car** n (BRIT) vagone m
ristorante
restless [ˈrɛstlɪs] adj agitato/a,
irrequieto/a
restoration [rɛstəˈreɪʃən] n restauro;
restituzione f
restore [rɪˈstɔːʳ] vt (building) restaurare; (sth
stolen) restituire; (peace, health) ristorare
restrain [rɪsˈtreɪn] vt (feeling) contenere,
frenare; (person): **to ~ (from doing)**
trattenere (dal fare); **restraint** n
(restriction) limitazione f; (moderation)
ritegno; (of style) contenutezza
restrict [rɪsˈtrɪkt] vt restringere, limitare;
restriction [rɪsˈtrɪkʃən] n: **restriction
(on)** restrizione f (di), limitazione f (di)
rest room n (US) toletta
restructure [riːˈstrʌktʃəʳ] vt ristrutturare
result [rɪˈzʌlt] n risultato ▷ vi: **to ~ in**
avere per risultato; **as a ~ (of)** in or di
conseguenza (a), in seguito (a)
resume [rɪˈzjuːm] vt, vi (work, journey)
riprendere
résumé [ˈreɪzjuːmeɪ] n riassunto; (US)
curriculum vitae m inv
resuscitate [rɪˈsʌsɪteɪt] vt (Med) risuscitare
retail [ˈriːteɪl] cpd al minuto ▷ vt vendere
al minuto; **retailer** n commerciante m/f al
minuto, dettagliante m/f
retain [rɪˈteɪn] vt (keep) tenere, serbare
retaliation [rɪtælɪˈeɪʃən] n rappresaglie fpl
retarded [rɪˈtɑːdɪd] adj (Med: col!)
ritardato/a

retire [rɪ'taɪəʳ] vi (give up work) andare in pensione; (withdraw) ritirarsi, andarsene; (go to bed) andare a letto, ritirarsi; **retired** adj (person) pensionato/a; **retirement** n pensione f; (act) pensionamento

retort [rɪ'tɔ:t] vi rimbeccare

retreat [rɪ'tri:t] n ritirata; (place) rifugio ▷ vi battere in ritirata

retrieve [rɪ'tri:v] vt (sth lost) recuperare, ritrovare; (situation, honour) salvare; (error, loss) rimediare a

retrospect ['rɛtrəspɛkt] n: **in ~** guardando indietro; **retrospective** [rɛtrə'spɛktɪv] adj retrospettivo/a; (law) retroattivo/a

return [rɪ'tə:n] n (going or coming back) ritorno; (of sth stolen etc) restituzione f; (Comm: from land, shares) profitto, reddito; **in ~ (for)** in cambio (di) ▷ cpd (journey, match) di ritorno; (BRIT: ticket) di andata e ritorno ▷ vi tornare, ritornare ▷ vt rendere, restituire; (bring back) riportare; (send back) mandare indietro; (put back) rimettere; (Pol: candidate) eleggere; **returns** npl (Comm) incassi mpl; profitti mpl; **by ~ of post** a stretto giro di posta; **many happy ~s (of the day)!** cento di questi giorni!; **return ticket** n (esp BRIT) biglietto di andata e ritorno

retweet [ri:'twi:t] vt (on Twitter) retwittare

reunion [ri:'ju:nɪən] n riunione f

reunite [ri:ju:'naɪt] vt riunire

revamp ['ri:'væmp] vt (firm) riorganizzare

reveal [rɪ'vi:l] vt (make known) rivelare, svelare; (display) rivelare, mostrare; **revealing** adj rivelatore/trice; (dress) scollato/a

revel ['rɛvl] vi: **to ~ in sth/in doing** dilettarsi di qc/a fare

revelation [rɛvə'leɪʃən] n rivelazione f

revenge [rɪ'vɛndʒ] n vendetta ▷ vt vendicare; **to take ~ on** vendicarsi di

revenue ['rɛvənju:] n reddito

Reverend ['rɛvərənd] adj (in titles) reverendo/a

reversal [rɪ'və:sl] n capovolgimento

reverse [rɪ'və:s] n contrario, opposto; (back) rovescio; (Aut: also: **~ gear**) marcia indietro ▷ adj (order) inverso/a; (direction) opposto/a ▷ vt (turn) invertire, rivoltare; (change) capovolgere, rovesciare; (Law: judgement) cassare; (car) fare marcia indietro con ▷ vi (BRIT Aut, person etc) fare marcia indietro; **reverse-charge call** [rɪ'və:stʃɑːdʒ-] n (BRIT Tel) telefonata con addebito al ricevente; **reversing lights** npl (BRIT Aut) luci fpl per la retromarcia

revert [rɪ'və:t] vi: **to ~ to** tornare a

review [rɪ'vju:] n rivista; (of book, film) recensione f; (of situation) esame m ▷ vt passare in rivista; fare la recensione di; fare il punto di

revise [rɪ'vaɪz] vt (manuscript) rivedere, correggere; (opinion) emendare, modificare; (study: subject, notes) ripassare; **revision** [rɪ'vɪʒən] n revisione f; ripasso

revival [rɪ'vaɪvəl] n ripresa; ristabilimento; (of faith) risveglio

revive [rɪ'vaɪv] vt (person) rianimare; (custom) far rivivere; (hope, courage, economy) ravvivare; (play, fashion) riesumare ▷ vi (person) rianimarsi; (hope) ravvivarsi; (activity) riprendersi

revolt [rɪ'vəult] n rivolta, ribellione f ▷ vi rivoltarsi, ribellarsi ▷ vt (far) rivoltare; **revolting** adj ripugnante

revolution [rɛvə'lu:ʃən] n rivoluzione f; (of wheel etc) rivoluzione, giro; **revolutionary** adj, n rivoluzionario/a

revolve [rɪ'vɔlv] vi girare

revolver [rɪ'vɔlvəʳ] n rivoltella

reward [rɪ'wɔ:d] n ricompensa, premio ▷ vt: **to ~ (for)** ricompensare (per); **rewarding** adj (fig) soddisfacente

rewind [ri:'waɪnd] vt (irreg: watch) ricaricare; (ribbon etc) riavvolgere

rewritable [ri:'raɪtəbl] adj (CD, DVD) riscrivibile

rewrite [ri:'raɪt] vt (irreg) riscrivere

rheumatism ['ru:mətɪzəm] n reumatismo

rhinoceros [raɪ'nɔsərəs] n rinoceronte m

rhubarb ['ru:bɑ:b] n rabarbaro

rhyme [raɪm] n rima; (verse) poesia

rhythm ['rɪðm] n ritmo

rib [rɪb] n (Anat) costola ▷ vt (tease) punzecchiare

ribbon ['rɪbən] n nastro; **in ~s** (torn) a brandelli

rice [raɪs] n riso; **rice pudding** n budino di riso

rich [rɪtʃ] adj ricco/a; (clothes) sontuoso/a; **to be ~ in sth** essere ricco di qc

rid (pt, pp **rid**) [rɪd] vt: **to ~ sb of** sbarazzare or liberare qn di; **to get ~ of** sbarazzarsi di

riddle ['rɪdl] n (puzzle) indovinello ▷ vt: **to be ~d with** (holes) essere crivellato/a di; (doubts) essere pieno/a di

ride (pt **rode**, pp **ridden**) [raɪd, rəud, 'rɪdn] n (on horse) cavalcata; (outing) passeggiata; (distance covered) cavalcata; corsa ▷ vi (as sport) cavalcare; (go somewhere: on horse, bicycle) andare (a cavallo or in bicicletta etc); (journey: on bicycle, motorcycle, bus) andare, viaggiare ▷ vt (a horse) montare, cavalcare; **to ~ a horse/bicycle/camel** montare a cavallo/in bicicletta/in groppa a un cammello; **to take sb for a ~** (fig) prendere in giro qn; fregare qn; **rider**

n cavalcatore/trice; (*jockey*) fantino; (*on bicycle*) ciclista *m/f*; (*on motorcycle*) motociclista *m/f*

ridge [rɪdʒ] *n* (*of hill*) cresta; (*of roof*) colmo; (*on object*) riga (in rilievo)

ridicule ['rɪdɪkjuːl] *n* ridicolo; scherno ▷ *vt* mettere in ridicolo; **ridiculous** [rɪ'dɪkjuləs] *adj* ridicolo/a

riding ['raɪdɪŋ] *n* equitazione *f*; **riding school** *n* scuola d'equitazione

rife [raɪf] *adj* diffuso/a; **to be ~ with** abbondare di

rifle ['raɪfl] *n* carabina ▷ *vt* vuotare

rift [rɪft] *n* fessura, crepatura; (*fig: disagreement*) incrinatura, disaccordo

rig [rɪg] *n* (*also:* **oil ~**: *on land*) derrick *m inv*; (*: at sea*) piattaforma di trivellazione ▷ *vt* (*election etc*) truccare

right [raɪt] *adj* giusto/a; (*suitable*) appropriato/a; (*not left*) destro/a ▷ *n* giusto; (*title, claim*) diritto; (*not left*) destra ▷ *adv* (*answer*) correttamente; (*not on the left*) a destra ▷ *vt* raddrizzare; (*fig*) riparare ▷ *excl* bene!; **to be ~** (*person*) aver ragione; (*answer*) essere giusto/aor corretto/a; **~ now** proprio adesso; subito; **~ away** subito; **by ~s** di diritto; **on the ~** a destra; **to be in the ~** aver ragione, essere nel giusto; **right angle** *n* angolo retto; **rightful** *adj* (*heir*) legittimo/a; **right-hand** *adj*: **right-hand drive** guida a destra; **the right-hand side** il lato destro; **right-handed** *adj* (*person*) che adopera la mano destra; **rightly** *adv* bene, correttamente; (*with reason*) a ragione; **right of way** *n* diritto di passaggio; (*Aut*) precedenza

right wing *n* (*Pol*) destra ▷ *adj*: **right-wing** (*Pol*) di destra

rigid ['rɪdʒɪd] *adj* rigido/a; (*principle*) rigoroso/a

rigorous ['rɪgərəs] *adj* rigoroso/a

rim [rɪm] *n* orlo; (*of spectacles*) montatura; (*of wheel*) cerchione *m*

rind [raɪnd] *n* (*of bacon*) cotenna; (*of lemon etc*) scorza

ring [rɪŋ] (*pt* **rang**, *pp* **rung**) *n* anello; (*of people, objects*) cerchio; (*of spies*) giro; (*of smoke etc*) spirale *f*; (*arena*) pista, arena; (*for boxing*) ring *m inv*; (*sound of bell*) scampanio ▷ *vi* (*person, bell, telephone*) suonare; (*also:* **~ out**: *voice, words*) risuonare; (*Tel*) telefonare; (*ears*) fischiare ▷ *vt* (BRIT *Tel: also:* **~ up**) telefonare a; (*bell, doorbell*) suonare; **to give sb a ~** (BRIT *Tel*) dare un colpo di telefono a qn; **ring back** *vt, vi* (*Tel*) richiamare; **ring off** *vi* (BRIT *Tel*) mettere giù, riattaccare; **ringing tone** *n* (BRIT *Tel*) segnale *m* di libero; **ringleader** *n* (*of gang*) capobanda *m*; **ring road** *n* (BRIT) raccordo anulare

ringtone *n* suoneria

rink [rɪŋk] *n* (*also:* **ice ~**) pista di pattinaggio

rinse [rɪns] *n* risciacquatura; (*hair tint*) cachet *m inv* ▷ *vt* sciacquare

riot ['raɪət] *n* sommossa, tumulto ▷ *vi* tumultuare; **a ~ of colours** un'orgia di colori; **to run ~** creare disordine

rip [rɪp] *n* strappo ▷ *vt* strappare ▷ *vi* strapparsi; **rip off** *vt* (*col: cheat*) fregare; **rip up** *vt* stracciare

ripe [raɪp] *adj* (*fruit, grain*) maturo/a; (*cheese*) stagionato/a

rip-off ['rɪpɔf] *n* (*col*): **it's a ~!** è un furto!

ripple ['rɪpl] *n* increspamento, ondulazione *f*; mormorio ▷ *vi* incresparsi

rise [raɪz] *n* (*slope*) salita, pendio; (*hill*) altura; (*increase: in wages*: BRIT) aumento; (*: in prices, temperature*) rialzo, aumento; (*fig: to power etc*) ascesa ▷ *vi* (*pt* **rose** [rəuz], *pp* **risen** ['rɪzn]) alzarsi, levarsi; (*prices*) aumentare; (*waters, river*) crescere; (*sun, wind, person: from chair, bed*) levarsi; (*also:* **~ up**) (*building*) ergersi; (*rebel*) insorgere; ribellarsi; (*in rank*) salire; **to give ~ to** provocare, dare origine a; **to ~ to the occasion** dimostrarsi all'altezza della situazione; **risen** ['rɪzn] *pp of* **rise**; **rising** *adj* (*increasing: number*) sempre crescente; (*: prices*) in aumento; (*tide*) montante; (*sun, moon*) nascente, che sorge

risk [rɪsk] *n* rischio; pericolo ▷ *vt* rischiare; **to take or run the ~ of doing** correre il rischio di fare; **at ~** in pericolo; **at one's own ~** a proprio rischio e pericolo; **risky** *adj* rischioso/a

rite [raɪt] *n* rito; **last ~s** l'estrema unzione

ritual ['rɪtjuəl] *adj*, *n* rituale (*m*)

rival ['raɪvl] *n* rivale *m/f*; (*in business*) concorrente *m/f* ▷ *adj* rivale; che fa concorrenza ▷ *vt* essere in concorrenza con; **to ~ sb/sth in** competere con qn/qc in; **rivalry** *n* rivalità; concorrenza

river ['rɪvər] *n* fiume *m* ▷ *cpd* (*port, traffic*) fluviale; **up/down ~** a monte/valle; **riverbank** *n* argine *m*

rivet ['rɪvɪt] *n* ribattino, rivetto ▷ *vt* (*fig*) concentrare, fissare

Riviera [rɪvɪ'eərə] *n*: **the (French) ~** la Costa Azzurra; **the Italian ~** la Riviera

road [rəud] *n* strada; (*small*) cammino; (*in town*) ▷ *cpd* stradale; **major/minor ~** strada con/senza diritto di precedenza; **roadblock** *n* blocco stradale; **road map** *n* carta stradale; **road rage** *n* comportamento aggressivo al volante; **road safety** *n* sicurezza sulle strade; **roadside** *n* margine *m* della strada; **roadsign** *n* cartello stradale; **road tax** *n* (BRIT) tassa di circolazione; **roadworks** *npl* lavori *mpl* stradali

roam [rəum] *vi* errare, vagabondare

roar [rɔːʳ] *n* ruggito; *(of crowd)* tumulto; *(of thunder, storm)* muggito; *(of laughter)* scoppio ▷ *vi* ruggire; tumultuare; muggire; **to ~ with laughter** scoppiare dalle risa; **to do a ~ing trade** fare affari d'oro

roast [rəust] *n* arrosto ▷ *vt* arrostire; *(coffee)* tostare, torrefare; **roast beef** *n* arrosto di manzo

rob [rɔb] *vt (person)* rubare; *(bank)* svaligiare; **to ~ sb of sth** derubare qn di qc; *(fig: deprive)* privare qn di qc; **robber** *n* ladro; *(armed)* rapinatore *m*; **robbery** *n* furto; rapina

robe [rəub] *n (for ceremony etc)* abito; *(also:* **bath~)** accappatoio; *(US: also:* **lap ~)** coperta

robin ['rɔbɪn] *n* pettirosso

robot ['rəubɔt] *n* robot *m inv*

robust [rəu'bʌst] *adj* robusto/a; *(material, economy)* solido/a

rock [rɔk] *n (substance)* roccia; *(boulder)* masso; roccia; *(in sea)* scoglio; *(US: pebble)* ciottolo; *(BRIT: sweet)* zucchero candito ▷ *vt (swing gently: cradle)* dondolare; *(: child)* cullare; *(shake)* scrollare, far tremare ▷ *vi* dondolarsi; oscillare; **on the ~s** *(drink)* col ghiaccio; *(marriage etc)* in crisi; **rock and roll** *n* rock and roll *m*; **rock climbing** *n* roccia

rocket ['rɔkɪt] *n* razzo

rocking chair *n* sedia a dondolo

rocky ['rɔkɪ] *adj (hill)* roccioso/a; *(path)* sassoso/a; *(marriage etc)* instabile

rod [rɔd] *n (metallic, Tech)* asta; *(wooden)* bacchetta; *(also:* **fishing ~)** canna da pesca

rode [rəud] *pt of* **ride**

rodent ['rəudnt] *n* roditore *m*

rogue [rəug] *n* mascalzone *m*

role [rəul] *n* ruolo; **role model** *n* modello (di comportamento)

roll [rəul] *n* rotolo; *(of banknotes)* mazzo; *(also:* **bread ~)** panino; *(register)* lista; *(sound: of drums etc)* rullo ▷ *vt* rotolare; *(also:* **~ up**: *string)* aggomitolare; rimboccare; *(cigarettes)* arrotolare; *(eyes)* roteare; *(also:* **~ out**: *pastry)* stendere; *(: lawn, road etc)* spianare ▷ *vi* rotolare; *(wheel)* girare; *(drum)* rullare; *(vehicle: also:* **~ along)** avanzare; *(ship)* rollare; **roll over** *vi* rivoltarsi; **roll up** *vi (col: arrive)* arrivare ▷ *vt (carpet, cloth, map)* arrotolare; **roller** *n* rullo; *(wheel)* rotella; *(for hair)* bigodino; **rollerblades®** ['rəuləbleɪdz] *npl* pattini *mpl* in linea; **roller coaster** [-'kəustəʳ] *n* montagne *fpl* russe; **roller skates** *npl* pattini *mpl* a rotelle; **roller-skating** *n* pattinaggio a rotelle; **to go roller-skating** andare a pattinare *(con i pattini a rotelle)*; **rolling pin** *n* matterello

ROM [rɔm] *n abbr (Comput:* = read-only memory) ROM *f*

Roman ['rəumən] *adj*, *n* romano/a; **Roman Catholic** *adj*, *n* cattolico/a

romance [rə'mæns] *n* storia *(or avventura or film m inv)* romantico/a; *(charm)* poesia; *(love affair)* idillio

Romania [rəu'meɪnɪə] *n* Romania

Romanian [rəu'meɪnɪən] *adj* romeno/a ▷ *n* romeno/a; *(Ling)* romeno

Roman numeral *n* numero romano

romantic [rə'mæntɪk] *adj* romantico/a; sentimentale

Rome [rəum] *n* Roma

roof [ruːf] *n (of tunnel, cave)* volta ▷ *vt* coprire (con un tetto); **~ of the mouth** palato; **roof rack** *n (Aut)* portabagagli *m inv*

rook [ruk] *n (bird)* corvo nero; *(Chess)* torre *f*

room [ruːm] *n (in house)* stanza; *(bedroom, in hotel)* camera; *(in school etc)* sala; *(space)* posto, spazio; **roommate** *n* compagno/a di stanza; **room service** *n* servizio da camera; **roomy** *adj* spazioso/a; *(garment)* ampio/a

rooster ['ruːstəʳ] *n* gallo

root [ruːt] *n* radice *f* ▷ *vi (plant, belief)* attecchire

rope [rəup] *n* corda, fune *f*; *(Naut)* cavo ▷ *vt (box)* legare; *(climbers)* legare in cordata; **to ~ sb in** *(fig)* coinvolgere qn; **to know the ~s** *(fig)* conoscere i trucchi del mestiere

rort [rɔːt] *n (AUSTR, NZ col)* truffa ▷ *vt* fregare

rose [rəuz] *pt of* **rise** ▷ *n* rosa; *(also:* **~ bush)** rosaio; *(on watering can)* rosetta

rosé ['rəuzeɪ] *n* vino rosato

rosemary ['rəuzmərɪ] *n* rosmarino

rosy ['rəuzɪ] *adj* roseo/a

rot [rɔt] *n (decay)* putrefazione *f*; *(col: nonsense)* stupidaggini *fpl* ▷ *vt*, *vi* imputridire, marcire

rota ['rəutə] *n* tabella dei turni

rotate [rəu'teɪt] *vt (revolve)* far girare; *(change round: jobs)* fare a turno ▷ *vi (revolve)* girare

rotten ['rɔtn] *adj (decayed)* putrido/a, marcio/a; *(dishonest)* corrotto/a; *(col: bad)* brutto/a; *(: action)* vigliacco/a; **to feel ~** *(ill)* sentirsi a pezzi

rough [rʌf] *adj (skin, surface)* ruvido/a; *(terrain, road)* accidentato/a; *(voice)* rauco/a; *(person, manner: coarse)* rozzo/a, aspro/a; *(: violent)* brutale; *(district)* malfamato/a; *(weather)* cattivo/a; *(sea)* mosso/a; *(plan)* abbozzato/a; *(guess)* approssimativo/a ▷ *n (Golf)* macchia; **to ~ it** far vita dura; **to sleep ~** *(BRIT)* dormire all'addiaccio; **roughly** *adv* (*handle*) rudemente, brutalmente; (*make*) grossolanamente; (*speak*) bruscamente; (*approximately*) approssimativamente

roulette [ruː'lɛt] *n* roulette *f*

round [raund] *adj* rotondo/a ▷ *n* (BRIT: *of toast*) fetta; (*duty: of police officer, milkman etc*) giro; (: *of doctor*) visite *fpl*; (*game: of cards, golf, in competition*) partita; (*Boxing*) round *m inv*; (*of talks*) serie *f inv* ▷ *vt* (*corner*) girare; (*bend*) prendere ▷ *prep* intorno a ▷ *adv*: **right ~, all ~** tutt'attorno; **the long way ~** il giro più lungo; **all the year ~** tutto l'anno; **in ~ figures** in cifra tonda; **it's just ~ the corner** (*also fig*) è dietro l'angolo; **to go ~ to sb's (house)** andare da qn; **go ~ the back** passi da dietro; **enough to go ~** abbastanza per tutti; **~ the clock** 24 ore su 24; **~ of ammunition** cartuccia; **~ of applause** applausi *mpl*; **~ of drinks** giro di bibite; **~ of sandwiches** sandwich *m inv*; **round off** *vt* (*speech etc*) finire; **round up** *vt* radunare; (*criminals*) fare una retata di; (*prices*) arrotondare; **roundabout** *n* (BRIT: *Aut*) rotatoria; (: *at fair*) giostra ▷ *adj* (*route, means*) indiretto/a; **round trip** *n* (*viaggio di*) andata e ritorno; **roundup** *n* raduno; (*of criminals*) retata

rouse [rauz] *vt* (*wake up*) svegliare; (*stir up*) destare; provocare; risvegliare

route [ruːt] *n* itinerario; (*of bus*) percorso

router ['ruːtə^r] *n* (*Comput*) router *m inv*

routine [ruː'tiːn] *adj* (*work*) corrente, abituale; (*procedure*) solito/a ▷ *n* (*pej*) routine *f*, tran tran *m*; (*Theat*) numero

row¹ [rəu] *n* (*line*) riga, fila; (*Knitting*) ferro; (*behind one another: of cars, people*) fila; (*in boat*) remata ▷ *vi* (*in boat*) remare; (*as sport*) vogare ▷ *vt* (*boat*) manovrare a remi; **in a ~** (*fig*) di fila

row² [rau] *n* (*noise*) baccano, chiasso; (*dispute*) lite *f*; (*scolding*) sgridata ▷ *vi* (*argue*) litigare

rowboat ['rəubəut] *n* (*US*) barca a remi

rowing ['rəuɪŋ] *n* canottaggio; **rowing boat** *n* (BRIT) barca a remi

royal ['rɔɪəl] *adj* reale; **royalty** ['rɔɪəltɪ] *n* (*royal persons*) (membri *mpl* della) famiglia reale; (*payment: to author*) diritti *mpl* d'autore

rpm *abbr* (= *revolutions per minute*) giri/min

RSVP *abbr* (= *répondez s'il vous plaît*) R.S.V.P.

Rt. Hon. *abbr* (BRIT: = *Right Honourable*) ≈ On.

rub [rʌb] *n*: **to give sth a ~** strofinare qc; (*sore place*) massaggiare qc ▷ *vt* strofinare; massaggiare; (*hands: also:* **~ together**) sfregarsi; **to ~ sb up** *or* (*US*) **~ sb the wrong way** lisciare qn contro pelo; **rub in** *vt* (*ointment*) far penetrare (massaggiando or

frizionando); **rub off** *vi* andare via; **rub out** *vt* cancellare

rubber ['rʌbə^r] *n* gomma; **rubber band** *n* elastico; **rubber gloves** *npl* guanti *mpl* di gomma

rubbish ['rʌbɪʃ] *n* (*from household*) immondizie *fpl*, rifiuti *mpl*; (*fig, pej*) cose *fpl* senza valore; robaccia; (*nonsense*) sciocchezze *fpl*; **rubbish bin** *n* (BRIT) pattumiera; **rubbish dump** *n* discarica

rubble ['rʌbl] *n* macerie *fpl*; (*smaller*) pietrisco

ruby ['ruːbɪ] *n* rubino

rucksack ['rʌksæk] *n* zaino

rudder ['rʌdə^r] *n* timone *m*

rude [ruːd] *adj* (*impolite: person*) scortese, rozzo/a; (: *word, manners*) grossolano/a, rozzo/a; (*shocking*) indecente

ruffle ['rʌfl] *vt* (*hair*) scompigliare; (*clothes, water*) increspare; (*fig: person*) turbare

rug [rʌg] *n* tappeto; (BRIT: *for knees*) coperta

rugby ['rʌgbɪ] *n* (*also:* **~ football**) rugby *m*

rugged ['rʌgɪd] *adj* (*landscape*) aspro/a; (*features, determination*) duro/a; (*character*) brusco/a

ruin ['ruːɪn] *n* rovina ▷ *vt* rovinare; **ruins** *npl* (*of building, castle etc*) rovine *fpl*, ruderi *mpl*

rule [ruːl] *n* regola; (*regulation*) regolamento, regola; (*government*) governo; (*ruler*) riga ▷ *vt* (*country*) governare; (*person*) dominare ▷ *vi* regnare; decidere; (*Law*) dichiarare; **as a ~** normalmente; **rule out** *vt* escludere; **ruler** *n* (*sovereign*) sovrano/a; (*for measuring*) regolo, riga; **ruling** *adj* (*party*) al potere; (*class*) dirigente ▷ *n* (*Law*) decisione *f*

rum [rʌm] *n* rum *m*

Rumania *etc* [ruː'meɪnɪə] = **Romania** *etc*

rumble ['rʌmbl] *n* rimbombo; brontolio ▷ *vi* rimbombare; (*stomach, pipe*) brontolare

rumour, (US) **rumor** ['ruːmə^r] *n* voce *f* ▷ *vt*: **it is ~ed that** corre voce che

▮ Be careful not to translate *rumour* by the Italian word *rumore*.

rump steak [rʌmp-] *n* bistecca di girello

run [rʌn] (*pt* **ran**, *pp* **run**) *n* corsa; (*outing*) gita (in macchina); (*distance travelled*) percorso, tragitto; (*series*) serie *f inv*; (*Theat*) periodo di rappresentazione; (*Ski*) pista; (*Cricket, Baseball*) meta; (*in tights, stockings*) smagliatura ▷ *vt* (*distance*) correre; (*operate: business*) gestire, dirigere; (: *competition, course*) organizzare; (: *hotel*) gestire; (: *house*) governare; (*Comput*) eseguire; (*water, bath*) far scorrere; (*force through: rope, pipe*) to **~ sth through** far passare qc attraverso; (*pass: hand, finger*): **to ~ sth over** passare qc su; (*Press: feature*) presentare ▷ *vi* correre; (*flee*) scappare; (*pass: road etc*) passare;

(work: machine, factory) funzionare, andare; (bus, train: operate) servizio; (: travel) circolare; (continue: play, contract) durare; (slide: drawer: flow: river, bath) scorrere; (colours, washing) stemperarsi; (in election) presentarsi come candidato; (nose) colare; **to go for a ~** andare a correre; (in car) fare un giro (in macchina); **to break into a ~** mettersi a correre; **a ~ of luck** un periodo di fortuna; **to have the ~ of sb's house** essere libero di andare e venire in casa di qn; **there was a ~ on ...** c'era una corsa a ...; **in the long ~** a lungo andare; **on the ~** in fuga; **to ~ a race** partecipare a una gara; **I'll ~ you to the station** la porto alla stazione; **to ~ a risk** correre un rischio; **run after** vt fus (to catch up) rincorrere; (chase) correre dietro a; **run away** vi fuggire; **run down** vi (clock) scaricarsi ▷ vt (Aut) investire; (criticize) criticare; (production) ridurre gradualmente; (factory, shop) rallentare l'attività di; **to be ~ down** (person) essere spossato/a; **run into** vt fus (meet: person) incontrare per caso; (: trouble) incontrare, trovare; (collide with) andare a sbattere contro; **run off** vi fuggire ▷ vt (water) far defluire; (copies) fare; **run out** vi (person) uscire di corsa; (liquid) colare; (lease) scadere; (money) esaurirsi; **run out of** vt fus rimanere a corto di; **run over** vt (Aut) investire, mettere sotto ▷ vt fus (revise) rivedere; **run through** vt fus (instructions) dare una scorsa a; (rehearse: play) riprovare, ripetere; **run up** vt (debt) lasciar accumulare; **to ~ up against** (difficulties) incontrare; **runaway** adj (person) fuggiasco/a; (horse) in libertà; (truck) fuori controllo

rung [rʌŋ] pp of **ring** ▷ n (of ladder) piolo

runner ['rʌnəʳ] n (in race) corridore m; (: horse) partente m/f; (on sledge) pattino; (for drawer etc) guida; **runner bean** n (BRIT) fagiolino; **runner-up** n secondo/a arrivato/a

running ['rʌnɪŋ] n corsa; direzione f; organizzazione f; funzionamento ▷ adj (water) corrente; (commentary) simultaneo/a; **6 days ~** 6 giorni di seguito; **to be in/out of the ~ for sth** essere/non essere più in lizza per qc

runny ['rʌnɪ] adj che cola

run-up ['rʌnʌp] n (BRIT): **~ to sth** (election etc) periodo che precede qc

runway ['rʌnweɪ] n (Aviat) pista (di decollo)

rupture ['rʌptʃəʳ] n (Med) ernia

rural ['ruərl] adj rurale

rush [rʌʃ] n corsa precipitosa; (hurry) furia, fretta; (of emotion) impeto; (Bot) giunco; (sudden demand): **~ for** corsa a; (current) flusso ▷ vt mandare or spedire velocemente; (attack: town etc) prendere d'assalto ▷ vi precipitarsi; **rush hour** n ora di punta

Russia ['rʌʃə] n Russia; **Russian** adj russo/a ▷ n russo/a; (Ling) russo

rust [rʌst] n ruggine f ▷ vi arrugginirsi

rusty ['rʌstɪ] adj arrugginito/a

ruthless ['ruːθlɪs] adj spietato/a

RV abbr (= revised version) versione riveduta della Bibbia ▷ n abbr (US) = **recreational vehicle**

rye [raɪ] n segale f

S

Sabbath ['sæbəθ] n (*Jewish*) sabato; (*Christian*) domenica
sabotage ['sæbətɑːʒ] n sabotaggio ▷ vt sabotare
saccharin(e) ['sækərɪn] n saccarina
sachet ['sæʃeɪ] n bustina
sack [sæk] n (*bag*) sacco ▷ vt (*dismiss*) licenziare, mandare a spasso; (*plunder*) saccheggiare; **to get the ~** essere mandato a spasso
sacred ['seɪkrɪd] adj sacro/a
sacrifice ['sækrɪfaɪs] n sacrificio ▷ vt sacrificare
sad [sæd] adj triste
saddle ['sædl] n sella ▷ vt (*horse*) sellare; **to be ~d with sth** (*col*) avere qc sulle spalle
sadistic [sə'dɪstɪk] adj sadico/a
sadly ['sædlɪ] adv tristemente; (*regrettably*) sfortunatamente; **~ lacking in** penosamente privo di
sadness ['sædnɪs] n tristezza
sae abbr (= stamped addressed envelope) busta affrancata e con indirizzo
safari [sə'fɑːrɪ] n safari m inv
safe [seɪf] adj sicuro/a; (*out of danger*) salvo/a, al sicuro; (*cautious*) prudente ▷ n cassaforte f; **~ from** al sicuro da; **~ and sound** sano/a e salvo/a; **(just) to be on the ~ side** per non correre rischi; **safely** adv sicuramente; prudentemente; **safe sex** n sesso sicuro
safety ['seɪftɪ] n sicurezza; **safety belt** n cintura di sicurezza; **safety pin** n spilla di sicurezza
saffron ['sæfrən] n zafferano
sag [sæg] vi incurvarsi; afflosciarsi
sage [seɪdʒ] n (*herb*) salvia; (*man*) saggio
Sagittarius [sædʒɪ'tɛərɪəs] n Sagittario
Sahara [sə'hɑːrə] n: **the ~ Desert** il Deserto del Sahara

said [sɛd] pt, pp of **say**
sail [seɪl] n (*on boat*) vela; (*trip*): **to go for a ~** fare un giro in barca a vela ▷ vt (*boat*) condurre, governare ▷ vi (*travel: ship*) navigare; (: *passenger*) viaggiare per mare; (*set off*) salpare; (*Sport*) fare della vela; **they ~ed into Genoa** entrarono nel porto di Genova; **sailboat** ['seɪlbəut] n (*us*) barca a vela; **sailing** n (*sport*) vela; **to go sailing** fare della vela; **sailing boat** n barca a vela; **sailor** n marinaio
saint [seɪnt] n santo/a
sake [seɪk] n: **for the ~ of** per, per amore di
salad ['sæləd] n insalata; **salad cream** n (*BRIT*) (tipo di) maionese f; **salad dressing** n condimento per insalata
salami [sə'lɑːmɪ] n salame m
salary ['sælərɪ] n stipendio
sale [seɪl] n vendita; (*at reduced prices*) svendita, liquidazione f; (*auction*) vendita all'asta; **sales** npl (*total amount sold*) vendite fpl; **"for ~"** "in vendita"; **on ~** in vendita; **on ~ or return** da vendere o rimandare; **sales assistant** n, (*us*) **sales clerk** n commesso/a; **salesman** n (*irreg*) commesso; (*representative*) rappresentante m; **salesperson** n (*irreg*) (*in shop*) commesso/a; (*representative*) rappresentante m/f di commercio; **sales rep** n rappresentante m/f di commercio; **saleswoman** n (*irreg*) commessa; (*representative*) rappresentante f
saline ['seɪlaɪn] adj salino/a
saliva [sə'laɪvə] n saliva
salmon ['sæmən] n (*pl inv*) salmone m
salon ['sælɔn] n (*hairdressing salon*) parrucchiere/a; (*beauty salon*) salone m di bellezza
saloon [sə'luːn] n (*us*) saloon m inv, bar m inv; (*BRIT Aut*) berlina; (*ship's lounge*) salone m
salt [sɔːlt] n sale m ▷ vt salare; **saltwater** adj di mare; **salty** adj salato/a
salute [sə'luːt] n saluto ▷ vt salutare
salvage ['sælvɪdʒ] n (*saving*) salvataggio; (*things saved*) beni mpl salvati or recuperati ▷ vt salvare, mettere in salvo
Salvation Army [sæl'veɪʃən-] n Esercito della Salvezza
same [seɪm] adj stesso/a, medesimo/a ▷ pron: **the ~** lo (la) stesso/a, gli (le) stessi/e; **the ~ book as** lo stesso libro di (or che); **at the ~ time** allo stesso tempo; **all** or **just the ~** tuttavia; **to do the ~ as sb** fare come qn; **and the ~ to you!** altrettanto a lei!
sample ['sɑːmpl] n campione m ▷ vt (*food*) assaggiare; (*wine*) degustare

sanction ['sæŋkʃən] n sanzione f ▷ vt sancire, sanzionare; **sanctions** npl (Pol) sanzioni fpl

sanctuary ['sæŋktjuəri] n (holy place) santuario; (refuge) rifugio; (for wildlife) riserva

sand [sænd] n sabbia ▷ vt (also: ~ down) cartavetrare

sandal ['sændl] n sandalo

sand: sandbox ['sændbɒks] n (us: for children) buca di sabbia; **sandcastle** ['sændkɑːsl] n castello di sabbia; **sand dune** n duna di sabbia; **sandpaper** ['sændpeɪpəʳ] n carta vetrata; **sandpit** ['sændpɪt] n (for children) buca di sabbia; **sands** npl spiaggia; **sandstone** ['sændstəun] n arenaria

sandwich ['sændwɪtʃ] n tramezzino, panino, sandwich m inv ▷ vt: **cheese/ham ~** sandwich al formaggio/prosciutto; **to be ~ed between** essere incastrato/a fra

sandy ['sændɪ] adj sabbioso/a; (colour) color sabbia inv, biondo/a rossiccio/a

sane [seɪn] adj (person) sano/a di mente; (outlook) sensato/a

sang [sæŋ] pt of **sing**

sanitary towel ['sænɪtərɪ-], (us) **sanitary napkin** n assorbente m (igienico)

sanity ['sænɪtɪ] n sanità mentale; (common sense) buon senso

sank [sæŋk] pt of **sink**

Santa Claus [sæntə'klɔːz] n Babbo Natale

sap [sæp] n (of plants) linfa ▷ vt (strength) fiaccare

sapphire ['sæfaɪəʳ] n zaffiro

sarcasm ['sɑːkæzm] n sarcasmo

sarcastic [sɑː'kæstɪk] adj sarcastico/a; **to be ~** fare del sarcasmo

sardine [sɑː'diːn] n sardina

Sardinia [sɑː'dɪnɪə] n Sardegna

SASE n abbr (us: = self-addressed stamped envelope) busta affrancata e con indirizzo

sat [sæt] pt, pp of **sit**

Sat. abbr (= Saturday) sab.

satchel ['sætʃl] n cartella

satellite ['sætəlaɪt] adj, n satellite m; **satellite dish** n antenna parabolica; **satellite television** n televisione f via satellite

satin ['sætɪn] n raso ▷ adj di or in raso

satire ['sætaɪəʳ] n satira

satisfaction [sætɪs'fækʃən] n soddisfazione f

satisfactory [sætɪs'fæktərɪ] adj soddisfacente

satisfied ['sætɪsfaɪd] adj (customer) soddisfatto/a; **to be ~ (with sth)** essere soddisfatto/a (di qc)

satisfy ['sætɪsfaɪ] vt soddisfare; (convince) convincere

satnav ['sætnæv] n abbr (= satellite navigation) navigatore m satellitare

Saturday ['sætədɪ] n sabato

sauce [sɔːs] n salsa; (containing meat, fish) sugo; **saucepan** n casseruola

saucer ['sɔːsəʳ] n sottocoppa m, piattino

Saudi Arabia ['saudɪ-] n Arabia Saudita

sauna ['sɔːnə] n sauna

sausage ['sɒsɪdʒ] n salsiccia; **sausage roll** n rotolo di pasta sfoglia ripieno di salsiccia

sautéed ['səuteɪd] adj saltato/a

savage ['sævɪdʒ] adj (cruel, fierce) selvaggio/a, feroce; (primitive) primitivo/a ▷ n selvaggio/a ▷ vt attaccare selvaggiamente

save [seɪv] vt (person, belongings, Comput) salvare; (money) risparmiare, mettere da parte; (time) risparmiare; (food) conservare; (avoid: trouble) evitare; (Sport) parare ▷ vi (also: ~ up) economizzare ▷ n (Sport) parata ▷ prep salvo, a eccezione di

saving ['seɪvɪŋ] n risparmio; **savings** npl risparmi mpl; **savings account** n libretto di risparmio; **savings and loan association** n (us) ≈ società di credito immobiliare

savoury, (us) **savory** ['seɪvərɪ] adj (dish: not sweet) salato/a

saw [sɔː] pt of **see** ▷ n (tool) sega ▷ vt (pt **sawed**, pp **sawed** or **sawn** [sɔːn]) segare; **sawdust** n segatura

sawn [sɔːn] pp of **saw**

saxophone ['sæksəfəun] n sassofono

say [seɪ] n: **to have one's ~** fare sentire il proprio parere; **to have a** or **some ~** avere voce in capitolo ▷ vt (pt, pp **said**) dire; **could you ~ that again?** potrebbe ripeterlo?; **that goes without ~ing** va da sé; **saying** n proverbio, detto

scab [skæb] n crosta; (pej) crumiro/a

scaffolding ['skæfəldɪŋ] n impalcatura

scald [skɔːld] n scottatura ▷ vt scottare

scale [skeɪl] n scala; (of fish) squama ▷ vt (mountain) scalare; **~ of charges** tariffa; **on a large ~** su vasta scala; **scales** [skeɪlz] npl (for weighing) bilancia

scallion ['skæljən] n cipolla; (us: shallot) scalogna; (: leek) porro

scallop ['skɒləp] n (Zool) pettine m; (Sewing) smerlo

scalp [skælp] n cuoio capelluto ▷ vt scotennare

scalpel ['skælpl] n bisturi m inv

scam [skæm] n (col) truffa

scampi ['skæmpɪ] npl scampi mpl

scan [skæn] vt scrutare; (glance at quickly) scorrere, dare un'occhiata a; (TV) analizzare; (Radar) esplorare ▷ n (Med) ecografia

scandal ['skændl] n scandalo; (gossip) pettegolezzi mpl

Scandinavia [skændɪ'neɪvɪə] n Scandinavia; **Scandinavian** adj, n scandinavo/a

scanner ['skænə'] n (Radar, Med) scanner m inv

scapegoat ['skeɪpɡəʊt] n capro espiatorio

scar [skaː'] n cicatrice f ▷ vt sfregiare

scarce [skɛəs] adj scarso/a; (copy, edition) raro/a; **to make o.s. ~** (col) squagliarsela; **scarcely** adv appena

scare [skɛə'] n spavento; panico ▷ vt spaventare, atterrire; **to ~ sb stiff** spaventare a morte qn; **there was a bomb ~ at the bank** hanno evacuato la banca per paura di un attentato dinamitardo; **scarecrow** n spaventapasseri m inv; **scared** adj: **to be scared** aver paura

scarf (pl **scarves**) [skɑːf, skɑːvz] n (long) sciarpa; (square) fazzoletto da testa, foulard m inv

scarlet ['skɑːlɪt] adj scarlatto/a

scarves [skɑːvz] npl of **scarf**

scary ['skɛərɪ] adj (col) che fa paura

scatter ['skætə'] vt spargere; (crowd) disperdere ▷ vi disperdersi

scenario [sɪ'nɑːrɪəʊ] n (Theat, Cine) copione m; (fig) situazione f

scene [siːn] n (Theat, fig etc) scena; (of crime, accident) scena, luogo; (sight, view) vista, veduta; **scenery** n (Theat) scenario; (landscape) panorama m; **scenic** adj scenico/a; panoramico/a

scent [sɛnt] n profumo; (sense of smell) olfatto, odorato; (fig: track) pista

sceptical, (us) **skeptical** ['skɛptɪkl] adj scettico/a

schedule ['ʃɛdjuːl, us 'skɛdjuːl] n programma m, piano; (of trains) orario; (of prices etc) lista, tabella ▷ vt fissare; **on ~** in orario; **to be ahead of/behind ~** essere in anticipo/ritardo sul previsto; **scheduled flight** n volo di linea

scheme [skiːm] n piano, progetto; (method) sistema m; (dishonest plan, plot) intrigo, trama; (arrangement) disposizione f, sistemazione f; (pension scheme etc) programma m ▷ vi fare progetti; (intrigue) complottare

schizophrenic [skɪtsə'frɛnɪk] adj, n schizofrenico/a

scholar ['skɒlə'] n studioso/a; **scholarship** ['skɒləʃɪp] n erudizione f; (grant) borsa di studio

school [skuːl] n (primary, secondary) scuola; (in university: us) scuola, facoltà f inv ▷ cpd scolare, scolastico/a ▷ vt (animal) addestrare; **schoolbook** n libro scolastico;

schoolboy n scolaro; **schoolchild** n (pl -children) scolaro/a; **schoolgirl** n scolara; **schooling** n istruzione f; **schoolteacher** n insegnante m/f, docente m/f; (primary) maestro/a

science ['saɪəns] n scienza; **science fiction** n fantascienza; **scientific** [saɪən'tɪfɪk] adj scientifico/a; **scientist** n scienziato/a

sci-fi ['saɪfaɪ] n abbr (col) = **science fiction**

scissors ['sɪzəz] npl forbici fpl

scold [skəʊld] vt rimproverare

scone [skɒn] n focaccina da tè

scoop [skuːp] n mestolo; (for ice cream) cucchiaio dosatore; (Press) colpo giornalistico, notizia (in) esclusiva

scooter ['skuːtə'] n (motorcycle) motoretta, scooter m inv; (toy) monopattino

scope [skəʊp] n (capacity: of plan, undertaking) portata; (: of person) capacità fpl; (opportunity) possibilità fpl

scorching ['skɔːtʃɪŋ] adj cocente, scottante

score [skɔː'] n punti mpl, punteggio; (Mus) partitura, spartito; (twenty) ▷ vt (goal, point) segnare, fare; (success) ottenere ▷ vi segnare; (Football) fare un goal; (keep score) segnare i punti; **on that ~** a questo riguardo; **~s of people** un sacco di gente; **to ~ 6 out of 10** prendere 6 su 10; **score out** vt cancellare con un segno; **scoreboard** n tabellone m segnapunti; **scorer** n marcatore/trice; (keeping score) segnapunti m inv

scorn [skɔːn] n disprezzo ▷ vt disprezzare

Scorpio ['skɔːpɪəʊ] n Scorpione m

scorpion ['skɔːpɪən] n scorpione m

Scot [skɒt] n scozzese m/f

Scotch tape® ['skɒtʃ-] n scotch® m

Scotland ['skɒtlənd] n Scozia

Scots [skɒts] adj scozzese; **Scotsman** n (irreg) scozzese m; **Scotswoman** n (irreg) scozzese f; **Scottish** ['skɒtɪʃ] adj scozzese; **the Scottish Parliament** il Parlamento scozzese

scout [skaut] n (Mil) esploratore m; (also: **boy ~**) giovane esploratore, scout m inv

scowl [skaul] vi accigliarsi, aggrottare le sopracciglia; **to ~ at** guardare torvo

scramble ['skræmbl] n arrampicata ▷ vi inerpicarsi; **to ~ out** etc uscire etc in fretta; **to ~** azzuffarsi per; **scrambled eggs** npl uova fpl strapazzate

scrap [skræp] n pezzo, pezzetto; (fight) zuffa; (also: **~ iron**) rottami mpl di ferro, ferraglia ▷ vt demolire; (fig) scartare ▷ vi: **to ~ (with sb)** fare a botte (con qn); **scraps** npl (waste) scarti mpl; **scrapbook** n album m inv di ritagli

scrape [skreɪp] vt, vi raschiare, grattare ▷ n: **to get into a ~** cacciarsi in un guaio

scrap paper n cartaccia

scratch [skrætʃ] n graffio ▷ cpd: **~ team** squadra raccogliticcia ▷ vt graffiare, rigare ▷ vi grattare; (paint, car) graffiare; **to start from ~** cominciare or partire da zero; **to be up to ~** essere all'altezza; **scratch card** n (BRIT) cartolina f gratta e vinci

scream [skri:m] n grido, urlo ▷ vi urlare, gridare

screen [skri:n] n schermo; (fig) muro, cortina, velo ▷ vt schermare, fare schermo a; (from the wind etc) riparare; (film) proiettare; (book) adattare per lo schermo; (candidates etc) passare al vaglio; **screening** n (Med) dépistage m inv; **screenplay** n sceneggiatura; **screensaver** n (Comput) screen saver m inv; **screenshot** n (Comput) screenshot m inv

screw [skru:] n vite f ▷ vt avvitare; **screw up** vt (paper, material) spiegazzare; (col: ruin) mandare a monte; **to ~ up one's eyes** strizzare gli occhi; **screwdriver** n cacciavite m

scribble ['skrɪbl] n scarabocchio ▷ vt scribacchiare ▷ vi scarabocchiare

script [skrɪpt] n (Cine etc) copione m; (in exam) elaborato or compito d'esame

scroll [skrəul] n rotolo di carta

scrub [skrʌb] n (land) boscaglia ▷ vt pulire strofinando; (reject) annullare

scruffy ['skrʌfɪ] adj sciatto/a

scrum(mage) ['skrʌm(ɪdʒ)] n mischia

scrutiny ['skru:tɪnɪ] n esame m accurato

scuba diving ['sku:bə-] n immersioni fpl subacquee

sculptor ['skʌlptəʳ] n scultore m

sculpture ['skʌlptʃəʳ] n scultura

scum [skʌm] n schiuma; (pej: people) feccia

scurry ['skʌrɪ] vi sgambare, affrettarsi

sea [si:] n mare m ▷ cpd marino/a, del mare; (ship, port, route, transport) marittimo/a; (bird, fish) di mare; **on the ~** (boat) in mare; (town) in riva al mare; **to go by ~** andare per mare; **out to ~** al largo; (out) **at ~** in mare; **seafood** n frutti mpl di mare; **sea front** n lungomare m; **seagull** n gabbiano

seal [si:l] n (animal) foca; (stamp) sigillo; (impression) impronta del sigillo ▷ vt sigillare; **seal off** vt (close) sigillare; (forbid entry to) bloccare l'accesso a

sea level n livello del mare

seam [si:m] n cucitura; (of coal) filone m

search [sə:tʃ] n (Law: at sb's home) perquisizione f ▷ vt frugare ▷ vi: **to ~ for** ricercare; **in ~ of** alla ricerca di; **search engine** n (Comput) motore m di ricerca; **search party** n squadra di soccorso

sea: seashore ['si:ʃɔ:ʳ] n spiaggia; **seasick** ['si:sɪk] adj che soffre il mal di mare; **seaside** ['si:saɪd] n spiaggia; **seaside resort** n stazione f balneare

season ['si:zn] n stagione f ▷ vt condire, insaporire; **seasonal** adj stagionale; **seasoning** n condimento; **season ticket** n abbonamento

seat [si:t] n sedile m; (in bus, train: place) posto; (Parliament) seggio; (buttocks) didietro; (of trousers) fondo ▷ vt far sedere; (have room for) avere or essere fornito/a di posti a sedere per; **to be ~ed** essere seduto/a; **seat belt** n cintura di sicurezza; **seating** n posti mpl a sedere

sea: sea water n acqua di mare; **seaweed** ['si:wi:d] n alghe fpl

sec. abbr = **second**

secluded [sɪ'klu:dɪd] adj isolato/a, appartato/a

second ['sɛkənd] num secondo/a ▷ adv (in race etc) al secondo posto ▷ n (unit of time) secondo; (BRIT Scol: degree) laurea con punteggio discreto; (Aut: also: **~ gear**) seconda; (Comm: imperfect) scarto ▷ vt (motion) appoggiare; **~ thoughts** ripensamenti mpl; **on ~ thoughts** (BRIT) or **thought** (US) ripensandoci bene; **secondary** adj secondario/a; **secondary school** n scuola secondaria; **second-class** adj di seconda classe ▷ adv: **to travel second-class** viaggiare in seconda (classe); **second-hand** adj di seconda mano, usato/a; **secondly** adv in secondo luogo; **second-rate** adj scadente

secrecy ['si:krəsɪ] n segretezza

secret ['si:krɪt] adj segreto/a ▷ n segreto; **in ~** in segreto

secretary ['sɛkrətrɪ] n segretario/a; **S~ of State (for)** (BRIT Pol) ministro (di)

secretive ['si:krətɪv] adj riservato/a

secret service n servizi mpl segreti

sect [sɛkt] n setta

section ['sɛkʃən] n sezione f

sector ['sɛktəʳ] n settore m

secular ['sɛkjuləʳ] adj secolare

secure [sɪ'kjuəʳ] adj sicuro/a; (firmly fixed) assicurato/a, ben fermato/a; (in safe place) al sicuro ▷ vt (fix) fissare, assicurare; (get) ottenere, assicurarsi

security [sɪ'kjuərɪtɪ] n sicurezza; (for loan) garanzia; **securities** npl (Stock Exchange) titoli mpl; **security guard** n guardia giurata

sedan [sə'dæn] n (US Aut) berlina

sedate [sɪ'deɪt] adj posato/a; calmo/a ▷ vt calmare

sedative ['sɛdɪtɪv] n sedativo, calmante m

seduce [sɪ'dju:s] vt sedurre; **seductive** [sɪ'dʌktɪv] adj seducente

see [si:] (pt **saw**, pp **seen**) vt vedere; (accompany): **to ~ sb to the door** accompagnare qn alla porta ▷ vi vedere; (understand) capire ▷ n sede f vescovile; **to ~ that** (ensure) badare che + sub, fare in modo che + sub; **~ you soon/later/tomorrow!** a presto/più tardi/domani!; **see off** vt salutare alla partenza; **see out** vt (take to the door) accompagnare alla porta; **see through** vt portare a termine ▷ vt fus non lasciarsi ingannare da; **see to** vt fus occuparsi di

seed [si:d] n seme m; (fig) germe m; (Tennis) testa di serie; **to go to ~** fare seme; (fig) scadere

seeing ['si:ɪŋ] conj: **~ (that)** visto che

seek [si:k] (pt, pp **sought**) vt cercare

seem [si:m] vi sembrare, parere; **there ~s to be ...** sembra che ci sia ...; **seemingly** adv apparentemente

seen [si:n] pp of **see**

seesaw ['si:sɔ:] n altalena a bilico

segment ['segmənt] n segmento

segregate ['segrɪgeɪt] vt segregare, isolare

seize [si:z] vt (grasp) afferrare; (take possession of) impadronirsi di; (Law) sequestrare

seizure ['si:ʒər] n (Med) attacco; (Law) confisca, sequestro

seldom ['seldəm] adv raramente

select [sɪ'lɛkt] adj scelto/a ▷ vt scegliere, selezionare; **selection** n selezione f, scelta; **selective** adj selettivo/a

self [sɛlf] n: **the ~** l'io m ▷ prefix auto...; **self-assured** adj sicuro/a di sé; **self-catering** adj (BRIT) in cui ci si cucina da sé; **self-centred**, (US) **self-centered** adj egocentrico/a; **self-confidence** n sicurezza di sé; **self-confident** adj sicuro/a di sé; **self-conscious** [sɛlf'kɔnʃəs] adj timido/a; **self-contained** adj (BRIT: flat) indipendente; **self-control** n autocontrollo; **self-defence**, (US) **self-defense** n autodifesa; (Law) legittima difesa; **self-drive** adj (BRIT: rented car) senza autista; **self-employed** adj che lavora in proprio; **self-esteem** n amor proprio m; **self-indulgent** adj indulgente verso se stesso/a; **self-interest** n interesse m personale; **selfish** adj egoista; **self-pity** n autocommiserazione f; **self-raising**, (US) **self-rising** adj: **self-raising flour** miscela di farina e lievito; **self-respect** n rispetto di sé, amor proprio; **self-service** n autoservizio, self-service m

selfie ['sɛlfɪ] n selfie m inv

sell (pt, pp **sold**) [sɛl, səʊld] vt vendere ▷ vi vendersi; **to ~ at** or **for 100 euros** essere in vendita a 100 euro; **sell off** vt svendere,

liquidare; **sell out** vt esaurire; **the tickets are all sold out** i biglietti sono esauriti; **sell-by date** ['sɛlbaɪ-] n data di scadenza; **seller** n venditore/trice

Sellotape® ['sɛləʊteɪp] n (BRIT) nastro adesivo, scotch® m

selves [sɛlvz] npl of **self**

semester [sɪ'mɛstər] n (US) semestre m

semi... ['sɛmɪ] prefix semi...; **semicircle** n semicerchio; **semidetached (house)** [sɛmɪdɪ'tætʃt-] n (BRIT) casa gemella; **semifinal** n semifinale f

seminar ['sɛmɪnɑ:r] n seminario

semi-skimmed ['sɛmɪ'skɪmd] adj (milk) parzialmente scremato/a

senate ['sɛnɪt] n senato; **senator** n senatore/trice

send [sɛnd] (pt, pp **sent**) vt mandare; **send back** vt rimandare; **send for** vt fus mandare a chiamare, far venire; **send in** vt (report, application, resignation) presentare; **send off** vt (goods) spedire; (BRIT Sport: player) espellere; **send on** vt (BRIT: letter) inoltrare; (luggage etc: in advance) spedire in anticipo; **send out** vt (invitation) diramare; **send up** vt (person, price) far salire; (BRIT: parody) mettere in ridicolo; **sender** n mittente m/f; **send-off** n: **to give sb a good send-off** festeggiare la partenza di qn

senile ['si:naɪl] adj senile

senior ['si:nɪər] adj (older) più vecchio/a; (of higher rank) di grado più elevato; **senior citizen** n persona anziana; **senior high school** n (US) ≈ liceo

sensation [sɛn'seɪʃən] n sensazione f; **sensational** adj sensazionale; (marvellous) eccezionale

sense [sɛns] n senso; (feeling) sensazione f, senso; (meaning) senso, significato; (wisdom) buonsenso ▷ vt sentire, percepire; **it makes ~** ha senso; **~ of humour** (senso dell')umorismo; **senseless** adj sciocco/a; (unconscious) privo/a di sensi

sensible ['sɛnsɪbl] adj sensato/a, ragionevole

> Be careful not to translate sensible by the Italian word sensibile.

sensitive ['sɛnsɪtɪv] adj sensibile; (skin, question) delicato/a

sensual ['sɛnsjʊəl] adj sensuale

sensuous ['sɛnsjʊəs] adj sensuale

sent [sɛnt] pt, pp of **send**

sentence ['sɛntns] n (Ling) frase f; (Law: judgement) sentenza; (: punishment) condanna ▷ vt: **to ~ sb to death/to 5 years** condannare qn a morte/a 5 anni

sentiment ['sɛntɪmənt] n sentimento; (opinion) opinione f; **sentimental** [sɛntɪ'mɛntl] adj sentimentale

Sep. abbr (= September) Sett.
separate adj ['sɛprɪt] separato/a ▷ vt ['sɛpəreɪt] separare ▷ vi ['sɛpəreɪt] separarsi; **separately** adv separatamente; **separates** npl (clothes) coordinati mpl; **separation** [sɛpə'reɪʃən] n separazione f
September [sɛp'tɛmbə'] n settembre m
septic ['sɛptɪk] adj settico/a; (wound) infettato/a; **septic tank** n fossa settica
sequel ['si:kwl] n conseguenza; (of story) seguito; (of film) sequenza
sequence ['si:kwəns] n (series) serie f inv; (order) ordine m
sequin ['si:kwɪn] n lustrino, paillette f inv
Serb [sə:b] adj, n = **Serbian**
Serbia ['sə:bɪə] n Serbia
Serbian ['sə:bɪən] adj serbo/a ▷ n serbo/a; (Ling) serbo
sergeant ['sɑ:dʒənt] n sergente m; (Police) brigadiere m
serial ['sɪərɪəl] n (Press) romanzo a puntate; (Radio, TV) trasmissione f a puntate, serial m inv; **serial killer** n serial killer mf inv; **serial number** n numero di serie
series ['sɪərɪːz] n (pl inv) serie f inv; (Publishing) collana
serious ['sɪərɪəs] adj serio/a, grave; **seriously** adv seriamente
sermon ['sə:mən] n sermone m
servant ['sə:vənt] n domestico/a
serve [sə:v] vt (employer etc) servire, essere a servizio di; (purpose) servire a; (customer, food, meal) servire; (apprenticeship) fare; (prison term) scontare ▷ vi (also Tennis) servire; (be useful): **to ~ as/for/to do** servire da/per/per fare ▷ n (Tennis) servizio; **it ~s him right** ben gli sta, se l'è meritata; **server** n (Comput) server m inv
service ['sə:vɪs] n servizio; (Aut: maintenance) assistenza, revisione f ▷ vt (car, washing machine) revisionare; **services** npl (BRIT: on motorway) stazione f di servizio; (Mil): **the S~s** le forze armate; **to be of ~ to sb** essere d'aiuto a qn; **~ included/ not included** servizio compreso/escluso; **service area** n (on motorway) area di servizio; **service charge** n (BRIT) servizio; **serviceman** n (irreg) militare m; **service station** n stazione f di servizio
serviette [sə:vɪ'ɛt] n (BRIT) tovagliolo
session ['sɛʃən] n (sitting) seduta, sessione f; (Scol) anno scolastico (or accademico)
set [sɛt] n serie f inv; (of cutlery etc) servizio; (Radio, TV) apparecchio; (Tennis) set m inv; (group of people) mondo, ambiente m; (Cine) scenario; (Theat: stage) scene fpl; (: scenery) scenario; (Math) insieme m; (Hairdressing) messa in piega ▷ adj (fixed) stabilito/a, determinato/a; (ready)

pronto/a ▷ vt (pt, pp set) (place) posare, mettere; (arrange) sistemare; (fix) fissare; (adjust) regolare; (decide: rules etc) stabilire, fissare ▷ vi (pt, pp set) (sun) tramontare; (jam, jelly) rapprendersi; (concrete) fare presa; **to be ~ on doing** essere deciso a fare; **to ~ to music** mettere in musica; **to ~ on fire** dare fuoco a; **to ~ free** liberare; **to ~ sth going** mettere in moto qc; **to ~ sail** prendere il mare; **set aside** vt mettere da parte; **set down** vt (bus, train) lasciare; **set in** vi (infection) svilupparsi; (complications) intervenire; **the rain has ~ in for the day** ormai pioverà tutto il giorno; **set off** vi partire ▷ vt (bomb) far scoppiare; (cause to start) mettere in moto; (show up well) dare risalto a; **set out** vi partire; **to ~ out to do** proporsi di fare ▷ vt (arrange) disporre; (state) esporre, presentare; **set up** vt (organization) fondare, costituire; **setback** n (hitch) contrattempo, inconveniente m; **set menu** n menù m inv fisso
settee [sɛ'ti:] n divano, sofà m inv
setting ['sɛtɪŋ] n (background) ambiente m; (of controls) posizione f; (of sun) tramonto; (of jewel) montatura
settle ['sɛtl] vt (argument, matter) appianare; (bill, account) regolare; (Med: calm) calmare ▷ vi (bird, dust etc) posarsi; (sediment) depositarsi; (also: ~ down) sistemarsi, stabilirsi; (become calmer) calmarsi; **to ~ for sth** accontentarsi di qc; **to ~ on sth** decidersi per qc; **settle in** vi sistemarsi; **settle up** vi: **to ~ up with sb** regolare i conti con qn; **settlement** n (payment) pagamento, saldo; (agreement) accordo; (colony) colonia; (village etc) villaggio, comunità f inv
setup ['sɛtʌp] n (arrangement) sistemazione f; (situation) situazione f
seven ['sɛvn] num sette; **seventeen** num diciassette; **seventeenth** [sɛvn'ti:nθ] num diciassettesimo/a; **seventh** num settimo/a; **seventieth** ['sɛvntɪɪθ] num settantesimo/a; **seventy** num settanta
sever ['sɛvə'] vt recidere, tagliare; (relations) troncare
several ['sɛvərl] adj, pron alcuni/e, diversi/e; **~ of us** alcuni di noi
severe [sɪ'vɪə'] adj severo/a; (serious) serio/a, grave; (hard) duro/a; (plain) semplice, sobrio/a
sew [səu] (pt sewed, pp sewn) vt, vi cucire
sewage ['su:ɪdʒ] n acque fpl di scolo
sewer ['su:ə'] n fogna
sewing ['səuɪŋ] n cucitura; cucito; **sewing machine** n macchina da cucire

sewn [səun] *pp of* **sew**

sex [sɛks] *n* sesso; **to have ~ with** avere rapporti sessuali con; **sexism** ['sɛksɪzəm] *n* sessismo; **sexist** *adj*, *n* sessista (*m/f*); **sexual** ['sɛksjuəl] *adj* sessuale; **sexual intercourse** rapporti *mpl* sessuali; **sexuality** [sɛksju'ælɪtɪ] *n* sessualità; **sexy** ['sɛksɪ] *adj* provocante, sexy *inv*

shabby ['ʃæbɪ] *adj* malandato/a; (*behaviour*) meschino/a

shack [ʃæk] *n* baracca, capanna

shade [ʃeɪd] *n* ombra; (*for lamp*) paralume *m*; (*of colour*) tonalità *f inv*; (*small quantity*): **a ~ (more/too large)** un po' (di più/troppo grande) ▷ *vt* ombreggiare, fare ombra a; **shades** *npl* (*US: sunglasses*) occhiali *mpl* da sole; **in the ~** all'ombra

shadow ['ʃædəu] *n* ombra ▷ *vt* (*follow*) pedinare; **shadow cabinet** *n* (*BRIT Pol*) governo *m* ombra *inv*

shady ['ʃeɪdɪ] *adj* ombroso/a; (*fig: dishonest*) losco/a, equivoco/a

shaft [ʃɑːft] *n* (*of arrow, spear*) asta; (*Aut, Tech*) albero; (*of mine*) pozzo; (*of lift*) tromba; (*of light*) raggio

shake [ʃeɪk] (*pt* **shook**, *pp* **shaken**) *vt* scuotere; (*bottle, cocktail*) agitare ▷ *vi* tremare; **to ~ one's head** (*in refusal, dismay*) scuotere la testa; **to ~ hands with sb** stringere *or* dare la mano a qn; **shake off** *vt* scrollare (via); (*fig*) sbarazzarsi di; **shake up** *vt* scuotere; **shaky** *adj* (*hand, voice*) tremante; (*building*) traballante

shall [ʃæl] *aux vb*: **I ~ go** andrò; **~ I open the door?** apro io la porta?; **I'll get some, ~ I?** ne prendo un po', va bene?

shallow ['ʃæləu] *adj* poco profondo/a; (*fig*) superficiale

sham [ʃæm] *n* finzione *f*, messinscena; (*jewellery, furniture*) imitazione *f*

shambles ['ʃæmblz] *n* confusione *f*, baraonda, scompiglio

shame [ʃeɪm] *n* vergogna ▷ *vt* far vergognare; **it is a ~ (that/to do)** è un peccato (che + *sub*/fare); **what a ~!** che peccato!; **shameful** *adj* vergognoso/a; **shameless** *adj* sfrontato/a; (*immodest*) spudorato/a

shampoo [ʃæm'puː] *n* shampoo *m inv* ▷ *vt* fare lo shampoo a

shandy ['ʃændɪ] *n* birra con gassosa

shan't [ʃɑːnt] = **shall not**

shape [ʃeɪp] *n* forma ▷ *vt* formare; (*statement*) formulare; (*sb's ideas*) condizionare; **to take ~** prendere forma

share [ʃɛər] *n* (*thing received, contribution*) parte *f*; (*Comm*) azione *f* ▷ *vt* dividere; (*have in common*) condividere, avere in comune; **shareholder** *n* azionista *m/f*

shark [ʃɑːk] *n* squalo, pescecane *m*

sharp [ʃɑːp] *adj* (*razor, knife*) affilato/a; (*point*) acuto/a, acuminato/a; (*nose, chin*) aguzzo/a; (*outline*) netto/a; (*cold, pain*) pungente; (*voice*) stridulo/a; (*person: quick-witted*) sveglio/a; (: *unscrupulous*) disonesto/a; (*Mus*): **C ~** do diesis ▷ *n* (*Mus*) diesis *m inv* ▷ *adv*: **at 2 o'clock ~** alle due in punto; **sharpen** *vt* affilare; (*pencil*) fare la punta a; (*fig*) acuire; **sharpener** *n* (*also*: **pencil sharpener**) temperamatite *m inv*; **sharply** *adv* (*abruptly*) bruscamente; (*clearly*) nettamente; (*harshly*) duramente, aspramente

shatter ['ʃætər] *vt* mandare in frantumi, frantumare; (*fig: upset*) distruggere; (: *ruin*) rovinare ▷ *vi* frantumarsi, andare in pezzi; **shattered** *adj* (*grief-stricken*) sconvolto/a; (*exhausted*) a pezzi, distrutto/a

shave [ʃeɪv] *vt* radere, rasare ▷ *vi* radersi, farsi la barba ▷ *n*: **to have a ~** farsi la barba; **shaver** *n* (*also*: **electric shaver**) rasoio elettrico

shaving cream *n* crema da barba

shaving foam *n* = **shaving cream**

shawl [ʃɔːl] *n* scialle *m*

she [ʃiː] *pron* ella, lei; **~-cat** gatta; **~-elephant** elefantessa

sheath [ʃiːθ] *n* fodero, guaina; (*contraceptive*) preservativo

shed [ʃɛd] *n* capannone *m* ▷ *vt* (*pt*, *pp* **shed**) (*leaves, fur etc*) perdere; (*tears, blood*) versare; (*workers*) liberarsi di

she'd [ʃiːd] = **she had**; **she would**

sheep [ʃiːp] *n* (*pl inv*) pecora; **sheepdog** *n* cane *m* da pastore; **sheepskin** *n* pelle *f* di pecora

sheer [ʃɪər] *adj* (*utter*) vero/a (e proprio/a); (*steep*) a picco, perpendicolare; (*almost transparent*) sottile ▷ *adv* a picco

sheet [ʃiːt] *n* (*on bed*) lenzuolo; (*of paper*) foglio; (*of glass*) lastra; (*of metal*) foglio, lamina

sheik(h) [ʃeɪk] *n* sceicco

shelf (*pl* **shelves**) [ʃɛlf, ʃɛlvz] *n* scaffale *m*, mensola

shell [ʃɛl] *n* (*on beach*) conchiglia; (*of egg, nut etc*) guscio; (*explosive*) granata; (*of building*) scheletro ▷ *vt* (*peas*) sgranare; (*Mil*) bombardare

she'll [ʃiːl] = **she will**; **she shall**

shellfish ['ʃɛlfɪʃ] *n* (*pl inv*: crab etc) crostaceo; (*scallop etc*) mollusco; (*as food*) crostacei; molluschi

shelter ['ʃɛltər] *n* riparo, rifugio ▷ *vt* riparare, proteggere; (*give lodging to*) dare rifugio *or* asilo a ▷ *vi* ripararsi, mettersi al riparo; **sheltered** *adj* riparato/a

shelves [ʃɛlvz] *npl of* **shelf**

shelving ['ʃelvɪŋ] n scaffalature fpl

shepherd ['ʃepəd] n pastore m ▷ vt (guide) guidare; **shepherd's pie** (BRIT) n timballo di carne macinata e purè di patate

sheriff ['ʃerɪf] (US) n sceriffo

sherry ['ʃerɪ] n sherry m inv

she's [ʃi:z] = **she is**; **she has**

Shetland ['ʃetlənd] n (also: **the ~s, the ~ Isles**) le (isole) Shetland

shield [ʃi:ld] n scudo; (trophy) scudetto; (protection) schermo ▷ vt: **to ~ (from)** riparare (da), proteggere (da or contro)

shift [ʃɪft] n (change) cambiamento; (of workers) turno ▷ vt spostare, muovere; (remove) rimuovere ▷ vi spostarsi, muoversi

shin [ʃɪn] n tibia

shine [ʃaɪn] (pt, pp shone) n splendore m, lucentezza ▷ vi (ri)splendere, brillare ▷ vt far brillare, far risplendere; (torch): **to ~ sth on** puntare qc verso

shingles ['ʃɪŋglz] n (Med) herpes zoster m

shiny ['ʃaɪnɪ] adj lucente, lucido/a

ship [ʃɪp] n nave f ▷ vt trasportare (via mare); (send) spedire (via mare); **shipment** n carico; **shipping** n (ships) naviglio; (traffic) navigazione f; **shipwreck** n relitto; (event) naufragio ▷ vt: **to be shipwrecked** naufragare, fare naufragio; **shipyard** n cantiere m navale

shirt [ʃə:t] n camicia; **in ~ sleeves** in maniche di camicia

shit [ʃɪt] excl (coll) merda (!)

shiver ['ʃɪvə'] n brivido ▷ vi rabbrividire, tremare

shock [ʃɔk] n (impact) urto, colpo; (Elec) scossa; (emotional) colpo, shock m inv; (Med) shock ▷ vt colpire, scioccare; scandalizzare; **shocking** adj scioccante, traumatizzante; (scandalous) scandaloso/a

shoe [ʃu:] n scarpa; (also: **horse~**) ferro di cavallo ▷ vt (pt, pp shod [ʃɔd]) (horse) ferrare; **shoelace** n stringa; **shoe polish** n lucido per scarpe; **shoeshop** n calzoleria

shone [ʃɔn] pt, pp of **shine**

shonky ['ʃɔŋkɪ] adj (AUST, NZ col: untrustworthy) sospetto/a

shook [ʃuk] pt of **shake**

shoot [ʃu:t] (pt, pp shot) n (on branch, seedling) germoglio ▷ vt (game) cacciare, andare a caccia di; (person) sparare a; (execute) fucilare; (film) girare ▷ vi (Football) sparare, tirare (forte); **to ~ (at)** (with gun) sparare (a), fare fuoco (su); (with bow) tirare (su); **shoot down** vt (plane) abbattere; **shoot up** vi (fig) salire alle stelle; **shooting** n (shots) sparatoria; (Hunting) caccia

shop [ʃɔp] n negozio; (workshop) officina ▷ vi (also: **go ~ping**) fare spese; **shop assistant** n (BRIT) commesso/a; **shopkeeper** n

negoziante m/f, bottegaio/a; **shoplifting** n taccheggio; **shopping** n (goods) spesa, acquisti mpl; **shopping bag** n borsa per la spesa; **shopping centre**, (US) **shopping center** n centro commerciale; **shopping mall** n centro commerciale; **shopping trolley** n (BRIT) carrello del supermercato; **shop window** n vetrina

shore [ʃɔ:'] n (of sea) riva, spiaggia; (of lake) riva ▷ vt: **to ~ (up)** puntellare; **on ~** a riva

short [ʃɔ:t] adj (not long) corto/a; (soon finished) breve; (person) basso/a; (curt) brusco/a, secco/a; (insufficient) insufficiente ▷ n (also: **~ film**) cortometraggio; **it is ~ for** è l'abbreviazione or il diminutivo di; **to be ~ of sth** essere a corto di or mancare di qc; **to run ~ of sth** rimanere senza qc; **in ~** in breve; **~ of doing** a meno che non si faccia; **everything ~ of** tutto fuorché; **to cut ~** (speech, visit) accorciare, abbreviare; **to fall ~ of** venire meno a; non soddisfare; **to stop ~** fermarsi di colpo; **to stop ~ of** non arrivare fino a; **shortage** n scarsezza, carenza; **shortbread** n biscotto di pasta frolla; **shortcoming** n difetto; **short(crust) pastry** n (BRIT) pasta frolla; **shortcut** n scorciatoia; **shorten** vt accorciare, ridurre; **shortfall** n deficit m inv; **shorthand** n stenografia; **short-lived** adj di breve durata; **shortly** adv fra poco; **shorts** npl (also: **a pair of shorts**) i calzoncini; **short-sighted** adj (BRIT) miope; **short-sleeved** ['ʃɔ:tsli:vd] adj a maniche corte; **short story** n racconto, novella; **short-tempered** adj irascibile; **short-term** adj (effect) di or a breve durata; (borrowing) a breve scadenza

shot [ʃɔt] pt, pp of **shoot** ▷ n sparo, colpo; (try) prova; (Football) tiro; (injection) iniezione f; (Phot) foto f inv; **like a ~** come un razzo; (very readily) immediatamente; **shotgun** n fucile m da caccia

should [ʃud] aux vb: **I ~ go now** dovrei andare ora; **he ~ be there now** dovrebbe essere arrivato ora; **I ~ go if I were you** se fossi in lei andrei; **I ~ like to** mi piacerebbe

shoulder ['ʃəuldə'] n spalla; **hard ~** corsia d'emergenza ▷ vt (fig) addossarsi, prendere sulle proprie spalle; **shoulder blade** n scapola

shouldn't ['ʃudnt] = **should not**

shout [ʃaut] n urlo, grido ▷ vt gridare ▷ vi (also: **~ out**) urlare, gridare

shove [ʃʌv] vt spingere; (col: put): **to ~ sth in** ficcare qc in

shovel ['ʃʌvl] n pala ▷ vt spalare

show [ʃəu] (pt showed, pp shown) n (of emotion) dimostrazione f, manifestazione f;

(*semblance*) apparenza; (*exhibition*) mostra, esposizione *f*; (*Theat, Cine*) spettacolo ▷ *vt* far vedere, mostrare; (*courage etc*) dimostrare, dar prova di; (*exhibit*) esporre ▷ *vi* vedersi, essere visibile; **to be on ~** essere esposto; **it's just for ~** è solo per far scena; **show in** *vt* (*person*) far entrare; **show off** *vi* (*pej*) esibirsi, mettersi in mostra ▷ *vt* (*display*) mettere in risalto; (*pej*) mettere in mostra; **show out** *vt* (*person*) accompagnare alla porta; **show up** *vi* (*stand out*) essere ben visibile; (*col: turn up*) farsi vedere ▷ *vt* mettere in risalto; **show business** *n* industria dello spettacolo

shower ['ʃauə'] *n* doccia; (*rain*) acquazzone *m*; (*of stones etc*) pioggia ▷ *vi* fare la doccia ▷ *vt*: **to ~ sb with** (*gifts, abuse etc*) coprire qn di; (*missiles*) lanciare contro qn una pioggia di; **to have** *or* **take a ~** fare la doccia; **shower cap** *n* cuffia da doccia; **shower gel** *n* gel *m* doccia *inv*

showing ['ʃəuɪŋ] *n* (*of film*) proiezione *f*

show jumping *n* concorso ippico (di salto ad ostacoli)

shown [ʃəun] *pp of* **show**

show: show-off *n* (*col: person*) esibizionista *m/f*; **showroom** *n* sala d'esposizione

shrank [ʃræŋk] *pt of* **shrink**

shred [ʃred] *n* (*gen pl*) brandello ▷ *vt* fare a brandelli; (*Culin*) sminuzzare, tagliuzzare

shrewd [ʃruːd] *adj* astuto/a, scaltro/a

shriek [ʃriːk] *n* strillo ▷ *vi* strillare

shrimp [ʃrɪmp] *n* gamberetto

shrine [ʃraɪn] *n* reliquario; (*place*) santuario

shrink [ʃrɪŋk] (*pt* **shrank**, *pp* **shrunk**) *vi* restringersi; (*fig*) ridursi; (*also*: **~ away**) ritrarsi ▷ *vt* (*wool*) far restringere ▷ *n* (*col, pej*) psicanalista *m/f*; **to ~ from doing sth** rifuggire dal fare qc

shrivel ['ʃrɪvl], **shrivel up** *vt* raggrinzare, avvizzire ▷ *vi* raggrinzirsi, avvizzire

shroud [ʃraud] *n* lenzuolo funebre ▷ *vt*: **~ed in mystery** avvolto/a nel mistero

Shrove Tuesday ['ʃrəuv-] *n* martedì *m* grasso

shrub [ʃrʌb] *n* arbusto

shrug [ʃrʌg] *n* scrollata di spalle ▷ *vt, vi*: **to ~ (one's shoulders)** alzare le spalle, fare spallucce; **shrug off** *vt* passare sopra a

shrunk [ʃrʌŋk] *pp of* **shrink**

shudder ['ʃʌdə'] *n* brivido ▷ *vi* rabbrividire

shuffle ['ʃʌfl] *vt* (*cards*) mescolare; **to ~ (one's feet)** strascicare i piedi

shun [ʃʌn] *vt* sfuggire, evitare

shut (*pt, pp* **shut**) [ʃʌt] *vt* chiudere ▷ *vi* chiudersi, chiudere; **shut down** *vt, vi* chiudere definitivamente; **shut up** *vi* (*col: keep quiet*) stare zitto/a, fare silenzio ▷ *vt*

(*close*) chiudere; (*silence*) far tacere; **shutter** *n* imposta; (*Phot*) otturatore *m*

shuttle ['ʃʌtl] *n* spola, navetta; (*space shuttle*) navetta (spaziale); (*also*: **~ service**) servizio *m* navetta *inv*; **shuttlecock** *n* volano

shy [ʃaɪ] *adj* timido/a

sibling ['sɪblɪŋ] *n* (*formal*) fratello/sorella

Sicily ['sɪsɪlɪ] *n* Sicilia

sick [sɪk] *adj* (*ill*) malato/a; (*humour*) macabro/a; **to be ~** (*vomiting*) vomitare; **to feel ~** avere la nausea; **to be ~ of** (*fig*) averne abbastanza di; **sickening** *adj* (*fig*) disgustoso/a, rivoltante; **sick leave** *n* congedo per malattia; **sickly** *adj* malaticcio/a; (*causing nausea*) nauseante; **sickness** *n* malattia; (*vomiting*) vomito

side [saɪd] *n* lato; (*of lake*) riva; (*team*) squadra ▷ *cpd* (*door, entrance*) laterale ▷ *vi*: **to ~ with sb** parteggiare per qn, prendere le parti di qn; **by the ~ of** a fianco di; (*road*) sul ciglio di; **~ by ~** fianco a fianco; **to take ~s (with)** schierarsi (con); **from ~ to ~** da una parte all'altra; **sideboard** *n* credenza; **sideboards** ['saɪdbɔːdz], (*US*) **sideburns** ['saɪdbəːnz] *npl* (*whiskers*) basette *fpl*; **sidelight** *n* (*Aut*) luce *f* di posizione; **sideline** *n* (*Sport*) linea laterale; (*fig*) attività secondaria; **side order** *n* contorno (*pietanza*); **side road** *n* strada secondaria; **side street** *n* traversa; **sidetrack** *vt* (*fig*) distrarre; **sidewalk** *n* (*US*) marciapiede *m*; **sideways** *adv* (*move*) di lato, di fianco

siege [siːdʒ] *n* assedio

sieve [sɪv] *n* setaccio ▷ *vt* setacciare

sift [sɪft] *vt* passare al crivello; (*fig*) vagliare

sigh [saɪ] *n* sospiro ▷ *vi* sospirare

sight [saɪt] *n* (*faculty*) vista; (*spectacle*) spettacolo; (*on gun*) mira ▷ *vt* avvistare; **in ~** in vista; **on ~** a vista; **out of ~** non visibile; **sightseeing** *n* giro turistico; **to go sightseeing** visitare una località

sign [saɪn] *n* segno; (*with hand etc*) segno, gesto; (*notice*) insegna, cartello ▷ *vt* firmare; (*player*) ingaggiare; **as a ~ of** in segno di; **it's a good/bad ~** è buon/ brutto segno; **to show ~s/no ~ of doing sth** accennare/non accennare a fare qc; **plus/minus ~** segno del più/meno; **to ~ one's name** firmare, apporre la propria firma; **sign for** *vt fus* (*item*) firmare per l'accettazione di; **sign in** *vi* firmare il registro (all'arrivo); **sign on** *vi* (*Mil etc*) arruolarsi; (*as unemployed*) iscriversi sulla lista (dell'ufficio di collocamento) ▷ *vt* (*Mil*) arruolare; (*employee*) assumere; **sign up** *vi* (*Mil*) *vt* (*player*) ingaggiare; (*recruits*) reclutare ▷ *vi* arruolarsi; (*for course*) iscriversi

signal ['sɪgnl] n segnale m ▷ vt (person) fare segno a; (message) comunicare per mezzo di segnali ▷ vi (Aut) segnalare, mettere la freccia; **to ~ to sb (to do sth)** far segno a qn (di fare qc); **to ~ a left/right turn**

signature ['sɪgnətʃəʳ] n firma

significance [sɪg'nɪfɪkəns] n significato; (of event) importanza

significant [sɪg'nɪfɪkənt] adj significativo/a

signify ['sɪgnɪfaɪ] vt significare

sign language n linguaggio dei muti

signpost ['saɪnpəust] n cartello indicatore

Sikh [siːk] adj, n sikh mf inv

silence ['saɪlns] n silenzio ▷ vt far tacere, ridurre al silenzio

silent ['saɪlnt] adj silenzioso/a; (film) muto/a; **to keep** or **remain ~** tacere, stare zitto/a

silhouette [sɪluːˈɛt] n silhouette f inv

silicon chip ['sɪlɪkən-] n chip m inv (al silicio)

silk [sɪlk] n seta ▷ cpd di seta

silly ['sɪlɪ] adj stupido/a, sciocco/a

silver ['sɪlvəʳ] n argento; (money) monete da 5, 10, 20 o 50 pence; (also: **~ware**) argenteria ▷ cpd d'argento; **silver-plated** adj argentato/a

SIM card ['sɪm-] n (Tel) SIM card f inv

similar ['sɪmɪləʳ] adj: **~ (to)** simile (a); **similarity** [sɪmɪˈlærɪtɪ] n somiglianza, rassomiglianza; **similarly** adv allo stesso modo; (as is similar) così pure

simmer ['sɪməʳ] vi cuocere a fuoco lento

simple ['sɪmpl] adj semplice; **simplicity** [sɪmˈplɪsɪtɪ] n semplicità; **simplify** vt semplificare; **simply** adv semplicemente

simulate ['sɪmjuleɪt] vt fingere, simulare

simultaneous [sɪməlˈteɪnɪəs] adj simultaneo/a; **simultaneously** adv simultaneamente, contemporaneamente

sin [sɪn] n peccato ▷ vi peccare

since [sɪns] adv da allora ▷ prep da ▷ conj (time) da quando; (because) poiché, dato che; **~ then, ever ~** da allora

sincere [sɪn'sɪəʳ] adj sincero/a; **sincerely** adv: **Yours sincerely** distinti saluti

sing [sɪŋ] (pt **sang**, pp **sung**) vt, vi cantare

Singapore [sɪŋgəˈpɔːʳ] n Singapore f

singer ['sɪŋəʳ] n cantante m/f

singing ['sɪŋɪŋ] n canto

single ['sɪŋgl] adj solo/a, unico/a; (unmarried: man) celibe; (: woman) nubile; (not double) semplice ▷ n (BRIT: also: **~ ticket**) biglietto di (sola) andata; (record) 45 giri m inv; **single out** vt scegliere; (distinguish) distinguere; **single bed** n letto a una piazza; **single file** n: **in single file** in fila indiana; **single-handed** adv senza aiuto, da solo/a; **single-minded** adj tenace, risoluto/a; **single parent** n ragazzo padre/ragazza madre; genitore m separato; **single parent family** famiglia monoparentale; **single room** n camera singola; **singles** npl (Tennis) singolo

singular ['sɪŋgjuləʳ] adj singolare ▷ n (Ling) singolare m

sinister ['sɪnɪstəʳ] adj sinistro/a

sink [sɪŋk] (pt **sank**, pp **sunk**) n lavandino, acquaio ▷ vt (ship) (fare) affondare, colare a picco; (foundations) scavare; (piles etc): **to ~ sth into** conficcare qc in ▷ vi affondare, andare a fondo; (ground etc) cedere, avvallarsi; **my heart sank** mi sentii venir meno; **sink in** vi penetrare

sinus ['saɪnəs] n (Anat) seno

sip [sɪp] n sorso ▷ vt sorseggiare

sir [səʳ] n signore m; **S~ John Smith** Sir John Smith; **yes ~** sì, signore

siren ['saɪərn] n sirena

sirloin ['səːlɔɪn] n controfiletto

sister ['sɪstəʳ] n sorella; (nun) suora; (BRIT: nurse) infermiera f caposala inv; **sister-in-law** n cognata

sit [sɪt] (pt, pp **sat**) vi sedere, sedersi; (assembly) essere in seduta; (for painter) posare ▷ vt (exam) sostenere, dare; **sit back** vi (in seat) appoggiarsi allo schienale; **sit down** vi sedersi; **sit on** vt fus (jury, committee) far parte di; **sit up** vi tirarsi su a sedere; (not go to bed) stare alzato/a fino a tardi

sitcom ['sɪtkɔm] n abbr (TV: = situation comedy) sceneggiato a episodi (comico)

site [saɪt] n posto; (also: **building ~**) cantiere m ▷ vt situare

sitting ['sɪtɪŋ] n (of assembly etc) seduta; (in canteen) turno; **sitting room** n soggiorno

situated ['sɪtjueɪtɪd] adj situato/a

situation [sɪtjuˈeɪʃən] n situazione f; (job) lavoro; (location) posizione f; **"~s vacant/wanted"** (BRIT) "offerte/domande di impiego"

six [sɪks] num sei; **sixteen** num sedici; **sixteenth** [sɪksˈtiːnθ] num sedicesimo/a; **sixth** num sesto/a; **sixth form** n (BRIT) ultimo biennio delle scuole superiori; **sixth-form college** n istituto che offre corsi di preparazione all'esame di maturità per ragazzi dai 16 ai 18 anni; **sixtieth** ['sɪkstɪɪθ] num sessantesimo/a ▷ pron (in series) sessantesimo/a; (fraction) sessantesimo; **sixty** num sessanta

size [saɪz] n dimensioni fpl; (of clothing) taglia, misura; (of shoes) numero; (glue) colla; **sizeable** adj considerevole

sizzle ['sɪzl] vi sfrigolare

skate [skeɪt] n pattino; (fish: pl inv) razza
▷ vi pattinare; **skateboard** ['skeɪtbɔːd]
n skateboard m inv; **skateboarding** n
skateboard m inv; **skater** n pattinatore/
trice; **skating** n pattinaggio; **skating rink**
n pista di pattinaggio

skeleton ['skɛlɪtn] n scheletro

skeptical ['skɛptɪkl] (US) adj = **sceptical**

sketch [skɛtʃ] n (drawing) schizzo, abbozzo;
(Theat etc) scenetta comica, sketch m inv
▷ vt abbozzare, schizzare

skewer ['skjuːəʳ] n spiedo

ski [skiː] n sci m inv ▷ vi sciare; **ski boot** n
scarpone m da sci

skid [skɪd] n slittamento ▷ vi slittare

ski: skier ['skiːəʳ] n sciatore/trice; **skiing**
['skiːɪŋ] n sci m

skilful, (US) **skillful** ['skɪlful] adj abile

ski lift n sciovia

skill [skɪl] n abilità f inv, capacità f
inv; **skilled** adj esperto/a; (worker)
qualificato/a, specializzato/a

skim [skɪm] vt (milk) scremare; (glide over)
sfiorare ▷ vi: **to ~ through** (fig) scorrere,
dare una scorsa a; **skimmed milk**, (US)
skim milk n latte m scremato

skin [skɪn] n pelle f ▷ vt (fruit etc) sbucciare;
(animal) scuoiare, spellare; **skinhead** n
skinhead mf inv; **skinny** adj molto magro/a,
pelle e ossa inv

skip [skɪp] n saltello; (BRIT) balzo;
(container) benna ▷ vi saltare; (with rope)
saltare la corda ▷ vt saltare

ski: ski pass n ski pass m inv; **ski pole** n
racchetta (da sci)

skipper ['skɪpəʳ] n (Naut, Sport) capitano

skipping rope ['skɪpɪŋ-], (US) **skip rope** n
corda per saltare

skirt [skəːt] n gonna, sottana ▷ vt
fiancheggiare, costeggiare

skirting board n (BRIT) zoccolo

ski slope n pista da sci

ski suit n tuta da sci

skull [skʌl] n cranio, teschio

skunk [skʌŋk] n moffetta

sky [skaɪ] n cielo

Skype® [skaɪp] (Internet, Tel) n Skype® m
▷ vt: **to s~ sb** chiamare qn con Skype

skyscraper n grattacielo

slab [slæb] n lastra; (of meat, cheese) fetta

slack [slæk] adj (loose) allentato/a; (slow)
lento/a; (careless) negligente; **slacks** npl
(trousers) pantaloni mpl

slain [sleɪn] pp of **slay**

slam [slæm] vt (door) sbattere; (throw)
scaraventare; (criticize) stroncare ▷ vi
sbattere

slander ['slɑːndəʳ] n calunnia; (Law)
diffamazione f

slang [slæŋ] n gergo, slang m

slant [slɑːnt] n pendenza, inclinazione f;
(fig) angolazione f, punto di vista

slap [slæp] n manata, pacca; (on face)
schiaffo ▷ vt dare una manata a;
schiaffeggiare ▷ adv (directly) in pieno;
~ a coat of paint on it dagli una mano di
vernice

slash [slæʃ] vt tagliare; (face) sfregiare; (fig:
prices) ridurre drasticamente, tagliare

slate [sleɪt] n ardesia; (piece) lastra di
ardesia ▷ vt (fig: criticize) stroncare,
distruggere

slaughter ['slɔːtəʳ] n strage f, massacro
▷ vt (animal) macellare; (people) trucidare,
massacrare; **slaughterhouse** n macello,
mattatoio

Slav [slɑːv] adj, n slavo/a

slave [sleɪv] n schiavo/a ▷ vi (also: **~ away**)
lavorare come uno schiavo; **slavery** n
schiavitù f

slay (pt **slew**, pp **slain**) [sleɪ, sluː, sleɪn] vt
(formal) uccidere

sleazy ['sliːzɪ] adj trasandato/a

sled [slɛd] (US) = **sledge**

sledge [slɛdʒ] n slitta

sleek [sliːk] adj (hair, fur) lucido/a, lucente;
(car, boat) slanciato/a, affusolato/a

sleep [sliːp] n sonno ▷ vi (pt, pp **slept**)
dormire; **to go to ~** addormentarsi; **sleep
in** vi (oversleep) dormire fino a tardi; **sleep
together** vi (have sex) andare a letto
insieme; **sleeper** n (BRIT Rail: on track)
traversina; (: train) treno di vagoni letto;
sleeping bag n sacco a pelo; **sleeping car**
n vagone m letto inv, carrozza f letto inv;
sleeping pill n sonnifero; **sleepover** n il
dormire a casa di amici, usato in riferimento
a bambini; **sleepwalk** vi camminare nel
sonno; (as a habit) essere sonnambulo/a;
sleepy adj assonnato/a, sonnolento/a;
(fig) addormentato/a

sleet [sliːt] n nevischio

sleeve [sliːv] n manica; (of record)
copertina; **sleeveless** adj (garment) senza
maniche

sleigh [sleɪ] n slitta

slender ['slɛndəʳ] adj snello/a, sottile; (not
enough) scarso/a, esiguo/a

slept [slɛpt] pt, pp of **sleep**

slew [sluː] vi (BRIT: also: **~ round**) girare
▷ pt of **slay**

slice [slaɪs] n fetta ▷ vt affettare, tagliare
a fette

slick [slɪk] adj (skilful) brillante ▷ n (also:
oil ~) chiazza di petrolio

slide [slaɪd] n scivolone m; (in playground)
scivolo; (Phot) diapositiva; (also: **hair ~**)
fermaglio (per capelli) ▷ vt (pt, pp **slid** [slɪd])

far scivolare ▷ *vi* (*pt, pp* **slid** [slɪd]) scivolare; **sliding** *adj* (*door*) scorrevole

slight [slaɪt] *adj* (*slim*) snello/a, sottile; (*frail*) delicato/a, fragile; (*trivial*) insignificante; (*small*) piccolo/a ▷ *n* offesa, affronto; **not in the ~est** affatto, neppure per sogno; **slightly** *adv* lievemente, un po'

slim [slɪm] *adj* magro/a, snello/a ▷ *vi* dimagrire; fare *or* seguire) una dieta dimagrante; **slimming** ['slɪmɪŋ] *adj* (*diet, pills*) dimagrante; (*food*) ipocalorico/a

slimy ['slaɪmɪ] *adj* (*also fig: person*) viscido/a; (*covered with mud*) melmoso/a

sling [slɪŋ] *n* (*Med*) fascia al collo; (*for baby*) marsupio ▷ *vt* (*pt, pp* **slung** [slʌŋ]) lanciare, tirare

slip [slɪp] *n* scivolata, scivolone *m*; (*mistake*) errore *m*, sbaglio; (*underskirt*) sottoveste *f*; (*paper*) foglietto; tagliando, scontrino ▷ *vt* (*slide*) far scivolare ▷ *vi* (*slide*) scivolare; (*decline*) declinare; **to ~ into/out of** (*move smoothly*) scivolare in/fuori da; **to give sb the ~** sfuggire qn; **a ~ of paper** un foglietto; **a ~ of the tongue** un lapsus linguae; **slip up** *vi* sbagliarsi

slipper ['slɪpəʳ] *n* pantofola

slippery ['slɪpərɪ] *adj* scivoloso/a

slip road *n* (BRIT: *to motorway*) rampa di accesso

slit [slɪt] *n* fessura, fenditura; (*cut*) taglio ▷ *vt* (*pt, pp* **slit**) fendere; tagliare

slog [slɔg] (BRIT) *n* faticata ▷ *vi* lavorare con accanimento, sgobbare

slogan ['sləʊɡən] *n* motto, slogan *m inv*

slope [sləʊp] *n* pendio; (*side of mountain*) versante *m*; (*ski slope*) pista; (*of roof*) pendenza; (*of floor*) inclinazione *f* ▷ *vi*: **to ~ down** declinare; **to ~ up** essere in salita; **sloping** *adj* inclinato/a

sloppy ['slɔpɪ] *adj* (*work*) tirato/a via; (*appearance*) sciatto/a

slot [slɔt] *n* fessura ▷ *vt*: **to ~ into** infilare in; **slot machine** *n* (BRIT: *vending machine*) distributore *m* automatico; (*for amusement*) slot-machine *f inv*

Slovakia [sləʊˈvækɪə] *n* Slovacchia

Slovene ['sləʊviːn] *adj* sloveno/a ▷ *n* sloveno/a; (*Ling*) sloveno

Slovenia [sləʊˈviːnɪə] *n* Slovenia; **Slovenian** *adj*, *n* = **Slovene**

slow [sləʊ] *adj* lento/a; (*watch*): **to be ~** essere indietro ▷ *adv* lentamente ▷ *vt, vi* (*also:* **~ down**, **~ up**) rallentare; **"~"** (*road sign*) "rallentare"; **slowly** *adv* lentamente; **slow motion** *n*: **in slow motion** al rallentatore

slug [slʌg] *n* lumaca; (*bullet*) pallottola; **sluggish** *adj* lento/a; (*business, market, sales*) stagnante

slum [slʌm] *n* catapecchia

slump [slʌmp] *n* crollo, caduta; (*economic*) depressione *f*, crisi *f inv* ▷ *vi* crollare

slung [slʌŋ] *pt, pp of* **sling**

slur [sləːʳ] *n* (*smear*): **~ (on)** macchia (su) ▷ *vt* pronunciare in modo indistinto

sly [slaɪ] *adj* (*smile, remark*) sornione/a; (*person*) furbo/a

smack [smæk] *n* (*slap*) pacca; (*on face*) schiaffo ▷ *vt* schiaffeggiare; (*child*) picchiare ▷ *vi*: **to ~ of** puzzare di

small [smɔːl] *adj* piccolo/a; **small ads** *npl* (BRIT) piccoli annunci *mpl*; **small change** *n* moneta, spiccioli *mpl*

smart [smɑːt] *adj* elegante; (*fashionable*) alla moda; (*clever*) intelligente; (*quick*) sveglio/a ▷ *vi* bruciare; **smartcard** *n* smartcard *f inv*, carta intelligente; **smartphone** *n* smartphone *m inv*

smash [smæʃ] *n* (*also:* **~-up**) scontro, collisione *f*; (*smash hit*) successone *m* ▷ *vt* frantumare, fracassare; (*Sport: record*) battere ▷ *vi* frantumarsi, andare in pezzi; **smashing** *adj* (col) favoloso/a, formidabile

smear [smɪəʳ] *n* macchia; (*Med*) striscio ▷ *vt* ungere; (*make dirty*) sporcare; (*fig*) denigrare, diffamare; **his hands were ~ed with oil/ink** aveva le mani sporche di olio/inchiostro; **smear test** *n* (BRIT *Med*) Pap-test *m inv*

smell (*pt, pp* **smelt** *or* **smelled**) [smɛl, smɛlt, smɛld] *n* odore *m*; (*sense*) olfatto, odorato ▷ *vt* sentire (l')odore di ▷ *vi* (*food etc*): **to ~ (of)** avere odore (di); (*pej*) puzzare, avere un cattivo odore; **smelly** *adj* puzzolente

smelt [smɛlt] *pt, pp of* **smell** ▷ *vt* (*ore*) fondere

smile [smaɪl] *n* sorriso ▷ *vi* sorridere

smirk [sməːk] *n* sorriso furbo; sorriso compiaciuto

smog [smɔg] *n* smog *m*

smoke [sməʊk] *n* fumo ▷ *vt, vi* fumare; **smoke alarm** *n* rivelatore *f* di fumo; **smoked** *adj* (*bacon, glass*) affumicato/a; **smoker** *n* (*person*) fumatore/trice; (*Rail*) carrozza per fumatori; **smoking** *n* fumo; **"no smoking"** (*sign*) "vietato fumare"; **smoky** *adj* fumoso/a; (*taste, surface*) affumicato/a

smooth [smuːð] *adj* liscio/a; (*sauce*) omogeneo/a; (*flavour, whisky*) amabile; (*movement*) regolare; (*person*) mellifluo/a ▷ *vt* lisciare, spianare; (*also:* **~ out**) (*difficulties*) appianare

smother ['smʌðəʳ] *vt* soffocare

SMS *n abbr* (= *short message service*) SMS *m*; **SMS message** *n* SMS *m inv*, messaggino

smudge [smʌdʒ] n macchia; sbavatura
▷ vt imbrattare, sporcare

smug [smʌg] adj soddisfatto/a,
compiaciuto/a

smuggle ['smʌgl] vt contrabbandare;
smuggling n contrabbando

snack [snæk] n spuntino; **snack bar** n
tavola calda, snack bar m inv

snag [snæg] n intoppo, ostacolo imprevisto

snail [sneɪl] n chiocciola

snake [sneɪk] n serpente m

snap [snæp] n (sound) schianto, colpo
secco; (photograph) istantanea ▷ adj
improvviso/a ▷ vt (far) schioccare; (break)
spezzare di netto ▷ vi spezzarsi con un
rumore secco; (fig: person) crollare; **to ~ at**
sb (dog) cercare di mordere qn; **to**
~ open/
shut aprirsi/chiudersi di scatto; **snap up** vt
afferrare; **snapshot** n istantanea

snarl [snɑːl] vi ringhiare

snatch [snætʃ] n (small amount): **~es of**
frammenti mpl di ▷ vt strappare (con
violenza); (steal) rubare

sneak [sniːk] ((Us) pt **snuck**) vi: **to ~ in/out**
entrare/uscire di nascosto ▷ n spione/a; **to**
~ up on sb avvicinarsi quatto quatto a qn;
sneakers npl scarpe fpl da ginnastica

sneer [snɪəʳ] vi sogghignare; **to ~ at sb/sth**
farsi beffe di qn/qc

sneeze [sniːz] n starnuto ▷ vi starnutire

sniff [snɪf] n fiutata, annusata ▷ vi tirare su
col naso ▷ vt fiutare, annusare

snigger ['snɪgəʳ] vi ridacchiare, ridere sotto
i baffi

snip [snɪp] n pezzetto; (bargain) (buon)
affare m, occasione f ▷ vt tagliare

sniper ['snaɪpəʳ] n (marksman) franco
tiratore m, cecchino

snob [snɔb] n snob mf inv

snooker ['snuːkəʳ] n tipo di gioco del biliardo

snoop [snuːp] vi: **to ~ about** curiosare

snooze [snuːz] n sonnellino, pisolino ▷ vi
fare un sonnellino

snore [snɔːʳ] vi russare

snorkel ['snɔːkl] n (of swimmer) respiratore
m a tubo

snort [snɔːt] n sbuffo ▷ vi sbuffare

snow [snəʊ] n neve f ▷ vi nevicare;
snowball n palla di neve ▷ vi (fig) crescere a
vista d'occhio; **snowstorm** n tormenta

snub [snʌb] vt snobbare ▷ n offesa, affronto

snug [snʌg] adj comodo/a; (room, house)
accogliente, comodo/a

KEYWORD

so [səʊ] adv **1** (thus, likewise) così; **if so** se è
così, quand'è così; **I didn't do it — you did**
so! non l'ho fatto io — sì che l'hai fatto!; **so**
do I, so am I anch'io; **it's 5 o'clock — so it**
is! sono le 5 — davvero!; **I hope so** lo spero;
I think so penso di sì; **so far** finora, fin qui;
(in past) fino ad allora

2 (in comparisons etc: to such a degree) così;
so big (that) così grande (che); **she's not**
so clever as her brother lei non è (così)
intelligente come suo fratello

3: **so much** adj tanto/a; adv tanto; **I've got**
so much work/money ho tanto lavoro/
tanti soldi; **I love you so much** ti amo
tanto; **so many** tanti/e

4 (phrases): **10 or so** circa 10; **so long!** (col:
goodbye) ciao!, ci vediamo!

▷ conj **1** (expressing purpose): **so as to do**
in modo or così da fare; **we hurried so as**
not to be late ci affrettammo per non fare
tardi; **so (that)** affinché + sub, perché + sub

2 (expressing result): **he didn't arrive so I**
left non è venuto così me ne sono andata;
so you see, I could have gone vedi, sarei
potuto andare

soak [səʊk] vt inzuppare; (clothes) mettere
a mollo ▷ vi (clothes) essere a mollo; **soak**
up vt assorbire; **soaking** adj (also: **soaking**
wet) fradicio/a

so-and-so ['səʊənsəʊ] n (somebody) un
tale; **Mr/Mrs ~** signor/signora tal dei tali

soap [səʊp] n sapone m; **soap opera** n soap
opera f inv; **soap powder** n detersivo

soar [sɔːʳ] vi volare in alto; (price, morale,
spirits) salire alle stelle; (building) ergersi

sob [sɔb] n singhiozzo ▷ vi singhiozzare

sober ['səʊbəʳ] adj non ubriaco/a;
(moderate) moderato/a; (colour, style)
sobrio/a; **sober up** vt far passare la sbornia
a ▷ vi farsi passare la sbornia

so-called ['səʊ'kɔːld] adj cosiddetto/a

soccer ['sɔkəʳ] n calcio

sociable ['səʊʃəbl] adj socievole

social ['səʊʃl] adj sociale ▷ n festa, serata;
socialism n socialismo; **socialist** adj, n
socialista m/f; **socialize** vi: **to socialize**
with socializzare con; **social life** n vita
sociale; **socially** adv socialmente, in
società; **social media** npl social media mpl;
social network n social network m inv;
social networking n il comunicare tramite
social network; **social networking site**
n social network m; **social security** n
previdenza sociale; **social services** npl
servizi mpl sociali; **social work** n servizio
sociale; **social worker** n assistente m/f
sociale

society [sə'saɪətɪ] n società f inv; (club)
società, associazione f; (also: **high ~**) alta
società

sociology [səʊsɪ'ɔlədʒɪ] n sociologia

sock [sɔk] n calzino
socket ['sɔkɪt] n cavità f inv; (of eye) orbita; (BRIT Elec: also: **wall ~**) presa di corrente
soda ['səudə] n (Chem) soda; (also: **~ water**) acqua di seltz; (US: also: **~ pop**) gassosa
sodium ['səudɪəm] n sodio
sofa ['səufə] n sofà m inv; **sofa bed** n divano m letto inv
soft [sɔft] adj (not rough) morbido/a; (not hard) soffice; (not loud) sommesso/a; (not bright) tenue; (kind) gentile; **soft drink** n analcolico; **soft drugs** npl droghe fpl leggere; **soften** ['sɔfn] vt ammorbidire; addolcire; attenuare ▷ vi ammorbidirsi; addolcirsi; attenuarsi; **softly** adv dolcemente; morbidamente; **software** ['sɔftwɛəʳ] n (Comput) software m
soggy ['sɔgɪ] adj inzuppato/a
soil [sɔɪl] n terreno ▷ vt sporcare
solar ['səuləʳ] adj solare; **solar power** n energia solare; **solar system** n sistema m solare
sold [səuld] pt, pp of **sell**
soldier ['səuldʒəʳ] n soldato, militare m
sold out adj (Comm) esaurito/a
sole [səul] n (of foot) pianta (del piede); (of shoe) suola; (fish: pl inv) sogliola ▷ adj solo/a, unico/a; **solely** adv solamente, unicamente; **I will hold you solely responsible** la considererò il solo responsabile
solemn ['sɔləm] adj solenne
solicitor [sə'lɪsɪtəʳ] n (BRIT: for wills etc) ≈ notaio; (in court) ≈ avvocato
solid ['sɔlɪd] adj (not hollow) pieno/a; (strong, sound, reliable, not liquid) solido/a; (meal) sostanzioso/a ▷ n solido
solitary ['sɔlɪtərɪ] adj solitario/a
solitude ['sɔlɪtjuːd] n solitudine f
solo ['səuləu] n assolo; **soloist** n solista m/f
soluble ['sɔljubl] adj solubile
solution [sə'luːʃən] n soluzione f
solve [sɔlv] vt risolvere
solvent ['sɔlvənt] adj (Comm) solvibile ▷ n (Chem) solvente m
sombre, (US) **somber** ['sɔmbəʳ] adj scuro/a; (mood, person) triste

◯ **KEYWORD**

some [sʌm] adj 1 (a certain amount or number of): **some tea/water/cream** del tè/ dell'acqua/della panna; **some children/ apples** dei bambini/delle mele
2 (certain: in contrasts) certo/a; **some people say that …** alcuni dicono che …, certa gente dice che …
3 (unspecified) un/a certo/a, qualche; **some woman was asking for you** una tale

chiedeva di lei; **some day** un giorno; **some day next week** un giorno della prossima settimana
▷ pron 1 (a certain number) alcuni/e, certi/e; **I've got some** (books etc) ne ho alcuni; **some (of them) have been sold** alcuni sono stati venduti
2 (a certain amount) un po'; **I've got some** (money, milk) ne ho un po'; **I've read some of the book** ho letto parte del libro
▷ adv: **some 10 people** circa 10 persone

somebody ['sʌmbədɪ] pron qualcuno
somehow ['sʌmhau] adv in un modo o nell'altro, in qualche modo; (for some reason) per qualche ragione
someone ['sʌmwʌn] pron = **somebody**
someplace ['sʌmpleɪs] adv (US) = **somewhere**
something ['sʌmθɪŋ] pron qualcosa, qualche cosa; **~ nice** qualcosa di bello; **~ to do** qualcosa da fare
sometime ['sʌmtaɪm] adv (in future) una volta o l'altra; (in past): **~ last month** durante il mese scorso; **sometimes** adv qualche volta
somewhat ['sʌmwɔt] adv piuttosto
somewhere ['sʌmwɛəʳ] adv in or da qualche parte
son [sʌn] n figlio
song [sɔŋ] n canzone f
son-in-law ['sʌnɪnlɔː] n genero
soon [suːn] adv presto, fra poco; (early) presto; **~ afterwards** poco dopo; **as ~ as possible** prima possibile; **sooner** adv (time) prima; (preference): **I would sooner do** preferirei fare; **sooner or later** prima o poi
soothe [suːð] vt calmare
sophisticated [sə'fɪstɪkeɪtɪd] adj sofisticato/a; raffinato/a; complesso/a
sophomore ['sɔfəmɔːʳ] n (US) studente/ essa del secondo anno
soprano [sə'prɑːnəu] n (voice) soprano m; (singer) soprano m/f
sorbet ['sɔːbeɪ] n sorbetto
sordid ['sɔːdɪd] adj sordido/a
sore [sɔːʳ] adj (painful) dolorante ▷ n piaga
sorrow ['sɔrəu] n dolore m
sorry ['sɔrɪ] adj spiacente; (condition, excuse) misero/a; **~!** scusa! (or scusi! or scusate!); **to feel ~ for sb** rincrescersi per qn
sort [sɔːt] n specie f, genere m ▷ vt (also: **~ out**) (papers) classificare; ordinare; (letters etc) smistare; (problems) risolvere; (Comput) ordinare
SOS n S.O.S. m inv
so-so ['səusəu] adv così così
sought [sɔːt] pt, pp of **seek**
soul [səul] n anima

sound [saund] *adj* (*healthy*) sano/a; (*safe, not damaged*) solido/a, in buono stato; (*reliable, not superficial*) solido/a; (*sensible*) giudizioso/a, di buon senso ▷ *adv*: ~ **asleep** profondamente addormentato ▷ *n* (*noise*) suono; rumore *m*; (*Geo*) stretto ▷ *vt* (*alarm*) suonare ▷ *vi* suonare; (*fig: seem*) sembrare; **to ~ like** rassomigliare a; **soundtrack** *n* (*of film*) colonna sonora

soup [su:p] *n* minestra; (*clear*) brodo; (*thick*) zuppa

sour ['sauə'] *adj* aspro/a; (*fruit*) acerbo/a; (*milk*) acido/a; (*fig*) arcigno/a, acido/a; **it's ~ grapes** è soltanto invidia

source [sɔ:s] *n* fonte *f*, sorgente *f*; (*fig*) fonte

south [sauθ] *n* sud *m*, meridione *m*, mezzogiorno ▷ *adj* del sud, sud *inv*, meridionale ▷ *adv* verso sud; **South Africa** *n* Sudafrica *m*; **South African** *adj*, *n* sudafricano/a; **South America** *n* Sudamerica *m*, America del sud; **South American** *adj*, *n* sudamericano/a; **southbound** ['sauθbaund] *adj* (*gen*) diretto/a a sud; (*carriageway*) sud *inv*; **southeastern** [sauθ'i:stən] *adj* sudorientale; **southern** ['sʌðən] *adj* del sud, meridionale; (*wall*) esposto/a a sud; **South Korea** *n* Corea *f* del Sud; **South Pole** *n* Polo Sud; **southward(s)** *adv* verso sud; **south-west** *n* sud-ovest *m*; **southwestern** [sauθ'westən] *adj* sudoccidentale

souvenir [su:və'nɪə'] *n* ricordo, souvenir *m inv*

sovereign ['sɔvrɪn] *adj*, *n* sovrano/a

sow¹ [səu] (*pt* **sowed**, *pp* **sown**) *vt* seminare

sow² [sau] *n* scrofa

soya ['sɔɪə], (*US*) **soy** *n*: ~ **bean** seme *m* di soia; ~ **sauce** salsa di soia

spa [spa:] *n* (*resort*) stazione *f* termale; (*US: also*: **health ~**) centro di cure estetiche

space [speɪs] *n* spazio; (*room*) posto; spazio; (*length of time*) intervallo ▷ *cpd* spaziale ▷ *vt* (*also*: ~ **out**) distanziare; **spacecraft** *n* (*pl inv*) veicolo spaziale; **spaceship** *n* astronave *f*, navicella spaziale

spacious ['speɪʃəs] *adj* spazioso/a, ampio/a

spade [speɪd] *n* (*tool*) vanga; pala; (*child's*) paletta; **spades** *npl* (*Cards*) picche *fpl*

spaghetti [spə'gɛtɪ] *n* spaghetti *mpl*

Spain [speɪn] *n* Spagna

spam [spæm] (*Comput*) *n* spamming *m* ▷ *vt*: **to ~ sb** inviare a qn messaggi pubblicitari non richiesti via email

span [spæn] *n* (*of bird, plane*) apertura alare; (*of arch*) campata; (*in time*) periodo; durata ▷ *vt* attraversare; (*fig*) abbracciare

Spaniard ['spænjəd] *n* spagnolo/a

Spanish ['spænɪʃ] *adj* spagnolo/a ▷ *n* (*Ling*) spagnolo; **the ~** *n pl* gli Spagnoli

spank [spæŋk] *vt* sculacciare

spanner ['spænə'] *n* (*BRIT*) chiave *f* inglese

spare [spɛə'] *adj* di riserva, di scorta; (*surplus*) in più, d'avanzo ▷ *n* (*part*) pezzo di ricambio ▷ *vt* (*do without*) fare a meno di; (*afford to give*) concedere; (*refrain from hurting, using*) risparmiare; **to ~** (*surplus*) d'avanzo; **spare part** *n* pezzo di ricambio; **spare room** *n* stanza degli ospiti; **spare time** *n* tempo libero; **spare tyre**, (*US*) **spare tire** *n* (*Aut*) gomma di scorta; **spare wheel** *n* (*Aut*) ruota di scorta

spark [spa:k] *n* scintilla

sparkle ['spa:kl] *n* scintillio, sfavillio ▷ *vi* scintillare, sfavillare

Spark plug *n* candela

sparrow ['spærəu] *n* passero

sparse [spa:s] *adj* sparso/a, rado/a

spasm ['spæzəm] *n* (*Med*) spasmo; (*fig*) accesso, attacco

spat [spæt] *pt*, *pp* of **spit**

spate [speɪt] *n* (*fig*): ~ **of** diluvio *or* fiume *m* di

spatula ['spætjulə] *n* spatola

speak (*pt* **spoke**, *pp* **spoken**) [spi:k, spəuk, 'spəukn] *vt* (*language*) parlare; (*truth*) dire ▷ *vi* parlare; **to ~ to sb/of** *or* **about sth** parlare a qn/di qc; ~ **up!** parli più forte!; **speaker** *n* (*in public*) oratore/trice; (*also*: **loudspeaker**) altoparlante *m*; (*Pol*): **the Speaker** *il presidente della Camera dei Comuni or* (*US*) *dei Rappresentanti*

spear [spɪə'] *n* lancia ▷ *vt* infilzare

special ['spɛʃl] *adj* speciale; **special delivery** *n* (*Post*): **by special delivery** per espresso; **special effects** *npl* (*Cine*) effetti *mpl* speciali; **specialist** *n* specialista *m/f*; **speciality** [spɛʃɪ'ælɪtɪ] *n* specialità *f inv*; **specialize** *vi*: **to specialize (in)** specializzarsi (in); **specially** *adv* specialmente, particolarmente; **special needs** *adj*: **special needs children** bambini *mpl* con difficoltà di apprendimento; **special offer** *n* (*Comm*) offerta speciale; **special school** *n* (*BRIT*) scuola speciale (*per portatori di handicap*); **specialty** *n* (*esp US*) = **speciality**

species ['spi:ʃi:z] *n* (*pl inv*) specie *f inv*

specific [spə'sɪfɪk] *adj* specifico/a; preciso/a; **specifically** *adv* esplicitamente; (*especially*) appositamente

specify ['spɛsɪfaɪ] *vt* specificare, precisare; **unless otherwise specified** salvo indicazioni contrarie

specimen ['spɛsɪmən] *n* esemplare *m*, modello; (*Med*) campione *m*

speck [spɛk] *n* puntino, macchiolina; (*particle*) granello

spectacle ['spɛktəkl] n spettacolo;
spectacles npl occhiali mpl; **spectacular**
[spɛk'tækjuləʳ] adj spettacolare

spectator [spɛk'teɪtəʳ] n spettatore/trice

spectrum (pl **spectra**) ['spɛktrəm, -rə] n
spettro

speculate ['spɛkjuleɪt] vi speculare; (try to
guess): **to ~ about** fare ipotesi su

sped [spɛd] pt, pp of **speed**

speech [spiːtʃ] n (faculty) parola; (talk,
Theat) discorso; (manner of speaking) parlata;
speechless adj ammutolito/a, muto/a

speed [spiːd] n velocità f inv; (promptness)
prontezza; **at full or top ~** a tutta velocità;
speed up vi, vt accelerare; **speedboat** n
motoscafo; **speeding** n (Aut) eccesso di
velocità; **speed limit** n limite m di velocità;
speedometer [spɪ'dɔmɪtəʳ] n tachimetro;
speedy adj veloce, rapido/a; (reply)
pronto/a

spell [spɛl] n (also: **magic ~**) incantesimo;
(period of time) (breve) periodo ▷ vt (pt, pp
spelt or **spelled**) (in writing) scrivere (lettera
per lettera); (aloud) dire lettera per lettera;
(fig) significare; **to cast a ~ on sb** fare un
incantesimo a qn; **he can't ~** fa errori di
ortografia; **spell out** vt (letter by letter)
dettare lettera per lettera; (explain): **to ~
sth out for sb** spiegare qc a qn per filo e per
segno; **spellchecker** ['spɛltʃɛkəʳ] n
correttore m ortografico; **spelling** n
ortografia

spelt [spɛlt] pt, pp of **spell**

spend (pt, pp **spent**) [spɛnd, spɛnt] vt
(money) spendere; (time, life) passare;
spending ['spɛndɪŋ] n: **government
spending** spesa pubblica

spent [spɛnt] pt, pp of **spend**

sperm [spəːm] n sperma m

sphere [sfɪəʳ] n sfera

spice [spaɪs] n spezia ▷ vt aromatizzare

spicy ['spaɪsɪ] adj piccante

spider ['spaɪdəʳ] n ragno

spike [spaɪk] n punta

spill (pt, pp **spilt** or **spilled**) [spɪl, -t, -d] vt
versare, rovesciare ▷ vi versarsi, rovesciarsi

spin [spɪn] (pt, pp **spun**) n (revolution of
wheel) rotazione f; (Aviat) avvitamento; (trip
in car) giretto ▷ vt (wool etc) filare; (wheel) far
girare ▷ vi girare

spinach ['spɪnɪtʃ] n spinacio; (as food)
spinaci mpl

spinal ['spaɪnl] adj spinale

spin doctor n (col) esperto di comunicazioni
responsabile dell'immagine di un partito
politico

spin-dryer [spɪn'draɪəʳ] n (BRIT)
centrifuga

spine [spaɪn] n spina dorsale; (thorn) spina

spiral ['spaɪərl] n spirale f ▷ vi (prices) salire
vertiginosamente

spire ['spaɪəʳ] n guglia

spirit ['spɪrɪt] n spirito; (ghost) spirito,
fantasma m; (mood) stato d'animo, umore
m; (courage) coraggio; **spirits** npl (drink)
alcolici mpl; **in good ~s** di buon umore

spiritual ['spɪrɪtjuəl] adj spirituale

spit [spɪt] n (for roasting) spiedo; (spittle)
sputo; (saliva) saliva ▷ vi (pt, pp **spat** [spæt])
sputare; (fire, fat) scoppiettare

spite [spaɪt] n dispetto ▷ vt contrariare, far
dispetto a; **in ~ of** nonostante, malgrado;
spiteful adj dispettoso/a

splash [splæʃ] n spruzzo; (sound) tonfo;
(of colour) schizzo ▷ vt spruzzare ▷ vi (also:
~ about) sguazzare; **splash out** (col) vi
(BRIT) fare spese folli

splendid ['splɛndɪd] adj splendido/a,
magnifico/a

splinter ['splɪntəʳ] n scheggia ▷ vi
scheggiarsi

split [splɪt] (pt, pp **split**) n spaccatura; (fig:
division, quarrel) scissione f ▷ vt spaccare;
(party) dividere; (work, profits) spartire,
ripartire ▷ vi (divide) dividersi; **split up**
vi (couple) separarsi, rompere; (meeting)
sciogliersi

spoil (pt, pp **spoilt** or **spoiled**) [spɔɪl, -t,
-d] vt (damage) rovinare, guastare; (mar)
sciupare; (child) viziare

spoilt [spɔɪlt] pt, pp of **spoil**

spoke [spəuk] pt of **speak** ▷ n raggio

spoken ['spəukn] pp of **speak**

spokesman ['spəuksmən] n (irreg)
portavoce m inv

spokesperson ['spəukspəːsn] n portavoce
m/f

spokeswoman ['spəukswumən] n (irreg)
portavoce f inv

sponge [spʌndʒ] n spugna; (also: **~ cake**)
pan m di Spagna ▷ vt spugnare, pulire con
una spugna ▷ vi: **to ~ on or off** scroccare a;
sponge bag n (BRIT) nécessaire m inv

sponsor ['spɔnsəʳ] n (Radio, TV, Sport etc)
sponsor m inv; (of enterprise, bill) promotore/
trice ▷ vt sponsorizzare; (bill) presentare;
sponsorship n sponsorizzazione f

spontaneous [spɔn'teɪnɪəs] adj
spontaneo/a

spooky ['spuːkɪ] adj (col) che fa
accapponare la pelle

spoon [spuːn] n cucchiaio; **spoonful** n
cucchiaiata

sport [spɔːt] n sport m inv; (person) persona
di spirito ▷ vt sfoggiare; **sport jacket**
n (US) = **sports jacket**; **sports car** n
automobile f sportiva; **sports centre** n
(BRIT) centro sportivo; **sports jacket** n

(BRIT) giacca sportiva; **sportsman** n (irreg) sportivo; **sportswear** n abiti mpl sportivi; **sportswoman** n (irreg) sportiva; **sporty** adj sportivo/a

spot [spɔt] n punto; (mark) macchia; (dot: on pattern) pallino; (pimple) foruncolo; (place) posto; (Radio, TV) spot m inv; (small amount): **a ~ of** un po' di ▷ vt (notice) individuare, distinguere; **on the ~** sul posto; **to do sth on the ~** fare qc immediatamente or su due piedi; **to put sb on the ~** mettere qn in difficoltà; **spotless** adj immacolato/a; **spotlight** n proiettore m; (Aut) faro ausiliario

spouse [spauz] n sposo/a

sprain [spreɪn] n storta, distorsione f ▷ vt: **to ~ one's ankle** storcersi una caviglia

sprang [spræŋ] pt of **spring**

sprawl [sprɔːl] vi sdraiarsi (in modo scomposto); (place) estendersi (disordinatamente)

spray [spreɪ] n spruzzo; (container) nebulizzatore m, spray m inv; (of flowers) mazzetto ▷ vt spruzzare; (crops) irrorare

spread [sprɛd] (pt, pp **spread**) n diffusione f; (distribution) distribuzione f; (Culin) pasta (da spalmare); (col: food) banchetto ▷ vt (cloth) stendere, distendere; (butter etc) spalmare; (disease, knowledge) propagare, diffondere ▷ vi stendersi, distendersi; spalmarsi; propagarsi, diffondersi; **spread out** vi (move apart) separarsi; **spreadsheet** n foglio elettronico

spree [spriː] n: **to go on a ~** fare baldoria

spring [sprɪŋ] n (leap) salto, balzo; (coiled metal) molla; (season) primavera; (of water) sorgente f ▷ vi (pt **sprang**, pp **sprung**) saltare, balzare; **spring up** vi (problem) presentarsi; **spring onion** n (BRIT) cipollina

sprinkle ['sprɪŋkl] vt spruzzare; spargere; **to ~ water etc on, ~ with water** etc spruzzare dell'acqua etc su

sprint [sprɪnt] n scatto ▷ vi scattare

sprung [sprʌŋ] pp of **spring**

spun [spʌn] pt, pp of **spin**

spur [spəː'] n sperone m; (fig) sprone m, incentivo ▷ vt (also: **~ on**) spronare; **on the ~ of the moment** lì per lì

spurt [spəːt] n (of water) getto; (of energy) esplosione f ▷ vi sgorgare

spy [spaɪ] n spia ▷ vi: **to ~ on** spiare ▷ vt (see) scorgere

sq. abbr = **square**

squabble ['skwɔbl] vi bisticciarsi

squad [skwɔd] n (Mil) plotone m; (Police) squadra

squadron ['skwɔdrn] n (Mil) squadrone m; (Aviat, Naut) squadriglia

squander ['skwɔndə'] vt dissipare

square [skwɛə'] n quadrato; (in town) piazza ▷ adj quadrato/a; (col: ideas, person) di vecchio stampo ▷ vt (arrange) regolare; (Math) elevare al quadrato; (reconcile) conciliare; **a ~ meal** un pasto abbondante; **2 metres ~** di 2 metri per 2; **1 ~ metre** 1 metro quadrato; **all ~** pari; **square root** n radice f quadrata

squash [skwɔʃ] n (vegetable) zucca; (Sport) squash m; **lemon/orange ~** (BRIT) sciroppo di limone/arancia ▷ vt schiacciare

squat [skwɔt] adj tarchiato/a, tozzo/a ▷ vi accovacciarsi; **squatter** n occupante m/f abusivo/a

squeak [skwiːk] vi squittire

squeal [skwiːl] vi strillare

squeeze [skwiːz] n pressione f; (also Econ) stretta ▷ vt premere; (hand, arm) stringere

squid [skwɪd] n calamaro

squint [skwɪnt] vi essere strabico/a ▷ n: **he has a ~** è strabico

squirm [skwəːm] vi contorcersi

squirrel ['skwɪrəl] n scoiattolo

squirt [skwəːt] vi schizzare; zampillare ▷ vt spruzzare

Sr abbr = **senior; sister**

Sri Lanka [srɪ'læŋkə] n Sri Lanka m

St abbr = **saint; street**

stab [stæb] n (with knife etc) pugnalata; (of pain) fitta; (col: try): **to have a ~ at (doing) sth** provare a fare qc ▷ vt pugnalare

stability [stə'bɪlɪtɪ] n stabilità

stable ['steɪbl] n (for horses) scuderia; (for cattle) stalla ▷ adj stabile

stack [stæk] n catasta, pila ▷ vt accatastare, ammucchiare

stadium ['steɪdɪəm] n stadio

staff [stɑːf] n (work force: gen) personale m; (: BRIT Scol) personale insegnante ▷ vt fornire di personale

stag [stæg] n cervo

stage [steɪdʒ] n (platform) palco; palcoscenico; **the ~** il teatro, la scena; (point) fase f, stadio ▷ vt (play) allestire, mettere in scena; (demonstration) organizzare; **in ~s** per gradi; a tappe

stagger ['stægə'] vi barcollare ▷ vt (person) sbalordire; (hours, holidays) scaglionare; **staggering** adj (amazing) sbalorditivo/a

stagnant ['stægnənt] adj stagnante

stag night, stag party n festa di addio al celibato

stain [steɪn] n macchia; (colouring) colorante m ▷ vt macchiare; (wood) tingere; **stained glass** [,steɪnd'glɑːs] n vetro colorato; **stainless** adj (steel) inossidabile

stair [stɛə'] n (step) gradino; **stairs** npl (flight of stairs) scale fpl, scala

staircase ['steəkeɪs], **stairway** ['steəweɪ] *n* scale *fpl*, scala

stake [steɪk] *n* palo, piolo; (*Comm*) interesse *m*; (*Betting*) puntata, scommessa ▷ *vt* (*bet*) scommettere; (*risk*) rischiare; **to be at ~** essere in gioco

stale [steɪl] *adj* (*bread*) raffermo/a; (*food*) stantio/a; (*air*) viziato/a; (*beer*) svaporato/a; (*smell*) di chiuso

stalk [stɔ:k] *n* gambo, stelo ▷ *vt* inseguire

stall [stɔ:l] *n* bancarella; (*in stable*) box *m inv* di stalla ▷ *vt* (*Aut*) far spegnere; (*fig*) bloccare ▷ *vi* (*Aut*) spegnersi, fermarsi; (*fig*) temporeggiare

stamina ['stæmɪnə] *n* vigore *m*, resistenza

stammer ['stæməʳ] *n* balbuzie *f* ▷ *vi* balbettare

stamp [stæmp] *n* (*postage stamp*) francobollo; (*implement*) timbro; (*mark, also fig*) marchio, impronta; (*on document*) bollo; timbro ▷ *vi* (*also:* **~ one's foot**) battere il piede ▷ *vt* battere; (*letter*) affrancare; (*mark with a stamp*) timbrare; **~ed addressed envelope** busta affrancata per la risposta; **stamp out** *vt* (*fire*) estinguere; (*crime*) eliminare; (*opposition*) soffocare

▎Be careful not to translate *stamp* by the Italian word *stampa*.

stampede [stæm'pi:d] *n* fuggi fuggi *m inv*

stance [stæns] *n* posizione *f*

stand [stænd] (*pt, pp* **stood**) *n* (*position*) posizione *f*; (*for taxis*) posteggio; (*structure*) supporto, sostegno; (*at exhibition*) stand *m inv*; (*in shop*) banco; (*at market*) bancarella; (*booth*) chiosco; (*Sport*) tribuna ▷ *vi* stare in piedi; (*rise*) alzarsi in piedi; (*be placed*) trovarsi ▷ *vt* (*place*) mettere, porre; (*tolerate, withstand*) resistere, sopportare; **to make a ~** prendere posizione; **to ~ for parliament** (*BRIT*) presentarsi come candidato (per il parlamento); **to ~ sb a drink/meal** offrire da bere/un pranzo a qn; **stand back** *vi* prendere le distanze; **stand by** *vi* (*be ready*) tenersi pronto/a ▷ *vt fus* (*opinion*) sostenere; **stand down** *vi* (*withdraw*) ritirarsi; **stand for** *vt fus* (*signify*) rappresentare, significare; (*tolerate*) sopportare, tollerare; **stand in for** *vt fus* sostituire; **stand out** *vi* (*be prominent*) spiccare; **stand up** *vi* (*rise*) alzarsi in piedi; **stand up for** *vt fus* difendere; **stand up to** *vt fus* tener testa a, resistere a

standard ['stændəd] *n* modello, standard *m inv*; (*level*) livello; (*flag*) stendardo ▷ *adj* (*size etc*) normale, standard *inv*; **standards** *npl* (*morals*) principi *mpl*, valori *mpl*; **~ of living** livello di vita

stand-by ['stændbaɪ] *n* riserva, sostituto; **to be on ~** (*gen*) tenersi pronto/a; (*doctor*) essere di guardia; **stand-by ticket** *n* (*Aviat*) biglietto senza garanzia

standing ['stændɪŋ] *adj* diritto/a, in piedi; (*permanent*) permanente ▷ *n* rango, condizione *f*, posizione *f*: **of many years' ~** che esiste da molti anni; **standing order** *n* (*BRIT: at bank*) ordine *m* di pagamento (permanente)

stand: standpoint ['stændpɔɪnt] *n* punto di vista; **standstill** ['stændstɪl] *n*: **at a standstill** fermo/a; (*fig*) a un punto morto; **to come to a standstill** fermarsi; giungere a un punto morto

stank [stæŋk] *pt of* **stink**

staple ['steɪpl] *n* (*for papers*) graffetta ▷ *adj* (*food etc*) di base ▷ *vt* cucire

star [stɑ:ʳ] *n* stella; (*celebrity*) divo/a ▷ *vi*: **to ~ (in)** essere il (or la) protagonista (di) ▷ *vt* (*Cine*) essere interpretato/a da; **the stars** *npl* (*Astrology*) le stelle

starboard ['stɑ:bəd] *n* dritta

starch [stɑ:tʃ] *n* amido

stardom ['stɑ:dəm] *n* celebrità

stare [steəʳ] *n* sguardo fisso ▷ *vi*: **to ~ at** fissare

stark [stɑ:k] *adj* (*bleak*) desolato/a ▷ *adv*: **~ naked** completamente nudo/a

start [stɑ:t] *n* inizio; (*of race*) partenza; (*sudden movement*) sobbalzo; (*advantage*) vantaggio ▷ *vt* cominciare, iniziare; (*car*) mettere in moto ▷ *vi* cominciare; (*on journey*) partire, mettersi in viaggio; (*jump*) sobbalzare; **to ~ doing sth** (in)cominciare a fare qc; **start off** *vi* cominciare; (*leave*) partire; **start out** *vi* (*begin*) cominciare; (*set out*) partire; **start up** *vi* cominciare; (*car*) avviarsi ▷ *vt* iniziare; (*car*) avviare; **starter** *n* (*Aut*) motorino d'avviamento; (*Sport: official*) starter *m inv*; (*BRIT Culin*) primo piatto; **starting point** *n* punto di partenza

startle ['stɑ:tl] *vt* far trasalire; **startling** *adj* sorprendente

starvation [stɑ:'veɪʃən] *n* fame *f*, inedia

starve [stɑ:v] *vi* morire di fame; soffrire la fame ▷ *vt* far morire di fame, affamare

state [steɪt] *n* stato ▷ *vt* dichiarare, affermare; annunciare; **to be in a ~** essere agitato/a; **statement** *n* dichiarazione *f*; **States** *npl*: **the States** (*USA*) gli Stati Uniti; **state school** *n* scuola statale; **statesman** *n* (*irreg*) statista *m*

static ['stætɪk] *n* (*Radio*) scariche *fpl* ▷ *adj* statico/a

station ['steɪʃən] *n* stazione *f* ▷ *vt* collocare, disporre

stationary ['steɪʃənərɪ] *adj* fermo/a, immobile

stationer ['steɪʃənəʳ] *n* cartolaio/a; **~'s shop** cartoleria

stationery ['steɪʃənərɪ] n articoli mpl di cancelleria

station wagon n (US) giardinetta

statistic [stə'tɪstɪk] n statistica; **statistics** n (science) statistica

statue ['stætjuː] n statua

stature ['stætʃəʳ] n statura

status ['steɪtəs] n posizione f, condizione f sociale; (prestige) prestigio; (legal, marital) stato; **status quo** [-'kwəu] n: **the status quo** lo statu quo

statutory ['stætjutərɪ] adj stabilito/a dalla legge, statutario/a

staunch [stɔːntʃ] adj fidato/a, leale

stay [steɪ] n (period of time) soggiorno, permanenza ▷ vi rimanere; (reside) alloggiare, stare; (spend some time) trattenersi, soggiornare; **to ~ put** non muoversi; **to ~ the night** passare la notte; **stay away** vi (from person, building) stare lontano (**from** da); (from event) non andare (**from** a); **stay behind** vi restare indietro; **stay in** vi (at home) stare in casa; **stay on** vi restare, rimanere; **stay out** vi (of house) rimanere fuori (di casa); **stay up** vi (at night) rimanere alzato/a

steadily ['stɛdɪlɪ] adv (firmly) saldamente; (constantly) continuamente; (fixedly) fisso; (walk) con passo sicuro

steady ['stɛdɪ] adj (not wobbling) fermo/a; (regular) costante; (person, character) serio/a; (: calm) calmo/a, tranquillo/a ▷ vt stabilizzare; calmare

steak [steɪk] n (meat) bistecca; (fish) trancia

steal (pt **stole**, pp **stolen**) [stiːl, stəul, 'stəuln] vt rubare ▷ vi rubare; (move) muoversi furtivamente

steam [stiːm] n vapore m ▷ vt (Culin) cuocere a vapore ▷ vi fumare; **steam up** vi (window) appannarsi; **to get ~ed up about sth** (fig) andare in bestia per qc; **steamy** adj (room) pieno/a di vapore; (window) appannato/a

steel [stiːl] n acciaio ▷ cpd di acciaio

steep [stiːp] adj ripido/a, scosceso/a; (price) eccessivo/a ▷ vt inzuppare; (washing) mettere a mollo

steeple ['stiːpl] n campanile m

steer [stɪəʳ] vt guidare ▷ vi (Naut: person) governare; (car) guidarsi; **steering** n (Aut) sterzo; **steering wheel** n volante m

stem [stɛm] n (of flower, plant) stelo; (of tree) fusto; (of glass) gambo; (of fruit, leaf) picciolo ▷ vt contenere, arginare; **stem cell** n cellula staminale

step [stɛp] n passo; (stair) gradino, scalino; (action) mossa, azione f ▷ vi: **to ~ forward/back** fare un passo avanti/indietro; **steps** npl (BRIT) = **stepladder**; **to be in/out of ~**

with stare/non stare al passo con; **step down** vi (fig) ritirarsi; **step in** vi fare il proprio ingresso; **step up** vt aumentare; intensificare; **stepbrother** n fratellastro; **stepchild** n figliastro/a; **stepdaughter** n figliastra; **stepfather** n patrigno; **stepladder** n scala a libretto; **stepmother** n matrigna; **stepsister** n sorellastra; **stepson** n figliastro

stereo ['stɛrɪəu] n (system) sistema m stereofonico; (record player) stereo m inv ▷ adj (also: **~phonic**) stereofonico/a

stereotype ['stɪərɪətaɪp] n stereotipo

sterile ['stɛraɪl] adj sterile; **sterilize** ['stɛrɪlaɪz] vt sterilizzare

sterling ['stɜːlɪŋ] adj (gold, silver) di buona lega ▷ n (Econ) (lira) sterlina; **a pound ~** una lira sterlina

stern [stɜːn] adj severo/a ▷ n (Naut) poppa

steroid ['stɪərɔɪd] n steroide m

stew [stjuː] n stufato ▷ vt cuocere in umido

steward ['stjuːəd] n (Aviat, Naut, Rail) steward m inv; (in club etc) dispensiere m; **stewardess** n assistente f di volo, hostess f inv

stick [stɪk] (pt, pp **stuck**) n bastone m; (of rhubarb, celery) gambo; (of dynamite) candelotto ▷ vt (glue) attaccare; (thrust): **to ~ sth into** conficcare or piantare or infiggere qc in; (col: put) ficcare; (: tolerate) sopportare ▷ vi attaccarsi; (remain) restare, rimanere; **stick out** vi sporgere, spuntare; **stick up** vi sporgere, spuntare; **stick up for** vt fus difendere; **sticker** n cartellino adesivo; **sticking plaster** n cerotto adesivo; **stick insect** n insetto in stecco inv; **stick shift** n (US Aut) cambio manuale

sticky ['stɪkɪ] adj attaccaticcio/a, vischioso/a; (label) adesivo/a; (fig: situation) difficile

stiff [stɪf] adj rigido/a, duro/a; (muscle) legato/a, indolenzito/a; (difficult) difficile, arduo/a; (cold) freddo/a, formale; (strong) forte; (high: price) molto alto/a ▷ adv: **bored ~** annoiato/a a morte

stifling ['staɪflɪŋ] adj (heat) soffocante

stigma ['stɪgmə] n stigma m

stiletto [stɪ'lɛtəu] n (BRIT: also: **~ heel**) tacco a spillo

still [stɪl] adj fermo/a; (quiet) silenzioso/a ▷ adv (up to this time, even) ancora; (nonetheless) tuttavia, ciò nonostante

stimulate ['stɪmjuleɪt] vt stimolare

stimulus (pl **stimuli**) ['stɪmjuləs, 'stɪmjulaɪ] n stimolo

sting [stɪŋ] (pt, pp **stung**) n puntura; (organ) pungiglione m ▷ vt pungere

stink [stɪŋk] n fetore m, puzzo ▷ vi (pt **stank**, pp **stunk**) puzzare

stir [stə:ʳ] *n* agitazione *f*, clamore *m* ▷ *vt* mescolare; (*fig*) risvegliare ▷ *vi* muoversi; **stir up** *vt* provocare, suscitare; **stir-fry** *vt* saltare in padella ▷ *n* pietanza al salto

stitch [stɪtʃ] *n* (*Sewing*) punto; (*Knitting*) maglia; (*Med*) punto (di sutura); (*pain*) fitta ▷ *vt* cucire, attaccare; suturare

stock [stɔk] *n* riserva, provvista; (*Comm*) giacenza, stock *m inv*; (*Agr*) bestiame *m*; (*Culin*) brodo; (*Finance*) titoli *mpl*, azioni *fpl*; (*descent, origin*) stirpe *f* ▷ *adj* (*fig: reply etc*) consueto/a, classico/a ▷ *vt* (*have in stock*) avere, vendere; **to have sth in ~** avere qc in magazzino; **out of ~** esaurito/a; **~s and shares** valori *mpl* di borsa; **stockbroker** ['stɔkbrəukəʳ] *n* agente *m* di cambio; **stock cube** *n* (*BRIT*) dado; **stock exchange** *n* Borsa (valori); **stockholder** ['stɔkhəuldəʳ] *n* (*Finance*) azionista *m/f*

stocking ['stɔkɪŋ] *n* calza

stock market *n* Borsa, mercato finanziario

stole [stəul] *pt of* **steal** ▷ *n* stola

stolen ['stəuln] *pp of* **steal**

stomach ['stʌmək] *n* stomaco; (*belly*) pancia ▷ *vt* sopportare, digerire; **stomach ache** *n* mal *m* di stomaco

stone [stəun] *n* pietra; (*pebble*) sasso, ciottolo; (*in fruit*) nocciolo; (*Med*) calcolo; (*BRIT: weight*) 6.348 *kg*; 14 *libbre* ▷ *cpd* di pietra ▷ *vt* lapidare; (*fruit*) togliere il nocciolo a

stood [stud] *pt, pp of* **stand**

stool [stu:l] *n* sgabello

stoop [stu:p] *vi* (*also:* **have a ~**) avere una curvatura; (*also:* **~ down**) chinarsi, curvarsi

stop [stɔp] *n* arresto; (*stopping place*) fermata; (*in punctuation*) punto ▷ *vt* arrestare, fermare; (*break off*) interrompere; (*also:* **put a ~ to**) porre fine a ▷ *vi* fermarsi; (*rain, noise etc*) cessare, finire; **to ~ doing sth** cessare or finire di fare qc; **to ~ dead** fermarsi di colpo; **stop by** *vi* passare, fare un salto; **stop off** *vi* sostare brevemente; **stopover** *n* breve sosta; (*Aviat*) scalo; **stoppage** ['stɔpɪdʒ] *n* arresto, fermata; (*of pay*) trattenuta; (*strike*) interruzione *f* del lavoro

storage ['stɔ:rɪdʒ] *n* immagazzinamento

store [stɔ:ʳ] *n* provvista, riserva; (*depot*) deposito; (*BRIT: department store*) grande magazzino; (*US: shop*) negozio ▷ *vt* immagazzinare; **in ~** di riserva; in serbo; **storekeeper** *n* (*US*) negoziante *m/f*

storey, (*US*) **story** ['stɔ:rɪ] *n* piano

storm [stɔ:m] *n* tempesta; temporale *m*, burrasca; uragano; (*fig*) infuriarsi ▷ *vt* prendere d'assalto; **stormy** *adj* tempestoso/a, burrascoso/a

story ['stɔ:rɪ] *n* storia; favola; racconto; (*US*) = **storey**

stout [staut] *adj* solido/a, robusto/a; (*supporter*) tenace; (*fat*) corpulento/a, grasso/a ▷ *n* birra scura

stove [stəuv] *n* (*for cooking*) fornello; (: *small*) fornelletto; (*for heating*) stufa

straight [streɪt] *adj* dritto/a; (*frank*) onesto/a, franco/a; (*plain, uncomplicated*) semplice ▷ *adv* diritto; (*drink*) liscio; **to put** *or* **get ~** mettere in ordine, mettere ordine in; **~ away**, **~ off** (*at once*) immediatamente; **straighten** *vt* (*also:* **straighten out**) raddrizzare; **straighteners** ['streɪtnəz] *npl* (*for hair*) piastra *f* per capelli; **straightforward** *adj* semplice; (*frank*) onesto/a, franco/a

strain [streɪn] *n* (*Tech*) sollecitazione *f*; (*physical*) sforzo; (*mental*) tensione *f*; (*Med*) strappo; distorsione *f*; (*streak, trace*) tendenza; elemento ▷ *vt* tendere; (*muscle*) stirare; (*ankle*) slogar; (*resources*) pesare su; (*food*) colare; passare; **strained** *adj* (*muscle*) stirato/a; (*laugh etc*) forzato/a; (*relations*) teso/a; **strainer** *n* passino, colino

strait [streɪt] *n* (*Geo*) stretto; **straits** *npl*: **to be in dire ~s** (*fig*) essere nei guai

strand [strænd] *n* (*of thread*) filo; **stranded** *adj* nei guai; senza mezzi di trasporto

strange [streɪndʒ] *adj* (*not known*) sconosciuto/a; (*odd*) strano/a, bizzarro/a; **strangely** *adv* stranamente; **stranger** *n* sconosciuto/a; (*from another place*) estraneo/a

strangle ['stræŋgl] *vt* strangolare

strap [stræp] *n* cinghia; (*of slip, dress*) spallina, bretella

strategic [strə'ti:dʒɪk] *adj* strategico/a

strategy ['strætɪdʒɪ] *n* strategia

straw [strɔ:] *n* paglia; (*drinking straw*) cannuccia; **that's the last ~!** è la goccia che fa traboccare il vaso!

strawberry ['strɔ:bərɪ] *n* fragola

stray [streɪ] *adj* (*animal*) randagio/a; (*bullet*) vagante; (*scattered*) sparso/a ▷ *vi* perdersi

streak [stri:k] *n* striscia; (*of hair*) mèche *f inv* ▷ *vt* striare, screziare ▷ *vi*: **to ~ past** passare come un fulmine

stream [stri:m] *n* ruscello; corrente *f*; (*of people, smoke etc*) fiume *m* ▷ *vt* (*Scol*) dividere in livelli di rendimento ▷ *vi* scorrere; **to ~ in/out** entrare/uscire a fiotti

street [stri:t] *n* strada, via; **streetcar** *n* (*US*) tram *m inv*; **street light** *n* lampione *m*; **street map** *n* pianta (di una città); **street plan** *n* pianta (di una città)

strength [streŋθ] *n* forza; **strengthen** *vt* rinforzare; fortificare; (*economy, currency*) consolidare

strenuous ['strɛnjuəs] adj vigoroso/a, energico/a; (tiring) duro/a, pesante

stress [strɛs] n (force, pressure) pressione f; (mental strain) tensione f; (accent) accento ▷ vt insistere su, sottolineare; accentare; **stressed** adj (tense: person) stressato/a; (Ling, Poetry: syllable) accentato/a; **stressful** adj (job) difficile, stressante

stretch [strɛtʃ] n (of sand etc) distesa ▷ vi stirarsi; (extend): **to ~ to** or **as far as** estendersi fino a ▷ vt tendere, allungare; (spread) distendere (al massimo); **stretch out** vi allungarsi, estendersi ▷ vt (arm etc) allungare, tendere; (spread) distendere

stretcher ['strɛtʃə'] n barella, lettiga

strict [strɪkt] adj (severe) rigido/a, severo/a; (precise) preciso/a, stretto/a; **strictly** adv severamente; rigorosamente; strettamente

stride [straɪd] n passo lungo ▷ vi (pt **strode**, pp **stridden**) camminare a grandi passi

strike [straɪk] (pt, pp **struck**) n sciopero; (of oil etc) scoperta; (attack) attacco m ▷ vt colpire; (oil etc) scoprire, trovare; (bargain) fare; (fig): **the thought** or **it ~s me that …** mi viene in mente che … ▷ vi scioperare; (attack) attaccare; (clock) suonare; **on ~** (workers) in sciopero; **to go on** or **come out on ~** mettersi in sciopero; **to ~ a match** accendere un fiammifero; **striker** n scioperante m/f; (Sport) attaccante m; **striking** adj impressionante

string [strɪŋ] n spago; (row) fila; sequenza; catena; (Mus) corda ▷ vt (pt, pp **strung**): **to ~ out** disporre di fianco; **to ~ together** (words, ideas) mettere insieme; **the strings** npl (Mus) gli archi; **to pull ~s for sb** (fig) raccomandare qn

strip [strɪp] n striscia ▷ vt spogliare; (paint) togliere; (also: **~ down**) (machine) smontare ▷ vi spogliarsi; **strip off** vt (paint etc) staccare ▷ vi (person) spogliarsi

stripe [straɪp] n striscia, riga; (Mil, Police) gallone m; **striped** adj a strisce or righe

stripper ['strɪpə'] n spogliarellista m/f

strip-search ['strɪpsə:tʃ] vt: **to ~ sb** perquisire qn facendolo/a spogliare ▷ n perquisizione f (facendo spogliare il perquisito)

strive (pt **strove**, pp **striven**) [straɪv, strəuv, 'strɪvn] vi: **to ~ to do** sforzarsi di fare

strode [strəud] pt of **stride**

stroke [strəuk] n colpo; (Med) colpo apoplettico; (Swimming) bracciata; (: style) stile m ▷ vt accarezzare; **at a ~** in un attimo

stroll [strəul] n giretto, passeggiatina ▷ vi andare a spasso; **stroller** n (us) passeggino

strong [strɒŋ] adj (gen) forte; (sturdy: table, fabric etc) robusto/a; **they are 50 ~** sono in 50; **stronghold** n (also fig) roccaforte f; **strongly** adv fortemente, con forza; energicamente

strove [strəuv] pt of **strive**

struck [strʌk] pt, pp of **strike**

structure ['strʌktʃə'] n struttura; (building) costruzione f, fabbricato

struggle ['strʌgl] n lotta ▷ vi lottare

strung [strʌŋ] pt, pp of **string**

stub [stʌb] n mozzicone m; (of ticket etc) matrice f, talloncino ▷ vt: **to ~ one's toe (on sth)** urtare or sbattere il dito del piede (contro qc); **stub out** vt schiacciare

stubble ['stʌbl] n stoppia; (on chin) barba ispida

stubborn ['stʌbən] adj testardo/a, ostinato/a

stuck [stʌk] pt, pp of **stick** ▷ adj (jammed) bloccato/a

stud [stʌd] n bottoncino; borchia; (also: **~ earring**) orecchino a pressione (of horses) scuderia, allevamento di cavalli; (also: **~ horse**) stallone m ▷ vt (fig): **~ded with** tempestato/a di

student ['stju:dənt] n studente/essa ▷ cpd studentesco/a; universitario/a; degli studenti; **student driver** n (us) conducente m/f principiante; **students' union** n (BRIT: association) circolo universitario; (: building) sede f del circolo universitario

studio ['stju:dɪəu] n studio; **studio flat**, (us) **studio apartment** n monolocale m

study ['stʌdɪ] n studio ▷ vt studiare; esaminare ▷ vi studiare

stuff [stʌf] n (substance) materiale m; (belongings) roba ▷ vt imbottire; (animal: for exhibition) impagliare; (Culin) farcire; (col: push) ficcare; **stuffing** n imbottitura; (Culin) ripieno; **stuffy** adj (room) mal ventilato/a, senz'aria; (ideas) antiquato/a

stumble ['stʌmbl] vi inciampare; **to ~ across** (fig) imbattersi in

stump [stʌmp] n ceppo; (of limb) moncone m ▷ vt: **to be ~ed** essere sconcertato/a

stun [stʌn] vt stordire; (amaze) sbalordire

stung [stʌŋ] pt, pp of **sting**

stunk [stʌŋk] pp of **stink**

stunned [stʌnd] adj (from blow) stordito/a; (amazed, shocked) sbalordito/a

stunning ['stʌnɪŋ] adj sbalorditivo/a; (girl, dress) stupendo/a

stunt [stʌnt] n bravata; trucco pubblicitario

stupid ['stju:pɪd] adj stupido/a; **stupidity** [stju:'pɪdɪtɪ] n stupidità f inv, stupidaggine f

sturdy ['stəːdɪ] adj robusto/a, vigoroso/a; solido/a

stutter ['stʌtər] n balbuzie f ▷ vi balbettare

style [staɪl] n stile m; (distinction) eleganza, classe f; **stylish** adj elegante; **stylist** n: **hair stylist** parrucchiere/a

sub... [sʌb] prefix sub..., sotto...; **subconscious** adj, n subcosciente m

subdued [səb'djuːd] adj pacato/a; (light) attenuato/a

subject n ['sʌbdʒɪkt] soggetto; (citizen etc) cittadino/a; (Scol) materia ▷ vt [səb'dʒɛkt]: **to ~ to** sottomettere a; esporre a; **to be ~ to** (law) essere sottomesso/a a; (disease) essere soggetto/a a; **subjective** [səb'dʒɛktɪv] adj soggettivo/a; **subject matter** n argomento; contenuto

subjunctive [səb'dʒʌŋktɪv] adj congiuntivo/a ▷ n congiuntivo

submarine [sʌbmə'riːn] n sommergibile m

submission [səb'mɪʃən] n sottomissione f; (to committee etc) richiesta

submit [səb'mɪt] vt sottomettere ▷ vi sottomettersi

subordinate [sə'bɔːdɪnət] adj, n subordinato/a

subscribe [səb'skraɪb] vi contribuire; **to ~ to** (opinion) approvare, condividere; (fund) sottoscrivere a; (newspaper) abbonarsi a; essere abbonato/a a

subscription [səb'skrɪpʃən] n sottoscrizione f; abbonamento

subsequent ['sʌbsɪkwənt] adj successivo/a, seguente; conseguente; **subsequently** adv in seguito, successivamente

subside [səb'saɪd] vi cedere, abbassarsi; (flood) decrescere; (wind) calmarsi

subsidiary [səb'sɪdɪərɪ] adj sussidiario/a; accessorio/a ▷ n filiale f

subsidize ['sʌbsɪdaɪz] vt sovvenzionare

subsidy ['sʌbsɪdɪ] n sovvenzione f

substance ['sʌbstəns] n sostanza

substantial [səb'stænʃl] adj solido/a; (amount, progress etc) notevole; (meal) sostanzioso/a

substitute ['sʌbstɪtjuːt] n (person) sostituto/a; (thing) succedaneo, surrogato ▷ vt: **to ~ sth/sb for** sostituire qc/ qn a; **substitution** [sʌbstɪ'tjuːʃən] n sostituzione f

subtle ['sʌtl] adj sottile

subtract [səb'trækt] vt sottrarre

suburb ['sʌbəːb] n sobborgo; **the ~s** la periferia; **suburban** [sə'bəːbən] adj suburbano/a

subway ['sʌbweɪ] n (us: underground) metropolitana; (brit: underpass) sottopassaggio

succeed [sək'siːd] vi riuscire; avere successo ▷ vt succedere a; **to ~ in doing** riuscire a fare

success [sək'sɛs] n successo; **successful** adj (venture) coronato/a da successo, riuscito/a; **to be successful (in doing)** riuscire (a fare); **successfully** adv con successo

succession [sək'sɛʃən] n successione f

successive [sək'sɛsɪv] adj successivo/a, consecutivo/a

successor [sək'sɛsər] n successore m

succumb [sə'kʌm] vi soccombere

such [sʌtʃ] adj tale; **~ books** tali libri, libri del genere; (so much): **~ courage** tanto coraggio; (of that kind): **~ a book** un tale libro, un libro del genere ▷ adv talmente, così; **~ a long trip** un viaggio così lungo; **~ a lot of** talmente o così tanto/a; **~ as** (like) come; **as ~** come o in quanto tale; **such-and-such** adj tale (after noun)

suck [sʌk] vt succhiare; (baby) poppare

Sudan [suː'dɑːn] n Sudan m

sudden ['sʌdn] adj improvviso/a; **all of a ~** improvvisamente, all'improvviso; **suddenly** adv bruscamente, improvvisamente, di colpo

sudoku [su'dəukuː] n sudoku m inv

sue [suː] vt citare in giudizio

suede [sweɪd] n pelle f scamosciata

suffer ['sʌfər] vt soffrire, patire; (bear) sopportare, tollerare ▷ vi soffrire; **to ~ from** soffrire di; **suffering** n sofferenza

suffice [sə'faɪs] vi essere sufficiente, bastare

sufficient [sə'fɪʃənt] adj sufficiente; **~ money** abbastanza soldi

suffocate ['sʌfəkeɪt] vi (have difficulty breathing) soffocare; (die through lack of air) asfissiare

sugar ['ʃugər] n zucchero ▷ vt zuccherare

suggest [sə'dʒɛst] vt proporre, suggerire; (indicate) indicare; **suggestion** [sə'dʒɛstʃən] n suggerimento, proposta; indicazione f

suicide ['suɪsaɪd] n (person) suicida m/f; (act) suicidio; **to commit ~** suicidarsi; **suicide bomber** n kamikaze mf inv, attentatore/trice suicida; **suicide bombing** n attentato suicida

suit [suːt] n (man's) vestito; (woman's) completo, tailleur m inv; (lawsuit) causa; (Cards) seme m, colore m ▷ vt andar bene a o per; essere adatto/a a o per; (adapt): **to ~ sth to** adattare qc a; **well ~ed** (couple) ben assortito/a; **suitable** adj adatto/a; appropriato/a; **suitcase** ['suːtkeɪs] n valigia

suite [swiːt] n (of rooms) appartamento; (Mus) suite f inv; (furniture): **bedroom/**

dining room ~ arredo or mobilia per la camera da letto/sala da pranzo

sulfur etc ['sʌlfər] (US) = **sulphur** etc

sulk [sʌlk] vi fare il broncio

sulphur, (US) **sulfur** ['sʌlfər] n zolfo

sultana [sʌl'tɑːnə] n (fruit) uva (secca) sultanina

sum [sʌm] n somma; (Scol etc) addizione f; **sum up**, vi riassumere

summarize ['sʌməraɪz] vt riassumere, riepilogare

summary ['sʌmərɪ] n riassunto

summer ['sʌmər] n estate f ▷ cpd d'estate, estivo/a; **summer holidays** npl vacanze fpl estive; **summertime** n (season) estate f

summit ['sʌmɪt] n cima, sommità; (Pol) vertice m

summon ['sʌmən] vt chiamare, convocare

sun [sʌn] n sole m

Sun. abbr (= Sunday) dom.

sun: sunbathe vi prendere un bagno di sole; **sunbed** n lettino solare; **sunblock** n crema solare a protezione totale; **sunburn** n (painful) scottatura; **sunburnt** ['sʌnbəːnt], **sunburned** ['sʌnbəːnd] adj abbronzato/a; (painfully) scottato/a dal sole

Sunday ['sʌndɪ] n domenica

Sunday paper n giornale m della domenica

sunflower ['sʌnflauər] n girasole m

sung [sʌŋ] pp of **sing**

sunglasses ['sʌnglɑːsɪz] npl occhiali mpl da sole

sunk [sʌŋk] pp of **sink**

sun: sunlight n (luce f del) sole m; **sun lounger** n sedia a sdraio; **sunny** adj assolato/a, soleggiato/a; (fig) allegro/a, felice; **sunrise** n levata del sole, alba; **sunroof** n (Aut) tetto apribile; **sunscreen** n (protective ingredient) filtro solare; (cream) crema solare protettiva; **sunset** n tramonto; **sunshade** n parasole m; **sunshine** n (luce f del) sole m; **sunstroke** n insolazione f, colpo di sole; **suntan** n abbronzatura; **suntan lotion** n lozione f solare; **suntan oil** n olio solare

super ['suːpər] adj (col) fantastico/a

superb [suː'pəːb] adj magnifico/a

superficial [suːpə'fɪʃəl] adj superficiale

superintendent [suːpərɪn'tɛndənt] n direttore/trice; (Police) ≈ commissario (capo)

superior [suː'pɪərɪər] adj, n superiore m/f

superlative [suː'pəːlətɪv] adj superlativo/a, supremo/a ▷ n (Ling) superlativo

supermarket ['suːpəmɑːkɪt] n supermercato

supernatural [suːpə'nætʃərəl] adj, n soprannaturale m

superpower ['suːpəpauər] n (Pol) superpotenza

superstition [suːpə'stɪʃən] n superstizione f

superstitious [suːpə'stɪʃəs] adj superstizioso/a

superstore ['suːpəstɔːr] n (BRIT) grande supermercato

supervise ['suːpəvaɪz] vt (person etc) sorvegliare; (organization) soprintendere a; **supervision** [suːpə'vɪʒən] n sorveglianza; supervisione f; **supervisor** n sorvegliante m/f; soprintendente m/f; (in shop) capocommesso/a

supper ['sʌpər] n cena

supple ['sʌpl] adj flessibile; agile

supplement n ['sʌplɪmənt] supplemento ▷ vt ['sʌplɪmɛnt] completare, integrare

supplier [sə'plaɪər] n fornitore m

supply [sə'plaɪ] vt: **to ~ sth (to sb)** (goods) fornire qc (a qn); **to ~ sth (with sth)** (system, machine) alimentare qc (con qc) ▷ n riserva, provvista; (supplying) approvvigionamento; (Tech) alimentazione f; **supplies** npl (food) viveri mpl; (Mil) sussistenza

support [sə'pɔːt] n (moral, financial etc) sostegno, appoggio; (Tech) supporto ▷ vt sostenere; (financially) mantenere; (uphold) sostenere, difendere; **supporter** n (Pol etc) sostenitore/trice, fautore/trice; (Sport) tifoso/a

▌ Be careful not to translate support by the Italian word sopportare.

suppose [sə'pəuz] vt supporre; immaginare; **to be ~d to do** essere tenuto/a a fare; **supposedly** [sə'pəuzɪdlɪ] adv presumibilmente; **supposing** conj se, ammesso che + sub

suppress [sə'prɛs] vt reprimere; sopprimere; occultare

supreme [suː'priːm] adj supremo/a

surcharge ['səːtʃɑːdʒ] n supplemento

sure [ʃuər] adj sicuro/a; (definite, convinced) sicuro/a, certo/a; **~!** (of course) senz'altro!, certo!; **~ enough** infatti; **to make ~ of** assicurarsi di; **surely** adv sicuramente; certamente

surf [səːf] n (waves) cavalloni mpl; (foam) spuma

surface ['səːfɪs] n superficie f ▷ vt (road) asfaltare ▷ vi risalire alla superficie; (fig: person, news, feeling) venire a galla

surfboard ['sə:fbɔ:d] n tavola per surfing
surfer ['sə:fəʳ] n (in sea) surfista m/f; (on the Internet) navigatore/trice
surfing ['sə:fɪŋ] n surfing m
surge [sə:dʒ] n (strong movement) ondata; (of feeling) impeto ▷ vi gonfiarsi; (people) riversarsi
surgeon ['sə:dʒən] n chirurgo
surgery ['sə:dʒərɪ] n chirurgia; (BRIT: room) studio or gabinetto medico, ambulatorio; (also: ~ hours) orario delle visite or di consultazione; **to undergo ~** subire un intervento chirurgico
surname ['sə:neɪm] n cognome m
surpass [sə:'pɑ:s] vt superare
surplus ['sə:pləs] n eccedenza; (Econ) surplus m inv ▷ adj eccedente, d'avanzo
surprise [sə'praɪz] n sorpresa; (astonishment) stupore m ▷ vt sorprendere; stupire; **surprised** [sə'praɪzd] adj (look, smile) sorpreso/a; **to be surprised** essere sorpreso, sorprendersi; **surprising** adj sorprendente, stupefacente; **surprisingly** adv (easy, helpful) sorprendentemente
surrender [sə'rɛndəʳ] n resa, capitolazione f ▷ vi arrendersi
surround [sə'raund] vt circondare; (Mil etc) accerchiare; **surrounding** adj circostante; **surroundings** npl dintorni mpl; (fig) ambiente m
surveillance [sə:'veɪləns] n sorveglianza, controllo
survey n ['sə:veɪ] quadro generale; (study) indagine f; (in housebuying etc) perizia; (of land) rilevamento, rilievo topografico ▷ vt [sə:'veɪ] osservare; esaminare; (building) fare una perizia di; (land) fare il rilevamento di; **surveyor** n perito; geometra m; (of land) agrimensore m
survival [sə'vaɪvl] n sopravvivenza; (relic) reliquia, vestigio
survive [sə'vaɪv] vi sopravvivere ▷ vt sopravvivere a; **survivor** n superstite m/f, sopravvissuto/a
suspect adj ['sʌspɛkt] sospetto/a ▷ n ['sʌspɛkt] persona sospetta ▷ vt [səs'pɛkt] sospettare; (think likely) supporre; (doubt) dubitare di
suspend [səs'pɛnd] vt sospendere; **suspended sentence** n condanna con la condizionale; **suspenders** npl (BRIT) giarrettiere fpl; (US) bretelle fpl
suspense [səs'pɛns] n apprensione f; (in film etc) suspense m; **to keep sb in ~** tenere qn in sospeso
suspension [səs'pɛnʃən] n (gen, Aut) sospensione f; (of driving licence) ritiro temporaneo; **suspension bridge** n ponte m sospeso

suspicion [səs'pɪʃən] n sospetto; **suspicious** [səs'pɪʃəs] adj (suspecting) sospettoso/a; (causing suspicion) sospetto/a
sustain [səs'teɪn] vt sostenere; sopportare; (Law: charge) confermare; (suffer) subire
SUV n abbr (= sports utility vehicle) SUV m inv
swallow ['swɔləu] n (bird) rondine f ▷ vt inghiottire; (fig: story) bere
swam [swæm] pt of **swim**
swamp [swɔmp] n palude f ▷ vt sommergere
swan [swɔn] n cigno
swap [swɔp] vt: **to ~ (for)** scambiare (con)
swarm [swɔ:m] n sciame m ▷ vi (bees) sciamare; (people) brulicare; (place): **to be ~ing with** brulicare di
sway [sweɪ] vi (tree) ondeggiare; (person) barcollare ▷ vt (influence) influenzare, dominare
swear [swɛəʳ] (pt **swore**, pp **sworn**) vi (curse) bestemmiare, imprecare ▷ vt: **to ~ to sth** giurare qc; **swear in** vt prestare giuramento a; **swearword** n parolaccia
sweat [swɛt] n sudore m, traspirazione f ▷ vi sudare
sweater ['swɛtəʳ] n maglione m
sweatshirt ['swɛtʃə:t] n felpa f
sweaty ['swɛtɪ] adj sudato/a; bagnato/a di sudore
Swede [swi:d] n svedese m/f
swede [swi:d] n (BRIT) rapa svedese
Sweden ['swi:dn] n Svezia; **Swedish** ['swi:dɪʃ] adj svedese ▷ n (Ling) svedese m
sweep [swi:p] (pt, pp **swept**) n spazzata; (also: **chimney ~**) spazzacamino ▷ vt spazzare, scopare; (current) spazzare ▷ vi (hand) muoversi con gesto ampio; (wind) infuriare
sweet [swi:t] n (BRIT: pudding) dolce m; (candy) caramella ▷ adj dolce; (fresh) fresco/a; (fig) piacevole; delicato/a, grazioso/a; (kind) gentile; **sweetcorn** n granturco dolce; **sweetener** ['swi:tnə'] n (Culin) dolcificante m; **sweetheart** n innamorato/a; **sweetshop** n (BRIT) ≈ pasticceria
swell [swɛl] (pt **swelled**, pp **swollen** or **swelled**) n (of sea) mare m lungo ▷ adj (US col: excellent) favoloso/a ▷ vt gonfiare, ingrossare; (numbers, sales etc) aumentare ▷ vi gonfiarsi, ingrossarsi; (sound) crescere; (Med: also: ~ **up**) gonfiarsi; **swelling** n (Med) tumefazione f, gonfiore m
swept [swɛpt] pt, pp of **sweep**
swerve [swə:v] vi deviare; (driver) sterzare; (boxer) scartare
swift [swɪft] n (bird) rondone m ▷ adj rapido/a, veloce

swim [swɪm] (*pt* **swam**, *pp* **swum**) *n*: **to go for a ~** andare a fare una nuotata ▷ *vi* nuotare; (*Sport*) fare del nuoto; (*head, room*) girare ▷ *vt* (*river, channel*) attraversare *or* percorrere a nuoto; (*length*) nuotare; **swimmer** *n* nuotatore/trice; **swimming** *n* nuoto; **swimming costume** *n* (*BRIT*) costume *m* da bagno; **swimming pool** *n* piscina; **swimming trunks** *npl* costume *m* da bagno (da uomo); **swimsuit** *n* costume *m* da bagno

swine flu *n* influenza suina

swing [swɪŋ] (*pt, pp* **swung**) *n* altalena; (*movement*) oscillazione *f*; (*Mus*) ritmo; (*also:* **~ music**) swing *m* ▷ *vt* dondolare, far oscillare; (*also:* **~ round**) far girare ▷ *vi* oscillare, dondolare; (*also:* **~ round**) (*object*) roteare; (*person*) girarsi, voltarsi; **to be in full ~** (*activity*) essere in piena attività; (*party etc*) essere nel pieno

swipe card *n* tessera magnetica

swirl [swəːl] *vi* turbinare, far mulinello

Swiss [swɪs] *adj, n* (*pl inv*) svizzero/a

switch [swɪtʃ] *n* (*for light, radio etc*) interruttore *m*; (*change*) cambiamento ▷ *vt* (*also:* **~ round, ~ over**) cambiare; scambiare; **switch off** *vt* spegnere; **switch on** *vt* accendere; (*engine, machine*) mettere in moto, avviare; **switchboard** *n* (*Tel*) centralino

Switzerland ['swɪtsələnd] *n* Svizzera

swivel ['swɪvl] *vi* (*also:* **~ round**) girare

swollen ['swəʊlən] *pp of* **swell**

swoop [swuːp] *n* incursione *f* ▷ *vi* (*also:* **~ down**) scendere in picchiata, piombare

swop [swɒp] *n, vt* = **swap**

sword [sɔːd] *n* spada; **swordfish** *n* pesce *m* spada *inv*

swore [swɔːʳ] *pt of* **swear**

sworn [swɔːn] *pp of* **swear** ▷ *adj* giurato/a

swum [swʌm] *pp of* **swim**

swung [swʌŋ] *pt, pp of* **swing**

syllable ['sɪləbl] *n* sillaba

syllabus ['sɪləbəs] *n* programma *m*

symbol ['sɪmbl] *n* simbolo

symbolic(al) [sɪm'bɔlɪk(l)] *adj* simbolico/a; **to be ~ of sth** simboleggiare qc

symmetrical [sɪ'mɛtrɪkl] *adj* simmetrico/a

symmetry ['sɪmɪtrɪ] *n* simmetria

sympathetic [sɪmpə'θɛtɪk] *adj* (*showing pity*) compassionevole; (*kind*) comprensivo/a; **~ towards** ben disposto/a verso

▍ Be careful not to translate *sympathetic* by the Italian word *simpatico*.

sympathize ['sɪmpəθaɪz] *vi*: **to ~ with sb** compatire qn; partecipare al dolore di qn; **to ~ with a cause** simpatizzare per una causa

sympathy ['sɪmpəθɪ] *n* compassione *f*

symphony ['sɪmfənɪ] *n* sinfonia

symptom ['sɪmptəm] *n* sintomo; indizio

synagogue ['sɪnəgɔg] *n* sinagoga

syndicate ['sɪndɪkɪt] *n* sindacato

syndrome ['sɪndrəʊm] *n* sindrome *f*

synonym ['sɪnənɪm] *n* sinonimo

synthetic [sɪn'θɛtɪk] *adj* sintetico/a

Syria ['sɪrɪə] *n* Siria

syringe [sɪ'rɪndʒ] *n* siringa

syrup ['sɪrəp] *n* sciroppo; (*also:* **golden ~**) melassa raffinata

system ['sɪstəm] *n* sistema *m*; (*order*) metodo; (*Anat*) apparato; **systematic** [sɪstə'mætɪk] *adj* sistematico/a; metodico/a; **systems analyst** *n* analista *m/f* di sistemi

t

ta [tɑː] *excl* (*BRIT col*) grazie!

tab [tæb] *n* (*loop: on coat etc*) laccetto; (*label*) etichetta; **to keep ~s on** (*fig*) tenere d'occhio

table ['teɪbl] *n* tavolo, tavola; (*Math, Chem etc*) tavola ▷ *vt* (*BRIT: motion etc*) presentare; **to lay** *or* **set the ~** apparecchiare *or* preparare la tavola; **tablecloth** *n* tovaglia; **table d'hôte** [tɑːbl'dəut] *adj* (*meal*) a prezzo fisso; **table lamp** *n* lampada da tavolo; **tablemat** *n* sottopiatto; **tablespoon** *n* cucchiaio da tavola; (*also*: **tablespoonful**: *as measurement*) cucchiaiata

tablet ['tæblɪt] *n* (*Med*) compressa; (*of stone*) targa; (*Comput*) tablet *m inv*

table tennis *n* tennis *m* da tavolo, ping-pong® *m*

tabloid ['tæblɔɪd] *n* (*newspaper*) tabloid *m inv* (*giornale illustrato di formato ridotto*); **the ~s, the ~ press** i giornali popolari

taboo [tə'buː] *adj*, *n* tabù *m inv*

tack [tæk] *n* (*nail*) bulletta; (*fig*) approccio ▷ *vt* imbullettare; imbastire ▷ *vi* bordeggiare

tackle ['tækl] *n* attrezzatura, equipaggiamento; (*for lifting*) paranco; (*Rugby*) placcaggio; (*Football*) contrasto ▷ *vt* (*difficulty*) affrontare; (*Rugby*) placcare; (*Football*) contrastare

tacky ['tækɪ] *adj* appiccicaticcio/a; scadente

tact [tækt] *n* tatto; **tactful** *adj* delicato/a, discreto/a

tactics ['tæktɪks] *n*, *npl* tattica

tactless ['tæktlɪs] *adj* che manca di tatto

tadpole ['tædpəul] *n* girino

taffy ['tæfɪ] *n* (*US*) caramella *f* mou *inv*

tag [tæg] *n* etichetta

tail [teɪl] *n* coda; (*of shirt*) falda ▷ *vt* (*follow*) seguire, pedinare; **tails** *npl* (*formal suit*) frac *m inv*

tailor ['teɪlə^r] *n* sarto

Taiwan [taɪ'wɑːn] *n* Taiwan *m*; **Taiwanese** [taɪwə'niːz] *adj*, *n* taiwanese

take [teɪk] (*pt* **took**, *pp* **taken**) *vt* prendere; (*gain: prize*) ottenere, vincere; (*require: effort, courage*) occorrere, volerci; (*tolerate*) accettare, sopportare; (*hold: passengers etc*) contenere; (*accompany*) accompagnare; (*bring, carry*) portare; (*exam*) sostenere, presentarsi a; **to ~ a photo/a shower** fare una fotografia/una doccia; **I ~ it that** suppongo che; **take after** *vt fus* assomigliare a; **take apart** *vt* smontare; **take away** *vt* portare via; togliere; **take back** *vt* (*return*) restituire; riportare; (*one's words*) ritirare; **take down** *vt* (*building*) demolire; (*letter etc*) scrivere; **take in** *vt* (*lodger*) prendere, ospitare; (*deceive*) imbrogliare, abbindolare; (*understand*) capire; (*include*) comprendere, includere; **take off** *vi* (*Aviat*) decollare; (*go away*) andarsene ▷ *vt* (*remove*) togliere; **take on** *vt* (*work*) accettare, intraprendere; (*employee*) assumere; (*opponent*) sfidare, affrontare; **take out** *vt* portare fuori; (*remove*) togliere; (*licence*) prendere, ottenere; **to ~ sth out of** (*drawer, pocket etc*) tirare qc fuori da; estrarre qc da; **take over** *vt* (*business*) rilevare ▷ *vi*: **to ~ over from sb** prendere le consegne *or* il controllo da qn; **take up** *vt* (*dress*) accorciare; (*occupy: time, space*) occupare; (*engage in: hobby etc*) mettersi a; **to ~ sb up on sth** accettare qc da qn; **takeaway** ['teɪkəweɪ] (*BRIT*) *n* (*shop etc*) ≈ rosticceria; (*food*) pasto per asporto; **taken** *pp of* **take**; **takeoff** *n* (*Aviat*) decollo; **takeout** ['teɪkaut] *adj*, *n* (*US*) = **takeaway**; **takeover** *n* (*Comm*) assorbimento; **takings** ['teɪkɪŋz] *npl* (*Comm*) incasso

talc [tælk] *n* (*also*: **~um powder**) talco

tale [teɪl] *n* racconto, storia; **to tell ~s** (*fig: to teacher, parent etc*) fare la spia

talent ['tælənt] *n* talento; **talented** *adj* di talento

talk [tɔːk] *n* discorso; (*gossip*) chiacchiere *fpl*; (*conversation*) conversazione *f*; (*interview*) discussione *f* ▷ *vi* parlare; **talks** *npl* (*Pol etc*) colloqui *mpl*; **to ~ about** parlare di; **to ~ sb out of/into doing** dissuadere qn da/convincere qn a fare; **to ~ shop** parlare di lavoro *or* di affari; **talk show** *n* talk show *m inv*

tall [tɔːl] *adj* alto/a; **to be 6 feet ~** ≈ essere alto 1 metro e 80

tambourine [tæmbə'riːn] *n* tamburello

tame [teɪm] *adj* addomesticato/a; (*fig: story, style*) insipido/a, scialbo/a

tamper ['tæmpə^r] *vi*: **to ~ with** manomettere

tampon ['tæmpɔn] n tampone m

tan [tæn] n (also: **sun~**) abbronzatura ▷ vi abbronzarsi ▷ adj (colour) marrone rossiccio inv

tandem ['tændəm] n tandem m inv

tangerine [tændʒə'ri:n] n mandarino

tangle ['tæŋgl] n groviglio; **to get in(to) a ~** aggrovigliarsi; (fig) combinare un pasticcio

tank [tæŋk] n serbatoio; (for fish) acquario; (Mil) carro armato

tanker ['tæŋkə'] n (ship) nave f cisterna inv; (truck) autobotte f, autocisterna

tankini [tæn'ki:nɪ] n tankini m inv

tanned [tænd] adj abbronzato/a

tantrum ['tæntrəm] n accesso di collera

Tanzania [tænzə'nɪə] n Tanzania

tap [tæp] n (on sink etc) rubinetto; (gentle blow) colpetto ▷ vt dare un colpetto a; (resources) sfruttare, utilizzare; (telephone) mettere sotto controllo; **on ~** (fig: resources) a disposizione; **tap-dancing** n tip tap m

tape [teɪp] n nastro; (also: **magnetic ~**) nastro (magnetico); (sticky tape) nastro adesivo ▷ vt (record) registrare (su nastro); (stick) attaccare con nastro adesivo; **tape measure** n metro a nastro; **tape recorder** n registratore m (a nastro)

tapestry ['tæpɪstrɪ] n arazzo; tappezzeria

tar [tɑ:'] n catrame m

target ['tɑ:gɪt] n bersaglio; (fig: objective) obiettivo

tariff ['tærɪf] n tariffa

tarmac ['tɑ:mæk] n (BRIT: on road) macadam m al catrame; (Aviat) pista di decollo

tarpaulin [tɑ:'pɔ:lɪn] n tela incatramata

tarragon ['tærəgən] n dragoncello

tart [tɑ:t] n (Culin) crostata; (BRIT col, pej: woman) sgualdrina ▷ adj (flavour) aspro/a, agro/a

tartan ['tɑ:tn] n tartan m inv

tartar(e) sauce n salsa tartara

task [tɑ:sk] n compito; **to take to ~** rimproverare

taste [teɪst] n gusto; (flavour) sapore m, gusto; (sample) assaggio; (fig: glimpse, idea) idea ▷ vt gustare; (sample) assaggiare ▷ vi: **to ~ of** or **like** (fish etc) sapere di, avere sapore di; **in good/bad ~** di buon/cattivo gusto; **you can ~ the garlic (in it)** (ci) si sente il sapore dell'aglio; **can I have a ~?** posso assaggiarlo?; **tasteful** adj di buon gusto; **tasteless** adj (food) insipido/a; (remark) di cattivo gusto; **tasty** adj saporito/a, gustoso/a

tatters ['tætəz] npl: **in ~** a brandelli

tattoo [tə'tu:] n tatuaggio; (spectacle) parata militare ▷ vt tatuare

taught [tɔ:t] pt, pp of **teach**

taunt [tɔ:nt] n scherno ▷ vt schernire

Taurus ['tɔ:rəs] n Toro

taut [tɔ:t] adj teso/a

tax [tæks] n (on goods) imposta; (on services) tassa; (on income) imposte fpl, tasse fpl ▷ vt tassare; (fig: strain: patience etc) mettere alla prova; **tax-free** adj esente da imposte

taxi ['tæksɪ] n taxi m inv ▷ vi (Aviat) rullare; **taxi driver** n tassista m/f; **taxi rank**, (US) **taxi stand** n posteggio dei taxi

tax payer n contribuente m/f

TB n abbr (= tuberculosis) TBC f

tea [ti:] n tè m inv; (BRIT: snack: for children) merenda; **high ~** (BRIT) cena leggera (presa nel tardo pomeriggio); **tea bag** n bustina di tè; **tea break** n (BRIT) intervallo per il tè

teach (pt, pp **taught**) [ti:tʃ, tɔ:t] vt: **to ~ sb sth, ~ sth to sb** insegnare qc a qn ▷ vi insegnare; **teacher** n insegnante m/f; (in secondary school) professore/essa; (in primary school) maestro/a; **teaching** n insegnamento

tea: tea cloth n (for dishes) strofinaccio; (BRIT: for trolley) tovaglietta da tè; **teacup** ['ti:kʌp] n tazza da tè; **tea leaves** npl foglie fpl di tè

team [ti:m] n squadra; (of animals) tiro; **team up** vi: **to ~ up (with)** mettersi insieme (a)

teapot ['ti:pɔt] n teiera

tear¹ [tɪə'] n lacrima; **in ~s** in lacrime

tear² [tɛə'] (pt **tore**, pp **torn**) n strappo ▷ vt strappare ▷ vi strapparsi; **tear apart** vt (also fig) distruggere; **tear down** vt (building, statue) demolire; (poster, flag) tirare giù; **tear off** vt (sheet of paper etc) strappare; (one's clothes) togliersi di dosso; **tear up** vt (sheet of paper etc) strappare; **tearful** ['tɪəful] adj piangente, lacrimoso/a; **tear gas** n gas m lacrimogeno

tearoom ['ti:ru:m] n sala da tè

tease [ti:z] vt canzonare; (unkindly) tormentare

tea: teaspoon n cucchiaino da tè; (also: **teaspoonful**) (as measurement) cucchiaino; **teatime** n ora del tè; **tea towel** n (BRIT) strofinaccio (per i piatti)

technical ['tɛknɪkl] adj tecnico/a

technician [tɛk'nɪʃən] n tecnico/a

technique [tɛk'ni:k] n tecnica

technology [tɛk'nɔlədʒɪ] n tecnologia

teddy (bear) ['tɛdɪ-] n orsacchiotto

tedious ['ti:dɪəs] adj noioso/a, tedioso/a

tee [ti:] n (Golf) tee m inv

teen [ti:n] adj = **teenage** ▷ n (US) = **teenager**

teenage ['ti:neɪdʒ] adj (fashions etc) per giovani, per adolescenti; **teenager** n adolescente m/f

teens [ti:nz] *npl*: **to be in one's ~** essere adolescente

teeth [ti:θ] *npl of* **tooth**

teetotal ['ti:'təutl] *adj* astemio/a

telecommunications ['tɛlɪkəmju:nɪ'keɪʃənz] *n* telecomunicazioni *fpl*

telegram ['tɛlɪgræm] *n* telegramma *m*

telegraph pole *n* palo del telegrafo

telephone ['tɛlɪfəun] *n* telefono ▷ *vt* (*person*) telefonare a; (*message*) comunicare per telefono; **telephone book** *n* elenco telefonico; **telephone box**, (*US*) **telephone booth** *n* cabina telefonica; **telephone call** *n* telefonata; **telephone directory** *n* elenco telefonico; **telephone number** *n* numero di telefono

telesales ['tɛlɪseɪlz] *n* vendita per telefono

telescope ['tɛlɪskəup] *n* telescopio

televise ['tɛlɪvaɪz] *vt* teletrasmettere

television ['tɛlɪvɪʒən] *n* televisione *f*; **on ~** alla televisione; **television programme** *n* programma *m* televisivo

tell [tɛl] (*pt, pp* **told**) *vt* dire; (*relate: story*) raccontare; (*distinguish*): **to ~ sth from** distinguere qc da ▷ *vi* (*talk*): **to ~ (of)** parlare (di); (*have effect*) farsi sentire, avere effetto; **to ~ sb to do** dire a qn di fare; **tell off** *vt* rimproverare, sgridare; **teller** *n* (*in bank*) cassiere/a

telly ['tɛlɪ] *n abbr* (*BRIT, col*: = **television**) tivù *f inv*

temp [tɛmp] *abbr* (*BRIT col*) = **temporary** ▷ *n* impiegato/a interinale

temper ['tɛmpəʳ] *n* (*nature*) carattere *m*; (*mood*) umore *m*; (*fit of anger*) collera ▷ *vt* (*moderate*) moderare; **to be in a ~** essere in collera; **to lose one's ~** andare in collera

temperament ['tɛmprəmənt] *n* (*nature*) temperamento; **temperamental** [tɛmprə'mɛntl] *adj* capriccioso/a

temperature ['tɛmprətʃəʳ] *n* temperatura; **to have** *or* **run a ~** avere la febbre

temple ['tɛmpl] *n* (*building*) tempio; (*Anat*) tempia

temporary ['tɛmpərərɪ] *adj* temporaneo/a; (*job, worker*) avventizio/a, temporaneo/a

tempt [tɛmpt] *vt* tentare; **to ~ sb into doing** indurre qn a fare; **temptation** [tɛmp'teɪʃən] *n* tentazione *f*; **tempting** *adj* allettante

ten [tɛn] *num* dieci

tenant ['tɛnənt] *n* inquilino/a

tend [tɛnd] *vt* badare a, occuparsi di ▷ *vi*: **to ~ to do** tendere a fare; **tendency** ['tɛndənsɪ] *n* tendenza

tender ['tɛndəʳ] *adj* tenero/a; (*sore*) dolorante ▷ *n* (*Comm: offer*) offerta; (*money*): **legal ~** moneta in corso legale ▷ *vt* offrire

tendon ['tɛndən] *n* tendine *m*

tenner ['tɛnəʳ] *n* (*BRIT col*) (banconota da) dieci sterline *fpl*

tennis ['tɛnɪs] *n* tennis *m*; **tennis ball** *n* palla da tennis; **tennis court** *n* campo da tennis; **tennis match** *n* partita di tennis; **tennis player** *n* tennista *m/f*; **tennis racket** *n* racchetta da tennis

tenor ['tɛnəʳ] *n* (*Mus*) tenore *m*

tenpin bowling ['tɛnpɪn-] *n* bowling *m*

tense [tɛns] *adj* teso/a ▷ *n* (*Ling*) tempo

tension ['tɛnʃən] *n* tensione *f*

tent [tɛnt] *n* tenda

tentative ['tɛntətɪv] *adj* esitante, incerto/a; (*conclusion*) provvisorio/a

tenth [tɛnθ] *num* decimo/a

tent: tent peg *n* picchetto da tenda; **tent pole** *n* palo da tenda, montante *m*

tepid ['tɛpɪd] *adj* tiepido/a

term [tə:m] *n* termine *m*; (*Scol*) trimestre *m*; (*Law*) sessione *f* ▷ *vt* chiamare, definire; **terms** *npl* (*conditions*) condizioni *fpl*; (*Comm*) prezzi *mpl*, tariffe *fpl*; **in the short/long ~** a breve/lunga scadenza; **to be on good ~s with** essere in buoni rapporti con; **to come to ~s with** (*problem*) affrontare

terminal ['tə:mɪnl] *adj* finale, terminale; (*disease*) terminale ▷ *n* (*Elec, Comput*) morsetto; (*Aviat, for oil, ore etc*) terminal *m inv*; (*BRIT: also*: **coach ~**) capolinea *m*

terminate ['tə:mɪneɪt] *vt* mettere fine a

termini ['tə:mɪnaɪ] *npl of* **terminus**

terminology [tə:mɪ'nɔlədʒɪ] *n* terminologia

terminus (*pl* **termini**) ['tə:mɪnəs, 'tə:mɪnaɪ] *n* (*for buses*) capolinea *m*; (*for trains*) stazione *f* terminale

terrace ['tɛrəs] *n* terrazza; (*BRIT: row of houses*) fila di case a schiera; **terraced** *adj* (*garden*) a terrazze

terrain [tɛ'reɪn] *n* terreno

terrestrial [tɪ'rɛstrɪəl] *adj* (*life*) terrestre; (*BRIT: channel*) terrestre

terrible ['tɛrɪbl] *adj* terribile; **terribly** *adv* terribilmente; (*very badly*) malissimo

terrier ['tɛrɪəʳ] *n* terrier *m inv*

terrific [tə'rɪfɪk] *adj* incredibile, fantastico/a; (*wonderful*) formidabile, eccezionale

terrified ['tɛrɪfaɪd] *adj* atterrito/a

terrify ['tɛrɪfaɪ] *vt* terrorizzare; **terrifying** *adj* terrificante

territorial [tɛrɪ'tɔ:rɪəl] *adj* territoriale

territory ['tɛrɪtərɪ] *n* territorio

terror ['tɛrəʳ] *n* terrore *m*; **terrorism** *n* terrorismo; **terrorist** *n* terrorista *m/f*

test [tɛst] *n* (*trial, check: of courage etc*) prova; (*Med*) esame *m*; (*Chem*) analisi *f inv*; (*exam: of intelligence etc*) test *m inv*; (: *in school*) compito in classe; (*also*: **driving ~**) esame *m* di guida ▷ *vt* provare; esaminare;

analizzare; sottoporre ad esame; **to ~ sb in history** esaminare qn in storia

testicle ['tɛstɪkl] n testicolo

testify ['tɛstɪfaɪ] vi (Law) testimoniare, deporre; **to ~ to sth** (Law) testimoniare qc; (gen) comprovare or dimostrare qc

testimony ['tɛstɪmənɪ] n (Law) testimonianza, deposizione f

test: test match n (Cricket, Rugby) partita internazionale; **test tube** n provetta

tetanus ['tɛtənəs] n tetano

text [tɛkst] n testo; (Tel) sms m inv, messaggino ▷ vt: **to ~ sb** (col) mandare un sms a ▷ vi messaggiarsi; **textbook** n libro di testo

textile ['tɛkstaɪl] n tessile m

text message n (Tel) sms m inv, messaggino

text messaging [-'mɛsɪdʒɪŋ] n il mandarsi sms

texture ['tɛkstʃə'] n tessitura; (of skin, paper etc) struttura

Thai [taɪ] adj tailandese ▷ n tailandese m/f; (Ling) tailandese m

Thailand ['taɪlænd] n Tailandia

Thames [tɛmz] n: **the ~** il Tamigi

than [ðæn, ðən] conj (in comparisons) che; (with numerals, pronouns, proper names) di; **more ~ 10/Maria/once** più di 10/Maria/una volta; **I have more/less ~ you** ne ho più/meno di te; **she has more apples ~ pears** ha più mele che pere; **she is older ~ you think** è più vecchia di quanto tu (non) pensi

thank [θæŋk] vt ringraziare; **~ you (very much)** grazie (tante); **thankfully** adv con riconoscenza; con sollievo; **thankfully there were few victims** grazie al cielo ci sono state poche vittime; **thanks** npl ringraziamenti mpl, grazie fpl ▷ excl grazie!; **thanks to** grazie a

Thanksgiving (Day) n giorno del ringraziamento

* **THANKSGIVING (DAY)**
*
* Negli Stati Uniti il quarto giovedì di
* novembre ricorre il *Thanksgiving (Day)*,
* festa nazionale in ricordo della celebrazione
* con cui i Padri Pellegrini, i puritani inglesi
* che fondarono la colonia di Plymouth nel
* Massachusetts, ringraziarono Dio del
* buon raccolto del 1621.

KEYWORD

that [ðæt ʃ] (pl **those**) adj (demonstrative) quel (quell', quello) m; quella (quell') f; **that man/woman/book** quell'uomo/quella donna/quel libro; (not "this") quell'uomo/quella donna/quel libro là; **that one** quello/a là

▶ pron **1** (demonstrative) ciò; (: not "this one") quello/a; **who's that?** chi è?; **what's that?** cos'è quello?; **is that you?** sei tu?; **I prefer this to that** preferisco questo a quello; **that's what he said** questo è ciò che ha detto; **what happened after that?** che è successo dopo?; **that is (to say)** cioè

2 (relative: direct) che; (: indirect) cui; **the book (that) I read** il libro che ho letto; **the box (that) I put it in** la scatola in cui l'ho messo; **the people (that) I spoke to** le persone con cui or con le quali ho parlato

3 (relative: of time) in cui; **the day (that) he came** il giorno in cui è venuto

▶ conj che; **he thought that I was ill** pensava che io fossi malato

▶ adv (demonstrative) così; **I can't work that much** non posso lavorare (così) tanto; **that high** così alto; **the wall's about that high and that thick** il muro è alto circa così e spesso circa così

thatched [θætʃt] adj (roof) di paglia

thaw [θɔː] n disgelo ▷ vi (ice) sciogliersi; (food) scongelarsi ▷ vt (food) (fare) scongelare

 KEYWORD

the [ðiː, ðə] def art **1** (gen) il (lo, l') m; la (l') f; I (gli) mpl; le fpl; **the boy/girl/ink** il ragazzo/la ragazza/l'inchiostro; **the books/pencils** i libri/le matite; **the history of the world** la storia del mondo; **give it to the postman** dallo al postino; **I haven't the time/money** non ho tempo/soldi; **the rich and the poor** i ricchi e i poveri

2 (in titles): **Elizabeth the First** Elisabetta prima; **Peter the Great** Pietro il Grande

3 (in comparisons): **the more he works, the more he earns** più lavora più guadagna

theatre, (US) **theater** ['θɪətə'] n teatro; (also: **lecture ~**) aula magna; (also: **operating ~**) sala operatoria

theft [θɛft] n furto

their [ðɛə'] adj il (la) loro; (pl) i (le) loro; **theirs** pron il (la) loro; (pl) i (le) loro; see also **my; mine¹**

them [ðɛm, ðəm] pron (direct) li(le); (indirect) gli, loro (after vb); (stressed, after prep: people) loro; (: people, things) essi/e; see also **me**

theme [θiːm] n tema m; **theme park** n parco a tema

themselves [ðəm'sɛlvz] pl pron (reflexive) si; (emphatic) loro stessi/e; (after prep) se stessi/e

then [ðɛn] adv (at that time) allora; (next) poi, dopo; (and also) e poi ▷ conj (therefore) perciò, dunque, quindi ▷ adj: **the ~ president** il presidente di allora; **by ~** allora; **from ~ on** da allora in poi

theology [θɪ'ɔlədʒɪ] n teologia

theory ['θɪərɪ] n teoria

therapist ['θɛrəpɪst] n terapista m/f

therapy ['θɛrəpɪ] n terapia

 KEYWORD

there [ðɛəʳ] adv **1**: **there is** c'è; **there are** ci sono; **there are 3 of them** (people) sono in 3; (things) ce ne sono 3; **there is no-one here** non c'è nessuno qui; **there has been an accident** c'è stato un incidente

2 (referring to place) là, lì; **up/in/down there** lassù/là dentro/laggiù; **he went there on Friday** ci è andato venerdì; **I want that book there** voglio quel libro là or lì; **there he is!** eccolo!

3: **there, there** (esp to child) su, su; **thereabouts** ['ðɛərəbauts] adv (place) nei pressi, da quelle parti; (amount) giù di lì, all'incirca; **thereafter** [ðɛər'ɑ:ftəʳ] adv da allora in poi; **thereby** [ðɛə'baɪ] adv con ciò; **therefore** ['ðɛəfɔ:ʳ] adv perciò, quindi; **there's** [ðɛəz] = **there is; there has**

thermal ['θə:ml] adj termico/a

thermometer [θə'mɔmɪtəʳ] n termometro

thermostat ['θə:məstæt] n termostato

these [ði:z] pl pron di questi/e

thesis (pl **theses**) ['θi:sɪs, 'θi:si:z] n tesi f inv

they [ðeɪ] pl pron essi(esse) (people only) loro; **~ say that ...** (it is said that) si dice che ...; **they'd** [ðeɪd] = **they would; they had; they'll** [ðeɪl] = **they will; they shall; they're** [ðɛəʳ] = **they are; they've** = **they have**

thick [θɪk] adj spesso/a; (crowd) compatto/a; (stupid) ottuso/a, lento/a ▷ n: **in the ~ of** nel folto di; **it's 20 cm ~** ha uno spessore di 20 cm; **thicken** vi ispessire ▷ vt (sauce etc) ispessire, rendere più denso/a; **thickness** n spessore m

thief (pl **thieves**) [θi:f, θi:vz] n ladro/a

thigh [θaɪ] n coscia

thin [θɪn] adj sottile; (person) magro/a; (soup) poco denso/a ▷ vt: **to ~ (down)** (sauce, paint) diluire

thing [θɪŋ] n cosa; (object) oggetto; (mania): **to have a ~ about** essere fissato/a con; **things** npl (belongings) cose fpl; **the best ~ would be to** la cosa migliore sarebbe di; **poor ~** poveretto/a

think (pt, pp **thought**) [θɪŋk, θɔ:t] vi pensare, riflettere ▷ vt pensare, credere; (imagine) immaginare; **to ~ of** pensare a; **what did you ~ of them?** cosa ne ha pensato?; **to ~ about sth/sb** pensare a qc/qn; **I'll ~ about it** ci penserò; **to ~ of doing** pensare di fare; **I ~ so/not** penso or credo di sì/no; **to ~ well of** avere una buona opinione di; **think over** vt riflettere su; **think up** vt ideare

third [θə:d] n terzo/a ▷ n terzo/a; (fraction) terzo, terza parte f; (Aut) terza; (BRIT Scol: degree) laurea col minimo dei voti; **thirdly** adv in terzo luogo; **third party insurance** n (BRIT) assicurazione f contro terzi; **Third World** n: **the Third World** il Terzo Mondo

thirst [θə:st] n sete f; **thirsty** adj (person) assetato/a, che ha sete

thirteen [θə:'ti:n] num tredici; **thirteenth** [-'ti:nθ] num tredicesmo/a

thirtieth ['θə:tɪɪθ] num trentesimo/a

thirty ['θə:tɪ] num trenta

 KEYWORD

this [ðɪs ʃ] (pl **these**) adj (demonstrative) questo/a; **this man/woman/book** quest'uomo/questa donna/questo libro; (not "that") quest'uomo/questa donna/questo libro qui; **this one** questo/a qui ▷ pron (demonstrative) questo/a; (: not "that one") questo/a qui; **who/what is this?** chi è/che cos'è questo?; **I prefer this to that** preferisco questo a quello; **this is where I live** io abito qui; **this is what he said** questo è ciò che ha detto; **this is Mr Brown** (in introductions, photo) questo è il signor Brown; (on telephone) sono il signor Brown ▷ adv (demonstrative): **this high/long** etc alto/lungo etc così; **I didn't know things were this bad** non sapevo andasse così male

thistle ['θɪsl] n cardo

thorn [θɔ:n] n spina

thorough ['θʌrə] adj (search) minuzioso/a; (knowledge, research) approfondito/a, profondo/a; (person) coscienzioso/a; (cleaning) a fondo; **thoroughly** adv (search) minuziosamente; (wash, study) a fondo; (very) assolutamente

those [ðəuz] pl pron quelli/e ▷ pl adj quei (quegli) mpl; quelle fpl

though [ðəu] conj benché, sebbene ▷ adv comunque

thought [θɔ:t] pt, pp of **think** ▷ n pensiero; (opinion) opinione f; **thoughtful** adj pensieroso/a, pensoso/a; (*considerate*) premuroso/a; **thoughtless** *adj* sconsiderato/a; (*behaviour*) scortese

thousand ['θaʊzənd] *num* mille; **one ~** mille; **~s of** migliaia di; **thousandth** *num* millesimo/a

thrash [θræʃ] *vt* picchiare; bastonare; (*defeat*) battere; **thrash about** *vi* dibattersi

thread [θrɛd] *n* filo; (*of screw*) filetto ▷ *vt* (*needle*) infilare

threat [θrɛt] *n* minaccia; **threaten** *vi* (*storm*) minacciare ▷ *vt*: **to threaten sb with sth/to do** minacciare qn con qc/di fare; **threatening** *adj* minaccioso/a

three [θriː] *num* tre; **three-dimensional** *adj* tridimensionale; (*film*) stereoscopico/a; **three-piece suite** *n* salotto comprendente un divano e due poltrone; **three-quarters** *npl* tre quarti *mpl*; **three-quarters full** pieno per tre quarti

threshold ['θrɛʃhəʊld] *n* soglia

threw [θruː] *pt of* **throw**

thrill [θrɪl] *n* brivido ▷ *vt* (*audience*) elettrizzare; **to be ~ed** (*with gift etc*) essere elettrizzato/a; **thrilled** *adj*: **I was thrilled to get your letter** la tua lettera mi ha fatto veramente piacere; **thriller** *n* thriller *m inv*; **thrilling** *adj* (*book, play etc*) pieno/a di suspense; (*news, discovery*) elettrizzante

thriving ['θraɪvɪŋ] *adj* fiorente

throat [θrəʊt] *n* gola; **to have a sore ~** avere (un *or* il) mal di gola

throb [θrɒb] *vi* palpitare; (*engine*) vibrare; (*with pain*) pulsare

throne [θrəʊn] *n* trono

through [θruː] *prep* attraverso; (*time*) per, durante; (*by means of*) per mezzo di; (*owing to*) a causa di ▷ *adj* (*ticket, train, passage*) diretto/a ▷ *adv* attraverso; **to put sb ~ to sb** (*Tel*) passare qn a qn; **to be ~** (*Tel*) ottenere la comunicazione; (*have finished*) avere finito; **"no ~ road"** (*BRIT*) "strada senza sbocco"; **throughout** *prep* (*place*) dappertutto in; (*time*) per *or* durante tutto/a ▷ *adv* dappertutto; sempre

throw [θrəʊ] *n* tiro; (*Sport*) lancio ▷ *vt* (*pt* **threw**, *pp* **thrown**) tirare, gettare; (*Sport*) lanciare; (*rider*) disarcionare; (*fig*) confondere; **to ~ a party** dare una festa; **throw away** *vt* gettare *or* buttare via; **throw in** *vt* (*Sport: ball*) rimettere in gioco; (*include*) aggiungere; **throw off** *vt* sbarazzarsi di; **throw out** *vt* buttare fuori; (*reject*) respingere; **throw up** *vi* vomitare

thru [θruː] *prep, adj, adv* (*US*) = **through**

thrush [θrʌʃ] *n* tordo

thrust [θrʌst] *vt* (*pt, pp* **thrust**) spingere con forza; (*push in*) conficcare

thud [θʌd] *n* tonfo

thug [θʌɡ] *n* delinquente *m*

thumb [θʌm] *n* (*Anat*) pollice *m*; **to ~ a lift** fare l'autostop; **thumbtack** *n* (*US*) puntina da disegno

thump [θʌmp] *n* colpo forte; (*sound*) tonfo ▷ *vt* (*person*) picchiare; (*object*) battere su ▷ *vi* picchiare; battere

thunder ['θʌndəʳ] *n* tuono ▷ *vi* tuonare; (*train etc*): **to ~ past** passare con un rombo; **thunderstorm** *n* temporale *m*

Thur(s). *abbr* (= Thursday) gio.

Thursday ['θəːzdɪ] *n* giovedì *m inv*

thus [ðʌs] *adv* così

thwart [θwɔːt] *vt* contrastare

thyme [taɪm] *n* timo

Tiber ['taɪbəʳ] *n*: **the ~** il Tevere

Tibet [tɪ'bɛt] *n* Tibet *m*

tick [tɪk] *n* (*sound, of clock*) tic tac *m inv*; (*mark*) segno; spunta; (*Zool*) zecca; (*BRIT col*): **in a ~** in un attimo ▷ *vi* fare tic tac ▷ *vt* spuntare; **tick off** *vt* spuntare; (*person*) sgridare

ticket ['tɪkɪt] *n* biglietto; (*in shop: on goods*) etichetta; (*for library*) scheda; **to get a (parking) ~** (*Aut*) prendere una multa (per sosta vietata); **a single/return ~ to ...** un biglietto di sola andata/di andata e ritorno per...; **ticket barrier** *n* (*BRIT Rail*) cancelletto d'ingresso; **ticket collector** *n* bigliettaio; **ticket inspector** *n* controllore *m*; **ticket machine** *n* distributore *m* di biglietti; **ticket office** *n* biglietteria

tickle ['tɪkl] *vt* fare il solletico a ▷ *vi*: **it ~s** mi (*or* gli etc) fa il solletico; **ticklish** ['tɪklɪʃ] *adj* che soffre il solletico; (*which tickles: blanket, cough*) che provoca prurito; (*problem*) delicato/a

tide [taɪd] *n* marea; (*fig: of events*) corso; **high/low ~** alta/bassa marea

tidy ['taɪdɪ] *adj* (*room*) ordinato/a, lindo/a; (*dress, work*) curato/a, in ordine; (*person*) ordinato/a ▷ *vt* (*also: ~ up*) riordinare, mettere in ordine

tie [taɪ] *n* (*string etc*) legaccio; (*BRIT: also: neck~*) cravatta; (*fig: link*) legame *m*; (*Sport: draw*) pareggio ▷ *vt* (*parcel*) legare; (*ribbon*) annodare ▷ *vi* (*Sport*) pareggiare; **to ~ sth in a bow** annodare qc; **to ~ a knot in sth** fare un nodo a qc; **tie down** *vt* legare, assicurare con una corda; **to ~ sb down to** (*price etc*) costringere qn ad accettare; **tie up** *vt* (*parcel, dog*) legare; (*boat*) ormeggiare; (*arrangements*) concludere; **to be ~d up** (*busy*) essere occupato *or* preso

tier [tɪəʳ] *n* fila; (*of cake*) piano, strato

tiger ['taɪɡəʳ] *n* tigre *f*

tight [taɪt] *adj* (*rope*) teso/a, tirato/a; (*money*) poco/a; (*clothes, budget, programme,*

bend) stretto/a; (*control*) severo/a, fermo/a; (*col: drunk*) sbronzo/a ▷ *adv* (*squeeze*) fortemente; (*shut*) ermeticamente;
tighten *vt* (*rope*) tendere; (*screw*) stringere; (*control*) rinforzare ▷ *vi* tendersi; stringersi;
tightly *adv* (*grasp*) bene, saldamente;
tights *npl* (BRIT) collant *m inv*

tile [taɪl] *n* (*on roof*) tegola; (*on floor, wall*) mattonella, piastrella

till [tɪl] *n* registratore *m* di cassa ▷ *vt* (*land*) coltivare ▷ *prep*, *conj* = **until**

tilt [tɪlt] *vt* inclinare, far pendere ▷ *vi* inclinarsi, pendere

timber ['tɪmbəʳ] *n* (*material*) legname *m*

time [taɪm] *n* tempo; (*epoch: often pl*) epoca, tempo; (*by clock*) ora; (*moment*) momento; (*occasion*) volta; (*Mus*) tempo ▷ *vt* (*race*) cronometrare; (*programme*) calcolare la durata di; (*fix moment for*) programmare; **a long ~** molto tempo; **for the ~ being** per il momento; **4 at a ~** 4 per o alla volta; **from ~ to ~** ogni tanto; **in ~** (*soon enough*) in tempo; (*after some time*) col tempo; (*Mus*) a tempo; **at ~s** a volte; **in a week's ~** fra una settimana; **in no ~** in un attimo; **any ~** in qualsiasi momento; **on ~** puntualmente; **5 ~s 5** 5 volte 5, 5 per 5; **what ~ is it?** che ora è?, che ore sono?; **to have a good ~** divertirsi; **time limit** *n* limite *m* di tempo; **timely** *adj* opportuno/a; **timer** *n* (*in kitchen*) contaminuti *m inv*; (*time switch*) temporizzatore *m*; **time-share** *adj*: **time-share apartment/villa** appartamento/villa in multiproprietà; **timetable** *n* orario; **time zone** *n* fuso orario

timid ['tɪmɪd] *adj* timido/a; (*easily scared*) pauroso/a

timing ['taɪmɪŋ] *n* (*fig*) scelta del momento opportuno; (*Sport*) cronometraggio

tin [tɪn] *n* stagno; (*also: ~ plate*) latta; (BRIT: *can*) barattolo (di latta), lattina; (*container*) scatola; **tin foil** *n* stagnola

tingle ['tɪŋgl] *vi* pizzicare

tinker ['tɪŋkəʳ]: **tinker with** *vt fus* armeggiare intorno a; cercare di riparare

tinned [tɪnd] *adj* (BRIT: *food*) in scatola

tin-opener ['tɪnəʊpnəʳ] *n* (BRIT) apriscatole *m inv*

tint [tɪnt] *n* tinta; **tinted** *adj* (*hair*) tinto/a; (*spectacles, glass*) colorato/a

tiny ['taɪnɪ] *adj* minuscolo/a

tip [tɪp] *n* (*end*) punta; (*gratuity*) mancia; (BRIT: *for rubbish*) immondezzaio; (*advice*) suggerimento ▷ *vt* (*waiter*) dare la mancia a; (*tilt*) inclinare; (*overturn: also: ~ over*) capovolgere; (*empty: also: ~ out*) scaricare; **tip off** *vt* fare una soffiata a

tiptoe ['tɪptəʊ] *n*: **on ~** in punta di piedi

tire ['taɪəʳ] *vt* stancare ▷ *vi* stancarsi ▷ *n* (US) = **tyre**; **tired** *adj* stanco/a; **to be tired of** essere stanco *or* stufo di; **tire pressure** *n* (US) = **tyre pressure**; **tiring** *adj* faticoso/a

tissue ['tɪʃuː] *n* tessuto; (*paper handkerchief*) fazzoletto di carta; **tissue paper** *n* carta velina

tit [tɪt] *n* (*bird*) cinciallegra; **to give ~ for tat** rendere pan per focaccia

title ['taɪtl] *n* titolo

T-junction ['tiː'dʒʌŋkʃən] *n* incrocio a T

TM *n abbr* = **trademark**

 KEYWORD

to [tuː, tə] *prep* **1** (*direction*) a; **to go to France/London/school** andare in Francia/a Londra/a scuola; **to go to Paul's/the doctor's** andare da Paul/dal dottore; **the road to Edinburgh** la strada per Edimburgo; **to the left/right** a sinistra/destra

2 (*as far as*) (fino) a; **from here to London** da qui a Londra; **to count to 10** contare fino a 10; **from 40 to 50 people** da 40 a 50 persone

3 (*with expressions of time*): **a quarter to 5** le 5 meno un quarto; **it's twenty to 3** sono le 3 meno venti

4 (*for, of*): **the key to the front door** la chiave della porta d'ingresso; **a letter to his wife** una lettera per la moglie

5 (*expressing indirect object*) a; **to give sth to sb** dare qc a qn; **to talk to sb** parlare a qn; **to be a danger to sb/sth** rappresentare un pericolo per qn/qc

6 (*in relation to*) a; **3 goals to 2** 3 goal a 2; **30 miles to the gallon** ≈ 11 chilometri con un litro

7 (*purpose, result*): **to come to sb's aid** venire in aiuto a qn; **to sentence sb to death** condannare a morte qn; **to my surprise** con mia sorpresa

▶ *with vb* **1** (*simple infinitive*): **to go/eat** *etc* andare/mangiare *etc*

2 (*following another vb*): **to want/try/start to do** volere/cercare di/cominciare a fare

3 (*with vb omitted*): **I don't want to** non voglio (farlo); **you ought to** devi (farlo)

4 (*purpose, result*) per; **I did it to help you** l'ho fatto per aiutarti

5 (*equivalent to relative clause*): **I have things to do** ho da fare; **the main thing is to try** la cosa più importante è provare

6 (*after adjective etc*): **ready to go** pronto/a a partire; **too old/young to ...** troppo vecchio/a/giovane per ...

▶ *adv*: **to push the door to** accostare la porta

toad [təud] n rospo; **toadstool** n fungo (velenoso)

toast [təust] n (Culin) pane m tostato; (drink, speech) brindisi m inv ▷ vt (Culin) tostare; (drink to) brindare a; **a piece** or **slice of ~** una fetta di pane tostato; **toaster** n tostapane m inv

tobacco [tə'bækəu] n tabacco

toboggan [tə'bɔgən] n toboga m inv

today [tə'deɪ] adv, n (also fig) oggi m inv

toddler ['tɔdlə'] n bambino/a che impara a camminare

toe [təu] n dito del piede; (of shoe) punta ▷ vt: **to ~ the line** (fig) stare in riga, conformarsi; **toenail** n unghia del piede

toffee ['tɔfɪ] n caramella

together [tə'geðə'] adv insieme; (at same time) allo stesso tempo; **~ with** insieme a

toilet ['tɔɪlət] n (BRIT: lavatory) gabinetto ▷ cpd (soap etc) da toletta; **toilet bag** n (BRIT) nécessaire m inv da toilette; **toilet paper** n carta igienica; **toiletries** npl articoli mpl da toletta; **toilet roll** n rotolo di carta igienica

token ['təukən] n (sign) segno ▷ cpd (substitute coin) gettone m; **book/record/gift ~** (BRIT) buono-libro/-disco/-regalo

Tokyo ['tɔukjəu] n Tokyo f

told [təuld] pt, pp of **tell**

tolerant ['tɔlərnt] adj: **~ (of)** tollerante (nei confronti di)

tolerate ['tɔləreɪt] vt sopportare; (Med, Tech) tollerare

toll [təul] n (tax, charge) pedaggio ▷ vi (bell) suonare; **the accident ~ on the roads** il numero delle vittime della strada; **toll call** n (US Tel) (telefonata) interurbana; **toll-free** (US) adj senza addebito, gratuito/a ▷ adv gratuitamente; **toll-free number** ≈ numero verde

tomato [tə'mɑːtəu] (pl **tomatoes**) n pomodoro; **tomato sauce** n salsa di pomodoro

tomb [tuːm] n tomba; **tombstone** ['tuːmstəun] n pietra tombale

tomorrow [tə'mɔrəu] adv, n (also fig) domani m inv; **the day after ~** dopodomani; **~ morning** domani mattina

ton [tʌn] n tonnellata (Brit = 1016 kg; 20 cwt; US = 907 kg; metric = 1000 kg); **~s of** (col) un mucchio or sacco di

tone [təun] n tono ▷ vi (also: **~ in**) intonarsi; **tone down** vt (colour, criticism, sound) attenuare

tongs [tɔŋz] npl tenaglie fpl; (for coal) molle fpl; (for hair) arricciacapelli m inv

tongue [tʌŋ] n lingua; **~ in cheek** (say, speak) ironicamente

tonic ['tɔnɪk] n (Med) ricostituente m; (also: **~ water**) acqua tonica

tonight [tə'naɪt] adv stanotte; (this evening) stasera ▷ n questa notte; questa sera

tonne [tʌn] n (BRIT: metric ton) tonnellata

tonsil ['tɔnsl] n tonsilla; **tonsillitis** [tɔnsɪ'laɪtɪs] n tonsillite f

too [tuː] adv (excessively) troppo; (also) anche; **~ much** adv troppo; adj troppo/a; **~ many** troppi/e

took [tuk] pt of **take**

tool [tuːl] n utensile m, attrezzo; **tool box** n cassetta f portautensili; **tool kit** n cassetta di attrezzi

tooth (pl **teeth**) [tuːθ, tiːθ] n (Anat, Tech) dente m; **toothache** n mal m di denti; **toothbrush** n spazzolino da denti; **toothpaste** n dentifricio; **toothpick** n stuzzicadenti m inv

top [tɔp] n (of mountain, page, ladder) cima; (of box, cupboard, table) sopra m inv, parte f superiore; (lid: of box, jar) coperchio; (: of bottle) tappo; (toy) trottola; (blouse etc) camicia (or maglietta etc) ▷ adj più alto/a; (in rank) primo/a; (best) migliore ▷ vt (exceed) superare; (be first in) essere in testa a; **on ~ of** sopra, in cima a; (in addition to) oltre a; **from ~ to bottom** da cima a fondo; **top up**, (US) **top off** vt riempire; (salary) integrare; **top floor** n ultimo piano; **top hat** n cilindro

topic ['tɔpɪk] n argomento; **topical** adj d'attualità

topless ['tɔplɪs] adj (bather etc) col seno scoperto

topping ['tɔpɪŋ] n (Culin) guarnizione f

topple ['tɔpl] vt rovesciare, far cadere ▷ vi cadere; traballare

top-up ['tɔpʌp] n (for mobile phone: also: **~ card**) ricarica

torch [tɔːtʃ] n torcia; (BRIT: electric) lampadina tascabile

tore [tɔː'] pt of **tear²**

torment n ['tɔːment] tormento ▷ vt [tɔː'ment] tormentare

torn [tɔːn] pp of **tear²**

tornado [tɔː'neɪdəu] (pl **tornadoes**) n tornado

torpedo [tɔː'piːdəu] (pl **torpedoes**) n siluro

torrent ['tɔrnt] n torrente m; **torrential** [tɔ'rɛnʃl] adj torrenziale

tortoise ['tɔːtəs] n tartaruga

torture ['tɔːtʃə'] n tortura ▷ vt torturare

Tory ['tɔːrɪ] adj, n (BRIT Pol) tory mf inv, conservatore/trice

toss [tɔs] vt gettare, lanciare; (head) scuotere; **to ~ a coin** fare a testa o croce; **to ~ up for sth** fare a testa o croce per qc; **to ~ and turn** (in bed) girarsi e rigirarsi

total ['təutl] *adj* totale ▷ *n* totale *m* ▷ *vt* (*add up*) sommare; (*amount to*) ammontare a
totalitarian [təutælɪ'tɛərɪən] *adj* totalitario/a
totally ['təutəlɪ] *adv* completamente
touch [tʌtʃ] *n* tocco; (*sense*) tatto; (*contact*) contatto ▷ *vt* toccare; **a ~ of** (*fig*) un tocco di; un pizzico di; **to get in ~ with** mettersi in contatto con; **to lose ~** (*friends*) perdersi di vista; **touch down** *vi* (*on land*) atterrare; **touchdown** *n* atterraggio; (*on sea*) ammaraggio; (*US Football*) meta; **touched** *adj* commosso/a; **touching** *adj* commovente; **touchline** *n* (*Sport*) linea laterale; **touch screen** *n* (*Tech*) schermo touch screen; **touch-screen** *adj* touch screen; **touch-screen mobile** telefono touch screen; **touch-screen technology** tecnologia touch screen; **touch-sensitive** *adj* sensibile al tatto
tough [tʌf] *adj* duro/a; (*resistant*) resistente
tour [tuə^r] *n* viaggio; (*also*: **package ~**) viaggio organizzato *or* tutto compreso (*of town, museum*) visita; (*by artist*) tournée *f inv* ▷ *vt* visitare; **tour guide** *n* guida turistica
tourism ['tuərɪzəm] *n* turismo
tourist ['tuərɪst] *n* turista *m/f* ▷ *adv* (*travel*) in classe turistica ▷ *cpd* turistico/a; **tourist office** *n* pro loco *f inv*
tournament ['tuənəmənt] *n* torneo
tour operator *n* (BRIT) operatore *m* turistico
tow [təu] *vt* rimorchiare; **"on ~"**, (US) **"in ~"** (*Aut*) "veicolo rimorchiato"
toward(s) [tə'wɔːd(z)] *prep* verso; (*of attitude*) nei confronti di; (*of purpose*) per
towel ['tauəl] *n* asciugamano; (*also*: **tea ~**) strofinaccio; **towelling** *n* (*fabric*) spugna
tower ['tauə^r] *n* torre *f*; **tower block** *n* (BRIT) palazzone *m*
town [taun] *n* città *f inv*; **to go to ~** andare in città; (*fig*) mettercela tutta; **town centre** *n* centro (città); **town hall** *n* ≈ municipio
tow truck *n* (US) carro *m* attrezzi *inv*
toxic ['tɒksɪk] *adj* tossico/a; **toxic asset** *n* (*Econ*) titolo tossico; **toxic bank** *n* (*Econ*) banca cattiva (*che investe in titoli tossici*)
toy [tɔɪ] *n* giocattolo; **toy with** *vt fus* giocare con; (*idea*) accarezzare, trastullarsi con; **toyshop** *n* negozio di giocattoli
trace [treɪs] *n* traccia ▷ *vt* (*draw*) tracciare; (*follow*) seguire; (*locate*) rintracciare
track [træk] *n* (*of person, animal*) traccia; (*on tape, Sport: path: gen*) pista; (: *of bullet etc*) traiettoria; (: *of suspect, animal*) pista, tracce *fpl*; (*Rail*) binario, rotaie *fpl* ▷ *vt* seguire le tracce di; **to keep ~ of** seguire; **track down** *vt* (*prey*) scovare; snidare; (*sth lost*) rintracciare; **tracksuit** *n* tuta sportiva
tractor ['træktə^r] *n* trattore *m*

trade [treɪd] *n* commercio; (*skill, job*) mestiere *m* ▷ *vi* commerciare; **to ~ with/in** commerciare con/in ▷ *vt*: **to ~ sth (for sth)** barattare qc (con qc); **trade in** *vt* (*old car etc*) dare come pagamento parziale; **trademark** *n* marchio di fabbrica; **trader** *n* commerciante *m/f*; **tradesman** *n* (*irreg*) fornitore *m*; (*shopkeeper*) negoziante *m*; **trade union** *n* sindacato
trading ['treɪdɪŋ] *n* commercio
tradition [trə'dɪʃən] *n* tradizione *f*; **traditional** *adj* tradizionale
traffic ['træfɪk] *n* traffico ▷ *vi*: **to ~ in** (*pej: liquor, drugs*) trafficare in; **traffic circle** *n* (US) isola rotatoria; **traffic island** *n* salvagente *m*, isola *f*, spartitraffico *inv*; **traffic jam** *n* ingorgo (del traffico); **traffic lights** *npl* semaforo; **traffic warden** *n* addetto/a al controllo del traffico e del parcheggio
tragedy ['trædʒədɪ] *n* tragedia
tragic ['trædʒɪk] *adj* tragico/a
trail [treɪl] *n* (*tracks*) tracce *fpl*, pista; (*path*) sentiero; (*of smoke etc*) scia ▷ *vt* trascinare, strascicare; (*follow*) seguire ▷ *vi* essere al traino; (*dress etc*) strusciare; (*plant*) arrampicarsi; strusciare; (*in game*) essere in svantaggio; **trailer** *n* (*Aut*) rimorchio; (US) roulotte *f inv*; (*Cine*) prossimamente *m inv*
train [treɪn] *n* treno; (*of dress*) coda, strascico ▷ *vt* (*apprentice, doctor etc*) formare; (*sportsman*) allenare; (*dog*) addestrare; (*memory*) esercitare; (*point: gun etc*): **to ~ sth on** puntare qc contro ▷ *vi* formarsi; allenarsi; **one's ~ of thought** il filo dei propri pensieri; **trainee** [treɪ'niː] *n* (*in trade*) apprendista *m/f*; **trainer** *n* (*Sport*) allenatore/trice; (*of dogs etc*) addestratore/trice; **trainers** *npl* (*shoes*) scarpe *fpl* da ginnastica; **training** *n* formazione *f*; allenamento; addestramento; **in training** (*Sport*) in allenamento; **training course** *n* corso di formazione professionale; **training shoes** *npl* scarpe *fpl* da ginnastica
train wreck *n* (*fig*) persona distrutta; (: *pej*) rottame *m*; **he's a complete ~** è completamente distrutto, è un rottame
trait [treɪt] *n* tratto
traitor ['treɪtə^r] *n* traditore/trice
tram [træm] *n* (BRIT: *also*: **~car**) tram *m inv*
tramp [træmp] *n* (*person*) vagabondo/a; (*col, pej: woman*) sgualdrina
trample ['træmpl] *vt*: **to ~ (underfoot)** calpestare
trampoline ['træmpəliːn] *n* trampolino
tranquil ['træŋkwɪl] *adj* tranquillo/a; **tranquillizer**, (US) **tranquilizer** *n* (*Med*) tranquillante *m*
transaction [træn'zækʃən] *n* transazione *f*

transatlantic [ˈtrænzətˈlæntɪk] adj transatlantico/a

transcript [ˈtrænskrɪpt] n trascrizione f

transfer n [ˈtrænsfəʳ] (gen, also Sport) trasferimento; (Pol: of power) passaggio; (picture, design) decalcomania; (: stick-on) autoadesivo ▷ vt [trænsˈfəːʳ] trasferire; passare; **to ~ the charges** (BRIT Tel) fare una chiamata a carico del destinatario

transform [trænsˈfɔːm] vt trasformare; **transformation** n trasformazione f

transfusion [trænsˈfjuːʒən] n trasfusione f

transit [ˈtrænzɪt] n: **in ~** in transito

transition [trænˈzɪʃən] n passaggio, transizione f

transitive [ˈtrænzɪtɪv] adj (Ling) transitivo/a

translate [trænzˈleɪt] vt tradurre; **translation** [trænzˈleɪʃən] n traduzione f; **translator** n traduttore/trice

transmission [trænzˈmɪʃən] n trasmissione f

transmit [trænzˈmɪt] vt trasmettere; **transmitter** n trasmettitore m

transparent [trænsˈpærnt] adj trasparente

transplant vt [trænsˈplɑːnt] trapiantare ▷ n [ˈtrænsplɑːnt] (Med) trapianto

transport n [ˈtrænspɔːt] trasporto ▷ vt [trænsˈpɔːt] trasportare; **transportation** [ˈtrænspɔːˈteɪʃən] n (mezzo di) trasporto

transvestite [trænzˈvɛstaɪt] n travestito/a

trap [træp] n (snare, trick) trappola; (carriage) calesse m ▷ vt prendere in trappola, intrappolare

trash [træʃ] n (col: goods) ciarpame m; (: nonsense) sciocchezze fpl; **trash can** n (US) secchio della spazzatura

trauma [ˈtrɔːmə] n trauma m; **traumatic** [trɔːˈmætɪk] adj traumatico/a

travel [ˈtrævl] n viaggio; viaggi mpl ▷ vi viaggiare ▷ vt (distance) percorrere; **travel agency** n agenzia (di) viaggi; **travel agent** n agente m di viaggio; **travel insurance** n assicurazione f di viaggio; **traveller**, (US) **traveler** n viaggiatore/trice; **traveller's cheque**, (US) **traveler's check** n assegno turistico; **travelling**, (US) **traveling** n viaggi mpl; **travel-sick** adj: **to get travel-sick** (in vehicle) soffrire di mal d'auto; (in aeroplane) soffrire di mal d'aria; (in boat) soffrire di mal di mare; **travel sickness** n mal m d'auto (or di mare or d'aria)

tray [treɪ] n (for carrying) vassoio; (on desk) vaschetta

treacherous [ˈtrɛtʃərəs] adj infido/a

treacle [ˈtriːkl] n melassa

tread [trɛd] n passo; (sound) rumore m di passi; (of stairs) pedata; (of tyre) battistrada m inv ▷ vi (pt **trod**, pp **trodden**) camminare; **tread on** vt fus calpestare

treasure [ˈtrɛʒəʳ] n tesoro ▷ vt (value) tenere in gran conto, apprezzare molto; (store) custodire gelosamente; **treasurer** [ˈtrɛʒərəʳ] n tesoriere/a

treasury [ˈtrɛʒərɪ] n: **the T~** (BRIT), **the T~ Department** (US) ≈ il Ministero del Tesoro

treat [triːt] n regalo ▷ vt trattare; (Med) curare; **to ~ sb to sth** offrire qc a qn; **treatment** [ˈtriːtmənt] n trattamento

treaty [ˈtriːtɪ] n patto, trattato

treble [ˈtrɛbl] adj triplo/a, triplice ▷ vt triplicare ▷ vi triplicarsi

tree [triː] n albero

trek [trɛk] n (hike) escursione f a piedi; (in car) escursione f in macchina; (tiring walk) camminata sfiancante ▷ vi (as holiday) fare dell'escursionismo

tremble [ˈtrɛmbl] vi tremare

tremendous [trɪˈmɛndəs] adj (enormous) enorme; (excellent) meraviglioso/a, formidabile

> Be careful not to translate *tremendous* by the Italian word *tremendo*.

trench [trɛntʃ] n trincea

trend [trɛnd] n (tendency) tendenza; (of events) corso; (fashion) moda; **trendy** adj (idea) di moda; (clothes) all'ultima moda

trespass [ˈtrɛspəs] vi: **to ~ on** entrare abusivamente in; **"no ~ing"** "proprietà privata", "vietato l'accesso"

trial [ˈtraɪəl] n (Law) processo; (test: of machine etc) collaudo; **to be on ~** (Law) essere sotto processo; **trial period** n periodo di prova

triangle [ˈtraɪæŋgl] n (Math, Mus) triangolo

triangular [traɪˈæŋgjuləʳ] adj triangolare

tribe [traɪb] n tribù f inv

tribunal [traɪˈbjuːnl] n tribunale m

tribute [ˈtrɪbjuːt] n tributo, omaggio; **to pay ~ to** rendere omaggio a

trick [trɪk] n trucco; (joke) tiro; (Cards) presa ▷ vt imbrogliare, ingannare; **to play a ~ on sb** giocare un tiro a qn; **that should do the ~** vedrai che funziona

trickle [ˈtrɪkl] n (of water etc) rivolo; gocciolio ▷ vi gocciolare

tricky [ˈtrɪkɪ] adj difficile, delicato/a

tricycle [ˈtraɪsɪkl] n triciclo

trifle [ˈtraɪfl] n sciocchezza; (BRIT Culin) ≈ zuppa inglese ▷ adv: **a ~ long** un po' lungo

trigger [ˈtrɪgəʳ] n (of gun) grilletto

trim [trɪm] adj (house, garden) ben tenuto/a; (figure) snello/a ▷ n (haircut etc) spuntata, regolata; (embellishment) finiture fpl; (on car) guarnizioni *fpl* ▷ *vt* spuntare; (*Naut: a sail*) orientare; (*decorate*): **to ~ (with)** decorare (con)

trio ['triːəu] *n* trio

trip [trɪp] *n* viaggio; (*excursion*) gita, escursione *f*; (*stumble*) passo falso ▷ *vi* inciampare; (*go lightly*) camminare con passo leggero; **on a ~** in viaggio; **trip up** *vi* inciampare ▷ *vt* fare lo sgambetto a

triple ['trɪpl] *adj* triplo/a

triplets ['trɪplɪts] *npl* bambini/e trigemini/e

tripod ['traɪpɔd] *n* treppiede *m*

triumph ['traɪʌmf] *n* trionfo ▷ *vi*: **to ~ (over)** trionfare (su); **triumphant** [traɪˈʌmfənt] *adj* trionfante

trivial ['trɪvɪəl] *adj* insignificante; (*excuse, comment*) banale

⬛ Be careful not to translate *trivial* by the Italian word *triviale*.

trod [trɔd] *pt of* **tread**

trodden ['trɔdn] *pp of* **tread**

trolley ['trɔlɪ] *n* carrello

trombone [trɔmˈbəun] *n* trombone *m*

troop [truːp] *n* gruppo; (*Mil*) squadrone *m*; **troops** *npl* (*Mil*) truppe *fpl*

trophy ['trəufɪ] *n* trofeo

tropical ['trɔpɪkəl] *adj* tropicale

trot [trɔt] *n* trotto ▷ *vi* trottare; **on the ~** (*BRIT fig*) di fila, uno/a dopo l'altro/a

trouble ['trʌbl] *n* difficoltà *f inv*, problema *m*; (*problems*) difficoltà *fpl*, problemi *mpl*; (*worry*) preoccupazione *f*; (*bother, effort*) sforzo; (*Pol*) conflitti *mpl*, disordine *m*; (*Med*): **stomach etc ~** disturbi *mpl* gastrici *etc* ▷ *vt* disturbare; (*worry*) preoccupare ▷ *vi*: **to ~ to do** disturbarsi a fare; **troubles** *npl* (*Pol etc*) disordini *mpl*; **to be in ~** avere dei problemi; **it's no ~!** di niente!; **what's the ~?** cosa c'è che non va?; **troubled** *adj* (*person*) preoccupato/a, inquieto/a; (*epoch, life*) agitato/a, difficile; **troublemaker** *n* elemento disturbatore, agitatore/trice; (*child*) disloco/a; **troublesome** *adj* fastidioso/a, seccante

trough [trɔf] *n* (*also*: **drinking ~**) abbeveratoio; (*also*: **feeding ~**) trogolo, mangiatoia; (*channel*) canale *m*

trousers ['trauzəz] *npl* pantaloni *mpl*, calzoni *mpl*; **short ~** calzoncini *mpl*

trout [traut] *n* (*pl inv*) trota

trowel ['trauəl] *n* cazzuola

truant ['truənt] *n*: **to play ~** (*BRIT*) marinare la scuola

truce [truːs] *n* tregua

truck [trʌk] *n* autocarro, camion *m inv*; (*Rail*) carro merci aperto; (*for luggage*) carrello *m* portabagagli *inv*; **truck driver** *n* camionista *m/f*

true [truː] *adj* vero/a; (*accurate*) accurato/a, esatto/a; (*genuine*) reale; (*faithful*) fedele; **to come ~** avverarsi

truly ['truːlɪ] *adv* veramente; (*truthfully*) sinceramente; **yours ~** (*in letter-writing*) distinti saluti

trumpet ['trʌmpɪt] *n* tromba

trunk [trʌŋk] *n* (*of tree, person*) tronco; (*of elephant*) proboscide *f*; (*case*) baule *m*; (*us Aut*) bagagliaio; **trunks** *npl* (*also*: **swimming trunks**) calzoncini *mpl* da bagno

trust [trʌst] *n* fiducia; (*Law*) amministrazione *f* fiduciaria; (*Comm*) trust *m inv* ▷ *vt* (*rely on*) contare su; (*entrust*): **to ~ sth to sb** affidare qc a qn; (*hope*): **to ~ (that)** sperare (che); **trusted** *adj* fidato/a; **trustworthy** *adj* fidato/a, degno/a di fiducia

truth (*pl* **truths**) [truːθ, truːðz] *n* verità *f inv*; **truthful** *adj* (*person*) sincero/a; (*description*) veritiero/a, esatto/a

try [traɪ] *n* prova, tentativo; (*Rugby*) meta ▷ *vt* (*Law*) giudicare; (*test: also*: **~ out**) provare; (*strain*) mettere alla prova ▷ *vi* provare; **to have a ~** fare un tentativo; **to ~ to do** (*seek*) cercare di fare; **try on** *vt* (*clothes*) provare; **trying** *adj* (*day, experience*) logorante, pesante; (*child*) difficile, insopportabile

T-shirt ['tiːʃəːt] *n* maglietta

tsunami [tsuˈnɑːmɪ] *n* tsunami *m inv*

tub [tʌb] *n* tinozza; mastello; (*bath*) bagno

tube [tjuːb] *n* tubo; (*BRIT: underground*) metropolitana, metrò *m inv*; (*for tyre*) camera d'aria

tuberculosis [tjubəːkjuˈləusɪs] *n* tubercolosi *f inv*

tube station *n* (*BRIT*) stazione *f* della metropolitana

tuck [tʌk] *n* piega ▷ *vt* (*put*) mettere; **tuck away** *vt* riporre; (*building*): **to be ~ed away** essere in un luogo isolato; **tuck in** *vt* mettere dentro; (*child*) rimboccare ▷ *vi* (*eat*) mangiare di buon appetito; abbuffarsi

tucker ['tʌkə'] *n* (*AUST, NZ col*) cibo

tuck shop *n* negozio di pasticceria (*in una scuola*)

Tue(s). *abbr* (= *Tuesday*) mar.

Tuesday ['tjuːzdɪ] *n* martedì *m inv*

tug [tʌg] *n* (*ship*) rimorchiatore *m* ▷ *vt* tirare con forza

tuition [tjuːˈɪʃən] *n* (*BRIT*) lezioni *fpl*; (*: private tuition*) lezioni *fpl* private; (*us: fees*) tasse *fpl* scolastiche (*or* universitarie)

tulip ['tjuːlɪp] *n* tulipano

tumble ['tʌmbl] *n* (*fall*) capitombolo ▷ *vi* capitombolare, ruzzolare; **to ~ to sth** (*col*) realizzare qc; **tumble dryer** *n* (*BRIT*) asciugatrice *f*

tumbler ['tʌmblə'] n bicchiere m senza stelo

tummy ['tʌmɪ] n (col) pancia

tumour, (us) **tumor** ['tjuːmə'] n tumore m

tuna ['tjuːnə] n (pl inv: also: **~ fish**) tonno

tune [tjuːn] n (melody) melodia, aria ▷ vt (Mus) accordare; (Radio, TV, Aut) regolare, mettere a punto; **to be in/out of ~** (instrument) essere accordato/a/ scordato/a; (singer) essere intonato/a/ stonato/a; **tune in** vi (Radio, TV): **to ~ in (to)** sintonizzarsi (su); **tune up** vi (musician) accordare lo strumento

tunic ['tjuːnɪk] n tunica

Tunisia [tjuː'nɪzɪə] n Tunisia

tunnel ['tʌnl] n galleria ▷ vi scavare una galleria

turbulence ['təːbjuləns] n (Aviat) turbolenza

turf [təːf] n terreno erboso; (clod) zolla ▷ vt coprire di zolle erbose

Turin [tjuə'rɪn] n Torino f

Turk [təːk] n turco/a

Turkey ['təːkɪ] n Turchia

turkey ['təːkɪ] n tacchino

Turkish ['təːkɪʃ] adj turco/a ▷ n (Ling) turco

turmoil ['təːmɔɪl] n confusione f, tumulto

turn [təːn] n giro; (change) cambiamento; (in road) curva; (tendency: of mind, events) tendenza; (performance) numero; (chance) turno; (Med) crisi f inv, attacco ▷ vt girare, voltare; (change): **to ~ sth into** trasformare qc in ▷ vi girare; (person: look back) girarsi, voltarsi; (reverse direction) girarsi indietro; (change) cambiare; (milk) andare a male; (become) diventare; **a good ~** un buon servizio; **it gave me quite a ~** mi ha fatto prendere un bello spavento; **"no left ~"** (Aut) "divieto di svolta a sinistra"; **it's your ~** tocca a lei; **in ~** a sua volta; a turno; **to take ~s (at sth)** fare (qc) a turno; **turn away** vi girarsi (dall'altra parte) ▷ vt mandar via; **turn back** vi ritornare, tornare indietro ▷ vt far tornare indietro; (clock) spostare indietro; **turn down** vt (refuse) rifiutare; (reduce) abbassare; (fold) ripiegare; **turn in** vi (col: go to bed) andare a letto ▷ vt (fold) voltare in dentro; **turn off** vi (from road) girare, voltare ▷ vt (light, radio, engine etc) spegnere; **turn on** vt (light, radio etc) accendere; **turn out** vt (light, gas) chiudere; spegnere ▷ vi (troops, doctor, voters etc) presentarsi; **to ~ out to be ...** rivelarsi ..., risultare ...; **turn over** vi (person) girarsi ▷ vt girare; **turn round** vi girare; (person) girarsi; **turn to** vt fus: **to ~ to sb** girarsi verso qn; **to ~ to sb for help** rivolgersi a qn per aiuto; **turn up** vi (person) arrivare, presentarsi; (lost object) saltar

fuori ▷ vt (collar, sound, gas etc) alzare; **turning** n (in road) curva; **turning point** n (fig) svolta decisiva

turnip ['təːnɪp] n rapa

turn: **turnout** ['təːnaut] n presenza, affluenza; **turnover** ['təːnəuvə'] n (Comm) giro di affari; (Culin): **apple** etc **turnover** sfogliatella alle mele etc; **turnstile** ['təːnstaɪl] n tornella; **turn-up** n (BRIT: on trousers) risvolto

turquoise [təˈkwɔɪz] n turchese m ▷ adj turchese

turtle ['təːtl] n testuggine f; **turtleneck (sweater)** ['təːtlnɛk-] n maglione m con il collo alto

Tuscany ['tʌskənɪ] n Toscana

tusk [tʌsk] n zanna

tutor ['tjuːtə'] n (in college) docente m/f (responsabile di un gruppo di studenti); (private teacher) precettore m; **tutorial** [tjuːˈtɔːrɪəl] n (Scol) lezione f con discussione (a un gruppo limitato)

tuxedo [tʌkˈsiːdəu] n (us) smoking m inv

TV [tiːˈviː] n abbr (= television) tivù f inv

tweed [twiːd] n tweed m inv

tweet [twiːt] n (on Twitter) post m su Twitter ▷ vt, vi (on Twitter) twittare

tweezers ['twiːzəz] npl pinzette fpl

twelfth [twelfθ] num dodicesimo/a

twelve [twɛlv] num dodici; **at ~** alle dodici, a mezzogiorno; (midnight) a mezzanotte

twentieth ['twɛntɪɪθ] num ventesimo/a

twenty ['twɛntɪ] num venti; **in ~ fourteen** nel duemilaquattordici

twice [twaɪs] adv due volte; **~ as much** due volte tanto; **~ a week** due volte alla settimana

twig [twɪg] n ramoscello ▷ vt, vi (col) capire

twilight ['twaɪlaɪt] n crepuscolo

twin [twɪn] adj, n gemello/a ▷ vt: **to ~ one town with another** fare il gemellaggio di una città con un'altra; **twin-bedded room** n stanza con letti gemelli; **twin beds** npl letti mpl gemelli

twinkle ['twɪŋkl] vi scintillare; (eyes) brillare

twist [twɪst] n torsione f; (in wire, flex) piega; (in story) colpo di scena; (bend) svolta, piega; (in road) curva ▷ vt attorcigliare; (ankle) slogare; (weave) intrecciare; (roll around) arrotolare; (fig) distorcere ▷ vi (road) serpeggiare

twit [twɪt] n (col) cretino/a

twitch [twɪtʃ] n tiratina; (nervous) tic m inv ▷ vi contrarsi

Twitter® ['twɪtə'] n Twitter® m

two [tuː] num due; **to put ~ and ~ together** (fig) fare uno più uno

type [taɪp] *n* (*category*) genere *m*; (*model*) modello; (*example*) tipo; (*Typ*) tipo, carattere *m* ▷ *vt* (*letter etc*) battere (a macchina), dattilografare; **typewriter** *n* macchina da scrivere

typhoid ['taɪfɔɪd] *n* tifoidea

typhoon [taɪ'fuːn] *n* tifone *m*

typical ['tɪpɪkl] *adj* tipico/a; **typically** *adv* tipicamente; **typically, he arrived late** come al solito è arrivato tardi

typing ['taɪpɪŋ] *n* dattilografia

typist ['taɪpɪst] *n* dattilografo/a

tyre, (*us*) **tire** ['taɪə'] *n* pneumatico, gomma; **I've got a flat ~** ho una gomma a terra; **tyre pressure** *n* pressione *f* (delle gomme)

UFO ['juːfəu] *n abbr* (= *unidentified flying object*) UFO *m inv*

Uganda [juː'gændə] *n* Uganda

ugly ['ʌglɪ] *adj* brutto/a

UHT *adj abbr* (= *ultra heat treated*) UHT *inv*, a lunga conservazione

UK *n abbr* = **United Kingdom**

ulcer ['ʌlsər] *n* ulcera; **mouth ~** afta

ultimate ['ʌltɪmɪt] *adj* ultimo/a, finale; (*authority*) massimo/a, supremo/a; **ultimately** *adv* alla fine; in definitiva, in fin dei conti

ultimatum (*pl* **ultimatums** *or* **ultimata**) [ʌltɪ'meɪtəm, -tə] *n* ultimatum *m inv*

ultrasound [ʌltrə'saund] *n* ultrasuono; (*Med*) ecografia

ultraviolet ['ʌltrə'vaɪəlɪt] *adj* ultravioletto/a

umbrella [ʌm'brelə] *n* ombrello

umpire ['ʌmpaɪər] *n* arbitro

UN *n abbr* (= *United Nations*) ONU *f*

unable [ʌn'eɪbl] *adj*: **to be ~ to** non potere, essere nell'impossibilità di; (*not to know how to*) essere incapace di

unacceptable [ʌnək'sɛptəbl] *adj* (*proposal, behaviour*) inaccettabile; (*price*) impossibile

unanimous [juː'nænɪməs] *adj* unanime

unarmed [ʌn'ɑːmd] *adj* (*person*) disarmato/a; (*combat*) senz'armi

unattended [ʌnə'tɛndɪd] *adj* (*car, child, luggage*) incustodito/a

unattractive [ʌnə'træktɪv] *adj* poco attraente

unavailable [ʌnə'veɪləbl] *adj* (*article, room, book*) non disponibile; (*person*) impegnato/a

unavoidable [ʌnə'vɔɪdəbl] *adj* inevitabile

unaware [ʌnə'wɛər] *adj*: **to be ~ of** non sapere, ignorare; **unawares** *adv* di sorpresa, alla sprovvista

unbearable [ʌn'bɛərəbl] *adj* insopportabile

unbeatable [ʌn'biːtəbl] *adj* imbattibile

unbelievable [ʌnbɪ'liːvəbl] *adj* incredibile

unborn [ʌn'bɔːn] *adj* non ancora nato/a

unbutton [ʌn'bʌtn] *vt* sbottonare

uncalled-for [ʌn'kɔːldfɔːʳ] *adj (remark)* fuori luogo *inv*; *(action)* ingiustificato/a

uncanny [ʌn'kænɪ] *adj* misterioso/a, strano/a

uncertain [ʌn'səːtn] *adj* incerto/a; dubbio/a; **uncertainty** *n* incertezza

unchanged [ʌn'tʃeɪndʒd] *adj* immutato/a

uncle ['ʌŋkl] *n* zio

unclear [ʌn'klɪəʳ] *adj* non chiaro/a; **I'm still ~ about what I'm supposed to do** non ho ancora ben capito cosa dovrei fare

uncomfortable [ʌn'kʌmfətəbl] *adj* scomodo/a; *(uneasy)* a disagio, agitato/a; *(unpleasant)* fastidioso/a

uncommon [ʌn'kɔmən] *adj* raro/a, insolito/a, non comune

unconditional [ʌn'kən'dɪʃənl] *adj* incondizionato/a, senza condizioni

unconscious [ʌn'kɔnʃəs] *adj* privo/a di sensi, svenuto/a; *(unaware)* inconsapevole, inconscio/a ▷ *n*: **the ~** l'inconscio

uncontrollable [ʌnkən'trəuləbl] *adj* incontrollabile; indisciplinato/a

unconventional [ʌnkən'vɛnʃənl] *adj* poco convenzionale

uncover [ʌn'kʌvəʳ] *vt* scoprire

undecided [ʌndɪ'saɪdɪd] *adj* indeciso/a

undeniable [ʌndɪ'naɪəbl] *adj* innegabile, indiscutibile

under ['ʌndəʳ] *prep* sotto; *(less than)* meno di; al disotto di; *(according to)* secondo, in conformità a ▷ *adv* (al) disotto; **~ there** là sotto; **~ repair** in riparazione; **undercover** *adj* segreto/a, clandestino/a; **underdone** *adj* (Culin) al sangue; *(pej)* poco cotto/a; **underestimate** *vt* sottovalutare; **undergo** *vt (irreg) (treatment)* sottoporsi a; **undergraduate** *n* studente/essa universitario/a; **underground** *n* (BRIT: *railway)* metropolitana; *(Pol)* movimento clandestino ▷ *adj* sotterraneo/a; *(fig)* clandestino/a ▷ *adv* sottoterra; **to go underground** *(fig)* darsi alla macchia; **undergrowth** *n* sottobosco; **underline** *vt* sottolineare; **undermine** *vt* minare; **underneath** [ʌndə'niːθ] *adv* sotto, disotto ▷ *prep* sotto, al di sotto di; **underpants** *npl* mutande *fpl*; slip *m inv*; **underpass** *n* (BRIT) sottopassaggio; **underprivileged** *adj* svantaggiato/a; **underscore** *vt* sottolineare; **undershirt** *n* (US) maglietta; **underskirt** (BRIT) *n* sottoveste *f*

understand [ʌndə'stænd] *(irreg: like* **stand**) *vt, vi* capire, comprendere; **I don't ~** non

capisco; **I ~ that ...** sento che ...; credo di capire che ...; **understandable** *adj* comprensibile; **understanding** *adj* comprensivo/a ▷ *n* comprensione *f*; *(agreement)* accordo

understatement [ʌndə'steɪtmənt] *n*: **that's an ~!** a dire poco!

understood [ʌndə'stud] *pt, pp of* **understand** ▷ *adj* inteso/a; *(implied)* sottinteso/a

undertake [ʌndə'teɪk] *vt (irreg: like* **take**) intraprendere; **to ~ to do sth** impegnarsi a fare qc

undertaker ['ʌndəteɪkəʳ] *n* impresario di pompe funebri

undertaking [ʌndə'teɪkɪŋ] *n* impresa; *(promise)* promessa

under: **underwater** [ʌndə'wɔːtəʳ] *adv* sott'acqua ▷ *adj* subacqueo/a; **underway** [ˌʌndə'weɪ] *adj*: **to be underway** essere in corso; **underwear** ['ʌndəwɛəʳ] *n* biancheria (intima); **underwent** [ʌndə'wɛnt] *vb see* **undergo**; **underworld** ['ʌndəwəːld] *n (of crime)* malavita

undesirable [ʌndɪ'zaɪərəbl] *adj* indesiderato/a

undisputed [ʌndɪs'pjuːtɪd] *adj* indiscusso/a

undo [ʌn'duː] *vt (irreg)* disfare

undone [ʌn'dʌn] *pp of* **undo**; **to come ~** slacciarsi

undoubtedly [ʌn'dautɪdlɪ] *adv* senza alcun dubbio

undress [ʌn'drɛs] *vi* spogliarsi

unearth [ʌn'əːθ] *vt* dissotterrare; *(fig)* scoprire

uneasy [ʌn'iːzɪ] *adj* a disagio; *(worried)* preoccupato/a; *(peace)* precario/a

unemployed [ʌnɪm'plɔɪd] *adj* disoccupato/a ▷ *npl*: **the ~** i disoccupati

unemployment [ʌnɪm'plɔɪmənt] *n* disoccupazione *f*; **unemployment benefit**, *(US)* **unemployment compensation** *n* sussidio di disoccupazione

unequal [ʌn'iːkwəl] *adj (length, objects)* disuguale; *(amounts)* diverso/a; *(division of labour)* ineguale

uneven [ʌn'iːvn] *adj* ineguale; *(heartbeat)* irregolare

unexpected [ʌnɪk'spɛktɪd] *adj* inatteso/a, imprevisto/a; **unexpectedly** *adv* inaspettatamente

unfair [ʌn'fɛəʳ] *adj*: **~ (to)** ingiusto/a (nei confronti di)

unfaithful [ʌn'feɪθful] *adj* infedele

unfamiliar [ʌnfə'mɪlɪəʳ] *adj* sconosciuto/a, strano/a; **to be ~ with sth** non avere familiarità con qc

unfashionable [ʌnˈfæʃnəbl] *adj* (*clothes*) fuori moda *inv*; (*district*) non alla moda

unfasten [ʌnˈfɑːsn] *vt* slacciare; sciogliere

unfavourable, (*us*) **unfavorable** [ʌnˈfeɪvərəbl] *adj* sfavorevole

unfinished [ʌnˈfɪnɪʃt] *adj* incompiuto/a

unfit [ʌnˈfɪt] *adj* (*ill*) non in forma; (*incompetent*): **~ (for)** incompetente (in); (*work, Mil*) inabile (a)

unfold [ʌnˈfəuld] *vt* spiegare ▷ *vi* (*story*) svelarsi

unforgettable [ʌnfəˈgɛtəbl] *adj* indimenticabile

unfortunate [ʌnˈfɔːtʃnɪt] *adj* sfortunato/a; (*event, remark*) infelice; **unfortunately** *adv* sfortunatamente, purtroppo

unfriend [ʌnˈfrɛnd] *vt* (*Internet*) cancellare dagli amici

unfriendly [ʌnˈfrɛndlɪ] *adj* poco amichevole, freddo/a

unfurnished [ʌnˈfəːnɪʃt] *adj* non ammobiliato/a

unhappiness [ʌnˈhæpɪnɪs] *n* infelicità

unhappy [ʌnˈhæpɪ] *adj* infelice; **~ about/ with** (*arrangements etc*) insoddisfatto/a di

unhealthy [ʌnˈhɛlθɪ] *adj* (*gen*) malsano/a; (*person*) malaticcio/a

unheard-of [ʌnˈhəːdɔv] *adj* inaudito/a, senza precedenti

unhelpful [ʌnˈhɛlpful] *adj* poco disponibile

unhurt [ʌnˈhəːt] *adj* incolume, illeso/a

unidentified [ʌnaɪˈdɛntɪfaɪd] *adj* non identificato/a

uniform [ˈjuːnɪfɔːm] *n* uniforme *f*, divisa ▷ *adj* uniforme

unify [ˈjuːnɪfaɪ] *vt* unificare

unimportant [ʌnɪmˈpɔːtənt] *adj* senza importanza, di scarsa importanza

uninhabited [ʌnɪnˈhæbɪtd] *adj* disabitato/a

unintentional [ʌnɪnˈtɛnʃənəl] *adj* involontario/a

union [ˈjuːnjən] *n* unione *f*; (*also*: **trade ~**) sindacato ▷ *cpd* sindacale, dei sindacati; **Union Jack** *n* bandiera nazionale britannica

unique [juːˈniːk] *adj* unico/a

unisex [ˈjuːnɪsɛks] *adj* unisex *inv*

unit [ˈjuːnɪt] *n* unità *f inv*; (*section: of furniture etc*) elemento; (*team, squad*) reparto, squadra

unite [juːˈnaɪt] *vt* unire ▷ *vi* unirsi; **united** *adj* unito/a; unificato/a; (*efforts*) congiunto/a; **United Kingdom** *n* Regno Unito; **United Nations (Organization)** *n* (Organizzazione *f* delle) Nazioni Unite; **United States (of America)** *n* Stati *mpl* Uniti (d'America)

unity [ˈjuːnɪtɪ] *n* unità

universal [juːnɪˈvəːsl] *adj* universale

universe [ˈjuːnɪvəːs] *n* universo

university [juːnɪˈvəːsɪtɪ] *n* università *f inv*

unjust [ʌnˈdʒʌst] *adj* ingiusto/a

unkind [ʌnˈkaɪnd] *adj* poco gentile, scortese

unknown [ʌnˈnəun] *adj* sconosciuto/a

unlawful [ʌnˈlɔːful] *adj* illecito/a, illegale

unleaded [ˈʌnˈlɛdɪd] *adj* senza piombo; **~ petrol** benzina verde *or* senza piombo

unleash [ʌnˈliːʃ] *vt* (*fig*) scatenare

unless [ʌnˈlɛs] *conj* a meno che (non) + *sub*

unlike [ʌnˈlaɪk] *adj* diverso/a ▷ *prep* a differenza di, contrariamente a

unlikely [ʌnˈlaɪklɪ] *adj* improbabile

unlimited [ʌnˈlɪmɪtɪd] *adj* illimitato/a

unlisted [ʌnˈlɪstɪd] *adj* (*us Tel*): **to be ~** non essere sull'elenco

unload [ʌnˈləud] *vt* scaricare

unlock [ʌnˈlɔk] *vt* aprire

unlucky [ʌnˈlʌkɪ] *adj* sfortunato/a; (*object, number*) che porta sfortuna

unmarried [ʌnˈmærɪd] *adj* non sposato/a; (*man only*) scapolo, celibe; (*woman only*) nubile

unmistak(e)able [ʌnmɪsˈteɪkəbl] *adj* inconfondibile

unnatural [ʌnˈnætʃrəl] *adj* innaturale; contro natura

unnecessary [ʌnˈnɛsəsərɪ] *adj* inutile, superfluo/a

UNO [ˈjuːnəu] *n abbr* (= *United Nations Organization*) ONU *f*

unofficial [ʌnəˈfɪʃl] *adj* non ufficiale; (*strike*) non dichiarato/a dal sindacato

unpack [ʌnˈpæk] *vi* disfare la valigia (*or* le valigie) ▷ *vt* disfare

unpaid [ʌnˈpeɪd] *adj* (*holiday*) non pagato/a; (*work*) non retribuito/a; (*bill, debt*) da pagare

unpleasant [ʌnˈplɛznt] *adj* spiacevole

unplug [ʌnˈplʌg] *vt* staccare

unpopular [ʌnˈpɔpjuləʳ] *adj* impopolare

unprecedented [ʌnˈprɛsɪdəntɪd] *adj* senza precedenti

unpredictable [ʌnprɪˈdɪktəbl] *adj* imprevedibile

unprotected [ˈʌnprəˈtɛktɪd] *adj* (*sex*) non protetto/a

unqualified [ʌnˈkwɔlɪfaɪd] *adj* (*in professions*) non abilitato/a; (*success*) assoluto/a, senza riserve

unravel [ʌnˈrævl] *vt* dipanare, districare

unreal [ʌnˈrɪəl] *adj* irreale

unrealistic [ʌnrɪəˈlɪstɪk] *adj* non realistico/a

unreasonable [ʌnˈriːznəbl] *adj* irragionevole

unrelated [ʌnrɪ'leɪtɪd] *adj:* ~ **(to)** senza rapporto (con); (*by family*) non imparentato/a (con)

unreliable [ʌnrɪ'laɪəbl] *adj* (*person, machine*) che non dà affidamento; (*news, source of information*) inattendibile

unrest [ʌn'rɛst] *n* agitazione *f*

unroll [ʌn'rəul] *vt* srotolare

unruly [ʌn'ruːlɪ] *adj* indisciplinato/a

unsafe [ʌn'seɪf] *adj* pericoloso/a, rischioso/a

unsatisfactory ['ʌnsætɪs'fæktərɪ] *adj* che lascia a desiderare, insufficiente

unscrew [ʌn'skruː] *vt* svitare

unsettled [ʌn'sɛtld] *adj* (*person, future*) incerto/a, indeciso/a; turbato/a; (*weather, market*) instabile

unsettling [ʌn'sɛtlɪŋ] *adj* inquietante

unsightly [ʌn'saɪtlɪ] *adj* brutto/a, sgradevole a vedersi

unskilled [ʌn'skɪld] *adj:* ~ **worker** operaio/a non specializzato/a

unspoiled ['ʌn'spɔɪld], **unspoilt** ['ʌn'spɔɪlt] *adj* (*place*) non deturpato/a

unstable [ʌn'steɪbl] *adj* (*gen*) instabile; (*mentally*) squilibrato/a

unsteady [ʌn'stɛdɪ] *adj* instabile, malsicuro/a

unsuccessful [ʌnsək'sɛsful] *adj* (*writer, proposal*) che non ha successo; (*marriage, attempt*) mal riuscito/a, fallito/a; **to be ~** (*in attempting sth*) non avere successo

unsuitable [ʌn'suːtəbl] *adj* inadatto/a; (*moment*) inopportuno/a; sconveniente

unsure [ʌn'ʃuə'] *adj:* ~ (**of** or **about**) incerto/a (su); **to be ~ of o.s.** essere insicuro/a

untidy [ʌn'taɪdɪ] *adj* (*room*) in disordine; (*appearance, work*) trascurato/a; (*person, writing*) disordinato/a

untie [ʌn'taɪ] *vt* (*knot, parcel*) disfare; (*prisoner, dog*) slegare

until [ʌn'tɪl] *prep* fino a; (*after negative*) prima di ▷ *conj* finché, fino a quando; (*in past, after negative*) prima che + *sub*, prima di + *infinitive*; ~ **he comes** finché or fino a quando non arriva; ~ **now** finora; ~ **then** fino ad allora

untrue [ʌn'truː] *adj* (*statement*) falso/a, non vero/a

unused [ʌn'juːzd] *adj* nuovo/a

unusual [ʌn'juːʒuəl] *adj* insolito/a, eccezionale raro/a; **unusually** *adv* insolitamente

unveil [ʌn'veɪl] *vt* scoprire; svelare

unwanted [ʌn'wɒntɪd] *adj* (*clothing*) smesso/a; (*child*) non desiderato/a

unwell [ʌn'wɛl] *adj* indisposto/a; **to feel ~** non sentirsi bene

unwilling [ʌn'wɪlɪŋ] *adj:* **to be ~ to do** non voler fare

unwind [ʌn'waɪnd] (*irreg: like* **wind²**) *vt* svolgere, srotolare ▷ *vi* (*relax*) rilassarsi

unwise [ʌn'waɪz] *adj* poco saggio/a

unwittingly [ʌn'wɪtɪŋlɪ] *adv* senza volerlo

unwrap [ʌn'ræp] *vt* disfare; (*present*) aprire

unzip [ʌn'zɪp] *vt* aprire (la chiusura lampo di); (*Comput*) dezippare

KEYWORD

up [ʌp] *prep:* **he went up the stairs/the hill** è salito su per le scale/sulla collina; **the cat was up a tree** il gatto era su un albero; **they live further up the street** vivono un po' più su nella stessa strada
▶ *adv* **1** (*upwards, higher*) su, in alto; **up in the sky/in the mountains** su nel cielo/in montagna; **up there** lassù; **up above** su in alto
2: **to be up** (*out of bed*) essere alzato/a; (*prices, level*) essere salito/a
3: **up to** (*as far as*) fino a; **up to now** finora
4: **to be up to** (*depending on*): **it's up to you** sta a lei, dipende da lei; (*equal to*): **he's not up to it** (*job, task etc*) non ne è all'altezza; (*be doing: col*): **what is he up to?** cosa sta combinando?
▶ *n*: **ups and downs** alti e bassi *mpl*

up-and-coming ['ʌpənd'kʌmɪŋ] *adj* pieno/a di promesse, promettente

upbringing ['ʌpbrɪŋɪŋ] *n* educazione *f*

update [ʌp'deɪt] *vt* aggiornare

upfront [ʌp'frʌnt] *adj* (*col*) franco/a, aperto/a ▷ *adv* (*pay*) subito

upgrade [ʌp'greɪd] *vt* (*job*) rivalutare; (*house*) rimodernare; (*employee*) avanzare di grado

upheaval [ʌp'hiːvl] *n* sconvolgimento; tumulto

uphill [ʌp'hɪl] *adj* in salita; (*fig: task*) difficile ▷ *adv*: **to go ~** andare in salita, salire

upholstery [ʌp'həulstərɪ] *n* tappezzeria

upload ['ʌpləud] *vt* caricare

up-market [ʌp'mɑːkɪt] *adj* (*product*) che si rivolge ad una fascia di mercato superiore

upon [ə'pɒn] *prep* su

upper ['ʌpə'] *adj* superiore ▷ *n* (*of shoe*) tomaia; **upper-class** *adj* dell'alta borghesia

upright ['ʌpraɪt] *adj* diritto/a; verticale; (*fig*) diritto/a, onesto/a

uprising ['ʌpraɪzɪŋ] *n* insurrezione *f*, rivolta

uproar ['ʌprɔː'] *n* tumulto, clamore *m*

upset *n* ['ʌpsɛt] (*to plan etc*) contrattempo ▷ *vt* [ʌp'sɛt] (*irreg: like* **set**) (*glass etc*) rovesciare; (*plan, stomach*) scombussolare; (*person: offend*) contrariare; (: *grieve*)

addolorare; sconvolgere ▷ *adj* [ʌp'sɛt]
contrariato/a, addolorato/a; (*stomach*)
scombussolato/a; **to have a stomach ~**
avere lo stomaco in disordine *or*
scombussolato
upside down ['ʌpsaɪd-] *adv* sottosopra
upstairs [ʌp'stɛəz] *adv, adj* di sopra, al
piano superiore ▷ *n* piano di sopra
up-to-date ['ʌptə'deɪt] *adj* moderno/a;
aggiornato/a
uptown ['ʌptaun] (*US*) *adv* verso i quartieri
residenziali ▷ *adj* dei quartieri residenziali
upward ['ʌpwəd] *adj* ascendente; verso
l'alto ▷ *adv* = **upwards**
uranium [juə'reɪnɪəm] *n* uranio
Uranus [juə'reɪnəs] *n* (*planet*) Urano
urban ['ə:bən] *adj* urbano/a
urge [ə:dʒ] *n* impulso; stimolo; forte
desiderio ▷ *vt*: **to ~ sb to do** esortare qn a
fare, spingere qn a fare; raccomandare a
qn di fare
urgency ['ə:dʒənsɪ] *n* urgenza; (*of tone*)
insistenza
urgent ['ə:dʒənt] *adj* urgente; (*tone, voice*)
insistente
urinal ['juərɪnl] *n* (*BRIT: building*)
vespasiano; (: *vessel*) orinale *m*, pappagallo
urinate ['juərɪneɪt] *vi* orinare
urine ['juərɪn] *n* orina
URL *n abbr* (= *uniform resource locator*)
URL *m inv*
us [ʌs] *pron* ci; (*stressed, after prep*) noi; *see
also* **me**
USA *n abbr* = **United States of America**
USB stick *n* pennetta USB
use *n* [ju:s] uso; impiego, utilizzazione *f* ▷ *vt*
[ju:z] usare, utilizzare, servirsi di; **she ~d to
do it** lo faceva (una volta), era solita farlo;
in ~ in uso; **out of ~** fuori uso; **to be of ~**
essere utile, servire; **it's no ~** non serve, è
inutile; **to be ~d to** avere l'abitudine di; **use
up** *vt* finire; (*left-overs*) consumare; **used**
adj (*car, object*) usato/a; **useful** *adj* utile;
useless *adj* inutile; (*person*) inetto/a; **user**
n utente *m/f*; **user-friendly** *adj* (*computer*)
di facile uso
username ['ju:zəneɪm] *n* (*Comput*) nome
m utente
usual ['ju:ʒuəl] *adj* solito/a; **as ~** come al
solito, come d'abitudine; **usually** *adv* di
solito
ute [ju:t] *n* (*AUST, NZ*) pick-up *m inv*
utensil [ju:'tɛnsl] *n* utensile *m*; **kitchen ~s**
utensili da cucina
utility [ju:'tɪlɪtɪ] *n* utilità; (*also:* **public ~**)
servizio pubblico
utilize ['ju:tɪlaɪz] *vt* utilizzare; sfruttare
utmost ['ʌtməust] *adj* estremo/a ▷ *n*: **to
do one's ~** fare il possibile *or* di tutto

utter ['ʌtər] *adj* assoluto/a, totale ▷ *vt*
pronunciare, proferire; emettere; **utterly**
adv completamente, del tutto
U-turn ['ju:tə:n] *n* inversione *f* a U

V

v *abbr* (= *verse*) v.; (= *vide*) v., vedi; (= *volt*) V.; (= *versus*) contro

vacancy ['veɪkənsɪ] *n* (*job*) posto libero; (*room*) stanza libera; **"no vacancies"** "completo"

> Be careful not to translate *vacancy* by the Italian word *vacanza*.

vacant ['veɪkənt] *adj* (*job, seat etc*) libero/a; (*expression*) assente

vacate [və'keɪt] *vt* lasciare libero/a

vacation [və'keɪʃən] *n* (*esp us*) vacanze *fpl*; **vacationer, vacationist** (*us*) *n* vacanziere/a

vaccination [væksɪ'neɪʃən] *n* vaccinazione *f*

vaccine ['væksiːn] *n* vaccino

vacuum ['vækjum] *n* vuoto; **vacuum cleaner** *n* aspirapolvere *m inv*

vagina [və'dʒaɪnə] *n* vagina

vague [veɪg] *adj* vago/a; (*blurred: photo, memory*) sfocato/a

vain [veɪn] *adj* (*useless*) inutile, vano/a; (*conceited*) vanitoso/a; **in ~** inutilmente, invano

Valentine's Day ['væləntaɪnzdeɪ] *n* San Valentino *m*

valid ['vælɪd] *adj* valido/a, valevole; (*excuse*) valido/a

valley ['vælɪ] *n* valle *f*

valuable ['væljuəbl] *adj* (*jewel*) di (grande) valore; (*time, help*) prezioso/a; **valuables** *npl* oggetti *mpl* di valore

value ['væljuː] *adj* valore *m* ▷ *vt* (*fix price*) valutare, dare un prezzo a; (*cherish*) apprezzare, tenere a; **values** *npl* (*principles*) valori *mpl*

valve [vælv] *n* valvola

vampire ['væmpaɪər] *n* vampiro

van [væn] *n* (*Aut*) furgone *m*; (*BRIT Rail*) vagone *m*

vandal ['vændl] *n* vandalo/a; **vandalism** *n* vandalismo; **vandalize** *vt* vandalizzare

vanilla [və'nɪlə] *n* vaniglia ▷ *cpd* (*ice cream*) alla vaniglia

vanish ['vænɪʃ] *vi* svanire, scomparire

vanity ['vænɪtɪ] *n* vanità

vapour, (*us*) **vapor** ['veɪpər] *n* vapore *m*

variable ['veərɪəbl] *adj* variabile; (*mood*) mutevole

variant ['veərɪənt] *n* variante *f*

variation [veərɪ'eɪʃən] *n* variazione *f*; (*in opinion*) cambiamento

varied ['veərɪd] *adj* vario/a, diverso/a

variety [və'raɪətɪ] *n* varietà *f inv*; (*quantity*) quantità, numero

various ['veərɪəs] *adj* vario/a, diverso/a; (*several*) parecchi/e, molti/e

varnish ['vɑːnɪʃ] *n* vernice *f*; (*nail varnish*) smalto ▷ *vt* verniciare; mettere lo smalto su

vary ['veərɪ] *vt, vi* variare, mutare

vase [vɑːz] *n* vaso

Vaseline® ['væsɪliːn] *n* vaselina

vast [vɑːst] *adj* vasto/a; (*amount, success*) enorme

VAT [væt] *n abbr* (*BRIT*: = *value added tax*) I.V.A. *f*

Vatican ['vætɪkən] *n*: **the ~** il Vaticano

vault [vɔːlt] *n* (*of roof*) volta; (*tomb*) tomba; (*in bank*) camera blindata ▷ *vt* (*also*: **~ over**) saltare (d'un balzo)

VCR *n abbr* = **video cassette recorder**

VDU *n abbr* = **visual display unit**

veal [viːl] *n* vitello

veer [vɪər] *vi* girare; virare

vegan ['viːgən] *n* vegetaliano/a

vegetable ['vedʒtəbl] *n* verdura, ortaggio ▷ *adj* vegetale

vegetarian [vedʒɪ'teərɪən] *adj, n* vegetariano/a

vegetation [vedʒɪ'teɪʃən] *n* vegetazione *f*

vehicle ['viːɪkl] *n* veicolo

veil [veɪl] *n* velo

vein [veɪn] *n* vena; (*on leaf*) nervatura

Velcro® ['velkrəu] *n* velcro® *m inv*

velvet ['velvɪt] *n* velluto ▷ *adj* di velluto

vending machine ['vendɪŋ-] *n* distributore *m* automatico

vendor ['vendər] *n* venditore/trice

vengeance ['vendʒəns] *n* vendetta; **with a ~** (*fig*) davvero; furiosamente

Venice ['venɪs] *n* Venezia

venison ['venɪsn] *n* carne *f* di cervo

venom ['venəm] *n* veleno

vent [vent] *n* foro, apertura; (*in dress, jacket*) spacco ▷ *vt* (*fig: one's feelings*) sfogare, dare sfogo a

ventilation [ventɪ'leɪʃən] *n* ventilazione *f*

venture ['vɛntʃəʳ] n impresa (rischiosa) ▷ vt rischiare, azzardare ▷ vi arrischiarsi; **a business ~** un'iniziativa commerciale

venue ['vɛnjuː] n luogo (designato) per l'incontro

Venus ['viːnəs] n (planet) Venere m

verb [vəːb] n verbo; **verbal** adj verbale; (translation) orale

verdict ['vəːdɪkt] n verdetto

verge [vəːdʒ] n bordo, orlo; **"soft ~s"** (BRIT) "banchina cedevole"; **on the ~ of doing** sul punto di fare

verify ['vɛrɪfaɪ] vt verificare; (prove the truth of) confermare

versatile ['vəːsətaɪl] adj (person) versatile; (machine, tool etc) (che si presta) a molti usi

verse [vəːs] n (stanza) stanza, strofa; (in bible) versetto; (no pl: poetry) versi mpl

version ['vəːʃən] n versione f

versus ['vəːsəs] prep contro

vertical ['vəːtɪkl] adj, n verticale (m)

very ['vɛrɪ] adv molto ▷ adj: **the ~ book which** proprio il libro che; **~ much** moltissimo; **the ~ last** proprio l'ultimo; **at the ~ least** almeno

vessel ['vɛsl] n (Anat) vaso; (Naut) nave f; (container) recipiente m

vest [vɛst] n (BRIT) maglia; (: sleeveless) canottiera; (US: waistcoat) gilè m inv

vet [vɛt] n abbr (BRIT: = veterinary surgeon) veterinario ▷ vt esaminare minuziosamente

veteran ['vɛtərn] n veterano; (also: **war ~**) veterano, reduce m

veterinary surgeon ['vɛtrɪnərɪ-], (US) **veterinarian** [vɛtrɪ'nɛərɪən] n veterinario

veto ['viːtəu] (pl **vetoes**) n veto ▷ vt opporre il veto a

via ['vaɪə] prep (by way of) via; (by means of) tramite

viable ['vaɪəbl] adj attuabile; vitale

vibrate [vaɪ'breɪt] vi: **to ~ (with)** vibrare (di); (resound) risonare (di)

vibration [vaɪ'breɪʃən] n vibrazione f

vicar ['vɪkəʳ] n pastore m

vice [vaɪs] n (evil) vizio; (Tech) morsa; **vice-chairman** n (irreg) vicepresidente m

vice versa ['vaɪsɪ'vəːsə] adv viceversa

vicinity [vɪ'sɪnɪtɪ] n vicinanze fpl

vicious ['vɪʃəs] adj (remark) cattivo/a; (dog) cattivo/a; (blow) violento/a

victim ['vɪktɪm] n vittima

victor ['vɪktəʳ] n vincitore m

Victorian [vɪk'tɔːrɪən] adj vittoriano/a

victorious [vɪk'tɔːrɪəs] adj vittorioso/a

victory ['vɪktərɪ] n vittoria

video ['vɪdɪəu] cpd video… ▷ n (video film) video m inv; (also: **~ cassette**) videocassetta; (also: **~ recorder**) videoregistratore m; **video call** n videochiamata; **video camera** n videocamera; **video game** n videogioco; **videophone** n videotelefono; **video shop** n videonoleggio; **video tape** n videotape m inv; **video wall** n schermo m multivideo inv

vie [vaɪ] vi: **to ~ with** competere con, rivaleggiare con

Vienna [vɪ'ɛnə] n Vienna

Vietnam [vjɛt'næm] n Vietnam m; **Vietnamese** adj, n vietnamita m/f

view [vjuː] n vista, veduta; (opinion) opinione f ▷ vt (also fig: situation) considerare; (house) visitare; **on ~** (in museum etc) esposto/a; **to be in** or **within ~ (of sth)** essere in vista (di qc); **in my ~** a mio parere; **in ~ of the fact that** considerato che; **viewer** n telespettatore/trice; **viewpoint** n punto di vista; (place) posizione f

vigilant ['vɪdʒɪlənt] adj vigile

vigorous ['vɪgərəs] adj vigoroso/a

vile [vaɪl] adj (action) vile; (smell) disgustoso/a, nauseante; (temper) pessimo/a

villa ['vɪlə] n villa

village ['vɪlɪdʒ] n villaggio; **villager** n abitante m/f di villaggio

villain ['vɪlən] n (scoundrel) canaglia; (BRIT: criminal) criminale m; (in novel etc) cattivo

vinaigrette [vɪneɪ'grɛt] n vinaigrette f inv

vine [vaɪn] n vite f; (climbing plant) rampicante m

vinegar ['vɪnɪgəʳ] n aceto

vineyard ['vɪnjɑːd] n vigna, vigneto

vintage ['vɪntɪdʒ] n (year) annata, produzione f ▷ cpd d'annata

vinyl ['vaɪnl] n vinile m

viola [vɪ'əulə] n viola

violate ['vaɪəleɪt] vt violare

violation [vaɪə'leɪʃən] n violazione f; **in ~ of sth** violando qc

violence ['vaɪələns] n violenza

violent ['vaɪələnt] adj violento/a

violet ['vaɪələt] adj (colour) viola inv, violetto/a ▷ n (plant) violetta; (colour) violetto

violin [vaɪə'lɪn] n violino

VIP n abbr (= very important person) V.I.P. m/f inv

viral ['vaɪərəl] adj (Comput) virale

virgin ['vəːdʒɪn] n vergine f ▷ adj vergine inv

Virgo ['vəːgəu] n (sign) Vergine f

virtual ['vəːtjuəl] adj effettivo/a, vero/a; (Comput, Physics) virtuale; (in effect): **it's a ~ impossibility** è praticamente impossibile; **the ~ leader** il capo all'atto pratico; **virtually** ['vəːtjuəlɪ] adv (almost) praticamente; **virtual reality** n (Comput) realtà f inv virtuale

virtue ['və:tju:] n virtù f inv; (advantage) pregio, vantaggio; **by ~ of** grazie a

virus ['vaɪərəs] n (also Comput) virus m inv

visa ['vi:zə] n visto

vise [vaɪs] n (Us Tech) = **vice**

visibility [vɪzɪ'bɪlɪtɪ] n visibilità

visible ['vɪzəbl] adj visibile

vision ['vɪʒən] n (sight) vista; (foresight, in dream) visione f

visit ['vɪzɪt] n visita; (stay) soggiorno ▷ vt (person: us: also: **~ with**) andare a trovare; (place) visitare; **visiting hours** npl (in hospital etc) orario delle visite; **visitor** n visitatore/trice; (guest) ospite m/f; **visitor centre**, (Us) **visitor center** n centro informazioni per visitatori di museo, zoo, parco ecc

visual ['vɪzjuəl] adj visivo/a; visuale; ottico/a; **visualize** ['vɪzjuəlaɪz] vt immaginare, figurarsi; (foresee) prevedere

vital ['vaɪtl] adj vitale

vitality [vaɪ'tælɪtɪ] n vitalità

vitamin ['vɪtəmɪn] n vitamina

vivid ['vɪvɪd] adj vivido/a

V-neck ['vi:nɛk] n maglione m con lo scollo a V

vocabulary [vəu'kæbjulərɪ] n vocabolario

vocal ['vəukl] adj (Mus) vocale; (communication) verbale

vocational [vəu'keɪʃənl] adj professionale

vodka ['vɔdkə] n vodka f inv

vogue [vəug] n moda; (popularity) popolarità, voga

voice [vɔɪs] n voce f ▷ vt (opinion) esprimere; **voice mail** n servizio di segreteria telefonica

void [vɔɪd] n vuoto ▷ adj (invalid) nullo/a; (empty): **~ of** privo/a di

volatile ['vɔlətaɪl] adj volatile; (fig) volubile

volcano [vɔl'keɪnəu] (pl **volcanoes**) n vulcano

volleyball ['vɔlɪbɔ:l] n pallavolo f

volt [vəult] n volt m inv; **voltage** n tensione f, voltaggio

volume ['vɔlju:m] n volume m

voluntarily ['vɔləntrɪlɪ] adv volontariamente; gratuitamente

voluntary ['vɔləntərɪ] adj volontario/a; (unpaid) gratuito/a, non retribuito/a

volunteer [vɔlən'tɪər] n volontario/a ▷ vt offrire volontariamente ▷ vi (Mil) arruolarsi volontario; **to ~ to do** offrire (volontariamente) di fare

vomit ['vɔmɪt] n vomito ▷ vt, vi vomitare

vote [vəut] n voto, suffragio; (cast) voto; (franchise) diritto di voto ▷ vi votare ▷ vt (propose): **to ~ that** approvare la proposta

che; **he was ~d secretary** è stato eletto segretario; **~ of thanks** discorso di ringraziamento; **voter** n elettore/trice; **voting** n scrutinio

voucher ['vautʃər] n (for meal, petrol) buono

vow [vau] n voto, promessa solenne ▷ vt: **to ~ to do/that** giurare di fare/che

vowel ['vauəl] n vocale f

voyage ['vɔɪɪdʒ] n viaggio per mare, traversata

vulgar ['vʌlgər] adj volgare

vulnerable ['vʌlnərəbl] adj vulnerabile

vulture ['vʌltʃər] n avvoltoio

W

waddle ['wɔdl] *vi* camminare come una papera

wade [weɪd] *vi*: **to ~ through** camminare a stento in; (*fig: book*) leggere con fatica

wafer ['weɪfə^r] *n* (*Culin*) cialda

waffle ['wɔfl] *n* (*Culin*) cialda; (*col*) ciance *fpl* ▷ *vi* cianciare

wag [wæg] *vt* agitare, muovere ▷ *vi* agitarsi

wage [weɪdʒ] *n* (*also:* **~s**) salario, paga ▷ *vt*: **to ~ war** fare la guerra

wag(g)on ['wægən] *n* (*horse-drawn*) carro; (*BRIT Rail*) vagone *m* (merci)

wail [weɪl] *n* gemito; (*of siren*) urlo ▷ *vi* gemere; urlare

waist [weɪst] *n* vita, cintola; **waistcoat** *n* (*BRIT*) panciotto, gilè *m inv*

wait [weɪt] *n* attesa ▷ *vi* aspettare, attendere; **to ~ for** aspettare; **~ for me, please** aspettami, per favore; **I can't ~ to …** (*fig*) non vedo l'ora di …; **to lie in ~ for** stare in agguato a; **wait behind** *vi* rimanere (ad aspettare); **wait on** *vt fus* servire; **waiter** *n* cameriere *m*; **waiting list** *n* lista d'attesa; **waiting room** *n* sala d'aspetto or d'attesa; **waitress** *n* cameriera

waive [weɪv] *vt* rinunciare a, abbandonare

wake [weɪk] (*pt* **woke, waked**, *pp* **woken, waked**) *vt* (*also:* **~ up**) svegliare ▷ *vi* (*also:* **~ up**) svegliarsi ▷ *n* (*for dead person*) veglia funebre; (*Naut*) scia

Wales [weɪlz] *n* Galles *m*

walk [wɔːk] *n* passeggiata; (*short*) giretto; (*gait*) passo, andatura; (*path*) sentiero; (*in park etc*) sentiero, vialetto ▷ *vi* camminare; (*for pleasure, exercise*) passeggiare ▷ *vt* (*distance*) fare or percorrere a piedi; (*dog*) accompagnare, portare a passeggiare; **10 minutes' ~ from** 10 minuti di cammino or a piedi da; **from all ~s of life** di tutte le condizioni sociali; **walk out** *vi* (*audience*) andarsene; (*strike*) scendere in sciopero; **walker** *n* (*person*) camminatore/trice; **walkie-talkie** ['wɔːkɪ'tɔːkɪ] *n* walkie-talkie *m inv*; **walking** *n* camminare *m*; **walking shoes** *npl* scarpe *fpl* da passeggio; **walking stick** *n* bastone *m* da passeggio; **Walkman®** ['wɔːkmən] *n* walkman® *m inv*; **walkway** *n* passaggio pedonale

wall [wɔːl] *n* muro; (*internal, of tunnel, cave*) parete *f*

wallet ['wɔlɪt] *n* portafoglio

wallpaper ['wɔːlpeɪpə^r] *n* carta da parati ▷ *vt* (*room*) mettere la carta da parati in

walnut ['wɔːlnʌt] *n* noce *f*; (*tree*) noce *m*

walrus ['wɔːlrəs] (*pl* **walrus** or **walruses**) *n* tricheco

waltz [wɔːlts] *n* valzer *m inv* ▷ *vi* ballare il valzer

wand [wɔnd] *n* (*also:* **magic ~**) bacchetta (magica)

wander ['wɔndə^r] *vi* (*person*) girare senza meta, girovagare; (*thoughts*) vagare ▷ *vt* girovagare per

want [wɔnt] *vt* volere; (*need*) aver bisogno di; **for ~ of** per mancanza di; **wanted** *adj* (*criminal*) ricercato/a; **"wanted"** (*in adverts*) "cercasi"

war [wɔː^r] *n* guerra; **to make ~ (on)** far guerra (a)

ward [wɔːd] *n* (*in hospital: room*) corsia; (*: section*) reparto; (*Pol*) circoscrizione *f*; (*Law: child: also:* **~ of court**) pupillo/a

warden ['wɔːdn] *n* (*of institution*) direttore/trice; (*of park, game reserve*) guardiano/a; (*BRIT: also:* **traffic ~**) addetto/a al controllo del traffico e del parcheggio

wardrobe ['wɔːdrəub] *n* (*cupboard*) guardaroba *m inv*, armadio; (*clothes*) guardaroba; (*Theat*) costumi *mpl*

warehouse ['wɛəhaus] *n* magazzino

warfare ['wɔːfɛə^r] *n* guerra

warhead ['wɔːhɛd] *n* (*Mil*) testata

warm [wɔːm] *adj* caldo/a; (*welcome, applause*) caloroso/a; (*person, greeting*) cordiale; **it's ~** fa caldo; **I'm ~** ho caldo; **warm up** *vi* scaldarsi, riscaldarsi ▷ *vt* scaldare, riscaldare; (*engine*) far scaldare; **warmly** *adv* (*applaud, welcome*) calorosamente; (*dress*) con abiti pesanti; **warmth** *n* calore *m*

warn [wɔːn] *vt*: **to ~ sb not to do sth** or **against doing sth** avvertire or avvisare qn di non fare qc; **to ~ sb that** avvertire or avvisare qn che; **warning** *n* avvertimento; (*notice*) avviso; (*signal*) segnalazione *f*; **warning light** *n* spia luminosa

warrant ['wɔrnt] *n* (*voucher*) buono; (*Law: to arrest*) mandato di cattura; (*: to search*) mandato di perquisizione

warranty ['wɒrəntɪ] n garanzia
warrior ['wɒrɪəʳ] n guerriero/a
Warsaw ['wɔːsɔː] n Varsavia
warship ['wɔːʃɪp] n nave f da guerra
wart [wɔːt] n verruca
wartime ['wɔːtaɪm] n: **in ~** in tempo di guerra
wary ['wɛərɪ] adj prudente
was [wɒz] pt of **be**
wash [wɒʃ] vt lavare ▷ vi lavarsi; (sea): **to ~ over/against sth** infrangersi su/contro qc ▷ n lavaggio; (of ship) scia; **to give sth a ~** lavare qc, dare una lavata a qc; **to have a ~** lavarsi; **wash up** vi (BRIT) lavare i piatti; (US: have a wash) lavarsi; **washbasin**, (US) **washbowl** n lavabo; **washcloth** n (US) pezzuola (per lavarsi); **washer** n (Tech) rondella; **washing** n (linen etc) bucato; **washing line** n (BRIT) corda del bucato; **washing machine** n lavatrice f; **washing powder** n (BRIT) detersivo (in polvere)
Washington ['wɒʃɪŋtən] n Washington f
wash: washing-up n (dishes) piatti mpl sporchi; **washing-up liquid** n detersivo liquido (per stoviglie); **washroom** n gabinetto
wasn't ['wɒznt] = **was not**
wasp [wɒsp] n vespa
waste [weɪst] n spreco; (of time) perdita; (rubbish) rifiuti mpl; (also: **household ~**) immondizie fpl ▷ adj (material) di scarto; (food) avanzato/a; (land, ground) incolto/a ▷ vt sprecare; **waste ground** n (BRIT) terreno incolto or abbandonato; **wastepaper basket** ['weɪstpeɪpə-] n cestino per la carta straccia
watch [wɒtʃ] n (wristwatch) orologio (da polso); (act of watching, vigilance) sorveglianza; (guard: Mil, Naut) guardia; (Naut: spell of duty) quarto ▷ vt (look at) osservare; (: match, programme) guardare; (spy on, guard) sorvegliare; (land, ground) guardare; (be careful of) fare attenzione a ▷ vi osservare, guardare; (keep guard) fare or montare la guardia; **watch out** vi fare attenzione; **watchdog** n cane m da guardia; **watch strap** n cinturino da orologio
water ['wɔːtəʳ] n acqua ▷ vt (plant) annaffiare ▷ vi (eyes) lacrimare; **in British ~s** nelle acque territoriali britanniche; **to make sb's mouth ~** far venire l'acquolina in bocca a qn; **water down** vt (milk) diluire; (fig: story) edulcorare; **watercolour**, (US) **watercolor** n acquerello; **watercress** n crescione m; **waterfall** n cascata; **watering can** n annaffiatoio; **watermelon** n anguria, cocomero; **waterproof** adj impermeabile; **water-skiing** n sci m acquatico

watt [wɒt] n watt m inv
wave [weɪv] n onda; (of hand) gesto, segno; (in hair) ondulazione f; (fig: of enthusiasm, strikes etc) ondata ▷ vi fare un cenno con la mano; (branches, grass) ondeggiare; (flag) sventolare ▷ vt (hand) fare un gesto con; (handkerchief) sventolare; (stick) brandire; **wavelength** n lunghezza d'onda
waver ['weɪvəʳ] vi esitare; (voice) tremolare
wavy ['weɪvɪ] adj ondulato/a; ondeggiante
wax [wæks] n cera ▷ vt dare la cera a; (car) lucidare ▷ vi (moon) crescere
way [weɪ] n via, strada; (path, access) passaggio; (distance) distanza; (direction) parte f, direzione f; (manner) modo, stile m; (habit) abitudine f; **which ~? — this ~** da che parte or in quale direzione? — da questa parte or per di qua; **on the ~** (en route) per strada; **to be on one's ~** essere in cammino or sulla strada; **to be in the ~** bloccare il passaggio; (fig) essere tra i piedi or d'impiccio; **to go out of one's ~ to do** (fig) mettercela tutta or fare di tutto per fare; **to be under ~** (work, project) essere in corso; **to lose one's ~** perdere la strada; **in a ~** in un certo senso; **in some ~s** sotto certi aspetti; **"~ in"** (BRIT) "entrata", "ingresso"; **"~ out"** (BRIT) "uscita"; **the ~ back** la via del ritorno; **"give ~"** (BRIT Aut) "dare la precedenza"; **no ~!** (col) neanche per idea!; **by the ~ …** a proposito …
WC n abbr (BRIT: = water closet) W.C. m inv, gabinetto
we [wiː] pl pron noi
weak [wiːk] adj debole; (health) precario/a; (beam etc) fragile; (tea, coffee) leggero/a; **weaken** vi indebolirsi ▷ vt indebolire; **weakness** n debolezza; (fault) punto debole, difetto; **to have a weakness for** avere un debole per
wealth [wɛlθ] n (money, resources) ricchezza, ricchezze fpl; (of details) abbondanza, profusione f; **wealthy** adj ricco/a
weapon ['wɛpən] n arma; **~s of mass destruction** armi di distruzione di massa
wear [wɛəʳ] (pt **wore**, pp **worn**) n (use) uso; (deterioration through use) logorio, usura; (clothing): **sports/baby ~** abbigliamento sportivo/per neonati ▷ vt (clothes) portare; (put on) mettersi; (damage: through use) consumare ▷ vi (last) durare; (rub etc through) consumarsi; **town/evening ~** abiti mpl or tenuta da città/sera; **wear off** vi sparire lentamente; **wear out** vt consumare; (person, strength) esaurire
weary ['wɪərɪ] adj stanco/a ▷ vi: **to ~ of** stancarsi di
weasel ['wiːzl] n (Zool) donnola

weather ['wɛðəʳ] *n* tempo ▷ *vt* (*storm, crisis*) superare; **what's the ~ like?** che tempo fa?; **under the ~** (*fig: ill*) poco bene; **weather forecast** *n* previsioni *fpl* del tempo, bollettino meteorologico

weave (*pt* **wove**, *pp* **woven**) [wi:v, wəuv, 'wəuvn] *vt* (*cloth*) tessere; (*basket*) intrecciare

web [wɛb] *n* (*of spider*) ragnatela; (*on foot*) palma; (*fabric, also fig*) tessuto; **the (World Wide) W~** la Rete; **web address** *n* indirizzo Internet; **webcam** *n* webcam *f inv*; **web page** *n* (*Comput*) pagina *f* web *inv*; **website** *n* (*Comput*) sito (Internet)

wed [wɛd] *vt* (*pt, pp* **wedded**) sposare ▷ *vi* sposarsi

Wed. *abbr* (= *Wednesday*) mer.

we'd [wi:d] = **we had; we would**

wedding ['wɛdɪŋ] *n* matrimonio; **wedding anniversary** *n* anniversario di matrimonio; **wedding day** *n* giorno delle nozze *or* del matrimonio; **wedding dress** *n* abito nuziale; **wedding ring** *n* fede *f*

wedge [wɛdʒ] *n* (*under door etc*) zeppa; (*of cake*) fetta ▷ *vt* (*fix*) fissare con zeppe; (*pack tightly*) incastrare

Wednesday ['wɛdnzdɪ] *n* mercoledì *m inv*

wee [wi:] *adj* (SCOTTISH) piccolo/a

weed [wi:d] *n* erbaccia ▷ *vt* diserbare; **weed-killer** *n* diserbante *m*

week [wi:k] *n* settimana; **a ~ on Tuesday** martedì a otto; **a ~ today** oggi a otto; **weekday** *n* giorno feriale; (*Comm*) giornata lavorativa; **weekend** *n* fine settimana *m inv or f inv*, weekend *m inv*; **weekly** *adv* ogni settimana, settimanalmente ▷ *adj*, *n* settimanale (*m*)

weep (*pt, pp* **wept**) [wi:p, wɛpt] *vi* (*person*) piangere

weigh [weɪ] *vt, vi* pesare; **to ~ anchor** salpare *or* levare l'ancora; **weigh up** *vt* valutare

weight [weɪt] *n* peso; **to put on/lose ~** ingrassare/dimagrire; **weightlifting** *n* sollevamento pesi

weir [wɪəʳ] *n* diga

weird [wɪəd] *adj* strano/a, bizzarro/a; (*eerie*) soprannaturale

welcome ['wɛlkəm] *adj* benvenuto/a ▷ *n* accoglienza, benvenuto ▷ *vt* dare il benvenuto a; (*be glad of*) rallegrarsi di; **you're ~** (*after thanks*) prego

weld [wɛld] *n* saldatura ▷ *vt* saldare

welfare ['wɛlfɛəʳ] *n* benessere *m*; **welfare state** *n* stato sociale

well [wɛl] *n* pozzo ▷ *adv* bene ▷ *adj*: **to be ~** (*person*) stare bene ▷ *excl* allora!; ma!; ebbene!; **~ done!** bravo/a!; **get ~ soon!** guarisci presto!; **to do ~** andare bene; **as ~** anche

we'll [wi:l] = **we will; we shall**

well: well-behaved *adj* ubbidiente; **well-built** *adj* (*person*) ben fatto/a; **well-dressed** *adj* ben vestito/a, vestito/a bene

wellies (*col*) ['wɛlɪz] *npl* (BRIT) stivali *mpl* di gomma

well: well-known *adj* noto/a, famoso/a; **well-off** *adj* benestante, danaroso/a; **well-paid** [wɛl'peɪd] *adj* ben pagato/a

Welsh [wɛlʃ] *adj* gallese ▷ *n* (Ling) gallese *m*; **Welshman** *n* (*irreg*) gallese *m*; **Welshwoman** *n* (*irreg*) gallese *f*

went [wɛnt] *pt of* **go**

wept [wɛpt] *pt, pp of* **weep**

were [wəːʳ] *pt of* **be**

we're [wɪəʳ] = **we are**

weren't [wəːnt] = **were not**

west [wɛst] *n* ovest *m*, occidente *m*, ponente *m* ▷ *adj* (a) ovest *inv*, occidentale ▷ *adv* verso ovest; **the W~** l'Occidente; **westbound** ['wɛstbaund] *adj* (*traffic*) diretto/a a ovest; (*carriageway*) ovest *inv*; **western** *adj* occidentale, dell'ovest ▷ *n* (Cine) western *m inv*; **West Indian** *adj* delle Indie Occidentali ▷ *n* abitante *m/f* (*or* originario/a) delle Indie Occidentali; **West Indies** [-'ɪndɪz] *npl*: **the West Indies** le Indie Occidentali

wet [wɛt] *adj* umido/a, bagnato/a; (*soaked*) fradicio/a; (*rainy*) piovoso/a ▷ *n* (BRIT Pol) politico moderato; **to get ~** bagnarsi; **"~ paint"** "vernice fresca"; **wet suit** *n* tuta da sub

we've [wi:v] = **we have**

whack [wæk] *vt* picchiare, battere

whale [weɪl] *n* (Zool) balena

wharf (*pl* **wharves**) [wɔːf, wɔːvz] *n* banchina

⭕ **KEYWORD**

what [wɔt] *adj* **1** (*in direct/indirect questions*) che; quale; **what size is it?** che taglia è?; **what colour is it?** di che colore è?; **what books do you want?** quali *or* che libri vuole? **2** (*in exclamations*) che; **what a mess!** che disordine!

▶ *pron* **1** (*interrogative*) che cosa, cosa, che; **what are you doing?** che *or* (*che*) cosa fai?; **what are you talking about?** di che cosa parli?; **what is it called?** come si chiama?; **what about me?** e io?; **what about doing …?** e se facessimo …?
2 (*relative*) ciò che, quello che; **I saw what you did** ho visto quello che hai fatto; **I saw what was on the table** ho visto cosa c'era sul tavolo
3 (*indirect use*) (che) cosa; **he asked me what she had said** mi ha chiesto

che cosa avesse detto; **tell me what you're thinking about** dimmi a cosa stai pensando
▶ *excl* (*disbelieving*) cosa!, come!

whatever [wɔt'ɛvəʳ] *adj*: ~ **book** qualunque *or* qualsiasi libro + *sub* ▷ *pron*: **do ~ is necessary/you want** faccia qualunque *or* qualsiasi cosa sia necessaria/lei voglia; ~ **happens** qualunque cosa accada; **no reason ~** *or* **whatsoever** nessuna ragione affatto *or* al mondo; **nothing ~** proprio niente
whatsoever [wɔtsəu'ɛvəʳ] *adj* = **whatever**
wheat [wi:t] *n* grano, frumento
wheel [wi:l] *n* ruota; (*Aut: also:* **steering ~**) volante *m*; (*Naut*) (ruota del) timone *m* ▷ *vt* spingere ▷ *vi* (*birds*) roteare; (*also:* ~ **round**) girare; **wheelbarrow** *n* carriola; **wheelchair** *n* sedia a rotelle; **wheel clamp** *n* (*Aut*): **wheel clamps** ganasce *fpl* (*per vetture in sosta vietata*)
wheeze [wi:z] *vi* ansimare

KEYWORD

when [wɛn] *adv* quando; **when did it happen?** quando è successo?
▶ *conj* **1** (*at, during, after the time that*) quando; **she was reading when I came in** quando sono entrato lei leggeva; **that was when I needed you** era allora che avevo bisogno di te
2 (*on, at which*): **on the day when I met him** il giorno in cui l'ho incontrato; **one day when it was raining** un giorno che pioveva
3 (*whereas*) quando, mentre; **you said I was wrong when in fact I was right** mi hai detto che avevo torto, quando in realtà avevo ragione

whenever [wɛn'ɛvəʳ] *adv* quando mai ▷ *conj* quando; (*every time that*) ogni volta che
where [wɛəʳ] *adv, conj* dove; **this is** ~ qui che; **whereabouts** *adv* dove ▷ *n*: **sb's whereabouts** luogo dove qn si trova; **whereas** *conj* mentre; **whereby** *adv* per cui; **wherever** [wɛəʳ'ɛvəʳ] *conj* dovunque + *sub*; (*interrogative*) dove mai
whether ['wɛðəʳ] *conj* se; **I don't know ~ to accept or not** non so se accettare o no; **it's doubtful ~** è poco probabile che; ~ **you go or not** che lei vada o no

KEYWORD

which [wɪtʃ] *adj* **1** (*interrogative, direct, indirect*) quale; **which picture do you**

want? quale quadro vuole?; **which one?** quale?; **which one of you did it?** chi di voi lo ha fatto?
2: **in which case** nel qual caso
▶ *pron* **1** (*interrogative*) quale; **which (of these) are yours?** quali di questi sono suoi?; **which of you are coming?** chi di voi viene?
2 (*relative*) che; (: *indirect*) cui, il (la) quale; **the apple which you ate/which is on the table** la mela che hai mangiato/che è sul tavolo; **the chair on which you are sitting** la sedia sulla quale *or* su cui sei seduto; **he said he knew, which is true** ha detto che lo sapeva, il che è vero; **after which** dopo di che

whichever [wɪtʃ'ɛvəʳ] *adj*: **take ~ book you prefer** prenda qualsiasi libro che preferisce; ~ **book you take** qualsiasi libro prenda
while [waɪl] *n* momento ▷ *conj* mentre; (*as long as*) finché; (*although*) sebbene + *sub*; **for a ~** per un po'
whilst [waɪlst] *conj* = **while**
whim [wɪm] *n* capriccio
whine [waɪn] *n* gemito ▷ *vi* gemere; uggiolare; piagnucolare
whip [wɪp] *n* frusta; (*for riding*) frustino; (*Pol: person*) capogruppo (*che sovrintende alla disciplina dei colleghi di partito*) ▷ *vt* frustare; (*Culin: cream, eggs etc*) sbattere; **whipped cream** *n* panna montata
whirl [wə:l] *vt* (far) girare rapidamente; (far) turbinare ▷ *vi* (*dancers*) volteggiare; (*leaves, water, dust*) sollevarsi in un vortice
whisk [wɪsk] *n* (*Culin*) frusta; frullino ▷ *vt* sbattere, frullare; **to ~ sb away** *or* **off** portar via qn a tutta velocità
whiskers ['wɪskəz] *npl* (*of animal*) baffi *mpl*; (*of man*) favoriti *mpl*
whisky, (*IRISH, US*) **whiskey** ['wɪskɪ] *n* whisky *m inv*
whisper ['wɪspəʳ] *n* sussurro ▷ *vt, vi* sussurrare
whistle ['wɪsl] *n* (*sound*) fischio; (*object*) fischietto ▷ *vi* fischiare
white [waɪt] *adj* bianco/a; (*with fear*) pallido/a ▷ *n* bianco; (*person*) bianco/a; **whiteboard** ['waɪtbɔ:d] *n* lavagna bianca; **interactive whiteboard** lavagna interattiva; **White House** *n*: **the White House** la Casa Bianca; **whitewash** *n* (*paint*) bianco di calce ▷ *vt* imbiancare; (*fig*) coprire
whiting ['waɪtɪŋ] *n* (*pl inv: fish*) merlango
Whitsun ['wɪtsn] *n* Pentecoste *f*
whittle ['wɪtl] *vt*: **to ~ away** *or* **down** ridurre, tagliare
whizz [wɪz] *vi*: **to ~ past** *or* **by** passare sfrecciando

○ KEYWORD

who [huː] *pron* **1** (*interrogative*) chi; **who is it?, who's there?** chi è?

2 (*relative*) che; **the man who spoke to me** l'uomo che ha parlato con me; **those who can swim** quelli che sanno nuotare

whoever [huːˈɛvəʳ] *pron*: **~ finds it** chiunque lo trovi; **ask ~ you like** lo chieda a chiunque vuole; **~ she marries** sposerà, non importa chi sposerà; **~ told you that?** chi mai gliel'ha detto?

whole [həʊl] *adj* (*complete*) tutto/a, completo/a; (*not broken*) intero/a, intatto/a ▷ *n* (*all*): **the ~ of** tutto/a il; (*not broken*) tutto; **the ~ lot (of it)** tutto; **the ~ of the town** tutta la città, la città intera; **on the ~, as a ~** nel complesso, nell'insieme; **wholefood(s)** *n(pl)* cibo integrale; **wholeheartedly** [həʊlˈhɑːtɪdlɪ] *adv* sentitamente, di tutto cuore; **wholemeal** [ˈhəʊlmiːl] *adj* (BRIT: *flour, bread*) integrale; **wholesale** *n* commercio *or* vendita all'ingrosso ▷ *adj* all'ingrosso; (*destruction*) totale; **wholewheat** *adj* = **wholemeal**; **wholly** *adv* completamente, del tutto

○ KEYWORD

whom [huːm] *pron* **1** (*interrogative*) chi; **whom did you see?** chi hai visto?; **to whom did you give it?** a chi lo hai dato? **2** (*relative*) che, *prep* + il (la) quale; **the man whom I saw** l'uomo che ho visto; **the man to whom I spoke** l'uomo al *or* con il quale ho parlato

whore [hɔːʳ] *n* (*col, pej*) puttana

○ KEYWORD

whose [huːz] *adj* **1** (*possessive, interrogative*) di chi; **whose book is this?, whose is this book?** di chi è questo libro?; **whose daughter are you?** di chi sei figlia? **2** (*possessive, relative*): **the man whose son you rescued** l'uomo il cui figlio hai salvato *or* a cui hai salvato il figlio; **the girl whose sister you were speaking to** la ragazza alla cui sorella stavi parlando ▷ *pron* di chi; **whose is this?** di chi è questo?; **I know whose it is** so di chi è

○ KEYWORD

why [waɪ] *adv* perché; **why not?** perché no?; **why not do it now?** perché non farlo adesso?

▷ *conj* perché; **I wonder why he said that** mi chiedo perché l'abbia detto; **that's not why I'm here** non è questo il motivo per cui sono qui; **the reason why** il motivo per cui ▷ *excl* (*surprise*) ma guarda un po'!; (*remonstrating*) ma (via)!; (*explaining*) ebbene!

wicked [ˈwɪkɪd] *adj* cattivo/a, malvagio/a; (*mischievous*) malizioso/a; (*terrible: prices, weather*) terribile

wicket [ˈwɪkɪt] *n* (*Cricket*) porta; area tra le due porte

wide [waɪd] *adj* largo/a; (*region, knowledge*) vasto/a; (*choice*) ampio/a ▷ *adv*: **to open ~** spalancare; **to shoot ~** tirare a vuoto *or* fuori bersaglio; **widely** *adv* (*different*) molto, completamente; (*believed*) generalmente; **widely spaced** molto distanziati/e; **widen** *vt* allargare, ampliare; **wide open** *adj* spalancato/a; **widescreen** *adj* (*television, TV*) a schermo panoramico; **widespread** *adj* (*belief etc*) molto *or* assai diffuso/a

widget [ˈwɪdʒɪt] *n* (*Comput*) widget *m inv*

widow [ˈwɪdəʊ] *n* vedova; **widower** *n* vedovo

width [wɪdθ] *n* larghezza

wield [wiːld] *vt* (*sword*) maneggiare; (*power*) esercitare

wife (*pl* **wives**) [waɪf, waɪvz] *n* moglie *f*

Wi-Fi [ˈwaɪfaɪ] *n* WiFi *m*

wig [wɪg] *n* parrucca

wild [waɪld] *adj* selvatico/a; (*countryside, appearance*) selvaggio/a; (*sea, weather*) tempestoso/a; (*idea, life*) folle; stravagante; (*applause*) frenetico/a; **wilderness** [ˈwɪldənɪs] *n* deserto; **wildlife** *n* natura; **wildly** *adv* selvaggiamente; (*applaud*) freneticamente; (*hit, guess*) a casaccio; (*happy*) follemente

○ KEYWORD

will [wɪl] *aux vb* **1** (*forming future tense*): **I will finish it tomorrow** lo finirò domani; **I will have finished it by tomorrow** lo finirò entro domani; **will you do it? — yes I will/ no I won't** lo farai? — sì (lo farò)/no (non lo farò)

2 (*in conjectures, predictions*): **he will** *or* **he'll be there by now** a quest'ora dovrebbe essere arrivato; **that will be the postman** sarà il postino

3 (*in commands, requests, offers*): **will you be quiet!** vuoi stare zitto?; **will you come?** vieni anche tu?; **will you help me?** mi aiuti?, mi puoi aiutare?; **will you have a cup of tea?** vorrebbe una tazza di tè?; **I won't put up with it!** non lo accetterò!

▶ vt (pt, pp **willed**): to will sb to do volere che qn faccia; **he willed himself to go on** continuò grazie a un grande sforzo di volontà
▶ n **1** volontà
2 (Law) testamento

willing ['wɪlɪŋ] adj volonteroso/a; ~ **to do** disposto/a a fare; **willingly** adv volentieri
willow ['wɪləu] n salice m
willpower ['wɪlpauə'] n forza di volontà
wilt [wɪlt] vi appassire
win [wɪn] (pt, pp **won**) n (in sports etc) vittoria ▷ vt (battle, prize, money) vincere; (popularity) guadagnare ▷ vi vincere; **win over** vt convincere
wince [wɪns] vi trasalire
wind¹ [wɪnd] n vento; (Med) flatulenza; (breath) respiro, fiato ▷ vt (take breath away) far restare senza fiato
wind² (pt, pp **wound**) vt attorcigliare; (wrap) avvolgere; (clock, toy) caricare ▷ vi (road, river) serpeggiare; **wind down** vt (car window) abbassare; (fig: production, business) diminuire; **wind up** vt (clock) caricare; (debate) concludere
windfall ['wɪndfɔːl] n (money) guadagno insperato
wind farm n centrale f eolica
winding ['waɪndɪŋ] adj (road) serpeggiante; (staircase) a chiocciola
windmill ['wɪndmɪl] n mulino a vento
window ['wɪndəu] n finestra; (in car, train, plane) finestrino; (in shop etc) vetrina; (also: ~ **pane**) vetro; **window box** n cassetta da fiori; **window cleaner** n (person) pulitore m di finestre; **window pane** n vetro; **window seat** n posto finestrino; **windowsill** n davanzale m
wind: **wind power** n energia eolica; **windscreen** ['wɪndskriːn], (US) **windshield** n parabrezza m inv; **windscreen wiper**, (US) **windshield wiper** n tergicristallo; **windsurfing** ['wɪndsəːfɪŋ] n windsurf m inv; **wind turbine** ['wɪndtəːbaɪn] n pala eolica; **windy** ['wɪndɪ] adj ventoso/a; **it's windy** c'è vento
wine [waɪn] n vino; **wine bar** n enoteca (per degustazione); **wine glass** n bicchiere m da vino; **wine list** n lista dei vini; **wine tasting** n degustazione f dei vini
wing [wɪŋ] n ala; (Aut) fiancata; **wing mirror** n (BRIT) specchietto retrovisore esterno
wink [wɪŋk] n occhiolino ▷ vi ammiccare, fare l'occhiolino; (light) baluginare
winner ['wɪnə'] n vincitore/trice
winning ['wɪnɪŋ] adj (team) vincente; (goal) decisivo/a; (charming) affascinante

winter ['wɪntə'] n inverno; **winter sports** npl sport mpl invernali; **wintertime** n inverno, stagione f invernale
wipe [waɪp] n pulita, passata ▷ vt pulire (strofinando); (erase: tape) cancellare; **wipe out** vt (debt) pagare, liquidare; (memory) cancellare; (destroy) annientare; **wipe up** vt asciugare
wire ['waɪə'] n filo; (Elec) filo elettrico; (Tel) telegramma m ▷ vt (house) fare l'impianto elettrico di; (also: ~ **up**) collegare, allacciare; (person) telegrafare a
wireless ['waɪəlɪs] adj wireless inv, senza fili; **wireless technology** n tecnologia wireless
wiring ['waɪərɪŋ] n impianto elettrico
wisdom ['wɪzdəm] n saggezza; (of action) prudenza; **wisdom tooth** n dente m del giudizio
wise [waɪz] adj saggio/a; (advice, remark) prudente; giudizioso/a
wish [wɪʃ] n (desire) desiderio; (specific desire) richiesta ▷ vt desiderare, volere; **best ~es** (on birthday etc) i migliori auguri; **with best ~es** (in letter) cordiali saluti, con i migliori saluti; **to ~ sb goodbye** dire arrivederci a qn; **he ~ed me well** mi augurò di riuscire; **to ~ to do/sb to do** desiderare or volere fare/che qn faccia; **to ~ for** desiderare
wistful ['wɪstful] adj malinconico/a
wit [wɪt] n (gen pl) intelligenza; presenza di spirito; (wittiness) spirito, arguzia; (person) bello spirito
witch [wɪtʃ] n strega

🔘 **KEYWORD**

with [wɪð, wɪθ] prep **1** (in the company of) con; **I was with him** ero con lui; **we stayed with friends** siamo stati da amici; **I'll be with you in a minute** vengo subito
2 (descriptive) con; **a room with a view** una camera con vista (sul mare or sulle montagne etc); **the man with the grey hat/blue eyes** l'uomo con il cappello grigio/gli occhi blu
3 (indicating manner, means, cause): **with tears in her eyes** con le lacrime agli occhi; **red with anger** rosso/a dalla rabbia; **to shake with fear** tremare di paura
4: **I'm with you** (I understand) la seguo; **to be with it** (col: up-to-date) essere alla moda; (: alert) essere sveglio/a; **I'm not really with it today** (col) oggi sono un po' fuori

withdraw (irreg: like draw) [wɪθ'drɔː] vt ritirare; (money from bank) ritirare; prelevare ▷ vi ritirarsi; **withdrawal** n ritiro; prelievo; (of army) ritirata; **withdrawal symptoms**

npl (*Med*) crisi f di astinenza; **withdrawn** *adj* (*person*) distaccato/a

withdrew [wɪθˈdruː] *pt of* **withdraw**

wither [ˈwɪðər] *vi* appassire

withhold [wɪθˈhəuld] *vt* (*irreg: like* **hold**) (*money*) trattenere; (*permission*): **to ~ (from)** rifiutare (a); (*information*) nascondere (a)

within [wɪðˈɪn] *prep* all'interno di; (*in time, distances*) entro ▷ *adv* all'interno, dentro; **~ reach (of)** alla portata (di); **~ sight (of)** in vista (di); **~ a mile of** entro un miglio da; **~ the week** prima della fine della settimana

without [wɪðˈaut] *prep* senza; **to go** or **do ~ sth** fare a meno di qc

withstand [wɪθˈstænd] *vt* (*irreg: like* **stand**) resistere a

witness [ˈwɪtnɪs] *n* (*person, also Law*) testimone *m/f* ▷ *vt* (*event*) essere testimone di; (*document*) attestare l'autenticità di

witty [ˈwɪtɪ] *adj* spiritoso/a

wives [waɪvz] *npl of* **wife**

wizard [ˈwɪzəd] *n* mago

wk *abbr* = **week**

wobble [ˈwɔbl] *vi* tremare; (*chair*) traballare

woe [wəu] *n* dolore *m*; disgrazia

woke [wəuk] *pt of* **wake**

woken [ˈwəukn] *pp of* **wake**

wolf (*pl* **wolves**) [wulf, wulvz] *n* lupo

woman (*pl* **women**) [ˈwumən, ˈwɪmɪn] *n* donna

womb [wuːm] *n* (*Anat*) utero

women [ˈwɪmɪn] *npl of* **woman**

won [wʌn] *pt, pp of* **win**

wonder [ˈwʌndər] *n* meraviglia ▷ *vi*: **to ~ whether/why** domandarsi se/perché; **to ~ at** essere sorpreso/a di; meravigliarsi di; **to ~ about** domandarsi di; pensare a; **it's no ~ that** c'è poco or non c'è da meravigliarsi che + *sub*; **wonderful** *adj* meraviglioso/a

won't [wəunt] = **will not**

wood [wud] *n* legno; (*timber*) legname *m*; (*forest*) bosco; **wooden** *adj* di legno; (*fig*) rigido/a; inespressivo/a; **woodwind** *npl* (*Mus*): **the woodwind** i legni; **woodwork** *n* (*craft, subject*) falegnameria

wool [wul] *n* lana; **to pull the ~ over sb's eyes** (*fig*) gettare fumo negli occhi a qn; **woollen**, (*US*) **woolen** *adj* di lana; (*industry*) laniero/a; **woolly**, (*US*) **wooly** *adj* di lana; (*fig: ideas*) confuso/a

word [wəːd] *n* parola; (*news*) notizie *fpl* ▷ *vt* esprimere, formulare; **in other ~s** in altre parole; **to have ~s with sb** avere un diverbio con qn; **to break/keep one's ~** non mantenere/mantenere la propria parola; **wording** *n* formulazione *f*; **word processing** *n* word processing *m*, elaborazione *f* testi; **word processor** *n* word processor *m inv*

wore [wɔːr] *pt of* **wear**

work [wəːk] *n* lavoro; (*Art, Literature*) opera ▷ *vi* lavorare; (*mechanism, plan etc*) funzionare; (*medicine*) essere efficace ▷ *vt* (*clay, wood etc*) lavorare; (*mine etc*) sfruttare; (*machine*) far funzionare; (*cause: effect, miracle*) fare; **to be out of ~** essere disoccupato/a; **how does this ~?** come funziona?; **the TV isn't ~ing** la TV non funziona; **to ~ loose** allentarsi; **work out** *vi* (*plans etc*) riuscire, andare bene ▷ *vt* (*problem*) risolvere; (*plan*) elaborare; **it ~s out at £100** fa 100 sterline; **worker** *n* lavoratore/trice; operaio/a; **work experience** *n* (*previous jobs*) esperienze *fpl* lavorative; (*student training placement*) tirocinio; **work force** *n* forza lavoro; **working class** *n* classe f operaia or lavoratrice; **working week** *n* settimana lavorativa; **workman** *n* (*irreg*) operaio; **work of art** *n* opera d'arte; **workout** *n* (*Sport*) allenamento; **work permit** *n* permesso di lavoro; **workplace** *n* posto di lavoro; **works** *n* (*BRIT: factory*) fabbrica ▷ *npl* (*of clock, machine*) meccanismo; **workshop** *n* officina; (*practical session*) gruppo di lavoro; **work station** *n* stazione *f* di lavoro; **work surface** *n* piano di lavoro; **worktop** *n* piano di lavoro

world [wəːld] *n* mondo ▷ *cpd* (*tour, champion*) del mondo; (*record, power, war*) mondiale; **to think the ~ of sb** (*fig*) pensare un gran bene di qn; **World Cup** *n* (*Football*) Coppa del Mondo; **world-wide** *adj* universale; **World-Wide Web** *n* World Wide Web *m*

worm [wəːm] *n* (*also:* **earth~**) verme *m*

worn [wɔːn] *pp of* **wear** ▷ *adj* usato/a; **worn-out** *adj* (*object*) consumato/a, logoro/a; (*person*) sfinito/a

worried [ˈwʌrɪd] *adj* preoccupato/a

worry [ˈwʌrɪ] *n* preoccupazione *f* ▷ *vt* preoccupare ▷ *vi* preoccuparsi; **worrying** *adj* preoccupante

worse [wəːs] *adj* peggiore ▷ *adv*, *n* peggio; **a change for the ~** un peggioramento; **worsen** *vt*, *vi* peggiorare; **worse off** *adj* in condizioni (economiche) peggiori

worship [ˈwəːʃɪp] *n* culto ▷ *vt* (*God*) adorare, venerare; (*person*) adorare; **Your W~** (*BRIT: to mayor*) signor sindaco; (*to judge*) signor giudice

worst [wəːst] *adj* il (la) peggiore ▷ *adv*, *n* peggio; **at ~** al peggio, per male che vada

worth [wəːθ] *n* valore *m* ▷ *adj*: **to be ~** valere; **it's ~ it** ne vale la pena; **it's not ~ the trouble** non ne vale la pena; **worthless** *adj* di nessun valore; **worthwhile** *adj* (*activity*) utile; (*cause*) lodevole

worthy ['wəːðɪ] adj (person) degno/a; (motive) lodevole; ~ **of** degno di

O **KEYWORD**

would [wud] aux vb **1** (conditional tense): **if you asked him he would do it** se glielo chiedesse lo farebbe; **if you had asked him he would have done it** se glielo avesse chiesto lo avrebbe fatto
2 (in offers, invitations, requests): **would you like a biscuit?** vorrebbe or vuole un biscotto?; **would you ask him to come in?** lo faccia entrare, per cortesia; **would you open the window please?** apra la finestra, per favore
3 (in indirect speech): **I said I would do it** ho detto che l'avrei fatto
4 (emphatic): **it WOULD have to snow today!** doveva proprio nevicare oggi!
5 (insistence): **she wouldn't do it** non ha voluto farlo
6 (conjecture): **it would have been midnight** sarà stata mezzanotte; **it would seem so** sembrerebbe proprio di sì
7 (indicating habit): **he would go there on Mondays** andava lì ogni lunedì

wouldn't ['wudnt] = **would not**
wound[1] [wuːnd] n ferita ▷ vt ferire
wound[2] [waund] pt, pp of **wind**[2]
wove [wəuv] pt of **weave**
woven ['wəuvn] pp of **weave**
wrap [ræp] vt (also: ~ **up**) avvolgere; (parcel) incartare; **wrapper** n (on chocolate) carta; (BRIT: of book) copertina; **wrapping** ['ræpɪŋ] n carta; **wrapping paper** n carta da pacchi; (for gift) carta da regali
wreath (pl **wreaths**) [riːθ, riːðz] n corona
wreck [rɛk] n (sea disaster) naufragio; (ship) relitto; (pej: person) rottame m ▷ vt demolire; (ship) far naufragare; (fig) rovinare; **wreckage** n rottami mpl; (of building) macerie fpl; (of ship) relitti mpl
wren [rɛn] n (Zool) scricciolo
wrench [rɛntʃ] n (Tech) chiave f; (tug) torsione f brusca; (fig) strazio ▷ vt strappare; storcere; **to ~ sth from** strappare qc a or da
wrestle ['rɛsl] vi: **to ~ (with sb)** lottare (con qn); **wrestler** n lottatore/trice; **wrestling** n lotta
wretched ['rɛtʃɪd] adj disgraziato/a; (col: weather, holiday) orrendo/a, orribile; (: child, dog) pestifero/a
wriggle ['rɪgl] vi (also: ~ **about**) dimenarsi; (snake, worm) serpeggiare, muoversi serpeggiando

wring (pt, pp **wrung**) [rɪŋ, rʌŋ] vt torcere; (wet clothes) strizzare; (fig): **to ~ sth out of** strappare qc a
wrinkle ['rɪŋkl] n (on skin) ruga; (on paper etc) grinza ▷ vt (nose) torcere; (forehead) corrugare ▷ vi (skin, paint) raggrinzirsi
wrist [rɪst] n polso
write (pt **wrote**, pp **written**) [raɪt, rəut, 'rɪtn] vt, vi scrivere; **write down** vt annotare; (put in writing) mettere per iscritto; **write off** vt (debt, plan) cancellare; **write out** vt mettere per iscritto; (cheque, receipt) scrivere; **write-off** n perdita completa; **writer** n autore/trice, scrittore/trice
writing ['raɪtɪŋ] n scrittura; (of author) scritto, opera; **in ~** per iscritto; **writing paper** n carta da lettere
written ['rɪtn] pp of **write**
wrong [rɔŋ] adj sbagliato/a; (not suitable) inadatto/a; (wicked) cattivo/a; (unfair) ingiusto/a ▷ adv in modo sbagliato, erroneamente ▷ n (injustice) torto ▷ vt fare torto a; **you are ~ to do it** ha torto a farlo; **you are ~ about that, you've got it ~** si sbaglia; **to be in the ~** avere torto; **what's ~?** cosa c'è che non va?; **to go ~** (person) sbagliarsi; (plan) fallire, non riuscire; (machine) guastarsi; **wrongly** adv (incorrectly, by mistake) in modo sbagliato; **wrong number** n: **you have the wrong number** (Tel) ha sbagliato numero
wrote [rəut] pt of **write**
wrung [rʌŋ] pt, pp of **wring**
WWW n abbr = **World Wide Web**; **the ~** la Rete

X y

XL *abbr* = **extra large**
Xmas ['ɛksməs] *n abbr* = **Christmas**
X-ray ['ɛks'reɪ] *n* raggio X; (*photograph*) radiografia ▷ *vt* radiografare
xylophone ['zaɪləfəun] *n* xilofono

yacht [jɔt] *n* panfilo, yacht *m inv*; **yachting** *n* yachting *m*, sport *m* della vela
yard [jɑːd] *n* (*of house etc*) cortile *m*; (*measure*) iarda (= 914 mm; 3 feet); **yard sale** (*us*) *n* vendita di oggetti usati nel cortile di una casa privata
yarn [jɑːn] *n* filato; (*tale*) lunga storia
yawn [jɔːn] *n* sbadiglio ▷ *vi* sbadigliare
yd. *abbr* = **yard**
yeah [jɛə] *adv* (*col*) sì
year [jɪəʳ] *n* anno; (*referring to harvest, wine etc*) annata; **she's three ~s old** ha tre anni; **an eight-~-old child** un(a) bambino/a di otto anni; **yearly** *adj* annuale ▷ *adv* annualmente
yearn [jəːn] *vi*: **to ~ for sth/to do** desiderare ardentemente qc/di fare
yeast [jiːst] *n* lievito
yell [jɛl] *n* urlo ▷ *vi* urlare
yellow ['jɛləu] *adj* giallo/a; **Yellow Pages®** *npl* pagine *fpl* gialle
yes [jɛs] *adv, n* sì (*m inv*); **to say ~ (to)** dire di sì (a)
yesterday ['jɛstədɪ] *adv, n* ieri (*m inv*); **~ morning/evening** ieri mattina/sera; **all day ~** ieri per tutta la giornata
yet [jɛt] *adv* ancora; già ▷ *conj* ma, tuttavia; **it is not finished ~** non è ancora finito; **the best ~** finora il migliore finora; **as ~** finora
yew [juː] *n* tasso (*albero*)
Yiddish ['jɪdɪʃ] *n* yiddish *m*
yield [jiːld] *n* produzione *f*, resa; reddito ▷ *vt* produrre, rendere; (*surrender*) cedere ▷ *vi* cedere; (*us Aut*) dare la precedenza
yob(bo) ['jɔb(əu)] *n* (*BRIT col*) bullo
yoga ['jəugə] *n* yoga *m*
yog(h)urt ['jəugət] *n* iogurt *m inv*
yolk [jəuk] *n* tuorlo, rosso d'uovo

you [juː] *pron* **1** *(subject)* tu; *(: polite form)* lei; *(: pl)* voi; *(: formal)* loro; **you Italians enjoy your food** a voi italiani piace mangiare bene; **you and I will go** andiamo io e te *(or lei ed io)*
2 *(object: direct)* ti; la; vi; loro *(after vb)*; *(: indirect)* ti; le; vi; loro *(after vb)*; **I know you** ti *(or la or vi)* conosco; **I gave it to you** te l'ho dato; gliel'ho dato; ve l'ho dato; l'ho dato loro
3 *(stressed, after prep, in comparisons)* te; lei; voi; loro; **I told YOU to do it** ho detto a TE *(or a LEI etc)* di farlo; **she's younger than you** è più giovane di te *(or lei etc)*
4 *(impers: one)* si; **fresh air does you good** l'aria fresca fa bene; **you never know** non si sa mai

you'd [juːd] = **you had; you would**
you'll [juːl] = **you will; you shall**
young [jʌŋ] *adj* giovane ▷ *npl (of animal)* piccoli *mpl*; **the ~** i giovani, la gioventù; **youngster** *n* giovanotto/a, ragazzo/a; *(child)* bambino/a
your [jɔːʳ] *adj* il (la) tuo/a; *(pl)* i (le) tuoi (tue); *(polite form)* il (la) suo/a; *(pl)* i (le) suoi (sue); *(pl)* il (la) vostro/a; *(pl)* i (le) vostri/e; *(: formal)* il (la) loro; *(pl)* i (le) loro
you're [juəʳ] = **you are**
yours [jɔːz] *pron* il (la) tuo/a; *(pl)* i (le) tuoi (tue); *(polite form)* il (la) suo/a; *(pl)* i (le) suoi (sue); *(pl)* il (la) vostro/a; *(pl)* i (le) vostri/e; *(: formal)* il (la) loro; *(pl)* i (le) loro; **~ sincerely/faithfully** *(in letter)* cordiali/ distinti saluti; *see also* **mine¹**
yourself [jɔːˈsɛlf] *pron (reflexive)* ti; *(: polite form)* si; *(after prep)* te; sé; *(emphatic)* tu stesso/a; lei stesso/a; **yourselves** *pl pron (reflexive)* vi; *(: polite form)* si; *(after prep)* voi; loro; *(emphatic)* voi stessi/e; loro stessi/e; *see also* **oneself**
youth [juːθ] *n* gioventù *f*; *(young man)* giovane *m*, ragazzo; **youth club** *n* centro giovanile; **youthful** *adj* giovane; da giovane; giovanile; **youth hostel** *n* ostello della gioventù
you've [juːv] = **you have**
Yugoslavia [juːgəʊˈslɑːviə] *n (formerly)* Jugoslavia

Z

zeal [ziːl] *n* zelo; entusiasmo
zebra [ˈziːbrə] *n* zebra; **zebra crossing** *n* (BRIT) (passaggio pedonale a) strisce *fpl*, zebre *fpl*
zero [ˈzɪərəʊ] *n* zero
zest [zɛst] *n* gusto; *(Culin)* buccia
zigzag [ˈzɪgzæg] *n* zigzag *m inv* ▷ *vi* zigzagare
Zimbabwe [zɪmˈbɑːbwɪ] *n* Zimbabwe *m*
zinc [zɪŋk] *n* zinco
zip [zɪp] *n* *(also:* **~ fastener***)* chiusura *f* or cerniera *f* lampo *inv* ▷ *vt* (Comput) zippare; *(also:* **~ up***)* chiudere con una cerniera lampo; **zip code** *n* (US) codice *m* di avviamento postale; **zipper** (US) *n* cerniera *f* lampo *inv*
zit [zɪt] *n* brufolo
zodiac [ˈzəʊdɪæk] *n* zodiaco
zone [zəʊn] *n* *(also Mil)* zona
zoo [zuː] *n* zoo *m inv*
zoology [zuːˈɒlədʒɪ] *n* zoologia
zoom [zuːm] *vi*: **to ~ past** sfrecciare; **zoom lens** *n* zoom *m inv*, obiettivo a focale variabile
zucchini [zuːˈkiːnɪ] *n* *(pl inv: US)* zucchina